THE GOLF GUIDE

PGA

WHERE TO PLAY
WHERE TO STAY

1994

Endorsed by
The Professional Golfers' Association

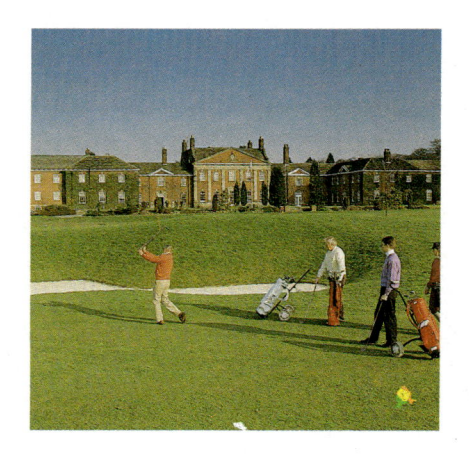

**FHG Publications
Paisley**

Acknowledgements

The Publishers wish to acknowledge the assistance of the Professional Golfers' Association, their staff at The Belfry and their golfing correspondents in the preparation of this, the 17th edition of *THE GOLF GUIDE*. Thanks are particularly due to Laraine Beeching, Jane Carter, Joanne Taylor and Mike Gray.

For colour illustrations we wish to acknowledge the PGA and photographer Ray Garnett (pp 37, 38, 39, 40 and front cover Ryder Cup Team inset), East Lothian Tourist Board (p 7), Yorkshire and Humberside Tourist Board (p 24), Bournemouth Tourism (p 27) and Michael Gedye (pp 30, 32, 33 and 36). We are also grateful to the PGA, Tourist Boards and others who have supplied additional information and illustrations.

Our Front Cover shows The Belfry, hotel and golf course and venue for the 1993 Ryder Cup. The Belfry is one of the De Vere group of hotels and other De Vere hotels featured in this edition are Mottram Hall (title page and back cover) and Belton Woods (p 25). These and other De Vere hotels have excellent golfing and leisure facilities and further details of the group are available on 0925 265050.

We wish to thank all our advertisers and, finally, the Club Secretaries, Professionals and others who have co-operated in the annual updating of the golf club directory entries which are the essential ingredient of *THE GOLF GUIDE: Where To Play/Where To Stay.*

Cover design: Ted Carden, Glasgow

Title page picture: Mottram Hall Hotel, Prestbury, Cheshire

ISBN 1 85055 180 4 © FHG Publications 1993-94

All rights reserved. No part of this publication may be reproduced, stored in a retrieval system or recorded by any means whatsoever without prior permssion from the Publishers.

Whilst every care has been taken to obtain and compile accurate and reliable information, the Publishers cannot accept liability for any errors or omissions in this publication.

Published by FHG Publications, a member of the U.N. Group, Abbey Mill Business Centre, Seedhill, Paisley PA1 1TJ (041-887 0428)

Distribution: **Book Trade:** WLM, 117 The Hollow, Littleover, Derby DE3 7BS
(Tel: 0332 272020 Fax: 0332 774287)
News Trade: UMD, Castle House, 37-45 Paul Street, London EC2A 4PB
(Tel: 071-490 2020 Fax: 071-490 1235)

Typeset by RD Composition Ltd., Glasgow
Printed and bound by Benham's Ltd., Colchester

PRINTED AND PUBLISHED IN BRITAIN

Foreword

The game of golf provides wonderful opportunities to explore the length and breadth of the country, discovering golf courses, old and new. No serious explorer should be without *THE GOLF GUIDE* which, with its accommodation entries, course descriptions and helpful advice, makes the ideal companion for any such journey.

Wherever you go in your golf travels, from the most luxurious and renowned establishments to those undiscovered gems in some quiet corner of the country, there will be a PGA Professional to welcome you. The Professional Golfers' Association, through its 4,000 members, act as custodians of this great game. They can offer advice, help and guidance to make the sport more enjoyable for everyone who takes part, whatever their ability.

I hope that when you visit one of the hundreds of golf courses listed in this guide you take the opportunity to meet the club professional who will undoubtedly have some words of advice to make your visit even more pleasant.

As well as playing the many courses, you will undoubtedly enjoy reading this guide and the informative articles it contains. The PGA's tournament year is covered in full, as is the jewel in our crown, the Ryder Cup by Johnnie Walker, played at The Belfry. It was a marvellous occasion which, even though the result was not as Europe may have hoped, still proved that the true spirit of this ancient game lives on!

On behalf of The Professional Golfers' Association may I wish you many happy hours exploring the pages of this guide, the many golf courses and hotels which it lists and above all, enjoyment of this wonderful sport!

Ross Whitehead
Captain
The Professional Golfers' Association

Whilst great care has been made to obtain accurate and reliable information, the Publisher cannot accept liability for any errors or omissions in this publication.

THE CADDYMATIC FAMILY

CADDYMATIC "Pedigree"
- Weight 12.0 kgs
- One-piece construction
- Fully folding
- Pace setter control
- Battery options:
  24 A/H,
  28 A/H,
  36 A/H

CADDYMATIC "Cub"
- Weight 11.9 kgs
- Two-piece construction
- Fully folding
- Pace setter control
- Battery options:
  24 A/H or 28 A/H

The NEW Revolutionary
CADDYMATIC "Cougar"
- Lightweight 8.0 kgs
- Two-piece construction
- Adjustable handle and bag support
- Pace setter control
- Battery options: 15 A/H or 24 A/H
- Unique lead or follow option
- Colour options: Black or Black and Silver
- Patent applied for
- Registered design

Options for Cub & Pedigree Models
- Available in four colours:
  Black, Red, Green, Burgundy
- Waterproof seat
- Over run control brake
- Caddymatic Umbrella
- Caddymatic Carry Bag

For Your Nearest CADDYMATIC Stockist Contact

Power Golf Limited, 31 Alexandra Way, Ashchurch Business Centre, Tewkesbury, Gloucestershire GL20 8NB
Telephone (0684) 296544 · Facsimile (0684) 850007 for information and free brochure

How to Use The Golf Guide

THE GOLF GUIDE Where to Play ● Where to Stay, contains up-to-date basic information on every course (as far as we know) in Britain. Details are provided by the clubs themselves. You will also find sections on Spain & Majorca, Portugal and France. The guide also carries entries from hotels, guest-houses and other accommodation convenient to specific courses or areas. These are generally 'paid' entries and usually follow a recommendation from a club. *THE GOLF GUIDE* itself is endorsed by the Professional Golfers' Association and is usually available for sale in golf clubs through the Professional and/or the Secretary – as well as bookshops etc.

Golf Course Information

For virtually every course you will find the following details, updated annually:

1. Name, address and telephone number.
2. Location.   3. Brief description.
4. Number of holes, length and Standard Scratch Score.   5. Green fees.
6. Details of facilities for visitors – individuals, groups and societies.
7. Name and telephone number of the Professional and the Secretary.

The accuracy of details published depends on the response of the clubs and to our best knowledge is correct at the time of going to press (October 1993). However, we cannot accept responsibility for errors or omissions and we recommend that you check important details with clubs before making any arrangements.

Choosing a Course

The golf clubs and courses are listed alphabetically by nearest town or village within the appropriate county section for England, Scotland, Wales, Ireland, the Isle of Man and the Channel Islands. Courses in Spain & Majorca, Portugal and France are also listed by region. We have chosen to classify by place-name rather than club or course name since this seems more straightforward and recognisable to the majority.

If you want to find a club or course by its name, you should simply refer to the Index where you will see the page number of the listing. In each entry the name of the club or course is always shown in bold type after the place-name heading.

Accommodation

Accommodation entries are placed as near a particular club or course as possible and there are also hotel displays in the front colour section. Most of the accommodation advertised has been recommended by the local golf club. A full index is provided.

Maps

At the back of *THE GOLF GUIDE* you will find a set of maps showing cities, towns and villages in Britain with counties, motorways and main roads. Although many of the place-names under which the courses are classified are on the maps, please note that the maps are not golf course or club location maps.

The location details supplied with each entry should get you there and if you are in any doubt at all you should ask directions from the club itself.

Please mention *THE GOLF GUIDE Where to Play ● Where to Stay* when you make a hotel booking or play at courses after using our guide.

The Golf break other golfers want to keep a secret

Country Club Hotels' Short Breaks are a closely guarded secret among people who really enjoy the game of golf...and want to play it on some of Britain's finest courses.

With all our venues located in beautiful countryside settings, Country Club Hotels offer the perfect environment to challenge friends to a rewarding game...entertain business clients or colleagues...or simply take a well-deserved break from home or office routine.

To help you relax and unwind, we provide a range of leisure activities – from tennis, swimming and squash to jacuzzis, saunas and fitness studios. So your partner is sure to enjoy a stay at Country Club Hotels as much as you do!

For full details on all 10 UK Country Club Hotels, call us now on the number below.

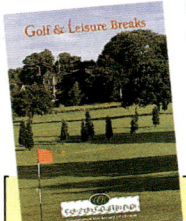

COUNTRY CLUB HOTELS

Experience the luxury of choice

CALL ☎ 0582 396969 AND QUOTE CG1302

Golfing around Edinburgh: in East Lothian on the Firth of Forth with the Bass Rock in the background.

Golfing Around Britain
Where to Play – Where to Stay

SCOTLAND, or more precisely, St Andrews, claims to be the home of golf and it's quite appropriate to start a brief review of golf and golfing accommodation north of the Border!

All over Scotland there are groups of courses with accompanying hotels for excellent golfing and family holidays. The Ayrshire coast, around the Dornoch Firth, Moray, Nairn, around Edinburgh, Angus from Dundee through Monifieth to Arbroath and Montrose. Perthshire abounds with picturesque inland courses such as Crieff and Comrie as does Inverness-shire, especially in the Spey Valley. Gleneagles and Turnberry have a justifiably high reputation and Turnberry's new clubhouse can only add to its standing.

It may come as a surprise that Arran supports seven golf courses. There are eighteen-hole courses at Brodick, Lamlash and Whiting Bay, none very long but some quite strenuous walking. Nine-hole courses are sited at Corrie, Lochranza and Machrie, not challenging but all good fun and ideal for beginners. The twelve-holer at Shiskine at Blackwaterfoot must be a throwback to the start of the game. Looking out on to Kilbrannan Sound, and beautifully maintained, Shiskine has the only par 5 of any of Arran's golf courses, plus a number of other challenging holes.

It's often forgotten that cities can have excellent golf facilities. If you were based at the 5-Crown Hospitality Inn in Glasgow you'd have over thirty courses

Scottish Golfing Breaks
with Mount Charlotte Thistle Hotels

Enjoy the beauty of Scotland and guaranteed tee-off times at some of Scotland's finest golf courses. Centered around 8 top grade, 4 and 5 crown hotels, Scottish Golfing Breaks are the ideal way to spend 3, 5 or 7 days away on a golf inclusive package.

Choose from:

Caledonian Thistle Hotel, **Aberdeen**
Altens Skean Dhu Hotel, **Aberdeen**
Hospitality Inn, **Irvine**
The Portpatrick Hotel, **Portpatrick**

The Angus Thistle, **Dundee**
King Malcom Thistle, **Dunfermline**
King James Thistle, **Edinburgh**
Johnstounburn Hotel, **Humbie**

Prices start at £195 for a 3 night "Hole in One" break, to £460 for the "Par Excellence" 7 night break, with special "Highlife" and "Weekaway" rates for non golfers.

For a FREE leaflet & booking form contact:

MOUNT CHARLOTTE THISTLE HOTELS

Golfing Co-Ordinator, Scottish Golfing Breaks,
Caledonian Thistle Hotel, Union Terrace, Aberdeen AB9 1HE
Telephone: 0224-640233   Fax: 0224-641627

BALBIRNIE HOUSE

AA ★★★★   **DELUXE**   **RAC** ★★★★

Balbirnie is a beautiful 18th century mansion fully restored as an outstanding luxury country house hotel. Surrounded by a 416 acre country park, the hotel is ideally situated a mere chip from the first tee of Balbirnie Park Golf Course, a challenging and beautifully landscaped 18 hole, 6210 yards, par 71 parkland course. At the heart of the home of golf, St. Andrews, Ladybank and Carnoustie are just a few of the 100 golf courses within one hour's drive of Balbirnie, making it the perfect destination for the golf enthusiast.

For further details please contact Alan Russell (Managing Director)

**BALBIRNIE PARK, MARKINCH, GLENROTHES, FIFE KY7 6NE
TELEPHONE: 0592 610066   FAX: 0592 610529**

within very easy reach and at the Aberdeen Skean Dhu hotels there's an equally impressive if smaller selection. In the same Mount Charlotte Hotels group the Hospitality Inn at Irvine will have its own nine-hole course and driving range.

The east coast of Fife and St Andrews with its famous courses and hotels is an essential visit for any golfer. But inland Fife, based for example amid the comforts of Balbirnie House Hotel near Markinch, offers attractive alternatives less affected by 'haar' sea-mists and obstructive winds.

At the other end of Britain is Cornwall, with its early Springs and late Winters. The West Cornwall Club at St Ives has an enviable outlook, equalled perhaps by the view from the Pedn Olva Hotel, which represents the range of excellent holiday golf accommodation in this area. The course at Carlyon Bay Hotel stretches along the cliff-tops towards Parr, looking over St Austell Bay and tests any

ALVIE ESTATE SCOTTISH HIGHLAND GOLFING HOLIDAYS

A Golfing Holiday on a traditionally run Highland Estate of 13,000 acres combined with many other activities such as clay pigeon shooting, skiing, fishing, shooting, microlight flying and gliding. Golf at any one of six courses nearby. A range of accommodation to suit most pockets, from full board in the shooting lodge to self catering cottages or caravans and chalets. Packages of accommodation and activities individually devised on request.

ALVIE ESTATE OFFICE (Ref PGA1),
Kincraig, by Kingussie, Inverness-shire PH21 1NE
Tel: 0540 651255/651249   Fax: 0540 651380

Alvie

NO QUEUES. NO CROWDS. NO TEE BOOKINGS.
8 Uncrowded Highland Courses

A freedom to enjoy your golf as you never believed possible. Our only distractions from the game here in the HIGHLANDS are the dramatic scenery, wildlife or the occasional burn or loch!
Less than 45 minutes' drive from any of these courses – Nairn, Boat of Garten, Abernethy, Grantown-on-Spey, Kingussie, Lossiemouth (Moray) and Forres. Garden pitch and putt. We will welcome you with log fires, award winning food, over 150 wines and 40 malt whiskies, whilst you enjoy our sensational views over the River Spey and the Abernethy Forest to the Cairngorm Mountains.
Ring Ian Kirk, 047 985 347 for further information on golf courses, tuition and our hotel. 7 Bedrooms. D,B&B £35-£62.

AUCHENDEAN LODGE HOTEL
Dulnain Bridge, Grantown on Spey,
Inverness-shire PH26 3LU

STB 3 Crowns Highly Commended – Taste of Scotland – Egon Ronay Good Hotel Guide – Good Food Guide

STOTFIELD HOTEL
LOSSIEMOUTH, MORAY IV31 6QS
Tel: 0343 812011   Fax: 0343 814820
**GROUPS AND SOCIETIES WELCOMED
CONFIRMED TEE TIMES ARRANGED**

Elegant Victorian Hotel overlooking Moray's premier 18-hole Championship Golf Course, also a second 18-hole course. Many fine golf courses a short drive away. The Hotel has 47 en-suite bedrooms, all with colour TV, video channel, tea and coffee making facilities, direct dial telephones, clock radio-alarms; a sauna and mini-gym are available. Excellent food. American Bar and Grill.   **Enquiries to Mike and Patricia Warnes, resident owners.**

QUALITY GOLF IN A MAGNIFICENT SETTING . . .

THE CARLYON BAY HOTEL and Golf Course is set amidst some of Cornwall's most breathtaking coastal scenery, the course itself stretching out along the cliff tops, enjoys magnificent views across St. Austell Bay and miles of golden sands.

Built in 1925 as a private enterprise, the course has been owned by the hotel since 1929. In its early days the glorious setting attracted the Duke of Windsor, probably the keenest of the all golfing Royals while Winston Churchill too spent a few of his finest hours at Carlyon Bay.

Considerable changes have occurred during the past decade or so. In 1978, golf architect Hamilton Stutt was commissioned to make alterations to various parts of the course, prior to the hotel coming under ownership of the Brend Family, whose emphasis has been on improving the quality of golf offered. The extensive clubhouse complex included spacious, modern locker rooms, bar, restaurant and lounge and the club professional's shop, offering a selection of equipment in addition to buggy hire and expert tuition.

The Hotel's location complements the interior, being unique with superb views of the bay. Set in two hundred and fifty acre ground and gardens, The Carlyon Bay Hotel has the perfect combination of luxury, location and leisure facilities, the highest standard of cuisine and personal attentive service.

From the moment of arrival, an atmosphere of relaxation and luxury greets you. Each bedroom has private bathroom facilities, colour TV, tea and coffee making facilities, direct dial telephone and most have sea views. Deluxe bedrooms offer very spacious accommodation with added luxuries, chocolates, bathrobes etc.

An excellent choice at all times.

"THE CREAM OF GOLF AT CORNWALLS FINEST..."

"...set in 250 spectacular acres."

The Carlyon Bay Hotel Golf Course has been owned by the hotel since 1929. Even in its earliest days, this spectacular location attracted the keenest golfers including the Duke of Windsor and Sir Winston Churchill.

Improved in 1978 by golf architect Hamilton Stutt, the emphasis of continual improvement has remained to this day. The Extensive clubhouse complex includes spacious modern locker rooms, bar, restaurant, lounge and club professionals shop.

The 6,505 yard course stretches through the beautiful countryside of Cornwall. The Carlyon Bay Course proves both interesting and challenging to golfers of all handicaps. A full course layout is available from The Brend Hotels Travel Centre 0271 44496.

- Spectacular Location
- One of Cornwalls Premier Courses
- 4 star luxury at Cornwalls finest Hotel
- Professionally managed course

The Carlyon Bay Hotel
AND GOLF COURSE
AA ★★★★ RAC
St.Austell, South Cornwall. PL25 8RD
Telephone: St.Austell 812304

Brend Hotels
A Member of The Brend Group of Exclusive Hotels

CREAM OF CORNISH GOLF

5 DIFFERENT COURSES WITH 4 NIGHTS STAY

All reservations and tee times booked for you.

4 course dinner full English breakfast. All rooms en-suite.

Facilities include: snooker, squash, tennis, swimming pool and late bar!

From £220 all inclusive

3 nights / 4 courses from £170

- **ST. MELLION**
  (£20 suppliment to play Nicklaus Course).
- **ST. ENODOC**
- **LAUNCESTON**
- **BODMIN**
- **BOWOOD PARK**
  Adjacent to the hotel

Golfing breaks of any duration can be arranged with an itinerary tailor-made to suit your requirements. We have special arrangements and concessionary green fees at most of the courses in Cornwall.

Tuition available at Bowood Park for beginners and refresher courses.

Lanteglos

Lanteglos Country House Hotel
Camelford, Cornwall, PL32 9RF

**Phone or Fax.
Camelford
(0840) 213551**

Pedn-Olva

HOTEL & RESTAURANTS

Guests are assured of a warm, friendly welcome, personal attention, comfort and good food at Pedn-Olva, situated just two minutes' walk from the harbour and the quaint, narrow streets of St. Ives.

The hotel has direct access to safe Porthminster beach for bathing, and arrangements can be made for water ski-ing, paragliding, windsurfing, fishing, clay-pigeon shooting and golf.

35 bedrooms with private facilities, tea-makers, TV and radio, telephone and baby listening. Car parking available.

* Open all year   * Fully licensed
* Heated swimming pool   * Sun terrace

AA ★★ RAC

Porthminster Beach, St. Ives, Cornwall TR26 2EA
Telephone (0736) 796222   Fax (0736) 797710

MORETONHAMPSTEAD:
a secret no longer!

"The ubiquitous motorways are not everyone's choice of road, but they have proved of benefit to holidaymakers and visitors seeking easier access to the more remote corners of the country, not least the West Country.

The M5 to Exeter has been a boon to that part of England, a green and tranquil corner where countryside on the edge of Dartmoor has remained unchanged for centuries, compelling in its beauty and serenity. Here are to be found dozens of lovely villages, all thatched roofs and flowerpots, and miles of golden beaches.

Golf here is a particular delight and nowhere is it better or more appealing than at Moretonhampstead, where the gracious old Manor House Hotel sits in regal splendour overlooking a golf course that is a sight for sore eyes at any time of year.

Only 17 miles from the ancient cathedral city of Exeter, near the village of North Bovey, the Manor House and its golf course was once the best-kept secret in British golf, the haunt for those to whom it represented all that was best in life.

Set on the edge of the Dartmoor National Park, the course provides a stunning combination of natural beauty and ideal golf terrain perhaps without peer. It is a rare mix of moor and parkland folded into the floor of a valley that winds around the 270 acre estate hidden from the eyes of the unknowing who pass the gatehouse lodge and the entrance to the mile-long driveway which splits the course and leads to the elegant hotel.

Formerly a country retreat for the rich and titled, the Manor is presently owned by 'Principal Hotels' and is currently undergoing an extensive refurbishment programme which aims to retain its former glory whilst providing the high standard of comfort and service you would expect.

Stand on the hotel's terrace and immediately below is the first tee. Down to the right, tucked into a bend of the River Bovey, lies the first green.

The river is a recurring feature of the first eight holes as it threads its way through the valley imposing its presence on virtually every shot played.

After your game relax in the recently re-opened 'Spikes Bar' with its 'pub like' atmosphere serving a selection of hot and cold snacks, plus the usual alcoholic beverages, it is the ideal spot to sit and discuss the finer points of your game.

Another bonus, and part of the formerly well-kept secret, is the elegant former country home that is now the Manor House, a hotel in the grand tradition with oak panelled lounges, lots of open fireplaces, wide sweeping staircases, superb cuisine and impeccable service.

The hotel also offers the additional sports of game and fly fishing, squash, tennis, croquet and a challenging par 3 course.

Add walks through countryside of matchless beauty where hidden villages offer a treasure trove of lovely restaurants and shops in a setting of total tranquillity, and the prospect is one of idyllic holidays you will want to re-live again and again''.

Richard Wade writing in 'Golf Holiday Digest'.

COME AND EXPERIENCE THE SECRET.

THE
MANOR HOUSE
HOTEL & GOLF COURSE
MORETONHAMPSTEAD

Moretonhampstead,
Devon, TQ13 8RE.
Tel: 0647 40355
Fax: 0647 40961

Formerly a 'gentleman's residence' and now a luxurious country house hotel.

The Manor House is situated in 270 acres of private estate. The River Bovey meanders through the picturesque grounds which encompass our challenging par 69, championship golf course, well known as one of the finest inland courses in England.

In addition to the superb golf, other country pursuits available include horse riding, game and fly-fishing, shooting, tennis and croquet. Alternatively, relax at your leisure with a clotted cream Tea in the oak-panelled lounges with their open log fires and enjoy traditional Devonshire hospitality.

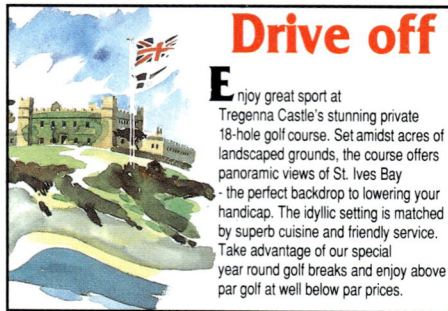

Drive off to a great break at TREGENNA CASTLE

Enjoy great sport at Tregenna Castle's stunning private 18-hole golf course. Set amidst acres of landscaped grounds, the course offers panoramic views of St. Ives Bay - the perfect backdrop to lowering your handicap. The idyllic setting is matched by superb cuisine and friendly service. Take advantage of our special year round golf breaks and enjoy above par golf at well below par prices.

from **£40** DB&B per person

The Hotel's extensive sporting facilities includes 6 tennis courts, heated outdoor swimming pool, bowling green, squash, badminton and much more.

0736 795254

TREGENNA CASTLE, ST. IVES, CORNWALL.

An Oasis of Tranquillity

ETB　　Highly Commended

Superb quality cottages with heated indoor pool, sauna, fitness room, views across Exmoor, yet only a few miles from the sea and a variety of golf courses, including Saunton Sands. Concessionary rates available at nearby driving range and Ilfracombe Golf Club. Free tee reservation service and for riding and fishing. The watermill and barn conversions have central heating, wood stoves, four posters, dishwashers and homemade meals. Bedlinen and maid service included. Open March to November. Short breaks and special golfing rates off season.

Wheel Farm Country Cottages,
Berrydown 15, Combe Martin, Devon EX34 0NT.
Tel: 0271-882100

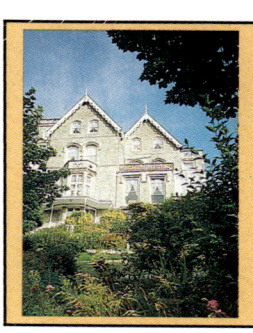

Merlin Court Hotel

Torrs Park, Ilfracombe, North Devon EX34 8AY
AA Listed   RAC Acclaimed   ETB

This beautiful detached hotel has its own large car park and lovely gardens. All rooms have colour TV, radio alarm - most ensuite. Excellent choice of menu. Well stocked bars and games room.

Golf Breaks arranged to suit own requirements. Tee times and tickets arranged from hotel for Ilfracombe, Saunton and Royal North Devon Golf Clubs.

For immediate reservation or colour brochure :
Telephone : 0271 862697

West Ridge, Devon

Seaton EX12 2TA "West Ridge", Harepath Hill, Mrs E. P. Fox (Seaton [0297] 22398).

"West Ridge" bungalow stands on elevated ground above the small coastal town of Seaton. It has 1½ acres of lawns and gardens and enjoys wide panoramic views of the beautiful Axe Estuary and the sea. The picture shows the view from the front garden and, one mile distant, situated on the hill in the background, is Axmouth Golf Course. Also within 30 minutes by car are golf courses at Lyme Regis, Bridport, Sidmouth, Budleigh Salterton and Honiton. This comfortably furnished accommodation is ideally suited for 3 to 5 persons. Available March to October. £125 to £295 weekly (fuel charges included). Full gas c/h. Colour T.V. English Tourist Board Three Keys Commended. S.A.E. for brochure.

golfer lucky enough to play there – and even luckier to be staying at the four-star hotel itself!

Cross the River Tamar into Devon and here on the edge of the Dartmoor Forest is a former private mansion now owned by Crown Hotels. The Manor House Hotel at Moretonhampstead is just 17 miles from the ancient cathedral city of Exeter, providing a luxurious country house hotel atmosphere with its mixed moorland and parkland golf course, regarded as one of the best-kept secrets in the whole south of England.

One could linger here or move on to North Devon to Westward Ho!, Saunton or Ilfracombe where Merlin Court and other hotels make golfers and their families very welcome. But the M5 draws us back towards the east, past Weston, Burnham and Bream in Somerset – look out for the comforts of Batch Farm – and onwards across the Severn to the well-known course and facilities of the St Pierre at Chepstow, one of Britain's major courses.

BATCH FARM COUNTRY HOTEL
LYMPSHAM, NR. WESTON-SUPER-MARE
☎ **Weston-Super-Mare (0934) 750371**
RAC★★ AA★★ Egon Ronay Recommended
Ashley Courtenay Recommended

★ Family run Hotel with friendly atmosphere and excellent food ★ Fully licensed Lounge Bar ★ Own grounds with unlimited parking, spacious lawns ★ All bedrooms en-suite with colour TV, tea/coffee making facilities ★ Golfers most welcome; Reduced terms for children. Credit cards accepted ★ Easy access from M5 motorway.

Weston, Burnham, Brean and Worlebury Golf Courses all within 10 minutes' drive
Weston-Super-Mare Hotels and Restaurants Merit Award

St. Pierre Hotel Golf & Country Club

St. Pierre Park, Chepstow, Gwent NP6 6YA
Tel: 0291 625261   Fax: 0291 629975
Telex: 497562

Inclusive Golf and Leisure Packages – Terms on application

Set within 400 acres of beautiful parkland the Hotel, a 14th century mansion and modern leisure complex, provides accommodation in well equipped and luxurious bedrooms, all ensuite. Guests can enjoy a large variety of leisure facilities including indoor swimming pool, solarium, sauna, jacuzzi, steam room, gymnasium, squash, badminton, tennis, bowling, croquet, snooker and beauty therapy. There are two challenging 18-hole golf courses to play, including the world famous championship 'Old Course'. By March 1994 a multi-million pound refurbishment programme will be completed, making St. Pierre the premier leisure resort in South Wales.

THE GOLF GUIDE 1994

The St Pierre is across the Wye as well as the Severn, and therefore in Wales, where true 'golf' hotels are few. The Coed-y-Mwstwr, however, at Coychurch near Bridgend, is ideally situated to tackle three of the finest courses in Mid-Glamorgan. Within ten miles of this superb 29-roomed country hotel are Royal Porthcawl, Southerndown and the relatively little known Pyle and Kenfig. The latter club is a mixture of links and downland, where the second nine holes meander through huge sand dunes.

'Royal' Porthcawl . . . then 'Royal' St David's near Harlech, then 'Royal' Birkdale at Southport and 'Royal' Lytham, near Blackpool. We are back in the north, looking over Morecombe Bay and the Irish Sea towards the Isle of Man. Here at Castletown Golf Links with its hotel, is another championship course and a popular family holiday centre.

Back to the Severn, and not far from St Pierre but looking out to the Cotswolds, is the woodland and parkland pleasure of the par-70 course at the Gloucester Hotel

---

Coed-y-Mwstwr Hotel

COYCHURCH, NR. BRIDGEND, MID GLAMORGAN, SOUTH WALES

★ *General Manager: Mr. Philip Thomas* ★

Three generations of family and 100 years of history combine to provide Coed-y-Mwstwr's guests with an ideal base for a Golfing Break in South Wales. 27 superbly appointed Guest Rooms and two Suites, plus a Guide Listed Restaurant and the benefits of an excellent cellar ensure that you are prepared for the challenges of the 14 courses that are only 20 minutes away.

*Reservations (0656) 860621 Fax: (0656) 863122
or through Johansens Room Service*

CASTLETOWN GOLF LINKS HOTEL

FORT ISLAND · DERBYHAVEN · ISLE OF MAN

TELEPHONE: 0624 822201
FAX: 0624 824633

* Superb 18 hole Championship Links Course
* Luxurious on-course hotel
* Excellent Banquet and Conference facilities
* Sauna, Solarium, Swimming Pool, Snooker Room with 2 Matchroom tables
* FREE MEMBERSHIP with immediate access to the Palace Hotel Casino with admission to Toffs Night Club, in nearby Douglas

Best Western WORLDWIDE HOTELS

The Tytherington Club
Macclesfield, Cheshire SK10 2JP

Magnificent 6750 yard, par 72 championship golf course in beautiful parkland setting. Headquarters of the Women Professional Golfers' European Tour and venue for the Ladies English Open.

Private dining and bar facilities, superb Society dining, gourmet restaurant, all day bar and golfers' snacks. Visitors very welcome; Societies and Company days by prior arrangement, Country Club facilities include pool, health and beauty, sauna, steam, gym, squash, tennis, bowls and snooker. Clay shoot by arrangement.

Green Fees: Societies – £22.00 per round, £33.00 per day
Visitors – £25 per round, £35 per week-day. Golf Carts and Trollies available.

Telephone: 0625 434562   **Fax: 0625 611076**

YOU'LL FIND US MORE THAN ACCOMMODATING

A challenging course designed by Peter Alliss and Clive Clark, complemented by superb facilities, at prices that will only add to your enjoyment. Visitors, Societies and Company Days welcome.
0253 838866

VILLAGE
hotel & leisure club
BLACKPOOL

18 Hole Championship Standard Golf Course, Floodlit Driving Range, 21m Swimming Pool, Tennis, Squash, Toning Salon, Gym, Aerobics Studio, Spa, Steam Room, Sauna.

There's More than Golf at Gloucester

Excellent golfing facilities are just one reason why the Gloucester Hotel and Country Club is well worth a visit – but there are many more attractions for the whole family.

Set in over 200 acres of beautiful Cotswold countryside, this modern hotel has 117 luxury bedrooms. An investment of over £3.5 million has ensured it offers a unique combination of sporting and leisure facilities including ski-ing, snooker, swimming, squash and tennis. With so much on offer, your golfing break could well turn into a family holiday.

For the keen golfer the 6,127 yard par 70, 18 hole course features a strategically laid out bunker formation. The natural hazards – trees, copses, small lakes and a variety of hillside undulations test all golfing skills.

The 9 hole par 3 course appeals to those who don't have time for a full round of golf, and the 12 bay floodlit driving range is always available for practising your swing.

Catering for all levels of golfing skills, tailored courses and special breaks are available, with tuition from the Club's 3 resident professionals.

For those learning the game, the residential beginners golf instruction week covers basic techniques, discussion of rules and etiquette by the experts, and, for fun, concludes with a competition on the 9 hole course.

Away from the fairways, members of the whole family may wish to try out the premier dry ski slopes in England – and the excellent "après-ski" facilities at the new Ski Lodge. Perhaps a game of tennis or squash for the more energetic, or chalk your cues for a game of snooker or pool. Warm and welcoming water attractions include an exciting leisure pool, complete with rapids, spa pool, steam room, sauna and jacuzzi to provide that period of relaxation.

Not only catering for leisure breaks, the Hotel has extensive conference facilities ranging from rooms for select confidential business meetings to a full scale delegation of 150 people. The Redwell Restaurant, a popular venue for business lunches offers haute cuisine standards and an extensive wine cellar.

Should you wish to make the most of your stay in this most attractive area, Gloucester boasts an excellent shopping centre, many surrounding sites of historic interest and scenic walking routes in the Cotswolds. Reception staff are fully informed on all seasonal activities in the area.

The complex enjoys easy access from the M5 motorway, and is just 1½ miles from the City Centre.

The Gloucester Hotel and Country Club is a member of the Jarvis Hotel Group.

A golfing break for people who hate golf.

Firstly, the bad news. At the Gloucester Hotel & Country Club, set among 280 acres of the Cotswolds you'll find a superb, if testing, 18-hole par 70 golf course, plus a pleasing 9-hole course, floodlit driving range and a well stocked shop.

But the good news is that this luxurious hotel also boasts a magnificent new leisure complex, complete with superb pool, whirl-pools, steam room, sauna and solarium.

Not to mention squash, twin tennis courts and a fully-equipped supervised gym.

Of course, all 117 bedrooms are appointed to the highest standards and our 'Redwell' à la carte restaurant can more than cater for the gourmet in you.

So whether golf is the love or bane of your life, call us on (0452) 525653 for more details about our great value short stay breaks.

GLOUCESTER HOTEL AND COUNTRY CLUB

Robinswood Hill, Gloucester GL4 9EA. Fax (0452) 307212.   Jarvis Hotels and Country Club. Less than two miles from Gloucester City, the Country Club is close to the M5 which leads into literally the "Heart of England" and the golf course which brought back Britain's pride in golf just a few years ago. It was at the Belfry, just outside Birmingham, that Tony Jacklin led the UK and European Team to victory in the Ryder Cup in 1989.

The Belfry is not a club, but a golf hotel, part of the De Vere group, and can be justly regarded as "famous". As well as the par 73 Brabazon, a less testing and shorter course, the Derby, is available to vary the play. To play the Ryder Cup course is an experience one should not miss. Teeing off at the 390-yard ninth requires an accurate shot to the middle of the fairway or slightly right to make the pitch over the lake on to the green, otherwise a watery end is a distinct possibility.

Also a De Vere hotel is the Belton

Abbey Park Golf & Country Club Hotel
Abbey Park, Dagnell End Road, Redditch, Worcs
Tel 0527 584140   Fax 0527 65872

Set within 230 acres of parkland and yet close to the M42 motorway with easy access to the National Exhibition Centre, Abbey Park provides the ideal Leisure/Conference venue. Our 31 luxuriously appointed rooms all have private facilities; there is an 18 hole championship golf course, a Leisure Suite comprising Swimming Pool, Spa Bath, Sauna, Solarium, Steam Room and Gymnasium. With a choice of 5 purpose built conference suites for 5-50 delegates.

ACCOMMODATION:		ROOM FACILITIES:		MEETING ROOMS: Seating Capacity			
				Room/Suite	Theatre Style	Banquet	Exhib.Sq.M
Twins	18	Phone	All	Westminster	60	40	82
Doubles	14	TV	All	Rievaulx	3		
Private Bath/Shower	All	Free Video channel	All	Tintern	10	–	26
Total	32	Tea/Coffee	All	Bordesley	15	–	26
(incl. 2 executive suites)		Hair dryers	All	Modern	15	–	22
		Trouser Press	All				

The Belfry Hotel, near Birmingham, venue of the 1993 Ryder Cup.

HAWKSTONE PARK
HOTEL, GOLF, HISTORIC PARK & FOLLIES

Golf Centre of Excellence in the Centre of the UK

10th Fairway Hawkstone Course – Unique Setting

'Where Sandy Lyle learned his game'

* New Golf Centre, complete with Golf Shop, Indoor Video Room and the Terrace Restaurant.
* The Hawkstone Centre, an 18 hole parkland golf course.
* New Weston Course (**Brian Huggett Design**), 9 holes to open 1st July 1994.
* New Practice Range facility now open.
* New Golf Academy (5 hole, par 3) opens Spring 1994.
* Corporate events are our speciality.
* Individual tuition, group coaching programmes and Golf School. Head Golf Professional – **Keith Williams**.
* **Hawkstone Park** is situated 14 miles north of Shrewsbury on the A49, and is 30 minutes from M54 and 40 minutes from M6.
* Golf Societies and green fees welcome.

New Golf Centre

Please write or telephone (0939) 200611 for a brochure.
Hawkstone Park Golf Centre, Weston-under-Redcastle, Shrewsbury, Shropshire SY4 5UY.

THE GOLF GUIDE 1994

Woods Hotel and Country Club near Grantham in Lincolnshire, whose two 18-hole courses are always a challenge. Lincolnshire has one of England's finest inland courses at Woodhall Spa and the nearby **Petwood House** has long provided the best of country house hotel hospitality for visiting golfers.

Yorkshire boasts courses too numerous to mention and offers a great variety of golfing experiences, from parkland to moorland. Further north is the 68-bedroomed Lumley Castle Hotel, adjacent to the Chester-le-Street Golf Club and within striking distance of County Durham's finest at Brancepeth Castle. The Great North Road links the hotel with the championship Northumberland golf course where most of the holes are inside the Newcastle Race Course.

Travel northwards to Bamburgh, where overlooking the castle, the golf course can be compared to a mini-Turnberry, including a hole where the tee shot is played out over the sea. For an evening out, or an oasis of shopping the City of Newcastle is fast becoming the best in Europe.

For those seeking something completely different, it must be the Old Thorns Golf Course at Liphook in Hampshire. One of Britain's newer courses, it was designed by Dave Thomas and John Harris and built under the

Sea view golf at Ganton, near Scarborough.

PETWOOD HOUSE HOTEL

A unique Country House Hotel, famous for its beautiful gardens and woodland covering 30 acres.

5 excellent golf courses within 30 minutes drive and 1½ miles from Woodhall Spa's Championship course.

★ 46 luxurious bedrooms, including four posters   ★ Superb Restaurant   ★ Snooker Room
★ Putting Green   ★ Croquet   ★ Golf Practice Area

PETWOOD HOUSE HOTEL
Woodhall Spa, Lincolnshire LN10 6QF
Telephone: (0526) 352411   Fax: (0526) 353473

HIGHLY COMMENDED

What will your wife do next time you want to play golf all weekend?

If you quiver at the thought, fear not. The Belton Woods Hotel, Lincolnshire, has the answer.

As sister hotel to the world famous Belfry, it aims to please both the serious golfer and his non-golfing partner.

So as well as having two superb championship length golf courses, it offers luxurious Leisure Club facilities such as a sauna, spa pool, heated indoor pool, sunbeds, beauty salon, tennis, aerobics and, of course, archery.

Going anywhere else could be more than your life's worth.

Belton Woods Hotel. **Tel: 0476 593200.**

DE VERE HOTELS

De Vere House, Chester Rd, Daresbury, Warrington, Cheshire WA4 4BN. **Tel: 0925 265050.**

THERE'S A FAIR WAY TO PLAY AT OLD THORNS

(You only pay when you play – no membership fees)

Splendid golf in superb surroundings on our challenging 18 hole par 72 Championship Course

Free Colour Brochure available on request

- Thorns à la carte Restaurant with English and French cuisine.
- Nippon Kan authentic Japanese Restaurant.
- 32 en-suite Guest Rooms, Direct Dial Phones, Teletext Televisions.
- Heated Indoor Swimming Pool, Sauna, Solarium, Shiatsu Massage and Tennis Courts.
- *Ideal location for:* Wedding Receptions and Functions, Business Meetings and Conferences, Golfing Holidays and Weekend Breaks.

KOSAIDO OLD THORNS
GOLF COURSE • HOTEL • RESTAURANTS

Longmoor Road, Liphook, Hampshire GU30 7PE
Tel: Liphook (0428) 724555   Fax: 0428 725036

Old Thorns Golf Course, Hotel and Restaurants complex is a unique combination of old and new creating a country estate appeal with the traditional beauty of the old tile hung farmhouse providing blazing log fires in winter and terraces which overlook the magnificent 200 acres of Hampshire downs. The regal oaks, beeches and Scotch pines have been painstakingly conserved and the superb course is enhanced by the creation of water features fed from natural water springs.

Our testing 18-hole championship course provides a fine challenge for the enthusiastic golfer. The fairways wind their way through parkland, over lakes and streams and some holes cut through the pines or over the heathered slopes. A fleet of 30 golf cars has a track carefully incorporated within the contours of the fairways. Mid-week enjoyment for societies and golfing weekends is ensured by a driving range and practice green on hand for the individual golfer and adds up to perfect golf for everyone.

Our resident teaching professional will assess, encourage and monitor golfing skills. Everything needed to play is available on hire from the Pro's shop which carries a very comprehensive selection of golfing accessories. A wide range of brand name items are stocked as well as a variety of prizes for societies.

The tranquillity and peace of Old Thorns is complemented by the elegant new Japanese Centre carefully developed to blend naturally into the background of the undulating countryside thus cleverly uniting Eastern and Western culture.

Within one hour's drive of London, Heathrow and Gatwick airports, Old Thorns can provide the perfect venue for any business or social function.

Holiday golf at Meyrick Park, Bournemouth.

direction of golf commentator, Peter Alliss, one of the original directors at Old Thorns. In 1984 the complex was bought by the London Kosaido Company, a subsidiary of a Japanese multi-national corporation.

Even nearer to the capital city, lies Selsdon Park at Sanderstead, South Croydon, set amid 200 acres of green rolling hills on the edge of the Surrey countryside. Selsdon Park, a mere 30 minutes away from London's shops and theatre-land, combines a traditional country house weekend with the facilities of an eighteen-hole championship golf course, all to the highest standards and amenities of an international hotel.

A golfing holiday in Kent has much to offer, with a mixture of some superb parkland and links courses throughout the county. The most famous must be Royal St Georges on Sandwich Bay, the only course in the South of England where the Open Championship is staged. Situated on the sea front at Westgate Bay, the Ivyside Hotel is within 20 minutes' drive from Sandwich or 15 minutes from the springy turf at North Foreland Golf Club.

For those who would venture beyond the magnetic appeal of such venues as Wentworth, Sunningdale and the like, the courses and golf hotels of East Sussex provide good sport and accommodation in rural surroundings which have much in common with the New Forest further west. As we have seen, the resorts of the west of England are no strangers to golf and none more so than Bournemouth where there are playing opportunities for all grades of golfers from rabbit to 'plus one' and where nineteenth hole and other après-golf facilities are fully provided.

'Where to Play' and 'Where to Stay' for golf in Britain is always likely to be a matter of choice and with more than enough choice to provide a lifetime experience.

IVYSIDE HOTEL

AA ★★ RAC
ETB 👑👑👑👑

Sea Road, Westgate on Sea, Kent   Tel: 0843-831082

Facing the golden sands of St. Mildred's Bay.
The ideal centre for 7 golf courses,
including 2 championship, all within 25 minutes.

1993 Sandwich Open Championship.

Royal St. Georges	SSS 72 – 12 ml	Westgate	SSS 65 – 1 ml
Prince's	SSS 72 – 12 ml	North Foreland	SSS 70 – 5 ml
Royal Cinque Ports	SSS 72 – 17 ml	St. Augustine's	SSS 70 – 6 ml
		Canterbury	SSS 70 – 13 ml

Badminton/tennis courts open all year – 1 ml.
4 Hardcourt tennis courts – ¼ ml.
Riding Stables 4 ml. Gliding and Flying 5 ml.

Hotel facilities:
* Heated indoor pool plus jacuzzi and weights
* Heated outdoor pool and children's pool
* Steam room, sauna, spa, solarium, masseuse
* 2 Squash courts (balconied)
* 72 en-suite rooms, colour TV, satellite, telephones – from £34 pp DB&B
* Conference and seminar suites

Excellent cuisine with extensive wine list, from excellent house wines to chateau bottles. Vegetarian and individual diets.

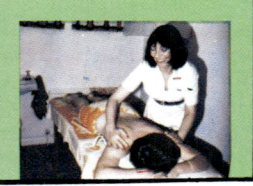

Featured on "WISH YOU WERE HERE".

NIZELS GOLF CLUB

Nizels Lane, Hildenborough, near Tonbridge, Kent TN11 8NX
Telephone: Tonbridge (0732) 833138

Our splendid Georgian Clubhouse complements our superb 18 hole Golf Course which features many water hazards. In addition to golf we have facilities for wedding receptions and private parties, also rooms for business meetings. Golf Societies and Corporate days are most welcome. Our bar and restaurant offer quality service and we are open every day. Breakfast from 7 a.m. Bar snacks at reasonable prices, plus full A La Carte. Why not call round and see the beautifully landscaped gardens with panoramic views and meet our Club Secretary, Tony Fensom for full membership details.

- **6408 yards Par 72**
- **Green Fees from £23**
- **Society/Corporate days**
- **Private Functions Room**
- **Well equipped Pro Shop**
- **Fantastic Club Atmosphere**

Nizels LTD

DALE HILL GOLF HOTEL
TICEHURST, WADHURST, EAST SUSSEX TN5 7DQ

One of England's finest new golfing hotels, complemented by a stunningly beautiful established parkland golf course. Individuals, green fees, societies and corporate business days all receive the warmest of welcomes at Dale Hill, fast becoming the place to be.

Bed, Breakfast and All Day Golf – £60 per person per night

- **6,066 Yds Par 69**
- **Green Fees £20/£25**
- **Society Days £45**
- **Executive Days £60**
- **Swimming Pool**
- **Most Activities/Sports**

Tel: 0580 200112
UNLIMITED GOLF

Valderrama, near Gibraltar, a championship course worthy of the Ryder Cup.

Holiday Golf in Spain

by Michael Gedye

COSTA DEL GOLF – no country in Europe has become more closely associated with holiday golf than Spain, particularly along its south-eastern coast bordering the Mediterranean. Fertile river valleys running down from a craggy mountain backdrop to sundrenched sandy beaches, cork oak and orange groves, rolling slopes of umbrella pine – all have played their part in turning a rural coastline into a golfing mecca for the ever-increasing demands of northern Europe. First the British, then more recently Germans, Swedes and many others have discovered this golfing treasure and their winter place in the sun.

In common with its near neighbour France, there has been golf in Spain since before the first World War; a limited number of clubs catering to an élite and wealthy local patronage. Unlike France, however, the attractions of Spain as a tourist destination only emerged with the advent of inexpensive charter flights in the 1950's. The country offered the promise of a tan (even in winter), affordable prices and a land rich in culture, history and colour. Northern Europe responded, especially the British, and the development of resort golf, specifically designed for the holiday visitor, soon followed.

In no other country in Europe has there been such an extensive development of facilities targeted at foreign players. Despite the international success of professionals like Ballesteros and Olazabal, the game is still only played by a relatively small proportion of Spaniards, with members' clubs mostly located close to major conurbations.

In contrast, the major share of new course construction during the last twenty years has been in popular holiday destinations, mainly along the Costa del Sol in Andalucia and Majorca. In a country where greensward and regular rainfall are not natural commodities, huge investment has been made with some of the world's most famous golf architects creating courses using the very latest techniques of construction and agronomy. Probably nowhere outside the United States, with its verdant golfing necklaces bordering Florida and the Carolinas, have so many top-class courses, manicured to perfection, been available to the holiday visitor.

However, the attractive location along southern Spain and the rising tide of players from the newer golfing nations of Germany and Sweden in particular, created situations in the mid-eighties none could have foreseen. Courses became overcrowded, green fees rose to unpalatable levels and, inevitably, some players started to look elsewhere. I am pleased to report that the situation is now well in hand. Even more courses have been opened, green fees have returned to acceptable levels and the future for holiday golf in Spain looks assured.

There is no doubting the pedigree of the golf available. Two World Cups have been staged on the Costa del Sol, countless Spanish and other Opens played on the courses included in this edition. There is now even a bid to stage the 1997 Ryder Cup at the showpiece setting of Valderrama, one of the most westerly courses almost in the shadow of Gibraltar. Many are the layouts with claims to championship calibre – created by such world-renowned names as Robert Trent Jones, Jack Nicklaus, Ron Kirby and Gary Player as well as the home-grown talents of Javier Arana and Pepe Gancedo. Demanding, immaculate, genuine tests for the competitive golfer with a wealth of choice on which to examine his skills.

But there are also many courses, equally attractive, which will cater to the less demanding games of higher handicappers, offering true holiday golf in delightful settings. All the courses we have chosen in this initial selection fall within the coastal crescent which runs from Cadiz, past Gibraltar and up round the Mediterranean shoreline to Valencia. On similar latitude, we have also included Majorca. A good variety of fine courses, often in great settings, all with full facilities and kept in superb condition.

Holiday Golf in Portugal

by Michael Gedye

THERE IS far more to Portugal than golf in the sun, just as there is far more golf than most intending visitors realise. In a country only a short flight south, rich in culture and history, there are more than thirty courses to play in a wide variety of locations. Ever since a group of expatriate port wine shippers established a links course near Oporto more than a century ago, the game has become established in some of the most delightful settings one may ever play in, with most in or close to popular holiday locations.

For the visiting golfer, the country has much in its favour. Bordering the Atlantic, just north of the African continent, it has

Val do Lobo, near Faro in the Algarve.

the benefit of year-round sunshine, temperate sea breezes and a wide range of topography. From inland mountains and wooded valleys, gently rolling slopes planted with fig, pomegranate, mimosa and eucalyptus or the natural beauty of craggy cliffs and broad white sand beaches – golf has been created throughout the land and its islands to captivate the holiday visitor. Add in some of the freshest fish and superb wines, a panoply of glories from the past, native charm and a friendly welcome – who could ask for more.

In the north, where it all began, three courses are found near Oporto by the sea in a region famous for some of the country's best wines. There is also a course at the mountain spa resort of Vidago.

Move south to Lisbon and the environs of the capital offer a golfing feast, as well as all the charms of a sophisticated and elegant city. West lies the internationally famous course at Estoril, plus three others including the new and palatial complex of Penha Longa. Drive south across the Tagus river and the Costa Azul offers three more, cut through pine forest, vineyards and along a tree-lined coastal sand bar. Two of them, the Portuguese Country Club at Aroeira and the splendid test at Troia, may well be the best two courses in the country.

For most overseas golfers, Portugal means the Algarve and there are certainly a wealth of courses along this fertile southern coast. Between Faro and Cape Vincent there are no less than seventeen courses in play, with more planned. Golf for all running along white sand beaches, across jagged ochre clifftops, greenly winding past umbrella pine, almond and cork oak or soaring up to distant mountain views. Newcomers include a fine 18 holes by Ronald Fream at Carvoeiro, its strategic layout winding through rolling olive groves, and the Pinheiros Altos course just west of the Quinta do Lago/San Lorenzo complex, which combines an elevated pine-clad front nine with the hazards of a low-lying lake bordered return. Within a two hour drive, there is more golf here than you can ever hope to play on any holiday.

Further afield, the Azores islands offer golf while on the semi-tropical isle of Madeira, two fine new courses at altitude have added a new dimension to this holiday garden location.

HOTEL PALACIO
Estoril

Rua do Parque 2765 ESTORIL/PORTUGAL (near Lisbon)
Tel: (010-351)-1-4680400; Telex 12757 PLAGE
Fax: (010-351)-1-4684867

The HOTEL PALACIO . . . a modern symbol of luxury and comfort in the tradition of the Old World . . . 200 rooms and suites of quiet elegance . . . Conference and Meeting Rooms, plus full convention facilities . . . swimming pool in spacious garden . . . magnificent beach . . . special privileges for international championship golf course . . . 18 clay tennis courts, nearby . . . Gambling Casino.

Golf in the French Alps, at Chamonix.

Holiday Golf in France

by Michael Gedye

HOLIDAY GOLF abroad is not a new phenomenon. Just as France has provided us with many of the better things in life such as haute cuisine, grand cru wines, great literature and a culture of romance, so our better-heeled late-Victorian forebears found summer solace on fairways facing us across the Channel. A further group, well-connected or socially mobile, would pack their clubs and exchange the chills of winter for the sunshine of Biarritz in the south-west of Cannes in the south-east. Long before the advent of package golf in the sun, France led the world as an overseas holiday golfing destination, albeit for an elite minority.

The British took golf to France initially with the formation of a club at Pau in 1856 and for many years the game remained the preserve of a privileged minority, a 'snob' activity for the rich.

HÔTEL DU PALAIS
Biarritz

Sister city with Augusta, Georgia

1 avenue de l'Impératrice, 64200 BIARRITZ France
Tel: (010 33) 59.41.64.00 Fax: (010 33) 59.24.36.43
London office: 071-630 1704

Enjoy the dignified luxury of this prestigious hotel on the Basque coast, the 'Mecca' of golf in France.

Within easy reach of six of France's leading courses, catering for all levels of golf, the Hotel du Palais offers the finest facilities for golfers and their families. Deluxe rooms, including 21 suites, all with mini-bar, multi-channel TV and direct-dial phone. Heated seawater pool, bars, restaurants, boutiques and hairdresser. Secure car-park. Tennis, riding and Casino nearby. Magnificent sea-front location.

PART OF THE CONCORDE HOTELS GROUP AND A MEMBER OF **THE LEADING HOTELS OF THE WORLD**

Latitudes Hotels*** on site

LATITUDES VALESCURE	LATITUDES LACANAU	LATITUDES MIDI-PYRENÉES	LATITUDES ARC 1800
GOLF	GOLF	GOLF	Hôtel du Golf
ESTEREL	DE L'ARDILOUSE	TOULOUSE-SEILH	GOLF DES ARCS
Complete golf accomodations	Complete golf accomodations	Complete golf accomodations	Complete golf accomodations
(010 33) 94 82 42 42	(010 33) 56 03 23 15	(010 33) 62 13 14 15	(010 33) 79 41 43 43

Latitudes
HOTELS & RESORTS

(010 33) 42 66 01 02

CÔTE D'AZUR	ATLANTIQUE	MIDI-PYRENÉES	SAVOIE	CAMARGUE	ARDÈCHE
18 holes	18 holes	two 18 holes	18 holes	6 holes	3 holes
9 holes			6 holes		

Yours best memories are waiting for you

Today, the situation could hardly be more different. In what can only be termed a golfing explosion, the last half-dozen years have seen the country transformed. Led by rising domestic interest in the sport and a shrewd awareness of its tourist potential, France has become the fastest growing country in the world of golf. There are now over four hundred and sixty places to play, more than in any other European country apart from England – a broad golfing canvas across a country rich in interest, much of it specifically geared to the visitor.

For the holiday golfer, such rapid expansion has brought bonus benefits. New clubs are normally built to the most modern specifications, with a well-equipped clubhouse (remember this is France) with superb restaurant and wine list as well as courses that are manicured and watered to very high standards. Golf membership is not cheap so top quality facilities can be expected as the norm. Green fees, however, are decidedly competitive, running at a general average of £17 to £25, much less than in some other vaunted holiday golfing destinations. A further advantage for the visitor is that, since most domestic players are beginners (such has been the speed of growth of the game), many will be hard at it having lessons on the practice ground and the course will be relatively free to play. Empty fairways in great condition at reasonable cost – the touring holiday player has it made.

Many of the country's most attractive courses, those in key resort locations, have joined together in an initiative started by the French Golf Federation and the French Ministry of Tourism. All are pledged to maintain the highest possible standards and offer a warm welcome to visitors. Highlighted under the banner of "France Golf International", this represents a landmark

---

Between sea and lake with the Pyrenees mountains as a background, in the exclusive setting of the Domaine du Golf de Saint-Cyprien

Le Mas d'Huston
GOLF HOTEL & SELF-CATERING APARTMENTS

Golf de Saint-Cyprien
66750 Saint-Cyprien Plage
68.21.01.71 *Fax:* **68.21.11.33**
or from March 1st 1994:
68.37.63.63 *Fax:* **68.37.64.64**

A luxury hotel with 50 air-conditioned rooms, large and spacious, decorated with a personal touch. Shops, bars and restaurants by the pool or overlooking the golf course.

Studios or 2 and 3 roomed apartments for comfortable self-catering.

After golf, enjoy the two swimming-pools, floodlit tennis, water sports on the private lake . . . or simply the peace of this privileged situation.

Short Breaks, Conferences, Golfing Holidays, *for the Connoisseur!*

Hôtel de la Plage

2 avenue de la mer,
85690 Notre-Dame-de-Monts,
Vendée, France
Telephone: 51 58 83 09

The hotel borders a sandy beach facing ile d'Yeu and ile de Noirmoutier. Some rooms have balconies overlooking the ocean. The restaurant offers a gastronomic variety of seafoods. Conference and function facilities. Enjoy a wide choice of leisure activities, from tennis and riding to windsurfing and sailing. This pleasant seaside resort has much to entertain younger holidaymakers while the adults enjoy a challenging round of golf. Special accommodation for golfers including green fees. Sea water therapy clinic nearby. Facilities for disabled guests.

in the world of tourist golf and a guarantee worth taking advantage of.

One of the attractions of golf in France is the wide variety of location, from coastal duneland to snow-capped mountain valleys, from rolling pineforest to sun-soaked southern vineyards. You can play cliff-top holes in Normandy, just across the Channel, or explore the rustic charms of rural Brittany. Further south, golf follows the silver ribbon of the Loire and its classic chateaux before you drive on to the rich pleasures of Aquitaine and the mixture of seaside and pinewood that runs from Bordeaux to Biarritz. Inland, you can wonder at the green fairways dwarfed by mountains in Savoy or the craggy colours of pastoral Provence. Historic or modern, there is a feast of golf for all, highly accessible either by car ferry or short flight.

Two recently opened facilities encapsulate the flavour of France. At Chateau des Vigiers Golf & Country Club, just east of Bordeaux, a Donald Steel designed course undulates around a classic chateau hotel, replete with stately trees, orchards and its own wine to enjoy at the 19th. In the south-east, Golf de Frègate at Bandol offers 27 holes carved by Ronald Fream from dramatic rolling headland overlooking the Mediterranean. Players even drive across the established Fregate vineyards at one hole, an anticipation of clubhouse delights to come.

The new course at Bandol, overlooking the Mediterranean.

The Ryder Cup 1993

by Jane Carter

The long-awaited Ryder Cup by Johnnie Walker in September 1993 may not have provided the result hoped for, but the true spirit of the contest and Samuel Ryder continues to live on.

Top: Nick Faldo, Open Champion and top of the rankings.

CLOSE but not close enough for the European team when they narrowly failed to win back the Ryder Cup by Johnnie Walker at The Belfry. Bernard Gallacher's gallant dozen gave their all over three days of magnificent golf played in the spirit for which the biennial contest is so famous in sporting circles.

Enormous crowds were taken from the peaks of ecstasy to the troughs of despair as first Europe forged ahead but then saw the gold trophy slip from their grasp as they crumbled in the final day's singles matches.

Nick Faldo, one of the mainstays of the European side, said: "We were a great team with a great team spirit but the Americans did a helluva good job today. Some guys had a tough time at the end but if you give your best – and everyone gave 100 per cent this week – then it's okay."

Hopes were higher than could have been imagined at the end of the first day when Europe took an overall one point lead. The mornings foursomes – traditionally the Achilles Heel of the European side – were halved two points each with Nick Faldo and Colin Montgomerie victorious against Ray Floyd and Fred Couples and Ian Woosnam and Bernhard Langer triumphant over Paul Azinger and Payne Stewart. The Montgomerie and Faldo partnership was every bit as good as it had promised to be and it was obvious that these two scalps were to be highly prized by the United States team.

The real disappointment was the failure of Jose Maria Olazabal and Seve Ballesteros to win their match against Tom Kite and David Love III and so end an unbeaten run in Ryder Cup foursomes matches.

It might have been an ominous warning, for the "Spanish Armada" – as they were nicknamed by the Americans – had been drafted in as wild cards by

Below: Ballesteros and Olazabal, Spanish favourites and a strong partnership.

Bernard Gallacher in order to provide the inspiration factor for which they have been famous in past encounters.

Europe reigned supreme in the afternoon's fourballs with Ian Woosnam and rookie Peter Baker beating Jim Gallacher and Lee Janzen by one hole and Seve Ballesteros and Jose Maria Olazabal repairing the damage of their morning's encounter by beating Love and Kite by the convincing margin of 4&3.

Severe fog had delayed the start by more than two hours and so the Faldo/Montgomerie pairing ran out of light before they could complete their match against Azinger and Couples. The score stood at four points to three in Europe's favour overnight with the final fourball facing an early start to play the 18th hole and complete their tussle. Montgomerie and Couples decided it was to be between Faldo and Azinger when they both lost their balls in the water. Azinger made certain of his four but a weak first putt by Faldo left him facing a 15-footer to halve the match and gain a valuable half point. The roar when it went in reverberated throughout the Brabazon course and Faldo's face said it all. "What a putt, what a man," was all Montgomerie could utter as the two hugged each other in celebration.

But there was still much work to be done. With the scoreline so close, Gallacher's men turned their attention to the morning foursomes in an effort to increase that margin. And increase it they did with one of their best performances in recent Ryder Cup history, winning three points out of four. Only the rookie partnership of Peter Baker and Barry Lane failed to win their match against Ray Floyd and Payne Stewart. The Spanish Armada sank the hopes of Love and Kite, while Faldo and Montgomerie beat Wadkins and Pavin and Langer and Woosnam beat Couples and Azinger.

There were now three points in it and all over the course the crowds were celebrating and cheering a magnificent European performance. The European team's spirits were soaring but in the afternoon fourballs it all began to go horribly wrong. Seve Ballesteros and Bernhard Langer had both requested to be dropped so they could rest. The rookies Constantino Rocca and Joakim Haeggman therefore found themselves in the gladiator's arena for the first time. It turned out to be a baptism of fire as James and Rocca could not contain the magician Corey Pavin who, together with Jim Gallagher Jnr, dished out a 5&4 thrashing. Jose Maria Olazabal and Joakim Haeggman held on longer before succumbing to Floyd and Stewart by 2&1 while only Ian Woosnam and Peter Baker gave the Europeans any hope with their 6&5 win over Couples and Azinger. It was a superb performance, particularly by Baker who rose to the challenge of his first Ryder Cup and is undoubtedly a new star for future teams.

Peter Baker, a successful Ryder Cup newcomer.

The crucial match, which in the post mortem was seen by the Americans as the turning point, featured Faldo and Montgomerie against John Cook and Chip Beck. Neither of the Americans had played all week and their rookie partnership was greeted by raised eyebrows in some quarters. The European duo were playing as confidently as ever but when Cook holed out at the first to match Faldo's birdie it was clear it was going to be another tough match. The European pairing on which so much depended led out the fourballs and were a hole up after five. From then on, it was downhill all the way to the 18th where, at one down, Faldo's birdie putt for a half point shied away from the hole leaving the Americans with an important scalp. Captain Tom Watson later said: "It was a turning point. Our spirits soared thanks to John and Chip's victory. The whole evening was a memorable one with fun, laughter and revelry all stemming from that one point."

There was little revelry in the European team room and even less when Bernard Gallacher broke the news that Scotland's Sam Torrance was unlikely to tee up the next day because of a toe infection. Torrance had been conspicuous by his absence both on the course and on the practice ground, losing his only match in Friday's foursomes with Mark James. The American captain Tom Watson now had the invidious decision of placing a name in the envelope of the team member who would step down if Torrance was unable to play. In the event Torrance was not fit and Lanny Wadkins stepped down as "the man in the envelope". It had been at his own request, preferring to allow all those who had qualified as of right rather than as a wild card to play their singles match.

The singles draw caused great discussion as Gallacher spread his experienced players throughout the field, finishing with Nick Faldo who found

Ian Woosnam, always a worthy competitor.

himself paired against Paul Azinger. Theirs promised to be a magnificent battle and many believed that yet another Ryder Cup encounter would come down to the final holes with the singles on the final day – and what two better players to leave it to. Sadly, they never had their chance as Europe's poor record in Ryder Cup singles continued.

In the early stages it seemed as though Europe might just pull it off. Ian Woosnam led from the front and at one point he, Barry Lane, Colin Montgomerie and Peter Baker were all ahead in their matches. In the lower half of the draw Europe were struggling. An unfit Langer, the out-of-form Olazabal, James and Ballesteros were seeing their American opponents steadily moving out of reach. Glances at the scoreboard – despite strict instructions from both captains not to scoreboard-watch – revealed Europe's fortunes starting to sway. Woosnam could only manage a half against Couples while Lane, who had at one time been three holes up, lost the 14th, 15th and 16th to Chip Beck. It all came down to the 18th and a poor drive by Lane found the bunker while his second, inevitably, found the water and the Americans received an unexpected bonus of one point they had surely written off. Colin Montgomerie and Peter Baker provided

USA:
Lanny Wadkins; Tom Kite; Raymond Floyd; Payne Stewart; Paul Azinger; Chip Beck; Fred Couples; Corey Pavin; Lee Janzen; John Cook; Davis Love III; Jim Gallagher Jnr.

Europe:
Severiano Ballesteros; Nick Faldo; Bernhard Langer; Jose Maria Olazabal; Ian Woosnam; Mark James; Sam Torrance; Colin Montgomerie; Constantino Rocca; Barry Lane; Peter Baker; Joakim Haeggman.

THE GOLF GUIDE 1994

RYDER CUP RESULTS
A Reminder

YEAR	VENUE	RESULT	
1927	Worcester, Mass.	9½ : 3½	USA
1929	Moortown, Leeds	7 : 5	GB
1931	Columbus, Ohio	9 : 3	USA
1933	Southport & Ainsdale	6½ : 5½	GB
1935	Ridgewood, NJ	9 : 3	USA
1937	Southport & Ainsdale	8 : 4	USA
1947	Portland, Oregon	11 : 1	USA
1949	Ganton, N. Yorks	7 : 5	USA
1951	Pinehurst, N. Carolina	9½ : 2½	USA
1953	Wentworth, Surrey	6½ : 5½	USA
1955	USA	8 : 4	USA
1957	Lindrick, S. Yorks	7½ : 4½	GB
1959	Eldorado, California	8½ : 3½	USA
1961	Lytham St. Annes, Lancs.	13 : 8	USA
1963	Atlanta, Georgia	20 : 6	USA
1965	Birkdale, Merseyside	18 : 11	USA
1967	Houston, Texas	21 : 6	USA
1969	Birkdale, Merseyside	13 : 13	–
1971	St. Louis, Missouri	16 : 11	USA
1973	Muirfield, Edinburgh	16 : 10	USA
1975	Laurel Valley, Pa.	18 : 8	USA
1977	Lytham St. Annes, Lancs.	12 : 7	USA
1979	Greenbier, West Va.	16 : 10	USA
1981	Walton Heath, Surrey	17 : 8	USA
1983	PGA National, Florida	21 : 11	USA
1985	The Belfry, W. Midlands	15 : 10	GB/EUR.
1987	Muirfield, Ohio	13 : 11	GB/EUR.
1989	The Belfry, W. Midlands	14 : 14	–
1991	Kiawah Island, S. Carolina	14½ : 13½	USA
1993	The Belfry, W. Midlands	15 : 13	USA

some hope with wins over Lee Janzen and Corey Pavin, while Joakin Haeggman justified Gallacher's faith with victory over John Cook by one hole.

Meanwhile, Ballesteros – at one point five down against Jim Gallagher – finally succumbed by 3&2 while Mark James who had a disappointing Ryder Cup, lost his singles to Payne Stewart by the same margin. Europe needed just two points from the final five matches to clinch victory and it looked as though they would come from Faldo and Rocca. The Italian was one up after 15 but three putts on the 17th for a bogey saw Davis Love pull back to all square. His missed four-footer must have lingered with Rocca as he hit a poor drive down the 18th. His second shot just clambered over the water while Love played the ball pin high on the right edge of the green. Rocca failed to get up and down in two and Davis's face as he holed his putt for a four and win said it all. That crucial point had retained the Cup for the Americans and Europe's only hope rested on a tie.

Olazabal staged a fightback against Floyd, coming from three down to one down playing the last but his hopes disappeared into a watery grave along with those of the European team. Faldo and Azinger were left to fight it out for pride's sake, although a hole in one by Faldo at the 14th – only the second in Ryder Cup history – gave the crowd every opportunity to roar. As it was they halved thanks to an Azinger birdie at the last to leave the scoreline at 15 points to 13 to the USA.

At the closing ceremony Bernard Gallacher bowed to the Americans' superior skill. "We did not lose the Cup, they won it."

In the final analysis the Americans, as their captain Tom Watson said, "had the guts which typifies all our teams. My reaction is one of pride, relief and satisfaction."

More than 30,000 people witnessed each day's play and marvelled at the immense amount of work which had gone into staging this memorable contest. The week got off on a good note when Johnnie Walker announced they would be sponsoring the contest and the PGA Cup matches for a further four years and the PGA unveiled plans for a national training academy at The Belfry.

Everyone is now looking forward to Ryder Cup USA 1995 and good luck to Bernard Gallacher's successor and whoever his team may be!

Publisher's Note

1993 has been a busy year for golf, culminating for the leading professionals, at least, in the Ryder Cup at the Belfry which is also the home of The Professional Golfers' Association. Regardless of such prestige events, however, the work of the club professional goes on, year after year and the strength of the club game in Britain is reflected by the significant number of new entries which you will find in this new edition of *THE GOLF GUIDE: Where to Play/Where to Stay*. Golf in Britain still represents good value for money, especially when costs are compared with some of the areas abroad where golfing facilities are being developed more with an eye to the purely commercial advantages of the sport than any great feeling for the game itself. Fortunately it is possible to reach a compromise and sensible developers know that their business is impossible without the support of the men and women for whom golf is regular week-to-week activity and are careful not to out-price this market.

Many golfers love to travel and to challenge courses and conditions which are a contrast to their home clubs. This new edition of *THE GOLF GUIDE* now features a selection of holiday courses in Spain (including Majorca) as well as up-dated entries for France and Portugal. There are certainly golfing attractions there but for choice, variety and convenience the appeal of the 'home' countries cannot be denied.

As well as new clubs and courses in Britain, we are pleased to welcome a wider range of accommodation choices for golfers, their families, friends and colleagues. Many of these advertising entries are recommended by golfers themselves and we are always happy to receive comments and new recommendations.

Enquiries and Bookings. It is quite normal to confirm a booking in writing and also to receive written confirmation – and a receipt for any advance payment. You should check prices and also any special requirements.

Cancellations. Any booking is a form of contract for both parties. If you have to cancel, try to give maximum notice. With reasonable notice the hotel should normally refund any advance payment but on short notice a full refund is not necessarily a legal entitlement.

Complaints. Most owners/managers are anxious to sort out problems on the spot so that you are a satisfied customer. If a problem persists you can get advice from a Citizens' Advice Bureau, Consumers' Association, Trading Standards Office, Tourist Board or indeed your own solicitor.

Serious complaints are unlikely to arise with the kind of accommodation you'll find on our pages. FHG Publications Ltd. do not inspect accommodation and an entry does not imply a firm recommendation. However, most of the advertisers have been recommended or proposed by local golf clubs and have standards which satisfy and in many cases far exceed those expected by inspecting authorities. In addition we will be pleased to hear from you if you have a serious complaint and although we cannot act as intermediaries or accept responsibility for our advertisers, we will record the complaint and follow it up with the advertiser in question.

We are grateful to all Club Secretaries and Club Professionals who assist in the supply and revision of entries and to the PGA for editorial support. We are happy to hear from any Club which for some reason does not already have an entry. We also thank accommodation proprietors and managers for their support and we welcome suggestions from golfers for new accommodation entries which can be considered.

When you make enquiries and bookings for golf, accommodation or both, please mention this latest edition of *THE GOLF GUIDE: Where to Play/Where to Stay*.

Peter Clark
Publishing Director

Contents

Foreword	3
How to Use *THE GOLF GUIDE*	5
Golfing Around Britain	7
Holiday Golf in Spain: *Michael Gedye*	30
Holiday Golf in Portugal: *Michael Gedye*	31
Holiday Golf in France: *Michael Gedye*	33
The Ryder Cup 1993	37
The PGA Year	45
Clubs and Courses	
ENGLAND	53
SCOTLAND	232
WALES	307
IRELAND	328
THE ISLE OF MAN	343
CHANNEL ISLANDS	344
FRANCE	346
PORTUGAL	357
SPAIN	362
Driving Ranges	370
Index of Clubs and Courses	377
Index of Advertisers/Hotels	401
MAPS: Routes and Towns	409

The golf break other golfers want to keep a secret

Country Club Hotels' Short Breaks are a closely guarded secret among people who really enjoy the game of golf...and want to play it on some of Britain's finest courses.

With all our venues located in beautiful countryside settings, Country Club Hotels offer the perfect environment to challenge friends to a rewarding game... entertain business clients or colleagues... or simply take a well-deserved break from home or office routine.

To help you relax and unwind, we provide a range of leisure activities – from tennis, swimming and squash to jacuzzis, saunas and fitness studios. So your partner is sure to enjoy a stay at Country Club Hotels as much as you do!

For full details on all 10 UK Country Club Hotels, call us now on the number below.

COUNTRY CLUB HOTELS
Experience the luxury of choice

CALL ☎ **0582 396969** AND QUOTE CG1302

THE GOLF FOUNDATION
57 London Road, Enfield, Middlesex EN2 6DU
Telephone: 081-367 4404

Established in 1952 The Golf Foundation has the specific aims of introducing more young people to the game of golf and of promoting and developing their skills and enjoyment of the game. The basis of the Foundation's work is the Coaching Scheme, whereby qualified members of the PGA give instruction to students at schools and universities. The Foundation also sponsors Open Coaching Centres during vacations, and implements a Coaching Award Scheme for teachers. A four-stage Merit Award Scheme operates successfully throughout the country, and Age Group Championships help raise the standard of junior golf by providing real competition at all levels of ability.

A newsletter "Tee to Green" is published, as well as other coaching material, visual aids and films.

The Golf Foundation is a non-profit-making organisation and a Registered Charity, relying on support from organisations within the game, commerce and industry, and individual Golf Clubs and club members. As the national body responsible for junior golf it plays a vital role in the future development of the game.

The PGA Year

THE PROFESSIONAL GOLFERS' ASSOCIATION was formed over 91 years ago with 50 members. Perhaps its potential membership and influence was reflected by the standing of its first president, the Rt Hon. James Balfour who was shortly afterwards to become the Prime Minister! The current president is the equally distinguished Lord Derby and the membership has grown to just under 4,000, including 800 working abroad and more than 1,000 trainees.

The working club professional continues to give lessons, repair clubs and run his shop and increasingly he has to play the "business" game as well as he plays golf! His time is very much taken up with pro-ams, company days and regional tournaments which have become vital to the economics and the image of professional golf. Other competitive demands on the professional have less to do with golf than with shopkeeping – in the shape of the trading competition he faces from retail sports shop chains and large supermarkets.

However, the club professional still has prestigious national tournaments where he can put his skills on more public show and compete against the best in his business in his own selected game – golf. It is with these annual and important events that our review of the PGA year deals.

THE TRUSTHOUSE FORTE PGA SENIORS' CHAMPIONSHIP

Brian Huggett called on all the competitive skills that once made him one of the toughest British Ryder Cup performers in winning the Forte PGA Seniors' Championship at Sunningdale. The 56-year-old Tour star of the 60s and 70s collected his fourth Seniors' title with a superb six-under-par total of 204. It gave him a three stroke margin over runner-up Bobby Verwey, South African winner of the British Seniors' title two years ago.

Brian Waites, Forte PGA Seniors' Champion in 1990 and 1991, scorched into third place on a sun-drenched final day with a record equalling six-under-par 64. It gave him a one-under-par total of 209 and confirmed his return to top form after recovering from his life-threatening car crash just two years ago.

Huggett's victory earned him £12,500 and lifted him to second place behind Tommy Horton in the Seniors Tour Order of Merit. It was built around his second day 65 which was bogey free and established a three stroke lead over the ever-threatening Verwey. And it was typical Huggett strategy and tenacity that held off the South African's last round challenge and preserved the margin.

Playing together there was no change for ten holes, both having reached the turn in level par 35. But at the short par-four 11th Huggett ran into his first crisis, pushing his tee shot into trouble. He could only pitch into a greenside bunker and took five while Verwey, just short of the putting surface with his drive, made a birdie.

Suddenly there was only one stroke in it. But Verwey handed a stroke back when he missed a two-foot tap in for par at the short 13th. Huggett needed no further encouragement. While Verwey

The PGA Year THE GOLF GUIDE 1994

FORTE P.G.A. SENIORS' CHAMPIONSHIP

Brian Huggett receives the Forte PGA Seniors trophy from The Hon. Rocco Forte.

required all five shots at the comfortable 477 yard 14th, the diminutive Welsh star coolly stroked a three iron to the heart of the green to secure the birdie that put him three in front once more. Solid regulation figures from both men over the final four holes kept it that way, both scoring level par 70s.

"That's just the way I planned it," said Huggett. "I knew if I could get it round in par, the others had to do it all to catch me. Well, I'm not a Faldo but that five at the 11th was my first bogey for 40 holes, so I'm delighted with the way I played."

Waites rued an opening 75 which precluded a realistic challenge on the final day. But his 64 really took this lovely layout apart, featuring eight birdies and just two bogeys – an overhit second at the 10th and a bunkered seven iron at the 13th. Waites required just 26 putts and was openly delighted to have achieved his first 64 in more than ten years. It equalled the Seniors Tour's lowest round by Jose Maria Rocca at La Bresse last year. "I'm highly encouraged, especially after making the cut and playing so well in distinguished company in the US Seniors," added Waites.

Peter Butler, winner of the Lawrence Batley the previous week, sandwiched a 68 between two 71s but a hat-trick of birdies over the final three holes left him in fourth place on level par. Tommy Horton's title defence was a struggle after a first round 72 and despite a good-looking 67 second time out he eventually had to settle for fifth place on 212.

The tournament, the longest running in British Seniors golf, was boosted by the return of Australia's Peter Thomson who won the title in 1988. It was a sentimental journey as he played over the course where he won the Dunlop Masters back in 1968, three years after the last of his five Open victories.

Thomson, now 63 admitted to being a little rusty after playing only social golf in recent years, but still managed scores of 76, 73 and 74 before dashing off to St Andrews to fulfil one of his growing course construction commitments.

Now part of the PGA European Tour, the Forte PGA Seniors dates from 1957 and past winners to add to the name of Peter Thomson are such still-remembered stars as Christy O'Connor, Dai Rees, Max Faulkner, Neil Coles and Ken Nagle.

Clive Hall, Glenmuir PGA Club Professional Champion with Malcolm Boyd of Glenmuir.

THE GLENMUIR PGA CLUB PROFESSIONAL CHAMPIONSHIP

Bulwell Forest's Chris Hall produced a remarkable final day performance to achieve a career best win in the Glenmuir Club Professional Championship at Coventry.

Runner-up at St Pierre the previous year, the 32-year-old set out on the final round eight shots behind leader, Mark Parker, hoping for nothing more than a high finish that would secure selection points for next year's European side for the PGA Cup matches against America.

But, nine birdies and an eagle later, the Nottingham man had equalled the course record of 64 and rocketed through the field to seal the £6,000 top cheque by three strokes with an 18 under par 274 total!

Parker, from Riverside Club at Thamesmeade in London, and two-time former winner, Russell Weir, shared second place another stroke further back.

Playing in the event for the first time, Parker had set out on the final round with a four stroke lead. The 26-year-old Cockney cruised through the opening rounds 68, 68, 66.

"I've been working with a sports psychologist, Chris Linstead, for the past month, and he's made a huge difference to my game," revealed Parker, who had given up a place in the Australian Open to compete in the £50,000 Glenmuir event.

"My concentration is so much better. He's got me to really focus on each individual shot. This week, I've been speaking to him on the 'phone every night."

The benefits were in evidence at the first hole in the final round. Parker split the fairway with a cracking drive at the

The PGA Glenmuir Club Professional Champion, Chris Hall, has the use of a new Volvo car for a year.

487 yard hole, creamed an eight iron to ten feet and holed for an eagle.

However, the pursuing pack was in no mood to settle for second place. Pay cheques and PGA Cup selection points are a potent lure.

Scot Russell Weir, who had finished second in a Tartan Tour "major" – the Sunderland of Scotland Masters – the previous week, was the first to make his mark.

The Cowal professional opened with an eagle 3 and went on to collect birdies at the 3rd, 4th and 6th in an outward half of 31. Further gains at the 10th and 13th put him within one shot of the top of the leaderboard.

However, his dream of becoming the first three-time winner of the Club Professional title disappeared with dropped shots at the 15th and 17th.

Hall then took up the challenge. After a birdie at the first had been followed by a bogey at the 2nd, he started his charge by reeling off four successive birdies from the 3rd – three from short range and a 20 footer falling at the 4th – as he made his way to the turn in 36.

And he kept on the roll coming home. An eagle – an eight iron struck to 30 feet – at the 495 yard 10th was followed by back to back birdies at the 12th and 13th, another at the 16th, and then the icing was added to the cake when his 10 foot effort slipped in for a final gain at the 18th.

THE GOLF GUIDE 1994

It all added up to a round of 64, and Hall had set a clubhouse target of 18-under-par 274 that no one could match.

Parker did still have a chance to at least force a play-off when he stood on the 17th tee at 18 under par. But he missed and took 4, and then ran up a disastrous double bogey six at the last when his approach rolled into an impossible lie at the back of a greenside bunker.

A member of the gallery witnessing Parker's sad finale at the 18th green, the moment of victory was sweet for Hall. But he did express his sympathy for the young Londoner.

"When I went out on the final day I never really thought I could still win," he said. "But I knew it would be difficult for Mark protecting a big lead. It's not an easy situation to be in. But, obviously, I'm absolutely delighted. This is the best win of my career."

Not that he is a total stranger to the staging of fighting comebacks – he came from six behind in the final round to win the Midland Masters at Patshull Park last year.

In the final round at Coventry he had just 25 shots on the greens, and, afterwards he attributed his victory to many hours spent practising his putting on the lounge carpet.

"Putting is the key to good scoring," he said. "I had disc trouble over the winter and couldn't work on my long game but spent a couple of hours every evening working on my putting. My wife was getting a bit fed up, but she should be happy now!

"This is the fifth time I've played in the Club Professional Championship and, after I finished second last year, I vowed to my caddy that one day I would win the title."

Hall now intends making a bid to win his European Tour card, and will attend the qualifying school in France in November. "I love competition, and playing on the European circuit is my ultimate ambition."

John Hoskison had an unfortunate start to his defence of the title when his West Surrey professional's shop suffered a break-in on the Monday of the Championship week.

However, having survived a cut on the final 145 mark, he went on to record closing rounds of 67 and 69 to finish joint ninth.

Edzell's Alastair Webster, the 1990 champion who had set the course record of 64 on the opening day and also led the halfway stage, started the final round as Parker's nearest challenger. But he closed with a 73 to finish joint fifth alongside Lee Fickling (Enfield) and Joe Higgins (Ketley Golf Club).

Among those to earn PGA Cup selection points were members who have already played in matches against America – Hall, Weir, Kevin Stables, Hoskison and Martin Gray.

All the competitors were grateful to Glenmuir, who were sponsoring the event for the first of a five-year agreement.

Craig Everett of Caldwell Golf Club near Glasgow; the PGA Assistants' Champion.

THE PGA ASSISTANTS' CHAMPIONSHIP

Craig Everett completed the conversion from a top class amateur career when he scored his first major professional victory in the PGA Assistants' Championship at Oaklands Golf and Country Club, Cheshire. The 25-year-old produced impressive rounds of 69, 69 and 68 to head the field by five shots after 54 holes, and a closing 74 earned the £3,750 top cheque by three shots from fellow Scot Colin Gillies and Jonathan Langmead.

It was a significant breakthrough for the Caldwell Assistant for whom the triumph secured an invitation to the US Assistants' Championship. Everett hopes also to make progress towards his ultimate ambition of a place on the Volvo European Tour.

"It's tremendous to win my first 72-hole professional title," stated the delighted youngster. "This win will give me a tremendous amount of confidence and I'm looking forward to the trip to the States."

Tied with Gillies at the halfway stage, it was his third round 68 that virtually sealed victory. The three under par round contained five birdies and he finished with a flourish by holing from the edge of the green for a four at the 18th.

On the final lap Everett went out with the aim of defending his lead with par figures. He did slip up by dropping a shot at the 8th, but by the time he made another error – a double-bogey at the 17th where his tee shot hit a tree and landed in water – the trophy and the cheque already bore his name.

Capped at all levels for Scotland and winner of the 1990 Scottish Amateur Championship, Everett moved into the paid ranks in 1991 and made an immediate mark on the Tartan Tour.

For Westerwood's Gillies, who finished third in the 1990 PGA Assistants'

The PGA Year THE GOLF GUIDE 1994

Championship, the share of second place was a welcome respite from a season ruined by a strength sapping throat virus. The 27-year-old, who has finished in the top ten in the Tartan Tour Order of Merit for the past three years and was third in the 1990 Assistants', suffered a throat infection in America in January and he admitted: "I feel tired all the time and it's been a really miserable season." However, he lifted his spirits with a second round 66 and, despite setting out on the final day with fingers crossed that he would complete the 36 holes, put together commendable rounds of 74 and 71 for his share of runner up spot.

On a rain interrupted opening day, it was 1991 Champion Simon Wood who set the pace with a 68.

Despite the unfavourable conditions – thunder, lightning and torrential rain caused two lengthy hold ups in play – the Herne Bay man grabbed five birdies, all from close range. While unable to sustain his lead, Wood brought the curtain down on his assistant's career with following rounds of 72, 71 and 75 to finish in the top ten.

With the sunshine making a welcome appearance on the second day, Gillies produced the golf to match with a sparkling five-under-par 66 that included eight birdies. Starting at the 11th, the Scot covered the opening seven holes in an uninspiring level par, birdies at the 14th and 16th being wiped out by a 5 at the short 17th.

However, he then came alight with a hat trick of gains from the 2nd – holing from 15 feet, 20 feet and 6 inches – and he enjoyed a similar run from the 8th. At the 9th he holed from fully 45 feet, while he signed off in style with an effort from 15 feet going down at the 10th. Unfortunately for Gillies, a shortened course was in use over the opening two days due to the adverse weather conditions, and so his brilliant effort did not count as an official course record.

However, James Cook did lay claim to that honour on the final day. The Leamington and County assistant who completed all four rounds in the 1993 Open Championship, shot a closing round of four-under-par 67 to finish joint 10th on 286.

Crowned Midland Assistants' Champion earlier in the week, Cook, a former British Boys' and Youths' Champion, made six birdies, the highlight coming when he chipped in from 35 yards at the 11th.

LORD DERBY'S KNOWSLEY SAFARI PARK TOURNAMENT

The Bolton Golf Club course at Lostock Park again played host to the Knowsley Safari Park Tournament which is sponsored by the PGA President, the Rt. Hon. the Earl of Derby MC. James Mellor, 23-year-old Midland Region Assistants' Champion from Worksop, turned his 1992 six-over-par in the 1992 event into a three-under-par play-off score in 1993.

Unlike many of his contemporaries who can be superstitious of such knowledge, Mellor wanted to know exactly where he stood as he approached the 13th tee and the closing holes of the final round. Without a leader board in sight, he consulted one of the spectators to be told that the target to beat was three-under-par.

It had been set earlier in the day in spectacular fashion by James Wright, a professional for less than four months, who broke the course record with a six-under-par 64.

Mellor responded with birdies at the 13th, where he wedged to three feet, and at the next, a short hole, where his eight iron left him a similar distance from the flag. That put him four under for the tournament but with two tricky holes out of the last four to negotiate in the strengthening wind. He misjudged his chip to the 16th to drop his third stroke of the day, made a safe par down the 17th but then had to call upon his powers of

THE GOLF GUIDE 1994

The PGA Year

Lord Derby (left), with John Mellor (centre), winner of the Lord Derby's Knowsley Safari Park Tournament in association with RAM Golf UK.

concentration to force a tie with the admirable Wright of West Herts.

Mellor pushed his two iron approach into the rough, leaving himself with a downhill lie and a pitch over the bunker to the green. He executed the shot perfectly, the ball pulling up six feet left of the pin from where he coolly rapped in his putt for his 64 and a tie.

Mellor said: "I like to know what I have to do when in contention." Wright, watching from the sidelines, was among the first to congratulate him – and the compliment was duly reciprocated by Mellor.

Wright after all had come from nowhere to post his 64 – shredding the old mark by three shots – for a three-under-par two round total of 137. The 21-year-old did not even have a practice round over the Lostock Park course, driving straight to Bolton from a pro-am.

Wright, a former England schoolboys' captain, strung together eight birdies in his 64 – three in succession from the 15th – and the only blemishes on his card were bogeys at the 10th, which he three-putted and at the 12th, where he found a greenside bunker.

The sudden death play off was all over in minutes. Wright found the rough on the left and failed to reach the green while Mellor, after a perfect drive, pitched to ten feet. Even then Wright had a chance to half, but his six footer slid past.

Dore and Totley's Robert Wagg was third with a brace of 69s. A stroke further back, at one under, was Paul Barrington of Weston-Super-Mare after rounds of 68 and 71. Overnight leader Cameron Smellie, of North Manchester, who followed up his 67 with a 73, was among a group of three players who tied fifth on level par.

Mellor later toasted his success with a double Magnum of Moet et Chandon and the prizes were presented by the Rt. Hon. Earl of Derby MC, President of the PGA.

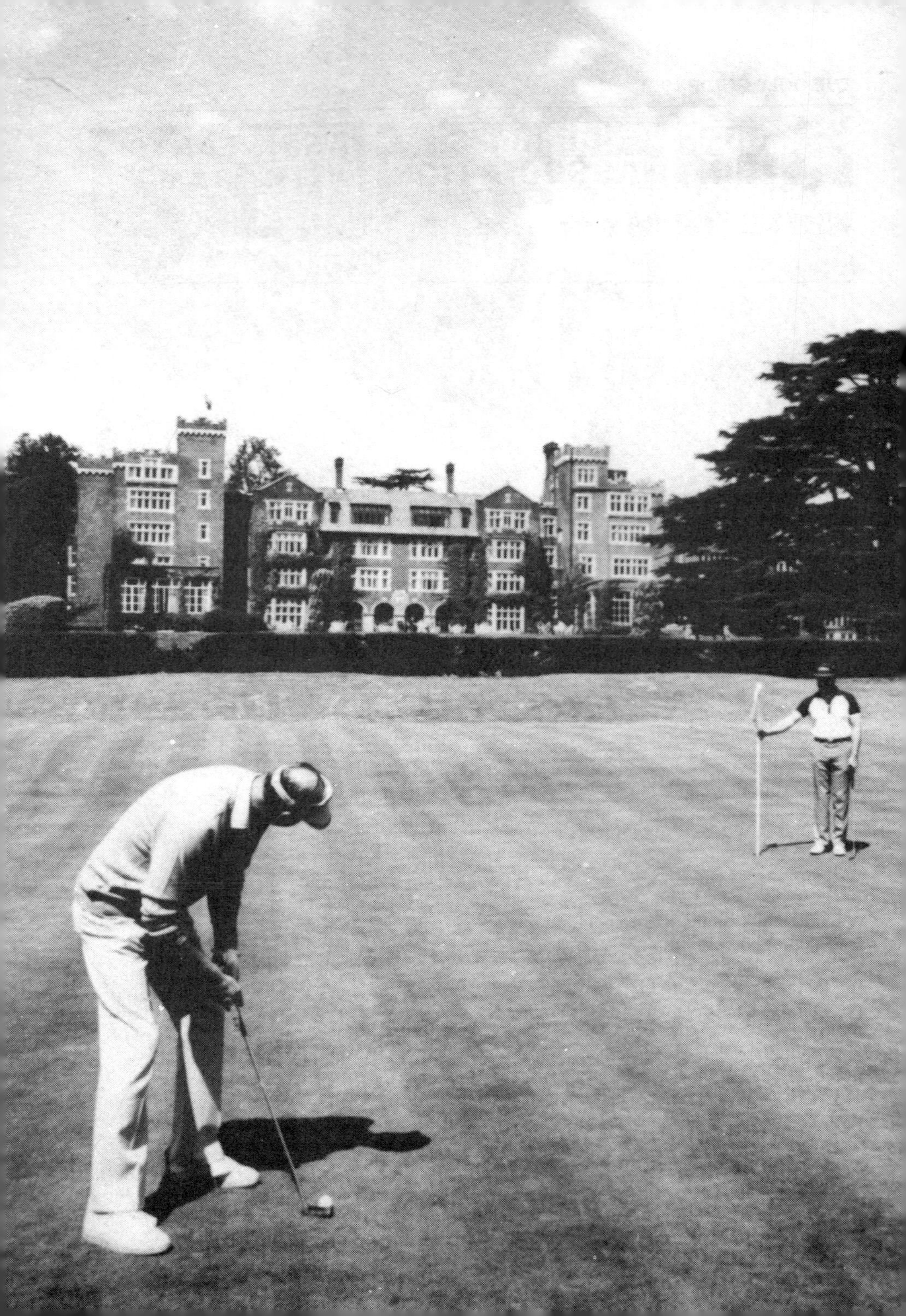

Golf in England
WHERE TO PLAY • WHERE TO STAY

ONE USUALLY associates hotels with holiday golf and there is, not surprisingly, the widest selection in the south-west. For those who prefer country air and a rural atmosphere, a possible choice would be Collacott Farm, Umberleigh or Batch Farm Country Hotel near Weston-super-Mare. For more of a golfing environment and perhaps the livelier amenities of a resort, choose between Burnham-on-Sea in Somerset, Bude or Falmouth in Cornwall, or Ilfracombe or Seaton in Devon. One would also think quite naturally of Moretonhampstead before moving east to Avon and Bristol and, of course, Gloucester.

The south, through Dorset and Hampshire, whose Old Thorns is always an attractive choice, offers both inland and seaside golfing interest with well-established golfing hotels in Sussex and Kent and such metropolitan favourites as Selsdon Park in Surrey.

A grand tour of England's courses would require volumes and we mustn't omit what is often a neglected golfing corner of the country – East Anglia.

A favourite must be the links at Hunstanton. This is a true championship course but it has never been considered for a major tournament only because getting there is so tedious. Several amateur events have been played there, including the Amateur Championship and the English Open.

Nearby is Brancaster, the Royal West Norfolk Club said to have been built at the suggestion of Edward VII when he

Selsdon Park Golfing Centre, Surrey.

was Prince of Wales, who used the land to shoot over when staying at Sandringham.

Ipswich has two great courses, Woodbridge laid out on sandy heathland two miles from the village and Purdis Heath designed by Fred Hawtree on the outskirts of the city. There are no bad holes, each is very distinctive in its own way and both clubs offer an alternative nine-holer for either the beginner, or the golfer short on time.

The county hosting the largest number of golf courses is Yorkshire, with around one hundred and fifty.

The Spa and Conference town of Harrogate is an excellent base for one of the finest weeks' golf to be enjoyed outside Scotland. Ample hotels, reasonably priced guest houses, combine with many first class restaurants and entertainment add to the pleasure.

As well as Moortown's marvellous moorland course, where Britain regained the Ryder Cup from the hands of the USA back in 1927, within the length of a par five is Sandmoor. Shorter than Moortown and spoilt somewhat by the opening holes, Sandmoor is nevertheless a pleasant course, with some memorable holes alongside the Fewston Reservoir.

On into North Yorkshire, Fulford is recommended, as is the York Golf Club at Strensall. This course is owned by the military, but also has a separate club membership of non-military personnel, who administer their own affairs.

Easingwold some ten miles north is a perfect treat, especially since the clubhouse has been extended. The

Golf in England   **THE GOLF GUIDE 1994**

course is in two parts, the old and the new, though each year it is played the distinction is fading.

Scarborough is now only an hour from Leeds since the road improvements around Malton have been completed. On the coast try both the North and South Cliff courses, or the super family course at Filey, a regular venue for societies and club outings.

Midland golf centres around famous golf courses such as the Belfry, venue of the Ryder Cup and also the headquarters of the PGA. Not far away is Patshull Park, Wolverhampton, where a complete leisure complex has been developed.

There are parts of England less traditionally associated with golf but where excellent facilities exist. In Cumbria, for example, Windermere Golf Club has an enviable location and a huge choice of accommodation. And at the other end of our islands, the Isle of Wight and the Channel Islands offer more than just golf with their relaxed and almost 'overseas' flavour.

ALADDIN'S

SUNDERLAND of Scotland   *Titleist*   POWAKaddy

Confidence   YONEX   Mizuno   MORTON KNIGHT

Taylor Made   STIX   RAM   Pringle SPORTS

GOLF HOUSE
AT THE CORNER OF UXBRIDGE ROAD
AND NICHOLLS AVE, HILLINGDON.
JUST 4 MILES FROM HEATHROW
TEL 0895 251691/271106
AN
OPEN INVITATION
TO VISIT THE WORLD'S LARGEST
STOCKED GOLF STORES.
NO. 1 FOR CHOICE · VALUE · EXPERT ADVICE ·
PART EXCHANGE

Wilson   SPALDING   PING   DUNLOP   FootJoy   LYNX   Callaway GOLF

818 Queens Drive, Liverpool 13 – end of M62 | AUCHTERLONIE of ST ANDREWS, FIFE, SCOTLAND
Tel: 051-228 9061 | **Tel: 0334 73253**

A warm welcome awaits you at all our stores
VISIT THE WORLD'S LARGEST STOCKED GOLF SHOPS
MON FRI 8.00am-8.00pm, SAT 8.00am-6.00pm, SUN 9.00am-5.00pm   Access, Visa and Switch Welcome

---

PUBLISHER'S NOTE

While every effort is made to ensure accuracy, we regret that FHG Publications cannot accept responsibility for errors, omissions or misrepresentation in our entries or any consequences thereof. Prices in particular should be checked because we go to press early. We will follow up complaints, but cannot act as arbiters or agents for either party.

England LONDON

London

ASHFORD. **Ashford Manor Golf Club,** Fordbridge Road, Ashford, Middlesex TW15 3RT (Ashford (0784) 252049). 18 holes, 6343 yards. S.S.S. 70. *Green Fees:* information not provided. *Visitors:* welcome with introduction. Professional: M. Finney (0784 255940). Secretary: B.J. Duffy.

BARNET. **North Middlesex Golf Club,** The Manor House, Friern Barnet Lane, Whetstone N20 0NL (081-445 1732). *Location:* five miles north of Finchley, A1000. 18 holes, 5611 yards. S.S.S. 67. *Green Fees:* weekday round/day £22.00; weekends and Bank Holidays £30.00. *Eating facilities:* luncheons, snacks and dining facilities. *Visitors:* welcome (with Official Handicap), weekends playing with a member and in possession of Official Handicap. Advisable to telephone Professional to book time. *Society Meetings:* catered for. Professional: A.S.R. Roberts (081-445 3060). General Manager/Secretary: M.C.N. Reding (081-445 1604).

BARNET. **Old Fold Manor Golf Club,** Hadley Green, Barnet, Herts EN5 4QN (081-440 9185). *Location:* Junction 23 M25. A1000 one mile north of Barnet. Heathland course. 18 holes, 6471 yards. S.S.S. 71. Practice nets and putting green. *Green Fees:* £27.00 per round, £30.00 per day, with a member £10.00 (Mondays and Wednesdays £7.50 per round); weekends with a member only £12.00. *Eating facilities:* restaurant and bar except Mondays and Wednesdays. *Visitors:* welcome weekdays. *Society Meetings:* catered for Thursdays and Fridays. Professional: Peter Jones (081-440 7488). Manager: A.W. Dickens (081-440 9185).

BEXLEY HEATH. **Barnehurst Golf Course,** Mayplace Road East, Bexley Heath, Kent DA7 6JU (0322 523746). *Location:* Just north of Crayford town centre. Mature inland course in traditional woodland setting. 9 greens (18 tees). S.S.S. 66. Designed by five times Open Champion, James Braid, in 1904. *Green Fees:* weekdays £5.70, weekends and Bank Holidays £9.20. Reduced rates for senior citizens and juniors. Membership available. *Eating facilities:* fully licensed bar and catering. *Visitors:* welcome. *Society Meetings:* catered for. Large function room. Professional: Patrick "Teach" Tallack.

BROMLEY. **Bromley Golf Club,** Magpie Hall Lane, Bromley. *Location:* off A21 Bromley to Farnborough road. Short, flat, open course with a few trees. 9 holes, 2745 yards. S.S.S. 35. Putting green and teaching facilities. *Green Fees:* information not available. *Eating facilities:* snacks available. *Visitors:* no booking required as this is public course. *Society Meetings:* by arrangement with Bromley District Council. Professional: Alan Hodgeson (081-462 7014).

CHINGFORD. **Chingford Golf Club,** 158 Station Road, Chingford E4 (081-529 2107). 18 holes, 6342 yards. S.S.S. 70. *Green Fees:* on application. *Visitors:* welcome weekdays only, an article of red must be worn. Professional: John Francis. Secretary: Bryan Sinden.

CHINGFORD. **Royal Epping Forest Golf Club,** Forest Approach, Chingford, London E4 7AZ (081-529 6407). *Location:* 200 yards east of Chingford (BR) Station. A private club on a public course. Wooded 18 holes, 6342 yards. S.S.S. 71. *Green Fees:* weekdays £8.00; weekends £11.00. *Eating facilities:* public snack bar. *Visitors:* may play course but may not use clubhouse. Must wear red garment (trousers or shirt/sweater). Professionals: Robin Gowers/John Francis (081-529 5708). Secretary: Mrs P. Runciman (081-529 2195).

CHINGFORD. **West Essex Golf Club,** Bury Road, Sewardstonebury, Chingford, London E4 7QL (081-529 0928). *Location:* two miles north of Chingford BR Station. M25 (Junction 26) and Waltham Abbey follow directions to Chingford (Daws Lane on left). Parkland, wooded, hilly. 18 holes, 6289 yards. S.S.S. 70. *Green Fees:* weekdays £30.00 per round, £38.00 per day; weekends with member only. *Eating facilities:* restaurant and bar facilities. *Visitors:* welcome weekdays except Tuesday mornings and Thursday afternoons; after 3pm competition days. Phone first. *Society Meetings:* catered for by arrangement Mondays, Wednesdays and Fridays. Professional: C. Cox (081-529 4367). Secretary: P.H. Galley MBE (081-529 7558).

DULWICH. **Dulwich and Sydenham Hill Golf Club,** Grange Lane, College Road, London SE21 (081-693 3961). *Location:* off South Circular, Dulwich Common. 18 holes, 6051 yards. S.S.S. 69. *Green Fees:* £25.00 per round. *Eating facilities:* lunch every day. *Visitors:* welcome, with reservation on weekdays. *Society Meetings:* catered for, maximum 30. Professional: David Baillie. Secretary: Mrs Susan Alexander.

EDMONTON. **Leaside Golf Club,** Pickett's Lock Sports Centre, Edmonton N9 0AS (081-803 4756). *Location:* near North Circular Road. Flat parkland. 9 holes, 2496 yards. S.S.S. 32. Driving range, putting green. *Green Fees:* information not available. Reductions weekdays for Senior Citizens and Juniors. *Eating facilities:* cafe and bar. *Visitors:* booking required at weekends. *Society Meetings:* by arrangement with Sports Centre. Professional: R. Gerken.

EDMONTON. **Lee Valley Leisure Golf Course,** Lee Valley Leisure, (Picketts Lock), Edmonton, London N9 0AS. *Location:* off Meridian Way near North Circular Road, Edmonton. Flat parkland course with lake and River Lea as water hazards. 18 holes, 4902 yards. S.S.S. 64. 20 bay floodlit driving range. *Green Fees:* weekdays £9.00; weekends £11.00. Senior Citizens and Junior weekday concessions. *Eating facilities:* snack bar and bar. *Visitors:* open to public every day, weekend booking advisable (contact Professional). *Society Meetings:* small Societies welcome weekdays. Professional: Richard Gerken (081-803 3611). Manager: John Houston (081-345 6666).

LONDON *England* THE GOLF GUIDE 1994

ELTHAM. **Eltham Warren Golf Club,** Bexley Road, Eltham SE9 2PE (081-850 1166). *Location:* A210 Eltham. Parkland. 9 holes, 5840 yards. S.S.S. 68. *Green Fees:* £25.00 per day; with member £10.00. *Eating facilities:* two bars, diningroom. *Visitors:* welcome weekdays only, weekends with member only. *Society Meetings:* by arrangement. Professional: R.V. Taylor (081-859 7909). Secretary: D.J. Clare (081-850 4477).

ELTHAM. **Royal Blackheath Golf Club,** The Clubhouse, Court Road, Eltham SE9 5AF. *Location:* M25, A20 exit London bound, second set of traffic lights turn right, 600 yards up hill on right. Parkland, wooded with water. 18 holes, 6219 yards. S.S.S. 70. Practice area. *Green Fees:* £40.00 per day (£15.00 with member). *Eating facilities:* excellent diningroom and two bars. *Visitors:* welcome weekdays, weekends only if introduced by and playing with member. Museum. *Society Meetings:* catered for midweek, prior booking essential. Professional: Ian McGregor (081-850 1763). Secretary: R. Barriball (081-850 1795; Fax: 081-859 0150).

ENFIELD. **Crews Hill Golf Club,** Cattlegate Road, Crews Hill, Enfield EN2 8AZ (081-363 0787). *Location:* off Junction 24 M25, follow directions to Enfield. Parkland. 18 holes, 6230 yards. S.S.S. 70. Practice area. *Green Fees:* on application. *Eating facilities:* restaurant by arrangement, bar. *Visitors:* welcome weekdays. Handicap Certificate required. Weekends by invitation of member. *Society Meetings:* by arrangement. Professional: J.R. Reynolds (081-366 7422). General Manager: E.J. Hunt (081-363 6674; Fax: 081-364 5641).

ENFIELD. **Enfield Golf Club,** Old Park Road South, Enfield, Middlesex EN2 7DA. *Location:* off Junction 24, M25; follow directions to Enfield. Parkland; designed by James Braid. 18 holes, 6200 yards. S.S.S. 70. *Green Fees:* on request. *Eating facilities:* full bar and catering facilities. *Visitors:* welcome weekdays only, with current Handicap Certificate. *Society Meetings:* catered for Mondays, Wednesdays and Fridays by prior arrangement. Professional: Lee Fickling (081-366 4492). Secretary: Nigel Challis (081-363 3970; Fax: 081-342 0381).

ENFIELD. **Whitewebbs Golf Club,** Clay Hill, Beggars Hollow, Enfield EN2 9JN (081-363 2951). *Location:* A10 off M25, north of Enfield. Parkland course. 18 holes, 5863 yards. S.S.S. 68. Practice area, separate 9 hole pitch and putt. *Green Fees:* £10.60 weekdays; £12.40 weekends. *Eating facilities:* public cafe on site. *Visitors:* welcome, public course, no restrictions. *Society Meetings:* contact the Secretary. Professional: D. Lewis (081-363 4454). Secretary: Victor Van Graan (081-363 2951).

FINCHLEY. **Finchley Golf Club,** Nether Court, Frith Lane, Finchley, London NW7 1PU (081-346 0883). *Location:* close A1/M1 Mill Hill East tube station. Wooded course. 18 holes, 6411 yards. S.S.S. 71. *Green Fees:* weekdays £28.00; weekends £37.00. *Eating facilities:* bar; diningroom open daily except Mondays. *Visitors:* welcome weekdays except Thursdays, weekends after mid-day. *Society Meetings:* catered for Wednesdays and Fridays. Professional: David Brown (081-346 5086). Secretary: John Pearce (081-346 2436).

GREENFORD. **Ealing Golf Club,** Perivale Lane, Greenford, Middlesex UB6 8SS (081-997 2595). *Location:* on Western Avenue A40 half a mile from Hanger Lane Gyratory System. Flat parkland. 18 holes, 6216 yards. S.S.S. 70. *Green Fees:* £30.00 weekdays; weekends with a member only. *Eating facilities:* men's bar, mixed lounge, restaurant – lunches and snacks. *Visitors:* welcome weekdays with reservation through Professional. *Society Meetings:* catered for on Monday, Wednesday and Thursday. Professional: A. Stickley (081-997 3959). Secretary: M. Scargill (081-997 0937).

GREENFORD. **Horsenden Hill Golf Club,** Whitton Avenue, Woodland Rise, Greenford UB6 0RD (081-902 4555). *Location:* off Whitton Avenue East, next door to Sudbury Golf Course. Very tough though short course. 9 holes, 1632 yards, 1490 metres. S.S.S. 55. Practice area, nets and putting green. *Green Fees:* weekdays £3.75 for 9 holes; weekends £5.60 for 9 holes. *Eating facilities:* restaurant and bar. *Visitors:* welcome at all times, unrestricted. Professional: Andrew Rogers and Anthony Ferrier. Secretary: Mr Jim Kelly.

GREENFORD. **Perivale Park Golf Club,** Stockdove Way, Greenford, Middlesex (081-575 7116). *Location:* A40, turn off at sign for Ealing and Perivale. Flat parkland. 9 holes, 2667 yards. S.S.S. 34. Excellent practice ground. *Green Fees:* information not provided. *Eating facilities:* cafeteria. *Visitors:* welcome – public course. Professional: Peter Bryant. Secretary: George Taylor.

HAMPSTEAD. **Hampstead Golf Club,** Winnington Road, London N2 0TU (081-455 0203). *Location:* down Hampstead Lane adjacent to Spaniards Inn. Undulating parkland with trees. 9 holes, 5812 yards. S.S.S. 68. *Green Fees:* £23.00 (£28.00 per day) weekdays; weekends £30.00. *Eating facilities:* bar; snacks and afternoon teas; lunches bookable. *Visitors:* welcome weekdays (not Tuesdays) if members of a golf club or have Handicap Certificate. Limited at weekends. 1993 is Club's Centenary Year. *Society Meetings:* small societies catered for weekdays by prior arrangement. Professional: Peter Brown (081-455 7089). Secretary: K.F. Young (081-455 0203).

ENFIELD GOLF CLUB
Old Park Road South, Enfield, Middlesex EN2 7DA Tel: 081-363 3970
A warm welcome awaits you at Enfield. Course designed by James Braid.
Casual green fees (with Handicap Certificate) and Society Days welcome.
Call Secretary for details.

England LONDON

HAMPTON HILL. Fulwell Golf Club, Wellington Road, Hampton Hill, Middlesex TW12 1JY (081-977 3188). *Location:* opposite Fulwell Railway Station and bus garage. Flat parkland course. 18 holes, 6544 yards. S.S.S. 71. Practice ground. *Green Fees:* weekdays £25.00; weekends £35.00. £12.00 with member. *Eating facilities:* lunches and teas. *Visitors:* welcome weekdays. *Society Meetings:* welcome Monday, Wednesday, Thursday and Fridays. Professional: D. Haslam (Tel & Fax: 081-977 3844). Secretary: C.A. Brown (081-977 2733).

HAMPTON WICK. Home Park Golf Club, Hampton Wick, Kingston-upon-Thames KT1 4AD (081-977 2658). *Location:* between Hampton Court and Kingston Bridge, entrance at Kingston Bridge roundabout. Flat parkland. 18 holes, 6598 yards. S.S.S. 71. *Green Fees:* weekdays £15.00 (£24.00 all day), weekends and Bank Holidays £20.00 (£30.00 all day). *Eating facilities:* full bar and dining facilities. *Visitors:* welcome – no advance booking. *Society Meetings:* catered for by arrangement. Professional: D.L. Roberts (081-977 2658). Secretary: Mr B.W. O'Farrell (081-977 2423).

HENDON. Hendon Golf Club, off Sanders Lane, Devonshire Road, Mill Hill, London NW7 1DG (081-346 8083). *Location:* leave M1 southbound at Junction 2. Turn off A1 into Holders Hill Road. 10 miles north of London. Parkland, wooded, well bunkered. 18 holes, 6266 yards. S.S.S. 70. *Green Fees:* weekdays £24.00 per round, £30.00 per day; weekends £35.00. *Eating facilities:* full bar and catering facilities. *Visitors:* welcome weekdays (limited at weekends and Bank Holidays), book through Pro Shop. *Society Meetings:* catered for by arrangement Tuesdays to Fridays, book through Secretary's office. Professional: Stuart Murray (081-346 8990). Secretary: David Cooper (081-346 6023).

HIGHGATE. Highgate Golf Club, Denewood Road, Highgate, London N6 4AH (081-340 1906). *Location:* near A1, turn down Sheldon Avenue, opposite Kenwood House and first left. Parkland. 18 holes, 5985 yards. S.S.S. 69. *Green Fees:* weekdays £27.00/£35.00; weekends only with member. *Eating facilities:* bar, restaurant. *Visitors:* welcome weekdays except Wednesdays before 3pm. *Society Meetings:* catered for Thursdays/Fridays. Professional: Robin Turner (081-340 5467). Secretary: Jack Lafford (081-340 3745).

HILLINGDON. Hillingdon Golf Club, 18 Dorset Way, Hillingdon, Uxbridge Middlesex UB10 0JR (Uxbridge (0895) 239810). *Location:* near A40, adjacent to RAF Uxbridge. Very undulating – well wooded course, sloping down to river. 9 holes, 5490 yards. S.S.S. 67. *Green Fees:* weekdays £17.50 for 18 holes, £25.00 per day. *Eating facilities:* bar meals available Tuesday to Saturday. *Visitors:* welcome Mondays, Tuesdays and Fridays; Thursdays – Ladies' Day, weekends with members only. *Society Meetings:* catered for by special arrangement only with Committee through club Secretary. Professional: Mr Neil Wichelow (0895 251980). Secretary: Mrs A.M. Cooper (0895 233956).

HOUNSLOW. Airlinks Golf Club, Southall Lane, Hounslow, Middlesex TW5 9PE (081-561 1418; Fax: 081-813 6284). *Location:* Junction 3 on M4, A312 to Hayes. Same entrance as D. Lloyd Tennis Centre. Flat parkland course with water holes and doglegs. 18 holes, 5885 yards. S.S.S. 68. Floodlit driving range. *Green Fees:* weekdays £10.40 per round, £18.50 per day; weekends £13.00. *Eating facilities:* full catering and bar facilities/restaurant area. *Visitors:* weekdays no restrictions, some restrictions weekends, bookings advised seven days in advance. *Society Meetings:* catered for all week. Professionals: Bill Mylward/Ken Wickham (081-813 6282). PR Manager: P.D. Watson.

HOUNSLOW. Hounslow Heath Municipal Golf Course, Staines Road, Hounslow TW4 5DS (081-570 5271). *Location:* Staines Road A315 between Hounslow and Bedfont. Heath course, some water hazards, tight fairways. 18 holes, 5820 yards, 5322 metres. S.S.S. 69. Practice area. *Green Fees:* weekdays £7.30 per round, £11.20 per day; weekends and Bank Holidays £10.20 per round, £14.50 per day. Reduced rates for Juniors and Senior Citizens weekdays except Bank Holidays (Council Leisure Card must be held). *Eating facilities:* snacks; tea, coffee, soft drinks. *Visitors:* welcome at all times, bookings required at weekends and Bank Holidays. *Society Meetings:* by arrangement. Secretary: Mr Bob Leslie.

ISLEWORTH. Wyke Green Golf Club, Syon Lane, Isleworth TW7 5PT (081-560 4874). *Location:* situated half a mile north of A4 near Gillettes Corner. Fairly flat parkland. 18 holes, 6242 yards. S.S.S. 70. *Green Fees:* weekdays £28 per day; weekends £48 per day (half price with member). *Eating facilities:* catering daily except Mondays. *Visitors:* welcome with reservation weekdays; weekends only with member until after 3pm. *Society Meetings:* catered for on Tuesdays, Wednesdays and Thursdays by arrangement, minimum 20. Professional: David Holmes (081-847 0685). Secretary: D. Wentworth-Pollock (081-560 8777).

LONDON. London Scottish Golf Club, Windmill Enclosure, Wimbledon Common SW19 5NQ (081-788 0135). *Location:* just off A3 – Tibbetts Corner – just south of Putney SW15. Parkland (no bunkers). 18 holes, 5438 yards. S.S.S. 67/68. *Green Fees:* information not provided. *Eating facilities:* bar and catering. *Visitors:* welcome weekdays only. Check with Professional recommended. Red top must be worn, no

---

AIRLINKS GOLF CLUB

18-hole Links-Style Golf Course; 36 Bay Driving Range; 7 Day Advance Booking. Full Bar and Catering facilities.

Southall Lane, Hounslow, Middlesex TW5 9PE
Tel: 081 561 1418   Fax: 081 813 6284

LONDON *England* THE GOLF GUIDE 1994

jeans or sweatshirts. *Society Meetings:* minimum 20 players. Professional: Matthew Barr (081-789 1207). Secretary: Jack Johnson (081-789 7517).

LONDON. **Mill Hill Golf Club,** 100 Barnet Way, Mill Hill, London NW7 3AL (081-959 2282). *Location:* A1, south half a mile before Apex Corner left into clubhouse car park – signposted. Flat wooded parkland. 18 holes, 6232 yards, 5697 metres. S.S.S. 70. Practice ground. *Green Fees:* weekdays £20.00 per round; weekends £30.00 per round. Special rates mid-November to mid-March – Mondays/Wednesdays/Fridays minimum of eight players coffee, golf, high tea £25.00. *Eating facilities:* restaurant and bar. *Visitors:* welcome Monday to Friday; weekends and Bank Holidays bookings only. Two snooker tables. *Society Meetings:* catered for Mondays, Wednesdays and Fridays with prior booking. Professional: Mr A. Daniel (081-959 7261). Secretary: Mr F.H. Scott (081-959 2339; Fax: 081-906 0731).

LONDON. **Springfield Park Golf Club,** Burntwood Lane, London SW17 0AT (081-871 2468; Fax: 081-871 2221). *Location:* Burntwood Lane off Garratt Lane in the former grounds of Springfield Hospital. Inland links course in rural setting in heart of London, beautiful feature trees. 9 greens (18 tees), 4400 yards. S.S.S 62. *Green Fees:* weekdays £6.00; weekends and Bank Holidays £7.00. Membership available. *Eating facilities:* fully licensed bar and catering facilities. *Visitors:* welcome except Saturday and Sunday mornings when members only. Bowling Club, snooker and function room. *Society Meetings:* welcome weekdays only. Professional (and Course Designer): Patrick "Teach" Tallack.

LONDON. **Trent Park Golf Club,** Bramley Road, Southgate, London N14 (081-366 7432). *Location:* opposite Oakwood Tube Station. Undulating parkland. 18 holes, 6008 yards. S.S.S. 69. Large practice area. *Green Fees:* on application. *Eating facilities:* bar and snacks. *Visitors:* open to public at all times. Bookings advised on weekdays and necessary at weekends. *Society Meetings:* welcome Monday to Thursday. Professional: Craig Easton. Secretary: F.L. Montgomery.

NORTHOLT. **The London Golf Centre,** Ruislip Road, Northolt, Middlesex UB5 6QZ (081-845 3180). *Location:* just off A40 at the Polish War Memorial roundabout. Undulating parkland with interesting water hazards. 9 holes, 5906 yards. S.S.S. 70/71. Floodlit driving range. *Green Fees:* information not provided. *Eating facilities:* two bars/bistro. *Visitors:* welcome at all times. Golf superstore. *Society Meetings:* catered for. Professional: Gary Newall (081-845 3180). Secretary: Nigel Sturgess (081-842 0442; Fax: 081-842 2097).

NORTHWOOD. **Northwood Golf Club Ltd,** Rickmansworth Road, Northwood, Middlesex HA5 2QW (0923 825329). *Location:* on A404 between Pinner and Rickmansworth. Parkland/wooded course. 18 holes, 6493 yards. S.S.S. 71. *Green Fees:* weekdays £20.00. *Visitors:* welcome weekdays only. *Society Meetings:* by arrangement. Professional: C.J. Holdsworth (0923 820112). Secretary: R.A. Bond.

NORTHWOOD. **Sandy Lodge Golf Club,** Sandy Lodge Lane, Northwood, Middlesex HA6 2JD (Northwood (0923) 825429). *Location:* adjacent Moor Park Underground Station. Inland links. 18 holes, 6340 yards. S.S.S. 71. *Green Fees:* weekdays £26.00 per round. *Eating facilities:* full catering and bar service available. *Visitors:* not weekends – telephone first. Handicap Certificate required. *Society Meetings:* catered for by prior arrangement. Professional: Alex M. Fox (0923 825321). Secretary: J.N. Blair (0923 825429; Fax: 0923 824319).

ORPINGTON. **Lullingstone Park Golf Club,** Park Gate, Chelsfield, Near Orpington, Kent (Knockholt (0959) 32928). *Location:* M25 Junction 4, fifth exit on left (signposted). Undulating parkland. 18 holes, 6779 yards. S.S.S. 72. 9 holes, 2432 yards. Par 33. Pitch and putt/putting green, driving range. *Green Fees:* weekdays £6.00 per 9 holes, £9.00 per 18 holes; weekends £7.00 per 9 holes, £13.50 per 18 holes. *Eating facilities:* cafeteria and bar. *Visitors:* welcome at all times. All players on 18-holes course must have recognised golf shoes. *Society Meetings:* catered for, phone the Professional. Professional: Dave Cornford (0959 34542; Fax: 0959 34012). Secretary: G.S. Childs (0959 34297).

PINNER. **Grim's Dyke Golf Club,** Oxhey Lane, Hatch End, Pinner, Middlesex HA5 4AL (081-421 1286). *Location:* on A4008 Watford to Harrow (2 miles west of Harrow). Undulating parkland, tree lined, testing greens. 18 holes, 5600 yards. S.S.S. 67. Practice area. *Green Fees:* weekdays £20.00 per round, £25.00 per day; weekends only with a member. *Eating facilities:* bar snacks, lunches available on request. No catering on Mondays. *Visitors:* must produce Certificate of Handicap. *Society Meetings:* catered for Tuesdays and Fridays. Professional: John Rule (081-428 7484). Secretary: P. Payne (081-428 4539).

PINNER. **Pinner Hill Golf Club,** Southview Road, Pinner Hill HA5 3YA (081-866 0963). *Location:* one mile west Pinner Green. 18 holes, 6280 yards. S.S.S. 70. *Green Fees:* £25.00 weekdays, £32.00 weekends by prior arrangement only; Public Days (no access to clubhouse), Wednesdays and Thursdays £8.10 per round, £11.15 per day. *Eating facilities:* light refreshments served at all times (except Wednesdays and Thursdays). *Visitors:* welcome with Handicap Certificate or letter of introduction. *Society Meetings:* Mondays, Tuesdays and Fridays. Professional: Mark Grieve (081-866 2109). Secretary: Jeremy Devitt (081-868 4817).

ROEHAMPTON. **Roehampton Club Ltd,** Roehampton Lane, London SW15 5LR (081-876 1621). *Location:* South Circular Road between Sheen and Putney. Parkland. 18 holes, 6011 yards. S.S.S. 69. *Green Fees:* weekdays £15.00, weekends £20.00. *Eating facilities:* bar and full restaurant available all week. *Visitors:* welcome if introduced by member, and must play with member at weekends. *Society Meetings:* catered for by arrangement, if introduced by member. Professional: Alan L. Scott (081-876 3858). Chief Executive: Martin Yates (081-876 5505; Fax: 081-392 2318).

THE GOLF GUIDE 1994

England LONDON

RUISLIP. **Ruislip Golf Club,** King's End, Ickenham Road, Ruislip, Middlesex HA4 7OQ (Ruislip (0895) 638081). *Location:* two and a half miles from Junction 1, M40, first left after M40/A40 merge, onto B467, then left at T-Junction onto B466. Parkland course. 18 holes, 5702 yards. S.S.S. 68. Driving range (40 bays). *Green Fees:* £9.25 weekdays, £12.50 weekends. Juniors and Senior Citizens on income support £6.25 weekdays. *Eating facilities:* full restaurant facilities. *Visitors:* welcome, booking system at all times. *Society Meetings:* welcome by arrangement. Professional: Derek Nash (0895 632004). Secretary: B.J. Channing (0895 638835).

SHEPPERTON. **Sunbury Golf Club,** Charlton Lane, Shepperton, Middlesex TW17 8QA (0932 772898). *Location:* just off Junction 1 of the M3. Flat parkland course. 9 holes, 6502 yards. S.S.S. 72. 32 bay floodlit range, green 8am to 10pm. *Green Fees:* information not provided. *Eating facilities:* two bars, restaurant. *Visitors:* welcome, no restrictions. *Society Meetings:* welcome. Professional: Alistair Hardaway. Secretary: Sally Clark.

SHOOTERS HILL. **Shooters Hill Golf Club Ltd,** "Lowood", Eaglesfield Road, Shooters Hill, London SE18 3DA (081-854 1216). *Location:* off A207 between Blackheath and Welling. Hilly wooded course. 18 holes, 5736 yards. S.S.S. 68. *Green Fees:* weekdays £30.00. *Eating facilities:* bar and diningroom. *Visitors:* members of other clubs welcome weekdays on production of letter of introduction, or official Handicap Certificate. Jacket, collar and tie required in clubhouse. *Society Meetings:* catered for Tuesdays and Thursdays only. Professional: M. Ridge (081-854 0073). Secretary: B.R. Adams (081-854 6368; Fax: 081-854 0469).

SOUTHALL. **West Middlesex Golf Club,** Greenford Road, Southall, Middlesex UB1 3EE (081-574 0166). *Location:* junction of Uxbridge Road (A4020) and Greenford Road. 18 holes, 6242 yards. S.S.S. 70. *Green Fees:* information not provided. *Visitors:* welcome without reservation. *Society Meetings:* catered for by prior arrangement. Professional: L. Farmer. Secretary: P.J. Furness (081-574 3450).

SOUTHWARK. **Aquarius Golf Club,** Beachcroft Reservoir, Marmora Road, Honor Oak, Southwark SE22 0RY (081-693 1626). *Location:* nearest main road – Forest Hill Road. The course is situated on and around a reservoir, testing first and eighth holes. 9 holes, 5246 yards. S.S.S. 66. *Green Fees:* £10.00. *Eating facilities:* limited. *Visitors:* welcome with member only. Professional: F. Private. Secretary: Mrs Marilyn Moss.

STANMORE. **Stanmore Golf Club,** 29 Gordon Avenue, Stanmore, Middlesex HA7 2RL (081-954 2599). *Location:* turn off A410 by church to Old Church Lane, Gordon Avenue is to the right. Wooded, parkland course. 18 holes, 5860 yards. S.S.S. 68. Practice and putting areas. *Green Fees:* Tuesday, Wednesday and Thursday £25.00; Public Days, Monday and Friday £8.10; weekends with a member only. *Eating facilities:* lunch and dinner available. *Visitors:* welcome Tuesdays, Wednesdays and Thursdays, Handicap Certificates required on Wednesday and Thursday. Jacket and tie after 7pm. *Society Meetings:* catered for Wednesday and Thursday by prior booking only. Professional: Vivian Law (081-954 2646). Secretary: L.J. Pertwee. Caterer: (081-954 4661).

TOTTERIDGE. **South Herts Golf Club,** Links Drive, Totteridge N20 (081-445 0117). *Location:* off Totteridge Lane one mile from Whetstone, nearest station Totteridge. Parkland. 18 holes, 6432 yards. S.S.S. 71. *Green Fees:* on application. *Eating facilities:* lunch, high tea (Dinner served by arrangement). *Visitors:* welcome with reservation Wednesday, Thursday, Friday; lunch, high tea, dinner. Professional: R. Livingstone (081-445 4633). Secretary: P.F. Wise (081-445 2035).

TWICKENHAM. **Strawberry Hill Golf Club,** Wellesley Road, Twickenham TW2 (081-894 1246). *Location:* near Strawberry Hill Station. Parkland. 9 holes, 2381 (x2) yards. S.S.S. 62. *Green Fees:* weekdays £18.00 per round, £25.00 per day; weekends with member only. *Eating facilities:* course bar/lounge bar, bar snacks, lunches. *Visitors:* welcome, restrictions weekends and competition days. *Society Meetings:* small numbers (maximum 24) catered for by arrangement. Professional: P. Buchan (081-898 2082). Secretary: F.E. Ingoldby (081-894 0165).

The Crescent Lodge Hotel is a family run hotel situated in a quiet crescent in Harrow, yet only a short distance from the West End, Wembley and Heathrow. All rooms have colour TV, video and satellite, fridge and tea/coffee facilities. Many boast en suite facilities. For the businessman we offer fax and photocopying facilities. Conference room. Pleasant dining room overlooking gardens. Comfortable lounge. Many historic places to visit around Harrow. Several golf courses close to hand. We aim to make your stay better than home from home.

**56-62 Welldon Crescent, Harrow, Middlesex HA1 1QR.
Telephone: 081-863 5491 Fax: 081-427 5965**

LONDON England

THE GOLF GUIDE 1994

TWICKENHAM. **Twickenham Golf Course,** Staines Road, Twickenham (081-783 1698). *Location:* just off A316. Parkland. 9 holes, 3050 yards. S.S.S 35. Practice area. *Green Fees:* information not provided. *Eating facilities:* Pavilion Bar and cafe. *Visitors:* welcome, public course. Function room available. *Society Meetings:* welcome, full banqueting facilities. Golf Director: Suzy Baggs (081-783 1698). Secretary: Norman Harnett (081-783 1748).

UPMINSTER. **Upminster Golf Club,** 114 Hall Lane, Upminster (Upminster (04022) 20249). *Location:* one mile from Upminster Station. Parkland/wooded – river runs through the course. 18 holes, 5931 yards. S.S.S. 68. *Green Fees:* £25.00 per round, £30.00 per day weekdays. *Eating facilities:* full catering at club, bookable. *Visitors:* welcome weekdays except Tuesday mornings and must produce evidence of handicap. *Society Meetings:* catered for Wednesdays, Thursdays and Fridays (max 40). Professional: Neil Carr (04022 20000). Secretary: Keith Moyse (04022 22788).

UXBRIDGE. **Uxbridge Golf Course,** The Drive, Harefield Place, Uxbridge UB10 8PA (Uxbridge (0895) 272457). *Location:* off Swakleys Junction – M40. Undulating parkland. 18 holes, 5753 yards. S.S.S. 68. *Green Fees:* information not provided. *Eating facilities:* bars, restaurant. *Visitors:* welcome anytime, booking required at weekends. Function suite. *Society Meetings:* welcome Thursdays. Professional: Phil Howard (0895 237287; Fax: 0895 810262). Secretary: Brian Russell.

WANSTEAD. **Wanstead Golf Club,** Overton Drive, Wanstead E11 2LW (081-989 0604). *Location:* one mile from junction of A12 and A406. Parkland bordering Epping Forest with featured lake. 18 holes, 6109 yards. S.S.S. 69. *Green Fees:* £25.00 per day weekdays; weekends as member's guest only. *Eating facilities:* dining room and bars. *Visitors:* welcome Mondays, Tuesdays and Fridays by prior arrangement with the Secretary. Handicap Certificate required. Weekends with member only. *Society Meetings:* welcome, apply Secretary. Professional: Gary Jacom (081-989 9876). Secretary: Keith Jones (081-989 3938).

WEMBLEY. **Sudbury Golf Club Ltd,** Bridgewater Road, Wembley, Middlesex HA0 1AL (081-902 3713). *Location:* junction of A4005 (Bridgewater Road) and A4090 (Whitton Ave East). Undulating parkland. 18 holes, 6282 yards. S.S.S. 70. Practice ground. *Green Fees:* weekdays £20.00 per round, £30.00 two rounds. *Eating facilities:* dining room and bars. *Visitors:* welcome weekdays with Handicap Certificate. *Society Meetings:* catered for. Professional: Neil Jordan (081-902 7910). General Manager: A.J. Poole.

WEST DRAYTON. **Holiday Inns Golf Club,** Stockley Road, West Drayton, Middlesex UB7 9NA (0895 444232). Flat parkland course. 18 holes, 3856 yards. S.S.S. 62. *Green Fees:* information not provided. Eating facilities: catering and bars. *Visitors:* welcome. *Society Meetings:* welcome except weekends. Professional: N. Coles. Secretary: P. Davies (081-561 3471).

WIMBLEDON. **Royal Wimbledon Golf Club,** 29 Camp Road, Wimbledon SW19 4UW. *Location:* one mile west of War Memorial in Wimbledon Village. 18 holes, 6300 yards. S.S.S. 70. *Visitors:* not permitted. *Society Meetings:* Wednesdays and Thursdays only, by arrangement. Professional: Hugh Boyle (081-946 4606). Secretary: Maj. G.E. Jones (081-946 2125). Caddiemaster (081-946 1118).

WIMBLEDON. **Wimbledon Common Golf Club,** 19 Camp Road, Wimbledon Common, Wimbledon SW19 4UW (081-946 0294). Links type wooded course. 18 holes, 5438 yards. S.S.S. 66. *Green Fees:* weekdays £13.50 per round, £20.00 per day. *Eating facilities:* light lunches available every day; bar. *Visitors:* welcome weekdays, but only with a member at weekends. *Society Meetings:* groups of up to 24 catered for. Professional: J.S. Jukes (081-946 0294). Secretary: B.K. Cox (081-946 7571).

WIMBLEDON. **Wimbledon Park Golf Club,** Home Park Road, London SW19 7HR. *Location:* Church Road, Arthur Road and Home Park Road from Wimbledon High Street, or by District Line to Wimbledon Park Station where signposted. 18 holes, 5465 yards. *Green Fees:* £25.00 per day. *Eating facilities:* dining room and bar snacks each day except Monday. *Visitors:* welcome weekdays, occasional weekends after 3.30 pm (check with Professional). *Society Meetings:* catered for. Professional: D. Wingrove (081-946 4053). Secretary: M.K. Hale (081-946 1250).

WINCHMORE HILL. **Bush Hill Park Golf Club,** Bush Hill, Winchmore Hill, London N21 2BU (081-360 5738). *Location:* Enfield, nine miles north of City. Parkland. 18 holes, 5825 yards. S.S.S. 68. Practice ground and nets. *Green Fees:* weekdays £20.00; weekends only with member. *Eating facilities:* full catering and bar facilities. *Visitors:* welcome weekdays, Handicap Certificate required. *Society Meetings:* catered for weekdays except Wednesdays. Professional: G. Low (081-360 4103). Secretary: Michael Burnand (081-360 5738).

WOOD GREEN. **Muswell Hill Golf Club,** Rhodes Avenue, Wood Green, London N22 4UT (081-888 2044; Fax: 081-889 9380). *Location:* North Circular/ Bounds Green tube station one mile. Parkland/ wooded. 18 holes, 6438 yards. S.S.S. 71. *Green Fees:* weekdays £23.00 per round, £33.00 per day; weekends £35.00 per round. Bookings through Secretary and Professional. *Eating facilities:* available in Clubhouse. *Visitors:* welcome weekdays, weekends pre-booked with Professional. *Society Meetings:* catered for Monday, Wednesday, Thursday and Friday, charges on request. Professional: I. Roberts (081-888 8046). Secretary: D.E. Beer (081-888 1764).

England AVON

Avon

BATH. **Bath Golf Club,** Sham Castle, North Road, Bath BA2 6JG (Bath (0225) 425182). *Location:* off A36, one mile south-east of Bath City Centre. 18 holes, 6369 yards, 5824 metres. S.S.S. 70. *Green Fees:* weekdays £25.00; weekends and Bank Holidays £30.00. *Eating facilities:* catering every day. *Visitors:* with bona fide handicap welcome. *Society Meetings:* catered for Wednesday and Friday. Professional: Peter Hancox (0225 466953). Secretary: P.B. Edwards (0225 463834).

BATH. **Entry Hill Golf Club,** Entry Hill, Bath BA2 5AN (0225 834248). *Location:* one mile south of city centre, off A367 road to Wells. Hilly parkland course with many young trees. 9 holes, 2103 yards, 1922 metres. S.S.S. 61 (18 holes). Practice net. *Green Fees:* weekdays £7.00; weekends £8.00. Weekdays: rounds completed before 12 noon £4.75. *Visitors:* no restrictions but pre-booking up to one week in advance essential. Well equipped Pro Shop. *Society Meetings:* as per visitors. Professional: T. Tapley (0225 834248). Secretary: J. Sercombe (0225 834248).

BATH. **Fosseway Country Club and Centurion Hotel,** Charlton Lane, Midsomer Norton, Bath BA3 4BD (0761 417711; Fax: 0761 418357). *Location:* off A367 10 miles south of Bath; midway between Bath and Wells. Flat parkland course. 9 holes, 4278 yards. S.S.S. 65. *Green Fees:* weekdays £10.00; weekends and Bank Holidays £15.00. *Eating facilities:* table d'hôte/à la carte restaurant, full bar meals. *Visitors:* welcome except Saturday and Sunday mornings and Wednesday evenings. Outdoor bowls, squash, snooker, heated indoor pool. *Society Meetings:* welcome. Secretary: R.F. Jones (0761 412214).

BATH. **Lansdown Golf Club,** Lansdown, Bath BA1 9BT (Bath (0225) 425007). *Location:* M4 junction 18 follow signs for Park and Ride. Flat, parkland, 800ft above sea-level, panoramic views. 18 holes, 6299 yards, 5759 metres. S.S.S. 70. Practice ground. *Green Fees:* weekdays £18.00 per round, £24.00 per day; weekends £30.00. *Eating facilities:* snacks at all times, lunch or dinner by arrangement with Steward. *Visitors:* welcome anytime, must have Handicap Certificate. *Society Meetings:* Mondays/Fridays only. Professional: T. Mercer (0225 420242). Secretary: Ron Smith (0225 422138).

BRISTOL. **Bristol and Clifton Golf Club,** Beggar Bush Lane, Failand, Bristol BS8 3TH (0275 393117). *Location:* two miles west of the Suspension Bridge or three miles south of the M5-Junction 19 access. 18 holes, 6294 yards. S.S.S. 70. Parkland course. *Green Fees:* weekdays £27.00; weekends £35.00. *Eating facilities:* available. *Visitors:* welcome weekdays without reservation, must have current golf club Handicap Certificate. *Society Meetings:* welcome. Professional: Peter Mawson (0275 393031). Secretary: D.E. Aitken (0275 393474).

BRISTOL. **Chipping Sodbury Golf Club,** Chipping Sodbury, Bristol BS17 6PU (Chipping Sodbury (0454) 312024). *Location:* 12 miles north of Bristol, nine miles from Junction No. 14 on M5 and three miles from Junction 18 on M4. Parkland course. 18 hole course, 6912 yards; 9 hole course, 3076 yards. S.S.S. 73. *Green Fees:* 18-hole course weekdays £20.00; weekends £25.00. 9 hole course £2.50 any day. *Eating facilities:* full catering available. *Visitors:* welcome except Saturday/Sunday morning and Bank Holidays. Must have Handicap Certificate. *Society Meetings:* catered for by prior arrangement weekdays only. Professional: Mike Watts (0454 314087). Secretary: K.G. Starr (0454 319042).

BRISTOL. **Filton Golf Club,** Golf Course Lane, Filton, Bristol BS12 7QS (Bristol (0272) 692021). *Location:* Off A38 north of Bristol. Parkland, 18 holes, 6277 yards. S.S.S. 70. Two practice fields. *Green Fees:* weekdays £20.00 per round, £25.00 per day, £12.00 with member; weekends £12.00 with member only. *Eating facilities:* meals available. *Visitors:* accepted daily subject to programme. *Society Meetings:* all catered for, subject to programme – must book well in advance. Professional: J.C.N. Lumb (0272 694158). Secretary: Mr M. Burns (0272 694169).

BRISTOL. **Henbury Golf Club,** Henbury Hill, Westbury-on-Trym, Bristol BS10 7QB (Bristol (0272) 500660). *Location:* north M5 Junction 17 A4018 to Westbury-on-Trym; next to Blaise Castle. Wooded parkland, 18 holes, 6039 yards. S.S.S. 70. *Green Fees:* weekdays £21.00 for 18 holes, £28.00 more than 18 holes; weekends with member only. *Eating facilities:* dining room and bar snacks. *Visitors:* welcome, restricted at weekends and Bank Holidays. *Society Meetings:* Tuesdays and Fridays by prior arrangement. Professional: Nick Riley (0272 502121). Managing Secretary: J.R. Leeming (0272 500044).

BRISTOL. **Knowle Golf Club,** Fairway, Bristol BS4 5DF (Bristol (0272) 776341). *Location:* three miles south of city centre, left off Wells Road. A4 – Bath. Parkland course. 18 holes, 6100 yards. S.S.S. 69. Practice field. *Green Fees:* weekdays £22.00 for 18 holes, £27.00 for 27 holes; weekends £27.00 for 18 holes, £32.00 for 27 holes. *Eating facilities:* bar and snacks, dinners by arrangement with Stewardess. *Visitors:* welcome with Handicap Certificate. *Society Meetings:* Thursdays only with Handicap Certificate. Professional: Mr Gordon M. Brand (0272 779193). Secretary: Mrs J.D. King (0272 770660).

BRISTOL. **Mangotsfield Golf Club,** Carsons Road, Mangotsfield, Bristol (Bristol (0272) 565501). *Location:* four miles M32 via Downend, one mile Warmley A420. Parkland, hilly course. 18 holes, 5337 yards, 4877 metres. S.S.S. 66. Small practice area. *Green Fees:* information not provided. *Eating facilities:* no restriction on food and drink. *Visitors:* welcome, no restric-

AVON England   THE GOLF GUIDE 1994

tions. *Society Meetings:* catered for weekdays only. Professional: Craig Trewin. Secretary: Terry Bindon (0272 755432 daytime, evenings 0272 697032).

BRISTOL. **Shirehampton Park Golf Club**, Park Hill, Shirehampton, Bristol BS11 0UL (Bristol (0272) 823059). *Location:* one mile from Junction 18 on M5 on B4054 to Shirehampton. Parkland course. 18 holes, 5498 yards. S.S.S. 67. *Green Fees:* weekdays £18.00, weekends £25.00 (check with Secretary/Professional). *Eating facilities:* lunches, snacks, teas, etc available daily. *Visitors:* welcome weekdays, with reservation (check with Secretary), not weekends or Public Holidays. *Society Meetings:* catered for on Mondays, application to Secretary. Professional: Brent Ellis (0272 822488). Secretary: Piers Drew-Wilkinson (0272 822083).

BRISTOL. **Tall Pines Golf Club**, Cooks Bridle Path, Downside, Backwell, Bristol BS19 3DJ (0275 472076). *Location:* off A38 next to Bristol Airport. Parkland. 18 holes, 5767 yards. S.S.S. 68. Practice ground. *Green Fees:* weekdays £10.00; weekends £12.50. Twilight ticket half price. *Eating facilities:* restaurant, bar. *Visitors:* welcome at all times, bookings at weekends. *Society Meetings:* welcome except weekends. Professional/Manager: Terry Murray (0275 472076).

BRISTOL. **The Long Ashton Golf Club**, The Club House, Long Ashton, Bristol BS18 9DW (0275 392229). *Location:* three miles south-west of Bristol on the B3129 Clevedon/Bristol Road. Wooded parkland. 18 holes, 6077 yards. S.S.S. 70. Practice ground. *Green Fees:* weekdays £22.00; weekends £30.00. *Eating facilities:* full catering daily, bar open Monday to Saturday (11am – 11pm). *Visitors:* welcome, must have current Handicap Certificate. *Society Meetings:* by arrangement with Secretary. Professional: Denis Scanlan (0275 392265). Secretary: B. Manning (0275 392316; Fax: 0275 394395).

BRISTOL. **Tracy Park Golf and Country Club**, Bath Road, Wick, Bristol BS15 5RN (0272 372251; Fax: 0272 374288). *Location:* M4 Junction 18, A46 towards Bath, A420 towards Bristol. Turn left at bottom of steep hill for Lansdown/Bath. Wooded parkland with water hazards. 27 holes, 6800, 6800, 6200 yards. S.S.S. 73, 73, 70. Practice ground. *Green Fees:* weekdays £15/£22, weekends £20/£30. *Eating facilities:* full catering available. *Visitors:* welcome – telephone ahead. *Society Meetings:* welcome. Tennis, swimming, squash, croquet, snooker available. Professional: Grant Aitken (0272 373521). Manager: Stephen Allen.

Penscot Farmhouse Hotel
SHIPHAM, NR. CHEDDAR, SOMERSET BS25 1TW

Set in superb Mendip countryside, the Penscot has 10 Golf Clubs within 10 mile radius, including Bristol and Clifton, Tall Pines, Long Ashton and Weston Super Mare. Concessionary rates at Puxton. The Hotel offers high standard, varied table d'hôte or à la carte menus, comfortable sitting room and lounge bar with log fires. Ensuite bedrooms with tea/coffee making facilities, direct dial telephones. Local trout fishing and clay pigeon shooting arranged. Ideal for small company conferences with personal attention assured. 2½ hours from London; 2 hours from Birmingham.
GROUP RATES AVAILABLE FOR PARTY BOOKINGS. TELEPHONE 0934-842659 for free brochure.

---

the commodore
and Worlebury & Weston Golf Clubs

Literally minutes from these quite differing and superb courses, The Commodore is a peaceful and stylish haven dedicated to fine food and service – you concentrate on your handicap whilst we concentrate on you!

Please telephone our sales office for details of year round special terms and preferential green fees. Group discounts.

The Commodore Hotel
Beach Road, Sand Bay, Kewstoke,
Weston-super-Mare, Avon BS22 9UZ.
Telephone: Weston-super-Mare
(0934) 415778   Fax: (0934) 636483

THE GOLF GUIDE 1994

England AVON/BEDFORDSHIRE

CLEVEDON. **Clevedon Golf Club,** Castle Road, Walton, Clevedon BS21 7AA (0275 873140). *Location:* two miles from M5 Junction 20; M5 Junction 19 (A369) four miles. Picturesque, beautiful parkland course, hilly. 18 holes, 5799 yards. S.S.S. 69. Practice green and net. *Green Fees:* weekdays £22.00, weekends and Bank Holidays £35.00. *Eating facilities:* available every day except Mondays (snacks only). *Visitors:* welcome except Wednesdays. Handicap Certificate must be produced; must phone in advance for availability. *Society Meetings:* catered for on Tuesdays only. Professional: Martin Heggie (0275 874704). Secretary: Capt. M. Sullivan (0275 874057; Fax: 0275 341228).

SALTFORD. **Saltford Golf Club,** Golf Club Lane, Saltford, Bristol BS18 3AA (Saltford (0225) 873220). *Location:* off A4 between Bristol and Bath. Wooded parkland course. 18 holes, 6081 yards. S.S.S. 69. Practice ground. *Green Fees:* weekdays £21.00 single round, £24.00 more than one round; weekends £25.00 single round summer only. *Eating facilities:* restaurant, bar service. *Visitors:* welcome. *Society Meetings:* accepted by arrangement. Professional: D. Millensted (0225 872043). Secretary: Valerie Radnedge (0225 873513).

WESTON-SUPER-MARE. **Weston-Super-Mare Golf Club,** The Clubhouse, Uphill Road North, Weston-Super-Mare BS23 4NQ (Weston-Super-Mare (0934) 621360). *Location:* M5 Junction 21 – on the sea front. Flat links course with excellent greens. 18 holes, 6251 yards. S.S.S. 70. Large practice area. *Green Fees:* weekdays £20.00, weekends £28.00. *Eating facilities:* full bar and catering facilities. *Visitors:* welcome weekdays and weekends. Handicap Certificate required. *Society Meetings:* catered for weekdays. Professional: Terence Murray (0934 633360). Secretary: D.R. Cooper (0934 626968).

WESTON-SUPER-MARE. **Worlebury Golf Club,** Monks Hill, Weston-Super-Mare BS22 9SX (Weston-Super-Mare (0934) 623214). *Location:* from the M5 (Junction 21) then A370 main road to the town for two miles, turn right into Baytree Road and continue to top of Milton Hill. Hill top with extensive views of the Severn Estuary and Wales. 18 holes, 5936 yards. S.S.S. 69. *Green Fees:* weekdays £20.00 per day, £12.00 with a member; weekends and Bank Holidays £30.00 per day, £17.00 with a member. *Eating facilities:* bar and restaurant. *Visitors:* welcome without reservation. *Society Meetings:* catered for by arrangement. Professional: Gary Marks (0934 418473). Secretary: Ralph Bagg (0934 625789).

Bedfordshire

AMPTHILL. **Millbrook Golf Course,** Millbrook, Ampthill MK45 2JB (0525 840252; Fax: 0525 405669). *Location:* one mile from town centre, M1 Junction 12 from south, Junction 13 from north, towards Ampthill (A507), located on A418. Hilly tree-lined parkland, one of the longest courses in Britain. 18 holes, 6779 yards. S.S.S. 73. Practice ground. *Green Fees:* weekdays £12.00 – £28.00; weekends £30.00 for 36 holes. Surcharge for non-handicap players. *Eating facilities:* bar snacks, meals available from 11am daily, booking required for main evening meals. *Visitors:* welcome weekdays all day except Thursdays (course closed), weekends after 12 noon. *Society Meetings:* by arrangement with course Secretary. Professional: T.K. Devine (0525 402269). Secretary: Mrs M.R. Brackley (Tel & Fax: 0525 840252).

BEADLOW. **Beadlow Manor Hotel, Golf and Country Club,** Beadlow, Near Shefford SG17 5PH (Silsoe (0525) 860800; Fax: 0525 861345). *Location:* from M1 (J12) take A5120 east to Ampthill, then A507 to Shefford. From A1 (J10) take A507 west to Ampthill. Challenging, rolling parkland with water hazards. Two courses, 36 holes, 6619 yards. S.S.S. 73. Covered 25 bay floodlit driving range, practice area. *Green Fees:* weekdays £14.00; weekends £27.00. Special rates from £7. *Eating facilities:* restaurant, three bars, snacks, refreshments, two function rooms. *Visitors:* welcome at all times. Integral Health Farm offers steam room, sauna, sunbeds, spa baths, beauty salon, gym. Residential Golf and Health Breaks available. Professional shop. Special mid-week and weekend Breaks for Society and Company Groups. All reservations through Sales and Marketing Office.

BEADLOW • MANOR
HOTEL GOLF AND COUNTRY CLUB
Beadlow, Near Shefford, Bedfordshire SG17 5PH
Telephone: 0525 860800/861292   Fax: 0525 861345
SEE OUR COLOUR ADVERTISEMENT ON THE INSIDE BACK COVER OF THIS GUIDE.

BEDFORDSHIRE England

BEDFORD. **Bedford and County Golf Club,** Green Lane, Clapham, Bedford (0234) 354010). *Location:* off A6 north of Bedford before Clapham Village. Parkland. 18 holes, 6290 yards. S.S.S. 70. *Green Fees:* weekdays £27.50, with member £11.00; weekends and Bank Holidays £16.00 with a member only. *Eating facilities:* full catering facilities and bar. *Visitors:* welcome without reservation except weekends. *Society Meetings:* catered for Mondays, Tuesdays, Thursdays and Fridays. Professional/Manager: Eddie Bullock (0234 359189/352617; Fax: 0234 357195).

BEDFORD. **Bedfordshire Golf Club,** Biddenham, Bedford MK40 4AF (Bedford (0234) 353241). *Location:* one mile west of Bedford town centre on the A428. Wooded parkland, flat. 18 holes, 6185 yards. S.S.S. 69. *Green Fees:* weekdays £20.00; £24.00 per day. *Eating facilities:* bar and catering; evening meals by arrangement. *Visitors:* welcome on weekdays, must be with members at weekends. *Society Meetings:* catered for weekdays. Professional: G. Buckle (0234 353653). Manager: J.K. White (0234 261669).

BEDFORD. **Mowsbury Golf Club,** Cleat Hill, Kimbolton Road, Bedford MK41 8DQ (0234 771493). *Location:* on B660 at northern limit of city boundary. 18 holes, 6510 yards. S.S.S. 71. Driving range. *Green Fees:* on request. *Eating facilities:* meals and bar snacks until 2pm; evening meals if booked in advance. *Visitors:* welcome. Squash courts. *Society Meetings:* not on Friday afternoons or weekends. Professional: Malcolm Summers (0234 216374), for tee reservations and fees. Secretary: L.W. Allan (0234 771041).

DUNSTABLE. **Dunstable Downs Golf Club,** Whipsnade Road, Dunstable LU6 2NB (Dunstable (0582) 604472). *Location:* on B4541; from the south, leave M1 at Markyate, A5 to centre of town, turn left at roundabout into West Street, turn left into Whipsnade Road at third roundabout, club half a mile on left. Downland course, 18 holes, 6184 yards. S.S.S. 70. *Green Fees:* on application. *Eating facilities:* catering Tuesday to Sunday. *Visitors:* weekdays if members of recognised Golf Club, weekends with member only. Handicap Certificate required. *Society Meetings:* Tuesdays and Thursdays. Professional: M. Weldon (0582 662806). Secretary: Lt Cdr J.R. Smith RN (Rtd) (0582 604472; Fax: 0582 478700).

DUNSTABLE. **Tilsworth Golf Centre,** Dunstable Road, Tilsworth, Leighton Buzzard LU7 9PU (Leighton Buzzard (0525) 210722). *Location:* two miles north of Dunstable off A5, Tilsworth turn-off. Parkland. 18 holes, 5303 yards. S.S.S. 66. 9 holes £5.00, 18 holes £8.00; *Green Fees:* weekdays 9 holes £5.00, 18 holes £8.00; weekends 9 holes £6.00, 18 holes £10.00. *Eating facilities:* bar snacks and restaurant available. *Visitors:* welcome any time (except Sundays before 11.45 am). Bookings taken up to seven days in advance. *Society Meetings:* welcome by prior arrangement. Professional: Nick Webb (0525 210721).

LEIGHTON BUZZARD. **Aylesbury Vale Golf Club,** Stewkley Road, Wing, Leighton Buzzard LU7 0UJ (0525 240196). *Location:* four miles west of Leighton Buzzard, on Stewkley to Wing road. Gently undulating course with lakes. 18 holes, 6622 yards. S.S.S. 72. 10

THE GOLF GUIDE 1994

bay driving range. *Green Fees:* weekdays £12.00, £8.50 with member; weekends £18.50, £14.00 with member. £10.00 after 4pm weekends. *Eating facilities:* downstairs bar and restaurant, upstairs bar with balcony, views over course. *Visitors:* welcome any time, no restrictions apart from correct dress. Indoor golf simulator. *Society Meetings:* all welcome. Professional: Lee Scarbrow (0525 240197). Secretary: Chris Wright (0525 240196).

LEIGHTON BUZZARD. **Leighton Buzzard Golf Club,** Plantation Road, Leighton Buzzard LU7 7JF (Leighton Buzzard (0525) 373812). *Location:* off A5 between Dunstable and Milton Keynes at village of Heath and Reach. Wooded parkland course. 18 holes, 6101 yards. S.S.S. 70. Practice ground. *Green Fees:* weekdays £18.00 per round, £25.00 per day; weekends with member only, £14.00. *Eating facilities:* available – dining room and two bars. *Visitors:* welcome weekdays with Handicap Certificate only. (Tuesday Ladies' Day). Weekends and Bank Holidays with member only. *Society Meetings:* catered for weekdays only, except Tuesdays. Professional: Lee Muncey (0525 372143). Secretary: J. Burchell (0525 373811).

LEIGHTON BUZZARD near. **Ivinghoe Golf Club,** The Wellcroft, Ivinghoe, Near Leighton Buzzard LU7 9EF (0296 668881). *Location:* four miles from Tring and Dunstable, seven miles from Aylesbury. Rolling parkland. 9 holes, 4508 yards. S.S.S. 62. *Green Fees:* weekdays £6.00, weekends £7.00. *Eating facilities:* bar meals (between 11am and 2pm). *Visitors:* no restrictions weekdays, some restrictions weekends. *Society Meetings:* all welcome and catered for. Professional: Bill Garrad (0296 668696; Fax: 0296 662755). Secretary: Mrs S. Garrad (0296 668696; Fax: 0296 662755).

LEIGHTON BUZZARD near. **Mentmore Golf and Country Club,** Mentmore, Near Leighton Buzzard LU7 0UA (0296 662020; Fax: 0296 662592). *Location:* Leighton Buzzard three miles, in village of Mentmore. Parkland – some water features and woodland. Two courses – Rothschild and Rosebery. 36 holes, 6777 & 6763 yards. S.S.S. 72. Driving range. *Green Fees:* £25.00, £15.00 with a member. *Eating facilities:* restaurant, two bars; function suite. *Visitors:* welcome. *Society Meetings:* welcome. Professional/Golf Director: Pip Elson.

LUTON. **South Beds. Golf Club,** Warden Hill Road, Luton LU2 7AA (0582 591500). *Location:* on east side A6, two and a half miles north of Luton. Undulating downland course. 18 holes, 6342 yards. S.S.S. 71. Also 9 holes, 4914 yards. S.S.S. 64. Practice fairway, hut and chipping area. *Green Fees:* 18 holes weekdays £26.00 per day, £17.00 per round; weekends £34.50 per day, £24.00 per round (not on Competition Days). 9 holes (twice round) weekdays £8.00, weekends £11.00. *Eating facilities:* full course meals (must be booked), snacks at all times. *Visitors:* welcome weekdays with reservation. Handicap Certificate essential. Tuesday afternoon is Ladies Day. *Society Meetings:* catered for by arrangement. Professional: Eddie Cogle (0582 591209). Secretary: S. Beaton (0582 591500).

THE GOLF GUIDE 1994

England   BEDFORDSHIRE/BERKSHIRE

LUTON. **Stockwood Park Golf Club,** London Road, Luton LU1 4LX (Luton (0582) 23241). *Location:* adjacent Exit 10 of M1 exit Luton Airport. Parkland. 18 holes, 5973 yards. S.S.S. 69. Driving range, mini golf course and pitch and putt. *Green Fees:* weekdays Luton residents £5.90, non residents £7.10; weekends Luton residents £8.10, non residents £9.30. Subject to review. *Eating facilities:* two bars and restaurant. *Visitors:* always welcome, municipal club. *Society Meetings:* catered for Mondays, Tuesdays and Thursdays by prior arrangement. Professional: G. McCarthy (0582 413704). Secretary: A.J. Bland.

MILTON KEYNES. **Aspley Guise and Woburn Sands Golf Club,** West Hill, Aspley Guise MK17 8DX (Milton Keynes (0908) 582264). *Location:* two miles west of Junction 13 M1, between Aspley Guise and Woburn Sands. Undulating parkland, 18 holes, 6135 yards, 5610 metres. S.S.S. 70. *Green Fees:* weekdays £21.00 per round, £26.00 per day. *Eating facilities:* full catering except Mondays. *Visitors:* welcome weekdays with bona fide handicaps – check with Secretary; only with a member at weekends. *Society Meetings:* Wednesdays and Fridays. Professional: Trevor Hill (0908 582974). Secretary: M.A. Beadle (0908 583596).

SANDY. **John O'Gaunt Golf Club,** Sutton Park, Sandy SG19 2LY (0767 260 360; Fax: 0767 261381). *Location:* on B1040 off A1 two miles north of Biggleswade. Parkland courses. Two 18 hole courses: John O'Gaunt Course 6513 yards S.S.S. 71 and Carthagena Course 5869 yards S.S.S. 68. Small practice area. *Green Fees:* weekdays £35.00, weekends £50.00. *Eating facilities:* restaurant and bar. *Visitors:* welcome. Handicap Certificate required at weekends. *Society Meetings:* welcome weekdays, with some limitations on Thursdays and Fridays. Professional: P. Round (0767 260094). Secretary: I.M. Simpson (0767 260360).

WYBOSTON. **Wyboston Lakes Golf Club,** Wyboston Lakes, Wyboston MK44 3AL (Huntingdon (0480) 218411). *Location:* one mile south of St. Neots, off A1 and A45. Parkland with play round five lakes. 18 holes, 5803 yards. S.S.S. 69. Driving range. *Green Fees:* weekdays £10.00 per 18 holes; weekends £14.00 per 18 holes. £20.00 per 36 holes weekdays only. Twilight Ticket (play till dark) £6.00 from 5pm. *Eating facilities:* clubhouse catering. *Visitors:* welcome weekdays, booking times required for weekends. Motel on site. *Society Meetings:* catered for weekdays only. Professional: P. Ashwell (0480 212501). Secretary: B. Chinn (0480 219200).

Berkshire

ASCOT. **Berkshire Golf CLub,** Swinley Road, Ascot SL5 8AY (Ascot (0344) 21495). *Location:* on A332 between Bagshot and Ascot. Heathland (wooded) course. 36 holes. Blue Course: 6260 yards, S.S.S. 70, Par 71. Red Course: 6369 yards, S.S.S. 70, Par 72. Practice facilities. *Green Fees:* £45.00 per round, £60.00 per day weekdays. *Eating facilities:* dining room open daily except Monday, snack bar open daily; bar open every day. *Visitors:* welcome weekdays only by application to the Secretary. *Society Meetings:* catered for by prior bookings. Professional: P. Anderson (0344 22351). Secretary: Major P.D. Clarke (0344 21496).

ASCOT. **Lavender Park Golf Centre,** Swinley Road, Ascot SL5 1BD (0344 890940). *Location:* one mile outside Bracknell on the A329. Flat, semi wooded course. 9 holes, 1104 yards. S.S.S. 28. 26 bay floodlit driving range. *Green Fees:* weekdays £3.25; weekends £4.25. *Eating facilities:* hot and cold food available. *Visitors:* welcome at all times. *Society Meetings:* welcome. Professional: Tony Bowers (0344 886096).

ASCOT. **Royal Ascot Golf Club,** Winkfield Road, Ascot SL5 7LJ (Ascot (0344) 22923). *Location:* Winkfield Road is off Ascot High Street (A329). Heathland. 18 holes, 5709 yards. S.S.S. 68. *Green Fees:* weekdays £11.00 as member's guest; weekends £13.00 as member's guest. *Eating facilities:* full catering available except Mondays. *Visitors:* welcome only as guests of members. *Society Meetings:* catered for Wednesdays and Thursdays, maximum 40. Professional: Garry Malia (0344 24656). Secretary: Derek Simmonds (0344 25175).

ASCOT. **Swinley Forest Golf Club,** Coronation Road, Ascot SL5 9LE (0344 20197). *Location:* between Ascot and Bagshot. 18 holes, 6001 yards. *Green Fees:* £65.00 only on the introduction of a member. *Eating facilities:* lunches served. *Visitors:* welcome only with a member. *Society Meetings:* catered for. Professional: R.C. Parker (0344 874811). Secretary: I.L. Pearce.

CROWTHORNE. **East Berkshire Golf Club,** Ravenswood Avenue, Crowthorne RG11 6BD (Crowthorne (0344) 772041). *Location:* M3 Junction 3 – Bracknell turn off follow signs to Crowthorne, Ravenswood Avenue opposite Railway Station. Heathland course. 18 holes, 6344 yards. S.S.S. 70. *Green Fees:* information not provided. *Eating facilities:* meals à la carte except Monday. *Visitors:* welcome weekdays, Handicap Certificate essential. *Society Meetings:* Thursdays and Fridays only. Professional: Arthur Roe (0344 774112). Secretary: W.H. Short (0344 772041; Fax: 0344 777378).

BERKSHIRE *England*   THE GOLF GUIDE 1994

MAIDENHEAD. **Maidenhead Golf Club,** Shoppenhangers Road, Maidenhead SL6 2PZ (Maidenhead (0628) 20545). *Location:* adjacent to Maidenhead Station (south side), one mile from M4. Flat parkland course. 18 holes, 6364 yards. S.S.S. 70. *Green Fees:* weekdays £27.00. *Eating facilities:* bar meals Monday to Friday. *Visitors:* welcome weekdays, no visitors after 12 noon Fridays, Handicap Certificate required. *Society Meetings:* welcome, main days Wednesdays and Thursdays. Professional: Clive Dell (0628 24067). Secretary: Iain Lindsay (0628 24693).

MAIDENHEAD near. **Hawthorn Hill Golf Centre,** Drift Road, Hawthorn Hill, Near Maidenhead SL6 3ST (0628 771030). *Location:* M4 Junction 8/9 to Maidenhead, A330 to Ascot. Parkland course. 18 holes. 38 bay floodlit driving range. *Green Fees:* £12.00 per round (£7.00 for 9 holes) weekdays; £15.00 per round (£8.00 for 9 holes) weekends. Juniors/Senior Citizens concessionary rates. *Eating facilities:* large clubhouse, restaurant, barbecue, private function hall. *Visitors:* always welcome, open every day except Christmas Day. Large Pro shop, Conference facilities. *Society Meetings:* always welcome. Professional: (0628 26035). Secretary: Alan Kibblewhite (0628 771030).

MAIDENHEAD. **Temple Golf Club,** Henley Road, Hurley, Near Maidenhead SL6 5LH (0628 824248). *Location:* on the A423 Maidenhead to Henley Road (exit 8/9 on M4) Parkland. 18 holes, 6206 yards. S.S.S. 70. Putting, pitching, net. *Green Fees:* £25.00 per round, £40.00 per day weekdays; £50.00 per day weekends. Society full day £58 including meals. *Eating facilities:* available. *Visitors:* welcome, not before 9.15am and 2.15pm. Handicap Certificate required. *Society Meetings:* must book a year in advance. Professional: Alan Dobbins (0628 824254). Secretary: D.W. Kirkland (0628 824795).

MAIDENHEAD. **Winter Hill Golf Club,** Grange Lane, Cookham SL6 9RP (Bourne End (0628) 527810). *Location:* M4 Junction 8/9, four miles from Maidenhead. Parkland. 18 holes, 6408 yards. S.S.S. 71. Large practice ground. *Green Fees:* £24.00 weekdays. *Eating facilities:* lunches/snacks available daily. *Visitors:* welcome weekdays – confirmatory telephone enquiry advisable. Dress – strictly no jeans/trainers/shell suits on course or in clubhouse. *Society Meetings:* welcome, main day Wednesday. Professional: Mr. Paul Hedges (0628 527610). Secretary: Mr G.B. Charters-Rowe (0628 527613).

NEWBURY. **Newbury and Crookham Golf Club Ltd,** Bury's Bank Road, Greenham, Newbury RG15 8BZ (0635 40035). *Location:* on north side of Newbury. Varied and interesting with woods or trees on almost every hole. 18 holes, 5880 yards, 5380 metres. S.S.S. 68. *Green Fees:* weekdays £27.50; weekends £15.00 with a member only. Reduced rates for groups over 25 in number. *Eating facilities:* restaurant/bar. *Visitors:* welcome, except weekends and Bank Holidays unless with a member. *Society Meetings:* welcome Wednesdays, Thursdays and Fridays. Professional: Mr David Harris (0635 31201). Secretary: Mrs J.R. Hearsey (0635 40035).

NEWBURY. **West Berkshire Golf Club,** Chaddleworth, Newbury RG16 0HS. *Location:* M4 Junction 14, SP RAF Welford, OS Map Ref SU411 762. Downland. 18 holes, 7069 yards. S.S.S. 74. *Green Fees:* £23.00 weekdays. *Eating facilities:* full catering available. *Visitors:* welcome weekdays, members and guests only at weekends. *Society Meetings:* catered for. Professional: (04882 8851). Secretary: (04882 574).

NORTH ASCOT. **Mill Ride Golf Club,** Mill Ride Estate, North Ascot SL5 8LT (0344 886777). *Location:* off Junction 3 of M3 or Junction 6 of M4, one mile from Ascot Racecourse. Parkland; designed by Donald Steel. 18 holes, 6750 yards. Par 72. Putting green, chipping green, driving range. *Green Fees:* information not provided. *Eating facilities:* lounge bar/restaurant/private dining room. *Visitors:* by reservation only at specified times. Gym/saunas/steam rooms. Accommodation. Pro shop. Professional: Suzy Baggs (0344 886777).

READING. **Calcot Park Golf Club,** Bath Road, Calcot, Reading RG3 5RN (0734 427124). *Location:* off Exit 12, M4 along A4 towards Reading, approximately one mile. Undulating wooded parkland. 18 holes, 6283 yards. S.S.S. 70. Limited practice areas. *Green Fees:* weekdays £30.00. *Eating facilities:* fully licensed restaurant, snacks available, two bars. *Visitors:* welcome on provision of Handicap Certificate. Not weekends or Bank Holidays. Advisable to ring first to check availability. *Society Meetings:* catered for Tuesday, Wednesday and Thursday. Professional: Albert MacKenzie (0734 427797). Secretary: A.L. Bray.

READING. **Hurst Golf Club,** Sandford Lane, Hurst, Reading (0734 344355). *Location:* five miles Reading towards Wokingham. Parkland by the side of a large lake. 9 holes, 3154 yards. S.S.S. 70. *Green Fees:* information not provided. *Eating facilities:* bar and bar snacks. *Visitors:* unrestricted, bookings accepted. *Society Meetings:* welcome. Professional: Paul Watson (0734 344355). Secretary E. Brewer (Fax: 0344 301020).

READING. **Reading Golf Club,** 17 Kidmore End Road, Emmer Green, Reading RG4 8SG (Reading (0734) 472169). *Location:* two miles north of Reading off the Peppard Road (B481). Parkland. 18 holes, 6212 yards. S.S.S. 70. Practice facilities. *Green Fees:* £28.00 per day, £14.00 with member. *Eating facilities:* available. *Visitors:* welcome Monday to Thursday if member of recognised club, with handicap of 24 or less. Friday to Sunday with member only. *Society Meetings:* catered for by arrangement Tuesdays, Wednesdays and Thursdays. Professional: Tim Morrison (0734 476115). Secretary: J. Weekes (0734 472909).

READING. **Sonning Golf Club,** Duffield Road, Sonning RG4 0GJ (Reading (0734) 693332). *Location:* left off A4 at Sonning Roundabout, then left again. Parkland. 18 holes, 6366 yards. S.S.S. 70. *Green Fees:* on application. *Eating facilities:* lunches served – advance booking necessary. *Visitors:* welcome Monday to Friday, must be member of a recognised golf club with an official handicap. *Society Meetings:* catered for. Professional: R.T. McDougall (0734 692910). Secretary: P.F. Williams.

England BERKSHIRE / BUCKINGHAMSHIRE

SINDLESHAM. **Bearwood Golf Club,** Mole Road, Sindlesham RG11 5DB (Arborfield Cross (0734) 761330). *Location:* on B3030 from Winnersh to Arborfield. Flat wooded course. 9 holes, 2802 yards. S.S.S. 68 (18 holes). 9 hole Pitch and Putt. *Green Fees:* weekdays £8.00 for 9 holes, £15.00 for 18 holes. *Eating facilities:* food available all day. *Visitors:* welcome weekdays, Handicap Certificate required. Weekends as guests of members only. *Society Meetings:* maximum of 18 catered for, Thursdays only. Professional/Manager: Barry Tustin (0734 760643). Secretary: C. Dyer OBE (0734 760060).

SLOUGH. **Datchet Golf Club,** Buccleuch Road, Datchet (Slough (0753) 543887). *Location:* within two miles of both Windsor and Slough. 9 holes, 5978 yards. S.S.S. 69. *Green Fees:* £16.00 per round, £22.00 per day. *Visitors:* welcome without reservation during week up to 3pm. Lessons and club repairs for non members. *Society Meetings:* small societies welcome. Professional: Bill Mainwaring (0753 542755). Secretary: Anne Perkins (0753 541872).

STREATLEY ON THAMES. **Goring and Streatley Golf Club,** Rectory Road, Streatley on Thames RG8 9QA (Goring (0491) 872688). *Location:* 10 miles north west of Reading off A417 Wantage Road. Parkland course on Berkshire Downs. 18 holes, 6255 yards. S.S.S. 70. *Green Fees:* £28.00 per day; £19.00 per round after 4pm except Weekends. Weekends only playing with a member. *Eating facilities:* full restaurant and bar meals. *Visitors:* welcome on weekdays by telephone booking. *Society Meetings:* catered for. Professional: Roy Mason (0491 873715).. Secretary: J. Menzies (0491 873229).

SUNNINGDALE. **Sunningdale Ladies' Golf Club,** Cross Road, Sunningdale SL5 9RX (0344 20507). *Location:* second left going west on A30, past Sunningdale level crossing. Heathland, 18 holes, 3622 yards. (Designed for Ladies' Golf). S.S.S. 60. *Green Fees:* £17.00/£22.00 weekdays; £19.00/£27.00 weekends. *Eating facilities:* snack lunches available except Sundays. *Visitors:* welcome, telephone first. Must have Handicap Certificate. *Society Meetings:* catered for (Ladies only). Secretary: John Darroch.

WOKINGHAM. **Downshire Golf Course,** Easthampstead Park, Wokingham RG11 3DH (Bracknell (0344) 302030). *Location:* between Bracknell and Crowthorne off Nine Mile Ride. Parkland. 18 holes, 6395 yards. S.S.S. 71. 9 hole pitch and putt, driving range and golf academy. *Green Fees:* weekdays £9.00 winter, £11.00 summer; weekends £11.00 winter, £13.00 summer. *Eating facilities:* bar meals, grills, free house bar and restaurant. *Visitors:* welcome. Membership available. *Society Meetings:* welcome. Professional: Paul Watson (0344 302030; Fax: 0344 301020). Secretary: (0344 422708).

Buckinghamshire

AYLESBURY. **Chiltern Forest Golf Club,** Aston Hill, Halton, Aylesbury (Steward: Aylesbury (0296) 630899). *Location:* five miles south-east of Aylesbury, signposted St. Leonards. Wooded, hilly course. 18 holes, 5765 yards. S.S.S. 70. *Green Fees:* £20.00 weekdays; £12.00 with a member weekends. *Visitors:* weekdays unrestricted, weekends with a member. *Society Meetings:* welcome, preferably Wednesdays. Professional: Christopher Skeet (0296 631817). Secretary: L.E.A. Clark (0296 631267).

AYLESBURY. **Ellesborough Golf Club,** Butlers Cross, Aylesbury HP17 0TZ (Wendover (0296) 622375). *Location:* on B4010 one and a half miles from Wendover. Chiltern Hills course. Undulating links. 18 holes, 6271 yards. S.S.S. 71. Practice net/ground. *Green Fees:* £30.00 per day. £20.00 per round weekdays. *Eating facilities:* available. *Visitors:* except weekends, Tuesday mornings and competition days, must provide Handicap Certificate. *Society Meetings:* catered for Wednesdays and Thursdays only by arrangement with Secretary. Professional: Paul Warner (0296 623126). Secretary: K.M. Flint (0296 622114).

AYLESBURY. **Weston Turville Golf & Squash Club,** New Road, Weston Turville, Near Aylesbury HP22 5QT (Aylesbury (0296) 24084). *Location:* two miles south east of Aylesbury off A41. Easy walking course at the foot of the Chiltern Hills. 18 holes, 6002 yards. S.S.S. 69. *Green Fees:* weekdays £15; weekends £20. *Eating facilities:* meals, snacks and visitors' bar. *Visitors:* truly welcome, booking advisable Saturday and Sundays. Squash courts available. *Society Meetings:* especially catered for. Professional: Tom Jones (0296 25949). General Manager: Mr Barry Hill (0296 24084).

BEACONSFIELD. **Beaconsfield Golf Club Ltd.** Seer Green, Near Beaconsfield HP9 2UR (Beaconsfield (0494) 676545/6). *Location:* from A40 at Beaconsfield, A355 Amersham Road, one mile turn right to Jordans, one mile signposted. Parkland course. 18 holes, 6469 metres. S.S.S. 71. Large practice ground. *Green Fees:* £40.00 per day, £33.00 per round. *Eating facilities:* dining room or bar menu; 2 bars. *Visitors:* welcome weekdays with accredited introduction – check with Pro. *Society Meetings:* catered for Tuesdays and Wednesdays. Professional: Mike Brothers (0494 676616). Secretary: P.I. Anderson (0494 676545/6; Fax: 0494 681148).

BUCKINGHAMSHIRE England   THE GOLF GUIDE 1994

BUCKINGHAM. **Buckingham Golf Club**, Tingewick Road, Buckingham MK18 4AG (0280 813282). *Location:* one and a half miles south west of Buckingham on A421. Undulating parkland – eight holes affected by river. 18 holes, 6082 yards. S.S.S. 69. Practice ground. *Green Fees:* weekdays £28.00; weekends as members' guests only. *Eating facilities:* seven day catering – bars, lunch and evening. *Visitors:* welcome weekdays only. *Society Meetings:* pre-booked on Tuesdays or Thursdays. Professional: Tom Gates (0280 815210). Secretary: David Rolph (0280 815566).

BURNHAM. **Burnham Beeches Golf Club**, Green Lane, Burnham, Slough SL1 8EG (Burnham (0628) 661150). *Location:* on M4 for Slough two miles, M40 seven miles. Wooded parkland course.18 holes, 6449 yards. S.S.S. 71. *Green Fees:* information not provided. *Eating facilities:* bar and restaurant, full catering available. *Visitors:* welcome weekdays, weekends only with a member. *Society Meetings:* welcome by arrangement. Professional/Secretary: A.J. Buckner (0628 661661 or 661448).

BURNHAM. **Lambourne Golf Club**, Dropmore Road, Burnham SL1 8NF (0628 666755; Fax: 0628 663301). *Location:* take M4 to Exit 7; take M40 to Exit 2. Parkland. 18 holes, 6746 yards. S.S.S. 72. Practice facilities available. *Green Fees:* weekdays £30.00 per round, weekends £30.00 only with a member. *Eating facilities:* bars and restaurants. *Visitors:* welcome. Handicap Certificate required weekdays; weekends only with a member. Golf Director: R.A. Newman (0628 662936). Secretary: C.J. Lumley.

CHALFONT ST. GILES. **Harewood Downs Golf Club**, Cokes Lane, Chalfont St. Giles HP8 4TA (Little Chalfont (0494) 762308). *Location:* off A413, two miles east of Amersham. Rolling, tree lined. 18 holes, 5958 yards, 5448 metres. S.S.S. 69. Practice ground. *Green Fees:*weekdays £20.00 per round, £27.00 per day; weekends £30.00. *Eating facilities:* lunches served at club. *Visitors:* welcome on weekdays with current handicap, weekends by prior arrangement only. *Society Meetings:* catered for by arrangement. Professional: G. Morris (0494 764102). Secretary: M.R. Cannon (0494 762184).

CHESHAM. **Chartridge Park Golf Club**, Chartridge, Chesham HP5 2TF (0494 791772 extension 3; Fax: 0494 786462). *Location:* situated on Chartridge Lane three miles from town. Flat parkland course with wooded areas and views over Chilterns. 18 holes, 5800 yards. S.S.S. 70. Practice ground. *Green Fees:* weekdays £13.50; weekends £17.50. *Eating facilities:* snacks and cooked food available seven days a week. *Visitors:* welcome mid-week except Thursday till 12 noon. *Society Meetings:* always welcome. Professional: Peter Gibbins (0494 791772 extension 2). Secretary: Anita Gibbins (0494 791772 extension 1).

CHESHAM. **Chesham and Ley Hill Golf Club**, Ley Hill, Chesham HP5 1UZ (0494 784541). *Location:* off A41 on B4504 and follow signs for Ley Hill, nearest town – Chesham. Wooded parkland. 9 holes, 5296 yards. S.S.S. 66. Putting green and practice net. *Green Fees:* weekdays £15.00 per round, £20.00 per day. *Eating facilities:* licensed bar, food available at certain times. *Visitors:* welcome Mondays and Thursdays all day; Wednesdays after 12 noon; Fridays till 1pm. *Society Meetings:* Thursdays only by prior arrangement. Secretary: J.R. Taylor (0494 784541).

DENHAM. **Denham Golf Club**, Tilehouse Lane, Denham UB9 5DE (Denham (0895) 832079). *Location:* one and a half miles from Uxbridge off the left hand side of the A412 en route to Watford. Parkland – undulating. 18 holes, 6451 yards, 6159 metres. S.S.S. 71. Practice ground. *Green Fees:* £32.00 per round, £48.00 per day weekdays; weekends with a member only. *Eating facilities:* diningroom, bar snacks. *Visitors:* welcome Monday to Thursday by prior arrangement only. Handicap Certificate. *Society Meetings:* catered for Tuesdays, Wednesdays and Thursdays. Professional: John Sheridan (0895 832801). Secretary: Wg Cdr D. Graham (0895 832022; Fax: 0895 835340).

GERRARDS CROSS. **Gerrards Cross Golf Club**, Chalfont Park, Gerrards Cross SL9 0DE (0753 883263; Fax: 0753 883593). *Location:* alongside A413 (to Amersham) about one mile from junction with A40 (London to Oxford road). Wooded parkland course. 18 holes, 6295 yards. S.S.S. 70. *Green Fees:* weekdays £28.00 per round, £35.00 per day. *Eating facilities:* lunch available to order, bar snacks at all times. *Visitors:* welcome except at weekends and Public Holidays but must produce a letter of introduction or current Handicap Certificate. *Society Meetings:* catered for Thursdays and Fridays, maximum number 50. Professional: M. Barr (0753 885300). Secretary/Manager: P.H. Fisher.

HIGH WYCOMBE. **Flackwell Heath Golf Club Limited**, Treadaway Road, Flackwell Heath, High Wycombe HP10 9PE (Bourne End (0628) 520027). *Location:* M4 Exit 3 from London, Exit 4 from Oxford. 2 miles High Wycombe. Heath and woodland, some hills. 18 holes, 6207 yards. S.S.S. 70. *Green Fees:* weekdays £27.00; weekends £10.00 with member only. *Eating facilities:* restaurant and bars daily (limited catering Mondays). *Visitors:* welcome weekdays only with Handicap Certificate. Weekends with member only. *Society Meetings:* catered for by arrangement Wednesdays and Thursdays. Professional: Steven Bryan (0628 523017). Secretary: Peter Jeans (0628 520929).

HIGH WYCOMBE. **Hazlemere Golf and Country Club**, Penn Road, Hazlemere, Near High Wycombe (High Wycombe (0494) 714722). *Location:* on B474 about half a mile from junction with A404 High Wycombe/Amersham Road – three miles from High Wycombe centre. Undulating parkland course. 18 holes, 5873 yards. S.S.S. 68. *Green Fees:* weekdays £25.00; weekends £34.00. *Eating facilities:* restaurant and bar. *Visitors:* restricted at weekends. Snooker table. *Society Meetings:* by prior arrangement. Professional: Steve Morvell (0494 718298). Secretary: D. Hudson (0494 714722).

IVER. **Iver Golf Course**, Hollow Hill Lane, Off Langley Park Road, Iver SL0 0JJ (Slough (0753) 655615). *Location:* situated off Langley Park Road leaving the town of Langley heading towards Iver. Flat parkland, easy walking with natural ditches and ponds.

68

THE GOLF GUIDE 1994 *England* BUCKINGHAMSHIRE

9 holes, 5988 yards (men), 5230 yards (ladies). S.S.S. 70 (men), 72 (ladies). Driving range and practice ground for short game. *Green Fees:* weekdays £5.00 for 9 holes, £8.50 for 18; weekends £6.80 for 9 holes, £12.00 for 18. Special rates available, please enquire. *Eating facilities:* lunch served 12 noon to 2.30pm seven days, snacks and rolls always available. *Visitors:* always welcome, best to phone on day of play for booking. *Society Meetings:* always welcome. Professional: Geraldine Isles (0753 655615). Secretary: James Rice.

LITTLE CHALFONT. **Little Chalfont Golf Club,** Lodge Lane, Little Chalfont HP8 4AJ (0494 764877). *Location:* Junction 18 M25, two miles towards Amersham on A404, first left past garden centre. Undulating parkland. 9 holes, 5852 yards S.S.S. 68. *Green Fees:* information not provided. *Eating facilities:* full bar and eating facilities. *Visitors:* always welcome. *Society Meetings:* welcome mid-week. Professional: B. Woodhouse and A. Philpott (0494 762942). Secretary: J.M. Dunne (0494 764877).

MILTON KEYNES. **Abbey Hill Golf Club,** Abbey Hill, Milton Keynes (Milton Keynes (0908) 562408). *Location:* 2 miles south of Stony Stratford. 18 holes, 5732 metres. S.S.S. 69. Short par 3 course available. *Green Fees:* on application. *Eating facilities:* available. *Visitors:* welcome. *Society Meetings:* catered for, apply Professional. Professional: S. Harlock. Secretary: Mr I.D. Grieve.

MILTON KEYNES. **Three Locks Golf Club,** Great Brickhill, Milton Keynes MK17 9BH (0525 270470). *Location:* A4146 Bletchley to Leighton Buzzard. Parkland with water hazards on eight holes. 9 holes, 3327 yards. S.S.S. 70. Practice ground. *Green Fees:* weekdays £8.50; weekends £10.00. *Eating facilities:* restaurant and bar. *Visitors:* welcome every day. Accommodation available in Club's hotel, free golf for residents. Pro shop. *Society Meetings:* all welcome. Secretary: Mrs Darby (0525 270470).

MILTON KEYNES. **Wavendon Golf Centre,** Lower End Road, Wavendon, Milton Keynes MK17 8DA (0908 281296; Fax: 0908 281257). *Location:* two minutes from Junction 13 M1, just off A421 link road. Parkland with six small lakes as hazards. 18 holes, 5479 yards. S.S.S. 67. 9 holes, 1424 yards. S.S.S. 27. 36 bay driving range, practice green and bunker. *Green Fees:* weekdays £9.00; weekends £12.00. Senior Citizens and Juniors half price, twilight evening rates. *Eating facilities:* 65 seater carvery restaurant and downstairs bar. *Visitors:* welcome. *Society Meetings:* welcome weekdays, weekends by arrangement. Professional: Nick Elmen (0908 281811). Secretary: Cynthia Caeney (0908 281297).

MILTON KEYNES. **Windmill Hill Golf Course,** Tattenhoe Lane, Bletchley, Milton Keynes MK3 7RB (0908 378623). *Location:* M1 Junction 13/14 A421 to Buckingham, 10 minutes from motorway. Flat parkland course, Henry Cotton design. 18 holes, 6773 yards. S.S.S. 72. 23 bay floodlit driving range. *Green Fees:* weekdays £6.00; weekends and Bank Holidays £8.50. Reduced rates Juniors and Senior Citizens; twilight ticket. *Eating facilities:* public bar and restaurant. *Visitors:* welcome at any time, booking seven days in advance. *Society Meetings:* welcome at all times. All bookings through Professional. Professional: C. Clingan (0908 378623; Fax: 0908 271478). Secretary: Pat Long.

MILTON KEYNES. **Woburn Golf and Country Club,** Bow Brickhill, Milton Keynes MK17 9LJ (Milton Keynes (0908) 370756; Fax: 0908 378436). *Location:* four miles west of junction 13 M1. Two courses: 36 holes, Duke's Course 6940 yards S.S.S. 74; Duchess' Course 6641 yards, S.S.S. 72. Two practice grounds. *Green Fees:* on application. *Eating facilities:* two restaurants; breakfasts, lunches and dinners. *Visitors:* welcome weekdays with prior arrangement. Members' guests only at weekends. *Society Meetings:* catered for, details on application. Professional: Alex Hay (0908 647987). Secretary: Mrs G. Beasley (0908 370756).

PRINCES RISBOROUGH. **Whiteleaf Golf Club Ltd,** The Clubhouse, Whiteleaf, Aylesbury HP17 0LY (08444 3097). *Location:* A4010 from Princes Risborough. 9 holes, 5359 yards. S.S.S. 66. *Green Fees:* information not provided. *Visitors:* welcome on weekdays only. *Society Meetings:* on application, Thursdays only. Professional: K.S. Ward (08444 5472). Secretary: D.G. Bullard (0844 274058).

SLOUGH. **Farnham Park Municipal Golf Course,** Park Road, Stoke Poges SL2 4PJ (0753 643335). *Location:* centrally situated between Stoke Poges and Farnham Royal, off Park Road. Parkland. 18 holes, 6172 yards. S.S.S. 69, 70 Ladies. *Green Fees:* weekdays £8.00; weekends £11.00. Reduced rates for Senior Citizens and Juniors. *Eating facilities:* available. *Visitors:* welcome. Professional: P. Harrison (0753 643332). Hon. Secretary: Maureen Brooker (0753 647065).

STOKE POGES. **Stoke Poges Golf Club,** North Drive, Park Road, Stoke Poges SL2 4PG (Slough (0753) 526385). *Location:* one mile north of Slough. 18 holes, 6654 yards. S.S.S. 72. *Green Fees:* weekdays £27.00 single round, £37.00 per day. *Eating facilities:* lunch and snack restaurant. *Visitors:* welcome weekdays only with Handicap Certificate or letter of introduction; weekends as members' guests only. *Society Meetings:* catered for. Professional: to be appointed. Secretary/Manager: R.C. Pickering.

THE SWAN REVIVED HOTEL

Highly Commended   AA ★★ RAC

Situated in this attractive North Bucks market town. Family run hotel, 16th century coaching inn, with modern facilities and a warm welcome. 40 ensuite bedrooms, 2 mews (family/executive) cottages. Lounge and local bars. Popular à la carte restaurant, plus chef's specialities.

High Street, Newport Pagnell, Milton Keynes, Bucks. Tel: 0908 610565
Fax: 0908 210995 (just 4 minutes from M1 Junction 14)

STOWE. **Silverstone Golf Club,** Silverstone Road, Stowe MK18 5LH (0280 850005). *Location:* 14 miles Northampton, 28 miles Oxford. Opposite Silverstone Racing circuit. Flat, bordered by woodland, newly planted copses. 18 holes, 6164 yards. S.S.S. 70. Unique practice course, driving range. *Green Fees:* weekdays £8.00 (£6.00 special offer); weekends £12.00 non members, £10.00 guests of members. *Eating facilities:* licensed bar, meals at all times. *Visitors:* welcome, booking 24 hours in advance. *Society Meetings:* welcome weekdays only. Secretary: Margaret Mears.

STOWE. **Stowe Golf Club,** Stowe, Buckingham MK18 5EH (0280 816264). *Location:* situated at Stowe School, four miles north of Buckingham. Parkland course with follies and lakes. 9 holes, 2189 yards. S.S.S. 63. *Green Fees:* information not provided.

Visitors: only as a guest of a member. *Society Meetings:* catered for by appointment. Secretary: Mrs S.A. Cross (0280 813650).

WEXHAM. **Wexham Park Golf Course,** Wexham Street, Slough SL3 6NB (0753 663271). *Location:* M40 to Beaconsfield, A40 to Gerrards Cross, direction to Fulmer on right hand side, near Wexham Park Hospital. Parkland. 18 holes, 5390 yards. S.S.S. 66. Also 9/18 hole course, 2851/5702 yards. S.S.S. 34/68; and 9 hole course, 2283 yards. S.S.S. 32. Driving range. *Green Fees:* weekdays £8.50 for 18 holes, £5.00 for 9 holes; weekends £12.00 for 18 holes, £6.90 for 9 holes. *Eating facilities:* clubhouse bar and full kitchen facilities. *Visitors:* welcome – Pay and Play, open to all. Hotel and sports complex. *Society Meetings:* weekdays only (except Bank Holidays), minimum 12 people. Professional: David Morgan (0753 663425). Secretary: P.J. Gale.

Cambridgeshire

CAMBRIDGE. **Cambridgeshire Moat House Hotel Golf Club,** Bar Hill, Cambridge CB3 8EU (Craftshill (0954) 780555). *Location:* five miles north from Cambridge on A604 Huntingdon Road. Undulating parkland with a lake, ditches and many trees. 18 holes, 6734 yards. S.S.S. 72. Practice grounds. *Green Fees:* weekdays £19.00; weekends and Public Holidays £25.00. Daily and weekend golf packages. *Eating facilities:* restaurant, bars, bar meals (Mon-Fri lunch). *Visitors:* welcome anytime by prior phone call. 100 Bedroom Hotel, Squash, Tennis, Residents' Health and Fitness Club and Indoor Heated Swimming Pool. *Society Meetings:* welcome weekdays. Resident Societies only at weekends. Professional: David Vernon (0954 780098). Secretary: (0954 780555).

CAMBRIDGE. **Girton Golf Club,** Dodford Lane, Girton, Cambridge CB3 0QE (Cambridge (0223) 276143). *Location:* two miles north of Cambridge. Flat parkland. 18 holes, 6085 yards. S.S.S. 69. *Green Fees:* £19.00 per day with Handicap Certificate, £25.00 without; weekends with a member only. *Eating facilities:* diningroom, lounge and bar. *Visitors:* weekdays only. *Society Meetings:* welcomed. Professional: S. Thomson (0223 276991). Secretary: Mrs M.A. Cornwell (0223 276169).

CAMBRIDGE. **Gog Magog Golf Club,** Shelford Bottom, Cambridge CB2 4AB (0223 247626; Fax: 0223 414990). *Location:* two miles from A11 – A604 roundabout. Colchester – Cambridge Road A604. Open, undulating. Two courses. 18 holes, 6386 yards. S.S.S. 70. 9 holes, 5805 yards. S.S.S. 68. *Green Fees:* Old Course £29.00 per round, £35.00 per day. 9-hole course £19.00 per day. *Eating facilities:* diningroom, bar meals, mixed and men's bar. *Visitors:* welcome,

only with members at weekends and Bank Holidays, Handicap Certificates required, Handicap limit on Old Course 22 and below. *Society Meetings:* catered for Tuesdays and Thurdays. Professional: I. Bamborough (0223 246058). Secretary: John E. Riches (0223 247626).

ELY. **Ely City Golf Course Ltd,** Cambridge Road, Ely CB7 4HX (Ely (0353) 663810). *Location:* on southern outskirts of city on A10 going to Cambridge. Parkland course, slightly undulating, magnificent views of the 12th century cathedral. 18 holes, 6602 yards. S.S.S. 72. Practice area. *Green Fees:* weekdays £22.00, weekends and Bank Holidays £30.00. *Eating facilities:* full bar and restaurant facilities. *Visitors:* welcome anytime with a member or if in possession of a valid Handicap Certificate. Jeans, T-shirts and trainers not allowed. Snooker. *Society Meetings:* welcome Tuesday to Friday inclusive by arrangement. Professional: F.C. Rowden (0353 663317). Secretary: Mr G.A. Briggs (0353 662751)

HUNTINGDON. **Brampton Park Golf Club,** Buckden Road, Brampton, Huntingdon PE18 8NF. *Location:* three quarter of a mile off A1, travelling north take first Huntingdon turn, south take second sign for "RAF Brampton". Picturesque parkland/meadowland with many water hazards and wooded areas. 18 holes, 6364 yards. S.S.S. 73. *Green Fees:* information not provided. *Eating facilities:* full a la carte restaurant, members bar, bar snacks. *Visitors:* welcome at all times, no restrictions save telephone for tee reservations at weekends. Accommodation and business conference facilities available. *Society Meetings:* welcome. Professional: Mike Torrens (0480 434705). Secretary: John Prout (0480 434700).

THE GOLF GUIDE 1994 *England* CAMBRIDGESHIRE

HUNTINGDON. **Lakeside Lodge Golf Club,** Fen Road, Pidley, Huntingdon PE17 3DD (Tel & Fax: 0487 740540). *Location:* on the B1040 St. Ives to Warboys Road. Course has 8 lakes and considerable landscaping. 18 holes, 6437 yards. S.S.S. 73. Driving range, 9 hole Par 3 course. *Green Fees:* weekdays £7.00 for 18 holes, £4.00 for 9 holes; weekends £14.00 for 18 holes, £7.00 for 9 holes. *Eating facilities:* full bar and restaurant open all day for snacks and à la carte restaurant. *Visitors:* everyone welcome anytime, no restrictions. *Society Meetings:* all welcome. Professional: Mr A.W. Headley PGA (0487 741541). Secretary: Mrs Jane Hopkins.

HUNTINGDON. **Ramsey Golf Club,** 4 Abbey Terrace, Ramsey, Huntingdon (Ramsey (0487) 813573). *Location:* 20 minutes from A1, 12 miles south of Peterborough, 10 miles north of Huntingdon. Parkland, 18 holes, 6133 yards. S.S.S. 70. Two practice grounds. *Green Fees:* weekdays £20.00 per round or day with Handicap Certificate. Weekends, Bank Holidays with member only. *Eating facilities:* full catering available. *Visitors:* welcome without reservation. *Society Meetings:* catered for by arrangement, weekdays only. Professional: S.J. Scott (0487 813022). Secretary: Mr R. Muirhead (0487 812600).

MARCH. **March Golf Club,** Frogs Abbey, Grange Road, March PE15 0YH (March (0354) 52364). *Location:* one mile south of town centre on west side of A141. Flat parkland. 9 holes, 6210 yards. S.S.S. 70 men, 71 ladies. *Green Fees:* weekdays £15.00 (£7.50 with a member); weekends £7.50 with a member only. *Eating facilities:* food available at weekends only, bar daily. *Society Meetings:* accepted. Professional: Nigel Pickerell (0354 52364). Secretary: J.B. Clapham.

PETERBOROUGH. **Elton Furze Golf Club,** Bullock Road, Haddon, Peterborough. *Location:* four miles west of Peterborough on old A604 Oundle to Peterborough road. New course opened April 1993. Scenic parkland, wooded. 18 holes, 6289 yards, 5715 metres. S.S.S. 70. Driving range. *Green Fees:* weekdays £20.00 per round, £30.00 per day. *Eating facilities:* limited until mid 1994. *Visitors:* welcome Tuesdays and Thursdays. *Society Meetings:* welcome Tuesdays and Thursdays – need to pre book. Professional: Frank Kiddie (0733 267701). Secretary: Peter Robinson (0733 232440).

PETERBOROUGH. **Orton Meadows Golf Club,** Ham Lane, Orton Waterville, Peterborough PE2 0UU (Peterborough (0733) 237478). *Location:* four miles west of Peterborough on A605. Parkland. 18 holes, 5800 yards. S.S.S. 68. Practice ground. *Green Fees:* weekdays £7.00; weekends £10.00. Weekday reductions for Juniors and Senior Citizens. *Eating facilities:* restaurant attached to course. *Visitors:* unrestricted – public course. *Society Meetings:* welcome. Professional: N. Grant (0733 237478). Secretary: K. Boyer.

PETERBOROUGH. **Peterborough Milton Golf Club,** Milton Ferry, Peterborough PE6 7AG (Peterborough (0733) 380204). *Location:* on A47 west of Peterborough, 3 miles east of A1. Parkland. 18 holes, 6431 yards, 5856 metres. S.S.S. 71. *Green Fees:* weekdays £20.00 per round, weekends £25.00 per round. Societies £30.00 per day. *Eating facilities:* available daily. *Visitors:* welcome weekdays; as member's guest at weekends. *Society Meetings:* Tuesdays, Wednesdays and Thursdays by arrangement with Secretary. Professional: Michael Gallagher (0733 380793). Secretary: Mrs D.K. Adams (0733 380489).

PETERBOROUGH. **Thorpe Wood Golf Course,** Thorpe Wood, Peterborough PE3 6SE (Peterborough (0733) 267701). *Location:* three miles west of town on A47. Parkland. 18 holes, 7086 yards. S.S.S. 74. Practice ground. *Green Fees:* weekdays £7.50; weekends and Bank Holidays £10.00. Weekday reductions for Senior Citizens and Juniors. *Eating facilities:* Public House attached to course. *Visitors:* unrestricted, booking required. Public Course. *Society Meetings:* welcome – book early. Professionals: Dennis and Roger Fitton (0733 267701; Fax: 0733 332774). Secretary: R. Palmer.

ST. IVES. **St. Ives (Hunts) Golf Club,** Westwood Road, St. Ives PE17 4RS (St. Ives (0480) 64459). *Location:* B1040 off A45. 9 holes, 6052 yards. S.S.S. 69. *Green Fees:* information not provided. *Eating facilities:* lunches at club, except Mondays. Order in advance. *Visitors:* no visitors weekends or Bank Holidays. *Society Meetings:* catered for. Professional: A. Currie (0480 66067). Secretary: Ray Hill (0480 68392).

ST. NEOTS. **St. Neots Golf Club,** Crosshall Road, St. Neots PE19 4AE (0480 474311). *Location:* A45 off A1, eastwards, one mile east of Great North Road. Undulating parkland with water hazards. 18 holes, 6027 yards. S.S.S. 69. *Green Fees:* on application. *Eating facilities:* full catering facilities. *Visitors:* at weekends/Bank Holidays with member only. *Society Meetings:* welcome. Professional: G. Bithrey (0480 476513). Secretary: R.J. Marsden (Tel & Fax: 0480 472363).

If you are writing, a stamped, addressed envelope is always appreciated.

Cheshire

ALDERLEY EDGE. Alderley Edge Golf Club, Brook Lane, Alderley Edge SK9 7RU (Alderley Edge (0625) 585583). *Location:* off A34. 9 holes, 5836 yards. S.S.S. 68. *Green Fees:* weekends £22.00, weekdays £18.00. *Eating facilities:* meals served in clubhouse. *Visitors:* subject to restrictions on Tuesdays, Wednesdays and weekends. *Society Meetings:* welcome on Thursdays. Professional: A. Sproston (0625 584493). Secretary: J.B. Page.

ALSAGER. Alsager Golf and Country Club, Audley Road, Alsager, Stoke-on-Trent ST7 2UR (0270 875700). *Location:* off M6 at Junction 16 onto A500, first left to Alsager, course is two and a half miles on right. Parkland. 18 holes, 6192 yards. S.S.S. 70. *Green Fees:* weekdays £20.00, weekends with member. *Eating facilities:* restaurant and bar snacks. *Visitors:* welcome weekdays without reservation. Disco, conference and banqueting facilities. *Society Meetings:* welcome, package available on request. Pro Shop (0270 877432). Secretary: A.E. Moffat (0270 875700).

ALTRINCHAM. Hale Golf Club, Rappax Road, Hale, Altrincham WA15 0NU (061-980 4225). Pleasant undulating parkland. 9 holes (2 rounds), 5780 yards. S.S.S. 68. *Green Fees:* weekdays £20.00 per round, £25.00 per day; weekends only with member. *Eating facilities:* by arrangement with Steward. *Visitors:* welcome weekdays (except Thursday) with reservation. *Society Meetings:* by arrangement with Hon. Secretary. Professional: Joy Jackson (061-904 0835). Secretary: J.W. Hughes (061-980 4320).

APPLETON. The Warrington Golf Club, Hill Warren, London Road, Appleton, Near Warrington WA4 5HR (0925 61620). *Location:* M56 exit 11, A49 Warrington one and a half miles. Parkland course. 18 holes, 6217 yards. S.S.S. 70. *Green Fees:* information not provided. *Eating facilities:* available except Monday lunchtime. *Visitors:* welcome with reservation. *Society Meetings:* Wednesdays only. Professional: A.W. Fryer (0925 65431). Secretary: R.O. Francis (0925 61775).

CHEADLE. Gatley Golf Club Ltd, Waterfall Farm, Styal Road, Heald Green, Cheadle SK8 3TW (061-437 2091). *Location:* from Gatley village to South down Styal Road and follow directions into Yew Tree Grove, then Motcombe Grove to Club entrance. Parkland course. 9 holes, 5934 yards. S.S.S. 68. *Green Fees:* weekdays £18.00 and £6.00 with member, weekends only if playing with member. Special rates by arrangement. *Eating facilities:* available except Monday, bar. *Visitors:* welcome Mondays, Wednesdays and Thursdays. *Society Meetings:* welcome Thursdays. Professional: S. Crake (061-436 2830). Secretary: P. Hannam F.C.A.(061-437 2091).

CHESTER. Chester Golf Club, Curzon Park, Chester CH4 8AR (0244 675130). *Location:* one mile south west of city centre. From Chester Castle take A483 (Wrexham) to first roundabout over Grovesnor Bridge. Turn right into Curzon Park North and follow signs. Parkland on two levels overlooking the River Dee. 18 holes, 6508 yards. S.S.S. 71. *Green Fees:* weekdays £21.00 per day; weekends £26.00. Reductions if playing with a member. *Eating facilities:* full restaurant and bar facilities except Mondays, when snacks only are served except by special arrangement. *Visitors:* welcome most days but advisable to telephone first. *Society Meetings:* catered for by prior arrangement. Professional: George Parton (0244 671185). Secretary: Peter Griffiths (0244 677760).

CHESTER. Upton-by-Chester Golf Club, Upton Lane, Chester CH2 1EE (Chester (0244) 381183). *Location:* off A41, near Zoo turn-off traffic lights. Flat parkland course. 18 holes, 5808 yards. S.S.S. 69. *Green Fees:* £20.00 per day weekdays; £25.00 per round weekends. *Eating facilities:* large restaurant and four bars. *Visitors:* no restrictions except Competition Days. *Society Meetings:* welcome except Mondays, Tuesdays and weekends. Minimum number 16. All day package £32.00, half day £29.00. Professional: P.A. Gardner (0244 381333). Secretary: John B. Durban (0244 381183).

CHESTER. Vicars Cross Golf Club, Tarvin Road, Great Barrow, Chester CH3 7HN (0244 335174). *Location:* four miles east of Chester on the A51. Wooded parkland course. 18 holes, 6243 yards. S.S.S. 70. Two practice grounds. *Green Fees:* weekdays £20.00 per day or round; weekends and Bank Holidays as member's guest only, £10.00. After 4pm £14.00 per round. *Eating facilities:* men's bar, mixed bar, restaurant. *Visitors:* welcome Monday to Thursday only for day ticket, after 4pm any day. *Society Meetings:* catered for Tuesdays and Thursdays only. Professional: John Forsyth (0244 335595). Secretary: Andrew Rogers.

Alsager Golf & Country Club
A Day's Golf to Remember & Much More!

GOLF SOCIETIES WELCOME. Visit this lovely 18 hole parkland course. Large and small function rooms available for private parties, weddings, conferences, etc. Excellent facilities including dance floor, stage and bar. Large car park. Business functions and conferences arranged for you by Andrew Galvin (Catering Manager). Menus to cover all tastes and pockets.

Audley Rd, Alsager, Cheshire ST7 2UR. Tel: 0270 875700 *(Just 2 miles from Junction 16 on M6)*

THE GOLF GUIDE 1994

England CHESHIRE

CONGLETON. **Astbury Golf Club,** Peel Lane, Astbury, Near Congleton CW12 4RE (Congleton (0260) 272772). *Location:* on A34 Congleton to Newcastle-under-Lyme road. Parkland. 18 holes, 6367 yards. S.S.S. 70. Large practice area. *Green Fees:* weekdays £25.00; £8.00 with member. *Eating facilities:* diningroom and bar. *Visitors:* welcome weekdays, weekends with a member only. Must be members of recognised golf club with bona fide Handicap. *Society Meetings:* Thursdays only. £20.00 per player. Professional: Nigel Griffith (0260 272772). Secretary: Mike Bates (0260 279139).

CONGLETON. **Congleton Golf Club,** Biddulph Road, Congleton CW12 3LZ (Congleton (0260) 273540). *Location:* one mile south of Congleton Railway Station on Biddulph Road. Parkland. 9 holes, 5080 yards. S.S.S. 65. *Green Fees:* weekdays £14.00 (£7.00 with a member); weekends £20.00 (£10.00 with a member). *Eating facilities:* lunches and evening meals served if ordered in advance. Snacks available except Monday evenings. *Visitors:* welcome. *Society Meetings:* catered for, one year's notice if accepted. Professional: John Colclough (0260 271083). Secretary: R. Walsh (0260 273540).

CREWE. **Crewe Golf Club Ltd,** Fields Road, Haslington, Crewe CW1 1TB (0270 584227). *Location:* off A534 between Crewe and Sandbach. Parkland course. 18 holes, 6201 yards. S.S.S. 70. *Green Fees:* £20.00 after 1pm, £25.00 before 1pm. Subject to review. *Eating facilities:* bar, diningroom. *Visitors:* welcome weekdays only, not Bank Holidays. Snooker room. *Society Meetings:* Tuesdays only. Professional: R.E. Rimmer (0270 585032). Secretary: David G. Elias B.Sc. (Tel & Fax: 0270 584099).

CREWE. **Onneley Golf Club,** Barrhill Road, Onneley, Near Crewe (Stoke-on-Trent (0782) 750577). *Location:* one mile from Woore off A51, two miles from Stoke-on-Trent. Parkland on gentle slope. 9 holes, 5584 yards. S.S.S. 67. *Green Fees:* weekdays £15.00 (£6.00 with member); Saturdays and Bank Holidays with member only. Juniors half normal price. *Eating facilities:* light bar snacks when bar is open in summer. *Visitors:* welcome weekdays unrestricted. *Society Meetings:* welcome, except Tuesdays and Fridays (£17.00 per day including meal). Hon. Secretary: L.A.C. Kennedy (0270 661842).

CREWE. **Queens Park Golf Course,** Queens Park Drive, Crewe CW2 7SB (0270 662378). *Location:* next to Queens Park, one mile from Crewe Station. Parkland. 9 holes x 2, 4920 yards. S.S.S. 64. *Green Fees:* information not provided. *Eating facilities:* bar with excellent bar snacks. *Visitors:* welcome, restrictions Sunday mornings to 11am. *Society Meetings:* welcome. Professional: (0270 666724). Secretary: K. Lear (0270 628352).

FRODSHAM. **Frodsham Golf Club,** Simons Lane, Frodsham WA6 6HE (0928 732159). *Location:* Frodsham 10 minutes M56 Junction 12 Cheshire. Parkland with views over Mersey estuary; undulating. 18 holes, 6289 yards. S.S.S. 70. Two practice areas with bunkers, putting green and nets. *Green Fees:* weekdays £18.00; weekends £25.00. *Eating facilities:* clubhouse, spike bar, lounge bar, dining areas. *Visitors:* welcome at all times, no parties at weekends. Self catering dormy house accommodation available. *Society Meetings:* welcome weekdays, groups 12 minimum. Professional: Graham Tonge (0928 739442). Secretary: Eric Roylance (0928 732159; Fax: 0928 739037).

HELSBY. **Helsby Golf Club,** Towers Lane, Helsby, Warrington WA6 0JB (Helsby (0928) 723407). *Location:* M56 Junction 14 take B5117 to Helsby. Through traffic lights one mile, first right into Primrose Lane, then first right into Towers Lane (200 yards). Flat parkland course. 18 holes, 6229 yards. S.S.S. 70. Practice area available. *Green Fees:* £20.00 weekdays. *Eating facilities:* full facilities, except Mondays. *Visitors:* welcome weekdays, weekends must play with a member. Snooker facilities. *Society Meetings:* welcome Tuesdays and Thursdays by arrangement. Professional: I. Wright (0928 725457). Secretary: G.A. Johnson (0928 722021).

KNUTSFORD. **Knutsford Golf Club,** Mere Heath Lane, Knutsford (Knutsford (0565) 633355). *Location:* one mile east of town centre. 9 holes, 6200 yards. S.S.S. 70. *Green Fees:* information not provided. *Eating facilities:* by prior arrangement with Steward. *Visitors:* welcome with reservation except Tuesdays and Wednesdays. To be introduced by member. *Society Meetings:* catered for by special arrangement with Hon. Secretary. Professional: A. Gillies. Secretary: D. Francis.

KNUTSFORD. **Mere Golf and Country Club,** Chester Road, Mere, Knutsford WA16 6LJ (0565 830155; Fax: 0565 830518). *Location:* two miles east of Junction 19 M6 and three miles west of Junction 7 M56. Parkland Championship course. 18 holes, 6817 yards. S.S.S. 73. Practice area, two 9-hole putting greens, driving range (April to October). *Green Fees:* £45.00 weekdays, £55.00 weekends. *Eating facilities:* bistro, restaurant, bar snacks. *Visitors:* welcome by prior arrangement only. *Society Meetings:* Mondays, Tuesdays and Thursdays only by arrangement. Professional: Peter Eyre (0565 830219). Secretary: Karen Bucksey.

Mere
Golf &
Country
Club

One of the finest inland Championship Golf Courses in the North of England.
Superb facilities.   Reservations essential.
CHESTER ROAD, KNUTSFORD, CHESHIRE WA16 6LJ
TELEPHONE: 0565 830155   FAX: 0565 830518

CHESHIRE England

KNUTSFORD. **Wilmslow Golf Club,** Great Warford, Mobberley, Knutsford WA16 7AY (0565 872148). *Location:* two miles from Wilmslow off the Knutsford road. Parkland course. 18 holes, 6611 yards. S.S.S. 72. Practice facility. *Green Fees:* weekdays £25.00 per round, £37.50 per day; weekends £40.00 per round, £50.00 per day. *Eating facilities:* full catering except Monday, two bars. *Visitors:* welcome, Ladies' Day Wednesday. *Society Meetings:* Tuesdays and Thursdays only. Professional: L.J. Nowicki (0565 873620). Secretary: A. Laurence (Tel & Fax: 0565 872148).

LYMM. **Lymm Golf Club,** Whitbarrow Road, Lymm WA13 9AN (0925 752177). *Location:* five miles south east of Warrington, one and a half miles from Junction 20 on M6 and Junction 9 on M56. Parkland. 18 holes, 6304 yards. S.S.S. 70. Practice ground. *Green Fees:* information not provided. *Eating facilities:* coffee, bar snacks, lunches and dinner, bar. *Visitors:* welcome with Handicap Certificates, no visitors on Thursdays until 1.30pm, weekends or Bank Holidays. *Society Meetings:* catered for Wednesdays with reservations. Professional: Steve McCarthy (0925 755054). Secretary: J.M. Pearson (0925 755020).

MACCLESFIELD. **Macclesfield Golf Club,** Hollins Road, Macclesfield SK11 7EA (0625 423227). *Location:* turn off A523 Leek Road into Windmill Street, half a mile fork right. Hilly course with extensive views. 18 holes, 5625 yards, 5388 metres. S.S.S. 67. *Green Fees:* £17.00 weekdays; £20.00 weekends and Bank Holidays. *Eating facilities:* full catering and bar facilities. *Visitors:* welcome by arrangement. *Society Meetings:* welcome by arrangement (Tuesdays and Wednesdays preferred). Professional: Tony Taylor (0625 616952). Secretary: N.H. Edwards (0625 615845).

MACCLESFIELD. **Prestbury Golf Club,** Macclesfield Road, Prestbury, Near Macclesfield (0625 829388). *Location:* on the Macclesfield road leaving Prestbury village. 18 holes, 6359 yards. S.S.S. 71. *Green Fees:* information not provided. *Eating facilities:* lunches, teas and dinners. *Visitors:* welcome on weekdays with official club handicap; Bank Holidays and weekends only with a member. *Society Meetings:* Thursdays only. Professional: Nick Summerfield (0625 828241). Secretary: J. Wright (0625 828241).

MACCLESFIELD. **Shrigley Hall Golf and Country Club,** Shrigley Park, Pott Shrigley, Near Macclesfield SK10 5SB (0625 575757; Fax: 0625 573323). *Location:* easily accessible by M56, M62/63, M6, A523 and A6. Parkland with magnificent views, home of the Norman Wisdom Classic. 18 holes, 6305 yards. S.S.S. 71. Driving range. *Green Fees:* weekdays £22.00; weekends £28.00. Special rates for residents and guests of members. *Eating facilities:* golf clubhouse and restaurant. *Visitors:* on availability. Handicap Certificate required. 156 bedroomed, four star hotel. *Society Meetings:* all welcome. Professional: Granville A. Ogden (0625 575626). Secretary: Sandra Major.

MACCLESFIELD. **The Tytherington Club,** Macclesfield SK10 2JP (0625 434562; Fax: 0625 611076). *Location:* one mile north of Macclesfield off A523. Championship course in beautiful parkland setting, Headquarters of WPGET. 18 holes, 6756 yards, 6136 metres. S.S.S. 72 (men) 74 (ladies). Practice area. *Green Fees:* £25.00 18 holes, £35.00 36 holes weekdays; £30.00 18 holes, £40.00 36 holes weekends. *Eating facilities:* bar snacks, bistro, à la carte restaurant, private diningrooms. *Visitors:* welcome, Handicap Certificates required, no other restrictions. Full Country Club facilities, pool, tennis. Accommodation arranged. *Society Meetings:* very welcome weekdays. Professional: Sandy Wilson. Managing Director: P. Dawson.

NORTHWICH. **Delamere Forest Golf Club,** Station Road, Delamere, Northwich CW8 2JE (Sandiway (0606) 882807). *Location:* opposite Delamere Station on the B5152 Tarporley to Frodsham Road. Heathland course. 18 holes, 6305 yards. S.S.S. 70. Two practice grounds and one indoor net. *Green Fees:* weekdays £25.00 per round, £35.00 per day; weekends and Bank Holidays £30.00 per round. *Eating facilities:* bar snacks, diningroom for parties of 30 plus. *Visitors:* welcome any day except Competition Days – advisable to check in advance. *Society Meetings:* welcome if 24 or more in number with prior booking – Tuesdays and Thursdays only. Professional: E.B. Jones (0606 883307). Secretary: R.H. Allardice (0606 883264).

Macclesfield Golf Club The Hollins, Macclesfield, Cheshire SK11 7EA
Telephones: Secretary 0625 615845   Steward & Members 0625 423227   Professional 0625 616952

Hilly course in quiet location with extensive views.
Inclusive packages for Societies. Excellent Bar and Catering.
Secretary N. H. Edwards. Professional A. Taylor

THE TYTHERINGTON CLUB
Manchester Road, Macclesfield, Cheshire SK10 2JP Telephone: 0625 434562   Fax: 0625 611076
Championship course in beautiful parkland setting, one mile north of Macclesfield on A523.
Green Fees: Societies – £22.00 per round, £33.00 per day.
Individuals – £28.00 per round, £38.00 per weekday. GOLF CARTS & TROLLIES AVAILABLE.
See Colour Advertisement on page 19.

THE GOLF GUIDE 1994   *England*   CHESHIRE

NORTHWICH. **Sandiway Golf Club,** Chester Road, Sandiway, Northwich CW8 2DJ (Sandiway (0606) 883247). *Location:* off A556, Northwich by-pass. Undulating heavily wooded parkland. 18 holes, 6435 yards. S.S.S. 72. *Green Fees:* weekdays £30.00 per round, £35.00 per day; weekends £35.00 per round, £40.00 per day. *Eating facilities:* lunches and teas served daily, full restaurant facilities. *Visitors:* welcome on weekdays with letter of introduction and Handicap Certificate from home club. *Society Meetings:* restricted to Tuesdays, parties up to 120. Professional: William Laird (0606 883180). Secretary: V.F.C. Wood. Caterer: (0606 882606).

PRESTBURY. **Mottram Hall Golf Course,** Wilmslow Road, Mottram St. Andrew, Prestbury SK10 4QT (0625 820064). *Location:* M56 and M6. Flat parkland/woodland course. 18 holes, 6905 yards, 6250 metres. S.S.S. 72. Practice area. *Green Fees:* £30.00 weekdays; £35.00 weekends. Reduced green fees for Hotel residents. *Eating facilities:* golf centre bar and restaurant. *Visitors:* no restrictions. Accommodation in 133 bedrooms. *Society Meetings:* no restrictions. Professional: Tim Rastall.

RUNCORN. **Runcorn Golf Club,** Clifton Road, Runcorn WA7 4SU (0928 572093). *Location:* signposted The Heath, A557. High parkland course. 18 holes, 6035 yards, 5514 metres. S.S.S. 69. *Green Fees:* weekdays £18.00 per round or day, weekends and Bank Holidays £22.00 per round/day. *Eating facilities:* bar snacks; meals by arrangement. *Visitors:* welcome weekdays except Tuesday mornings. No visitors weekends or Bank Holidays except with a member. Handicap Certificate required. *Society Meetings:* by arrangement Mondays and Fridays. Professional: S. Dooley (0928 564791). Secretary: W.B. Reading (0928 574214).

SANDBACH. **Malkins Bank Golf Club,** Betchton Road, Malkins Bank, Sandbach CW11 0XN (0270 767878). *Location:* M6, Junction 17 south, one mile via Sandbach. Countryside course. 18 holes, 6071 yards. S.S.S. 69. Practice area. *Green Fees:* information not provided. *Eating facilities:* bar and meals available. *Visitors:* welcome at all times, pre-booking advised weekends via club Professional. *Society Meetings:* welcome by prior arrangement. Professional: David Wheeler (0270 765931). Secretary: Ken Lea.

SANDBACH. **Sandbach Golf Club,** 117 Middlewich Road, Sandbach CW11 9EA (Crewe (0270) 762117). *Location:* two miles from Junction 17 of M6 on Middlewich Road. Meadowland course. 9 holes, 5593 yards. S.S.S. 67. Practice field. *Green Fees:* weekdays £16.00 per day, £8.00 with member; weekends and Bank Holidays must be accompanied by a member. *Eating facilities:* available except Mondays and Thursdays. *Visitors:* welcome weekdays, weekends by invitation only. *Society Meetings:* catered for only by advance arrangement with Hon. Secretary. Secretary: A.F. Pearson.

SOUTH WIRRAL. **Ellesmere Port Golf Club,** Chester Road, Hooton, South Wirral L66 1QH (051-339 7502). *Location:* approximately six miles north of Chester on main A41 trunk road to Birkenhead. Wooded with a lot of ponds. 18 holes, 6432 yards. S.S.S. 71. *Green Fees:* weekdays £4.80; weekends £5.60. Special fees for Juniors and Senior Citizens, and concessions for unemployed during weekdays. *Eating facilities:* catering is booked through clubhouse. *Visitors:* welcome weekdays, weekends must be booked; booking fee of £1. *Society Meetings:* catered for Monday and Friday only. Professional: Mr D. Yates (051-339 7689). Secretary: Mr B. Turley (051-335 8800).

STALYBRIDGE. **Stamford Golf Club,** Oakfield House, Heyheads, Huddersfield Road, Stalybridge SK15 3PY (0457 832126). *Location:* on B6175 off A6018. Hilly moorland course. 18 holes, 5701 yards. S.S.S. 68. *Green Fees:* weekdays £17.50; weekends after 3pm £23.00. *Eating facilities:* meals lunchtime and evening (except Monday). *Visitors:* welcome without restrictions. *Society Meetings:* catered for by appointment only. Golf Shop: Brian Badger (0457 834829). Secretary: F.E. Rowles.

STOCKPORT. **Davenport Golf Club,** Middlewood Road, Poynton, Near Stockport SK12 1TS (0625 877321). *Location:* A6 from Stockport, Macclesfield Road at Hazel Grove, left at Poynton Church. Undulating parkland course. 18 holes, 6065 yards. S.S.S. 69. *Green Fees:* weekdays £24.00 (£8.00 with member), weekends £30.00 (£10.00 with a member). *Eating facilities:* bar snacks daily except Mondays, full meals by

---

18 holes worthy of an *Open*?

Mottram Hall

DE VERE HOTELS

Play the Mottram Hall course, 6905 yard, par 72.
Expertly designed by Dave Thomas. Set in 270 acres of mature Cheshire park and woodland, the course surrounds Mottram Hall Hotel.
Book now and experience a championship standard 18 holes.
(See our advertisement inside the front cover for further details).

MOTTRAM HALL HOTEL,
WILMSLOW ROAD,
MOTTRAM ST. ANDREW,
PRESTBURY, CHESHIRE SK10 4QT.
Telephone: 0625 828135.

CHESHIRE England

arrangement. *Visitors:* welcome, tee booking in operation after consultation with Club Professional. *Society Meetings:* catered for Tuesdays and Thursdays only. Professional: Wyn Harris (0625 877319). Secretary: B. Commins (0625 876951).

TARPORLEY. **Oaklands Golf Club,** Forest Road, Tarporley CW6 0JA (0829 733884; Fax: 0829 733666). *Location:* half a mile from Tarporley on A49. Undulating parkland with lovely views. 18 holes, 6169 yards. S.S.S. 72. *Green Fees:* weekdays £21.00 per round, £30.00 per day. *Eating facilities:* spike bar, bar meals. *Visitors:* welcome except weekends. Snooker. *Society Meetings:* catered for. Professionals: B. Rimmer/Miss J. Stratham. Secretary: Roy Hitchen.

WARRINGTON. **Birchwood Golf Club,** Kelvin Close, Birchwood, Warrington WA3 7PB (Warrington (0925) 818819). *Location:* Junction 11, two miles Leigh – Warrington road M62. Parkland with water. 18 holes, 6810 yards. S.S.S. 73. *Green Fees:* information not provided. *Eating facilities:* full restaurant facilities and bar snacks. Must book in advance. *Visitors:* conference and banqueting facilities for 200. *Society Meetings:* catered for weekdays except Fridays. Package deals available. Professional: Derrick Cooper. Secretary: R.G. Jones (0925 818819).

WARRINGTON. **Leigh Golf Club,** Kenyon Hall, Broseley Lane, Culcheth, Warrington WA3 4BG (0925 763130). *Location:* off A580 East Lancs Road to Culcheth Village. Parkland – tree lined fairways. 18 holes, 5876 yards. S.S.S. 68. Three practice areas, practice nets. *Green Fees:* weekdays £24.00, £8.00 playing with member; weekends and Bank Holidays £30.00. *Eating facilities:* two bars and restaurant. *Visitors:* check with Professional. *Society Meetings:* catered for Mondays (except Bank Holidays) and Tuesdays. Professional: Andrew Baguley (0925 762013). Secretary: G.D. Riley (0925 762943).

WARRINGTON. **Poulton Park Golf Club Ltd,** Dig Lane, Cinnamon Brow, Warrington (0925 812034/ 825220). *Location:* off A574 (Warrington/Leigh, Crab Lane). 9 holes, 4937 metres. S.S.S. 66. *Green Fees:* weekdays £16.00, in winter £12.00; weekends £18.00. *Eating facilities:* available except Mondays. *Visitors:* welcome. *Society Meetings:* catered for except weekends. Golf Society Package £24.00. Professional: A. Cuppello. Secretary: J. Reekie.

WARRINGTON. **Walton Hall Golf Club,** Warrington Road, Higher Walton, Warrington WA4 5LU (Warrington (0925) 266775). *Location:* two miles south of Warrington off A56. Wooded parkland. 18 holes, 6849 yards. S.S.S. 73. Practice ground. *Green Fees:* weekdays £6.00; weekends £7.50. Reduced rates 9-hole evening rounds; Juniors and Senior Citizens. *Eating facilities:* licensed clubhouse, meals and bar snacks. *Visitors:* unrestricted. *Society Meetings:* welcome. Professional: Peter Maton (0925 263061). Secretary: Maurice Youd (0925 266775).

WIDNES. **St.Michael's Jubilee Golf Club,** Dundalk Road, Widnes WA8 8BS (051-424 6230). *Location:* five minutes from M56 and M62. Undulating parkland. 18 holes, 5612 yards. S.S.S. 67. Putting and practice areas. *Green Fees:* information not available. *Eating facilities:* bar, meals in restaurant. *Visitors:* unrestricted. *Society Meetings:* by arrangement with Professional. Professional: B. Bilton. Secretary: W. Hughes.

WIDNES. **Widnes Golf Club,** Highfield Road, Widnes WA8 7DT (051-424 2440; Fax: 051-495 2849). *Location:* near town centre, five miles from M56 and M62. Parkland course. 18 holes, 5471 yards. S.S.S. 68 White, 69 Yellow, 69 Ladies. *Green Fees:* weekdays £20.00; weekends £30.00. *Eating facilities:* two bars and full catering service. *Visitors:* welcome, Wednesdays by prior arrangement. *Society Meetings:* catered for by arrangement. Professional: Mr S. Forster (051-420 7467). Secretary: Margaret M. Cresswell (051-424 2995).

WIDNES. **Widnes Municipal,** Dundalk Road, Widnes (051-424 6230). 18 holes, 5638 yards. S.S.S. 67, Par 69. *Visitors:* unrestricted. Secretary: W. Hughes. Professional: Bob Bilton.

WINSFORD. **Knights Grange Golf Course,** Sports Complex, Grange Lane, Winsford CW7 2PT. *Location:* signposted "Sports Complex" from traffic lights Winsford Town Centre. 6 miles from M6. Very flat but a challenging course. 9 holes, 2860 yards. S.S.S. 35/37. Practice area. *Green Fees:* £2.55 for 9 holes, £3.40 for 18 holes weekdays; £3.80 for 9 holes, £5.10 for 18 holes weekends. *Eating facilities:* snacks and hot drinks from golf shop, public house adjacent. *Visitors:* unrestricted (Municipal Course), 24 hour advance booking available 0606 552780. Bowls, tennis, football, athletics and crazy golf. *Society Meetings:* welcomed – booking in writing in advance. Professional: G. Moore. Manager: R. Wright (0606 552780).

SHRIGLEY HALL

Shrigley Hall is a Regency-style Country House built in 1825 with its own 18-hole Championship Golf Course within the 262-acre estate overlooking the Cheshire Plain and Peak District. Golfing Breaks are available all year and include full use of the Country Club with swimming, sauna, squash, snooker, spa bath and gymnasium. Special Breaks for golfing parties.

Shrigley Hall Hotel, Shrigley Park, Pott Shrigley, near Macclesfield, Cheshire SK10 5SB. Tel: 0625 575757 Fax: 0625 573923

Cleveland

BILLINGHAM. **Billingham Golf Club,** Sandy Lane, Billingham TS22 5NA (Stockton (0642) 554494). *Location:* off A19 trunk road, one mile west of Billingham town centre. Undulating parkland. 18 holes, 6460 yards. S.S.S. 71. Practice area including pitching green and putting greens. *Green Fees:* weekdays £20.00, £10.00 with member; weekends £33.00, £17.00 with member. *Eating facilities:* full catering Tuesdays to Saturdays. Snacks only on Mondays. *Visitors:* welcome weekdays, proof of membership of another club or Handicap Certificate required. Prior booking advised. *Society Meetings:* catered for with prior arrangement with Secretary. Professional: P.S. Bradley (0642 557060). Secretary: G.I. Douglas (0642 533816).

BROTTON. **Hunley Hall Golf Club,** Brotton, Saltburn TS12 2QQ (0287 76216). *Location:* situated off A174 at McLean Road, signposted. 18 holes, 6918 yards. S.S.S. 73. *Green Fees:* weekdays £18.00, with a member £9.00; weekends and Bank Holidays £25.00, with a member £12.50. *Eating facilities:* full catering and bar facilities. *Visitors:* welcome. *Society Meetings:* welcome by arrangement. Professional: Andrew Brook (0287 77444).

EAGLESCLIFFE. **Eaglescliffe Golf Club Ltd,** Yarm Road, Eaglescliffe, Stockton-on-Tees TS16 0DB (Eaglescliffe (0642) 780098). *Location:* on A135 one mile north of Yarm and three miles south of Stockton. Hilly parkland course, sloping to River Tees. 18 holes, 6275 yards. S.S.S. 70. Practice area and putting green. *Green Fees:* weekdays £20.00, weekends and Bank Holidays £26.00. *Eating facilities:* two bars, meals available except Mondays, separate diningroom. *Visitors:* welcome weekdays, restriction on Tuesdays and Fridays. *Society Meetings:* catered for except weekends. Professional: N. Gilks (0642 790122). Secretary: A.H. Painter (0642 780238).

HARTLEPOOL. **Castle Eden and Peterlee Golf Club,** Castle Eden, Hartlepool TS27 4SS (Wellfield (0429) 836220). *Location:* two miles south of Peterlee, use exits from A19. Picturesque parkland course. 18 holes, 6262 yards. S.S.S. 70. Practice ground. *Green Fees:* weekdays £20.00; weekends and Bank Holidays £30.00. *Eating facilities:* restaurant, lounge and bar. *Visitors:* welcome weekdays. Hours 9.30am – 11.30am, 1.45pm – 3.30pm. Tuesday Ladies' day. No visiting parties weekends or Bank Holidays. *Society Meetings:* weekdays only with reservation. Professional: Graham J. Laidlaw (0429 836689). Secretary: Peter Robinson (0429 836510).

HARTLEPOOL. **Hartlepool Golf Club Ltd,** Hart Warren, Hartlepool (Hartlepool (0429) 274398). *Location:* off A1086 at Hart Station (north of town). Seaside links course, 18 holes, 6255 yards. S.S.S. 70. Practice ground. *Green Fees:* weekdays £17.00; weekends £24.00, £9.00 if playing with a member. *Eating facilities:* meals and snacks available. *Visitors:* welcome (excluding Sunday) without reservation. *Society Meetings:* catered for by prior arrangement. Professional: M. E. Cole (0492 267473). Hon. Secretary: W.E. Storrow (0492 870282).

HARTLEPOOL. **Seaton Carew Golf Club,** Tees Road, Seaton Carew, Hartlepool (Hartlepool (0429) 266249). *Location:* two miles south of Hartlepool on A178. Seaside links. 22 holes. Old Course: 6604 yards. S.S.S. 72. Brabazon Course: 6802 yards. S.S.S. 73. *Green Fees:* to be arranged. *Eating facilities:* available. *Visitors:* welcome, some weekend restrictions. *Society Meetings:* catered for by arrangement. Professional: W. Hector (0429 266249). Secretary: P.R. Wilson (0429 261473).

MIDDLESBROUGH. **Middlesbrough Golf Club,** Brass Castle Lane, Marton, Middlesbrough TS8 9EE (0642 311515 and 316430). *Location:* five miles south of Middlesbrough west of the A172. Parkland course. 18 holes, 6111 yards. S.S.S. 69. *Green Fees:* weekdays £25.00; weekends £30.00. *Eating facilities:* lunches, teas and dinners. *Visitors:* welcome with reservation. *Society Meetings:* catered for. Professional: D.J. Jones (0642 311766). Secretary: J.M. Jackson (0642 311515 and 316430).

MIDDLESBROUGH. **Middlesbrough Municipal Golf Centre,** Ladgate Lane, Middlesbrough TS5 7YZ (0642 315533; Fax: 0642 300726). *Location:* three miles south of Middlesbrough on A174. Parkland course with featured streams. 18 holes, 6333 yards. S.S.S. 71. Floodlit driving range, practice area and putting green. *Green Fees:* weekdays £7.50 adult, £4.50 Senior Citizen/Junior; weekends £9.50 adult, £8.50 Senior Citizen/Junior. *Eating facilities:* bar meals provided, lunches available seven days. *Visitors:* welcome anytime, but starting times must be booked in advance. *Society Meetings:* by prior arrangement, special golf packages available. Professionals: Alan Hope and Dave Symington (0642 300720). Manager: Mr M. Gormley (0642 315533). Secretary: John Dilworth (0642 319416).

REDCAR. **Cleveland Golf Club,** Queen Street, Redcar TS10 1BT (Redcar (0642) 483693). *Location:* south bank of River Teesmouth by A174 then A1042 into Redcar. 18 holes, 6707 yards. S.S.S. 72. *Green Fees:* weekdays £16.00; weekends £25.00. Societies £25.00. *Eating facilities:* all week except Monday. *Visitors:* welcome but not on weekends or Bank Holidays. *Society Meetings:* catered for by prior arrangement weekdays only. Professional: M. Nutter (0642 483462). Secretary: L.R. Manley (0642 471798).

CLEVELAND *England* **THE GOLF GUIDE 1994**

REDCAR. **Wilton Golf Club**, Wilton Castle, Wilton, Redcar TS10 4QY (0642 454626). *Location:* eight miles east of Middlesbrough A174, four miles west of Redcar. Wooded parkland course. 18 holes, 6145 yards. S.S.S. 69. Small practice area. *Green Fees:* weekdays £18.00, £9.00 with member; Sundays and Bank Holidays £24.00 (£11.00 with a member). *Eating facilities:* lunches, except Sundays; evening meals by arrangement. *Visitors:* not on Saturdays or Tuesdays. Snooker, squash by arrangement. *Society Meetings:* by arrangement with Secretary. Secretary: J.C.P. Elder (0642 465265).

SALTBURN BY THE SEA. **Saltburn by the Sea Golf Club Ltd**, Hob Hill, Saltburn by the Sea TS12 1NJ (Guisborough (0287) 622812). *Location:* from Saltburn take Guisborough Road, one mile out of town on left. 18 holes, 5846 yards. S.S.S. 68. *Green Fees:* weekdays £19.00 per day, weekends and Bank Holidays £22.00 per day. *Eating facilities:* available except Mondays. *Visitors:* welcome, limited Sundays and Thursdays and no visitors Saturdays. *Society Meetings:* catered for by arrangement. Professional: David Forsythe (0287 24653). Secretary: David Becker (0287 622812).

STOCKTON-ON-TEES. **Teesside Golf Club**, Acklam Road, Thornaby, Stockton-on-Tees TS17 7JS (Stockton (0642) 676249). *Location:* A19 – A1130 to Thornaby, 0.7 miles on right hand side. Flat parkland, partly tree lined. 18 holes, 6504 yards. S.S.S. 71. Practice ground. *Green Fees:* weekdays £18.00, £9.00 with a member; weekends £24.00, £13.00 with a member. Parties over 10 £14.00. *Eating facilities:* catering except Mondays, bars 11am to 11pm. *Visitors:* welcome mid-week up to 4.30pm, weekend after 11am subject to starting sheet. *Society Meetings:* catered for midweek only. Professional: K. Hall (0642 673822). Secretary: Mr W. Allen (0642 616516).

HUNLEY HALL GOLF CLUB

★ 18 Hole Course
★ Floodlit Driving Range
★ Professional's Shop
★ Tuition Available ★ Spike Bar
★ Visitors Welcome ★ Restaurant
★ Members Lounge ★ Lounge

Brotton, Saltburn-by-Sea, Cleveland TS12 2PP Tel: 0287 76216

BLACK LION HOTEL

Special rates for all those playing at Hunley Hall Golf Club

High Street, Staithes, North Yorkshire TS13 5BQ
Telephone: 0947 841132

Moorlands Hotel
ETB ♛♛♛ Egon Ronay Recommended

Situated in the picturesque village of Castleton in the heart of the North Yorkshire Moors National Park. Commands superb views of the Esk Valley and heather clad moors. Comfortable hotel with an atmosphere of warmth and friendliness. Dales and Moors are ideal for walking, riding and cycling. Yorkshire Heritage Coast nearby. The hotel has ten bedrooms and is a freehouse. All twin and double rooms are ensuite, with colour TV and tea/coffee making. Extensive bar and restaurant menus. Many challenging golf courses within easy reach.
Contact Angie & Alan Abrahams for further details.
Moorlands Hotel, Castleton, North Yorkshire YO21 2DB
Telephone: 0287 660206

England CORNWALL

Cornwall

BODMIN. **Lanhydrock Golf Club,** Lanhydrock, Near Bodmin PL30 5AQ (0208 73600; Fax: 0208 77325). *Location:* one-and-a-half miles outside Bodmin on B3269. Parkland with brooks and natural water hazards. 18 holes, 6142 yards. S.S.S. 69. Putting green and practice area. *Green Fees:* £22.00; any five consecutive days (unlimited golf) £80.00. Concessions arranged with several hotels. *Eating facilities:* bar, limited catering. *Visitors:* welcome, please book tee times. *Society Meetings:* welcome by arrangement. General Manager: Graham Bond.

BUDE. **Bude and North Cornwall Golf Club,** Burn View, Bude EX23 8BY (Bude (0288) 352006). *Location:* seaside links course situated in the centre of the town adjacent to beaches. 18 holes, 6202 yards. S.S.S. 77. Practice net and grounds. *Green Fees:* weekdays £20.00 per round or day; weekends £25.00 (subject to review). *Eating facilities:* catering and bar snacks. *Visitors:* welcome without reservation. Snooker, billiards and pool. *Society Meetings:* catered for by bookings. Professional: John Yeo (0288 353635). Secretary: Kevin Brown (0288 352006).

CAMBORNE. **Tehidy Park Golf Club,** Camborne TR14 0HH (Portreath (0209) 842208). *Location:* A30 via Blackwater and Camborne by-passes to sign for Portreath. Parkland, wooded, 3 new lakes. 18 holes, 6241 yards. S.S.S. 70. *Green Fees:* weekdays £21.00 per round, £27.00 per day; weekends £26.00 per round, £32.00 per day. *Eating facilities:* bar snacks, à la carte restaurant except Mondays. *Visitors:* welcome with Handicap Certificate. *Society Meetings:* by arrangement; early booking essential. Professional: J. Dumbreck (0209 842914). Secretary: John Prosser (0209 842208).

CAMELFORD. **Bowood Golf Club,** Valley Truckle, Camelford PL32 9RT (0840 213017). *Location:* M4, M5, A30, A39 through Camelford, half a mile out turn right for Tintagel/Boscastle. First left after garage. Parkland set in an old deer park, once owned by the Black Prince. Plenty of wild life, trees and water and American style greens. Rating 10/10 Golf Monthly (October 1992). 18 holes, 6692 yards. S.S.S. 72. Teaching/practice areas, driving range. *Green Fees:* weekdays £23.00 per round, £30.00 per day; weekends £25.00 per round. *Eating facilities:* catering and bar all year round. *Visitors:* welcome, phone for tee reservations. *Society Meetings:* welcome by prior booking. Professional: Bryan Patterson. Secretary: Tony Japes. Proprietor: Ross Cobbledick.

FALMOUTH. **Budock Vean Golf and Country House Hotel,** Near Mawnan Smith, Falmouth TR11 5LG (0326 250288). *Location:* between Helford and Falmouth, area of Helford River. 9 holes/18 tees, 5222 yards. Par 68. S.S.S. 65. *Green Fees:* weekdays and Saturdays £14.00; Sundays and Bank Holidays £18.00 for non-residents, Hotel Guests Free. *Eating facilities:* catering and bars available. *Visitors:* daily only for outside visitors who are most welcome, but must have Handicap Certificate. Hotel accommodation. Secretary: F.G. Benney. Golf Manager: A. Ramsden.

LANHYDROCK GOLF CLUB

A superb parkland course with many water features. Enjoyed by golfers of all standards. Fully stocked golf shop with excellent range of both ladies and gents clothes and equipment. Visitors welcome. Brochures, etc. available on request.

Lostwithiel Road, near Lanhydrock, Bodmin, Cornwall PL30 5AQ. Telephone: 0208 73600

Lanteglos Country House Hotel
Camelford, Cornwall PL32 9RF Tel: (0840) 213551

Lantegos is a fine country house set amidst 15 acres of lovely garden in the heart of unspoilt North Cornwall and directly adjacent to Bowood Park Golf Club. Lanteglos offers freedom, space and a relaxed atmosphere where everyone can enjoy their holiday. Heated swimming pool. Solarium. Games room. Tennis. Satellite TV. Enjoy the comfort of Lanteglos after a day's golf at any of Cornwall's fine courses.

CORNWALL *England* THE GOLF GUIDE 1994

PENMERE MANOR HOTEL

*A*fter a hard day's golf relax in the delights of the Fountain Leisure Club. Facilities include indoor and outdoor heated swimming pools, sauna, solarium and, if you're not too exhausted, a mini-gym. The croquet lawn and 3/4 sized snooker table are there for those who have not lost their competitive edge. If the golf didn't go so well, there is a practice net in the hotel grounds alongside the Woodland Fitness Trail. Alternatively do absolutely nothing but enjoy the excellent cuisine accompanied by fine wines and ports and revel in the luxury of our Georgian Country House Hotel. Please ask for details of our golfing holidays.

Mongleath Road, Falmouth, Cornwall TR11 4PN
Tel: (0326) 211411 Fax: (0326) 317588

Cobblers Cottage

Nantithet, Cury, Helston TR12 7RB
Telephone: 0326 241342

Delightful 18th century cottage (once a cobbler's shop and Kiddlewink) with a large garden and ample parking, situated 2 miles from Mullion Golf Course which stretches between the coves of Poldhu and Gunwalloe, giving panoramic views of the sea and surrounding countryside. High class accommodation, en-suite bedrooms, good home cooking, tea/coffee facilities, oak beams, log fires. Sorry, no dogs or reductions for children as only small number of guests catered for.

BROCHURE FROM MRS H. E. LUGG

Mayrose Farm

HELSTONE, CAMELFORD,
CORNWALL PL32 9RN
TELEPHONE: (0840) 213509

17th century farmhouse and four converted cottages in a designated area of outstanding natural beauty, overlooking wooded valley. Each cottage has its own private garden with barbecue. Private heated swimming pool. Spring-fed lake with trout. Large variety of farm animals. National Trust coastline four miles with sandy beaches and surfing. Ideal base for enjoying some of Cornwall's wealth of golf courses, many within easy reach.

Contact Ann & Clive Ahrens

THE WHITE HART HOTEL
Launceston, Cornwall Tel: Launceston (0566) 772013

Restaurant Open 12 noon-2 pm & 7 pm-10 pm
Lunchtime "Specials available, Salad Buffet running throughout. Special Sunday lunch menu
Dinner A la Carte & Table d'Hote menus
Bar Food from 12 noon-2 pm & 6 pm-10 pm
Bars open from 11 am-3 pm & 5 pm-11 pm
"Happy Hour" 5 pm-7 pm weekdays
Three Function Suites, Conference facilities for 3 to 250 delegates.
Hot meals, Fork & Finger Buffets from 20 to 200 guests

BAKERS ARMS

Meeting Room available.

★ ★ ★

Happy Hour

★ ★ ★

Accommodation

LOSTWITHIEL
Hotel
GOLF & COUNTRY CLUB

Superb golf & leisure hotel set in magnificent countryside near former Cornish capital of Lostwithiel. 18 hole parkland course in richly wooded hills above the banks of the river Fowey. 18 bedrooms of great charm & character converted from traditional stone farm buildings. Tennis, heated indoor swimming pool, bar & restaurant. Only a short drive to beautiful coast.

Tel: 0208 873550
LOSTWITHIEL CORNWALL PL22 0HQ

England — CORNWALL

FALMOUTH. Falmouth Golf Club, Swanpool Road, Falmouth TR11 5BQ (0326 311262).*Location:* quarter-of-a- mile west of Swanpool Beach, Falmouth, on the road to Maenporth. Wooded parkland course with magnificent views. 18 holes, 5680 yards, 5192 metres. S.S.S. 67. Five acres of practice ground. *Green Fees:* on application. *Eating facilities:* catering and bar all year round. *Visitors:* welcome at all times, except during major competitions. *Society Meetings:* are always welcome, four weeks' notice required. Professional: David Short (0326 316229). Secretary: D.J. de C. Sizer (0326 40525).

HELSTON. Mullion Golf Club, Cury, Helston TR12 7BP (Mullion (0326) 240276). *Location:* from Helston on the A3083 past Culdrose Air Station, take first right past roundabout; signposted three miles. Cliff top and links. 18 holes, 6022 yards. S.S.S. 69. *Green Fees:* £18.00 from 1st April to 30 September; £14.00 from 1st October to 31st March. *Eating facilities:* bar and catering available each day. Caterers: (0326 241231). *Visitors:* welcome, with handicap only. *Society Meetings:* by prior arrangement. Professional: R. Goodway (0326 241176). Secretary/Treasurer: D. Watts, F.C.A. (0326 240685).

LAUNCESTON. Launceston Golf Club, St. Stephens, Launceston PL15 8HF (0556 773442). *Location:* one mile north of town on Bude road (B3254). Parkland. 18 holes, 6407 yards. S.S.S. 71. *Green Fees:* weekdays £20.00 per day. *Eating facilities:* available. *Visitors:* welcome without reservation, no visitors weekends between March 1st and October 31st. *Society Meetings:* catered for. Professional: J. Tozer (0566 775359). Secretary: B.J. Grant (0566 773442).

LOOE. Looe Golf Club, Bin Down, Looe PL13 1PX (Widegates (05034) 239). *Location:* three miles east of Looe on A387. Downland/parkland, fabulous views of S.E. Cornwall and beyond; designed by Harry Vardon. 18 holes, 5940 yards. S.S.S. 68. Large practice ground. *Green Fees:* on application. Five and seven day membership available. *Eating facilities:* full catering facilities available. *Visitors:* welcome, phone for tee reservations. Clubs for hire. Golf tuition available. *Society Meetings:* welcome by arrangement. Professional: Alistair MacDonald. Manager: Graham Bond.

NEWQUAY. Merlin Golf Club, Mawgan Porth, Newquay TR8 4AD (0841 540222). *Location:* on coast road between Newquay and Padstow. Fairly flat course. 18 holes, 5495 yards. S.S.S. 69. Driving range. *Green Fees:* £10.00. Special rates on request. *Eating facilities:* snacks. *Visitors:* most welcome. *Society Meetings:* all welcome. Secretary: N. Oliver (0841 540222; Fax: 0637 881057).

NEWQUAY near. Carvynick Golf and Country Club, Carvynick, Summercourt, Near Newquay (0872 510716). *Location:* turn off the A30 at Summercourt then take B3058 towards Newquay. Half a mile on left. Parkland and wooded course. 9 holes, 1246 yards. S.S.S. 27. *Green Fees:* information not provided. *Eating facilities:* at 16th century village inn and restaurant. *Visitors:* welcome all year. Sauna, gym, indoor swimming pool and badminton court. Holiday cottages available. Secretary: Peter Barton.

LOOE GOLF CLUB

Three miles east of Looe on A387. Downland/parkland course with fabulous views of S.E. Cornwall and beyond. Visitors welcome all year. Five and seven day membership available. Green fees on application. Diningroom, two bars. Bar snacks.

Bin Down, Looe, Cornwall PL13 1PX. Tel: (05034) 239.

NEWQUAY GOLF CLUB

Undulating 18 hole seaside lonks with 107 bunkers and splendid sea views. Relax after a round in the bar where lunches and snacks are on offer. Visitors are welcome at all times, although Societies are welcome every day except Sundays. Green fees from £18. Handicap certificate required.

Newquay Golf Club, Tower Road, Newquay TR7 1LT. Telephone/Fax: 0637 874354

CORNWALL *England*

NEWQUAY. **Newquay Golf Club,** Tower Road, Newquay TR7 1LT (0637 872091). *Location:* 400yards from Newquay Town Centre. Seaside links with 107 bunkers. 18 holes, 6140 yards, 5526 metres. S.S.S. 69. *Green Fees:* weekdays £18.00 per round, weekends £20.00 per round. £70.00 per week. *Eating facilities:* lunches and bar snacks, evening meal by arrangement with the caterer on 0637 872091. *Visitors:* welcome at all times. *Society Meetings:* catered for except Sundays (£14.00). Professional: P. Muscroft (0637 874830). Secretary: G. Binney (0637 874354).

NEWQUAY. **Treloy Golf Club,** Newquay TR7 4JN (0637 878554). *Location:* five minutes' drive from Newquay on the A3059 Newquay to St. Columb Major road. Parkland, seaside. 9 hole Executive golf course. First of its kind in Cornwall – sculptured greens, American Pencross grass, extensive mouldings and bunkers. 9 holes, 2143 yards, 1955 metres. S.S.S. 31. Practice green. *Green Fees:* 9 holes £7.50, 18 holes £11.50. *Eating facilities:* vending machines. *Visitors:* welcome. *Society Meetings:* welcome. Changing facilities, golf shop, club hire and professional tuition will be available on site. Secretary: Jim Reid.

PADSTOW. **Trevose Golf and Country Club,** Constantine Bay, Padstow PL28 8JB (0841 520208; Fax: 0841 521057). *Location:* off B3276, four miles west of Padstow at Constantine Bay. Seaside links course. 18 holes, 6461 yards. S.S.S. 71. *Green Fees:* weekdays £20.00 to £30.00 depending on season. Weekly and fortnightly rates available. *Eating facilities:* restaurant, bar open 11am to 11pm. *Visitors:* welcome if checked by telephone beforehand; Handicap Certificate required. Tennis, summer swimming pool available, also self catering accommodation. *Society Meetings:* by application. Professional: G. Alliss (0841 520261). Secretary: L. Grindley (0841 520208).

PENZANCE. **Cape Cornwall Golf and Country Club,** Cape Cornwall, St. Just, Penzance TR19 7NL (0736 788611). *Location:* signposted from St. Just-in-Penwith, seven miles west of Penzance. Cliff top course with spectacular coastal views. 18 holes, 5462 yards. S.S.S. 68. Practice putting green and golf area. *Green Fees:* weekdays £14.00; weekends £17.00. Special rates available for parties/societies over 15. *Eating facilities:* restaurant facilities lunchtime and evenings, bar all day. *Visitors:* welcome, telephone booking recommended. Heated indoor swimming pool, function room, games room. *Society Meetings:* welcome. Professional: Mr B. Hamilton. Clubhouse Manager: Graham Addison.

PENZANCE. **Praa Sands Golf Club,** Germoe Crossroads, Near Penzance TR20 9TQ (0736 763445; Fax: 0736 763399). *Location:* midway between Helston and Penzance on A394. Seaside, parkland – beautiful sea views from all holes. 9 holes, 4104 yards. S.S.S. 60 Par 62. Putting green – net. *Green Fees:* £12.50 per round. *Eating facilities:* restaurant, bar snacks. *Visitors:* welcome every day except Sunday mornings and Friday evenings after 5pm. *Society Meetings:* catered for by arrangement. Professional: Mike Singleton. Secretary: Ray Hudson. Proprietors: Kate and David Phillips.

TREVOSE GOLF & COUNTRY CLUB
Constantine Bay, Padstow, North Cornwall PL28 8JJ
Telephone: (0841) 520208   Fax: (0841) 521057

Trevose offers not only Golf (Championship 18 hole Course, 9 hole Short Course plus a second 9 hole Course par 35, length 3100 yds) but also first class Club House and Restaurant, 3 hard all-weather Tennis Courts; Heated Outdoor Swimming Pool from mid May to mid September; a Pro-shop and a Boutique. Accommodation is in Bungalows, Chalets, Luxury Flats, and Double and Single Dormy Suites. Send for our detailed full colour brochure.

BOSCAWEN

Two single storey detached cottages with panoramic sea views, standing in own grounds between the 9th and 10th holes. All golf facilities, restaurant, swimming pool, cottages open all year. One cottage sleeps three, whilst the other sleeps four. Both have modern facilities and are comfortably furnished.
First class stamp for full details to Mrs Rawlinson.
Boscawen, Carn Bosavern, St. Just, Penzance. Telephone: 0736 788671

PRAA SANDS GOLF CLUB

PRAA SANDS,
GERMOE CROSS ROADS,
PENZANCE, CORNWALL.
TEL. PENZANCE (0736) 763445

Proprietors: David & Kate Phillips

This 9-hole golf course offers outstanding views and a deceptively challenging par 62. Situated on the main A394 Helston to Penzance Holiday Route (7 miles east of Penzance), David and Kate offer a warm welcome to one and all. After playing why not relax further in the licensed bar and enjoy a quiet meal or snack with your family? Clubs for hire. Green fees from £12.50, weekly ticket £72.

Contact Kate and Dave Phillips for further details.

THE GOLF GUIDE 1994   England   CORNWALL

White Lodge Hotel

MAWGAN PORTH BAY, NEAR NEWQUAY, CORNWALL TR8 4BN
Tel: St. Mawgan (STD 0637) 860512

AA Listed   RAC Listed

REDUCED GREEN FEES AT 10 EXCELLENT CORNISH COURSES!

Special low price inclusive golfing holidays at WHITE LODGE HOTEL overlooking beautiful Mawgan Porth Bay, near Newquay, Cornwall.

★ 7 days (6 nights) dinner, bed and breakfast and also 5 ROUNDS OF GOLF INCLUDED at any 5 of the following 9 superb Cornish Golf Courses:

● BOWOOD PARK (CAMELFORD) ● LANHYDROCK (BODMIN) ● LOOE ● LOSTWITHIEL
● MERLIN (MAWGAN PORTH) ● PERRANPORTH ● ST. MELLION (OLD COURSE)
● TRELOY ● TRURO *from only £220 to £245 including V.A.T.*

★ £75 reduction for non-golfers ★ NO HANDICAP CERTIFICATES REQUIRED
★ Fantastic sea views ★ Direct access to Sandy Beach ★ Some en-suite rooms
★ DOGS MOST WELCOME – FREE OF CHARGE ★ Reduced green fees also available for the NICKLAUS OPEN CHAMPIONSHIP COURSE at ST. MELLION.

Weekly terms excluding green fees from only £161 to £189 including V.A.T. for 5-course evening dinner, bed and 4-course breakfast with CHOICE OF MENU.

Phone **John or Diane Parry on 0637 860512** for free colour brochure.

CORNWALL *England* THE GOLF GUIDE 1994

WHY NOT PLAY THE PORT GAVERNE WAY?

INCLUSIVE GOLF AT FOUR OF CORNWALL'S FINEST COURSES

Play ST MELLION OLD COURSE (supplement for the Nicklaus Championship Course); ST ENODOC; BODMIN and BOWOOD PARK from £199 fully inclusive dinner, bed, breakfast and golf including VAT.

2, 3 and 5 day breaks also available to individual requirements. Stay in an early 17th century Cornish Coastal Inn situated in unique position on the edge of a sheltered cove and offering memorable dining and personal service.

PORT GAVERNE HOTEL
Near Port Isaac, Cornwall PL29 3SQ

For brochure and details –
Mrs Ross (0208) 880244

"THE CREAM OF GOLF AT CORNWALLS FINEST..."

"...set in 250 spectacular acres."

This spectacular clifftop 6,505 yard course stretches through the beautiful countryside of Cornwall. The Carlyon Bay Hotel Golf Course proves both interesting and challenging to golfers of all handicaps. Telephone for information and a full course layout.

- Spectacular Location
- One of Cornwalls Premier Courses
- 4 star luxury at Cornwalls finest Hotel
- Professionally managed course

The Carlyon Bay Hotel
AND GOLF COURSE
AA ★★★★ RAC
St.Austell, South Cornwall. PL25 8RD
Telephone: St.Austell 812304

Brend Hotels
A Member of The Brend Group of Exclusive Hotels

THE GOLF GUIDE 1994 *England* CORNWALL

PERRANPORTH. **Perranporth Golf Club**, Budnick Hill, Perranporth TR6 0AB (Truro (0872) 572454). Seaside course overlooking Perranporth and beach. 18 holes, 6208 yards. S.S.S. 70. Par 72. *Green Fees:* information on request. *Eating facilities:* lunch and dinner. *Visitors:* welcome without reservation. Concessionary rates from selected holiday accommodation. *Society Meetings:* catered for with advance notice; concessionary rates. Professional: D. Michell (0872 572317). Secretary: P.D.R. Barnes (0872 573701).

REDRUTH. **Radnor Golf and Ski Centre**, Radnor Road, Treleigh, Redruth TR16 5EL (Redruth (0209) 211059). *Location:* two miles north east of Redruth, signposted from A3047 at Treleigh and North Country crossroads. Purpose-built Par 3 – interesting layout. 9 holes, 1312 yards. S.S.S. 52. Covered floodlit 18-bay driving range. *Green Fees:* £4.00 for 9 holes, £6.00 for 18 holes. *Eating facilities:* available. *Visitors:* welcome. Indoor ski training machine. Professional: Gordon Wallbank.

SALTASH. **St. Mellion Golf and Country Club**, Near Saltash PL12 6SD (Liskeard (0579) 50101). *Location:* Tamar Bridge. Old Course: 18 holes, 5927 yards, par 70. S.S.S. 68. Nicklaus Course. 18 holes, 6626 yards, par 72, S.S.S. 72. *Green Fees:* on application. *Eating facilities:* many within club complex. *Visitors:* welcome, Handicap Certificate required. *Society Meetings:* welcome. Hotel accommodation: 24 rooms, full facilities (badminton, squash, swimming, tennis, sauna, solarium, multi-gym). Golf Director: D.M. Webb. Professional: Tony Moore (0579 50724).

ST. AUSTELL. **Carlyon Bay Hotel Golf Course**, Carlyon Bay, St. Austell. *Location:* St. Austell A390. Clifftop course running into parkland. 18 holes, 6505 yards. S.S.S. 71. Six acre practice ground. *Green Fees:* £20.00. Subject to review. *Eating facilities:* bar open 11.30am to 10.30pm, food available 11.30am to 9pm. *Visitors:* welcome, must phone Professional for starting times. Accommodation available in four star hotel. *Society Meetings:* catered for by arrangement with the Professional. Professional: Nigel Sears (072681 4228; Fax: 072681 5604).

ST. AUSTELL. **St. Austell Golf Club**, Tregongeeves, Tregongeeves Lane, St. Austell PL26 7DS (St. Austell (0726) 72649). *Location:* one mile west of St. Austell on A390 St. Austell to Truro road. Parkland course. 18 holes, 6089 yards, 5569 metres. S.S.S. 69. *Green Fees:* information on request. *Eating facilities:* full service; arrange for Hot Meals before play. *Visitors:* welcome with reservation, must be club members and hold Handicap Certificate. *Society Meetings:* catered for weekdays by arrangement. Professional: M. Rowe (0726 68621). Secretary: S.H. Davey (0726 74756).

ST. IVES. **Tregenna Castle Hotel Golf Club**, Trelyon Avenue, St. Ives TR26 2DE (0736 795254; Fax: 0736 796066). *Location:* on the main road between Carbis Bay and St. Ives, half a mile from town centre. Seaside links course, wooded, with panoramic views overlooking St. Ives Harbour and Atlantic coast. 18 holes, 3549 yards. S.S.S. 59. *Green Fees:* £10.00 per round, £15.00 per day. *Eating facilities:* bar serving light snacks and refreshments. *Visitors:* welcome. 85 bedroom Hotel with restaurant, bar and wide range of leisure facilities. *Society Meetings:* prices on application; day packages available. Professional: Miss Ingrid Kemp.

ST IVES. **West Cornwall Golf Club**, Church Lane, Lelant, St. Ives TR26 3DZ (0736 753319). *Location:* two miles from St. Ives. Seaside links – wonderful coastal views. 18 holes, 5884 yards. S.S.S. 69. Practice ground. *Green Fees:* weekdays £20.00; weekends £25.00. Five Day ticket £60.00, Seven Day ticket £80.00. *Eating facilities:* bar and restaurant. *Visitors:* must be golf club members with Handicap Certificate. Snooker table. *Society Meetings:* on written application. Professional: P. Atherton (0736 753177). Secretary: M. Lack (0736 753401).

TORPOINT. **Whitsand Bay Hotel Golf Club**, Portwrinkle, Torpoint PL11 3BU (St. Germans (0503) 30276). *Location:* on coast six miles from Torpoint. Clifftop course. 18 holes, 5796 yards. S.S.S. 68. *Green Fees:* weekdays £12.50; weekends £15.00. *Eating facilities:* clubhouse and hotel. *Visitors:* welcome at all times with Handicap Certificate. Swimming/leisure complex. *Society Meetings:* catered for and hotel accommodation arranged on application to hotel. Professional: D.S. Poole (0503 30778). Secretary: G.G. Dyer (0503 30418). Hotel: (0503 30276).

TREGENNA CASTLE

Set amidst acres of landscaped grounds, Tregenna Castle's stunning 18 hole golf course is the ideal place to perfect your game, with splendid views of St. Ives Bay.
A wide range of sporting facilities are available. Special year round Golf Breaks.
See our Colour Advertisement on page 16.
Tregenna Castle, St. Ives, Cornwall. Telephone: **0736 795254**

Pedn-Olva
HOTEL & RESTAURANTS
*Porthminster Beach,
St. Ives, Cornwall TR26 2EA
Tel: 0736 796222
Fax: 0736 797710*

Pedn-Olva sits on a rocky promontory overlooking St. Ives harbour. The Hotel has 35 bedrooms, all with panoramic views of the sea. All rooms have private facilities and are very comfortably furnished. Guests can enjoy the sun on the sun soaked terrace with heated pool overlooking the beach. For further details see our colour advertisement on page 15.

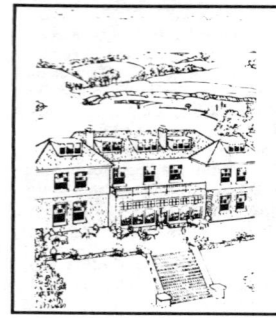

CORNWALL/ISLES OF SCILLY *England*   THE GOLF GUIDE 1994

ST. ENODOC HOTEL
Rock, Near Wadebridge
Cornwall PL27 6LA

Situated in its own grounds adjoining the St. Enodoc Golf Club with its two eighteen-hole courses, this well established Hotel provides comfortable accommodation with private bath, colour TV and telephone in all bedrooms. Full central heating. Wide choice of freshly prepared food using much local produce.
Special terms for golfing societies. Open all year.
Our own Leisure Club has a heated swimming pool, two glass-backed squash courts, two full-size snooker tables, sauna, jacuzzi, solarium and exercise room.

Please telephone for brochure and tariff.
(020 886) 3394 Fax (0208) 863394

TRURO. **Killiow Golf Club,** Killiow, Kea, Truro (0872 70246; Fax: 0872 40915). *Location:* three miles from Truro on A39 Truro/Falmouth road. Wooded parkland, picturesque setting with water features. 18 holes, 3542 yards. S.S.S. 60. All-weather floodlit driving range, practice bunker and putting green. *Green Fees:* contact reception. *Eating facilities:* soft drinks, sandwiches, etc. *Visitors:* course restricted to members until 10.30am at weekends otherwise available to visitors – check with reception. Professional: (visiting) D. Short. Secretary: John Crowson (0872 72768).

TRURO. **Truro Golf Club,** Treliske, Truro TR1 3LG (Truro (0872) 72640). *Location:* two miles west of Truro on A390 to Redruth. Undulating parkland. 18 holes, 5357 yards. S.S.S. 66. *Green Fees:* weekdays £18.00 per day or round, weekends and Bank Holidays £22.00 per day or round. *Eating facilities:* available. *Visitors:* welcome with Handicap Certificates but restrictions on competition days, Tuesdays and weekends. *Society Meetings:* catered for on weekdays. Professional: N.K. Bicknell (0872 76595). Secretary: B.E. Heggie (0872 78684).

WADEBRIDGE. **St. Enodoc Golf Club,** Rock, Wadebridge PL27 6LB (0208 863216). *Location:* take the B3314 from Wadebridge, signposted Rock (three miles). Seaside links. Two courses: Church Course 18 holes, 6243 yards. S.S.S. 69; Holywell Course 18 holes, 4134 yards. S.S.S. 61. Practice range, putting greens, etc. *Green Fees:* Church Course – weekdays £22.00 per round, £35.00 per day; weekends £27.00 per round, £40.00 per day. Holywell Course – £12.00 per round, £18.00 per day. *Eating facilities:* restaurant and bar snacks. *Visitors:* Handicap Certificates (24 and below) required for Church Course; no restrictions for Holywell Course. *Society Meetings:* all welcome by arrangement with the Secretary. Professional: Nick Williams (0208 862402). Secretary: Mr L. Guy.

Isles of Scilly

ST MARY'S. **Isles of Scilly Golf Club,** St. Mary's, Isles of Scilly (0720 22692). *Location:* one mile from Hugh Town, St. Mary's. Heathland by the sea with magnificent views. 9 holes, 3025 yards, 2791 metres. S.S.S. 69. Par 73. *Green Fees:* information not provided. *Eating facilities:* lunches and evening meals available. *Visitors:* welcome weekdays; Sunday play with member only. Secretary: Steve Watt (0720 22536).

Cumbria

ALSTON. **Alston Moor Golf Club,** The Hermitage, Middleton in Teesdale Road, Alston CA9 3DB (0434 381675). *Location:* one-and-three-quarter miles from Alston on B6277 to Barnard Castle. Parkland with panoramic views (highest golf course in England). 10 holes, 5456 yards. S.S.S. 66. Practice ground. *Green Fees:* weekdays £7.00; weekends £10.00. Juniors half price. *Eating facilities:* 19th Hole bar, catering available by prior notice. *Visitors:* welcome anytime, prior notice required for groups. *Society Meetings:* welcome by arrangement. Secretary: A. Dodd (0434 381242).

APPLEBY. **Appleby Golf Club,** Brackenber Moor, Appleby-in-Westmorland (Appleby (07683) 51432). *Location:* off A66 at Coupland Beck, two miles south of Appleby. Moorland course. 18 holes, 5914 yards. S.S.S. 68. *Green Fees:* weekdays £11.00; weekends £15.00. *Eating facilities:* available except Tuesdays. *Visitors:* welcome without reservation. *Society Meetings:* catered for by prior arrangement. Secretary: B.W. Rimmer.

ASKAM-IN-FURNESS. **Dunnerholme Golf Club,** Duddon Road, Askam-in-Furness LA16 7AW (Dalton (0229) 62675). *Location:* A590 onto A595. Seaside links. 10 holes (18 tees), 6181 yards. S.S.S. 69. Practice area. *Green Fees:* as on notice board. Special rates for parties of 12 or more. *Eating facilities:* by request for parties. *Visitors:* welcome without reservation, excluding competition days. *Society Meetings:* catered for. Secretary: J.H. Mutton (0229 62979).

BARROW-IN-FURNESS. **Barrow Golf Club,** Rakesmoor Lane, Hawcoat, Barrow-in-Furness LA14 4QB (Barrow (0229) 825444). *Location:* one mile from Barrow town centre, turn right first traffic lights into town (St. Pauls Church on right), then one mile. 18 holes, 6209 yards, 5679 metres. S.S.S. 70. *Green Fees:* weekdays £15.00 per day, £8.00 if playing with a member; weekends and Bank Holidays £25.00. *Eating facilities:* available. *Visitors:* welcome without reservation, must be member of recognised golf club. *Society Meetings:* up to 40 catered for by prior arrangement. Professional: N. Hyde (0229 831212). Secretary: J. Slater (0229 826968).

BARROW-IN-FURNESS. **Furness Golf Club,** Central Drive, Walney Island, Barrow-in-Furness LA14 3LN (Barrow (0229) 471232). *Location:* A590 into Barrow, follow sign to Walney Island, over bridge, straight on at lights. Clubhouse half a mile on right hand side. Seaside links. 18 holes, 6363 yards. S.S.S. 71. Practice area. *Green Fees:* weekdays £15.00, (£10.00 with member); Societies £8.00 per head for parties numbering over 12. *Eating facilities:* by arrangement with Steward. *Visitors:* parties by prior arrangement, others without reservation. Ladies' Day – Wednesdays; Competition Days – Saturdays or Sundays in summer. *Society Meetings:* welcome (tee reservation by prior arrangement). Professional: K. Bosward. Secretary: W.T. French.

Swim, Bubble and Golf!

Enjoy your par 68 round on Appleby's eighteen beautiful moorland holes (5915 yds), then it's five-minutes by car to return to your favourite Country House Hotel for a refreshing swim and a relaxing jacuzzi in the indoor leisure club.

Phone now for a free colour brochure with full details of the hotel, leisure club and prices:

APPLEBY·MANOR COUNTRY HOUSE HOTEL

Roman Road, Appleby - in - Westmorland, Cumbria CA16 6JD. Tel: Appleby (07683) 51571

If you are writing, a stamped, addressed envelope is always appreciated.

CUMBRIA England

BRAMPTON. **Brampton Golf Club,** Talkin Tarn, Brampton CA8 1HN (Brampton (06977) 2255). *Location:* situated on the Brampton-Castle Carrock road (B6413), approximately one and a half miles from Brampton. Rolling fell countryside, excellent views. 18 holes, 6420 yards. S.S.S. 71. *Green Fees:* on application. Practice facilities available plus snooker and pool tables. *Eating facilities:* catering available every day during playing season and on most days during winter period. *Visitors:* welcome without reservation, but should avoid Sunday, Monday, Wednesday and Thursday mornings. *Society Meetings:* catered for, limited numbers at weekends. Contact for visiting Societies, J.F. Swift (0228 36699). Professional: S. Harrison (06977 2000). Secretary: Ian J. Meldrum (0228 23155).

CARLISLE. **Carlisle Golf Club,** Aglionby, Carlisle CA4 8AG (Carlisle (0228) 513303). *Location:* on A69 Newcastle Road, half a mile from Junction 43 of M6. Parkland. 18 holes, 6278 yards. S.S.S. 70. Practice area. *Green Fees:* weekdays £20.00 per round, £27.50 per day; £30.00 Sundays only. Package deals for parties of 12 or more on application. *Eating facilities:* snacks, lunches, dinners and high teas. *Visitors:* welcome Mondays to Fridays and Sundays. *Society Meetings:* catered for Mondays, Wednesdays and Fridays, parties of 12 of more. Professional: John S. Moore (0228 513241). Administrator/Secretary: J. Hook.

CARLISLE. **Dalston Hall Golf Club,** Dalston Hall, Dalston, Carlisle CA5 7JX (0228 710165). *Location:* leave M6 at Exit 42, take road to Dalston at Dalston turn onto B5299, course on the right after one mile. Scenic parkland course. 9 holes, 5294 yards. S.S.S. 67. Practice area. *Green Fees:* weekdays £4.00 per 9 holes, £7.00 per 18 holes; weekends £5.00 per 9 holes, £8.00 per 18 holes. *Eating facilities:* full catering and bar facilities. *Visitors:* welcome, tee reservation is required at weekends and after 4pm during the week. *Society Meetings:* welcome by prior arrangement. Secretary: Jane Simpson (0228 710165).

CARLISLE. **Newby Grange Golf Club,** Newby Grange Hotel, Crosby on Eden, Carlisle (0228 573645; Fax: 0228 573420). *Location:* M6 three miles. Parkland course beside the Eden with six lakes. 18 holes, 7146 yards. S.S.S. 73. *Green Fees:* information not provided. *Eating facilities:* full hotel facilities. *Visitors:* welcome at all times. 20 bedroomed hotel, conference facilities. *Society Meetings:* welcome by prior arrangement with Professional. Professional: Phil Harrison (0228 573645 extension 221). Secretary: Denis Wiley.

CARLISLE. **Stoneyholme Municipal Golf Club,** St. Aidans Road, Carlisle (Carlisle (0228) 33208). *Location:* off A69 between M6 Junction 42 and town. Parkland course, 18 holes, 6000 yards. S.S.S. 68. Large practice area, changing rooms. *Green Fees:* information not available. *Eating facilities:* bar and restaurant. *Visitors:* welcome without reservation, but booking advisable weekends and Bank Holidays. *Society Meetings:* welcome by prior arrangement. Professional: Stephen Ling (0228 34856).

The Blacksmiths Arms

Situated one mile from Brampton, with its superb 18 hole golf course, in the peaceful and beautiful village of Talkin. (Winner of Carlisle and district best-kept small village for the past two years). The Blacksmiths Arms is the ideal base for Golfing at Brampton and Carlisle. A freehouse with a selection of real ales available. Accommodation comprises 5 bedrooms ensuite. Bar meals and full restaurant facilities available.

Talkin Village, Brampton, Cumbria CA8 1LE.
Telephone: 069 773452 Farm Holiday Guide Diploma Winner
ETB 👑👑 AA *QQQ*

AA & RAC 2 Star. Egon Ronay.

Tarn End House Hotel is situated in its own grounds of 1½ acres running down to the shores of the Tarn, and is only 500 yards from Brampton Golf Club where discounted fees have been arranged for our guests. Many other courses in the vicinity. Our bar, restaurant and residents' lounge all overlook the Lake as do most of the bedrooms, all of which have colour TV and tea/coffee facilities. Other relaxations include fishing, birdwatching, sailing and walking. As resident proprietors, we offer you a warm welcome, really good food and every hospitality. Special golf party rates are available.

THE TARN END HOUSE HOTEL

Talkin Tarn, Brampton, Carlisle, Cumbria. Telephone: (06977) 2340 Fax: (06977) 2089

DALSTON HALL CARAVAN PARK
Dalston, Near Carlisle CA5 7JX Tel: (0228) 710165

Set in peaceful surroundings, ideally situated for the Lake District border counties, Solway Firth and historic city of Carlisle. Facilities include: * Shop
* Launderette * Children's Play Area * Hard standings with electric hook-ups * Restaurant/Bar * 9-hole Golf Course * Fishing * Holiday homes for sale * Dogs welcome – but must be kept on a lead! *Phone for details.*

THE GOLF GUIDE 1994

England CUMBRIA

EMBLETON. Cockermouth Golf Club, The Clubhouse, Embleton, Near Cockermouth CA13 9SG (Bassenthwaite Lake (07687) 76223). *Location:* second exit A66 to Embleton across Old Road and up 1:5 hill. Scenic fell land course. 18 holes, 5457 yards. S.S.S. 67. *Green Fees:* weekdays £12.00; weekends and Bank Holidays £18.00. *Eating facilities:* meals by arrangement with Stewardess. *Visitors:* welcome; with members at weekends. *Society Meetings:* catered for mid week only. Secretary: R.D. Pollard (0900 822650).

GRANGE-OVER-SANDS. Grange Fell Golf Club, Fell Road, Grange-over-Sands LA11 6HB (05395 32536). *Location:* Cartmel Road from Grange one mile. Hillside course with panoramic views. 9 holes, 4826 metres. S.S.S. 66. *Green Fees:* weekdays £10.00, weekends and Bank Holidays £15.00. *Visitors:* welcome without reservation. *Society Meetings:* not catered for. Secretary: J.B. Asplin (05395 32021).

GRANGE-OVER-SANDS. Grange-over-Sands Golf Club, Meathop Road, Grange-over-Sands LA11 6QX (Grange-over-Sands (05395) 33180). *Location:* leave the A590 at roundabout signposted Grange, take the B5277 for approximately three miles. Flat parkland. 18 holes, 5938 yards, 5430 metres. S.S.S. 69. Practice area. *Green Fees:* weekdays £15.00 per round, £20.00 per day; weekends and Bank Holidays £20.00 per round, £25.00 per day. *Eating facilities:* diningroom, bar open every day except Tuesdays. *Visitors:* welcome without reservation weekdays and most weekends. *Society Meetings:* by arrangement with Secretary. Professional: Steve Sumner-Roberts. Secretary: J.R. Green (05395 33754).

KENDAL. Kendal Golf Club, The Heights, Kendal (0539 724079). *Location:* off A6 at Town Hall, signposted. 18 holes, 5515 yards. S.S.S. 67. *Green Fees:* £16.00 (£8.00 with member), weekends £20.00 (£10.00 with member). *Eating facilities:* meals available any day except Mondays. *Visitors:* welcome without reservation. Professional: D.J. Turner (0539 723499). Secretary/Manager: D. Leack (0539 733708).

KESWICK. Keswick Golf Club, Threlkeld Hall, Keswick CA12 4SX (Threlkeld (07687) 79013). *Location:* four miles from Keswick on A66 road to Penrith. Scenic fell and parkland course. 18 holes, 6175 yards. S.S.S. 72, Par 71. Extensive practice area. *Green Fees:* weekdays £15.00; weekends £20.00. Societies 12 or more £12.00 weekdays, £15.00 weekends and Public Holidays. *Eating facilities:* daily by arrangement; bar. *Visitors:* welcome, Ladies' Day Thursdays 12 noon to 1.30pm. *Society Meetings:* welcome by arrangement, unrestricted weekdays, 11.30am to 12.30pm weekends. Professional: Nigel Burkitt (07687 79010). Secretary: Richard Bell (07687 79324).

KIRKBY LONSDALE. Kirkby Lonsdale Golf Club, Scalebar Lane, Barbon, Kirkby Lonsdale, Carnforth (0468 36366). *Location:* three and a half miles from Kirkby Lonsdale on the A638 Sedbergh Road. Parkland, over Barbon Beck and sweeping down to the River Lune. 18 holes, 6280 yards. S.S.S. 70. Practice area. *Green Fees:* information not provided. *Eating facilities:* limited dining and bar facilities. *Visitors:* welcome. Tee reserved for members until 9.30am and between noon and 1.30pm. Accommodation and meals can be arranged at local hotels. *Society Meetings:* by arrangement. Secretary: P. Jackson (0468 36365).

MARYPORT. Maryport Golf Club, Bankend, Maryport (0900 812605). *Location:* adjacent to beach. Links course. 11 holes, 18 tees, 6272 yards. S.S.S. 71. *Green Fees:* weekdays £10.00 per day; weekends £15.00. *Eating facilities:* by arrangement. *Visitors:* welcome without reservation. *Society Meetings:* catered for. Secretary: A. Carlton (0900 822680).

MILLOM. Silecroft Golf Club, Silecroft, Millom LA18 4NX (0229 774250). *Location:* junction of A595 and A5093, eight miles north of Broughton-in-Furness. 9 holes, 18 tees, 5712 yards. S.S.S. 68. Large practice area near 9th/18th green. *Green Fees:* £10 per day. *Visitors:* welcome without reservation except Bank Holidays. Secretary: D. MacLardie (0229 774342).

PENRITH. Penrith Golf Club, Salkeld Road, Penrith CA11 8SG (Penrith (0768) 62217). *Location:* one mile from A6 to east of town. 18 holes, 6026 yards, 5510 metres. S.S.S. 69. *Green Fees:* weekdays £18.00 per round, £21.00 per day; weekends and Bank Holidays £25.00 per day. *Eating facilities:* dining facilities, excellent cuisine. *Visitors:* welcome with Handicap Certificate. Tee reservation is required at weekends and telephone enquiries advisable weekdays. No visitors to start before 9.15am or after 4pm. *Society Meetings:* catered for, restricted at weekends. Professional: C.B. Thomson. Secretary: D. Noble (0768) 62217).

Middle Ruddings Country Inn & Restaurant

BRAITHWAITE, CUMBRIA CA12 5RY. TEL: 07687 78436 FAX: 07687 78438

Family run hotel standing in 2½ acres of natural gardens, with magnificent mountain range views. Free golf at Keswick Golf Club, also free bowls and lawn tennis. Ideally situated for touring the Lakes – from only £25 per person per night for Bed and Breakfast.

★★★ RAC   ★★ AA   ETB 🌷🌷🌷 Commended

CUMBRIA   *England*

SEASCALE. Seascale Golf Club, The Banks, Seascale CA20 1QL (Seascale (09467) 28202). *Location:* B5344 off A595 to north of village. Links. 18 holes, 6416 yards. S.S.S. 71. 16-acre practice ground. *Green Fees:* weekdays £18.00; weekends £22.00. Three-day rate £40.00. 10% reduction for parties up to 12. *Eating facilities:* catering limited on Mondays and Tuesdays, bar available every day. *Visitors:* welcome when no tee reservations in force. *Society Meetings:* catered for by arrangement with Secretary. Secretary: C. Taylor.

SEDBERGH. Sedbergh Golf Club, Catholes – Abbot Holme, Sedbergh LA10 5SS (05396 20993). *Location:* one mile out of Sedbergh on road to Dent, well signposted. Superbly scenic course in Yorkshire Dales National Park. 9 holes, 5588 yards. S.S.S. 68. *Green Fees:* weekdays £14.00; weekends £18.00. *Eating facilities:* catering and bar. *Visitors:* welcome most weekdays without booking; weekends booking essential. Good local accommodation easily arranged via Secretary. *Society Meetings:* very welcome by prior arrangement. Secretary: A.D. Lord (05396 20993).

SILLOTH. Silloth on Solway Golf Club, The Clubhouse, Silloth, Carlisle (06973 31304). *Location:* M6 Junction 41 – B5305 to Wigton, B5302 Silloth. Seaside links, rated in the best five links courses in England. 18 holes, 6357 yards. S.S.S. 72. Practice facilities. *Green Fees:* weekdays £22.50 per round; weekends and Bank Holidays £27.50 per round. Restriction, only one round allowed per day at weekends. *Eating facilities:* full bar and catering. *Visitors:* welcome without reservation. *Society Meetings:* maximum 40 catered for weekends, one round per day. Professional: John Burns. Secretary: John G. Proudlock.

ULVERSTON. Ulverston Golf Club Ltd, Bardsea Park, Ulverston LA12 9QJ (Ulverston (0229) 52824). *Location:* Exit 36, M6. A590 to Barrow then A5087 to Bardsea village. Wooded parkland. 18 holes, 6142 yards. S.S.S. 69. *Green Fees:* weekdays £22.00,

THE GOLF GUIDE 1994

weekends and Bank Holidays £27.00. November to February £16.00 and £20.00; Juniors half price. Subject to review. *Eating facilities:* lunch and bar snacks (except Mondays and Fridays after 1.45pm). *Visitors:* welcome except Saturdays (competition day), and Tuesdays (Ladies' day). Must be members of accredited golf club and have a handicap. *Society Meetings:* welcome, write with reservation to the Match Secretary. Professional: M.R. Smith (0229 52806). Secretary: I.D. Procter.

WHITEHAVEN. St. Bees Golf Club, Whitehaven (0946) 822695). *Location:* four miles south of Whitehaven. 9 holes, 5079 yards. S.S.S. 65. *Green Fees:* information not provided. *Visitors:* unrestricted. Secretary: J.B. Campbell, Rhoda Grove, Rheda, Frizington CA26 3TE (0946 812105).

WINDERMERE. Windermere Golf Club, Cleabarrow, Windermere LA23 3NB (05394 43123). *Location:* one mile from Bowness-on-Windermere on Crook road, B5284. Idyllic National Park setting. 18 holes, 5006 yards. S.S.S. 65. Practice ground. *Green Fees:* weekdays £23.00; weekends £28.00. *Eating facilities:* restaurant. *Visitors:* welcome with bona fide handicaps and if members of recognised golf clubs. *Society Meetings:* catered for by prior arrangement with Secretary, numbers from twelve to 50, corporate days by arrangement. Professional: W.S.M. Rooke (05394 43550). Secretary: K.R. Moffat (05394 43123).

WORKINGTON. Workington Golf Club Ltd, Branthwaite Road, Workington (Workington (0900) 603460). *Location:* on A596, two miles east of town. Meadowland. 18 holes, 6252 yards. S.S.S. 70. *Green Fees:* weekdays £15.00, weekends and Bank Holidays £20.00. *Eating facilities:* lunches and dinners except Mondays and Thursdays. *Visitors:* welcome without reservation, must be members of recognised golf club. *Society Meetings:* welcome by prior arrangement. Professional: A. Drabble (0900 67828). Secretary: J.K. Walker (0900 605420).

LOOKING FOR A GUIDE?

If you have found *THE GOLF GUIDE* useful, you will also enjoy other titles in the FHG range including:

Recommended Country Hotels of Britain	£3.60
Recommended Wayside Inns of Britain	£3.60
Recommended Short Break Holidays in Britain	£3.60

You'll find our guides in most bookshops and in larger newsagents. In case of difficulty you can post or fax your order direct to FHG Publications in Paisley. You'll find an Order Form showing all prices, including postage, on the back pages of this book.

England   CUMBRIA

Scawfell Hotel, Seacale – fully licensed, most rooms en suite, all with colour T.V, tea and coffee making facilities and intercom. Why not stay and enjoy the relaxing atmosphere of Scawfell Hotel along with 3 days golf at the challenging Seascale Golf Club course (links). Package includes arriving Friday, golf in the afternoon, followed by dinner at the hotel, golf Saturday morning & afternoon followed by dinner, plus golf Sunday morning prior to departure. Mid week packages can also be arranged. The hotel is the largest in the area providing a full measure of comfort, and is situated only 500 yards from the golf course, which is a 6416 yards championship links course.

The **Scawfell** *Hotel*
SEASCALE, CUMBRIA
TELEPHONE: 09467 28400

STANLEY ARMS HOTEL

The Stanley Arms is a 17th century coaching inn, situated in the picturesque village of Calder Bridge. Scafell Pike (highest mountain in England) is nearby, as are Eskdale and Ennerdale. The famous Hardknott Fort and Pass are only a short drive away. All of the bedrooms are ensuite, with usual facilities. The restaurant is a converted stable, with charming old beams and a tempting menu. The River Calder runs through the garden where you can enjoy a memorable barbecue. The Stanley Arms is an ideal base for a golfing holiday, with many courses close by. Call Mike and Molly for further details.

Mike & Molly Porteous, Stanley Arms Hotel, Calderbridge, Seascale, Cumbria CA20 1DN. Tel: (0946) 841235 Fax: (0946) 841759

CALDER HOUSE (Private Hotel)
The Banks, Seascale, Cumbria CA20 1QP

Family-run, fully licensed hotel with darts and pool table. Standing in a quiet residential area of Seascale 100 yards from the beach and on the edge of the Lake District. Hotel offers 19 bedrooms, some with ensuite facilities, most with sea views. With annexe accommodation we can accommodate 36 golfers. There is a Fax facility and the car park holds 27 cars. There is also a 50 cover diningroom. We successfully run three-day Golfing Weekend Breaks from £110, in conjunction with the Seascale Golf Club, only 150 yards away. Two days' Half Board and three days' golf over the challenging 6416 yards links course are included in the package. For further information please ring **W.H. & G.L.J. Neal (Resident Proprietors). Tel. 09467 28538/27491; Fax: 09467 28265.**

Birdie, Eagle, Albatross . . .
. . . or even if you're looking for the elusive 'hole in one', Windermere is the place.
Situated only a mile from this 18 hole course, The Wild Boar with it's olde worlde charm offers you a friendly and welcome atmosphere in a tranquil setting.
Reflect whilst sampling our excellent cuisine and extensive wine list, on the 67 par round.
All rooms are ensuite and are equipped with every modern day facility to ensure your stay is an enjoyable one!
For your free colour brochure, telephone Windermere (05394) 45225 or fax (05394) 42498.
Discounted green fees, plus free golf balls.

Wild Boar Hotel Crook, Nr. Windermere, Cumbria LA23 3NF.   AA ★★★ RAC

Derbyshire

ALFRETON. **Alfreton Golf Club,** Wingfield Road, Alfreton (Alfreton (0773) 832070). *Location:* B6024 (Matlock Road) one mile from Alfreton. 9 holes, 5012 yards. S.S.S. 65. *Green Fees:* £12.00 per round, £15.00 per day weekdays; weekends only with member. *Eating facilities:* lunches except Mondays. *Visitors:* welcome with reservation. *Society Meetings:* catered for. Secretary: F.I. Lees.

ASHBOURNE. **Ashbourne Golf Club Ltd,** Clifton, Ashbourne (Ashbourne (0335) 42078). *Location:* on A515 Ashbourne to Lichfield, one and a half miles out of Ashbourne. Undulating parkland. 9 holes, 4960 yards. S.S.S. 66. *Green Fees:* weekdays £14.00. *Eating facilities:* catering available by prior arrangement with Steward; bar. *Visitors:* welcome most weekdays. *Society Meetings:* by arrangement. Secretary: N.P.A. James (0335 42077).

BAKEWELL. **Bakewell Golf Club,** Station Road, Bakewell (Bakewell (0629) 812307). *Location:* Sheffield Road out of Bakewell, turn right over River Bridge. Parkland, scenic hillside course. 9 holes, 5830 yards. S.S.S. 68. *Green Fees:* weekdays £12.00; weekends £16.00 by arrangement only. *Eating facilities:* available except Mondays. *Visitors:* welcome weekdays only unless accompanied by a member. *Society Meetings:* welcome, but available weekdays only. Professional: T.E. Jones. Secretary: T.P. Turner.

BURTON-ON-TRENT. **Burton-on-Trent Golf Club,** 43 Ashby Road East, Burton-on-Trent DE15 0PS (Burton-on-Trent (0283) 68708). *Location:* three miles east of Burton-on-Trent on the left hand side of the A50. Undulating and mature parkland course. 18 holes, 6555 yards. S.S.S. 71. Practice ground. *Green Fees:* weekdays £20.00 per round, £25.00 per day, weekends and Bank Holidays £25.00 per round, £30.00 per day. *Eating facilities:* bar open daily, diningroom/bar snacks except Mondays. *Visitors:* welcome during the week, not weekends. Ladies' day Tuesday, therefore some restrictions. *Society Meetings:* catered for, write to enquire. Professional: Gary Stafford (0283 62240). Secretary: D. Hartley (0283 44551).

BUXTON. **Buxton and High Peak Golf Club,** Town End, Buxton SK17 7EN (Buxton (0298) 23453). *Location:* A6 one mile north of Buxton. Gently undulating open Peak District countryside. 18 holes, 5980 yards. S.S.S. 69. *Green Fees:* weekdays £20.00; weekends £25.00. *Eating facilities:* full catering facilities except Thursdays. *Visitors:* welcome without reservation, ring at weekends. *Society Meetings:* up to 40 welcome. Contact Mrs S. Arnfield. Professional: A. Hoyles (0298 23112). Secretary: J.M. Williams (0298 26263).

BUXTON. **The Cavendish Golf Club Ltd,** Gadley Lane, Buxton SK17 6XD (0298 23494). *Location:* three quarters of a mile from town centre, on Leek Road A53, signposted. Parkland/moorland course, designed by Dr Alastair McKenzie who designed Augusta. 18 holes, 5833 yards. S.S.S. 68. Practice ground. *Green Fees:* £22.00 per round weekdays; £33.00 per round weekends. Juniors half price and visitors half price if playing with a member. *Eating facilities:* usual bar hours, snacks available, meals by prior booking. *Visitors:* apply to Professional, weekends only with a member. Snooker. *Society Meetings:* catered for weekdays only except Thursdays, apply to the Professional for booking arrangements. Professional: Paul Hunstone (0298 25052). Secretary: D.N. Doyle-Davidson (0298 23256).

CHAPEL-EN-LE-FRITH. **Chapel-en-le-Frith Golf Club,** The Cockyard, Manchester Road, Chapel-en-le-Frith SK12 6UH (0298 812118). *Location:* midway between Sheffield and Manchester, 25 miles from each on the B5470. Parkland, scenic. 18 holes, 6119 yards. S.S.S. 69. Practice ground. *Green Fees:* weekdays £18.00, weekends £30.00. *Eating facilities:* all meals daily except Mondays. *Visitors:* welcome, small numbers without reservation. *Society Meetings:* catered for by arrangement. Professional: D. Cullen (0298 812118). Secretary: J.W. Dranfield (0298 813943).

CHESTERFIELD. **Chesterfield Golf Club Ltd,** The Clubhouse, Walton, Chesterfield S42 7LA (Chesterfield (0246) 279256). *Location:* two miles from town centre on Chesterfield to Matlock road (A632). Parkland. 18 holes, 6326 yards. S.S.S. 70. Practice ground. *Green Fees:* weekdays £20.00 per round, £25.00 per day; weekends £10.00 with member only. *Eating facilities:* full catering, two bars. *Visitors:* weekdays only. *Society Meetings:* catered for on application except weekends. Professional: Michael McLean (0246 276297). Secretary: A. Bonsall (0246 279256).

CHESTERFIELD. **Chesterfield Municipal Golf Course,** Murray House, Crow Lane, Chesterfield S41 0EQ (0246 203960). *Location:* behind railway station. Wooded parkland course. 18 hole course and 9 hole pitch and putt course. 27 holes, 6025 yards. S.S.S. 69. *Green Fees:* weekdays £5.50, £3.00 9 holes; weekends £7.00, £4.00 9 holes. Concessions for unemployed and retired persons. *Eating facilities:* bar open to the public; restaurant. *Visitors:* welcome. Professional: Carl Weatherhead. Secretary: Mr J. Hearnshaw.

CHESTERFIELD. **Grassmoor Golf Centre,** North Wingfield Road, Grassmoor, Chesterfield S42 5EA (0246 856044; Fax: 0246 856200). *Location:* Grassmoor near Chesterfield, M1 Junction 29 or A61.

THE GOLF GUIDE 1994

England DERBYSHIRE

Heathland course incorporating many water hazards. 18 holes, 5715 yards. S.S.S. 68. *Green Fees:* non members £7.50, members £5.00 weekdays; non members £10.00, members £6.50 weekends. *Eating facilities:* available 8am to 11pm seven days a week. *Visitors:* welcome. *Society Meetings:* all welcome including at weekends. Professional: Darren Webster-Clarke. Secretary: Michael Shattock (0246 856200).

CHESTERFIELD. **Stanedge Golf Club,** Walton Hay Farm, Chesterfield S45 0LW (Chesterfield (0246) 566156). *Location:* five miles south-west of Chesterfield, off B5057 near "Red Lion" public house. 9 holes, 4867 yards. S.S.S. 64. *Green Fees:* weekdays £15.00, £7.50 with member; Saturdays and Bank Holidays £15.00, must be playing with member. *Visitors:* welcome by prior arrangement. Must book in by 2pm Monday to Fridays. No visitors on Sundays until 4 p.m. and they must be with member. *Society Meetings:* catered for by prior arrangement. Secretary: W.A. Tyzack (0246 276568).

CHESTERFIELD. **Tapton Park Golf Club,** Murray House, Crow Lane, Chesterfield (0246 203960). *Location:* head for Chesterfield railway station, turn left onto Crow Lane, 250 yards on. Parkland course. 18 holes, 6025 yards. S.S.S. 69. Also 9 hole course, 2478 yards. *Green Fees:* information not provided. *Eating facilities:* meals and bar all day. *Visitors:* welcome without reservation. Coaching by qualified PGA staff. *Society Meetings:* welcome with reservations. Municipal course, open to general public. Professional: Carl Weatherhead. Secretary: G.C. Howard (0246 854588).

CODNOR. **Ormonde Fields Golf Club,** Nottingham Road, Codnor, Ripley DE5 9RG (0773 744157). *Location:* five miles M1 Junction 26 towards Ripley on A610. Parkland. 18 holes, 6011 yards. S.S.S. 69. Practice area, putting green. *Green Fees:* £15.00 weekdays, £20.00 weekends. *Eating facilities:* full restaurant available. *Visitors:* unrestricted. *Society Meetings:* catered for; book through Secretary. Secretary: R.N. Walters (0773 742987).

DERBY. **Allestree Park Golf Club,** Allestree Hall, Allestree, Derby (Derby (0332) 552971). *Location:* 2 miles north of city centre on A6. Municipal course – hilly parkland. 18 holes, 5749 yards. S.S.S. 68. *Green Fees:* information not provided. *Eating facilities:* full bar, catering arranged with Steward. *Visitors:* booking sheet at weekends, weekday bookings available for parties through Professional. Professional: C. Henderson (0332 550616). Secretary: G. Rawson.

DERBY. **Breadsall Priory Hotel, Golf and Country Club,** Moor Road, Morley DE7 6DL (0332 832534 leisure club; Fax: 0332 833509). *Location:* turn off the A61 towards Breadsall, proceed on Croft Lane, turn left into Rectory Lane, then bear right onto Moor Road, continue past the Church for approximately one mile. Two courses – Priory is a parkland course and Moorland is a contrast of open moorland. Priory – 18 holes, 5871 yards. S.S.S. 68 off yellow tees; Moorland – 18 holes, 5820 yards. S.S.S.S. 68 off yellow tees. Practice area and putting green. *Green Fees:* £23.00 weekdays; £27.00 weekends. Golf Packages available. *Eating facilities:* Hotel – Priory Restaurant and cocktail bar; leisure club – poolside bar and Mullarkeys Restaurant. *Visitors:* welcome any time subject to availability. *Society Meetings:* catered for by prior arrangement, rates on application. Hotel has 91 bedrooms, leisure club and conference facilities. Professional: Andrew Smith (0332 834425). Golf Manager: Pat Wolf (0332 832534).

DUFFIELD. **Chevin Golf Club,** Golf Lane, Duffield DE56 4EE (0332 840497). *Location:* five miles north of Derby on A6 at Duffield village. Hilly course. 18 holes, 6057 yards, 5451 metres. S.S.S. 69. Two practice areas. *Green Fees:* £25.00 per day. *Eating facilities:* bar snacks and diningroom. *Visitors:* welcome weekdays, Handicap Certificates required. Snooker. *Society Meetings:* welcome weekdays, but never weekends. Professional: W. Bird (0332 841112). Secretary: C.P. Elliott (0332 841864).

GLOSSOP. **Glossop and District Golf Club,** Sheffield Road, Glossop SK13 9PU (0457 865247). *Location:* off A57, one mile from town centre. Moorland course. 11 holes, 5800 yards. S.S.S. 68. *Green Fees:* weekdays £15.00 per round; weekends £20.00 per round. *Eating facilities:* full catering facilities available. *Visitors:* welcome with reservation through Professional, except Saturdays during playing season. *Society Meetings:* welcome, same restrictions as visitors. Professional: Gary S. Brown (0457 853117). Secretary: D.M. Pridham (061-339 3959).

HORSLEY. **Horsley Lodge Golf Club,** Smalley Mill Road, Horsley DE21 5BL (0332 780838; Fax: 0332 781118). *Location:* north of Derby on A61, past Little Eaton, right turn signposted. Parkland. 18 holes, 6432 yards, 5901 metres. S.S.S. 71. Driving range. *Green Fees:* £17.00; £12.00 societies. Free golf for residents. *Eating facilities:* two bars, bar meals, dinners; function room seats 140. *Visitors:* welcome weekdays and some weekends but not on competition days. Four bedroom accommodation available. *Society Meetings:* by appointment. Professional: Simon Berry (0332 781400). Company Secretary: Richard Salt. Hon. Secretary (club): George Johnson (0332 880599).

ILKESTON. **Erewash Valley Golf Club Ltd,** Stanton-by-Dale, Near Ilkeston DE7 4QR (0602 323258). *Location:* Junction 25 of the M1, Stanton-by-Dale village. Parkland with two holes in an old quarry. 18 holes, 6487 yards. S.S.S. 71. *Green Fees:* weekdays £22.00 per round, £27.00 per day; weekends and Bank Holidays £27.00 per round. DUGC Card half price. *Eating facilities:* bar snacks available at all times, diningroom service on request. *Visitors:* welcome all week subject to club events and society bookings. *Society Meetings:* welcome weekdays only. Professional: Mike Ronan (0602 324667). Secretary: J.A. Beckett (0602 322984).

ILKESTON. **Ilkeston Borough Golf Club,** Peewit Municipal Golf Course, West End Drive, Ilkeston (0602 304550). *Location:* one mile west of Ilkeston market place. Slightly hilly meadowland. 9 holes, 4116 yards. S.S.S. 60. *Green Fees:* information not available. *Eating facilities:* not available. *Visitors:* welcome, no restrictions. Secretary: S.J. Rossington (0602 320304).

DERBYSHIRE *England*

MATLOCK. **Matlock Golf Club Ltd,** Chesterfield Road, Matlock DE4 5LF (Matlock (0629) 582191). *Location:* Matlock-Chesterfield road, A632, one mile out of Matlock, left hand side main road. Moorland with extensive views. 18 holes, yellow tees, 5801 yards. S.S.S. 68. *Green Fees:* weekdays £25.00; weekends and Bank Holidays £12.50 with a member only. *Eating facilities:* snacks available, luncheons and evening meals by arrangement (except on Mondays). *Visitors:* welcome weekdays. *Society Meetings:* catered for Tuesday to Friday. Professional: M. Deeley (0629 584934). Secretary: A.J. Box.

MICKLEOVER. **Mickleover Golf Club,** Uttoxeter Road, Mickleover, Derby DE3 5AD (Derby (0332) 513339). *Location:* three miles west of Derby on the A516/B5020 to Uttoxeter. Undulating. 18 holes, 5708 yards, 5222 metres. S.S.S. 68. *Green Fees:* weekdays £18.00, weekends and Bank Holidays £25.00. Society rates on request. *Eating facilities:* bar snacks available. *Visitors:* welcome, no restrictions – telephone Professional before arrival. *Society Meetings:* Tuesdays and Thursdays. Professional: Paul Wilson (0332 518662). Secretary: Doug Rodgers (0332 516011).

MICKLEOVER. **Pastures Golf Club,** Pastures Hospital, Mickleover (0332 513921 extension 419). *Location:* four miles west of Derby. Undulating meadowland. 9 holes, 5005 yards. S.S.S. 64. Practice area. *Green Fees:* £10.00 weekdays and Saturdays, no green fees Sundays. *Eating facilities:* bar facilities/snacks. *Visitors:* welcome every day except Sundays and must be with a member. *Society Meetings:* by arrangement. Secretary: S. McWilliams (0332 513921 extension 348).

QUARNDON. **Kedleston Park Golf Club,** Kedleston, Quarndon, Derby DE22 5JD. *Location:* four miles north of Derby on Kedleston Hall Estate – National Trust. Parkland with lakes. 18 holes, 6636 yards, 6068 metres. S.S.S. 72. *Green Fees:* weekdays £25.00 per round, £35.00 per day. *Eating facilities:* full catering, bars. *Visitors:* welcome Monday to Friday; weekends with member. *Society Meetings:* welcome Monday to Friday. Professional: J. Hetherington (0332 841685). Secretary: K. Wilson (0332 840035).

SHEFFIELD. **Renishaw Park Golf Club,** Golf House, Station Road, Renishaw, Sheffield S31 9UZ (Eckington (0246) 432044). *Location:* A616 Barlborough (Junction 30 M1) to Sheffield. Parkland/meadowland. 18 holes, 6253 yards. S.S.S. 70. Practice net. *Green Fees:* weekdays £20.00 per round, £28.00 per day; weekends £33.00 per round/day. *Eating facilities:* bar meals, full restaurant. *Visitors:* welcome without reservation (advisable to ring Pro prior to arrival). *Society Meetings:* by prior arrangement. Full day package available. Professional: S. Elliott (0246 435484). Secretary: L.T. Hughes (0246 432044).

SHEFFIELD. **Sickleholme Golf Club,** Bamford, Sheffield S30 2BH (Hope Valley (0433) 651306). *Location:* A625 west of Sheffield, right at Marquis of Granby, Bamford. 18 holes, 6064 yards. S.S.S. 69. *Green Fees:* information not available. *Eating facilities:* by arrangement. *Visitors:* must be members of a recognised Golf Club. *Society Meetings:* catered for by arrangement. Professional/Manager: P. H. Taylor (0433 651252).

SHIRLAND. **Shirland Golf Club,** Lower Delves, Shirland DE5 6AU (Alfreton (0773) 834969/834935). *Location:* one mile north of Alfreton off A61, three miles from M1 Junction 28 via A38. Tree-lined rolling parkland, 18 holes, 6072 yards. S.S.S. 69. Par 71. Two practice grounds. *Green Fees:* £15.00 per round, £25.00 per day weekdays; £20.00 per round, £30.00 per day weekends. *Eating facilities:* full restaurant, bar meals. Conference and banquet rooms. *Visitors:* unrestricted weekdays, but must book through Professional at weekends. County standard bowling green available. *Society Meetings:* welcome. Professional: Mrs C.S. Fincham (0773 832515). Secretary: Mrs C.S. Fincham (0773 832515).

SINFIN. **Derby Golf Club,** Shakespeare Street, Sinfin, Derby DE24 9HD (Derby (0332) 766323). *Location:* two miles town centre, access via Wilmore Road. Parkland. 18 holes, 6144 yards, 5618 metres. S.S.S. 69. Practice area. *Green Fees:* on request. *Eating facilities:* bar and catering available. *Visitors:* welcome weekdays. *Society Meetings:* welcome weekdays. Professional: Andrew Carnell (0332 766462). Secretary: P. Davidson.

STOCKPORT. **New Mills Golf Club,** Shaw Marsh, New Mills (New Mills (0663) 743485). *Location:* off A6015. 9 holes, 5633 yards. S.S.S. 67. *Green Fees:* £15.00 weekdays only. *Eating facilities:* catering except Thursdays. *Visitors:* welcome weekdays with reservation, weekends with members. No visitors competition days. *Society Meetings:* no catering Thursdays, catered for by appointment. Professional: Edward Litchfield. Secretary: R. Tuson.

PUBLISHER'S NOTE

While every effort is made to ensure accuracy, we regret that FHG Publications cannot accept responsibility for errors, omissions or misrepresentation in our entries or any consequences thereof. Prices in particular should be checked because we go to press early. We will follow up complaints, but cannot act as arbiters or agents for either party.

Devon

AXMOUTH. **Axe Cliff Golf Club,** Squires Lane, Axmouth, Seaton EX12 4AZ (0297 20499). *Location:* A35 from Lyme Regis, turn left on to B3172 at junction with A358 Seaton. Seaside wooded course. 18 holes, 5057 yards. S.S.S. 65. *Green Fees:* weekdays £14.00; weekends £17.00. *Eating facilities:* dining room. Hot meals/snacks, etc. *Visitors:* welcome without reservation, course closed until 11 am on Sundays and Wednesdays. *Society Meetings:* catered for, apply Secretary. Secretary: Mrs D. Rogers (0297 24371).

BIDEFORD near. **Clovelly Golf and Country Club,** Woolsery, Near Bideford EX39 5RA (0237 431442; Fax: 0237 431734). *Location:* between Bideford and Bude A39, signposted from main A39 road. Parkland with pond and lakes. 18 holes, 5641 yards. S.S.S. 67. *Green Fees:* £12.00. *Eating facilities:* restaurant and bar. *Visitors:* welcome at all times. Heated swimming pool, sauna, solarium, jacuzzi, fitness room. *Society Meetings:* welcome. Secretary: T. Woolnough.

BIGBURY. **Bigbury Golf Club Ltd,** Bigbury, Kingsbridge TQ7 4BB (Bigbury on Sea (0548) 810207). *Location:* off main Plymouth to Kingsbridge road, turn right at Harraton Cross. Two courses: No 1 – 18 holes, 5902 yards. S.S.S. 68. No. 2 (Comp) – 18 holes, 6076 yards. S.S.S. 69. *Green Fees:* weekdays £20.00; weekends £24.00. *Eating facilities:* buffet catering always available; medium to full catering order in advance. *Visitors:* welcome, Handicap Certificate required. *Society Meetings:* catered for by prior arrangement. Professional: Simon Lloyd. Secretary: B.J. Perry (0548 810557).

BRAUNTON. **Saunton Golf Club,** Saunton, Braunton (0271 812436; Fax: 0271 814241). *Location:* eight miles west of Barnstaple on Linksland at north side of Barnstaple Bay. East course 18 holes, 6708 yards. S.S.S. 73. West course 18 holes, 6356 yards. S.S.S. 71. *Green Fees:* weekdays £28.00, weekends £33.00. Subject to review. *Eating facilities:* full catering available. *Visitors:* welcome with reservation, must be members of other golf club and must be able to produce Handicap Certificate. *Society Meetings:* catered for by arrangement. Professional: J.A. McGhee (0271 812013). Secretary: W.E. Geddes (0271 812436).

BRIXHAM. **Churston Golf Club Ltd,** Churston, Near Brixham TQ5 0LA (0803 842218). *Location:* Torquay – follow road signs to Brixham. Seaside course overlooking Torbay. 18 holes, 6243 yards. S.S.S. 70. *Green Fees:* weekdays £22.00, weekends £27.00. *Eating facilities:* available all day. *Visitors:* welcome, must be members of recognised club. Handicap Certificate required. *Society Meetings:* catered for by arrangement. Professional: Richard Penfold (0803 842218). Manager/Secretary: A.M. Chaundy (0803 842751; Fax: 0803 845738).

The Broadsands Links Hotel

BASCOMBE ROAD · CHURSTON FERRERS
BRIXHAM · DEVON · TQ5 0JT
Telephone: Churston (0803) 842360

The Broadsands Links Hotel enjoys a unique position on the headland overlooking Torbay, with unrivalled sea views and offers comfortable, tastefully decorated rooms, excellent food, a superb wine cellar and attentive discreet service.
All rooms ensuite, with central heating and tea making facilities. All rooms have colour TV. Fine, well-stocked cocktail bar, residents' lounge and a small intimate cosy lounge, very popular with guests.
Situated in approximately two acres of grounds, with a private path to the beach road, you can sail, swim, windsurf or just soak up some of Torbay's famous sunshine.
Adjacent to the Hotel is Churston Golf Club, a marvellous course, 6238 yard par 70, with two fine par 5's and some delightful short holes. Societies welcome. Please phone or write for brochure & tariff.

WEST RIDGE

See colour advertisement on page 16.

"West Ridge" bungalow stands on elevated ground above the small coastal town of Seaton. It has 1½ acres of lawns and gardens and is just a mile from Axmouth Golf Course. Several other golf courses nearby. Accommodation is suitable for 3 to 5 persons. Available March to October.
£125 to £295 weekly. Gas c/h. Colour TV.
SAE for brochure to: Mrs E. P. Fox, "West Ridge", Harepath Hill, Seaton EX12 2TA
Telephone and Fax: Seaton (0297) 22398   ETB Three Keys Commended

DEVON *England* THE GOLF GUIDE 1994

BUDLEIGH SALTERTON. **East Devon Golf Club,** North View Road, Budleigh Salterton EX9 6DQ (Budleigh Salterton (0395) 442018). *Location:* three miles from Exmouth. Heathland, 18 holes, 6214 yards. S.S.S. 70. *Green Fees:* weekdays £23.50; weekends £28 20. *Eating facilities:* full bar and catering facilities (no catering Mondays). *Visitors:* welcome with letter of introduction, Handicap Certificate or Devon County card. *Society Meetings:* catered for by arrangement. Professional: Trevor Underwood (0395 445195). Secretary: J.C. Tebbet (0395 443370).

CHULMLEIGH. **Chulmleigh Golf Course** Leigh Road, Chulmleigh EX18 7BL (Chulmleigh (0769) 80519). *Location:* midway between Barnstaple and Crediton on A377. Undulating course. 18 holes, 1450 yards. S.S.S. 54. Mid December to end of March 9 holes x 2, 2352 yards. *Green Fees:* £5.00 per round, 2 rounds £7.50. Day ticket £10.00. Reductions for Juniors. *Eating facilities:* snacks, bar. *Visitors:* welcome. Large luxury apartment available. Giant TV screen for watching all major tournaments and own videos made on premises. *Society Meetings:* welcome by prior arrangement. Owner/Secretary: P.N. Callow.

CREDITON. **Downes Crediton Golf Club,** Hookway, Crediton (Crediton (0363) 773991). *Location:* off Crediton-Exeter road. Part flat, part hilly course featuring woods and water. 18 holes, 5917 yards. S.S.S. 68. *Green Fees:* £16.00 weekdays, £22.00 weekends. *Eating facilities:* available from 11.30am to one hour before bar closes. *Visitors:* welcome, advisable to phone first and must produce Handicap Certificate. *Society Meetings:* by arrangement. Professional: Howard Finch (0363 774464). Secretary: W.J. Brooks (0363 773025).

CULLOMPTON. **Padbrook Park Golf Club,** Padbrook Park, Cullompton (0884 38286; Fax: 0884 38359). *Location:* Junction 28 of M5, one mile away. Parkland. 9 holes (18 tees), 6108 yards. S.S.S. 70. Nets. *Green Fees:* weekdays £7.00 for 9 holes, £10.00 for 18 holes; weekends £8.00 for 9 holes, £16.00 for 18 holes. Juniors half price. *Eating facilities:* two bars and restaurant. *Visitors:* always welcome. Indoor bowls, fishing. *Society Meetings:* welcome by prior arrangement. Professional: Stewart Adwick. General Manager: Richard Chard.

DAWLISH. **Warren Golf Club,** Dawlish EX7 0NF (0626 862738). *Location:* 12 miles south of Exeter off A379. Links golf course lying on a spit of land between the sea and Exe Estuary. 18 holes, 5973 yards. S.S.S. 69. *Green Fees:* weekdays £19.00, weekends and Bank Holidays £21.00 (half price with a member). *Eating facilities:* bar and full catering available. *Visitors:* welcome with Handicap Certificate.*Society Meetings:* welcome by arrangement, Special Packages available. Professional: Geoff Wicks (0626 864002). Secretary: D.G. Daniell (0626 862255).

EXETER. **Exeter Golf and Country Club,** Countess Wear, Exeter EX2 7AE (Tel & Fax: 0392 874139). *Location:* near M5, exit Junction 30. Parkland course. 18 holes, 6000 yards. S.S.S. 69. Large practice ground. *Green Fees:* £22.00. *Eating facilities:* sports bar, lounge bar, diningroom. *Visitors:* welcome except Tuesdays (Ladies' Day) and weekends (very busy with members), booking number 0392 876303). *Society Meetings:* catered for Thursdays only. Professional: Mike Rowett (0392 875028). Secretary: C.H.M. Greetham (0392 874023).

EXETER near. **Fingle Glen Golf and Leisure Complex,** Tedburn St. Mary, Near Exeter EX6 6AF (0647 61817; Fax: 0647 61135). *Location:* A30 five miles from Exeter on the Okehampton Road. Parkland with streams and lakes. 9 holes, 2466 yards. S.S.S. 63 (18 holes). Golf academy, 12 bay floodlit driving range. *Green Fees:* weekdays £5.00 9 holes, £9.00 18 holes; weekends £7.00 9 holes, £13.00 18 holes. *Eating facilities:* restaurant, bar snacks, family area, sun terrace. *Visitors:* welcome at all times. 3 star accommodation available. *Society Meetings:* welcome at all times. Professional: Stephen Gould. Golf Manager: Gary Chown (0647 61817).

EXETER near. **Woodbury Park Golf and Country Club,** Woodbury Castle, Near Exeter EX5 1JJ (0395 233382; Fax: 0395 233384). Parkland, wooded with lakes. 18 hole championship course and 9 hole course. *Green Fees:* weekdays £20.00; weekends £25.00. *Eating facilities:* full bar, snacks and catering for societies. *Visitors:* welcome at anytime – tee reservations essential. *Society Meetings:* welcome, special rates. Professional: Alan Richards. Secretary: Malcolm Davies.

EXETER near. **Woodbury Park Golf and Country Club,** Woodbury Castle, Woodbury, Near Exeter EX5 1JJ (0395 233382; Fax: 0395 233384). *Location:* Junction 30 M5, A3052 towards Sidmouth, turn right B3052. Seven miles from motorway. Parkland through mature woodland with several water features. 18 hole championship course and 9 hole course. 18 holes, 6707 yards. S.S.S. 72. 12 bay driving range. *Green Fees:* weekdays £20.00 for 18 holes, £8.00 for 9 holes; weekends £25.00 for 18 holes, £9 for 9 holes. *Eating facilities:* bar snacks; meals available if requested. *Visitors:* welcome at all times. *Society Meetings:* welcome, please ring; Golf Packages available. Professional: Alan Richards. Secretary: Basil Warren.

Venn Ottery Barton
A 16th CENTURY COUNTRY HOTEL
Family run. Superb home cooking, cosy bedrooms, log fires, full central heating, well stocked bar. Ideally situated near 6 Golf Courses, including the challenging East Devon Golf Course at Budleigh Salterton.
Venn Ottery, Ottery St. Mary, Devon EX11 1RZ Tel: (040481) 2733

THE GOLF GUIDE 1994   England   DEVON

HOLSWORTHY. Holsworthy Golf Club, Kilatree, Holsworthy (Holsworthy (0409) 253177). *Location:* leave Holsworthy on Bude road, A3072; one mile on left. Parkland, 18 holes, 6012 yards. S.S.S. 69. *Green Fees:* weekdays £15.00; weekends £20.00. *Eating facilities:* snacks at bar, diningroom. *Visitors:* welcome without reservation, (after 2.30pm Sundays). *Society Meetings:* catered for by arrangement. Professional: Tim McSherry (0409 254771). Secretary: Barry Megson (0409 253177).

HONITON. Honiton Golf Club, Middlehills, Honiton EX14 8TR (0404 47167). *Location:* one mile south of town proceed from New Street to Farway. Flat parkland. 18 holes, 5940 yards. S.S.S. 68. Small practice ground. *Green Fees:* weekdays £18.00 per day, weekends and Bank Holidays £23.00. *Eating facilities:* bar and restaurant. *Visitors:* bona fide members of other clubs welcome, with restrictions on Wednesdays (ladies' day) and weekends (club competitions). *Society Meetings:* bookable on Thursdays only. Professional: Adrian Cave (0404 42943). Secretary: J.L. Carter (0404 44422).

ILFRACOMBE. Ilfracombe Golf Club, Hele Bay, Ilfracombe EX34 9RT (0271 862050). *Location:* on main coastal road between Ilfracombe and Combe Martin. Undulating parkland with spectacular views of sea and moors from every tee and green. 18 holes, 5893 yards. S.S.S. 69. Practice area and green. *Green Fees:* weekdays £17.00; weekends £20.00. *Eating facilities:* full catering available; normal club bar hours. *Visitors:* welcome (Handicap/membership Certificate preferred), members only 12 noon to 2pm daily and

---

St. Brannocks House Hotel
Golfing breaks from £185 D,B&B inc. 5 days golf

Friendly family run hotel. Walking distance of town and seafront. ★ Ensuite rooms; ★ Parking;
★ Licensed bar; ★ All rooms tea/coffee making facilities & TV; ★ Pets welcome; ★ Open all year

St. Brannocks Road, Ilfracombe, North Devon EX34 8EQ
Telephone (0271) 863873

RAC Acclaimed   ETB

Enjoy your Golfing Holiday at the Cream of Devon's Golf Courses!

Stay at the **FLOYDE HOTEL, Brookdale Avenue, ILFRACOMBE** – the Golfer's choice. Our Golfing Proprietor arranges all golf tees, all you do is arrive and enjoy yourself. BE OUR GUEST – NOT JUST A ROOM NUMBER! See you at the Golfers' Favourite 19th hole SOON! 7 nights BB&EM, 5 days' golf from £199; 4 nights' BB&EM, 3 days' golf from £117 – or days to suit. *Phone Jeff or Sue Whitmore.*   **Tel: 0271 862594**

Merlin Court Hotel

RAC Acclaimed   Torrs Park, Ilfracombe, North Devon EX34 8AY   AA Listed

Detached hotel, own large car park, lovely grounds. Colour TV, radio alarm. Ensuites available. See Colour advertisement on page 16 for more details.

Telephone 0271 862697 for Reservation or Brochure   ETB

The Darnley Hotel   Belmont Road, Ilfracombe, Devon EX34 8DR

Small licensed hotel of charm and character serving probably the best food in Devon allied to friendly personal service in a relaxed atmosphere. Tea making facilities in all rooms; most ensuite! Live entertainment in the Bar one night per week. Six nights' Bed, Breakfast and Evening Meal, with five days' GOLF at Ilfracombe from £160. Holidays also arranged with Golf at Saunton & Royal North Devon, Westward Ho! Two, three or four day Breaks available. Open all year including Christmas and New Year.

Telephone: (0271) 863955

DEVON England

before 10am weekends. *Society Meetings:* welcome, but book in advance. Professional: David Hoare (0271 863328). Secretary: Rodney C. Beer (0271 862176; Fax: 0271 867731).

MORETONHAMPSTEAD. **Manor House Hotel and Golf Course,** Moretonhampstead TR13 8RE (Moretonhampstead (0647) 40355). *Location:* Junction 31 from M5, B3212 for two miles. Parkland with rivers. 18 holes, 6016 yards. S.S.S. 69. Extensive practice facilities. Practice ground, Par 3 course. *Green Fees:* weekdays £22.50; weekends £28.00. *Eating facilities:* brunch service, cream teas, two bars. *Visitors:* welcome. Please book in advance. Accommodation (Hotel), squash courts, tennis courts. *Society Meetings:* by prior arrangement. Professional/Golf Manager: Richard Lewis (0647 40355)).

NEWTON ABBOT. **Dainton Park Golf Club,** Dainton Park, Ipplepen, Newton Abbot. *Location:* midway between Newton Abbot and Totnes. Downland. 18 holes, 6200 yards. S.S.S. 70. Practice ground. *Green Fees:* weekdays £10.00; weekends £14.00. Special rates for weekly tickets. *Visitors:* unrestricted. Professional: Richard Stevenson.

NEWTON ABBOT. **Newton Abbot (Stover) Golf Club,** Bovey Road, Newton Abbot TQ12 6QQ (Newton Abbot (0626) 52460). *Location:* A382 three miles north of Newton Abbot. Wooded parkland with river. 18 holes, 5886 yards. S.S.S. 68. *Green Fees:* £22.00; half price with a member. *Eating facilities:* full catering daily from 11.00am. *Visitors:* welcome, must produce proof of membership of a county affiliated golf club. *Society Meetings:* catered for on Thursdays, parties of 24 and over. Professional: M. Craig (0626 62078). Secretary: R. Smith (0626 52460).

OKEHAMPTON. **Okehampton Golf Club,** Off Tors Road, Okehampton EX20 1EF (0837 52113) *Location:* from A30 take turning from centre of Okehampton then follow the signposts. Parkland. 18 holes, 5191 yards. S.S.S. 67. *Green Fees:* weekdays £15.00; Saturdays £20.00, Sundays £17.00. *Eating facilities:* by arrangement; bar. *Visitors:* welcome. *Society Meetings:* catered for. Professional: Philip Blundell (0837 53541). Secretary: S. Chave (0837 52113).

PLYMOUTH. **Elfordleigh Hotel, Golf and Country Club,** Near Colebrook, Plympton, Plymouth PL7 5EB (0752 336428). *Location:* one mile from Plympton. Woodland course in picturesque countryside. 9 holes, 5470 yards (twice round). S.S.S. 67. Practice area. *Green Fees:* £15.00 weekdays, £20.00 weekends. Special rates available on request. *Eating facilities:* bar meals available from Country Club bar. *Visitors:* welcome. Hotel accommodation available. *Society Meetings:* catered for by arrangement. Secretary: Mrs P. Parfitt (0752 348425; Fax: 0752 344581).

PLYMOUTH. **Staddon Heights Golf Club,** Staddon Heights, Plymstock, Plymouth PL9 9SP. *Location:* from Plymouth city follow signs to Plymstock. Seaside links. 18 holes, 5874 yards. S.S.S. 68. Practice area. *Green Fees:* weekdays £15.00; weekends £20.00. *Eating facilities:* diningroom open daily. *Visitors:* welcome except when tee booked for club competitions. *Society Meetings:* by arrangement with Secretary. Professional: John Cox (0752 492630). Secretary: Mike Holliday (0752 402475).

SIDMOUTH. **Sidmouth Golf Club,** Cotmaton Road, Peak Hill, Sidmouth EX10 8SX (0395 513023). *Location:* half a mile from town centre, 12 miles south east of M5 Junction 30. Parkland with breathtaking views over Sid Valley and Lyme Bay. 18 holes, 5109 yards. S.S.S. 65. *Green Fees:* £18.00 per day. *Eating facilities:* catering available except Mondays. All day bar Saturdays. *Visitors:* welcome anytime other than club competition, tee reservations. *Society Meetings:* catered for, contact Secretary. Professional: M. Kemp (0395 516407). Secretary: I.M. Smith (0395 513451).

SOUTH BRENT. **Wrangaton Golf Club,** Golf Links Road, Wrangaton, South Brent TQ10 9HJ (South Brent (0364) 73001). *Location:* heading south take next exit off A38 after South Brent. Undulating parkland/moorland course. 18 holes, 6041 yards. S.S.S 69. Practice area and net. *Green Fees:* weekdays £16.00 per day, weekends and Bank Holidays £20.00. *Eating facilities:* full catering and bar facilities available. *Visitors:* welcome, restricted on club competition days; phoning beforehand advised during season. *Society Meetings:* all welcome, written notice required. Professional: John Cox (0364 72161). Secretary/Manager: Richard R. Hine (0364 73229).

TAVISTOCK. **Hurdwick Golf Club,** Tavistock Hamlets, Tavistock PL19 8PZ (0822 612746). *Location:* one mile north of Tavistock on the Brentor Road. Parkland. 18 holes, 4800 yards. S.S.S. 64. *Green Fees:* weekdays £14.00 per round, £20.00 all day; weekends £16.00 per round, £25.00 all day. *Eating facilities:* fresh sandwiches, licensed bar. *Visitors:* welcome anytime. *Society Meetings:* (10 or more) 36 holes and buffet for £20 a head. Professional: available. Secretary: Major Roger Cullen.

TAVISTOCK. **Tavistock Golf Club,** Down Road, Tavistock PL19 9AQ (0822 612049). *Location:* Whitchurch Down one mile from Tavistock. 18 holes, 6250 yards. S.S.S. 70. *Green Fees:* £17.00 weekdays, £22.00 weekends and Bank Holidays. *Eating facilities:* full catering facilities. *Visitors:* welcome with reservation. *Society Meetings:* catered for. Professional: R.M. Cade (0822 612316). Secretary: B. G. Steer (0822 612344).

TEIGNMOUTH. **Teignmouth Golf Club,** Haldon Moor, Teignmouth (0626 773614). *Location:* two miles north of Teignmouth on the Exeter Road – B3192. Level heathland course, panoramic views. 18 holes, 6227 yards. S.S.S. 71. *Green Fees:* £22.00. *Eating facilities:* full catering service midday to 6pm. *Visitors:* welcome with reservation if members of another club with Handicap Certificate. *Society Meetings:* catered for weekdays only. Professional: P. Ward (0626 772894). Secretary: D. Holloway (0626 774194).

THE GOLF GUIDE 1994   *England* DEVON

THURLESTONE. **Thurlestone Golf Club**, Thurlestone, Kingsbridge TQ7 3NZ (0548 560221). *Location:* turn off A379 near Kingsbridge. Downland with superb views. 18 holes, 6303 yards, 5818 metres. S.S.S. 70. Practice area. *Green Fees:* £24.00 per day. *Eating facilities:* catering available from 10.00am until 5.30pm daily. *Visitors:* must produce Handicap Certificate, please telephone in advance. *Society Meetings:* not catered for. Professional: Neville Whitley (0548 560715). Secretary: R.W. Marston (0548 560405).

WHEEL FARM COUNTRY COTTAGES

Superb quality cottages, heated indoor pool, sauna and fitness room; across Exmoor, yet only a few miles from the sea and a variety of golf courses, including Saunton Sands. Concessionary rates available at nearby driving range and Ilfracombe Golf Club. Free tee reservation service and for riding and fishing. The watermill and barn conversions have central heating, wood stoves, four posters, dishwashers and homemade meals. Bedlinen and maid service included. Open March to November. Short breaks and special golfing rates off season.

Mr. & Mrs. Massey, Wheel Farm Country Cottages,
Berrydown 15, Combe Martin, Devon EX34 0NT.

Tel: 0271-882100
See our colour advertisement on page 16.

THE MANOR HOUSE HOTEL
Moretonhampstead,
Devon TQ13 8RE
Tel: (0647) 40355

Experience traditional Devonshire hospitality in our beautiful Hotel with superb food and exquisite furnishings, own 18 hole course in the picturesque grounds, as well as shooting, riding, tennis, game and fly fishing! Details on request.

See our full page advertisement on page 15.

The Bel Alp House
COUNTRY HOTEL

A.A.   R.A.C.
★★★   ★★★

With all three "Merit Awards" at ★★★ from both the AA and RAC,
and "Highly Commended" at 🌹🌹🌹 from the Tourist Board

HAYTOR, NEAR BOVEY TRACEY, SOUTH DEVON TQ13 9XX
TELEPHONE: (0364) 661217

A warm welcome awaits you from the Resident Owners, Roger and Sarah Curnock, at their small elegant Country House Hotel on the South Eastern edge of Dartmoor, where they provide a remarkable standard of Food, Comfort and Hospitality, in one of the most spectacular settings in the West Country, with dramatic views to the sea 15 miles away.

Enjoy the atmosphere of a Private House with large, beautifully furnished rooms, magnificent views, and superb five-course dinners. All nine bedrooms have en-suite bathrooms, colour TV, radio and telephone. There are 2 ground-floor bedrooms, a lift, billiard table, games room and lovely grounds. Riding arranged locally. Excellent golf at Stover, Newton Abbot (4 miles), the Manor House, Moretonhampstead (6 miles) and other good South Devon Courses.

DEVON England   THE GOLF GUIDE 1994

TIVERTON. **Tiverton Golf Club,** Post Hill, Tiverton EX16 4NE (Tiverton (0884) 252114). *Location:* three miles east of Tiverton, Junction 27 of M5, proceed through Sampford Peverell and Halberton. Parkland, tree-lined fairways. 18 holes, 6263 yards. S.S.S. 71. *Green Fees:* on application. *Eating facilities:* snacks, lunches and teas; evening meals by arrangement. *Visitors:* welcome with reservation, Handicap Certificate or introduction required. Professional: D. Sheppard (0884 254836). Secretary: M. Crouch (0884 252187).

TORQUAY. **Torquay Golf Club,** 30 Petitor Road, St Marychurch, Torquay TQ1 4QF (0803 327471). *Location:* north east of Torquay. St. Marychurch. Parkland. 18 holes, 6192 yards. S.S.S. 69. *Green Fees:* on application. *Eating facilities:* lunches, teas and evening meals available. *Visitors:* welcome if members of a golf club with Handicap Certificate. *Society Meetings:* catered for. Professional: M. Ruth (0803 329113). Secretary: B.G. Long (0803 314591).

TORRINGTON. **Torrington Golf Club,** Weare Trees, Torrington EX38 7EZ (Torrington (0805) 22229). *Location:* one mile north of Torrington on Weare Giffard road. Exposed common land with excellent views. 9 holes, 4418 yards, 4044 metres. S.S.S. 61. *Green Fees:* weekdays £10.00; weekends £14.00. Reduced rates if playing with a member. *Eating facilities:* light meals and bar snacks available during bar hours. *Visitors:* welcome except on Saturday and Sunday mornings and during club and open competitions. *Society Meetings:* catered for by arrangement. Secretary: Geoffrey S.C. Green (0237 472792).

TOTNES. **Dartmouth Golf and Country Club,** Blackawton, Totnes TQ9 7DG (080-421 686; Fax: 080-421 628). *Location:* five miles from Dartmouth on the A3122. Undulating inland course with lakes, rock faces and multiple tees. Club Course: 9 holes, 2583 yards. S.S.S. 33; Championship Course: 18 holes, 7191 yards. S.S.S 74. 15 bay driving range. *Green Fees:* weekdays £32.00; weekends £35.00. *Eating facilities:* bar, bar snacks and restaurant. *Visitors:* welcome at all times except weekends when restrictions will apply. Accommodation can be arranged. *Society Meetings:* welcome weekdays, details of golf packages available on request. Professional: Peter Laugher. Secretary: Howard Fagan.

UMBERLEIGH. **Highbullen Hotel Golf Course,** Chittlehamholt, Umberleigh EX37 9HG (0769 540561). *Location:* M5 Tiverton Exit 27, A361 to South Molton, B3226 five miles. Right uphill to Chittlehamholt. Pleasant parkland setting amongst mature specimen trees and water hazards, spectacular views. *Green Fees:* non-residents only (free to hotel guests) £8.00 weekdays; £10.00 weekends. £2.00 reduction after 5pm. *Eating facilities:* in hotel – including snack lunches. *Visitors:* welcome anytime. *Society Meetings:* welcome, small numbers only. Professional: Paul Weston (0769 540530). Secretary: Martin Neil (hotel).

UMBERLEIGH. **Libbaton Golf Club,** High Bickington, Umberleigh EX37 9BS (0769 60269). *Location:* situated on B3217, one and a half miles south High Bickington, close to A377. Parkland, rolling countryside, NOT steep up and down slopes. 18 holes, 6428 metres. S.S.S. 72. Floodlit driving range. *Green Fees:* weekdays £12.00; weekends £15.00. *Eating facilities:* bar food served 10am to 9pm. *Visitors:* always welcome, after 9.30am weekends. Three bedroomed house to let. *Society Meetings:* welcome by prior arrangement. Special Society Packages. Professional: John N. Phillips. Secretary: Jack H. Brough.

"TEE OFF FROM TIVERTON"

Small family-run hotel and restaurant, seven miles from Tiverton Golf Club, offering double and twin en-suite rooms with colour television and tea making facilities. Full à la carte dinner menu and friendly comfortable bar surroundings. Please ring Edward or Pauline.

**The Courtyard, Fore Street, Bampton, Tiverton, Devon
Telephone: Bampton (0398) 331536**

This traditional inn is the nearest licensed accommodation to the Dartmouth Golf & Country Club (1½ miles). Four comfortable ensuite bedrooms in which to stay. Excellent food plus local beers and wines to enjoy in a friendly atmosphere after your golf.

The Normandy Arms
A Fully Licensed Freehouse

Blackawton, near Totnes, Devon TQ9 7BN. Tel: 0803 712316

If you are writing, a stamped, addressed envelope is always appreciated.

England   DEVON/DORSET

Yelverton Golf Club
GOLF LINKS ROAD, YELVERTON, DEVON PL20 6BN

Attractive moorland course, 18 holes, 6293 yards. Situated 8 miles from Plymouth. Green fees £20 per day or round. Practice area. Societies welcome, by arrangement. Full catering facilities and licensed.

Clubhouse: 0822 853618 **Professional:** 0822 853593 **Secretary:** 0822 852824

WESTWARD HO!. **Royal North Devon Golf Club,** Golf Links Road, Westward Ho!, Bideford EX39 1HD (0237 473824). *Location:* A39 Tiverton. Links course. 18 holes, 6662 yards, 6089 metres. S.S.S. 72. Practice area. *Green Fees:* on application. *Eating facilities:* full catering available. *Visitors:* welcome with Handicap Certificate. Tee reservations should be made in advance. *Society Meetings:* catered for. Professional: G. Johnston (0237 477598). General Manager/Secretary: J.E. Linaker (0237 473817).

YELVERTON. **Yelverton Golf Club,** Golf Links Road, Yelverton PL20 6BN (Yelverton (0822 853618). *Location:* eight miles north of Plymouth on A386 road. Moorland course. 18 holes, 6293 yards. S.S.S. 70. Practice ground. *Green Fees:* £20.00 per day or round. *Eating facilities:* full catering available, licensed. *Visitors:* welcome if member of a recognised golf club or golf society. Handicap Certificate required. *Society Meetings:* catered for, welcome by arrangement with Secretary. Professional: Mr Iain Parker (0822 853593). Secretary: D.R. Bettany (0822 852824).

Dorset

BLANDFORD. **Ashley Wood Golf Club,** Wimborne Road, Blandford DT11 9HN (Blandford (0258) 450190). *Location:* half a mile south of Blandford on B3082. Downland with magnificent views. 18 holes, 6227 yards. S.S.S. 70. Practice ground, putting green. *Green Fees:* weekdays £17.00; weekends £25.00. *Eating facilities:* hot and cold snacks all day; restaurant. *Visitors:* welcome, Ladies only Tuesday mornings. Handicap Certificate or EGU Affiliation required. *Society Meetings:* welcome by arrangement with Secretary. Professional: Spencer Taylor (0258 480379). Secretary: Peter Lillford (0258 452253).

BOURNEMOUTH. **Bournemouth & Meyrick Park Golf Club,** (playing over Municipal course), Meyrick Park, Bournemouth BH2 6LH (Bournemouth (0202) 290307). *Location:* one mile from town centre. Beautiful woodland. 18 holes, 5663 yards. S.S.S. 68. Practice area. *Green Fees:* information not provided. *Eating facilities:* clubhouse restaurant and bar available if signed in by member; public cafe. *Visitors:* welcome at anytime (pay as you play) but must be signed in by members. *Society Meetings:* catered for. Bookings (0202 290871). Professional: J. Waring (0202 290862). Secretary: Ms. J. Bennett (0202 290307).

BOURNEMOUTH. **Knighton Heath Golf Club,** Francis Avenue, Bournemouth BH11 8NX (Bournemouth (0202) 577870). *Location:* A348 and A3049 roundabout exit Francis Avenue. Undulating heathland, 18 holes, 5987 yards. S.S.S. 69. *Green Fees:* on application. *Eating facilities:* meals and bar snacks available daily, except Monday. *Visitors:* wel-

GOLFERS WELCOME

With so many fine courses in and around the town, why not stay at the Tralee Hotel on Bournemouth's West Cliff. A traditional favourite with golfers, the Tralee has 90 bedrooms with private facilities, colour/satellite TV and telephone, and is close to the town centre for shops, shows and the Bournemouth International Centre leisure pool.

- Indoor heated swimming pool.
- Sauna, solarium and sundeck.
- Games room, garden & patio.
- Beauty Salon, masseuse.
- Dancing, entertainment and trad jazz.
- Attractive bars and real ale.

TRALEE HOTEL
WEST HILL ROAD · WEST CLIFF
BOURNEMOUTH BH2 5EQ
TELEPHONE 0202 556746

SIMPLY THE BEST VALUE IN BOURNEMOUTH

DORSET *England*

come with reservation, after 9.30am weekdays. Restrictions on competition days. Not at weekends unless with a member. Handicap Certificate required. *Society Meetings:* catered for if arranged in advance. Professional: Jane Miles (0202 578275). Secretary: R.C. Bestwick (0202 572633).

BOURNEMOUTH. **Queens Park Golf Club,** Queens Park West Drive, Bournemouth BH8 9BY (0202 394466). *Location:* off Wessex Way. Parkland course in centre of Bournemouth. 18 holes, 6072 yards. S.S.S. 72. Small practice area. *Green Fees:* £11.20. *Eating facilities:* restaurant and bar. *Visitors:* welcome anytime, last tee off times Sundays 12 noon. *Society Meetings:* catered for. Professional: R. Hill (0202 396817). Secretary: M.J. Poole (0202 302611).

BRIDPORT. **Bridport and West Dorset Golf Club,** East Cliff, West Bay, Bridport DT6 4EP (Bridport (0308) 422597). *Location:* one and a half miles south of Bridport, east of West Bay harbour. Clifftop links course. 18 holes, 5246 yards, 4795 metres. S.S.S. 66. Practice area. *Green Fees:* weekdays £18.00 (£12.00); weekends £22.00 (£18.00). *Eating facilities:* lounge and diningroom. *Visitors:* welcome. Members only 8am – 9.30am and 12.30pm to 2pm. *Society Meetings:* catered for by prior arrangement. Professional: John Parish (0308 421491). Secretary: P.J. Ridler (0308 421095).

AA★★ FIRCROFT HOTEL RAC★★
OWLS ROAD, BOURNEMOUTH, BH5 1AE

★ All 49 rooms ensuite, col TV, tea mkg.   ★ Choice of menu   ★ Large ballrooms
★ Indoor pool, Jacuzzi, Sauna & Full sports facilities (9am-5pm)
★ 3 full size snooker tables   ★ Entertainment   ★ Out of season 3/4/5 day breaks
★ Special rates for children
FREE £100 of Entertainment Vouchers for every weekly booking
Many local Golf Courses nearby
FOR DETAILS TELEPHONE **0202 309771** FAX: **0202 395644**

BRIDPORT ARMS HOTEL
WEST BAY, BRIDPORT, DORSET DT6 4EN   TEL: 0308 22994
The nearest hotel to Bridport and West Dorset Golf Club

FOR THE MUTUAL GUIDANCE OF GUEST AND HOST

Every year literally thousands of holidays, short-breaks and overnight stops are arranged through our guides, the vast majority without any problems at all. In a handful of cases, however, difficulties do arise about bookings, which often could have been prevented from the outset.

It is important to remember that when accommodation has been booked, both parties — guests and hosts — have entered into a form of contract. We hope that the following points will provide helpful guidance.

GUESTS: When enquiring about accommodation, be as precise as possible. Give exact dates, numbers in your party and the ages of any children. State the number and type of rooms wanted and also what catering you require — bed and breakfast, full board, etc. Make sure that the position about evening meals is clear — and about pets, reductions for children or any other special points.

Read our reviews carefully to ensure that the proprietors you are going to contact can supply what you want. Ask for a letter confirming all arrangements, if possible.

If you have to cancel, do so as soon as possible. Proprietors do have the right to retain deposits and under certain circumstances to charge for cancelled holidays if adequate notice is not given and they cannot re-let the accommodation.

HOSTS: Give details about your facilities and about any special conditions. Explain your deposit system clearly and arrangements for cancellations, charges, etc, and whether or not your terms include VAT.

If for any reason you are unable to fulfil an agreed booking without adequate notice, you may be under an obligation to arrange alternative suitable accommodation or to make some form of compensation.

THE GOLF GUIDE 1994

England DORSET

BROADSTONE. **Broadstone (Dorset) Golf Club,** Wentworth Drive, Broadstone BH18 8DQ (Broadstone (0202) 693363). *Location:* off A349 to B3072 to Broadstone. Heathland. 18 holes, 6315 yards. S.S.S. 70. *Green Fees:* weekdays £27.00 per round, £33.00 per day. *Eating facilities:* full catering available. *Visitors:* welcome, after 9.30am weekdays by arrangement, current Handicap Certificate required. No visitors weekends. *Society Meetings:* welcome by arrangement. Professional: Nigel Tokely (Tel & Fax: 0202 692835). Secretary: C.T. Manktelow (Tel & Fax: 0202 692595).

CHRISTCHURCH. **Highcliffe Castle Golf Club,** 107 Lymington Road, Highcliffe on Sea, Christchurch BH23 4LA (Highcliffe (0425 272953). *Location:* on the coastal road linking Lymington and Christchurch. Flat, wooded course. 18 holes, 4686 yards, 4284 metres. S.S.S. 63. *Green Fees:* weekdays £18.00, after 4pm £11.00; weekends before noon £27.00; afternoon £22.00, after 4pm £15.00. Must be in possession of Handicap Certificate.*Eating facilities:* full catering available. *Visitors:* welcome after 9.30am if member of recognised golf club, after 3.00pm on competition days. *Society Meetings:* catered for Tuesdays only by prior arrangement, all must be members of recognised golf clubs. Professional: R.E. Crockford (0425 276640). Secretary: Mrs E. Thompson (0425 272210).

CHRISTCHURCH. **Iford Bridge Golf Club,** Barrack Road, Christchurch BH23 2BA (0202 473817). *Location:* on the Christchurch/Bournemouth borders, on the bank of the River Stour. 9 greens (18 tees), S.S.S. 63. Driving range. *Green Fees:* weekdays £5.40; weekends and Bank Holidays £6.10. Reduced rates for Senior Citizens and Juniors. *Visitors:* welcome. Membership available. *Society Meetings:* welcome. Resident Golf Professional: Peter Troth.

DORCHESTER. **Came Down Golf Club,** Came Down, Dorchester DT2 8NR (Dorchester (0305) 812531). *Location:* two miles south of Dorchester. Downland course. 18 holes, 6224 yards, 5914 metres. S.S.S. 71. Practice area and nets. *Green Fees:* £20.00 weekdays; £25.00 weekends and Bank Holidays. *Eating facilities:* full catering available; bar. *Visitors:* welcome without reservation except Sunday mornings – phone in advance. All visitors must have Handicap.

Society Meetings: Wednesday only. Professional: R. Preston (0305 812670). Secretary: David E. Matthews (0305 813494).

DORCHESTER. **Lyons Gate Golf Club,** Lyons Gate, Dorchester DT2 7AZ (03005 239). *Location:* on A352 going north from Dorchester about 11 miles, or south from Sherborne about seven miles. Parkland with spectacular views, probably England's most spectacular 9 hole course, famous for its wild flowers. 9 holes, 2000 yards. S.S.S. 30. Practice nets, greens. *Green Fees:* £4.50 for 9 holes, £7.50 for 18 holes. Children under 17 years half price. *Eating facilities:* snacks in shop, vending machine. *Visitors:* welcome, no restrictions, dogs on leads. *Society Meetings:* by arrangement. Secretary: Mr H. Wood.

FERNDOWN. **Dudsbury Golf Club,** Christchurch Road, Ferndown BH22 8ST (0202 593499; Fax: 0202 594555). *Location:* Ferndown town centre. Follow signs for Poole on A348, turn left at first mini roundabout, turn left to Hurn Airport, 200 yards. Club on right hand side. Parkland course designed by Donald Steel, three lakes in beautiful Dorset countryside rolling gently down to the River Stour. 18 holes, 6208 yards. S.S.S 70. Par 71. 5 hole teaching academy practice range. *Green Fees:* weekdays £22.50 per round, £30.00 per day; weekends £30.00 per round. *Eating facilities:* two bars, spikes bar snacks, à la carte Clocktower Restaurant. *Visitors:* welcome. Handicap Certificate required. *Society Meetings:* welcome Monday to Friday, Handicap required. Professional: Andy Greig (0202 594488). General Manager: Ken Heathcote.

FERNDOWN. **Ferndown Golf Club,** 119 Golf Links Road, Ferndown BH22 8BU (Ferndown (0202) 872022). *Location:* off A31. Wooded heathland. 18 holes, 6452 yards. S.S.S. 71. 9 holes, 5604 yards. S.S.S. 68. Practice ground. *Green Fees:* Old Course: £35.00 weekdays, £40.00 weekends. President's Course: £15.00 weekdays, £20.00 weekends. Societies £50.00 for the day. *Eating facilities:* available. *Visitors:* welcome but prior permission recommended. Handicap Certificate required from a recognised golf club. Professional: D.N. Sewell (0202 873825). Secretary: E. Robertson (0202 874602).

THE DORMY HOTEL   DE VERE ● HOTELS
ADJOINING FERNDOWN GOLF COURSE

Excellent accommodation, imaginative cuisine and friendly, attentive service, the delightful atmosphere of a roaring log fire – just a few of the features that make the Dormy first choice for golfers and such a favourite with our guests.

- Snooker.
- Superb Leisure Club with heated indoor pool, squash & tennis courts, gym, solarium, sauna and more.
- Choice of bars and restaurants.
- Ample free parking.

AA★★★★RAC

FERNDOWN · NR. BOURNEMOUTH · DORSET · BH22 8ES · TEL: (0202) 872121 · FAX: (0202) 895388

DORSET *England*

LYME REGIS. Lyme Regis Golf Club, Timber Hill, Lyme Regis DT7 3HQ (Lyme Regis (0297) 442043). *Location:* between Lyme Regis and Charmouth. Cliff top course (not hilly) with fine coastal views. 18 holes, 6220 yards. S.S.S. 70. *Green Fees:* £24.00 per day, £20.00 after 2pm. Concession £4.00 for guests of certain hotels. *Eating facilities:* restaurant and bar. *Visitors:* welcome, but not before 9.30am and restrictions Thursday and Sundays; best to check with Professional. Handicap Certificate or proof of membership of a golf club required. *Society Meetings:* minimum for Tee Booking 12. Professional: Mr A. Black (0297 443822). Secretary: Mr R.G. Fry (0297 442963).

OKEFORD FITZPAINE. **Mid-Dorset Golf Club,** Belchalwell, Okeford Fitzpaine, Blandford DT11 0EG (0258 861386). *Location:* A357 Sturminster Newton, Bulbarrow Hill. Parkland/wooded course. 18 holes, 6503 yards. S.S.S. 71. Large practice ground. *Green Fees:* weekdays £15.00 per day; weekends £20.00. *Eating facilities:* dining room, bar and restuarant. *Visitors:* welcome all week. *Society Meetings:* welcome. Reduction in green fees for groups of 30 or more. Professional: Spencer Taylor (0258 861184). Secretary: David Astill (0258 861386; Fax: 0258 860656).

POOLE near. **Bulbury Woods Golf Club,** Halls Road, Lytchett Matravers, Near Poole BH16 6EP (092945 574). *Location:* Poole – Bere Regis Road. Wooded parkland. 18 holes, 6020 yards. S.S.S. 69. Practice ground. *Green Fees:* £15.00 per round. *Eating facilities:* bar and restaurant. *Visitors:* welcomed; dress requirements – recognised golf attire, no jeans, vests or training shoes. *Society Meetings:* welcome by prior arrangement. Professional: J. Sharkey. Secretary: T.I. Williams.

POOLE. **Parkstone Golf Club,** Links Road, Parkstone, Poole BH14 9JU (0202) 707138). *Location:* off A35 Bournemouth to Poole. Wooded heathland. 18 holes, 6250 yards. S.S.S. 70. *Green Fees:* £24.00 per round, £32.00 per day weekdays; £30.00 per round, £40.00 per day weekends and Bank Holidays (subject to review). *Eating facilities:* catering available daily. *Visitors:* welcome with reservation and Handicap Certificate. *Society Meetings:* catered for as above. Professional: Mark Thomas (0202 708092). Secretary: A.S. Kinnear (0202 707138).

SHERBORNE. **Sherborne Golf Club,** Higher Clatcombe, Sherborne DT9 4RN (Sherborne (0935) 812475). *Location:* one mile north of town on B3145 to Wincanton. Parkland. 18 holes, 5949 yards. S.S.S. 68. Practice facilities. *Green Fees:* £20.00 weekdays, £25.00 weekends and Bank Holidays. *Eating facilities:* snacks, lunches, suppers, teas; dinners to order. *Visitors:* as commitment allows, telephone in advance. Handicap Certificates required. Thursday is Ladies' Day. *Society Meetings:* catered for Tuesdays and Wednesdays. Professional: Stewart Wright (0935 812274). Secretary/Manager: Mrs J.M.C. Guy (0935 814431).

STUDLAND. **Isle of Purbeck Golf Club,** Studland, Swanage BH19 3AB (0929 44210). *Location:* A351 towards Swanage, at Corfe Castle turn onto B3351 to Studland. Heathland courses with wonderful views. Purbeck – 18 holes, 6248 yards, 5823 metres. S.S.S. 71. Dene – 9 holes, 2022 yards. S.S.S. 30. *Green Fees:* £22.50 per round, £30.00 per two rounds weekdays; £27.50 per round, £35.00 per two rounds weekends. *Eating facilities:* bar and restaurant. *Visitors:* welcome. *Society Meetings:* catered for by arrangement, minimum 8. Professional: Kevin Spurgeon (0929 44354). Secretary: Mrs J. Robinson (0929 44361).

AA ★★ RAC
Blue Ribbon
👑👑👑 Highly Commended

EAT WELL AT KERSBROOK!

We can't guarantee you will play well at the FIVE Courses close to the Hotel, but you will be assured of delicious food prepared by our international Chef! We arrange tee-off times and even a chauffeur-driven car. Needless to say, our bedrooms are of the highest standard, and you can relax and discuss the day's play in one of our two lounges. Lyme Regis with its seaside amenities is within easy walking distance. Telephone: (02974) 42596.

KERSBROOK HOTEL, POUND ROAD, LYME REGIS, DORSET DT7 3HX

Springfield Country Hotel
• AND SPORTS & LEISURE CLUB •

GRANGE ROAD, STOBOROUGH, WAREHAM, DORSET BH20 5AL.
Telephone: (0929) 552177 Fax: (0929) 551862

Family-run hotel in six acres of landscaped gardens at the foot of the Purbeck Hills. 32 en-suite bedrooms, all with colour TV, radio, telephone, tea/coffee making facilities. Excellent a la carte Restaurant. New Leisure Club with indoor swimming pool, spa, saunas, steam rooms, solariums, gymnasium, squash courts, games room, snooker and billiards. Outdoor heated pool and tennis court. 3 golf courses nearby. Special discount arranged at one club.

AA ★★★   ETB 👑👑👑 COMMENDED   RAC ★★★

SELF-CATERING GOLF BREAKS IN DORSET

WEST FARM LODGES

West Farm Lodges, Romford,
Verwood, Dorset BH31 7LE

We are committed to letting you arrange your golfing holiday to suit your requirements. In one of our attractive farm lodges you can do just that, being based at Crane Valley Golf Club, and set in our magnificent and relaxing part of Dorset. Prices from £8.50.
Call us now for details on 0202 822263.

EAST DORSET GOLF CLUB

In the Beautiful Dorset Countryside
- LAKELAND AND WOODLAND COURSES
- PRACTICE GROUND
- VISITORS WELCOME
- FLOODLIT DRIVING RANGE
- BEAUTIFUL CLUBHOUSE
- DORMY BUNGALOW FOR LETTING
- THE ULTIMATE GOLF SHOP

Near Wareham, Dorset. Tel: 0929 472544 Fax: 0929 471294

VERWOOD. **Crane Valley Golf Club,** Verwood BH31 6LE (0202 814088; Fax: 0202 813407). *Location:* on B3081 Verwood to Cranborne Road. Parkland featuring lakes and River Crane. 18 holes, 6400 yards. S.S.S. 71. 9 hole course, 2100 yards..Covered driving range. *Green Fees:* weekdays £18.00; weekends £24.00. *Eating facilities:* restaurant and spikes bar. *Visitors:* welcome at all times except weekend mornings. Accommodation adjoining course at West Farm. *Society Meetings:* by appointment. Professional: Alan Egford. Secretary: Martin Wilson.

WAREHAM. **East Dorset Golf Club,** Hyde, Wareham BH20 7NT (0929 472244). *Location:* take A352 off Wareham by-pass, enter Puddletown Road, Worgret Heath. Proceed four miles, turn right immediately before ARC Blockworks (signposted), 200 yards to clubhouse. Two courses: Lakeland Course 18 holes, 6556 yards. S.S.S. 71. Woodland Course 18 holes, 4853 yards. S.S.S. 64. Driving range and Pro Shop. *Green Fees:* weekdays £25.00; weekends £35.00. *Eating facilities:* excellent bar and restaurant. *Visitors:* welcome anytime with prior tee reservation. New dormy bungalow overlooking course for parties of four to eight people. *Society Meetings:* welcome by advance booking. Professional: Kim Thomas (0929 472272). Secretary: Brian R. Lee (0929 472244; Fax: 0929 471294).

WAREHAM. **Wareham Golf Club,** Sandford Road, Wareham BH20 4DH (Wareham (0929) 554156). *Location:* adjoining A351 near railway station. Partly wooded course. 18 holes, 5603 yards. S.S.S. 67. *Green Fees:* weekdays £18.00 per day; weekends with a member only £8.00. *Eating facilities:* bar and restaurant. *Visitors:* welcome, after 9.30am weekdays only. *Society Meetings:* catered for by arrangement. Secretary: Major J.L. Hollaway (0929 554147).

WEYMOUTH. **Wessex Golf Centre,** Rapipole Lane, Weymouth (Weymouth (0305) 784737). *Location:* on bypass road by Weymouth Football Club. Flat public course. 9 holes, 1385 yards. Par 3. Driving range. *Green Fees:* information not available. *Visitors:* welcome; public course.

WEYMOUTH. **Weymouth Golf Club Ltd,** Links Road, Weymouth DT4 0PF (0305 784994). *Location:* A354 from Dorchester, take last exit at Manor roundabout then second left at Chafeys roundabout. Undulating parkland. 18 holes, 6030 yards. S.S.S. 69 (Par 70). Practice area. *Green Fees:* weekdays £18.00, weekends and Bank Holidays £24.00. Half price playing with a member. Juniors half price. *Eating facilities:* full restaurant and bar. *Visitors:* welcome, but only with Handicap Certificate. *Society Meetings:* catered for Tuesdays and Thursdays, arrange with Secretary. Professional: Mr Des Lochrie (0305 773997). Secretary: Mr Colin Robinson (0305 773981).

WIMBORNE. **Sturminster Marshall Golf Club,** Moor Lane, Sturminster Marshall, Wimborne BH21 4AH (0258 858444). *Location:* Wimborne to Bere Regis Road. Parkland. 9 holes, 2325 yards. S.S.S. 63. Practice net. *Green Fees:* £5.00 for 9 holes, £8.00 for 18 holes. *Eating facilities:* tea, coffee and soft drinks; snack meals. *Visitors:* welcome, no restrictions. *Society Meetings:* not catered for. Professional: Mr J. Sharkey. Secretary: Mr K. Iball.

Please mention this guide when you write or phone to enquire about accommodation.

COUNTY DURHAM *England*

County Durham

BARNARD CASTLE. Barnard Castle Golf Club, Harmire Road, Barnard Castle DL12 8QN (Barnard Castle (0833) 37237). *Location:* one mile north of Barnard Castle Town Centre on the B6278. Open parkland, 18 holes, 5838 yards. S.S.S. 68. *Green Fees:* weekdays £15.00 per day, £18.00 per round, weekends and Bank Holidays £24.00. Reduced rates playing with member. *Eating facilities:* full catering – limited on Mondays. *Visitors:* welcome, but booking system at weekends and Bank Holidays. *Society Meetings:* catered for by prior arrangement. Professional: J. Harrison (0833) 31980). Secretary: A.W. Lavender (0833 38355).

BISHOP AUCKLAND. **Bishop Auckland Golf Club,** High Plains, Durham Road, Bishop Auckland DL14 8DL (Bishop Auckland (0388) 602198). *Location:* leave Bishop Auckland Market Place on route to Spennymoor/Durham, half a mile on left. Parkland, 18 holes, 6420 yards, 6124 metres. S.S.S. 71 (Par 72). Practice fairways. *Green Fees:* weekdays £18.00 per round, £22.00 per day; weekends £24.00 per round. Visiting parties over 20 have day reduction to £18.00. *Eating facilities:* bar, full catering facilities except Mondays. *Visitors:* welcome mid-week only. Ladies' day Tuesday. Two snooker tables. *Society Meetings:* catered for on application, not weekends and Christmas period, and official Handicap required. Professional: Mr D. Skiffington (0388 661618). Secretary: Mr G. Thatcher (0388 663648).

BRANCEPETH. **Brancepeth Castle Golf Club,** Brancepeth DH7 8EA (091-378 0075). *Location:* four miles west of Durham city on A690. Parkland. 18 holes, 6415 yards. S.S.S. 71. Practice ground. *Green Fees:* weekdays £23.00 per day, weekends by prior booking £30.00. *Eating facilities:* available every day – limited Mondays. *Visitors:* welcome weekdays, weekends by prior arrangement. *Society Meetings:* catered for Monday to Friday only. Professional: D.C. Howdon (091-378 0183). Secretary: J.T. Ross (091-378 0075).

CHESTER-LE-STREET. **Chester-le-Street Golf Club,** Lumley Park, Chester-le-Street DH3 4NS (Chester-le-Street (091-388) 3218). *Location:* Off A1 adjacent to Lumley Castle, half a mile east of Chester-le-Street. Parkland, 18 holes, 6054 yards, 5535 metres. S.S.S. 69. *Green Fees:* weekdays £20.00, weekends and Public Holidays £30.00. *Eating facilities:* lunches, snacks, dinners, bar. *Visitors:* welcome weekdays with letter of introduction or Handicap Certificate, but some restrictions weekends and Public Holidays. *Society Meetings:* catered for but not weekends and Public Holidays. Professional: A. Hartley (091-389 0157). Secretary: W.B. Dodds (091-388 3218).

CHESTER-LE-STREET. **Roseberry Grange Golf Club,** Grange Villa, Chester-le-Street DH2 3NF (091-370 0670). *Location:* three miles west of Chester-le-Street on A693. Parkland course. 18 holes, 5809 yards. S.S.S. 68. Driving range. *Green Fees:* weekdays £7.60 per round, £10.50 per day; weekends £10.30 per round, £13.00 per day ticket. Half price weekdays for Juniors and Senior Citizens. *Eating facilities:* bar meals 12 noon to 2.00pm and 7.00pm to 9.30pm. *Visitors:* welcome, no restrictions. Professional: A. Hartley (091-370 0660). Secretary: Raymond McDermott (091-370 2047).

CONSETT. **Consett and District Golf Club,** Elmfield Road, Consett DH8 5NN (Consett (0207) 502186). *Location:* A691 from Durham (12 miles), A692 from Gateshead (12 miles). 18 holes, 6013 yards. S.S.S. 69. *Green Fees:* information not provided. *Eating facilities:* full catering available. *Visitors:* most welcome without reservation. *Society Meetings:* catered for by arrangement, enquiries welcomed. Professional: S. Corbally (0207 580210). Secretary: Mr J. Horrill (0207 562261).

CROOK. **Crook Golf Club,** Low Jobs Hill, Crook DL15 9AA (Bishop Auckland (0388) 762429). *Location:* six miles west of Durham City on A689. Hilly, demanding parkland course. 18 holes, 6075 yards. S.S.S. 69. Practice nets and fairway. *Green Fees:* weekdays £12.00; weekends £20.00. *Eating facilities:* full catering facilities. *Visitors:* at any time other than when club competitions are held. Caravan Club Site (5 Vans) adjacent clubhouse. *Society Meetings:* catered for by arrangement with Secretary. Secretary: Peter N. Willis (0388 762429; Fax: 091-378 9711).

DARLINGTON. **Blackwell Grange Golf Club,** Briar Close, Blackwell, Darlington DL3 8QX (0325 464464). *Location:* one mile south of Darlington on A66 turn into Blackwell. Signposts to Club. Parkland course. 18 holes, 5621 yards. S.S.S. 67. *Green Fees:* weekdays £15.00 per round, £18.00 per day; weekends and Bank Holidays £20 per round. *Eating facilities:* full menu except Sundays and Mondays. *Visitors:* welcome without reservation except weekends. *Society Meetings:* catered for except Wednesday and weekends. Professional: Ralph Givens (0325 462088). Secretary: F. Hewitson (0325 464458).

DARLINGTON. **Dinsdale Spa Golf Club,** Neasham Road, Middleton-St-George, Darlington DL2 1DW (Dinsdale (0325) 332222). *Location:* near Teesside Airport. Parkland. 18 holes, 6090 yards. S.S.S. 70. *Green Fees:* weekdays £16.00 per round, £20.00 per day; weekends with a member only (£8.00). *Eating facilities:* bar, catering except Mondays. *Visitors:* welcome weekdays except Tuesdays (Ladies Day). *Society Meetings:* catered for Wednesday, Thursday and Friday by advance booking. Professional: C. Imlah (Tel & Fax: 0325 332515). Secretary: Mr P.J. Wright (0325 332297).

THE GOLF GUIDE 1994   *England*   COUNTY DURHAM

DARLINGTON. **Stressholme Golf Club,** Snipe Lane, Darlington (0325 353073). *Location:* one mile south of Darlington town centre near junction of A66 and A167. 18 holes, 6511 yards, 5953 metres. S.S.S. 71. Practice ground. *Green Fees:* information not provided. *Eating facilities:* two bars, three course meals to snacks. *Visitors:* always welcome anytime. *Society Meetings:* all welcome any time – reserved tees available. Professional: Tim Jenkins (0325 461002). Secretary: Graham A. Patrick (0325 466587).

DARLINGTON. **The Darlington Golf Club (Members) Ltd,** Haughton Grange, Darlington DL1 3JD (0325 363936). *Location:* northern outskirts of town, A1150 off A167, approximately 800 yards. Flat wooded parkland. 18 holes, 6271 yards. S.S.S. 70. Large practice ground. *Green Fees:* weekdays £22.00 per day; weekends with member only. *Eating facilities:* first class catering, Men's Bar, lounge bar available. *Visitors:* welcome weekdays with reservation, must be members of recognised golf club. *Society Meetings:* by arrangement weekdays, no more than 40 members. Professional: Mr I. Todd (0325 462996). Secretary: Mr N. Adair (0325 355324).

DURHAM. **Durham City Golf Club,** Littleburn, Langley Moor, Durham DH7 8HL (Durham (091) 3780806). *Location:* from Durham City take A690 to Crook – course signposted in Langley Moor. Parkland with river. 18 holes, 6326 yards. S.S.S. 70. Large practice area. *Green Fees:* weekdays £18.00, weekends £24.00. Half fees if playing with a member. £14.00 per person for parties of 20 or more. *Eating facilities:* no catering Mondays or Thursday evenings. *Visitors:* welcome, no restrictions when club competitions are being held – ring Professional for details. *Society Meetings:* welcome, but restricted to weekdays. Professional: S. Corbally (091 3780029). Secretary: I. Wilson (091 3780069).

DURHAM. **Mount Oswald Golf Club,** South Road, Durham DH1 3TQ (091-386 7527; Fax: 091-384 0975). *Location:* A1(M) Junction marked Bowburn. A177 Durham City A1050. Parkland, partial wooded. 18 holes, 6101 yards. S.S.S. 69. *Green Fees:* weekdays £10.50 per round, weekends and Bank Holidays £12.50 per round. *Eating facilities:* bar meals, Sunday lunches, set meals, etc. *Visitors:* welcome except Sunday mornings before 10am (members only). Bookings only at weekends and Bank Holidays. *Society Meetings:* welcome, same restrictions as visitors, must order food. General Manager: S.E. Reeve (091-386 7527).

NEWTON AYCLIFFE. **Aycliffe Golf Club,** Oak Leaf Sports Complex, School Aycliffe Lane, Newton Aycliffe DL5 4EF (0325 300600). *Location:* three miles from A1M and A68. Rolling parkland. 18 holes, 5422 yards. S.S.S. 67. Driving range (floodlit). *Green Fees:* information not provided. Reduced rates for Senior Citizens and under 16's. *Eating facilities:* bar, limited eating facilities. Contact Stewardess (0325 300700). *Visitors:* welcome anytime (booking system), slight restrictions weekends. *Society Meetings:* all welcome by prior arrangement. Professional: Robert Lister (0325 310820). Secretary: W.J. Findley (0325 312994).

NEWTON AYCLIFFE. **Woodham Golf and Country Club,** Burnhill Way, Newton Aycliffe DL5 4PN (Newton Aycliffe (0325) 320574; Fax: 0325 315254). *Location:* A167, one mile north of Newton Aycliffe on the Shildon road. Parkland, wooded with lakes. 18 holes, 6727 yards. S.S.S. 72. Practice grounds, putting green. *Green Fees:* weekdays £15.00 per round, £20.00 per day; weekends £20.00 per round, £25.00 per day. *Eating facilities:* bar snacks, meals and restaurant available. *Visitors:* unlimited weekdays; tee restrictions weekends and Bank Holidays. *Society Meetings:* welcome by arrangement. Professional: Ernie Wilson (0325 315257). Secretary: John D. Jenkinson. Steward: (0325 301551).

SEAHAM. **Seaham Golf Club,** Shrewsbury Street, Seaham SR7 7RD (091-5812354). *Location:* Dawdon, two miles north east of A19 leave for Seaham. Heathland. 18 holes, 6017 yards. S.S.S. 69. Practice area. *Green Fees:* weekdays £15.00 (£7.00 playing with a member); weekends and Bank Holidays £18.00 (£9.00 playing with a member). *Eating facilities:* snacks available, meals on request. *Visitors:* welcome, unrestricted weekdays, booking for weekends. *Society Meetings:* welcome on application. Professional: D. Patterson (091-5130837). Secretary: Vincent Smith (091-5815413).

STANLEY. **Beamish Park Golf Club,** Beamish, Stanley DH9 0RH (Durham (091-370) 1382). *Location:* follow directions to Beamish Museum. Parkland, 18 holes, 6205 yards. S.S.S. 70. Two practice areas. *Green Fees:* weekdays £16.00 per round, £20.00 per day; weekends £24.00 per round, £30.00 per day. *Eating facilities:* bar and à la carte menu. *Visitors:* welcome, Monday to Friday. Professional: C. Cole (091-370 1984). Secretary: L. Gilbert (091-370 1382).

STANLEY. **South Moor Golf Club,** The Middles, Craghead, Stanley DH9 6AG (Stanley (0207) 232848). *Location:* eight miles north-west of Durham, seven miles north-west of A1 (M) from Chester-le-Street. Parkland and moorland. 18 holes, 6445 yards. S.S.S. 71. *Green Fees:* weekdays £14.00 per round, £21.00 per day; with a member £10 per round, £15.00 per day; Weekends and Bank Holidays £25.00 per day; with a member £12.00 per round, £18.00 per day. *Eating facilities:* available. *Visitors:* members only before 9.30am and 12 – 2pm. No casual visitors weekends or Bank Holidays unless with member. *Society Meetings:* catered for except Sundays. Professional: S. Cowell (0207 283525). Secretary: B. Davison (0207 232848).

If you are writing, a stamped, addressed envelope is always appreciated.

ESSEX *England*

Essex

BASILDON. **Basildon Golf Club,** Clay Hill Lane, Basildon (Basildon (0268) 533297). *Location:* off A13 or A127 on A176 – Kingswood Roundabout. Undulating woodland. 18 holes, 6122 yards. S.S.S. 69. Practice area. *Green Fees:* £8.70 weekdays; £13.50 weekends. *Eating facilities:* snack meals/bar. *Visitors:* welcome anytime, booking system at weekends and Bank Holidays. *Society Meetings:* catered for – apply to Basildon Council. Professional: Mr G. Hill (0268 533352). Secretary: A. M. Burch (0268 533849).

BASILDON. **Pipps Hill Country Club,** Cranes Farm Road, Basildon SS14 3DG (Basildon (0268) 523456). *Location:* A127 – Basildon. Flat course. 9 hole course, 5658 yards. *Green Fees:* on request. *Eating facilities:* Golfer Arms Public House nearby. *Visitors:* unrestricted at all times. Golf days catered for.

BILLERICAY. **Stock Brook Manor Golf Club,** Queens Park Avenue, Stock, Near Billericay CM11 0SP (0277 633063). *Location:* nearest main road A12, Billericay. Parkland – gently undulating with featured lakes. 18 holes, 6728 yards. S.S.S. 72. Manor – 9 holes, 2997 yards. Driving range, putting green and three par 3 practice holes. *Green Fees:* weekdays £25.00; weekends £30.00. *Eating facilities:* available. *Visitors:* welcome. Handicap Certificate required. *Society Meetings:* welcome. Professional: Kevin Merry (0277 653616). Secretary: Kevin Roe.

BRAINTREE. **Braintree Golf Club,** Kings Lane, Stisted, Braintree CM7 8DA (Braintree (0376) 24117). *Location:* A120 to Colchester, 300 yards east of Braintree by-pass, signposted Stisted and Golf Club. Parkland, with slopes down to the river. 18 holes, 6153 yards, S.S.S. 69. Practice ground, pitching area. *Green Fees:* £27.00 weekdays, £45.00 Saturdays only. *Eating facilities:* available. *Visitors:* welcome Monday to Fridays (Fridays must have Handicap Certificate). *Society Meetings:* catered for Mondays, Wednesdays and Thursdays. Professional: A.K. Parcell (0376 343465). Secretary: G.J. Bardsley (0376 346079).

BRAINTREE. **Towerlands Golf Club,** Panfield Road, Braintree CM7 5BJ (0376 326802; Fax: 0376 552487). *Location:* off A120 into Braintree, then B1053. Undulating course. 9 holes, 2703 yards. S.S.S. 66. Golf range. *Green Fees:* weekdays £8.50 for 9 holes, £10.50 for 18 holes; weekends and Bank Holidays £12.50 for 18 holes only after 12 noon. *Eating facilities:* full bar and restaurant. *Visitors:* welcome. Wide range of other sports facilities. *Society Meetings:* by arrangement. Teaching Professional: A. Boulter (0376 347951). Secretary: Mr K. Cooper (0376 513519).

BRENTWOOD. **Hartswood Golf Club, (Play on Brentwood Municipal),** King George's Playing Fields, Ingrave Road, Brentwood (Brentwood (0277) 217128). *Location:* one mile south of Brentwood on A128. Parkland, 18 holes, 6238 yards. S.S.S. 70. *Green Fees:* information not provided. *Eating facilities:* full catering available. *Visitors:* welcome without reservation. *Society Meetings:* limited number of society bookings. Professional: J. Stanion (0277 230474). Secretary: A.D. Jevans (0277 218850).

BRENTWOOD. **The Warley Park Golf Club,** Magpie Lane, Little Warley, Brentwood CM13 3DX (0277) 224891). *Location:* leave M25 at Intersection 29. A127 towards Southend. Turn left three-quarters-of-a-mile Little Warley, Hall Lane. Turn left into Magpie Lane. Parkland, 3 Courses, (27 holes). S.S.S. 70-70-69. Large practice area, putting greens. *Green Fees:* weekdays £20.00 per round, £30.00 per day. *Eating facilities:* lounge bar and restaurant/spike bar. *Visitors:* welcome Monday to Friday, must produce club Handicap Certificate. *Society Meetings:* catered for. Professional: P. O'Connor (0277 212552). Secretary: K. Regan (0277 224891).

BRENTWOOD. **Thorndon Park Golf Club Ltd,** Thorndon Park, Ingrave, Brentwood CM13 3RH (0277 811666). *Location:* three miles south of Brentwood on A128. 18 holes, 6481 yards. S.S.S. 71. *Green Fees:* £40.00 per day, £25.00 per round weekdays, weekends with members only. *Eating facilities:* lunches served at club. *Visitors:* welcome with reservation, weekdays subject to prior permission. *Society Meetings:* catered for. Professional: Brian White (0277 810736). Secretary: J.E. Leggitt (0277 810345).

BRENTWOOD.**Bentley Golf Club,** Ongar Road, Brentwood CM15 9SS (Coxtie Green (0277) 373179). *Location:* situated on A128 approximately five miles from Junction 28 of M25. Flat parkland course. 18 holes, 6709 yards, 6136 metres. S.S.S. 72. Practice field. *Green Fees:* weekdays £20.00 per round, £26.00 day ticket; weekends with a member only. Reductions for Senior Citizens and under 18s. *Eating facilities:* food and bar available all day. *Visitors:* welcome weekdays; Bank Holidays after 11am. *Society Meetings:* welcome by prior arrangement. Professional: Keith Bridges (0277 372933). Secretary: J.A. Vivers (0277 373179).

BULPHAN. **The Langdon Hills Golf Club,** Lower Dunton Road, Bulphan RM14 3TY (0268 548444; Fax: 0268 548065). *Location:* 8 miles from M25, Dartford River crossing, Basildon three miles before A127 and A13. Gently undulating parkland. 18 holes, 6485 yards. S.S.S. 71. 9 hole course, 22 bay floodlit driving range, large shortgame practice area. *Green Fees:* weekdays £18.50 per round, £26.50 per day; weekends £25.00 per round. *Eating facilities:* restaurant, two bars and private function room. *Visitors:* welcome most times, ring for details. 25 bedroomed hotel. *Society Meetings:* welcomed. Professional: John Slinger (Golf Director). Secretary: Mrs C. Hammond.

THE GOLF GUIDE 1994

England ESSEX

BURNHAM-ON-CROUCH. **Burnham-on-Crouch Golf Club Ltd,** Ferry Road, Creaksea CM0 8PQ (Maldon (0621) 782282). *Location:* one mile west of Burnham-on-Crouch, turn right off B1010. Undulating meadowland. 18 holes, 6056 yards. S.S.S. 70. Practice ground. *Green Fees:* £20.00 weekdays. *Eating facilities:* full bar, lunch and evening meals. *Visitors:* no visitors weekends and Bank Holidays. Must commence play Mondays to Fridays (except Thursdays) 9.30am to 2pm. Thursdays 12 noon to 2pm. *Society Meetings:* catered for, weekdays preferred. Secretary: W.F. Miller.

CANVEY ISLAND. **Castle Point Golf Club,** Somnes Avenue, Canvey Island SS8 9FG (0268 511149). *Location:* A13 to Southend, A130 to Canvey Island, opposite sports centre. Links course, flat; views of Hadleigh Downs and Castle. 18 holes, 6176 yards. S.S.S. 69. Driving range. *Green Fees:* weekdays £8.75; weekends £13.00. Juniors and Senior Citizens £4.50 weekdays. *Eating facilities:* restaurant and bar available. *Visitors:* welcome anytime, booking required at weekends. Changing facilities, showers. *Society Meetings:* welcome, catered for weekdays only. Professional: John Hudson (0268 510830). Secretary: Vic Russell (0268 698909).

CHELMSFORD. **Channels Golf Club,** Belsteads Farm Lane, Little Waltham, Chelmsford CM3 3PT (0245 440005). *Location:* three miles north east of Chelmsford on A130. 9 holes parkland, 18 holes on re-claimed gravel workings, many lakes and hazards. 18 holes, 5636 yards. S.S.S. 68. 9 hole pitch and putt, 2971 yards. S.S.S. 35. *Green Fees:* £28.00 per day weekdays; weekends only with a member. Juniors and Senior Citizens £15.00 per round, £22.00 per day weekdays. *Eating facilities:* excellent restaurant in 13th century clubhouse. *Visitors:* welcome weekdays only. *Society Meetings:* catered for weekdays. Professional: I.B. Sinclair (0245 441056). Secretary: Mr A.M. Squire (0245 440005; Fax: 0245 442032).

CHELMSFORD. **Chelmsford Golf Club,** Widford Road, Chelmsford (0245 250555). *Location:* close to Widford roundabout on A1016. 18 holes, 5944 yards. S.S.S. 68. *Green Fees:* information not provided. *Eating facilities:* dining room and bar. *Visitors:* welcome Monday to Friday with reservation. Professional: D. Bailey. Manager: Wg. Cdr. B.A. Templeman-Rooke DSO, DFC, AFC, RAF (Retd.) (0245 256483).

CHIGWELL. **Chigwell Golf Club,** The Clubhouse, High Road, Chigwell IG7 5BH (081-500 2059). *Location:* on A113, 14 miles from London, seven miles Waltham Abbey exit M25. Testing undulating parkland course. 18 holes, 6279 yards. S.S.S. 70. Practice shed and ground. *Green Fees:* weekdays £28.00 per round, £35.00 per day; weekends with introduction by member only. *Eating facilities:* restaurant and bars available. *Visitors:* weekdays by prior arrangement, Handicap Certificate required and membership of authorised Golf Club. *Society Meetings:* weekdays by arrangement. Professional: R. Beard (081-500 2384). Secretary: Mr M. McL. Farnsworth (081-500 2059).

CHIGWELL. **Hainault Forest Golf Club,** Romford Road, Chigwell IG7 4QW (081-500 2097). *Location:* off A12 towards Chigwell-Hainault. Flat wooded course with several lakes. 18 holes, 6600 yards. S.S.S. 71. 18 holes, 5754 yards. S.S.S. 67. Practice field and putting green. *Green Fees:* weekdays £9.20; weekends £11.50. *Eating facilities:* course restaurant; bars in private club. *Visitors:* public course. *Society Meetings:* weekdays by arrangement with Secretary. Professional: T. Dungate (081-500 2131).

CLACTON. **Clacton Golf Club,** West Road, Clacton (0255 421919). Seaside course. 18 holes, 6244 yards. S.S.S. 71. *Green Fees:* £20.00 weekdays, £30.00 weekends and Bank Holidays. *Eating facilities:* full catering by prior arrangement. *Visitors:* welcome with reservation and current Handicap Certificate. Weekends and Bank Holidays not before 11.00am. *Society Meetings:* Monday to Friday catered for by arrangement. Professional: S.J. Levermore. Secretary: H.F. Lucas.

COLCHESTER. **Birch Grove Golf Club,** Layer Road, Colchester CO2 0HS (0206 734276). *Location:* on B1026, two miles south of town. Parkland – small but challenging. 9 holes, 4038 yards. S.S.S. 60. *Green Fees:* £10.00 weekdays, £12.00 weekends and Bank Holidays for 18 holes. *Eating facilities:* hot meals and snacks are available during opening hours. *Visitors:* welcome without reservation Monday to Saturday and after 1pm Sundays. *Society Meetings:* catered for weekdays. Secretary: Mrs M. Marston.

COLCHESTER. **Colchester Golf Club,** Braiswick, Colchester CO4 5AU (Colchester (0206) 852946). *Location:* one mile north-west of Colchester North Station, on A133. Parkland. 18 holes, 6319 yards. S.S.S. 70. *Green Fees:* £25.00 per day weekdays; £30.00 weekends. *Eating facilities:* catering available all day. *Visitors:* welcome except Saturday and Sunday mornings. *Society Meetings:* catered for by prior arrangement. Professional: Mark Angel (0206 853920). Secretary: Mrs J. Boorman (0206 853396; Fax: 0206 852698).

COLCHESTER. **Earls Colne Golf and Leisure Centre,** Earls Colne, Colchester CO6 2NS (0787 224466; Fax: 0787 224410). *Location:* we are on the B1024 Earls Colne – Coggeshall Road, four miles A12, two miles A120 (Euro-Route), one mile A604. Flat parkland courses (3). 4 hole teaching course; The Honeywood Course – 9 holes, 3100 yards. Par 34; 18 hole course 6715 yards. Par 73. *Green Fees:* weekdays £12.00; weekends £15.00. *Eating facilities:* à la carte restaurant, poolside grill and spike bar, two bars. *Visitors:* pay and play course – visitors welcome anytime. Full leisure centre including gym, swimming pool, whirlpool spa. *Society Meetings:* welcome anytime. Professional: Owen McKenna. Secretary: Sally Blackwell.

ESSEX *England*

COLD NORTON. Three Rivers Golf and Country Club, Stow Road, Cold Norton, Purleigh, Near Chelmsford CM3 6RR (0621 828631; Fax: 0621 828060). *Location:* B1012, three miles from South Woodham Ferrers, 12 miles from Chelmsford. Parkland with some water hazards. 18 holes, 6609 yards. S.S.S. 72. 9 hole Par 3 course. *Green Fees:* weekdays £25.00. *Eating facilities:* comprehensive. *Visitors:* welcome Monday to Friday without reservation. En suite accommodation available (inc. swimming pool, snooker, saunas, 2 squash courts, 3 tennis courts). *Society Meetings:* catered for mainly Tuesdays and Thursdays, some Wednesdays or Fridays. Professional: Graham Packer. General Manager: Stephen Evans.

EPPING. **Theydon Bois Golf Club**, Theydon Road, Epping CM16 4EH. *Location:* M25 Waltham Abbey/ Epping A121 London to Cambridge, turn right at Bell Hotel. Wooded course. 18 holes, 5472 yards. S.S.S. 68. Practice area. *Green Fees:* (1993 rates) £23.00 per day, £34.00 at weekends. *Eating facilities:* restaurant and bar. *Visitors:* welcome except Wednesday and Thursday morning. Not available November to March. *Society Meetings:* Monday and Tuesday £32 per person plus catering per day. Professional: R.T. Joyce (0992 812460). Secretary: Ian McDonald (0992 813054).

FRINTON-ON-SEA. **Frinton Golf Club**, 1 The Esplanade, Frinton-on-Sea CO13 9EP. *Location:* 17 miles east of Colchester, A12 – A133, B1033. Flat seaside links course, strength of wind always a feature. 18 holes, 6265 yards. S.S.S. 70. Short Course 2508 yards, no Handicap Certificate required. Practice facilities. *Green Fees:* £22.00. *Eating facilities:* snack and restaurant facilities. *Visitors:* welcome, check with Secretary. Handicap Certificate required. *Society Meetings:* catered for Wednesday and Thursday by arrangement. Professional: Peter Taggart (Tel & Fax: 0255 671618). Secretary: Lt Col R.W. Attrill (0255 674618).

HARLOW. **Canons Brook Golf Club**, Elizabeth Way, Harlow CM19 5BE (Harlow (0279) 25142). *Location:* A414. 18 holes, 6745 yards. S.S.S. 73. *Green Fees:* £25.00 per weekday. *Eating facilities:* full catering except Mondays. *Visitors:* welcome weekdays. *Society Meetings:* catered for except Mondays. Professional: Alan McGinn (0279 418357). Secretary: G.E. Chambers (0279 421482).

HARWICH. **Harwich and Dovercourt Golf Club**, Station Road, Parkeston, Harwich CO12 4NZ (Harwich (0255) 3616). *Location:* A604 thence to sign Parkeston Quay. Course marked on left hand side of Parkeston Road. 9 holes, 5862 yards. S.S.S. 68. *Green Fees:* information not provided. No visitors Saturdays, Sundays and Bank Holidays unless playing with a member. *Eating facilities:* order before playing. *Visitors:* welcome with Handicap Certificates. *Society Meetings:* catered for. Secretary: Mr B.Q. Dunham.

ILFORD. **Fairlop Waters**, Forest Road, Barkingside, Ilford IG6 3JA (081-500 9911). *Location:* two miles north of Ilford, half a mile from A12, one and a half miles from southern end of M11. Parkland course. 18 holes, 6281 yards. S.S.S. 70. *Green Fees:* £7.50 weekdays; £11.00 weekends. Pay as you play, no membership required. *Eating facilities:* Daltons American Diner open from breakfast till late 7 days a week, lunchtime bar food. *Visitors:* welcome all week. Banqueting for 250 and conferences. Professional: Tony Bowers (081-501 1881). Manager: Keith Robson.

ILFORD. **Ilford Golf Club**, 291 Wanstead Park Road, Ilford RG1 3TR (081-554 5174). *Location:* at end of M11. Parkland with winding river. 18 holes, 5787 yards. S.S.S. 68. *Green Fees:* weekdays £13.50, weekends £16.00. *Eating facilities:* restaurant and bar. *Visitors:* welcome weekdays, restricted times at weekends. *Society Meetings:* welcome. Professional: S. Dowsett (081-554 0094). Secretary: P.H. Newson (081-554 2930).

LEIGH-ON-SEA. **Belfairs Golf Club**, Eastwood Road North, Leigh-on-Sea SS9 4LR (Southend (0702) 526911). Park front 9, heavy woodland back 9; easy walking but challenging golf. Play over Belfairs municipal course. 18 holes, 5857 yards. S.S.S. 68. *Green Fees:* weekdays £13.20, weekends and Bank Holidays £16.80 (approximately). *Visitors:* unrestricted on the course but no clubhouse facilities available. Bookings required at weekends, Bank Holidays and during school holidays. Professional: Roger Foreman (0702 520202). Secretary: J.W. Pacey (0702 520322).

LOUGHTON. **Loughton Golf Club**, Clay's Lane, Debden Green, Loughton IG10 2RZ (081-502 2923). *Location:* just north of Loughton, on edge of Epping Forest. Hilly parkland, wooded. 9 holes, 4700 yards. S.S.S. 63. Practice range. *Green Fees:* weekdays £5.00 9 holes, £8.00 18 holes; weekends £6.00 for 9 holes, £10.00 for 18 holes. *Eating facilities:* bar, snacks available. *Visitors:* welcome, telephone to book. *Society Meetings:* welcome. Professional/Manager: Brian Davies.

MALDON. **Bunsay Downs Golf Club**, Little Baddow Road, Woodham Walter, Maldon CM9 6RW (0245 222648). *Location:* 7 miles east of Chelmsford off A414 at Woodham Walter, left onto Little Baddow Road. Undulating landscaped course. 9 holes, 2913 yards. S.S.S. 68. Par 3 course, indoor range. *Green Fees* information not supplied. *Eating facilities:* bar/grill restaurant. *Visitors:* welcome at all times. Gift shop. *Society Meetings:* small societies welcome. Professional: Mickey Walker (0245 224662). Secretary: (0245 222369).

MALDON. **Forrester Park Golf and Tennis Club**, Beckingham Road, Great Totham, Near Maldon CM9 8EA (Maldon (0621) 891406). *Location:* three miles off A12 Rivenhall turn-off, on B1022 in Great Totham, near Maldon between Compasses and Bull. Parkland course. 18 holes, 6073 yards. S.S.S. 69. *Green Fees:* weekdays £15.00, weekends £20.00. *Eating facilities:* full catering and bar facilities. *Visitors:* welcome, but not before 9.30am Tuesdays and Wednesdays and not before 12.30pm Saturdays and Sundays. *Society Meetings:* welcome subject to prior booking. Professional: Gary Pike (0621 893456). Manager: Tim Forrester-Muir (0621 891406).

THE GOLF GUIDE 1994

England   ESSEX

MALDON. **Maldon Golf Club,** Beeleigh, Langford, Maldon CM9 6LL (Maldon (0621) 853212). *Location:* B1019 two miles north west of Maldon, turn off at the Essex Waterworks. Flat parkland. 9 holes, 6197 yards, 5667 metres. S.S.S. 69. *Green Fees:* 18 holes £15.00, all day £20.00 weekdays; weekends 18 holes £12.00, all day £17.00 with a member only. *Eating facilities:* by prior arrangement only; bar. *Visitors:* welcome weekdays, Handicap Certificates required. *Society Meetings:* catered for by arrangement. Secretary: G.R. Bezant.

MALDON. **Quietwaters Hotel, Golf and Country Club,** Colchester Road, Tolleshunt Knights, Maldon CM9 8HX (Maldon (0621) 868888; Fax: 0621 869696). *Location:* eight miles from Colchester on B1026. Links type courses. (Two courses). Links Course – 18 holes, 6222 yards, 5690 metres. S.S.S. 70. Lakes Course – 18 holes, 6767 yards, 6186 metres. S.S.S. 72. *Green Fees:* Links – weekdays £18.00, weekends £22.50; Lakes – weekdays and weekends £30.00. *Eating facilities:* full catering available in hotel restaurant, bar snacks. *Visitors:* welcome at most times except Sunday mornings. *Society Meetings:* catered for. Director of Golf: P.D. Keeble (0621 868888).

MALDON. **Warren Golf Club,** Woodham Walter, Maldon CM9 6RW (Danbury (0245) 223198/223258; Fax: 0245 223989). *Location:* close to Chelmsford. A414 turn off to Maldon. Undulating wooded course. 18 holes, 6211 yards. S.S.S. 70. Large practice area. *Green Fees:* weekdays £28.00 18 holes, £35.00 36 holes. *Eating facilities:* restaurant, bar, bar snack menu. *Visitors:* welcome with reservation weekdays except Wednesdays am. Handicap Certificate required. Golf Academy. *Society Meetings:* catered for weekdays – up to 40 players. Professional: Mickey Walker (0245 224662). Manager: M.F.L. Durham.

OCKENDON. **Belhus Park Golf Club,** Belhus Park, Aveley By-Pass, South Ockendon RM15 4QR (0708 852248 complex, 0708 854748 office). *Location:* on A13 London – Southend Road, approximately one mile from Dartford Tunnel. Parkland. 18 holes, 5188 yards. S.S.S. 68. Driving range. *Green Fees:* information not provided. *Eating facilities:* cafe and bar. *Visitors:* welcome anytime (municipal course), but booking essential weekends and Bank Holidays. Swimming pool. *Society Meetings:* by arrangement with complex. Professional: Gary Lunn (0708 854260). Secretary: D.A. Faust (07084 46224).

ONGAR. **Toot Hill Golf Club,** School Road, Toot Hill, Ongar CM5 9PU (0277 365523). *Location:* between Epping and Ongar. Rolling Essex countryside. 18 holes, 6053 yards. S.S.S. 69. Practice ground. *Green Fees:* £25.00. Society Days (Tuesday and Thursdays): 18 holes £31.00, 27 holes £42.00. *Eating facilities:* available. *Visitors:* welcome during week. *Society Meetings:* welcome. Professional: Geof Bacon (0277 365747). Secretary: Mrs C. Cameron.

ORSETT. **Orsett Golf Club,** Brentwood Road, Orsett RM16 3DS (0375 891352). *Location:* A13 junction roundabout with A128. South towards Chadwell St. Mary on A128. Heathland, parkland course. 18 holes, 6614 yards. S.S.S. 72. *Green Fees:* £30.00 per round or day. *Eating facilities:* full catering available. *Visitors:* welcome on weekdays only. Must be members of a club and have Handicap. Proof must be produced. *Society Meetings:* welcome on Mondays, Tuesdays and Wednesdays. Professional: Robert Newberry (0375 891797). Secretary: P.M. Pritchard (0375 891226).

ROCHFORD near. **Ballards Gore Golf Club,** Gore Road, Canewdon, Near Rochford SS4 2DA (0702 258917). *Location:* Southend Airport three miles, London via A127, club two miles from Rochford. Parkland with lakes. 18 holes, 7062 yards. S.S.S. 74. Practice area. *Green Fees:* £20.00 weekdays. *Eating facilities:* diningroom (100 covers). *Visitors:* welcome weekdays only. *Society Meetings:* catered for by arrangement. Professional: Ian Marshall (0702 258924). Secretary: N.G. Patient (0702 258917).

ROMFORD. **Maylands Golf and Country Club,** Harold Park, Romford RM3 0AZ (0708 342055). *Location:* directly on A12 between Romford and Brentwood. 18 holes, 6182 yards. S.S.S. 70. Practice field and putting green. *Green Fees:* £20.00 per round, £30.00 per day. *Eating facilities:* bar, spike bar, restaurant and bar snacks. *Visitors:* welcome mid-week if members of recognised clubs with Handicap Certificates. *Society Meetings:* catered for Mondays, Wednesdays and Fridays. Professional: John Hopkin (0708 346466). Secretary/Proprietor: P. S. Taylor (0708 373080).

ROMFORD. **Risebridge Golf Centre,** Risebridge Chase, Romford RM1 4DG (0708 727376). *Location:* Gallows Corner, Strait Road, left turn into Lower Bedfords Road, first left Risebridge Chase. Parkland. 18 holes, 6342 yards. S.S.S. 70. Par 3 course. Practice range. *Green Fees:* weekdays £8.65; weekends £10.65. *Eating facilities:* cafe *Visitors:* welcome without reservation. Professional: Paul Jennings. Secretary: Jean Pettite.

SAFFRON WALDEN. **Saffron Walden Golf Club,** Windmill Hill, Saffron Walden CB10 1BX (Saffron Walden (0799) 22786). *Location:* end of town on A130 to Cambridge. 18 holes, 6609 yards. S.S.S. 72. *Green Fees:* £28.00 per day or round (weekdays only). *Eating facilities:* lunches and snacks available. *Visitors:* welcome with current Handicap Certificate. *Society Meetings:* catered for Mondays, Wednesdays and Thursdays. Professional: Philip Davis. General Manager: David Smith.

SOUTH BENFLEET. **Boyce Hill Golf Club Ltd,** Vicarage Hill, South Benfleet SS7 1PD (Benfleet (0268) 793625). *Location:* one-and-a-half-miles from A13 or A127. Hilly course, 18 holes. S.S.S. 68. *Green Fees:* weekdays £20.00 per round, £25.00 per day. *Eating facilities:* full dining facilities. *Visitors:* welcome, except Tuesday mornings. *Society Meetings:* catered for Thursdays only. Professional: G. Burroughs (0268 752565). Secretary: J.E. Atkins (0268 793625).

SOUTHEND-ON-SEA. **Southend-on-Sea Golf Club,** Belfairs Park, Eastwood Road North, Leigh-on-Sea SS9 4LR (0702 524836). *Location:* A127 London to Southend Road. Parkland/wooded course (Belfairs Municipal course). 18 holes, 5857 yards. S.S.S. 68.

ESSEX/GLOUCESTERSHIRE *England*

Green Fees: information not provided. *Eating facilities:* restaurant in the park. *Visitors:* welcome, unrestricted, but bookings required for weekends and Bank Holidays. Booking by phone to Starters Hut (0702 525345). Professional: Roger Foreman (0702 520202). Secretary: N.A. Dye (0702 340472).

SOUTHEND-ON-SEA. **Thorpe Hall Golf Club,** Thorpe Hall Avenue, Thorpe Bay, Southend-on-Sea. *Location:* one mile east of Southend-on-Sea. Parkland. 18 holes, 6286 yards. S.S.S. 71. *Green Fees:* on application. *Eating facilities:* restaurant open every day except Mondays. *Visitors:* welcome weekdays with Handicap Certificate, weekends with members only. *Society Meetings:* catered for. Professional: Gary Harvey (0702 588195). Secretary: G.R.G. Winckless (0702 582205).

STANFORD LE HOPE. **St. Cleres Golf Club,** St. Cleres Hall, Stanford le Hope (0375 361565). Downland course. 18 holes, 6500 yards. S.S.S. 71. Practice ground. *Green Fees:* weekdays £15.00; weekends £20.00. *Visitors:* unrestricted. *Society Meetings:* welcome.

STAPLEFORD ABBOTTS. **Stapleford Abbotts Golf Club,** Horsemans Side, Tysea Hill, Stapleford Abbotts RM4 1JU. *Location:* three miles from Junction 28 M25. Off main Romford – Ongar Road B175 at Stapleford Abbotts, Essex. Parkland with many water hazards. Abbotts – 18 holes, 6684 yards. S.S.S. 71. Priors – 18 holes, 6005 yards. S.S.S. 70. Friars – 9 holes, 1140 yards. S.S.S. 27. Two practice areas. *Green Fees:* Abbotts – £20.00 per round; Priors £15.00 per round; Friars £5.00 per round. *Eating facilities:* stud bar and restaurant. *Visitors:* midweek no restrictions. *Society Meetings:* ring for booking brochure. Professional: Dominic Eagle (0708 381278). Secretary: Keith Fletcher (0708 381108). Tee Reservations: Abbotts (0708 370040), Priors (0277 373344).

STAPLEFORD TAWNEY. **Abridge Golf and Country Club,** Epping Lane, Stapleford Tawney RM4 1ST (0708 688388). *Location:* A113 from London through Chigwell to Abridge, left at White Hart, right after 300 yards. Two miles on. Parkland. 18 holes, 6690 yards. S.S.S. 72. *Green Fees:* on application. *Eating facilities:* restaurant Saturdays to Thursdays, lunch; bar Saturday to Thursday, drinks and snacks; no service Fridays. *Visitors:* welcome but must be a member of a recognised golf club and produce evidence of current Handicap, weekdays only. Tennis courts and heated swimming pool. *Society Meetings:* catered for on Mondays and Wednesdays only by arrangement. Professional: Mike Herbert (0708 688333). Secretary: P.G. Pelling (0708 688396).

WOODFORD GREEN. **Woodford Golf Club,** Sunset Avenue, Woodford Green (081-504 4254). *Location:* near Castle Public House, Woodford High Road. Public forest land. 9 holes, 5806 yards. S.S.S. 68. *Green Fees:* £15.00 per round. *Eating facilities:* bar. *Visitors:* no green fees Tuesday or Thursday mornings and Sundays after 12.30pm. Red (scarlet) clothing must be worn – trousers or top. *Society Meetings:* welcome. Professional: A. Johns (081-504 4254). Secretary: G.J. Cousins (081-504 3330).

Gloucestershire

BROADWAY. **Broadway Golf Club,** Willersey Hill, Broadway WR12 7LG (0386 853683). *Location:* one-and-a-half-miles east Broadway (A44). 18 holes, 6211 yards. S.S.S. 70 *Green Fees:* on application. *Eating facilities:* available daily (except Monday). *Visitors:* welcome; reservation advised. Handicap Certificates required. Saturdays (April/September) with member only before 3pm. October/March no restrictions. *Society Meetings:* by arrangement. (Wednesday, Thursday and Friday). Professional: Martyn Freeman (0386 853275). Managing Secretary: B. Carnie (0386 853683).

CHELTENHAM. **Cleeve Cloud Golf Club,** Cleeve Hill, Near Cheltenham (0242 672025). *Location:* three miles north of Cheltenham on B4632. Inland links with gorse. 18 holes, 6411 yards. S.S.S. 71. *Green Fees:* information not provided. *Eating facilities:* full restaurant and bar snacks every day. *Visitors:* welcome. *Society Meetings:* welcome with reservation. Professional: D. Finch (0242 672592). Secretary: R. East (0242 672025).

CHELTENHAM. **Lilley Brook Golf Club,** Cirencester Road, Charlton Kings, Cheltenham GL53 8EG (Cheltenham (0242) 526785). *Location:* two miles south-east of Cheltenham on main Cirencester road (A435). Parkland, 18 holes, 6226 yards, 5979 metres. S.S.S. 70. Practice field. *Green Fees:* weekdays £20.00. *Eating facilities:* full catering available. *Visitors:* welcome weekdays, weekends as a guest of a member only. Handicap Certificates required. *Society Meetings:* by arrangement. Professional: Forbes E. Hadden (0242 525201). Secretary: K.A. Skeen (0242 526785).

England GLOUCESTERSHIRE

CHELTENHAM near. **Cotswold Hills Golf Club Ltd,** Ullenwood, Near Cheltenham GL53 9QT (Cheltenham (0242) 522421). *Location:* at Ullenwood, off the A436 south of Cheltenham (two miles from town). Undulating Cotswold country course, excellent drainage. 18 holes, 6750 yards. S.S.S. 72. Large practice ground. *Green Fees:* weekdays £21.00 per round; weekends £26.00 per round. *Eating facilities:* full restaurant and bars. *Visitors:* no restrictions as a rule, but it is wise to telephone. *Society Meetings:* catered for by arrangement with Secretary. Professional: Noel Boland (0242 515263). Secretary: Andrew O'Reilly (0242 515264).

CIRENCESTER. **Cirencester Golf Club,** Cheltenham Road, Cirencester (0285 653939; Fax: 0285 650665). *Location:* one mile north of Cirencester on A435 Cheltenham road. 18 holes, 6108 yards. S.S.S. 69. *Green Fees:* weekdays £20.00, weekends and Bank Holidays £25.00. *Eating facilities:* lunches and suppers by arrangement. Hot and cold snacks always available. *Visitors:* welcome, Handicap Certificate required. *Society Meetings:* catered for Tuesday, Wednesday and Friday only. Professional: Geoff Robbins (0285 656124). Secretary: N.D. Jones (0285 652465).

COLEFORD. **Forest Hills Golf Club Ltd.,** Mile End Road, Coleford (0594 810620). *Location:* 10 miles from Severn Bridge, six miles from Monmouth M5, M50. Coleford town centre on Gloucester Road. Parkland with panoramic views to Welsh hills. 18 holes, 6000 yards. S.S.S. 68. Practice ground. *Green Fees:* weekdays £13.00; weekends £15.00. All-inclusive packages available. *Eating facilities:* bar, restaurant. *Visitors:* welcome, no restrictions. *Society Meetings:* very welcome. Professional: T. Morgan. Secretary: Mrs H. Richards.

BEECHMOUNT

Small friendly Guest House situated in the village of Birdlip. Conveniently situated for a number of Golf Clubs, i.e. Cotswold Hills, Painswick, Lillybrook, Gloucester Country Club, Cirencester, Tewkesbury Park, Minchinhampton and Anberly. Also an ideal centre for a walking or touring holiday. All bedrooms equipped to a high standard. Some en suite, all with colour TVs, radio alarms, tea and coffee making facilities, shoe cleaning, hand basins, etc. Key provided. Car parking and large garden. Evening meals by arrangement. Highly recommended, competitive rates. Fire certificate held.

Mrs P.M. Carter, Beechmount, Birdlip, Gloucestershire GL4 8JH. Tel: 0452 862262.

**Charlton Kings Hotel
Cheltenham GL52 6UU
Telephone: 0242 231061
ETB 👑👑👑 Commended**

Enjoy playing a round in the Cotswolds, spectacular scenery, a choice of magnificent clubs all within a few miles of Cheltenham. Stay in a newly refurbished (1991) hotel situated in an area of outstanding natural beauty. All rooms have views of the Cotswold Hills. If you have a non-golfing partner bring him/her as well – our room information folder lists over 200 sights and activities. During your stay you will be tempted to try our cosy restaurant offering an imaginative and varied menu. Above all, we offer a standard of service only a small private hotel can provide.

A double ensuite room from £37pp for 1 night, £32pp for 2 nights or £28pp for 5 nights inclusive of full English Breakfast.

**Poolway House
16th Century Manor**

ETB 👑👑👑   AA ★★

The Anstice family invite you to their 16th Century Manor Hotel and Restaurant, situated in the Ancient Forest of Dean, a Golfer's and Walker's Paradise Enjoy their hospitality and good food, and the seven local golf courses, discover the challenging and famous or the sympathetic and less demanding. (Championship courses; Rolls of Monmouth and St Pierre). All our bedrooms are ensuite, with TV, tea/coffee and direct dial telephone. Inclusive golf packages. Please phone for comprehensive brochure and tariff.

**Poolway House, Gloucester Road, Coleford GL16 8BN
Telephone: 0594 833937**

GLOUCESTERSHIRE England

COLEFORD. **Royal Forest of Dean Golf Club**, Lords Hill, Coleford GL16 8BD (Dean (0594) 832583; Fax: 0594 832584). *Location:* quarter of a mile from Coleford town centre on B4431 Coleford to Parkend Road, 10 miles from Severn Bridge, M4, M5 and M50. Parkland course in Forest of Dean. 18 holes, 5535 yards. S.S.S. 67. Practice area. *Green Fees:* weekdays £14.00, weekends £16.00. Society Days – 36 holes golf, snack lunch, dinner only £24.00 available Mondays to Thursdays. *Eating facilities:* food available all day – breakfast, coffee, lunches, teas and dinner. Table d'hôte restaurant, bar open all day. *Visitors:* always welcome, please book teeing-off times with Professional. Own 32 bedroom Hotel (all en-suite), outdoor swimming pool, tennis court, bowling green, golf cars available. *Society Meetings:* welcome. Professional: John Nicol (0594 833689). Secretary: Mrs K. Cave (0594 832583).

DURSLEY. **Stinchcombe Hill Golf Club**, Stinchcombe Hill, Dursley GL11 6AQ (Dursley (0453) 542015). *Location:* M5 between Junctions 13 and 14, A38 to Dursley. At traffic lights in centre of Dursley enter May Lane, continue to top of Hill and turn right onto Golf Course. A gently undulating course situated on a hilltop at the southern edge of the Cotswolds, extensive views. 18 holes, 5723 yards. S.S.S. 68. Practice and teaching areas. *Green Fees:* £20.00 weekdays (£10.00 with member); £25.00 weekends and Bank Holidays (£12.50 with member). *Eating facilities:* full catering and bar service available. *Visitors:* welcome with recognised handicaps, time restrictions at weekends and Bank Holidays. *Society Meetings:* catered for by arrangement. Professional: Brendan Wynne (0453 543878). Secretary: John R. Clarke (0453 542015).

GLOUCESTER. **Gloucester Hotel, Golf and Country Club**, Matson Lane, Gloucester GL4 9EA (Gloucester (0452) 525653 Ext. 316). *Location:* situated on Robinswood Hill, turn off Gloucester to Painswick Road and head for Ski slopes. Parkland-type. Back 9 holes on top of hill. 18 holes, 6137 yards, 5613 metres. S.S.S. 69. 9 holes Par 3 course, driving range. *Green Fees:* information not provided. *Eating facilities:* full catering available. *Visitors:* welcome any time but booking recommended by telephoning Secretary. *Society Meetings:* welcome weekdays, weekends by special arrangement. Professional/Manager: P. Darnell (0452 411331).

LYDNEY. **Lydney Golf Club**, The Links, off Lakeside Avenue, Lydney GL15 5QA (Dean (0594) 842614). *Location:* on front left-hand side of town when entering on A48 Chepstow Road from Gloucester. Flat meadowland with views over the River Severn. 9 holes, 5382 yards. S.S.S. 66. Small practice area. *Green Fees:* £12.00 per day weekdays; weekends with a member only. Reduction of £3.00 when playing with a member. *Eating facilities:* snack meals only. *Visitors:* welcome weekdays, only with a member at weekends/Bank Holidays. *Society Meetings:* welcome by prior arrangement (maximum 36). Hon. Secretary: D.A. Barnard (0594 843940).

Bells Hotel AND THE Royal Forest of Dean Golf Club

LORDS HILL, COLEFORD, GLOS. GL16 8BD   Tel: (0594) 832583   Fax: (0594) 832584

Set adjacent to the 1st Tee, this family owned hotel and golf course, established 20 years offers you:

- **Restaurant & Bar Open all day**
- **Weekend Break** inclusive of all golf & Sunday Lunch only **£92.00**
- **Society Day** – Days golf, Snack Lunch and 3 Course Dinner only **£24.00**
- **Winter Daily Break** – Brunch, Golf, and 3 Course Dinner only **£20.00**
- **Half Board Rates** – from **£39.50** inclusive of Golf

THE BEST PLACE IN GLOUCESTER TO WORK, REST OR PLAY

- 18 hole Golf Course and Driving Range.
- 2 Dry Ski Slopes.
- Extensive Leisure Facilities, including Superb
- new Leisure Complex with Squash Courts and magnificent Swimming Pool.
- Excellent Restaurant.
- Superb Conference Venue.
- Ideal for Weddings and Private functions.

GLOUCESTER HOTEL AND COUNTRY CLUB
Robinswood Hill, Gloucester GL4 9EA
Telephone (0452) 525653 Fax (0452) 307212

See our Colour Advertisement on Page 21

Jarvis□Hotels

BARNHILL FARMHOUSE

The Archers welcome you to their comfortable Grade II Listed farmhouse. Large guest house with inglenook and television. Two bedrooms with TV, one ensuite and one with private bathroom. Generous home cooking. Ample parking. Ideal for business or pleasure. Many challenging golf courses within easy reach, including The Belfry, Cotswold Hills and Royal Forest of Dean.

Barnhill Farmhouse, Bredons Norton, near Tewkesbury, Gloucestershire GL20 7HB
Telephone/Fax: 0684 72704

MINCHINHAMPTON. **Minchinhampton Golf Club**, New Course, Minchinhampton, Stroud (0453 833858 for New Course, 0453 832642 for Old Course). *Location:* New Course between Minchinhampton and Avening. Old Course between Minchinhampton and Stroud. Both courses 18 holes. New Course 6675 yards. Old Course 6295 yards. S.S.S. New Course 72, Old Course 70. *Green Fees:* New Course: weekdays £24.00 day, weekends and Bank Holidays £30.00 day. Old Course: weekdays £10.00 day, weekends and Bank Holidays £13.00. *Eating facilities:* normal catering at both New Course and Old Course Clubhouses. *Visitors:* New Course: welcome, must have handicap. Old Course: welcome. *Society Meetings:* both courses cater for groups by arrangement. Professional: New and Old Courses C. Steele (0453 833860). Secretary: D.R. Vickers (0453 833866). Old Course Pro Shop: (0453 836382).

PAINSWICK. **Painswick Golf Club**, Painswick, Near Stroud (Painswick (0452) 812180). *Location:* three miles north-east of Stroud on A46. 18 holes, 4900 yards. S.S.S. 64. *Green Fees:* weekdays £10.00; Saturdays £15.00. *Eating facilities:* lunches at Club (prior notice requested). *Visitors:* welcome weekdays and Saturday mornings. Saturday afternoons and Sunday mornings only with member. *Society Meetings:* catered for, welcome most days. Secretary: R. Power.

TETBURY. **Westonbirt Golf Course**, c/o Bursar, Westonbirt School Ltd, Westonbirt, Near Tetbury GL8 8QP (0666 880 242). *Location:* three miles south from Tetbury on A433, A439 to Bath on Bath road. Parkland. 9 holes, 4504 yards. S.S.S. 61. Practice area.

Green Fees: information not provided. *Eating facilities:* available. *Visitors:* welcome without reservation. *Society Meetings:* catered for, limited facilities. Professional: C. Steele (visiting from Minchinhampton Golf Club). Secretary: Mr Nolan.

TEWKESBURY. **Tewkesbury Park Hotel, Golf and Country Club**, Lincoln Green Lane, Tewkesbury GL20 7DN (0684 295405; Fax: 0684 292386). *Location:* leave Junction 9 of M5, continue into Tewkesbury onto Gloucester Road. Parkland. 18 holes, 6533 yards. S.S.S. 72. 9 holes, Par 3 course. *Green Fees:* weekdays £25.00; weekends £30.00. Special rates available by arrangement. *Eating facilities:* full facilities available. *Visitors:* welcome, reservation required weekends. Valid Handicap Certificate required. Leisure complex. 78 bedroomed hotel. *Society Meetings:* all welcome by prior arrangement. Professional: Mr Robert Taylor (0684 294892). Secretary: Mr Bob Nichol (0684 299452).

WOTTON-UNDER-EDGE. **Cotswold Edge Golf Club**, Upper Rushmire, Wotton-under-Edge GL12 7PT (Dursley (0453) 844167). *Location:* eight miles from Junction 14 M5, on B4058 Tetbury road. Fairly flat course with magnificent views. 18 holes, White Tees – 6170 yards. S.S.S. 70; Yellow Tees – 5816 yards. S.S.S. 68. *Green Fees:* weekdays £15.00. Subject to review. *Eating facilities:* good catering service, usual bar facilities. *Visitors:* welcome weekdays. Telephone call in advance advisable. *Society Meetings:* by arrangement with Secretary. Professional: David Gosling (0453 844398). Secretary: N.J. Newman (0453 844167).

Hampshire

ALDERSHOT. **Army Golf Club**, Laffan's Road, Aldershot GU11 2HF (0252 540638; Fax: 0252 376562). Clubhouse (0252 541104). Pro's Shop (0252 547232). *Location:* access from Eelmoor Bridge off A323 Aldershot Fleet Road. 18 holes, 6533 yards. S.S.S. 71. *Green Fees:* special rates for servicemen. *Eating facilities:* a range of catering is available by arrangement with the Secretary. *Visitors:* weekdays only, members' guests anytime. *Society Meetings:* catered for. Professional: Mr Nigel Turner. Secretary/Manager: R.T. Crabb.

ALRESFORD. **Alresford Golf Club**, Cheriton Road, Tichborne Down, Alresford SO24 0PN. *Location:* one mile south of A31 (Winchester/Alton). Two miles north A272 (Winchester/Petersfield). Rolling downland, wooded. 18 holes, 5905 yards. S.S.S. 68. Practice area. *Green Fees:* weekdays £16.50; weekends and Bank Holidays £32.00 per round (not before 12 noon). *Eating facilities:* full catering except Mondays. *Visitors:* welcome but not before 12 noon weekends/Bank Holidays. Handicap Certificate required. *Society Meetings:* catered for by prior arrangement. Professional: Malcolm Scott (0962 733998). Secretary: Peter Kingston (0962 733746).

115

HAMPSHIRE *England*

ALTON. **Alton Golf Club**, Old Odiham Road, Alton GU34 4BU (Alton (0420) 82042). *Location:* off A32, two miles north of Alton. Odiham six miles. Undulating wooded course. 9 holes, Alternate tees. 5744 yards. S.S.S. 68. Practice area. *Green Fees:* weekdays £12.00 per round, £16.00 per day; weekends £20.00 per round, £30.00 per day. Half green fees if with a member. *Eating facilities:* bar. *Visitors:* weekdays welcome without reservation, except on competition days. Weekends and Bank Holidays with member or 18 Handicap maximum. *Society Meetings:* welcome weekdays only, catering provided. Professional: Mr A. Lamb (0420 86518). Secretary: W.J. Cleveland (Home: 0420 84774; Office: 0420 82042).

AMPFIELD. **Ampfield Par Three Golf and Country Club**, Winchester Road, Ampfield, Near Romsey SO51 9BQ (Braishfield (0794) 68480). *Location:* A31 Winchester to Romsey road, next door to White Horse Public House. Parkland course designed by Henry Cotton. All holes par 3. 18 holes, 2478 yards. S.S.S. 53. *Green Fees:* on application. *Eating facilities:* light meals and snacks, bar facilities. *Visitors:* welcome, but best to phone first. Handicap Certificate required at weekends and Bank Holidays. Recognised golf shoes must be worn. *Society Meetings:* catered for by prior arrangement. Professional: Richard Benfield (0794 68750). Secretary: Mrs Stella Baker.

ANDOVER. **Andover Golf Club**, 51 Winchester Road, Andover SP10 2EF (Andover (0264) 323980). *Location:* half-mile south of town centre on the A3057 Winchester/Stockbridge road. Parkland. 9 holes, 5933 yards. S.S.S. 68. *Green Fees:* £12.00 weekdays, £22.00 weekends. *Eating facilities:* full catering available. *Visitors:* welcome but not before 12 noon weekends and Bank Holidays. *Society Meetings:* catered for with prior arrangement. Professional: A. Timms (0264 324151). Secretary: D.A. Fairweather (0264 358040). Clubhouse Manager: (0264 323980).

BARTON-ON-SEA. **Barton-on-Sea Golf Club**, Milford Road, New Milton BH25 5PP (0425 615308; Fax: 0425 621457). *Location:* one mile from centre of New Milton on B3058 towards Milford-on-Sea. Flat landscaped course on cliff edge – superb views of Isle of Wight and Christchurch Bay to Swanage. 27 holes. S.S.S. 72 any 18 holes. *Green Fees:* £25.00 per day weekdays; £30.00 weekends. *Eating facilities:* lunch, snacks and teas daily, full bar service. *Visitors:* welcome after 8.30am weekdays; weekends and Bank Holidays after 11.15am. Handicap Certificate required. *Society Meetings:* welcome by arrangement Mondays, Wednesdays and Fridays. Professional: P. Coombs (0425 611210). General Manager: A. Ross.

BASINGSTOKE. **Basingstoke Golf Club**, Kempshott Park, Basingstoke RG23 7LL (Basingstoke (0256) 465990). *Location:* on A30, three miles west of town on road to Winchester; from Winchester leave M3 at Exit 7. Parkland course. 18 holes, 6259 yards. S.S.S. 70. *Green Fees:* information not provided. *Eating facilities:* lunches and teas in clubhouse. *Visitors:* welcome on weekdays if member of a golf club, visitors at weekends and Bank Holidays only if playing with a member. *Society Meetings:* Wednesdays and Thursdays. Professional: I. Hayes (0256 51332). Secretary: K.G. Maplesden (Tel & Fax: 0256 465990).

BASINGSTOKE. **Bishopswood Golf Club**, Bishopswood Lane, Tadley, Basingstoke RG26 6AT (Tadley (0734) 812200). *Location:* six miles north of Basingstoke off the A340. Parkland/wooded course. 9 holes, 6474 yards. S.S.S. 71. 12 bay floodlit driving range open seven days a week. *Green Fees:* weekdays £8.00 for 9 holes, £13.00 for 18 holes. *Eating facilities:* lounge and spike bars – snacks, bar meals and 50 seater restaurant facility. *Visitors:* welcome weekdays only by prior booking. *Society Meetings:* welcome by arrangement. Professional: S. Ward (0734 815213). Manager: M.W. Phillips (0734 812200).

BASINGSTOKE. **Sandford Springs Golf Club**, Wolverton, Basingstoke (0635 297881; Fax: 0635 298065). *Location:* A339 Basingstoke to Newbury at Kingsclere. Wooded parkland course with lakes. 27 holes. Three loops of 9 holes. S.S.S. 69/70/69. *Green Fees:* weekdays £21.00. *Eating facilities:* available all day; also conference and banqueting facilities. *Visitors:* welcome weekdays. *Society Meetings:* always welcome weekdays. Professional: G. Edmunds. Secretary: G. Tipple. Professional/Managing Director: K. Brake.

BASINGSTOKE. **Test Valley Golf Club**, Micheldever Road, Overton, Basingstoke RG25 3DS (0256 771737). *Location:* on the C79, one mile north of M3/A303 signposted Overton. Downland in the style of the traditional Scottish/Irish links with hidden pot bunkers, etc. 18 holes, 6811 yards. S.S.S. 73. Full practice facilities. *Green Fees:* weekdays £14.00; weekends £20.00. *Eating facilities:* snacks in spike bar; breakfast, full meals, etc in diningroom. *Visitors:* welcome but may be restricted weekend mornings. *Society Meetings:* welcome (from £18.00 per person). Professional: Terry Notley. Secretary: Mrs J. McDonagh.

BASINGSTOKE. **Tylney Park Golf Club**, Rotherwick, near Basingstoke (Hook (0256) 762079). *Location:* one mile Hook A30. Parkland. 18 holes, 6135 yards. S.S.S. 69, Par 70. *Green Fees:* weekdays £20.00; weekends £28.00. *Eating facilities:* catering available. *Visitors:* weekdays unrestricted, weekends with Handicap Certificate or member. Professional: C. DeBruin. Secretary: A.D. Bewley.

The Wheatsheaf
Market Square, Alton. Tel: (0420) 83316

Mr and Mrs Rooney welcome you to the Wheatsheaf. They offer a vast extensive menu which is available for lunch and evening meals seven days a week. Accommodation available all year round. Telephone for further details and bookings.

THE GOLF GUIDE 1994   *England*   HAMPSHIRE

BORDON. **Blackmoor Golf Club,** Bordon GU35 0XA (0420 472775). *Location:* lies midway between Petersfield and Farnham on A325. 18 holes, 6213 yards. S.S.S. 70. *Green Fees:* £35.00 per day, after 1pm £26.00. *Eating facilities:* dining room. *Visitors:* welcome with reservation, Handicaps necessary. *Society Meetings:* catered for all day. Morning coffee, lunch, evening meal. Professional: Stephen Clay (0420 472345; Fax: 0420 476110). Secretary: Major (Retd.) H.R.G. Spiller (0420 472775; Fax: 0420 487666).

BORDON near. **Kingsley Golf Club,** Main Road, Kingsley, Near Bordon GU35 9NG (0420 476118). *Location:* B3004 off A325 (Farnham to Petersfield Road). Parkland public course, a challenging short course. 9 holes, 1797 yards. S.S.S. Men 53, Ladies 60. *Green Fees:* information not provided. *Eating facilities:* bar and cafeteria. *Visitors:* no visitors on Sundays without prior booking. Driving range, indoor computerised driving bay, equipment superstore, golf school for tuition. *Society Meetings:* by prior arrangement. Professional: Richard Adams (0420 488478). Secretary: Alex Cook (0420 476118).

BROCKENHURST. **Brokenhurst Manor Golf Club,** Sway Road, Brockenhurst SO4 7SG (Lymington (0590) 22383). *Location:* from M27 take A337 to Brockenhurst then B3055 (to Sway). Approximately one mile to golf club. Beautiful New Forest course – wet in winter. 18 holes, 6222 yards. S.S.S. 70. *Green Fees:* weekdays £25.00 per round, £35.00 per day; weekends and Bank Holidays £40.00. *Eating facilities:* full catering and bar facilities. *Visitors:* welcome any day but please book in advance as there are restrictions on some days. Club Handicap Certificate required. *Society Meetings:* Thursdays by arrangement, small groups catered for by arrangement Mondays, Wednesdays and Fridays. Professional: B. Plucknett (0590 23092). Secretary: A.S. Craven (0590 23332).

CRONDALL. **Oak Park Golfing Complex,** Heath Lane, Crondall, Near Farnham, Surrey GU10 5PB (0252 850880; Fax: 0252 850851). *Location:* one and a half miles off A287 Farnham-Odiham road, five miles from Junctions 4 and 5 of M3 motorway. Gently undulating parkland course. 18 holes, 6437 yards. S.S.S. 71. Putting green and 16 bay covered driving range. *Green Fees:* weekdays £16.00 per round, £25.00 per day (reductions for Juniors); weekends £22.50 per round, £40 per day. *Eating facilities:* à la carte restaurant: Mon to Fri lunchtime and Sunday lunch. Tues to Sat evenings. Bar snacks available. *Visitors:* welcome; must book through Professional; reserved tee system weekends and Public Holidays. *Society Meetings:* by arrangement with Secretary, welcome every day subject to availability. Professional: Simon Coaker (0252 850066). Secretary: Mrs R. Smythe (0252 850850).

DIBDEN. **Dibden Golf Centre,** Main Road, Dibden, Southampton (Hythe (0703) 845060). *Location:* half-mile off A326 Totton to Fawley road at Dibden very close to New Forest. 18 holes, 6206 yards. S.S.S. 70. 9 hole course and 19 bay driving range. *Green Fees:* summer rate: weekdays £6.50, weekends £9.50. *Eating facilities:* available. *Visitors:* welcome without reservation. *Society Meetings:* catered for. Professional: Alan Bridge (0703 845596). Course administration by Professional.

EASTLEIGH. **Fleming Park Golf Club,** Magpie Lane, Eastleigh (0703 643671). *Location:* two miles off M27 Eastleigh Airport turning. Parkland. 18 holes, 4376 yards. S.S.S. 61. *Green Fees:* information not provided. *Eating facilities:* bar. *Visitors:* welcome, book on day or one week in advance. *Society Meetings:* all welcome. Professional: D. Miller (0703 612797). Secretary: D. Ainsworth-Lay (0703 612797).

FAREHAM. **Southwick Park Golf Club,** Pinsley Drive, Southwick, Fareham PO17 6EL. *Location:* near Southwick village, within HMS Dryad. Parkland. 18 holes, 5972 yards. S.S.S. 68. Practice area, pitch and putt. *Green Fees:* information not provided. *Eating facilities:* bar and snacks available. *Visitors:* weekdays only. *Society Meetings:* Tuesdays only, book through Manager. Professional: J. Green (0705 380442). Manager: N.W. Price (0705 380131).

FARNBOROUGH. **Southwood Golf Course,** Ively Road, Cove, Farnborough GU14 0LJ (0252 515139). *Location:* approximately half a mile west of A325. Flat parkland. 18 holes, 5553 yards. S.S.S. 67. Putting green. *Green Fees:* weekdays £11.00; weekends £14.00. *Eating facilities:* bar and diningroom available. *Visitors:* welcome, bookable at all times. *Society Meetings:* catered for by arrangement. Professional: Bob Hammond (0252 548700).

FLEET. **Hartley Wintney Golf Club,** London Road, Hartley Wintney, Basingstoke RG27 8PT (0252 842214). *Location:* on A30 between Camberley and Basingstoke. Parkland, wooded. 9 holes, 6096 yards. S.S.S. 69. Practice area. *Green Fees:* under review. *Eating facilities:* full catering facilities available except Mondays. *Visitors:* restricted Wednesdays Ladies' Day; weekends and Bank Holidays with member only. *Society Meetings:* catered for Tuesdays and Thursdays on application. Professional: Martin Smith (0252 843379). Secretary: B.D. Powell (0252 844211).

FLEET. **North Hants Golf Club,** Minley Road, Fleet GU13 8RE (0252 616443). *Location:* B3013 off A30, M3 Junction 4a. 400 yards from railway station. Heathland. 18 holes, 6257 yards. S.S.S. 70. Practice ground. *Green Fees:* weekdays £23.00 per round, £29.00 per two rounds. *Eating facilities:* lunch, daily,

---

THE WATERSPLASH HOTEL
BROCKENHURST

The Watersplash Hotel is recommended for its excellent food, friendly service and accommodation. Brockenhurst Manor Golf Club, situated just half a mile away, is one of ten courses within easy reach of the hotel.

Personally supervised by resident proprietors Robin and Judy Foster who specialise in catering for the individual and small golf parties. Well-stocked bar and extensive wine list. All 23 bedrooms have private bathrooms, colour TV, tea and coffee making facilities, direct-dial telephones and room radios. Heated outdoor pool. For further details ask for our colour brochure.

The Watersplash Hotel, The Rise, Brockenhurst, Hampshire SO42 7ZP   **Tel: (0590) 22344 Fax: (0590) 24047**

HAMPSHIRE *England*

evening meals by prior arrangement. *Visitors:* welcome weekday only by prior arrangement, Handicap Certificates required, Thursdays ladies day. *Society Meetings:* Tuesdays and Wednesdays only, maximum 42. Professional: Steve Porter (0252 616655). Secretary: I.R. Goodliffe (0252 616443; Fax: 0252 811627).

GOSPORT. **Fleetlands Golf Club,** RNAY Fleetlands, Fareham Road, Gosport PO13 0AW. *Location:* two miles south of Fareham on Fareham/Gosport Road. Flat/wooded course. 9 holes, 4852 yards. S.S.S. 64. *Green Fees:* £4.00 weekdays; £6.00 weekends. *Eating facilities:* bar/clubhouse. *Visitors:* by appointment with member only. *Society Meetings:* by appointment with member only. Secretary: Mr A. Eade (0705 822351 extension 44384).

GOSPORT. **Gosport and Stokes Golf Club,** off Fort Road, Haslar, Gosport (Gosport (0705) 581625). *Location:* A32 to Gosport, course is one mile east of Stokes Bay, near Gilkicker Point. Water course, natural hazards. 9 holes, 5800 yards. S.S.S. 68. Nets and putting green. *Green Fees:* information not provided. *Eating facilities:* bar snacks, meal by arrangement. *Visitors:* welcome all week, restricted Sundays and Thursdays. *Society Meetings:* by arrangement. Secretary: A.P. Chubb (0705 527941).

HAVANT. **Rowlands Castle Golf Club,** 31 Links Lane, Rowlands Castle PO9 6AE (Portsmouth (0705) 412216). *Location:* four miles north of Havant or Horndean/Rowlands Castle Junction from A3M. Flat parkland, wooded course. 18 holes, 6627 yards White Tees, 6381 yards Yellow Tees. S.S.S. 72 (White), 70 (Yellow). *Green Fees:* weekdays £22.00 per round/day; weekends £27.00. Subject to review. *Eating facilities:* full catering available except Mondays. *Visitors:* welcome, except Saturdays unless playing with a member, maximum 12 visitors on a Sunday and Bank Holidays. *Society Meetings:* catered for Tuesdays and Thursdays, bookings through Secretary. Professional: Peter Klepacz (0705 412785). Secretary: Captain A.W. Aird (0705 412784).

HAYLING ISLAND. **Hayling Golf Club,** Links Lane, Hayling Island PO11 0BX (Hayling Island (0705) 463777). *Location:* A3023 five miles south of Havant. Seaside links. 18 holes, 6489 yards. S.S.S. 71. *Green Fees:* £25.00 per day, weekends £35.00. *Eating facili-*

ties: lunches and afternoon teas available. *Visitors:* welcome with current Handicap Certificate and must be members of recognised clubs. *Society Meetings:* Tuesdays and Wednesdays only by arrangement with the Secretary. Professional: Ray Gadd (0705 464491). Secretary: R.C.W. Stokes (0705 464446).

LEE-ON-THE-SOLENT. **Lee-On-The-Solent Golf Club,** Brune Lane, Lee-on-the-Solent PO13 9PB (0750 550207). *Location:* M27 Exit 9, three miles south of Fareham on the B3385 then signposted. Flat parkland course. 18 holes, 5959 yards. S.S.S. 69. Practice range. *Green Fees:* weekdays £21.00; weekends £26.00. *Eating facilities:* catering and bar. *Visitors:* welcome weekdays, Handicap Certificate required. *Society Meetings:* Thursdays and Fridays by arrangement. Professional: Mr. John Richardson (0705 551181). Secretary: R. Evans (0705 551170).

LIPHOOK. **Liphook Golf Club,** Wheatsheaf Enclosure, Liphook GU30 7EH (Liphook (0428) 723271). *Location:* one mile south of Liphook off the old A3 Portsmouth road. Heathland. 18 holes, 6250 yards. S.S.S. 70. *Green Fees:* on application. *Eating facilities:* bar and restaurant. *Visitors:* welcome, Handicap Certificate required, check with Secretary. *Society Meetings:* catered for. Professional: Ian Large (0428 723271). Secretary: Major J.B. Morgan MBE (0428 723785).

LIPHOOK. **Old Thorns Golf Course and Hotel,** Longmoor Road, Liphook GU30 7PE (Liphook (0428) 724555). *Location:* A3 to Griggs Green exit then 500 yards. Parkland, wooded, with natural streams and lakes. 18 holes, 6529 yards. S.S.S. 72. Practice ground and putting green. *Green Fees:* £24.00 per round, £42.00 per weekday. £40.00 per round weekends. Telephone to arrange a starting time. *Eating facilities:* full catering available. Choice of European or Japanese cuisine. *Visitors:* welcome at all times. *Society Meetings:* welcome all week. Society Days £52.00. Company Days £65.00. Facilities: 33 en suite bedrooms, indoor heated swimming pool, sauna, solarium, massage, 2 tennis courts, conference and banqueting rooms. Professional: Philip Loxley. General Manager: G.M. Jones.

LYNDHURST. **Bramshaw Golf Club,** Brook, Lyndhurst (Soton (0703) 813433). *Location:* M27 (Inter-

KOSAIDO OLD THORNS
GOLF COURSE·HOTEL·RESTAURANTS

Griggs Green, Liphook, Hampshire. Telephone: Liphook (0428) 724555. *See Colour Advertisement on Page 26.*

AA **The Penny Farthing Hotel** RAC
Romsey Rd, Lyndhurst, Hampshire SO43 7AA
Tel: 0703 2884422 Fax: 0703 284488

Set in the heart of the New Forest this tastefully refurbished hotel offers ensuite, colour TV and tea/coffee facilities. Only a minute's walk from Lyndhurst High Street's charming selection of shops and restaurants. We also provide a large car park, licensed bar and residents lounge.
Call for a brochure and tariff.

THE GOLF GUIDE 1994   England HAMPSHIRE

change 1) one mile from M27 (north) at Brook. Two courses: one parkland, one woodland. Both 18 holes. Forest Course 5774 yards. S.S.S. 68. Manor Course 6233 yards. S.S.S. 70. Practice facilities. *Green Fees:* £30.00 weekdays, weekends with member only or Bell Inn Hotel guest. *Eating facilities:* clubhouse and restaurant, also Bell Inn close by. *Visitors:* welcome Monday to Friday. No visitors at weekends unless playing with a member or Bell Inn resident. Accommodation in 22 bedroomed hotel. *Society Meetings:* catered for by arrangement. Professional: Clive Bonner (0703 813434). General Manager: Bob Tingey (0703 813433).

LYNDHURST. **New Forest Golf Club,** Southampton Road, Lyndhurst SO43 7BU (0703 282752). *Location:* on the A35 between Ashurst and Lyndhurst. Forest heathland course. 18 holes, 5742 yards. S.S.S. 68. Practice area and net. *Green Fees:* weekdays £12.00; weekends and Bank Holidays £14.00. *Eating facilities:* bar and lounge, dining room, garden. *Visitors:* welcome, weekdays after 9am, Saturdays after 10am and Sundays after 2.30pm. *Society Meetings:* advance booking only; maximum number of 24. Professional: Mr Ken Gilhespy (0703 282752). Secretary: Mrs W. Swann (0703 282752).

PETERSFIELD. **Petersfield Golf Club,** Heath Road, Petersfield GU31 4EJ (Petersfield (0730) 263725). *Location:* turn off A3 in town centre, clubhouse one mile east. Heathland and parkland. 18 holes, 5649 yards. S.S.S. 67. *Green Fees:* £15.00 weekdays, £21.00 weekends. *Eating facilities:* available Tuesday to Saturday. *Visitors:* welcome weekdays, also Saturday and Sunday afternoon. *Society Meetings:* welcome except at weekends. Professional: Greg Hughes (0730 267732). Secretary: Neil Garfoot (0730 262386; Fax: 0730 262386).

PORTSMOUTH. **Great Salterns Municipal Golf Course,** Burrfields Road, Portsmouth PO3 5HH. *Location:* south on A2030 off M27 signposted "Southsea". Flat links course. 18 holes, 5894 yards. S S.S. 68. Floodlit driving range. *Green Fees:* summer £9.40, winter £6.90. Senior Citizens/Under 18's summer £5.70, winter £4.20. *Eating facilities:* full bar and catering service at Farmhouse Pub next door. *Visitors:* always welcome, tee time booking required, phone day in advance. *Society Meetings:* welcome. Professional: Terry Healy (0705 664549; Fax: 0705 650525).

PORTSMOUTH. **Portsmouth Golf Club (1926),** Crookhorn Lane, Widley, Portsmouth PO7 5QL (0705 375999). *Location:* two thirds of a mile from junction of B2177 and A3. Hilly course with good views. 18 holes, 6139 yards. S.S.S. 69. Practice area. *Green Fees:* £9.40. *Eating facilities:* full restaurant and bar. *Visitors:* welcome, tee bookings required. *Society Meetings:* welcome by prior arrangement with Pro Shop. Professional: Ian Roper (0705 372210; Fax: 0705 200766). Secretary: D. Houlihan (0705 201827).

PORTSMOUTH. **Southsea Golf Club,** Eastern Road, Portsmouth. *Location:* half a mile from M27 exit A2030 Southsea. Plays over Great Salterns Golf Course. Flat parkland. 18 holes, 6050 yards. S.S.S. 68. Floodlit golf driving range. *Green Fees:* information not provided. *Eating facilities:* at adjacent farmhouse bar/restaurant. *Visitors:* welcome – public course. Professional: Terry Healy (0705 690816). Secretary: K. Parker (0705 812435).

PORTSMOUTH. **Waterlooville Golf Club,** Cherry Tree Avenue, Cowplain, Waterlooville PO8 8AP. *Location:* off A3 or A3 (M), 10 miles north of Portsmouth. Parkland course. 18 holes, 6647 yards. S.S.S. 72. *Green Fees:* £20.00 per round, £30.00 per day, weekdays only. *Eating facilities:* full catering service available, bar facilities. *Visitors:* welcome weekdays, weekends as members' guests only. *Society Meetings:* catered for by prior arrangement. Professional: John Hay (0705 256911). Secretary: Mr C. Chamberlain (Tel & Fax: 0705 263388).

RINGWOOD. **Burley Golf Club,** Cott Lane, Burley, Ringwood BH24 4BB (Burley (0425) 403737). *Location:* A31 from Ringwood and turn right at Picket Post and on through Burley Street. Heathland course, 9 holes, 6149 yards. S.S.S. 69. *Green Fees:* weekdays £13.00, weekends £15.00. Under 18's half price. *Visitors:* welcome, but not before 4pm Saturdays and 1.45pm Wednesdays. *Society Meetings:* not catered for. Secretary: Major G.R. Kendall (0425 402431).

RINGWOOD. **Moors Valley Golf Centre,** Horton Road, Ashley Heath, Ringwood BH24 2ET. *Location:* signposted from A338/A31 roundabout. Public heathland course. 18 holes, 6270 yards. S.S.S. 72. 14 bay floodlit driving range. *Green Fees:* weekdays £5.00 9 holes, £8.50 18 holes; weekends £6.00 9 holes, £11.00 18 holes. Youth rates available. *Eating facilities:* snack bar and bar. *Visitors:* welcome. *Society Meetings:* welcome by arrangement. Professional: Michael Torrens (Tel & Fax: 0425 479776).

ROMSEY. **Dunwood Manor Golf Club,** Shootash Hill, Near Romsey SO51 0GF (0794 40549). *Location:* four miles from Romsey off A27. Undulating parkland. 18 holes, 6004 yards. S.S.S. 69. Practice area. *Green Fees:* £20.00 round, £30.00 day weekdays; £30.00 per round weekends. Society rates from £28.00. *Eating facilities:* full catering, all day bar. *Visitors:* welcome, by arrangement. *Society Meetings:* welcome, by arrangement. Professional: Richard Pilbury (0794 40663). Secretary: Hazel Johnson (0794 40549; Fax: 0794 41215).

SHEDFIELD. **Meon Valley Hotel, Golf and Country Club,** Sandy Lane, Shedfield SO3 2HQ (0329 833455; Fax: 0329 834411). *Location:* leave M27 at exit 7, take A334 to Botley then towards Wickham. Sandy Lane is 2 miles on the left. Wooded course. 18 holes, 6519 yards. S.S.S. 71. 9 holes, 2714 yards. S.S.S. 34. *Green Fees:* weekdays £24.00 per round; weekends £30.00. *Eating facilities:* Treetops Restaurant, poolside grillroom and three bars. *Visitors:* welcome, no restrictions. Handicap Certificates required to play. *Society Meetings:* catered for. Professional: Mr John Stirling (0329 832184). Secretary: Mr George McMenemy.

SOUTHAMPTON. **Botley Park Golf Club,** Winchester Road, Botley, Southampton SO3 2UA (0489 780888; Fax: 0489 789242). *Location:* approximately

HAMPSHIRE/HEREFORD & WORCESTER England

two miles from Junction 7 on M27. Parkland. 18 holes, 5714 yards. S.S.S. 69. Driving range. *Green Fees:* £23.00. *Eating facilities:* two bars, main restaurant and club lounge. *Visitors:* welcome by prior booking by phone. Handicap Certificate required. 100 bedroomed hotel on site; tennis, squash, swimming, sauna, solarium, steam room, fitness suite, snooker. *Society Meetings:* Wednesdays and Thursdays only. Professional: Tim Barter. Secretary: Keith Pearson.

SOUTHAMPTON. **Corhampton Golf Club,** Sheeps Pond Lane, Droxford, Southampton SO3 1QZ (Droxford (0489) 877279). *Location:* one mile from Corhampton on the Bishops Waltham – Corhampton road (B3135). 18 holes, 6088 yards. S.S.S. 69. *Green Fees:* weekdays £20.00 per round, £28.00 per day; weekends £10.00 with a member only. *Eating facilities:* full catering, except Tuesdays. *Visitors:* welcome Monday to Friday; weekends and Bank Holidays with a member. *Society Meetings:* Mondays and Thursdays. Professional: Garry Stubbington (0489 877638). Secretary: P. Taylor (0489 877279). Steward: J. Smith (0489 878749).

SOUTHAMPTON. **Stoneham Golf Club,** Bassett Green Road, Bassett, Southampton SO2 3NE (Southampton (0703) 768151; Fax: 0703 769272). *Location:* A33/M27 north of Southampton find Chilworth roundabout, take road to Airport (A27), half mile on left. Hilly heathery course. 18 holes, 6310 yards.

S.S.S. 70. *Green Fees:* £27.00 per round or day; weekends £30.00. Telephone re availability. *Eating facilities:* full catering, bar open all day. *Visitors:* welcome, except competition days. *Society Meetings:* catered for. Professional: Ian Young (0703 768397). Secretary: Mrs. A. M. Wilkinson (0703 769272).

WINCHESTER. **Hockley Golf Club,** Twyford, Near Winchester SO21 1PL (Winchester (0962) 713461). *Location:* on A333 (Twyford road), two miles south east of Winchester off M3. Parkland course. 18 holes, 6279 yards. S.S.S. 70. Practice areas. *Green Fees:* £25.00 per day or round. *Eating facilities:* restaurant and bar available. *Visitors:* welcome weekdays, weekends with members only. Check first with Professional. *Society Meetings:* welcome, catered for Wednesdays only. Professional: Terry Lane (0962 713678). Secretary: J.R. Digby (0962 713165).

WINCHESTER. **Royal Winchester Golf Club,** Sarum Road, Winchester SO22 5QE (Winchester (0962) 851694). *Location:* exit Winchester on Romsey Road, Hospital on left, right at roundabout, first left into Sarum Road. Downland. 18 holes, 6212 metres. S.S.S. 70. *Green Fees:* weekdays £26.00. Weekends with member only. *Eating facilities:* full catering available. *Visitors:* welcome weekdays, Handicap Certificate required. *Society Meetings:* by prior arrangement. Professional: Steven A. Hunter (0962 862473). Secretary: D.P. Williams (0962 852462).

Hereford & Worcester

BELMONT. **Belmont Lodge and Golf Course,** Belmont, Hereford HR2 9SA (0432 352666; Fax: 0432 358090). *Location:* 15 miles south of Hereford. Parkland running alongside the River Wye. 18 holes, 6500 yards. S.S.S. 71. *Green Fees:* weekdays £14.00 per round, £24.00 per day, £7.00 twilight ticket; weekends £18.00 per round, £28.00 per day, £12.00 twilight ticket. *Eating facilities:* restaurant and bar (snacks). *Visitors:* welcome at all times. 30 bedroomed hotel – bowls, snooker, tennis, fishing, meeting rooms. *Society Meetings:* catered for. Professional: Mike Welsh (0432 352717).

BEWDLEY. **Little Lakes Golf Club,** Lye Head, Bewdley, Worcester (Rock (0299) 266385). *Location:* two miles west of Bewdley off A456, turn left opposite Alton Glasshouses. 9 holes, 6247 yards. S.S.S. 72. *Green Fees:* weekdays £15.00 per round, £18.00 per day, weekends only by invitation of a member. *Eating facilities:* full restaurant service. *Visitors:* no restrictions weekdays. *Societies:* welcome by prior arrangement. Professional: M. Laing. Secretary: R.A. Norris (0502 67495).

BLACKWELL. **Blackwell Golf Club,** Blackwell, Near Bromsgrove B60 1PY (021-445 1470). *Location:* approximately 10 miles south of Birmingham and three miles east of Bromsgrove. Parkland. 18 holes, 6202

yards. S.S.S. 71. *Green Fees:* £36.00 per day. *Eating facilities:* full catering by prior arrangement. *Visitors:* welcome Monday to Friday without reservation. *Society Meetings:* catered for by arrangement through Secretary. Professional: N. Blake (021-445 3113). Secretary: R.W.A. Burns (021-445 1994).

BLAKEDOWN. **Churchill and Blakedown Golf Club,** Churchill Lane, Blakedown, Near Kidderminster DY10 3NB (Kidderminster (0562) 700200). *Location:* off A456 Birmingham/Kidderminster road at Blakedown. Elevated, hilly parkland, partially wooded course. 9 holes, 6472 yards. S.S.S. 71. *Green Fees:* £15.00 weekdays. *Eating facilities:* snacks and full meals except Monday. *Visitors:* welcome with reservation. Weekends with member only. *Society Meetings:* weekdays only by arrangement through the Hon. Secretary. Professional: Mr Keith Wheeler (0562 700454). Secretary: (0562 700018).

BRANSFORD. **Bransford Golf Club,** Bank House Hotel, Bransford WR6 5JD. *Location:* on A4103 Hereford Road, four miles south west of Worcester, at Bank House Hotel. Flat, undulating course incorporating 14 lakes – "Florida" style course – island greens, etc. 18 holes, 6175 yards. S.S.S. 69. 20 bay floodlit driving range. *Green Fees:* weekdays £15.00 per 18 holes; weekends £15.00 or £20.00 for day. *Eating facilities:* available in Bank House Hotel. *Visitors:*

THE GOLF GUIDE 1994   *England*   HEREFORD & WORCESTER

welcome after 10am. Handicap Certificates required. Smart golf attire. Accommodation in hotel. *Society Meetings:* welcome after 9.30am – accommodation and meals available. Professional: Graham Hawkings (0886 833621). Secretary: Patrick A.D. Holmes (0886 833551; Fax: 0886 832461).

BROMYARD near. **Sapey Golf Club**, Upper Sapey, Worcester WR6 6XT (08867 288; Fax: 08867 485). *Location:* situated six miles north of Bromyard on B4203. Parkland course with trees, ditches and water; outstanding views over Malvern Hills. 18 holes, 5885 yards. S.S.S. 69. Driving range. *Green Fees:* weekdays £15.00; weekends £20.00. *Eating facilities:* bar and restaurant meals available Wednesday to Sunday. *Visitors:* always welcome. *Society Meetings:* catered for Wednesdays to Sundays. Professional: Chris Knowles. Secretary: Shirley Dykes.

DROITWICH. **Droitwich Golf and Country Club Ltd**, Westford House, Ford Lane, Droitwich WR9 0BQ (Droitwich (0905) 770129). *Location:* between Junction 5 of M5 and Droitwich just off A38. Parkland – undulating – wooded. 18 holes, 6040 yards. S.S.S. 69. Practice area. *Green Fees:* £24.00 weekdays, with a member £8.00; £10.00 weekends playing with a member only. *Eating facilities:* full catering available. *Visitors:* welcome without reservation Mondays to Fridays, weekends with member only. *Society Meetings:* catered for Wednesdays or Fridays. Professional: C.S. Thompson (0905 770207). Secretary: M.J. Taylor (0905 774344).

DROITWICH near. **Ombersley Golf Club**, Bishops Wood Road, Lineholt, Ombersley, Near Droitwich WR9 0LE (0905 620747; Fax: 0905 621016). *Location:* A449. High undulating course above the Severn Valley. 18 holes, 6289 yards. S.S.S. 68. Practice range £1.40 per 40 balls. *Green Fees:* £9.60 weekdays (£7.00 veterans and Juniors); £12.80 weekends. *Eating facilities:* bar facilities, snacks and meals available. *Visitors:* all visitors welcome. *Society Meetings:* welcome by arrangement. Professional: Mr Graham Glenister. Secretary: Mr Robert Dowty.

EVESHAM. **Evesham Golf Club**, Craycombe Links, Fladbury Cross, Pershore WR10 2QS (Evesham (0386) 860395). *Location:* M5 at Junction 6, A4538 and B4084 to Evesham approximately 10 miles. Evesham take B4084 towards Worcester about three miles.

Meadowland, heavily bunkered, tree-lined fairways. 9 holes (18 tees), 6415 yards, 5866 metres. S.S.S. 71. Practice area. *Green Fees:* £15.00 or £7.00 per round if playing with member. *Eating facilities:* diningroom and bar, except Mondays. *Visitors:* must be members of recognised club and have a certified Handicap. On Tuesdays, Ladies' Day, play is not possible in Summer until after 3.15pm approx. *Society Meetings:* catered for by prior arrangement. Professional: Charles Haynes (0386 861144). Hon. Secretary: Frank G. Vincent (home 0386 552373). Steward: J.A. Webber.

HAGLEY. **Hagley Country Club Golf Club**, Wassell Grove, Hagley (Hagley (0562) 883701). *Location:* Wassell Grove is off A456 Birmingham to Kidderminster Road. 18 holes, 6353 yards. S.S.S. 72. *Green Fees:* £20.00 per round, £25.00 per day weekdays. *Eating facilities:* à la carte Restaurant and bar snacks, Tuesday to Saturday. *Visitors:* welcome. Society Meetings: welcome by prior arrangement. Professional: Iain Clark (0562 883852). Secretary: Graham F. Yardley.

HEREFORD. **Burghill Valley Golf Club**, Tillington Road, Burghill, Hereford HR4 7RW (Hereford [0432] 760456; Fax: 0432 760315). *Location:* three miles west of Hereford on minor road to Weobley. Pleasantly undulating parkland including two lakes, and easy walking with some interesting holes through mature cider orchards. 18 holes, 6239 yards. S.S.S. 70. Large practice area. *Green Fees:* weekdays £12.00; weekends £14.00. *Eating facilities:* bar and light refreshments. *Visitors:* welcome at any time, must book tee time at weekends. *Society Meetings:* by prior arrangement with the Professional. Professional: Tim Morgan PGA. Secretary: Mrs P. Barnett.

HEREFORD. **The Herefordshire Golf Club**, Ravens Causeway, Wormsley, Hereford HR4 8LY. *Location:* six miles north-west of Hereford on a B road to Weobley. Undulating parkland course. 18 holes, 6036 yards. S.S.S. 69. *Green Fees:* £14.00 per round, £20.00 per day weekdays; £18.00 per round, £26.00 per day weekends and Bank Holidays. As members' guests weekdays £9.00 per round, £15.00 per day; weekends £11.00 per round, £19.00 per day. *Eating facilities:* catering available, limited on Mondays. *Visitors:* welcome. *Society Meetings:* catered for. Early application advised, weekends restricted. Professional: David Hemming (0432 830465). Secretary: W.J. Bullock (0432 830219).

Hagley Country Club, Wassell Grove, Hagley, West Midlands DY9 9JW
Telephone: 0562 883701

HAGLEY COUNTRY CLUB

The Hagley Country Club, located in the hamlet of Wassell Grove, facing the beautiful Clent Hills is the ideal setting for that golfing day out. The 18 hole golf course is set in superb undulating countryside with woodland streams and a small lake; the course has been professionally landscaped to give golvers an interesting and challenging game. This is complemented by a well-furnished clubhouse which can cater for all your needs in comfort.

HEREFORD & WORCESTER *England*

KIDDERMINSTER. **Habberley Golf Club**, Habberley, Kidderminster DY11 5LG (0562 822381). *Location:* north west side of Kidderminster. Hilly parkland course. 9 holes, 5481 yards. S.S.S. 68. *Green Fees:* information not provided. *Eating facilities:* food and bar available. *Visitors:* welcome weekdays, without reservation; weekends with member only. *Society Meetings:* by negotiation. Secretary: Mr D.B. Lloyd (0562 745756).

KIDDERMINSTER. **Kidderminster Golf Club**, Russell Road, Kidderminster DY16 3HT (Kidderminster (0562) 822303). *Location:* signposted off A449 Worcester-Wolverhampton Road. Wooded parkland course. 18 holes, 6405 yards. S.S.S. 71. Practice ground. *Green Fees:* £22.00 weekdays. *Eating facilities:* bar and restaurant available. *Visitors:* welcome weekdays only if bona fide member of another club, weekends if guest of member. Snooker room with bar. *Society Meetings:* catered for Thursdays only. Professional: N.P. Underwood (0562 740090). Secretary: Alan Biggs (0562 822303; Fax: 0562 862041).

KINGTON. **Kington Golf Club**, Bradnor Hill, Kington (Kington (0544) 230340). *Location:* one mile out of Kington, on B4355 to Presteigne. Hill course, with views of seven counties. Highest 18 hole course in England and Wales. 18 holes, 5820 yards. S.S.S. 68. *Green Fees:* £13.00 per round, £16.00 per day weekdays; weekends and Bank Holidays £18.00 per round, £22.00 per day. *Eating facilities:* meals at club. *Visitors:* welcome. Please contact Professional to ensure course is available. *Society Meetings:* catered for by arrangement. Professional: Dean Oliver (0544 231320). Hon. Secretary: G.E. Long (0497 820542).

LEOMINSTER. **Leominster Golf Club**, Ford Bridge, Leominster HR6 0LE (Leominster (0568) 612863). *Location:* three miles south of Leominster on A49 bypass, clearly signed. Undulating parkland with some holes alongside River Lugg. 18 holes, 6045 yards. S.S.S. 69. Small practice area and putting green, driving range adjacent to course. *Green Fees:* weekdays £17.00 per day, weekends £21.00. *Eating facilities:* full bar and catering daily except Mondays. *Visitors:* welcome weekdays, weekends on checking with club Professional. *Society Meetings:* most welcome Tuesdays to Fridays inclusive, some weekends available by prior booking. £25.00 golf and catering. Professional: Gareth Bebb (0568 611402). Secretary: J.A. Ashcroft (0432 880493).

MALVERN WELLS. **The Worcestershire Golf Club**, Wood Farm, Malvern Wells WR14 4PP (Malvern (0684) 575992). *Location:* two miles south of Great Malvern, near junction of A449 and B4209. Exceptionally scenic – Malvern Hills and Vale of Evesham. 18 holes, 6449 yards. S.S.S. 71. *Green Fees:* £25.00 weekdays; £30.00 weekends. With member £10. Seven Day ticket £80. *Eating facilities:* available. *Visitors:* visitors unaccompanied by a member must provide evidence of Golf Club membership. Weekends after 10am. *Society Meetings:* catered for Thursdays and Fridays only on application. Professional: G.M. Harris (0684 564428). Secretary: G.R. Scott (0684 575992).

PERSHORE. **The Vale Golf and Country Club**, Hill Furze Road, Bishampton, Near Pershore WR10 2LZ (0386 82781; Fax: 0386 82597). *Location:* off the B4084 Evesham to Worcester road, Fladbury crossroads. Feature lakes and wooded surrounds. Two courses: 1: The Lenches, 9 holes, 2628 to 2918 yards. S.S.S 66 to 68. 2: The International Championship Course, 18 holes, 7114 yards. S.S.S. 74. Driving range. *Green Fees:* weekdays £18.00 International, £6.50 Lenches; weekends £24.00 International, £8.50 Lenches. Twilight fee on International £10.00 after 6pm. *Eating facilities:* Vale restaurant, spike bar, Sir William Lyons Suite. *Visitors:* welcome anytime on the Lenches, not before 10.30am weekends on International. *Society Meetings:* welcome any time, possible restriction at weekends. Professional: Caroline Griffiths (0386 82520; Fax: 0386 82660). General Manager: Robin Fischer.

REDDITCH. **Abbey Park Golf and Country Club**, Abbey Park, Dagnell End Road, Redditch B98 7BD (0527 63918; Fax: 0527 65872). *Location:* leave M42 at A435 Evesham – through Beoley towards Redditch (B4101) or off A441 Birmingham to Redditch. Parkland. 18 holes, 6411 yards, 5827 metres. S.S.S. 71. Driving range. *Green Fees:* weekdays £10.00; weekends £12.50. *Eating facilities:* restaurant and bars. *Visitors:* welcome, no restrictions. Booking advisable. 31 bedroomed hotel, leisure facilities including swimming pool. *Society Meetings:* welcome, including weekends. Professional: R.K. Cameron (0527 68006). Secretary: M.E. Bradley.

REDDITCH. **Redditch Golf Club**, Green Lane, Lower Grinsty, Callow Hill, Redditch B97 5PJ (Redditch (0527) 543309). *Location:* three miles west of Redditch town centre, off Redditch to Bromsgrove road (A448), or Astwood Bank to Redditch (A441), take Windmill Drive, look for Callow Hill signs. First 9 holes parkland, second 9 holes wooded. White – 18 holes, 6671 yards. S.S.S. 72; Yellow – 18 holes, 6285 yards. S.S.S. 70. Two practice areas. *Green Fees:* £27.50 weekdays; weekends £8.00 with member only. *Eating facilities:* restaurant and bar with bar snacks except Mondays. *Visitors:* welcome, weekends with member. *Society Meetings:* catered for by arrangement. Professional: Mr F. Powell (0527 546372). Secretary: Mr C. Holman.

ABBEY PARK GOLF & COUNTRY CLUB HOTEL
Abbey Park, Dagnell End Road, Redditch, Worcs.   Tel: 0527 584140   Fax: 0527 65872
Set in 230 acres of parkland, yet close to M42 motorway, Abbey Park provides the ideal leisure/conference venue. All bedrooms have private facilities and there is a Leisure Suite with swimming pool, spa bath, sauna, solarium, steam room and gymnasium. **There is also an 18-hole championship golf course.**
ALSO SEE OUR COLOUR ADVERTISEMENT ON PAGE 22

Rocks Place

Rocks Place, Yatton, Ross-on-Wye, Herefordshire HR9 7RD
Tel: 053 184 218 Fax: 053 184 460
Resident Proprietors: Peter & Mollie Cotton

Situated quarter-mile off A449 midway between Ross-on-Wye and Ledbury. Beautiful small hotel purposely designed from half-timbered 16th century barn. All en-suite. ♣♣♣ Licensed Restaurant.

21 courses within 25 mile radius.
Brochure with course locations on request.

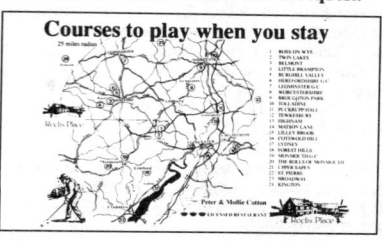

Courses to play when you stay

REDDITCH. **Redditch Kingfisher Golf Club,** Plymouth Road, Redditch (0527 541054). *Location:* bus station, traffic lights. Parkland, wooded course. 9 holes, 4527 yards. S.S.S. 62. Practice nets. *Green Fees:* weekdays £4.00 9 holes, £5.50 18 holes; weekends £4.50 9 holes, £6.50 18 holes. Senior Citizens £3.50 18 holes, £2.50 9 holes weekdays. *Eating facilities:* full catering and bar facilities. *Visitors:* welcome at all times. Showers/changing rooms. *Society Meetings:* welcome at all times. Professional: Mr David Stewart (0527 541054). Secretary: J.A. Pullen (0527 541043).

ROSS-ON-WYE. **Ross-on-Wye Golf Club,** Two Park, Gorsley, Ross-on-Wye HR9 7UT (098982 457). *Location:* adjacent Junction 3 M50, five miles north of Ross-on-Wye. Parkland course. 18 holes, 6500 yards. S.S.S. 73. Large and small practice areas. *Green Fees:* weekdays £25.00; weekends £30.00. *Eating facilities:* full catering, restaurant. *Visitors:* welcome any day if prior arrangement made with Professional or Secretary. Snooker tables (2). *Society Meetings:* welcome Wednesdays to Fridays. Professional: Nick Catchpole (098982 439). Secretary: G.H. Cason (098982 267).

WORCESTER. **Tolladine Golf Club,** The Fairway, Tolladine Road, Worcester WR4 9BA (Worcester (0905) 21074). *Location:* M5, exit 6. Warndon turn off, one mile. Hilly course. 9 holes, 5630 yards (for 18 holes). S.S.S. 67. *Green Fees:* £12.00 weekdays, £5.00 with member; £6.00 weekends with member only. *Eating facilities:* bar (limited opening). *Visitors:* welcome weekdays, not after 2pm Wednesdays. *Society Meetings:* welcome Mondays. Golf Shop: (0905 726180). Secretary: K.T. Reveley (0905 27416).

WORCESTER. **Worcester Golf and Country Club,** Boughton Park, Worcester WR2 4EZ (Worcester (0905) 421132). *Location:* one-and-a-quarter miles west of city on A4103 (to Hereford). Parkland. 18 holes, 5946 yards. S.S.S. 68. Practice ground. *Green Fees:* £23.00 per weekday. Weekends only with a member. *Eating facilities:* full catering available. *Visitors:* welcome weekdays. Handicap Certificate required. *Society Meetings:* catered for. Professional: Colin Colenso (0905 422044). Secretary: J.M. Kennedy (0905 422555). Caterer: Mrs M. Frutos.

WYTHALL. **Fulford Heath Golf Club Ltd,** Tanners Green Lane, Wythall (Wythall (0564) 822806). *Location:* one mile from Alcester Road, via Tanners Green Lane. 18 holes, 6216 yards. S.S.S. 70. *Green Fees:* weekdays £25.00 (Societies £20). *Eating facilities:* available. *Visitors:* welcome weekdays with reservation, not at weekends and Bank Holidays. *Society Meetings:* catered for on application. Professional: Mr. K. Hayward (0564 822730). Secretary: R. Bowen (0564 824758).

Hertfordshire

HADLEY WOOD GOLF CLUB

★ Visitors & Societies Welcome
★ Beautiful 18 Hole Course
★ Splendid Georgian Club House
★ Renowned for Catering
★ Limited Sunday Green Fees
★ Professional Shop/Coaching

Beech Hill, Near Barnet, Hertfordshire EN4 0JJ Tel: 081-449 4328
See entry under BARNET for full details.

HERTFORDSHIRE England

BARNET. **Arkley Golf Club,** Rowley Green Road, Barnet EN5 3HL (081-449 0394). *Location:* A1 from London, turn by Elstree Moat House, two miles from Barnet. Parkland. 9 holes, 6045 yards. S.S.S. 69. *Green Fees:* weekdays £20.00 per round or £25.00 day; weekends with a member only. *Eating facilities:* available, no catering Mondays. *Visitors:* welcome weekdays, please phone, weekends with member only. *Society Meetings:* catered for Wednesdays, Thursdays and Fridays. Professional: M. Squire (081-440 8473). Secretary: G.D. Taylor (081-499 0394).

BARNET. **Hadley Wood Golf Club,** Beech Hill, Near Barnet (081-449 4328). *Location:* off the exit from M25 at Junction 24 on to A111 Cockfosters. Down hill, third turning on the right. Very attractive undulating parkland with lakes. 18 holes, 6473 yards. S.S.S. 71. Two practice areas and putting area. *Green Fees:* on application. *Eating facilities:* available weekdays. *Visitors:* welcome weekdays, (not Tuesday a.m.), with club Handicap Certificate or letter of introduction. *Society Meetings:* catered for weekdays except Tuesday mornings. Professional: Peter Jones (081-449 3285). Secretary/General Manager: P.S. Bryan (Fax: 081-364 8633).

BERKHAMSTED. **Ashridge Golf Club,** Little Gaddesden, Berkhamsted (044284 2244). *Location:* five miles north west of Berkhamsted. 18 holes, 6547 yards. S.S.S. 72. *Green Fees:* on application. *Eating facilities:* daily. *Visitors:* welcome with reservation. Professional: Geoffrey Pook. Secretary: Mrs Maggie West.

BERKHAMSTED. **Berkhamsted Golf Club,** The Common, Berkhamsted HP4 2QB (Berkhamsted (0442) 863730). *Location:* A41 to Berkhamsted, up past the castle to the common. Heathland, wooded, grass bunkers. 18 holes, 6605 yards. S.S.S. 72. Two practice grounds. *Green Fees:* weekdays £20.00 per round, £35.00 per day; weekends £35.00 per day. *Eating facilities:* daily although limited on Mondays. *Visitors:* welcome most days by reservation. Handicap Certificate required. *Society Meetings:* catered for Wednesdays and Fridays (maximum 45). Professional: B.J. Proudfoot (0442 865851). Secretary: Colin Hextall (0442 865832).

BISHOP'S STORTFORD. **Bishop's Stortford Golf Club,** Dunmow Road, Bishop's Stortford CM23 5HP (Bishop's Stortford (0279) 654027). *Location:* M11 Junction 8, follow signs for Bishop's Stortford, after third (mini) roundabout entrance about half a mile on left hand side of road. Parkland. 18 holes, 6440 yards. S.S.S. 71. *Green Fees:* weekdays £21.00, with a member £10.50; weekends £16.00 (with full member only). *Eating facilities:* restaurant and bar meals. *Visitors:* welcome weekdays; weekends and Public Holidays with member only. *Society Meetings:* catered for weekdays except Tuesdays (minimum 15, maximum 40). Professional: Vince Duncan (0279 651324). Secretary: Major C. Rolls (0279 654715).

BUNTINGFORD. **East Herts Golf Club Ltd,** Hamels Park, Buntingford SG9 9NA (Ware (0920) 821978). *Location:* one mile north of Puckeridge on A10. 18 holes, 6416 yards. S.S.S. 71. *Green Fees:* details on application. *Eating facilities:* separate restaurant. *Visitors:* welcome, with members only at weekends. *Society Meetings:* catered for weekdays. Professional: J. Hamilton (0920 821922). Secretary: G.N. Taylor (Fax: 0920 821978).

BUSHEY. **Bushey Hall Golf Club,** Bushey Hall Drive, Bushey WD2 2EP (Watford (0923) 229759). *Location:* Bushey Hall Road, Aldenham Road roundabout, one mile from M1. Parkland. 18 holes, 6099 yards. S.S.S. 69. *Green Fees:* weekdays £21.00; weekends £13.50 with member only. *Eating facilities:* full catering available, two bars. *Visitors:* welcome weekdays with Handicap Certificate. *Society Meetings:* catered for Monday, Tuesday, Thurday and Friday. Professional: D. Fitzsimmons (0923 222253). Secretary: Colin M. Brown (0923 225802).

BUSHEY HEATH. **Hartsbourne Golf and Country Club,** Hartsbourne Avenue, Bushey Heath WD2 1JW. *Location:* five miles south east of Watford. Parkland. 18 holes, 6305 yards. S.S.S. 70. 9 holes, 5342 yards. S.S.S. 66. *Green Fees:* information not supplied. *Eating facilities:* restaurant and snack bar available. *Visitors:* guests of members only. *Society Meetings:* catered for Mondays and Fridays. Professionals: Geoff Hunt and Martin Hattam (081-950 2836). Secretary: David J. Woodman (081-950 1133 or 4346).

CHORLEYWOOD. **Chorleywood Golf Club Ltd.,** Common Road, Chorleywood WD3 5LN (Chorleywood (0923) 282009). *Location:* half a mile off A404, three miles from Rickmansworth. Flat common land with woods. 9 holes, 5676 yards. S.S.S. 67. *Green Fees:* £14.00 weekdays, £17.50 weekends. *Eating facilities:* meals served if ordered by phone. *Visitors:* welcome weekdays except Tuesday and Thursday mornings, restricted at weekends. Secretary: R.M. Lennard.

DAGNALL. **Whipsnade Park Golf Club,** Studham Lane, Dagnall HP4 1RH (Little Gaddesden (044-284) 2330/2331; Fax: 044-284 2090). *Location:* between Dagnall and Studham. Junction 11 M1 (from north), Junction 9 (from south). Parkland. 18 holes, 6800 yards. S.S.S. 72. Large practice area. *Green Fees:* £20.00 per round, £30.00 per day weekdays, weekends with member only. *Eating facilities:* restaurant open daily, 2 bars. *Visitors:* welcome weekdays with reservation. *Society Meetings:* welcome with reservation. Professional: Mike Lewendon (044-284 2310). Secretary: Andrea King (044-284 2330).

GRAVELEY. **Chesfield Downs Family Golf Centre,** Jack's Hill, Graveley, Near Hitchin SG4 7EQ (0462 482929). *Location:* just off Junction 8 of the A1 (M), approximately two miles along the B197. Inland links/downland. Two Courses: Chesfield Downs – 18 holes, 6630 yards. S.S.S. 72. Par 71. Lannock Links – 9 holes, 975 yards. S.S.S. 27. 25 bay floodlit driving range, putting green. *Green Fees:* weekdays £12.25 (£3.50 for 9 hole course); weekends £17.50 (£4.50). Special rates for over 50's every Monday and Tuesday 10am to 1pm. *Eating facilities:* "Chesfields Restaurant and Bar". *Visitors:* welcome, advance booking system available to reserve tee-off times. Golf Superstore, Golf

THE CHESFIELD DOWNS
A FAMILY GOLF CENTRE

VISITORS WELCOME
Open Daily from 7.00 a.m. – 11.00 p.m.

- Superb 18 hole Chesfield Downs Course.
- 9 hole Lannock Links Course.
- 25 Bay floodlit, covered Driving Range, equipped with top grade two-piece range balls and superior quality practice mats.
- Well stocked Family Golf Superstore. Huge Choice – Competitive Prices – Expert Advice.
- The Family Golf Academy, featuring individual and group tuition from our team of Professionals.
- Hire Clubs available.
- Chesfields Restaurant & Bar.
- 18 Hole Putting Green.
- Purpose built and well designed modern Clubhouse, including changing facilities and a fully equipped Function Room.
- Golf Societies and Corporate Golf Days available.
- Specialist Repair Centre.
- Creche and Adventure Playground.

☎ 0462 482929

The Chesfield Downs F.G.C.
Jack's Hill
Graveley
Herts
SG4 7EQ

FAX: 0462 482930

HERTFORDSHIRE England

Academy, changing facilities, creche/playground. *Society Meetings:* catered for by arrangement. Professional: Beverly Huke. Secretary: David C.M. Carter.

HARPENDEN. **Harpenden Golf Club,** Hammonds End, Redbourn Lane, Harpenden (Harpenden (0582) 712580). *Location:* turn off A1081, four miles after St. Albans on B487. Parkland course. 18 holes, 6363 yards. S.S.S. 70. *Green Fees:* £30 per day. *Eating facilities:* lunches at club, order in advance. *Visitors:* welcome by arrangement. *Society Meetings:* by arrangement only. Professional: Doug Smith. Secretary: J.R. Newton.

HARPENDEN. **Harpenden Common Golf Club,** East Common, Harpenden AL5 1BL (0582 712856). *Location:* on A1081 between Harpenden and St. Albans. Flat heathland. 18 holes, 5613 yards, 5133 metres. S.S.S. 67. *Green Fees:* weekdays £20.00 per round, £25.00 per day; weekends £25.00 per day. *Eating facilities:* bar and restaurant daily. *Visitors:* welcome weekdays only with reservation (not Tuesdays). Weekends with member only. *Society Meetings:* Thursday and Friday only. Professional: B. Puttick (0582 460655). Secretary: R.D. Parry (0582 715959). Fax: 0582 715959).

HATFIELD. **Brookmans Park Golf Club,** Golf Club Road, Brookmans Park, Hatfield AL9 7AT (Potters Bar (0707) 652459). *Location:* between A1 and A1000, also just off M25, exit for Potters Bar. Parkland. 18 holes, 6454 yards, 5901 metres. S.S.S. 71. Practice ground and putting green. *Green Fees:* weekdays £27.00 per round, £32.00 per day. Handicap Certificate required. *Eating facilities:* bar snacks and lunches weekdays. *Visitors:* welcome weekdays; weekends with member only. *Society Meetings:* catered for Wednesdays and Thursdays. Professionals: M.M.R. Plumbridge and I. Jelley (0707 652468). Secretary: P.A. Gill (0707 652487; Fax: 0707 661851).

HATFIELD. **Hatfield London Country Club,** Bedwell Park, Essendon, Hatfield AL9 6JA (0707 642624 or 442626). *Location:* four miles south of Junction 4 A1(M), five miles north east of Junction 24 M25 Potters Bar. 18 holes, 6385 yards, Par 72. 9 holes Pitch and Putt. *Green Fees:* from £14.00. *Eating facilities:* lunch except Mondays. *Visitors:* welcome, advance bookings only. Tennis courts. *Society Meetings:* catered for. Professional: Norman Greer.

HEMEL HEMPSTEAD. **Boxmoor Golf Club,** 18 Box Lane, Boxmoor, Hemel Hempstead HP1 1DZ (Hemel Hempstead (0442) 242434). *Location:* two miles from Hemel Hempstead, three-quarters of a mile from Hemel Hempstead Station on A41. Hilly/moorland course, 9 holes, 4112 yards. S.S.S. 62. *Green Fees:* £10.00 weekdays; £15.00 weekends. Half fee if playing with member. *Eating facilities:* ring Steward. *Visitors:* welcome without reservation, except on Sundays. *Society Meetings:* catered for on application. Secretary: E. Duell.

HEMEL HEMPSTEAD. **Little Hay Golf Complex,** Box Lane, Bovingdon, Hemel Hempstead HP3 0DQ (0442 833783). *Location:* just off A41, along Chesham Road from Hemel Hempstead. 18 holes, 6678 yards.

THE GOLF GUIDE 1994

S.S.S. 72. 9 hole pitch & putt course, 18 hole putting green, floodlit driving range. *Green Fees:* information not provided. *Eating facilities:* open from 8am to 10pm seven days a week. *Visitors:* all members of the public welcome. *Society meetings:* made most welcome, special rates. Professional: David Johnson and Stephen Proudfoot (0442 833798). Director of Golf: David Johnson (0442 833798).

HERTFORD. **Brickendon Grange Golf and Country Club,** Brickendon, Near Hertford SG13 8PD (0992 511411). *Location:* three miles south of Hertford, one mile from Bayford Railway Station. Undulating parkland with specimen trees. 18 holes, 6315 yards. S.S.S. 70. Excellent practice area. *Green Fees:* weekdays £30.00 day ticket, £24.00 per round. *Eating facilities:* bar and restaurant, snack meals available lunchtimes. *Visitors:* welcome weekdays only. Handicap Certificate required. *Society Meetings:* catered for by arrangement. Professional: J. Hamilton (0992 511218). Secretary: C.T. MacDonald (0992 511258).

KNEBWORTH. **Knebworth Golf Club,** Deards End Lane, Knebworth SG3 6NL (Stevenage (0438) 814681). *Location:* one mile south of Stevenage. Parkland. 18 holes, 6492 yards. S.S.S. 71. *Green Fees:* details on application. *Eating facilities:* available. *Visitors:* welcome (with members only at weekends). *Society Meetings:* welcome Mondays, Tuesdays and Thursdays only. Professional: R.Y. Mitchell (0438 812757). Secretary: J.C. Wright (0438 812752).

LETCHWORTH. **Letchworth Golf Club,** Letchworth Lane, Letchworth SG6 3NQ. *Location:* two miles from A1 (M) near village of Willian, adjacent to Letchworth Hall Hotel. Parkland course. 18 holes, 6181 yards. S.S.S. 69. Practice ground. *Green Fees:* weekdays £23.50 per round, £32.50 per day; weekend accompanied only. Special rates Mondays – £12.00 per round, £20.00 per day. *Eating facilities:* bars and restaurant except Mondays. *Visitors:* weekdays Handicap Certificate required, weekends accompanied only. *Society Meetings:* catered for Wednesdays, Thursdays and Fridays. Professional: John Mutimer (0462 682713). Secretary: A.R. Bailey (0462 683203).

POTTERS BAR. **Potters Bar Golf Club,** Darkes Lane, Potters Bar EN6 1DF (0707 652020; Fax: 0707 655051). *Location:* one mile north of M25 exit 24 signposted Potters Bar, turn right at second traffic lights, club on left at end of shopping centre. Parkland course, well wooded, undulating, with streams. 18 holes, 6279 yards. S.S.S. 71. Small practice ground. *Green Fees:* weekdays £18.00 per round, £27.50 per day; weekends with member only. *Eating facilities:* luncheons and bar available from 11.30am. *Visitors:* weekdays only, must produce valid Handicap Certificate. *Society Meetings:* Mondays/Tuesdays/Fridays only. Professional: Kevin Hughes (0707 652987). Secretary: Arthur Williams (0707 652020).

RADLETT. **Porters Park Golf Club,** Shenley Hill, Radlett WD7 7AZ (0923 856262). *Location:* approximately 3 miles south west of Junction 22 (M25), 3 miles north-east Junction 5 (M1), half a mile north of Radlett Station on Shenley Hill. Park-type course with fine trees and a brook. 18 holes, 6313 yards. S.S.S. 70. Two practice areas, putting. *Green Fees:* £28.00 per round, £42.00 per day. Societies £65 inclusive. *Eating facili-*

THE GOLF GUIDE 1994 — England HERTFORDSHIRE

ties: full diningroom and bar snack menus. *Visitors:* welcome weekdays if pre-booked, with members only at weekends and Bank Holidays. Handicap Certificate required. *Society Meetings:* catered for Wednesday and Thursday March to October only. Professional: David Gleeson (0923 854366). Manager: J.H. Roberts (0923 854127).

RICKMANSWORTH. **Moor Park Golf Club,** Moor Park, Rickmansworth WD3 1QN (0923 773146; Fax: 0923 777109). *Location:* A404 to Northwood Hills, Batchworth Heath. Course no. 1: 18 holes, 6695 yards. S.S.S. 72. Course no. 2: 18 holes, 5823 yards. S.S.S. 68. *Green Fees:* weekdays High Course – £30.00, West Course – £25.00; £50.00 per day for either. *Eating facilities:* full catering always available at club. *Visitors:* welcome on weekdays by prior arrangement, and on weekends with a member. Professional: L. Farmer (0923 774113). Secretary: J.A. Davies.

RICKMANSWORTH. **Rickmansworth Public Golf Course,** Moor Lane, Rickmansworth WD3 1QL (Rickmansworth (0923) 773163). *Location:* from town centre along A404 to Waterworks, left along B4504, then first right. Testing, undulating parkland course. 18 holes, 4500 yards, 4115 metres. S.S.S. 62. *Green Fees:* weekdays £8.00, Juniors and Senior Citizens £4.00; weekends £11.50 (subject to review). *Eating facilities:* bars, restaurant. *Visitors:* no restrictions. *Society Meetings:* catered for, contact Professional. Professional: Iain Duncan (0923 775278). Secretary: W.F. Stokes (0923 772948).

ROYSTON. **Royston Golf Club,** Baldock Road, Royston SG8 5BG (0763 242177). *Location:* alongside the A505 on right hand side when approaching from Baldock, clubhouse at top of hill before entering town. Links – undulating heathland. 18 holes, 6032 yards. S.S.S. 69 yellow, 67 white. Practice fairway. *Green Fees:* £20.00 weekdays; weekends with a member only £12.50. *Eating facilities:* lounge bar – 19th bar, diningroom and bar meals. *Visitors:* welcome weekdays; weekends only with member. *Society Meetings:* weekdays only, book through Secretary. Professional: M. Hatcher (0763 243476). Secretary: Mrs S. Morris (0763 242696).

SAWBRIDGEWORTH. **The Manor of Groves Golf and Country Club,** High Wych, Sawbridgeworth CM21 0LA (0279 722333; Fax: 0279 726972). *Loca-*

tion: one mile north of Harlow off the A1184. Parkland course. 18 holes, 6198 yards. S.S.S. 70. *Green Fees:* £16.00 weekdays; £20.00 Saturdays, £22.00 Sundays. *Eating facilities:* restaurant and bar. *Visitors:* welcome anytime weekdays, after 11am weekends. Must have Handicap Certificate or proficiency certificate. Accommodation available in our 35 bedroomed Hotel. *Society Meetings:* welcome anytime. Professionals: S. James and L. Jones. Secretary: S. Sharer.

ST. ALBANS. **Batchwood Hall Golf Club,** Batchwood Drive, St. Albans (St. Albans (0727) 833349). *Location:* north west corner of town. 18 holes, 6463 yards. S.S.S. 71. *Green Fees:* on application from Pro's shop. *Eating facilities:* bar meals. *Visitors:* welcome with reservation (0727 44250) except 0630 to 1000 hours weekends. *Society Meetings:* not catered for. Professional: J. Thomson (0727 52101). Secretary: B.R. Mercer (Tel & Fax: 0582 79 3215).

ST. ALBANS. **Mid-Herts Golf Club,** Gustard Wood, Wheathampstead, St. Albans (0582 833385). *Location:* B651, six miles north of St. Albans. Heathland, short and tight course. 18 holes, 6094 yards. S.S.S. 69. Course record 67. *Green Fees:* weekdays £21.00 per round; weekends and Bank Holidays with member only. *Eating facilities:* by arrangement. *Visitors:* welcome weekdays with reservation; Handicap Certificate required. *Society Meetings:* catered for by arrangement. Professional: N. Brown (0582 832788). Secretary: R.J.H. Jourdan (0582 832242).

ST. ALBANS. **Verulam Golf Club,** 226 London Road, St. Albans AL1 1JG (0727 839016). *Location:* M25/A1081 to St. Albans, near railway bridge over London Road (A1081). Easy walking parkland course. 18 holes, 6457 yards. S.S.S. 71. Practice nets/ground. *Green Fees:* Mondays £11.00 per round, £18.00 per day, rest of weekdays £20.00 per round, £26.00 per day; weekends with member only (£12.00). *Eating facilities:* bar snacks from 7.30am to close, other dining by prior arrangement. *Visitors:* welcome all day Mondays, rest of weekdays unintroduced with Handicap Certificate. *Society Meetings:* welcome by arrangement with Secretary Tuesdays, Thursdays and Fridays. Professional: Nick Burch (0727 861401). Secretary: A.R. Crichton-Smith (0727 853327; Fax: 0727 812201).

MANOR OF GROVES GOLF CLUB & COUNTRY MANOR HOTEL
High Wych, Sawbridgeworth, Hertfordshire CM21 0LA Tel: (0279) 722333 Fax: (0279) 726972

Attractive parkland and meadowland 18-hole golf course adjoining luxury 32 bedroom Georgian Manor hotel. All bedrooms have ensuite marble bathrooms. The Colonnade Restaurant and glassed loggia overlook the terrace and offer splendid views across the lawns to the golf course.

VERULAM GOLF CLUB
Parkland course designed by James Braid 1905 · Par 72 · *Easy walking with good views*
HISTORIC CONNECTION WITH THE RYDER CUP
Presented by Samuel Ryder, Captain 1911, 1926, 1927
Visitors and Societies by arrangement · Easy access from M1/M10/M25   **Tel: 0727 853327**

HERTFORDSHIRE England

THE GOLF GUIDE 1994

ST. ALBANS. **Redbourn Golf Club**, Kinsbourne, Green Lane, Redbourn, Near St. Albans AL3 7QA (Bar (0582) 793363). *Location:* four miles north of St. Albans, 4 miles south of Luton, one mile south of M1 Junction 9. Parkland. 18 holes, 6407 yards. S.S.S. 71. 9 holes, 1361 yards. S.S.S. 27. Driving range. *Green Fees:* £14.00 weekdays, £18.00 weekends and Bank Holidays. *Eating facilities:* licensed bar, snacks and hot meals readily available. *Visitors:* welcome weekdays except between 4.15pm – 6pm, weekends and Bank Holidays after 3.00pm. *Society Meetings:* catered for by arrangement Mondays to Thursdays. Professional: Dale Brightman (0582 793493). Secretary: Chris Gyford (0582 792150).

STEVENAGE. **Stevenage Golf Centre**, Aston Lane, Stevenage SG2 7EL (0438 880424). *Location:* turn off A1(M) at Stevenage South Junction onto A602 to Hertford. 18 holes, 6451 yards. S.S.S. 71. Par 72. 20-bay driving range. *Green Fees:* telephone the Professional for details. *Eating facilities:* restaurant and bar. *Visitors:* welcome, advance booking system available to reserve tee-off times. Shower facilities. *Society Meetings:* catered for by arrangement. Professional: K. Bond.

WALTHAM CROSS. **Cheshunt Golf Club**, The Clubhouse, Park Lane, Cheshunt EN7 6QD (Waltham Cross (0992) 29777). *Location:* M25 Junction 25, then A10 towards Hertford, second set of traffic lights turn left, right at mini roundabout. Flat parkland course. 18 holes, 6608 yards. S.S.S. 71. Practice ground. *Green Fees:* weekdays £8.00; weekends and Bank Holidays £10.50. Senior Citizens, UB40s, Juniors £4.00 weekdays only. *Eating facilities:* public cafe. *Visitors:* welcome any time. For tee-off times phone Pro's shop (0992 24009). *Society Meetings:* catered for by arrangement through Pro Shop. Professional: Mr A.C. Newton (0992 24009). Secretary: Mr J.G. Duncan (0992 29777).

WARE. **Chadwell Springs Golf Club**, Hertford Road, Ware SG12 9LE (0920 461447). *Location:* A10 Hertford or Ware. Heathland. 9 holes, 6418 yards. S.S.S. 71. *Green Fees:* £14.00 weekdays; weekends £10.00 with a member only. *Eating facilities:* bar meals. *Visitors:* welcome weekdays; weekends with member only. *Society Meetings:* by arrangement. Professional: Adrian Shearn (0920 462075). Secretary: D. Evans (0920 461447).

WARE. **Whitehill Golf Club**, Whitehill Golf Centre, Dane End, Ware SG12 0JS (0920 438495; Fax: 0920 438891). *Location:* turn off A10 at Happy Eater, High Cross. Undulating course. 18 holes, 6636 yards. S.S.S. 72. 25 bay floodlit driving range. *Green Fees:* weekdays £15.00 per round, £20.00 per day; weekends £18.00. *Eating facilities:* bar, restaurant,

function room. *Visitors:* welcome, must have Handicap Certificate. Snooker room. *Society Meetings:* catered for, groups of 12 or more. Professional: Robert Green (0920 438326). Secretary: Andrew Smith.

WATFORD. **Aldenham Golf and Country Club**, Church Lane, Aldenham, Near Watford WD2 8AL (Radlett (0923) 853929; Fax: 0923 858472). *Location:* Junction 5 on M1, take A41 to South Watford, turn left at first roundabout to Church Lane. Flat parkland. 18 holes, 6500 yards. S.S.S. 71. New 9 hole course, 2500 yards. Practice area. *Green Fees:* weekdays £20.00; weekends £28.00. 9 hole course £10.00. *Eating facilities:* three bars, snack bar, restaurant. *Visitors:* welcome weekdays, weekends not before 12 noon. Teaching. Swing Analyser video. *Society Meetings:* by arrangement. Professional: Alistair McKay (0923 857889). Secretary: Mrs J.I. Phillips (0923 853929).

WATFORD. **West Herts Golf Club**, Cassiobury Park, Watford WD1 7SL (Watford (0923) 226911). *Location:* just off A412 at Croxley Green. Parkland. 18 holes, 6488 yards. S.S.S. 71. *Green Fees:* weekdays £20.00; weekends £30.00. *Eating facilities:* catering (including breakfast) available seven days a week. *Visitors:* welcome weekdays only. Handicap Certificate required. *Society Meetings:* catered for Wednesdays and Fridays. Professional: C.S. Gough (0923 220352). General Manager: A.D. Bluck (0923 236484).

WELWYN GARDEN CITY. **Panshanger Golf Complex**, Old Herns Lane, Panshanger, Welwyn Garden City AL7 2ED (Welwyn Garden (0707) 333312). *Location:* Junction 6 A1(M), 10 minutes from M25. Parkland set in the Mimram Valley. 18 holes, 6347 yards. S.S.S. 70. Practice ground, 9 hole pitch and putt. *Green Fees:* information not provided. *Eating facilities:* Fairway Tavern pub and servery. *Visitors:* municipal course, pay as you play, all welcome, dress conditions. *Society Meetings:* welcome. Professionals: Bryan Lewis and Mick Corlass (0707 333350). Secretary: Sheila (0707 332837).

WELWYN GARDEN CITY. **Welwyn Garden City Golf Club Ltd.**, Mannicotts, High Oaks Road, Welwyn Garden City AL8 7BP (Welwyn Garden (0707) 322722). *Location:* from north Junction 5 on A1M and take B197 to Valley Road. From south Junction 4 on A1M to Lemsford Lane and Valley Road. Undulating parkland. 18 holes, 6200 yards. S.S.S. 69. Practice ground. *Green Fees:* £25.00 weekdays. *Eating facilities:* by order for lunches; sandwiches available. *Visitors:* welcome weekdays with Handicap Certificate; weekends with member only. *Society Meetings:* Wednesdays and Thursdays only (£48.00 per person per day). Professional: Simon Bishop (0707 325525). Secretary/Manager: J.K. McIver (0707 325243).

BRIGGENS HOUSE HOTEL
Briggens Park, Stanstead Road (A414)
Stanstead Abbotts, Ware, Herts SG12 8LD
Telephone: (0279) 792416
♦♦♦♦♦ RAC ★★★★
RAC 'R' Merit Award for Restaurant

Elegance and tranquillity are to be found at this 18th century stately home set in 80 acres of softly rolling countryside. Own 9 hole golf course with full time Golf Pro. Outdoor swimming pool, 2 tennis courts, croquet, boules and putting lawns. Further details on request.

Humberside

BEVERLEY. **Beverley and East Riding Golf Club,** Westwood, Beverley HU17 8RG (0482 867190). *Location:* one mile from Beverley town centre. Common pastureland. 18 holes, 6127 yards. S.S.S. 68. *Green Fees:* £11.00 weekdays, £15.00 weekends and Bank Holidays. *Eating facilities:* lunch and evening meals by prior ordering. *Visitors:* welcome except weekends. *Society Meetings:* catered for, prior notice for approval of committee. Professional: Ian Mackie (0482 869519). Secretary: A. Walker (0482 868757).

BEVERLEY. **Hainsworth Park Golf Club,** Brandesburton, Near Driffield YO25 8RT (Tel & Fax: 0964 542362). *Location:* eight miles north east of Beverley on A165 road to Bridlington. Well drained parkland course with mature trees. 18 holes, 6003 yards. S.S.S. 69. Practice area. *Green Fees:* weekdays £10.00 per round, £15.00 per day; weekends £15.00. *Eating facilities:* bar and full catering. *Visitors:* welcome anytime. Hotel accommodation. *Society Meetings:* welcome. General Manager: Major R. Kilpatrick (0964 542362).

BRIDLINGTON. **Bridlington Golf Club,** Belvedere Road, Bridlington YO15 3NA (0262 672092). *Location:* A165 Bridlington to Hull. Flat parkland. 18 holes, 6491 yards. S.S.S. 71. Practice area. *Green Fees:* weekdays £10.00 per round, £15.00 per day; weekends and Bank Holidays £20.00. Reductions for parties over 25 in number. *Eating facilities:* full catering, bar meals, etc. *Visitors:* welcome most days but limited on Wednesdays/Sundays. Advisable to book in advance. *Society Meetings:* catered for. Professional: (0262 674721). Hon. Secretary: Clive Wilson (0262 606367).

BRIDLINGTON. **Flamborough Head Golf Club,** Flamborough, Bridlington (Bridlington (0262) 850333). *Location:* five miles north-east of Bridlington on B1255. 18 holes, 5438 yards. S.S.S. 66. *Green Fees:* weekdays £12.00 per day; weekends and Bank Holidays £16.00 per day. *Visitors:* welcome, limited Sunday and Wednesday mornings. *Society Meetings:* catered for, apply to Secretary. Secretary: W.R. Scarle (0262 676494).

BRIGG. **Elsham Golf Club,** Barton Road, Elsham, Brigg, South Humberside DN20 0LS (0652 688382). *Location:* off M180 at Barnetby Top or A15 through Brigg to Barton. Flat parkland. 18 holes, 6411 yards. S.S.S. 71. Indoor and outdoor practice ground. *Green Fees:* weekdays £22.00, with a member £12; weekends only with a member £18.00. *Eating facilities:* full catering. *Visitors:* welcome weekdays except Thursdays. *Society Meetings:* catered for on weekdays except Thursdays. Steward (0652 688382). Professional: Stuart Brewer (0652 680432). Secretary: B.P. Nazer (0652 680291).

BROUGH. **Brough Golf Club,** Cave Road, Brough HU15 1HB (0482-667374). *Location:* 10 miles west of Hull off A63. Parkland. 18 holes, 6153 yards. S.S.S. 69. Practice facilities. *Green Fees:* information not provided. *Eating facilities:* snacks etc. *Visitors:* welcome Monday to Friday subject to club events, no weekends or Bank Holidays. Wednesdays only after 2pm. *Society Meetings:* catered for. Professional: G. Townhill (0482 667483). Secretary/Manager: W.G. Burleigh (0482 667291).

BROUGH. **Cave Castle Hotel Golf Club,** South Cave, Brough HU15 2EU (0430 422245; Fax: 0430 421118). *Location:* end of M62 east, 10 miles from Hull. Parkland at the foot of the wolds with views of the River Humber. 18 holes, 6400 yards. S.S.S. 71. *Green Fees:* £12.50 per round, £18.00 per day weekdays; £18.00 per round, £25.00 per day weekends. *Eating facilities:* golf bar plus hotel à la carte, banqueting and conference facilities for 300. *Visitors:* welcome, no restrictions. Hotel has 70 bedrooms. *Society Meetings:* welcome. Professional: Chris Gray (0430 421286). Secretary: Mr J.R. Bean (0430 421286).

CLEETHORPES. **Cleethorpes Golf Club Ltd.,** Golf House, Kings Road, Cleethorpes DN35 0PN (0472 812059). *Location:* approximately one mile south of Cleethorpes. Flat meadowland crossed by large dykes. 18 holes, 6018 yards, 5503 metres. S.S.S. 69. Restricted practice area. *Green Fees:* weekdays £18.00; weekends £25.00. Reductions if with member. *Eating facilities:* lunch time hot and cold snacks, evening meals by arrangement. *Visitors:* welcome except Wednesdays, but must be member of another golf club. Ladies do not play Saturday afternoon and Sunday morning. Men do not play Wednesday afternoon. *Society Meetings:* weekdays only by arrangement with the Secretary. Professional: P. Davies (0472 814060). Secretary: G.B. Standaloft (0472 814060).

CONISTON. **Ganstead Park Golf Club,** Longdales Lane, Coniston, Near Hull HU11 4LB (0482 811280). *Location:* A165 to Bridlington. Flat course with lakes. 18 holes, 6495 yards. S.S.S. 71. Practice area. *Green Fees:* weekdays £18.00; weekends £24.00. *Eating facilities:* full catering facilities. *Visitors:* welcome without reservation except Wednesday 9.00 – 11.00am and Sunday 8.00am – 1.00pm. *Society Meetings:* catered for subject to availability. Professional: Mike Smee (0482 811121).

COTTINGHAM. **Hessle Golf Club,** Westfield Road, Raywell, Cottingham (Hull (0482) 659187). *Location:* three miles south west of Cottingham. Parkland. 18 holes, 6290 yards, S.S.S. 70. Two practice areas. *Green Fees:* £20.00 per round, £25.00 per day weekdays; weekends and Bank Holidays £25.00 per

HUMBERSIDE England

round. *Eating facilities:* snack lunches Tuesday to Sunday, set lunches by arrangement. *Visitors:* midweek unrestricted except Tuesdays 9am – 1pm. Weekends visitors may play after 11am at Professional's discretion. *Society Meetings:* catered for weekdays only by arrangement. Professional: G. Fieldsend (0482 650190). Secretary: R. L. Dorsey (0482 650171).

DRIFFIELD. **Driffield Golf Club,** Sunderlandwick, Driffield YO25 9AD (Driffield (0377) 43116). *Location:* one mile south of Driffield off the A161. Parkland. 18 holes, 6199 yards. S.S.S. 70. Practice area. *Green Fees:* weekdays £18.00; weekends £28.00. *Eating facilities:* bar, dining facility. *Visitors:* welcome weekdays, Ladies' Day Tuesdays, restrictions weekends. *Society Meetings:* catered for by prior arrangement. Secretary: M. Winn (0377 44167).

GRIMSBY. **Grimsby Golf Club Ltd,** Littlecoats Road, Grimsby DN34 4LU (Grimsby (0472) 342823). *Location:* one mile west of Grimsby town centre off A18. 18 holes, 6058 yards. S.S.S. 69. Practice area. *Green Fees:* weekdays £17.00, £12 with member; weekends £22.00, £12.00 with member. *Eating facilities:* snack lunches most days, set lunches by arrangement, afternoon teas most days, evening meals by arrangement with Steward. *Visitors:* welcome weekdays, must be members of golf clubs. Ladies do not play Saturday between 1.00pm – 5.00pm and Sunday mornings. *Society Meetings:* catered for Mondays and Fridays by arrangement with Secretary (Club ladies' day Tuesday, club ladies have priority). Professional: Mike Grantham (0472 356981). Secretary: A.D. Houlihan (0472 342630).

HORNSEA. **Hornsea Golf Club,** Rolston Road, Hornsea HU18 1XG (Hornsea (0964) 535488). *Location:* follow signs for Hornsea Pottery – Golf Course 200 yards past Pottery. Parkland. 18 holes, 6475 yards. S.S.S. 71. Practice area. *Green Fees:* weekdays £18.50; weekends after 3pm £30.00. *Eating facilities:* available every day. *Visitors:* welcome, please ring Professional for a time. Ladies' Day Tuesdays. Snooker room. *Society Meetings:* catered for by arrangement with the Secretary. Professional: B. Thompson (0964 534989). Secretary: B.W. Kirton (0964 532020).

HOWDEN. **Boothferry Golf Club,** Spaldington Lane, Howden, Near Goole DN14 7NG (0430 430371). *Location:* M62 Junction 37 - Howden - B1228 towards Bubwith Road. Flat meadowland, with ditches and ponds. 18 holes, 6651 yards. S.S.S. 72. Large practice area and driving range. *Green Fees:* weekdays £6.50 per round, weekends £10.50 per round. *Eating facilities:* restaurant and bar facilities available. *Visitors:* always welcome with prior booking. Certain dress restrictions for play on golf course. *Society Meetings:* all societies welcome with prior booking. Special rates for visiting parties over 12 players. Professional: Stewart Wilkinson (0430 430364; Fax: 0430 430567). Secretary: Graham Cole (0430 430364; Fax: 0430 430567).

HULL. **Hull Golf Club (1921) Ltd.,** The Hall, 27 Packman Lane, Kirk Ella, Hull HU10 7TJ (Hull (0482) 653026). *Location:* five miles west of Hull. Parkland and wooded. 18 holes, 6242 yards. S.S.S. 70. *Green Fees:* on application. *Eating facilities:* available. *Visitors:* welcome weekdays except Wednesday. *Society Meetings:* by prior arrangement. Professional: D. Jagger (0482 653074). General Manager: R. Toothill (0482 658919).

HULL. **Springhead Park Golf Club,** Willerby Road, Hull HU5 5JE (Hull (0482) 656309). *Location:* west boundary. Parkland. 18 holes, 6402 yards. S.S.S. 71. *Green Fees:* weekdays £5.00 per round, weekends £6.50 per round. *Visitors:* welcome, restricted Sundays from dawn to 2pm. Professional: B. Herrington (0482 594969). Secretary: B.W. Taylor.

HULL. **Sutton Park Municipal Golf Club,** Saltshouse Road, Hull HU8 9HF (Hull (0482) 74242). *Location:* three miles east of city centre on A164. Parkland course. 18 holes, 6295 yards, 5719 metres. S.S.S. 70. *Green Fees:* weekdays £5.00; weekends £6.50. Reductions for Juniors and Senior Citizens. *Eating facilities:* available, parties by pre-booking. *Visitors:* no restrictions except Sunday mornings. *Society Meetings:* by application to Hull Corporation Leisure Services Dept. Professional: Paul Rushworth (0482 711450). Secretary: Mr Platten (0482 706088).

IMMINGHAM. **Immingham Golf Club,** St. Andrews Lane, off Church Lane, Immingham DN40 2EU (Immingham (0469) 575298). *Location:* two miles off A180, behind St. Andrew's Church, Immingham. Flatridge and furrow, wide and deep dykes. 18 holes, 6161 yards, 5633 metres. S.S.S. 72. Small practice area. *Green Fees:* weekdays £14.00 per round; weekends £20.00. *Eating facilities:* full catering facilities, normal bar. *Visitors:* welcome anytime except Thursday pm, Saturday pm and Sunday am. *Society Meetings:* catered for if booked in advance. £14.00 per player (minimum 16). Professional: Mr N. Harding (0469 575493). Secretary: (0469 575298).

SCUNTHORPE. **Grange Park Golf Club,** Butterwick Road, Messingham, Scunthorpe DN17 3PP (0724 762945). *Location:* five miles south of Scunthorpe between Messingham and East Butterwick, four miles south of Junction 3 of M180. New parkland course. 9

Boothferry Golf Club
Welcomes Golf Societies in 1994 – Weekdays and Weekends

Book now while dates are still available. A day's outing comprises 27/36 holes of Golf, morning coffee and biscuits, snack lunch, 3-course evening meal at an inclusive price. Pleasant meadowland course on Vale of York. GREEN FEES £7.50 weekdays; £11.00 weekends.

Contact: Stewart Wilkinson (Professional/Manager), Boothferry Golf Club, Spalding, Goole DN14 7NG
Telephone: (0430) 430364

THE GOLF GUIDE 1994   *England*   HUMBERSIDE

holes, 2970 yards. S.S.S. 69. Par 35. Driving range. *Green Fees:* £4.00 weekdays; £6.00 weekends. Juniors half price. *Eating facilities:* coffee bar. *Visitors:* welcome at all times. Pro shop. Manager: Ian Cannon.

SCUNTHORPE. **Holme Hall Golf Club,** Holme Lane, Bottesford, Scunthorpe DN16 3RF (Scunthorpe (0724) 849185). *Location:* M180 Exit 4 (Scunthorpe East). Heathland with sandy subsoil. 18 holes, 6475 yards. S.S.S. 71. *Green Fees:* £18.00 per round or day. *Eating facilities:* daily except Mondays. Bar meals or restaurant. *Visitors:* welcome if members of affiliated clubs, not weekends or Bank Holidays unless with a member. *Society Meetings:* catered for by arrangement with Secretary. Professional: Richard McKiernon (0724 851816). Secretary: Mr G.D. Smith (0724 862078).

SCUNTHORPE. **Normanby Hall Golf Club,** Normanby Park, Near Scunthorpe DN15 9HU (Scunthorpe (0724) 720252). *Location:* five miles north of Scunthorpe on B1130. Follow signs for Normanby Country Park. Parkland. 18 holes, 6500 yards. S.S.S. 71. Practice area. *Green Fees:* weekdays £9.50 per round, £15.00 per day; weekends £11.50 per round. *Eating facilities:* fully licensed Clubhouse with restaurant, Societies should notify Catering Manager in advance. *Visitors:* welcome on most occasions, check times in advance with golf Professional. *Society Meetings:* bookings taken for weekdays, except Bank Holidays and Friday pm. Professional: Mr Chris Mann (0724 720226). Bookings Secretary: I.D. Reekie (0724 280444). Secretary: Mr Graham Kirk (0724 844303).

SCUNTHORPE. **Scunthorpe Golf Club,** Burringham Road, Scunthorpe DN17 2AB (Scunthorpe (0724) 842913). *Location:* M181 – Burringham Road opposite Asda Superstore. Flat wooded course. 18 holes, 6281 yards. S.S.S. 71. *Green Fees:* weekdays £20.00 per round, £24.00 per day. *Eating facilities:* full catering and bar available. *Visitors:* welcome weekdays only. *Society Meetings:* catered for weekdays. Professional: A. Lawson (0724 868972). Secretary: E. Willsmore (0724 866561).

WITHERNSEA. **Withernsea Golf Club,** Chestnut Avenue, Withernsea HU19 2PG (0964 612258). *Location:* 25 miles north-east of Kingston-upon-Hull. Seaside links. 9 holes, 5112 yards. S.S.S. 64. *Green Fees:* weekdays £8.00 per day, £5.00 if with a member; weekends £8.00 with a member only. *Eating facilities:* bar and meals available. *Visitors:* welcome any day except weekends unless playing with a member. *Society Meetings:* by reservation. Special rates. Professional: G. Harrison. Secretary: F. Buckley (0964 612214).

Briggate Lodge Inn
HOTEL, RESTAURANT AND BARS
Ermine Street, Broughton, Nr Scunthorpe, North Lincolnshire
Tel: (0652) 650770 Fax: (0652) 650495
♣♣♣♣ Highly Commended   AA RAC ★★★

The Briggate Lodge Inn is a friendly, family run country hotel. Set in 5 acres of woodland and landscaped gardens. 50 luxury bedrooms with full ensuite facilities. Bar meals served daily. A la Carte or Table d'Hote in the exquisite restaurant. Breakfast served daily from 7.00 am. 27 hole Championship Course expected to open 1995. Five excellent courses within 8 miles of hotel. Please call or fax for brochure.

LOOKING FOR A GUIDE?

If you have found *THE GOLF GUIDE* useful, you will also enjoy other titles in the FHG range including:

Recommended Country Hotels of Britain	£3.60
Recommended Wayside Inns of Britain	£3.60
Recommended Short Break Holidays in Britain	£3.60

You'll find our guides in most bookshops and in larger newsagents. In case of difficulty you can post or fax your order direct to FHG Publications in Paisley. You'll find an Order Form showing all prices, including postage, on the back pages of this book.

Isle of Wight

COWES. Cowes Golf Club, Crossfield Avenue, Cowes, Isle of Wight PO31 8HN (Cowes (0983) 292303). *Location:* entrance adjacent Cowes High School. Parkland with sea views. 9 holes, 5934 yards. S.S.S. 68. *Green Fees:* weekdays £15.00; weekends £18.00. *Eating facilities:* snack meals available in bar in summer. Bar open 11am to 2pm summer months. *Visitors:* welcome except Sunday before 1pm and Thursday, Ladies' Day (11.30am to 3pm). *Society Meetings:* by arrangement with Secretary. Society rates by arrangement. Secretary: D.C. Weaver.

EAST COWES. **Osborne Golf Club,** Osborne House, East Cowes PO32 6JX (Cowes (0983) 295421). *Location:* off A3027 north of East Cowes, in Osborne Estate. Parkland. 9 holes, 6286 yards. S.S.S. 70. Practice area. *Green Fees:* weekdays £18.00; weekends and Bank Holidays £20.00. *Eating facilities:* catering available each day. *Visitors:* welcome except on Saturdays and Sundays before 12.00 noon and Tuesdays before 1.00pm. *Society Meetings:* catered for (24 maximum). Professional: Andrew Scullion (0983 295649). Secretary: Roy Jones.

FRESHWATER. **Freshwater Bay Golf Club,** Afton Down, Freshwater (Freshwater (0983) 752955). *Location:* western end of Island, approximately half-a-mile east of Freshwater Bay on coast road to Ventnor. 18 holes, 5662 yards. S.S.S. 68. *Green Fees:* £18.00 per day, £22.00 weekends and Bank Holidays. *Eating facilities:* licensed bar, catering. *Visitors:* welcome. *Society Meetings:* by arrangement. Secretary: G. Smith.

NEWPORT. **Newport (Isle of Wight) Golf Club,** St. Georges Down, Near Shide, Newport, Isle of Wight (Newport (0983) 525076). *Location:* one mile south east of Newport. 9 holes, 5704 yards. S.S.S. 68. *Green Fees:* £15.00 per day weekdays; £17.50 weekends. *Eating facilities:* snacks available. *Visitors:* welcome, except Saturday after 3.30pm and Sunday afternoons. *Society Meetings:* welcome by arrangement weekdays except Wednesday afternoons. Secretary: Mr P.J. Mills (0983 525076).

RYDE. **Ryde Golf Club,** Binstead Road, Ryde, Isle of Wight PO33 3NF (Ryde (0983) 614809). *Location:* on A3054 very close to town. Parkland course. 9 holes, 5287 yards. S.S.S. 66. Practice area. *Green Fees:* weekdays £15.00 per day; weekends and Bank Holidays £20.00. *Eating facilities:* available during bar hours. *Visitors:* welcome, restrictions Wednesdays and Sundays. *Society Meetings:* catered for. Professional: Mark Wright. Secretary: (0983 614809).

SANDOWN. **Shanklin and Sandown Golf Club,** The Fairway, Lake, Sandown PO36 9PR (0983 403170). *Location:* one mile from Sandown. Heathland. 18 holes, 6068 yards. S.S.S. 69. Practice ground. *Green Fees:* £22/£27 weekdays; £27/£30 weekends. Three day ticket weekdays £50. *Eating facilities:* available 10/11am to dusk. *Visitors:* welcome, restrictions weekends. Handicap Certificate preferred. Bona fide golfers only. *Society Meetings:* by arrangement. Professional: Peter Hammond (0983 404424). Secretary: G.A. Wormald (0983 403217).

UPPER VENTNOR. **Ventnor Golf Club,** Steephill Down Road, Upper Ventnor (Ventnor (0983) 853326). *Location:* north-west boundary of Ventnor. Downland undulating with side slopes windy. 12 holes, 5767 yards. S.S.S. 68. *Green Fees:* weekdays £12.00; weekends £14.00. Ladies £2.00 less; Juniors under 16 half price. *Eating facilities:* bar snacks only. *Visitors:* welcome, Sundays after 1pm, Ladie's Day Fridays 12 noon to 3pm. Secretary: J.C. Hill (0983 883784).

FARRINGFORD HOTEL

RAC ★★★   ONCE THE HOME OF TENNYSON

"Situated just one mile from Freshwater Bay Golf Course"

Set in 33 acres of private parkland. All rooms in the main hotel have bathrooms en suite. 24 two bedroomed self-catering suites with bathroom, kitchen, lounge and colour T.V. Dancing on Saturdays, heated swimming pool, children's play area, putting, croquet, tennis, NINE HOLE GOLF COURSE and baby listening – all free to residents.

SPRING AND AUTUMN "MINI BREAKS" AVAILABLE. CHRISTMAS PROGRAMMES AVAILABLE ON REQUEST.

Farringford Hotel, Freshwater Bay, Isle of Wight PO40 9PE

For colour brochure Tel: 0983 752500/752700 Fax: 0983 756515

Kent

ASHFORD. **Ashford (Kent) Golf Club,** Sandyhurst Lane, Ashford TN25 4NT (Ashford (0233) 620180). *Location:* just off A20, one and a half miles west of Ashford. Parkland – stream cutting through course. 18 holes, 6246 yards. S.S.S. 70. *Green Fees:* weekdays £27.00, weekends and Bank Holidays £42.00 (November to February reduced green fees). *Eating facilities:* every day. *Visitors:* welcome. Handicap Certificate required. *Society Meetings:* catered for Tuesdays and Thursdays by arrangement. Professional: Hugh Sherman (0233 629644). Secretary: A.H. Story (0233 622655).

ASHFORD. **Chart Hills Golf Club,** Biddenden, Ashford TN27 8JX (0580 292222; Fax: 0580 292233). Wooded course designed by Nick Faldo. 18 holes, 7086 yards. S.S.S. 72. Extensive practice facilities. *Green Fees:* on application. *Eating facilities:* restaurant, bar snacks, bar, conference facilities. *Visitors:* restricted play – please contact the Pro Shop. *Society Meetings:* contact Pro Shop. Secretary: Mr J. Levine.

BECKENHAM. **Beckenham Place Park Golf Club,** Beckenham Hill Road, Beckenham. *Location:* on A222 north of Bromley. Parkland. 18 holes, 5672 yards. S.S.S. 68. Practice ground, nets, putting green. *Green Fees:* information not available. *Eating facilities:* bar and cafeteria. *Visitors:* welcome without reservation on weekdays, but must book for weekends. *Society Meetings:* not catered for. Other facilities include tennis courts and putting green. Professional: B. Woodman (081-658 5374). Secretary: K. Tregunno (081-778 4116).

BECKENHAM. **Braeside Golf Club,** Beckenham Place Park, Beckenham Hill, Beckenham (081-650 2292). Parkland course. 18 holes, 5722 yards, 5230 metres. S.S.S. 68. Practice area and nets. *Green Fees:* information not provided. *Eating facilities:* cafe and bar. *Visitors:* welcome any time. Professional: Bill Woodman (081-658 5374). Secretary: R. Oliver (081-304 3818).

BECKENHAM. **Langley Park Golf Club,** Barnfield Wood Road, Beckenham BR3 2SZ (081-650 2090). *Location:* one mile from Bromley South station. Flat wooded parkland. 18 holes, 6488 yards, 5931 metres. S.S.S. 71. Practice areas and nets. *Green Fees:* weekdays £35.00 per round or day; weekends with member only. *Eating facilities:* bar snacks, restaurant/dining room. *Visitors:* welcome weekdays by arrangement with Pro Shop. *Society Meetings:* Wednesdays and Thursdays only by arrangement with Secretary. Professional: George Ritchie (081-650 1663). Secretary: J.L. Smart (081-658 6849).

BEXLEY HEATH. **Bexley Heath Golf Club,** Mount Road, Bexley Heath DA6 8JS (081-303 6951). *Location:* adjacent to A2. Hilly parkland. 9 holes, 5239 yards, 4788 metres. S.S.S. 66. *Green Fees:* £15.00 (approximately). Weekends with member only. *Eating facilities:* catering available. *Visitors:* weekdays only. Professional: To be appointed. Secretary: S.E. Squires.

BIGGIN HILL. **Cherry Lodge Golf Club,** Jail Lane, Biggin Hill, Near Westerham TN16 3AX (0959 572250; Fax: 0959 540672). *Location:* A233 to M25 Junction 5, nearest town Bromley, eight miles. Parkland. 18 holes, 6652 yards, 6084 metres. S.S.S. 72. Extensive practice ground. *Green Fees:* weekdays £18.00 per round, £28.00 per day; weekends with member only. *Eating facilities:* restaurant, lounge snacks, full bar. *Visitors:* welcome weekdays except Bank Holidays. *Society Meetings:* welcome weekdays only by arrangement. Professional: Nigel Child (0959 572987). General Manager: Christopher F. Dale (0959 576712).

BROADSTAIRS. **North Foreland Golf Club,** The Clubhouse, Convent Road, Broadstairs CT10 3PU (Thanet (0843) 862140). *Location:* outside Broadstairs, near North Foreland Lighthouse. Seaside downland. 18 holes, 6382 yards. S.S.S. 71. Short Course: 18 holes, 1752 yards. Par 3. *Green Fees:* £25.00 per round; £35.00 per day weekdays. Short Course: £5.50 weekdays, £6.50 weekends and Public Holidays. *Eating facilities:* bar and dining room. *Visitors:* weekdays and weekend afternoons with current Handicap Certificate. Tennis. *Society Meetings:* Wednesdays and Fridays by prior arrangement with Secretary. Professional: Mike Lee (0843 869628). Secretary: B.J. Preston (0843 862140).

BROMLEY. **Shortlands Golf Club,** Postal Meadow Road, Shortlands, Bromley BR2 0PB (081-460 2471). *Location:* car park and entrance in Ravensbourne Avenue, off the main Beckenham to Bromley Road, adjacent Shortlands B.R. Station. 9 holes, 5261 yards. S.S.S. 66. *Green Fees:* no green fees allowed except when introduced and playing with a member £10.00. *Eating facilities:* available. *Visitors:* restricted to playing with a member. *Society Meetings:* only when member involved. Professional: J. Bates (081-464 6182). Hon. Secretary: Mrs Leah Burrows (081-460 8828 or 2471).

BROMLEY. **Sundridge Park Golf Club,** Garden Road, off Plaistow Lane, Bromley BR1 3NE (081-460 1822). *Location:* five minutes walk from Sundridge Park station. Wooded parkland. 36 holes. East 6467 yards. West 6007 yards. S.S.S. 71 and 69. Two practice grounds. *Green Fees:* £36.00 per day weekdays. *Eating facilities:* restaurant, spike bar, lounge bar, members bar. *Visitors:* welcome weekdays only, with Handicap Certificate. *Society Meetings:* catered for by arrangement. Professional: Bob Cameron (081-460 5540). Secretary: Derek Lowton (081-460 0278).

KENT *England*

BROMLEY.Magpie Hall Lane Municipal Golf Club, Magpie Hall Lane, Bromley (081-462 7014). *Location:* off Bromley Common on A21. 9 holes, 5538 yards. S.S.S. 67. *Green Fees:* information not provided. *Visitors:* welcome without reservation. Professional: A. Hodgson (081-462 7014). Clubhouse (081-462 8001).

CANTERBURY. Broome Park Golf and Country Club, Broome Park Estate, Barham, Near Canterbury CT4 6QX (0227 831701; Fax: 0227 831973). *Location:* off the A2 in the direction of Folkestone, half a mile on right. Undulating parkland, lake in front of 18th green. 18 holes, 6610 yards, S.S.S. 72. Practice ground. *Green Fees:* £25.00 weekdays; £30.00 weekends. *Eating facilities:* available all week. *Visitors:* weekdays subject to prior booking. Handicap Certificate required. *Society Meetings:* weekdays only. Professional: Tienie Britz (0227 831701 extension 264). Hon. Secretary: John Cowling (0227 831701 extension 298).

CANTERBURY. Canterbury Golf Club, Scotland Hills, Littlebourne Road, Canterbury CT1 1TW (0227 781871). *Location:* one mile from town centre on the A257 road to Sandwich. 18 holes, 6209 yards. S.S.S. 70. *Green Fees:* weekdays £27.00 per round, £36.00 per day; weekends £36.00 per round. Saturday/Sunday after 3pm only. *Eating facilities:* snacks, sandwiches, lunches, dinners daily. *Visitors:* welcome without reservation. *Society Meetings:* catered for Tuesday and Thursday. Professional: Paul Everard (0227 462865). Secretary: E.L. Ruckert (0227 453532).

THE GOLF GUIDE 1994

CHISLEHURST. Chislehurst Golf Club, Camden Park Road, Chislehurst BR7 5HJ (081-467 3055). *Location:* between Bromley and junction of A222 and Sidcup bypass. Parkland. 18 holes, 5128 yards. S.S.S. 65. *Green Fees:* £25.00 weekdays; £10.00 weekends with member only. *Eating facilities:* catering available. Large parties by prior arrangement. *Visitors:* welcome but restricted to weekdays (except Wednesday mornings) and only with a member at weekends. *Society Meetings:* catered for by arrangement, 36 hole Societies only on Thursdays. Professional: Mark Lawrence (081-467 6798). Secretary: N.E. Pearson (081-467 2782; Fax: 081-295 0874).

CRANBROOK. Cranbrook Golf Club Ltd., Benenden Road, Cranbrook TN17 4AL (0580 712833; Fax: 0580 714274). *Location:* situated between Sissinghurst and Benenden. Parkland – tree lined. 18 holes, 6351 yards. S.S.S. 70. Practice area. *Green Fees:* weekdays £19.00, £11.00 with a member; weekends £27.50, £16.00 with a member. *Eating facilities:* clubhouse facilities open all day. *Visitors:* welcome anytime weekdays except before 9.30am Tuesdays and before 10.30am Thursdays; weekends welcome 12 noon to 12.30pm and after 3.30pm. *Society Meetings:* company days available. Secretary: (0580 712833).

DARTFORD. Corinthian Golf Club, Valley Road, Fawkham, Dartford DA3 8LZ (0474 707559). *Location:* off the A2 east of Dartford/off A20 north of Brands Hatch. Wooded with 18 artificial tees and 9 grass greens during summer; artificial greens during winter. 9 holes, 6045 yards. S.S.S. 70. Practice area. *Green Fees:*

KING WILLIAM IV

4 HIGH STREET, LITTLEBOURNE, NEAR CANTERBURY, KENT   TELEPHONE: 0227 721244

15 minutes drive to Royal St. George Golf Course and close to Canterbury, Chesterfield and Broome Park Golf Courses. Four miles east of Canterbury, just off M2 motorway. 17th century inn with excellent food and recently renovated bedrooms with ensuite facilities.

The Tanner of WINGHAM

Family run 16th Century Restaurant with bed and breakfast accommodation, centrally placed for 10 golf courses. Sandwich and Canterbury just 6 miles away. Imaginative monthly changing menus with full vegetarian alternative. **ETB Approved.**
44 High Street, Wingham, Canterbury, Kent. Tel: 0227 720532

BROOME PARK GOLF & COUNTRY CLUB

Broome Park was built in 1635, the former home of Lord Kitchener, standing in 268 acres of rolling Kentish countryside. Facilities include 18 hole championship length golf course, tennis, squash, croquet, snooker, outdoor swimming pool, Busybodies Health & Fitness Centre, 2 bars, 2 restaurants, Dizzys Jazz Bar & Creole Restaurant. Accommodation available throughout the year in self catering villas and hotel apartments from £150 per person for three nights to include free golf and half board.

**Broome Park Golf & Country Club,
The Broome Park Estate, Barham, Canterbury, Kent CT4 6QX.
Telephone: 0227 831701 Fax: 0227 831973**

THE GOLF GUIDE 1994

£14.00, with a member £7.50. *Eating facilities:* bar food available, catering by arrangement. *Visitors:* welcome except weekend and Bank Holiday mornings. *Society Meetings:* welcome Mondays, Wednesdays and Fridays. Secretary: Mark Harris.

DARTFORD. **Dartford Golf Club Ltd.,** The Clubhouse, Dartford Heath, Dartford DA1 2TN (Dartford (0322) 223616). *Location:* backing on to A2, one mile from Dartford Tunnel and M25. Flat parkland. 18 holes, 5914 yards. S.S.S. 68. *Green Fees:* weekdays £28.00. *Eating facilities:* catering available. *Visitors:* welcome on weekdays with reservation, must be member of another golf club. *Society Meetings:* welcome on Mondays and Fridays by prior arrangement with Secretary. Professional: G. Cooke (0322 226409). Secretary: Margaret Gronow (0322 226455).

DEAL. **Royal Cinque Ports Golf Club,** Golf Road, Deal (Deal (0304) 374007; Fax: 0304 379530). *Location:* A258 from Sandwich. In Upper Deal leave for Middle Deal Road, left turn into Albert Road, Western Road, on to Golf Road (or from Dover, A258 via seafront and Godwin Road). Links course. 18 holes, Championship 6785 yards, Medal 6406 yards. S.S.S. 71. *Green Fees:* weekdays £45.00 per day, £35.00 per round after 1pm. No fees accepted at weekends. *Eating facilities:* hot snacks provided Monday to Friday, through bar. *Visitors:* welcome with reservation, introduction preferred. *Society Meetings:* catered for on application. Professional: A.W. Reynolds (0304 374170). Secretary: N.S. Phillips.

DEAL. **Walmer and Kingsdown Golf Club,** The Leas, Kingsdown, Deal CT14 8EP (Deal (0304) 373256). *Location:* on A258 from Dover (A2) to Deal, club signposted at village of Ringwood. Seaside links on clifftop near Dover. 18 holes, 6451 yards. S.S.S. 71. *Green Fees:* weekdays £22.00 per round, £28.00 per day; weekends £24.00 per round, £30.00 per day. *Eating facilities:* full catering and bar service. *Visitors:* welcome without reservation if members of another club. *Society Meetings:* catered for except Saturdays and Sundays. Professional: Ian Coleman (0304 363017). Secretary: B.W. Cockerill.

DEANGATE. **Deangate Ridge Golf Club,** Hoo, Rochester (Medway (0634) 250374). *Location:* three miles from Rochester off A228 towards Isle of Grain. Wooded. 18 holes, 6300 yards. S.S.S. 70. 9 hole Pitch and Putt. *Green Fees:* £8.60 weekdays, £11.30 weekends. *Eating facilities:* available. *Visitors:* welcome without reservation, bookings required for weekends. *Society Meetings:* catered for. Professional: Barry Aram (0634 251180). Secretary: R. Worthington (0634 271749).

EDENBRIDGE. **Edenbridge Golf and Country Club,** Crouch House Road, Edenbridge TN8 5LQ (Edenbridge (0732) 865097). *Location:* from M25 take A25, at Limpsfield take B2026 to Edenbridge. Parkland. 18 holes, 6643 yards. S.S.S. 73. Second Course 18 holes, 5671 yards. S.S.S. 67. 16 bay floodlit driving range. *Green Fees:* weekdays £15.00 per round, weekends and Bank Holidays £18.00 per round; Skeynes Course £12.00 weekdays, £15.00 weekends. *Eating facilities:* bar and restaurant. *Visitors:* welcome, call for start time. *Society Meetings:* welcome by arrangement. Professional: B. Hemsley (0732 865202). Secretary: Judith Scully (0732 867381; Fax: 0732 867029).

EYNSFORD. **Austin Lodge Golf Club,** Upper Austin Lodge Road, Eynsford DA4 0HU (0322 862944; Fax: 0322 862406). *Location:* Eynsford - 10 minutes' drive from Junction 3 of M25, M20, A20. Secluded rolling countryside with lakes. 18 holes, 6575 yards Yellow Tees, 7118 yards White Tees. S.S.S. 73. Practice ground. *Green Fees:* weekdays £15.00; weekends £20.00. *Eating facilities:* bar, restaurant with light meals all day. *Visitors:* welcome weekdays, possibly after 2pm weekends, telephone booking only. *Society Meetings:* welcome, telephone booking only. Professional: Nigel Willis. Secretary: S. Bevam.

FARNBOROUGH. **High Elms Golf Club,** High Elms Road, Downe (0689 858175). *Location:* two miles from Farnborough Hospital on A21, turn right at Shire Lane, second on left. Beautiful parkland. 18 holes, 5626 metres. S.S.S. 70. *Green Fees:* weekends £11.00. *Eating facilities:* food by arrangement with publican, ring (0689 50177). Professional: Bob Lee. Secretary: Mrs P. O'Keeffe.

Sutherland House
Private Hotel & Restaurant
186 London Road, Deal CT14 9PT
Tel: (0304) 362853 Fax: (0304) 361268
ETB Commended

Fine cuisine and comfortable accommodation in a charming Edwardian house. Channel ports readily accessible. *International Golf Courses only 10 minutes' drive – Royal Cinque Ports, Royal St. Georges, Princes Golf Club.* Private car park.
Guest Accom Good Room Award. Terms on application.

KENT *England*

FAVERSHAM. **Faversham Golf Club Ltd.**, Belmont Park, Faversham ME13 0HB (0795 890251). *Location:* M2 Faversham Exit (A251) to A2 junction, left to Brogdale Road, left to Belmont. 18 holes, 6021 yards. S.S.S. 69. *Green Fees:* weekdays £23.00 per round, £30.00 all day; weekends with members only £24.00 per round, £32.00 per day. Societies £25.00 per round, £32.00 per day. Fees subject to review. *Eating facilities:* by arrangement with Steward. *Visitors:* welcome with member. *Society Meetings:* Wednesdays and Fridays catered for, Tuesdays limited numbers. Professional: G. Nixon (0795 890275). Secretary: D.B. Christie (0795 890561).

FOLKESTONE. **Sene Valley Golf Club Ltd.**, Blackhouse Hill, Sene, Folkestone CT18 8BZ (0303 266726). *Location:* A20 then B2065 towards Hythe. Downland course overlooking sea. 18 holes, 6287 yards. S.S.S. 70. Practice ground. *Green Fees:* weekdays £25.00; weekends £30.00. *Eating facilities:* bar and restaurant (no catering Mondays). *Visitors:* welcome with Handicap Certificate (preferably not weekends or Bank Holidays). *Society Meetings:* welcome Wednesdays to Fridays. Professional: P. Moger (0303 268514). Secretary: R.W. Leaver (0303 268513).

GILLINGHAM. **Gillingham Golf Club Ltd.**, Woodlands Road, Gillingham ME7 2AP (Medway (0634) 850999; Fax: 0634 574749). *Location:* A2 Gillingham. Parkland. 18 holes, 5879 yards. S.S.S. 68. Practice nets/ground. *Green Fees:* weekdays with a member £11.00 per round, £16.50 per day; without a member £22.00 per round or day. Weekends only with a member £11.00 per round, £16.50 per day. *Eating facilities:* available Wednesday – Sunday. *Visitors:* only with a member at weekends; during week must have proof of Handicap or membership of another club. *Society Meetings:* welcome, maximum 30 players. Professional: Brian Impett (0634 855862). Secretary: L.P. O'Grady (0634 853017).

GRAVESEND. **Mid-Kent Golf Club**, Singlewell Road, Gravesend DA11 7RB (Gravesend (0474) 352387). *Location:* A227 off A2. Parkland. 18 holes, 6206 yards. S.S.S. 70. *Green Fees:* weekdays £28.00 per round, £35.00 per day; weekends with member only. *Eating facilities:* breakfast, dinner by arrangement, lunch every day, bar 11am to 11pm. *Visitors:* welcome weekdays except competition days with Handicap Certificate. *Society Meetings:* catered for Tuesdays only. Professional: Neil Hansen (0474 332810). Secretary: T. Potter (0474 568035; Fax: 0474 564218).

HAWKHURST. **Hawkhurst Golf Club**, High Street, Hawkhurst TN18 4JS (Hawkhurst (0580) 752396). *Location:* on A268 from Hawkhurst to Flimwell. Parkland. 9 holes, 5769 yards. S.S.S. 68. *Green Fees:* £18.00 weekdays; weekends £10.00 only with member. *Eating facilities:* all facilities, prior notice for societies. *Visitors:* welcome weekdays, weekends with member only. *Society Meetings:* weekdays, catered for with prior notice. Professional: Tony Collins (0580 753600). Secretary: Richard C. Fowles (0580 830287).

HEADCORN. **Weald of Kent Golf Course**, Maidstone Road, Headcorn TN27 9PT (0622 891671; Fax: 0622 891793). *Location:* M20 Maidstone, Kent. Some holes flat, with mature trees, various trenches, natural and man made lakes with fountains. 18 holes. *Eating facilities:* 60 cover à la carte and table d'hôte restaurant and bar meals. *Visitors:* welcome at anytime. Banqueting and conference facilities from 30 to 200 covers. *Society Meetings:* welcome; minimum 12, maximum 60.

HERNE BAY. **Herne Bay Golf Club**, Canterbury Road, Herne Bay (Herne Bay (0227) 373964). 18 holes, 5466 yards. S.S.S. 67. *Green Fees:* weekdays £18.00 per round, £25.00 per day; weekends £25.00. *Eating facilities:* available except Monday. *Visitors:* welcome weekdays unrestricted. Weekends and Bank Holidays after 12 noon only. Handicap Certificate required. *Society Meetings:* catered for weekdays. Professional: D. Lambert. Secretary: B. Warren.

HEVER. **Hever Golf Club**, Hever TN8 7NG (0732 70778). *Location:* at Junction 6 take A22 turning to Godstone, then turn left onto the A25 to Sevenoaks, after three and a half miles take the Edenbridge road. Follow signs for Hever Castle. Go past the entrance to castle and the club is one mile further on the right. Parkland, wooded. 18 holes, 6951 yards, 6319 metres. S.S.S. 73. Large practice area. *Green Fees:* on application. *Eating facilities:* available in the clubhouse. *Visitors:* members only. *Society Meetings:* on application. Professional/Secretary: John Powell (0732 70785 or 70771; Fax: 0732 70775).

HYTHE. **Hythe Imperial Golf Club**, Princes Parade, Hythe CT21 6AE (0303 267441). *Location:* come off M20 Junction 11 directions for Hythe A261. Flat seaside course. 9 holes, 5533 yards. S.S.S. 67. Practice ground. *Green Fees:* £15.00 weekdays. Reductions if playing with a member. *Eating facilities:* available at the hotel. *Visitors:* welcome weekdays, no fees accepted weekends up to 1pm. *Society Meetings:* welcome weekdays only. Professional: Gordon Ritchie (0303 267441). Secretary: Mr R. Barrett (0303 267554).

Lovely Edwardian house in its own attractive grounds close to the English Channel. Tasteful and comfortable bedrooms (some ensuite) with excellent views. Delicious breakfasts and dinners in the charming dining room and a spacious guest lounge with satellite TV. Ample parking. Ideally situated for a golfing holiday in the lovely Kent area, with its many challenging golf courses.

Contact Peter and Frances Fern for further details.

FERN HOUSE
87 SEABROOK ROAD, HYTHE, KENT CT21 5QP   TELEPHONE: 0303 267315

THE GOLF GUIDE 1994   *England* KENT

MAIDSTONE. **Bearsted Golf Club**, Ware Street, Bearsted, Maidstone ME14 4PQ (0622 38389). *Location:* Junction 7 off M20. Secluded parkland course with view of North Downs. 18 holes, 6253 yards, 5715 metres. S.S.S. 70. Practice area/net. *Green Fees:* £22.00 per round weekdays only. *Eating facilities:* bar/restaurant. *Visitors:* welcome on proof of membership of bona fide golf club. Handicap Certificate required. Weekends with member only. *Society Meetings:* catered for Tuesdays and Thursdays, limited numbers Wednesday/Fridays. Professional: T. Simpson (0622 38024). Secretary: Mrs L.M. Siems (0622 38198).

MAIDSTONE. **Cobtree Manor Park Golf Club**, Chatham Road, Sandling, Maidstone ME14 3AZ (0622 681560). *Location:* M20, A229 Chatham (not Maidstone). Undulating course with trees, and interesting 6th hole over lake. 18 holes, 5716 yards. S.S.S. 68. Tuition, practice, putting. *Green Fees:* information not available. *Eating facilities:* restaurant and bar. *Visitors:* welcome, book one week in advance through Professional. *Society Meetings:* weekdays by arrangement only. Professional: Martin Drew (0622 753276).

MAIDSTONE. **Leeds Castle Golf Course**, Leeds Castle, Leeds, Maidstone ME17 1PL (0622 880467). *Location:* M20-A20 near Maidstone. Situated in the grounds of Leeds Castle, parkland. 9 holes, 2790 yards S.S.S. 34. Practice putting green and nets. *Green Fees:* weekdays £8.50; weekends £9.50. Reduced second 9 holes weekdays £6.50; Senior Citizens and Juniors £6.50 9 holes. *Eating facilities:* Park Gate Inn (situated in golf course car park). *Visitors:* welcome anytime, bookings taken from six days in advance. Correct dress must be worn – no denim jeans allowed, golf shoes preferred. *Society Meetings:* welcome midweek. Professional: Chris Miller PGA. Secretary: Jill Skinner.

MAIDSTONE. **Tudor Park Golf and Country Club**, Ashford Road, Bearsted ME14 4NQ (Maidstone (0622) 735891). *Location:* east of Maidstone, on A20 at Bearsted. Off Junction 8 of M20. Parkland. 18 holes, 6041 yards. S.S.S. 69. Practice area. *Green Fees:* information not provided. *Eating facilities:* restaurants and bars. *Visitors:* current Handicap Certificate required. Hotel, leisure and conference facilities. *Society Meetings:* societies and company days catered for. Professional: Marc Boggia (0622 39412). Secretary: Christopher May (0622 34334).

MAIDSTONE. **West Malling Golf Club**, London Road, Addington, West Malling ME19 5AR (West Malling (0732) 844785). *Location:* A228 turn off M20. Parkland, 18 holes, 6142 yards. S.S.S. 70 (Spitfire Course). 18 holes, 6300 yards. S.S.S. 70 (Hurricane Course). *Green Fees:* weekdays £20.00 per round, £28.00 per day; weekends £30.00 per round after 12 noon. *Eating facilities:* restaurant available. *Visitors:* welcome except Bank Holidays or before 12 noon weekends. Conference/function facilities available. *Society Meetings:* catered for. Professional: Paul Foston (0732 844022). Secretary: Mike Ellis (0732 844785).

NEW ROMNEY. **Littlestone Golf Club**, St. Andrews Road, Littlestone, New Romney TN28 8RB (New Romney (0679) 62310). *Location:* A20 to Ashford, B2070 to New Romney, one mile from New Romney. Seaside links course. 18 holes, 6417 yards. S.S.S. 71. Driving range. *Green Fees:* £25.00 per round, £35.00 per day weekdays; £30.00 per round, £40.00 per day weekends. *Eating facilities:* available. *Visitors:* Handicap Certificate required, visitors not allowed at weekends in Winter, in Summer only after 3pm. Weekdays by prior arrangement with the Secretary. Professional: Stephen Watkins (0679 62231). Secretary: J.D. Lewis (0679 63355).

NEW ROMNEY. **Romney Warren Golf Club**, St. Andrews Road, New Romney TN28 8RB (0679 63355). *Location:* A20 to Ashford, B2070 to New Romney. Traditional links course. 18 holes, 5100 yards. S.S.S. 64. *Green Fees:* weekdays £9.50 per round, £19.00 per day. *Eating facilities:* available. *Visitors:* welcome. *Society Meetings:* catered for. Professional: Stephen Watkins (0679 62231). Secretary: J.D. Lewis.

ORPINGTON. **Cray Valley Golf Club**, Sandy Lane, St. Paul's Cray, Orpington BR5 3HY (Orpington (0689) 831927). *Location:* Ruxley roundabout A20; turn off into Sandy Lane, half-a-mile on left. Parkland. 18 holes, 5624 yards. S.S.S. 67. *Green Fees:* weekdays £11.00, weekends £16.80. Also 9 hole course: weekdays £4.00, weekends £5.50. *Eating facilities:* hot meals available lunchtimes, also bar. *Visitors:* welcome all week. *Society Meetings:* welcome weekdays. Professional: Mr John Gregory (0689 837909). Secretary: Ron Hill (0689 839677).

ORPINGTON. **Hewitts Golf Centre**, Court Road, Orpington BR6 9BX (0689 896266; Fax: 0689 824577). *Location:* M25 Junction 4, take A224 Orpington (Court Road), quarter of a mile on left. Parkland with archways throughout, two lakes. 18 holes, 6077 yards, 5556 metres. S.S.S. 69. 9 hole par 3 course, 40 bay floodlit driving range. *Green Fees:* weekdays £13.00; weekends £16.00. *Eating facilities:* bar snacks and restaurant. *Visitors:* welcome anytime except during members' tee-off times at weekends (please ring for times). *Society Meetings:* all welcome, contact Centre Manager. Professional: Head Teaching Professional Nigel Lee. Centre Manager: Gareth Watkins.

ORPINGTON. **Ruxley Park Golf Centre**, Sandy Lane, St. Paul's Cray, Orpington BR5 3HY (Orpington (0689) 871490). *Location:* off Ruxley roundabout on the old A20. Parkland course. 18 holes, 6031 yards, 5388 metres. S.S.S. 69. Floodlit driving range. *Green Fees:* weekdays £10.30; weekends £15.50. Weekend afternoon rate £11.00. *Eating facilities:* bar snacks and bar facilities. *Visitors:* welcome. *Society Meetings:* welcome. Professional: Mark Woodman. Secretary: Paul Davis.

KENT *England*

ORPINGTON. West Kent Golf Club, West Hill, Downe, Near Orpington BR6 7JJ (0689 853737). *Location:* from Downe village south along Luxted Lane, 600 yards turn right into West Hill. 18 holes, 6399 yards. S.S.S. 70. *Green Fees:* £25.00 per round, £40.00 per day. *Eating facilities:* meals by arrangement. *Visitors:* welcome with letter of introduction and recognised handicap. Casual golfers must phone at least 24 hours in advance. *Society Meetings:* catered for. Professionals: R.S. Fidler and G. Ryan (0689 856863). Secretary: A.J. Messing (0689 851323).

RAMSGATE. St. Augustine's Golf Club, Cottington Road, Cliffsend, Ramsgate CT12 5JN (Thanet (0843) 590333). *Location:* two miles south-west of Ramsgate – approaching from A253 or A256 follow signs to St. Augustine's Cross. Entrance 75 yards beyond Cross by railway bridge. Mainly parkland, flat – tight and challenging course. 18 holes, 4999 yards, 4572 metres. S.S.S. 64. *Green Fees:* £20.00 weekdays; £22.00 weekends and Bank Holidays. Weekly £65.00, monthly £195. *Eating facilities:* full catering except Mondays when sandwiches and beverages only, usual bar facilities. *Visitors:* welcome, proof of Handicap required, advisable to ring Professional the day before to check periods booked for competitions, societies, etc. *Society Meetings:* catered for, book through Secretary. Professional: D. Scott (0843 590222). Secretary: R.E. Freeman (0843 590333).

ROCHESTER. Rochester and Cobham Park Golf Club, Park Pale, by Rochester ME2 3UL (Shorne (047 482) 3411). *Location:* on A2, 2 miles east of Gravesend turn-off. 18 holes, 6467 yards. S.S.S. 71. *Green Fees:* on application. *Eating facilities:* lunch, tea, dinner and snacks available, lunches should be ordered in advance. *Visitors:* with Handicap Certificates – welcome without reservation on weekdays. *Society Meetings:* catered for on Tuesdays and Thursdays. Professional: Matt Henderson (047 482 3658). Manager: J.W. Irvine (047 482 3411).

SANDWICH BAY. Prince's Golf Club, Sandwich Bay (Sandwich (0304) 611118). *Location:* four miles from Sandwich through the Sandwich Bay Estate. Seaside links. 27 holes. arranged as 3 loops of 9 holes named "Dunes", "Himalayas", "Shore". D & H 6262 – 6776 yards Par 71, S.S.S. 70-73. H & S 6238 – 6813 yards, Par 71, S.S.S. 70-73. S & D 6466-6947 yards, Par 72, S.S.S. 71-73. Driving range, full practice facilities. *Green Fees:* weekdays £29.50 round, £34.00 day; Saturdays £34.00 round, £39.00 day; Sundays £34.00 round, £44.00 day. Special package rates October to May. *Eating facilities:* breakfast, lunch, dinner available every day (pre-booking advisable); bar buffet/Ploughman's lunchtime & evenings; light snacks throughout the day. *Visitors & Societies:* welcome without restriction, Company days and private parties our speciality. Brochure available on request. Starting Times: Philip Sparks Professional: (0304 613797). Information & Bookings: Bob Duncan (0304 611118).

SANDWICH LEISURE PARK Situated in the medieval cinque port of Sandwich and within easy reach of Royal St. Georges, Princes, Royal Cinque Ports, Walmer and Kingsdown, North Foreland, and St. Augustines Golf Clubs - The ideal golfing holiday retreat.

YOUR OWN HOME ON HOLIDAY FROM ONLY **£4250** HOLIDAYS FOR YOUR FAMILY WHENEVER YOU WANT

OR WHY NOT STOP ON OUR TOURING FIELD **EXCELLENT FACILITIES**

Coast & Country CARAVANS

Say you saw us in the "PGA Guide"

TEL: 0304 612681

Woodnesborough Road, Sandwich, Kent CT13 0AA

THE GOLF GUIDE 1994 — England KENT

SANDWICH. Royal St. Georges Golf Club, Sandwich CT13 9PB (0304 617308; Fax: 0304 611245). *Location:* one mile from Sandwich on the road to Sandwich Bay. From Canterbury A257, from Dover A258. Links. 18 holes, Championship 6903 yards, Medal 6534 yards. S.S.S. Championship 74. Medal 72. Large practice ground. *Green Fees:* £50.00 per round, £70.00 per day weekdays. *Eating facilities:* snack bar and dining room. *Visitors:* welcome weekdays only. Must have Handicap Certificate and be member of club with membership of E.G.U. *Society Meetings:* catered for by arrangement. All players must meet requirements for visitors. Professional: Niall Cameron (0304 615236). Secretary: Gerald E. Watts (0304 613090).

SEVENOAKS. Darenth Valley Golf Course, Station Road, Shoreham, Near Sevenoaks TN14 7SA (0959 522944). *Location:* A225 between Otford and Eynsford, approximately four miles north of Sevenoaks. Parkland course. 18 holes, 6356 yards. S.S.S. 72. Practice area, putting greens. *Green Fees:* weekdays £11.00; weekends and Bank Holidays £15.00. *Eating facilities:* bar snacks, diningroom, functions up to 100 covers. *Visitors:* welcome with reservation through Pro's shop. *Society Meetings:* catered for by arrangement. Professional: Scott Fotheringham (0959 522922). Clubhouse Manager/Steward: Neil Morgan.

SEVENOAKS. Knole Park Golf Club, Seal Hollow Road, Sevenoaks TN15 0HJ (Sevenoaks (0732) 452709). *Location:* one mile south-east of Sevenoaks town. Parkland. 18 holes, 6249 yards, 5711 metres. S.S.S. 70. *Green Fees:* weekdays only, £25.50 per round, £36.00 for two rounds. *Eating facilities:* full catering and bar. *Visitors:* by appointment only, must have a club handicap. *Society Meetings:* catered for by arrangement only. Professional: P.E. Gill (0732 451740). Secretary: D.J.L. Hoppe (0732 452150).

SEVENOAKS. Wildernesse Golf Club, Park Lane, Seal, Sevenoaks TN15 0JE (Sevenoaks (0732) 761526). *Location:* A25 between Sevenoaks and Borough Green. Park and woodland. 18 holes, 6478 yards, 5924 metres. S.S.S. 72. Large practice ground.

Green Fees: £26.00/£37.00 weekdays. *Eating facilities:* by arrangement. *Visitors:* welcome, weekdays only by prior arrangement; letter of introduction. *Society Meetings:* catered for Mondays and Thursdays. Professional: Bill Dawson (0732 761527). Secretary: K.L. Monk (0732 761199).

SEVENOAKS. Woodlands Manor Golf Club, Tinkerpot Lane, Woodlands, Near Otford, Sevenoaks TN15 6AB (Otford (09592) 3805). *Location:* Junction 3, M25 take "Brands Hatch" sign on A20, seven miles. Parkland. 18 holes, 6000 yards. S.S.S. 68. Six acre practice ground. *Green Fees:* on application. *Eating facilities:* bar daily. *Visitors:* welcome weekdays, Handicap Certificate required at weekends after 1pm. *Society Meetings:* welcome by arrangement Monday to Friday. Professional: Nick Allen (09592 4161). Secretary: E.F. Newman (09592 3806).

SEVENOAKS. Wrotham Heath Golf Club, Seven Mile Lane, Comp, Sevenoaks TN15 8QZ (Borough Green (0732) 884800). *Location:* on B2016 half-a-mile south of junction with A20. Woods and heather. 9 holes with alternate tees for 18. 5918 yards. S.S.S. 68. *Green Fees:* weekdays £20.00; weekends only with a member. *Eating facilities:* bar and snacks, meals by arrangement, except Mondays. *Visitors:* welcome on weekdays with Handicap Certificate, but not Bank Holidays. *Society Meetings:* catered for Fridays only, no more than 30 people. Professional: H. Dearden (0732 883854). Secretary: L.J. Byrne (0732 884800).

SHEERNESS. Sheerness Golf Club, Power Station Road, Sheerness ME12 3AE (Sheerness (0795) 662585). *Location:* follow A249 then A250 towards Sheerness. Flat marshland/meadowland — numerous water hazards. 18 holes, 6460 yards. S.S.S. 71. Practice area. *Green Fees:* weekdays £15.00 (£8.00) per round, £20.00 (£12.00) per day; weekends £12.00 only if playing with a member. *Eating facilities:* available. *Visitors:* weekdays only except with member. *Society Meetings:* catered for Tuesdays, Wednesdays and Thursdays by previous arrangement. (16-40). Professional: Darran Clark (0795 666840). Secretary: J.W. Gavins.

Butts Hill FARM

**WROTHAM – MID KENT – ENGLAND
2 & 3 BEDROOM TIMBER LODGES
OVER 20 LOCAL GOLF COURSES AND
OVER 100 WITHIN EASY REACH**

Each lodge can sleep 4 to 6 persons and is fully equipped with all modern conveniences for self catering. These include microwave, fridge, cooker and well-equipped kitchen with dining area. Large bathroom. Comfortably furnished lounge with radio, TV and large gas fire. Good quality bed linen and towels are included. Safe car parking, peaceful location.

Sheila and Gerry Morel, Butts Hill Farm, Labour-in-Vain Road, Wrotham, Kent TN15 7PA
Telephone & Fax: 0732 822415
(close to Junction of M20 and M26)

English Tourist Board HIGHLY COMMENDED

KENT *England*

SIDCUP. Sidcup Golf Club (1926) Ltd, 7 Hurst Road, Sidcup DA15 9AE (081-300 2150). *Location:* three minutes' walk from Sidcup Station. Parkland. 9 holes, 5722 yards. S.S.S. 69. Practice area. *Green Fees:* weekdays £18.00. *Eating facilities:* restaurant and bar. *Visitors:* welcome weekdays except Bank Holidays. *Society Meetings:* (up to 30 members) catered for by arrangement. Professional: Nick Terry (081-309 0679). Secretary: Sandy Watt (081-300 2150).

SITTINGBOURNE near. Upchurch River Valley Golf Courses, Oak Lane, Upchurch, near Sittingbourne ME9 7AY (0634 360626; Fax: 0634 387784). *Location:* M2, Junction 4 (A278) A2 Rainham 2.5 miles L, Upchurch (opposite Little Chef). Undulating parkland with ponds and panoramic views. 18 holes, 6160 yards. S.S.S. 69. Driving range. *Green Fees:* weekdays £9.50 18 holes, £6.00 9 holes; weekends £12.50 18 holes, £7.00 9 holes. Reductions for Senior Citizens. *Eating facilities:* 120 seater à la carte restaurant, all day food and drinks lounge. *Visitors:* unrestricted. Swimming pool. *Society Meetings:* welcome weekdays. Professional: Martin Daniels (0634 379592). Secretary: (Members only) A.J. New ACIB (0634 260594). Course Controller: URVGC Ltd.

SITTINGBOURNE. Sittingbourne and Milton Regis, Wormdale, Newington, Sittingbourne ME9 7PX (Newington (0795 842261). *Location:* Junction 5 M2, A249 to Sheerness three quarters of a mile. Undulating course with trees. 18 holes, 6279 yards, 5760 metres. S.S.S. 70. *Green Fees:* £20.00 (18 holes), £32.00 (36 holes) weekdays. No green fees weekends. *Eating facilities:* available. *Visitors:* welcome weekdays, Handicap Certificate or letter of introduction required. *Society Meetings:* catered for Tuesdays and Thursdays by arrangement. Professional: J. Hearn (0795 842775). Manager: H.D.G. Wylie.

SNODLAND. Oastpark Golf Club, Malling Road, Snodland ME6 5LG (0634 242661). *Location:* quarter of a mile off Junction 4 of M20 (Snodland A228). Easy walking, good test of golf, lots of water/sand/trees. 18 holes, 6173 yards. S.S.S. 69. Extensive practice facilities. *Green Fees:* weekdays £9.00, £7.00 members; weekends £12.00, £9.00 members. Twilight ticket available two and a half hours before dusk. *Eating facilities:* full bar and catering service. *Visitors:* welcome, no restrictions. No jeans, tracksuits; golf shoes must be worn. *Society Meetings:* all welcome. Professional: Terry Cullen. Secretary: B.J. Townsend (0634 242818).

TENTERDEN. Tenterden Golf Club, Woodchurch Road, Tenterden TN30 7DR. *Location:* one mile south east of Tenterden on B2067. Parkland course. 18 holes, 6030 yards. S.S.S. 69. *Green Fees:* weekdays £20.00. *Eating facilities:* catering available. *Visitors:* welcome except weekends and Bank Holidays. *Society Meetings:* by prior arrangement. Professional: Garry Potter (0580 762409). Secretary: J.B. Shaw (0580 763987).

TONBRIDGE. Nizels Golf Club, Nizels Lane, Hildenborough, Near Tonbridge TN11 8NX (0732 833138; Fax: 0732 833764). *Location:* five minutes from M25 between Sevenoaks and Tonbridge. Lakes and woodland. 18 holes, 6408 yards. S.S.S. 71. Par 72. *Green Fees:* weekdays £25.00 per round. *Eating facilities:* open all day, high class catering. *Visitors:* welcome weekdays, bookings taken. *Society Meetings:* weekdays. Professional: M.S. Jarvis (0732 838926). Secretary: T.J. Fensom (0732 833138).

TONBRIDGE. Poult Wood Public Golf Course, Higham Lane, Tonbridge (Tonbridge (0732) 364039 – Golf Shop). *Location:* A227, two miles north of town centre. Wooded, 18 holes, 5569 yards. S.S.S. 67. Practice ground. *Green Fees:* £8.00 per round (£4.60 Juniors/Senior Citizens) weekdays; £12.00 per round weekends. Day ticket (Society) £22.00, £11.00 for 18 holes. *Eating facilities:* full catering available. *Visitors:* all welcome. *Society Meetings:* by arrangement with Clubhouse Manager. Other facilities, squash courts, meeting room, showers, toilets, changing, lockers. Non- Resident Professional: Ken Adwick. Club House Manager: (0732 366180).

TUNBRIDGE WELLS. Lamberhurst Golf Club, Church Road, Lamberhurst TN3 8DT (Lamberhurst (0892) 890241). *Location:* A21 from Tunbridge Wells to Hastings, turn left prior to descending hill to Lamberhurst then first right. Attractive parkland course. 18 holes, 6232 yards. S.S.S. 70. Small practice ground. *Green Fees:* weekdays £20.00 per round, £30.00 per day; £36.00 weekends and Bank Holidays. *Eating facilities:* full catering by arrangement. *Visitors:* welcome after 8am weekdays, 12 noon weekends and Bank Holidays. Handicap Certificate required. *Society Meetings:* catered for Tuesdays, Wednesdays and Thursdays by arrangement. Professional: M. Travers (0892 890552). Secretary: Mr P. Gleeson (Tel & Fax: 0892 890591).

TUNBRIDGE WELLS. Nevill Golf Club, Benhall Mill Road, Tunbridge Wells TN2 5JW (0892 527820). *Location:* off Forest Road, follow signs. 18 holes, 6336 yards. S.S.S. 70. *Green Fees:* £33.00 weekdays; £46.00 weekends and Bank Holidays. *Eating facilities:* lunches at club by prior arrangement. *Visitors:* welcome with reservation. Handicap Certificate required. *Society Meetings:* catered for. Professional: Paul Huggett (0892 532941). Secretary: Miss K.N.R. Pudner (0892 525818).

NIZELS GOLF CLUB

Nizels Lane, Hildenborough, near Tonbridge, Kent TN11 8NX Telephone: Tonbridge (0732) 833138

Superb 18 hole golf course, featuring many water hazards is complemented by our lovely Georgian Clubhouse. The bar and restaurant offer quality of service and delicious meals and snacks. Society/Corporate days. Functions catered for.

See our colour display on page 29.

England KENT/LANCASHIRE

IVYSIDE HOTEL
Westgate on Sea,
Kent CT8 8SB
0843-831082   AA**RAC

♛♛♛♛
The ideal centre for seven different golf courses,
including two Championship,
all within 25 minutes.

See our Display entry in colour section page 28.

TUNBRIDGE WELLS. **Tunbridge Wells Golf Club**, Langton Road, Tunbridge Wells (Tunbridge Wells (0892) 523034). *Location:* behind Marchants Garages. Parkland. 9 holes, 4525 yards. S.S.S. 62. *Green Fees:* weekdays £22.00. *Eating facilities:* snacks at bar or by arrangement. *Visitors:* welcome weekdays except Tuesdays. Weekends with member only. *Society Meetings:* only by previous arrangement. Professional: K. Smithson (0892 541386). Secretary: P.F. Janes (0892 536918).

WESTGATE ON SEA. **Westgate and Birchington Golf Club,** 176 Canterbury Road, Westgate on Sea CT8 8LT (0843 833905). Seaside course between Westgate on Sea and Birchington (A28). Seaside links course. 18 holes, 4926 yards, 4547 metres. S.S.S. 64. *Green Fees:* weekdays £14.00 per day (after 10am), weekends and Bank Holidays £17.00 (after 11 am, Sun after 12 noon). *Eating facilities:* full service available except Mondays and Fridays. *Visitors:* welcome if members of a recognised golf club. *Society Meetings:* by arrangement with Secretary. Professional: R. Game (0843 831115). Secretary: J.M. Wood (0843 831115).

WHITSTABLE. **Chestfield (Whitstable) Golf Club,** 103 Chestfield Road, Chestfield, Whitstable CT5 3LU (0227 792243). *Location:* half a mile south of Thanet Way (A299). Seaside links with woods – slightly hilly. 18 holes, 6181 yards. S.S.S. 70. *Green Fees:* £22.00 weekdays. *Eating facilities:* full catering facilities. *Visitors:* welcome weekdays with Handicap Certificate, weekends with member only. *Society Meetings:* catered for weekdays. Professional: John Brotherton (0227 793563). Secretary: M.A. Sutcliffe (0227 79441).

WHITSTABLE. **Whitstable and Seasalter Golf Club,** Collingwood Road, Whitstable CT5 1EB (0227 272020). *Location:* course adjoins town centre, take Nelson Road turning off main street. Flat seaside links. 9 holes, 5276 yards. S.S.S. 63. Practice net. *Green Fees:* £15.00, green fees are accepted at weekends only if accompanied by a member. *Eating facilities:* bar snacks. *Society Meetings:* welcome (limited in size). Secretary: Mr G.A. Hodson.

Lancashire

ACCRINGTON. **Accrington and District Golf Club,** New Barn Farm, West End, Oswaldtwistle, Accrington (Accrington (0254) 232734). *Location:* on A679, 2 miles from Blackburn. 18 holes, 5954 yards. S.S.S. 69. *Green Fees:* weekdays £15.00, weekends £18.00. *Eating facilities:* lunches and evening meals. *Visitors:* welcome without reservation. *Society Meetings:* prior bookings catered for. Professional: Bill Harling (0254 231091). Hon Secretary: J. Pilkington (0254 232734).

ACCRINGTON. **Green Haworth Golf Club,** Green Haworth, Accrington (Accrington (0254) 237580). *Location:* off A679, one mile Town Centre, via Willows Lane, turn left 300 yards beyond Red Lion Inn. Moorland. 9 holes, 5513 yards. S.S.S. 67. *Green Fees:* weekdays £10.00; weekends and Bank Holidays £14.00. *Eating facilities:* full catering and bar facilities. *Visitors:* welcome, no visitors on Sundays March to October. *Society Meetings:* catered for weekdays only. Secretary: Mr John K.S. Allan.

BACUP. **Bacup Golf Club,** Bankside Lane, Bacup (Bacup (0706) 3170). *Location:* one mile from Bacup centre. 9 holes, 6008 yards. S.S.S. 69. *Green Fees:* information not provided. *Eating facilities:* by arrangement except Mondays. *Visitors:* welcome without reservation except Mondays. Secretary: J. Garvey (0706 874485).

BLACKBURN. **Blackburn Golf Club,** Beardwood Brow, Blackburn BB2 7AX. *Location:* off A677 within easy reach of M6 (Junction 31), M61 and M65; west end of Blackburn. Meadowland with superb views of Lancashire coast and Pennine hills. 18 holes, 6140 yards, 5614 metres. S.S.S. 70. Par 71. Outdoor practice ground and indoor net. *Green Fees:* weekdays £19.00 (£7.00 with a member); weekends and Bank Holidays £22.00 (£8.00 with a member). Special rates for parties of 20 or more. *Eating facilities:* full catering and bar facilities (restricted Mondays). *Visitors:* welcome without reservation except on competition days. *Society Meetings:* catered for by arrangement (not Tuesdays or weekends). Professional: Alan Rodwell (0254 55942). Secretary: P.D. Haydock (0254 51122).

LANCASHIRE *England*

BLACKBURN. Great Harwood Golf Club, Harwood Bar, Great Harwood, Blackburn BB6 7TE (Great Harwood (0254) 884391). Flat wooded course. 9 holes, 6411 yards, 5862 metres. S.S.S. 71. Practice area. *Green Fees:* weekdays £13.00; weekends £16.00. *Eating facilities:* all meals catered for, bar hours 12-2pm, 4-11pm. *Visitors:* welcome Tuesday – Friday. *Society Meetings:* catered for by advance bookings. Secretary: A. Garraway (0254 886802).

BLACKBURN. Pleasington Golf Club, Pleasington, Near Blackburn (Blackburn (0254) 202177). *Location:* M6 north to Junction 31. Blackburn eight miles. Undulating woodland. 18 holes, 6445 yards. S.S.S. 71. *Green Fees:* weekdays £26.00, weekends and Bank Holidays £30.00. *Eating facilities:* full catering available. *Visitors:* welcome by prior arrangement. *Society Meetings:* Mondays, Wednesdays, Fridays by arrangement. Professional: G.J. Furey (0254 201630). Secretary: J. Hacking (0254 202177).

BLACKBURN. Rishton Golf Club, Eachill Links, Rishton (Great Harwood (0254) 884442). *Location:* three miles east of Blackburn. 9 holes, 6098 yards. S.S.S. 69. *Green Fees:* weekdays £12.00, £7.00 with a member; weekends £8.00 with a member. *Eating facilities:* full catering by prior arrangement. *Visitors:* welcome on weekdays and with a member at weekends and on Bank Holidays. *Society Meetings:* visiting parties welcome by prior arrangement, special rates can be obtained. Secretary: I. Baron.

BLACKBURN. Whalley Golf Club, Portfield Lane, Whalley, Blackburn BB6 9DR (Whalley (0254) 822236). *Location:* seven miles east of Blackburn on A59. Parkland. 9 holes, 5912 yards, 5406 metres. S.S.S. 69. *Green Fees:* weekdays £15.00 (with a member £8.00); weekends £20.00 (with a member £12.00). *Eating facilities:* full catering and bar facilities. *Visitors:* welcome except Thursday afternoons and Saturdays April to September. *Society Meetings:* welcome by appointment. Professional: H. Smith (0254 824766). Secretary: R. Bolsover (0254 824259).

BLACKBURN. Wilpshire Golf Club Ltd, Whalley Road, Wilpshire, Blackburn (Blackburn (0254) 248260 or 249691). *Location:* A666 three miles north of Blackburn on Blackburn to Whalley road. 18 holes, 5911 yards. S.S.S. 68. *Green Fees:* £22.00 weekdays; £27.00 weekends. *Eating facilities:* lunch, high tea, dinner except Mondays. *Visitors:* welcome without reservation except competition days. *Society Meetings:* catered for by prior booking through the Secretary. Professional: W. Slaven. Secretary: B. Grimshaw.

BLACKPOOL. Blackpool North Shore Golf Club, Devonshire Road, Blackpool FY1 2LZ (0253 51017). *Location:* north Blackpool on A587 behind North Prom. Undulating parkland. 18 holes, 6431 yards. S.S.S. 71. *Green Fees:* £21.00 weekdays; £23.00 weekends. Special Package – day's golf with meals £30.00. *Eating facilities:* full catering and bar facilities. *Visitors:* welcome except Saturdays. *Society Meetings:* welcome except Thursdays and weekends. Professional: Brendan Ward (0253 54640). Secretary: Mr R. Yates (0253 52054).

BLACKPOOL. Blackpool Park Golf Club, North Park Drive, Blackpool FY3 8LS (Blackpool (0253) 393960). *Location:* one mile west of Tower. Parkland course. 18 holes, 6060 yards. S.S.S. 69. *Green Fees:* £7.50 weekdays; £9.50 weekends. Bookings for tee reservation must be made to Blackpool Borough Council. *Eating facilities:* full catering services except Tuesday, bar. *Visitors:* welcome. *Society Meetings:* welcome (booking to be made through Blackpool Borough Council). Professional: B. Purdie (0253 391004). Secretary: Diane Woodman (0253 397916).

BLACKPOOL. Herons Reach. The Village Hotel and Leisure Club, East Park Drive, Blackpool FY3 8LL (0253 838866). *Location:* from Junction 4 off M55 follow signs for Blackpool Zoo, complex is opposite Stanley Park and next to the Zoo. Championship standard parkland course incorporating links features and 10 lakes. 6416 yards. S.S.S. 71. 18 bay floodlit driving range. *Green Fees:* weekdays £20.00 per round; weekends and Bank Holidays £30.00 per round. *Eating facilities:* Spikes Bar, leisure bar, grill restaurant. *Visitors:* welcome. Must hold current Handicap Certificate. 166 bedroomed hotel, leisure facilities, conference and banqueting facilities. Hotel Reservations (0253 838866; Fax: 0253 798800). *Society Meetings:* welcome. Golf Packages available. Professional: Richard Hudson. Manager: David Hughes.

BLACKPOOL. Knott End Golf Club Ltd, Wyre Side, Knott End, Poulton-le-Fylde FY6 0AA (Knott End (0253) 810254). *Location:* M55 Exit 3, A585 Fleetwood Road then A588 to Knott End, or by passenger ferry from Fleetwood. Scenic riverside course, slight undulations. 18 holes, 5852 yards. S.S.S. 68. Practice ground. *Green Fees:* £20.00 per day weekdays, weekends £24.00. *Eating facilities:* full catering and bar. *Visitors:* welcome, time sheet in use, contact Professional with 24 hours notice. *Society Meetings:* by arrangement weekdays only. Professional: Paul Walker (0253 811365). Secretary: Keith E. Butcher (0253 810576).

BLACKPOOL. Poulton-le-Fylde Golf Club, Myrtle Farm, Breck Road, Poulton-le-Fylde, Blackpool FY6 7HJ (Blackpool (0253) 893150). *Location:* three miles east of Blackpool. 9 holes, 2972 yards. *Green Fees:* £5.50 weekdays, £7.50 weekends per round. *Eating*

VILLAGE HOTEL & LEISURE CLUB

Play our challenging 18-hole course, complemented by superb facilities to enhance your enjoyment.
Visitors, Societies and Company Days welcome. Floodlit Driving Range. Swimming pool, tennis and squash courts, gym, aerobics studio, spa, steam room, sauna and toning salon.
See our colour display advertisement on page 19.
Village Hotel and Leisure Club, Blackpool. Telephone: 0253 838866

THE GOLF GUIDE 1994   *England* LANCASHIRE

facilities: meals at lunch time and light snacks available all day. *Visitors:* welcome without reservation. *Society Meetings:* catered for by prior booking. Professional: D. Spencer (0253 892444). Secretary: K. Audis.

BOLTON. **Bolton Municipal Golf Course,** Links Road, Chorley New Road, Bolton BL2 9XX (Bolton (0204) 844170). *Location:* midway between Horwich and Bolton, A673. Fairly flat parkland. 18 holes, 6336 yards, 5570 metres. S.S.S. 70. Practice ground. *Green Fees:* weekdays £5.00; weekends £6.50. *Eating facilities:* snack and meal facilities available and bar. *Visitors:* welcome at any time. *Society Meetings:* advance booking. Mid-week Society package available. Professional: Bob Longworth (0204 42336). Secretary: K. Taylor (0204 652882).

BURNLEY. **Burnley Golf Club,** Glen View, Burnley BB11 3RW (Burnley (0282) 21045). *Location:* 300 yards from junction of A56 and A646. Moorland. 18 holes, 5899 yards, 5391 metres. S.S.S. 69. *Green Fees:* weekdays £18.00; weekends and Bank Holidays £24.00. *Eating facilities:* available except Wednesdays from lunchtime and Mondays. *Visitors:* welcome except Saturdays. *Society Meetings:* catered for. Professional: W.P. Tye (Tel & Fax: 0282 455266). Secretary: G.J. Butterfield (0282 451281).

BURNLEY. **Towneley Golf Club,** Todmorden Road, Burnley (0282 451636). *Location:* east of Burnley centre. Parkland course, mostly flat. 18 holes, 5862 yards, 5357 metres. S.S.S. 68, Par 70. 9 hole course. Small practice area. *Green Fees:* £4.50 weekdays, £5.50 weekends. *Eating facilities:* clubhouse with diningroom, lounge bar and games room. *Visitors:* welcome, reservations recommended and tee reservation advisable. *Society Meetings:* contact Steward at clubhouse for catering requirements (0282 451636). Secretary: I. Kippax (0282 33972).

CARNFORTH. **Silverdale Golf Club,** Redbridge Lane, Silverdale, Carnforth LA5 0SP (Silverdale (0524) 701300). *Location:* M6 to Carnforth, then two miles west, adjacent to railway station. Testing heathland course with rock outcrops and excellent views. 12 holes, 5417 yards. S.S.S. 67. *Green Fees:* weekdays £12.00, weekends and Bank Holidays £17.00. *Eating facilities:* not available. *Visitors:* welcome except Sundays in the Summer unless with a member. *Society Meetings:* welcome by arrangement with Secretary.

Professional: S. Sumner Roberts. Secretary: P.J. Watts (0524 701307).

CHORLEY. **Chorley Golf Club,** Hall o' the' Hill, Heath Charnock, Chorley PR6 9HX (0257 480263). *Location:* south of Chorley, just off the A673 at the junction with the A6. Scenic course. 18 holes, 6317 yards. S.S.S. 70. *Green Fees:* weekdays £20.00 per round, £22.50 per day. *Eating facilities:* restaurant and lounge bar. *Visitors:* welcome by prior arrangement not Mondays, Bank Holidays or weekends. *Society Meetings:* catered for by arrangement. Professional: Paul Wesselingh (0257 481245). Secretary: A.K. Tyrer. Catering: (0257 474664).

CHORLEY. **Duxbury Park Golf Club (Municipal),** Duxbury Hall Road, Duxbury Park, Chorley PR7 4AS (02572 41634). *Location:* one mile south of town centre off A6. Wooded parkland with water hazards on several holes. 18 holes, 6390 yards, 5843 metres. S.S.S. 70. Small practice area. *Green Fees:* weekdays £6.50; weekends £8.50. *Eating facilities:* can be arranged. *Visitors:* welcome, book seven days in advance. *Society Meetings:* weekdays. Professional: David Clarke (02572 65380). Secretary: Reg Blease (02572 68665).

CHORLEY. **Shaw Hill Hotel Golf and Country Club,** Preston Road, Whittle-le-Woods, Chorley PR6 7PP (0257 269221; Fax: 0257 261223). *Location:* one mile north of Junction 8 on M61 and two miles M6 Junction 28. Championship course in superb parkland with the clubhouse in a beautiful Georgian mansion. 18 holes, 6405 yards. S.S.S. 71. Practice area. *Green Fees:* weekdays £30.00 per round; weekends £40.00 per round. *Eating facilities:* spike bar and formal bar, à la carte restaurant. *Visitors:* welcome all week, must hold current Handicap Certificate. Accommodation available. Golf trolleys and buggies also available. *Society Meetings:* catered for midweek only. Professional: David Clarke (0257 279222). General Manager: Mr G. Tyrer. Secretary: Mr F. Wharton.

CLITHEROE. **Clitheroe Golf Club,** Whalley Road, Pendleton, Clitheroe BB7 1PP (Clitheroe (0200) 22618). *Location:* A59, junction A671 (south of Clitheroe); 300m turn left (signposted Barrow) clubhouse 100m on right. Parkland with extensive countryside views. 18 holes, 6326 yards, 5785 metres. S.S.S. 71. Practice ground and range. *Green Fees:* weekdays

SHAWHILL
Hotel, Golf and Country Club

Whittle-le-Woods, near Chorley, Lancashire PR6 7PP
Telephone: Chorley (0257) 269221
Fax: Chorley (0257) 261223

Mini breaks are available all the year round.

Magnificent Georgian hotel retaining many original features, well known for its fine cuisine and excellent wine list.

All bedrooms are ensuite. Suites also available.

Lessons available from our Professional.

Ring for a brochure. Prices from £95 per person for 2 days' dinner, bed and breakfast and a complimentary round of golf per day.

LANCASHIRE England

£25.00; weekends and Bank Holidays £30.00. With a member £7.00. *Eating facilities:* full service available. *Visitors:* welcome but restricted to times available. No jeans, trainers, track/shell suits. *Society Meetings:* catered for, maximum 40 on Mondays, Tuesdays and Wednesdays, maximum 25 on Thursdays, Fridays and Sundays. No parties Saturdays or Bank Holidays. Professional: John E. Twissell (0200 24242). Secretary: G. Roberts JP (0200 22292).

COLNE. **Colne Golf Club,** Law Farm, Skipton Old Road, Colne BB8 7EB (Colne (0282) 863391). *Location:* come off eastern end of M65. Carry on one mile to next roundabout and take first exit on left. Goup Hill. Flat scenic moorland course with trees. 9 holes, 5961 yards, 5451 metres. S.S.S. 69. Full practice facilities. *Green Fees:* £12.00 weekdays, £16.00 weekends and Bank Holidays (subject to review). Parties of 12 or more £11.00 per person (not at weekends, Thursdays or competition days). *Eating facilities:* available daily except Mondays. *Visitors:* welcome except on competition days; two-balls only on Thursdays. *Society Meetings:* welcome except weekends, Thursdays and competition days. Secretary: A. Wharton.

DARWEN. **Darwen Golf Club,** Winter Hill, Darwen BB3 0LB (0254 701287). *Location:* one and a half miles from Darwen centre. Moorland. 18 holes, 5752 yards. S.S.S. 68. Large practice area. *Green Fees:* weekdays £15.00; weekends and Bank Holidays £20.00. *Eating facilities:* full catering. *Visitors:* welcome, except Saturdays. *Society Meetings:* welcome, except Saturdays. Professional: Wayne Lennon (0254 776370). Secretary: J. Kenyon (0254 704367).

FLEETWOOD. **Fleetwood Golf Club Ltd.,** The Golf House, Princes Way, Fleetwood FY7 8AF (0253 873114). *Location:* on Fylde Coast, eight miles from Blackpool, Coast Road Blackpool to Fleetwood, two miles west of Fleetwood Centre. Seaside, true links. White course 18 holes, 6723 yards, S.S.S. 72; Yellow course 18 holes, 6433 yards, S.S.S. 71. *Green Fees:* weekdays £20.00; weekends £25.00. *Eating facilities:* full catering and bar service. *Visitors:* welcome with Handicap Certificate. *Society Meetings:* catered for by arrangement. Professional: C.T. Burgess (0253 873661). Secretary: H. Fielding (0253 873661).

HEYSHAM. **Heysham Golf Club,** Trumacar Park, Middleton Road, Heysham LA3 3JH (Lancaster (0524) 851240). *Location:* five miles from M6 via Lancaster and Morecambe. Parkland, flat, part-wooded. 18 holes, 6338 yards. S.S.S. 70. Two practice grounds. *Green Fees:* weekdays £17.00 per round, £22.00 per day; weekends and Bank Holidays £27.00. Special rates for parties on application. *Eating facilities:* full catering seven days. *Visitors:* welcome without reservation. Tee reserved for members 1 to 1.45pm. *Society Meetings:* catered for by arrangement with Secretary. Professional: S. Fletcher (0524 852000). Secretary: F.A. Bland (0524 851011).

LANCASTER. **Lancaster Golf and Country Club Ltd,** Ashton Hall, Ashton-with-Stodday, Lancaster LA2 0AJ (0524 752090). *Location:* three miles south of Lancaster on A588. Parkland. 18 holes, 6282 yards. S.S.S. 71. *Green Fees:* weekdays £26.00. *Eating facilities:* available (Caterer: 0524 751105). *Visitors:* welcome weekdays only unless staying in the Dormy House. Club has a Dormy House (part of Ashton Hall) which accommodates 18 persons, 2 night minimum stay. *Society Meetings:* catered for weekdays only. Professional: David Sutcliffe (0524 751802). Secretary: Mr D.D.J. Palmer (0524 751247).

LANCASTER. **Lansil Golf Club,** Caton Road, Lancaster LA1 3PE (Lancaster (0524) 39269). *Location:* A683, towards Lancaster from Junction 34 M6. Parkland, quite hilly. 9 holes, 5608 yards. S.S.S. 67. *Green Fees:* £12.00 (£8.00 with a member). *Eating facilities:* light refreshments only by arrangement. *Visitors:* welcome, not before 1pm Saturday and Sunday. *Society Meetings:* catered for by arrangement weekdays only. Secretary: Derrick Crutchley (0524 418007).

LEYLAND. **Leyland Golf Club Ltd.,** Wigan Road, Leyland, Preston PR5 2UD (Leyland (0772) 421359). *Location:* leave M6 at Exit 28, turn right to traffic lights, (200 yards) turn right onto the A49, course located one mile on left. Flat parkland. 18 holes, 6123 yards. S.S.S. 69. *Green Fees:* £24.00 weekdays. *Eating facilities:* full catering except Mondays. *Visitors:* welcome weekdays only unless with a member. *Society Meetings:* welcome by arrangement with Secretary. Professional: C. Burgess (0772 423425). Secretary: G.D. Copeman (0772 436457).

LYTHAM ST. ANNES. **Fairhaven Golf Club Ltd.,** Lytham Hall Park, Ansdell, Lytham St. Annes FY8 4JU (Lytham (0253) 736741). *Location:* on B5261, two miles from Lytham, eight miles from Blackpool. 18 holes, 6880 yards. S.S.S. 73. Practice ground and net. *Green Fees:* weekdays £25.00 per round, £32.00 per day; weekends £30.00 per round. *Eating facilities:* full catering except Mondays. *Visitors:* welcome with reservation. *Society Meetings:* catered for by arrangement Mondays, Tuesdays, Wednesdays and Fridays. Professional: Mr I. Howieson (0253 736976). Secretary: Brian Hartley.

LYTHAM ST. ANNES. **Lytham Green Drive Golf Club,** Ballam Road, Lytham St. Annes FY8 4LE (Lytham (0253) 737390). *Location:* one mile from Lytham Square. 18 holes, 6159 yards. S.S.S. 69. *Green Fees:* £19.00 per round, £24.00 per day weekdays; £31.00 per round weekends. *Eating facilities:* catering available daily. *Visitors:* welcome without reservation. *Society Meetings:* catered for mid-week. Professional: A. Lancaster (0253 737379). Secretary: R. Kershaw.

LYTHAM ST. ANNES. **Royal Lytham and St. Annes Golf Club,** Links Gate, Lytham St. Annes FY8 3LQ (0253 724206; Fax: 0253 780946). *Location:* within one mile of the centre of St. Annes on Sea. Seaside links course. 18 holes, 6673 yards. S.S.S. 73. Practice ground. *Green Fees:* information not provided. *Eating facilities:* restaurant and bar. *Visitors:* welcome weekdays, limited Sundays times by arrangement. Dormy House accommodation available. *Society Meetings:* by arrangement. Professional: Eddie Birchenough (0253 720094). Secretary: Major A.S. Craven.

THE GOLF GUIDE 1994

England LANCASHIRE

LYTHAM ST. ANNES. **St. Annes Old Links Golf Club,** Highbury Road, Lytham St. Annes FY8 2LD (St. Annes (0253) 721826). *Location:* M55 via Blackpool South Shore, following airport signs. Past airport down to coast road, turn left and first left at next real traffic lights. The only true links course in Lancashire. 18 holes, 6616 yards. S.S.S. 72. Practice ground, putting and chipping greens. *Green Fees:* £25.00 weekdays; £30.00 weekends. *Eating facilities:* restaurant and snack facilities, bar. *Visitors:* welcome, not Saturdays, restricted Sundays. Tuesday is ladies day. *Society Meetings:* restricted to those with Handicaps and membership of other clubs. Professional: G.G. Hardiman (0253 722432). Secretary: P.W. Ray (0253 723597).

MORECAMBE. **Morecambe Golf Club Ltd.,** The Club House, Bare, Morecambe LA4 6AJ (Morecambe (0524) 418050). *Location:* on A589 leaving Morecambe towards Carnforth. Parkland course affected by sea breezes and offering superb views. 18 holes, 5766 yards. S.S.S. 68. *Green Fees:* weekdays £21.00 per day; weekends and Bank Holidays £26.00 per day. *Eating facilities:* diningroom and bar snacks, except Mondays. *Visitors:* welcome at all times, tee reserved for members up to 9.30am and from 12 noon to 1.30pm. *Society Meetings:* welcome at all times. Professional: P. De Valle (0524 415596). Secretary: T.H. Glover (0524 412841).

NELSON. **Marsden Park Golf Club,** Nelson Municipal Golf Course, Townhouse Road, Nelson BB9 8DG (0282 67525). *Location:* just off M65, heading towards Colne. Hilly parkland. 18 holes, 5806 yards. S.S.S. 68. *Green Fees:* information not available. *Eating facilities:* bar, meals to order. *Visitors:* welcome without restriction. Shop (0282 617525). *Society Meetings:* by arrangement. Secretary: J.L. Beck (0282 699181).

NELSON. **Nelson Golf Club,** King's Causeway, Brierfield, Nelson BB9 0EU (Nelson (0282) 614583). *Location:* on A682 two miles north of Burnley, one mile from Junction 12 M65. Moorland with trees. 18 holes, 5967 yards. S.S.S. 69. *Green Fees:* information not provided. Eating facilities: lunches, dinners by arrangement except Mondays. *Visitors:* weekdays except Thursdays, no Saturdays, Sundays by arrangement. *Society Meetings:* weekdays except Thursdays. Professional: M.J. Herbert (0282 617000). Secretary: R.W. Baldwin (0282 611234).

ORMSKIRK. **Ormskirk Golf Club,** Cranes Lane, Lathom L40 5UJ (Ormskirk (0695) 572112). *Location:* two miles east of Ormskirk. 18 holes, 6358 yards. S.S.S. 70. *Green Fees:* information not provided. *Eating facilities:* available except Monday. *Visitors:* welcome, Handicap Certificates required, notice advised with reservation. *Society Meetings:* catered for, book in advance. Professional: J. Hammond. Secretary: P.D. Dromgoole.

PRESTON. **Ashton and Lea Golf Club Ltd,** Tudor Avenue, off Blackpool Road, Lea, Preston PR4 0XA (Preston (0772) 726480). *Location:* on A583, three miles west of Preston, turn right opposite Pig and Whistle Hotel. Parkland with water features. 18 holes, 6289 yards. S.S.S. 70. Small practice ground. *Green Fees:* Mondays to Thursdays £18.00, Fridays £20.00; weekends and Bank Holidays £24.00. Reduced rates if playing with member. *Eating facilities:* full catering every day. *Visitors:* welcome but please telephone to reserve tee time. *Society Meetings:* catered for weekdays only. Professional: Mr M.R. Greenough (0772 720374). Secretary: Mr M.G. Gibbs (0772 735282).

PRESTON. **Fishwick Hall Golf Club,** Glenluce Drive, Farringdon Park, Preston PR1 5TD (Preston (0772) 798300). *Location:* two minutes from Exit 31 M6, off A49 Blackburn to Preston Road. Parkland, part wooded, bounded by river. 18 holes, 6028 yards. S.S.S. 69. Practice ground and net. *Green Fees:* weekdays £20.00; weekends and Public Holidays £25.00. Reductions if playing with members. *Eating facilities:* bar, full catering available. *Visitors:* welcome by arrangement. *Society Meetings:* catered for by arrangement. Professional: S. Bence (0772 795870). Secretary: R.R. Gearing (0772 798300).

PRESTON. **Ingol Golf Club,** Tanterton Hall Road, Ingol, Preston PR7 1BY (Preston (0772) 734556). *Location:* two miles from Junction 32 M6 (joins M55). Parkland. 18 holes, 5868 yards. S.S.S. 68. *Green Fees:* weekdays £20.00 (reduction with member), weekends and Bank Holidays £25.00 (reduction with member). Reductions for parties. *Eating facilities:* bar/restaurant. *Visitors:* welcome anytime, please telephone to check tee reservations. Snooker, pool and squash. *Society Meetings:* welcome by arrangement. Professional: S. Laycock. Secretary: Amanda Parker.

PRESTON. **Longridge Golf Club,** Fell Barn, Jeffrey Hill, Longridge, Preston PR3 2TU (Longridge (0772) 783291). *Location:* eight miles north-east of Preston off B6243. Moorland with extensive spectacular views. 18 holes, 5726 yards. S.S.S. 68. *Green Fees:* £18.00 Mondays to Thursdays, £21.00 Fridays, Saturdays, Sundays and Bank Holidays. *Eating facilities:* full catering except Mondays. *Visitors:* welcome at all times. *Society Meetings:* welcome by arrangement. Professional: Neil James. Secretary: J. Greenwood (0772 782765 evenings).

PRESTON. **Penwortham Golf Club Ltd.,** Blundell Lane, Penwortham, Preston PR1 0AX (Preston (0772) 743207). *Location:* one mile west of Preston on main Southport to Liverpool road. Parkland. 18 holes, 5667 yards. S.S.S. 68. *Green Fees:* £22.00 weekdays, £28.00 weekends. *Eating facilities:* lunches and dinners served at Club. *Visitors:* weekdays only. *Society Meetings:* catered for by arrangement. Professional: J. Wright (0772 742345; Fax: 0772 741677). Secretary: J. Parkinson (0772 744630).

PRESTON. **Preston Golf Club,** Fulwood Hall Lane, Fulwood, Preston PR2 4DD (0772 700011). *Location:* exit 32 on M6 marked Preston & Garstang, partway to Preston turning at Watling Street Road. Parkland course. 18 holes, 6267 yards. S.S.S. 70. *Green Fees:* weekdays £22.00 per round, £27.00 per day. *Eating facilities:* first class diningroom, bars. *Visitors:* welcome Mondays, Wednesdays and Fridays, maximum 48, Thursdays maximum 32, Tuesdays maximum 16. *Society Meetings:* catered for, Handicap Certificate required. Professional: P. Wells (0772 700022). Secretary: J.R. Spedding (0772 700011).

LANCASHIRE/LEICESTERSHIRE England   THE GOLF GUIDE 1994

ROSSENDALE. **Rossendale Golf Club Ltd.**, Ewood Lane Head, Haslingden, Rossendale BB4 6LH (Rossendale (0706) 213056). *Location:* 14 miles north of Manchester, easy access from M66 and A56. 18 holes, 6260 yards. S.S.S. 70. *Green Fees:* weekdays £20.00; weekends and Bank Holidays £25.00. *Eating facilities:* full catering except Mondays; bar. *Visitors:* welcome except Saturdays during season. *Society Meetings:* special terms including full catering available. Professional: S.J. Nicholls (0706-213616). Secretary: J.R. Swain (0706 831339).

SKELMERSDALE. **Beacon Park Golf Club,** Beacon Lane, Dalton, Upholland WN8 7RU (Upholland (0695) 622700). *Location:* M6 Junction 26, follow signs for Upholland. Parkland, tree lined – undulating. 18 holes, 5995 yards. S.S.S. 72. Large practice ground, 24 bay floodlit driving range. *Green Fees:* information not provided. *Eating facilities:* bar/restaurant. *Visitors:* welcome anytime. Public course, open seven days. *Society Meetings:* Society and Group bookings available on request. Professional: Ray Peters (0695 622700; Fax: 0695 633066).

UPHOLLAND. **Dean Wood Golf Club,** Lafford Lane, Upholland, Skelmersdale WN8 0QZ (0695 622980). *Location:* Exit 26 from M6 signposted for Southport. Follow A577 to Upholland, first right after church. Wooded parkland course. 18 holes, 6137 yards. S.S.S. 70. *Green Fees:* weekdays £26.00; weekends £30.00. *Eating facilities:* daily catering available, bar. *Visitors:* welcome with reservation, not before 10.30am weekends and Bank Holidays. *Society Meetings:* catered for by prior arrangement. Professional: Tony Coop. Secretary: T.F. Hehir (0695 622219).

Leicestershire

ASHBY DE LA ZOUCH. **Willesley Park Golf Club,** Tamworth Road, Ashby de la Zouch (0530 411532). *Location:* on B5006 towards Tamworth, one mile from centre of Ashby. Wooded park, semi-heathland. 18 holes, 6304 yards. S.S.S. 70. *Green Fees:* weekdays £27.50 per round/day, weekends and Bank Holidays £32.50. *Eating facilities:* dining room and bar, no catering Mondays. *Visitors:* welcome with reservation. *Society Meetings:* catered for Wednesday, Thursday and Friday. Professional: C.J. Hancock (0530 414820). Secretary: N.H. Jones (0530 414596).

BIRSTALL. **Birstall Golf Club,** Station Road, Birstall LE4 3BB (Leicester (0533) 674450). *Location:* 3 miles north of Town just off the A6 Leicester to Derby. Parkland. 18 holes, 6222 yards. S.S.S. 70. Practice ground and net. *Green Fees:* weekdays £25.00 per day. *Eating facilities:* bar, diningroom. No catering Mondays. *Visitors:* welcome Mondays, Wednesdays and Fridays. *Society Meetings:* minimum 20, catered for by prior arrangement £20.00 per person. Professional: D. Clark (0533 675245). Secretary: Mrs S.E. Chilton (0533 674322).

COSBY. **Cosby Golf Club,** Chapel Lane, off Broughton Road, Cosby, Leicester (Leicester (0533) 864759). *Location:* eight miles south of Leicester, four miles from Junction 21 M1. Undulating parkland. 18 holes, 6418 yards. S.S.S. 71. *Green Fees:* weekdays £20.00 per round, £22.00 per day; weekends £8.00 but only with a member. Special rates for societies over 20 in number. *Eating facilities:* bar and food available by arrangement with the Steward. *Visitors:* no visitors after 4pm weekdays or weekends. Handicap Certificates may be required for all visitors. *Society Meetings:* welcome, prior booking essential. Professional: (0533 848275). Secretary: M.D. Riddle.

ENDERBY. **Enderby Golf Club,** Enderby Golf Course, Enderby Leisure Centre, Mill Lane, Enderby (0533 849388). *Location:* two miles from M1/M69 junction 21 roundabout. Flat parkland course. 9 holes, 2178 yards. S.S.S. 61. *Green fees:* information not provided. *Eating facilities:* bar open normal bar hours, light snacks available at lunchtime. *Visitors:* welcome at all times. Full range of recreational facilities available – swimming, squash, indoor bowls, sauna, solarium, badminton, snooker, etc. Professional: Chris d'Araujo.

HINCKLEY. **Hinckley Golf Club,** Leicester Road, Hinckley LE10 3DR (Hinckley (0455) 615124). *Location:* situated one mile from Hinckley on A47 Leicester-Hinckley road. Parkland with lakeside features. 18 holes, 6517 yards, 5959 metres. S.S.S. 71. Practice area for members. *Green Fees:* weekdays £20.00 per round, £25.00 per day. *Eating facilities:* bar; meals daily except Sunday evenings. *Visitors:* welcome except Tuesdays and weekends. *Society Meetings:* Mondays and Wednesdays by appointment. Professional: R. Jones (Tel & Fax: 0455 615014). Secretary: J. Toon (0455 615124).

KIRBY MUXLOE. **Kirby Muxloe Golf Club,** Station Road, Kirby Muxloe LE9 9EP (Leicester (0533) 393107). *Location:* four miles west of Leicester on A47. M1 Exit 21. Undulating parkland with lake. 18 holes, 6303 yards, 5766 metres. S.S.S. 70. Practice area and tuition from Professional. *Green Fees:* weekdays £20.00 per round, £25.00 per day; weekends with member or by Captain's permission only. *Eating facilities:* bars, dining room. *Visitors:* welcome weekdays. Advisable to phone in advance. *Society Meetings:* Wednesdays, Thursdays, Friday afternoons only. Professional: R.T. Stephenson (0533 392813). Secretary: S.F. Aldwinckle (0533 393457).

THE GOLF GUIDE 1994   *England*   LEICESTERSHIRE

LEICESTER. **Humberstone Heights Golf Club,** Gipsy Lane, Leicester (Leicester (0533) 761905). *Location:* opposite Towers Hospital, Uppingham side of Leicester. Parkland. 18 holes, 6343 yards. S.S.S. 70. Practice area, pitch and putt course. *Green Fees:* weekdays £6.00 per round; weekends £7.50 (reduced rates for Juniors). *Eating facilities:* bar, snacks. *Visitors:* welcome (Municipal Golf Course). Green Fee ticket gains entry to Clubhouse. *Society Meetings:* welcome. Professional: Philip Highfield (0533 764674). Secretary: Stephen Day (0533 761905).

LEICESTER. **Kibworth Golf Club Ltd.,** Weir Road, Kibworth Beauchamp, Leicester LE8 0LP (0533 792301). *Location:* A6, four miles Market Harborough, 12 miles Leicester. Flat wooded course. 18 holes, 6298 yards. S.S.S. 70. *Green Fees:* £21.00. *Eating facilities:* restaurant – book through Steward in advance avoiding Monday. *Visitors:* welcome, Handicap Certificate required or introduction from club member. *Society Meetings:* catered for if booked. Professional: Alan Strange (0533 792283). Secretary: A. Towers (0533 792301).

LEICESTER. **Leicestershire Golf Club,** Evington Lane, Leicester LE5 6DJ (Leicester (0533) 736035). *Location:* two miles from city centre off A6 road. Parkland. 18 holes, 6312 yards. S.S.S. 70. *Green Fees:* weekdays £25.00, weekends £30.00. *Eating facilities:* bar snacks, full catering available by order. *Visitors:* welcome, Handicap Certificate required. *Society Meetings:* by arrangement. Professional: John R. Turnbull (0533 736730). Secretary: J.L. Adams (0533 738825).

LEICESTER. **Scraptoft Golf Club,** Beeby Road, Scraptoft, Leicester LE7 9SJ (Leicester (0533) 419000). *Location:* off A47 Peterborough. Undulating. 18 holes, 6166 yards. S.S.S. 69. *Green Fees:* £20.50 weekdays, £25.50 weekends. Sunday mornings with club member only. *Eating facilities:* full restaurant service except Mondays. *Visitors:* welcome, proof of Handicap required. *Society Meetings:* catered for on application weekdays only. Professional: Simon Sherratt (0533 419138). Secretary: A.M. Robertson (0533 418863).

LEICESTER. **Western Park Golf Club,** Scudamore Road, Braunstone Frith, Leicester (0533 876158). *Location:* four miles west of Junction 21 on M1 motorway. Flat, wooded course. 18 holes, 6532 yards. S.S.S. 71. Practice area. *Green fees:* information not available. *Eating facilities:* full catering facilities. *Visitors:* contact Professional. *Society Meetings:* contact Professional. Professional: Bruce Whipham (0533 872339). Secretary: Brian Wells (0533 773543).

LEICESTER. **Whetstone Golf Club and Driving Range,** Cambridge Road, Cosby (Leicester (0533) 861424). *Location:* south of Leicester between Cosby and Whetstone. Parkland. 18 holes, 5795 yards. S.S.S. 68. Driving range, putting green. *Green Fees:* weekdays £12.00; weekends £13.00. *Eating facilities:* bar/lounge serving full range of meals. *Visitors:* welcome midweek and after 1pm Saturday and Sunday. *Society Meetings:* welcome by prior arrangement. Professionals: N. Leatherland and D. Raitt. Secretary: Mr D.H. Dalby.

LOUGHBOROUGH. **Charnwood Forest Golf Club,** Breakback Road, Woodhouse Eaves, Near Loughborough LE12 8TA(Woodhouse Eaves (0509) 890259). *Location:* Beacon Hill, Charnwood Forest. A6 to B591 two miles. M1 Junction 22 two miles east. Rocks, bracken, heather, woods – in the heart of Charnwood Forest. No bunkers. 9 holes, 5960 yards. S.S.S. 69. *Green Fees:* for 18 holes: weekdays £20.00 (£10.00 with member); weekends £25.00 (£12.50 with member). *Eating facilities:* full catering except Mondays, snacks available. *Visitors:* welcome, but not Tuesdays (Ladies' Day). *Society Meetings:* not more than 40 catered for by prior arrangement. Professional: Mr A. Stokes (0509 890509). Secretary: A.G. Stanley (0509 890259).

LOUGHBOROUGH. **Longcliffe Golf Club,** Snell's Nook Lane, Nanpantan, Loughborough (0509 216321). *Location:* two miles west of Loughborough Town Centre, 13 miles north of Leicester. Approximately one mile from Exit 23, M1. 18 holes, 6551 yards. S.S.S. 71. *Green Fees:* £22.00 per round, £27.00 per day. *Eating facilities:* full catering facilities, except Tuesdays. *Visitors:* restricted, must be introduced and playing with member at weekends and Bank Holidays. *Society Meetings:* by arrangement only accepted on Mondays, Wednesdays, Thursdays and Fridays. Professional: I. Bailey (0509 231450). Secretary: G. Harle (0509 239129).

LUTTERWORTH. **Lutterworth Golf Club,** Rugby Road, Lutterworth, Leicester LE17 5HN (Lutterworth (0455) 557141). *Location:* on A4114. Hilly parkland-type course – open fairways. 18 holes, 5570 yards. S.S.S. 67. *Green Fees:* £16.00 per round, £22.00 per day. *Eating facilities:* lunches and evening meals available every day. *Visitors:* welcome on weekdays and with a member at weekends. Professional: N. Melvin (0455 557199). Secretary: Mrs Tranter (0455 552532). Steward: C.D. Sholl (0455 557141).

LUTTERWORTH near. **Ullesthorpe Court Golf Club,** Frolesworth Road, Ullesthorpe, Near Lutterworth LE17 5BZ (0455 209023; Fax: 0455 202537). *Location:* 10/15 minutes M1, M69, M6, between Leicester and Coventry. 18 holes, 6650 yards. S.S.S. 72. *Green Fees:* £19.00 weekdays. Golf Day Specials from £22.00. *Eating facilities:* restaurant, bar snacks and functions. *Visitors:* welcome weekdays except Bank Holidays. 40 bedroomed hotel and leisure centre. *Society Meetings:* catered for weekdays except Bank Holidays. Professional: David Bowrins. Secretary: Mrs P. Woolley.

MARKET HARBOROUGH. **Market Harborough Golf Club,** Great Oxendon Road, Market Harborough (0858 463684). *Location:* one mile south of Market Harborough on A508. Parkland. An excellent testing new 9 holes were opened in May 1993. 18 holes, 6022 yards. S.S.S. 69. Practice ground. *Green Fees:* weekdays £16.00 per round, £22.00 per day; weekends £14.00 with a member. *Eating facilities:* bar snacks and full meals available. *Visitors:* welcome weekdays; weekends only with a member. *Society Meetings:* welcome on application. Professional: F. Baxter. Secretary: J. Lord (0536 771771).

147

MELTON MOWBRAY. **Melton Mowbray Golf Club,** Thorpe Arnold, Melton Mowbray LE14 4SD (Melton Mowbray (0664) 62118). *Location:* A607 road two miles north-east of Melton Mowbray. 18 holes, 6222 yards, S.S.S. 70. Practice ground. *Green Fees:* weekdays £17.50; weekends £25.00. *Eating facilities:* full catering and bar facilities. *Visitors:* welcome before 3pm. *Society Meetings:* by prior arrangement weekdays only. Professional: Tony Westwood (0664 69629). Secretary: E.A. Sallis.

OADBY. **Glen Gorse Golf Club,** Glen Road, Oadby LE2 4RF (Leicester (0533) 712226). *Location:* on A6, four and a half miles south of Leicester. Flat but wooded course. 18 holes, 6615 yards, 6048 metres. S.S.S. 72. Par 72. *Green Fees:* weekdays £22.00 per round, £25.00 per day (£7.50 with member); weekends £7.50 with member only. *Eating facilities:* bar and meals/snacks (not Mondays). *Visitors:* welcome weekdays without reservation, weekends with members only. *Society Meetings:* welcome Tuesday to Friday by prior arrangement. Professional: Bob Larratt (0533 713748). Secretary: M. Goodson (0533 714159).

OADBY. **Oadby Golf Club,** Leicester Road, Oadby, Leicester LE2 4AB (Leicester (0533) 700215). *Location:* on A6 south of Leicester, one mile from City boundary, at Leicester Racecourse. Parkland. 18 holes, 6376 yards, 5827 metres. S.S.S. 70. Practice ground, coaching. *Green Fees:* information not provided. *Eating facilities:* snacks always available, bar with meals

on prior notice. *Visitors:* welcome on application to the Professional or booked through Oadby and Wigston Borough Council. *Society Meetings:* booking as for Visitors (weekdays only). Professional: Simon Ward (0533 709052). Hon. Secretary: C. Chamberlain (0533 889862 home).

ROTHLEY. **Rothley Park Golf Club,** Westfield Lane, Rothley, Leicester LE7 7LH (Leicester (0533) 302019). *Location:* off A6, north of Leicester. Parkland. 18 holes, 6481 yards. S.S.S. 71. *Green Fees:* £25.00 per round, £30.00 per day (mid-week). *Eating facilities:* available except Mondays. *Visitors:* welcome except Tuesdays, weekends and Bank Holidays, must be members of recognised golf club with handicap. *Society Meetings:* catered for Wednesdays and Thursdays. Professional: P.J. Dolan (0533 303023). Secretary: Bernard Durham (0533 302809).

WOODHOUSE EAVES. **Lingdale Golf Club,** Joe Moore's Lane, Woodhouse Eaves, Near Loughborough LE12 8TF (Woodhouse Eaves (0509) 890035). *Location:* on B5300, Anstey-Shepshed road, three miles from Exit 23 on M1. Woodland and parkland – set in Charnwood Forest. 18 holes, 6545 yards. S.S.S. 71. Practice ground. *Green Fees:* weekdays £18.00 per day; weekends £20.00. Societies £15.00. *Eating facilities:* full catering available. *Visitors:* welcome, but please telephone first. *Society Meetings:* catered for Mondays, Wednesdays, Thursdays and Fridays (one month's notice required). Professional: P. Sellears (0509 890684). Secretary: M. Green (0509 890703).

Lincolnshire

BOSTON. **Boston Golf Club Ltd,** Cowbridge, Horncastle Road, Boston PE22 7EL (Boston (0205) 362306). *Location:* two miles north of Boston on B1183. Look for sign to right if travelling north. Parkland with featured water. 18 holes, 6566 yards, 6060 metres. S.S.S. 71. *Green Fees:* weekdays £16.00 per round, £22.00 per day; weekends and Bank Holidays £22.00 per round, £30.00 per day. *Eating facilities:* daily by arrangement with resident Steward (0205 352533). *Visitors:* welcome without reservation. *Society Meetings:* small groups catered for midweek. Professional: T.R. Squires (0205 362306). Secretary: D.E. Smith (Tel & Fax: 0205 350589).

GAINSBOROUGH. **Gainsborough Golf Club,** Gainsborough DN21 1PZ (Gainsborough (0427) 613088). *Location:* one mile north east of Gainsborough, between A159 and A631. Flat parkland. 18 holes, 6620 yards. S.S.S. 72. Putting green and driving range. *Green Fees:* weekdays £20.00 per round, £25.00 per day. *Eating facilities:* restaurant and coffee shop. *Visitors:* welcome weekdays without reservation;

weekends with member only. *Society Meetings:* welcome if booked in advance. Professional: S. Cooper (0427 612278). Manager: D.J. Garrison (0427 613088).

GRANTHAM. **Belton Park Golf Club,** Belton Lane, Londonthorpe Road, Grantham NG31 9SH (0476 67399; Fax: 0476 592078). *Location:* two miles from Grantham. 250 acre Deer Park adjacent to the historical Belton House. Three courses as follows: Brownlow Course 6420 yards (Championship). S.S.S. 71. Ancaster Course 6252 yards. S.S.S. 70. Belmont Course 6016 yards. S.S.S. 69. Two large practice areas. *Green Fees:* weekdays £18.00 per round, half price if playing with member; weekends and Bank Holidays £28.00 per round, half price with member. All including VAT. *Eating facilities:* full restaurant facilities every day; three bars. *Visitors:* welcome without reservation. *Society Meetings:* catered for by arrangement weekdays only (except Tuesday). Special day package. Professional: B. McKee (0476 63911). Secretary and General Manager: T. Measures (0476 67399 – all enquiries; Fax: 0476 592078).

THE GOLF GUIDE 1994 — England LINCOLNSHIRE

GRANTHAM near. **Belton Woods Hotel and Country Club,** Belton, Near Grantham NG32 2LN (0476 593200). *Location:* two miles north of Grantham on A607 to Lincoln. Five minutes off A1 at Gonerby Moor. Parkland course. Three courses – Lancaster Course: 18 holes, 7021 yards. S.S.S. 74; Wellington Course: 18 holes, 6875 yards. S.S.S. 73; Spitfire Course: 9 holes, 1184 yards. 24-bay driving range. *Green Fees:* on application. Special rates for Societies and groups. *Eating facilities:* three bars, two restaurants. *Visitors:* welcome with advance booking. Accommodation in Hotel, 96 luxurious bedrooms and suites, with extensive leisure and conference facilities. Golfing Breaks and Society Meetings a speciality. Golf and Leisure Manager: Richard Woolston. Golf Professional: Tony Roberts (0476 79101).

GRANTHAM. **Stoke Rochford Golf Club,** Stoke Rochford, Near Grantham NG33 5EW (Great Ponton (047-683 275). *Location:* five miles south of Grantham on A1. Entrance at "A.J.S." service area. Parkland. 18 holes, 6251 yards. S.S.S. 70. Small practice ground. *Green Fees:* £17.00 per round, £24.00 per day weekdays (estimated); weekends and Bank Holidays £26.00 per round, £35.00 per day (estimated). If playing with a member £8.00 weekdays, £10.00 weekends. *Eating facilities:* meals available daily, to be booked before playing. *Visitors:* cannot commence play before 10.30am at weekends or on Public Holidays. No visitors at weekends November, December and January. *Society Meetings:* by prior arrangement. Professional: A.E. Dow (047-683 218). Secretary: J.M. Butler (0476) 67030).

HORNCASTLE near. **Horncastle Golf Club,** West Ashby, Near Horncastle LN9 5PP (0507 526800). *Location:* just off A158 between Horncastle and Baumber. Parkland course – water features on 14 holes. 18 holes, 5800 yards. S.S.S. 70. Floodlit golf range. *Green Fees:* weekdays £11.00 per round, £17.00 per day; weekends £12.50 per round, £20.00 per day. *Eating facilities:* bar, restaurant. *Visitors:* welcome anytime. Special package available golf range, golf course, food and drink. Ballroom and conference facilities. Accommodation available in 24 bedrooms. Fishing lake. *Society Meetings:* please phone in advance. Professional: E.C. Wright. Secretary: T. Bullimore.

LINCOLN. **Blankney Golf Club,** Blankney, near Metheringham, Lincoln LN4 3AZ (0526 320263). *Location:* on B1188, 10 miles south of Lincoln. Parkland, slightly undulating. 18 holes, 6378 yards. S.S.S. 71. Practice area. *Green Fees:* weekdays £15.00 per round, £25.00 per day; weekends £20.00 per round, £30.00 per day. *Eating facilities:* bar meals and snacks, dining room by prior arrangement. *Visitors:* welcome – telephone beforehand. *Society Meetings:* by advance booking only. Professional: Graham Bradley (0526 320202). General Manager: D.A. Priest (0526 320263; Fax: 0526 322521).

LINCOLN. **Canwick Park Golf Club,** Canwick Park, Washingborough Road, Lincoln LN4 1EF (Lincoln (0522) 522166). *Location:* one and a half miles approximately east of Lincoln, first left (turning) off Canwick Road from Lincoln is Washingborough Road. Wooded parkland course. 18 holes, 6257 yards, 5726 metres, S.S.S. 70. Practice ground. *Green Fees:* £13.00 per round, £20.00 per day weekdays; £14.00 per round, £22.00 per day weekends. *Eating facilities:* bar snacks and meals to order. *Visitors:* welcome weekdays; weekends after 3.00pm. Professional: Steve Williamson (0522 536870). Secretary: Mr A.C. Hodgkinson (0522 791757).

LINCOLN. **Carholme Golf Club,** Carholme Road, Lincoln LN1 1SE (Lincoln (0522) 523725). *Location:* one mile from city centre on A57 to Worksop. Flat parkland. 18 holes, 6150 yards. S.S.S. 69. *Green fees:* on application; no green fees weekends. *Eating facilities:* full service except Mondays. *Visitors:* welcome (not Sundays). *Society Meetings:* by prior arrangement only. Professional: G. Leslie (0522 536811). Secretary: Mr D.R. Motts (0522 523725).

LINCOLN. **Lincoln Golf Club,** Torksey, Lincoln (Torksey (042 771) 210). *Location:* East Lincolnshire, between Lincoln, Gainsborough and Newark. Flat testing inland course with quick drying sandy subsoil. 18 holes, 6438 yards. S.S.S. 71. *Green Fees:* £18.00 per round, £23.00 per day. *Eating facilities:* full facilities except Tuesday (ladies day). *Visitors:* welcome by arrangement, weekends with members only. *Society Meetings:* catered for. Professional: Ashley Carter (042 771 273). Secretary: D. Boag (042 771 721).

LOUTH. **Louth Golf Club,** 59 Crowtree Lane, Louth LN11 9LJ (Louth (0507) 602554). *Location:* western outskirts of Louth. Undulating parkland. 18 holes, 6477 yards. S.S.S. 71. Practice ground. *Green Fees:* £15.00 per round, £18.00 per day weekdays; £18.00 per round, £20.00 per day weekends and Bank Holidays. *Eating facilities:* full catering 10am to 10pm (to order). *Visitors:* welcome without reservation. Squash courts. *Society Meetings:* catered for. Professional: A.J. Blundell (0507 604648). Secretary: P.C. Bell (Tel & Fax: 0507 603681). Manager: M. Covey (0507 604864). Manager's Assistant: T. Curtis.

MABLETHORPE. **Sandilands Golf Club,** Roman Bank, Sandilands, Sutton-on-Sea LN12 2RJ (0521 41432). *Location:* A52 one mile south of Sutton-on-Sea. Seaside links adjacent to sea and sand. 18 holes, 5995 yards, 5483 metres. S.S.S. 69. *Green Fees:*

BELTON WOODS HOTEL

As sister hotel to the world famous Belfry, Belton Woods aims to please both the serious golfer and his non-golfing partner. As well as having two superb courses, it offers luxurious leisure club facilities, from sauna, spa and sunbeds to the beauty salon, tennis and archery.   DE VERE 🞛 HOTELS

See our Colour Display Advertisement on page 25.

Belton, near Grantham, Lincolnshire NG32 2LN. Telephone: 0476 593200 Fax: 0476 74547

LINCOLNSHIRE England   THE GOLF GUIDE 1994

weekdays £12.00 round, £18.00 day; weekends and Bank Holidays £18.00 per round. *Eating facilities:* meals and drinks in clubhouse. *Visitors:* welcome. *Society Meetings:* catered for weekdays. Professional: (0521 41600). Secretary: D. Mumby (0521 41617).

MARKET RASEN. **Market Rasen and District Golf Club,** Legsby Road, Market Rasen LN8 3DZ (Market Rasen (0673) 842319). *Location:* A46 to Market Rasen – one mile east of town. Wooded course. 18 holes, 6043 yards, 5527 metres. S.S.S. 69. Practice ground. *Green Fees:* weekdays £20.00 per day, £15.00 per round; weekends only with member. *Eating facilities:* by arrangement with the Steward, but not Mondays. *Visitors:* welcome with reservation, must be member of bona fide golf club. Not Wednesdays after 10.30am. Weekends with members only. *Society Meetings:* catered for Tuesdays and Fridays. Professional: A.M. Chester (0673 842416). Secretary: J.A. Brown (0673 842319).

SKEGNESS. **North Shore Hotel and Golf Club,** North Shore Road, Skegness PE25 1DN (Skegness (0754) 763298). *Location:* north of town one mile. Half seaside links, half parkland overlooking the sea. 18 holes, 6134 yards. S.S.S. 71. *Green Fees:* information not provided. *Eating facilities:* hotel on the course. *Visitors:* welcome, prior notice essential. *Society Meetings:* welcome. Professional: Golf instruction given by John Cornelius (0754 764822).

SKEGNESS. **Seacroft Golf Club,** Seacroft, Skegness PE25 3AU (Skegness (0754) 763020). *Location:* towards Gibraltar Nature Reserve. Seaside links course. 18 holes, 6490 yards. S.S.S. 71. *Green Fees:* weekdays £20.00 per day, £28.00 per day; weekends and Bank Holidays £25.00 round, £35.00 per day. *Eating facilities:* available on prior booking. *Visitors:* welcome after 9.30am if members of recognised club, Handicap Certificate required; not between 12noon and 2pm. *Society Meetings:* catered for, limited to 24 at weekends. Professional: R. Lawie (0754 769624). Secretary: H.K. Brader (0754 763020).

SLEAFORD. **Sleaford Golf Club,** Willoughby Road, South Rauceby, Sleaford NG34 8PL (South Rauceby (0529) 488273). *Location:* off A153, two miles west of Sleaford. Inland links-type course, fairly flat and lightly wooded. 18 holes, 6443 yards, 5947 metres. S.S.S. 71. Practice field, 6 hole pitch and putt. *Green Fees:* weekdays £20.00 per round/day; weekends £28.00. *Eating facilities:* full catering except Mondays. Bar open seven days. *Visitors:* welcome without reservation, except winter Sundays. Handicap Certificate required and must be members of a recognised club. *Society Meetings:* catered for weekdays only by prior arrangement. Professional: J.N. Wilson (0529 488644). Secretary: D.B.R. Harris (0529 488326).

SOUTH KYME. **South Kyme Golf Club,** Skinners Lane, South Kyme LN4 4AE (0526 861113). *Location:* approximately four miles off A153 road from Sleaford to Horncastle, turn right before North Kyme. Six miles off A17 from Sleaford to Boston, turn left before East Heckington. A long and testing fenland course. 18 holes, 6597 yards. S.S.S. Men 71, Ladies 70. 6 hole pitch and putt. *Green Fees:* weekdays £10.00;

weekends £12.00. £2.00 reduction when playing with a member. *Eating facilities:* bar and restaurant. Snacks available all day. Lunch menu available from 1pm to 2.30pm. *Visitors:* no restrictions at present but advisable to check at weekends in case of competitions. *Society Meetings:* welcome with prior booking. Secretary: Anne Maplethorpe.

SPALDING near. **Gedney Hill Golf Course,** West Drove, Gedney Hill, Near Spalding PE12 0NT (0406 330183). *Location:* six miles from Radar Tower near Crowland, off B1073 follow signs or follow 1066 off A47. Flat, testing conditions; playing characteristics of a links course with fen winds. 18 holes, 5429 yards. S.S.S. 66. 10 bay driving range. *Green Fees:* weekdays £5.75; weekends £9.75. *Eating facilities:* two bars (one casual spike bar), restaurant (80 seater). *Visitors:* welcome by arrangement, no restrictions. Full snooker room/snookerette table. *Society Meetings:* by arrangement. Professional: David Creek (0406 330922). Secretary: Steve McGregor (0406 330922).

SPALDING. **Sutton Bridge Golf Club,** New Road, Sutton Bridge, Spalding (Holbeach (0406) 350323). *Location:* off A17, 18 miles east of Spalding. 9 holes, 5804 yards. S.S.S. 68. *Green Fees:* weekdays £15.00. *Eating facilities:* available. *Visitors:* welcome, except weekends, Bank Holidays and match or competition days. *Society Meetings:* not catered for. Professional: R. Wood (0406 351080). Secretary: K.C. Buckle (0945 870455).

SPALDING. **The Spalding Golf Club,** Surfleet, Spalding PE11 4EA (0775 85234). *Location:* four miles from Spalding on A16 to Boston. Parkland. 18 holes, 6435 yards. S.S.S. 71. *Green Fees:* £20.00 weekdays; £25.00 weekends. *Visitors:* welcome, Handicap Certificates required. *Society Meetings:* catered for on Thursdays only April to October. Professional: John W. Spencer (0775 85474). Secretary: T.I. Chambers (0775 85386).

STAMFORD. **Burghley Park (Stamford) Golf Club,** St. Martins Without, Stamford PE9 3JX (0780 53789). *Location:* leave A1 at roundabout for Stamford, club one mile on right. Flat parkland. 18 holes, 6236 yards. S.S.S. 70. *Green Fees:* weekdays £20.00, weekends as members' guests only. Half price after 5pm May to September. *Eating facilities:* restaurant and bar. *Visitors:* welcome weekdays. Handicap Certificates required. *Society Meetings:* Wednesdays and Thursdays only. Professional: Glenn Davies (0780 62100). Secretary: Howard Mulligan (0780 53789).

STAMFORD. **Luffenham Heath Golf Club,** Ketton, Stamford PE9 3UU (Stamford (0780) 720218). *Location:* one-and-a-half miles south-west of Ketton on A6121. Undulating heathland, in conservation area for flora and fauna. 18 holes, 6254 yards. S.S.S. 70. *Green Fees:* weekdays £30.00 per day/per round; weekends £35.00 per day/per round. *Eating facilities:* catering available by arrangement. *Visitors:* welcome, advisable to contact Professional first. Handicap Certificate required. Changing room/showers. *Society Meetings:* by arrangement through the Secretary. Professional: J.A. Lawrence (0780 720298). Secretary: Ian F. Davenport (0780 720205).

England LINCOLNSHIRE

THE DOWER HOUSE HOTEL
MANOR ESTATE, WOODHALL SPA, LINCS
Only a short par four to the first tee.   Special rates for golfing parties.
Under personal management of the proprietors.
Reservations: (0526) 352588

THE PETWOOD HOUSE HOTEL
WOODHALL SPA
After an enjoyable day's golf at the Woodhall Spa Golf Course, Petwood is the ideal setting in which to relax.

Tel: 0526 352411   *See our colour display advertisement on page 24*   Fax: 0526 353473

STAMFORD. **Rutland County Golf Club,** Great Casterton, Stamford PE9 4AQ (0780 86239). *Location:* five miles north of Stamford on A1 Great North Road. Open rolling fairways, heavily bunkered, some water, inland links style. 27 holes, 6189 yards. S.S.S. 70. 20 bay driving range, grass practice area, putting green, practice bunker. *Green Fees:* weekdays £14.50; weekends £16.50. £20.00 day ticket, £25.00 weekend. *Eating facilities:* coffee bar, dining lounge, players bar. *Visitors:* welcome. Must have Handicap Certificate or be signed in by Pro. *Society Meetings:* welcome except weekends. Professional: James Darroch. Secretary: Steve Cowe (0780 86330).

WOODHALL SPA. **Woodhall Spa Golf Club,** Woodhall Spa LN10 6PU (0526 352511; Fax: 0526 352778). *Location:* 19 miles from Lincoln, Boston, Sleaford; 33 miles from Skegness; 50 miles from Nottingham. Flat, wooded heathland. 18 holes, 6907 yards. S.S.S. 73. Practice ground and driving net. *Green Fees:* weekdays £24.00 per round, £35.00 per day; weekends and Bank Holidays £28.00 per round, £40.00 per day (all fees are estimates). *Eating facilities:* full catering available. *Visitors:* welcome with reservation. Handicap Certificates required (maximum handicap permitted Gents 20, Ladies 30). *Society Meetings:* catered for if booked in advance. Professional: P. Fixter (0526 353229). Secretary: B.H. Fawcett.

FOR THE MUTUAL GUIDANCE OF GUEST AND HOST

Every year literally thousands of holidays, short-breaks and overnight stops are arranged through our guides, the vast majority without any problems at all. In a handful of cases, however, difficulties do arise about bookings, which often could have been prevented from the outset.

It is important to remember that when accommodation has been booked, both parties — guests and hosts — have entered into a form of contract. We hope that the following points will provide helpful guidance.

GUESTS: When enquiring about accommodation, be as precise as possible. Give exact dates, numbers in your party and the ages of any children. State the number and type of rooms wanted and also what catering you require — bed and breakfast, full board, etc. Make sure that the position about evening meals is clear — and about pets, reductions for children or any other special points.

Read our reviews carefully to ensure that the proprietors you are going to contact can supply what you want. Ask for a letter confirming all arrangements, if possible.

If you have to cancel, do so as soon as possible. Proprietors do have the right to retain deposits and under certain circumstances to charge for cancelled holidays if adequate notice is not given and they cannot re-let the accommodation.

HOSTS: Give details about your facilities and about any special conditions. Explain your deposit system clearly and arrangements for cancellations, charges, etc, and whether or not your terms include VAT.

If for any reason you are unable to fulfil an agreed booking without adequate notice, you may be under an obligation to arrange alternative suitable accommodation or to make some form of compensation.

While every effort is made to ensure accuracy, we regret that FHG Publications cannot accept responsibility for errors, omissions or misrepresentation in our entries or any consequences thereof. Prices in particular should be checked because we go to press early. We will follow up complaints but cannot act as arbiters or agents for either party.

Greater Manchester

ALTRINCHAM. **Altrincham Golf Course,** Stockport Road, Timperley, Altrincham, Cheshire (061-928 0761). *Location:* one mile east of Altrincham on A560. Parkland. 18 holes, 6190 yards, 5659 metres. S.S.S. 69. *Green Fees:* £5.50 weekdays; £6.50 weekends. *Eating facilities:* Old Hall Hotel attached to course. *Visitors:* welcome any time, book one week in advance. Public course. Professional: John Jackson. Secretary: Lewis Cunningham.

ALTRINCHAM. **Dunham Forest Golf and Country Club,** Oldfield Lane, Altrincham WA14 4TY (061-928 2605; Fax: 061-929 8975). *Location:* approximately 9 miles south of Manchester off A56. Wooded parkland. 18 holes, 6772 yards. S.S.S. 72. *Green Fees:* weekdays £25.00, weekends and Bank Holidays £30.00. *Eating facilities:* clubhouse restaurant and bar open daily. *Visitors:* welcome, but should telephone to check availability. *Society Meetings:* welcome by prior arrangement. Professional: I. Wrigley (061-928 2727). Secretary: Mrs S. Klaus (061-928 2605).

ALTRINCHAM. **The Ringway Golf Club Ltd,** Hale Mount, Hale Barns, Altrincham WA15 8SW (061-904 9609). *Location:* Junction 6, M56 then A538 towards Altrincham for one mile. Parkland. 18 holes, 6494 yards. S.S.S. 71. *Green Fees:* weekdays £26.00, weekends and Bank Holidays £32.00. *Eating facilities:* full diningroom facilities available. *Visitors:* generally not on Tuesdays or Saturdays which are Ladies' and Gentlemen's Competition Days, or Fridays (members only). *Society Meetings:* catered for by arrangement. Professional: Nick Ryan (061-980 8432). Secretary: D. Wright (061-980 2630).

ASHTON-IN-MAKERFIELD. **Ashton-in-Makerfield Golf Club Ltd,** Garswood Park, Liverpool Road, Ashton-in-Makerfield (Wigan (0942) 727269). *Location:* M6, Junction 23 from south, M6 Junction 24 from north. Wooded course. 18 holes, 6205 yards. S.S.S. 70. *Green Fees:* £21.00. *Eating facilities:* available, except Mondays. *Visitors:* welcome mid-week (except Wednesday) with reservation but not before 9.45am. *Society Meetings:* catered for Tuesdays and Thursdays by prior appointment. Professional: P. Allan (0942 724229). Secretary: J.R. Hay (0942 719330).

ASHTON-UNDER-LYNE. **Ashton-under-Lyne Golf Club,** Gorsey Way, Ashton-under-Lyne OL6 9HT (061-330 1537). *Location:* three miles from town centre, Mossley Road, left at Queens Road, right at Nook Lane, Clubhouse top of St. Christopher's Road. Wooded course. 18 holes, 6209 yards. S.S.S. 70. *Green Fees:* weekdays £20.00 per day, weekends with member only. *Eating facilities:* full catering except Mondays. *Visitors:* welcome weekdays except Wednesdays; members of recognised golf clubs welcome without reservation. *Society Meetings:* catered for on application: special daily rates. Professional: C. Boyle (061-308 2095). Secretary: G.J. Musgrave (061-339 8655).

BOLTON. **Bolton Golf Club Ltd,** Lostock Park, Chorley New Road, Bolton BL6 4AJ (Bolton (0204) 843278). *Location:* off main road half-way between Bolton and Horwich. 18 holes, 6215 yards. S.S.S. 70. *Green Fees:* weekdays £25.00 per round, £28.00 per day; weekends £28.00 per round, £32 per day. *Eating facilities:* luncheons (evening meals except Monday and Sunday). *Visitors:* welcome with reservation. *Society Meetings:* catered for on Thursdays and Fridays. Professional: R. Longworth (0204 843073). Secretary: H. Cook (0204 843067).

BOLTON. **Breightmet Golf Club,** Red Bridge, Ainsworth, Bolton (Bolton (0204) 27381). *Location:* leave Bolton on main road to Bury, turn left two miles on Milnthorpe road for the bridge. 9 holes, 6418 yards. S.S.S. 71. *Green Fees:* weekdays £15.00, weekends and Bank Holidays £18.00 (half-price with a member). *Eating facilities:* lunches and light refreshments. *Visitors:* welcome, preliminary phone call advisable. *Society Meetings:* catered for on application. Secretary: R. Weir.

BOLTON. **Deane Golf Club,** Broadford Road, Deane, Bolton (Bolton (0204) 61944). *Location:* one mile east of Junction 5 of M61 towards Bolton Centre. Rolling parkland with number of small ravines to cross. 18 holes, 5583 yards, 5105 metres. S.S.S. 67. *Green Fees:* weekdays £17.50; weekends £22.50. *Eating facilities:* lunches and evening meals by arrangement. *Visitors:* welcome. *Society Meetings:* Tuesdays, Thursdays and Fridays only. Secretary: P. Flaxman (0204 651808).

BOLTON. **Dunscar Golf Club Ltd,** Longworth Lane, Bromley Cross, Bolton BL7 9QY (Bolton (0204) 303321). *Location:* one and a half miles north of Bolton on A666. Parkland, moorland course. 18 holes, 6085 yards. S.S.S. 69. Practice facilities available. *Green Fees:* weekdays £20.00; weekends and Bank Holidays £30.00. With a member £10.00. *Eating facilities:* available. *Visitors:* welcome except weekends. *Society Meetings:* catered for by arrangement. Professional: Gary Treadgold (0204 592992). Secretary: Thomas Michael Yates (0204 301090).

BOLTON. **Great Lever and Farnworth Golf Club Ltd,** Lever Edge Lane, Bolton BL3 3EN (Bolton (0204) 62582). *Location:* A666 or M61 (Junction 4), one and a half miles from Bolton town centre. Flat parkland. 18 holes, 5859 yards. S.S.S. 69. Practice ground. *Green Fees:* weekdays £12.00; weekends £19.00. *Eating facilities:* restaurant and bar every day except Mondays. *Visitors:* welcome, preferably by appointment. *Society Meetings:* catered for by arrangement weekdays. Professional: Donald Stirling (0204 656650). Secretary: Mrs J. Ivill (0204 656137).

THE GOLF GUIDE 1994
England GREATER MANCHESTER

BOLTON. **Harwood Golf Club,** Roading Brook Road, Harwood, Bolton BL2 4JD (Bolton (0204) 22878). *Location:* three miles east of Bolton – A58 to Bury, turn left through Ainsworth village. Flat meadowland. 9 holes, 5958 yards. S.S.S. 69. Small practice area. *Green Fees:* £15.00, £5.00 with a member. *Eating facilities:* bar not open during weekdays, except Wednesdays; catering on request. *Visitors:* welcome weekdays only, weekends only with a member. Should be members of recognised golf club or society. *Society Meetings:* catered for on written application to Secretary. Professional: Max Evans (0204 398472). Secretary: D. Bamber (0204 22878 or 061-761 6022).

BOLTON. **Old Links (Bolton) Ltd,** Chorley Old Road, Montserrat, Bolton BL1 5SU (0204 840050). *Location:* on B6226, 400 yards north of roundabout on ring road. Championship course, moorland. 18 holes, 6410 yards. S.S.S. 72. Practice facilities. *Green Fees:* weekdays £26.00, weekends £30.00. Special rates for groups over 20. *Eating facilities:* available. *Visitors:* welcome, not Saturdays until 4pm. *Society Meetings:* catered for not Wednesdays or weekends. Professional: P. Horridge (0204 843089). Secretary: E. Monaghan (0204 842307).

BOLTON. **Regent Park Golf Club Ltd,** Links Road, Lostock, Bolton BL6 4AF (0204 844170). *Location:* midway between Bolton and Horwich off Chorley New Road. Parkland. 18 holes, 6217 yards. S.S.S. 70/71. Practice area. *Green Fees:* weekdays £5.00; weekends £6.75. *Eating facilities:* meals/bar available. *Visitors:* welcome seven days, telephone Professional to book time slot. *Society Meeetings:* welcome midweek, book in advance. Professional: Bob Longworth (0204 842336/495421). Secretary: K.J. Taylor (0204 652882).

BOLTON. **Turton Golf Club,** Wood End Farm, Chapeltown Road, Bromley Cross, Bolton (0204 852235). *Location:* three miles north of Bolton on the A666. Moorland course with extensive views. 9 holes, 5805 yards. S.S.S. 68. Practice area. *Green Fees:* £15.00 per day. *Eating facilities:* to order except Mondays. *Visitors:* welcome, restrictions Wednesdays (Ladies Day). *Society Meetings:* welcome on Tuesdays and Thursdays by arrangement. Secretary: B.E. Stanley (0204 306881).

BRAMHALL. **Bramhall Golf Club,** The Clubhouse, Ladythorn Road, Bramhall, Stockport SK7 2EY (061-439 4057). *Location:* three quarters of a mile from Bramhall Railway Station, half a mile from Bramhall Moat House Hotel. Parkland. 18 holes, 6361 yards, 5816 metres. S.S.S. 70. *Green Fees:* information not provided. *Eating facilities:* Steward will provide meals on request, subject to club and visiting party occasions. *Visitors:* welcome except Thursdays and Competition Days. *Society Meetings:* catered for Wednesday, minimum 24. Professional: Brian Nield (061-439 1171). Secretary: J.G. Lee (061-439 6092).

BURY. **Bury Golf Club,** Unsworth Hall, Blackford Bridge, Bury (061-766 4897). *Location:* A56 eight miles north of Manchester. Undulating parkland. 18 holes, 5961 yards. S.S.S. 69. *Green Fees:* information not provided. *Eating facilities:* grill room service except Mondays. *Visitors:* welcome without reservation but Handicap Certificate will be required. *Society Meetings:* catered for. Professional: M. Peel (061-766 2213). Secretary: J. Meikle.

BURY. **Greenmount Golf Club,** Greenhaigh Fold Farm, Greenmount, Bury (Tottington (0204 88 3712). *Location:* three miles north of Bury. Undulating parkland. 9 holes, 4920 yards. S.S.S. 64. *Green Fees:* £12.00, £5.00 with member. *Eating facilities:* lunches at club except on Thursdays. *Visitors:* welcome, weekends with members only, Tuesday – ladies' day. *Society Meetings:* catered for by arrangement with Secretary. Professional: G. Pearson. Secretary: G.J. Lowe.

BURY. **Lowes Park Golf Club Ltd.,** Hill Top, Walmersley, Bury BL9 6SU (061-674 1231). *Location:* take A56 north from Bury, turn right at Bury General Hospital into Lowes Road. Hilly course, usually windy. 9 holes, 6009 yards. S.S.S. 69. *Green Fees:* information not provided. *Eating facilities:* full catering except Mondays. *Visitors:* welcome weekdays except Wednesdays (Ladies' Day), not Saturday, Sunday by appointment. *Society Meetings:* catered for weekdays (not Saturday), Sundays by appointment. Secretary: E. Brierley (0706 67331).

BURY. **Walmersley Golf Club,** Garretts Close, Walmersley, Bury (061-764 1429). *Location:* leave A56 approximately two miles north of Bury at Walmersley Post Office into Old Road, right at Masons Arms Inn. Moorland course. 9 holes, 6114 yards, 5588 metres. S.S.S. 70. *Green Fees:* £12.00 per day, £6.00 with member. *Eating facilities:* lunches and evening meals served except Mondays. *Visitors:* welcome weekdays except Tuesdays 12.30pm to 5.30pm. *Society Meetings:* catered for weekdays. Secretary: C. Stock (061-764 5057).

CHEADLE. **Cheadle Golf Club,** Shiers Drive, Cheadle SK8 1HW (061-428 2160). *Location:* one-and-a-half miles Junction 11 M63. Parkland. 9 holes, 5006 yards. S.S.S. 65. *Green Fees:* information not provided. *Eating facilities:* by arrangement with the Steward. *Visitors:* welcome, must be members of a bona fide golf club; current Handicap Certificate to be produced; no visitors on Tuesdays or Saturdays. *Society Meetings:* catered for by arrangement with the Secretary. Professional: A.G. Collins (061-428 9878). Secretary: P.P. Webster (061-491 4452).

DAVYHULME. **Davyhulme Park Golf Club,** Gleneagles Road, Davyhulme, Urmston M31 2SA (061-748 2856). *Location:* one mile from M63/M62. Wooded parkland course. 18 holes, 6237 yards. S.S.S. 70. *Green Fees:* information not provided. *Eating facilities:* lunches and dinners. *Visitors:* welcome except Competition days. *Society Meetings:* catered for by prior arrangement. Professional: Hugh Lewis (061-748 3931). Secretary: H.A. Langworthy (061-748 2260).

DENTON. **Denton Golf Club,** Manchester Road, Denton M34 2NU (061-336 3218). *Location:* A57, five miles from Piccadilly, Manchester. 18 holes, 6290 yards. S.S.S. 70. *Green Fees:* information not provided. *Eating facilities:* meals catered for except all day Monday and Thursday afternoon. *Visitors:* welcome

GREATER MANCHESTER England

with club members and handicap, without reservation weekdays only. *Society Meetings:* catered for on weekdays except Tuesday by application. Professional: Roger Vere. Secretary: R. Wickham.

DUKINFIELD. **Dukinfield Golf Club,** Lyne Edge, Dukinfield (061-338 2340). *Location:* six miles east of Manchester via Ashton-under-Lyne. Hillside with wooded areas. 18 holes, 5556 yards. S.S.S. 67. *Green Fees:* weekdays £16.50. *Visitors:* welcome except Wednesdays and weekends. *Society Meetings:* catered for by prior arrangement. Secretary: K.P. Parker (061-338 2669).

ECCLES. **Worsley Golf Club,** Stableford Avenue, Monton, Eccles M30 8AP (061-789 4202). *Location:* one mile from Junction 13 M62. Parkland. 18 holes, 6200 yards. S.S.S. 70. *Green Fees:* weekdays £20.00; weekends and Bank Holidays £25.00 (£12.00 with member). *Eating facilities:* snacks, lunches and evening meals. *Visitors:* welcome, if past or present members of recognised golf clubs. *Society Meetings:* catered for Mondays, Wednesdays and Thursdays. Professional: Ceri Cousins. Secretary: B. Dean.

FLIXTON. **Acre Gate Golf Club,** Pennybridge Lane, Flixton, Manchester M31 (061-748 1226). *Location:* off Flixton Road. Flat parkland course. 18 holes, 4395 yards. S.S.S. 61. *Green Fees:* weekdays £4.60; weekends £6.50. *Eating facilities:* not available to visitors unless with member. *Visitors:* course is municipal (William Wroe Municipal Course) therefore no restrictions, book 24 hours in advance. *Society Meetings:* small groups welcome on application to the Club Secretary. Secretary: D.J. Bostock.

HYDE. **Werneth Low Golf Club Ltd,** Werneth Low Road, Hyde, Cheshire SK14 3AF (061-368 2503). *Location:* A560 from Junction 4 of M67. Scenic, hilly course with excellent greens. 11 holes, 6550 yards. S.S.S. 69. *Green Fees:* weekdays £18.00; weekends £23.00 (Saturdays only). *Eating facilities:* light refreshments normally available except Wednesdays. *Visitors:* welcome any time except Sunday before 4pm and Tuesday mornings and evenings. *Society Meetings:* catered for by prior arrangement. Professional: T. Bacchus (061-336 6908). Secretary: R. Clapham (061-366 0837).

LEIGH. **Pennington Golf Club (Municipal),** Pennington Golf Course, Pennington Country Park, off St. Helens Road, Leigh. *Location:* Junction 17 on M6 to Leigh. Flat parkland with water coursing through. 9 holes, 2919 yards. S.S.S. 34. *Green Fees:* on request. *Eating facilities:* snack bar facilities. *Visitors:* welcome without reservation. Professional: Mr T. Kershaw (0942 607278). Secretary: Mr P.A. Cartwright (061-794 5316).

LITTLEBOROUGH. **Whittaker Golf Club,** Whittaker Lane, Littleborough OL15 0LH (Littleborough (0706) 378310). *Location:* one mile from town centre along Blackstone Edge Old Road. Moorland course. 9 holes, 5632 yards. S.S.S. 67. *Green Fees:* weekdays £10.00; weekends £12.00. *Eating facilities:* bar only. *Visitors:* welcome without reservation, except Tuesday afternoons and Sundays. *Society Meetings:* weekdays and Saturdays only by prior arrangement with Secretary. Secretary: Mr G.A. Smith (0484 428546).

MANCHESTER. **Blackley Golf Club,** Victoria Avenue East, Blackley, Manchester M9 2HW (061-643 2980). *Location:* five miles north from City Centre. Parkland. 18 holes, 6237 yards, 5708 metres. S.S.S. 70. *Green Fees:* £15.00 weekdays. *Eating facilities:* diningroom/bar. *Visitors:* welcome, Thursdays and weekends with member only. *Society Meetings:* catered for. Professional: Martin Barton (061-643 3912). Secretary: C.B. Leggott (061-654 7770).

MANCHESTER. **Brookdale Golf Club Ltd,** Ash Bridge, Woodhouses, Failsworth, Manchester (061-681 4534). *Location:* five miles north of Manchester. 18 holes, 6040 yards. S.S.S. 68. *Green Fees:* weekdays £18.00; weekends and Bank Holidays £21.00. *Eating facilities:* available with ample notice. *Visitors:* welcome, only with a member weekends. *Society Meetings:* welcome except Tuesdays (Ladies Day). Package Deal £29.00 by arrangement. Professional: Mr Jason Spibey (061-681 2655). Secretary: Mr Bernard Rimmer.

MANCHESTER. **Chorlton-cum-Hardy Golf Club,** Barlow Hall Road, Chorlton-cum-Hardy M21 2JJ (061-881 3139). *Location:* near junction of A5145 and A5103 (M63 Junction 9). Meadowland. 18 holes, 6003 yards. S.S.S. 69. *Green Fees:* weekdays £20.00; weekends and Bank Holidays £25.00. *Eating facilities:* catering provided – seasonal limited hours, sandwiches only Mondays. *Visitors:* welcome without reservation, except on Competition days, must provide proof of recognised handicap. *Society Meetings:* catered for Thursdays only by arrangement with Secretary. Professional: David Screeton (061-881 9911). Secretary: Mrs H.M. Stuart (061-881-5830).

MANCHESTER. **Didsbury Golf Club Ltd,** Ford Lane, Northenden, Manchester M22 4NQ (061-998 2743). *Location:* Junction 3 on M56 to Palatine Road, to Church Road, to Ford Lane. Parkland. 18 holes, 6276 yards. S.S.S. 70. Good practice facilities. *Green Fees:* weekdays £22.00; weekends £25.00. *Eating facilities:* fully-equipped bar and restaurant. *Visitors:* Thursday/Friday – Tuesday small societies. *Society Meetings:* catered for. Professional: P. Barber (061-998 2811). Secretary/Manager: C.B. Turnbull (061-998 9278).

MANCHESTER. **Ellesmere Golf Club,** Old Clough Lane, Worsley, Manchester M28 4EP (061-790 2122). *Location:* off A580 East Lancs Road, adjacent to M62 northbound, (eastbound) access. Wooded parkland. 18 holes, 5954 yards. S.S.S. 69. *Green Fees:* weekdays £18.00 per round, £24.00 per day; weekends £25.00. *Eating facilities:* bar; catering available, with or without reservation. *Visitors:* members of recognised golf clubs welcome, but not during club competitions or Bank Holidays, contact Professional for restrictions. *Society Meetings:* catered for by appointment. Professional: Terry Morley (061-790 8591). Hon. Secretary: A.C. Kay (061-799 0554).

THE GOLF GUIDE 1994

England GREATER MANCHESTER

MANCHESTER. Fairfield Golf and Sailing Club, "Boothdale", Booth Road, Audenshaw, Manchester M34 5GA (061-370 1641). *Location:* off A635, five miles east of Manchester. Parkland bounded in part by reservoir. 18 holes, 4956 yards. S.S.S. 68. *Green Fees:* weekdays £16.00; weekends £20.00. *Eating facilities:* available. *Visitors:* welcome, restrictions Wednesdays, Thursdays and weekends. *Society Meetings:* catered for by prior arrangement mid-week. Professional: N. Harding (061-370 2292). Hon. Secretary: J. Humphries (061-336 3950).

MANCHESTER. Flixton Golf Club, Church Road, Flixton, Urmston (061-748 2116). *Location:* five miles from Manchester. Parkland. 9 holes, 6410 yards. S.S.S. 71. *Green Fees:* £17.50 weekdays; £10.00 weekends, Bank Holidays and Christmas and New Year holiday period (playing with a member only). *Eating facilities:* daily except Tuesdays. *Visitors:* welcome with reservation. *Society Meetings:* catered for by arrangement. Professional: B. Ling (061-746 7160). Hon. Secretary: J.G. Frankland (061-747 0296). Catering: (061-748 7545).

MANCHESTER. Heaton Park Golf Club, Heaton Park, Prestwich, Manchester (061-798 0295). *Location:* north Manchester, M62 to Exit 19 M66 to A576, right to park entrance (200 yards). Undulating parkland. 18 holes, 5840 yards. S.S.S. 68. *Green Fees:* weekdays £5.50, weekends and Bank Holidays £6.60 per round. *Visitors:* welcome, book week in advance. Secretary: F. Lewis (061-773 1113).

MANCHESTER. Houldsworth Golf Club Ltd, Houldsworth Street, Reddish, Stockport SK5 6HY (061-442 1815). *Location:* off A6 between Manchester and Stockport, adjacent to M63 and M6. Flat parkland with water hazards. 18 holes, 6234 yards. S.S.S. 70. Practice area. *Green Fees:* weekdays £13.00 per round, £14.00 per day; weekends £16.00 per round. Reduced rates for parties. *Eating facilities:* bar snacks, or full restaurant service. *Visitors:* must be pre-arranged with Professional or Hon. Secretary. *Society Meetings:* catered for on application. Professional: David Naylor (061-224 4571). Secretary: S.W. Zielinski (061-224 5055).

MANCHESTER. Manchester Golf Club, Hopwood Cottage, Middleton, Manchester M24 2QP (061-643 2718). *Location:* Exit 20 from M62, three minutes from motorway. Moorland/parkland. 18 holes, 6454 yards, 5895 metres. S.S.S. 72. Large practice ground. Driving range. *Green Fees:* weekdays £25.00 per day, weekends £30.00 per day. *Eating facilities:* two bars and first class restaurant. *Visitors:* welcome weekdays. *Society Meetings:* parties up to 120 catered for by arrangement. Professional: B. Connor (061-643 2638). Secretary: K.G. Flett (061-643 3202).

MANCHESTER. New North Manchester Golf Club Ltd, Rhodes House, Manchester Old Road, Middleton, Manchester (061-643 2941). *Location:* A576, less than one mile from Junction 18 on M62/M66. Undulating and sometimes hilly terrain. 18 holes, 6527 yards, 5987 metres. S.S.S. 72. Large practice ground. *Green Fees:* £20.00 per round £25.00 per day. *Eating facilities:* catering every day. *Society Meetings:* welcome. Professional: P.J. Lunt (061-643 7094). Secretary: (061-643 9033).

MANCHESTER. Northenden Golf Club, Palatine Road, Northenden, Manchester M22 4FR (061-998 4079). *Location:* half a mile off Junction 9 M56. Parkland with plenty of trees. 18 holes, 6469 yards. S.S.S. 71. Practice net. *Green Fees:* £25.00 weekdays, £27.50 weekends. Reduced rates if playing with a member. *Eating facilities:* available (061-998 4079). *Visitors:* welcome most days, preferably with reservation. Restrictions 8.30am to 9.15am tuesdays and 12 noon to 1.15pm Fridays. *Society Meetings:* catered for Tuesdays and Fridays only. Professional: W. McColl (061-945 3386). Manager: R.N. Kemp (061-998 4738; Fax: 061-945 5592). Steward: Mr P. Massey.

MANCHESTER. Pikefold Golf Club, Cooper Lane, Blackley, Manchester M9 2QQ (061-740 1136). *Location:* four miles north of city centre off Rochdale Road A664, then A6104 Victoria Avenue, located rear of St. Clares RC church. Undulating wooded parkland course. 9 holes, 5789 yards. S.S.S. 68. *Green Fees:* weekdays £12.00 per day (£5.00 with member); Saturdays and Bank Holidays £7.00, must play with member. No visitors Sundays. *Eating facilities:* available by arrangement. *Visitors:* welcome weekdays without reservation. *Society Meetings:* catered for weekdays and Saturday mornings. Secretary: F.J. Ashworth.

MANCHESTER. Prestwich Golf Club, Hilton Lane, Prestwich, Manchester (061-773 2544). *Location:* on A6044, one mile from junction with A56. 18 holes, 4757 yards. S.S.S. 63. *Green Fees:* information not provided. *Eating facilities:* by arrangement. *Visitors:* welcome weekdays. *Society Meetings:* catered for weekdays, special rates for parties of 16 and over. Professional: Gary Coope. Secretary: V. Trees.

MANCHESTER. Stand Golf Club, The Dales, Ashbourne Grove, Whitefield, Bury, Manchester M25 7NL (061-766 2388). *Location:* M62 Exit 17, A56/A665 one mile. Undulating parkland with sandy subsoil, playable all year round. 18 holes, 6426 yards. S.S.S. 71. *Green Fees:* weekdays £20.00; weekends £25.00. Reduced rates for societies over 20. *Eating facilities:* meals served daily and bar except Mondays, order in advance. *Visitors:* welcome Monday to Friday; weekends by prior arrangement. *Society Meetings:* welcome Wednesday/Friday by prior arrangement. Professional: Mark Dance (061-766 2214). Hon. Secretary: Eric B. Taylor (061-766 3197).

MANCHESTER. Swinton Park Golf Club, East Lancashire Road, Swinton, Manchester M27 1LX (061-794 1785). *Location:* on the A580 Manchester to Liverpool road, five miles from Manchester centre. Parkland. Three courses. Practice area. *Green Fees:* on application. *Eating facilities:* available. *Visitors:* welcome Tuesdays, Wednesdays and Fridays, Tee reservations 10am-noon, 2pm-4pm. *Society Meetings:* catered for by prior arrangement. Professional: J. Wilson (061-793 8077). General Secretary: F. Slater (061-794 0861).

155

GREATER MANCHESTER England

MANCHESTER. **Withington Golf Club,** 243 Palatine Road, West Didsbury, Manchester M20 8UD (061-445 3912). *Location:* three miles from Manchester city centre, adjacent M56 and M63. Flat parkland. 18 holes, 6410 yards. S.S.S. 71. *Green Fees:* (1993) weekdays only (except Thursdays) £21.00 per round, £24.00 per day. *Eating facilities:* lunches and evening meals to order. Snacks available at all times except Mondays. *Visitors:* ring Professional for times. *Society Meetings:* catered for by arrangement with the Secretary. Professional: R.J. Ling (061-445 4861). Secretary/Manager: A. Larsen (061-445 9544).

MARPLE. **Marple Golf Club,** Barnsfold Road, Marple, Stockport SK6 7EL (061-427 2311). *Location:* off A6 at Hawk Green sign. Parkland. 18 holes, 5565 yards. S.S.S. 67. Practice area. *Green Fees:* weekdays £20.00 per day, £8.50 with member; weekends £30.00 per day (when no competitions), £11.00 with member. *Eating facilities:* full meals available except Mondays when bar snacks only. *Visitors:* welcome, not competition days or Thursday between 11am and 3.30pm. *Society Meetings:* all welcome by arrangement with Professional. Professional: Nick Hamilton (061-449 0690). Secretary: F.W. Ogden (061-427 1125).

OLDHAM. **Crompton and Royton Golf Club Ltd,** High Barn, Royton, Oldham OL2 6RW (061-624 2154). *Location:* A671 Oldham to Rochdale, turn off in Royton. Heathland. 18 holes, 6215 yards. S.S.S. 70. Practice ground and nets. *Green Fees:* weekdays £24.00; weekends £30.00. *Eating facilities:* lunches and meals served, except Mondays. *Visitors:* welcome without reservation, not at weekends. *Society Meetings:* catered for by arrangement with Secretary. Professional: D.A. Melling (061-624 2154). Secretary: Ron Butler (061-624 0986).

OLDHAM. **Oldham Golf Club,** Lees New Road, Oldham (061-624 4986). *Location:* B6194 between Ashton-under-Lyne and Oldham. Moorland course, no bunkers. 18 holes, 5045 yards. S.S.S. 65. *Green Fees:* weekdays £12.00; weekends £18.00. *Eating facilities:* full catering. *Visitors:* welcome, telephone to check for competitions, especially weekends. *Society Meetings:* catered for by prior arrangement with Secretary. Professional's shop (061-626 8346). Secretary: J. Brooks (061-624 1955).

OLDHAM. **Saddleworth Golf Club,** Mountain Ash, Ladcastle Road, Uppermill, Near Oldham OL3 6LT (0457 872059). *Location:* five miles from Oldham – M62. A moorland course with superb views of the Pennines. 18 holes, 5976 yards. S.S.S. 69. Practice area. *Green Fees:* weekdays £22.00 (£7.00 per day with member), weekends and Bank Holidays £25.00 (£10.00 per day with member). Visiting parties £30 per day. *Eating facilities:* snacks and meals available. *Visitors:* welcome. *Society Meetings:* groups of 12 or more catered for except weekends. Professional: T. Shard (0457 873653). Secretary: H.A. Morgan (0457 873653).

OLDHAM. **Werneth Golf Club,** 124 Green Lane, Garden Suburb, Oldham (061-624 1190). Semi moorland. 18 holes, 5363 yards. S.S.S. 66. Practice ground. *Green Fees:* £16.00 weekdays only. *Eating facilities:* full catering service available. *Visitors:* welcome Mondays and Wednesdays, ring for details. *Society Meetings:* catered for, ring for details. Professional: Roy Penny. Secretary: J.H. Barlow.

ROCHDALE. **Lobden Golf Club,** Whitworth, Near Rochdale (Rochdale (0706) 343228). *Location:* take A671 from Rochdale, turn right at Dog and Partridge Pub in Whitworth. Moorland. 9 holes, 2885 yards. S.S.S. 68. *Green Fees:* weekdays £10.00; weekends £12.00. *Eating facilities:* by prior arrangement. *Visitors:* welcome all week except Saturday. *Society Meetings:* catered for by arrangement. Secretary: C. Buchanan (0706 343197).

ROCHDALE. **Rochdale Golf Club,** The Clubhouse, Edenfield Road, Bagslate, Rochdale OL11 5YR (Rochdale (0706) 46024). *Location:* M62 at Exit 20, three miles on A680. Parkland. 18 holes, 6002 yards. S.S.S. 69. *Green Fees:* on request. *Eating facilities:* meals available, order in advance, sandwiches only Mondays. *Visitors:* welcome, Summer period – Sundays not before 10.30am, Mondays, Wednesdays, Fridays not between 1pm and 2pm, Tuesdays not between 12 noon and 7pm, Thursdays not between 12.30pm and 6pm, Saturdays not before 4pm. *Society Meetings:* catered for by arrangement Wednesdays and Fridays. Professional: A. Laverty (0706 522104). Secretary: S. Cockroft (0706 43818).

ROCHDALE. **Springfield Park Golf Club,** Springfield Park, Marland, Rochdale (0706 56401). *Location:* A58 out of Rochdale, along Bolton Road on right. Parkland. 18 holes, 5237 yards. S.S.S. 66. *Green Fees:* on request. *Eating facilities:* none available. *Visitors:* welcome, no restrictions. Professional: D. Wills (0706 49801). Secretary: B. Wynn (0706 526064).

SALE. **Ashton-on-Mersey Golf Club,** Church Lane, Ashton-on-Mersey, Sale M33 5QQ (061-973 3220). *Location:* M63, two miles from Sale Station. Parkland course. 9 holes, 6242 yards. S.S.S. 69. *Green Fees:* £16.00 weekdays, £8.00 with a member. *Eating facilities:* available weekdays except Mondays. *Visitors:* welcome on weekdays. Saturdays, Sundays and Bank Holidays only with member. *Society Meetings:* Thursdays. Professional: P. Preston (061-962 3727). Secretary: J.H. Edwards (061-976 4390).

SALE. **Sale Golf Club,** Sale Lodge, Golf Road, Sale M33 5RH (061-973 3404). *Location:* Junction 8 M63, A6144. Parkland. 18 holes, 6346 yards. S.S.S. 71. *Green Fees:* £20.00 weekdays, £30.00 weekends. *Eating facilities:* dining room daily. *Visitors:* welcome weekdays, weekends and Bank Holidays with a member. *Society Meetings:* by arrangement. Professional: M. Stewart (061-973 1730). Manager: Harry Prow (061-973 1638).

SALFORD. **Brackley Golf Club** Bullows Road (off Captain Fold Road), Little Hulton, Worsley (061-790 6076). *Location:* M61 to Junction 4 onto A6, left at roundabout onto A6 (Walkden), half a mile turn left at White Lion pub. Flat parkland course. 9 holes, 3003 yards, 2747 metres. S.S.S. 70. *Green Fees:* weekdays £3.00; £5.00 weekends. Senior Citizens £2.50. *Visitors:* welcome anytime. *Society Meetings:* welcome. Secretary: B. Heyes.

England GREATER MANCHESTER

STOCKPORT. **Bramall Park Golf Club,** 20 Manor Road, Bramhall, Stockport (061-485 3119). *Location:* 10 miles south of Manchester, 3 miles south of Stockport, half a mile from Cheadle Hulme. Parkland. 18 holes, 6214 yards. S.S.S. 70. *Green Fees:* weekdays £25.00; weekends and Bank Holidays £35.00. *Eating facilities:* full eating facilities except Fridays. *Visitors:* welcome, apply to Professional. *Society Meetings:* catered for. Professional: M. Proffitt (061-485 2205). Secretary: J.C. O'Shea (061-485 3119).

STOCKPORT. **Disley Golf Club Ltd,** Stanley Hall Lane, Disley, Stockport SK12 2JX (Disley (0663) 762071). *Location:* off Jacksons Edge Road. Parkland, hillside course. 18 holes, 6015 yards, 5832 metres. S.S.S. 69. *Green Fees:* weekdays £20.00; weekends £30.00. *Eating facilities:* available except Mondays. *Visitors:* welcome except Thursdays and Saturdays. *Society Meetings:* catered for by arrangement. Professional: A.G. Esplin (0663 764001). Secretary: R.A. Clayton (0663 762884).

STOCKPORT. **Hazel Grove Golf Club,** Buxton Road, Hazel Grove, Stockport SK7 6LU (061-483 3217). *Location:* A6 to Buxton out of Hazel Grove, three miles south of Stockport. Flat parkland with tree-lined fairways. 18 holes, 6366 yards. S.S.S. 71. *Green Fees:* weekdays £22.50; Friday, Saturday, Sunday and Bank Holidays £27.50. *Eating facilities:* available daily except Mondays. *Visitors:* welcome, ring for booking of tee times. *Society Meetings:* catered for on Thursdays and Fridays. Professional: M.E. Hill (061-483 7272). Secretary: H.A.G. Carlisle (061-483 3978).

STOCKPORT. **Heaton Moor Golf Club,** Mauldeth Road, Heaton Mersey, Stockport SK4 3NX (061-432 2134). *Location:* A34 off M56. Flat parkland course, tree lined fairways. 18 holes, 5909 yards. S.S.S. 68. Practice area. *Green Fees:* weekdays £22.00; weekends £30.00. *Eating facilities:* lunches and evening meals by arrangement; bar. *Visitors:* welcome weekdays. *Society Meetings:* catered for. Professional: Clive Loydall (061-432 0846). Secretary: A.D. Townsend.

STOCKPORT. **Mellor and Townscliffe Golf Club Ltd,** Gibb Lane, Tarden, Mellor, Stockport SK6 5NA (061-427 2208). *Location:* seven miles south east of Stockport off A626. Parkland with trees/moorland. 18 holes, 5925 yards. S.S.S. 69. *Green Fees:* weekdays £18.00 per day, £8.00 with a member; weekends and Bank Holidays £25.00, with a member £10.00. *Eating facilities:* available daily except Tuesdays. *Visitors:* welcome weekdays, no casual visitors weekends. *Society Meetings:* catered for by prior arrangement. Professional: Michael J. Williams (061-427 5759). Secretary: D.A. Ogden.

STOCKPORT. **Reddish Vale Golf Club,** Southcliffe Road, Reddish, Stockport SK5 7EE (061-480 2359). *Location:* one mile north east of Stockport. Varied undulating heathland course, designed by Dr A. MacKenzie. 18 holes, 6086 yards. S.S.S. 69. *Green Fees:* weekdays £22.00. *Eating facilities:* bar and catering. *Visitors:* welcome on weekdays (not 12.30 – 1.30pm). *Society Meetings:* catered for by arrangement. Professional: Richard Brown (061-480 3824). Secretary: J.L. Blakey.

STOCKPORT. **Romiley Golf Club Ltd,** Goosehouse Green, Romiley, Stockport SK6 4LJ (061-430 2392). *Location:* B6104 off A560, signposted from Romiley village. Parkland. 18 holes, 6421 yards. S.S.S. 71. *Green Fees:* weekdays £24.00 per round, £30.00 per day; weekends and Bank Holidays £36.00 per round, £49.00 per day. Reduced rates for visitors by arrangement: over 30 in number £22.00 per round, £28.00 per day. *Eating facilities:* full catering by arrangement except Mondays. *Visitors:* welcome any day. *Society Meetings:* catered for by prior arrangement with Secretary. Professional: Gary Butler (061-430 7122). Secretary: Frank Beard (061-430 7257).

STOCKPORT. **Stockport Golf Club Ltd,** Offerton Road, Offerton, Stockport, Cheshire SK2 5HL (061-427 2001). *Location:* one mile from lights at Hazel Grove, along Torkington Road. Parkland. 18 holes, 6326 yards. S.S.S. 71. *Green Fees:* weekdays £30.00 per round, £45.00 per day. *Eating facilities:* available, excellent. *Visitors:* welcome, not weekends. *Society Meetings:* catered for. Professional: T.S. Le Brocq (061-427 2421). Secretary: P. Moorhead (Tel & Fax: 061-427 8369).

TRAFFORD. **William Wroe Municipal Golf Course,** Pennybridge Lane, off Flixton Road, Flixton, Trafford M31 3DL (061-748 8680). Course and shop managed by Trafford Borough Council, Acre Gate Golf Club play over the course. *Location:* M63 Exit 4, B5124 to Davyhulme Circle then one mile on B5158, left at Bird-in-Hand Pub. Flat course. 18 holes, 4395 yards. S.S.S. 61. *Green Fees:* weekdays £5.00 adults, £2.50 juniors; weekends £7.00 everyone. *Visitors:* welcome anytime, but advisable to book the day before. Teaching Professional: Roland West. Secretary: Mrs P. Rowan. Golf Course Manager: Mr B. Davies.

WESTHOUGHTON. **Westhoughton Golf Club,** Long Island, School Street, Westhoughton, Bolton BL5 2BR (Westhoughton (0942) 811085). *Location:* four miles south west of Bolton on A58. Parkland. 9 holes, 5702 yards. S.S.S. 68. *Green Fees:* weekdays £15.00 per day; weekends with a member only £5.00. *Eating facilities:* bar meals and home cooking. *Visitors:* welcome, Tuesdays Ladies' Day. Snooker room.

ALMA LODGE You get the best of both worlds at the Alma Lodge – a modern business venue meeting the needs of conferences, combined with all the style and elegance of a bygone era. The Library Room Restaurant offers traditional English dishes and an à la carte menu. There are also two pleasant bars. There are 60 comfortable bedrooms, including Executive rooms and some 'no smoking' rooms for those who prefer. Guests can be sure of a warm welcome at Alma Lodge and of friendly and attentive service. Brochure on request.

149 Buxton Road, Stockport SK2 6EL. Tel: 061-483 4431   RAC ★★★ ETB 🌙🌙🌙🌙 Commended

Society Meetings: welcomed on Thursdays, maximum 32. Professionals: P.Wesselingh/A. Franklin. Secretary: D.J. Kinsella.

WHITEFIELD. **Whitefield Golf Club,** Higher Lane, Whitefield, Manchester (061-766 2728). *Location:* Exit 17, off M62 then take road to Radcliffe for half a mile. 18 holes, 6041 yards. S.S.S. 69. *Green Fees:* on application. *Eating facilities:* restaurant facilities every day. *Visitors:* welcome. *Society Meetings:* catered for. Professional: P. Reeves. Secretary: Mrs R. L. Vidler (061-766 2904).

WIGAN. **Gathurst Golf Club,** 62 Miles Lane, Shevington, Wigan WN6 8EW. *Location:* one mile south of Junction 27 M6. Parkland. 9 holes, 6308 yards. S.S.S. 70. *Green Fees:* weekdays £20.00. *Eating facilities:* available bar hours, daily except Monday. *Visitors:* welcome Monday, Tuesday, Thursday and Friday with reservation. *Society Meetings:* catered for by appointment. Professional: D. Clarke (0257 254909). Secretary: H. Marrow (0257 255235).

WIGAN. **Haigh Hall Golf Club,** Haigh Country Park, Aspull, Near Wigan WN2 1PE (Wigan (0942) 833337). *Location:* Junction 27 M6, at Standish. Parkland. 18 holes, 6400 yards. S.S.S. 71. Practice area. *Green Fees:* weekdays £5.80; weekends £8.40. *Eating facilities:* cafeteria. *Visitors:* welcome, book by telephone. Professional: Mr I. Lee (0942 831107) Secretary: Mr J.M. Parker.

WIGAN. **Hindley Hall Golf Club,** Hall Lane, Hindley, Wigan (Wigan (0942) 55131). *Location:* two miles east of Wigan, Junction 6 M61, or A58 to Ladies Lane/Hall Lane. 18 holes, 5841 yards. S.S.S. 68. *Green Fees:* £20.00 weekdays; £27.00 weekends and Bank Holidays. *Eating facilities:* book before playing. *Visitors:* welcome without reservation if members of a recognised golf club. *Society Meetings:* catered for by arrangement with the Secretary. Professional: N. Brazell (0942 55991). Secretary: R. Bell.

WIGAN. **Wigan Golf Club,** Arley Hall, Haigh, Near Wigan WN1 2UH (Standish (0257) 421360). *Location:* M6 Exit 27, two miles on B5329, east of Standish. Parkland. 9 holes, 6058 yards. S.S.S. 69. *Green Fees:* information not provided. *Eating facilities:* meals and bar available. *Visitors:* welcome anytime except Tuesdays and Saturdays. *Society Meetings:* catered for on Thursdays and Fridays. Secretary: E. Walmsley (0942 43455).

Merseyside

BIRKENHEAD. **Arrowe Park Golf Course,** Arrowe Park, Birkenhead. *Location:* Mersey Tunnel into Brough Road, then Woodchurch Road, head for Arrowe Park roundabout, bear left approximately 400 yards, turn right into Arrowe Park. Parkland. 18 holes, 6435 yards, 5885 metres. S.S.S. 71. 9 hole pitch and putt, putting green. *Green Fees:* £4.70 per round. *Eating facilities:* cafe – bar. *Visitors:* EVERYBODY WELCOME! *Society Meetings:* by arrangement through Professional. Professional: Clive Scanlon (051-677 1527). Secretary: K. Finlay.

BIRKENHEAD. **Prenton Golf Club,** Golf Links Road, Prenton, Birkenhead L42 8LW (051-608 1053). *Location:* M53 Junction 3, off A552 towards Birkenhead. Parkland course. 18 holes, 6411 yards. S.S.S. 71. *Green Fees:* £23.00 weekdays; £25.00 weekends. *Eating facilities:* full catering facilities available. *Visitors:* welcome, reservation advisable. *Society Meetings:* catered for Wednesdays and Fridays. Professional: Robin Thompson (051-608 1636). Secretary: W.F.W. Disley.

BIRKENHEAD. **The Wirral Ladies' Golf Club Ltd,** 93 Bidston Road, Oxton, Birkenhead (051-652 5797). *Location:* on boundary of town, Bidston Hill area. 18 holes, 4966 yards (Ladies), 5170 yards (Men). S.S.S. 70 (Ladies), S.S.S. 66 (Men). *Green Fees:* information not

THE GOLF GUIDE 1994   England   MERSEYSIDE

provided. *Eating facilities:* meals during day to order. *Visitors:* welcome with reservation. Introduction from Club Secretary. Professional: Philip Chandler (051-652 2468). Secretary: D.P. Cranston-Miller (051-652 1255).

BLUNDELLSANDS. **West Lancashire Golf Club,** Hall Road West, Blundellsands, Liverpool L23 8SZ (051-924 4115). *Location:* A565 Liverpool – Southport to Crosby, follow signposts for club or Waterloo Rugby Club. Links course. 6756 yards. S.S.S. 73. *Green Fees:* £33.00 per day, £22.00 per round; £40.00 per round weekends. *Eating facilities:* lunch, tea and dinner every day. *Visitors:* welcome on weekdays. Electric trolleys by prior agreement only. *Society Meetings:* catered for by advance application. Professional: D.G. Lloyd (051-924 5662). Secretary: D.E. Bell (051-924 1076; Fax: 051-931 4448).

BOOTLE. **Bootle Golf Club,** 3 Dunnings Bridge Road, Bootle L30 2PP (051-928 6196). *Location:* five miles north of Liverpool, one mile from M57 and M58. Links course. 18 holes, 6362 yards. S.S.S. 70. *Green Fees:* £3.60 weekdays; £5.05 weekends. *Eating facilities:* full catering as required by arrangement. *Visitors:* welcome weekdays and afternoons at weekends. *Society Meetings:* by appointment. Professional: Gary Brown (051-928 1371). Secretary: John F. Morgan (051-922 4792).

BROMBOROUGH. **Bromborough Golf Club,** Raby Hall Road, Bromborough, Wirral, Merseyside L63 0NN (051-334 2155). *Location:* Exit 4 Wirral Motorway M53. Parkland. 18 holes, 6650 yards, 6080 metres. S.S.S. 73. *Green Fees:* weekdays £25.00, weekends £30.00, reduced rates for Societies over 24. *Eating facilities:* bar and full catering facilities. *Visitors:* welcome without reservation weekdays, but essential to ring in advance for weekends and Bank Holidays. *Society Meetings:* catered for by prior arrangement. Professional: G. Berry (051-334 4499). Secretary: J.T. Barraclough (051-334 2978).

EASTHAM. **Eastham Lodge Golf Club,** 117 Ferry Road, Eastham, Wirral, Merseyside L62 0AP (051-327 1483). *Location:* exit Junction 5 M53 into Eastham village from A41, follow signs for Eastham Country Park. Flat pleasant parkland course with many trees. 15 holes, 5864 yards (for 18). S.S.S. 68. *Green Fees:* weekdays £22.00; weekends with a member only £10.00. *Eating facilities:* bar snacks, full restaurant (book in advance). *Visitors:* welcome weekdays, with member weekends. *Society Meetings:* welcome mainly Tuesdays, some Mondays/Fridays by special arrangement; £22.00 per day, £18.00 per round. Professional: Bob Boobyer (051-327 3008). Secretary: C.S. Camden (051-327 3003).

FORMBY. **Formby Golf Club,** Golf Road, Formby, Liverpool L37 1LQ (07048 72164; Fax: 07048 33028). *Location:* one mile west of A565 by Freshfield Station. Seaside links, wooded. 18 holes, 6781 yards. S.S.S. 73. *Green Fees:* £40.00 weekdays only. *Eating facilities:* available. *Visitors:* welcome, except Wednesdays, weekends and Bank Holidays. Accommodation available. *Society Meetings:* catered for. Professional: C.F. Harrison (07048 73090). Secretary: A. Thirlwell (07048 72164).

FORMBY. **Formby Ladies' Golf Club,** Golf Road, Formby, Liverpool L37 1YH (Formby (07048) 74127). Seaside links. 18 holes, 5374 yards, 4914 metres. S.S.S. 71. Practice area. *Green Fees:* weekdays £25.00; weekends £31.00. *Eating facilities:* light lunches, afternoon teas. *Visitors:* welcome with prior reservation, contact the Secretary. *Society Meetings:* catered for with prior reservation. Professional: C. Harrison (07048 73090). Secretary: Mrs V. Bailey (07048 73493).

HESWALL. **Heswall Golf Club,** Cottage Lane, Gayton, Wirral L60 8PB (051-342 2193). *Location:* off A540, eight miles north-west of Chester. Parkland on the banks of River Dee estuary overlooking Welsh coast and hills. 18 holes, 6472 yards, 5909 metres. S.S.S. 72. Large practice area. *Green Fees:* weekdays £30.00, weekends and Bank Holidays £35.00. *Eating facilities:* bar snacks, full meals by arrangement. *Visitors:* welcome anytime subject to availability. Must have accredited Handicaps. *Society Meetings:* catered for fully on Wednesdays and Fridays only, minimum 24 players. Professional: Alan Thompson (051-342 7431). Secretary: (051-342 1237). Catering (051-342 2193).

Tree Tops Country House

Restaurant and Hotel

♥♥♥♥ Johansens Recommended
Ashley Courtenay Highly Recommended

Where better to relax than Tree Tops in its country setting with heated pool and patio area (available May to September), yet close to Southport with its famous Lord Street for shopping, theatres, cinemas and all sporting activities including five championship golf courses.

All accommodation is to a high standard with every comfort for our guests. The restaurant, which is exquisitely furnished is renowned in the area for its cuisine offering both à la carte and table d'hôte menu. SPECIAL BREAKS – 2 nights Dinner, Bed and Breakfast only £99 per person.

SOUTHPORT OLD ROAD, FORMBY, MERSEYSIDE. TEL: 07048 79651.

MERSEYSIDE *England*

HOYLAKE. Royal Liverpool Golf Club, Meols Drive, Hoylake, Wirral, Merseyside L47 4AL (051-632 3101). *Location:* 10 miles south-west of Liverpool on Wirral Peninsula. Approach from M6, M56 and M53 Junction 2. Championship links. 18 holes, 6804 yards. S.S.S. 74. Large practice area. Visitors welcome weekdays except Thursday mornings (Ladies' Day). Very limited play at weekends. Proof of handicap required. Caddies available. *Green Fees (1993):* £35.00 per round, £50.00 per day. *Eating facilities:* full Dining Room (jacket and tie) or soup/snacks in locker room bar. *Society Meetings:* catered for Tuesdays to Fridays. Professional: John Heggarty (051-632 5868). Secretary: Group Captain C.T. Moore OBE (051-632 3101).

HUYTON. **Bowring Golf Club,** Bowring Park, Roby Road, Huyton (051-489 1901). 9 holes, 5580 yards. S.S.S. 66. *Green Fees:* on application. *Visitors:* unrestricted. Secretary: E. Hatton. Professional: Michael Sarsfield.

HUYTON. **Huyton and Prescot Golf Club Ltd,** Hurst Park, Huyton Lane, Huyton, Liverpool L36 1UA (051-489 1138). *Location:* Liverpool Road to Prescot town centre. Parkland. 18 holes, 5779 yards. S.S.S. 68 white, 67 yellow. *Green Fees:* weekdays £22.00; weekends £8.00 (one visitor with member only). *Eating facilities:* catering 11am to 5pm; normal bar hours. *Visitors:* welcome, midweek days 9.30am to 12.30pm, 2pm to 4pm. *Society Meetings:* catered for Mondays, Wednesdays, Thursdays and Friday afternoons. Professional: Mr I. Sephton (051-489 2022). Secretary: Mrs E. Holmes (051-489 3948).

LIVERPOOL. **Allerton Park Golf Club,** Allerton Road, Liverpool L18 3JT (051-428 4074). *Location:* Menlove Avenue. Parkland. 18 holes, 5800 yards. S.S.S. 67. *Green Fees:* £4.75. *Eating facilities:* lunches at club. *Visitors:* welcome. Professional: Barry Large. Secretary: H.G. Drew.

LIVERPOOL. **Dudley Golf Club,** Allerton Municipal Golf Course, Menlove Avenue, Allerton, Liverpool 18 (051-428 8510). *Location:* end of M62, then two miles on Allerton road. Wooded parkland. 18 holes, 5459 metres. S.S.S. 67. 9 holes, 1685 metres. S.S.S. 34. *Green Fees:* information not provided. *Eating facilities:* hot meals available in clubhouse. *Visitors:* welcome at any time. *Society Meetings:* welcome. Professional: Barry Large (051-428 1046). Secretary: Terry Tollitt (051-427 6189).

LIVERPOOL. **Lee Park Golf Club,** Childwall Valley Road, Liverpool L27 3YA (051-487 9861). *Location:* Queens Drive, Childwall Valley Road. Parkland. 18 holes, 6074 yards. Medal tees: 5569 yards. Front tees: S.S.S. 68. Ladies' tee: 5650 yards. S.S.S. 72. *Green Fees:* information not provided. *Eating facilities:* restaurant and bar snacks daily. *Visitors:* welcome anytime except between 12.15pm and 2.15pm daily (reserved for members). *Society Meetings:* catered for. Secretary: Mrs Doris Barr (051-487 3882).

LIVERPOOL. **The Childwall Golf Club Ltd.,** Naylors Road, Gateacre, Liverpool L27 2YB (051-487 9982). *Location:* Exit 6 M62 to Liverpool follow Huyton A5080 to second set of traffic lights, turn left into Wheathill Road. Parkland, flat, designed by James Braid. 18 holes, 6425 yards. S.S.S. 72. Practice area.

ROYAL LIVERPOOL GOLF CLUB, HOYLAKE
Founded 1869

Visitors and Societies are welcome to use the full facilities of this long established Club, the home of the first Amateur Championship in 1885 and the venue for ten Open Championships. Hoylake offers the challenge of a magnificent Championship links as well as the chance to experience the history of a traditional Clubhouse with its impressive displays of golfing memorabilia. Green fees on application. Full dining facilities by prior arrangement.

Meols Drive, Hoylake, Wirral L47 4AL. Telephone: 051-632 3101

KING'S GAP COURT HOTEL
Valentia Road, Hoylake, Wirral L47 2AN
Telephone: 051 632 2073

Set in pleasant gardens within easy reach of eight golf courses, beach, marina and railway station. Most rooms en-suite; colour TV, tea and coffee making facilities. Full central heating. Large car park. Reduced terms for golfers or sailing enthusiasts Monday to Friday (4 nights).
LICENSED BAR & RESTAURANT.

THE GOLF GUIDE 1994
England MERSEYSIDE

Green Fees: £19.50 weekdays; £28.00 weekends. *Eating facilities:* bar, snacks and restaurant. *Visitors:* no visitors weekends and Tuesdays. *Society Meetings:* catered for on weekdays, contact the Secretary. Groups over 20, £17.50. Professional: Mr N.M. Parr (051-487 9871). Secretary: Mr L. Upton (051-487 0654).

LIVERPOOL. **West Derby Golf Club,** Yew Tree Lane, West Derby, Liverpool L12 9HQ. Flat parkland course. 18 holes, 6346 yards. S.S.S. 70. *Green Fees:* weekdays £20.00 per round, £22.50 per day; weekends £30.00. *Eating facilities:* soup and sandwiches, light meals available at lunch. Evening meals by prior arrangement. *Visitors:* welcome if members of a recognised golf club. *Society Meetings:* catered for only by arrangement with Secretary. Professional: Nick Brace (051-220 5478). Secretary/Manager: S. Young (051-254 1034).

LIVERPOOL. **Woolton Golf Club,** Doe Park, Speke Road, Woolton, Liverpool L25 7TZ (051-486 1601). *Location:* south Liverpool, one mile from Woolton Village. Parkland. 18 holes, 5706 yards. S.S.S. 68. *Green Fees:* weekdays £20.00; weekends £28.00. *Eating facilities:* bar snacks daily. *Visitors:* welcome without reservation, except Tuesdays. *Society Meetings:* catered for by arrangement. Professional Shop: (051-486 1298). Secretary: K.G. Jennions (051-486 2298).

MORETON. **Bidston Golf Club,** Scoresby Road, Leasowe, Moreton L46 1QQ (051-638 3412). *Location:* leave M53 Junction 1 (from Chester), Wallasey, Leasowe, one mile left Catholic Church, approximately one mile. Flat course. 18 holes, 6204 yards. S.S.S. 70. Practice ground. *Green Fees:* information not provided. *Eating facilities:* available. *Visitors:* welcome weekdays with prior notification. *Society Meetings:* catered for, early application by letter required. Professional: J. Law (051-630 6650). Secretary/Manager: L.A. Kendrick (051-638 8685).

MORETON. **Leasowe Golf Club,** Leasowe Road, Moreton, Wirral, Merseyside L46 3RD (051-677 5852). *Location:* one mile west of Wallasey Village and one mile from M53. Flat seaside links. 18 holes, 6204 yards. S.S.S. 70. *Green Fees:* £20.00 weekdays; weekends only with a member. *Eating facilities:* catering and bar. *Visitors:* welcome on weekdays, weekends with a member. *Society Meetings:* catered for weekdays by arrangement. Professional: Neil Sweeney (061-678 5460). Secretary: T. Lee.

NEWTON-LE-WILLOWS. **Haydock Park Golf Club,** Newton Lane, Newton-le-Willows WA12 0HX (Newton-le-Willows (0925) 224389). *Location:* off East Lancs Road (A580) and M6, three quarters of a mile from Newton-le-Willows High Street. Flat, wooded parkland course in beautiful setting. 18 holes, 6043 yards. S.S.S. 69. Large practice ground. *Green Fees:* weekdays £25.00. *Eating facilities:* restaurant and two bars. *Visitors:* welcome weekdays except Tuesdays, identification (club membership card) or letter of introduction required. *Society Meetings:* catered for by arrangement. Professional: P. Kenwright (0925 226944). Secretary: G. Tait (0925 228525).

SOUTHPORT. **Hesketh Golf Club,** Cockle Dicks Lane, Cambridge Road, Southport PR9 9QQ (Southport (0704) 530226). *Location:* one mile north of town centre. Seaside links Championship course. 18 holes, 6478 yards. S.S.S. 72. Practice ground. *Green Fees:* weekdays £25.00 per round, £35.00 per day; weekends and Bank Holidays £40.00 per day. *Eating facilities:* bar snacks and dining room; three bars. *Visitors:* welcome by prior arrangement with Secretary. *Society Meetings:* catered for by arrangement with Secretary. Professional: John Donoghue (0704 530050). Secretary: Peter B. Seal (0704 536897; Fax: 0704 539250).

SOUTHPORT. **Hillside Golf Club,** Hastings Road, Hillside, Southport PR8 2LU (0704 69902). *Location:* three miles south of town centre, Hillside station one mile. Links. Championship course used for R&A, EGU and PGA events. 18 holes, 6850 yards. S.S.S. 74. Practice ground. *Green Fees:* weekdays £45.00 per day, £35.00 per round; weekends £45.00 per round. *Eating facilities:* diningroom, bars and lounges. *Visitors:* welcome Mondays, Wednesdays, Thursdays and Fridays, Tuesday pm only, limited times available Sundays. *Society Meetings:* welcome with prior reservations. Professional: Brian Seddon (0704 68360). Secretary: John G. Graham (0704 67169; Fax: 0704 63192).

SOUTHPORT. **Park Golf Club,** Park Road West, Southport (Southport (0704) 530133). Play over Southport Municipal Links. S.S.S. 69. Secretary: J.A.V. Turner. Professional: (0704) 535286).

SOUTHPORT. **Royal Birkdale Golf Club,** Waterloo Road, Birkdale, Southport PR8 2LX (0704 67920; Fax: 0704 62327). *Location:* one mile south of Southport town centre. Classic Links on the Open Championship rota. 18 holes, 6703 yards. S.S.S. 73. *Green Fees:* contact the Secretary. *Visitors:* welcome by arrangement with Secretary, official golf Handicap required. *Society Meetings:* catered for, package prices for 20 plus, diningroom facilities. Professional: Richard Bradbeer (0704 68857). Secretary: Norman Crewe (0704 67920).

Metropole Hotel
Portland Street, Southport,
Merseyside PR8 1LL
Tel: 0704 536836; Fax: 0704 549041
AA ★★ RAC   Fully Licensed

Within five minutes of Royal Birkdale and four Championship courses. Fully licensed, privately owned family hotel run by Golfing Proprietors who can make golf arrangements if required. All rooms have colour TV's, tea/coffee makers, direct-dial telephones. Majority have private facilities. Full sized snooker table available in the hotel. Late bar facilities for residents. Party reductions. Phone now for your full colour brochure.

MERSEYSIDE *England*   THE GOLF GUIDE 1994

SOUTHPORT. **Southport and Ainsdale Golf Club,** Bradshaw's Lane, Off Liverpool Road, Ainsdale, Southport PR8 3LG (Southport (0704) 570892). *Location:* south of Southport on A565. Links course. 18 holes, 6615 yards. S.S.S. 73. *Green Fees:* weekdays £30.00 per round, £40.00 per day; weekends £45.00 per day. *Eating facilities:* full catering available. *Visitors:* advance booking recommended. *Society Meetings:* catered for by arrangement. Professional: M. Houghton (0704 577316). Secretary: I.F. Sproule (0704 578000; Fax: 0704 570896).

SOUTHPORT. **Southport Municipal Golf Club,** Park Road West, Southport (Southport (0704) 55130). *Location:* Park Road West, north end of Promenade, near Marine Lake, Southport. Flat seaside links. 18 holes, 6139 yards. S.S.S. 70. *Green Fees:* information not available. *Eating facilities:* licensed cafe. *Visitors:* booking system operates up to seven days in advance (visitors unrestricted). *Society Meetings:* welcome, book in advance. Professional: William Fletcher (0704 35286).

SOUTHPORT. **Southport Old Links Golf Club,** Moss Lane, Churchtown, Southport PR9 7QS (0704 28207). *Location:* end of Roe Lane, Churchtown, at the rear of Meols Hall. Tree lined links course. 9 holes, 6378 yards (x2). S.S.S. 71. *Green Fees:* weekdays £18.00 per round, £25.00 per day; weekends and Bank Holidays £25.00 per round only. Weekly ticket £75.00 to play any five out of seven days. For minimum number of 12 £30.00 per day including coffee on arrival, soup and sandwiches, three-course evening meal and two rounds of golf – £10 deposit. *Eating facilities:* available daily. *Visitors:* welcome except

---

Atlantic Hotel   17 Bath Street, Southport. Tel: 0704 530344.

ONLY MINUTES AWAY FROM 5 CHAMPIONSHIP GOLF COURSES INCLUDING ROYAL BIRKDALE

Close to Promenade, Pleasure Beach and famed Lord Street Shopping Centre, the Hotel is noted for its warm, friendly welcome, personal attention, cuisine and comfort. *En-suite rooms with a hairdryer; *Tea/coffee facilities; *Pool table, sauna, sunbed; *Access at all times; *Colour TV lounge; *Video library; *Open all year; *Coach parties welcome.

DUKES FOLLY
HOTEL · AND · RESTAURANT

DUKE STREET, SOUTHPORT PR8 1LS. TELEPHONE: (0704) 533355 FAX: (0704) 530065

Southport golfing breaks situated in the heart of Southport just over one mile from Royal Birkdale and within easy reach of all major courses. All rooms ensuite, car park and restaurant.

Please write or ring Michael or Jill Peterson for further details.

"GOLFERS' MECCA"

Play **ROYAL BIRKDALE** or ony of the 7 golf courses within a 6 mile radius and stay at the only hotel in Birkdale. The hotel is family-run with an outstanding reputation for a friendly atmosphere, cleanliness, service and excellent food.

★ All rooms are en suite ★ All rooms fitted with TV, tea/coffee facilities.
★ Car park ★ Licensed Bar ★ Full size snooker table ★ Drying facilities
★ Direct dial telephones ★ Assistance given with "Tee-off" times.

For brochure contact Denise or Brian.

BELGRAVIA HOTEL
11 Trafalgar Road, Birkdale, Southport PR8 2EA
Telephone: 0704 65298

AA ★★   RAC ★★   Highly Recommended   Inspection Invited

THE GOLF GUIDE 1994 *England* MERSEYSIDE

Wednesdays, Sundays and Bank Holidays. *Society Meetings:* catered for by arrangement, letter of application required. Professional: Mr P. Atkiss (0704 28207). Secretary: Mr J.A. Lord (0704 24294).

ST. HELENS. **Grange Park Golf Club,** Prescot Road, St. Helens WA10 3AD (St. Helens (0744) 22980). *Location:* one and a half miles south west of St. Helens on A58. Wooded parkland. 18 holes, 6429 yards. S.S.S. 71. Practice area. *Green Fees:* weekdays £21.00; weekends £26.00. *Eating facilities:* full catering and bar facilities. *Visitors:* welcome anytime but times are often not available at weekends/Bank Holidays; reservation through Professional recommended. *Society Meetings:* catered for Mondays, Wednesdays or Thursdays by advance reservation through Secretary. Professional: Paul Evans (0744 28785). Secretary: David A. Wood (0744 26318).

ST. HELENS. **Sherdley Park Golf Club,** St. Helens (0744 813149). Clubhouse (0744 815518). *Location:* two miles east of town on A570. 18 holes, 5941 yards. S.S.S. 69. *Green Fees:* information not provided. *Visitors:* unrestricted. Professional: P.R. Parkinson. Secretary: B.M. Healiss.

WALLASEY. **Wallasey Golf Club,** Bayswater Road, Wallasey L45 8LA (051-639 3630). *Location:* via M53 through Wirral or 15 minutes from Liverpool centre via Wallasey Tunnel. Seaside links. 18 holes, 6607 yards, 6038 metres. S.S.S. 73. *Green Fees:* weekdays £25.00 per round, £30.00 per day; weekends and Bank Holidays £30.00 per round, £35.00 per day. *Eating facilities:* snacks and full catering facilities. *Visitors:* welcome with reservation. *Society Meetings:* catered for by arrangement. Professional: Mike Adams (051-638 3888). Secretary: Mrs L.M. Dolman (051-691 1024).

WALLASEY. **Warren Golf Club,** The Grange, Grove Road, Wallasey (051-639 8293). *Location:* 300 yards Grove Road Station. Links course. 9 holes, 5914 yards.

S.S.S. 68. *Green Fees:* £5.40. Special rates for Senior Citizens and Juniors. *Visitors:* welcome. *Society Meetings:* welcome. Professional: Kenneth Lamb (051-639 5730). Secretary: Paul Warrington.

WIRRAL. **Brackenwood Golf Club,** Bracken Lane, Bebington, Wirral (051-608 5394). *Location:* M53 Junction 7 Clatterbridge turnoff. Parkland. 18 holes, 6285 yards, 5747 metres. S.S.S. 70. *Green Fees:* £6.00. There is a charge of £1.00 per person individual booking. *Eating facilities:* snacks available. *Visitors:* welcome anytime weekdays through the Professional, bookings at weekends. *Society Meetings:* welcome. Professional: Colin Disbury (051-608 3093). Secretary: N.D. Taylor.

WIRRAL. **Hoylake Golf Club,** Carr Lane, Hoylake, Wirral (051-632 2956). *Location:* turn at roundabout Hoylake town centre, over railway. Part flat semi links. 18 holes, 6313 yards, 5780 metres. S.S.S. 70. *Green Fees:* £6.00. *Eating facilities:* cafe and bar. Phone Steward (M. Down) in advance (051-632 4883). *Visitors:* welcome, booking fee required in advance. *Society Meetings:* weekdays only. Professional: S.N. Hooton (051-632 2956). Secretary: M.E. Down (051-632 4883).

WIRRAL. **The Caldy Golf Club Ltd,** Links Hey Road, Caldy, Wirral L48 1NB (051-625 5515). *Location:* one mile south of West Kirby on the River Dee, 10 miles from Chester. Undulating parkland, links, open aspect with views across the Dee to the North Wales hills. 18 holes, 6675 yards, 6105 metres. S.S.S. 73. Practice ground and putting green. *Green Fees:* weekdays £28.00 per round, £32.00 per day; weekends with member only. *Eating facilities:* bars and restaurant throughout the day. *Visitors:* welcome weekdays with advance booking and Handicap Certificate. Restrictions Tuesdays and Wednesdays. Jeans not allowed on course or in Clubhouse. *Society Meetings:* Thursdays by prior arrangement. Professional: Kevin Jones (051-625 1818). Secretary: T.D.M. Bacon (051-625 5660).

THE GOLF FOUNDATION
57 London Road, Enfield, Middlesex EN2 6DU
Telephone: 081-367 4404

Established in 1952 The Golf Foundation has the specific aims of introducing more young people to the game of golf and of promoting and developing their skills and enjoyment of the game. The basis of the Foundation's work is the Coaching Scheme, whereby qualified members of the PGA give instruction to students at schools and universities.

The Golf Foundation is a non-profit-making organisation and a Registered Charity, relying on support from organisations within the game, commerce and industry, and individual Golf Clubs and club members.

NORFOLK *England*   THE GOLF GUIDE 1994

Norfolk

CROMER. **Links Country Park Hotel and Golf Club,** Sandy Lane, West Runton, Cromer NR27 9QH (0263 838383). *Location:* midway between Cromer and Sheringham on the A149, turn left opposite the village inn. Undulating parkland with narrow fairways and tricky greens. 9 holes, 4814 yards, S.S.S. 64. *Green Fees:* £19.00 per day weekdays, £23.00 weekends. *Eating facilities:* grill room, snacks, hotel restaurant table d'hôte and à la carte. *Visitors:* welcome weekdays, restrictions weekends. Adjoining Hotel offers free golf to residents; sauna, solarium, swimming pool etc. *Society Meetings:* welcome weekdays and some weekends. Professional: Mike Jubb (0263 838215). Hon. Secretary: S. Mansfield (0263 838383).

CROMER. **Royal Cromer Golf Club,** 145 Overstrand Road, Cromer NR27 0JH (Cromer (0263) 512219). *Location:* one mile east of town centre on coast road. Undulating seaside course. 18 holes, 6508 yards. S.S.S. 71. Large practice ground. *Green Fees:* £25.00 weekdays, £30.00 weekends. *Eating facilities:* full catering and bar snacks. *Visitors:* welcome, booking essential from 1st April to 31st October, Handicap Certificates required. *Society Meetings:* welcome except weekends. Professional: Robin J. Page (0263 512267). Secretary: B.A. Howson (0263 512884).

DEREHAM. **Dereham Golf Club,** Quebec Road, Dereham NR19 2DS (Dereham (0362) 695900). *Location:* three-quarters-of-a mile from town centre on B1110. Wooded parkland. 9 holes (double tees), 6625 yards. S.S.S. 70. *Green Fees:* weekdays £16.00; weekends with member only £10. *Eating facilities:* full restaurant (limited Mondays). *Visitors:* welcome weekdays with prior notice, not weekends; players must produce proof of Handicap and club membership. *Society Meetings:* catered for with advance booking. Professional: Gary Kitley (0362 695631). Secretary: George Dalrymple (0362 695900).

DISS. **Diss Golf Club,** Stuston Common, Diss (0379 642847). The course is in Suffolk but Postal Address is Diss, Norfolk. *Location:* B1077 off A140, half-a-mile from Diss railway station, one mile from town centre. Flat common land. 18 holes, 6238 yards. S.S.S. 70. *Green Fees:* £20.00, £10.00 if playing with a member. *Eating facilities:* excellent facilities – newly refurbished. *Visitors:* welcome without reservation. *Society Meetings:* all welcome and catered for. Professional: N. Taylor (0379 644399). Secretary: J.A. Bell (0379 641025).

DOWNHAM MARKET. **Ryston Park Golf Club,** Ely Road, Denver, Downham Market PE38 0HH (Downham (0366) 382133).*Location:* one mile south Downham Market on A10. 36 miles north Cambridge. Parkland. 9 holes, 6292 yards. S.S.S. 70. Practice

NORFOLK COAST

F Use of own 9-hole golf course.
R Accommodation for children under 16 years.
E Use of indoor heated swimming pool.
E Use of all-weather tennis court.
   Use of sauna & solarium

Golf Societies Welcomed

The **Links**
Country Park Hotel & Golf Club

WEST RUNTON, CROMER, NORFOLK NR27 9QH
TEL: (0263) 838383 FAX: (0263) 838264

ground. *Green Fees:* weekdays £20.00, £8.00 with a member. *Eating facilities:* meals served to order. *Visitors:* welcome weekdays, one guest per member weekends. *Society Meetings:* restricted, catered for by arrangement. Secretary: A.J. Wilson (0366 383834).

FAKENHAM. **Fakenham Golf Club,** Gallow Sports Centre, Hempton Road, Fakenham (Fakenham (0328) 862867). *Location:* half-a-mile town centre on Swaffham Road. Parkland. 9 holes, 5992 yards. S.S.S. 69. Large practice area. *Green Fees:* weekdays £14.00, weekends and Bank Holidays £18.00 after 3pm. 10% reduction for Societies. *Eating facilities:* available in Sports Centre. *Visitors:* welcome by appointment. *Society Meetings:* welcome, reduced rates. Professional: J. Westwood (0328 863534). Secretary: G.G. Cocker (0328 855665).

GREAT YARMOUTH. **Caldecott Hall Golf Club,** Beccles Road, Fritton, Great Yarmouth NR31 9EY (0493 488488; Fax: 0493 488561). *Location:* on A143 just north of the village of Fritton. Parkland. 9 holes, 1650 yards. S.S.S. 27. Driving range, pitching and

164

THE GOLF GUIDE 1994

England NORFOLK

putting greens. *Green Fees:* weekdays £12.00 for 18 holes; weekends £16.00 for 18 holes. Group discounts. *Eating facilities:* bar, restaurant. *Visitors:* welcome at all times, starting sheets weekends and Bank Holidays. *Society Meetings:* welcome by arrangement. Professional: Frank Hill. Secretary: D. Brooks.

GREAT YARMOUTH. **Gorleston Golf Club,** Warren Road, Gorleston, Great Yarmouth NR31 6JT (Great Yarmouth (0493) 661082). *Location:* A12 Lowestoft to Great Yarmouth. Seaside links. 18 holes, 6400 yards. S.S.S. 71. *Green Fees:* weekdays £20.00; weekends and Public Holidays £25.00 (weekly £60.00). Reductions if playing with member. *Eating facilities:* restaurant/bars open seven days. *Visitors:* welcome, advisable to check in advance for details of restrictions. *Society Meetings:* catered for by prior arrangement (membership of recognised club required). Professional: Nick Brown (0493 662103). Secretary: C.B. Court (0493 661911).

GREAT YARMOUTH. **Great Yarmouth and Caister Golf Club,** Beach House, Caister-on-Sea, Great Yarmouth NR30 5TD (Great Yarmouth (0493) 720214). *Location:* A149 coast road, two miles north of Great Yarmouth. Links. 18 holes, 6235 yards. S.S.S. 70. Practice ground. *Green Fees:* £23.50, £15.00 after 3.30pm weekdays; £28.00, £18.00 after 3.30pm weekends. Members' guests 50 per cent. *Eating facilities:* full range of catering; bar. *Visitors:* welcome, not before 10.30am Saturdays and not before 11.30am Sundays. *Society Meetings:* catered for. Professional: R. Foster (0493 720421). Secretary: Mrs H.M. Marsh (0493 728699).

HELLESDON. **Royal Norwich Golf Club,** Drayton High Road, Hellesdon, Norwich NR6 5AH (Norwich (0603) 429928). *Location:* centre of city and thence by A1067 Fakenham or via Ring Road, then 500 yards along A1067. 18 holes, 6603 yards. S.S.S. 72. *Green Fees:* £26.00 per round or day. *Eating facilities:* lunches and teas served at club. *Visitors:* welcome during week only, but must have membership card of a recognised golf club and a bona fide handicap. Professional: Alan Hemsley (0603 408459). General Manager: John Meggy.

HUNSTANTON. **Hunstanton Golf Club,** Golf Course Road, Old Hunstanton PE36 6JQ (Hunstanton (0485) 532811). *Location:* off A149. Adjoins Old Hunstanton village, approximately half a mile north east of Hunstanton. Championship links course with excellent fast greens. 18 holes, 6670 yards. S.S.S. 72. Practice ground. *Green Fees:* weekdays £30.00; weekends £36.00. Special rates in winter, also after 4pm all year. *Eating facilities:* catering and bar facilities. *Visitors:* welcome but limited times available at weekends. Prior booking advisable. Visitors must be member of recognised golf club and hold a current Handicap. *Society Meetings:* welcome. Professional: J. Carter (0485 532751). Secretary: (0485 532811).

KINGS LYNN. **Eagles Golf Club,** 39 School Road, Tilney All Saints, Kings Lynn PE34 4RS (0553 827147). *Location:* off A47 road between Kings Lynn and Wisbech. Parkland. 9 holes, 4284 yards. S.S.S. 61. Par 3 course, driving range. *Green Fees:* weekdays £5.50 per 9 holes; weekends £6.50 per 9 holes. *Eating facilities:* bar/restaurant. *Visitors:* welcome, no restrictions. *Society Meetings:* apply to Secretary. Secretary: David W. Horn.

KING'S LYNN. **King's Lynn Golf Club,** Castle Rising, King's Lynn PE31 6BD (0553 631227). *Location:* four miles north-east of King's Lynn. Undulating wooded course. 18 holes, 6646 yards. S.S.S. 72. Practice areas. *Green Fees:* weekdays £30.00, weekends £38.00. *Eating facilities:* snacks, lunches, teas available; dinners by arrangement; two bars. *Visitors:* welcome on production of Handicap Certificate. *Society Meetings:* catered for by prior arrangement. Professional: C. Hanlon (0553 631655). Secretary: G.J. Higgins (0553 631654; Fax: 0553 631036).

KING'S LYNN. **Royal West Norfolk Golf Club,** Brancaster, Near King's Lynn PE31 8AX (Brancaster (0485) 210223). *Location:* one mile off A149, Beach Road junction, seven miles east of Hunstanton. Seaside links. 18 holes, 6428 yards. S.S.S. 71. *Green Fees:* weekdays £30.00 per day; weekends £40.00 per day. *Eating facilities:* available. *Visitors:* all visitors to be members of a recognised Golf Club, hold an official Handicap and must make prior arrangements with the Secretary to play. No visitors prior to 10.00am Sundays

---

IDEAL LOCATION FOR GOLF ON THE DELIGHTFUL NORFOLK COAST

THE LODGE HOTEL
Old Hunstanton, Norfolk PE36 6HX

Where a warm, friendly atmosphere, and good food enhance the pleasure of a good round and compensate for an unfortunate one. Close to three superb golf courses; full size snooker table, real ales, log fires, colour TV, radio, tea/coffee making facilities, direct dial telephones to all rooms.

SPECIAL RATES FOR GOLF PARTIES   TEL: 0485 532896

RAC ★★★

Le Strange Arms Hotel
OLD HUNSTANTON

ETB

Situated only 250 yards from Hunstanton Golf Club.   * Hotel lawns sweep down to the beach
* Full size snooker table   * Fine Restaurant and private dining rooms
Telephone: (0485) 534411   Fax: (0485) 534724

NORFOLK *England*

and no visitors during last week in July and until first week in September. Professional: R.E. Kimber (0485 210616). Secretary: Major N.A. Carrington Smith (0485 210087).

NORWICH. **Barnham Broom Hotel, Golf and Country Club**, Honingham Road, Norwich NR9 4DD (0603 759393; Fax: 0603 358224). *Location:* A11 to Norwich follow brown tourist signs marked "Barnham Broom" from Wymondham; A47 to Norwich follow brown tourist signs, 10 miles from Norwich. River valley parkland and hill courses. Two courses: Valley 18 holes, 6470 yards. S.S.S. 71; Hill 18 holes, 6628 yards. S.S.S. 72. Practice facilities. *Green Fees:* weekdays £25.00 per round, £30.00 per day; weekends on application. *Eating facilities:* all day buffet/bar and full restaurant. *Visitors:* welcome anytime, on application at weekends. 52 bedroomed hotel (en-suite). Golfing "Getaway" Breaks, residential Peter Ballingall Golf Schools, overnight stay tuition breaks. *Society Meetings:* welcome on application. Professional: Steve Beckham (0603 759393 ext. 279). Director of Golf: Peter Ballingall (0603 759393).

NORWICH. **Bawburgh Golf Club**, Long Lane, Bawburgh, Norwich NR9 3LX (0603 746390; Fax: 0603 811110). *Location:* directly off the new Norwich Southern Bypass/rear Royal Norfolk Showground. Undulating heathland and parkland. 18 holes, 6066 yards. S.S.S. 69. Driving range – covered and floodlit, group tuition. *Green Fees:* weekdays £14.00, weekends £17.00 on application. *Eating facilities:* bar snacks and licensed bar. *Visitors:* restricted at weekend mornings and Bank Holidays, advisable to ring in advance. Ladies have preference Monday mornings. Member of "The Buggy Club" for disabled golfers. *Society Meetings:* welcome on application. Professional: C. Potter (0603 742323). Secretary: R.J. Mapes (0953 606776).

THE GOLF GUIDE 1994

NORWICH. **Costessey Park Golf Course**, Old Costessey, Norwich NR8 5AL (Norwich (0603) 746333). *Location:* off the A47 Norwich to King's Lynn road, in the village of Old Costessey (adjacent to Norwich). Set in river valley with some parkland. 18 holes, 5964 yards. S.S.S. 69. Par 72. Practice area. *Green Fees:* information not provided. *Eating facilities:* bar and bar snacks; carvery and set meals available. *Visitors:* welcome anytime except weekends when visitors allowed only after 11.30am. Golf cart available for hire by physically handicapped golfers. *Society Meetings:* catered for by arrangement. Professional: Simon Cook (0603 747085). Secretary: Colin House.

NORWICH. **Eaton (Norwich) Golf Club**, Newmarket Road, Norwich NR4 6SF (Norwich (0603) 52881). *Location:* half a mile from A11, approximately one and a half miles from Norwich city centre. Parkland course. 18 holes, 6135 yards. S.S.S. 69. Practice areas available. *Green Fees:* £28.00 weekdays, £35.00 weekends and Bank Holidays. *Eating facilities:* snacks, lunches; dinners by arrangement. *Visitors:* welcome; only after 11.30am weekends. Handicap Certificate required. *Society Meetings:* on application. Professional: Mr Nigel Bundy (0603 52478). Secretary: Mr David Sochon (Tel & Fax: 0603 51686).

NORWICH. **Mundesley Golf Club**, Links Road, Mundesley, Norwich NR11 8ES (Mundesley (0263) 720297). *Location:* one mile from village centre. Undulating fairly exposed parkland course with fine panoramic views. 9 holes, 5410 yards, 4949 metres. S.S.S. 66. Small practice area. *Green Fees:* on application. *Eating facilities:* full catering facilities. *Visitors:* welcome, but course reserved for members until 11.30am at weekends and 12 noon to 3.30pm Wednesdays. *Society Meetings:* catered for, restriction as for visitors. Professional: T.G. Symmons (0831 455461). Secretary: Peter Hampel (0263 720095).

Self Catering at BURNHAM OVERY STAITHE, NORFOLK

FLAGSTAFF HOUSE – right on the quay, the old home of Captain Woodgett of the *Cutty Sark*. Each half of the house sleeps 5 in 3 bedrooms. Also available **FLAGSTAFF BARN** and **COTTAGE** in the garden all with superb views over the creeks and saltings. The **Garden House** is fully equipped for two and the **Summerhouse** sleeps an additional two. All properties fully equipped with all modern conveniences, including colour TV and video, telephone, washing machine and dishwasher. Ideal for all outdoor activities, and an ideal base for Norfolk's superb golf courses. ETB Commended. For Brochure contact: **Mr C. W. C. Green, Red House Farm, Badingham, Woodbridge, Suffolk IP13 8LL.**
Tel: (until Jan/Feb 1994) Badingham (072875) 637; Fax: Badingham (072875) 638

BARNHAM BROOM HOTEL

NORWICH NR9 4DD
Tel: (060545) 393 Fax: (060545) 8224
Changing from February 1994 to
Tel: (0603) 759 393 Fax: (0603) 75 8224
8 miles west of Norwich off A47

AA ★★★   ETB 🌸🌸🌸   Best Western   *M.D. Alan Long*

Set in 250 acres. Two 18 hole Courses. Complete leisure complex: Squash, Tennis, Swimming, Fitness Centre, Sauna, Solarium, Hairdressing Salon and Beautician. Full conference facilities. Getaway and Golfing Breaks from £108. Residential Golf Schools Spring to Autumn by Peter Ballingall, Director of Golf and Golf Monthly teaching Professional. 52 bedroom Hotel all with private bath/shower, colour TV, radio, telephone and tea/coffee making facilities. Restaurant, Buttery and Bars. Come and enjoy the friendship of Barnham Broom.

England NORFOLK

NORWICH. **Sprowston Park Golf Club,** Wroxham Road, Norwich NR7 8RP (0603 409188). *Location:* A1151 Norwich to Wroxham. Parkland with plenty of trees. 18 holes, 5982 yards. S.S.S. 70. Driving range, putting green, chipping green, bunker practice area. *Green Fees:* weekdays £12.00 per round; weekends £14.00 per round. *Eating facilities:* Fairways Bar and Restaurant. *Visitors:* always welcome. *Society Meetings:* catered for anytime with notice. Professional: P.G. Grice PGA (0603 417264). Secretary: J.A. Butterfield (Mrs) (0603 410657; Fax: 0603 788884).

NORWICH. **Wensum Valley Golf Club,** Beech Avenue, Taverham, Norwich NR8 6HP (0603 261012). *Location:* out of Norwich on the A1067 to Taverham. Two courses. Parkland and very picturesque set in the valley. Wensum Course – 4862 yards, 4447 metres. S.S.S. 66. Valley Course – 18 holes, 6000 yards, 5486 metres. S.S.S. 69. Driving range. *Green Fees:* weekdays £12.00; weekends £15.00. *Eating facilities:* full catering and bar facilities. *Visitors:* always welcome, restrictions at weekends and Bank Holidays. Accommodation for 14 people available. *Society Meetings:* all welcome; package available. Professional: Peter Briggs (0603 261012 extension 5). Secretary: Bridgette Todd (0603 261012 extension 2).

SHERINGHAM. **Sheringham Golf Club,** Weybourne Road, Sheringham NR26 8HG (Sheringham (0263) 822038). *Location:* one mile west of town on Weybourne Road (A149). Clifftop course. 18 holes, 6464 yards. S.S.S. 71. Large practice area. *Green Fees:* weekdays £28.00; weekends and Bank Holidays £33.00. *Eating facilities:* full catering to order. *Visitors:* welcome, telephone first, with reservation for members of other clubs, Handicap Certificate required. Accommodation in Dormy House, details from Secretary. *Society Meetings:* catered for by prior arrangement with Secretary except weekends from 1st April to 31st October. Professional: R.H. Emery (0263 822980). Secretary: M.J. Garrett (0263 823488; Fax: 0263 825189).

SWAFFHAM. **Swaffham Golf Club,** Cley Road, Swaffham PE37 8AE (Swaffham (0760) 721611). *Location:* two miles south-west of Swaffham Market Place (signposted) on Cley Road. Heathland course. 9 holes, 6252 yards. S.S.S. 70. Practice ground. *Green Fees:* £18.00 weekdays. *Eating facilities:* full catering except Mondays and Tuesdays, bar snacks all week. *Visitors:* welcome without reservation weekdays, weekends only if playing with member. *Society Meetings:* catered for subject to prior notice being given. Professional: Peter Field. Secretary: R. Joslin.

THETFORD. **Thetford Golf Club,** Brandon Road, Thetford IP24 3NE (Thetford (0842) 752258). *Location:* half a mile from A11. Wooded heathland course. 18 holes, 6879 yards. S.S.S. 73. *Green Fees:* £26.00 weekdays. *Eating facilities:* bar snacks, teas, meals available. *Visitors:* welcome weekdays. *Society Meetings:* catered for weekdays if members of golf clubs. Professional: N. Arthur (0842 752662). Secretary: R.J. Ferguson (0842 752169).

Sprowston Park Golf Club

Attractive 18-hole course set in parkland with trees. The Fairways Bar and Restaurant is a pleasant location to unwind after a challenging round. Visitors are welcome at all times, as are Societies.

Sprowston Park Golf Club, Wroxham Road, Norwich NR7 8RP Telephone: 0603 410567

BEAUMARIS HOTEL
15 South Street, Sheringham, Norfolk NR26 8LL
AA★★   FULLY LICENSED   Ashley Courtenay

Just three minutes' walking distance to Sheringham's exhilarating cliff-top Golf Course.
The same family has owned and run Beaumaris since 1947 so you can be assured of excellent food and personal service.
All rooms have Colour TV, early morning tea/coffee making facilities, Radio/Telephone and most have en suite facilities.
SPECIAL BREAKS offered Spring & Autumn
Access · Visa · American Express · Diners   CAR PARK
Telephone: Mrs. H. Stevens (0263) 822370 for Colour Brochure and details.

Please mention this guide when you write or phone to enquire about accommodation.

Northamptonshire

CORBY. **Corby Public Golf Course,** Priors Hall Complex, Corby (Corby (0536) 400497). *Location:* off A43 Kettering to Stamford Road one mile east of village of Weldon. 18 holes, 6677 yards. S.S.S. 72. *Green Fees:* information not provided. *Eating facilities:* available, and licensed bar. *Society Meetings:* by arrangement with Professional. Professional: M. Summers (0536 60756). Secretary: Jack Marr.

CORBY near. **Priors Hall Golf Club,** Stamford Road, Weldon, Near Corby NN17 3JH (0536 400497). *Location:* on the A43, four miles from Corby on the Stamford Road. 18 holes, 6700 yards. S.S.S. 72. Practice nets and ground. *Green Fees:* weekdays £7.00; weekends £8.30. *Eating facilities:* bar meals. *Visitors:* no restrictions mid week, booking system. *Society Meetings:* no restrictions mid week. Professional: Garry Brown (0536 60756). Secretary: J. Marr.

DAVENTRY. **Daventry and District Golf Club,** Norton Road, Daventry (Daventry (0327) 702829). 9 holes, 5812 yards. S.S.S. 67. *Green Fees:* weekdays £9.00; weekends £12.00. *Visitors:* welcome weekdays and weekends. Summer all welcome except Sunday before 11.00am. Professional: Mike Higgins. Secretary: F. Higham.

DAVENTRY. **Staverton Park Hotel and Golf Club,** Daventry Road, Staverton, Near Daventry NN11 6JT (Tel & Fax: 0327 311428). *Location:* one mile from Daventry on A425 to Leamington Spa. Easy access from M1 Junctions 16 or 18. Undulating parkland. 18 holes, 6661 yards. S.S.S. 72. Driving range, practice range, two putting greens. *Green Fees:* weekdays £19.50 per round; weekends and Bank Holidays £22.50 per round. After 4pm summer £16.00 (not bookable in advance). *Eating facilities:* full catering available at all times. *Visitors:* welcome, no restrictions. 52 bedroomed hotel with leisure facilities. Residential golf packages available. *Society Meetings:* welcome, please enquire about our Society Package. Professional: Richard Mudge (0327 705506). General Manager: John Daymore (0327 311428).

HELLIDON. **Hellidon Lakes Golf Club,** Hellidon NN11 6LN (0327 62550; Fax: 0327 62559). *Location:* six miles from Daventry off A361. Parkland. 18 holes, 6700 yards. S.S.S. 72. Driving range, putting green. *Green Fees:* information not provided. *Eating facilities:* bar with food available all day, à la carte restaurant. *Visitors:* always welcome, Handicap Certificates required at weekends. Accommodation available. *Society Meetings:* all welcome. Professional: Neil Dainton. Secretary: Mrs J.A. Nicoll.

KETTERING. **Kettering Golf Club,** Headlands, Kettering NN15 6XA (0536 512074). *Location:* course is at south end of Headlands which is continuation from High Street. Flat parkland. 18 holes, 6035 yards, 5515 metres. S.S.S. 69. *Green Fees:* weekdays £20.00 day/round; weekends £10.00 with member only. *Eating facilities:* by prior arrangement. *Visitors:* welcome weekdays only. *Society Meetings:* catered for Wednesdays and Fridays only by arrangement. Professional: K. Theobald (0536 81014). Secretary: D.G. Buckby (0536 511104).

NORTHAMPTON. **Cold Ashby Golf Club,** Cold Ashby, Northampton NN6 7EP (Tel & Fax: 0604 740548). *Location:* midway between Rugby, Leicester and Northampton, with easy access M1 Junction 18. Undulating parkland. 18 holes (additional 9 holes opening 1994), 6004 yards. S.S.S. 69. *Green Fees:* midweek £12.00 per round, £18.00 per day; weekends £15.00 per round. *Eating facilities:* meals and bar snacks available daily. *Visitors:* welcome midweek anytime, weekends after 2pm. *Society Meetings:* catered for weekdays. Professional: Shane Rose (0604 740099). Secretary: David Croxton.

HELLIDON LAKES HOTEL & COUNTRY CLUB
Hellidon, near Daventry, Northamptonshire NN11 6LN
Telephone: 0327 62550　　Fax: 0327 62559

Luxury four-star hotel nestles in 240 acres of Northamptonshire/Warwickshire countryside yet with easy access to M1, M6 and M40. Full leisure facilities including spectacular 6,700 acre 18 hole golf course with further 9 holes opening Spring 1994, lakeside driving range, putting green, horseriding, health and beauty studio with 2 beauty therapists, 12 station gym, sunbed, sauna, swimspa, fishing, clay pigeon shooting (by arrangement), tennis and snooker.

• 27 BEAUTIFULLY APPOINTED BEDROOMS • 100 SEAT LAKEVIEW RESTAURANT •
• CONFERENCE FACILITIES •
SOCIETY AND CORPORATE DAYS A SPECIALITY

England NORTHAMPTONSHIRE

NORTHAMPTON. **Collingtree Park Golf Course,** Windingbrook Lane, Northampton NN4 0XN (0604 700000). *Location:* take Junction 15 off M1-A508 Northampton. 18 holes, 6692 yards. S.S.S. 72. 18th hole is an island green, set in parkland. *Green Fees:* weekdays: £30.00 18 holes, £60.00 36 holes; weekends: £40.00 18 holes, £80.00 36 holes. *Eating facilities:* Conservatory Restaurant, à la carte and table d'hôte, and bar snacks at all times. *Visitors:* welcome – advised to book in advance, members only before 12.30pm at weekends. *Society Meetings:* corporate golf packages available. Golf Academy which includes two par 4 and one par 3 practice holes, as well as 16 driving range bays. Hi-tech indoor teaching rooms also. The finest teaching facility for golf, 5 special programmes available. Professional: John Cook. Secretary: Gill Peters (Fax: 0604 702600).

NORTHAMPTON. **Delapre Park Golf Club,** Eagle Drive, Nene Valley Way, Northampton NN4 0DU (Northampton (0604) 764036; Fax: 0604 763957). *Location:* two and a half miles from Junction 15 (M1), A45 to Wellingborough (exit at Swallow Hotel). Parkland. 18 holes, 6943 yards. S.S.S. 70. Additional 9 holes, 2146 yards. S.S.S. 32. Floodlit covered driving range, 40 bays; Par 3 courses, pitch and putt course. *Green Fees:* weekdays £6.80; weekends and Bank Holidays £8.50; 9 hole course £4.75 weekdays; £5.70 weekends and Bank Holidays. Pitch and putt £1.15 weekdays; £1.35 weekends. Par 3 courses £3.00 weekdays; £3.30 weekends. *Eating facilities:* meals available all day 9am to 9.30pm, bar – regular hours. *Visitors:* welcome without reservation, except 18 hole and 9 hole course. Start times bookable and must be paid and booked in advance unless vacancies occur on the day. *Society Meetings:* catered for by appointment and advance payment. Professional/Secretary: John Corby (0604 763957).

NORTHAMPTON. **Kingsthorpe Golf Club,** Kingsley Road, Northampton NN2 7BU (Northampton (0604) 711173). *Location:* off M1 and A43. Undulating parkland. 18 holes, 6006 yards. S.S.S. 69. *Green Fees:* (provisional) weekdays £20.00 per round/day; weekends £10.00 per round/day (must play with member). *Eating facilities:* full catering. *Visitors:* welcome weekdays, but must have a Certificate of Handicap. Weekends must be guest of member. *Society Meetings:* catered for by arrangement Mondays and Thursdays only. Professional: Paul Armstrong (0604 719602). Secretary: P.L. Voke (0604 710610).

NORTHAMPTON. **Northampton Golf Club,** Harlestone, Northampton NN7 4EF (Northampton (0604) 845102). *Location:* on A428 north-west of the village of Harlestone. Parkland with a lake coming into play 16th and 18th holes. 18 holes, 6534 yards. S.S.S. 71. Practice ground. *Green Fees:* £25.00 weekdays, weekends must play with a member. *Eating facilities:* restaurant and bar snacks. *Visitors:* welcome weekdays but must have a Certificate of Handicap. *Society Meetings:* weekdays except Wednesdays. Inclusive packages available. Professional: Mark Chamberlain (0604 845167). Secretary: I.M. Kirkwood (0604 845155).

Play & Stay at
COLLINGTREE PARK

PGA EUROPEAN TOUR COURSE

- Play 36 Holes at Collingtree Park Golf Course
- 1 Nights accommodation, Bed & Breakfast in the 4 Star Stakis Country Court Hotel with use of Club Tropics Leisure Club
- For only £60 per person sharing a twin room (groups up to 16 persons only)

**COLLINGTREE PARK GOLF COURSE
THE ULTIMATE GOLFING EXPERIENCE**

Please ask for our Golf Day Brochure

Windingbrook Lane
Northampton
NN4 0XN
Tel: 0604 700000
Fax: 0604 702600

NORTHAMPTON. **Northamptonshire County Golf Club,** Sandy Lane, Church Brampton, Northampton NN6 8AZ (Northampton (0604) 842170). *Location:* four miles north of Northampton between A50 and A428. Heathland with woods, gorse and stream. 18 holes, 6503 yards, 5946 metres. S.S.S. 71. Practice ground, indoor net. *Green Fees:* £35.00 (£10.00 with a member). *Eating facilities:* restaurant and bar. *Visitors:* by prior arrangement, must have Club Handicap. *Society Meetings:* catered for Wednesdays, some Thursdays and Mondays. Professional: T. Rouse (0604 842226). Secretary: M.E. Wadley (0604 843025).

OUNDLE. **Oundle Golf Club,** Benfield Road, Oundle, Peterborough PE8 4EZ (Oundle (0832) 273167). *Location:* one mile from Oundle on Corby Road A447. Undulating course. 18 holes, 5900 yards. S.S.S. 67. *Green Fees:* weekdays £18.00 per day; weekends £25.00. *Eating facilities:* full meals service. *Visitors:* welcome, after 10.30am weekends. *Society Meetings:* welcome by arrangement. Professional: R. Keys (0832 272273). Secretary: R.K. Davis.

RUSHDEN. **Rushden Golf Club,** Kimbolton Road, Chelveston, Wellingborough NN9 6AN (Rushden (0933) 312581). *Location:* on A45 two miles east of Higham Ferrers. Undulating parkland. 10 holes, 6335 yards. S.S.S. 70. Small practice area. *Green Fees:* weekdays £15.00 per round/day, £10.00 with member; no visitors weekends. *Eating facilities:* bar and dining area – no catering Mondays. *Visitors:* welcome except Wednesday afternoons, weekends must play with member. *Society Meetings:* small societies catered for weekdays. Secretary: E.W. Richardson (0933 314910).

TOWCESTER near. **West Park Golf and Country Club,** Whittlebury, Near Towcester NN12 8XW (0327 858092; Fax: 0327 858009). *Location:* 15 minutes from M1 and M40, from A43 onto A413, via Whittlebury. 36-hole championship quality course, comprising 3 standard 9-holes and a dedicated 9-hole Academy Course. Many 18-hole combinations of over 6700 yards. S.S.S. 72. Mature oak parkland with freshwater lakes and ancient copses. Large range/practice ground plus unique 9-hole Indoor Golf Course. *Green Fees:* weekdays £20.00 per round; weekends/ bank holidays £25.00. *Eating facilities:* bar/bistro within clubhouse plus special functions suites. *Visitors:* 'pay and play' or corporate guests welcome seven days. Other sports and activities offered. Accommodation planned. *Society Meetings:* welcome seven days, by arrangement. Secretary: R. Jones. *Bookings:* please contact Events Management team on 0327 858092.

WELLINGBOROUGH. **Wellingborough Golf Club,** Great Harrowden Hall, Wellingborough NN9 5AD (Wellingborough (0933) 673022). *Location:* one mile out of Wellingborough on A509, turn right at crossroads by Great Harrowden Church. Undulating parkland. 18 holes, 6617 yards, 6039 metres. S.S.S. 72. Practice ground. *Green Fees:* £22.00 per round, £27.00 per day weekdays; weekends as member's guest only. *Eating facilities:* bar with casual lunch or dinner menu, restaurant. *Visitors:* weekdays only by appointment and with Handicap Certificate. *Society Meetings:* welcome by appointment. Conference facilities available. Professional: David Clifford (0933 678752). Secretary: Roy Tomlin (0933 677234).

Northumberland

ALNMOUTH. **Alnmouth Golf Club Ltd,** Foxton Hall, Lesbury, Alnwick NE66 3BE (Alnmouth (0665) 830687). *Location:* four miles east of Alnwick. 18 holes, 6414 yards, 5855 metres. S.S.S. 71. *Green Fees:* weekdays £25.00 per day. *Eating facilities:* diningroom and bars. *Visitors:* welcome Mondays, Tuesdays, Thursdays by prior arrangement, Handicap Certificate required. Dormy House accommodation available. *Society Meetings:* maximum numbers 30 catered for on Mondays, Tuesdays and Thursdays only. Secretary: Charles Jobson (0665 830231).

ALNMOUTH. **Alnmouth Village Golf Club,** Marine Road, Alnmouth (0665 830370; Fax: 0665 603395). *Location:* leave A1 from Alnwick to Alnmouth. Seaside links course. 9 holes, 6090 yards, 5572 metres. S.S.S. 70. *Green Fees:* weekdays £15.00 per 18 holes; weekends £20.00 per 18 holes. *Eating facilities:* available. *Visitors:* welcome, restrictions on club competition days. *Society Meetings:* book in advance and only with official Golf Club Handicaps. Secretary: W. MacLean (0665 602096).

ALNWICK. **Alnwick Golf Club,** Swansfield Park, Alnwick (Alnwick (0665) 602632). *Location:* south-west of town, top of Swansfield Park Road, off A1. Mature wooded parkland. 9 holes (extending to 18 holes for 1994), 5387 yards. S.S.S. 66. *Green Fees:* weekdays £10.00 per round, £15.00 per day; weekends and Bank Holidays £15.00 per round, £20.00 per day. Half price with member at any time. *Eating facilities:* available on request; bar. *Visitors:* welcome without reservation, some restrictions on competition days. *Society Meetings:* welcome by prior arrangement. Secretary: L.E. Stewart (0665 602499).

ALNWICK. **Dunstanburgh Castle Golf Club,** Embleton, Alnwick NE66 3XQ (Embleton (0665) 576562). *Location:* eight miles off A1, to the north-east of Alnwick. Seaside links course in area of outstanding natural beauty. 18 holes, 6298 yards. S.S.S. 70. *Green Fees:* weekdays £12.50 per day; weekends £15.00 per round, £17.50 per day. *Eating facilities:* snacks, lunches, high teas; bar. *Visitors:* welcome without reservation. Clubs for hire. *Society Meetings:* catered for. Secretary: P.F.C. Gilbert.

THE GOLF GUIDE 1994   England NORTHUMBERLAND

BAMBURGH. **Bamburgh Castle Golf Club,** Bamburgh NE69 7DE (Bamburgh (06684) 378). *Location:* north of Alnwick on A1, take B1341 or B1342 to Bamburgh. Links course with outstanding coastal views. 18 holes, 5621 yards, 5132 metres. S.S.S. 67. Practice area. *Green Fees:* weekdays £23.00 per day or round; weekends £30.00 per round, £35.00 per day. Five-day ticket £60.00. All rates reduced for Juniors. *Eating facilities:* full catering and bar. *Visitors:* welcome, except Bank Holidays and Competition weekends. Handicap Certificate required. Buggy hire available. *Society Meetings:* by written application. Hon. Secretary: T.C. Osborne (06684 321).

BEDLINGTON. **Bedlingtonshire Golf Club,** Acorn Bank, Bedlington NE22 6AA (Bedlington (0670) 822457). *Location:* one mile south west of Bedlington on A1068. Parkland. 18 holes, 6546 metres. S.S.S. 73. Practice ground and putting green. *Green Fees:* weekdays £13.00 per round, £17.00 per day; weekends £16.00 per round, £19.00 per day (estimated). *Eating facilities:* catering available seven days a week. *Visitors:* welcome, but not before 10.30am weekends. *Society Meetings:* welcome, contact the Professional. Professional: Marcus Webb (0670 822087). Secretary: A.J. Gray (0670 826235).

BELFORD. **Belford Golf Club,** South Road, Belford NE70 7DP (0668 213433). *Location:* turn off A1 at sign for Belford, first turning on right. Parkland. 9 holes, 6304 yards, 5768 metres. S.S.S. 70. Floodlit driving range. *Green Fees:* weekdays £12.00 per round, £15.00 per day; weekends £15.00 per round, £20.00 per day. *Eating facilities:* meals and bar seven days a week. *Visitors:* welcome after 10am. *Society Meetings:* welcome. Secretary: A.M. Gilhome (0668 213587).

BERWICK-UPON-TWEED. **Berwick-upon-Tweed (Goswick) Golf Club,** Beal, Berwick-upon-Tweed TD15 2RW (0289 87256). *Location:* signposted off A1, seven miles south of Berwick-upon-Tweed. Seaside links. 18 holes, 6425 yards, 5871 metres. S.S.S. 71. Practice ground. *Green Fees:* weekdays £24.00 per day, £18.00 per round; weekends £32.00 per day, £24.00 per round. *Eating facilities:* catering except Mondays, bar meals. *Visitors:* welcome anytime, parties by arrangement, after 9.30am weekdays, after 10am weekends. *Society Meetings:* catered for by arrangement. Professional: P. Terras (0289 87380). Secretary: A.E. French (0289 87256).

BERWICK-UPON-TWEED. **Magdalene Fields Golf Club,** Magdalene Fields, Berwick-upon-Tweed TD15 1NE (0289 306384). *Location:* to coast from town centre, A1 Scotland/England border. Seaside, parkland course in clifftop setting. 18 holes, 6300 yards. S.S.S. 71. Practice area. *Green Fees:* weekdays £15.00; weekends £17.00. Discount for party bookings. Fees subject to review. *Eating facilities:* bar and eating facilities. *Visitors:* welcome Monday to Saturday, restrictions on Sundays. *Society Meetings:* all welcome. Secretary: R. Patterson (0289 305758). Green Ranger: (0289 330700).

BLYTH. **Blyth Golf Club Ltd,** New Delaval, Blyth NE24 9DB (Blyth (0670) 367728). *Location:* 12 miles north of Newcastle near the coast. Flat parkland, water hazards. 18 holes, 6533 yards, 6300 metres. S.S.S. 71. Large practice area. *Green Fees:* £16.00 per round, £18.00 per day (with a member £6.00) weekdays; weekends only with a member £6.00. *Eating facilities:* bar and full catering. *Visitors:* welcome weekdays before 3pm, weekends with member only. *Society Meetings:* welcome weekdays only by prior arrangement. Professional: B. Rumney (0670 356514). Secretary: Miss J. Tate (0670 540110).

CARLISLE. **Haltwhistle Golf Course,** Banktop, Greenhead, Via Carlisle (06977 47367). *Location:* off the A69 at the village of Greenhead, two and a half miles west of Haltwhistle. Undulating parkland course with wooded areas. 12 holes, 6154 yards over 18 holes. S.S.S. 69. Practice area. *Green Fees:* £10.00 per day. £30.00 weekly ticket for bona fide holidaymakers. *Eating facilties:* clubhouse bar, catering by prior arrangement. *Visitors:* welcome, no restrictions except on club competition days when course is closed until 4.00pm. *Society Meetings:* welcome by arrangement. Professional: Joe Metcalfe. Secretary: Bill Barnes (0434 320337).

A MIXED THREESOME . . .

The Beautiful Bamburgh Castle Golf Club (5465 yds S.S.S. 68). The Testing Goswick Links Championship Course (6425 yds S.S.S. 71) and in the middle The Superb **Blue Bell Hotel** at Belford.
The quality of Northumberland's Courses is undisputable. The high standard of service at the perfectly situated **Blue Bell** is unquestionable. Combine the two and the value becomes unbeatable. The Hotel, a Four Crown Highly Commended, A.A. and R.A.C. 3 Star Coaching Inn offers delightful en-suite accommodation with cuisine recommended by Ashley Courtenay, Johansens and Egon Ronay to name but a few – D.B.B. from £40 per night to include complimentary round at Belford Golf Club, other packages arranged. Societies or individuals welcome.

⛳ THE BLUE BELL HOTEL ⛳   Phone **0 6 6 8   2 1 3 5 4 3** for your brochure.

NORTHUMBERLAND England

HEXHAM. **Allendale Golf Club.** High Studdon, Allenheads Road, Allendale, Hexham. *Location:* 10 miles south of Hexham on B6295. Parkland course, hilly but not too severe. 9 holes, 5044 yards. S.S.S. 65. Driving net and putting green. *Green Fees:* weekdays £5.00; weekends and Bank Holidays £7.00. Special rates for visiting parties. *Eating facilities:* no catering apart from tea-making facilities, but several good hotels and pubs in Allendale. *Visitors:* welcome anytime except Sunday mornings and August Bank Holiday Monday. *Society Meetings:* catered for by arrangement. Secretary: Jim Hall (091-267 5875).

HEXHAM. **Bellingham Golf Club,** Boggle Hole, Bellingham, Hexham NE48 2DT (0434 220152). *Location:* four miles west of A68. Parkland with panoramic views of North Tyne Valley. 9 holes (18 tees), 5245 yards. S.S.S. 66. Large practice ground. *Green Fees:* weekdays £10.00; weekends and Bank Holidays £15.00. *Eating facilities:* meals available. *Visitors:* welcome, no visitors till 5pm Sundays and all visitors must adhere to starting sheet when in operation. *Society Meetings:* welcome by prior booking. Secretary: Mr R. Calladine (0434 220530).

HEXHAM. **Hexham Golf Club,** Spital Park, Hexham NE46 3RZ (Hexham (0434) 602057). *Location:* 20 miles west of Newcastle upon Tyne, one mile west of Hexham town centre. 18 holes, 6272 yards. S.S.S. 70. *Green Fees:* weekdays £20.00; weekends and Bank Holidays £26.00. *Eating facilities:* lunch, high tea and dinner. *Visitors:* welcome without reservation. Preliminary booking advisable. *Society Meetings:* catered for Monday to Friday by arrangement. Professional: M.W. Forster (0434 604904). Secretary: J.C. Oates (0434 603072; Fax: 0434 601865).

HEXHAM. **Tynedale Golf Club,** Tynegreen, Hexham (0434 608154). *Location:* off A69 towards Hexham over Tyne Bridge; immediate right along riverside. Flat, private course owned by Tynedale Council. 9 holes, 5640 yards. S.S.S. 67. *Green Fees:* weekdays £10.00; weekends £12.00. Reductions for Juniors and Senior Citizens. *Eating facilities:* full catering available. *Visitors:* welcome, restricted Sunday mornings 7.30am to 11am. *Society Meetings:* welcome. Professional: C. Brown. Secretary: J. McDiarmid.

MORPETH. **The Morpeth Golf Club,** The Common, Morpeth NE61 2BT (Morpeth (0670) 519980). *Location:* turn off A1 for Morpeth, A167 south side of town. Easy walking parkland. 18 holes, 6206 yards. S.S.S. 70. Practice area. *Green Fees:* weekdays £20.00 per round, £25.00 per day; weekends £25.00 per round, £33.00 per day. *Eating facilities:* restaurant/bar meals/snacks etc. *Visitors:* welcome, weekdays after 9.30am. Handicap Certificates may be asked for. *Society Meetings:* catered for weekdays by prior arrangement. Professional: M.R. Jackson (0670 515675). Secretary: G. Hogg (0670 504942; Fax: 0670 504918).

MORPETH. **Warkworth Golf Club,** The Links, Warkworth, Morpeth NE65 0SW (Alnwick (0665) 711596). *Location:* off A1 to B6345 at Felton, on to A1068 to Warkworth. Links course. 9 holes, 5817 yards. S.S.S. 66 (medal 68). Practice area. *Green Fees:* weekdays £10.00 per day; weekends £15.00 per day. Half price

THE GOLF GUIDE 1994

with member. *Eating facilities:* by arrangement with Stewardess. *Visitors:* welcome, avoid Tuesdays and Saturdays. *Society Meetings:* welcome by arrangement. Secretary: J.W. Anderson (0665 575608).

NEWBIGGIN-BY-THE-SEA. **Newbiggin-by-the-Sea Golf Club.** Clubhouse, Prospect Place, Newbiggin-by-the-Sea NE64 6DW (Ashington (0670) 817344). *Location:* take signpost for Newbiggin off A189 (spine road from Tyne Tunnel). Clubhouse at most easterly point of village, adjacent to Church Point Caravan Park. Seaside links. 18 holes, 6452 yards. S.S.S. 71. Practice area. *Green Fees:* weekdays £12.00, £8.00 with a member; weekends £17.00, £12.00 with a member. *Eating facilities:* bar, lounge bar, dining room. *Visitors:* welcome, not before 10am or on competition days, check by telephone with Professional. *Society Meetings:* catered for by prior arrangement with Secretary. Professional: D. Fletcher (0670 817833). Secretary: Derek Lyall (0670 520236).

NEWCASTLE. **Arcot Hall Golf Club Ltd,** Arcot Hall, Dudley, Cramlington NE23 7QP (091-236 2794). *Location:* seven miles north of Newcastle. Turn off A1 for Ashington and then signposted. 18 holes, 6389 yards, 5840 metres. S.S.S. 70. *Green Fees:* weekdays £22.00; weekends £25.00 by invitation only. *Eating facilities:* lunch and high tea. *Visitors:* welcome without reservation midweek only. Clubs for hire. *Society Meetings:* catered for on application to Secretary. Professional: Graham Cant (091-236 2147). Secretary: A.G. Bell (091-236 2794).

NEWCASTLE-UPON-TYNE. **Ponteland Golf Club,** Bell Villas, Ponteland, Newcastle-upon-Tyne NE20 9BD (0661 822689). *Location:* A696, one and a half miles north of Newcastle Airport. Parkland. 18 holes, 6524 yards. S.S.S. 71. Large practice area. *Green Fees:* £22.50 per day or round (inclusive VAT). *Eating facilities:* full menu in restaurant and bar. *Visitors:* welcome Monday to Thursday, must be members' guest Friday, weekends and Bank Holidays. Handicap Certificate required. *Society Meetings:* Tuesdays or Thursdays, catered for with pre-booking agreed by Secretary/Manager. Professional: Alan Crosby (0661 822689). Secretary: Mr John Hillyer (0661 822689).

PRUDHOE. **Prudhoe Golf Club,** Eastwood Park, Prudhoe NE42 5DX (Prudhoe (0661) 832466). *Location:* 10 miles west of Newcastle upon Tyne, A695 to Hexham. Undulating parkland, highly rated course. 18 holes, 5856 yards, 5319 metres. S.S.S. 68. Large practice area. *Green Fees:* £18.00 weekdays; £25.00 weekends after 4.30pm only. Special rates for parties over 20. *Eating facilities:* bar snacks, dining room and evening meals. *Visitors:* welcome midweek with reservation (contact Professional); weekends after 4.30pm. *Society Meetings:* catered for weekdays with prior booking. Professional: John Crawford (0661 836188). Secretary: G.B. Garratt. Bookings Secretary: W. Wray.

ROTHBURY. **Rothbury Golf Club,** Old Race Course, Thornton Road, Rothbury, Morpeth (0669 21271). *Location:* 15 miles north of Morpeth, take A697 turn off at Weldon Bridge for Rothbury. Flat on Haugh course alongside river. 9 holes, 5560 yards. S.S.S. 67. *Green Fees:* £10.00 weekdays, £15.00 weekends. *Eating*

The Links Hotel
8 King Street, Seahouses, Northumberland

Small family run, fully licensed hotel, less than ½ mile from Seahouses Golf Club and within easy driving distance of ten other courses. Special discounts available for parties.

Telephone: 0665 720062 Fax: 0665 721305

---

facilities: none available, but there are plenty of good hotels in Rothbury. Our bar is open each night except Monday. *Visitors:* welcome during weekdays, but limited at weekends due to club competitions. *Society Meetings:* catered for weekdays by arrangement only. Hon. Secretary: W.T. Bathgate (0669 20718).

SEAHOUSES. **Seahouses Golf Club,** Beadnell Road, Seahouses NE68 7XT (Alnwick (0665) 720794). *Location:* 15 miles north of Alnwick, turn off A1 for B1340. Flat seaside links with water hazard. 18 holes, 5462 yards. S.S.S. 67. Practice ground. *Green Fees:* weekdays £15.00 per day; weekends £20.00 per day. Juniors under 16 half rates. *Eating facilities:* full catering and bar. *Visitors:* welcome with no restrictions, please telephone clubhouse. *Society Meetings:* by arrangement. Secretary: J.A. Stevens (0665 720809).

STOCKSFIELD. **Stocksfield Golf Club,** New Ridley, Stocksfield NE43 7RE (Stocksfield (0661) 843041). *Location:* 15 miles west of Newcastle on A69, and three miles east of A68. Wooded parkland. 18 holes, 5594 yards. S.S.S. 68. Practice area. *Green Fees:* weekdays £20.00, weekends and Bank Holidays £25.00. *Eating facilities:* available, also bar. *Visitors:* welcome weekdays and after 4.30pm at weekends. *Society*

Meetings: catered for. Professional: Stephen McKenna. Secretary: D.B. Moon.

TYNEMOUTH. **Tynemouth Golf Club Ltd,** Spital Dene, Tynemouth (North Shields (091) 257 4578). *Location:* on A695. 18 holes, 6403 yards. S.S.S. 71. *Green Fees:* weekdays £20.00; weekends and Bank Holidays must be signed in and play with a member. *Eating facilities:* lunches and high teas served at club. *Visitors:* welcome with reservation. *Society Meetings:* catered for. Professional: John McKenna. Secretary: W. Storey.

WOOLER. **Wooler Golf Club,** Dod Law, Doddington, Wooler. *Location:* situated on the high ground named Dod Law to the east of the B6525 Wooler – Berwick road. The route is signposted from Doddington village. 9 holes (18 tees), 6358 yards. S.S.S. 70. Limited practice area. *Green Fees:* weekdays £10.00 per day; weekends and Bank Holidays £15.00 per day. Juniors £2.00 per round. Sunday parties (10 plus) £12.50 per day. *Eating facilities:* bar open evenings (operated voluntarily). *Visitors:* always welcome except during all day competitions, check with Secretary. *Society Meetings:* welcome by arrangement with Secretary. Secretary: James Henry Curry (0668 81956).

Nottinghamshire

BULWELL. **Bulwell Forest Golf Club,** Hucknall Road, Bulwell (0602 770576) *Location:* A610 north of Nottingham, M1 Junction 26, three miles from course. Parkland, very tight course. 18 holes, 5572 yards. S.S.S. 67. *Green Fees:* weekdays £6.50; weekends £8.10. *Eating facilities:* meals served at all times. *Visitors:* welcome except Tuesdays and weekends, time sheets in operation every day. *Society Meetings:* catered for, but book well in advance. Professional: C. D. Hall (0602 763172). Secretary: D. Stubbs.

CALVERTON. **Ramsdale Park Golf Centre,** The Clubhouse, Oxton Road, Calverton NG14 6NU (0602 655600; Fax: 0602 654105). *Location:* course alongside B6386 between Calverton and Oxton north east of Nottingham. Flat first 9 holes then undulating back 9. 18 holes, 6546 yards, 5985 metres. S.S.S. 71. 25 bay floodlit driving range. *Green Fees:* £11.50. *Eating facilities:* full catering/bar available. *Visitors:* no restrictions. *Society Meetings:* welcome. Professional: Robert Macey. Secretary: Brian Jenkinson.

EAST LEAKE. **Rushcliffe Golf Club,** Stocking Lane, East Leake, Near Loughborough LE12 5RL (0509 852209). *Location:* on A60 signposted eight miles south of Nottingham. Wooded hills on edge of the Wolds. 18 holes, 6057 yards, 5539 metres. S.S.S. 70. Practice ground. *Green Fees:* weekdays £22.00; weekends £25.00. *Eating facilities:* full catering except Mondays when bar snacks only. *Visitors:* welcome with reservation, weekends without a member between 9.30am to 11am and 3pm to 4.30pm. *Society Meetings:* catered for Mondays, Wednesdays, Thursdays and Fridays strictly by prior booking. Professional: Tim Smart (0509 852701). Secretary: D.J. Barnes (0509 852959).

EDWALTON. **Edwalton Municipal Golf and Social Club,** Wellin Lane, Edwalton (0602 234713). *Location:* follow Nottingham ring road, course signposted from island on ring road. Gently sloping parkland. 9 holes, 3342 yards. S.S.S. 72. Also 9 hole par 3 course. Large practice ground. *Green Fees:* £4.20 for 9 holes.

NOTTINGHAMSHIRE England

Students, Senior Citizens, disabled and UB40's £2.50 before 5pm, weekdays only. Par 3 course £2.40, special rate £1.40. *Eating facilities:* first class catering, bar open all day. *Visitors:* welcome anytime except club competitions (contact Professional for dates). Professional: J.A. Staples (0602 234775). Secretary: E. Watts (0602 231576).

KIRKBY-IN-ASHFIELD. **Notts. Golf Club Ltd,** Hollinwell, Kirkby-in-Ashfield, Nottingham NG17 7QR (Mansfield (0623) 753225). *Location:* three miles from Exit 27 on M1, turn off M1 then left on A611. Testing heathland championship course. 18 holes, 7020 yards. S.S.S. 74. *Green Fees:* on application. *Visitors:* welcome on production of Handicap Certificate (weekends and Bank Holidays with member only). Advisable to book beforehand. *Society Meetings:* catered for Mondays and Tuesdays. Professional: Brian Waites. Secretary: J.R. Walker.

MANSFIELD. **Coxmoor Golf Club,** Coxmoor Road, Sutton in Ashfield, Mansfield NG17 5LF (Mansfield (0623) 559878). *Location:* exit Junction 27 M1, A611 for three miles. Heathland, undulating. 18 holes, 6251 yards, 5944 metres. S.S.S. 72. Practice area and nets. *Green Fees:* weekdays £27.00. *Eating facilities:* restaurant and bars. *Visitors:* welcome except weekends and Bank Holidays, pre-book through Professional. (Tuesday Ladies' Day). *Society Meetings:* catered for by prior application to Secretary. Professional: D. Ridley (0623 559906). Secretary: Mr J.W. Tyler (0623 557359).

MANSFIELD. **Mansfield Woodhouse Golf Club,** Leeming Lane North, Mansfield Woodhouse NG19 9EU (0623 23521). *Location:* Junction 27 of M1, A60 Mansfield-Warsop. Flat parkland. 9 holes, 2446 yards. S.S.S. 64. *Green Fees:* £2.95 9 holes, £4.30 18 holes. *Eating facilities:* bar snacks. *Visitors:* welcome, unrestricted – pay and play. Professional: L. Highfield Jnr. (0623 23521). Secretary: T. Mason.

MANSFIELD. **Sherwood Forest Golf Club,** Eakring Road, Mansfield NG18 3EW (Mansfield (0623) 23327). *Location:* leave M1 at Exit 27, take signs for Mansfield, proceed via Southwell Road and Oak Tree Lane. Traditional heathland course designed by James Braid (Championship standard). 18 holes, 6710 yards. S.S.S. 73. Two practice grounds. *Green Fees:* weekdays £30.00 per round, £35.00 per day; weekends and Bank Holidays £35.00 per round. *Eating facilities:* two dining rooms, gents' bar and mixed lounge. *Visitors:* welcome Mondays, Thursdays and Fridays, must be member of a golf club with a handicap. *Society Meetings:* catered for Mondays, Thursdays and Fridays. Professional: K. Hall (Tel & Fax: 0623 27403). Secretary: K. Hall (0623 26689).

MAPPERLEY. **Mapperley Golf Club,** Central Avenue, Plains Road, Mapperley NG3 5RH (Nottingham (0602) 265611). *Location:* B684, four miles north east of centre of Nottingham. Hilly picturesque course. 18 holes, 6283 yards. S.S.S. 70. Practice ground. *Green Fees:* weekdays £15.50 per round, £18.50 per day; weekends £17.50 per round, £20.50 per day. With a member £10 per round, £12.00 per day. *Eating facilities:* bar open all day. *Visitors:* welcome except on match and competition days; Ladies Day Tuesdays. *Society Meetings:* catered for. Professional: Paul Richmond (0602 202227). Secretary: A. Newton.

NEWARK. **Newark Golf Club,** Coddington, Newark NG24 2QX (0636 626241). *Location:* off the A17 Sleaford road four miles east of Newark. Parkland, wooded course. 18 holes, 6486 yards. S.S.S. 71. Practice ground. *Green Fees:* £18.00 per round, £24.00 per day weekdays; weekends £24.00. *Eating facilities:* full catering, bar all day. *Visitors:* welcome with reservation. Handicap Certificates will be required. Restriction at peak times Saturday and Sunday, Ladies' Day Tuesday. Snooker. Professional tuition and computer/video analysis. *Society Meetings:* welcome except Tuesdays, weekends. Booking fee payable. Professional: H.A. Bennett (0636 626492). Secretary: A.W. Morgans (0636 626282).

NOTTINGHAM. **Beeston Fields Golf Club,** Old Drive, Wollaton Road, Beeston NG9 3DD (Nottingham (0602) 257062). *Location:* Wollaton road off A52 Derby road, M1, Exit 25. Parkland. 18 holes, 6414 yards. S.S.S. 71. Practice ground and net available. *Green Fees:* weekdays £20.00; weekends £30.00. *Eating facilities:* available daily. *Visitors:* welcome with reservation, Tuesday not until 2.30pm. *Society Meetings:* catered for Mondays and Wednesdays. Professional: Alun Wardle (0602 220872). Secretary: J.E.L. Grove (0602 257062).

NOTTINGHAM. **Chilwell Manor Golf Club,** Meadow Lane, Chilwell, Nottingham NG9 5AE (Nottingham (0602) 258958). *Location:* four miles from Nottingham on main Nottingham to Birmingham road. 18 holes, 6379 yards. S.S.S. 70. *Green Fees:* £18.00. *Eating facilities:* available. *Visitors:* welcome weekdays with reservation, restricted at certain busy times. *Society Meetings:* societies catered for by appointment (minimum 30). Professional: E. McCausland. Hon. Secretary: G.A. Spindley.

NOTTINGHAM. **Nottingham City Golf Club,** Lawton Drive, Bulwell, Nottingham NG6 8BL (Nottingham (0602) 278021). *Location:* exit 26 M1, at first roundabout follow signs for Bulwell. Parkland. 18 holes, 6218 yards. S.S.S. 70. Practice area. *Green Fees:* weekdays £8.00 per round; weekends £10.00.

PINE LODGE HOTEL   Mansfield   Nottinghamshire

Fully Licensed Private Hotel (Est. 1969)   AA★★ RAC★★

A fine hotel of simple excellence, offering fresh wholesome food at its best. **Close to the Coxmoor, Hollinwell and Sherwood Forest Golf Courses.** Private car parking, garden, sauna/solarium room. Double, twin and single rooms with bathrooms/showers ensuite all with colour TV. Satellite TV, Direct-dial telephone and complimentary tea/coffee making facilities. **For reservations please telephone (0623) 22308.**

England NOTTINGHAMSHIRE

Eating facilities: available. *Visitors:* welcome, Saturdays to 2pm – telephone for times. *Society Meetings:* welcome by prior arrangement. Professional: C.R. Jepson (0602 272767). Secretary: Laurie Whyte (0602 276916 mornings).

NOTTINGHAM. **Ruddington Grange Golf Club,** Wilford Road, Ruddington, Nottingham NG11 6NB (0602 214139). *Location:* M1 Junction 24 Nottingham road, A52 to Nottingham Knight island, right to Ruddington, half a mile outside Ruddington. Parkland. 18 holes, 6490 yards, 5935 metres. S.S.S. 71. *Green Fees:* information not provided. *Eating facilities:* full restaurant. *Visitors:* welcome all the time but at weekends members have priority. Swimming pool. *Society Meetings:* welcome. Professional: Robert Ellis (0602 211951). Secretary: R.L. Westgate (0602 846141).

NOTTINGHAM. **Wollaton Park Golf Club,** Wollaton Park, Nottingham (0602 787574). *Location:* turning off Ring Road Middleton Boulevard. 18 holes, 6545 yards. S.S.S. 71. *Green Fees:* weekdays £19.00 per round, weekends £22.00 per round. *Eating facilities:* meals and bar snacks available. *Visitors:* welcome, contact Professional for availability. *Society Meetings:* catered for Tuesdays and Fridays. Professional: J. Lower (0602 784834). Secretary: O.B. Kirk.

RADCLIFFE-ON-TRENT. **Radcliffe-on-Trent Golf Club,** Dewberry Lane, Cropwell Road, Radcliffe-on-Trent NG12 2JH (0602 333125). *Location:* A52 from Nottingham turn right at traffic lights on Cropwell Road. Flat, wooded parkland. 18 holes, 6423 yards. S.S.S. 71. Two large practice areas. *Green Fees:* weekdays £21.00 per day, weekends £26.00 per day (reductions for members' guests). *Eating facilities:* snacks, meals and bar. *Visitors:* welcome, confirm course availability with Professional or Secretary. *Society Meetings:* catered for on Wednesdays. Professional: Robert Ellis (0602 332396). Secretary: Les Wake (0602 333000).

RETFORD. **Retford Golf Club Ltd,** Brecks Road, Ordsall, Retford DN22 7UA (0777 703733). *Location:* south off A620. 18 holes, 6301 yards. S.S.S. 71. *Green Fees:* weekdays £15.00 per round (£8.00 with a member), £20.00 per day; weekends and Bank Holidays £8.00 (must be accompanied by a member). *Eating facilities:* meals at club. *Visitors:* welcome. Professional: S. Betteridge (0777 703733). Secretary: A. Harrison (0777 860682).

SOUTHWELL. **Oakmere Park Golf Club,** Oaks Lane, Oxton, Near Southwell NG25 0RH (0602 653545; Fax: 0602 655628). *Location:* eight miles north east of Nottingham on A614. Parkland course with longest Par 5 in Nottinghamshire. North Course – 18 holes, 6041 yards. S.S.S. 72. South Course – 9 holes, 3193 yards. S.S.S. 37. 30 bay floodlit driving range. *Green Fees:* North – weekdays £16.00; weekends £20.00. South – weekdays £6.00; weekends £8.00. *Eating facilities:* clubhouse bar, spike bar, restaurant, resident chef. *Visitors:* welcome but should make reservations weekends. *Society Meetings:* welcome, weekend require maximum notice possible. Professional: S. Meade. Operations Director: M. Gibson.

STANTON-ON-THE-WOLDS. **Stanton-on-the-Wolds Golf Club,** Stanton-on-the-Wolds NG12 5BH (0602 372044). *Location:* seven miles south of Nottingham, one mile west of main Nottingham – Melton road. Agricultural land. 18 holes, 6437 yards, 5886 metres. S.S.S. 71. Practice ground. *Green Fees:* weekdays £24.00; weekends with member only. *Eating facilities:* restaurant and bar. *Visitors:* welcome by prior arrangement with Secretary, weekends with member only. *Society Meetings:* catered for by arrangement with Secretary. Professional: Nick Hernon (0602 372390). Secretary: H.G. Gray, F.C.A. (0602 372006).

WORKSOP. **Kilton Forest Golf Club,** Blyth Road, Worksop S81 0TL (0909 472488). *Location:* one mile north of Worksop on B6045. Undulating parkland. 18 holes, 6569 yards. S.S.S. 72. Practice area. *Green Fees:* weekdays £7.00; weekends £8.50. *Eating facilities:* bar meals served until 2pm. *Visitors:* welcome, club competitions some Sundays – check with Professional. *Society Meetings:* by arrangement with Professional. Professional: P.W. Foster (0909 486563). Secretary: E.L. James (0909 477427).

WORKSOP. **Lindrick Golf Club,** Lindrick, Worksop S81 8BH (Worksop (0909) 485802). *Location:* on A57 four miles west of Worksop. M1 junction 31 on to A57 Worksop. Heathland. 18 holes, 6615 yards, 6048 metres. S.S.S. 72. Two practice areas. qo04Green Fees: weekdays £40.00 per day; weekends £45.00 per round. *Eating facilities:* diningroom. *Visitors:* welcome weekdays, except Tuesday mornings. Prior booking required. *Society Meetings:* catered for weekdays. Professional: P. Cowen (0909 475820). Secretary: G. Bywater (0909 475282; Fax: 0909 488685).

WORKSOP. **Worksop Golf Club,** Windmill Lane, Worksop S80 2SQ (Worksop (0909) 472696). *Location:* just off Worksop bypass (A57), one mile south east of town centre. Heathland with gorse, broom, birch and oak; easy walking. 18 holes, 6651 yards. S.S.S. 73. Practice ground. *Green Fees:* £18.00 per round, £25.00 per day weekdays; £25.00 per round weekends and Bank Holidays. *Eating facilities:* dining room and bar. *Visitors:* welcome, except weekends November to March without member. Advise preliminary phone call to Professional. Snooker table. *Society Meetings:* weekdays only by arrangement with Professional. Not Bank Holidays. Professional: J.R. King (0909 477732). Secretary: P.G. Jordan (0909 477731).

If you are writing, a stamped, addressed envelope is always appreciated.

Oxfordshire

ABINGDON. **Frilford Heath Golf Club,** Abingdon OX13 5NW (Frilford Heath (0865) 390864). *Location:* on A338 Oxford/Wantage Road seven miles south-west of Oxford, four miles west of Abingdon. Flat, wooded heathland. Red course: 18 holes, 6768 yards. S.S.S. 73; Green course: 18 holes, 5763 yards. S.S.S. 69. Two practice areas. *Green Fees:* weekdays £40.00; weekends and Bank Holidays £50.00; after 5pm £25.00 all week. *Eating facilities:* first class restaurant and bars. *Visitors:* welcome weekdays with Handicap Certificate, phone ahead for weekends and Bank Holidays. *Society Meetings:* welcomed Mondays, Wednesdays and Fridays. Professional: D.C. Craik (0865 390887). Secretary: J. Kleynhans (0865 390864).

BANBURY. **Cherwell Edge Golf Club,** C/o Cherwell Edge Public Course, Chacombe, Banbury (0295 711591). *Location:* half a mile off M40 at Banbury. Flat parkland. 18 holes, 5840 yards. S.S.S. 68. Practice area. *Green Fees:* weekdays £9.50; weekends £12.00. *Eating facilities:* restaurant. *Visitors:* welcome, some time restrictions. *Society Meetings:* welcome, some time restrictions. Professional: Mr R. Jefferies (0295 711591). Secretary: Mr R.A. Beare (0295 275679 home).

BANBURY. **Tadmarton Heath Golf Club,** Wiggin-ton, Banbury OX15 5HL (0608 737278). *Location:* off M40, off A41, off B4035, five miles west of Banbury. Heathland. 18 holes, 5917 yards. S.S.S. 69. Practice area. *Green Fees:* by application. *Eating facilities:* full catering. *Visitors:* welcome weekdays (restrictions Thursdays); weekends with member only. Must be member of another golf club with Handicap Certificate. *Society Meetings:* welcome weekdays except Thurs-days. Professional: Les Bond (0608 730047). Sec-retary: R.E. Wackrill (0608 737278).

BICESTER. **Chesterton Golf Club,** Chesterton, Near Bicester OX6 8TE (Bicester (0869) 241204). *Location:* one mile off A421, Bicester/Oxford. Two miles south-west of Bicester. 18 holes, 6224 yards. S.S.S. 70. Practice ground and putting green. *Green Fees:* weekdays £12.00 per round, £15.00 per day; weekends and Bank Holidays £18.00 per round, £24.00 per day. *Eating facilities:* bars and lunchtime bar food, diningroom by arrangement. *Visitors:* welcome weekdays without reservation, weekends may book through Pro shop. Snooker room. *Society Meetings:* catered for except weekends. Professional: Jack Wilkshire (0869 242023). Secretary: Brian Carter (0869 241204).

BURFORD. **Burford Golf Club,** Burford OX18 4JG (Burford (0993 822583). *Location:* A40 – Burford roundabout. Flat parkland. 18 holes, 6405 yards, 6083 metres. S.S.S. 71. *Green Fees:* £25.00 per day weekdays. *Eating facilities:* full catering. *Visitors:* wel-come weekdays only by arrangement. *Society Meet-ings:* catered for on application to Secretary. Professional: Norman Allen (0993 822344). Secretary: Richard Cane (0993 822583).

CHIPPING NORTON. **Chipping Norton Golf Club,** Southcombe, Chipping Norton OX7 5QH (0608 641150). *Location:* Junction of A3400 and A34, 18 miles from Oxford. 20 miles from Stratford-on-Avon. Downland, with many planted trees and lake. 18 holes, 6280 yards, 5743 metres. S.S.S. 70. Practice ground and putting green. *Green Fees:* weekdays £22.00; weekends only with a member £10.00. £38.00 per day for Societies, including catering. *Eating facilities:* diningroom and bar. *Visitors:* welcome Monday to Friday but not Bank Holidays. *Society Meetings:* Mon-days, Tuesdays, Wednesdays and some Fridays. Pro-fessional: Robert Gould (0608 643356). Secretary: John Norman (0608 642383).

CHIPPING NORTON. **Lyneham Golf Club,** Lyne-ham, Chipping Norton OX7 6QQ (0993 831841). *Location:* six miles off the A40 at Burford. One and a half miles off the A361 Chipping Norton to Burford Road. Tourism flag in position. Parkland. 18 holes, 6669 yards, 6099 metres. S.S.S. 72. Short 9 hole course under construction. *Green Fees:* weekdays £12.00; weekends £15. *Eating facilities:* bar, function room. *Visitors:* welcome, can book start time three days

The Crown & Cushion Hotel & Leisure Centre
Nr. Oxford, Chipping Norton OX7 5AD.

500 year old Coaching Inn, tastefully modernised to provide 40 excellent en-suite bedrooms. Some 4 Poster suites. "Old World Bar", log fires, real ale, good food. Indoor pool, Squash court, Multi gym, Solarium, (full sized snooker table subject to availability). A fully equipped modern conference centre. Hotel located in a picturesque Cotswold town midway between Oxford and Stratford-upon-Avon. Convenient for London, Heathrow Airport and M40 Motorway. Blenheim Palace, Warwick Castle, Broadway, Bourton-on-the-Water, Bibury, Stow-on-the-Wold, Shakespeare Country are all nearby. Price Busters start at just £19.50 or B&B plus full Restaurant Dinner at just £32. Lyncham Golf Club (18 hole, Tel: 0993 831841) is just 4 miles away and costs £12 midweek, £15 weekends per round. Chipping Norton Golf Club (18 hole, Tel: 0608 642383) costs £22 mid-week.

For colour brochure, freephone 0800 585251 or fax: 0608 642926   ETB ⚜⚜⚜⚜ Commended

in advance. *Society Meetings:* welcome. Professional: Mark Stancer. Secretary: Cyril Howkins.

HENLEY-ON-THAMES. **Badgemore Park Golf Club,** Badgemore, Henley-on-Thames RG9 4NR (0491 573667). *Location:* just west of Henley-on-Thames, on B290 Henley-Peppard road. Flat but wooded course. 18 holes, 6112 yards. S.S.S. 69. *Green Fees:* weekdays £26.00 per day; weekends £29.00. *Eating facilities:* full catering and bar facilities. *Visitors:* welcome though must play with a member weekends and Bank Holiday mornings. Handicap Certificate required. *Society Meetings:* complete Company and Society Golf Days available. Professional: J. Dunn (0491 574175). Manager: R. Park (0491 572206; Fax: 0491 567899).

HENLEY-ON-THAMES. **Henley Golf Club,** Harpsden, Henley-on-Thames RG9 4HG (Henley (0491) 573304). *Location:* from centre of Henley-Reading, one mile from Harpsden Way to clubhouse. Parkland with many trees. 18 holes, 6329 yards. S.S.S. 70. *Green Fees:* £30.00; weekends with member only £10. *Eating facilities:* bar snacks at all times, meals by arrangement. *Visitors:* welcome with reservation weekdays, not at weekends or Bank Holidays (Handicap Certificate holders only). *Society Meetings:* catered for Wednesdays and Thursdays only. Professional: Mark Howell (0491 575710). Secretary: John Hex (0491 575742).

HENLEY-ON-THAMES. **Huntercombe Golf Club,** Nuffield, Henley-on-Thames RG9 5SL (0491 641207). *Location:* A432, six miles west of Henley-on-Thames. Downland wooded course. 18 holes, 6301 yards. S.S.S. 70. Practice ground. *Green Fees:* £31.50 per day weekdays, £31.50 per round weekends. *Eating facilities:* catering and bar facilities. *Visitors:* welcome by prior arrangement only. *Society Meetings:* Tuesdays and Thursdays by arrangement. Professional: J.B. Draycott (0491 641201). Secretary: Lt Col T.J. Hutchinson.

MAPLEDURHAM. **Mapledurham Golf Club,** Chazey Heath, Mapledurham, Reading RG4 7UD (0734 463353; Fax: 0734 463363). *Location:* leave Reading on A4074 towards Mapledurham, Woodcote and Wallingford, club is on the right immediately after leaving built up area. Parkland. 18 holes, 5621 yards. S.S.S. 66. Practice ground. *Green Fees:* weekdays £13.00; weekends £16.00. *Eating facilities:* bar/lounge, food available. *Visitors:* welcome, no restrictions. *Society Meetings:* welcome. Professional: Douglas Burton. Manager: Kevin Bailey.

OXFORD. **North Oxford Golf Club,** Banbury Road, Oxford OX2 8ED (Oxford (0865) 54415). *Location:* just north of Oxford on the Banbury Road to Kidlington. 18 holes, 5805 yards, S.S.S. 67. *Green Fees:* on request. *Eating facilities:* limited on Mondays. *Visitors and Societies:* welcome. Professional: Bob Harris (0865 53977). Secretary: G.W. Pullin (0865 54924).

OXFORD. **Southfield Golf Club,** Hill Top Road, Oxford OX4 1PF. *Location:* one mile from Rover Works, along Cowley Road, turn right into Southfield Road, then right at end of road. Hilly parkland. 18 holes, 6328 yards. S.S.S. 70. *Green Fees:* £24.00 per day weekdays. *Eating facilities:* full catering except Mondays, bar open seven days. *Visitors:* welcome except weekends and Public Holidays. Handicap Certificates required. *Society Meetings:* welcome by arrangement (not weekends or Bank Holidays). Professional: Tony Rees (0865 244258). Secretary: A.G. Hopcraft (0865 242158).

WALLINGFORD near. **RAF Benson,** Near Wallingford OX10 6AA. *Location:* three and a half miles north-east of Wallingford, follow signposts to RAF Benson. Airfield course, through airfield installations. 9 holes, 4395 yards. S.S.S. 61. *Green Fees:* information not provided. *Visitors:* casual visitors not permitted, must be accompanied by members. Secretary: Flt Lt J.W. (Taff) Williams (0491 35376).

Shropshire

BRIDGNORTH. **Bridgnorth Golf Club,** Stanley Lane, Bridgnorth WV16 4SF (Bridgnorth (0746) 763315). *Location:* one mile from town centre on Broseley road. Parkland, alongside River Severn. 18 holes, 6627 yards. S.S.S. 72. Practice ground. *Green Fees:* £18.00 – £22.00 weekdays; £25.00 – £30.00 weekends and Bank Holidays. *Eating facilities:* full catering available except Mondays. *Visitors:* welcome weekdays except Wednesday with Handicap Certificate or if bona fide club member. *Society Meetings:* catered for Tuesday, Thursday, Friday only. Professional: Paul Hinton (0746 762045). Secretary: K.D. Cole (0746 764179).

CHURCH STRETTON. **Church Stretton Golf Club,** "Hunters Moon", Trevor Hill, Church Stretton SY6 6JH (Church Stretton (0694) 722281). *Location:* one mile west of A49, adjacent to Carding Mill Valley. Hillside, heathland course. 18 holes, 5008 yards. S.S.S. 65. *Green Fees:* £12.00 weekdays, £18.00 weekends and Bank Holidays. *Eating facilities:* snacks and meals by arrangement; bar. *Visitors:* welcome, Saturday not 9am to 10.30am or 1pm to 3pm, Sundays not before 10.30am or between 12.30pm and 3pm.*Society Meetings:* catered for by arrangement with Secretary. Hon. Secretary: R. Broughton (0694 722633).

LUDLOW. **Ludlow Golf Club,** Bromfield, Ludlow SY8 2BT (0584 77285). *Location:* A49 one mile north of Ludlow bypass, turn right onto the Bridgnorth road. Well signposted. Parkland with hills to north east; two quarry holes. 18 holes, 6239 yards. S.S.S. 70. Practice ground. *Green Fees:* weekdays £18.00; weekends £24.00 (£8.00 with member). *Eating facilities:* full catering and bar service. *Visitors:* welcome weekdays with prior booking, weekends with member only.

SHROPSHIRE *England*

TELFORD
HOTEL
Golf & Country CLUB

GREAT HAY, SUTTON HILL, TELFORD TF7 4DT.
TEL: 0952 585642 · FAX: 0952 582836 · TELEX: 35481

Spend some time at one of Shropshire's premier Hotel and Golf complexes and enjoy a range of Golfing Packages, each one designed to make your visit one to remember.

The challenging 18 hole championship golf course stands along with our 9 hole par 3 course, high above the splendour of the Ironbridge Gorge. Telford offers amenities such as buggy hire, pro shop, 8 bay floodlit driving range and expert video tuition to name but a few.

Lying to the south of Telford the Hotel complex is close to Junctions 4 and 5 of the M54, giving easy access to both the M1 and M6 motorways.

We have 86 comfortable double/twin bedded rooms, each having en-suite bathroom and shower, colour television, direct dial telephone and tea and coffee making facilities. The Hotel prides itself on its golf course, but why not make use of our excellent indoor heated pool, squash courts, snooker and sauna, steam room, gymnasium, spa pool and solariums, before choosing from our à la carte or table d'hôte menus.

For more information on our Special Golf Weekend Classic, Summer Saver Packages, Company Golf Days, and Society Golf Days please contact the Golf Co-ordinator on (0952) 585642 or Fax (0952) 582836. Conference and meeting facilities available.

Please note we now have full course irrigation.

Please rush details to me on the following:

Special Golf Weekend Classic	☐	Company Golf Days	☐
Summer Saver Packages	☐	Society Golf Days	☐

Name ....

Address ....

....

Great Hay, Sutton Hill, Telford TF7 4DT
Telephone: (0952) 585642   Fax: (0952) 582836   Telex: 35481

THE GOLF GUIDE 1994   *England*   SHROPSHIRE

Society Meetings: catered for Wednesdays and Thursdays April to October. Professional: Russell Price (0584 77366). Administrator: M. Cropper.

MARKET DRAYTON. **Market Drayton Golf Club,** Sutton, Market Drayton (Market Drayton (0630) 652266). *Location:* south of town leaving by Walkmill Road one mile past the swimming baths. Parkland with exceptional views. 18 holes, 6214 yards, 5702 metres. S.S.S. 70. *Green Fees:* weekdays £20.00; weekends only with a member. Reduced fees if playing with member. *Eating facilities:* bar with high class catering open all day. *Visitors:* welcome weekdays only. Tuesday Ladies' Day, first tee closed 9am to 11am. Bungalow (sleeps 6) available for letting. *Society Meetings:* catered for weekdays by prior arrangement. Professional: R. Clewes. Secretary: C. Price (0630 657496).

NEWPORT. **Lilleshall Hall Golf Club,** Lilleshall, Near Newport TF10 9AS (Telford (0952) 603840). *Location:* at Lillyhurst turn north off Abbey Road, which joins Wellington Road near Lilleshall and the B4379 near Sheriffhales. Wooded parkland. 18 holes, 5906 yards. S.S.S. 68. Practice ground. *Green Fees:* weekdays £18.00 (half price with member), weekends £15.00 only with member. Bank Holidays and following day plus Christmas holiday week £30.00 (half price with a member). *Eating facilities:* meals served 9am to 5pm, order in advance. *Visitors:* welcome on weekdays, check with Professional for tee restrictions. *Society Meetings:* catered for by prior arrangement with Secretary. Professional: N.W. Bramall (0952 604104). Secretary: B.G. Weaver (0952 604776).

OSWESTRY. **Llanymynech Golf Club,** Pant, Near Oswestry SY10 8LB (Llanymynech (0691) 830542). *Location:* one mile west of A483 Welshpool to Oswestry, six miles south of Oswestry. Turn by Cross Guns Inn, Pant signposted to club. Upland course with extensive views. 18 holes, 6114 yards, 5899 metres. S.S.S. 69. Practice area. *Green Fees:* weekdays £18.00 per day, £13.00 per round; weekends £23.00 per day, £19.00 per round. Half price with member. Reductions for Juniors. *Eating facilities:* restaurant and bar (not Mondays). *Visitors:* welcome weekdays; some weekends by prior arrangement. *Society Meetings:* by arrangement with the Secretary. Professional: A.P. Griffiths (0691 830879). Secretary: N. Clews (0691 830983).

OSWESTRY. **Oswestry Golf Club,** Aston Park, Oswestry SY11 4JJ (Queens Head (069188) 221). *Location:* four miles south-east of Oswestry on A5. Parkland course. 18 holes, 6038 yards. S.S.S. 69. *Green Fees:* weekdays £18.00; weekends £25.00. *Eating facilities:* diningroom and bar. *Visitors:* welcome; must be members of another club or playing with a member. *Society Meetings:* catered for Wednesday and Friday, by arrangement, application necessary. Professional: D. Skelton (069188 448). Secretary: Mrs. P.M. Lindner (069188 535).

SHIFNAL. **Shifnal Golf Club,** Decker Hill, Shifnal TF11 8QL (Telford (0952) 460330). *Location:* one mile north east of Shifnal, one mile from A5. Junction 4 M54. Parkland course. 18 holes, 6504 yards. S.S.S. 71. *Green Fees:* £22.00 per round, £30.00 per day; weekends with member only. *Eating facilities:* full catering service except Mondays. *Visitors:* welcome, phone first, not weekends or Bank Holidays. *Society Meetings:* catered for by arrangement with Secretary. Professional: J. Flanagan (0952 460457). Secretary: P.W. Holden (0952 460330).

SHREWSBURY. **Hawkstone Park Leisure Ltd,** Weston-under-Redcastle, Shrewsbury SY4 5UY (0939 200611; Fax: 0939 200311). Where Sandy Lyle, '85 Open Champion, learned his game. *Location:* 14 miles north of Shrewsbury off A49. Parkland course set in wonderful Shropshire countryside. 18 holes, 6465 yards. S.S.S. 71. Golf Centre and school, practice range, 5 holes par 3 Academy. *Green Fees:* from £20.00 per round. *Eating facilities:* terrace restaurant and bar. *Visitors:* welcome, book in advance. *Society Meetings:* comprehensive 'super-value' packages available. Buggies for hire. Head Professional: Keith Williams. Golf Manager: Sean Clarke.

SHREWSBURY. **Shrewsbury Golf Club,** Condover, Shrewsbury SY5 7BL (0743 872776). *Location:* A49 two miles south west of Shrewsbury. Parkland. 18 holes, 6212 yards. S.S.S. 70. Large practice ground. *Green Fees:* £15.00 per round, £20.00 per day weekdays; £25.00 per day or round weekends and Bank Holidays. *Eating facilities:* full restaurant facilities available seven days. *Visitors:* welcome at all times. *Society Meetings:* by arrangement if over 16 players, not Wednesdays, preferably Mondays and Fridays, some Sundays. Professional: Peter Seal (0743 873751). Secretary: Mrs S.M. Kenny (0743 872977).

TELFORD. **Telford Hotel, Golf and Country Club,** Great Hay, Sutton Hill, Telford TF7 4DT (0952 585642; Fax: 0952 586602). *Location:* turn off A442 between Bridgnorth and Telford, two miles to M54 Junction 4. Rolling wooded parkland with lake features. 18 holes, 6766 yards, 6187 metres. S.S.S. 72. 9 hole par 3 course. All-weather driving range. *Green Fees:* £25.00 weekdays; £30.00 weekends. *Eating facilities:* clubroom, coffee bar and restaurant, also private rooms for Societies. *Visitors:* welcome anytime but advance booking essential. Handicap Certificates or membership of bona fide golf club essential. Leisure Centre with swimming pool, gym, etc. *Society Meetings:* by arrangement with Golf Co-ordinator extension

---

HAWKSTONE PARK GOLF CENTRE
Where Sandy Lyle Learned his game

Don't miss our colour advertisement on page 23

The perfect setting, less than an hour from M6, M54 and M56. 18 holes of superb golf with green fees from £20. New Golf Centre, practice range. Expert tuition and golf clinics available. Residential golf breaks from £49.55 p.p. The new Hawkstone Park is more than a golfing hotel – it's unique.

Weston-under-Redcastle, Shrewsbury, Shropshire SY4 5UY Tel: (0939) 200611 Fax: (0939) 200311

SHROPSHIRE *England* THE GOLF GUIDE 1994

Patshull Park Hotel

Leisure and Beauty packages for the golf widow!

The Perfect Retreat for Golf & Leisure

Patshull Park Hotel Golf and Leisure complex – geared to residential Golf or Leisure Breaks throughout the year – will welcome you to the unspoilt beauty of Shropshire.

* Residential Golf & Leisure Breaks * Swimming, Gymnasium, Saunas, Fishing
* Executive & Company Golf Days * Conferences, Business Lunches & Dinner
*Lakeside Restaurant & Coffee Shop * Easy access M54, M6, A5 and A41. For further details contact:

PATSHULL PARK HOTEL GOLF & COUNTRY CLUB
Pattingham, Wolverhampton WV6 7HR
Telephone: (0902) 700100

---

297. Professional: Graham Farr (0952 586052). Secretary: Dave Paterson (0952 585642 ext. 274).

TELFORD. **Wrekin Golf Club,** Ercall Woods, Wellington, Telford (Telford (0952) 244032). *Location:* end of M54, turn back along Holyhead road to golf club sign. Undulating parkland. 18 holes, 5699 yards. S.S.S. 67. Small practice ground. *Green Fees:* weekdays £20.00; weekends £25.00 numbers limited. *Eating facilities:* by arrangement with Stewardess. *Visitors:* welcome except weekends and Bank Holidays. *Society Meetings:* by arrangement. Professional: K. Houseden (0952 223101). Secretary: S. Leys (0952 255586 after 7pm).

WHITCHURCH. **Hill Valley Golf and Country Club,** Terrick Road, Whitchurch SY13 4JZ (0948 663584; Fax: 0948 665927). *Location:* fully signposted off A49/A41 trunk road in Whitchurch. Undulating parkland courses. No 1 Course – 18 holes, 6050 yards. S.S.S. 69, Par 72. No 2 Course – 18 holes, 5283 yards. S.S.S. 65, Par 66. *Green Fees:* No 1 Course – weekdays £18.00, weekends and Bank Holidays £24.00; No 2 Course – weekdays £9.00, weekends and Bank Holidays £12.00. *Eating facilities:* full restaurant and bar facilities 8am – 9pm. *Visitors:* welcome without reservation. Motel accommodation, squash, tennis, snooker room. *Society Meetings:* fully catered for every day. Professional: A.R. Minshall (0948 663032). Secretary: R.B. Walker (0948 663584).

WOLVERHAMPTON. **Patshull Park Hotel, Golf and Country Club,** Patshull Park, Pattingham, Near Wolverhampton WV6 7HR (Tel/Fax: 0902 700100/ 700874). *Location:* take Junction 3 off M54 turn, left on A41 back towards Wolverhampton and fork right into Albrighton. From the main crossroads turn right along Cross Road, taking T-junction with the A464 Wolverhampton/Shifnal Road and turning right towards Shifnal. Signposted Patshull Park Golf Course. Set in glorious parkland landscaped by Capability Brown; John Jacobs designed course. 18 holes, 6412 yards. S.S.S. 72. Excellent practice area. *Green Fees:* information not provided. *Eating facilities:* available, one restaurant and three bars, coffee shop. *Visitors:* welcome on application. 48 bedroomed hotel, leisure club and swimming pool, fishing lakes (80 acres). Residential Breaks. *Society Meetings:* corporate and society meetings welcome; special group rates and facilities. Professional: Duncan J. McDowall (0902 700342).

WORFIELD. **Worfield Golf Club,** Bridgnorth Road, Worfield, Near Bridgnorth WV15 5HE (07464 541). *Location:* A454 Wolverhampton to Bridgnorth Road, three miles from Bridgnorth. Parkland and seaside links. 18 holes, 6801 yards. S.S.S. 73. Large practice range, chipping and bunker green. *Green Fees:* weekdays £15.00 per round, £20.00 per day; weekends £20.00 per round, £25 per day. *Eating facilities:* dining room and bar. *Visitors:* no visitors until after 10am weekends. *Society Meetings:* all welcome. Professional: Steve Russell (07464 372). Secretary: William Weaver (07464 541).

England SOMERSET

Somerset

BRIDGWATER. **Enmore Park Golf Club**, Enmore, Bridgwater TA5 2AN (0278 671244). *Location:* M5 Exit 23, left at lights in town for one mile, course signposted two miles on left. Wooded parkland course on Quantock foothills. 18 holes, 6406 yards, 5910 metres. S.S.S. 71. Large practice area. *Green Fees:* £18.00 per round, £25.00 per day weekdays; £25.00 per round £30.00 per day weekends. *Eating facilities:* lunch and evening meal available. *Visitors:* welcome weekdays, weekends if no competitions. *Society Meetings:* welcome by arrangement. Professional: Nigel Wixon (0278 671519). Secretary: David Weston (0278 671481).

BURNHAM-ON-SEA. **Brean Golf Club**, Coast Road, Brean, Burnham-on-Sea TA8 2RF (0278 751595; Fax: 0278 751539). *Location:* leave M5 at Junction 22, follow Brean signs for five miles; three miles north of Burnham-on-Sea. Flat moorland. 18 holes, 5714 yards. S.S.S. 68 (Par 69). Practice putting green. *Green Fees:* weekdays £12.00 per round; weekends £15.00 per round. *Eating facilities:* bar snacks at Clubhouse; meals at adjoining Leisure Centre on request. *Visitors:* welcome, Saturdays and Sundays after 1pm. *Society Meetings:* welcome by arrangement. Professional: Sue Spencer (0278 751570). Secretary: Bill Martin (0278 751409). Manager: Albert Clarke.

BURNHAM-ON-SEA. **Burnham and Berrow Golf Club**, St. Christopher's Way, Burnham-on-Sea TA8 2PE (Burnham-on-Sea (0278) 783137). *Location:* one mile north of Burnham-on-Sea. Leave M5 at Exit 22. Seaside links. 18 holes, 6327 yards. S.S.S. 72. *Green Fees:* £28.00 weekdays, £40.00 weekends and Bank Holidays. *Eating facilities:* catering available daily 11.00am to 6.00pm (other meals by arrangement). *Visitors:* welcome with reservation if members of a recognised golf club and with Handicap Certificate. *Society Meetings:* catered for. Professional: M. Crowther-Smith (0278 784545). Secretary: Mrs E.L. Sloman (0278 785760).

CHARD. **Windwhistle Golf, Squash and Country Club Ltd**, Cricket St. Thomas, Near Chard TA20 4DG (0460 30231; Fax: 0460 30055). *Location:* on A30 between Chard and Crewkerne, opposite Cricket St. Thomas Wildlife Park, follow signs. Unique elevated course with unsurpassed panoramic scenery, flora and fauna. 18 holes, 6500 yards. S.S.S. 71, Par 73. Practice areas. *Green Fees:* on application. *Eating facilities:* comprehensive and extensive clubhouse facilities. *Visitors:* welcome weekdays, weekends and holidays, booking preferred. Senior PGA tuition available. Trolley hire. *Society Meetings:* catered for – comprehensive arrangements available. Professional: visiting. Secretary/Manager: Ian Neville Dodd.

Friarn Court Hotel
37 St. Mary Street, Bridgwater
Somerset TA6 3LX
Tel: 0278-452859
Fax: 0278-452988

♛♛♛♛ AA ★★
Conveniently central for Taunton, Burnham and Enmore. Cosy bar.
A la carte restaurant. Weekend discounts.
Club storage and drying room.

AA**
Egon Ronay
Recommended

BATCH FARM COUNTRY HOTEL
Lympsham, Near Weston-super-Mare
Tel: (0934) 750371

RAC**
Ashley Courtenay
Recommended

A family-run Hotel with a friendly atmosphere, set in its own grounds, with all bedrooms ensuite with colour TV and tea/coffee facilities. Parking. A la carte and table d'hôte menus. Fully licensed. Panoramic views.
GOLFERS MOST WELCOME: WESTON, BURNHAM, BREAN & WORLEBURY – 10 minutes' drive.
See our display advertisement in the Colour Section on page 17.

When in Somerset . . .

. . . treat yourself to a stay at the Burnham and Berrow Golf Club. Championship links golf course and accommodation at the Dormy House for £55 per night inc. breakfast and Green Fees.

BURNHAM BERROW & *Golf Club*
St. Christopher's Way
Burnham on Sea TA8 2PE
Telephone 0278 785760

SOMERSET England

MINEHEAD. **Minehead and West Somerset Golf Club,** The Warren, Minehead TA24 5SJ (Minehead (0643) 705095). *Location:* beside the beach at eastern end of the town, three-quarters of a mile from town centre. Flat seaside links. 18 holes, 6137 yards. S.S.S. 70. *Green Fees:* weekdays £19.50; weekends and Bank Holidays £23.00. *Eating facilities:* available at clubhouse, bar open every day. *Visitors:* welcome with tee reservation at Pro's shop. *Society Meetings:* catered for, subject to prior arrangement with the Secretary. Society groups numbering 15 or more qualify for 10 per cent discount. Wide wheel trolleys only. Professional: Ian Read (0643 704378). Secretary: Laurie Harper (0643 702057).

SHEPTON MALLET. **Mendip Golf Club Ltd.,** Gurney Slade, Shepton Mallet, Near Bath BA3 4UT (Oakhill (0749) 840570). *Location:* three miles north of Shepton Mallet (A37). Downland, undulating course. 18 holes, 6330 yards. S.S.S. 70. Practice ground. *Green Fees:* weekdays £20.00 per round, £25.00 per day (with a member £8.00); weekends and Bank Holidays £30.00 per day (with a member £10.00). *Eating facilities:* bar and restaurant open seven days a week. *Visitors:* welcome every day, telephone Professional to check availability. *Society Meetings:* catered for Mondays to Fridays by arrangement. Professional: R.F. Lee (0749 840793). Secretary: Mrs J.P. Howe (0749 840570).

STREET. **Kingweston Golf Club,** (Millfield School), Street (0458 43921). *Location:* one mile south of Butleigh Village, near Street, Somerset. Flat course – trees. 9 holes, 2378 yards. S.S.S. 62. Practice area. *Green Fees:* £4.00. *Eating facilities:* pub half a mile. *Visitors:* welcome only with a member. Secretary: J.G. Willetts (0458 43921).

TAUNTON. **Oake Manor Golf Club,** Oake, Near Taunton TA4 1BA (0823 461993; Fax: 0823 461995). *Location:* off B3227, village of Oake between Taunton and Wellington or Wiveliscombe. Parkland course with lakes. 18 holes, 6109 yards. S.S.S. 69. *Green Fees:* weekdays £12.00; weekends £15.00. *Eating facilities:* bar, restaurant, lounge. *Visitors:* always welcome. No dogs allowed. *Society Meetings:* by arrangement. Professional: R. Gardner.

TAUNTON. **Taunton and Pickeridge Golf Club,** Corfe, Taunton TA3 7BY (0823 42240). *Location:* B3170 four miles south of Taunton, first left. Undulating parkland course. 18 holes, 5921 yards. S.S.S. 68. Practice ground. *Green Fees:* information not provided. *Eating facilities:* bar and diningroom. *Visitors:* by arrangement with Secretary, must produce Handicap Certificates. *Society Meetings:* catered for by arrangement. Professional: Graham Glew (0823 42790). Secretary: G.W. Sayers (0823 42537).

TAUNTON. **Taunton Golf Club,** Vivary Park, Taunton (Taunton (0823) 81946). 18 holes, 4280 yards. S.S.S. 62. *Green Fees:* information not provided.

TAUNTON. **Vivary Park Public Golf Course,** Vivary Park, Fons George, Taunton TA1 3JW. *Location:* one

---

Battleborough Grange Country Hotel
Brent Knoll, Somerset

RAC ★★   *Les Routiers*

Surrounded by Somerset countryside, the hotel and restaurant nestles in its own grounds at the foot of the historic iron age fort known as Brent Knoll and is an excellent centre for touring Bristol, Bath, Wells, Cheddar, Glastonbury, Longleat and Exmoor. 6 miles Weston. 3 miles Burnham-on-Sea golf course. Ample car parking. The excellent accommodation comprises double, twin and four poster bedrooms with en-suite facilities, spa baths, colour TV, direct dial telephones and tea and coffee making facilities. Night porter. Full central heating, residents' lounge, licensed bar lounge, with the restaurant offering an excellent selection of freshly prepared à la carte dishes. Carvery also available. Conferences and Functions catered for.

Telephone & Fax: (0278) 760208

Anchor Cottages

Set in glorious rural Somerset, 'twixt Taunton and Wellington, lies the famous 17th century Anchor Inn, known for miles around for its charm, atmosphere and sumptuous food. The inn has three self catering cottages, each sleeping up to four people. Double glazed, with central heating, colour TV and bathroom, they are tastefully furnished. Each cottage has a private garden and ample parking space. The Anchor is only half a mile from Taunton's newest 18 hole golf course at Oake Manor. This is an ideal base for a golfing holiday, with many challenging courses within easy reach. Fishing and riding nearby. Details from Tony and Les Webber.

Anchor Cottages, The Anchor Inn, Hillfarrance, Taunton, Somerset TA4 1AW. Telephone: 0823 461334

THE GOLF GUIDE 1994 *England* SOMERSET/STAFFORDSHIRE

mile from town centre off main Wellington road. Access to course is through Vivary Park in central Taunton. Pleasant parkland course with spectacular water hazards. 18 holes, 4620 yards. S.S.S. 63. Practice ground. *Green Fees:* information not available. *Eating facilities:* restaurant and bar available. *Visitors:* always welcome but will need to book on the day of play. *Society Meetings:* catered for by prior arrangement. Professional: Jeremy Wright (0823 33875).

WELLS. **Wells (Somerset) Golf Club Ltd,** East Horrington Road, Wells BA5 3DS (Wells (0749) 672868). *Location:* one mile east of city centre opposite Mendip Hospital. Parkland, wooded. 18 holes, 6046 yards, 5528 metres. S.S.S. 69. Practice area. *Green Fees:* weekdays £16.00 per round, £19.00 per day; weekends and Bank Holidays £20.00 per round, £22.00 per day. *Eating facilities:* restaurant and bar. *Visitors:* welcome, Handicaps required weekends and no play before 9.30am weekends and Public Holidays.

Caravan park adjacent. *Society Meetings:* catered for weekdays. Professional: Andrew England (0749 679059). Secretary: George Ellis (0749 675005).

YEOVIL. **Yeovil Golf Club,** Sherborne Road, Yeovil BA21 5BW (Yeovil (0935) 75949). *Location:* on A30, one mile from town centre towards Sherborne on right before Babylon Hill. Parkland. 18 holes, 6144 yards. S.S.S. 70. 9 holes, 5016 yards. S.S.S. 66. Practice ground and putting green. *Green Fees:* 18 hole course weekdays £20.00 per round, £30.00 per day, 9 hole course £12.00 per round, £20 per day; weekends and Bank Holidays 18 holes £30.00, 9 holes £20.00. *Eating facilities:* bars and dining room. Tuesdays 11.45am to 4.45pm only. *Visitors:* midweek unrestricted subject to Society bookings; weekends players with current handicaps only. Telephone Pro Shop to check. *Society Meetings:* welcome Mondays, Wednesdays and Thursdays. Professional: G. Kite (0935 73763; Fax: 0935 78605). Secretary/Manager: J. Riley (0935 22965).

Staffordshire

BARLASTON. **Barlaston Golf Club,** Meaford Road, Stone ST15 8UX (0782 372795). *Location:* one mile south of Barlaston off A34. 18 holes, 5800 yards. S.S.S. 68. *Green Fees:* weekdays £18.00; £22.50 weekends. *Eating facilities:* available on request in advance. *Visitors:* welcome anytime except before 10am at weekends and Bank Holidays. Professional: Ian Rogers. Secretary: M.J. Degg (0782 372867).

BURTON UPON TRENT. **Craythorne Golf Centre,** Craythorne Road, Stretton, Burton upon Trent DE13 0AZ (Burton upon Trent (0283) 64329). *Location:* A38 (Burton North) A5121 signposted Stretton. Parkland. 18 holes, 5243 yards. S.S.S. 66. Floodlit driving range. *Green Fees:* £12.00 weekdays, £14.00 Saturdays, £16.00 Sundays and Bank Holidays. *Eating facilities:* bars and restaurant open daily. *Visitors:* welcome every day, booking necessary at weekends. 9 hole pitch and putt. *Society Meetings:* welcome. Professional: Steve Hadfield (0283 33745). Secretary/General Manager: John Bissell (0283 37992; Fax: 0283 511908).

BURTON-ON-TRENT. **Branston Golf Club,** Burton Road, Branston, Burton-on-Trent DE14 3DP (Burton-on-Trent (0283) 43207). *Location:* A38 Junction A5121. Parkland. 18 holes, 6541 yards, 5978 metres. S.S.S. 71. Driving range, practice area. *Green Fees:* weekdays £19.00, weekends £23.00. *Eating facilities:* dining room and bar. *Visitors:* welcome, weekend restrictions only. *Society Meetings:* welcome, special rates. Professional: S.D. Warner (0283 43207). Secretary: K.L. George (0283 43207; Fax: 0283 66984).

CANNOCK. **Beau Desert Golf Club,** Hazel Slade, Hednesford, Cannock WS12 5PJ (0543 422773). *Location:* A460 Hednesford, signposted. Heathland course. 18 holes, 6279 yards. S.S.S. 71. Practice ground. *Green Fees:* £30.00 weekdays. *Eating facilities:* full catering and bar. *Visitors:* welcome Monday to Thursday. *Society Meetings:* catered for. Professional: Barrie Stevens (0543 422492). Secretary: A.J.R. Fairfield (0543 422626).

THE RIVERSIDE HOTEL & GOLF CLUB
AA/RAC ★★★ (Egon Ronay Recommended)
Facilities include 22 bedrooms, a superb restaurant, a bar that stays open till you go to bed.
Affiliated 18 hole golf course a short walk away.
Send for our brochure and special weekend golf package.
TELEPHONE: 0283 511234
Riverside Drive, Branston, Burton-on-Trent, Staffordshire DE14 3EP
Host: BRUCE ELLIOTT-BATEMAN

STAFFORDSHIRE England

CANNOCK. Cannock Park Golf Club, Stafford Road, Cannock WS11 2AL. *Location:* on the A34 Stafford Road. Quarter of a mile from Cannock town centre. Parkland course, playing alongside Cannock Chase. 18 holes, 5048 yards. S.S.S. 65. *Green Fees:* £6.00 weekdays, £7.50 weekends. Phone bookings same day midweek for after 12 noon, weekends personal bookings before 12 noon. Reductions for Juniors. *Eating facilities:* available. *Visitors:* welcome every day. Golf shop, inside leisure centre. *Society Meetings:* welcome weekdays. Professional/Secretary: David Dunk (Tel & Fax: 0543 578850).

LEEK. Leek Golf Club, Birchall, Cheddleton Road, Leek (Leek (0538) 385889). *Location:* one mile south of Leek on A520. Undulating semi-moorland. 18 holes, 6240 yards. S.S.S. 70. *Green Fees:* weekdays £25.00; weekends £35.00. *Eating facilities:* full bar facilities 11.30am-2pm and 4-11.30pm. Light refreshments from 9am. *Visitors:* welcome most times by prior arrangement. *Society Meetings:* catered for by arrangement Wednesdays only. Professional: P.A. Stubbs (0538 384767). Secretary: Frank Cutts B.E.M. (0538 384779).

LEEK. Westwood Golf Club, Newcastle Road, Leek ST13 7AA (Leek (0538) 398385). *Location:* A53 south of Leek. Moorland/parkland. 18 holes, 6156 yards. S.S.S. 69. *Green Fees:* weekdays £18.00. *Eating facilities:* full facilities. *Visitors:* welcome weekdays, Saturdays with member, no visitors Sundays. *Society Meetings:* Mondays and Thursdays by arrangement with Secretary. Professional: Colin Smith (0538 398897). Secretary: Don Peacock (0538 398385).

LICHFIELD near. The Seedy Mill Golf Club, Elmhurst, Near Lichfield WS13 8HE (0543 417333; Fax: 0543 418098). *Location:* A51 three miles north of Lichfield. Parkland with lakes, ponds and streams. The Mill – 18 holes, 6247 yards. S.S.S. 70; The Spires – 9 holes, Par 3. 26 bay floodlit driving range. *Green Fees:* weekdays £12.00; weekends £18.00. *Eating facilities:* full clubhouse facilities open 7.30am to 11pm. *Visitors:* welcome at all times. *Society Meetings:* welcome weekdays and weekends. Professional: Andrew Bolton. Director of Golf: Simon Lloyd.

LICHFIELD. Whittington Barracks Golf Club, Tamworth Road, Lichfield WS14 9PW (0543 432212). *Location:* on A51 Tamworth-Lichfield Road. Wooded heathland. 18 holes, 6457 yards. S.S.S. 71. *Green Fees:* weekdays £32.00. *Eating facilities:* lunches served at club. *Visitors:* welcome with prior notification and Handicap Certificate or letter of introduction. *Society Meetings:* catered for Wednesdays and Thursdays by arrangement. Professional: Adrian Sadler (0543 432261). Secretary: D.W.J. Macalester (0543 432317).

NEWCASTLE. Newcastle-under-Lyme Golf Club, Whitmore Road, Newcastle (0782 616583). *Location:* M6 Junction 15, one mile from Newcastle-under-Lyme. Parkland. 18 holes, 6404 yards. S.S.S. 71 white, 70 yellow. *Green Fees:* weekdays £25.00; weekends with a member only (£7.50). *Eating facilities:* restaurant and bar meals. *Visitors:* welcome. Restrictions at weekends. *Society Meetings:* Wednesdays 10am to 12 noon then 2pm to 4pm; Thursdays 2pm to 4pm. Professional: P. Symonds (0782 618526). Secretary: D.B. Saunders (0782 617006).

NEWCASTLE-UNDER-LYME. Newcastle-under-Lyme Municipal Golf Club, Keele Road, Newcastle-under-Lyme (0782 627596). *Location:* A525 Newcastle to Whitchurch, opposite University of Keele. Undulating parkland. 18 holes, 6300 yards, 5822 metres. S.S.S. 70. Driving range. *Green Fees:* weekdays £6.50, Juniors £3.00; weekends £8.00, Juniors £6.50. *Eating facilities:* available. *Visitors:* welcome, no restrictions but start times must be pre-booked. Professional: Mr M. Shryane. Secretary: Mr G.A. Bytheway (0782 619317).

RUGELEY. Lakeside Golf Club, Rugeley Power Station, Armitage Road, Rugeley WS15 1PR (0889 57200). *Location:* nearest town Rugeley (between Lichfield and Stafford), course over power station grounds. Flat parkland adjacent River Trent. 18 holes, 5508 yards, 5037 metres. S.S.S. 67. Limited practice area. *Green Fees:* £6.00 with member. *Eating facilities:* evening snacks and bar facilities. *Visitors:* must be accompanied by member. *Society Meetings:* by arrangement. Secretary: Mr E.G. Jones (0889 584472).

STAFFORD. Brocton Hall Golf Club, Brocton, Stafford ST17 0TH (Stafford (0785) 662627). *Location:* off A34 Stafford to Cannock four miles south of Stafford. Undulating parkland. 18 holes, 6095 yards. S.S.S. 69. *Green Fees:* weekdays £25.00; weekends and Bank Holidays £30.00. *Visitors:* by arrangement. *Society Meetings:* by arrangement Tuesdays and Thursdays. Professional: Bob Johnson (0785 661485). Secretary: W.R. Lanyon (0785 661901).

STAFFORD. Ingestre Park Golf Club, Ingestre, Near Stafford (Weston (0889) 270061). *Location:* six miles east of Stafford. Parkland. 18 holes, 6334 yards. S.S.S. 70. *Green Fees:* 18 holes £17.00, 27 holes £22.00, 36 holes £27.00; before 3.30pm Handicap Certificate required. *Eating facilities:* lunch and dinner menu. *Visitors:* welcome weekdays. *Society Meetings:* welcome with reservation except Wednesday. Professional: Danny Scullion (0889 270304). Manager: D.D. Humphries (0889 270845).

STAFFORD. Stafford Castle Golf Club, Newport Road, Stafford ST16 1BP (Stafford (0785) 223821). *Location:* M6 junction 13 or 14, 2 miles from club. Parkland course. 9 holes, 6071 yards. S.S.S. 69, Par 71. *Green Fees:* £14.00 weekdays; £18.00 weekends. *Eating facilities:* snacks and full catering available except Mondays. *Visitors:* welcome except Sunday mornings. Handicap Certificate required. *Society Meetings:* catered for by arrangement. Secretary: D.H. Fellowes.

STOKE ON TRENT. Parkhall Golf Course, Hulme Road, Weston Coyney, Stoke on Trent ST3 5BH (0782 599584). *Location:* one mile outside Longton. Parkland. 18 holes, 2335 yards, 2136 metres. S.S.S. 54. *Green Fees:* information not provided. *Visitors:* welcome. Seven days advance booking required for weekends and Bank Holidays. *Society Meetings:* welcome. Professional: T. Clingan.

THE GOLF GUIDE 1994

England STAFFORDSHIRE

STOKE-ON-TRENT. **Burslem Golf Club Ltd,** Wood Farm, High Lane, Tunstall, Stoke-on-Trent ST6 7ST (Stoke-on-Trent (0782) 837006). *Location:* leave Burslem centre by Hamil Road, turn left at High Lane junction, 2 miles on right. 9 holes, 5800 yards. S.S.S. 68. *Green Fees:* information not provided. *Eating facilities:* meals and refreshments by arrangement except Wednesday and Sunday. *Visitors:* welcome weekdays with reservation. Bona fide golf club members only. *Society Meetings:* catered for. Secretary: F. Askey.

STOKE-ON-TRENT. **Trentham Golf Club,** 14 Barlaston Old Road, Trentham, Stoke-on-Trent ST3 8HB (Stoke-on-Trent (0782) 642347). *Location:* off A34 travelling south of Newcastle (Staffs.). Turn left at Trentham Gardens on Longton Road. Turn right at National Westminster Bank. Parkland with a sprinkling of trees. 18 holes, 6644 yards. S.S.S. 72. Practice ground. *Green Fees:* £25.00 weekdays; Sundays 12 noon onwards £30.00. Playing with member £8.00. *Eating facilities:* lunches and dinners available. *Visitors:* welcome weekends, only can play from 12 noon onwards. Handicap Certificate required. *Society Meetings:* limited numbers catered for. Professional: Mark Budz (0782 657309). Secretary: R.B. Irving (0782 658109).

STOKE-ON-TRENT. **Trentham Park Golf Club,** Trentham Park, Trentham, Stoke-on-Trent ST4 8AE (0782 642245). *Location:* off A34 adjoining Trentham Gardens near Junction 15 on M6. 18 holes, 6403 yards. S.S.S. 71. *Green Fees:* £20.00 weekdays, £25.00 weekends. *Eating facilities:* available at clubhouse except Mondays. *Visitors:* welcome weekdays with reservation. *Society Meetings:* catered for Wednesdays and Fridays only. Professional: Jim McLeod (0782 642125). Secretary: R.N. Portas (0782 658800).

STONE. **Stone Golf Club,** Filleybrooks, Stone ST15 0NB (Stone (0785) 813103). *Location:* one mile north of Stone on the A34 adjacent to the Wayfarer Hotel. Parkland. 9 holes, 6299 yards. S.S.S. 70. *Green Fees:* weekdays £15.00 per round £20.00 per day. *Eating facilities:* full meals to order, snacks always available, bar. *Visitors:* welcome weekdays only except Bank Holidays. *Society Meetings:* catered for by arrangement. Secretary: M.G. Pharaoh (08897 224).

STOURBRIDGE. **Enville Golf Club Ltd,** Highgate Common, Enville, Stourbridge DY7 5BN (Kinver (0384) 872551). *Location:* leave A449 at Stewpony Hotel taking Bridgnorth Road A458, fork right after Fox Inn following signs for Halfpenny Green Airport. Two flat wooded heathland courses. Highgate Course – 18 holes, 6556 yards. S.S.S. 72; Lodge Course – 18 holes, 6217 yards. S.S.S. 70. *Green Fees:* weekdays £22.00 18 holes, £26.50 27 holes, £32.00 36 holes. *Eating facilities:* meals available except Mondays. *Visitors:* welcome weekdays with Handicap Certificate, advisable to phone prior to visit. Ladies' day Thursday; weekends with members only. *Society Meetings:* welcome except Thursdays and weekends. Professional: S. Power (0384 872585). Secretary/Manager: R.J. Bannister (0384 872074).

STREETLY. **Little Aston Golf Club,** Streetly, Sutton Coldfield B74 3AN (021-353 2066). *Location:* off A454. Parkland course. 18 holes, 6724 yards. S.S.S. 73. *Green Fees:* on application. *Eating facilities:* lunches and dinner except Mondays. *Visitors:* welcome on weekdays by prior arrangement, weekends with a member. *Society Meetings:* catered for on weekdays only. Professional: John Anderson (021-353 2942). Secretary: N.H. Russell (021-353 2942).

TAMWORTH. **Drayton Park Golf Club,** Drayton Park, Tamworth B78 3TN (Tamworth (0827) 251139). *Location:* two miles south of Tamworth on A4091, next to Drayton Manor Leisure Park. Parkland with wooded areas. 18 holes, 6214 yards. S.S.S. 70. Practice area. *Green Fees:* weekdays £27.00 per round/day. Special rates for Societies over 12. *Eating facilities:* full catering facilities. *Visitors:* welcome weekdays, weekends with member only. *Society Meetings:* catered for Tuesdays and Thursdays, booked through Secretary. Professional: M.W. Passmore (0827 251478). Secretary: A.O. Rammell (0827 251139).

TAMWORTH. **Tamworth Municipal Golf Club,** Eagle Drive, Amington, Tamworth B77 4EG (Tamworth (0827) 53858). *Location:* Junction 10 M42 direction – Amington, Tamworth, signposted. Parkland course. 18 holes, 6083 metres. S.S.S. 72. Practice area. *Green Fees:* information not provided. *Eating facilities:* bar and catering all week. *Visitors:* welcome every day, no restrictions. *Society Meetings:* welcome. Professional/Manager: Barry Jones (0827 53850).

UTTOXETER. **Uttoxeter Golf Club,** Woodgate Farm, Wood Lane, Uttoxeter ST14 7LZ (Uttoxeter (0889) 565108). *Location:* quarter of a mile past racecourse, about half a mile from town centre. Undulating parkland, very picturesque scenery. 18 holes, 5468 yards. S.S.S. 68. Par 68. Practice net and putting area. *Green Fees:* £13.00 per round, £20.00 per day weekdays; £17.00 per round weekends and Bank Holidays. *Eating facilities:* by arrangement with Steward (not Mondays). *Visitors:* always welcome, but not on major competition days. *Society Meetings:* welcome (groups of four and over). Rates for visiting parties £25.00 per day including refreshments. Professional: Mr John Pearsall (0889 564884). Secretary: Mrs G. Davies (0889 566552).

WOLSTANTON. **Wolstanton Golf Club,** Dimsdale Old Hall, Hassam Parade, Wolstanton, Newcastle (Newcastle (0782) 616995). *Location:* one mile north of Newcastle, turn right off A34 (Dimsdale Parade), first right (Hassam Parade) then right again 75 yards. Flat parkland. 18 holes, 5807 yards. S.S.S. 68. *Green Fees:* weekdays £18.00, £7.00 as member's guest; weekends as member's guest only £18.00. *Eating facilities:* full catering service and bar. *Visitors:* welcome weekdays; weekends only as member's guest. *Society Meetings:* catered for by arrangement. Professional: (0782 622718). Secretary: D. Shelley (0782 622413).

Suffolk

ALDEBURGH. **Aldeburgh Golf Club,** Aldeburgh IP15 5PE (Aldeburgh (0728) 452408). *Location:* one mile from town centre on A1094. Heathland course. 18 holes, 6366 yards. S.S.S. 71; also 9 holes, 2114 yards. S.S.S. 32. *Green Fees:* weekdays £30.00 per day, £20.00 after 12 noon; weekends £36.00 per day, £25.00 after 12 noon. *Eating facilities:* available, no evening meals. *Visitors:* welcome, to play on 18 hole course must have club Handicap Certificate. No three or four balls allowed. *Society Meetings:* by arrangement. Professional: K.R. Preston (0728 453309). Secretary: R.C. Van de Velde (0728 452890).

BECCLES. **Wood Valley (Beccles) Golf Club,** The Common, Beccles NR34 9BX (Beccles (0502) 712244). *Location:* A146 Norwich, Lowestoft, River Waveney, Church Tower, Safeway. Flat heathland. 9 holes, 5558 yards, 5084 metres. S.S.S. 67. *Green Fees:* weekdays £10.00 (with member £7.00); weekends and Bank Holidays £12.00 (with member £8.00). *Eating facilities:* two bars, snacks available. Meals to order. *Visitors:* welcome, must play with member on Sundays and Bank Holidays, course closed Sunday 1.30pm-5.30pm April to September. *Society Meetings:* catered for (not weekends or Bank Holidays). Secretary: Mrs L.W. Allen (0502 712479).

BUNGAY. **Bungay and Waveney Valley Golf Club,** Outney Common, Bungay NR35 1DS (Bungay (0986) 892337). *Location:* a quarter mile from town centre and alongside A143. Flat, links-type course. 18 holes, 5950 yards. S.S.S. 68. *Green Fees:* £18.00 per day. *Eating facilities:* available except Mondays. *Visitors:* welcome weekdays, weekends with member only. *Society Meetings:* by arrangement with Secretary. Professional: N. Whyte (0986 892337). Secretary: W.J. Stevens (0986 892337).

BURY ST. EDMUNDS. **Bury St. Edmunds Golf Club,** Tut Hill, Bury St. Edmunds IP28 6LG (0284 755977). *Location:* B1106 just off A45. Flat parkland. 18 holes, 6615 yards. S.S.S. 72; 9 holes, 4664 yards. S.S.S. 63. Practice facilities. *Green Fees:* weekdays £23.00 on 18 hole course, £11.00 on 9 hole course; weekends 9 hole course Saturdays only £12.00. *Eating facilities:* available. *Visitors:* welcome Monday to Friday on both courses; Saturday on 9 hole course. *Society Meetings:* catered for. Professional: Mark Jillings (0284 755978). Secretary: John C. Sayer (0284 755979).

BURY ST. EDMUNDS. **Flempton Golf Club,** Flempton, Bury St. Edmunds IP28 6EQ (0284 728291). *Location:* follow A1101 from Bury St. Edmunds towards Mildenhall for about four miles, course on right. 9 holes, 6240 yards. S.S.S. 70. *Green Fees:* weekdays £18.50 per round of 18 holes, £24.00 per day, weekends only with member. *Eating facilities:* by arrangement. *Visitors:* not weekends or Bank Holidays. Must produce Handicap Certificate. Professional: Jamie Perks (0284 728817). Secretary: P.H. Nunn.

BURY ST. EDMUNDS. **Fornham Park Golf and Country Club,** The Street, Fornham All Saints, Bury St. Edmunds IP28 6JQ (0284 706777; Fax: 0284 706721). *Location:* two miles from Bury St. Edmunds (A45), off A1101 to Mildenhall, village of Fornham All Saints. Flat parkland, interesting water hazards. 18 holes, 6209 yards. S.S.S. 70. Practice ground and putting green. *Green Fees:* phone for details. *Eating facilities:* bar and food available all week. *Visitors:* welcome weekdays except Tuesdays pm; after 1pm weekends. *Society Meetings:* welcome by prior arrangement. Professional/General Manager: Sean Clark (0284 706777; Fax: 0284 706721).

BURY ST. EDMUNDS. **Royal Worlington and Newmarket Golf Club,** Worlington, Bury St. Edmunds IP28 8SD (Mildenhall (0638) 712216). *Location:* six miles north east of Newmarket, signposted off A11 just south of Barton Mills roundabout. 9 holes, 3105 yards. S.S.S. 70 (18 holes). Practice ground. *Green Fees:* weekdays £30.00. *Eating facilities:* lunch and tea available with prior notice; no evening meals. *Visitors:* welcome weekdays, Handicap Certificate or letter of introduction from home club required. *Society Meetings:* catered for Tuesdays or Thursdays – booking well in advance essential. Professional: M. Hawkins (0638 715224). Secretary: Colin P. Simpson (0638 712216).

COLCHESTER. **Stoke by Nayland Golf Club,** Keepers Lane, Leavenheath, Colchester CO6 4PZ (Nayland (0206) 262836). *Location:* just off A134 on B1068 towards Stoke by Nayland. Undulating parkland with water hazards. Two courses (1) Gainsborough – 18 holes, 6516 yards. S.S.S. 71. (2) Constable – 18 holes, 6544 yards. S.S.S. 71. Practice range. *Green Fees:* weekdays £28.00 (36 holes); weekends £35.00 (handicap golfers only). *Eating facilities:* full catering and bar. *Visitors:* welcome weekdays, phone call advisable; weekends after 10.30am, must produce Handicap Certificate. Squash courts and sauna also available. *Society Meetings:* welcome weekdays, book well in advance. Professional: Kevin Lovelock (0206 262769). Secretary: Jonathan Loshak (0206 262836). Manager: Allan McLundie.

FELIXSTOWE. **Felixstowe Ferry Golf Club,** Ferry Road, Felixstowe IP11 9RY (0394 283060). *Location:* near Felixstowe Ferry, one mile north of Felixstowe. Links course. 18 holes, 6308 yards. S.S.S. 70. Practice area. *Green Fees:* £20.00 per day, weekends and Bank Holidays £24.00. *Eating facilities:* diningroom and bar. *Visitors:* welcome, but advisable to check first. Two self catering flats available, free golf included in charges. *Society Meetings:* catered for Tuesdays, Wednesdays and Fridays. Professional: Ian MacPherson (0394 283975). Secretary: Ian H. Kimber (0394 286834).

FRAMLINGHAM. **Cretingham Golf Club,** Cretingham, Woodbridge IP13 7BA (0728 685275). *Location:* A1120 to Earl Soham, Cretingham Golf Club

THE GOLF GUIDE 1994

England SUFFOLK

signposted. Wooded inland course, undulating terrain. 9 holes, 4024 yards (for 18 holes). S.S.S. 62. Practice area. *Green Fees:* weekdays £7.00, £6.00 with a member; weekends and Bank Holidays £10.00, £9.00 with a member. *Eating facilities:* full bar and catering available. *Visitors:* always welcome, no handicap required, smart casual dress. Caravan park. *Society Meetings:* welcome. Professional: Colin Jenkins. Secretary: Marion Jenkins.

HAVERHILL. **Haverhill Golf Club Ltd,** Coupals Road, Haverhill CB9 7UW (0440 61951; Fax: 0440 714883). *Location:* A604 Sturmer road turn into Chalkestone Way, near railway viaduct, right into Coupals Road. Club is one mile on right. Undulating parkland with river features. 9 holes, 5707 yards. S.S.S. 68. Practice ground. *Green Fees:* weekdays £15.00; weekends and Bank Holidays £21.00. *Eating facilities:* bar. *Visitors:* welcome at all times except when first tee booked for matches and societies. *Society Meetings:* by arrangement with Secretary. Professional: Mr S.P. Mayfield (0440 712628). Secretary: Mrs J. Webster (0440 61951).

IPSWICH. **Fynn Valley Golf Club,** Witnesham, Ipswich IP6 9JA (0473 785202). *Location:* two miles due north of Ipswich on B1077. Rolling, undulating parkland along the Fynn Valley. 18 holes, 5850 yards, 5400 metres. S.S.S. 68. Par 3 9 hole course. Golf range. *Green Fees:* £7.50 9 holes, £12.00 18 holes; £15.00 per day. *Eating facilities:* bar, bar meals and restaurant or full menu. *Visitors:* welcome, members only Sunday mornings, Ladies Thursday mornings. Weekly residential courses available at all levels. *Society Meetings:* welcome weekdays. Professional: Robin Mann (Tel & Fax: 0473 785463). Secretary: Merryn Tyrrell (0473 785267; Fax: 0473 785632).

IPSWICH. **Hintlesham Hall Golf Club,** Hintlesham, Ipswich IP8 3NS (0473 87761). *Location:* four miles west of Ipswich on the A1071 to Sudbury. Parkland, championship standard – Architect: Martin Hawtree. 18 holes, 6630 yards. S.S.S. 72. Full practice facilities. *Green Fees:* weekdays £26.00. *Eating facilities:* full catering facilities. *Visitors:* please telephone for tee off times. Accommodation available at Hintlesham Hall Hotel. *Society Meetings:* telephone enquiries welcome. We have a growing national reputation for the organisation of golf days. Professional: Alastair Spink.

IPSWICH. **Ipswich Golf Club,** Purdis Heath, Bucklesham Road, Ipswich IP3 8UQ (Ipswich (0473) 727474). *Location:* three miles east of Ipswich on Bucklesham Road, A12 and A45. Heathland. 18 holes, 6405 yards. S.S.S. 71. 9 holes, 1930 yards. S.S.S. 59. *Green Fees:* 18 hole course £30.00 weekdays, £36.00 weekends per day. 9 hole course £7.50 per day, £10.00 weekends and Bank Holidays. *Eating facilities:* full catering facilities available for visitors to 18 hole course only. *Visitors:* by prior arrangement for 18 hole course, and must produce Handicap Certificate or letter of introduction. No restriction for 9 hole course. *Society Meetings:* by special reservation only and on Society terms. Professional: S.J. Whymark (0473 724017). Secretary: Brig. A.P. Wright MBE (0473 728941).

IPSWICH. **Rushmere Golf Club,** Rushmere Heath, Woodbridge Road, Ipswich IP4 5QQ (Ipswich (0473) 727109). *Location:* off A12 north from Ipswich, 300 yards signposted. Heathland course. 18 holes, 6287 yards. S.S.S. 70. Practice facilities. *Green Fees:* £18.00. *Eating facilities:* full catering available. *Visitors:* welcome except 4.30 – 5.30pm, weekends after 2.30pm. Handicap Certificate required. *Society Meetings:* welcome. Professional: N.T.J. McNeill (0473 728076). Secretary: R.W. Whiting (0473 725648).

LOWESTOFT. **Rookery Park Golf Club,** Beccles Road, Carlton Colville, Lowestoft (Lowestoft (0502) 574009). *Location:* west of Lowestoft on A146. Flat parkland. 18 holes, 6898 yards, S.S.S. 72. 9 holes par 3 course. Practice ground. *Green Fees:* weekdays £20.00; weekends £25.00. Half price when playing with a member. *Eating facilities:* full catering and two bars. *Visitors:* welcome if members of recognised golf club, please telephone before coming. *Society Meetings:* welcome. Professional: M. Elsworthy (0502 515103). Secretary: S.R. Cooper (0502 560380).

NEWMARKET. **Links Golf Club,** Cambridge Road, Newmarket CB8 0TG (Newmarket (0638) 662708). *Location:* one and a half miles south of Newmarket High Street, opposite racecourse. Relatively flat parkland. 18 holes, 6424 yards. S.S.S. 71. Two practice grounds. *Green Fees:* weekdays £24.00 weekdays, £28.00 weekends and Bank Holidays. *Eating facilities:* full service available daily. *Visitors:* current Handicap Certificate required weekdays/weekends except for members of organised golf societies. Not before

• HINTLESHAM HALL •

Hintlesham, Ipswich, Suffolk IP8 3NS
Tel (0473) 652334/652268   Fax (0473) 652463
Golf Club direct Tel (0473) 652761

Under two hours' drive from central London this superb championship standard 18 hole golf course, designed by Hawtree and Son, will delight and challenge golfers of all abilities.

The course blends harmoniously with the ancient parkland surrounding this magnificent 16th century Hall, one of the most elegant and prestigious manor house hotels in England.

Hintlesham also offers 33 luxurious bedrooms, conference facilities, clay pigeon and game shooting, trout fishing, billiards, croquet, tennis and riding.

Contact Alastair Spink for further details.

11.30am Sunday unless member's guest. *Society Meetings:* mid-week only by prior arrangement. Professional: Mr John Sharkey (Tel & Fax: 0638 662395). Secretary: Mrs T. MacGregor (0638 663000).

SOUTHWOLD. **Southwold Golf Club,** The Common, Southwold (Southwold (0502) 723234). *Location:* from A12 Blythburgh turn off on A1095 to Southwold. Flat common land with sea views. 9 holes, 6050 yards. S.S.S. 69. *Green Fees:* £14.00 per round weekdays; £18.00 weekends. *Visitors:* welcome, phone for availability. *Society Meetings:* welcome, subject to availability. Professional: B.G. Allen (0502 723790). Secretary: Mr D.F. Randall (0502 723248).

STOWMARKET. **Stowmarket Golf Club Ltd,** Lower Road, Onehouse, Stowmarket IP14 3DA (0449 736473). *Location:* on B1508 from Stowmarket to Onehouse. Parkland. 18 holes, 6101 yards. S.S.S. 69. Driving range. *Green Fees:* weekdays £19.00 per round, £24.00 per day; weekends £25.00 per round, £33.00 per day. *Eating facilities:* lunches except Monday and Tuesday, snacks all week. *Visitors:* welcome, avoid Wednesdays. Handicap Certificate required at weekends. *Society Meetings:* catered for Thursdays and Fridays only. Professional: C. S. Aldred (0449 736392). Secretary: H.P. Monkley (0449 736473).

SUDBURY. **Newton Green Golf Club,** Newton Green, Sudbury (Sudbury (0787) 377501). *Location:* on A134 east of Sudbury. Flat course. 9 holes, 5488 yards, 5022 metres. S.S.S. 67. *Green Fees:* £15.00, weekends only with member. *Eating facilities:* available. *Visitors:* welcome Monday to Friday (except Tuesday). *Society Meetings:* not more than 20 persons. Professional: K. Lovelock (0787 210910). Secretary: G. Bright (0787 377217).

THORPENESS. **Thorpeness Golf Club and Hotel,** Thorpeness, Leiston IP16 4NH (0728 452176; Fax: 0728 453868). *Location:* leave A12 at Aldeburgh turnoff. Gorse and heather inland course. 18 holes, 6241 yards. S.S.S. 71. *Green Fees:* weekdays £20.00 per round, £30.00 per day; weekends £25.00 per round, £40.00 per day. *Visitors:* welcome without reservation. Accommodation available – 22 bedrooms. *Society Meetings:* catered for. Professional: T. Pennock (0728 452524). General Manager: N. Griffin.

WOODBRIDGE. **Ufford Park Hotel, Golf and Leisure Centre,** Yarmouth Road, Ufford, Woodbridge IP12 1QW (0394 383555). *Location:* A12 northwards to A1152 to Melton. In Melton turn left at traffic lights one mile on the right hand side. Parkland course with 10 water hazards. 18 holes, 6078 yards (6335 Medal). S.S.S. 71. *Green Fees:* weekdays £12.00; weekends £18.00. *Eating facilities:* spikes bar, restaurant, bar and patio. *Visitors:* welcome anytime. Hotel, conference and banqueting. Large leisure centre and indoor swimming pool. *Society Meetings:* welcome. Golf Director: Jon Marks (0394 382836). Golf Co-ordinator: David Cotton.

WOODBRIDGE. **Waldringfield Heath Golf Club,** Newbourne Road, Waldringfield, Woodbridge IP12 4PT (0473 36 426). *Location:* three miles north of Ipswich off old A12. Flat easy walking heathland course. 18 holes, 6153 yards. S.S.S. 69. Limited practice area. *Green Fees:* weekdays £10.00 per round, £15.00 per day; weekends £12.00 per round. Special rates available by arrangement. *Eating facilities:* full service. *Visitors:* welcome weekdays, weekends after 12 noon. *Society Meetings:* welcome weekdays by arrangement. Professional: A. Dobson (0473 36 417). Secretary: L.J. McWade (0473 36 768).

WOODBRIDGE. **Woodbridge Golf Club,** Bromeswell Heath, Woodbridge IP12 2PF (01394 383212). *Location:* leave A12 at Melton Roundabout. After traffic lights, follow A1152 over level crossing, fork left at roundabout. Club is 400 yards on right. Heathland. 18 holes, 6314 yards. S.S.S. 70. 9 holes, 2243 yards. S.S.S. 62. Large practice ground. *Green Fees:* £25.00 weekdays. Societies £28.00 per round or day. *Eating facilities:* main bar, casual bar and restaurant. *Visitors:* not before 9.30am, not at weekends. Handicap Certificates mandatory. Telephone call advisable. *Society Meetings:* by prior arrangement, maximum number 36. Professional: L.A. Jones (01394 383213). Secretary: Capt L.A. Harpum RN (01394 382038).

UFFORD PARK HOTEL GOLF & LEISURE

Yarmouth Road, Ufford, Woodbridge IP12 1QW. Tel: (0394) 383555 Fax: (0394) 383582
AA ★★★   RAC ★★★   ETB 🌸🌸🌸🌸 Highly Commended   Best Western

Ideally situated, just a short drive from the region's Heritage Coastline, and the historic market town of Woodbridge. 18 hole parkland golf course. Extensive leisure facilities including: fitness studio, indoor deck level swimming pool, steam room, sauna, spa bath, solarium, creche, beautician and hair salon. Full conference facilities available for up to 150. Getaway and Golfing Breaks from £98 per person. 25 bedroomed hotel with all en-suite facilities, colour TV, trouser press, radio, telephone and tea/coffee making facilities, most rooms with balcony overlooking course. Additional self-contained accommodation is available in the golfers lodge for groups up to twenty.

England SURREY

Surrey

BAGSHOT. **Pennyhill Park Hotel and Country Club,** London Road, Bagshot GU19 5ET (0276 471774; Fax: 0276 475570). *Location:* just off A30 at Bagshot. Wooded, hilly course. 9 holes, 2000 yards. S.S.S. 64. *Green Fees:* weekdays £10.00; weekends £15.00. *Eating facilities:* on site bar and light snacks – in Hotel full à la carte restaurant. *Visitors:* welcome anytime, booking Sunday advisable. Hotel with 76 Deluxe rooms; tennis, horse riding, clay pigeon shooting, etc. *Society Meetings:* welcome anytime. Professional: lessons on request. Manager: Sharon Millen.

BANSTEAD. **Cuddington (Banstead) Golf Club Ltd,** Banstead Road, Banstead SM7 1RD (081-393 0952; Fax: 081-786 7265). *Location:* 200 yards from Banstead Railway Station. 18 holes, 6394 yards. S.S.S. 70. *Green Fees:* on application. *Visitors:* welcome with reservation. *Society Meetings:* catered for on Thursdays. Professional: J. Morgan. Secretary: D. M. Scott.

BLETCHINGLEY. **Bletchingley Golf Club,** Church Lane, Bletchingley (0883 744775). *Location:* off A25, three miles Junction 6 M25. Attractive undulating course, part wooded, sand base. 18 holes, 6510 yards. S.S.S. 71/72. Excellent practice facilities. *Green Fees:* on application. *Eating facilities:* bar, dining. *Visitors:* welcome weekdays, weekend afternoons. Handicap Certificate or competence check. *Society Meetings:* welcome. Secretary: A. Richardson (081-390 6566).

BROOKWOOD. **West Hill Golf Club,** Bagshot Road, Brookwood GU24 0BH (0483 472110). *Location:* M3, Junction 3, A322 entrance adjacent railway bridge Brookwood. Heather, heathland, wooded course. 18 holes, 6368 yards. S.S.S. 70. Practice range and net. *Green Fees:* weekdays £42.00 per day. *Eating facilities:* bar snacks available, meals including dinner by prior arrangement. *Visitors:* by arrangement through the Professional. *Society Meetings:* catered for by arrangement through the Secretary. Professional: J.C. Clements (0483 473127). Secretary: W.D. Leighton (0483 474365).

CAMBERLEY. **Camberley Heath Golf Club,** Golf Drive, Portsmouth Road, Camberley GU15 1JG (0276 23258; Fax: 0276 692505). *Location:* adjacent to Ravenswood roundabout on the A325. Heathland and pine, designed by Harry Colt – his best. 18 holes, 6337 yards. S.S.S. 70. Practice ground. *Green Fees:* weekdays £30.00 per round, Saturdays accompanied by a member, £40.00 per round. *Eating facilities:* restaurants and Teppan Yaki (Japanese cuisine). *Visitors:* welcome weekdays only. *Society Meetings:* welcome by prior arrangement weekdays only. Professional: Gary Smith (0276 27905). Secretary/General Manager: J. Greenwood (0276 23258).

CARSHALTON. **Oaks Sports Centre Ltd,** Woodmansterne Lane, Carshalton SM5 4AN (081-643 8363; Fax: 081-770 7303). *Location:* on the B2032 past Carshalton Beeches Station, Oaks Sports Centre signposted north of A2022, half way between A217 and A237. Meadowland course. 18 holes, 5975 yards. S.S.S 69. 9 holes, 1590 yards. S.S.S 28. 18 bay golf range. *Green Fees:* £9.00 18 hole, £4.25 9 hole weekdays; £11.00 18 hole, £5.20 9 hole weekends. *Eating facilities:* bar lounge, restaurant (no smoking). *Visitors:* public course, everyone welcome. Five squash courts, changing rooms. *Society Meetings:* by arrangement. Professional: Mr G.D. Horley. Secretary: Mr J. Bremer.

CHERTSEY. **Barrow Hill Golf Club,** Longcross, Chertsey KT16 0DS. *Location:* four miles west of Chertsey. 18 holes, 3090 yards. S.S.S. 53. *Green Fees:* information not provided. *Visitors:* only with a member. *Society Meetings:* not accommodated. Secretary: R.W. Routley (0932 848117).

CHERTSEY. **Laleham Golf Club,** Laleham Reach, Mixnams Lane, Chertsey KT16 8RP (Chertsey (0932) 564211). *Location:* M25 take directions to Thorpe Park, entrance opposite through Penton Park. Parkland course. 18 holes, 6203 yards. S.S.S. 70. *Green Fees:* weekdays £25.00 per round or day (£16.00 1st November – 31st March); weekends with member only. *Eating facilities:* lunches and snacks available. *Visitors:* welcome weekdays only. *Society Meetings:* catered for Mondays to Wednesdays April to October; Monday, Wednesday and Friday November to March. Professional: T. Whitton (0932 562877). Secretary: D.G. Lee (0932 564211).

CHESSINGTON. **Chessington Golf Club,** Garrison Lane, Chessington KT9 2LW (081-391 0948). *Location:* off A243, 500 yards from Chessington World of Adventure. Opposite Chessington South Station, Junction 9 M25. Flat course. 9 holes, 1530 yards, 1401 metres. S.S.S. 28. Covered floodlit driving range. *Green Fees:* weekdays £3.50; weekends and Bank Holidays £4.25 (for 9 holes). Reductions for Juniors and Senior Citizens. *Eating facilities:* public bar and food available. *Visitors:* welcome, must book for weekend mornings. Facilities open to public 8am until 10pm seven days a week. *Society Meetings:* welcome. Professional: (081-391 0948). Secretary: Tony Maxted (081-974 1705).

CHESSINGTON. **Surbiton Golf Club,** Woodstock Lane, Chessington KT9 1UG (081-398 2056; Fax: 081-339 0992). *Location:* two miles east of Esher, off A3 at Ace of Spades roundabout. Undulating parkland. 18 holes, 6211 yards. S.S.S. 70. Limited practice area. *Green Fees:* £27.00 per round, £40.50 per day. *Eating facilities:* snacks and lunches to order by reservation weekdays. *Society Meetings:* catered for Monday and Friday only. Professional: Paul Milton (081-398 6619). Secretary: G.A. Keith MBE (081-398 3101).

CHIDDINGFOLD. **Shillinglee Park Golf Club,** Chiddingfold, Godalming GU8 4TA (Haslemere (0428) 653237; Fax: 0428 644391). *Location:* off A283 near

SURREY England

Chiddingfold. Parkland. 9 holes, 5300 yards. S.S.S. 64. 6 hole pitch and putt course, ideal for learners. Well equipped Pro Shop. *Green Fees:* weekdays £7.50 for 9 holes, £10.00 for 18; weekends £7.50 for 9 holes, £13.00 for 18 holes. Daily rate, plus Senior Citizens' and Junior rates. Season tickets and club membership available. Gradually reducing twilight green fees – the later you play the less you pay. *Eating facilities:* excellent menu from snacks to à la carte. *Visitors:* welcome at all times, advisable to book. Instruction available. *Society Meetings:* always welcome. Professional/Secretary: Roger Mace.

CHIPSTEAD. **Chipstead Golf Club Ltd,** How Lane, Coulsdon CR5 3PR (0737 551053). *Location:* by Chipstead Station (Tattenham Corner Line). Parkland. 18 holes, 5454 yards, 4351 metres. S.S.S. 67. *Green Fees:* £25.00 before 2.00pm, £20.00 after 2.00pm. *Eating facilities:* available. *Visitors:* welcome weekdays only. *Society Meetings:* catered for Thursdays. Professional: Gary Torbett (0737 554939). Secretary: S. Spencer-Skeen (0737 555781).

COBHAM. **Silvermere Golf and Leisure Complex.** Redhill Road (Cobham (0932) 866007). Individual bookings (0932) 867275). Open for the public seven days a week. Administration enquiries for Society bookings and Company days (Cobham (0932) 866007). *Location:* from junction 10, M25 take B366 to Byfleet, half a mile on right. From London take Cobham turn-off then A245 to Byfleet, half a mile on left into Redhill Road. London 25 minutes, Heathrow 15 minutes, Gatwick 25 minutes. Seven holes tight heathland, 10 holes open parkland, one hole (17th) completely over water. 18 holes, 6333 yards. S.S.S. 71. 34 bay floodlit (till 10.00pm) driving range. *Green Fees:* weekdays £16.50; weekends £21.00 bookable by telephone. Members only Saturday/Sunday mornings. Professional's Golf Superstore open seven days till 10.00pm. All top named brands stocked. Clubs may be tried on range prior to purchase. *Eating facilities:* full service from 7.00am – breakfast, lunch, snacks and dinner; bar facilities seven days a week. *Society Meetings:* welcome, £47.50 for full day including dinner. All enquiries to Secretary. Professional: Doug McClelland PGA (0932 867275). Secretary: Mrs Pauline Devereux (0932 866007).

COULSDON. **Coulsdon Court Golf Course,** Coulsdon Road, Coulsdon CR5 2LL (081-668 0414). *Location:* off M23/M25 A23 London to Brighton road. Parkland. 18 holes, 6030 yards. S.S.S. 68. *Green Fees:* information not available. *Eating facilities:* elegant restaurant offering table d'hôte and à la carte menus. Two relaxing bars with top quality bar food. *Visitors:* welcome. *Society Meetings:* welcome. Extensive banquet and conference facilities, 35 luxurious bedrooms, all en-suite. Professional: Mike Homewood (081-660 6083). General Manager: Mr MacArthur.

COULSDON. **Woodcote Park Golf Club Ltd,** Meadow Hill, Bridle Way, Coulsdon CR5 2QQ (081-660 2577). *Location:* south of Croydon, on B2030. 18 holes, 6669 yards. S.S.S. 72. *Green Fees:* information not available. *Eating facilities:* meals by arrangement, bar snacks. *Visitors:* welcome with reservation. *Society Meetings:* up to 60 catered for, by arrangement. Professional: Mr David Hudspith (081-668 1843). Secretary: Brian Dunn (Tel & Fax: 081-668 2788).

CRANLEIGH. **Fernfell Golf and Country Club,** Barhatch Lane, Cranleigh GU6 7NG (0483 268855). *Location:* Guildford A281 Horsham take Cranleigh turn-off. Interesting parkland course. 18 holes, 5599 yards. S.S.S. 67. Par 68. *Green Fees:* £20.00 per round, £30.00 per two rounds weekdays. *Eating facilities:* bar, bar snacks, banqueting facilities available. *Visitors:* welcome weekdays only. Tennis. *Society Meetings:* welcome weekdays (£45.00). Professional: Trevor Longmuir (0483 277188). Secretary: Catherine Kimberley (0483 268855; Fax: 0483 267251).

CROYDON. **Addington Court Golf Courses,** Featherbed Lane, Addington, Croydon CR0 9AA (081-657 0281-3). *Location:* two miles east of Croydon. Leave B281 at Addington Village. Undulating. Four courses – Old Championship 5577 yards, S.S.S. 67. New Falconwood 5513 yards, S.S.S. 66. Lower 9 hole course 1812 yards, S.S.S 62. 18 hole, Par 3 course. *Green Fees:* £2.50 – £12.00. *Eating facilities:* full range available. *Visitors:* golfers and non-golfers welcome. *Society Meetings:* catered for weekdays only. Professional/Managing Director: G.A. Cotton.

CROYDON. **Addington Palace Golf Club,** Gravel Hill, Addington, Croydon CR0 5BB (081-654 3061). *Location:* two miles East Croydon Station. 18 holes, 6262 yards. S.S.S. 71. *Green Fees:* weekdays £25.00. *Visitors:* welcome weekdays, weekends and Bank Holidays must be accompanied by a member. Sec-

---

FERNFELL
Golf and Country Club

Barrhatch Lane,
Cranleigh,
Surrey GU6 7NG
Telephone: (0483) 268855
Fax: (0483) 267251

A 5,599 yards Par 68 Parkland Golf Course set in beautiful Surrey countryside.

Green Fees £20 per round.

Golf Society Day from £45.

Golf Societies Welcome

Telephone: Trevor Longmuir –
Golf Professional for details 0483 277188

England SURREY

SELSDON PARK

More than just a golf course...

GOLFING BREAKS
PGA PROFESSIONALS
GOLF SHOP, GOLF TUITION
18 HOLE GOLF COURSE
LEISURE CLUB
ALL WEATHER AND GRASS TENNIS COURTS
GOLF SOCIETIES
CORPORATE LEISURE DAYS
SAM TORRANCE: SELSDON PARK TOURING PROFESSIONAL

Addington Road • Sanderstead • South Croydon • Surrey • CR2 8YA
Telephone: 081 657 8811 • Facsimile: 081 651 6171

SURREY England

retary: Mr J. Robinson. Professional: J. M. Pilkington (081-654 1786).

CROYDON. **Croham Hurst Golf Club,** Croham Road, South Croydon CR2 7HJ (081-657 2075). *Location:* midway between Croydon and Selsdon. Parkland. 18 holes, 6286 yards. S.S.S. 70. *Green Fees:* weekdays £32.00; weekends £42. *Eating facilities:* lunches, teas, snacks. *Visitors:* welcome with reservation on weekdays. *Society Meetings:* catered for booked one year ahead. Professional: E. Stillwell (081-657 7705). Secretary: Ray Passingham (081-657 5581).

CROYDON. **Selsdon Park Hotel Golf Course,** Sanderstead, South Croydon, Surrey CR2 8YA (081-657 8811; Fax: 081-651 6171). *Location:* three miles south of Croydon on A2022 Purley-West Wickham road. Parkland course, designed by J.H. Taylor. 18 holes, 6402 yards, 5854 metres. S.S.S. 71. Practice ground. *Green Fees:* weekdays £20.00 (18), £30.00 (36); Saturdays £30.00, Sundays and Bank Holidays £35.00. Reduced rates if starting after twilight. Reduced fees for resident guests. *Eating facilities:* hotel bars, restaurant and grill. *Visitors:* welcome all week with pre-bookable tee-off times, some times reserved for hotel guests. *Society Meetings:* welcome by prior arrangement. P.G.A. Professionals: Iain Naylor, Tom O'Keefe; Sam Torrance Touring Golf Professional (081-657 4129). Golf Reservations: (081-657 8811).

CROYDON. **Shirley Park Golf Club Ltd,** 194 Addiscombe Road, Croydon CR0 7LB (081-654 1143). *Location:* on A232 one and a half miles from East Croydon Station. Parkland. 18 holes, 6210 yards. S.S.S. 70. Practice area. *Green Fees:* £26.00 weekdays. *Eating facilities:* breakfast/snack lunch/dinner, two bars. *Visitors:* welcome weekdays 9.30am/12 noon and 1pm/4pm; weekends only with a member. *Society Meetings:* catered for Tuesdays and half day Mondays, Thursdays and Fridays (afternoon). Professional: Hogan Stott (081-654 8767). Secretary: Andrew Baird (081-654 1143).

DORKING. **Betchworth Park Golf Club (Dorking) Ltd,** Reigate Road, Dorking (Dorking (0306) 885929). *Location:* on A25 half a mile east of Dorking on Reigate Road. Parkland course. 18 holes, 6266 yards. S.S.S. 70. *Green Fees:* weekdays £31.00; weekends (when permitted) £43.00. *Eating facilities:* lunches to order, bar snack and bar facilities daily. *Visitors:* welcome all day Mondays and Thursdays, pm Tuesdays and Wednesdays, restricted on Fridays. Handicap Certificate required. *Society Meetings:* welcome Mondays and Thursdays. Professional: Rick Blackie (0306 884334). Secretary: D.A.S. Bradney (0306 882052).

DORKING. **Dorking Golf Club,** Chart Park, Dorking RH5 4BX (Dorking (0306) 886917). *Location:* on A24 half-a-mile south of junction with A25. Parkland/downland. 9 holes, alternative tees second 9, 5106 yards. S.S.S. 65. *Green Fees:* £16.00 per round. *Eating facilities:* full catering except Mondays. *Visitors:* weekdays only without reservation. *Society Meetings:* catered for up to 24, over this number by arrangement. Professional: P. Napier. Secretary: R. Payne.

DORKING. **Gatton Manor Hotel, Golf and Country Club,** Standon Lane, Ockley, Near Dorking RH5 5PQ (0306 627555; Fax: 0306 627713). *Location:* one and a half miles off A29 at Ockley, nine miles south of Dorking on A24, midway between London and South Coast. Undulating course, wooded and scenic water holes. 18 holes, 6903 yards. S.S.S. 72. *Green Fees:* weekdays £26.00 per day, £15.00 per round, £10.00 after 4pm; weekends £40.00 per day, £20.00 per round, £15.00 after 4pm. *Eating facilities:* bar meals and à la carte restaurant. *Visitors:* welcome every day except Sunday mornings. Hotel, conference suites. Fishing, tennis, bowls available. *Society Meetings:* welcome weekdays. Professional: Rae Sargent (0306 627557). Secretary: David G. Heath.

EAST HORSLEY. **Drift Golf Club,** The Drift, East Horsley, Leatherhead KT24 5HD (0483 284641). *Location:* the club is located just off the Drift Road which runs between Ockham Road and Forest Road, East Horsley. 18 holes, 6414 yards. S.S.S. 71. *Green Fees:* weekdays £30.00 before 1pm, £20.00 after 1pm; weekends with a member only. *Eating facilities:* restaurant/buffet service. *Visitors:* welcome Monday to Friday. *Society Meetings:* catered for. Professional: Joe Hagan (0483 284772). Secretary: Charles Rose (0483 284641).

EFFINGHAM. **Effingham Golf Club,** Guildford Road, Effingham KT24 5PZ (0372 452203; Fax: 0372 459959). *Location:* A246 between Guildford and Leatherhead. Downland course with magnificent views towards London. 18 holes, 6542 yards. S.S.S. 71. Large practice ground. *Green Fees:* weekdays £35.00. Weekends with members only. *Eating facilities:* full bar and catering (not Public Holidays). *Visitors:* welcome with reservation Monday-Friday. *Society Meetings:* Wednesdays, Thursdays, Fridays catered for. Professional: S. Hoatson (0372 452606). Secretary: Lt Col (Rtd) S.C. Manning OBE (0372 452203).

EPSOM. **Epsom Golf Club,** Longdown Lane South, Epsom KT17 4JR (Epsom (0372) 723363). *Location:* off A240 into B288, 200 yards south of Epsom Downs Station. Downland, links-type course with very fast, undulating greens. 18 holes, 6800 yards. S.S.S. 68. Practice nets and putting green. *Green Fees:* weekdays £12.00 per round, £18.00 per day; weekends £14.00

GATTON MANOR HOTEL, GOLF & COUNTRY CLUB LIMITED

Ockley
Near DORKING
Surrey RH5 5PQ
Tel: 0306 627555

An 18th century Manor House set in the heart of the Surrey countryside. Ensuite accommodation; large bar and à la carte restaurant. Fully equipped Conference Suites. 18 hole Championship length Golf Course, Practice Range. Fishing; Bowling; Tennis.

after 12 noon. *Eating facilities:* lounge and 19th hole bar with bar snack menu, two diningrooms with full catering facilities. *Visitors:* always welcome except Tuesday am (Ladies' Day), Saturday and Sunday before 12 noon (members and their guests only). *Society Meetings:* very welcome. Professional: R. Wynn (0372 721666). Secretary: Mr R.R. Fry (0372 741867).

EPSOM. **Horton Park Country Club,** Hook Road, Epsom KT19 8QG (081-393 8400; Fax: 081-394 1369). *Location:* A3, M25 (Junction 9). Parkland. 18 holes, 5197 yards. S.S.S. 65. Driving range, putting green. *Green Fees:* weekdays £11.00; weekends £13.00. *Eating facilities:* bars, restaurant and function suite. *Visitors:* welcome. *Society Meetings:* welcome except weekends. Professional: Gary Clements (081-394 2626). Secretary: Mr P.R. Hart.

ESHER. **Moore Place Golf Club,** Portsmouth Road, Esher KT10 9LN (0372 463533). *Location:* half a mile from Esher town centre on Portsmouth Road. Undulating parkland course with featured trees. 9 holes, 2093 yards. S.S.S. 32. Large practice ground. *Green Fees:* weekdays £5.00; weekends £7.00. *Eating facilities:* two bars, snack bar and restaurant. *Visitors:* unrestricted. *Society Meetings:* welcome anytime. Professional: David Allen (0372 463533). Hon. Secretary: K.J. Sargeant (081-941 1168).

ESHER. **Sandown Golf Centre,** More Lane, Esher KT10 8AN (Esher (0372) 463340). *Location:* centre of Sandown Park racecourse. Parkland. 9 holes, 2829 yards. S.S.S. 67 (18 holes). 9-hole par 3; 9-hole Pitch and Putt. Floodlit 33-bay driving range, open until 10.30pm. *Green Fees:* £5.00 weekdays; £6.50 weekends. Subject to review. *Eating facilities:* bar and coffee shop. *Visitors:* welcome. *Society Meetings:* welcome. Professional: Neal Bedward. General Manager: Peter Barriball.

ESHER. **Thames Ditton and Esher Golf Club,** Marquis of Granby, Portsmouth Road, Esher (081-398 1551). 9 holes played twice from different tees. 5190 yards. S.S.S. 65. *Green Fees:* £10.00 weekdays, £12.00 weekends. *Eating facilities:* breakfast-lunches, evening meals served on advance bookings by arrangement. *Society Meetings:* welcome except Sundays. Professional: R. Hutton. Secretary: D.I. Kaye.

FARNHAM. **Farnham Golf Club Ltd,** The Sands, Farnham GU10 1PX (0252 783163). *Location:* off A31 Crooksbury Road, Near "Jolly Farmer", signposted. Mixture of wooded parkland and heathland. 18 holes, 6313 yards. S.S.S. 70. Large practice ground. *Green Fees:* weekdays £25.00 round, £30.00 day; weekends with a member £10.00 per round, £12.00 per day. *Eating facilities:* two bars and diningroom, full high standard catering. *Visitors:* welcome weekdays with Handicap Certificate. *Society Meetings:* welcome Wednesday to Friday by prior booking. Professional: Grahame Cowlishaw (0252 782198). Secretary: James Pevalin (0252 782109).

FARNHAM. **Hankley Common Golf Club,** Tilford Road, Tilford, Farnham GU10 2DD (Frensham (025 125) 3145). *Location:* off A3, right at lights at Hindhead. Off A31 (Farnham by-pass) left at lights, three miles beyond level crossing on A287. Heathland, dry and sandy links-type course. 18 holes, 6418 yards. S.S.S. 71. Practice ground. *Green Fees:* information not provided. *Eating facilities:* full range available, restaurant and two bars. *Visitors:* welcome weekdays, weekends after 2pm only. Handicap Certificate required. *Society Meetings:* catered for on Tuesdays and Wednesdays. Professional: Peter Stow (025125 3761). Secretary: J.K.A. O'Brien (025125 2493).

GODALMING near. **Hurtmore Golf Club,** Hurtmore Road, Hurtmore, Near Godalming GU7 2RN (0483 426492; Fax: 0483 426121). *Location:* four miles south of Guildford on A3. Undulating parkland with large lakes. 18 holes, 5500 yards. S.S.S. 66. *Green Fees:* weekdays £13.00; weekends £16.00. Discounts for Senior Citizens and juniors. *Eating facilities:* bar, restaurant. *Visitors:* welcome, pay as you play course with 200 members. *Society Meetings:* welcome by prior booking. Professional: Tony White. Secretary: Neil Spinney.

GODALMING. **West Surrey Golf Club,** Enton Green, Godalming GU8 5AF (Godalming (0483) 421275). *Location:* off the A3 south of Guildford, half mile past Milford Station/crossing. Wooded parkland. 18 holes, 6259 yards, 5722 metres. S.S.S. 70. Practice ground. *Green Fees:* weekdays £23.50 and £33.50; weekends £41.00. *Eating facilities:* bar, diningroom. *Visitors:* welcome, must be member of recognised golf club and have current Handicap Certificate. *Society Meetings:* catered for by prior arrangement. Professional: J. Hoskison (0483 417278). Secretary: R.S. Fanshawe (0483 421275).

GUILDFORD. **Bramley Golf Club,** Bramley, Near Guildford GU5 0AL (0483 893042). *Location:* three miles south of Guildford on the Horsham road, A281. Parkland. 18 holes, 5990 yards. S.S.S. 67. Practice area, driving range. *Green Fees:* weekdays £25.00 per round, £30.00 per day; weekends with member only. *Eating facilities:* bar, breakfast from 8am, lunches, snacks, evening meals. *Visitors:* welcome Monday to Friday. *Society Meetings:* by prior arrangement with Secretary. Professional: Gary Peddie (0483 893685). Secretary: Ms M. Lambert (0483 892696).

GUILDFORD. **Guildford Golf Club,** High Path Road, Merrow, Guildford (Guildford (0483) 63941). Steward: (0483 31842). *Location:* from Guildford take Epsom Road (A246) turn right at the third set of traffic lights. Downland course. 18 holes, 6080 yards. S.S.S. 70. Practice area. *Green Fees:* £25.00 per round, £35.00 per day weekdays; weekends with a member only. *Eating facilities:* snacks and restaurant service. *Visitors:* welcome weekdays, with member weekends. *Society Meetings:* catered for Monday to Friday. Professional: P. G. Hollington (0483 66765). Secretary: R.E. Thomas (0483 63941).

GUILDFORD. **Puttenham Golf Club,** Guildford GU3 1AL (Guildford (0483) 810498). *Location:* Farnham and Guildford, 600 yards south of Hog's Back (A31). Wooded/heathland course. 18 holes, 6220 yards. S.S.S. 70. *Green Fees:* on application. *Visitors:* welcome weekdays only by prior arrangement. (Weekends playing with a member). *Society Meetings:* catered for Wednesdays and Thursdays. Secretary and Professional: Gary Simmons.

HINDHEAD. **Hindhead Golf Club,** Churt Road, Hindhead GU26 6HX (Hindhead (0428) 604614). *Location:* one and a half miles north of Hindhead on A287 to Farnham. The Course is played over heathland and wooded valleys. 18 holes, 6373 yards. S.S.S. 70. *Green Fees:* £35.00 per day weekdays; £42.00 weekends. *Eating facilities:* restaurant, snack bar, summer bar and members' bar. *Visitors:* welcome with Handicap Certificate, weekends by appointment. *Society Meetings:* Wednesdays and Thursdays only. Professional: Neil Ogilvy (0428 604458). General Manager: D. Browse.

KINGSTON-UPON-THAMES. **Coombe Hill Golf Club,** Golf Club Drive, off Coombe Lane West, Kingston KT2 7DG (081-942 2284). *Location:* from A3 take A238 to Kingston. Hilly and tree lined. 18 holes, 6040 yards. S.S.S. 71. *Green Fees:* weekdays £45.00. *Eating facilities:* diningroom 11.30am to 5pm, bar (varying hours). *Visitors:* weekdays only. *Society Meetings:* please contact Secretary. Professional: Craig De Foy (081-949 3713). Secretary: D.G. Seward.

KINGSTON-UPON-THAMES. **Coombe Wood Golf Club,** George Road, Kingston Hill KT2 7NS (081-942 3828). *Location:* on A307. Wooded course. 18 holes, 5296 yards, 4842 metres. S.S.S. 66. *Green Fees:* weekdays £26.00; weekends with member only. *Eating facilities:* catering all week. *Visitors:* welcome weekdays. *Society Meetings:* by arrangement Wednesday to Friday. Professional: D. Butler (081-942 6764). Secretary: T. Duncan (081-942 0388).

KINGSWOOD. **Kingswood Golf and Country Club Ltd,** Sandy Lane, Kingswood, Tadworth KT20 6NE (0737 833316; Fax: 0737 833920). *Location:* five miles south of Sutton just off A217/Junction 8 M25. 18 holes, 6855 yards. S.S.S. 73. Large practice area. *Green Fees:* weekdays £30.00 per round; weekends £42.00 per round. *Eating facilities:* full range available. *Visitors:* welcome anytime, restricted times at weekends. Squash courts, snooker tables. *Society Meetings:* catered for. Professional: Mr Martin Platts (0737 832334). Administrator: Miss Lynn Thompson (0737 832188).

LEATHERHEAD. **Leatherhead Golf Club,** Kingston Road, Leatherhead KT22 0EE (0372 843966; Fax: 0372 842241). *Location:* off Junction 9 of M25, onto A243 to Kingston. Parkland, many mature trees. 18 holes, 6157 yards. S.S.S. 71. Practice ground, putting green. *Green Fees:* weekdays £30.00 one round, £35.00 two rounds; weekends £42.50 one round afternoons only. *Eating facilities:* à la carte restaurant, cafe/brasserie and lounge bar. *Visitors:* welcome, no visitors Saturday or Sunday mornings. *Society Meetings:* welcome, from 16 to 100 by reservation. Professional: Richard Hurst (0372 843966). Secretary: W.G. Betts (0372 843966).

LEATHERHEAD. **Pachesham Golf Centre,** Oaklawn Road, Leatherhead KT22 0BT (0372 843453; Fax: 0372 844076). *Location:* half a mile outside Leatherhead on A244, quarter of a mile off Junction 9 M25. Flat parkland. 9 holes, 1756 yards. S.S.S. 56. 33 bay driving range, putting green, chipping area. *Green Fees:* weekdays £6.50 9 holes; weekends £7.50 9 holes. *Eating facilities:* fully licensed bar, restaurant. *Visitors:* welcome, bookings taken two days in advance. Must wear golf shoes. *Society Meetings:* welcome. Professional/Secretary: Phil Taylor.

LEATHERHEAD. **Tyrrells Wood Golf Club Ltd,** Leatherhead KT22 8QP (Leatherhead (0372) 376025). *Location:* south-east on A24 Leatherhead by-pass after A.A. caravan, one mile left to Headley, then 200 yards right into M25. Hillside, wooded course with glorious views. 18 holes, 6234 yards. S.S.S. 70. Small practice ground. *Green Fees:* weekdays £32.00 per round, £48.00 per day; Sunday afternoons only, £42.00. *Eating facilities:* catering by arrangement with Manager. *Visitors:* no visitors Saturday or Sunday mornings. *Society Meetings:* catered for by arrangement with Manager. Professional: Philip Taylor (0372 375200). Manager: B.C.L. Rumary (0372 376025).

LINGFIELD. **Lingfield Park Golf Club,** Racecourse Road, Lingfield Park, Lingfield RH7 6PQ (0342 834602). *Location:* A22 turn off at Blindley Heath, six miles from M25 Junction 6. Parkland/wooded. 18 holes, 6500 yards. S.S.S. 72. Driving range and practice ground. *Green Fees:* weekdays £20.00 per round, £30.00 per day; weekends no casual green fees. *Eating facilities:* snacks available all day, other catering by arrangement. *Visitors:* welcome weekdays only. Horse racing. *Society Meetings:* catered for weekdays only. Professional: C.K. Morley (0342 832659). Manager: Greer Milne.

MITCHAM. **Mitcham Golf Club,** Carshalton Road, Mitcham Junction, Mitcham CR4 4HN (081-648 1508). *Location:* Carshalton Road, aim for Mitcham Junction Station. Flat course. 18 holes, 5517 yards. S.S.S. 67. *Green Fees:* £10.00; Senior Citizens £5.50. *Eating facilities:* meals and snacks daily. *Visitors:* welcome, book via Professional. *Society Meetings:* catered for, book through Secretary. Professional: J.A. Godfrey (081-640 4280). Secretary: C.A. McGahan (081-648 4197).

NEW MALDEN. **Malden Golf Club,** Traps Lane, New Malden KT3 4RS (081-942 0654). *Location:* half a mile from Malden Station – near A3, between Wimbledon and Kingston. Parkland. 18 holes, 6295 yards. S.S.S. 70. *Green Fees:* weekdays £20.00 per round, £30.00 per day; weekends £45.00. *Eating facilities:* restaurant and bar. *Visitors:* welcome weekdays, weekends restricted. Advisable to telephone Professional. *Society Meetings:* catered for Wednesday, Thursday and Friday. Professional: Robert Hunter (081-942 6009). Secretary: Peter G. Fletcher (081-942 6433).

OTTERSHAW. **Foxhills Country Club,** Stonehill Road, Ottershaw KT16 0EL (0932 872050; Fax: 0932 874762). *Location:* Exit 11 M25, follow signs to Woking, right at roundabout, left at next roundabout, left at junction into Stonehill Road. Parkland course (Chertsey) 18 holes, 6734 yards, S.S.S. 72. Wooded course (Longcross) 18 holes, 6417 yards, S.S.S. 71. Par 3 course (9 holes). *Green Fees:* weekdays £45.00 per round, £65 per day; weekends £55.00 per round. *Eating facilities:* clubhouse restaurant (lunch only except Saturdays), Manor Restaurant (lunch and dinner, closed Sunday night, Monday and Tuesday lunch). *Visitors:* welcome from 7.30am weekdays and after 12 noon at weekends. 16 rooms; tennis, squash, gym, swimming pools. *Society Meetings:* bookings for weekdays only. Professional: Bernard Hunt MBE (0932 873961).

OXTED. **Limpsfield Chart Golf Club,** Westerham Road, Limpsfield, Oxted RH8 0SL (0883 723405). *Location:* on A25 between Westerham and Oxted. Heathland, fairly flat course. 9 holes – alternate tees for 18 holes, 5718 yards. S.S.S. 68 men, 70 ladies. *Green Fees:* weekdays £18.00, weekends £20.00 with a member only. *Eating facilities:* by prior arrangement. *Visitors:* welcome weekdays except Thursday (Ladies' Day) when only after 3.30pm. *Society Meetings:* catered for by prior arrangement. Secretary: W.G. Bannochie (0883 723405).

OXTED. **Tandridge Golf Club,** Oxted (Oxted (0883) 712274). *Location:* A25 between Godstone and Sevenoaks. 18 holes, 6260 yards. S.S.S. 70. *Green Fees:* information not provided. *Eating facilities:* full catering facilities. *Visitors:* welcome Monday, Wednesday and Thursday only. *Society Meetings:* catered for Mondays, Wednesdays and Thursdays. Professional: A. Farquhar (0883 713701). Secretary: A.S. Furmival.

PIRBRIGHT. **Goal Farm Golf Course,** Golf Road, Pirbright, Woking GU24 0PZ (0483 433183). *Location:* between Woking and Guildford, off A322. Challenging, picturesque course. 9 holes, 1273 yards. S.S.S. 48. Practice net, putting green, bunker. *Green Fees:* information not provided. *Eating facilities:* bar, light refreshments. *Visitors:* welcome, restrictions Saturday and Thursday mornings (Club Competitions) Professional: Kevin Warn. Secretary: Bruce Tapsfield.

PURLEY. **Purley Downs Golf Club,** 106 Purley Downs Road, Purley, South Croydon CR2 0RB (081-657 1231). *Location:* three miles south of Croydon, one mile east of A235. Downland (hilly). 18 holes, 6212 yards. S.S.S. 70. Practice area, nets. *Green Fees:* weekdays £28.00. Visitors are not allowed to play at weekends unless with a Full Member of the club. *Eating facilities:* diningroom, bar snacks, two bars. *Visitors:* welcome weekdays, Handicap Certificate required. *Society Meetings:* catered for Mondays and Thursdays. Professional: G. Wilson (081-651 0819). Secretary: P.C. Gallienne (081-657 8347).

REDHILL. **Redhill and Reigate Golf Club,** Clarence Lodge, Pendleton Road, Redhill (Reigate (0737) 244626). *Location:* one mile south of Reigate between A23 and A25. Well wooded course. 18 holes, 5261 yards. S.S.S. 66. Small practice area. *Green Fees:* weekdays £12.00 per round; weekends £18.00 per round. No green fees before 11.00am at weekends. No play after 2.00pm Sundays June to September. *Eating facilities:* available but very limited on Mondays. *Visitors:* welcome without reservation most days. Telephone enquiry advised weekends. *Society Meetings:* catered for by arrangement with Secretary. Professional: Barry Davies (0737 244433). Secretary: Frank R. Cole (0737 240777).

REIGATE. **Reigate Heath Golf Club,** The Clubhouse, Reigate Heath, Reigate RH2 8QR (Reigate (0737) 242610). *Location:* south of A25 on western boundary of Reigate. Heathland. 9 holes, 5554 yards. S.S.S. 67. *Green Fees:* on application. *Eating facilities:* meals by arrangement with Steward. Light lunches and snacks available except Mondays. *Visitors:* welcome weekdays, advisable to telephone before coming. *Society Meetings:* catered for Wednesdays or Thursdays. Professional: G. Gow (0737 243077). Secretary: R.J. Perkins (0737 226793).

RICHMOND. **Richmond Golf Club,** Sudbrook Park, Petersham, Richmond TW10 7AS (081-940 1463). *Location:* off A307 two miles south of Richmond, end of Sudbrook Lane. Parkland. 18 holes, 6007 yards, 6566 metres. S.S.S. 69. Practice driving range. *Green Fees:* weekdays £38.00. *Eating facilities:* lunches available Monday to Friday; teas daily. *Visitors:* welcome weekdays without reservation. *Society Meetings:* welcome Tuesdays, Thursdays and Fridays by arrangement with Secretary. Professional: Nicholas Job (081-940 7792). Secretary: R.L. Wilkins (081-940 4351).

RICHMOND. **Royal Mid-Surrey Golf Club,** Old Deer Park, Richmond TW9 2SB (081-940 1894). *Location:* in Old Deer Park off A316 at Richmond. Parkland course. Two 18 hole courses, Inner – 5544 yards, S.S.S. 67 men, 5446 yards, S.S.S. 71 ladies; Outer – 6337 yards, S.S.S. 70 men, 5755 yards, S.S.S. 73 ladies. *Green Fees:* weekdays £43.00 Summer, £30.50 Winter. *Eating facilities:* The Buttery daily, the diningroom daily except Mondays, the bar daily. *Visitors:* welcome weekdays only, accompanied by introduction from own club. *Society Meetings:* welcome by prior arrangement. Professional: D. Talbot (081-940 0459). Secretary: M.S.R. Lunt.

SUNNINGDALE. **Sunningdale Golf Club,** Ridgemount Road, Sunningdale, Ascot SL5 9RR (0344 21681; Fax: 0344 24154). *Location:* 350 yards west of station, off A30, 25 miles from London. Heathland, 36 holes, 2 courses. *Green Fees:* weekdays £80.00 day ticket. Subject to review. *Eating facilities:* diningroom and three bars. *Visitors:* require introduction from Secretary of own club on weekdays. At weekends with member only. *Society Meetings:* accepted Tuesday,

HEATHSIDE HOTEL
A217 Brighton Road, Burgh Heath, Surrey KT20 6BW
73 Bedrooms with Private Bath. Special Week-end Rates, Easy Reach of Walton Heath, Kingswood and Cuddington Golf Courses.
TELEPHONE: BURGH HEATH (0737) 353355

SURREY *England*

Wednesday, Thursday only, by arrangement. Professional: Keith Maxwell (0344 20128). Secretary: Stewart Zuill. Caddiemaster for bookings (0344 26064).

SUTTON. **Banstead Downs Golf Club,** Burdon Lane, Belmont, Sutton SM2 7DD (081-642 2284). *Location:* A217 (10 minutes from Belmont Station). 18 holes, 6190 yards. S.S.S. 69. *Green Fees:* weekdays £30.00 mornings, £20.00 afternoons. *Eating facilities:* lunches served at Club except on Mondays. *Visitors:* welcome on weekdays with letter of introduction, at weekends with member. *Society Meetings:* catered for all day Thursdays. Professional: Ian Marr (081-642 6884). Secretary/Manager: A.W. Schooling.

TADWORTH. **Walton Heath Golf Club,** Deans Lane, Walton-on-the-Hill, Tadworth KT20 7TP (Tadworth (0737) 812060). *Location:* Junction 8 M25, A217 towards London, B2032 towards Dorking, turning right hand side Deans Lane. Two 18 hole heathland courses. Old – 6883 yards, S.S.S. 73. New – 6659 yards. S.S.S. 72. Large putting green; indoor and outdoor practice facilities. *Green Fees:* £57.00 weekdays, after 11.30am £47.00. Special rates November – mid March. *Eating facilities:* restaurant and two bars. *Visitors:* welcome by previous arrangement, Handicap Certificate or letter of introduction required. *Society Meetings:* catered for by arrangement. A variety of packages available for both summer and winter. Professional: Ken MacPherson (0737 812152). Secretary: G.R. James (0737 812380).

VIRGINIA WATER. **Wentworth Club Ltd,** Wentworth Drive, Virginia Water GU25 4LS (0344 842201/2/3; Fax: 0344 842804). *Location:* 21 miles south-west of London, just off the A30 at junction with A329 to Ascot. M25 and M3 three miles. Wooded heathland. West course – 18 holes, 6945 yards, S.S.S. 74; East course – 18 holes, 6176 yards, S.S.S. 70; Edinburgh course – 18 holes, 6979 yards, S.S.S. 73; Executive course – 9 holes. Driving range. *Green Fees:* weekdays from £60 – £80 including VAT. *Eating facilities:* dining room, private rooms, bar. *Visitors:* welcome weekdays only by appointment. Accommodation available.

Society Meetings: welcome by prior arrangement. Professional: Bernard Gallacher (0344 843353). General Manager: Keith Williams (0344 842201).

WALTON-ON-THAMES. **Burhill Golf Club,** Walton-on- Thames KT12 4BL (Walton (0932) 227345). *Location:* off A3 to A245, right into Seven Hills Road and again into Burwood Road or from Walton Railway Bridge through Burwood Park. 18 holes, 6224 yards. S.S.S. 70. *Green Fees:* information not provided. Professional: Lee Johnson. Secretary: M.B. Richards.

WEST BYFLEET. **West Byfleet Golf Club,** Sheerwater Road, West Byfleet KT14 6AA (Byfleet (0932) 343433). *Location:* Junction 10 M25 onto A245 – half a mile west of West Byfleet. Flat, wooded course. 18 holes, 6211 yards. S.S.S. 70. *Green Fees:* weekdays £27.00 per round, £33.00 per day. *Eating facilities:* lunches, bar snacks, teas and evening meals available. Catering: 0932 353525. Bar 0932 352501. *Visitors:* welcome weekdays with reservation, weekends with member only. *Society Meetings:* catered for, advance bookings, minimum group size 25. Professional: David Regan (0932 346584). Secretary: D. Lee (0932 343433).

WEST CLANDON. **Clandon Regis Golf Club,** Epsom Road, West Clandon (0483 211781). Parkland, undulating with feature lakes. Course designed by David Williams. 18 holes, 6500 yards. S.S.S. 71/72. Excellent practice facilities. *Green Fees:* on application. *Eating facilities:* bar, diningroom. *Visitors:* welcome weekdays, weekend afternoons. Handicap Certificate or competence test. *Society Meetings:* welcome. Professional: S. Brady. Secretary: M. Thomas.

WEYBRIDGE. **New Zealand Golf Club,** Woodham Lane, Woodham, Addlestone KT15 3QD (Byfleet (0932) 345049). *Location:* junction Woodham Lane and Sheerwater Road on A245. 18 holes, 6012 yards. S.S.S. 69. *Green Fees:* information on request. *Eating facilities:* lunch available Tuesdays to Fridays. *Visitors:* welcome Monday to Friday with reservation. *Society Meetings:* catered for Tuesday, Wednesday, Thursday and Friday. Professional: V.R. Elvide. Secretary: Cdr J. Manley OBE RN.

Wentworth

Wentworth Club, set in glorious countryside, offers one 9 and three 18-hole golf courses, tennis, and a heated outdoor swimming pool. Complementing its prestigious sporting reputation with comfortable and friendly ambience the Club is charmingly informal. Residential golfing breaks are available.

Wentworth Club, Wentworth Drive, Virginia Water, Surrey GU25 4LS
Telephone 0344 84 2201

THE GOLF GUIDE 1994   *England* SURREY/EAST SUSSEX

WEYBRIDGE. **St. George's Hill Golf Club**, St. George's Hill, Weybridge KT13 0NL (0932 842406). *Location:* M25, Junction 10 take A3 off toward London, turn left is Byfleet, Outer estate at S.P's St. George's Hill. Hilly, Surrey heathland – well wooded with plentiful heather and rhododendron. 27 holes, 6569 yards. S.S.S. 71. *Green Fees:* information not provided. *Eating facilities:* diningroom, two bars. *Visitors:* by prior arrangement. *Society Meetings:* catered for on Wednesdays, Thursdays and Fridays by prior arrangement. Professional: A.C. Rattue (0932 843523). Secretary: M.R. Tapsell (0932 847758).

WOKING. **Hoebridge Golf Centre**, Old Woking Road, Old Woking GU22 8JH (0483 722611). Parkland with some trees. 18 holes, 6536 yards. S.S.S. 71. Par 3 course. (9 hole intermediate course). Covered driving range. *Green Fees:* Main Course £12.50; Intermediate £6.75; 18-hole Par 3 £6.00. *Eating facilities:* large dining room and bar, open all day. *Visitors:* welcome. *Society Meetings:* welcome weekdays. Professional: Tim Powell.

WOKING. **Windlemere Golf Club**, Windlesham Road, West End, Near Woking (0276 858727). *Location:* off A322. Well designed parkland course. 9 holes, 2673 yards. S.S.S. 33. Floodlit 12-bay driving range. *Green Fees:* information not provided. *Eating facilities:* bar with light menu, normal clubhouse facilities. *Visitors:* always welcome, may book up to one week in advance. Snooker, pool facilities. *Society Meetings:* welcome to book. Professionals: Dave Thomas and Alistair Kelso. Secretary: Simon Hodsdon (0276 857405).

WOKING. **Woking Golf Club**, Pond Road, Hook Heath, Woking GU22 0JZ (Woking (0483) 760053). *Location:* via Hollybank Road, just south of first road bridge over Woking/Brookwood railway. 18 holes, 6365 yards. S.S.S. 70. *Green Fees:* on application. *Eating facilities:* lunches and snacks available. *Visitors:* welcome with reservation, please telephone. *Society Meetings:* catered for. Professional: J. Thorne (0483 769582). Secretary: A.W. Riley.

WOKING. **Worplesdon Golf Club**, Heath House Road, Woking. *Location:* off A322 Guildford, Bagshot Road, Heath House Road, first left south of West Hill G.C. Wooded heathland course. 18 holes, 6440 yards. S.S.S. 71. *Green Fees:* £50.00 per day. *Eating facilities:* lunches served at club. *Visitors:* weekdays only. *Society Meetings:* by arrangement. Professional: Jim Christine (0483 473287). Secretary: Major R.E.E. Jones (0483 472277; Fax: 0483 473303).

WOLDINGHAM. **North Downs Golf Club**, Northdown Road, Woldingham, Caterham CR3 7AA (0883 653298). *Location:* Eastbourne Road roundabout at Caterham. 2 miles Woldingham road. 18 holes, 5843 yards, S.S.S. 68. *Green Fees:* enquire from Professional. *Eating facilities:* full restaurant facilities. *Visitors:* welcome with Handicap Certificate. *Society Meetings:* catered for. Professional: P. Ellis (0883 653004). Secretary: J.A.L. Smith (0883 652057).

East Sussex

BEXHILL-ON-SEA. **Cooden Beach Golf Club**, Cooden Sea Road, Bexhill-on-Sea TN39 4TR (Cooden (04243) 2040). *Location:* A259 Eastbourne to Hastings road, follow 'Cooden Beach' sign at Little Common roundabout (one mile). Seaside course, slightly undulating. 18 holes, 6450 yards. S.S.S. 71. Practice facilities. *Green Fees:* £24.00 weekdays, weekends and Bank Holidays £30.00. *Eating facilities:* catering and bar every day. *Visitors:* welcome, preferably by prior arrangement. Accommodation for five in Club's own guest house alongside 18th green. *Society Meetings:* prior booking necessary. Professional: Jeffrey Sim (04243 3938). Secretary: T.E. Hawes (04243 2040). Caterers: (04243 3936).

BEXHILL-ON-SEA. **Highwoods Golf Club**, Ellerslie Lane, Bexhill-on-Sea TN39 4LJ (0424 212625). *Location:* off A259 north west of town. Parkland, wooded course. 18 holes, 6218 yards. S.S.S. 70. *Green Fees:* information not provided. *Eating facilities:* snacks always available, lunch by prior arrangement. *Visitors:* Handicap Certificate required. Sunday mornings with member only. *Society Meetings:* welcome Thursdays by arrangement. £24.00 per play green fee plus coffee/ploughmans/evening meal £13.50 approximately per head. Professional: M. Andrews (0424 212770). Secretary: J.K. McIver (0424 212625).

BRIGHTON. **Brighton and Hove Golf Club**, Dyke Road, Brighton BN1 8YJ (Brighton (0273) 507861). *Location:* south from A23, at Patcham traffic lights turn right and right again at mini roundabout to Devil's Dyke. Downland course. 9 holes, 5722 yards. S.S.S. 68. *Green Fees:* (18 holes) weekdays £12.50; weekends and Bank Holidays £21.00. *Eating facilities:* every day except Mondays and Tuesdays. *Visitors:* welcome without reservation. *Society Meetings:* catered for. Professional: (0273 540560). Secretary: C. S. Cawkwell (0273 556482).

BRIGHTON. **Dyke Golf Club**, Dyke Road, Brighton BN1 8YJ (0273 857230). *Location:* off A23 on to A2038 on entering Brighton; follow signs to Devil's Dyke. Downland course. 18 holes, 6611 yards. S.S.S. 72. Practice fairway and putting green. *Green Fees:* weekdays £21.00 per round, £31.00 per day, after 4.30pm £10.50; weekends and Bank Holidays £31.00 per round. *Eating facilities:* full restaurant and bar available. *Visitors:* welcome with reservation, not before 12 noon Sundays. *Society Meetings:* catered for by appointment, £45.00 for full day inclusive of lunch and dinner. Professional: Mr P. Longmore (0273 857260). Secretary: Mr T.R. White (0273 857296; Fax: 0273 857078).

EAST SUSSEX *England* THE GOLF GUIDE 1994

BRIGHTON. **East Brighton Golf Club,** Roedean Road, Brighton BN2 5RA (Brighton (0273) 603989). *Location:* east end of Brighton just off A259, behind the Marina. Undulating downland course. 18 holes, 6346 yards, 5802 metres. S.S.S. 70. *Green Fees:* weekdays £21.00, weekends and Bank Holidays £30.00. *Eating facilities:* diningroom and bars, lunches and teas served. *Visitors:* welcome from 9am weekdays, after 11am weekends. *Society Meetings:* catered for weekdays (not Wednesdays) on application. Professional: W. Street (0273 603989). Secretary: K.R. Head (0273 604838).

BRIGHTON. **Hollingbury Park Golf Club,** Ditchling Road, Brighton (0273 552010). *Location:* between A23 and A27. 18 holes, 6502 yards. S.S.S. 71. *Green Fees:* weekdays £13.00 per round, £18.00 per day; weekends £15.00 per round. *Eating facilities:* full catering service seven days. *Visitors:* welcome without reservation. *Society Meetings:* catered for weekdays only. Professional: Peter Brown (0273 500086). Secretary: J. Walling.

BRIGHTON. **Pyecombe Golf Club,** Clayton Hill, Pyecombe BN4 7FF (0273 844176). *Location:* four miles north of Brighton on A273 Burgess Hill Road. Downland with magnificent views. 18 holes, 6278 yards. S.S.S. 70. Two practice areas. *Green Fees:* weekdays £15.00 per round, £18.00 per day; weekends and Bank Holidays £25.00. *Eating facilities:* catering 10.30am to 6pm every day or as booked. *Visitors:* welcome, after 9.15am weekdays, after 2pm weekends. *Society Meetings:* catered for on Mondays, Wednesdays and Thursdays. Professional: C.R. White (0273 845398). Secretary: W.M. Wise (0273 845372).

BRIGHTON. **Waterhall Golf Club,** Seddlescombe Road, off Devils Dyke Road, Brighton BN1 8YN (Brighton (0273) 508658). *Location:* three miles north of Brighton. Downland course. 18 holes, 5773 yards, 5328 metres. S.S.S. 68. Practice area. *Green Fees:* weekdays £11.00; weekends £14.00. *Eating facilities:* catering available every day except Tuesdays. *Visitors:* welcome except weekends. *Society Meetings:* catered for Tuesdays, weekends or Bank Holidays by prior arrangement with Secretary. Professional: Paul Charman-Mitchell. Secretary: Peter Verner.

CROWBOROUGH. **Crowborough Beacon Golf Club,** Beacon Road, Crowborough (Crowborough (0892) 661511). *Location:* nine miles south of Tunbridge Wells on the A26. Heathland. 18 holes, 6279 yards. S.S.S. 70. Practice ground. *Green Fees:* £22.50 per round, £34.00 per day weekdays. *Eating facilities:* available. *Visitors:* welcome after 9.30am weekdays, not allowed at weekends. *Society Meetings:* catered for. Professional: D. Newnham (0892 653877). Secretary: M.C. Swatton (0892 661511).

EAST GRINSTEAD near. **Royal Ashdown Forest Golf Club (Old Course),** Forest Row, Near East Grinstead RH18 5LR (0342 8222018/823014). *Location:* four miles south of East Grinstead; take B2110 (off A22) on Forest Row and then turn right into Chapel Lane, bear left at top of Chapel Lane. Undulating heathland/forest. 18 holes, 6477 yards. S.S.S. 71.

Play Golf in picturesque Sussex
7 Courses to choose from!

Take a break when you need it most – away from the hustle and bustle and play a few rounds of golf.
Any 2 days from 1 October 1993 until 31 December 1994. The break includes 2 days' unlimited golf with green fees paid, accommodation, a newspaper, English breakfast, a light lunch at the golf club, with a 4-course Dinner and coffee at the Hotel. Handicap Certificates required. You can play, subject to availability, at any of the following golf clubs in the area – all 18 hole –
Royal Eastbourne (6109/70); Willingdon (Eastbourne) (6049/68); Eastbourne Downs (6635/71); Hailsham (5717/68); Highwoods (Bexhill) (6218/70); Cooden Beach (Bexhill) (6450/69); Lewes (5951/69).

The Lansdowne Hotel is privately owned, licensed and with 127 bedrooms, all of which have private bath or shower en-suite. There is an attractive Regency Bar, 2 snooker rooms, 23 lock-up garages and a drying room. Premier seafront position.
The cost of your golf break from 1 October 1993 to 31 March 1994 is £142;
1 April to 31 May 1994, £144. From 1 June to 30 September 1994, £148;
1 October to 31 December 1994, prices on request.
1 December 1993 to 28 February 1994, £132. Extra days available pro-rata.

Please write or 'phone G. G. Hazell, our General Manager, for full details.

Lansdowne Hotel   AA/RAC ★★★
King Edward's Parade, Eastbourne, East Sussex BN21 4EE
Telephone: (0323) 725174   Fax: (0323) 739721

THE GOLF GUIDE 1994

England   EAST SUSSEX

Green Fees: weekdays £27.00 per round, £35.00 per day; weekends £32.00 per round, £40.00 per day. *Eating facilities:* lunch and tea (prior arrangement), bar snacks. *Visitors:* welcome but always phone beforehand. *Society Meetings:* catered for – prior reservation essential. Professional: M. Landsborough (0342 822247). Secretary: D.J. Scrivens.

EASTBOURNE. **Eastbourne Downs Golf Club,** East Dean Road, Eastbourne BN20 8ES (Eastbourne (0323) 21844). *Location:* five minutes from town centre via Old Town on A259. Downland. 18 holes, 6635 yards. S.S.S. 72. Practice area. *Green Fees:* weekdays £20.00; weekends £15.00. *Eating facilities:* food available except Monday and Tuesday, two bars. *Visitors:* welcome weekdays, after 1pm weekends. *Society Meetings:* catered for by arrangement. Professional: Terry Marshall (0323 32264). Secretary: D.J. Eldrett (0323 20827).

EASTBOURNE. **Eastbourne Golfing Park,** Lottbridge Drove, Eastbourne BN23 6QJ (0323 520400). *Location:* half a mile south of Hampden Park and one mile north of the sea. Parkland course with water on seven holes. 9 holes, 5046 yards. S.S.S. 65. 24 bay floodlit driving range. *Green Fees:* weekdays £13.00; weekends £16.00; plus cheaper 9 hole rounds, look out for specials. *Eating facilities:* all day snack bar and order by intercom from the course. *Visitors:* very welcome on a Pay As You Play basis, please book tee times. *Society Meetings:* welcome. Professional/Secretary: David Ashton.

EASTBOURNE. **Royal Eastbourne Golf Club,** Paradise Drive, Eastbourne BN20 8BP (0323 730412). *Location:* one mile from town centre via Meads Road and Compton Place Road. (a) 18 holes, 6109 yards. S.S.S. 69. (b) 9 holes, 2147 yards 2. S.S.S. 61. *Green Fees:* weekdays £20.00; weekends and Bank Holidays £25.00. *Eating facilities:* full catering. *Visitors:* welcome. Handicap Certificate required Long Course only. Cottage accommodation for four people. *Society Meetings:* catered for. Professional: Richard Wooller (Tel & Fax: 0323 736986). Secretary: P. Robins (0323 729738).

EASTBOURNE. **Willingdon Golf Club,** Southdown Road, Eastbourne BN20 9AA (Eastbourne (0323) 410983). *Location:* north of Eastbourne, one mile from station, just off A22 at traffic lights (signposted). Downland course of particular beauty. 18 holes, 6113 yards, 5589 metres. S.S.S. 69. Practice ground and nets. *Green Fees:* weekdays £24.00; Saturdays and Bank Holidays £27.00. *Eating facilities:* diningroom, lounge and casual bar. *Visitors:* welcome after 9.00am weekdays, Saturdays check for tee bookings, not Sunday mornings, check for tee bookings. *Society Meetings:* welcome – book well in advance. Professional: J. Debenham (0323 410984). Secretary: Brian Kirby (0323 410981).

FOREST ROW. **Ashdown Forest Hotel and Royal Ashdown Forest New Course,** Chapel Lane, Forest Row RH18 5BB (0342-82 4866; Fax: 0342-82 4869). *Location:* three miles south of East Grinstead on A22 in village of Forest Row. Take Tunbridge Wells road. Chapel Lane is fourth turning on right. Undulating forest and heathland course – no sand bunkers! Adjoins Royal Ashdown Forest Old Course. 18 holes, 5549 yards. S.S.S. 67. *Green Fees:* information on request. *Eating facilities:* bar snacks, restaurant, banqueting up to 100. *Visitors:* welcome seven days of the week, best to phone in advance, specific tee time can be reserved three days in advance by Access/Visa. 15 rooms available. *Society Meetings:* welcome. Professional: Martyn Landsborough (0342-82 2247). Proprietors: Mr R.L. Pratt and Mr A.J. Riddick.

HAILSHAM near. **Wellshurst Golf and Country Club,** North Street, Hellingly, Near Hailsham BN27 4EE (04353 3636; Fax: 04353 2444). *Location:* two miles north of the A22 roundabout at Hailsham on the A267. Parkland course. 18 holes, 5717 yards. S.S.S. 68. 16 bay driving range with two bunker bays. *Green Fees:* weekdays £12.00 per 18 holes; weekends £16.00 per 18 holes, £26.00 per day. *Eating facilities:* bar and restaurant open seven days a week. *Visitors:* no restrictions, pay as you play course; advisable to book at weekends. *Society Meetings:* all welcome at any time, good rates. Professional: Mr C. Patey (04353 3456). Secretary: Mr M. Adams.

HASTINGS. **Beauport Park Golf Club** (Associated to Hastings Golf Course), Battle Road, St. Leonards on Sea TN38 0TA (Hastings (0424) 851165). *Location:* A2100 Battle to Hastings Road. Parkland, wooded, hilly course. 18 holes, 6248 yards, 5767 metres. S.S.S. 70. Driving range. *Green Fees:* weekdays £10.00; weekends £12.50. *Eating facilities:* dining room. *Visitors:* welcome at all times. *Society Meetings:* catered for weekdays. Professional: M. Barton (0424 852981). Secretary: P.S. Irwin (0424 852977).

HEATHFIELD. **Horam Park Golf Course,** Chiddingly Road, Horam, Near Heathfield TN21 0JJ (04353 3477; Fax: 04353 3677). *Location:* 13 miles north of Eastbourne, seven miles east of Uckfield. Follow signs to Heathfield and turn right onto the Eastbourne Road A267, go through Horam village, club on right hand side. A delightful parkland course with wooded areas and several lakes and ponds. 9 holes (18 tees), 5864 yards. S.S.S. 69. Floodlit driving range, practice ground, par 3 9-hole course. *Green Fees:* £8.50 for 9 holes, £12.50 for unlimited play. *Eating facilities:* restaurant and bar facilities open all day seven days a week, also spike bar. *Visitors:* all facilities

THE CHEQUERS INN HOTEL
(15th century), The Square, Forest Row, East Sussex

The Chequers Inn

Privately owned 25 bedroom hotel with all rooms en-suite. The hotel stands within the vicinity of 6 Golf Courses and 2 are available with concessions on Green Fees via the hotel.

Prices are available on request. Please telephone (0342) 823333.

EAST SUSSEX   *England*   THE GOLF GUIDE 1994

at Horam Park are open to the general public with no restrictions, everybody welcome. *Society Meetings:* welcome seven days per week, special cheap rates from January/March every year. Golf and food £23.00 per person April onwards. Professional: Mr Liam Greasley. Secretary: Mrs Carole Johnson.

HOVE. **West Hove Golf Club,** Church Farm, Hangleton Valley, Hove BN3 8AN (Brighton (0273) 413411). *Location:* A27 Brighton bypass, second exit going east to Worthing from London Road A23. Downland course overlooking the sea. 18 holes, 6201 yards. S.S.S. 70. Practice range. *Green Fees:* £15.00 weekdays; £20.00 weekends. After 4.30pm in summer £8.00. *Eating facilities:* catering and bar. *Visitors:* welcome at all times. *Society Meetings:* welcome at all times; 36 holes, lunch and evening meal £40.00. Professional: D. Mills (0273 413494). Secretary: Nicholas G. Hill (0273 419738; Fax: 0273 439988).

LEWES. **Lewes Golf Club,** Chapel Hill, Lewes BN7 2BB (Lewes (0273) 473245). *Location:* A27 – A22. Undulating downland with panoramic views. 18 holes, 6204 yards. S.S.S. 70. Practice area. *Green Fees:* £15.50 weekdays; £26.00 weekends. *Eating facilities:* full catering. *Visitors:* welcome without reservation. *Society Meetings:* catered for by prior arrangement. Professional: Paul Dobson (0273 483823). Secretary: R.B.M. Moore (0273 483474).

NEWHAVEN. **Peacehaven Golf Club,** The Clubhouse, Brighton Road, Newhaven BN9 9UH (0273 514049). *Location:* one mile from Newhaven on the right hand side of A259 towards Brighton. Downland course, short but challenging. 9 holes, 5305 yards. S.S.S. 66. *Green Fees:* weekdays £12.00; weekends £16.00. *Eating facilities:* snacks (other catering by prior booking). *Visitors:* welcome except Saturday and Sunday mornings. *Society Meetings:* catered for up to 20. Professional: G. Williams. Secretary: A.A. Kemsley (0273 512571).

ROTHERFIELD. **Dewlands Manor Golf Course,** Rotherfield TN6 3JN. *Location:* three-quarters of a mile south of village of Rotherfield, just off B2101. Challenging undulating course on second highest point of Sussex. Fine bent and fescue greens. 9 holes, 3186 yards (18 – 6372 yards). Par 72. *Green Fees:* information not provided. *Eating facilities:* bar lunches/snacks on request. *Visitors:* welcome at all times by appointment. Handicap not required. Dress and etiquette a prerequisite. *Society Meetings:* Company Days a speciality. Professional: Nick Godin ETPD. Course Directors: Russell and Anna Page (0892 852266).

RYE. **Rye Golf Course,** Camber, Rye (Rye (0797) 225241). *Location:* A259 from Rye, take Camber road to coast. Seaside links. 18 holes, 6310 yards. S.S.S. 71.

9 holes, 6141 yards. S.S.S. 71. *Green Fees:* information not provided. *Eating facilities:* lunch and tea only, but not Tuesdays. Bars. *Visitors:* welcome, only playing with a member or on introduction by a member. *Society Meetings:* very limited. Professional: Peter Marsh (0797 225218). Secretary: Commander J.M. Bradley (0797 225241).

SEAFORD. **Seaford Golf Club,** East Blatchington, Seaford BN25 2JD (Seaford (0323) 892442). *Location:* turn inland at War Memorial in Seaford, follow the road for one and a quarter miles. Downland course. 18 holes, 6233 yards, 5700 metres. S.S.S. 70. Practice ground. *Green Fees:* weekdays £30.00 (£24.00 after 12 noon, £14.00 after 3pm). *Eating facilities:* diningroom for all meals and bar snacks available in the bar. *Visitors:* welcome weekdays other than Tuesdays. Telephone first. *Society Meetings:* catered for Wednesdays, Thursdays and Fridays if club members with Handicap Certificates. Residential accommodation for 18 guests. Professional: P. Stevens (0323 894160). Secretary: M.B. Hichisson (0323 892442).

SEDLESCOMBE. **Aldershaw Golf Club,** Sedlescombe TN33 0SD (0424 870898; Fax: 0424 870855). *Location:* A21 near Sedlescombe. Gently undulating parkland. 9 holes (18 tee positions), 3142 yards. S.S.S. 71. Driving range. *Green Fees:* £8.50 9 holes, £12.50 18 holes. Reduced rates for Senior Citizens and Juniors. *Eating facilities:* bar and restaurant facilities available all day seven days a week. *Visitors:* welcome, no restrictions. *Society Meetings:* welcome. Special rates golf and food all day £21.00 per person. Reduced rates January/March. Professional: Mr Ian Pearson. Secretary: Mrs Carole Johnson.

UCKFIELD. **East Sussex National Golf Club,** Little Horsted, Uckfield TN22 5ES (0825 880088; Fax: 0825 880066). *Location:* off the A22 Eastbourne road following the Uckfield by-pass, 30 minutes from Gatwick. American style, wooded, bent grasses. Two courses; 1: 18 holes, 7138 yards. S.S.S. 74 Championship; 2: 18 holes, 7154 yards. S.S.S. 74 Championship. 3 hole teaching academy, driving range. *Green Fees:* April to November: £65.00 per round, £85.00 per day weekdays; weekends £75.00 per round, £95.00 per day. November to March: £50.00 per day. Special rates on request. *Eating facilities:* full restaurant facilities. *Visitors:* welcome anytime booking six months in advance. Luxury country house hotel accommodation. *Society Meetings:* booking allowed one year in advance. Director of Golf: Mr Greg Dukart. C E O: Hon. John Sinclair.

UCKFIELD. **Piltdown Golf Club,** Piltdown, Uckfield TN22 3XB (0825 722033). *Location:* one mile west of Maresfield off A272, signposted Isfield. Undulating gorse and heather. 18 holes, 6070 yards. S.S.S. 69.

DALE HILL GOLF HOTEL

Set amidst a stunning parkland course, Dale Hill offers golfers a warm welcome. Green Fees £20/£25. Society Days £45, Executive Days £60. Bed, Breakfast and all day golf £60 p.p.p.n. Enjoy a wealth of activities at this fine new golfing hotel.

Ticehurst, Wadhurst TN5 7DQ. Tel: (0580) 200112

See our colour advertisement on page 32.

Practice ground, putting green. *Green Fees:* any day round or day £27.50. County cards £18.00 per round. *Eating facilities:* bar, full catering – please telephone to book. *Visitors:* welcome but must bring Handicap Certificate or letter of introduction from own club Secretary. Some time restrictions. Jacket and tie obligatory in lounge and diningroom. Smart dress on course. *Society Meetings:* catered for by prior arrangement Mondays, Wednesdays and Fridays only. Professional: John Amos (0825 722389). Secretary: J.C. Duncan (0825 722033).

WADHURST. **Dale Hill Golf Club,** Ticehurst, Wadhurst TN5 7DQ (0580 200113). *Location:* on B2087, one mile off A21, 50 miles south of London. 16 miles north of Hastings. Wood/parkland course. 18 holes, men 6063 yards (ladies 5221). S.S.S. 69 (ladies 70). Practice area and green, indoor practice area. *Green Fees:* information not provided. *Eating facilities:* breakfast and dinner to order, lunches and snacks always available. *Visitors:* welcome with reservation, handicap players only at weekends. 27 room luxury hotel with leisure centre. *Society Meetings:* catered for by prior arrangement. Professional: Ian Connelly (Director of Golf) (0580 201090). Secretary: L.E. Irvine (0580 200112).

West Sussex

ALBOURNE. **Singing Hills Golf Course Ltd.,** Albourne BN6 9AJ (0273 835353; Fax: 0273 835444). *Location:* on the B2117 between Hurstpierpoint and Shaves Thatch. 27 holes (two courses). S.S.S. 70. 15 bay practice range. *Green Fees:* weekdays £20.00; weekends £25.00. £2 voucher to use in bar/restaurant included in above prices. *Eating facilities:* The Pavilion Restaurant offering catering all day, large bar. *Visitors:* welcome, not before 9.00am weekends. *Society Meetings:* welcome. Professional: Kyle Kelsall. Club Director: Derek T. Howe.

ANGMERING. **Ham Manor Golf Club Ltd,** Angmering BN16 4JE (0903 783288). *Location:* on A259 between Worthing and Littlehampton. 18 holes, 6216 yards. S.S.S. 70. *Green Fees:* on application. *Eating facilities:* lunches served at club except on Mondays. *Visitors:* welcome with reservation. Handicap Certificate required. *Society Meetings:* catered for weekdays only. Professional: Simon Buckley. Secretary: P.H. Saubergue.

BOGNOR REGIS. **Bognor Regis Golf Club,** Downview Road, Felpham, Bognor Regis PO22 8JD (Bognor Regis (0243) 865867). *Location:* turn north at traffic lights on A259 at Felpham village. Flat parkland. 18 holes, 6238 yards. S.S.S. 70. Practice area. *Green Fees:* £25.00 weekdays, £30.00 weekends and Bank Holidays. *Eating facilities:* bar snacks available most days. *Visitors:* welcome weekdays, weekends only with a member. Handicap Certificate required. *Society Meetings:* catered for, minimum 20. Professional: R. Day (0243 865209). Secretary: B.D. Poston (0243 821929).

CHICHESTER. **Goodwood Golf Club,** Goodwood, Chichester PO18 0PN (Chichester (0243) 774105; Fax: 0243 536650). *Location:* one mile north of roundabout at east end of Chichester Bypass (A27). Parkland, wooded. 18 holes, 6401 yards. S.S.S. 71. Practice ground, nets, putting greens. *Green Fees:* weekdays £25.00, weekends and Bank Holidays £35.00. Sussex County Cards 50% off normal charges. *Eating facilities:* full catering and bar. *Visitors:* welcome, must show Handicap Certificate. *Society Meetings:* all welcome on Wednesdays and Thursdays only. Professional: Keith MacDonald (0243 774944). Secretary: Colin Pickup (0243 774968).

CHICHESTER. **Selsey Golf Club,** Golf Links Lane, Selsey, Chichester (0243 602203/602165). *Location:* B2145, seven miles south of Chichester. Flat course. 9 holes playing 18, 5932 yards. S.S.S. 68. *Green Fees:* information not available. *Eating facilities:* lunches served at club. *Visitors:* welcome weekends and Bank Holidays only if holding a bona fide Handicap Certificate or playing with a member. *Society Meetings:* catered for weekdays only. Professional: P. Grindley. Secretary: E.C. Rackstraw (0243 602029).

CRAWLEY. **Copthorne Golf Club,** Borers Arms Road, Copthorne, Crawley RH10 3LL (Copthorne (0342) 712033). *Location:* off Exit 10 M23, one mile on A264 towards East Grinstead. Flat wooded course. 18 holes, 6505 yards. S.S.S. 71. Practice area. *Green Fees:* weekdays £25.00 per round, £33.00 per day; weekends £30.00 after 2pm. Half fees if playing with member. *Eating facilities:* catering all day, bar. *Visitors:* welcome weekdays without reservation, after 1pm weekends. *Society Meetings:* welcome with advance bookings. Professional: Joe Burrell (0342 712405). Secretary: I.J. Evans (0342 712508; Fax: 0342 717682).

CRAWLEY. **Cottesmore Country Club,** Buchan Hill, Pease Pottage, Crawley RH19 1AT (0293 528256; Fax: 0293 522819). *Location:* Junction 11 off M23 to Pease Pottage and Horsham. Undulating Sussex countryside lined by Rhododendrons and Birch, four holes over lakes. Old Course 18 holes, 6280 yards. S.S.S. 70; New Course 18 holes, 5489 yards. S.S.S. 68. *Green Fees:* Old Course – weekdays £30.00; weekends £38.00. New Course – weekdays £20.00; weekends £25.00. *Eating facilities:* three bars, two diningrooms, licensed Spike Bar with snacks. *Visitors:* welcome; only members' guests and residents may use the course at weekends before 11am. Indoor heated

WEST SUSSEX England

pool, health club, tennis, squash club; en-suite accommodation available. *Society Meetings:* catered for. Professional: Steve Laycock (0293 535399). Secretary: M.F. Rogerson (0293 529196).

CRAWLEY. **Ifield Golf and Country Club,** Rusper Road, Ifield, Crawley RH11 0LW (0293 520590; Fax: 0293 612973). *Location:* outskirts of Crawley near A23 to Gossops Green. Parkland. 18 holes, 6314 yards. S.S.S. 70. Practice area. *Green Fees:* £27.00 per round or day, £20.00 after 1pm. *Eating facilities:* all day bar and catering. *Visitors:* welcome Monday, Tuesday and Wednesday afternoons, Thursday, Friday till 3.30pm. *Society Meetings:* catered for. Professional: Jon Earl (0293 523088). Secretary: Brian Gazzard (0293 520222).

CRAWLEY. **Tilgate Forest Golf Centre,** Titmus Drive, Tilgate, Crawley RH10 5EU (0293 530103). *Location:* Crawley, five minutes from junction 11 M23. Wooded parkland. 18 holes, 6167 yards, 5643 metres. Par 72. 35 bay floodlit driving range. Par 3 course. *Green Fees:* weekdays £11.50; weekends £15.75. *Eating facilities:* restaurant and bar. *Visitors:* welcome at all times but there is a booking system in operation weekends. *Society Meetings:* welcome Mondays to Thursdays. Professional: Sean Trussell (0293 545411; Fax: 0293 523478).

EAST GRINSTEAD. **Chartham Park,** Lingfield Road, Felcourt, East Grinstead RH19 2JT (0342 870340; Fax: 0342 870719). *Location:* Lingfield Road off A22 on north side of East Grinstead. Parkland. 18 holes, 6680 yards. S.S.S. 72. Practice area, putting green. *Green Fees:* information not provided. *Eating facilities:* light snacks and refreshments available all day. *Visitors:* pre-booking required. Golf carts and trolleys can be hired. *Society Meetings:* by prior arrangement. Secretary: Lindsey Irvine.

EAST GRINSTEAD. **Holtye Golf Club,** Holtye Common, Cowden, Near Edenbridge TN8 7ED (0342 850635). *Location:* four miles east of East Grinstead on A264, seven miles west of Tunbridge Wells. Undulating forest course; alternate tees. 9 holes, 5325 yards. S.S.S. 66. Large practice ground. *Green Fees:* information not available. *Eating facilities:* available every lunchtime, some evenings in summer season. *Visitors:* welcome, restrictions Thursday and weekend mornings. *Society Meetings:* catered for. Professional: Kevin Hinton (0342 850635). Secretary: J.P. Holmes (0342 850576).

EFFINGHAM. **Effingham Park Golf Club,** Copthorne Effingham Park Hotel, Copthorne (0342 716528). *Location:* Junction 10 M23, two miles east on A264. Wooded parkland around lake. 9 holes, 1750 yards. S.S.S. 57. *Green Fees:* information not provided. *Eating facilities:* Wellingtonia Restaurant, McLaren Restaurant and Charlie's Bar. *Visitors:* not before 1pm at weekends or on a Tuesday evening. Four star Hotel on site and leisure club. *Society Meetings:* catered for on request. Professional: I. Dryden. Secretary: Mr J.O'Donovan.

HAYWARDS HEATH. **Haywards Heath Golf Club,** High Beech Lane, Haywards Heath RH16 1SL (Haywards Heath (0444) 414310). *Location:* two miles north of Haywards Heath. Parkland. 18 holes, 6204 yards. S.S.S. 70. Practice area. *Green Fees:* weekdays £22.00 per round £27.00 for more than 18 holes; weekends and Bank Holidays £30.00 per round, £35.00 for more than 18 holes. *Eating facilities:* bar and catering both available. *Visitors:* welcome, by arrangement, phone Professional and members of other golf club only. *Society Meetings:* catered for Wednesdays and Thursdays only, numbers over 20. Professional: M. Henning (0444 414866). Secretary: John Duncan (0444 414457).

HORSHAM. **Mannings Heath Golf Club,** Goldings Lane, Mannings Heath, Near Horsham RH13 6JU (Horsham (0403) 210228; Fax: 0403 270974). *Location:* three miles south-east of Horsham off A281, seven miles west of M23. Undulating wooded course with featured streams. 18 holes, 6402 yards. S.S.S. 71.

COTTESMORE
Country Club

GOLF SOCIETIES WELCOME · WEEKEND & MIDWEEK BREAKS · CONFERENCE CENTRE

Two mature 18-hole Golf Courses set in beautiful undulating Sussex countryside. A superb Health Club surrounds an indoor heated Swimming Pool. All only 10 minutes from Gatwick Airport.

Contact: The Secretary, Cottesmore Country Club, Buchan Hill, Pease Pottage, Crawley, West Sussex RH11 9AT. Telephone: (0293) 528256

CHARTHAM PARK GOLF CLUB

Picturesque parkland course designed by Neil Coles, set in 225 acres of mature park and woodland. Green Fees per round: £25 midweek, £35 weekends, Day ticket £40 midweek. Golf carts and trolleys available for hire. Societies welcome.
Lingfield Road, Felcourt, East Grinstead RH19 2JT
Tel: 0342 870340 Fax: 0342 870719

THE GOLF GUIDE 1994   *England*   WEST SUSSEX

Practice net and practice ground with putting. *Green Fees:* weekdays £27.00 per 18 holes, £36 per day; weekends £35.00 per round, £52.00 per day. *Eating facilities:* restaurant and bar – bar hours 8am-11pm. Caterers: (0403 210168). *Visitors:* welcome, must give seven days notice at most. Handicap Certificate essential. *Society Meetings:* welcome during week, full or half day. Professional: Peter Harrison. Director of Golf: J.D. Owen. Golf Administrator: J.D. Windwood. Manager: Danny Pecorelle.

HORSHAM near. **Slinfold Park Golf and Country Club**, Stane Street, Slinfold, Near Horsham RG13 7RE (0403 791154). *Location:* A29 Slinfold, near Horsham. Wooded parkland with lakes and streams. 18 holes. S.S.S. 72. 9 hole course, driving range, practice course. *Green Fees:* weekdays £18.00 18 hole course, £6.00 9 hole course; weekends £25.00 18 hole course, £8.00 9 hole course. *Eating facilities:* full restaurant and bar facilities. *Visitors:* welcome at all times. Pro shop. *Society Meetings:* all welcome. Professional: George McKay (0403 791555). Manager: Nigel Caplin.

LITTLEHAMPTON. **Littlehampton Golf Club**, 170 Rope Walk, Riverside West, Littlehampton BN17 5DL (Littlehampton (0903) 717170). *Location:* leave A259 one mile west of Littlehampton at sign. Seaside links. 18 holes, 6244 yards. S.S.S. 70. *Green Fees:* £24.00 weekdays, £30.00 weekends. *Eating facilities:* restaurant and two bars. *Visitors:* welcome weekdays, weekends after midday, but phone prior to arrival. *Society Meetings:* recognised societies only. Professional: to be appointed (0903 716369). Secretary: Keith Palmer.

MIDHURST. **Cowdray Park Golf Club**, Midhurst GU29 0BB (0730) 812088). *Location:* one mile east of Midhurst on A272. Undulating parkland. 18 holes, 6212 yards. S.S.S. 70. Two practice grounds. *Green Fees:* £20.00 weekdays, £25.00 weekends. Reduction when playing with member. *Eating facilities:* available. *Visitors:* welcome weekends only after 11.00am. *Society Meetings:* catered for except Tuesdays, Fridays, weekends and Bank Holidays. Professional: Stephen Hall. Secretary: Mrs J.D. Huggett (0730) 813599).

PULBOROUGH. **West Sussex Golf Club**, Golf Club Lane, Wiggonholt, Pulborough RH20 2EN (0798 872563). *Location:* between Storrington and Pulborough on the A283. Heathland. 18 holes, 6221 yards. S.S.S. 70. Large practice ground. *Green Fees:* on application. *Eating facilities:* lunch and tea daily, bars. *Visitors:* welcome by prior arrangement (not Fridays and weekends). No three or four balls. *Society Meetings:* catered for Wednesdays and Thursdays. Professional: T. Packham (0798 872426). Secretary: G.R. Martindale (0798 872563).

WEST CHILTINGTON. **West Chiltington Golf Club**, Broadford Bridge Road, West Chiltington RH10 2YA (0798 813574; Fax: 0798 812631). *Location:* A29 Bognor from London Road, left at Adversane village B2132 then signposted. Gently undulating parkland with spectacular views of South Downs. 18 holes, 6389 yards. S.S.S. 69. 9 holes, 1360 yard short pitch and putt course ideal for beginners. 13 bay driving range. *Green Fees:* weekdays £14.00; weekends £19.00. *Eating facilities:* bar and restaurant open all day every day. *Visitors:* always welcome, smart dress. *Society Meetings:* welcome, apply to Secretary. Professionals: Brian Barnes/Roland Tisdall (0798 812089). Secretary: S.G. Coulson.

WORTHING. **Hill Barn Golf Course**, Hill Barn Lane, Worthing BN14 9AX (Worthing (0903) 233918). *Location:* signposted on the roundabout at the top of Broadwater, Worthing on the A27. Downland course with a few trees but generally fairly open. 18 holes, 6224 yards. S.S.S. 70. Small practice area (balls not provided) and putting green. *Green Fees:* weekdays £10.50, weekends £12.50. Juniors £4.50 weekdays only. *Eating facilities:* clubhouse and bar. *Visitors:* welcome at all times. *Society Meetings:* catered for by pre-booking, 25 people minimum. Professional/Secretary: A.P. Higgins (0903 237301).

WORTHING. **Worthing Golf Club**, Links Road, Worthing BN14 9QZ (Worthing (0903) 260801; Fax: 0903 694664). *Location:* on A27 near junction with A24 (Offington Roundabout). Two downland courses. Lower course: 18 holes, 6519 yards. S.S.S. 72. Upper course: 5243 yards. S.S.S. 66. *Green Fees:* weekdays £28.00 per day, weekends and Bank Holidays £35.00 per day. *Eating facilities:* first class restaurant facilities. *Visitors:* welcome, check in advance with Secretary. No visitors during December, January and February. *Society Meetings:* catered for by arrangement. Professional: Stephen Rolley (0903 260718). Secretary: Major R.B. Carroll (0903 260801).

AA   **RAC**   *South Lodge Hotel* is proud to be associated with *Mannings Heath Golf Club*. This challenging 18 hole, par 71 course, is located less than 3 miles from the Hotel. *South Lodge Hotel* is a luxurious country house, set in 90 acres of parkland, offering fine dining, and superb meeting facilities. Corporate Golfing Events and Short Golfing Breaks can be arranged.

SOUTH LODGE HOTEL

For reservations, please contact:
SOUTH LODGE HOTEL, Brighton Road, Lower Beeding, Near Horsham, West Sussex RH13 6PS
Telephone: (0403) 891711 Fax: (0403) 891766

ExclusivE ·HOTELS·

Tyne & Wear

BIRTLEY. **Birtley Golf Club,** Birtley Lane, Birtley (091-4102207). *Location:* just off old Durham road and main A1. Parkland. 9 holes, 5500 yards. S.S.S. 67. *Green Fees:* weekdays £12.00; weekends £12.00 with members only. *Eating facilities:* bar only after 7.30pm. *Visitors:* welcome weekdays except Friday afternoons; weekends with a member only. *Society Meetings:* welcome, limited. Secretary: T. Stobbart (091-4104021).

CHOPWELL. **Garesfield Golf Club,** Chopwell NE17 7AP (Ebchester (0207) 561278). *Location:* leave A694 at Rowlands Gill, follow signposts for Chopwell, approximately three miles. Parkland, wooded. 18 holes, 6203 yards. S.S.S. 70. Practice nets and area. *Green Fees:* weekdays £13.00 per round, £15.00 per day; weekends and Bank Holidays after 4.30pm, £15.00. Reduced for parties over 20 with prior booking. *Eating facilities:* full catering and bar service. *Visitors:* welcome weekdays, weekends after 4.30pm. *Society Meetings:* by arrangement with Secretary. Secretary: J.R. Peart (0207 561309).

EAST BOLDON. **Boldon Golf Club Ltd,** Dipe Lane, East Boldon (Wearside) (091-536) 4182). *Location:* near Sunderland approximately one mile from roundabout at junction of A19 and A1 highways. Fairly flat parkland. 18 holes, 6348 yards. S.S.S. 70. *Green Fees:* information not provided. *Eating facilities:* bar snacks and restaurant. *Visitors:* welcome, not between 9am and 10am, 12.30pm and 1.30pm and 4.30pm and 6.00pm. Not before 3.30pm at weekends. *Society Meetings:* catered for. Professional: Phipps Golf (091-536 5835). Hon. Secretary: R.E. Jobes (091-536 5360).

GATESHEAD. **Heworth Golf Club,** Gingling Gate, Heworth, Gateshead (091-469 2137). *Location:* A1 (M) south east boundary of Gateshead. Flat wooded course. 18 holes, 6437 yards. S.S.S. 71. Practice area. *Green Fees:* £15.00 weekdays; £18.00 weekends. Special rates for parties over 20. *Eating facilities:* diningroom, two bars. *Visitors:* weekdays up to 4pm, no visitors Saturdays; but after 10am on Sundays. *Society Meetings:* welcome mid-week only up to 4pm. Secretary: G. Holbrow (091-469 9832).

GATESHEAD. **Ravensworth Golf Club Ltd,** Moss Heaps, Wrekenton, Gateshead NE9 7UU (091-4876014). *Location:* two miles south of Gateshead town centre. 18 holes, 5872 yards, 5374 metres. S.S.S. 68. *Green Fees:* £15.00 per round weekdays; £23.00 weekends and Bank Holidays. *Eating facilities:* meals served with reasonable notice (not Mondays). *Visitors:* welcome without reservation. *Society Meetings:* catered for. Professional: David Race. Secretary: L. Winter.

HEDDON-ON-THE-WALL. **Close House Golf Club,** Heddon-on-the-Wall, Newcastle-upon-Tyne NE15 0HT (0661 852953). *Location:* nine miles west of city on A69. Parkland/part wooded. 18 holes, 5587 yards. S.S.S. 67. Private golf club. *Eating facilities:* by arrangement with Close House Mansion (0661 852427). *Visitors:* with member only. *Society Meetings:* weekdays only by arrangement with Secretary. Secretary: J. Pearson (0661 852953).

HOUGHTON-LE-SPRING. **Houghton-le-Spring Golf Club,** Copt Hill, Houghton-le-Spring (Tyneside (091) 5841198). *Location:* off A690 Durham Road, take Houghton to Seaham road, course is situated at the top of Copt Hill bank. Testing hillside course. 18 holes, 6416 yards, 5867 metres. S.S.S. 71. *Green Fees:* information not provided. *Eating facilities:* available most days, bar open every day. *Visitors:* welcome most days but not on competition days (Sundays). *Society Meetings:* catered for by arrangement. Professional: S.J. Bradbury (091-584 7421). Secretary: N. Wales (091-528 5481).

NEWCASTLE UPON TYNE. **City of Newcastle Golf Club,** Three Mile Bridge, Gosforth, Newcastle upon Tyne NE3 2DR (091-285 1775). *Location:* B1318 three miles north of city. Flat parkland. 18 holes, 6510 yards. S.S.S. 71. *Green Fees:* weekdays £19.00; weekends and Bank Holidays £21.00. *Eating facilities:* bar, meals. *Visitors:* welcome without reservation, restricted times Fridays and no visitors on men's competition days. *Society Meetings:* very welcome. Professional/Secretary: A.J. Matthew (091-285 5481).

NEWCASTLE UPON TYNE. **Gosforth Golf Club,** Broadway East, Gosforth, Newcastle upon Tyne NE3 5ER (091-285 6710). *Location:* three miles north of Newcastle city centre, on A6127. Parkland with stream. 18 holes, 6030 yards. S.S.S. 69. *Green Fees:* information not provided. *Eating facilities:* full catering except Mondays, order in advance. *Visitors:* welcome weekdays. *Society Meetings:* catered for by arrangement with the Secretary. Not weekends or Bank Holidays. Professional: D. Race (091-285 0553). Secretary: A. Sutherland (091-285 3495).

NEWCASTLE UPON TYNE. **Newcastle United Golf Club,** 60 Ponteland Road, Cowgate, Newcastle upon Tyne NE5 3JW (Tyneside (091-2864693). *Location:* two miles west of city centre in direction of airport. Moorland. 18 holes, 6573 yards, 6010 metres. S.S.S. 71. Practice area. *Green Fees:* information not provided. *Eating facilities:* bar meals available. *Visitors:* no restrictions midweek, welcome weekends if no competitions. *Society Meetings:* welcome, book through Secretary. Professional: Brian Hall. Golf Shop: (091-2869998). Secretary: J. Simpson.

THE GOLF GUIDE 1994

England TYNE & WEAR

NEWCASTLE UPON TYNE. **Parklands Golf Club,** High Gosforth Park, Newcastle upon Tyne NE3 5HQ (091-236 4867). *Location:* just off A1 north of Newcastle, follow signs for Gosforth Park. Parkland. 18 holes, 6060 yards, 5530 metres. S.S.S. 69. 9 holes pitch and putt, 45 bay floodlit driving range. *Green Fees:* weekdays £9.00, weekends £13.00. *Eating facilities:* restaurant and bar. *Visitors:* welcome, no restrictions. *Society Meetings:* catered for. Professional: Grahame Garland (091-236 4480). Secretary: Brian Woof (091-236 4480).

NEWCASTLE UPON TYNE. **The Northumberland Golf Club Ltd,** High Gosforth Park, Newcastle upon Tyne NE3 5HT (Tyneside (091-236 2498). *Location:* off A1. 18 holes, 6629 yards. S.S.S. 72. *Green Fees:* information not provided. *Visitors:* welcome with prior reservation or introduction. *Society Meetings:* catered for except on Mondays, Wednesdays and weekends. Secretary: M.E. Anderson (091-236 2498).

NEWCASTLE UPON TYNE. **Tyneside Golf Club Ltd,** Westfield Lane, Ryton NE40 3QE (091-413 2177). *Location:* seven miles west of Newcastle upon Tyne, off A695 in Ryton Village. Parkland, hilly with water hazards. 18 holes, 6042 yards, 5522 metres. S.S.S. 69. Practice field. *Green Fees:* weekdays £16.00, weekends £25.00. *Eating facilities:* full catering. *Visitors:* bona fide golfers welcome. *Society Meetings:* by arrangement with Secretary, weekdays only. Professional: M. Gunn (091-413 1600). Secretary: J.R. Watkin (091-413 2742).

NEWCASTLE UPON TYNE. **Westerhope Golf Club,** Whorlton Grange, Westerhope, Newcastle-upon-Tyne NE5 1PP (Tyneside (091-2869125). *Location:* A69, Jingling Gate Public House. Parkland/wooded. 18 holes, 6468 yards, 5912 metres. S.S.S. 71. Two practice areas. *Green Fees:* weekdays £16.00, £8.00 with a member per round, £22.00, £12.00 with a member per day; weekends £10.00 per round with a member only. *Eating facilities:* lunches and high teas. *Visitors:* welcome weekdays, weekends and Bank Holidays with a member only. *Society Meetings:* by appointment. Professional: N. Brown (091-2860594). Secretary: J.W. Hedley (091-2867636).

NEWCASTLE-UPON-TYNE. **Hobson Municipal Golf Club,** Hobson, Burnopfield, Newcastle-upon-Tyne (0207 71605). *Location:* on main Newcastle to Consett road. Fairly flat, well designed course. 18 holes, 6582 yards, 6018 metres. S.S.S. 71. Practice area. *Green Fees:* weekdays £8.50 per round; weekends £11.00 per round. *Eating facilities:* bar, lounge and restaurant. *Visitors:* no restrictions; booking system at weekends. *Society Meetings:* by prior arrangement with Professional (all bookings). Professional: J.W. Ord (0207 71605). Secretary: R.J. Handrick (0207 570189).

NEWCASTLE-UPON-TYNE. **Whickham Golf Club,** Hollinside Park, Whickham, Newcastle-upon-Tyne NE16 5BA (091-488 7309). *Location:* five miles south west of Newcastle. Parkland. 18 holes, 6179 yards. S.S.S. 69. *Green Fees:* weekdays £20.00; weekends £25.00. *Eating facilities:* lunches, teas, evening meals available by prior order. *Visitors:* welcome without reservation. *Society Meetings:* catered for by arrangement. Professional: Brian Ridley (091-488 8591). Secretary/Manager: M.J. Musto (091-488 1576).

RYTON. **Ryton Golf Club,** Dr. Stanners, Clara Vale, Ryton NE40 3TD (091-413 3737). *Location:* off A695 eight miles west of Newcastle at Crawcrook to Clara Vale. Flat parkland, wooded, running alongside River Tyne. 18 holes, 6304 yards. S.S.S. 69. *Green Fees:* weekdays £16.00 per day; weekends £16.00 per round. *Eating facilities:* available by arrangement with Steward. *Visitors:* welcome weekdays, weekends with member or by prior arrangement. *Society Meetings:* catered for by arrangement with Secretary. Secretary: Mr F.R. Creed (091-413 3253).

SHIREMOOR. **Backworth Golf Club,** The Hall, Backworth, Shiremoor (Tyneside (091) 2681048). *Location:* from Newcastle to Shiremoor Crossroads then left for one mile. 9 holes, 5930 yards. S.S.S. 69. *Green Fees:* information not provided. *Visitors:* welcome by arrangement.

SOUTH SHIELDS. **South Shields Golf Club Ltd,** Cleadon Hills, South Shields NE34 8EG (Tyneside (091-456) 0475). *Location:* near A19 and A1 M, Cleadon Chimney prominent landmark. 18 holes, 6264 yards, 5729 metres. S.S.S. 70. *Green Fees:* weekdays £20.00; weekends and Bank Holidays £25.00. *Eating facilities:* meals available at all times, bar. *Visitors:* welcome at all times without reservation. *Society Meetings:* catered for. Professional: Gary Parsons (091-456 0110). Secretary: W.H. Loades (091-456 8942).

SOUTH SHIELDS. **Whitburn Golf Club,** Lizard Lane, South Shields NE34 7AF (Wearside (091-529) 2144). *Location:* between Sunderland and South Shields adjoining Coast Road. Parkland. 18 holes, 5773 yards, 5275 metres. S.S.S. 68. *Green Fees:* weekdays £15.00, introduced by and playing with member £8.00. Saturdays, Sundays and Bank Holidays £20.00, introduced by and playing with a member £10.00. *Eating facilities:* available. *Visitors:* welcome except on Saturday or Sunday when competitions being held and restricted Tuesdays (Ladies' Day). *Society Meetings:* catered for on weekdays by prior reservations. Professional: D. Stephenson (091-529 4210). Secretary: Mrs V. Atkinson (091-529 4944).

SUNDERLAND. **Wearside Golf Club,** Cox Green, Sunderland SR4 9JT (091-534 2518). *Location:* on south bank of River Wear, one mile west of A19. From A19 exit for A183, direction Chester-le-Street, at 200 yards turn right, signposted Offerton/Cox Green, then left at T junction, down hill over humped bridge. Parkland, bordered on north by River Wear, deep wooded gully traverses course. 18 holes, 6323 yards. S.S.S. 70. 4 holes par 3 field and separate practice tees. *Green Fees:* weekdays £24.00 per day; weekends and Bank Holidays £30.00. *Eating facilities:* full catering and bar service. *Visitors:* welcome most times, telephone Professional for information. *Society Meetings:* by advance application. Professional: Mr Steven Wynn (091-534 4269). Secretary: N. Hildrew (091-534 2518).

TYNE & WEAR/WARWICKSHIRE England   THE GOLF GUIDE 1994

Washington Moat House

INTERNATIONAL HOTELIERS

A Golfers' Haven, with an 18-hole Championship 6604 yards, Par 73 Course, a 9 hole Par 3 Course, and a 21-bay Floodlit Driving Range.
Our resident Golf Professional will be pleased to arrange either individual tuition or group clinics. Our fully stocked Golf Shop also offers hire of equipment.
A luxuriously furnished three star hotel. Leisure facilities include pool, sauna, solarium, squash, multi gym and snooker. Host to the **Sunderland Masters Pro-Am Golf Tournament.**

Stone Cellar Road, High Usworth, District 12, Washington NE37 1PH
Telex: 537143WSHMH   Tel: (091) 417 2626   Fax: (091) 415 1166

WALLSEND. **Wallsend Golf Club,** Bigges Main, Wallsend. *Location:* western boundary. Parkland. 18 holes, 6608 yards, 6043 metres. S.S.S. 72. *Green Fees:* weekdays £10.50; weekends £12.50. *Eating facilities:* meals available on request. *Visitors:* restricted weekends – not before 12.30pm April to October. *Society Meetings:* weekdays only. Professional: K. Phillips (091-262 2431). Secretary: D. Souter (091-262 1973).

WASHINGTON. **Washington Moat House Golf Club,** Stonecellar Road, Washington NE37 1PH (091-417 2626). *Location:* half a mile from A1 M junction A94. Parkland. 18 holes, 6604 yards, 6038 metres. S.S.S. 72. 21 bay floodlit driving range, 9 hole pitch and putt. *Green Fees:* weekdays £15.00; weekends £22.00. *Eating facilities:* fully licensed hotel on site.

Visitors: by arrangement. Special rates for visiting parties of over 15 mid-week. Hotel with 105-plus bedrooms. *Society Meetings:* by arrangement. Professional: Warren Marshall (091-417 8346). Secretary: Christopher Gonzalez (091-416 2609). Leisure Manager: B. Wardle.

WHITLEY BAY. **Whitley Bay Golf Club,** Claremont Road, Whitley Bay NE26 3UF (Tyneside (091-252 0180). *Location:* north side of town. Undulating parkland. 18 holes, 6617 yards. S.S.S. 72. *Green Fees:* information not provided. *Eating facilities:* available except Mondays. *Visitors:* welcome with reservation weekdays, weekends only with member. *Society Meetings:* catered for by arrangement with Secretary. Professional: W.J. Light (091-252 5688). Secretary: B. Dockar (091-252 0180).

Warwickshire

ATHERSTONE. **Atherstone Golf Club,** The Outwoods, Coleshill Road, Atherstone CV9 2RL (Atherstone (0827) 713110). *Location:* five miles north of Nuneaton and seven miles south of Tamworth. Undulating parkland. 11 holes (18 played), 6239 yards. S.S.S. 70. Practice ground. *Green Fees:* £17.00 per day/round weekdays, £8.00 with a member; Saturdays with member only. *Eating facilities:* bar and dining room. *Visitors:* welcome weekdays without reservation, Saturdays with member only, not Sundays. Ladies' Day Wednesday. 1994 is Club's Centenary Year. *Society Meetings:* on application to Secretary. Professional: (0827 713110). Secretary: V.A. Walton (0827 892568).

BRAILES. **Brailes Golf Club Ltd,** Sutton Lane, Brailes, Banbury OX15 5BB (0608 85336). *Location:* between Banbury and Shipston-on-Stour, just off the B4035. Parkland course. 18 holes, 6270 yards. S.S.S. 70. *Green Fees:* weekdays £18.00 per day; weekends

£22.00. *Eating facilities:* modern clubhouse; full restaurant facilities. *Visitors:* welcome. Large car park. *Society Meetings:* welcome subject to availability. Professional: M. Bendall (0608 85633). Manager: B.A. Hull.

KENILWORTH. **Kenilworth Golf Club Ltd,** Crew Lane, Kenilworth (0926 54038). *Location:* A429 Coventry to Kenilworth adjacent to A46 Coventry to Warwick Road. Parkland and wooded course. 18 holes, 6413 yards. S.S.S. 72. Practice ground and 9 hole Par 3 course. *Green Fees:* £26.00 weekdays; £37.00 weekends and Bank Holidays. *Eating facilities:* diningroom, bar snacks, two bars. *Visitors:* must be members of another club with official Handicap Certificate. *Society Meetings:* groups (under 20 in number) weekdays, Societies (over 20) Wednesday only. Professional: S. Yates (0926 512732). Secretary: J.H. McTavish (Tel & Fax: 0926 58517).

THE GOLF GUIDE 1994

England WARWICKSHIRE

LEAMINGTON SPA. Leamington and County Golf Club, Golf Lane, Whitnash, Leamington Spa (Leamington Spa (0926) 420298). *Location:* two miles south of town centre of Royal Leamington Spa. 18 holes, 6430 yards, 5878 metres. S.S.S. 71. *Green Fees:* weekdays £25.00 per round, £28.00 per day; weekends £37.00 per round. *Eating facilities:* luncheons, teas, evening meals and snacks. *Visitors:* welcome without reservation. *Society Meetings:* catered for. Professional: I. Grant (0926 428014). Secretary: S.M. Cooknell (0926 425961).

LEAMINGTON SPA. Newbold Comyn Golf Club, Newbold Terrace East, Leamington Spa (0926 421157). *Location:* signposted off Willes Road. Parkland, front 9 hilly, back 9 flat. 18 holes, 6315 yards. S.S.S. 70. Practice area. *Green Fees:* weekdays £6.00; weekends £8.50. *Visitors:* welcome, unrestricted. *Society Meetings:* catered for, book through Professional. Professional: D.R. Knight (0926 421157). Secretary: A.A. Pierce (0926 422660).

NORTH WARWICKSHIRE. Purley Chase Golf and Country Club "1990", Ridge Lane, Near Nuneaton CV10 0RB (Chapel End (0203) 397468). *Location:* three miles off A5 between Atherstone and Nuneaton. Slightly undulating. 18 holes, 6650 yards, 6040 metres. S.S.S. 71. Driving range. *Green Fees:* information not provided. *Eating facilities:* restaurant. *Visitors:* welcome all the time. *Society Meetings:* all welcome, special rates. Professional/Secretary: David Llewellyn (0203 395348 or 393118).

NUNEATON. Nuneaton Golf Club, Golf Drive, Whitestone, Nuneaton CV11 6QF (Nuneaton (0203 383281). *Location:* Junction 3 off M6. Wooded course. 18 holes, 6429 yards. S.S.S. 71. Practice ground. *Green Fees:* weekdays £22.00, with a member £6.00; weekends £22.00 playing with a member only. *Eating facilities:* catering available except Mondays; bar open usual hours. *Visitors:* welcome weekdays. *Society Meetings:* Wednesdays and Fridays only, must clear tee by 2pm on Fridays. Professional: (0203 340201). Secretary/Manager: G. Pinder (0203 347810).

RUGBY. Rugby Golf Club, Clifton Road, Rugby CV21 3RD (0788 542306). *Location:* one mile from Rugby town centre on the Clifton road. Parkland course. 18 holes, 5457 yards. S.S.S. 67. Practice ground. *Green Fees:* weekdays £20.00 per day; weekends with a member only. *Eating facilities:* bar and dining facilities daily except Tuesdays. *Visitors:* welcome weekdays; weekends and Bank Holidays only with a member. Ladies' Day Wednesday. Snooker room. *Society Meetings:* welcome if pre-booked. Professional: D. Sutherland (0788 575134). Secretary: R. Scott.

STRATFORD-UPON-AVON. Stratford Oaks Golf Club, Bearly Road, Snitterfield, Stratford-upon-Avon CV37 0JH (0789 731892). *Location:* from Junction 15 off M40 head south to Stratford-upon-Avon, take signpost to Snitterfield and club is between Snitterfield and Bearly. Flat parkland with lakes. 18 holes, 6100 yards. S.S.S. 69. 26 bay floodlit driving range. *Green Fees:* weekdays £12.00; weekends £15.00. Juniors half price. *Eating facilities:* available. *Visitors:* welcome, no restrictions. *Society Meetings:* catered for, no restrictions. Professional: Fraser Leek (0789 731571). Secretary: Simon Millington (0789 731571).

STRATFORD-UPON-AVON. Stratford-on-Avon Golf Club, Tiddington Road, Stratford-upon-Avon CV37 7BA (0789 297296). *Location:* half a mile from town on B4086. Flat parkland. 18 holes, 6309 yards. S.S.S. 70. Practice ground. *Green Fees:* information not provided. *Eating facilities:* full catering/bar service. *Visitors:* welcome any time subject to domestic commitments. *Society Meetings:* catered for Tuesdays and Thursdays. Professional: N.D. Powell (0789 205677). Secretary: J.H. Stanbridge (0789 205749).

Flattish parkland 18 hole course, eight holes water in play. Floodlit driving range. Lounge bar and newly opened spike bar. Restaurant. Visitors welcome at all times. Company/Society meetings welcome.

Call Lesley Newitt for further details.

Purley Chase Golf and Country Club "1990"
Ridge Lane, near Nuneaton, Warwickshire CV10 0RB. Telephone: (0203) 393118

The Crown & Cushion Hotel & Leisure Centre
Nr. Oxford, Chipping Norton OX7 5AD.

500 year old Coaching Inn, tastefully modernised to provide 40 excellent en-suite bedrooms. Some 4 Poster suites. "Old World Bar", log fires, real ale, good food. Indoor pool, Squash court, Multi gym, Solarium, (full sized snooker table subject to availability). A fully equipped modern conference centre. Hotel located in a picturesque Cotswold town midway between Oxford and Stratford-upon-Avon. Convenient for London, Heathrow Airport and M40 Motorway. Blenheim Palace, Warwick Castle, Broadway, Bourton-on-the-Water, Bibury, Stow-on-the-Wold, Shakespeare Country are all nearby. Price Busters start at just £19.50 or B&B plus full Restaurant Dinner at just £32. Lyneham Golf Club (18 hole, Tel: 0993 831841) is just 4 miles away and costs £12 midweek, £15 weekends per round. Chipping Norton Golf Club (18 hole, Tel: 0608 642783) costs £22 mid-week.

For colour brochure, freephone 0800 585251 or fax: 0608 642926   ETB ❦❦❦ Commended

WARWICKSHIRE/WEST MIDLANDS *England*

STRATFORD-UPON-AVON. **Welcombe Hotel Golf Course,** Warwick Road, Stratford-upon-Avon CV37 0NR (0789 299012). *Location:* exit M40 at Junction 15, follow signs to Stratford. Club is on A439 after five miles. Or take A439 out of town and club is on left after one mile. Undulating parkland with lakes and waterfall. 18 holes, 6217 yards. S.S.S. 70. Practice area and putting green. *Green Fees:* weekdays £32.50; weekends and Bank Holidays £40.00. *Eating facilities:* bar serving pub style food. *Visitors:* welcome subject to availability. Hotel on site, four star facilities. *Society Meetings:* weekdays by prior arrangement, rates on request. Golf Manager: (0789 295252).

WARWICK. **Warwick Golf Club,** Warwick Golf Centre, Racecourse, Warwick (0926) 494316). *Location:* off M40, from A41/A46 junction, travel half a mile towards Warwick, turn right into racecourse. Flat parkland. 9 holes, 2682 yards. S.S.S. 66. Driving range (floodlit). *Green Fees:* weekdays £3.80 per 9 holes, weekends £5.50 per 9 holes. *Eating facilities:* bar open 7-10.30pm weekdays, no catering. *Visitors:* welcome any time except Sunday mornings. Professional: (0926 491284). Secretary: R. Dunkley.

West Midlands

BIRMINGHAM. **Brandhall Golf Club,** Heron Road, Oldbury, Warley B68 8AQ (021-552 7475). *Location:* Junction 2 M5, A4123, right at traffic lights, signposted from there. Wooded course. 18 holes, 5734 yards, 5243 metres. S.S.S. 68. Practice area. *Green Fees:* information not provided. *Eating facilities:* cafe and bar. *Visitors:* welcome, no restriction except weekends. Tee reserved for club members only Saturdays 8-10am and Sundays 8-10.30am. *Society Meetings:* phone Pro Shop (021-552 2195) to book times. Professional: Garry Mercer. Secretary: D. Wood (0676 42482).

BIRMINGHAM. **Cocks Moors Woods Golf Club,** Alcester Road, Kings Heath, Birmingham B14 4ER (021-444 3584). *Location:* A435 Kings Heath, nearest motorway M42. Parkland/wooded course. 18 holes, 5820 yards. S.S.S. 68. *Green Fees:* £6.60 weekdays and weekends. *Eating facilities:* full catering and bars. *Visitors:* welcome at all times. Full range of leisure facilities within complex. *Society Meetings:* not catered for. Professional: Steve Ellis. Secretary: Glyn Williams.

BIRMINGHAM. **Edgbaston Golf Club Ltd,** Church Road, Edgbaston, Birmingham B15 3TB (021-454 1736). *Location:* from centre of city take A38 (Bristol Road). After one mile and at second traffic lights turn right into Priory Road, at end turn left into Church Road, club entrance 100 yards on left. Undulating parkland course designed by H.S. Colt. Clubhouse in historic Edgbaston Hall. 18 holes, 6118 yards, 5594 metres. S.S.S. 69. *Green Fees:* weekdays Summer £32.00, Winter £25.00; weekends Summer £42.00, Winter £35.00. Playing with a member £7.50. *Eating facilities:* fully licensed, lunches and teas daily, other meals by prior arrangement. *Visitors:* welcome. Must have Handicap Certificate. Facilities for business meetings/seminars. *Society Meetings:* welcome by arrangement with Secretary. Professional: A.H. Bownes (021-454 3226; Fax: 021-454 8295). Secretary: Andrew D. Mollett.

BIRMINGHAM. **Gay Hill Golf Club,** Hollywood Lane, Hollywood, Birmingham B47 5PP (021-430 6523). *Location:* M42 Junction 3, three miles. Flat course. 18 holes, 6532 yards. S.S.S. 71. Practice area. *Green Fees:* £28.50 weekdays. *Eating facilities:* available. *Visitors:* welcome all week; weekends by invitation only. *Society Meetings:* catered for by arrangement Thursdays. Professional: Andrew Hill (021-474 6001). Secretary: Mrs E.K. Devitt (021-430 8544).

BIRMINGHAM. **Great Barr Golf Club,** Chapel Lane, Great Barr, Birmingham B43 7BA (021-357 1232). *Location:* six miles north-west of Birmingham M6 Junction 7. 18 holes, 6545 yards. S.S.S. 72. *Green Fees:* £25.00 weekdays and weekends. *Eating facilities:* meals served, order in advance. *Visitors:* welcome weekdays, restricted at weekends. Weekends maximum handicap 18. Handicap Certificate required. *Society Meetings:* small groups catered for. Professional: (021-357 5270). Secretary: Mrs J.S. Pembridge (021-358 4376).

BIRMINGHAM. **Handsworth Golf Club,** 11 Sunningdale Close, Handsworth Wood, Birmingham B20 1NP (021-554 0599). *Location:* M5 Junction 1. A41 left at first lights, left at next set of lights, second left, second left/M6 Junction 7. A34 Birmingham Road, Old Walsall Road, Vernon Avenue, Westover Road, Craythorne Avenue. Parkland course. 18 holes, 6272 yards, 5733 metres. S.S.S 70. Large practice area and putting green. *Green Fees:* £25.00 per day, £7.00 with a member; weekends with member only, £10.00. *Eating facilities:* bar snacks to à la carte menu in restaurant. *Visitors:* welcome weekdays with Handicap Certificate. *Society Meetings:* catered for by arrangement with Secretary. Special packages available. Professional: Mr L. Bashford (021-523 3594). Secretary: P.S. Hodnett (021-554 3387).

THE GOLF GUIDE 1994 *England* WEST MIDLANDS

BIRMINGHAM. **Harborne (Church Farm) Golf Club**, Vicarage Road, Harborne, Birmingham B17 0SN (021-427 1204). *Location:* signposted from Harborne Centre. Parkland. 9 holes, 4062 yards. S.S.S. 63. *Green Fees:* 9 holes £3.30, 18 holes £6.00. *Eating facilities:* canteen serves hot and cold snacks. *Visitors:* welcome anytime. *Society Meetings:* by arrangement with the Professional. Professional: Mr Mark Hampton (021-427 1204). Secretary: Mr William Flanagan (021-426 5270).

BIRMINGHAM. **Harborne Golf Club**, 40 Tennal Road, Harborne, Birmingham B32 2JE (021-427 1728). *Location:* A4123, A456, B4124 three miles west Birmingham city centre. Undulating parkland/moorland. 18 holes, 6235 yards. S.S.S. 70. *Green Fees:* weekdays £29.00; weekends and Bank Holidays £10.00 (must play with a member). *Eating facilities:* bar and dining area daily. *Visitors:* must be members of golf club with Handicap Certificate. *Society Meetings:* Wednesday to Friday. Special rates for parties over 20 players. Professional: A. Quarterman (021-427 3512). Secretary: E.J. Humphreys (021-427 3058).

BIRMINGHAM. **Harborne Municipal Golf Club**, Vicarage Road, Harborne, Birmingham B17 0SN (021-427 1204). *Location:* A456 to Harborne Village then course is signposted. Parkland course, beware of brooks! 9 holes, 2457 yards. S.S.S. 63. *Green Fees:* 9 holes £3.30, 18 holes £6.00. *Eating facilities:* restaurant. *Visitors:* welcome anytime, must pre book. Free car parking. *Society Meetings:* welcome anytime. Professional: M.J. Hampton (021-427 1204; Fax: 021-428 3126). Secretary: W. Flanagan (021-427 1204).

BIRMINGHAM. **Hatchford Brook Golf Club**, Coventry Road, Sheldon, Birmingham B26 3PY (021-743 9821). *Location:* A45 next to Birmingham Airport, M6 Exit 4. North of M42 Junction 6. Parkland. 18 holes, 6157 yards. S.S.S. 69. Practice ground. *Green Fees:* £6.60 per round. *Eating facilities:* cafe/restaurant. *Visitors:* welcome without reservation. Professional: P. Smith. Secretary: D. Williams (0676 23383).

BIRMINGHAM. **Hilltop Public Golf Course**, Park Lane, Handsworth, Birmingham B21 8LJ (021-554 4463). *Location:* M5 exit West Bromwich, take Birmingham road first left past W.B.A. football ground. Parkland, gently sloping fairways, large greens. 18 holes, 6114 yards. S.S.S. 69. *Green Fees:* information not provided. *Eating facilities:* cafe serving drinks and hot meals. *Visitors:* welcome anytime, Municipal course. *Society Meetings:* bookings available through Professional. Professional: Kevin Highfield. Secretary: M. Adams.

BIRMINGHAM. **Kings Norton Golf Club Ltd**, Brockhill Lane, Weatheroak, Alvechurch, Birmingham B48 7ED (Wythall (0564) 822821). *Location:* M42 Junction 3, towards Birmingham. Sign on left to Weatheroak, follow for two miles, over first crossroads. Club on left hand side. Parkland. 27 holes, 7000 yards. S.S.S. 72. *Green Fees:* £27.00 per round; £29.50 per day. *Eating facilities:* available. *Visitors:* welcome weekdays only, weekends with member. *Society Meetings:* catered for weekdays only. Professional: to be appointed (0564 822822). Secretary: L.N.W. Prince (0564 826789).

BIRMINGHAM. **Maxstoke Park Golf Club**, Castle Lane, Coleshill, Birmingham B46 2RD (Coleshill (0675) 462158). *Location:* three miles north east of Coleshill on B4114, turn right for Maxstoke. Parkland with trees and lake. Water filled moat surrounding Maxstoke Castle. 18 holes, 6478 yards, 5925 metres. S.S.S. 71. Two practice areas. *Green Fees:* £22.00 per round, £32.00 per day. *Eating facilities:* restaurant and bar. *Visitors:* welcome weekdays only, weekends with member. *Society Meetings:* catered for. Professional: R.A. Young (0675 464915). Secretary: D. Haywood (0676 42082).

BIRMINGHAM near. **Rose Hill Golf Club**, Rose Hill, Rednal, Near Birmingham (021-453 7600). *Location:* M5 Exit 4 to Birmingham South. Parkland, wooded. 18 holes, 5866 yards. S.S.S. 68. *Green Fees:* £6.60 per round. *Eating facilities:* cafe in clubhouse. *Visitors:* welcome without reservation. Professional: M. March (021-453 3159). Secretary: M. Billingham.

BIRMINGHAM. **North Worcestershire Golf Club**, Frankley Beeches Road, Northfield, Birmingham B31 5LP (021-475 1026). *Location:* A38 from Birmingham City Centre. Parkland, established inland course. 18 holes, 5959 yards. S.S.S. 69. *Green Fees:* £19.50 weekdays; weekends with a member only. *Eating facilities:* catering facilities on request, normal bar opening hours. *Visitors:* welcome weekdays. *Society Meetings:* catered for Tuesdays and Thursdays. Professional: K.E. Jones (021-475 5721). Secretary: B.C. Lediard (021-475 1047).

BIRMINGHAM. **The Moseley Golf Club**, Springfield Road, Kings Heath, Birmingham B14 7DX (021-444 2115). *Location:* close by A435 (south Birmingham). Parkland. 18 holes, 6227 yards. S.S.S. 70. *Green Fees:* £30.00. *Eating facilities:* in clubhouse. *Visitors:* welcome only by prior arrangement with Secretary. *Society Meetings:* catered for by prior arrangement with the Secretary. Professional: G. Edge (021-444 2063). Secretary: R.A. Jowle (021-444 4957; Fax: 021-441 4662).

COVENTRY. **Ansty Golf Centre**, Brinklow Road, Ansty, Coventry CV7 9HZ (0203 621347). *Location:* Junction 2 M6, head towards Ansty/Shilton, turn right onto Brinklow Road. Parkland. 18 holes, 5628 yards, 5146 metres. S.S.S. 67. Driving range. *Green Fees:* weekdays £9.00; weekends £11.00. Reductions for Juniors and Senior Citizens. *Eating facilities:* full restaurant/bar. *Visitors:* always welcome. John Reay Golf Shop. *Society Meetings:* welcome. Professional: John Reay (0203 621305). Secretary: R. Challis (0203 621341).

COVENTRY. **Brandon Wood Golf Course**, Brandon Lane, Wolston, Near Coventry CV8 3GQ (0203 543133). *Location:* six miles south of Coventry off southbound carriageway A45. Parkland on banks of River Avon. 18 holes, 6610 yards, 6043 metres. S.S.S. 72. 11 bay floodlit driving range. *Green Fees:* telephone Professional for details. *Eating facilities:* bar and

WEST MIDLANDS *England*

THE GOLF GUIDE 1994

restaurant. *Visitors:* unrestricted. *Society Meetings:* phone for details. Professional/Secretary: Chris Gledhill (0203 543141; Fax: 0203 545108).

COVENTRY. **City of Coventry Golf Club,** Brandon Lane, Wolston, Near Coventry CV8 3GQ (Coventry [0203] 543133). *Location:* six miles south-east from City centre off A45. Parkland on banks of River Avon. 18 holes, 6610 yards. S.S.S. 72. Floodlit driving range. *Green Fees:* please telephone Secretary for details. *Eating facilities:* licensed bar and restaurant. *Visitors:* anytime – advance bookings available anyday up to seven days in advance on payment of one green fee – telephone bookings available 24 hours in advance. *Society Meetings:* telephone Professional for details. Professional/Secretary: C. Gledhill (0203 543141).

COVENTRY. **Coventry Golf Club,** Finham Park, Coventry CV3 6PJ (Coventry (0203) 411123). *Location:* on A444 south of A45, one mile on left. Parkland, wooded. 18 holes, 6613 yards. S.S.S. 72. Practice ground. *Green Fees:* on application. *Eating facilities:* available. *Visitors:* welcome weekdays only, without reservation. *Society Meetings:* catered for on Wednesdays and Thursdays by arrangement. Rates dependent on numbers. Professional: P. Weaver (0203 411298). Secretary: J.E. Jarman (0203 414152).

COVENTRY. **Coventry Hearsall Golf Club,** Beechwood Avenue, Coventry CV5 6DF (Coventry (0203) 675809). *Location:* off A46 south of Coventry, one mile south of city centre. 18 holes, 5983 yards. S.S.S. 69. *Green Fees:* Mondays to Fridays £23.00, weekends only as guest of a member. *Eating facilities:* full restaurant facilities. *Visitors:* welcome weekdays. *Society Meetings:* limited. Professional: (0203 713156). Secretary: W.G. Doughty (0203 713470).

COVENTRY. **Forest of Arden Hotel, Golf and Country Club,** Maxstoke Lane, Meriden, Coventry CV7 7HR (0676 22335). *Location:* three miles from Junction 6 off M42, three miles from Junction 4 off M6; very close to N.E.C. Two 18 hole parkland courses. The Arden – 6915 yards. S.S.S. 73; The Aylesford – 6525 yards. S.S.S. 71. *Green Fees:* on application. *Eating facilities:* bars and restaurant available. *Visitors:* residential visitors only at weekends before 1pm. 152 bedroom four star hotel with extensive conference and luxurious leisure facilities. *Society Meetings:* enquiries welcome. Professional: M. Tarn (0676 22118). Golf Operations Manager: Richard Woolston (0676 22335 extension 421; Fax: 0676 23711).

COVENTRY. **G.P.T. Golf Club,** Copeswood, Coventry (Coventry (0203) 451465). *Location:* three miles from centre of Coventry on A427/A428 road to Rugby, Lutterworth. 9 holes, 6002 yards. S.S.S. 69. *Green Fees:* weekdays £10.00 per round, Sundays £15.00 per round. *Visitors:* welcome except Saturdays, weekday evenings or Sunday mornings. Secretary: E. Soutar.

COVENTRY. **North Warwickshire Golf Club Ltd,** Hampton Lane, Meriden, Coventry CV7 7LL (Meriden (0676) 22259). *Location:* on B4102, one mile from Stonebridge on A45, approximately midway between Birmingham and Coventry. 9 holes, 6352 yards. S.S.S. 70. *Green Fees:* £18.00 weekdays; weekends £18.00 with member only. *Eating facilities:* full catering and bar. *Visitors:* welcome without reservation except Thursdays. *Society Meetings:* catered for by prior arrangement, limited numbers. Professional: Simon Edwin (0676 22259). Secretary: E.G. Barnes (0676 22915).

COVENTRY. **Windmill Village Hotel and Golf Club,** Birmingham Road, Allesley, Coventry CV5 9AL (0203 407241). *Location:* six miles from NEC Birmingham Airport on the A45 westbound. Parkland. 18 holes, 5131 yards. S.S.S. 67. Par 70. *Green Fees:* weekdays £9.40; weekends £10.50. *Eating facilities:* 180 seater restaurant, cellar bar, varied menus. *Visitors:* welcome, no restrictions. Leisure Club, 100 rooms all en-suite available at hotel, sauna, jaccuzi, etc. *Society Meetings:* welcome. Professional: Mr Rob Hunter. Secretary: Marc Harrhy.

DUDLEY. **Dudley Golf Club Ltd,** Turners Hill, Rowley Regis, Warley (Dudley (0384) 253719). *Location:* one mile south of Dudley town centre on Blackheath Road. 18 holes, 6000 yards. S.S.S. 68. *Green Fees:* £18.00 weekdays. *Eating facilities:* full catering facilities available. *Visitors:* welcome but only with a member at weekends. *Society Meetings:* by prior arrangement. Professional: Paul Taylor (0384 254020). Secretary: R.P. Fortune (0384 233877).

FOREST OF ARDEN HOTEL
GOLF & COUNTRY CLUB

Set above tree-fringed trout lakes, the Forest of Arden offers two golf courses and a wide range of sports and leisure facilities, including squash, tennis, indoor pool, sauna, dance studio, solarium and beauty salon. Host to the English Open 1993. The interior has a welcoming ambience with its warm terracotta tiles and spectacular circular atrium. Each bedroom has views across the lake, golf course or landscaped courtyard.

The Broadwater Restaurant offers a first class menu and there is also the Poolside Grill and several bars to relax in. Conference facilities. Parking for 300 cars.

**Forest of Arden Hotel, Golf and Country Club,
Maxstoke Lane, Meriden, Coventry, Warwickshire CV7 7HR
Telephone: 0676 22335 Fax: 0676 23711**

THE GOLF GUIDE 1994

England WEST MIDLANDS

DUDLEY. **Himley Hall Golf Centre,** Log Cabin, Himley Park, Himley Road, Dudley DY3 4DF (0902 895207). *Location:* just off A449 at Himley near Dudley. Parkland. 9 holes, 3145 yards. S.S.S. 35 for 9 holes. Practice ground, pitch and putt. *Green Fees:* weekdays £3.80 for 9 holes, £5.50 for 18 holes; weekends £4.20 for 9 holes, £6.00 for 18 holes. Juniors and Senior Citizens reduced rate. *Eating facilities:* snacks – hot and cold. *Visitors:* welcome weekdays, weekends with booking. *Society Meetings:* mid-week only. Secretary: Mr M. Harris (0384 239929).

DUDLEY near. **Swindon Golf Club,** Bridgnorth Road, Swindon, Near Dudley DY3 4PU (0902 897031). *Location:* B4176 Dudley/Bridgnorth Road, three miles from A449 at Himley. Woodland and parkland course with exceptional views. 27 holes, 9 – 1135 yards, 18 – 6042 yards. S.S.S. 18 – 69, 9 – Par 3. *Fees:* £15.00 per round, £25.00 per day weekdays; £25.00 per round, £40.00 per day weekends and Bank Holidays. *Eating facilities:* fully licensed bar and restaurant. *Visitors:* always welcome, booking not required. Buggies available. Fishing. *Society Meetings:* by arrangement weekdays only. Secretary: Rosemary Pope (0902 897031).

DUDLEY. **Sedgley Golf Centre,** Sandyfields Road, Sedgley, Dudley DY3 3DL (0902 880503). *Location:* half a mile from Sedgley town centre near Cotwall End Valley Nature Reserve, just off the A463. Undulating contours and mature trees with extensive views over surrounding countryside. 9 holes, 3147 yards. S.S.S. 71 (18 holes). Covered and floodlit golf range. *Green Fees:* £3.50 9 holes, £5.50 18 holes weekdays; £4.00 9 holes, £6.00 18 holes weekends. Reductions weekdays for Juniors and Senior Citizens. *Eating facilities:* snacks and limited bar facilities. *Visitors:* pay and play course throughout the week, booking advisable at weekends. *Society Meetings:* weekdays preferred by prior arrangement. Professional: David Fereday (0384 287996). Secretary: J.A. Cox (0902 672452).

DUDLEY. **Swindon Ridge Driving Range and Golf Club,** Bridgnorth Road, Swindon, Dudley DY3 4PU (0902 896765). *Location:* B4176 Bridgnorth/Dudley Road, three miles from Himley A449. Wooded. 18 holes, 6026 yards. S.S.S. 69. *Green Fees:* £15.00 per round weekdays; £25.00 per round weekends. *Eating facilities:* restaurant/bar. *Visitors:* welcome at all times. *Society Meetings:* welcome. Professionals: Phil Lester and Simon Price (0902 896191). Secretary: Rosemary Pope (0902 897031).

HALESOWEN. **Halesowen Golf Club,** The Leasowes, Leasowes Lane, Halesowen B62 8QF (021-550 1041). *Location:* exit Junction 3 M5, A456 (Kidderminster) two miles, Halesowen town centre one mile. Parkland course. 18 holes, 5754 yards. S.S.S. 68. *Green Fees:* weekdays £16.00 per round, £23.00 per day; weekends must play with a member. *Eating facilities:* no catering Mondays. *Visitors:* welcome Secretary. Professional: David Down (021-503 0593). Secretary: Mrs M. Bateman (021-501 3606).

REDNAL. **Lickey Hills (Municipal) Golf Club,** Old Birmingham Road, Rednal, Near Birmingham (021-453 3159). *Location:* M5 Exit 4 on city boundary. 18 holes, 5721 yards. S.S.S. 67. *Green Fees:* information not provided. *Eating facilities:* restaurant at club. *Visitors:* welcome.

SOLIHULL. **Copt Heath Golf Club,** 1220 Warwick Road, Knowle, Solihull B93 9LN (Knowle (0564) 772650). *Location:* on A4141 half a mile south of Junction 5 with M42. Flat parkland. 18 holes, 6500 yards. S.S.S. 71. Full practice facilities available. *Green Fees:* weekdays £35.00. Weekends and Public Holidays must be introduced by a member. *Eating facilities:* lunch and evening meal available except Mondays. *Visitors:* no restrictions weekdays. *Society Meetings:* by arrangement with Secretary. Professional: Brian Barton. Secretary: W. Lenton.

SOLIHULL. **Ladbrook Park Golf Club Ltd,** Poolhead Lane, Tanworth-in-Arden, Solihull B94 5ED (Tanworth-in-Arden (05644) 2220). *Location:* south from Junction 3 M42. Parkland gently undulating. 18 holes, 6427 yards. S.S.S. 71. *Green Fees:* weekdays £30.00 per day; weekends with a member only. *Eating facilities:* excellent dining. *Visitors:* welcome weekdays, prior telephone call suggested. Weekends with member only. *Society Meetings:* catered for by prior arrangement with Secretary. Professional: Steve Harrison (05644 2581). Secretary: E.W. Gadd (05644 2264).

SOLIHULL. **Olton Golf Club Ltd,** Mirfield Road, Solihull B91 1JH (021-705 1083; Fax: 021-711 2010). *Location:* approximately two miles off Junction 5 (M42), A41 – Birmingham. Parkland. 18 holes, 6229 yards, 5694 metres. S.S.S. 71. *Green Fees:* £35.00 weekdays. *Eating facilities:* by arrangement. *Visitors:* welcome weekdays only except Wednesdays. *Society Meetings:* catered for by arrangement. Professional: David Playdon (021-705 7296). Secretary: M.A. Perry (021-704 1936 am).

SOLIHULL. **Robin Hood Golf Club,** St. Bernards Road, Solihull B92 7DJ (021-706 0159). *Location:* eight miles south of Birmingham, off A41 Birmingham to Warwick road. Flat parkland. 18 holes, 6635 yards, 6067 metres. S.S.S. 72. *Green Fees:* £28.00 per round, £33.00 per day weekdays. *Eating facilities:* by prior arrangement with Steward (021-706 0159). *Visitors:* welcome weekdays only subject to limitations. Arrange with Professional. *Society Meetings:* catered for. Professional: R.S. Thompson (021-706 0806). Secretary: A.J. Hanson (021-706 0061).

SOLIHULL. **Shirley Golf Club,** Stratford Road, Monkspath, Shirley, Solihull (021-744 7024). *Location:* 8 miles from Birmingham on A34 to Stratford. 18 holes, 6411 yards. S.S.S. 71. *Green Fees:* £25.00 per round, £35.00 per day. *Eating facilities:* meals at club except Mondays. *Visitors:* welcome weekdays without reservation. *Society Meetings:* catered for weekdays. Professional: Chris Wicketts (021-745 4979). Secretary: A.J. Phillips (021-744 6001).

WEST MIDLANDS *England*

SOLIHULL. **Whitelakes Golf Club,** Tilehouse Lane, Tidbury Green, Solihull B90 1PT (0564 824414). *Location:* two miles from Shirley and three miles off the M42. To play over numerous ponds, lakes and the River Coal. 9 holes, 987 yards. S.S.S. 27. 15-bay golf range. *Green Fees:* information not available. *Eating facilities:* excellent bar and restaurant facilities. *Visitors:* welcome, no restrictions. Facilities for fishing, clay pigeon shooting, archery, swimming pool available. *Society Meetings:* catered for.

SOLIHULL. **Widney Manor Golf Club,** Saintbury Drive, Widney Manor, Solihull B91 3SZ (021-711 3646; Fax: 021-711 3884). *Location:* adjacent Widney Manor railway station. Small but interesting course. 18 holes. *Green Fees:* weekdays £7.00; weekends £10.00. *Eating facilities:* available. *Visitors:* welcome. *Society Meetings:* catered for. Professional: Tim Atkinson. Manager: Andrew Rosser.

STOURBRIDGE. **Stourbridge Golf Club,** Worcester Lane, Pedmore, Stourbridge DY8 2RB (Stourbridge (0384) 393062). *Location:* situated between Hagley and Stourbridge on Worcester road. Parkland. 18 holes, 6231 yards. S.S.S. 70. Small practice ground. *Green Fees:* weekdays £22.00; weekends with a member only £10.00. *Eating facilities:* bar meals available, lunch, dinner if booked. *Visitors:* welcome weekdays, weekends with member. *Society Meetings:* catered for mainly Tuesdays. Professional: W.H. Firkins (0384 393129). Secretary: Ms M.A. Cooper (0384 395566).

SUTTON COLDFIELD. **Boldmere Municipal Golf Club,** Monmouth Drive, Sutton Coldfield (021-354 3379). *Location:* A34, seven miles from centre of Birmingham. 18 holes, 4463 yards. S.S.S. 61. *Green Fees:* information not provided. *Eating facilities:* meals daily. *Visitors:* welcome without reservation. *Society Meetings:* not catered for. Professional: T.J. Short. Secretary: D. Dufty.

SUTTON COLDFIELD. **Moor Hall Golf Club Ltd,** Moor Hall Drive, Sutton Coldfield B75 6LN (021-308 0103). *Location:* one mile east of Sutton Coldfield, A446. Parkland. 18 holes, 6249 yards. S.S.S. 70. Practice area. *Green Fees:* £25.00 per round, £32.00 day ticket. *Eating facilities:* available weekdays except for Mondays. *Visitors:* welcome weekdays only (not Thursday mornings). *Society Meetings:* catered for Tuesdays and Wednesdays only. Professional: Alan Partridge (021-308 5106). Secretary: R.V. Wood (021-308 6130).

SUTTON COLDFIELD. **Pype Hayes Golf Club,** Eachelhurst Road, Walmley, Sutton Coldfield B76 8EP (021-351 1014). *Location:* off the A38 Kingsbury Road by M6 Junction 5, one and a half miles from Junction 9 M42. Wooded course. Smallish demanding greens as well as four demanding Par 3 holes. 18 holes, 5972 yards. S.S.S. 69. *Green Fees:* £6.90. *Eating facilities:* available. *Visitors:* welcome, booking by Link Card is now required and can be used on eight courses in Birmingham area. Professional: J. Bayliss. Secretary: K. Haden (021-779 2357).

SUTTON COLDFIELD. **Sutton Coldfield Golf Club,** Thornhill Road, Streetly, Sutton Coldfield B74 3ER (021-353 9633; Fax: 021-353 5503). *Location:* situated in Sutton Park, one mile off A452, seven miles from centre of Birmingham. Natural heathland. 18 holes, 6541 yards. S.S.S. 71. *Green Fees:* weekdays £30.00. *Eating facilities:* by arrangement with Steward. *Visitors:* welcome without reservation. Handicap Certificate required. *Society Meetings:* catered for by arrangement with Secretary. Professional: J.K. Hayes. Administrator: Mrs T. Thomas.

SUTTON COLDFIELD. **Walmley Golf Club,** Brooks Road, Wylde Green, Sutton Coldfield B72 1HR (021-373 0029). *Location:* Birmingham/Sutton Coldfield main road, turn right at Green Hill Road. Flat parkland. 18 holes, 6537 yards. S.S.S. 72. Practice area. *Green Fees:* weekdays £25.00 18 holes, £30.00 18+ holes; weekends playing with member only. *Eating facilities:* lunch and evening meals available except Mondays by arrangement with Steward. *Visitors:* welcome weekdays but should check with Professional prior to attending, weekends with a member only. *Society Meetings:* catered for weekdays except Mondays. 10% reductions on green fees if numbers are 30 or more. Professional: Mike Skerritt (021-373 7103). Secretary: J.P.G. Windsor (021-377 7272).

WALSALL. **Bloxwich Golf Club (1988) Ltd,** 136 Stafford Road, Bloxwich, Walsall WS3 3PQ (Bloxwich (0922) 405724). *Location:* off main Walsall-Cannock road (A34). Semi parkland. 18 holes, 6286 yards. S.S.S. 70. *Green Fees:* weekdays £20.00 per round, £25.00 per day. *Eating facilities:* available. *Visitors:* welcome with or without reservation except weekends and Bank Holidays. *Society Meetings:* catered for preferably midweek, reduced rates for 20 or more. Professional: Mr G. Broadbent (0922 476889). Secretary: Mrs J.N. Loveridge (0922 476593).

WALSALL. **Calderfields Golf Club Ltd,** Aldridge Road, Walsall WS4 2JS (0922 640540). *Location:* A454. Parkland, lake. 18 holes, 6700 yards, 6100 metres. S.S.S. 73. Practice hole and putting green. *Green Fees:* weekdays £12.00; weekends £16.00. *Eating facilities:* restaurant and bar. *Visitors:* always welcome. *Society Meetings:* very welcome, package deals available. Professional: Roger Griffin (0922 32243). Secretary: Mr Colin Andrew (0922 640540; Fax: 0922 38787).

— MOXHULL HALL HOTEL —

Luxury ★★★ Country House Hotel in eight acres of gardens and woodland. All rooms with bath or shower, colour television, telephone, etc.

Only one mile from international golf course at The Belfry.

HOLLY LANE, WISHAW, SUTTON COLDFIELD, WARWICKSHIRE B76 9PE Tel: 021-329 2056

WALSALL. Druids Heath Golf Club, Stonnall Road, Aldridge, Walsall WS9 8JZ (Aldridge (0922) 55595). *Location:* between Sutton Coldfield and Walsall, near A452. 18 holes, 6914 yards. S.S.S. 73. *Green Fees:* £25.00 weekdays; £33.00 weekends. *Eating facilities:* diningroom and bar snacks. *Visitors:* welcome without reservation weekdays, with member at weekends. Ladies' Day Thursdays. *Society Meetings:* catered for on weekdays. Professional: M.P. Daubney (0922 59523). Secretary: P.M. Halldron.

WALSALL. Walsall Golf Club, The Broadway, Walsall WS1 3EY (0922 20014 or 22710). *Location:* one and a half miles from M6/M5 junction. Wooded course. 18 holes, 6243 yards. S.S.S. 70. *Green Fees:* £33.00 per round, £40.00 per day. Reduced rates for organised Societies, minimum 16. *Eating facilities:* all facilities available. *Visitors:* welcome weekdays only. *Society Meetings:* catered for. Professional: R. Lambert (0922 26766). Secretary: E. Murray (0922 613512).

WARLEY. Warley Golf Club, Lightwood Hill, Warley (021-429 2440). *Location:* five miles west of Birmingham centre, just off main Hagley Road West. 9 holes, 2606 yards. S.S.S. 64. *Green Fees:* £6.00. *Eating facilities:* cafe. *Visitors:* welcome without reservation. *Society Meetings:* catered for, but not advised (Municipal Golf Course). Professional: David Owen. Secretary: C. Lowndes.

WEST BROMWICH. Dartmouth Golf Club, Vale Street, West Bromwich (021-588 2131). *Location:* one mile from West Bromwich town centre, rear of Churchfields High School, All Saints Way. Part flat, part undulating course. 9 holes, 6060 yards. S.S.S. 70. *Green Fees:* weekdays £17.50; weekends only with a member £14.00. *Eating facilities:* bar open mid-day and evenings except Tuesday and Sunday evenings. Meals by arrangement. *Visitors:* welcome weekdays, and on some Sundays with member. *Society Meetings:* welcome by prior arrangement. Professional: Carl R. Yates (021-588 2131). Secretary: M. Morton (021-588 2131).

WEST BROMWICH. Sandwell Park Golf Club Ltd., Birmingham Road, West Bromwich (021-553 0260). *Location:* on A41 to Birmingham close to Junction 1 M5. 18 holes, 6470 yards. S.S.S. 72. Two practice areas. *Green Fees:* weekdays £32.50. *Eating facilities:* full restaurant facilities and two bars. *Visitors:* welcome except weekends and Bank Holidays. Handicap Certificate required. *Society Meetings:* by prior arrangement, rates on request. Professional: N. Wylie (021-553 4384). Secretary: J.B. Mawby (021-553 4637).

WISHAW. The Belfry, Lichfield Road, Wishaw, Near Sutton Coldfield B76 9PR (Curdworth (0675) 470301; Fax: 0675 470178). *Location:* M42 Junction 9 just off the Lichfield Road (A446). Two parkland courses. Championship Brabazon: 18 holes, 6905 yards. Par 72, S.S.S. 72. Derby: 18 holes, 6103 yards. Par 70, S.S.S. 70. Driving range and putting green. *Green Fees:* Brabazon: £50.00; Derby: £25.00. Reduced winter rates on request. *Eating facilities:* eight bars, four restaurants. *Visitors:* welcome, non residential golf can be booked 24 hours in advance during summer months. Residential Golf Packages from £72.50 per person. 4 Star Hotel, 16 conference rooms, magnificent leisure complex and the Bel Air Night Club in the Hotel grounds. *Society Meetings:* welcome at all times. Professional: Peter McGovern. Assistant Professional: Glenn Williams.

WOLVERHAMPTON. Oxley Park Golf Club Ltd, Stafford Road, Bushbury, Wolverhampton WV10 6DE (0902 20506). *Location:* one and a half miles M54/A449 junction. One and a half miles Wolverhampton town centre. Undulating parkland. 18 holes, 6168 yards, 5639 metres. S.S.S. 69. *Green Fees:* weekdays £18.00 per round, £22.00 per day; weekends £20.00 per round, £24.00 per day. *Eating facilities:* each day except Monday. *Visitors:* welcome weekdays, weekends by arrangement with Professional. *Society Meetings:* catered for Wednesdays only. Professional: Leslie Burlison (0902 25445). Secretary: Mrs Kathryn Mann (0902 25892).

WOLVERHAMPTON. Penn Golf Club, Penn Common, Penn, Wolverhampton (Wolverhampton (0902) 341142). *Location:* two miles south west of Wolverhampton, off A449. Heathland. 18 holes, 6462 yards. S.S.S. 71. *Green Fees:* £22.00. *Eating facilities:* available, excluding Sunday and Monday. *Visitors:* welcome weekdays, without advance booking. *Society Meetings:* catered for. Professional: A. Briscoe (0902 330472). Secretary: P.W. Thorrington (0384 256220).

Near Belfry
BUXTON HOTEL,
65 Coleshill Street, Fazeley,
Tamworth, Staffs B78 3RG
Tel: 0827 284842/285805

Family run hotel, ideally situated for Golf, N.E.C. or Birmingham International Airport on A4091 – 200 yards A5. Excellent ensuite bedrooms, lounge, bar, also conference facilities available.

The Belfry
Wishaw,
N. Warwickshire B76 9PR
Tel: 0675 470301
Fax: 0675 470178

MORE THAN JUST A HOTEL
Play and stay at the Belfry. The Champion's Course!
See Outside Front Cover and also our advertisement inside the Front Cover for further details.

DE VERE HOTELS

WOLVERHAMPTON. **Perton Park Golf Club,** Wrottesley Park Road, Perton, Wolverhampton WV6 7HL (0902 380103). *Location:* just off the A454 Bridgnorth Road or A41 Wolverhampton to Newport road. Flat meadowland. 18 holes, 7007 yards. S.S.S. 71. Driving range, putting green. *Green Fees:* Mondays to Thursdays £5.00, Fridays £6.00; weekends and Bank Holidays £10.00. *Eating facilities:* available also bar. *Visitors:* pay as you play course. *Society Meetings:* catered for. Secretary: E.G.J. Greenway (0902 380073).

WOLVERHAMPTON. **South Staffordshire Golf Club,** Danescourt Road, Tettenhall, Wolverhampton WV6 9BQ (Wolverhampton (0902) 751065). *Location:* A41 out of Wolverhampton. Parkland. 18 holes, 6513 yards. S.S.S. 71. Practice area. *Green Fees:* weekdays £25.00 per round or day; weekends £30.00 by prior arrangement. *Eating facilities:* excellent catering facilities – Steward: Hugh Campbell (0902 756401). *Visitors:* use of first tee weekdays after 9.30am and 2pm except Tuesdays (Ladies' Day) after 2pm. *Society Meetings:* by arrangement with the Secretary. Professional: J. Rhodes (0902 754816). Secretary: John Macklin (0902 751065).

WOLVERHAMPTON. **Wergs Golf Club,** Keepers Lane, Tettenhall, Wolverhampton WV6 8UA (0902 742225; Fax: 0902 744748). *Location:* from centre of Wolverhampton, take A41 (to Newport), after two and a half miles turn right, half a mile on right. Open parkland. 18 holes, 6949 yards. S.S.S. 73. *Green Fees:* weekdays £12.50; weekends £15.00. *Eating facilities:* full catering and bar facilities. *Visitors:* always welcome. *Society Meetings:* welcome anytime during week, after 10am at weekends. Secretary: Mrs G. Parsons.

Wiltshire

CALNE. **Bowood Golf and Country Club,** Derry Hill, Calne SN11 9PQ (0249 822228; Fax: 0249 822218). `Location:* A4 between Marlborough and Chippenham, signposted off M4. Grade I listed, Capability Brown landscaped, parkland. 18 holes, 7317, 6890, 6566: 6229 yards. S.S.S: 74, 73, 71: 77. 3 academy holes, driving range. *Green Fees:* weekdays £27.00 per round, £40.00 per day; weekends £32.00 per round. *Eating facilities:* private diningrooms, public restaurant. *Visitors:* welcome at all times except before 12 noon at weekends. Four bedroomed house in centre of course. *Society Meetings:* welcome. Director of Golf: Nigel Blenkarne. Professional: Ian Brake. Chief Executive: Sally-Jane Coode.

CASTLE COMBE. **Castle Combe Golf Club,** Castle Combe SN14 7PL. *Location:* five miles south M4 between Junction 17 and 18. Parkland course in an area of outstanding natural beauty. 18 holes. 6340 yards. S.S.S. 71. *Green Fees:* information not provided. Eating facilities: bar and catering available all day. *Visitors:* welcome, book in advance. Snooker and sauna facilities. *Society Meetings:* welcome, book in advance. Professional: Christine Langford (0249 783101). Secretary: Stephen Wright (0249 782982; Fax: 0249 782992).

CHIPPENHAM. **Chippenham Golf Club,** Malmesbury Road, Chippenham SN15 5LT (Chippenham (0249) 652040). *Location:* A429 one mile from Chippenham, two miles from M4 (Junction 17). Parkland. 18 holes, 5540 yards. S.S.S. 67. *Green Fees:* weekdays £20.00, weekends £25.00. *Eating facilities:* snacks and evening à la carte (not Mondays). *Visitors:* welcome; current Handicap Certificate required. Prior arrangement necessary. *Society Meetings:* catered for weekdays only. Professional: Bill Creamer (0249 655519). Secretary: D. Maddison (0249 652040).

CORSHAM. **Kingsdown Golf Club,** Corsham SN14 9BS (Box (0225) 742530). *Location:* five miles east of Bath. Heathland. 18 holes, 6445 yards, 5891 metres. S.S.S. 71. *Green Fees:* weekdays £22.00. *Eating facilities:* lounge bar and diningroom. *Visitors:* welcome except at weekends and Bank Holidays and mu:t have current Handicap Certificate. *Society Meetings:* catered for by arrangement. Professional: Andrew Butler (0225 742634). Secretary: S.H. Phipps (0225 743472).

DEVIZES. **Erlestoke Sands Golf Club,** Erlestoke, Devizes SN10 5UA (0380 830507). *Location:* six miles east of Westbury on B3098. Downland course, on two levels with green 100 feet below, spectacular 7th hole, 170 yards Par 3, one of the finest short holes in the West Country. 18 holes, 6619 yards. S.S.S. 72, Par 71. Large practice ground. *Green Fees:* weekdays £12.00; weekends £16.00. *Eating facilities:* full catering service, lounge, bar and diningroom. *Visitors:* welcome, booking advisable. *Society Meetings:* catered for by prior arrangement. Stewards: Pauline and Trevor Head (0380 830507). Professional/Manager: Tony Valentine (0380 831027). Secretary: J. Hobbs (0380 831069).

DEVIZES. **North Wilts Golf Club,** Bishop's Cannings, Devizes SN10 2LP (Cannings (0380 860257). *Location:* one and a half miles from A4 east of Calne. Four miles from Devizes. Downland, undulating course with spectacular views. 18 holes, 6451 yards, 5898 metres. S.S.S. 71. Practice ground. *Green Fees:* weekdays £18.00 per round, £25.00 per day; weekends £30.00 when accepted. *Eating facilities:* full catering service. *Visitors:* welcome all weekdays, some weekends but not December to March. *Society Meetings:* catered for by prior arrangement. Professionals: Graham Laing and Richard Blake (0380 860330; Fax: 0380 860061). Secretary: Stuart Musgrove (0380 860627).

THE GOLF GUIDE 1994

England WILTSHIRE

HIGHWORTH. **Highworth Community Golf Centre,** Swindon Road, Highworth SN6 7SJ. *Location:* on A361 just south of the town. Undulating parkland. 9 holes, 3120 yards, 2851 metres. Par 35. 9 hole pitch and putt, practice ground. *Green Fees:* information not provided. *Eating facilities:* vending machines. *Visitors:* municipal course, no restrictions. *Society Meetings:* welcome any day. Professional: Kevin Pickett (0793 766014).

HIGHWORTH. **Wrag Barn Golf Club,** Shrivenham Road, Highworth SN6 7QQ (0793 861327). *Location:* Junction 15 M4, take A419 Cirencester Road to Highworth roundabout fourth exit B14000. Undulating, set in beautiful Wiltshire countryside, three lakes and moat around 17th green. 18 holes, 6548 yards. S.S.S. 71. Excellent practice facilities. *Green Fees:* weekdays £15.00; weekends £22.00 after 11.30am. *Eating facilities:* good bar snacks available all day and bar – à la carte Friday, Saturday, Sunday and Sunday lunch. *Visitors:* welcome but members have priority, no green fee players at weekends before 11.30am. *Society Meetings:* welcome any weekday. Two rounds, coffee, lunch, dinner £35.00 per head, minimum of 20 players. Professional: Barry Loughrey (0793 766027). Secretary: Mrs Suzanne Manners (0793 861327; Fax: 0793 861325).

MARLBOROUGH. **Marlborough Golf Club,** The Common, Marlborough SN8 1DU (Marlborough (0672) 512147). *Location:* about one mile from town centre on A345 travelling towards Swindon. Downland. 18 holes, 6241 yards. S.S.S. 70. Practice ground and putting green. *Green Fees:* weekdays only £19.50 per round, £29.00 per day; weekends £40.00 per round. *Eating facilities:* restaurant serving snacks and full meals open most of day. *Visitors:* welcome generally, but it is best to telephone in advance as course may be too busy to allow green fees; some weekends course is closed to green fees. *Society Meetings:* catered for with advance notice. Professional: L. Ross (0672 512493). General Manager: Laurence Ross (0672 512147).

PEWSEY. **Upavon (RAF) Golf Club,** Upavon, Pewsey SN9 6BQ (0980 630787). *Location:* off A342 south and east of Upavon one and a half miles. Parkland/downland course with two testing Par 3s across a ravine. 9 holes, 5589 yards, 5116 metres. S.S.S. 67. Practice area. *Green Fees:* weekdays £14.00; weekends £17.00. £7.00 with a member. *Eating facilities:* available by prior arrangement. *Visitors:* welcome at all times subject to club competitions, etc. Handicap Certificate required Sunday mornings. *Society Meetings:* welcome midweek by prior arrangement. Professional: Richard Blake (0980 630787). Secretary: Les Mitchell (0980 630787).

SALISBURY. **Hamptworth Golf and Country Club,** Elmtree Farmhouse, Hamptworth, Salisbury SP5 2DU (0794 390155; Fax: 0794 390022). *Location:* off A36 Salisbury to Southampton Road. Parkland. 18 holes, 6600 yards. S.S.S. 72. 9-hole Par 3 course. *Green Fees:* weekdays £16.00; weekends £25.00. *Eating facilities:* bar snacks. *Visitors:* welcome. *Society Meetings:* welcome. Secretary: Mark Pierson.

SALISBURY. **High Post Golf Club Ltd,** Great Durnford, Salisbury SP4 6AT (0722 73231). *Location:* midway between Salisbury and Amesbury on A345. Downland and blackthorn. 18 holes, 6267 yards, 5730 metres. S.S.S. 70. Large practice ground. *Green Fees:* weekdays £20.00 per round, £25.00 per day; weekends £25.00 per round, £30.00 per day. *Eating facilities:* full catering and bars available. *Visitors:* welcome with valid Handicap Certificate. *Society Meetings:* catered for mid-week by arrangement. Professional: Tony Harman (072 273 219). Secretary: W. Goodwin (072 273 356).

SALISBURY. **Salisbury and South Wilts Golf Club,** Netherhampton, Salisbury SP2 8PR (Salisbury (0722) 742131). *Location:* on A3094, two miles Salisbury, Wilton, opposite Netherhampton village. Parkland. 27 holes, 6528 yards. S.S.S. 71. Practice ground. *Green Fees:* weekdays £25.00 per day, weekends and Bank Holidays £40.00 per day. *Eating facilities:* full catering service and bar. *Visitors:* welcome without reservation at all times, but preliminary phone call advised. *Society Meetings:* catered for by prior arrangement. Professional: G. Emerson (0722 742929). Secretary: John Newcomb (0722 742645).

SHRIVENHAM. **Shrivenham Park Golf Course,** Penny Hooks, Near Swindon SN6 8EX (0793 783853; Fax: 0793 782999). *Location:* M4 exit 15. Follow signs to Shrivenham, go through village, golf club on right. A delightful parkland course in excellent condition. 18 holes, 5553 yards. S.S.S 69 (men), 71 (ladies). Practice area. *Green Fees:* £10.00 per round weekdays; £13.00 per round weekends. Discounts for Senior Citizens and Juniors. *Eating facilities:* restaurant and bar facilities open all day seven days a week. *Visitors:* all facilities at Shrivenham Park are open to the general public with no restrictions, everybody welcome. *Society Meetings:* welcome seven days a week. Special cheap rates January/March every year. Golf and food all day £19.00 April onwards. Professional: Mr Simon Jefferies. Secretary: Mrs Trudy Mace (0428 653237) and Mrs Carole Johnson (04353 3477). Manager: Mr V. Sedgwick.

SWINDON. **Broome Manor Golf Complex,** Pipers Way, Swindon SN3 1RG (Swindon (0793) 495761). *Location:* two miles from Junction 15, M4 (follow signs for "Golf Complex"). Wooded parkland. 18 holes, 6359 yards, 5815 metres. S.S.S. 71. 9 holes, 5610 yards, 5130 metres. S.S.S. 67. Floodlit covered driving range. *Green Fees:* weekdays £4.60 for 9 holes, £7.70 for 18 holes; weekends £5.70 for 9 holes, £9.40 for 18 holes. *Eating facilities:* full facilities. *Visitors:* welcome, no restrictions, booking essential for 18 hole course. *Society Meetings:* catered for Monday to Thursday. Professional: Barry Sandry (0793 532403). Manager: Tom Watt (0793 495761). Catering: (0793 490939).

SWINDON. **Swindon Golf Club,** Ogbourne St. George, Marlborough SN8 1TB (Ogbourne St. George (067-284) 217). *Location:* A345, four miles south of Junction 15 (M4), two miles north of Marlborough. Downland course. 18 holes, 6226 yards. S.S.S. 70. Practice area. *Green Fees:* on application weekdays; with a member only at weekends. *Eating facilities:* full daily catering available, full bar service. *Visitors:* welcome with reservation weekdays. Weekends and Bank Holidays with member only. Handicap Certificates required. *Society Meetings:* catered for Mondays, Wednesdays and Fridays only by prior arrangement with Secretary. Professional: Colin Harraway (067-284 287). Secretary: P.V. Dixon (067-284 327).

TIDWORTH. **Tidworth Garrison Golf Club,** Bulford Road, Tidworth SP9 7AF (0980 42321). *Location:* A338 Salisbury to Marlborough Road, golf course off Bulford Road. Undulating downland course. 18 holes, 6075 yards. S.S.S. 69. Practice driving area, chipping and putting greens. *Green Fees:* £18.00. *Eating facilities:* full bar and catering facilities except for Mondays (sandwiches only). *Visitors:* welcome at all times, but normally after 2pm at weekends and Bank Holidays. *Society Meetings:* catered for Tuesdays, Thursdays and Fridays. Professional: T. Gosden (0980 42393). Secretary: Lt. Col. (retd) D.F.T. Tucker RE (0980 42301).

WARMINSTER. **West Wilts Golf Club,** Elm Hill, Warminster BA12 0AU (Warminster (0985) 212702).

Location: on A350 half-a-mile out of Warminster on Westbury Road. Downland. 18 holes, 5709 yards. S.S.S. 68. *Green Fees:* weekdays £24.00; weekends £35.00. *Eating facilities:* full meals and snacks available at all times (restricted winter evenings). *Visitors:* welcome, but must produce a Handicap Certificate. Afternoons only at weekends. *Society Meetings:* catered for Wednesday to Friday. Professional: John Jacobs (0985 212110). Secretary: I.D. Wheater (0985 213133).

WESTBURY near. **Thoulstone Park Golf Club,** Chapmanslade, Near Westbury BA13 4AQ (0373 832825; Fax: 0373 832821). *Location:* on A36, three miles north west of Warminster. Parkland course with trees and two lakes. 18 holes, 6312 yards. S.S.S. 70. Driving range, practice putting green. *Green Fees:* weekdays £12.00; weekends £17.50. *Eating facilities:* Spikes Bar (with bar snacks), restaurant, function room. *Visitors:* welcome anytime except Sunday mornings before 11am. *Society Meetings:* welcome weekdays. Professional: Derek Thomson. General Manager: Peter Livesey.

North Yorkshire

ALDWARK. **Aldwark Manor Golf Club,** Aldwark, Alne, York YO6 2NF (0347 838146). *Location:* in village of Aldwark, five miles from A1 and five miles from A19. Flat parkland. 18 holes, 6171 yards. S.S.S. 69. Practice ground. *Green Fees:* weekdays £16.00 per round, £20.00 per day; weekends and Bank Holidays £20.00 per round, £24.00 per day. *Eating facilities:* two restaurants and two bars. *Visitors:* always welcome weekdays, restricted weekends. 20 bedroomed hotel. *Society Meetings:* always welcome, restricted weekends. Professional: Gary M. Platt (0347 838353). Golf Director: Geoff Platt (0347 838353; Fax: 0347 838867).

BEDALE. **Bedale Golf Club,** Leyburn Road, Bedale (Bedale (0677) 422568). *Location:* close to northern boundary of town. Parkland. 18 holes, 6565 yards. S.S.S. 71. *Green Fees:* £18.00 weekdays, £27.00 weekends. *Eating facilities:* caterer employed. *Visitors:* welcome without reservation. *Society Meetings:* catered for on application. Professional: A.D. Johnson (0677 422443). Secretary: G.A. Shepherdson (0677 422451).

BENTHAM. **Bentham Golf Club,** Robin Lane, Bentham, Near Lancaster LA2 7AG (Bentham (05242) 61018). *Location:* B6480 north-west of Lancaster towards Settle. Parkland with magnificent views. 9 holes, 5760 yards. S.S.S. 69. *Green Fees:* weekdays £14.00, Juniors £7.00; weekends and Bank Holidays £20.00, Juniors £9.00. Weekly tickets £40.00, Juniors £20.00. *Eating facilities:* hot and cold snacks and meals available. *Visitors:* welcome all week without reservation. *Society Meetings:* welcome – contact Secretary. Secretary: J.M. Philipson (05242 62455).

CATTERICK. **Catterick Garrison Golf Club,** Leyburn Road, Catterick Garrison, Catterick DL9 3QE (Richmond (0748) 833401). *Location:* six miles south-west Scotch Corner, A1 turn off to Catterick Garrison. Undulating parkland/moorland with spectacular views. 18 holes, 6331 yards, 5789 metres. S.S.S. 70. Practice ground. *Green Fees:* weekdays £16.00; weekends and Bank Holidays £24.00. *Eating facilities:* bar and restaurant. *Visitors:* welcome without reservation. *Society Meetings:* catered for by appointment only. Professional: Andy Marshall (0748 833671). Secretary: J.K. Mayberry (0748 833268).

ALDWARK MANOR GOLF HOTEL

18 hole par 71 parkland style course. Excellent club facilities.
20 bedroom Victorian Manor House. Golf breaks available.
Aldwark Manor Golf Hotel, Aldwark, York Y06 2NF
A member of the Best Western Hotels   Telephone: (0347) 838146 Fax: (0347) 838867

THE GOLF GUIDE 1994

England NORTH YORKSHIRE

EASINGWOLD. **Easingwold Golf Club,** Stillington Road, Easingwold, York YO6 3ET (Easingwold (0347) 21486). *Location:* 12 miles north of York, course one mile along Stillington Road. Flat, wooded parkland. 18 holes, 5679 metres. S.S.S. 70. *Green Fees:* weekdays £22.00 per day; weekends and Bank Holidays £27.00. £10.00 playing with a member at any time. *Eating facilities:* catering except Mondays, order in advance. *Visitors:* welcome without reservation. *Society Meetings:* weekdays only, prior booking essential. Contact G.C. Young. Professional: John Hughes (0347 21964). Secretary: K.C. Hudson (0347 22474).

FILEY. **Filey Golf Club,** The Clubhouse, West Avenue, Filey YO14 9BQ (Scarborough (0723) 513116). *Location:* one mile from town centre. Seaside links. 18 holes, 5742 yards. S.S.S. 67. Practice area. *Green Fees:* weekdays £18.00, weekends £23.00. *Eating facilities:* full dining and bar facilities. *Visitors:* welcome most days if members of a golf club and hold current Handicap Certificate. *Society Meetings:* welcome, must be pre-arranged. Professional: D. England (0723 513134). Secretary: T.M. Thompson (0723 513293).

HARROGATE. **Crimple Valley Golf Club,** Hookstone Wood Road, Harrogate HG2 8PN (0423 883485; Fax: 0423 881018). *Location:* one mile south from town centre. Turn off A61 at Appleyards Garage on to Hookstone Road, signposted to right. Gently sloping fairways in rural setting. 9 holes, 2500 yards. S.S.S. 33. *Green Fees:* information not provided. *Eating facilities:* licensed bar, lunches available weekdays, breakfasts weekends. *Visitors:* welcome at all times. Professional: R.A. Lumb. Secretary: A.M. Grange.

HARROGATE. **Harrogate Golf Club Ltd,** Forest Lane Head, Harrogate HG2 7TF (Harrogate (0423) 863158). *Location:* two miles from Harrogate on the A59 Harrogate/Knaresborough road. Parkland. 18 holes, 6204 yards. S.S.S. 70. Practice ground, net. *Green Fees:* weekdays £26.00 per round, £30.00 per day; weekends £40.00. *Eating facilities:* full catering by chef, full bar facilities. *Visitors:* welcome but prior enquiry advised. *Society Meetings:* catered for. Professional: P. Johnson (0423 862547). Secretary: Mr Peter H. Ince (0423 862999). Caterer: (0423 860278).

DELAINE HOTEL

A friendly family run hotel, set in beautiful gardens. Ideally situated for town centre and local golf courses. All en-suite bedrooms with colour TV, telephones and teatray. Evening meals available on request. Private car park and residential licence. For further details please phone. RAC Acclaimed. AA QQQQ Selected.

**Delaine Hotel, 17 Ripon Road, Harrogate HG1 2JL.
Telephone: 0423 567974**

Aston Hotel

Come and relax in this beautifully appointed family run hotel, situated in a peaceful tree-lined street, yet just minutes from town centre. All 15 rooms have shower/w.c., tea/coffee trays, direct dial telephones, radio alarms and colour TV. Beautifully furnished residents' lounge and bar. Traditional English Breakfast, all freshly cooked to order and served in our pretty dining room. The Aston Hotel has an excellent reputation for cleanliness and friendliness, just try us and see. From £36 per person per night, Dinner, Bed and Breakfast. Or weekly from £230. Terms apply all year except at Conference/Exhibition times.

**7/9 Franklin Mount, Harrogate HG1 5EJ.
Telephone: (0423) 564262   Fax: (0423) 505542**

AA ★ RAC

The Langham Hotel
**Valley Drive, Harrogate HG2 0JL
Tel: (0423) 502179 Fax: (0423) 502347**

Beautiful old hotel, owned and managed by the Ward families. Also exquisite restaurant offering superb cuisine. Special deals for golfing parties. Courses within ½ an hour's drive – Pannal, Fulford, Alwoodley, Moor Allerton, Ilkley, Moortown, Harrogate. We can arrange courses and tee-off times for you should you so wish. For brochure and details contact: Stephen Ward.

holiday COTTAGES and LODGES

Luxury Cottages and Lodges situated in an attractive setting near the picturesque village of Follifoot. All cottages have been restored retaining their traditional charm and are equipped to the highest standard. Facilities within the private country estate include heated swimming pool, mini golf course, children's playground and games room.

Please send for illustrated brochure.

RUDDING holiday PARK

Rudding Holiday Park, Follifoot, Harrogate, HG3 1JH. Tel: (0423) 870439

HARROGATE. **Oakdale Golf Club**, Oakdale Glen, Harrogate HG1 2LN (Harrogate (0423) 502806). *Location:* off Ripon road into Kent Road follow signs. Parkland, with featured stream. 18 holes, 6456 yards. S.S.S. 71. Practice ground and nets. *Green Fees:* weekdays £22.00 per round, £29.50 per day; weekends £27.50 per round. *Eating facilities:* first class restaurant, bar. *Visitors:* welcome at all times, Tuesday Ladies' Day. *Society Meetings:* welcome weekdays by arrangement. Professional: Richard Jessop (0423 560510). Secretary: Frank Hindmarsh (0423 567162).

HARROGATE. **Pannal Golf Club**, Follifoot Road, Pannal, Harrogate HG3 1ES (Harrogate (0423) 871641; Fax; 0423 870043). *Location:* two miles south of Harrogate A61 (Leeds Road). 18 holes, 6659 yards. S.S.S. 72. Large practice ground. *Green Fees:* weekdays £29.00 per round, £35.00 per day; weekends and Bank Holidays £35.00 per round. *Eating facilities:* lunch available daily, dinner by arrangement. *Visitors:* welcome Monday to Friday without reservation, enquiry advised. *Society Meetings:* catered for Monday, Tuesday (pm only), Wednesday and Thursday, Friday (limited to 16 only). Professional: Murray Burgess (0423 872620). Secretary: T.B. Davey MBE (0423 872628).

KIRKBYMOORSIDE. **Kirkbymoorside Golf Club**, Manor Vale, Kirkbymoorside, York YO6 6EG (0751 31525). *Location:* on A170 through Kirkbymoorside. Undulating parkland. 18 holes, 6000 yards, 4932 metres. S.S.S. 69. *Green Fees:* £15.00 weekdays, £20.00 weekends and Public Holidays. Reduced fees in winter when temporary greens and shortened course in use. *Eating facilities:* available except Mondays, bar. *Visitors:* welcome all days except weekend medal competitions. Handicap Certificates required. *Society Meetings:* catered for by arrangement with Steward except weekends. Secretary: D.G. Saunders.

KNARESBOROUGH. **Knaresborough Golf Club**, Boroughbridge Road, Knaresborough HG5 0QQ (Harrogate (0423) 863219). *Location:* one-and-a-half miles from town centre, direction A1 Boroughbridge. Wooded parkland. 18 holes, 6232 yards. S.S.S.70. Large practice area. *Green Fees:* weekdays £17.00 per round, £22.00 per day; weekends £23.00 per round, £28.00 per day. *Eating facilities:* resident Steward provides full catering. *Visitors:* welcome without reservation. *Society Meetings:* catered for. Professional: Keith Johnstone (0423 864865). Secretary/Manager: J.I. Barrow (0423 862690).

MALTON. **Malton and Norton Golf Club**, Welham Park, Malton YO17 9QE (Malton (0653) 692959). *Location:* off A64 to Malton between York and Scarborough. One mile south on Welham road turn right at Norton level crossing. 18 holes, 6411 yards. S.S.S. 71. Medal course: 6141 yards. S.S.S. 69 (club). Practice ground. *Green Fees:* weekdays £20.00; weekends and Public Holidays £25.00. *Eating facilities:* full bar and catering available. *Visitors:* welcome without reservation except club match days, and weekends from 1st November to 31st March unless with member. *Society Meetings:* catered for by arrangement with Secretary. Professional: S. Robinson (0653 693882). Secretary: W.G. Wade (0653 697912).

NORTHALLERTON. **Romanby Golf Course**, Yafforth Road, Northallerton DL7 0PE. *Location:* west of Northallerton on the B6271 Richmond Road. Parkland course with formidable "Great Lake Complex" on the 2nd, 11th and 12th. 18 holes, 6666 yards. 12 bay floodlit driving range. *Green Fees:* on application. *Visitors:* always welcome, best to telephone for tee off times. Professional: Fred Thorpe (0609 779988; Fax: 0609 779084).

RICHMOND. **Richmond (Yorkshire) Golf Club**, Bend Hagg, Richmond DL10 5EX (0748 825319). *Location:* Scotch Corner (A1). Wooded, parkland, some hills. 18 holes, 5704 yards. S.S.S. 68. *Green Fees:* weekdays £16.00; weekends £25.00. *Eating facilities:* bar and catering. *Visitors:* welcome except not before 12 noon Sundays. *Society Meetings:* catered for, book with Professional. Professional: Paul Jackson (0748 822457). Secretary: B.D. Aston (0748 825319).

RIPON. **Masham Golf Club**, Masham, Ripon (Ripon (0765) 689379). *Location:* nine miles north of Ripon. 9 holes, 5308 yards. S.S.S. 66. *Green Fees:* £15.00 U/A. *Visitors:* welcome weekdays but must be accompanied by a member weekends and Bank Holidays. Party visits by arrangement. Secretary: Mrs M.A. Willis (0765 689491).

THE GOLF GUIDE 1994   *England*   NORTH YORKSHIRE

RIPON. **Ripon City Golf Club,** Palace Road, Ripon HG4 1UW (Ripon (0765) 603640). *Location:* Masham Road out of Ripon. 9 holes hilly parkland and new 9 holes flat parkland. 18 holes. S.S.S. 70. *Green Fees:* weekdays £18.00; weekends £25.00. Half price if with a member. *Eating facilities:* available every day except Mondays. *Visitors:* welcome anytime. *Society Meetings:* catered for, apply in writing. Professional: T. Davis (0765 600411). Secretay: J.L. Wright (0765 603640).

SCARBOROUGH. **Ganton Golf Club Ltd,** Ganton, Near Scarborough YO12 4PA. *Location:* on A64, nine miles west of Scarborough. 18 holes, 6693 yards. *Green Fees:* on request. *Eating facilities:* available. *Visitors:* welcome by prior arrangement. *Society Meetings:* catered for with reservation. Professional: Gary Brown. Secretary: Air Vice-Marshal R.G. Price, CB.

SCARBOROUGH. **Raven Hall Country House Hotel Golf Course,** Ravenscar, Near Scarborough YO13 0ET (0723 870353; Fax: 0723 870072). *Location:* off main A171 (Whitby Road), 10 miles north of Scarborough. Open links, clifftop with a fair gradient. 9 holes, 3762 yards. S.S.S. 64. 18 hole putting green. *Green Fees:* £12.00 per day, every day. *Eating facilities:* Hotel bar and restaurant, Coach House bar facility. *Visitors:* welcome. 53 en-suite bedrooms plus a host of additional leisure facilities. *Society Meetings:* it is advisable for large societies to book in advance through Nick Davies or Caroline Connelly. Secretary: Mr Nicholas Davies.

SCARBOROUGH. **Scarborough North Cliff Golf Club,** North Cliff Avenue, Scarborough YO12 6PP (Scarborough (0723) 360786). *Location:* two miles north of Scarborough on coastal road to Whitby. Parkland. 18 holes, 6425 yards. S.S.S. 71. Practice area. *Green Fees:* weekdays £21.00 per day, weekends and Bank Holidays £26.00. *Eating facilities:* available. *Visitors:* welcome (restrictions on competition days, not allowed Sundays before 10am.). *Society Meetings:* catered for, from 12 to 40. Prior booking through Secretary. Professional: S.N. Deller (0723 365920). Secretary: J.R. Freeman (0723 360786).

SCARBOROUGH. **Scarborough South Cliff Golf Club Ltd,** Deepdale Avenue, Scarborough YO11 2UE (Scarborough (0723) 360522). *Location:* one mile south of Scarborough off Filey road. Parkland and clifftop with panoramic sea views. 18 holes, 6039 yards. S.S.S. 69. Practice ground. *Green Fees:* weekdays £20.00 18 holes, £25.00 per day; £25.00 per round, £30.00 per day weekends and Bank Holidays. *Eating facilities:* full catering facilities. *Visitors:* welcome when course available. *Society Meetings:* catered for by prior arrangement. Professional: (0723 365150). Secretary: R. Bramley BEM MBIM (0723 374737).

SELBY. **Selby Golf Club,** Mill Lane, Brayton Barff, Selby YO8 9LD (0757 228622). *Location:* three miles south of Selby off A19 Selby-Doncaster road. Inland links type course, very well drained. 18 holes, 6246 yards. S.S.S. 70. Large practice ground. *Green Fees:* weekdays £22.00 per round, £25.00 per day;

Raven Hall ★ ★ ★
Country House Hotel & Golf Course

Historic Country House with panoramic views across Robin Hood's Bay and CHALLENGING PRIVATE CLIFF TOP GOLF COURSE

53 ensuite bedrooms · 6 conference suites
Extensive leisure facilities freely available to guests.
100 acres of landscaped gardens & battlements.

TELEPHONE: (0723) 870353   FAX: (0723) 870072

RAVEN HALL HOTEL, RAVENSCAR, SCARBOROUGH, N. YORKS YO13 0ET

The Royal Hotel SCARBOROUGH
Golf on the Yorkshire Coast

The ideal centre of Society and individual golfers. Eight courses within easy reach including the championship course, Ganton. Special golf packages available. The Royal Oasis indoor swimming pool and Fitness Centre includes jacuzzi, steam room, sauna, solarium and exercise area. First class food. Snooker room. Private rooms for presentation of prizes.

The Royal Hotel offers so much more – and more.

Royal Hotel, St. Nicholas Street, Scarborough YO11 2HE
Telephone: **(0723) 364333**   Fax: (0723) 500618

NORTH YORKSHIRE *England*   THE GOLF GUIDE 1994

weekends casual visitors not accepted. *Eating facilities:* pleasant restaurant and bar. *Visitors:* welcome Wednesdays, Thursdays and Fridays. Tuesdays Ladies Day, Mondays no catering. All visitors must have Handicap Certificates. Snooker. *Society Meetings:* same as visitors; £25.00 per day including £2 evening meal voucher. Professional: Mr C.A.C. Smith (0757 228785). Secretary: Mr B.L.C. Moore.

SETTLE. **Settle Golf Club,** Buck Haw Brow, Giggleswick, Settle (Settle (0729) 825288). *Location:* one mile north of Settle on main A65. Moorland. 9 holes, 4600 yards. S.S.S. 62. *Green Fees:* £10.00. *Eating facilities:* bar facilities open Sundays only. *Visitors:* welcome, restrictions Sundays. *Society Meetings:* welcome, must book in advance through Secretary. Secretary: R.G. Bannier (0729 823596).

SKIPTON. **Skipton Golf Club,** off North West Bypass, Skipton BD23 1LL (Skipton (0756) 793922). *Location:* one and a half miles from Skipton centre on the northern bypass A65. Undulating, with panoramic views, some water hazards. 18 holes, 6200 yards. S.S.S. 70. Practice ground. *Green Fees:* weekdays £22.00; weekends and Bank Holidays £26.00. Half-price for Juniors (under 18) or if playing with a member. *Eating facilities:* available every day except Mondays. *Visitors:* welcome at all times, some restrictions weekends and Thursdays. *Society Meetings:* welcome, accepted with prior booking. Professional: P. Robinson (0756 793257). Secretary/Manager: D. Farnsworth (0756 795657).

THIRSK. **Thirsk and Northallerton Golf Club,** Thornton-le-Street, Thirsk YO7 4AB (0845 522170). *Location:* off the A168 Northallerton Road, two miles north of Thirsk. Flat parkland with excellent views. 9 holes, 6257 yards. S.S.S. 70. Small practice area. *Green Fees:* weekdays £15.00 per round, £20.00 per day; Saturdays and Public Holidays £25.00; Sundays only with a member. *Eating facilities:* bars open normal times, food available except Tuesdays. *Visitors:* must be members of a recognised golf club and have a handicap. Not at weekends. Dress regulations must be strictly followed. *Society Meetings:* application must be made in writing to, and confirmed by, the Secretary well in advance of a society visit. Not at weekends. Professional: Andrew Wright (0845 526216). Secretary: S. Weatherall (0845 525115).

THORNTON-IN-CRAVEN. **Ghyll Golf Club,** Ghyll Brow, Barnoldswick, Colne, Lancs BB8 6JQ (Earby (0282) 842466). *Location:* M65 to Colne. Parkland, hilly course. 9 holes, 5706 yards, 5213 metres. S.S.S. 68. *Green Fees:* weekdays £14.00 (£7.00 with member), weekends and Bank Holidays £18.00 restricted (£12.00 with member). *Eating facilities:* bar, evening only. *Visitors:* welcome except Sundays and some Saturdays. *Society Meetings:* catered for by arrangement. Secretary: John L. Gill (0756 798592).

WHITBY. **Whitby Golf Club,** Low Straggleton, Whitby YO21 3SR (Whitby (0947) 602768). *Location:* Sandsend Road (A174) out of Whitby. Coastal course. 18 holes, 5963 yards. S.S.S. 69. *Green Fees:* weekdays £17.50, weekends and Bank Holidays £25.00. Half price when playing with member. *Eating facilities:* meals available daily except Mondays, bar facilities. *Visitors:* welcome, parties over 12 by prior reservation, all must be bona fide golfers. *Society Meetings:* catered for by prior arrangement. Professional: (0947 602719). Secretary: Alan Dyson (0947 600660).

YORK. **Forest Park Golf Club,** Stockton on Forest, York YO3 9UX (0904 400425). *Location:* one and a half miles from East End of York bypass, follow signs for Stockton on Forest. Flat parkland type course with stream running through. 18 holes, 6200 yards. S.S.S. 70. Driving range and practice area. *Green Fees:* weekdays £14.00 per round, £18.00 per day; weekends £19.00 per round, £23.00 per day. *Eating facilities:* full bar and all golf club type meals. *Visitors:* welcome mid week, limited availability weekends. *Society Meetings:* welcome by prior arrangement. Secretary: David Crossley (0904 400688).

YORK. **Fulford (York) Golf Club Ltd,** Heslington Lane, York YO1 5DY (York (0904) 413579). *Location:* A19 (Selby) from city, turn left to Heslington (signposted to University). Heathland. 18 holes, 6775 yards. S.S.S. 72. Practice ground. *Green Fees:* weekdays £20.00 per round, £30.00 per day, £35.00 corporate fee. *Eating facilities:* lounge, diningroom and bar. *Visitors:* welcome Monday to Friday, prior reservation recommended. *Society Meetings:* Monday to Friday by arrangement with Secretary. Professional: B. Hessay (0904 412882). Secretary: Mrs Judith Hayhurst (0904 413579; Fax: 0904 416918).

AA LISTED   ❦❦❦ **Commended**   **RAC ACCLAIMED**

Ideally situated near Fulford Golf Club or for touring Historic York.

Four Poster Lodge

68 HESLINGTON ROAD, BARBICAN ROAD, YORK YO1 5AU
Telephone: 0904 651170   Proprietor: JUDITH JONES

A warm welcome, hearty Breakfast and relaxing lounge bar. Fourposter beds. Brochure on request.

ORILLIA HOUSE   ETB ❦❦

89 The Village, Stockton on Forest, YORK YO3 9UP Tel: (0904) 400600 or 738595

A warm welcome awaits at ORILLIA HOUSE, 3 miles NE of York, one mile from A64. This 17th century house has been restored to a high standard of comfort with modern facilities, yet retains all its original charm and character. All rooms have private facilities, colour TV and tea/coffee making. Private car park. Our local pub serves excellent Evening Meals. Bed and Breakfast from £15.00. Telephone for our brochure.

THE GOLF GUIDE 1994 *England* NORTH YORKSHIRE/SOUTH YORKSHIRE

YORK. **Heworth Golf Club,** Muncaster House, Muncastergate, York YO3 9JX (York (0904) 424618). *Location:* within city boundaries, adjacent A1036 (A64) for Malton/Scarborough. Parkland. 11 holes, 6141 yards. S.S.S. 69. *Green Fees:* weekdays £14.00; weekends and Bank Holidays £18.00. *Eating facilities:* available every day except Monday. *Visitors:* generally welcome except Sunday mornings and competition days, but advisable to telephone. *Society Meetings:* only by written application. Professional: Gregg Roberts (0904 422389). Secretary: J.R. Richards (0904 426156).

YORK. **Pike Hills Golf Club,** Tadcaster Road, Askham Bryan, York YO2 3UW (York (0904) 706566). *Location:* four miles from York on Tadcaster Road, right hand side going west. Flat parkland surrounding wildlife reserve. 18 holes, 6120 yards. S.S.S. 69. *Green Fees:* £21.00 per day. *Eating facilities:* newly opened restaurant and bar facilities. *Visitors:* welcome but not weekends or summer evenings. *Society Meetings:* welcome by arrangement. Professional: Ian Gradwell (0904 708756). Secretary: G. Rawlings (0904 706566).

YORK. **York Golf Club,** Lordsmoor Lane, Strensall, York YO3 5XF (York (0904) 490304). *Location:* two miles north of York Ring Road (A1237). Wooded heathland. 18 holes, 6285 yards. S.S.S. 70. Practice ground; Professional shop. *Green Fees:* £25.00 weekdays; £30.00 weekends and Bank Holidays. *Eating facilities:* full catering except Fridays. *Visitors:* welcome, but advisable to ring before visiting. *Society Meetings:* catered for Mondays, Wednesdays, Thursdays and Sundays. Professional: A.B. Mason (0904 490304). Secretary: Gp Captain F. Appleyard (0904 491840; Fax: 0904 491852).

South Yorkshire

BARNSLEY. **Barnsley Golf Club,** Wakefield Road, Staincross, Barnsley S75 6JZ (Barnsley (0226) 382856). *Location:* A61 three miles north of Barnsley, five miles south of Wakefield. Parkland course. 18 holes, 6048 yards, 5529 metres. S.S.S. 69. *Green Fees:* information not provided. *Eating facilities:* meals available. *Visitors:* welcome, no restrictions. *Society Meetings:* course extremely busy and not suitable for Societies. Professional: M. Melling (0226 382954). Secretary: L.E. Lammas (0226 382856).

BARNSLEY. **Silkstone Golf Club,** Field Head, Elmhirst Lane, Silkstone, Barnsley S75 4OD (Barnsley (0226) 790328). *Location:* one mile beyond Dodworth village on the A628 and one mile from M1. Parkland. 18 holes, 6045 yards. S.S.S. 70. Practice area. *Green Fees:* weekdays £22.00 per day. *Eating facilities:* available. *Visitors:* welcome weekdays only. *Society Meetings:* by arrangement. Package £32.00. Professional: Kevin Guy (0226 790328). Secretary: L. Depledge (0226 287053).

DONCASTER. **Austerfield Park Golf Club,** Cross Lane, Austerfield, Doncaster DN10 6RF (Doncaster (0302) 710841). *Location:* two miles from Bawtry on the A614. Parkland. 18 holes, 6828 yards. S.S.S. 73. 10 bay floodlit golf range, flat bowling green. *Green Fees:* midweek £12.00 per round, £16.00 per day; weekends £16.00 per round, £20.00 per day. *Eating facilities:* bar snacks and full restaurant. *Visitors:* welcome without reservation. *Society Meetings:* welcome, special package rates. Professional: Trevor Parkinson (0302 710850). Secretary: Alan Bradley (0709 540928).

DONCASTER. **Crookhill Park (Municipal) Golf Club,** Crookhill Park, Conisborough, Doncaster (Rotherham (0709) 862974). *Location:* leave A1(M) Doncaster by-pass, on to A630 Sheffield, after two miles turn left in Conisborough on to B60694. 18 holes, 5846 yards. S.S.S. 68. Practice area. *Green Fees:* £7.50. *Eating facilities:* buffet lunches at club. *Visitors:* welcome. Professional: Richard Swaine (0709 862979). Hon. Secretary: M. Belk.

DONCASTER. **Doncaster Town Moor Golf Club,** Bawtry Road, Belle Vue, Doncaster DN4 5HU (Doncaster (0302) 535286). *Location:* clubhouse approximately 300 yards from racecourse roundabout travelling south towards Bawtry, same entrance as Doncaster Rovers Football Club. Flat wooded parkland. 18 holes, 6094 yards. S.S.S. 69. *Green Fees:* weekdays £13.00, £7.00 with a member per round; £15.00, £8.00 with a member per day; weekends and Public Holidays £15.00, £8.00 with a member per round, £17.00, £9.00 with a member per day. *Eating facilities:* restaurant and bar meals. *Visitors:* welcome without reservation, not before 11.30am Sundays. *Society Meetings:* catered for by arrangement with Secretary. Professional: Steve Poole (0302 535286). Secretary: Gerry Sampson (0302 538423).

DONCASTER. **Hickleton Golf Club,** Hickleton, Near Doncaster (Rotherham (0709) 892496). *Location:* six miles from Doncaster on A635 to Barnsley. In Hickleton village turn right to Thurnscoe, 500 yards on right. Undulating parkland. 18 holes, 6403 yards. S.S.S. 71. Practice facilities. *Green Fees:* weekdays £17.00; weekends £20.00, Bank Holidays £25.00. *Eating facilities:* available by arrangement with Steward/ess. *Visitors:* welcome by arrangement, restricted times at weekends. *Society Meetings:* welcome by arrangement. Professional: Paul Shepherd (0709 895170; Fax: 0709 888436). Secretary: R. Jowett (0709 896081 office).

SOUTH YORKSHIRE *England*   THE GOLF GUIDE 1994

DONCASTER. **Serlby Park Golf Club,** Serlby, Doncaster DN10 6BA (Retford (0777) 818268). *Location:* 12 miles south of Doncaster, between A614 and A638. Parkland, wooded course. 9 holes, 5370 yards. S.S.S. 66. *Green Fees:* weekdays £8.00 per round; weekends £11.00 per round. *Eating facilities:* catering and bar. *Visitors:* welcome only if playing with member. *Society Meetings:* some visiting parties allowed. Hon. Secretary: R. Wilkinson.

DONCASTER. **Thorne Golf Club,** Kirkton Lane, Thorne, Near Doncaster (Thorne (0405) 815173). *Location:* A18, Parkland. 18 holes, 5366 yards. S.S.S. 66. Practice ground. *Green Fees:* weekdays £7.60 per round; weekends and Bank Holidays £8.60 per round. *Eating facilities:* snacks or full meals booked in advance. *Visitors:* welcome, no restrictions. *Society Meetings:* welcome, please book in advance. Professional: R.D. Highfield (0405 812084). Secretary: Mrs C. Highfield (0405 812084).

DONCASTER. **Wheatley Golf Club,** Armthorpe Road, Doncaster DN2 5QB (Doncaster (0302) 831655). *Location:* follow East Coast route alongside Racecourse boundary to water tower at first crossroads. Flat parkland, water hazards between 10th and 18th holes. 18 holes, 6209 yards. S.S.S. 70 (yellow markers); 6405 yards. S.S.S. 71 (white markers). Practice area and putting green. *Green Fees:* information not provided. *Eating facilities:* restaurant and bars. *Visitors:* welcome if member of another club. Non-members may play in the company of a member. *Society Meetings:* catered for weekdays only on written application. Professional: S. Fox. Secretary: T.A.D. Crumpton.

ROTHERHAM. **Grange Park Golf Club,** Upper Wortley Road, Kimberworth Park, Rotherham (Rotherham (0709) 558884). Municipal golf course, private clubhouse. *Location:* A629 from Rotherham, easy access from M1. Parkland. 18 holes, 6353 yards. S.S.S. 71. Practice ground. *Green Fees:* £6.00 weekdays; £7.00 weekends. *Eating facilities:* licensed bar and full catering. *Visitors:* welcome without restriction. *Society Meetings:* contact Professional in first instance. Professional: Eric Clark (0709 559497). Secretary: R. Charity (0709 583400).

ROTHERHAM. **Phoenix Golf Club,** Pavilion Lane, Brinsworth, Rotherham (Rotherham (0709) 363864). *Location:* M1 Tinsley roundabout, Bawtry Road, Pavilion Lane one mile on left. 18 holes, 6145 yards. S.S.S. 69. *Green Fees:* weekdays £18.00 per day, £7.00 with a member; weekends £24.00, £10.00 with a member. *Eating facilities:* snacks or full meals. *Visitors:* welcome weekdays. *Society Meetings:* welcome, reduced rates for parties. Professional: A. Limb (0709 382624). Secretary: J. Burrows (0709 370759).

ROTHERHAM. **Rotherham Golf Club Ltd,** Thrybergh Park, Thrybergh, Rotherham S65 4NU (Rotherham (0709) 850466). *Location:* three and a half miles east of Rotherham on A630. Wooded parkland. 18 holes, 6234 yards, 5701 metres. S.S.S. 70. Practice ground. *Green Fees:* weekdays £25.00; weekends £30.00. Reductions for societies over 16. *Eating facili-* *ties:* full catering, bar and restaurant. *Visitors:* welcome all day with limitations. *Society Meetings:* catered for weekdays only except Wednesdays. Professional: Simon Thornhill (0709 850480). Secretary: F. Green (0709 850812).

ROTHERHAM. **Sitwell Park Golf Club,** Shrogswood Road, Rotherham S60 4BY (Wickersley (0709) 700799). *Location:* A631 off M18, Bramley turn off to Rotherham thence to Sheffield, exit 33 off M1, follow A631 to Bawtry. Undulating parkland. 18 holes, 6203 yards. S.S.S. 70. Practice ground. *Green Fees:* weekdays £20.00 per day, £24.00 per day; weekends and Bank Holidays £24.00 per round, £28.00 per day. *Eating facilities:* restaurant and bar. *Visitors:* welcome with reservation, Saturdays only with member, Sundays after 11.30am. *Society Meetings:* catered for if pre-arranged with Secretary. Not Saturdays; Sundays after 11.30am only. Professional: N. Taylor (0709 540961). Secretary: G. Simmonite (0709 541046).

ROTHERHAM. **Wath Golf Club,** Abdy, Rawmarsh, Rotherham S62 7SJ (Rotherham (0709) 872149). *Location:* A633 from Rotherham, through Rawmarsh, taking B6090 towards Wentworth, right along B6089 taking signed road to Clubhouse 300 yards on right. Flat parkland course with small green, dykes and two ponds. 18 holes, 5857 yards. S.S.S. 68. Limited practice area. *Green Fees:* weekdays £16.00; weekends with a member £16.00. *Eating facilities:* lounge bar and dining area with seating for up to 150 people. *Visitors:* weekdays only. No jeans or collarless shirts allowed. *Society Meetings:* welcome weekdays only by prior arrangement. Golf/meal Package £25.00. Professional: Chris Bassett (0709 878677). Secretary: John Pepper (0709 873153 day, 873730 evening; Fax: 0709 760179).

SHEFFIELD. **Abbeydale Golf Club,** Twentywell Lane, Dore, Sheffield S17 4QA (Sheffield (0742) 360763). *Location:* A621 five miles south of Sheffield. Parkland. 18 holes, 6419 yards. S.S.S. 71. Practice ground. *Green Fees:* weekdays £27.50, weekends and Bank Holidays £32.50. *Eating facilities:* restaurant and bar meals. *Visitors:* welcome by arrangement. Starting time restrictions April-October. *Society Meetings:* catered for Tuesdays and Fridays by arrangement. Professional: N. Perry (0742 365633). Secretary: Mrs K.M. Johnston (0742 360763).

SHEFFIELD. **Beauchief Golf Club,** Abbey Lane, Beauchief, Sheffield S8 0DB (0742 620040). *Location:* the entrance to course is on the Sheffield Outer Ring Road, between the A621 Bakewell Road and the A61 Chesterfield Road. Mainly flat parkland with some hilly holes. 18 holes, 5452 yards, 4984 metres. S.S.S. 66. Practice area available (small charge). *Green Fees:* £7.50 per round. Juniors half price. *Eating facilities:* cafe/bar, open from 11am to dusk each day. *Visitors:* welcome anytime. It is a very busy course at weekends (advisable to book early). *Society Meetings:* weekdays only, can be booked through Sheffield City Council Recreation Department, Meersbrook Park, Sheffield S8 9FL. Professional: B.T. English (0742 620648). Bookings: (0742 338 7274). Secretary: J.G. Pearson (0742 306720).

SHEFFIELD. **Birley Wood Golf Club,** Birley Lane, Sheffield S12 3BP (0742 647262). *Location:* four and a half miles south east of city centre, off A616 from Mosbrough. Undulating meadowland course with well varied features, open plan and good views. 18 holes, 5452 yards. S.S.S. 67. Practice field near course. *Green Fees:* £6.90 per round. *Eating facilities:* bar and snacks at nearby Fairway Inn. *Visitors:* welcome with prior notice. *Society Meetings:* by prior arrangement. Professional: P. Ball (0742 647262). Secretary: T.C. Jacobs (0742 582449).

SHEFFIELD. **Concord Park Golf Club,** Shiregreen Lane, Sheffield S5 6AE. *Location:* one-and-a-half miles from M1 Junction 34. Hilly wooded parkland. 18 holes, 4321 yards, 3929 metres. S.S.S. 62. *Green Fees:* £6.00. *Eating facilities:* available at adjacent Sports Centre. *Visitors:* welcome any time. Secretary: B. Shepherd (0742 456806).

SHEFFIELD. **Dore and Totley Golf Club,** The Clubhouse, Bradway Road, Bradway, Sheffield S17 4QR (Sheffield (0742) 360492). *Location:* leave M1 at Junction 33. Parkland. 18 holes, 6265 yards. S.S.S. 70. *Green Fees:* weekdays £25.00 per round or day; weekends with a member only. *Eating facilities:* bar available, catering facilities available except Mondays. *Visitors:* unintroduced visitors restricted to the hours of 9.30am to 12 noon and after 2pm. Restrictions also exist on Wednesday (Ladies' Day). Handicap Certificates must be produced. *Society Meetings:* catered for Tuesday, Thursday, Friday by prior arrangement. Professional: Neil Cheetham (0742 366844). Secretary: Mrs C. Ward (0742 369872).

SHEFFIELD. **Hallamshire Golf Club Ltd,** Sandygate, Sheffield S10 4LA (Sheffield (0742) 301007). *Location:* A57 out of Sheffield, four miles out of city then fork left for Lodge Moor. Moorland course. 18 holes, 6359 yards, 5815 metres. S.S.S. 71. *Green Fees:* £27.00 weekdays; £34.00 weekends. *Eating facilities:* full catering except Tuesdays – prior notice required. *Visitors:* welcome weekdays by arrangement, some weekends. Snooker table. *Society Meetings:* catered for by arrangement with Secretary. Professional: Geoffrey Tickell (0742 305222). Secretary: D.G. Duckenfield (0742 302153).

SHEFFIELD. **Hallowes Golf Club,** Hallowes Lane, Dronfield, Near Sheffield S18 6UA (Dronfield (0246) 413734). *Location:* six miles south of Sheffield on old A61 (not by-pass to Chesterfield). Moorland/parkland. 18 holes, 6342 yards. S.S.S. 70. Large practice area. *Green Fees:* weekdays £20.00 per round, £27.00 per day. *Eating facilities:* bars, dining room (no catering Mondays). *Visitors:* weekdays only, no visitors at weekends and Bank Holidays except with members. *Society Meetings:* E.G.U. registered societies welcome. Professional: Philip Dunn (0246 411196). Secretary: L.F. Smith (0246 413734).

SHEFFIELD. **Hillsborough Golf Club Ltd,** Worral Road, Sheffield S6 4BE (Sheffield (0742) 343608). *Location:* three miles from city centre. Worrall Road via Middlewood Road, Dykes Hall Road. Undulating wooded parkland and heath. 18 holes, 6035 yards. S.S.S. 70. Practice field. *Green Fees:* weekdays £28.

Eating facilities: snacks available; lunches, teas, evening meals by arrangement (not Fridays). *Visitors:* welcome weekdays, weekends with a member only. *Society Meetings:* catered for by arrangement with Secretary/ Manager. Professional: G. Walker (0742 332666). Secretary/Manager: G. White (0742 343608).

SHEFFIELD. **Lees Hall Golf Club Ltd,** Hemsworth Road, Norton, Sheffield S8 8LL (0742 554402). *Location:* three miles south of Sheffield, between A61 and A6102 ring road. Undulating parkland with extensive views over Sheffield. 18 holes, 6137 yards. S.S.S. 69. *Green Fees:* information not provided. *Eating facilities:* available daily except Tuesdays. *Visitors:* welcome, except Saturday and Sunday before 10.30am. *Society Meetings:* by arrangement only. Professional: J.R. Wilkinson (0742 554402). Secretary: N.E. Westworth (0742 552900).

SHEFFIELD. **Stocksbridge and District Golf Club Ltd,** 30 Royd Lane, Deepcar S30 5RZ (Sheffield (0742) 882003). *Location:* 10 miles from Sheffield on A616 heading towards Manchester. Parkland course. 18 holes, 5200 yards. S.S.S. 65. Practice ground. *Green Fees:* weekdays £15.00; weekends £24.00. *Eating facilities:* available. *Visitors:* welcome weekdays, restrictions weekends. *Society Meetings:* catered for by arrangement. Secretary: Stuart Lee (0742 882408).

SHEFFIELD. **Tankersley Park Golf Club,** High Green, Sheffield S30 4LG (Sheffield (0742) 468247). *Location:* M1 north to Junction 35a, A616, golf club on right. M1 south Junction 36, A61 Sheffield, left on A616, golf club on left. Parkland. 18 holes, 6212 yards. S.S.S. 70. Practice area. *Green Fees:* £17.00 per round, £22.00 per day weekdays; £22.00 weekends. *Eating facilities:* sandwiches, bar meals, full evening meals. *Visitors:* welcome on weekdays without reservation but not before 3pm weekends. *Society Meetings:* catered for by prior arrangement. Professional: I. Kirk (0742 455583). Secretary: Mr P.A. Bagshaw (0742 468247).

SHEFFIELD. **Tinsley Park Golf Club (Municipal),** High Hazels Park, Darnall, Sheffield (0742 560237). *Location:* three miles from Junction 33 M1, exit – A6102. Wooded course. 18 holes, 6086 yards. S.S.S. 69. Practice facilities. *Green Fees:* £6.95. *Eating facilities:* cafe (closed Tuesday); meals if ordered from Stewardess. Time must be booked on arrival. *Visitors:* welcome without restriction, no booking facilities. *Society Meetings:* book through Sheffield City Council. Professional: Mr A.P. Highfield (0742 560237). Secretary: Mr C.E. Benson (0742 873110).

SHEFFIELD. **Wortley Golf Club,** Hermit Hill Lane, Wortley, Near Sheffield S30 7DF (Sheffield (0742) 882139). *Location:* leave M1 Junction 36 or 35A – A61 to A629 west of Wortley Village. Parkland. 18 holes, 5983 yards, 5469 metres. S.S.S. 69. *Green Fees:* £21.00 per day or round weekdays; £25.00 weekends and Bank Holidays. *Eating facilities:* order in advance, not Mondays. *Visitors:* welcome by arrangement. *Society Meetings:* parties catered for by arrangement Wednesdays and Fridays. Professional: Jeremy Tilson (0742 886490). Secretary: J. Lewis Dalby (0742 885294).

West Yorkshire

BINGLEY. **Bingley (St. Ives) Golf Club,** The Mansion, St. Ives, Harden, Bingley (Bradford (0274) 562436). Parkland/moorland. 18 holes, 6480 yards. S.S.S. 71. Practice ground. *Green Fees:* weekdays £20.00; weekends and Bank Holidays £25.00. *Eating facilities:* daily except Mondays. *Visitors:* welcome weekdays, limited availability weekends. *Society Meetings:* welcome, book through Professional. Professional: R.K. Firth (0274 562506). Secretary: Mary Welch (0274 562436).

BRADFORD. **Clayton Golf Club,** Thornton View Road, Clayton, Bradford BD14 6JX (Bradford (0274) 880047). *Location:* two miles south west of Bradford, via Thornton Road, then Listerhills Road. Moorland course, testing par 3 at third hole. 9 holes, 5515 yards. S.S.S. 67. *Green Fees:* weekdays £8.00 (£6.00 with a member); weekends £10.00 (£8.00 with a member). *Eating facilities:* diningroom – meals and snacks daily; evening meals by arrangement. *Visitors:* welcome at all times except before 4.00pm on Sundays. *Society Meetings:* catered for by arrangement. Secretary: F. V. Wood (0274 574203).

BRADFORD. **East Bierley Golf Club,** South View Road, East Bierley, Bradford (Bradford (0274) 681023). *Location:* situated about three miles east of Bradford on the Wakefield/Heckmondwike Road. Turn off at Bierley Bar and down South View Road. Undulating semi-moorland course. 9 holes, 4308 metres. S.S.S. 63. *Green Fees:* £10.00 per round weekdays; Saturdays £12.50. *Eating facilities:* lunchtime and evening catering. *Visitors:* welcome, not Sunday or Mondays after 4pm. Secretary: M. Welch (0274 683666). Steward: (0274 680450).

BRADFORD. **Headley Golf Club,** Headley Lane, Thornton, Bradford BD13 3LX (Bradford (0274 833481). *Location:* five miles west of Bradford. Hilly parkland. 9 holes, 4914 yards. S.S.S. 64. *Green Fees:* weekdays £10.00, £5.00 if playing with a member. *Eating facilities:* dining and bar. *Visitors:* weekdays only. *Society Meetings:* restricted facilities. Hon. Secretary: J.P. Clark (0274 832571).

BRADFORD. **Northcliffe Golf Club,** High Bank Lane, Shipley BD18 4LJ (Bradford (0274) 584025). *Location:* three miles west of Bradford on A650 Bradford-Keighley. Undulating wooded parkland. 18 holes, White Tees 6104 yards. S.S.S. 69; Yellow Tees 5839 yards. S.S.S. 68. *Green Fees:* weekdays £20.00; weekends and Bank Holidays £25.00. *Eating facilities:* bars, dining room (no catering Mondays). *Visitors:* unlimited apart from weekends (Competition Days). *Society Meetings:* welcome Tuesdays to Fridays. Handicap Certificate required. Professional: M. Hillas (0274 587193). Secretary: H.R. Archer (0274 596731).

BRADFORD. **Queensbury Golf Club,** Brighouse Road, Queensbury, Bradford BD13 1QF (Bradford (0274) 882155). *Location:* M62 Junction 25, A644 to Brighouse, Hipperholme and Queensbury. Wooded course. 9 holes, 5024 yards. S.S.S. 65. *Green Fees:* weekdays £13.00; weekends £20.00. *Eating facilities:* lunches, teas except Monday. Bar available. *Visitors:* welcome any day, must have Handicap. No parties at weekends. *Society Meetings:* by arrangement. Professional: Mr Geoff Howard (0274 882956). Secretary: Mr H. Andrew (0422 201565).

BRADFORD. **Shipley Golf Club,** Beckfoot Lane, Cottingley Bridge, Bingley BD16 1LX (Bradford (0274) 563212). *Location:* off A650 at Cottingley Bridge, Bradford six miles, Bingley one mile (from Bradford left before Cottingley Bridge). Slightly undulating parkland. 18 holes. S.S.S. 70. Practice area and net putting green. *Green Fees:* weekdays £25.00; weekends and Bank Holidays £33.00. *Eating facilities:* available by arrangement with Steward, except Mondays. *Visitors:* welcome (Tuesdays after 2pm, Saturdays after 4pm). *Society Meetings:* catered for by arrangement. Professional: J.R. Parry (0274 563674). Secretary: G. Martin Shaw (0274 568652).

BRADFORD. **South Bradford Golf Club,** Pearson Road, Odsal, Bradford BD12 0EA (Bradford (0274) 679195). *Location:* follow signs for Odsal Stadium, then turn right down towards club entrance. Parkland type course with some hilly sections. 9 holes, 6004 yards. S.S.S. 69. Practice ground. *Green Fees:* weekdays £12.00 per day (£7.00 with member); weekends £20.00 per day (£10.00 with member). *Eating facilities:* bar meals available except Mondays. *Visitors:* welcome; not before 3.30pm on weekends and Bank Holidays. Must conform with club rules on dress. Parties accommodated when possible on application. *Society Meetings:* catered for on request. Professional: M. Hillas (0274 673346). Secretary: John Canning (0274 679195).

BRADFORD. **The Manor Golf Club,** Bradford Road, Drighlington, Bradford (0532 852644). *Location:* between Leeds and Bradford, just off M62. Parkland. 18 holes, 6550 yards. S.S.S 72. Driving range, pitch and putt course. *Green Fees:* information not provided. *Eating facilities:* clubhouse. *Visitors:* welcome at all times. *Society Meetings:* welcome. Professional: Geoff Robertshaw. Secretary: Mr B. Cook.

BRADFORD. **West Bowling Golf Club Ltd,** Newall Hall, Rooley Lane, Bradford BD5 8LB (Bradford (0274) 724449). *Location:* junction of M606 (off M62) and Bradford ring road (east). Parkland. 18 holes, 5657 yards. S.S.S. 67. Practice facilities. *Green Fees:* weekdays £23.00 (£19.00 with Handicap Certificate);

weekends and Bank Holidays £30.00 (restricted). *Eating facilities:* available daily. *Visitors:* by arrangement with Professional for individuals, with Secretary for parties. Weekends severely restricted, no parties. *Society Meetings:* by arrangement as above. Professional: A. Swaine (0274 728036). Secretary: M.E. Lynn (0274 393207).

BRADFORD. **West Bradford Golf Club Ltd,** Chellow Grange Road, Haworth Road, Bradford BD9 6NP (Bradford (0274) 542767). *Location:* three miles west of city centre off Haworth Road. Undulating course. 18 holes, 5788 yards. S.S.S. 68. *Green Fees:* £15.00 weekdays; £22.00 weekends, including VAT. *Eating facilities:* available every day except Mondays. *Visitors:* welcome, except Saturdays. *Society Meetings:* welcome Wednesday to Friday. Golf package deals Wednesday to Friday £16.00. Professional: Nigel A. Barber (0274 542102). Secretary: D. Ingham (0274 820417).

BRIGHOUSE. **Castlefields Golf Club,** Rastrick Common, Rastrick, Brighouse HD6 3HL. *Location:* one mile out of Brighouse on A643. Parkland. 7 holes, 2406 yards. S.S.S. 50, Par 54. *Green Fees:* weekdays £4.00; weekends £5.00 (Juniors £2.00). *Eating facilities:* Globe Inn 200 yards away. *Visitors:* welcome at all times but must be accompanied by a member. Secretary: B.J. Davies (0422 376687).

CLECKHEATON. **Cleckheaton and District Golf Club Ltd,** Bradford Road, Cleckheaton BD19 6BU (0274 874118). *Location:* four miles south of Bradford on A638, 200 yards from Junction 26 M62. Parkland course. 18 holes, 5679 yards. S.S.S. 68. Practice area. *Green Fees:* £22.00 weekdays (winter £17.00); £25.00 weekends and Bank Holidays (winter £22.00). *Eating facilities:* available (except Mondays). *Visitors:* welcome all year, suggest prior enquiry. *Society Meetings:* catered for by prior arrangement except Saturdays. Professional: Mike Ingham (0274 851267). Secretary: Herbert Thornton (0274 851266).

DEWSBURY. **Hanging Heaton Golf Club,** White Cross Road, Dewsbury WF12 7DT (Dewsbury (0924) 461606). *Location:* one mile from town centre on main A653 Dewsbury to Leeds road. 9 holes, 5870 yards (for 18 holes). S.S.S. 67. *Green Fees:* weekdays £12.00 (£8.00 with member); weekends with member £10.00. Green fees not taken weekends or Bank Holidays without member's introduction. *Eating facilities:* available. *Visitors:* welcome without reservation, except weekends. *Society Meetings:* catered for by arrangement with Steward. Professional: (0924 467077). Secretary: S.M. Simpson (0924 430100).

ELLAND. **Elland Golf Club,** Hammerstones, Leach Lane, Elland HX5 0QP (0422 372505). *Location:* M62 Junction 24 exit off roundabout for Blackley. Parkland. 9 holes, 5630 yards. S.S.S. 66. *Green Fees:* weekdays £12.00; weekends £20.00. *Eating facilities:* meals/bar snacks except Mondays. *Visitors:* welcome mid-week. *Society Meetings:* by arrangement. Professional: M. Allison (0422 374886). Secretary: A.D. Blackburn (0422 372014).

GUISELEY. **Bradford Golf Club,** Hawksworth Lane, Guiseley, Leeds LS20 8NP (Guiseley (0943) 877239). *Location:* Shipley to Ilkley road, left at top of Hollins Hill, one mile up Hawksworth Lane. Moorland/parkland. 18 holes, 6259 yards. S.S.S. 71. *Green Fees:* weekdays £20.00 per round, £25.00 per day; weekends £32.00 (half price with member). *Eating facilities:* every day, preferably by prior arrangement. *Visitors:* welcome without reservation weekdays, not on weekends without prior arrangement. *Society Meetings:* catered for on weekdays (except Tuesdays) by prior arrangement. Professional: Sydney Weldon (0943 873719). Secretary: P. Atkinson (0943 875570).

HALIFAX. **Bradley Hall Golf Club,** Holywell Green, Halifax (0422 374108). *Location:* three miles south of Halifax on B6112. Moorland, undulating. 18 holes, 6213 yards. S.S.S. 70. Practice ground. *Green Fees:* weekdays £17.00 per round, £20.00 per day; weekends £25.00 per round, £30.00 per day. *Eating facilities:* full catering by arrangement except Tuesdays, seven day bar. *Visitors:* welcome. Snooker. *Societies:* welcome with prior reservation weekdays. Professional: P. Wood (0422 372103). Secretary: P.M. Pitchforth (0422 376626 evenings).

HALIFAX. **Halifax Golf Club Ltd,** Union Lane, Ogden, Halifax (Halifax (0422) 244171). *Location:* three miles out of Halifax, A629 towards Keighley. Moorland. 18 holes, 6037 yards. S.S.S. 70. *Green Fees:* weekdays £20.00; weekends £30.00. *Eating facilities:* luncheons and dinners served. Good restaurant facilities. *Visitors:* welcome most days by arrangement. All-in Day £22.00. *Society Meetings:* catered for by arrangement – mid-week £32.00; weekends £40.00. Professional: Mr Steve Foster (0422 240047). Secretary: Mr J.P. Clark (0422 244171).

HALIFAX. **Lightcliffe Golf Club,** Knowle Top Road, Lightcliffe, Halifax (Halifax (0422) 202459). *Location:* three miles east of Halifax on A58 (Leeds) road. Parkland. 9 holes, 5368 metres. S.S.S. 68 *Green Fees:* information not provided. *Eating facilities:* bar snacks and meals (except Mondays). *Visitors:* welcome without reservation but must confirm with Professional. Not Wednesdays. *Society Meetings:* catered for. Professional: D.W. Lockett (0422 202459). Secretary: T.H. Gooder (0422 201051).

HALIFAX. **Ryburn Golf Club,** The Shaw, Norland, Near Halifax (Halifax (0422) 831355). *Location:* Station Road Halifax to Sowerby Bridge, turn right up hill, right towards Hobbit Inn (signposted), left after cottages. Demanding, hilly, windy course. 9 holes, 4907 yards. S.S.S. 64. *Green Fees:* information not available. *Eating facilities:* good catering facilities and bar. *Visitors:* welcome weekdays, weekends by prior arrangement. *Society Meetings:* welcome by prior arrangement. Secretary: Jack Hoyle (0422 843070 home).

HALIFAX. **West End Golf Club (Halifax) Ltd,** Paddock Lane, Highroad Well, Halifax HX2 0NT (Halifax (0422) 353608). *Location:* two miles west of town centre. Parkland. 18 holes, 6003 yards. S.S.S. 69. *Green Fees:* weekdays £15.00 per round, £20.00 per day; weekends and Bank Holidays £18.00 per round,

£25.00 per day. *Eating facilities:* full bar and catering except Mondays. *Visitors:* welcome – please check with Professional. *Society Meetings:* catered for by arrangement with Secretary. Professional: D. Rishworth (0422 363293). Secretary: B.R. Thomas (0422 341878).

HEBDEN BRIDGE. **Hebden Bridge Golf Club,** Wadsworth, Hebden Bridge HX7 8PH (Hebden Bridge (0422) 842896). *Location:* one mile upwards past Birchcliffe Centre. Moorland with superb Pennine views. 9 holes, 5202 yards. S.S.S. 65. *Green Fees:* weekdays £7.50 (with a member £5.00); weekends £10.00 (with a member £5.00). *Eating facilities:* bar and diningroom facilities. *Visitors:* welcome, please check first at weekends. *Society Meetings:* welcome by prior arrangement. Secretary: Dr R.G. Pogson.

HUDDERSFIELD. **Bradley Park Municipal Golf Course,** Off Bradley Road, Huddersfield HD2 1PZ (Huddersfield (0484) 539988). *Location:* M62 Junction 25, one mile up A6107. Parkland, rolling hills with panoramic views. 18 holes, 6220 yards. S.S.S. 70. Floodlit driving range, 9 hole Par 3 course. *Green Fees:* weekdays £8.00; weekends £10.00. *Eating facilities:* full catering. *Visitors:* no restrictions except booking at weekends. *Society Meetings:* all welcome. Professional: P.E. Reilly. Secretary: D.W. Miller.

HUDDERSFIELD. **Crosland Heath Golf Club Ltd,** Felk Stile Road, Crosland Hill, Huddersfield HD4 7AF (0484 653216). *Location:* three miles from town centre off A62 Oldham road. Flat heathland with extensive views. 18 holes, 5963 yards. S.S.S. 70. Practice facilities. *Green Fees:* on application. *Eating facilities:* full catering except Mondays. *Visitors:* welcome, suggest prior enquiry. *Society Meetings:* catered for by arrangement. Professional: Christopher Gaunt (0484 653877). Secretary: D. Walker (0484 653426).

HUDDERSFIELD. **Huddersfield Golf Club,** Fixby Hall, Lightridge Road, Fixby, Huddersfield HD2 2EP (Huddersfield (0484) 420110). *Location:* M62 Junction 24; A643 from Hilton Hotel; turn right first traffic lights by Sun Inn. Parkland course. 18 holes, 6402 yards. S.S.S. 71. Practice ground. *Green Fees:* weekdays £30.00 for 18 holes, £40.00 for 27/36 holes; weekends and Public Holidays £40.00 for 18 holes, £50.00 for 27/36 holes. £10.00 playing with a member. *Eating facilities:* available. *Visitors:* always welcome, reservation advised but not essential. Tuesday is Ladies' day and no visitors Saturdays. Snooker. *Society and Company days:* catered for except weekends, well appointed private rooms. Catering to suit all occasions. Professional: P. Carman (0484 426463). Secretary: Mrs D. Lockett (0484 426203). General Manager: D.L. Bennett (0484 426203).

HUDDERSFIELD. **Longley Park Golf Club,** Maple Street, Aspley, Huddersfield HD5 9AX (Huddersfield (0484) 426932). *Location:* one mile town centre, Wakefield side. 9 holes, 5324 yards. S.S.S. 66. *Green Fees:* weekdays £12.00; weekends and Bank Holidays £15.00. *Eating facilities:* available. *Visitors:* welcome Mondays, Tuesdays and Fridays. *Society Meetings:* welome only by previous arrangement with Secretary. Professional: Neil Suckling (0484 422304). Secretary: D. Palliser.

HUDDERSFIELD. **Marsden Golf Club,** Hemplow, Marsden, Huddersfield HD7 6JL (Huddersfield (0484) 844253). *Location:* eight miles south of Huddersfield on A62 to Manchester. Moorland. 9 holes, 5702 yards. S.S.S. 68. *Green Fees:* weekdays £10.00. *Eating facilities:* lunches and snacks available except Tuesdays. *Visitors:* welcome weekdays, with a member only weekends. *Society Meetings:* catered for by arrangement. Professional: A. Bickerdike. Secretary: D. Horncastle (0484 647433).

HUDDERSFIELD. **Woodsome Hall Golf Club,** Woodsome Hall, Fenay Bridge, Huddersfield HD8 0LQ (Huddersfield (0484) 602971). *Location:* leave Huddersfield A629. Parkland. 18 holes, 6080 yards. S.S.S. 69. Practice ground. *Green Fees:* weekdays £25.00; weekends and Public Holidays £30.00. *Eating facilities:* available. *Visitors:* welcome Wednesday, Thursday and Fridays. *Society Meetings:* welcome. Professional: M. Higginbottam (0484 602034). Secretary: W.D.N. Woodhouse (0484 602739).

ILKLEY. **Ben Rhydding Golf Club,** High Wood, Ben Rhydding, Ilkley (0943 608759). *Location:* one mile south-east of Ilkley town centre along Ben Rhydding Road. Parkland course with fine panoramic views over Wharfedale and surrounding moors. 9 holes, 4711 yards (18 holes). S.S.S. 64. *Green Fees:* weekdays £10.00 per round/day; Bank Holiday Mondays £15.00. *Visitors:* welcome weekdays and Bank Holidays; as members' guests only at weekends. Secretary: P. Atkinson (0943 876442).

ILKLEY. **Ilkley Golf Club,** Nesfield Road, Ilkley (Ilkley (0943) 607277). *Location:* 15 miles north of Bradford. Flat course. 18 holes, 6262 yards. S.S.S. 70. *Green Fees:* weekdays £30.00; weekends £35.00. Subject to review. *Eating facilities:* by arrangement. *Visitors:* welcome by arrangement. *Society Meetings:* catered for by arrangement. Professional: J. L. Hammond (0943 607463). Secretary: G. Hirst (0943 600214).

KEIGHLEY. **Branshaw Golf Club,** Branshaw Moor, Oakworth, Keighley BD22 7ES (Haworth (0535) 643235). *Location:* one mile from Haworth. Moorland with extensive views. 18 holes, 5858 yards. S.S.S. 69. *Green Fees:* weekdays £15.00 per day; weekends £20.00. Juniors half price. *Eating facilities:* meals and bar snacks served (except Monday). *Visitors:* welcome anytime by prior arrangement with the Professional. *Society Meetings:* catered for weekdays only, contact Professional. Professional: John Nolan (Tel & Fax: 0535 647441). Secretary: Mr D.A. Town (0535 605003).

KEIGHLEY. **Keighley Golf Club,** Howden Park, Utley, Keighley BD20 6DH (Keighley (0535) 603179). *Location:* one mile west of Keighley on A629. Parkland. 18 holes, 6149 yards. S.S.S. 70. *Green Fees:* weekdays £25.00 per day, £21.00 per round; weekends £23.00 per round, £27.00 per day. *Eating facilities:* full catering available. *Visitors:* welcome by prior arrangement. Ladies' day, Tuesday. *Society Meetings:* catered for by arrangement. Professional: Mike Bradley (0535 665370). Secretary: C.L. Hodge (0535 604778).

England WEST YORKSHIRE

KEIGHLEY. **Riddlesden Golf Club,** Howden Rough, Riddlesden, Keighley BD20 5QN (Keighley (0535) 602148). *Location:* A650 Keighley-Bradford road, left into Bar Lane, left on Scott Lane, which leads on to Scott Lane West and Elam Wood Road, approximately two miles. Moorland, with spectacular par 3s. 18 holes, 4247 yards. S.S.S. 61. *Green Fees:* weekdays £10.00 (£5.00 with member); weekends £15.00 (£8.00 with a member). *Eating facilities:* catering available during bar hours – weekdays 12 noon to 3pm then 7pm onwards, weekends noon onwards. *Visitors:* welcome except between 10am – 2pm Saturdays and until after 2pm Sundays. *Society Meetings:* catered for by prior arrangement. Secretary: Mrs K.M. Brooksbank (0535 607646).

KEIGHLEY. **Silsden Golf Club,** High Brunthwaite, Silsden, Near Keighley BD20 0NH (Sleeton (0535) 652998). *Location:* five miles north of Keighley. Undulating downland. 14 holes, 4870 yards. S.S.S. 64. Practice area and putting green. *Green Fees:* £10.00 weekdays; £16.00 weekends. *Eating facilities:* licensed bar, food available. *Visitors:* restrictions at weekends – details from Secretary. *Society Meetings:* by arrangement with Secretary. Secretary: G. Davey (0943 601490).

KNOTTINGLEY. **Ferrybridge "C" P.S. Golf Club,** PO Box 39, Stranglands Lane, Knottingley WF11 8SQ. *Location:* off the A1 at Ferrybridge and quarter of a mile towards Castleford on the B6136. Undulating land within the boundaries of and surrounding the power station. 9 holes, 5138 yards. S.S.S. 65. Practice ground. *Green Fees:* £5.00 weekdays; £6.00 weekends. *Visitors:* welcome when accompanied by a member, only because of security restrictions. *Society Meetings:* by special arrangement in parties of not more than 12. Secretary: Mr N.E. Pugh (0977 793884).

LEEDS. **Alwoodley Golf Club,** Wigton Lane, Alwoodley, Leeds LS17 8SA (Leeds (0532) 681680). *Location:* five miles north of Leeds on A61 (Leeds to Harrogate). 18 holes, 6686 yards. S.S.S. 72. *Green Fees:* £35.00 weekdays; £45.00 weekends. *Eating facilities:* available. *Visitors:* welcome by arrangement. *Society Meetings:* catered for by arrangement. Professional: J. Green (0532 689603). Secretary: R.C.W. Banks.

LEEDS. **Calverley Golf Club,** Woodhall Lane, Pudsey, Leeds LS28 5QY (0532 564362). *Location:* Leeds seven miles, Bradford four miles. Parkland. 27 holes: 18 holes – 5527 yards, 9 holes – 2581 yards. S.S.S. 67. *Green Fees:* weekdays 18 holes £10.00, 9 holes £6.00; weekends 18 holes £15.00, 9 holes £6.00. *Eating facilities:* available. *Visitors:* welcome, must book 18 hole course. *Society Meetings:* welcome. Professional: Derek Johnson (0532 569244). Secretary: W. Gardner.

LEEDS. **Garforth Golf Club Ltd,** Long Lane, Garforth, Leeds LS25 2DS (Leeds (0532) 862021). *Location:* six miles east of Leeds on A63, then turn left on to A642. Flat parkland. 18 holes, 6306 yards. S.S.S. 70. Practice area. *Green Fees:* information not provided. *Eating facilities:* available. *Visitors:* welcome, but not before 9.30am or between 12 noon and 2.30pm or after 4.30pm. Weekend as members' guest only. *Society Meetings:* catered for. Professional: K. Findlater (0532 862063). Secretary/Manager: F.A. Readman (0532 863308).

LEEDS. **Gotts Park Municipal Golf Club,** Gotts House, Gotts Park, Armley Ridge Road, Leeds LS12 2QX (Leeds (0532) 310492). *Location:* three miles east of city centre off A647 Stanningley Road. Parkland, hilly, hard walking. 18 holes, 4960 yards. S.S.S. 64. Practice ground, lessons available. *Green Fees:* under review. *Eating facilities:* snack bar cafe, bar evenings only. *Visitors:* unrestricted except at weekends when booking system applies – no phone bookings. Professional: J.K. Simpson (0532 636600). Secretary: M. Gill (0532 562994).

LEEDS. **Headingley Golf Club,** Back Church Lane, Adel, Leeds LS16 8DW (Leeds (0532) 673052). *Location:* leave Leeds/Otley road (A660) at Church Lane, Adel about five miles from city centre. 18 holes, 6298 yards. S.S.S. 70. *Green Fees:* £25.00 per round, £30.00 per day weekdays; £36.00 per round or day weekends and Bank Holidays. *Eating facilities:* full catering except Fridays. *Visitors:* members of other golf clubs welcome, preferably with prior reservation. *Society Meetings:* catered for by arrangement. Professional: Andrew Dyson (0532 675100). Secretary: R.W. Hellawell (0532 679573).

LEEDS. **Horsforth Golf Club Ltd,** Layton Road, Layton Rise, Horsforth, Leeds LS18 5EX (0532 586819). *Location:* north-west of Leeds on A65 to Ilkley. 18 holes, 6293 yards. S.S.S. 70. *Green Fees:* £24.00 weekdays, £30.00 weekends and Bank Holidays. *Eating facilities:* full catering (except Monday), order in advance for dinner. *Visitors:* welcome, must be bona fide member of another club. *Society Meetings:* catered for by arrangement with Secretary. Professional: L. Turner (0532 585200). Secretary: E. Smurthwaite (0532 586819).

LEEDS. **Howley Hall Golf Club,** Scotchman Lane, Morley, Leeds (Batley (0924) 472432). *Location:* turn off the A650 Bradford/Wakefield road at the Halfway House Public House, take the B6123 towards Batley – the course is on the left. Parkland. 18 holes, 6058 yards, 5540 metres. S.S.S. 69. Practice ground. *Green Fees:* weekdays £18.00 per round, £22.00 per day; weekends £25.00. *Eating facilities:* dining room, meals available up to 7pm. *Visitors:* welcome. *Society Meetings:* catered for by reservation. Professional: S.A. Spinks. Secretary: Mrs A. Pepper.

LEEDS. **Leeds Golf Centre,** Wike Ridge Lane, Shadwell, Leeds LS17 9JW (0532 886186; Fax: 0532 738128). *Location:* eight miles north of Leeds, in village of Wike. Rolling heathland – built to USGA Spec. Donald Steel design. 18 holes, 6780 yards. S.S.S. 72. 9 hole Par 3 course. 18 bay driving range and golf academy. Membership currently available. *Green Fees:* weekdays £15.00; weekends £20.00. *Eating facilities:* lounge bar and grill. *Visitors:* welcome. *Society Meetings:* welcome weekdays. Professional (Golf Academy): David Leadbetter. Secretary: C. Brockbank.

WEST YORKSHIRE *England*

LEEDS. **Leeds Golf Club,** Cobble Hall, Elmete Lane, Leeds LS8 2LJ (Leeds (0532) 658775). *Location:* Leeds ring road to A58, turn left if from east, right if from west, fork right at next roundabout, turn right after 250 yards. 18 holes, 6097 yards. S.S.S. 69. *Green Fees:* £25.00 per day, £19.00 per round weekdays, weekends with member only. *Eating facilities:* full catering, apply in advance. *Visitors:* welcome. *Society Meetings:* catered for. Professional: J. Longster. Secretary: G.W. Backhouse.

LEEDS. **Middleton Park (Municipal) Golf Club,** Ring Road, Beeston, Middleton, Leeds LS10 4NX (0532 700449). *Location:* ring road to Middleton off A653 (Water Tower). Parkland, wooded course. 18 holes, 5036 yards. S.S.S. 66. Practice ground. *Green Fees:* on request – fixed by Leeds County Council. *Visitors:* weekdays, contact the Professional. *Society Meetings:* contact the Professional. Professional: David Bulmer (0532 709506). Secretary: Fred Ramsey (0532 533993).

LEEDS. **Moor Allerton Golf Club,** Coal Road, Wike, Leeds LS17 9NH (0532 661154; Fax: 0532 371124). *Location:* accessible from A61 at Alwoodley or from Harvester Scarcroft on A58. Undulating parkland, designed by Robert Trent Jones. 18 holes, 6552 yards. S.S.S. 72. 9 holes, 3541 yards. S.S.S. 37. 6 bay driving range, practice field. *Green Fees:* £35.00 per day weekdays, Saturdays only £45.00 per day. Winter rate November to March. *Eating facilities:* bars, full restaurant and snack facilities. *Visitors:* no visitors Sundays; restricted to small parties Saturdays. Crown green bowling, sauna. *Society Meetings:* can cater for up to 250 for golf and banqueting. Richard Lane (0532 665209). Secretary: Mr S. Mack (0532 661154). Executive Vice-President: J.J. Harris.

LEEDS. **Moortown Golf Club,** Harrogate Road, Alwoodley, Leeds LS17 7DB (Leeds (0532) 681682). *Location:* five miles north of Leeds centre, A61 Leeds to Harrogate road. 18 holes, 6515 yards. S.S.S. 72. Large practice field. *Green Fees:* weekdays £35.00 per round, £40.00 per day, weekends £40.00 per round, £45.00 per day. *Eating facilities:* lunches except Mondays, evening meals Tuesday to Saturday. *Visitors:* welcome weekdays, some tee-off time restrictions. *Society Meetings:* catered for. Professional: B. Hutchinson (0532 683636). Secretary: T. Hughes (0532 686521).

LEEDS. **Rawdon Golf and Lawn Tennis Club,** Buckstone Drive, Micklefield Lane, Rawdon, Leeds LS19 6BD (Leeds (0532) 506040). *Location:* eight miles north of Leeds on A65, left at Rawdon traffic lights on to Micklefield Lane. Undulating parkland, with trees a special feature. 9 holes (18 tees), 5964 yards. S.S.S. 69. *Green Fees:* information not provided. *Eating facilities:* meals and bar snacks except Mondays.

Visitors: welcome, weekends must play with a member. Facilities for tennis, visitors welcome with members. *Society Meetings:* catered for on application to Secretary. Professional: Syd Wheldon (of Bradford Golf Club) (0532 505017). Secretary: Ray Adams (0532 506064).

LEEDS. **Roundhay Golf Club,** Park Lane, Leeds LS8 3QW (Leeds (0532) 662695). *Location:* four miles north of Leeds city centre, leave A58 to Wetherby at Oakwood. Wooded parkland. 9 holes, 5322 yards. S.S.S. 65. Practice ground. *Green Fees:* weekdays £6.00; weekends and Bank Holidays £6.45. *Eating facilities:* bar for members and guests, restaurant in evenings. *Visitors:* welcome without reservation. *Society Meetings:* arrangements to be made with Leeds City Council. Professional: J. Pape (0532 661686). Hon Secretary: R.H. McLauchlan (0532 492523).

LEEDS. **Sand Moor Golf Club,** Alwoodley Lane, Leeds LS17 7DJ (Leeds (0532) 681685). *Location:* five miles north of Leeds off A61. Moorland, overlooking picturesque Wharfedale. 18 holes, 6429 yards, 5876 metres. S.S.S. 71. *Green Fees:* weekdays £28.00 per round, £35.00 per day; weekends £35.00 per round. *Eating facilities:* lunches daily, evening meals Tuesday to Friday. *Visitors:* welcome most weekdays by arrangement. *Society Meetings:* catered for. Professional: J.R. Foss (0532 683925). Secretary: B.F. Precious (0532 685180).

LEEDS. **Scarcroft Golf Club,** Syke Lane, Leeds LS14 3BQ (Leeds (0532) 892263). *Location:* A58 Wetherby road; turn left at New Inn, Scarcroft village seven miles north of Leeds. Undulating parkland. 18 holes, 6426 yards. S.S.S. 71. Practice ground and indoor net. *Green Fees:* £25.00 per round, £30.00 per day weekdays; £35.00 per round weekends. *Eating facilities:* bar and restaurant except Mondays. *Visitors:* casuals after 9.30am. *Society Meetings:* accepted Tuesdays to Fridays April to October. Must have official Handicaps. Party rates for groups of 20 or more. Professional: Martin R. Ross (0532 892780). Secretary: R.D. Barwell (0532 892311).

LEEDS. **South Leeds Golf Club,** Parkside Links, Gipsy Lane, Leeds LS11 5TU (Leeds (0532) 700479). *Location:* M62 and M1 within five minutes' drive, Leeds City Centre five minutes' drive. Parkland course with undulating fairways. 18 holes, 5769 yards. S.S.S. 68. Practice fairway. *Green Fees:* £18.00 weekdays, £26.00 weekends and Bank Holidays (rates may change). Special rates for visiting parties over 30. *Eating facilities:* full catering except Mondays; bar. *Visitors:* welcome most days and after 2pm on Sundays. *Society Meetings:* catered for by prior arrangement. Professional: Mike Lewis (0532 702598). Secretary: J. Neal (0532 771676).

THE HAREWOOD ARMS HOTEL
Harrogate Road, Harewood, Leeds LS17 9LH Tel: 0532 886566 Fax: 0532 886064
Centrally situated for many of the North's leading Golf Courses, this Hotel of outstanding character – formerly a coaching inn – offers a high standard of accommodation. All rooms en-suite with colour TV and telephone. The restaurant caters for the most discerning diner with a varied menu and an international wine list.

AA ★★★

THE GOLF GUIDE 1994　　　　　　　　　　　　　　　　　　　　　　　　*England* 　WEST YORKSHIRE

LEEDS. Temple Newsam Golf Club, Temple Newsam, Leeds 15 (Leeds (0532) 645624). *Location:* easily reached by public transport from City (to Temple Newsam or Halton). Two 18 hole courses. No. 1 Course 6448 yards. S.S.S. 71. No. 2 Course 5731 yards. S.S.S. 70. *Green Fees:* as decided by City Council. *Eating facilities:* cafe open Saturdays and Sundays 7.30am till 4.00pm. *Visitors:* welcome without reservation, except that parties must book in advance. *Society Meetings:* catered for. Professional: David Bulmer (0532 641464). Secretary: G. Gower.

MELTHAM. Meltham Golf Club, Thick Hollins Hall, Meltham, Huddersfield HD7 3DQ (Huddersfield (0484) 850227). *Location:* half mile east of Meltham, six miles south west of Huddersfield (B6107). Gently sloping course in wooded valley. 18 holes, 6202 yards, 5673 metres. S.S.S. 70. Restricted practice area. *Green Fees:* weekdays £20.00; weekends £25.00. *Eating facilities:* lunches, dinners (with reservation). *Visitors:* welcome weekdays and Sundays without reservation, not Saturdays. *Society Meetings:* catered for by arrangement. Professional: P. Davies (0484 851521). Secretary: J. Holdsworth.

MIRFIELD. Dewsbury District Golf Club, The Pinnacle, Sands Lane, Mirfield WF14 8HJ (0924 492399). *Location:* turn off A644 opposite Swan Inn, two miles west of Dewsbury. Undulating moorland/parkland with panoramic views over surrounding countryside. 18 holes, 6256 yards. S.S.S. 71. *Green Fees:* £22.00 weekdays. *Eating facilities:* full catering except Monday – order in advance. *Visitors:* welcome without reservation except weekends unless with member. Two full size snooker tables. *Society Meetings:* welcome. Professional: N.P. Hirst (0924 496030). Secretary: D.M. Scott.

NORMANTON. Normanton Golf Club, Snydale Road, Normanton WF6 1PA (Wakefield (0924) 892943). *Location:* Junction 30 M62, A655 towards Wakefield, left at lights, half a mile on left. Flat course with internal out of bounds. 9 holes, 5823 yards. S.S.S. 66. Large practice area. *Green Fees:* weekdays £10.00, £6.00 with a member; Saturday and Bank Holidays £17.50, £10.00 with a member. No green fees Sundays. *Eating facilities:* full catering and bar facilities. *Visitors:* welcome, no visitors on Sundays. *Society Meetings:* catered for weekdays only. Professional: Martin Evans (0924 220134). Secretary: Jack McElhinney (0977 702273).

OTLEY. Otley Golf Club, West Busk Lane, Otley LS21 3NG (0943 461015). *Location:* off main Bradford to Otley road. Parkland with magnificent views across Wharfedale. 18 holes, 6229 yards. S.S.S. 70. Good practice ground. *Green Fees:* weekdays £23.00; weekends £28.00. *Eating facilities:* large dining rooms. *Visitors:* welcome without reservation except Tuesday mornings and Saturdays. *Society Meetings:* catered for by arrangement. Professional: Simon Poot (0943 463403). Secretary/Manager: Mrs Pat Bates (0943 465329).

OUTLANE. Outlane Golf Club, Slack Lane, off New Hey Road, Outlane, Near Huddersfield (Halifax (0422) 374762). *Location:* from Huddersfield (A640) through Outlane Village, entrance on left just after bus terminus. Semi moorland course, part wooded. Offers panoramic views and is challenge to the amateur. 18 holes, 6003 yards. S.S.S. 69. Practice areas and nets available. *Green Fees:* £18.00 mid week; £27.00 weekends and Bank Holidays. Reduced rates playing with member and after 3pm Sunday. *Eating facilities:* full catering available except Mondays. *Visitors:* welcome except Saturdays; Sundays by arrangement. *Society Meetings:* welcome with reservation. Professional: D. Chapman. Secretary: J.S. Donnelly.

POLLARD LANE. Bradford Moor Golf Club, Scarr Hill, Pollard Lane, Bradford BD2 4RW (Bradford (0274) 638313). *Location:* A658 two miles from top of M606. Moorland, undulating course. 9 holes, 5854 yards. S.S.S. 68. *Green Fees:* weekdays £12.00 (with a member £6.00); weekends with a member only (£8.00). *Eating facilities:* available except Tuesdays. *Visitors:* welcome weekdays. *Society Meetings:* welcome weekdays. Professional: Mr R.J. Hughes (0274 870108). Secretary: Mr Chris Bedford (0274 626107).

PONTEFRACT. Pontefract and District Golf Club, Park Lane, Pontefract WF8 4QS (Pontefract (0977) 792241). *Location:* M62 Exit 32, one mile from Pontefract on B6134. Parkland. 18 holes, 6227 yards. S.S.S. 70. Practice ground. *Green Fees:* weekdays £24.00; weekends £30.00. *Eating facilities:* available except Mondays. *Visitors:* welcome, must be members of a golf club. *Society Meetings:* catered for Tuesdays, Thursdays and Fridays by arrangement. Professional: J. Coleman (0977 706806). Secretary: W. T. Smith (0977 792115).

PUDSEY. Fulneck Golf Club Ltd, Fulneck, Pudsey LS28 8NT (Pudsey (0532) 565191). *Location:* between Leeds and Bradford. Undulating wooded parkland course. 9 holes, 5564 yards. S.S.S. 67. *Green Fees:* £12.00 (£6.00 with member) weekdays, weekends with a member only. *Society Meetings:* catered for by arrangement. Secretary: J.A. Brogden (0532 574049).

PUDSEY. Woodhall Hills Golf Club Ltd, Woodhall Road, Calverley, Pudsey (Leeds (0532) 564771). *Location:* one mile from Pudsey roundabout on A647 Leeds to Bradford road, signposted Calverley. 18 holes, 6102 yards. S.S.S. 69. *Green Fees:* weekdays £20.50 per round/day, weekends and Bank Holidays £25.50. Juniors £10.50 any day. *Eating facilities:* available daily except Mondays. *Visitors:* welcome without reservation. *Society Meetings:* catered for by previous arrangement. Professional: D. Tear (0532 562857). Secretary: D. Harkness (0532 554594).

SHIPLEY. Baildon Golf Club, Moorgate, Baildon BD17 5PP (0274 584266). *Location:* five miles northwest of Bradford via Shipley. Hilly, moorland course. 18 holes, 6085 yards, 5692 metres. S.S.S. 70. *Green Fees:* weekdays £14.00, weekends and Bank Holidays £22.00. Reduced rates for groups of 12 and over. *Eating facilities:* catering except Mondays. Bar and separate restaurant. *Visitors:* welcome, restricted at weekends and Tuesdays. *Society Meetings:* welcome weekdays only, by written application. Professional: R. Masters (0274 595162). Secretary: A. Beuridge (0274 592320).

WEST YORKSHIRE *England*

TODMORDEN. Todmorden Golf Club, Rive Rocks, Cross Stone Road, Todmorden (Todmorden (0706) 812986). *Location:* A646 Halifax Road, one mile left Cross Stone Road, one mile, bear left at top. Moorland. 9 holes, 5818 yards. S.S.S. 68. *Green Fees:* weekdays £15.00; weekends and Bank Holidays £20.00. Packages for parties of four or more. *Eating facilities:* available, order in advance. *Visitors:* welcome without reservation. *Society Meetings:* catered for Monday to Friday by prior arrangement. Secretary: P.H. Eastwood.

WAKEFIELD. City of Wakefield Golf Club, Lupset Park, Horbury Road, Wakefield WF2 8QS (0924 367442). *Location:* one mile from city centre, two miles from M1 Junctions 39/40. Undulating partially wooded parkland. 18 holes, 6299 yards, 5760 metres. S.S.S. 70/71. *Green Fees:* weekdays £7.20; weekends and Bank Holidays £9.60. Juniors weekdays £3.60; weekends and Bank Holidays £4.80. *Eating facilities:* full or snack catering, bar available, except Thursdays. *Visitors:* weekdays ball chute operates, weekends – booked times only. *Society Meetings:* only by arrangement with Stewardess (0924 367242). Professional: Roger Holland (0924 360282). Secretary: Mrs P. Ambler (0924 367442 club or 0924 375008 home).

WAKEFIELD. Low Laithes Golf Club Ltd, Parkmill Lane, Flushdyke, Ossett, Wakefield WF5 9AP (Wakefield (0924) 273275). *Location:* one mile from Junction 40 M1, or along A638 Dewsbury to Wakefield road. Parkland, undulating. 18 holes, 6456 yards. S.S.S. 71. Practice area. *Green Fees:* £20.00 weekdays. *Eating facilities:* bar and catering. *Visitors:* welcome weekdays after 9.30am, no visitors weekends and Bank Holidays. *Society Meetings:* by arrangement, not weekends or Bank Holidays. Professional: Paul Browning (0924 274667). Secretary: Donald Wilford (Tel & Fax: 0924 378263).

WAKEFIELD. Painthorpe House Golf and Country Club, Painthorpe Lane, Crigglestone, Wakefield WF4 3HE (Wakefield (0924) 255083). *Location:* half a mile from Junction 39 M1. Undulating parkland. 9 holes, 4520 yards. S.S.S. 62. *Green Fees:* weekdays £5.00; Saturdays £7.00. *Eating facilities:* extensive catering for private functions. Two ballrooms (one holding 450, the other 60), Saturday dinner dances. *Visitors:* welcome weekdays. Bowling green. *Society Meetings:* by arrangement. Secretary: H. Kershaw (0924 274527).

WAKEFIELD. Wakefield Golf Club, Woodthorpe Lane, Sandal, Wakefield WF2 6JH (Wakefield (0924) 255104). *Location:* leave M1 at Junction 39, golf club off Barnsley Road. Parkland. 18 holes, 6611 yards. S.S.S. 72. *Green Fees:* weekdays £25.00, with a member £12.00; weekends and Bank Holidays £27.00, with a member £13.00. *Eating facilities:* full catering available. *Visitors:* visiting parties by arrangement Mondays, Wednesdays, Thursdays and Fridays, no catering Mondays. *Society Meetings:* catered for by arrangement. Professional: I.M. Wright (0924 255380). Secretary: D.T. Hall (0924 258778).

WETHERBY. Wetherby Golf Club, Linton Lane, Linton, Wetherby LS22 4JF (0937 582527). *Location:* three quarters of a mile west from A1 roundabout. Parkland course adjoining River Wharfe. 18 holes, 6235 yards. S.S.S. 70. Two practice grounds. *Green Fees:* weekdays £22.00 per round, £27.50 per day; weekends £33.00 per round/day. *Eating facilities:* available seven days a week. *Visitors:* welcome, advisable to phone first. *Society Meetings:* catered for weekdays except Tuesdays (April to September). Professional: D. Padgett (0937 583375). Secretary/Manager: J.R. Nicholson (0937 580089).

GOLF IN SCOTLAND

Golf – St. Andrews, Fife.

Golf in Scotland
WHERE TO PLAY • WHERE TO STAY

TO SAMPLE all the delights of Scottish golf would take more than a year. Edinburgh itself has twenty-eight courses inside the city boundaries, six owned and controlled by the municipal authorities, though this in no way detracts from the high standards, envied by some of the private clubs.

Eastwards along the coast is another golfing complex comprising the three courses at Gullane, the courses at Longniddry, Luffness and North Berwick and the championship links at Muirfield. Muirfield is not only a severe test of everything required in golf but as the Honourable Club of Edinburgh Golfers is one of the founder clubs, the clubhouse is literally steeped in history.

Travelling northwards we can stop off at Boat of Garten "Golf and Tennis Clubs" whose course is another of Braid's compositions, this time with some holes carved out of the silver birch forest, the others on springy moorland turf.

The links at Nairn are well worth a visit as this is regarded as a championship course. The greens can be like lightning in the middle of summer, but true and firm.

If the Royal Dornoch were situated anywhere else, other than 600 miles from London, it would have to be the most exclusive golf course in Britain. Only distance from the centres of population (Inverness, Scotland's most northerly city, is 50 miles to the south) has denied most the ultimate experience of a golfing paradise.

A long drive south now to the Ayrshire coast. Using Troon as a base, a number of fine links and parkland courses are easily accessible. The best known is Royal Troon, one of the few courses in Britain where male chauvinism still rules. The fairer sex are not permitted on the Old Course and no visitors are allowed on Fridays, Saturdays or Sundays, though the Portland is available.

Nearby Prestwick is on soil almost as hallowed as St. Andrews, as it was here that the Open Championships began with three rounds in a day over the existing twelve holes. The club came off the Open rota in 1925 because of the difficulty of coping with the increasing number of people who flocked to see the

FOR THE LATEST DEVELOPMENTS IN GROUNDCARE EQUIPMENT CONTACT *PowerShift*
YOU'LL SOON GET THE PICTURE!

Our Wide Range of Quality Groundcare Equipment has an added extra, No-one else can offer - THE POWERSHIFT CUSTOMER SERVICE COMMITMENT - this includes a wide range of new and used equipment in stock ready for immediate delivery, low cost flexible finance to suit your cash flow requirements, a computerised parts system linked with England, Germany & the USA and a fleet of service vans to carry out servicing and repairs 'on site' throughout Scotland. For more details on our products and services simply call us on the number below or cut out the coupon.

PowerShift
GROUNDCARE EQUIPMENT SPECIALISTS
UNIT 1, ANCHOR MILL, WEST HENDERSONS WYND, DUNDEE DD1 5BI
TEL: 0382 24152 FAX: 0382 202119

NAME	
ADDRESS	
	TEL
PLEASE SEND ME INFORMATION ON	

Golf in Scotland

- Feasibility studies
- Course extensions/modifications
- Architectural services
- Computer aided design
- In house surveying
- Construction
- Project management
- New 9 and 18 hole course
- Design

G. TAYLOR ASSOCIATES
Mill three, New Lanark, Lanarkshire ML11 9DB. Telephone: 0555 666116 Fax: 0555 665738

"A proven record in golf course development consultancy"

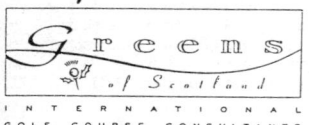

Greens of Scotland
INTERNATIONAL GOLF COURSE CONSULTANTS

Paul Campbell (Manager)
Greens of Scotland,
Craibstone Estate, Bucksburn,
Aberdeen AB2 9TR
Tel: 0224 714288 Fax: 0224 714591

Our extensive range of expertise and technical back-up provides a comprehensive service to Designers, Developers, Financiers, Constructors and Course Managers.

Providing the client with:
- Feasibility studies
- Financial planning
- Contract supervision
- Computer aided design
- Turf management consultancy
- Specifications for construction
- Building design
- Site surveys

---

international annual combat to claim the championship crown.

St. Andrews is the heart of golf. The headquarters of the governing body, the Royal and Ancient, overlook the first tee on the "Old Course", but all five courses at St. Andrews are under the control of a Links Management Committee whose duty it is to administer and maintain the courses for public use.

As well as the "Old Course" where the major championships are played, three additional links – the Eden, the Jubilee and the "New Course" – offer alternatives and there is also a nine-hole "Beginners" course within the complex.

Plans are in hand to add a sixth course in the conceivable future.

Southerness is aptly named as Scotland's most southerly course. Greatly underestimated, it is off the beaten track on the side of the Solway Firth, some 16 miles from Dumfries.

With the support of Tourist Boards such as Dumfries and Galloway, Scottish Borders, North-East, Fife, and the Lothians for example, golfing tourism is an important part of Scotland's economy. Well promoted as such by the Scottish Tourist Board, there is still just enough 'tee-time' left for Scotland's own thriving golf population!

LOOKING FOR A GUIDE?

If you have found *THE GOLF GUIDE* useful, you will also enjoy other titles in the FHG range including:

Recommended Country Hotels of Britain	£3.60
Recommended Wayside Inns of Britain	£3.60
Recommended Short Break Holidays in Britain	£3.60

You'll find our guides in most bookshops and in larger newsagents. In case of difficulty you can post or fax your order direct to FHG Publications in Paisley. You'll find an Order Form showing all prices, including postage, on the back pages of this book.

ABERDEENSHIRE *Scotland*

Aberdeenshire

ABERDEEN. **Auchmill Golf Course,** Aberdeen District Council, Aberdeen Leisure, Howes Road, Bucksburn, Aberdeen. *Location:* approximately four miles from city centre, turn off A96 into Aberdeen at Howes Road. Open, fairly flat. 18 holes, 5952 yards, 5439 metres. S.S.S. 69. *Green Fees:* information not provided. *Visitors:* welcome. Contact: Outdoor Activities Officer, Aberdeen Leisure, Bon Accord Baths, Justice Mill Lane, Aberdeen AB1 2EQ (0224 587920).

ABERDEEN. **Balnagask Golf Course,** Aberdeen District Council, Aberdeen Leisure. Grey Hope Road, Aberdeen. *Location:* on coast beside Girdleness Lighthouse between Aberdeen Harbour and Nigg Bay, south east side of city. Seaside links. 18 holes, 5986 yards, 5472 metres. S.S.S. 69. *Green Fees:* information not provided. *Visitors:* welcome. Contact: Outdoor Activities Officer, Aberdeen Leisure, Bon Accord Baths, Justice Mill Lane, Aberdeen AB1 2EQ (0224 587920).

ABERDEEN. **Bon Accord Municipal Golf Club,** 19 Golf Road, Aberdeen (0224 633464). *Location:* next to Pittodrie Stadium at Aberdeen beach. Seaside links. 18 holes, 6433 yards, 5880 metres. S.S.S. 71. *Green Fees:* information not provided. *Eating facilities:* meals on request. *Society Meetings:* bookings in advance. Secretary: J.B. Miller (0224 879204).

ABERDEEN. **Caledonian Golf Club,** Kings Links, Aberdeen (Aberdeen (0224) 632443). 18 holes, 6396 yards. S.S.S. 71. *Green Fees:* information not provided. *Visitors:* welcome.

ABERDEEN. **Deeside Golf Club,** Golf Road, Bieldside, Aberdeen (Aberdeen (0224) 867697). *Location:* A93 from Aberdeen to Braemar. Wooded parkland. 18 holes, 6000 yards. S.S.S. 71. Also 9 hole course. Practice area. *Green Fees:* £20.00 per day weekdays; £25.00 weekends and Public Holidays. Weekly tickets available. *Eating facilities:* full meal service and bar. *Visitors:* welcome any day except Saturdays (after 4pm). *Society Meetings:* by arrangement, Thursdays only. Professional: F.G. Coutts (0224 861041). Secretary: Dr N.M. Scott (0224 869457).

ABERDEEN. **Hazlehead Golf Course,** Aberdeen District Council, Aberdeen Leisure, Groats Road, Aberdeen. *Location:* situated on west edge of city, four miles from city centre. From A944 into Aberdeen turn off into Groats Road. No. 1 course, 18 holes, 6204 yards, 5673 metres. S.S.S. 70. No 2 course, 9 holes, 2770 yards, 2531 metres. S.S.S. 34. *Green Fees:* details available from Starter's Box (0224 321830). *Eating facilities:* restaurant adjoining park. *Visitors:* welcome. Professional: Iain Smith (0224 317336). Contact: Outdoor Activities Officer, Aberdeen Leisure, Bon Accord Baths, Justice Mill Lane, Aberdeen AB1 2EQ (0224 587920).

ABERDEEN. **Murcar Golf Club,** Murcar, Bridge of Don, Aberdeen AB2 8BD (0224 704345). *Location:* off A92 approximately five miles from Aberdeen centre. Seaside links. White Markers – 18 holes, 6241 yards. S.S.S. 70; Yellow Markers – 18 holes, 5809 yards. S.S.S. 68. *Green Fees:* weekdays £16.00 per round, £20.00 per day; weekends £22.50 after 4pm Saturdays, after 12 noon Sundays. *Eating facilities:* dining-room/bars. *Visitors:* welcome, restrictions Wednesdays and weekends. *Society Meetings:* catered for. Professional: A. White (Tel & Fax: 0224 704370). Secretary: R. Matthews (0224 704354).

ABERDEEN. **Nigg Bay Golf Club,** St. Fitticks Road, Torry, Aberdeen (0224 871286). *Location:* Junction of Victoria Road and St. Fitticks Road. Seaside links. 18 holes, 5986 yards, 5472 metres. S.S.S. 69. 9 hole pitch and putt. *Green Fees:* £6.00. *Eating facilities:* private club. *Visitors:* welcome anytime (municipal course); golfers welcome in clubhouse after playing. Secretary: Arthur Taylor.

ABERDEEN. **Northern Golf Club,** 22 Golf Road, Aberdeen AB2 1QB (0224 636440).*Location:* Adjacent to beach esplanade near Pittodrie Stadium. Kings Links course, 18 holes, 6347 yards, S.S.S.71. *Green Fees:* £6 per round. *Eating facilities:* not Tuesdays and Thursdays. *Visitors:* welcome Monday to Friday. *Society Meetings:* by prior arrangement only. Secretary: F. Sutherland. Steward: (0224 632443).

ABERDEEN. **Royal Aberdeen Golf Club,** Links Road, Balgownie, Bridge of Don AB23 8AT (0224 702571; Fax: 0224 826591). *Location:* on A92, north side of Aberdeen, cross Bridge of Don, second right. Seaside links. Two Courses – Championship (Balgownie): 18 holes, 6372 yards, 5828 metres. S.S.S. 71; Silverburn: 18 holes, 4033 yards, 3717 metres. S.S.S. 60. Practice area. *Green Fees:* weekdays £30.00 per round, £38.00 per day; weekends and Public Holidays

Scottish Golfing Breaks

Enjoy some of Scotland's best golf courses, whilst staying at one of eight top hotels. Special Golfing Breaks are the ideal way to spend your holidays. Prices start from £195, with special rates for non golfers.
Call for a brochure and booking form.
Golfing Co-Ordinator, Scottish Golfing Breaks, Caledonian Thistle Hotel, Union Terrace,
Aberdeen AB9 1HE. Telephone: 0224 640233 Fax: 0224 641627
See our colour advertisement on page 8.

THE GOLF GUIDE 1994　　　　　　　　　　　Scotland ABERDEENSHIRE

after 3.30pm only £38.00 per round. (Silverburn course green fees are half those quoted for Balgownie). *Eating facilities:* two bars and full catering. *Visitors:* welcome weekdays 9.30am to 12 noon and 2pm to 4pm, weekends after 3.30pm. Letter of introduction and Handicap Certificate required. *Society Meetings:* welcome. Professional: R.A. MacAskill (0224 702221). Secretary: Mrs Sandra Nicolson (0224 702571; Fax: 0224 826591).

ABERDEEN. **Tarland Golf Club,** Aberdeen Road, Tarland, Aboyne (033 98 81413). *Location:* from Aberdeen – A944 then A974. Parkland/wooded, easy walking, difficult upland course. 9 holes, 5816 yards for 18 holes, S.S.S. 68. Small practice area. *Green Fees:* weekdays £10.00; weekends £12.00. Weekly and fortnightly tickets available. (all rates to be reviewed). *Eating facilities:* catering available, bar 11am to midnight. *Visitors:* welcome without reservation, phone call advisable due to club competitions. *Society Meetings:* catered for except weekends. Secretary: Mr J.H. Honeyman.

ABOYNE. **Aboyne Golf Club,** Formaston Park, Aboyne (03398 86328). *Location:* A93, 30 miles west of Aberdeen. Part parkland, part hilly with lovely views. 18 holes, 5910 yards. S.S.S. 68. Practice ground. *Green Fees:* weekdays £14.00 per round, £18.00 per day; weekends £21.00 per day. *Eating facilities:* full restaurant and bar facilities. *Visitors:* welcome without reservation. *Society Meetings:* by arrangement with Secretary. Professional: Innes Wright (03398 86328). Secretary: Mrs M. MacLean (03398 87078).

ALFORD. **Alford Golf Club,** Montgarrie Road, Alford AB33 8AE (09755 62178). *Location:* A944, 26 miles west of Aberdeen. Flat course. 18 holes, 5290 yards. S.S.S. 66, ladies 70. Practice area. *Green Fees:* £8.00 per round, £12.00 per day weekdays; £12.00 per round, £16.00 per day weekends. *Eating facilities:* snacks available, meals to order, bar. *Visitors:* always welcome, enquiries advised weekends during playing season. Changing rooms. *Society Meetings:* catered for by arrangement. Secretary: Mrs M.J. Ball (09755 62843).

BALLATER. **Ballater Golf Club,** Victoria Road, Ballater AB35 5QX (03397 55200). *Location:* Aberdeen 42 miles east, Perth 62 miles south. Flat parkland course. 18 holes, 5638 yards. S.S.S. 69. Practice ground, putting. *Green Fees:* £15.00 per round, £22.50 per day weekdays; £18.00 per round, £27.00 per day weekends. Half rates for players aged under 18. *Eating facilities:* dining room April to October; bar lounge. *Visitors:* welcome, book through Pro's shop. *Society Meetings:* all welcome, book well in advance. Professional: Joe Blair (03397 55658). Secretary: Bert Ingram (Tel & Fax: 03397 55567).

BRAEMAR. **Braemar Golf Club,** Cluniebank Road, Braemar AB35 5XX (03397 41618). *Location:* about one mile from centre of the village, signposted opposite Fife Arms Hotel. Flat parkland, highest 18 hole course on mainland Great Britain, course split in two by River Clunie. 18 holes, 5011 yards. S.S.S. 64. Small practice area. *Green Fees:* weekdays £10.00 per round, £13.00 per day; weekends £13.00 per round, £16.00 per day.

Weekly ticket £50.00. *Eating facilities:* meals served until 7pm, bar open 11am to midnight. *Visitors:* no restrictions, best phone day prior for weekends. *Society Meetings:* welcome by booking through Secretary. Secretary: John Pennet (0224 704471).

ELLON. **McDonald Golf Club,** Hospital Road, Ellon AB41 9AW (Ellon (0358) 20576). *Location:* A92 from Aberdeen to Ellon. One mile down A948, on left. Flat parkland with trees and stream. 18 holes, 5986 yards. S.S.S. 69. Putting green and practice nets. *Green Fees:* on application. *Eating facilities:* full catering except Mondays, bar all week. *Visitors:* welcome at all times weekdays, after 10am and booking advisable at weekends. *Society Meetings:* must book in advance. Professional: Ronnie Urquhart (0358 22891). Secretary: Ken Clouston (0358 20576).

ELLON. **Newburgh-on-Ythan Golf Club,** c/o Andrew C. Stevenson, 51 Mavis Bank, Newburgh, Ellon, Aberdeen AB4 0FB (03586 89438). *Location:* 12 miles north of Aberdeen. Seaside links course. 9 holes, 6300 yards, 5758 metres. S.S.S. 70. *Green Fees:* weekdays £10.00; weekends £12.00. Reduction of £2 for Senior Citizens. *Eating facilities:* at local hotels. *Visitors:* welcome, but tee reserved Tuesday evenings (Club competitions), Monday evenings (Juniors have priority) and Wednesday evenings (Ladies have priority). *Society Meetings:* by arrangement. Secretary: Andrew C. Stevenson.

FRASERBURGH. **Fraserburgh Golf Club,** Corbie Hill, Fraserburgh (0346 518287). *Location:* turn right at roundabout on entry to town from Aberdeen then first right. Seaside links. 18 holes, 6279 yards. S.S.S. 70. Practice area. *Green Fees:* weekdays £11.00; weekends £15.00. Weekly £44; fortnightly £77. *Eating facilities:* full catering provided Tuesday to Sunday, bar open seven days. *Visitors:* welcome, some restrictions weekends. *Society Meetings:* welcome, book in advance. Secretary: J. Grant (0346 516616).

HUNTLY. **Huntly Golf Club,** Cooper Park, Huntly AB54 4SH (0466 792643). *Location:* north side of Huntly, 38 miles from Aberdeen on A96. Open parkland course between Rivers Deveron and Bogie. 18 holes, 5399 yards. S.S.S. 66. Practice area. *Green Fees:* weekdays £10.00 day ticket; weekends £15.00. Weekly ticket £50.00. *Eating facilities:* full catering by arrangement, lounge bar. *Visitors:* welcome, no restriction except Wednesday and Thursday evenings. *Society Meetings:* by arrangement with Secretary, maximum of 40. Secretary: Gordon Alexander (0466 792877).

INSCH. **Insch Golf Club,** Golf Terrace, Insch (0464 20363). *Location:* A96 from Aberdeen. Parkland – trees, water hazards. 9 holes, 5632 yards. S.S.S. 67. *Green Fees:* £7.00 per day weekdays; £8.00 weekends. *Eating facilities:* by arrangement. *Visitors:* welcome. Mondays from 4.30pm Ladies, Tuesdays from 5pm Gents and Wednesdays from 4pm Juniors. *Society Meetings:* welcome. Secretary: James G. McCombie (0464 20291).

ABERDEENSHIRE *Scotland*

INVERALLOCHY. **Inverallochy Golf Club,** Inverallochy, Fraserburgh (0346 582000). *Location:* three miles south of Fraserburgh. Seaside links course. 18 holes, 5137 yards. S.S.S. 65. *Green Fees:* weekdays £8.00; weekends £10.00. *Eating facilities:* limited, unlicensed, advance booking required. *Visitors:* welcome. *Society Meetings:* catered for on limited basis. Secretary: R.A. Mutch.

INVERURIE. **Inverurie Golf Club,** Davah Wood, Blackhall Road, Inverurie (Inverurie (0467) 20207). *Location:* main Aberdeen/Inverness trunk road, 16 miles west of Aberdeen. Parkland, partly wooded course. 18 holes, 6000 yards. S.S.S. 66. Practice area. *Green Fees:* weekdays £10.00; weekends £15.00. *Eating facilities:* bar lounge, catering. *Visitors:* welcome anytime – reserve through Golf Shop (0467 20193). *Society Meetings:* catered for. Secretary: David L. Taylor.

INVERURIE. **Kintore Golf Club,** Balbithan Road, Kintore, Inverurie AB5 0UR (0467 32631). *Location:* off A96 12 miles north of Aberdeen. Undulating moorland course. 18 holes, 5985 yards. S.S.S. 69. *Green Fees:* weekdays £10.00 per day; weekends £15.00 per day. Evenings after 6pm £6.00. Weekly tickets available. *Eating facilities:* bar available, catering if booked in advance. *Visitors:* welcome daily except Mondays, Wednesdays and Fridays after 4pm. *Society Meetings:* welcome weekdays. Secretary: Jim Smith.

KEMNAY. **Kemnay Golf Club,** Monymusk Road, Kemnay (Kemnay (0467) 42225). *Location:* from A96 main Aberdeen/Inverness road. Take B994 signposted Kemnay and pass through village of Kemnay to find golf course on left hand side on leaving village. Parkland. 9 holes (extending to 18 holes early 1994), 5502 yards. S.S.S. 67. *Green Fees:* weekdays £8.00; weekends £10.00. Half price in winter. *Eating facilities:* light snacks available at the bar. *Visitors:* welcome all week, Sundays if starting times available. *Society Meetings:* weekdays and weekends by arrangement, maximum number 25. Secretary: D. Imrie (0467 43047).

NEWMACHAR. **Newmachar Golf Club,** Swailend, Newmachar AB2 0UU (0651 863002). *Location:* two and a half miles north of Dyce on A947. Championship standard wooded parkland course with ponds being main feature. 18 holes, 6605 yards. S.S.S. 73. *Green Fees:* weekdays £16.00 per round; weekends £20.00 per round. *Eating facilities:* fully licensed clubhouse, catering available. *Visitors:* welcome by prior arrangement. Handicap Certificate required. *Society Meetings:* welcome by prior arrangement. Professional: Glenn Taylor (0651 862127). Manager: George McIntosh.

OLDMELDRUM. **Oldmeldrum Golf Club,** Kirk Brae, Oldmeldrum, Inverurie AB51 0DJ (0651 872648). *Location:* 17 miles north-west of Aberdeen on A947 to Banff. First on right entering from Aberdeen direction. Undulating parkland with tree-lined fairways and water features. 18 holes, 5988 yards, 5479 metres. S.S.S. 69. Practice area. *Green Fees:* weekdays £10.00 per day, weekends £15.00. *Eating facilities:* catering by arrangement, bar. *Visitors:* welcome, advisable to phone first. *Society Meetings:* catered for by arrangement. Secretary: Douglas Petrie (0651 872383).

PETERHEAD. **Cruden Bay Golf Club,** Aulton Road, Cruden Bay, Peterhead AB42 7NN (Cruden Bay (0779) 812285; Fax: 0779 812945). *Location:* seven miles south of Peterhead, 23 miles north east of Aberdeen. Traditional seaside links with magnificent views near Bay of Cruden. 18 holes, 6370 yards, 5859 metres. S.S.S. 71; 9 holes, 4710 yards. S.S.S. 62. Ample practice facilities. *Green Fees:* weekdays £20.00; weekends £28.00. *Eating facilities:* full bar and catering facilities. *Visitors:* welcome but restricted at weekends, telephone for details. *Society Meetings:* welcome weekdays only. Professional: Robbie Stewart (0779 812414). Secretary: George Donald MBE (0779 812285). Manager: Ian A.D. MacPherson (0779 812285; Fax: 0779 812945).

PETERHEAD. **Peterhead Golf Club,** Craigewan Links, Peterhead AB42 6LT (Peterhead (0779) 72149). *Location:* off Golf Road at north end of town at mouth of River Ugie. Seaside links. Old Course – 18 holes, 6189 yards. S.S.S. 70; New Course – 9 holes, 2263 yards. S.S.S. 62. Practice area. *Green Fees:* £12.00 per day weekdays, £16.00 weekends. *Eating facilities:* meals and snacks available, lounge bar. *Visitors:* welcome, no restrictions for individual visitors. *Society Meetings:* catered for anytime except Saturdays, prior booking necessary. Handicap Certificate required. Secretary: Mrs M. Bennions.

ROSEHEARTY. **Rosehearty Golf Club,** C/o Secretary, 24 Brucklay Street, Rosehearty AB43 4JN. *Location:* south of Rosehearty on Fraserburgh Road. Seaside links. 9 holes, 3368 yards. Par 58 (18 holes). *Green Fees:* £5.00 all day. *Eating facilities:* Masons Arms adjacent to course. *Visitors:* always welcome. Secretary: T. Keith Bruce (0346 571645).

TORPHINS. **Torphins Golf Club,** Bog Road, Torphins, Banchory AB3 4JT (03398 82115). *Location:* Torphins is five miles north-west of Banchory, well signposted. 9 holes, 4684 yards (for 18 holes). S.S.S. 63. *Green Fees:* £10.00 weekdays; £12.00 weekends. Juniors half price, after 6.30pm £6.00. *Eating facilities:* light refreshments, unlicensed. *Visitors:* no play on

Cruden Bay Golf Club

Attractive 18 hole course situated by the Bay of Cruden. Full bar and catering facilities. Visiting parties from Monday to Friday only. 9 hole course also. Call for further details.

Professional – R. Stewart: Tel 0779 0812414   Secretary: Tel 0779 812285

Aulton Road, Cruden Bay, Aberdeenshire AB42 7NN

medal days (alternate Saturdays or Sundays); members only Tuesday evenings. *Society Meetings:* no restrictions. Secretary: Mrs Sue Mortimer (03398 82563).

TURRIFF. **Turriff Golf Club,** Rosehall, Turriff AB53 7HB (0888 62745). *Location:* A947 signposted on south side of Turriff. Wooded parkland course. 18 holes, 5877 yards. S.S.S. 69. Small practice area, small putting green. *Green Fees:* weekdays £12.00 per round, £15.00 per day; weekends £15.00 per round, £20.00 per day. *Eating facilities:* catering by arrangement, licensed 11am to 11pm. *Visitors:* no visitors before 10am weekends, slight restrictions Wednesdays. Tee reservation by contacting Professional – during the week up to four days in advance, weekends on day only. *Society Meetings:* by arrangement with Secretary.

Professional: Robin Smith (0888 63025). Secretary: James D. Stott (0888 62982).

WESTHILL. **Westhill Golf Club,** Westhill Heights, Westhill, Skene (0224 743361). *Location:* six miles from Aberdeen on A944. Undulating parkland course (hilly in places). 18 holes, 5921 yards. S.S.S. 69. Practice ground. *Green Fees:* weekdays £10.00 per round, £13.00 per day; weekends and Public Holidays £13.00 per round, £16.00 per day. Special package Monday-Friday for parties of 20 or more £18.00. *Eating facilities:* lounge bar with dining area. *Visitors:* welcome weekdays except betweem 4pm and 7pm, no visitors on Saturdays. *Society Meetings:* welcome per visitors' times by arrangement. Professional: Ronnie McDonald (0224 740159). Secretary: John L. Webster (0224 740957).

Angus

ARBROATH. **Arbroath Golf Course,** Elliot, By Arbroath (Arbroath (0241) 72069). *Location:* one mile south on Dundee to Arbroath Road A92. Seaside links. 18 holes, 6095 yards. S.S.S 69. Practice area, putting green and new sprinkler system. *Green Fees:* weekdays £10.00 per round, £15.00 per day; weekends £16.00 per round, £24.00 per day. *Eating facilities:* full catering and bar facility. *Visitors:* welcome, no visitors before 10am weekends. *Society Meetings:* all welcome (good rates midweek). Professional: L. Ewart (0241 75837). Secretary: Gary Pyott (0241 74946).

BARRY. **Panmure Golf Club,** Burnside Road, Barry, By Carnoustie DD7 7RT (0241 53120). *Location:* two miles west of Carnoustie, south in centre at Barry village, then 200 yards turn right. Championship links. 18 holes, 6317 yards, 5776 metres. S.S.S. 70. *Green Fees:* £21.00 per round, £32.00 per day. *Eating facilities:* bar and diningroom. Steward's day off on Monday – snack lunch of soup and sandwiches only available that day. *Visitors:* welcome daily – no visiting parties on Saturdays. *Society Meetings:* catered for. Professional: A. Cullen. Secretary: D.A. Chidley.

AA ★★ RAC

HOTEL SEAFORTH

Dundee Road, Arbroath DD11 1QF

20 ensuite bedrooms. On the seafront, a short drive from many fine Golf Courses. Hotel's facilities include Lounge Bar, Restaurant and Leisure Centre with indoor pool, jacuzzi, and sunbed. Snooker tables.

Telephone: (0241) 72232   Fax: (0241) 77473

ANGUS   *Scotland*   **THE GOLF GUIDE 1994**

BRECHIHN. **Brechin Golf and Squash Club,** Trinity, By Brechin DD9 6BJ (Brechin (0356) 622383). *Location:* Trinity Village, one mile north of Brechin on A94. Rolling parkland. 18 holes, 6123 yards. S.S.S. 69. *Green Fees:* weekdays £12.00 per round, £18.00 per day; weekends £16.00 per round, £28.00 per day. *Eating facilities:* excellent catering available at all times; large bar. *Visitors:* welcome without reservation. Squash courts, pool table available. *Society Meetings:* catered for, but prior booking necessary. Midweek packages for parties of 12 or more. Professional: Steven Rennie (0356 625270). Secretary: A.B. May (0356 622326).

CARNOUSTIE. **Carnoustie Golf Links,** Links Parade, Carnoustie DD7 7JE (0241 53789; Fax: 0241 52720). *Location:* 12 miles east of Dundee. Three 18-hole courses. Championship Course 6936 yards. S.S.S. 74; Burnside Course 6020 yards. S.S.S. 69; Buddon Links 5196 yards. S.S.S. 66. Golf trolleys permitted from May to October only. *Green Fees:* (1993 only) Weekly tickets for play over three courses £136.00. Three-day tickets for play over three courses £102.00. Championship Course: Single round £34.00. Burnside Course: Single round £13.00. Buddon Links Course: Single round £8.00. *Eating facilities:* catering facilities can be arranged with the local golf clubs. *Visitors:* welcome, times must be booked and ballot system in operation. Handicap Certificates required for play on Championship Course. *Society Meetings:* catered for by arrangement. Secretary: Earle J.C. Smith.

DUNDEE. **Caird Park Golf Club,** Mains Loan, Dundee DD4 9BX (0382 453606). *Location:* northern edge of city, off Kingsway. Wooded parkland. 18 holes, 6273 yards, 5740 metres. S.S.S. 70. Practice range on course. *Green Fees:* information not available; telephone Starter 0382 451147. *Eating facilities:* at clubhouse. *Visitors:* welcome, must book in advance to ensure game. *Society Meetings:* see Dundee District Council, Parks Department. Professional: Jackie Black (0382 459438). Secretary: Greg Martin.

DUNDEE. **Camperdown Golf Club,** Camperdown House, Camperdown Park, Dundee (Dundee (0382) 623398). *Location:* two miles north-west of city, enter at Kingsway/Coupar Angus road junction. Wooded parkland. 18 holes, 6561 yards. S.S.S. 72 par 71. *Green Fees:* information not provided. *Eating facilities:* (must be ordered beforehand) all year round. *Visitors:* welcome, bookable all week, contact Art and Recreation Division, Leisure Centre, Dundee. *Society Meetings:* by arrangement, catered for once booked by Parks Dept. for date and times. Professional: R. Brown (0382 623398). Secretary: K. McCreery (0382 642925).

DUNDEE. **Downfield Golf Club,** Turnberry Avenue, Dundee DD2 3QP (0382 825595). *Location:* north end Dundee off A923 (Timex Circle). Map available on request. By rail Dundee Tay Bridge Station. Undulating wooded heathland course. 18 holes, 6804 yards. S.S.S. 73. Extensive practice ground. *Green Fees:* £36.00 per day, £24.00 per round. *Eating facilities:* full catering available. *Visitors:* welcome, weekend play arrange through Professional on day of play only.

Society Meetings: catered for (reservation). Professional: C. Waddell (0382 89246). Managing Secretary: Brian F. Mole (0382 825595; Fax: 0382 813111).

EDZELL. **Edzell Golf Club,** High Street, Edzell DD9 7TF (0356 648235). *Location:* turn left onto B966 from A94 north of Brechin by-pass on Forfar to Aberdeen road. Undulating heathland course. 18 holes, 6348 yards. S.S.S. 70. Practice area and putting green. *Green Fees:* weekdays £16.00 per round, £24.00 per day; weekends £22.00 per round, £33.00 per day. *Eating facilities:* dining room, lounge and bar. *Visitors:* welcome with some restrictions. *Society Meetings:* welcome with some restrictions, apply to Secretary. Professional: Alistair J. Webster (0356 648462). Secretary: J.M. Hutchison (0356 647283). Steward and Caterer: Mr and Mrs G. Milne.

FORFAR. **Forfar Golf Club,** Cunninghill, Forfar (Forfar (0307) 62120). *Location:* one mile from Forfar on A932 to Arbroath. Undulating wooded heathland course. 18 holes, 5497 metres. S.S.S. 69. *Green Fees:* weekdays £15.00 per round, £20.00 per day; Sundays £25.00 per day. *Visitors:* welcome. *Society Meetings:* catered for. Professional: Peter McNiven. Secretary: W. Baird (0307 63773).

KIRRIEMUIR. **Kirriemuir Golf Club Ltd,** Northmuir, Kirriemuir DD8 4LN (0575 72144). *Location:* on A926 and A928, just on edge of Kirriemuir. Parkland and heathland course, relatively flat. 18 holes, 5591 yards, 5336 metres. S.S.S. 67. Practice area for members only. *Green Fees:* £18.00; weekends with member only. *Eating facilities:* fully licensed, all catering facilities. *Visitors:* welcome weekdays only unless accompanied by a member. *Society Meetings:* weekdays only. Professional: A. Caira (0575 73317; Fax: 0575 74608). Secretary: Mrs Joan Knight (0575 73317; Fax: 0575 74608).

MONIFIETH. **Broughty Golf Club,** 6 Princes Street, Monifieth, Dundee DD5 4AW (0382 532147). Starter (0382 532767). *Location:* eight miles east of Dundee, in village of Monifieth. Seaside links, some fairways fringed with trees. Medal Course: 18 holes, 6657 yards, 6087 metres. S.S.S. 72. Ashludie Course: 18 holes, 5123 yards. S.S.S. 66. Practice area. *Green Fees:* Medal Course £22.00 per round, £32.00 per day; Sundays £24.00 per round, £36.00 per day. Ashludie Course £14.00 per round, £20.00 per day; Sundays £15.00 per round, £22.00 per day. *Eating facilities:* full catering; no catering Tuesdays or Thursdays. *Visitors:* no visitors before 2pm on Saturdays or before 10am Sundays. All tee times must be booked through Starters Box (0382 532767). *Society Meetings:* by arrangement. Secretary: Samuel J. Gailey (0382 730014).

MONIFIETH. **Monifieth Golf Links,** Princes Street, Monifieth, Dundee DD5 4AW (0382 532767). *Location:* seven miles east of Dundee, Monifieth High Street. Seaside links. Medal Course 18 holes, 6657 yards. S.S.S. 72; Ashludie Course 18 holes, 5123 yards. S.S.S. 64. *Green Fees:* Medal Course £22.00 per round, £32.00 per day; Ashludie Course £14.00 per round, £20.00 per day – Mondays to Fridays; Medal Course £24.00 per round, £36.00 per day Saturdays/

THE GOLF GUIDE 1994   *Scotland*   ANGUS

THE NORTHERN HOTEL
24 Clerk Street, Brechin DD9 6AE. Telephone: 035662 2156

Centrally situated, this old coaching inn is an excellent base for business or pleasure. All bedrooms have private facilities, TVs and telephones. A full range of meals, with a choice of delicious Scottish fare. Golfers have a choice of courses, from Brechin to Edzell, with a further 18 courses in the Angus area. *Proprietor: Norman Anderson*

STATION HOTEL
Station Road, Carnoustie • Reservations 0241-52447

Long established family run hotel offering friendly service, excellent food and accommodation.
GOLFING PARTIES WELCOME

Glencoe HOTEL

LINKS PARADE
CARNOUSTIE
TEL: 0241 53273 FAX: 0241 55319
AA ★★   "*Par excellence*"   RAC ★★

The '**Golf Hotel**' in Carnoustie, directly opposite the last green of the **championship golf course**. Family run hotel, offering excellent cuisine and accommodation. **Golfing parties welcome**.

The Glenesk Hotel, Edzell, Angus

AA ★★★   RAC ★★★

This splendid family-run hotel is situated in it own grounds ADJOINING THE 18 HOLE GOLF COURSE. 25 comfortable bedrooms all with modern facilities. Recommended by both golf parties and families who enjoy the friendly atmosphere and Scottish hospitality given by resident directors.

ENJOY OUR LEISURE COMPLEX
Indoor Pool, Sauna, Jacuzzi, Solarium and Games Room. Special Breaks always available.

Scottish Tourist Board COMMENDED

Telephone: (0356) 648319   Fax: (0356) 647333

PANMURE ARMS HOTEL
AA ★★   Les Routiers Recommended

Edzell, Angus DD9 7TA   Telephone: 0356 648 420   Fax: 0356 648 588

A warm welcome is extended to all golfers at this fully licensed, family-owned and run Private Hotel. 24 bedrooms with private bath or shower, CTV, telephone, radio, tea/coffee facilities and hairdryers. Guests have full use of our Leisure Complex with heated indoor Dip Pool, Sauna and Jacuzzi. Many excellent Golf Courses within easy reach, including ST. ANDREWS and CARNOUSTIE.

ANGUS Scotland

Sundays. Ashludie Course £15.00 per round, £22.00 per day Saturdays/Sundays. Composite ticket available, one round on each course – weekdays £24.00, weekends £28.00. *Eating facilities:* clubs and Hotel. *Visitors:* welcome Monday to Friday at any time except before 9.30am; Saturdays after 2pm; Sundays after 10am. *Society Meetings:* parties over 12 must provide club Handicap Certificates. Professional: Ian McLeod (0382 532945). Secretary: H.R. Nicoll (0382 535553).

MONTROSE. **Montrose Links Trust,** Traill Drive, Montrose DD10 8SW (Montrose (0674) 72932). *Location:* A92 runs from Dundee to Aberdeen, through Montrose. Links Medal Course 6443 yards. Par 71. S.S.S. 71. Broomfield Course 4815 yards. Par 66. S.S.S. 63. *Green Fees:* April 1993/March 1994. Medal: weekdays £22.00 per day, £13.00 per round, Juniors £6.50 per round; weekends £30.00 per day, £19.00 per round, Juniors £9.50 per round; weekly tickets £70.00 adult, £35.00 Juniors. Broomfield: weekdays £12.00 per day, £8.00 per round, Juniors £2.50 per round; weekends £18.00 per day, £12.00 per round,

Juniors £4.50 per round; weekly ticket £46.00 adult, £23.00 Junior. 'Special Deal' to parties for two rounds plus catering, details on request. *Eating facilities:* catering facilities available by arrangement in golf clubs. *Visitors:* welcome, except on Medal Course Saturdays and before 10am Sundays. *Society Meetings:* welcome by arrangement. Temporary membership available at the following clubs: Caledonia Golf Club (0674 72313); Mercantile Golf Club (0674 72408); Royal Montrose (0674 72376). Professional: Kevin Stables. Secretary: Mrs Margaret Stewart (0674 72932; Fax: 0674 72634).

MONTROSE. **Royal Montrose Golf Club,** Dornard Road, Montrose DD10 8SW (Montrose (0674) 72376). *Location:* A92 north from Dundee. Private club playing over the Montrose courses. 18 holes, 6442 yards. S.S.S. 71. *Green Fees:* information not provided. *Eating facilities:* available. *Visitors:* apply Montrose Links Trust. *Society Meetings:* apply Montrose Links Trust. Hon. Secretary: J D. Sykes (0674 73956).

GOLF PACKAGES

Links Hotel

24 Bedroomed Hotel . Groups / Clubs - a complete golf package tailored to your budget and requirements. Call for brochure.
DB&B from £36 per person per day. STB ♛♛♛♛ Commended.
Mid Links · Montrose · Angus DD10 8QT · Tel 0674 72288 · Fax 0674 72698

A Welcome Change

PARK HOTEL, Montrose

Situated a short distance from the Montrose Medal Course (Par 71) is the Park Hotel. Most of the 59 well appointed bedrooms are en suite and all have colour TV. Two nights Bed and Breakfast with Evening Meal, four rounds of golf and light lunch in the clubhouse from £130 per person.

The Park Hotel, John Street, Montrose
Angus DD10 8RJ
Telephone: Montrose (0674) 73415
Fax: (0674) 77091

MONTROSE LINKS TRUST
MONTROSE GOLF COURSES

Two Links Courses: Medal Par 71 (major improvements completed) and Broomfield Par 66, available throughout the year for clubs, societies and parties.

Prices for 1994 range from £21 MID-WEEK to £37 WEEKEND inclusive of day's golf, morning coffee and bacon roll, light lunch (soup and sandwiches) and full high tea.

Venue for British Boys' Championship in 1991.

Enquiries to:

The Secretary, Montrose Links Trust, Traill Drive, Montrose, DD10 8SW
Telephone (0674) 72932

Scotland ARGYLL

Argyll

CAMPBELTOWN. **Machrihanish Golf Club,** Machrihanish, by Campbeltown PA28 6PT (Machrihanish (058 681) 213). *Location:* five miles west of Campbeltown on B843 road. Championship standard, seaside links course. 18 holes, 6228 yards. S.S.S. 70. Also 9 holes, 2395 yards. Practice area. *Green Fees:* weekdays £15.00 per round, £20.00 per day; weekends day ticket only, £20.00. Discounts for parties of 12 and over. Advance booking necessary. *Eating facilities:* full catering and bar facilities. *Visitors:* welcome without reservation. (Some restrictions on competition days. Open competitions in summer). Special Flight/Golf packages available through Loganair, Glasgow Airport, Paisley. *Society Meetings:* as visitors. Professional: Ken Campbell (058 681 277). Secretary: Mrs Anna Anderson.

CARRADALE. **Carradale Golf Club,** Carradale PA28 6QT. *Location:* 15 miles north of Campbeltown on B842. Seaside, short but very demanding, unbelievable views. 9 holes, 2700 yards. S.S.S. 63 (18 holes). *Green Fees:* £5.00 per day. *Eating facilities:* hotel at first tee. *Visitors:* all welcome, no restrictions. Secretary: J.A. Duncan (05833 387).

DALMALLY. **Dalmally Golf Club,** Old Saw Mill, Dalmally PA33 1AS. *Location:* alongside the A85, two miles west of Dalmally. Flat course alongside River Orchy. 9 holes, 2217 yards. S.S.S. 62. *Green Fees:* £5.00. *Visitors:* welcome at all times. *Society Meetings:* all welcome. Secretary: A.J. Burke (08382 370).

DUNOON. **Blairmore and Strone Golf Club,** Strone, By Dunoon (Kilmun (036-984) 676). *Location:* on high road above Strone village, nine miles north of Dunoon on A880. Scenic hilly course, heavily wooded. 9 holes, 2112 yards, 1933 metres. S.S.S. 62. *Green Fees:* weekdays £8.00 per day; weekends £10.00 per day. *Eating facilities:* bar only. *Visitors:* welcome except Saturday afternoons. Secretary: R.J.K. Dunlop (036-984 260).

DUNOON. **Cowal Golf Club,** Ardenslate Road, Kirn, Dunoon PA23 8LT (Dunoon (0369) 5673). *Location:* quarter mile off A815 at Kirn (north-east boundary of Dunoon). Wooded parkland. 18 holes, 6251 yards. S.S.S. 70. *Green Fees:* weekdays £13.00 per round, £20.00 per day; weekends £20.00 per round, £30.00 per day (prices may be subject to increase). *Eating facilities:* bar snacks all day, lunches and dinners to order. *Visitors:* welcome weekdays, some restrictions weekends. *Society Meetings:* welcome at special rates in groups of 12 (minimum) to 24 (maximum). Professional: R.D. Weir (0369 2395). Secretary: Brian Chatham (0369 5673).

DUNOON. **Innellan Golf Club,** Innellan, By Dunoon (0369 83242). *Location:* four miles west of Dunoon. In elevated position overlooking Firth of Clyde. 9 holes, 2343 yards. S.S.S. 63. *Green Fees:* weekdays £8.00; weekends £10.00. *Eating facilities:* bar and snacks; new clubhouse. *Visitors:* welcome, except Monday evenings. *Society Meetings:* catered for on application. Secretary: J.G. Arden (0369 3546).

LOCHGILPHEAD. **Lochgilphead Golf Club,** Blairbuie Road, Lochgilphead PA31 8LE (0546 602340). *Location:* next to Argyll and Bute hospital, Lochgilphead. Parkland. 9 holes, 2500 yards. S.S.S. 63. Practice fairway. *Green Fees:* weekdays £7.00; weekends £10.00. *Eating facilities:* limited – weekends and most evenings. *Visitors:* welcome but some restriction on competition days. *Society Meetings:* welcome by arrangement. Secretary: Mr A. Law.

ARGYLL ARMS HOTEL
Main Street, Campbeltown, Argyll PA28 6AB

Hector Thomson cordially invites you to a Golf Break in the Mull of Kintyre. Enjoy all aspects of golf on the peninsula's three courses – Machrihanish, Dunaverty and Carradale. Relax at night in a comfortable well appointed Hotel with all modern facilities.
For details phone 0586 553431 Fax: 0586 553594

BRAEMAR HOTEL
Shore Road, Inellan,
by Dunoon PA23 7SP
Telephone: 0369 83792

All rooms have en-suite colour TV and tea/coffee making. Extensive range of food and drink on offer. Children's play area and pets corner. Sea views. Golf at Cowal or Inellan Golf Clubs. Reductions for groups. Fully licensed.
Terms from £17.00 to £23.50

ARGYLL/AYRSHIRE *Scotland* THE GOLF GUIDE 1994

ARDCHONNEL FARMS

Nestling amongst Argyll's most breathtaking scenery, this newly renovated, spacious, single storey, self-catering cottage sleeps 8 persons in 4 bedrooms, and is ideally situated to allow guests to visit a different course each day for a week, all within one hour's drive. Fishing in Loch Awe, bird-watching, hill climbing and walking. Open all year. Full central heating. Two bathrooms. All facilities. All linen supplied. Telephone for brochure and enquiries.

Ardchonnel Farms, by Dalmally, Argyll PA33 1BW Tel: 08664 242 (Mrs J Mackay)

OBAN. **Glencruitten Golf Club,** Glencruitten Road, Oban (Oban (0631) 62868). *Location:* one mile from town centre. Hilly parkland. 18 holes, 4452 yards. S.S.S. 63. Practice area. *Green Fees:* weekdays £9.50 per round, £11.50 per day; weekends £11.50 per round, £13.50 per day. Weekly £45.00. *Eating facilities:* full catering and bar facilities. *Visitors:* welcome, restrictions on Saturdays and Thursdays during competition times. *Society Meetings:* welcome. Professional: D. Black (0631 64115). Starter: (0631 64115). Secretary: A.G. Brown (0631 64604 after 6pm).

SOUTHEND. **Dunaverty Golf Club,** Southend, By Campbeltown (0586 83 677). *Location:* about 10 miles south of Campbeltown on B842. Scenic seaside course. 18 holes, 4799 yards. S.S.S. 64. *Green Fees:* £8.00 per round, £11.00 per day. *Eating facilities:* snacks, tea and coffee. *Visitors:* welcome all times except during competition ballot times (mainly Saturdays), telephone above number. *Society Meetings:* catered for on limited basis on prior application. Secretary: J. Galbraith (0586 83698).

TARBERT. **Tarbert Golf Club,** Kilberry Road, Tarbert PA29 6XX (0880 820565). *Location:* approximately one mile south of Tarbert on B8024. Hilly wooded parkland. 9 holes, 4460 yards. S.S.S. 64. *Green Fees:* £5.00 9 holes, £6.00 18 holes. *Eating facilities:* licensed clubhouse, open weekends. *Visitors:* welcome at all times. *Society Meetings:* by arrangement. Secretary: Peter Cupples (0880 820536).

TAYNUILT. **Taynuilt Golf Club,** Taynuilt. *Location:* 12 miles east of Oban on A85. Parkland course, gently undulating with unrivalled views. 9 holes, 4018 yards, 3674 metres. S.S.S. 62. *Green Fees:* £4.00 9 holes, £5.00 per day Adults; £1.00 9 holes, £3.00 per day Juniors. Weekly ticket (Mon-Fri) £20.00 Adults, £12.00 Juniors. *Visitors:* welcome, some restrictions Tuesday afternoons, Saturday and Sundays for competitions. Secretary: Mairead MacLeod (086 62429).

TIGHNABRUAICH. **Kyles Of Bute Golf Club,** Copeswood, Tighnabruaich PA21 2BS. *Location:* access from Dunoon and Strachur. Clubhouse by Kames Farm, turn south off B8000 Kames to Millhouse road. Hillside course with magnificent views. 9 holes, 4778 yards. S.S.S. 64. *Green Fees:* £6.00 per day. *Eating facilities:* no bar, but snacks and soft drinks available. *Visitors:* welcome, except Sunday mornings. *Society Meetings:* by special arrangement only. Secretary: J.A. Carruthers (0700 811601).

Ayrshire

AYR. **Belleisle Golf Course,** Doonfoot Road, Ayr KA7 4DU (Alloway (0292) 441258). *Location:* follow main road south through Ayr. Gently sloping parkland course with fine mature trees. 18 holes, 6477 yards. S.S.S. 71. Practice area. *Green Fees:* £15.00. One round Belleisle, one round Seafield £22.00. *Eating facilities:* hotel and bars with catering. *Visitors:* no restrictions but booking in advance advisable. Juniors under 17 must have handicap of 12 or under. *Society Meetings:* catered for, groups up to 40. Professional: David Gemmell (Tel & Fax: 0292 441314). Starter: (0292 441258).

AYR. **Dalmilling (Municipal) Golf Club,** Westwood Avenue, Ayr KA8 0QY (0292 263893; Fax: 0292 610543). *Location:* A77, on north-east boundary, one mile from town centre. Parkland. 18 holes, 5724 yards. S.S.S. 68. Practice area. *Green Fees:* £10.00 per round, £18.00 per day. *Eating facilities:* snacks/ lunches/high teas, table licence. *Visitors:* welcome, not before 9.30am weekends, telephone to ensure availability. *Society Meetings:* welcome by arrangement. Professional: Philip Cheyney. Secretary: Stewart Graham.

THE ELMS·COURT HOTEL
Family owned and run. Well situated in Ayr town, within easy travelling distance of all the major Golf Courses in Ayrshire. Extensive car parking. Twenty bedrooms with en-suite facilities, TV, telephone, tea-making, trouser press, hairdryer, radio and shoe-shining facilities. Attractive lounge bar. Excellent restaurant and wine cellar. Night Porters. Golf reservations can be arranged.
For further information and our new comprehensive brochure please contact:
GUY or MARGARET GREGOR, Miller Road, Ayr   Tel: (0292) 264191/282332
♥♥♥♥ Commended   AA ★★   IBA Les Routiers Recommended

THE GOLF GUIDE 1994

Scotland AYRSHIRE

GREAT GOLF IN SOUTH AYRSHIRE

BELLEISLE
Address: Belleisle Park, Ayr
Telephone: 0292 441258
SSS 71
Length: 6477 yards
PRO: David Gemmell
Telephone: 0292 441314

This 18 hole Parkland Course in Ayr is the flagship of Kyle and Carrick Golf, considered by many as one of the finest public courses in Scotland. Host to some top Scottish and European Competitions, the long fairways are flanked by hundreds of tall beech trees and crowned by a winding burn. With only two par 4's under 400 yards and one of the hardest par 3's on Ayrshire golf, it is a true golfing challenge.

SEAFIELD
Address: Belleisle Park, Ayr
Telephone: 0292 441258
SSS 68
Length: 5498 yards
PRO: David Gemmell
Telephone: 0292 441314

Seafield runs adjacent to Belleisle within the bounds of the old racecourse in Ayr and shares all the facilities. It is an 18 hole course and though shorter than its Championship companion, offers an interesting mixture of 10 parkland and 8 links holes.

DALMILLING
Address: Westwood Avenue, Ayr
Telephone: 0292 263893
SSS 68
Length: 5724 yards
PRO: Philip Cheyney

The course opened in 1961 and is situated next to Ayr's famous racecourse. The outward nine holes have been completely redesigned, with the new fourth hole a short par 3 surrounded by the burn running into the River Ayr.

GIRVAN
Address: Golf Course Road, Girvan
Telephone: Starter's Office: 0465 4346, Clubhouse 0465 4272
SSS 64
Length: 5095 yards

A 'pugnacious little course' with the opening eight holes running alongside the seashore. Crossing over the road the final 10 parkland holes are deserted by trees. The elevated tee on the 171 yard, par three, fifth hole is stunning, framed by Ailsa Craig, characterising Ayrshire and Burns Country.

LOCHGREEN
Address: Harling Drive, Troon
Telephone: 0292 312464
SSS 72
Length: 6785 yards
PRO: Gordon McKinlay

One of the three main golf courses in a single setting in Troon. Lochgreen favours the long hitters. It has been used several times as a qualifying course for the Open Championship and has several testing holes which are reminiscent of Royal Troon.

DARLEY
Address: Harling Drive, Troon
Telephone: 0292 312464
SSS 70
Length: 6501 yards
PRO: Gordon McKinlay

If you would like a challenge, this is the course for you. Of the links variety, it demands work from the renowned Scottish hazards of heather, gorse and whins and though not as long as Lochgreen, a tough test of golf demanding the straightest of tee shots.

FULLARTON
Address: Harling Drive, Troon
Telephone: 0292 312464
SSS 64
Length: 4919 yards
PRO: Gordon McKinlay

This course is ideal for beginners and those who may not wish to spend as long on the course as both Lochgreen and Darley demand. The longest hole is the first at 441 yards. Of the others, there are eight par 3 holes demanding great precision and accuracy.

MAYBOLE
Address: Memorial Park, Maybole
SSS 33
Length: 2635 yards

This is the shortest course, nine holes with the longest just 371 yards. However, the setting in the heart of Ayrshire's beautiful Carrick Hills makes it well worth a visit.

KYLE AND CARRICK LEISURE SERVICES

· AYRSHIRE ·
Scotland's Famous Golfing Coast

TURNBERRY – VENUE FOR 1994 BRITISH OPEN GOLF CHAMPIONSHIP

ROYAL TROON • LARGS • TURNBERRY • PRESTWICK OLD COURSE

and many more exciting and challenging courses are waiting to test your skill.

There's lots to do once you leave the 19th hole, or just relax in our comfortable accommodation. Whether you choose a luxury 4-star hotel or homely bed and breakfast, self-catering or a holiday home you'll be delighted with the choice available. Send now for our free colour brochure to:

DEPT. P.G.A.
Ayrshire Tourist Board, Suite 105, Prestwick Airport, Prestwick, Ayrshire KA9 2PL
Telephone: (0292) 79000   Fax: (0292) 78874

243

AYRSHIRE Scotland

AYR. Seafield Golf Course, Doonfoot Road, Ayr KA7 4DU (0292 441258). *Location:* follow main road south through Ayr. Parkland and links, gently sloping. 18 holes, 5498 yards. S.S.S. 66. *Green Fees:* £10.00. One round Seafield, one round Belleisle £22.00. *Eating facilities:* hotel and bars with catering. *Visitors:* welcome, no restrictions but booking in advance advisable. Juniors under 17 must have handicap of 12 or under. *Society Meetings:* catered for, groups up to 40. Professional: David Gemmell (Tel & Fax: 0292 441314). Starter: (0292 441258).

BEITH. **Beith Golf Club,** Threepwood Road, Beith (05055 3166). *Location:* off Beith by-pass road. Wooded and hilly course. 9 holes, 3400 yards, 3115 metres. S.S.S. 67. Practice area available. *Green Fees:* weekdays £8.00 per round, £10.00 per day; weekends £12.00. *Eating facilities:* meals are available and bar open between 11am and 11pm. *Visitors:* welcome except no visitors on Saturdays and last visitors before 1pm on Sundays. *Society Meetings:* all welcome. Secretary: J. Glen (050-55 3166).

GALSTON. **Loudoun Gowf Club,** Galston KA4 8PA (Galston (0563) 820551). *Location:* five miles east of Kilmarnock on A71. Flat parkland. 18 holes, 5844 yards. S.S.S. 68. *Green Fees:* £15.00 per round, £25.00 per day weekdays. *Eating facilities:* full catering. *Visitors:* welcome weekdays only. *Society Meetings:* welcome by arrangement. Secretary: T.R. Richmond (0563 821993).

GIRVAN. **Girvan Golf Club,** Golf Course Road, Girvan (Girvan (0465) 4272). *Location:* A77 from Glasgow, through Ayr, on coast road to Stranraer. Links/parkland course with testing Par 3 holes and scenic views of Firth of Clyde. 18 holes, 5132 yards. S.S.S. 65. Practice area. *Green Fees:* information not available. *Eating facilities:* full catering available in clubhouse. *Visitors:* welcome, book through Starter (0465 4346). *Society Meetings:* welcome, book through Starter. Secretary: W.B. Tait (0465 2011).

IRVINE. **Glasgow Golf Club,** Gailes, Irvine KA11 5AE (0294 311347). *Location:* six miles from Kilmarnock, three miles south of Irvine, four miles north of Troon. Links. 18 holes, 6502 yards. S.S.S. 72. *Green Fees:* weekdays £27.00 per round, £33.00 per day; Saturdays and Sunday afternoons £30.00 per round. *Eating facilities:* full catering and bar facilities. *Visitors:* welcome weekdays, and Saturday and Sunday afternoons if no club competitions. *Society Meetings:* by application to Club Secretary. Professional: Jack Steven (041-942 8507). Secretary: D.W. Deas (041-942 2011; Fax: 041-942 0770).

IRVINE. **Irvine Ravenspark Golf Club,** Municipal Clubhouse, Kidsneuk Lane, Irvine KA12 0SR (Irvine (0294) 71293). *Location:* on A78 between Irvine and Kilwinning at Ravenspark Academy. Flat parkland course. 18 holes, 6453 yards. S.S.S. 71. *Green Fees:* weekdays £5.00 per round, £8.00 per day; weekends £8.00 per round, £14.50 per day. *Eating facilities:* diningroom, bar. *Visitors:* welcome, after 2.30pm on Saturdays from April to September. No jeans or training shoes allowed in the clubhouse. *Society Meetings:* welcome, by arrangement weekends. Professional: P. Bond (0294 76467). Secretary: G. Robertson (0294 54617).

IRVINE. **The Irvine Golf Club,** Bogside, Irvine KA12 8SN (Irvine (0294) 275979). *Location:* through Irvine going towards Kilwinning, turn left at Ravenspark Academy. Flat links course. 18 holes, 6408 yards. S.S.S. 71. Practice ground. *Green Fees:* weekdays £25.00 per round, £35.00 per day; weekends £35.00. *Eating facilities:* full catering every day except Mondays. *Visitors:* welcome, after 3pm weekends. *Society Meetings:* catered for. Professional: Keith Erskine (0294 275626). Secretary: Andrew Morton (0294 275979).

THE ROBLIN HOTEL

Fully licensed hotel, situated in town centre. Own car park. Only 3 minutes from beach. Golf and fishing parties are very welcome. 11 ground floor rooms, 2 en-suites. Pool room adjoining bar. Colour TV lounge. Live music entertainment on Thursday–Sunday inclusive. Mini bus available with driver. Reasonable terms. Bar meals available Saturday and Sunday.

Miss Linda Maider, 11 Barns Street, Ayr KA7 1XB. Tel: (0292) 267595.

Finlayson Arms Hotel

COYLTON, AYR KA6 6JT
TEL: (0292) 570298
Proprietors: Murdo & Rena Munro
EGON RONAY RECOMMENDED

Country Inn four miles east of Ayr. All rooms ensuite shower room and toilet, TV, teamaker and telephone. Full Scottish Breakfast; Evening Meals à la carte. All Ayrshire's Golf Courses within half an hour's drive. GOLF TIMES ARRANGED MOST COURSES. Under private ownership. Personal attention. Bed & Breakfast from £26 per person; group discounts.

* **Bar Lunches**   * **Beer Garden**   * **All Functions Catered For**

THE GOLF GUIDE 1994

Scotland AYRSHIRE

IRVINE. **Western Gailes Golf Club,** Gailes, By Irvine KA11 5AE (0294 311649). *Location:* three miles north of Troon. Seaside links. 18 holes, 6664 yards, 6094 metres. S.S.S. 72. *Green Fees:* weekdays £35.00 per round, £43.00 per day. *Eating facilities:* full bar and catering facilities. *Visitors:* welcome Monday, Tuesday, Wednesday and Friday, must contact club in advance. Handicap Certificate required. *Society Meetings:* welcome by arrangement with Secretary. Secretary: Andrew M. McBean C.A.

KILBIRNIE. **Kilbirnie Place Golf Club,** Largs Road, Kilbirnie (Kilbirnie (0505) 683398). *Location:* on main Kilbirnie to Largs Road, left hand side just outside town boundary. Parkland. 18 holes, 5116 yards. S.S.S. 69. *Green Fees:* weekdays £10.00; weekends £17.50. Party bookings on application. *Eating facilities:* catering and bar. *Visitors:* welcome weekdays. No visitors Saturdays, no visiting parties Sundays. Secretary: J.C. Walker (0505 683283).

KILMARNOCK. **Annanhill Golf Club,** Irvine Road, Kilmarnock KA3 2RT (0563 21644). *Location:* between Kilmarnock and Crosshouse on road to Irvine. Parkland course with excellent views. 18 holes, 6285 yards. S.S.S. 70. *Green Fees:* weekdays £10.00; weekends £15.00. *Eating facilities:* full catering available. *Visitors:* no parties on Saturdays, but welcome Sundays and weekdays by reservation. *Society Meetings:* catered for. Secretary: Mr D. McKie.

KILMARNOCK. **Caprington Golf Club,** Ayr Road, Kilmarnock (0563 23702). Parkland/wooded course. *Green Fees:* information not available. *Eating facilities:* available. *Visitors:* welcome except Saturdays. *Society Meetings:* all welcome. Secretary: F. McCulloch (0563 25848).

LARGS. **Inverclyde National Golf Training Centre,** Scottish Sports Council, Burnside Road, Largs KA30 8RW (Largs (0475) 674666). *Location:* Largs-Greenock-Glasgow (M8). Parkland, links, training bunkers. 6 holes, driving range. *Green Fees:* on application. *Eating facilities:* cafeteria, dining room, accommodation and bar. *Visitors:* two and four day courses for groups and individuals, pre booking required. Professionals: Bob Torrance, Jack Steven, David Scott. Secretary: John Kent (Deputy Director).

LARGS. **Largs Golf Club,** Irvine Road, Largs KA30 8EU (Largs (0475) 673594). *Location:* on A78 28 miles from Glasgow. Parkland with scenic views. 18 holes, 6220 yards. S.S.S. 70. *Green Fees:* weekdays £24.00 per day, £18.00 per round; weekends £24.00 per round or day. *Eating facilities:* full catering and bar. *Visitors:* welcome, no restrictions except on competition days and weekends. *Society Meetings:* catered for Tuesdays and Thursdays only by prior arrangement. Professional: R. Collinson (0475 686192). Secretary: F. Gilmour (0475 672497).

LARGS. **Routenburn Golf Club,** Routenburn, Largs (Largs (0475) 673230). Hilly moorland course. 18 holes, 5765 yards. S.S.S. 67. *Green Fees:* information not provided. *Eating facilities:* lunches at club except Thursdays, order in advance. *Visitors:* welcome with reservation. *Society Meetings:* catered for on application to club. Professional: Greig McQueen (0475 687240). Secretary: J.E. Smeaton.

MAUCHLINE. **Ballochmyle Golf Club,** Mauchline KA5 6LE (Mauchline (0290) 50469). *Location:* on B705 off A76, one mile south of Mauchline. Wooded parkland course. 18 holes, 5952 yards. S.S.S. 69. *Green Fees:* £25.00 per day weekdays; £30.00 per day weekends. *Eating facilities:* all day bar opening from 1st April until 30th Sept, snacks and meals available during

---

Mr and Mrs P. Gibson
BUSBIEHILL GUEST HOUSE
Knockentiber, Kilmarnock KA2 0AJ. Tel: 0563 32985

Homely country guest house in the heart of "Burns Country" and ideally placed for Ayrshire's many golf courses – also handy for touring Loch Lomond, the Trossachs, Edinburgh and the Clyde Coast. Two single rooms, four family suites, two double rooms with bathroom. Bed and Breakfast from £10 per person, Evening Meal £4. 10% discount for Senior Citizens.

KILMARNOCK and LOUDOUN district council
LEISURE SERVICES

When in Ayrshire why not play a round at one of our fine municipal courses.
ANNANHILL GOLF COURSE, IRVINE ROAD, KILMARNOCK. TELEPHONE: 0563 21512
CAPRINGTON GOLF COURSE, AYR ROAD, KILMARNOCK. TELEPHONE: 0563 21915
For personal bookings telephone the Starters on the numbers listed above or for party bookings contact:
The Leisure Administration Office, John Finnie Street, Kilmarnock. Telephone: 0563 21140.

❦❦ Commended
HILLHOUSE FARM
GRASSYARDS ROAD, KILMARNOCK KA3 6HG TELEPHONE: 0563 23370

Centrally situated for Ayrshire Golf Courses, 2 miles east of Kilmarnock and easy access to A77. Excellent Bed and Breakfast accommodation in large, comfortable, heated farmhouse with home baking. Also, two self-catering houses, sleeping 6 and 9, fully equipped. Each has three bedrooms, living room, kitchen, bathroom and shower, storage heaters and phone. Enquiries to Mrs Mary Howie.

AYRSHIRE   *Scotland*   **THE GOLF GUIDE 1994**

bar hours. *Visitors:* welcome every day except Saturdays. Dress regulations both on and off the course must be adhered to. Two full size snooker tables and squash court. *Society Meetings:* all welcome to a total of 30 per party. Secretary: Douglas Munro (0290 50469).

MAYBOLE. **Maybole Golf Club**, Memorial Park, Kirkoswald Road, Maybole (0292 281511). *Location:* A77 from Glasgow. By-pass Ayr to Girvan road, on main Girvan road at Maybole. Hilly parkland. 9 holes, 5270 yards. S.S.S. 65. *Green Fees:* municipal rates. *Visitors:* welcome. *Society Meetings:* welcome.

NEW CUMNOCK. **New Cumnock Golf Club**, Lochhill, Cumnock Road, New Cumnock. *Location:* A76, half a mile north of New Cumnock. Parkland. 9 holes, 5176 yards (18). S.S.S. 65. *Green Fees:* £8.00 adults. Senior Citizens residing within Cumnock and Doon Valley £1.00. *Eating facilities:* clubhouse open for tea/coffee, filled rolls. *Visitors:* welcome at all times except Sunday competition days before 4pm. *Society Meetings:* welcome, contact Secretary. Secretary: Jim Bryce (0290 32037).

PATNA. **Doon Valley Golf Club**, Hillside, Patna (0292 531607). *Location:* 10 miles from Ayr on road to Castle Douglas. Parkland. 9 holes, 5654 yards. S.S.S. 68. *Green Fees:* £5.00 per round, £8.00 per day. *Eating facilities:* can be arranged. *Visitors:* welcome, groups of six or more need to apply for tee off times. *Society Meetings:* welcome. Secretary: J. Green (0292 531925).

PRESTWICK. **Prestwick Golf Club**, Links Road, Prestwick (Prestwick (0292) 77404). *Location:* one mile from Prestwick airport, 40 minutes by car from Turnberry Hotel, 10 minutes from Troon, 15 minutes from Ayr. 18 holes, 6544 yards. (No LGU tees). S.S.S. 72. *Green Fees:* information not provided. *Eating facilities:* dining room (male only: prior booking required) open from 12.30pm. to 2.30pm. Cardinal Room (light lunches) open to ladies and gentlemen from 10.00am. until 4.00pm. *Visitors:* welcome with reservation. *Society Meetings:* catered for. Professional: F.C. Rennie. Secretary: D.E. Donaldson.

PRESTWICK. **Prestwick St. Cuthbert Golf Club**, East Road, Prestwick KA9 2SX (0292 77101). *Location:* south-east area of Prestwick near A77 and Prestwick Airport. Flat, some trees; semi-parkland. 18 holes, 6470 yards, 6063 metres. S.S.S. 71. Limited practice area. *Green Fees:* £24.00 per day weekdays only. *Eating facilities:* full catering and bar service. *Visitors:* welcome except weekends unless introduced by and playing with member. *Society Meetings:* catered for. Secretary: R. Morton (0292 77101).

PRESTWICK. **Prestwick St. Nicholas Golf Club**, Grangemuir Road, Prestwick KA9 1SN (0292 77608). *Location:* proceed down Grangemuir Road from main street Prestwick. 18 holes, 5952 yards, 5441 metres. S.S.S. 69. *Green Fees:* weekdays £30.00 per day, £18.00 per round. *Eating facilities:* full service. *Visitors:* welcome most weekdays with club introduction, reserved for members at weekends. *Society Meetings:* catered for by arrangement. Professional: S. Smith (0292 79755). Secretary: J.R. Leishman (0292 77608).

SKELMORLIE. **Skelmorlie Golf Club**, Beithglass Road, Skelmorlie PA17 5ES (Wemyss Bay (0475) 520152). *Location:* two/three miles from Wemyss Bay Pier. Hillside course. 13 holes, 5056 yards. S.S.S. 65. *Green Fees:* weekdays £9.00 per round, £12.00 per day; Sundays only £10.00 per round, £15.00 per day. No visitors Saturdays. Discounts to local hotel residents. *Eating facilities:* bar with snacks available. *Visitors:* welcome except Saturdays before 4pm. *Society Meetings:* welcome by arrangement. Parties at discounted "all-in" rate. Secretary: Mrs A. Fahey (0475 520774).

STEVENSTON. **Ardeer Golf Club**, Greenhead, Stevenston KA20 4JX (0294 64542). *Location:* north of Ayr. Rural parkland, undulating fairways. 18 holes, 6630 yards. S.S.S. 72. *Green Fees:* weekdays £12.00 (£18.00 daily); weekends £14.00 (£24.00 daily). *Eating facilities:* restaurant and bars. *Visitors:* welcome except Saturdays and medal Sundays. *Society Meetings:* catered for. Professional: Bob Rodgers (0294 601327). Secretary: T. Cumming (0294 63538).

TROON. **Kilmarnock (Barassie) Golf Club**, 29 Hillhouse Road, Barassie, Troon KA10 6SY (Troon (0292) 311077). *Location:* two miles north of Troon.

Manor Park Hotel

A warm welcome awaits guests at The Manor Park Hotel where all bedrooms are ensuite and have TV, teasmaid and telephones. The Hotel has recently been refurbished and the new 'Reflections' Restaurant offers excellent food and fine wines in elegant surroundings.
Royal Troon, Old Prestwick and many other golf courses are within 10 minutes of the Hotel, as is Prestwick Airport. Contact: Mr Murray, Manor Park Hotel, by Prestwick Airport, Ayrshire. Telephone/Fax: (0292) 79765.

St. Nicholas Hotel
41 Ayr Road, Prestwick – Fully Licensed

STB ✦✦✦ Commended
AA ★★   RAC ★★

Situated on the main Ayr/Prestwick road and within ½ mile of St. Nicholas and Old Prestwick Courses, and 10 minutes from Ayr and Troon. All bedrooms have private facilities including colour TV, tea/coffee facilities, telephone etc. The hotel has full central heating and is fully double glazed. Bar lunches 1200-1400 hours, high tea or dinner 1700-2100 hours. Indoor bowling, tennis courts and swimming pool at rear. Ample parking.

Telephone: Prestwick (0292) 79568   Fax: (0292) 76726

THE GOLF GUIDE 1994   *Scotland* AYRSHIRE

Links course. 18 holes, Medal 6473 yards, Visitors 6177 yards. S.S.S. 71. Practice ground. *Green Fees:* £35.00 per day weekdays. *Eating facilities:* coffee, lunches, snacks, high teas. *Visitors:* welcome Mondays, Tuesdays, Thursdays and Friday afternoons. All visitors must adhere to club dress code – no denim, trainers, etc. *Society Meetings:* catered for Tuesdays and Wednesdays. Professional: W.R. Lockie (Tel & Fax: 0292 311322). Secretary: Robert L. Bryce (0292 313920).

TROON. **Royal Troon Golf Club,** Craigend Road, Troon KA10 6EP (0292 311555). *Location:* three miles from A77 (Glasgow/Ayr trunk road). Old Course 18 holes, 7097 yards. S.S.S. 74. Portland Course 18 holes, 6274 yards, 5738 metres. S.S.S. 71. *Green Fees:* £75.00 (Old); £45.00 (Portland). *Eating facilities:* full restaurant service available, including bar snacks. *Visitors:* Mondays, Tuesdays and Thursdays between 9.30 and 11.00am and 14.30 and 15.00pm. Letter of introduction from own club and Handicap Certificate (maximum of 20). (No ladies or those under 18 years on Old Course). *Society Meetings:* parties in excess of 24 not accepted. Professional: R. Brian Anderson (0292 313281), Secretary/Manager: J.D. Montgomerie (0292 311555 Fax: 0292 318204).

TROON. **Troon Municipal Golf Course,** Harling Drive, Troon (0292 312464). *Location:* adjacent to railway station, one mile off the Ayr-Glasgow road. Three 18 hole courses. Lochgreen 6687 yards. S.S.S. 72. Darley 6327 yards. S.S.S. 70. Fullerton 4784 yards.

S.S.S. 65. *Green Fees:* information not provided. *Eating facilities:* hot snacks, 8am – 6pm. Bar snacks and lunches, evening meals bookings only. *Visitors:* catered for. Broad wheeled trolleys only. *Society Meetings:* catered for. Caterer: John Darge. Professional: Gordon McKinley. Advance booking should be made in writing to Starter's Office, Troon Municipal Golf Courses, Harling Drive, Troon, Ayrshire.

TURNBERRY. **Turnberry Hotel Golf Courses,** Turnberry KA26 9LT (0655 31000; Fax: 0655 31706). *Location:* on main A77 between Girvan and Maybole. 2 Championship Links Courses, Arran 18 holes, 6408 yards. S.S.S. 72; Ailsa 18 holes, 6014 yards. S.S.S. 69. Large practice area. *Green Fees:* on application. *Eating facilities:* new clubhouse, restaurant and bar. *Visitors:* written requests only. *Society Meetings:* same as visitors. Professional: Bob Jamieson (0655 31000 extension 342). Club Manager: E.C. Bowman (0655 31000 extension 300).

WEST KILBRIDE. **West Kilbride Golf Club,** 33-35 Fullerton Drive, Seamill, West Kilbride KA23 9HT (0294 823128). *Location:* on A78 Greenock to Ayr Road, leave at Seamill. Seaside links course. 18 holes, 6452 yards. S.S.S. 71. Practice area. *Green Fees:* on application. *Eating facilities:* diningroom and bar. *Visitors:* welcome weekdays only. *Society Meetings:* catered for Tuesdays and Thursdays. Certificates required. Professional: Gregor Howie (0294 823042). Secretary: E.D. Jefferies (0294 823911).

CRAIGLEA HOTEL
Troon KA10 6EG · Tel/Fax: (0292) 311366   AA**   RAC**

Ideal for a golfing break this 22 bedroom family run hotel overlooks the Firth of Clyde. We are adjacent to all the Troon Courses (including Royal Troon) and minutes away from Prestwick, Barassie and Western Gailes Golf Courses. Special all year round rates for Golf Parties. Cocktail bar – Restaurant – Rooms with ensuite facilities, tea/coffee makers – TV – Radio – Direct dial telephones etc.

Partners: The Misses J. and M. Calderwood and R. L. Calderwood.

South Beach Hotel
Troon, Ayrshire KA10 6EG. Tel. (0292) 312033 Fax. (0292) 318278
FULLY LICENSED   Commended RAC ★★★

Privately owned Hotel with a high reputation for friendly and efficient service with health and fitness facilities. All rooms ensuite. In the immediate surrounding area there are 5 Championship Courses including the famous Royal Troon. Another 15 courses within a 20 mile radius. Phone for details.

Please mention this guide when you write or phone to enquire about accommodation.

BANFFSHIRE *Scotland*   **THE GOLF GUIDE 1994**

The Seafield Arms Hotel

RAC ★★★

This fine old coaching hotel, which is family run, offers a warm welcome to all its visitors. 25 en-suite bedrooms tastefully decorated and a most relaxing restaurant and lounge bar with open fire. This is the ideal place for relaxation. There are 18 golf courses within a radius of twenty miles. Lying on the sunny southern shores of the Moray Firth, the uncrowded district of Moray offers an excellent range of golf to challenge the most dedicated golfer. From traditional links to parkland and moorland, all courses welcome visitors and most participate in the inclusive golf ticket. If you feel able to foresake your clubs in favour of sightseeing, the only Malt Whisky Trail in the world is on your doorstep, besides a variety of things to do and see for all the family, while the Castle Trail, Loch Ness and the Cairngorms are all within easy reach for a half day excursion. Bed and Breakfast from £26. For that special holiday or golf break please telephone for a tariff or brochure.

The Seafield Arms Hotel, Cullen AB56 2SG. Tel: 0542 40791 Fax: 0542 40736

Banffshire

BANFF. **Duff House Royal Golf Club,** The Barnyards, Banff AB45 3SX (0261 812062). *Location:* two minutes from town centre, A97, A98. Level parkland. 18 holes, 6161 yards. S.S.S. 69. *Green Fees:* weekdays £10.00 per round, £15.00 per day; weekends £16.00 per round, £21.00 per day. *Eating facilities:* lounge bar and full catering service. *Visitors:* welcome weekdays without reservation; restricted weekends. *Society Meetings:* catered for by prior arrangement. Professional: R.S. Strachan (0261 812075). Secretary: H. Liebnitz (0261 812062).

BUCKIE. **Buckpool Golf Club (Buckie),** Barhill Road, Buckie AB56 1DU (0542 32236). *Location:* turn off A98 signposted Buckpool. Links course with superlative view over Moray Firth. 18 holes, 6257 yards. S.S.S. 70. *Green Fees:* weekdays £10.00 per day, £6.00 (single rounds only) after 3.30pm; weekends £15.00 per day, £10.00 (single rounds only) after 3.30pm. *Eating facilities:* full catering daily, normal bar hours. *Visitors:* no restrictions except when there are scheduled competitions. Squash, snooker and indoor bowling. *Society Meetings:* welcome by prior arrangement. Secretary: Miss M. Coull.

Marine Hotel
Luxury Accommodation – Fine Dining – Full Services
JASMINE'S RESTAURANT – COMMODORE LOUNGE – DODGERS SPORTS BAR
Sauna – Jacuzzi – Multigym – Snooker – Free Car Parking
Golf Packages – 6 nights, Dinner, Bed and Breakfast & 5 Days' Golf £350 (Single)
Marine Place, Buckie, Banffshire AB56 1UT. Tel: (0542) 832249 Fax: (0542) 834949

THE GOLF GUIDE 1994   *Scotland*   BANFFSHIRE/BERWICKSHIRE

BUCKIE. **Strathlene Golf Club,** Strathlene, Buckie AB56 2DJ (0542 31798). *Location:* equidistant between Aberdeen and Inverness. Raised links course which follows the natural contours of the land. 18 holes. Practice facilities. *Green Fees:* weekdays £10.00 per round, £12.00 per day; weekends £12.00 per round, £15.00 per day. *Eating facilities:* full catering facilities available, bar open all day. *Visitors:* prior booking essential; avoid Saturday and Sunday mornings. Locker room. *Society Meetings:* booking required. Secretary: G. Clark (0542 34170).

CULLEN. **Cullen Golf Club,** The Links, Cullen, Buckie AB56 2SN (0542 40685). *Location:* off A98 midway between Aberdeen and Inverness, on Moray Firth coast. Seaside links with elevated section, natural rock landscaping and sandy beach coming into play at several holes. 18 holes, 4610 yards. S.S.S. 62. Putting green and net area. *Green Fees:* day tickets: weekdays £8.00; weekends £11.00. Subject to review. Weekly and fortnightly tickets available. Member of District Council's Rover Golf Ticket scheme. *Eating facilities:* catering and bar facilities. *Visitors:* welcome, may be restrictions Wednesdays and Saturdays (club competitions). *Society Meetings:* catered for. Secretary: I. Findlay (0542 40174).

DUFFTOWN. **Dufftown Golf Club,** Mether Cluny, Tomintoul Road, Dufftown AB55 4BX (Dufftown (0340) 20325). *Location:* one mile from Dufftown on Tomintoul Road. Hilly course, spectacular views. 18 holes, 5308 yards. S.S.S. 67. *Green Fees:* £10.00 per round, £12.00 per day. Weekly (five day) ticket £35.00. Reductions for parties of 12 or more. Juniors half price. *Eating facilities:* bar and snacks daily, meals by arrangement. *Visitors:* welcome at all times. *Society Meetings:* welcome by arrangement, catering available. Secretary: J.A. Goodall (0340 20546).

KEITH. **Keith Golf Club,** Fife Park, Keith AB55 3DF (0542 882469). *Location:* main road – A96 Keith. Parkland. 18 holes, 5614 yards. S.S.S. 68. *Green Fees:* Day ticket: weekdays £9.00, with a member £4.00; weekends £12.00 all summer. *Eating facilities:* catering available by arrangement, full bar facilities. *Visitors:* welcome anytime, advisable to ring – club competitions and various outings during peak season. *Society Meetings:* all welcome, applications to Hon. Secretary. Hon. Secretary: G. Edwards.

MACDUFF. **Royal Tarlair Golf Club,** Buchan Street, Macduff (Macduff (0261) 32897). *Location:* A98 Fraserburgh to Inverness trunk road – A947. Seaside links. 18 holes, 5866 yards, 5373 metres. S.S.S. 68. *Green Fees:* weekdays £8.00 per round, £12.00 per day; weekends £10.00 per round, £15.00 per day. *Eating facilities:* full catering and bar available. *Visitors:* welcome. *Society Meetings:* catered for (bookings through Secretary). Secretary: Mrs T. Watt.

Berwickshire

COLDSTREAM. **Hirsel Golf Club,** Kelso Road, Coldstream TD12 4NJ (0890 882678). *Location:* A697 west end of Coldstream. Parkland. 9 holes, 6050 yards. S.S.S. 69. *Green Fees:* weekdays £10.00; weekends £15.00. Weekly tickets £45.00. Subject to review. *Eating facilities:* bar and catering facilities March/October. *Visitors:* welcome, no restrictions; groups of over 10 players must pre book. *Society Meetings:* catered for by arrangement. Secretary: John C. Balfour (0890 883052).

DUNS. **Duns Golf Club,** Hardens Road, Duns. *Location:* about one mile west of Duns just off A6105. 9 holes, 5826 yards (2913 x 2). S.S.S. 68. Practice ground. *Green Fees:* £10.00. Half-price 1st November to 15th March. *Eating facilities:* lounge/bar open weekday evenings and weekends during season, snacks available. *Visitors:* welcome without reservation. *Society Meetings:* catered for. Secretary: A. Campbell (0361 82717).

EYEMOUTH. **Eyemouth Golf Club,** Gunsgreeen House, Eyemouth (Eyemouth (08907) 50551). *Location:* six miles north of Berwick-on-Tweed, off the A1 towards the coast. Seaside on cliff tops with panoramic views, spectacular hole over North Sea inlet. 9 holes, 5000 metres. S.S.S. 65. *Green Fees:* information not provided. *Eating facilities:* no eating facilities, normal bar hours in the evenings. *Visitors:* welcome most weekdays; after 10.30am on Saturdays and after 12 noon Sundays. *Society Meetings:* by prior arrangement with Secretary. Secretary: I. Fairbairn (08907 50074).

LAUDER. **Lauder Golf Club,** Galashiels Road, Lauder. *Location:* off A68, 28 miles south of Edinburgh. Undulating course, originally designed by W. Park of Musselburgh, on Lauder Hill. 9 holes, 6002 yards. S.S.S. 70. Practice ground. *Green Fees:* information not provided. *Eating facilities:* none – good Hotels in Lauder. *Visitors:* welcome without reservation. Secretary: D. Dickson (05782 526).

Caithness

LYBSTER. **Lybster Golf Club**, Main Street, Lybster. *Location:* 14 miles south from Wick on A9, half-way down village street. One of smallest courses in Scotland, heathland/parkland. 9 holes, 1896 yards. S.S.S. 62. *Green Fees:* £3.00. *Eating facilities:* at nearby hotels in village. *Visitors:* welcome anytime. *Society Meetings:* welcome anytime. Secretary: N. Fraser (084 784 215).

THURSO. **Reay Golf Club**, Clubhouse, Reay, By Thurso (Reay (084781) 288). *Location:* 12 miles west of nearest main town of Thurso. Natural seaside links. 18 holes, 5884 yards. S.S.S. 68. Practice area. *Green Fees:* £10.00 per day. Rates available for week/fortnight – information from Secretary. *Eating facilities:* bar lunches May to September, bar available every evening. *Visitors:* welcome anytime, restricted during competitions (Saturday mornings May to September). *Society Meetings:* welcome, advance bookings via Secretary. Captain: Evan Sutherland (0847-81 439). Secretary: Miss P. Peebles (084781 537).

THURSO. **Thurso Golf Club**, Newlands of Geise, By Thurso (Thurso (0847) 63807). *Location:* two miles south west of Railway Station. Flat parkland, wonderful views of Pentland Firth and Orkneys. 18 holes, 5610 yards. S.S.S. 69. *Green Fees:* £10.00, with member £5.00 (clubs provided). *Eating facilities:* all day during summer months. *Visitors:* welcome without reservation. *Society Meetings:* catered for. Shop Manager: J. Newton. Secretary: Wendy Meiklejohn (0847 65024).

WICK. **Wick Golf Club**, Reiss, By Wick KW1 4RW (0955 2726). *Location:* three miles north of Wick on A9. Seaside links course. 18 holes, 5976 yards. S.S.S. 69, Ladies 72. Practice area. *Green Fees:* weekdays £10.00 per day; weekends £12.00 per day. *Eating facilities:* licensed; snacks available. *Visitors:* welcome. *Society Meetings:* catered for. Secretary: Mrs M.S.W. Abernethy (0955 2702).

Enjoy golf at three excellent courses, all within easy reach. 42 modern chalets with private facilities, direct dial phones, colour TV and tea/coffee making. 5 nights Bed and Breakfast £95 (based on 2 sharing). 5 nights Dinner, Bed and Breakfast £120 (based on 2 sharing). Prices include free golf at Thurso and a 50% reduction on green fees at Wick and Reay links.

Call Jim Youngson for further details.

**The Weigh Inn Motel,
Burnside, Thurso KW14 7UG.
Telephone: 0847 63722 Fax: 0847 62112**

The Weigh Inn Motel
Telephone: Thurso 63722
The Weigh Inn made us welcome

NOTE

All the information in this book is given in good faith in the belief that it is correct. However, the publishers cannot guarantee the facts given in these pages, neither are they responsible for changes in policy, ownership or terms that may take place after the date of going to press. Readers should always satisfy themselves that the facilities they require are available and that the terms, if quoted, still apply.

Clackmannanshire

ALLOA. **Alloa Golf Club,** Shawpark, Sauchie (Alloa (0259) 722745). *Location:* on A908 between Alloa and Tillicoultry. Parkland. 18 holes, 6240 yards. S.S.S. 70. Two practice grounds. *Green Fees:* weekdays £12.00 per round, £20.00 per day. *Eating facilities:* dining room, bar meals. *Visitors:* welcome. *Society Meetings:* catered for. Professional: Bill Bennett (0259 724476). Secretary: A.M. Frame (0259 50100).

ALLOA. **Braehead Golf Club,** Cambus, By Alloa FK10 2NT (0259 722078). *Location:* one mile west of Alloa on A907. Gently undulating parkland course with scenic views and a variety of challenging holes. 18 holes, 6013 yards. S.S.S. 69. Practice area. *Green Fees:* weekdays £12.00 per round, £18.00 per day; weekends £18.00 per round, £24.00 per day. *Eating facilities:* bar/full catering available all day during Summer months; slightly restricted during Autumn/Spring. *Visitors:* no restrictions but advisable to telephone in advance. *Society Meetings:* catered for with prior booking. Professional: Paul Brookes. Secretary: Paul MacMichael.

ALVA. **Alva Golf Club,** Beauclerc Street, Alva FK12 5LH (0259 760431). *Location:* seven miles from Stirling on A91 Stirling to St Andrews Road – course lies at foot of Ochil Hills. Inland wooded hillside course with fast greens. 9 holes, 2423 yards, 2213 metres. S.S.S. 64. *Green Fees:* on application. *Eating facilities:* bar snacks only. *Visitors:* welcome at all times. Lounge and changing rooms available. Secretary: (0259 760431).

DOLLAR. **Dollar Golf Club,** Brewlands House, Dollar (Dollar (0259) 42400). *Location:* on A91. Hillside course. 18 holes, 5144 yards. S.S.S. 66. *Green Fees:* weekdays £7.00 round, £11.00 day, weekends £15.00. *Eating facilities:* full catering except Tuesdays. *Visitors:* welcome. *Society Meetings:* catered for. Secretary: J.C. Brown.

DOLLAR. **Muckhart Golf Club,** Muckhart, By Dollar FK14 7JH (Muckhart (0259) 781423). *Location:* off A91, three miles east of Dollar. Undulating heathland. 18 holes, 6034 yards. S.S.S. 70. Practice ground. *Green Fees:* weekdays £12.00; weekends £18.00. *Eating facilities:* catering and bar available all day, every day. *Visitors:* welcome except before 10am and from 12 noon to 3pm weekends and Public Holidays. *Society Meetings:* catered for. Professional: Keith Salmoni (0259 781493). Secretary: A.B. Robertson.

STIRLING. **Tillicoultry Golf Club,** Alva Road, Tillicoultry FK13 6EB (Tillicoultry (0259) 50124). *Location:* on A91, nine miles from Stirling. Parkland. 9 holes, 5358 yards. S.S.S. 66. *Green Fees:* weekdays £8.00 per round, £11.00 after 4pm; weekends £13.50 per round. *Eating facilities:* licensed bar, bar lunches, snacks, etc from 12 noon to 2pm daily, bookings taken for evenings. *Visitors:* welcome at all times outwith competitions. No children under 15 weekends until 4.00pm. *Society Meetings:* catered for on application to the Secretary. Secretary: R. Whitehead (0259 51337/50124).

Dumfriesshire

ANNAN. **Powfoot Golf Club,** 27 Bank Street, Annan DG12 6AU (04617 227). *Location:* off Annan/Dumfries Road B724, signpost to course miles from Annan. Semi-links course on Solway shore with outstanding views. 18 holes, 6283 yards, 5745 metres. S.S.S. 70. Practice ground. *Green Fees:* weekdays £23.00 per day, £15.00 per round. Sundays after 2.45pm £16.00. *Eating facilities:* morning coffee, lunches and teas in clubhouse – ordering in advance essential for large parties. *Visitors:* welcome weekdays but restrictions at weekends, no formal introduction required. *Society Meetings:* catered for weekdays by prior arrangement (up to 40 in number). Professional: Gareth Dick (04617 327). Secretary: R.G. Anderson (0461 202866/7).

DALBEATTIE. **Dalbeattie Golf Club,** C/o 7 Galla Drive, Dalbeattie (0556 611421). *Location:* outskirts of Dalbeattie. Slightly hilly parkland. 9 holes, 2100 yards. S.S.S. 60. *Green Fees:* £10.00 per round. Reductions for parties. *Eating facilities:* bar and food available. *Visitors:* welcome everyday but restricted on three nights – Monday, Wednesday and Thursday. *Society Meetings:* all welcome. Secretary: T. Moffat (0556 610682).

DUMFRIES. **Crichton Royal Golf Club,** Bankend Road, Dumfries DG1 4TH (0387 55301). *Location:* directly across the road from Dumfries and Galloway Royal Infirmary, one mile outside Dumfries on Bankend Road. Wooded parkland. 9 holes, 5952 yards. S.S.S. 69. *Green Fees:* weekdays £12.00; weekends £15.00. *Eating facilities:* lunch, tea available in clubhouse. *Visitors:* welcome, restrictions depending on club competitions, Tuesdays gents' competitions. *Society Meetings:* on application. Secretary: Alastair B. McKay (0387 55301 extension 2122).

DUMFRIESSHIRE *Scotland*

DUMFRIES. **Dumfries and County Golf Club**, Nunfield, Edinburgh Road, Dumfries DG1 1JX (Dumfries (0387) 53585). *Location:* one mile north-east town centre on A701. 18 holes, 5928 yards. S.S.S. 68. Limited practice facilities. *Green Fees:* £21.00 weekdays; £25.00 weekends. *Eating facilities:* restaurant and bar snacks. *Visitors:* welcome except on Saturdays. *Society Meetings:* catered for by arrangement. Professional: G. Gray (0387 68918). Secretary: E.C. Pringle (0387 53585).

DUMFRIES. **Dumfries and Galloway Golf Club**, 2 Laurieston Avenue, Dumfries DG2 7NY (Dumfries (0387) 53582). *Location:* on Castle Douglas/Stranraer road, A75. Parkland course. 18 holes, 5803 yards. S.S.S. 68. Practice area. *Green Fees:* weekdays £16.00; weekends £20.00. *Eating facilities:* full catering during bar hours except Mondays. *Visitors:* welcome, except on competition days. *Society Meetings:* catered for weekdays, except Tuesdays. Secretary: Jack Donnachie (0387 63848). Professional: Joe Fergusson (0387 56902).

DUMFRIES. **Southerness Golf Club**, Southerness, Kirkbean, Dumfries DG2 8AZ (Kirkbean (038 788) 677). *Location:* 16 miles south west of Dumfries on A710 (Solway Coast Road). Natural challenging Championship links, designed by MacKenzie Ross with panoramic views of Solway Firth and Galloway hills. Hosted British Ladies' Amateur 1989 and British Youths' 1990. 18 holes, 6564 yards. S.S.S. 72. Large practice area. *Green Fees:* weekdays £23.00 per day; weekends £30.00 per day. Weekly (Monday to Friday) ticket £92.00. *Eating facilities:* full bar and catering facilities. *Visitors:* welcome 10am to 12 noon, 2pm to 4.30pm. Thursdays 11am to 1pm, 2.30pm to 4.30pm; weekends 10am to 11.30am, 2.30pm to 4.30pm. *Society Meetings:* on application to Secretary. Secretary: W.D. Ramage.

LANGHOLM. **Langholm Golf Club**, Whitaside, Langholm DG13 0JS (Langholm (03873) 80559). *Location:* on A7 Carlisle-Edinburgh road. Turn off at market place in centre of town. Hillside. 9 holes, 5744 yards. S.S.S. 68. Practice area available. *Green Fees:* £10.00; £5.00 playing with a member. *Eating facilities:* on request. *Visitors:* welcome without reservation; restrictions Saturday 9am to 9.45am, 1pm to 1.45pm, Sunday 9am to 10am and 1pm (Competition times). *Society Meetings:* apply in writing to Secretary. Secretary: W.J. Brown (03873 80395).

LOCKERBIE. **Lochmaben Golf Club**, Castlehillgate, Lochmaben, Lockerbie DG11 1NT (Lochmaben (0387) 810552). *Location:* Lockerbie four miles, Dumfries eight miles. Parkland with excellent views. 9 holes, 5304 yards, 4616 metres. S.S.S. 66. *Green Fees:* weekdays £12.00; weekends £14.00. *Eating facilities:* catering and bar. *Visitors:* welcome Monday to Saturday except on competition days and not after 5pm. Local hotel 50 yards from course. *Society Meetings:* welcome. Secretary: J.M. Dickie (0387 810713).

LOCKERBIE. **Lockerbie Golf CLub**, 89 High Street, Lockerbie DG11 2ND (0576 203363). *Location:* A74 to Lockerbie, take Corrie Road, 500 yards on right. Parkland featuring the only pond hole in area which is in play on three holes. 18 holes, 5418 yards. S.S.S. 66. Practice area, practice putting green. *Green Fees:* weekdays £16.00; weekends £20.00. Juniors £4.00. *Eating facilities:* catering 8am – 8pm, bar 11am – 11pm. *Visitors:* welcome, restricted on Sundays. *Society Meetings:* welcome by arrangement. Secretary: Mr J. Thomson (0576 202462).

PAUL JONES HOTEL

Situated by the Solway Firth, only 100 yards from the shore. All seven bedrooms are ensuite and have colour TV. Only a few minutes' walk from championship links at Southerness Golf Club, and several challenging courses nearby.

Paul Jones Hotel, Southerness, by Dumfries DG2 8AZ. Tel: 0387 88 205

GOLFING BREAKS IN SOUTH WEST SCOTLAND

Daily Golfing Rates from £55 per person

Superb leisure facilities at this privately owned Hotel include a 14m Heated Indoor Swimming Pool; Sauna; Steam Room; Hot Spa Bath; Gymnasium; Toning Tables, Sunbeds; Health and Beauty Salon. Enjoy a Dinner Dance every Saturday night or our popular Sunday Night Ceilidh throughout the summer months.

Daily Golfing Rate includes Dinner, Bed & Breakfast plus Golf on all local courses subject to availability.

AA ★★★   STB ✤✤✤ Commended   RAC ★★★

Group reductions by arrangement. For further details please contact Dept. P.G.A.

CAIRNDALE HOTEL AND LEISURE CLUB
ENGLISH STREET, DUMFRIES DG1 2DF   Tel: 0387 54111   Fax: 0387 50555

AA/RAC★★ ANNANDALE ARMS HOTEL
High Street, Moffat DG10 9HF
Telephone: Moffat (0683) 20013   Fax: (0683) 21395

This fine old Coaching Hotel stands in the centre of the beautiful Spa town of Moffat, amidst wonderful scenery. **Moffat's 18 hole Golf Course, where visitors are welcome, stands on a hill overlooking the Hotel, and we are just a few minutes away from this scenic hill course.** There are many golf courses within the Moffat area and a brochure showing those within a 40 mile radius is available from the Annandale Arms Hotel.

The Hotel offers excellent accommodation in 24 bedrooms, many of which have private facilities. Fine food is served in our Restaurant from 7.00 – 9.00 pm and in our comfortable panelled bar from 12.00 noon – 2.00 pm and 5.30 – 9.00 pm.

MOFFAT. **The Moffat Golf Club,** Coatshill, Moffat DG10 9SB (Moffat (0683) 20020). *Location:* leave A74 at Beattock on A701, club notice one mile on left. Scenic moorland course. 18 holes, 5218 yards. S.S.S. 66. Putting green; small practice area. *Green Fees:* weekdays £16.00 per day; weekends £24.00 per day. £24.00 weekdays, £32.00 weekends for parties of eight and over – package includes coffee, snack lunch, evening meal and two rounds of golf. *Eating facilities:* bar meals served all day. *Visitors:* welcome without reservation, except Wednesday after 12 noon. *Society Meetings:* catering provided. Secretary: T.A. Rankin (0683 20020). Clubmaster: Mr Ian Preston.

SANQUHAR. **Sanquhar Golf Club,** Euchan Course, Sanquhar (Sanquhar (0659) 50577). *Location:* situated quarter-of-a-mile from A76 Dumfries-Kilmarnock trunk road. Undulating parkland. 9 holes, 5144 metres. S.S.S. 68. *Green Fees:* weekdays £8.00 per round, weekends £10.00 per round. *Eating facilities:* bar available if requested in advance. *Visitors:* welcome without reservation. *Society Meetings:* catered for with advance notice. Licensed clubhouse with full-size snooker table. Secretary: Mrs J. Murray (0659 58181).

THORNHILL. **Thornhill Golf Club,** Blacknest, Thornhill DG3 5DW (Thornhill (0848) 30546) *Location:* 14 miles north of Dumfries on A76. Parkland/open moorland. 18 holes, 6011 yards. S.S.S. 69. Practice ground (two areas). *Green Fees:* weekdays £16.00; weekends £20.00. Weekly ticket £75.00. *Eating facilities:* catering available, except Mondays, bar facility. *Visitors:* welcome without reservation, but please contact club steward re competitions, etc. *Society Meetings:* welcome, contact club Steward. Secretary: R.L. Kerr (0848 30218).

Dunbartonshire

ALEXANDRIA. **Vale of Leven Golf Club,** Northfield Road, Bonhill, Alexandria (0389) 52351). *Location:* A82 to Dumbarton, follow signs at roundabout at Dumbarton for Bonhill then club signs. Moorland with splendid views of Loch Lomond. 18 holes, 5165 yards. S.S.S. 66. *Green Fees:* weekdays £10.00 per round, £15.00 per day; weekends £12.00 per round, £20.00 per day. *Eating facilities:* catering and bar available. *Visitors:* welcome except Saturdays between April 1st and September 30th. Full changing and locker facilities. *Society Meetings:* on application to Secretary. Secretary: W. McKinlay (0389 52508).

CARDROSS. **Cardross Golf Club,** Main Street, Cardross G82 5LB (Cardross [0389] 841213). *Location:* on A814 west of Dumbarton. Parkland course. 18 holes, 6469 yards. S.S.S. 71. Practice ground. *Green Fees:* weekdays £18.00 per round, £30.00 day ticket. *Eating facilities:* lunches/bar snacks available during bar hours. *Visitors:* weekdays only (by phoning Professional to book time). *Society Meetings:* catered for weekdays by arrangement. Professional: Robert Craig (0389 841350). Secretary: P.A. Laing (0389 841754).

CLYDEBANK. **Clydebank and District Golf Club,** Glasgow Road, Hardgate, Clydebank G81 5QY (0389 73289). *Location:* Hardgate village. Off A82 10 miles west of Glasgow (off Great Western Road). 18 holes, 5832 yards, 5325 metres. S.S.S. 68. *Green Fees:* £12.00 per round. *Eating facilities:* catering as required. *Visitors:* welcome weekdays only. Professional: David Pirie (0389 78686). Secretary: W. Manson (0389 72832).

CLYDEBANK. **Clydebank Municipal Golf Course,** Overtoun Road, Clydebank G81 3RE (041-952 8698). *Location:* one mile west of Clydebank centre off Duntocher Road. Parkland course – one of the best Par 3's in Scotland. 18 holes, 5349 yards. S.S.S. 66. *Green Fees:* information not provided. *Eating facilities:* tearoom. *Visitors:* municipal course, tee closed Saturdays in Summer 11am to 2pm. *Society Meetings:* contact District Council. Professional: Richard Bowman (041-952 6372). Secretary: District Council (041-941 1331).

DUNBARTONSHIRE Scotland

CUMBERNAULD. **Palacerigg Golf Club,** Palacerigg Country Park, Cumbernauld, Near Glasgow G67 3HU (0236 734969). *Location:* Palacerigg Road, three miles south of Cumbernauld off B8039 Lenziemill Road. Wooded parkland with good views to Campsie Hills. 18 holes, 6444 yards, 5894 metres. S.S.S. 71. Practice area, nearby golf range. *Green Fees:* £7.00 per day weekdays; £8.00 per day weekends. *Eating facilities:* bar seven days, all day opening from March to October; meals available Wednesdays to Sundays or by arrangement. *Visitors:* welcome weekdays only. *Society Meetings:* by letter to Secretary. Secretary: David S.A. Cooper. Starter: (0236 721461).

CUMBERNAULD. **Westerwood Golf Club,** Westerwood, Cumbernauld (0236 51171; Fax: 0236 738478). *Location:* off M80 towards Dullatur. Undulating wooded course designed by Seve Ballesteros and Dave Thomas. 18 holes, 6721 yards. S.S.S. 73. *Green Fees:* information not provided. *Eating facilities:* clubhouse, restaurant and bar. *Visitors:* welcome at all times, no restrictions. Advance booking of tee-off times recommended. Hotel golf packages available. *Society Meetings:* welcome by arrangement. Golf Professional: Tony Smith (0236 725281; Fax: 0236 738478).

DUMBARTON. **Dumbarton Golf Club,** Broadmeadow, Dumbarton G82 2BQ (Dumbarton (0389) 32830). *Location:* A814, three-quarters of a mile north west of town. Flat parkland. 18 holes, 6071 yards. S.S.S. 69. Small practice area. *Green Fees:* £15.00 weekdays. *Eating facilities:* bar available, meals by previous arrangement with Caterer. *Visitors:* welcome, Monday to Friday only. No jeans or shellsuits on course or in clubhouse. *Society Meetings:* all welcome with prior bookings. Secretary: R. Turnbull.

HELENSBURGH. **Helensburgh Golf Club,** 25 East Abercromby Street, Helensburgh G84 9JD (Helensburgh (0436) 74173). *Location:* A82 Dumbarton. Moorland course with panoramic views. 18 holes, 6058 yards. S.S.S. 69. Practice area. *Green Fees:* £15.00 per round, £23.00 per day weekdays. *Eating facilities:* full catering and bar. *Visitors:* welcome weekdays only, dress in recognised golfing attire. Professional: Robert Farrell (0436 75505). Secretary: Mrs A. McEwan (0436 74173).

KIRKINTILLOCH. **Kirkintilloch Golf Club,** Campsie Road, Kirkintilloch G66 1RN (041-776 1256). *Location:* from Glasgow to Bishopbriggs, then straight on to Kirkintilloch. Undulating, parkland course. 18 holes, 5269 yards. S.S.S. 66. Par 70. Putting green and practice areas. *Green Fees:* on application. *Eating facilities:* dining room and bar. *Visitors:* weekdays only, must be introduced by member. *Society Meetings:* catered for Mondays and Tuesdays, information from Secretary including catering. Secretary: I.M. Gray (041-775 2387).

LENZIE. **Lenzie Golf Club,** 19 Crosshill Road, Lenzie, Glasgow (041-776 1535). *Location:* six miles north-east of Glasgow. 18 holes, 5977 yards. S.S.S. 69. *Green Fees:* weekdays only, £12.50 per round, £20.00 per day. *Eating facilities:* dining room available. *Visitors:* welcome with introduction or prior reservation. *Society Meetings:* welcome. Professional: Jim McCallum (041-777 7748) Secretary: J.A. Chisholm (041-776 6020).

GOLFING PACKAGES AT WESTERWOOD

No golfing holiday in Scotland is complete without a visit to our superb parkland course designed by Seve Ballesteros and Dave Thomas.

Our fabulous 15th, a par 3, which has you driving at a waterfall tumbling 40 feet down a rock face, will take your breath away. Couple this with our Hotel and Country Club and your golfing holiday will be one to remember. Prices start from £45 per person per day for a THREE-DAY GOLF PACKAGE sharing a twin room, Bed and Breakfast including golf and leisure. Alternatively, join one of our Golf Schools, with tuition in our indoor golf facility.

– THE –
WESTERWOOD
HOTEL, GOLF & COUNTRY CLUB

WESTERWOOD HOTEL, GOLF & COUNTRY CLUB
St. Andrews Drive, Cumbernauld G68 0EW
Telephone: (0236) 457171   Fax: (0236) 738478

Edinburgh and the Lothians

Club golf at North Berwick, East Lothian.

MELVILLE GOLF RANGE

LOTHIAN'S LONGEST RANGE · 300 YDS

- A range built to lower your handicap
- 22 all weather covered bays and 12 outdoor mats
- Open Mon – Fri 9am – 10pm, Weekends 9am – 8pm
- Floodlit
- Favourable wind and sun direction, facing east
- 3 minutes from Edinburgh City Bypass, Exit A7 (Galashiels).

- 2 piece balls, costs from £1.60, various concessions
- Resident Professional, tuition available, individual and groups
- Club repair and hire
- Trial clubs
- Golf shop with men's and ladies' equipment and Golf Wear
- Target Golf and Grass Mats
- Hot and Cold beverages available

For further information
031-663 8038

SOUTH MELVILLE, LASSWADE,
NEAR DALKEITH,
MIDLOTHIAN EH18 1AN

EDINBURGH AND THE LOTHIANS *Scotland*

ABERLADY. Kilspindie Golf Club, The Clubhouse, Aberlady EH32 0QD (087 57 216). *Location:* off A198 North Berwick Road at Aberlady. Seaside course. 18 holes, 5417 yards, 4957 metres. S.S.S. 66. Large practice area. *Green Fees:* weekdays £20.00 per round, £27.00 per day; Saturday and Sunday £25.00 per round, £32.00 per day. *Eating facilities:* diningroom and bar. *Visitors:* welcome after 9.15am and before 4pm weekdays, after 11am weekends on non-competition days. *Society Meetings:* welcome subject to above restrictions (no catering Fridays). Professional: Graham Sked (087 57 695). Secretary: Hugh F. Brown (087-57 358).

ABERLADY. Luffness New Golf Club, Aberlady EH32 0QA (0620 843114; Fax: 0620 842933). *Location:* A198 – 17 miles east of Edinburgh. One mile from Gullane. Links course, 18 holes, 6122 yards. S.S.S. 69. *Green Fees:* provided on application. *Eating facilities:* dining room except Mondays. *Visitors:* weekdays only (require introduction). *Society Meetings:* by prior arrangement. Secretary: Lt. Col. J.G. Tedford (0620 843336; Fax: 0620 842933).

BATHGATE. Bathgate Golf Club, Edinburgh Road, Bathgate EH48 1BA (0506 52232; Fax: 0506 636775). *Location:* three miles from M8, 400 yards east of George Square, the town centre. Flat course. 18 holes, 6328 yards. S.S.S. 70. Practice area. *Green Fees:* weekdays £15.00 per round, £20.00 per day; weekends £25.00 per day. *Eating facilities:* diningroom open all week. *Visitors:* welcome without reservation except on Competition days at weekends. Professional: Sandy Strachan (0506 630553). Secretary: W. Gray (0506 630505).

DALKEITH. Newbattle Golf Club Ltd, Abbey Road, Dalkeith (031-663 2123). *Location:* approximately seven miles south-east of Edinburgh A7 to Eskbank Toll (Newbattle exit). Parkland, wooded course. 18 holes, 6012 yards, 5498 metres. S.S.S. 69. Small practice area. *Green Fees:* 14.00 per round, £20.00 per day. *Eating facilities:* full catering available on request. *Visitors:* weekdays only. No jeans/trainers on course or in clubhouse. *Society Meetings:* restricted. Professional: D. Torrance (031-660 1631). Secretary: H.G. Stanners (031 663 1819).

DUNBAR. Dunbar Golf Club, East Links, Dunbar EH42 1LP (Dunbar (0368) 62317). *Location:* on coast half a mile east of Dunbar. Seaside links, used for final qualifying 1992 Open Championship. 18 holes, 6426 yards. S.S.S. 71. *Green Fees:* weekdays £25.00 per day; weekends £40.00. *Eating facilities:* full catering facilities. *Visitors:* no visitors on Thursdays or before 9.30am and between 12.30pm and 2pm weekdays; or before 10am and between 12 noon and 2pm weekends. *Society Meetings:* welcome. Professional: Derek Small (0368 62086). Secretary: Don Thompson (0368 621317; Fax: 0368 65202).

GOLF HOTEL
Main Street, Aberlady, East Lothian EH32 0RF

This small family-run hotel is situated in a coastal village in the heart of East Lothian's golfing country. There are 14 golf courses within 10 miles radius of the hotel.

All rooms are en suite, with TV, telephone and tea/coffee making facilities.

Relax in our friendly traditional bar and enjoy excellent cuisine in our comfortable restaurant. STB ☆☆☆ Commended.

Golf Packages are our speciality. Dinner, Bed and Breakfast from £35 per person.

Telephone Tom Hill on 08757 503 for more details.

GOLDENSTONES HOTEL
QUEEN'S ROAD, DUNBAR

High Teas, Bar Lunches 7 Days, Fully Licensed, Accommodation.
Weddings, Engagements, 18th & 21st Birthdays, Presentations, and Anniversaries. Buffets a speciality.
Where: Service, Comfort and YOU really matter

☎ 0368 62356   Prop: J. QUINN
2-LANE SKITTLE ALLEY

Scotland **EDINBURGH AND THE LOTHIANS**

DUNBAR. **Winterfield Golf Club**, North Road, Dunbar (0368 62280). Seaside course. 18 holes, 4686 metres. S.S.S. 65. *Green Fees:* information not available. *Eating facilities:* available. *Visitors:* welcome without reservation. The Pro Shop: (0368 63562). Professional: Keven Phillips. Secretary: Michael O'Donnell (0368 62280/65119).

EDINBURGH. **Baberton Golf Club**, Baberton Avenue, Juniper Green, Edinburgh EH14 5DU (031-453 3361). *Location:* five miles west of Edinburgh on the A70. 18 holes, 6098 yards. S.S.S. 69. *Green Fees:* weekdays £17.00 per round, £25.00 per day. *Eating facilities:* by arrangement (phone Mrs Goodsir 031-453 3361). *Visitors:* welcome by arrangement with Secretary. *Society Meetings:* catered for. Professional: K. Kelly (031-453 3555). Secretary: E.W. Horberry (031-453 4911).

EDINBURGH. **Braids United Golf Club**, 22 Braid Hills Approach, Morningside, Edinburgh EH10 6JY (031-452 9408). *Location:* Braid Hills on south side of Edinburgh. Two 18 hole courses. No. 1 – 5880 yards. S.S.S. 68. No. 2 – 4495 yards. S.S.S. 64. *Green Fees:* £6.60. *Visitors:* welcome without reservation. (Accommodation in Braid Hills Hotel – 400 yards). Public courses, clubs on hire. Sunday golf on No. 2 course only. Professional: John Boath. Hon. Secretary: Gerald Hind (031-445 2044).

EDINBURGH. **Broomieknowe Golf Club Ltd**, 36 Golf Course Road, Bonnyrigg (031-663 9317). *Location:* south of Edinburgh, A6094 from Dalkeith. 18 holes, 5754 yards. S.S.S. 68. *Green Fees:* weekdays £15.00 per round, £25.00 per day; £25.00 per round at weekends. *Eating facilities:* lunches, high teas except Mondays. *Visitors:* welcome Monday to Friday, weekends by prior arrangement. *Society Meetings:* catered for Monday to Friday by arrangement. Professional: Mark Patchett (031-660 2035). Secretary: I.J. Nimmo.

EDINBURGH. **Bruntsfield Links Golfing Society**, The Clubhouse, 32 Barnton Avenue, Edinburgh EH4 6JH (031-336 2006). *Location:* off A90 to Davidson's Mains. Parkland course. 18 holes, 6402 yards. S.S.S. 71. *Green Fees:* information not provided. *Eating facilities:* lunches served at club. *Visitors:* welcome on weekdays if playing with a member, or if suitably introduced. *Society Meetings:* catered for. Professional: Brian MacKenzie (031-336 4050). Secretary: Lieut. Col. M.B. Hext (031-336 1479).

EDINBURGH. **Craigmillar Park Golf Club**, 1 Observatory Road, Edinburgh EH9 3HG (031-667 2837). *Location:* A702 from City centre on Mayfield Road, right at King's Buildings. Parkland. 18 holes, 5846 yards. S.S.S. 68. *Green Fees:* £12.00 per round, £18.00 per day. *Eating facilities:* lunches, snacks, high teas and dinners. *Visitors:* welcome with reservation on production of Handicap Certificate. Weekdays only before 3.30pm. *Society Meetings:* catered for by previous arrangement. Professional: B. McGee (031-667 0047). Secretary: J. Brough (031-667 0047).

WE'LL KEEP A WELCOME IN . . . **THE HILLSIDE HOTEL**
3 Queen's Road, Dunbar EH42 1LA Telephone **(0368) 862071**

Overlooking the East Lothian coast at the fishing port of Dunbar, close to the Lammermuir Hills and 30 minutes from Edinburgh. Two golf courses (one a championship course), sea fishing, walking and climbing. Scuba diving a short walk from hotel. Excellent restaurant and bar. Ensuite accommodation.
Telephone **Joan & Barrie Bussey** for brochure and reservation.

The Redheugh Hotel   AA/RAC ★★   Les Routiers
                            STB ♥♥♥   Commended
Bayswell Park, DUNBAR EH42 1AE. Tel: **(0368) 62793**

Cliff top location. Small licensed hotel with emphasis on personal attention and good food. Menu changed daily. Groups welcome. Tee times can be arranged on 14 different courses within half-hour's drive. Also ideal for visiting Edinburgh and touring the Borders. **GOLF BREAKS** from **£39.50 per person per night** Dinner, Bed and Breakfast. Phone **(0368) 62793** for more details.

The Courtyard
Hotel and Restaurant

WOODBUSH BRAE, DUNBAR, EAST LOTHIAN
SCOTLAND EH42 1HB   TEL: 0368 64169

As reviewed and approved by 'Golf World' July 1992
The sea washes against the walls of these fisherman's cottages which have been sympathetically converted to a small hotel and restaurant which have dramatic seascape views and located just three hundred paces from Dunbar golf course. The Courtyard is set in the heart of golf country and is also ideal for touring the border country with its wild and beautiful coastline – yet only 28 miles from the Edinburgh city lights.

AA ❀ Rosette for Food
Scottish Tourist Board   Taste of Scotland
– all Approved and Recommended
'BARGAIN BREAKS' THROUGHOUT THE YEAR
including specially priced 5 Day, 5 Round East Lothian Golfing Ticket

EDINBURGH AND THE LOTHIANS *Scotland* THE GOLF GUIDE 1994

EDINBURGH. **Duddingston Golf Club Ltd,** Duddingston Road West, Edinburgh EH15 3QD (031-661 1005). *Location:* adjacent to A1 Willowbrae Road, turn right at Duddingston crossroads then one mile on Duddingston Road West. Undulating parkland with stream. 18 holes, 6647 yards. S.S.S. 72. *Green Fees:* weekdays only £20.00 per round, £26.00 per day. *Eating facilities:* full catering and bar facilities. *Visitors:* welcome weekdays only. *Society Meetings:* catered for Tuesdays and Thursdays (rates on request). Professional: Alistair McLean (031-661 4301). Secretary: John C. Small (031-661 7688).

EDINBURGH. **Kingsknowe Golf Club,** 326 Lanark Road, Edinburgh EH14 2JD (031-441 1144). *Location:* on Edinburgh Corporation Bus No. 44 route. Parkland course. 18 holes, 5979 yards, 5466 metres. S.S.S. 69. Practice area. *Green Fees:* weekdays £16.00 per round, £20.00 per day; weekends £25.00 per round. *Eating facilities:* lounge bar, snacks and meals available. *Visitors:* welcome Monday to Friday, also weekends subject to availability. *Society Meetings:* catered for. Professional: Andrew Marshall (031-441 4030). Secretary: R. Wallace (031-441 1145)

EDINBURGH. **Liberton Golf Club,** 297 Gilmerton Road, Edinburgh EH16 5UJ (031-664 8580). *Location:* Corporation transport to Lodge Gate, buses 3 and 8 from Edinburgh. By car on A7 (Visitors' car park). Parkland, rolling. 18 holes, 5299 yards, 4845 metres. S.S.S. 66. *Green Fees:* weekdays £15.00 per round, £25.00 per day; weekends £25.00. *Eating facilities:* full catering and bar service. *Visitors:* not before 1.30pm weekends. *Society Meetings:* catered for by arrangement except Fridays or weekends. Professional: I. Seath (031-664 1056). Secretary: A. Poole (031-664 3009).

EDINBURGH. **Lothianburn Golf Club,** 106a Biggar Road, Edinburgh EH10 7DU (031-445 2206). *Location:* south on the A702 approximately four miles from city centre or easily reached from Edinburgh by pass road coming off at Lothianburn junction. Hill course close to Pentland Hills. 18 holes, 5750 yards. S.S.S. 69. Two practice grounds. *Green Fees:* weekdays £11.00 per round, £16.00 per day; weekends £15.00 per round, £20.00 per day. Special rates November to February on application. *Eating facilities:* normal bar hours, no hot food on Wednesdays. *Visitors:* welcome mid-week, weekends restricted. *Society Meetings:* catered for by prior arrangement with the Secretary. Professional: Paul Morton (031-445 2288). Secretary: W.F.A. Jardine (031-445 5067).

EDINBURGH. **Merchants Of Edinburgh Golf Club,** Craighill Gardens, Edinburgh EH10 5PY (031-447 1219). *Location:* car park Glenlockhart Road, Edinburgh EH10. Hilly parkland. 18 holes, 4889 yards. S.S.S. 64. *Green Fees:* weekdays £12.00. *Eating facilities:* by arrangement with Clubmaster, J. Wilson. *Visitors:* welcome weekdays until 4pm, not weekends. *Society Meetings:* catered for except weekends. Professional: C.A. Imlah (031-447 8709). Secretary: A.M. Montgomery.

EDINBURGH. **Mortonhall Golf Club,** 231 Braid Road, Edinburgh EH10 6PB (031-447 2411). *Location:* take A702 south from City to Morningside traffic lights, up Braid Road one mile, course on left. 18 holes, 6548 yards, 5987 metres. S.S.S. 71. *Green Fees:* information not provided. *Eating facilities:* lunch, tea and snacks every day (no lunches Mondays). *Visitors:* welcome with introduction. *Society Meetings:* catered for (not at weekends). Professional: D. Horn. Secretary: Mrs C.D. Morrison (031-447 6974).

EDINBURGH. **Murrayfield Golf Club,** 43 Murrayfield Road, Edinburgh EH12 6EU (031-337 1009). *Location:* two miles west of city centre. Parkland on east side of Corstorphine Hill. 18 holes, 5725 yards. S.S.S. 68. Practice area, net and putting green. *Green Fees:* weekdays £20.00 per round, £26.00 per day. *Eating facilities:* lunch each day, snacks in casual bar, also full bar facilities. *Visitors:* welcome playing with member or by prior arrangement only. No visitors weekends. *Society Meetings:* catered for by prior arrangement. Professional: J.J. Fisher (031-337 3479). Secretary: J.P. Bullen (031-337 3478).

EDINBURGH. **Portobello Golf Club,** Stanley Street, Portobello, Edinburgh EH15 1JJ (031-669 4361). *Location:* on A1 at Milton Road East. Parkland course. 9 holes, 2400 yards, 2195 metres. S.S.S. 32. *Green Fees:* £3.30 per round (9 holes). Reductions for Juniors and Senior Citizens. *Visitors:* welcome, restrictions on competition days. *Society Meetings:* not catered for. Professional: J. Boath. Secretary: A. Cook (031-669 5271).

EDINBURGH. **Prestonfield Golf Club,** 6 Priestfield Road North, Edinburgh EH16 5HS (031-667 1273). *Location:* off Dalkeith Road, near Royal Commonwealth Pool on A68. Parkland. 18 holes, 6216 yards. S.S.S. 70. Practice area. *Green Fees:* weekdays £17.00 per round, £25.00 per day; weekends and Bank Holidays £25.00 per round, £35.00 per day. *Eating facilities:* full catering. *Visitors:* welcome weekdays anytime, not between 8am and 10.30am and 12 noon to 1.30pm Saturdays, not before 11.30am Sundays. *Society Meetings:* welcome weekdays. Professional: Brian Commins (031-667 8597). Secretary: Michael D.A.G. Dillon (031-667 9665).

EDINBURGH. **Ravelston Golf Club Ltd,** 24 Ravelston Dykes Road, Blackhall, Edinburgh EH4 5NZ (031-315 2486). *Location:* A90 Queensferry Road (leading to Forth Road Bridge) Left pedestrian crossing, Blackhall, into Craigcrook Road, then second left. Parkland course. 9 holes, 2600 yards, 2377 metres. S.S.S. 66. *Green Fees:* £12.50 weekdays. *Eating facilities:* tea, coffee, soft drinks and light snacks. *Visitors:* welcome during quiet period. *Society Meetings:* permitted by special application only. Secretary: Frank Philip (031-312 6850).

EDINBURGH. **Royal Burgess Golfing Society of Edinburgh,** 181 Whitehouse Road, Barnton, Edinburgh EH4 6BY. *Location:* A90 to Queensferry, behind Barnton Hotel. Parkland. 18 holes, 6494 yards. S.S.S. 71. *Green Fees:* on request. *Eating facilities:* snacks and lunches available. *Visitors:* welcome weekdays, male only. *Society Meetings:* male only, catered for Tuesdays, Thursdays and Fridays. Professional: George Yuille (031-334 6474). Secretary: John Audis (031-339 2075).

EDINBURGH: **Silverknowes Golf Club,** Silverknowes, Parkway, Edinburgh EH4 5ET (031-336 5359). *Location:* nearest main road Queensferry Road; signs Davidson Mains, Silverknowes. Parkland, flat. 18 holes, 6216 yards. S.S.S. 71. *Green Fees:* £6.60 per round. *Eating facilities:* clubhouse – by invitation/Lauriston Farm restaurant. *Visitors:* only by invitation of club member. *Society Meetings:* by arrangement weekdays only. Secretary: D.W. Scobie.

EDINBURGH. **Swanston Golf Club,** 111 Swanston Road, Edinburgh EH10 7DS (031-445 2239). *Location:* five miles from centre of Edinburgh, west of Biggar Road (A702) on the lower slopes of the Pentland Hills. Parkland course. 18 holes, 5024 yards. S.S.S. 66. *Green Fees:* weekdays £8.00 per round, £12.00 day ticket; weekends £10.00 per round, £15.00 per day. *Eating facilities:* full catering facilities. *Visitors:* welcome without reservation weekdays, weekends restricted. *Society Meetings:* catered for. Professional: (031-445 4002). Secretary: John Allan (031-445 2239).

EDINBURGH. **Torphin Hill Golf Club,** Torphin Road, Edinburgh EH13 0PG (031-441 1100). *Location:* south west of Colinton Village at terminus of No. 9 and No. 10 bus. Holes 5 to 15 on plateau with outstanding views of Edinburgh. 18 holes, 5087 yards, 4652 metres. S.S.S. 66. Practice area. *Green Fees:* weekdays £7.00 per round, £12.00 per day; weekends £10.00 per round, £18.00 per day. *Eating facilities:* dining room and bar snacks. *Visitors:* welcome without reservation except on Competition Days. *Society Meetings:* catered for weekdays only. Reduced rates for parties over 20. Secretary: E.H. Marchant (031-441 4061).

EDINBURGH. **Turnhouse Golf Club,** Turnhouse, Edinburgh (031-339 1014). *Location:* to Glasgow first right at Maybury roundabout. 18 holes, 6171 yards. S.S.S. 69. *Green Fees:* weekdays £14.00 per round, £20.00 per day. *Eating facilities:* full service. *Visitors:* welcome only as a group/society or playing with member. Not at weekends, Bank Holidays or Competition days. Professional: John Murray (031-339 7701). Secretary: A.B. Hay (031-539 5937).

FAULDHOUSE. **Greenburn Golf Club,** 6 Greenburn Road, Fauldhouse EH47 9AY (Fauldhouse (0501) 70292). *Location:* four miles south of Junctions 4 and 5 of M8 motorway. Flat moorland with elevated railway line running through, supported by viaduct. 18 holes, 6055 yards. S.S.S. 70. Practice area. *Green Fees:* £11.00 per round, £16.50 per day weekdays; £13.00 per round, £19.50 per day weekends. *Eating facilities:* catering available except Tuesdays (catering on Tuesdays for visiting parties by prior arrangement only). *Visitors:* welcome by prior arrangement. Normal times 9am to 10am and 2pm to 3pm. *Society Meetings:* welcome with prior arrangement. Professional: Mr H. Ferguson (0501 71187). Secretary: Mr Alexander Stein (0501 741967).

GULLANE. **Gullane Golf Club,** Gullane EH31 2BB (0620 842255). *Location:* 18 miles east of Edinburgh on A198 Edinburgh to North Berwick Road. Links. Three 18 hole courses. No. 1 – 6466 yards, 5913 metres. S.S.S. 71. No. 2 – 6244 yards, 5676 metres. S.S.S. 70. No. 3 – 5166 yards, 4696 metres. S.S.S. 65. *Green Fees:* (1993)No. 1 course £35.00, No. 2 course £16.00, No. 3 course £10.00 weekdays; No. 1 course £45.00, No. 2 course £20.00, No. 3 course £12.00 weekends. *Eating facilities:* new Visitor Centre with bar, snacks, etc. *Visitors:* welcome with reservation. *Society Meetings:* catered for. Professional: Jimmy Hume (0620 843111). Secretary: A.J.B. Taylor (0620 842255). Starters: (0620 843115).

The Mallard
East Links Road, Gullane EH31 2AF
Telephone: (0620) 843288

Overlooking Gullane's famous courses, this family-run Hotel has a reputation for hospitality and service. 18 bedrooms, all ensuite, with colour TV, radio, telephone and tea/coffee making. Restaurant with a growing reputation for its food and wines. After a day on the golf course or touring, The Mallard is the perfect place to relax. Please phone for further details/brochure. GOLF PACKAGES AVAILABLE.

BISSETS HOTEL
**Main Street, Gullane,
East Lothian, EH31 2AA
Telephone: (0620) 842230**

This small, homely hotel with the personal touch is ideally situated in the heart of Gullane, close to the golf courses and a short walk from a lovely one mile long sandy beach. Good wholesome, freshly prepared food available all day, served in the dining area or bar.

Golfing holidays are a speciality – 16 courses within a 10 mile radius. Comfortable rooms with bathroom, TV and tea/coffee making facilities.

EDINBURGH AND THE LOTHIANS Scotland

GULLANE. **The Honourable Company Of Edinburgh Golfers**, Muirfield, Gullane EH31 2EG (0620 842123; Fax: 0620 842977). *Location:* 20 miles from Edinburgh along the coast road to North Berwick. 18 holes, 6601 yards. *Green Fees:* (1993) £48.00 per round, £64.00 per day. *Eating facilities:* morning coffee, lunches, afternoon teas, if ordered in advance. *Visitors:* welcome Tuesdays and Thursdays, maximum Handicap 18 for men, 24 for ladies. Secretary: Group Captain J.A. Prideaux.

HADDINGTON. **Haddington Golf Club**, Amisfield Park, Haddington, East Lothian EH41 4PT (062-082 3627). *Location:* on A1 Edinburgh. Wooded parkland, slightly undulating. 18 holes, 6280 yards, 5764 metres. S.S.S. 70. Practice area. *Green Fees:* weekdays £10.00 per round, £14.00 per day; weekends £14.00 per round, £18.00 day. Fees subject to increase. *Eating facilities:* two bars and diningroom. *Visitors:* welcome, midweek no restrictions, weekends permitted 10am-12 noon, 2-4pm. *Society Meetings:* catered for. Professional: J. Sandilands (062-082 2727); Secretary: A.S.F. Watt.

HADDINGTON near. **Gifford Golf Club**, Edinburgh Road, Gifford, Near Haddington (062 081 591). *Location:* quarter of a mile south of village. Undulating parkland with burn crossing the course. 9 holes, 6101 yards. S.S.S. 69. *Green Fees:* weekdays £10.00 per day, weekends £10.00 per 9/18 holes. Juniors (under 16's) £3.00 per day, £10.00 weekends. *Visitors:* closed to visitors from 4pm Tuesdays and Wednesdays and from 12 noon weekends. Closed all day first Sunday in the month April to October. Secretary: Donald A. Fantom (062 081 267).

KIRKNEWTON. **Dalmahoy Hotel, Golf and Country Club**, Kirknewton, Midlothian EH27 8EB (031-333 4105; Fax: 031-335 3203). *Location:* seven miles west of Edinburgh on A71. Two courses: East Course, Championship parkland course, host to many major tournaments. 18 holes, 6677 yards. S.S.S. 72. West Course, parkland course featuring two spectacular crossings of Gogar Burn. 18 holes, 5185 yards. S.S.S. 66. Extensive practice area. *Green Fees:* East Course: weekdays £33.00 per round; West Course: weekdays £22.00 per round. *Eating facilities:* Terrace Restaurant and Club Bar in Country Club, restaurant and bars in Hotel also. *Visitors:* welcome weekdays; weekends members and Hotel residents only. Hotel accommodation. Golf carts, buggies and clubs for hire. *Society Meetings:* welcome weekdays only. Director of Golf: Brian Anderson. Secretary: Jennifer Wilson.

LINLITHGOW. **Linlithgow Golf Club**, Braehead, Linlithgow EH49 6QF (Linlithgow (0506) 671044). *Location:* M8, M9, 20 miles west of Edinburgh, west end of Linlithgow – fork left. Parkland and wooded course with panoramic views. 18 holes, 5729 yards. S.S.S. 68. Small practice area and net. *Green Fees:* weekdays £10.00 per round, £15.00 per day; Sunday £15.00 per round, £20.00 per day. Weekly tickets £35. *Eating facilities:* full facilities available. *Visitors:* welcome except Saturdays. *Society Meetings:* welcome. Professional: Derek Smith (0506 844356). Secretary: Tommy Thomson (0506 842585).

𝕳𝖆𝖗𝖛𝖊𝖘𝖙𝖊𝖗𝖘 𝕳𝖔𝖙𝖊𝖑

... in pursuit of excellence

Georgian house of character, offering good food, fine wines and extremely comfortable en suite accommodation at attractive rates. East Lothian is a mecca for golfers, with many challenging courses on the doorstep, and the *Harvesters* is ideally placed for easy access to 15 of them, including Muirfield.

We're a touch better!

**EAST LINTON,
EAST LOTHIAN EH40 3DP
TELEPHONE: (0620) 860395**

AA ★★ RAC   Ashley Courtenay

The Queen's Hotel
Gullane, East Lothian
Telephone: 0620 842275

* Only eighteen miles east of Edinburgh * Nine golf courses within a radius of ten miles * Ideal base for walking or touring in the Border Country * New wing with twenty-two bedrooms, sixteen of which have private bathrooms, six with showers * TVs * Telephones * Tea/coffee making facilities in all bedrooms * Renowned for fine cuisine * Fully licensed * Dogs allowed * Reductions for children under twelve years sharing parents' room * Open all year.   RAC ★★

Scotland EDINBURGH AND THE LOTHIANS

GOLF HOTEL   34 DIRLETON AVENUE
NORTH BERWICK

Family-run hotel offering good food and comfortable bedrooms, most with private bathroom and television. **Ideally situated for all 16 of East Lothian's Golf Courses.** Half hour from Edinburgh. Families welcome. Children's course 5 minutes away. **Golf can be arranged if required.** Contact: Simon Searle. Telephone: (0620) 2202.

CRAIGESK GUEST HOUSE
10 Albert Terrace, Musselburgh EH21 7LR

Attractive stone villa overlooking racecourse, golf course and sea and near all other East Lothian golf courses. Double, single and family bedrooms, all with washbasins, colour TV and tea/coffee facilities. Children and pets welcome. Private parking. B&B from £14. Further details on request, SAE, please.
Miss A. R. Mitchell   Tel: 031-665 3344 or 3170

LINLITHGOW. **West Lothian Golf Club**, Airngath Hill, Bo'ness EH49 7RH (Bo'ness (0506) 826030). *Location:* situated midway between Linlithgow and Bo'ness. Undulating parkland course. 18 holes, 6629 yards. S.S.S. 71. Practice area. *Green Fees:* information not provided. *Eating facilities:* available by arrangement. *Visitors:* welcome, no restrictions before 3.30pm midweek. After 3.30pm and at weekends by arrangement only. *Society Meetings:* by arrangement. Secretary: T.B. Fraser (0506 825476).

LIVINGSTON. **Deer Park Golf & Country Club**, Golf Course Road, Livingston EH54 8PG (0506 31037; Fax: 0506 35608). *Location:* Junction 3 of M8. Parkland course, first 9 holes flat, back 9 holes hilly. 18 holes, 6688 yards. S.S.S. 72. *Green Fees:* £15.00 per round weekdays; £25.00 per round weekends. *Eating facilities:* four bars, catering seven days. *Visitors:* welcome. Snooker, ten pin bowling, pool, sauna, steam room. *Society Meetings:* catered for. Professional: W.J. Yule (0506 38843). Secretay: Alec Stathearn.

LIVINGSTON. **Pumpherston Golf Club**, Drumshoreland Road, Pumpherston, Livingston EH53 0LF (0506 32869). *Location:* one mile east of Livingston, one and a half miles south of M8. Undulating parkland course, well bunkered. 9 holes, 5154 yards, 4712 metres. S.S.S. 65. Small practice area. *Green Fees:* information not supplied. *Eating facilities:* snack meals, lounge bar. *Visitors:* only when introduced by member. *Society Meetings:* Mondays to Thursdays, maximum number 24. Secretary: A.H. Docharty (0506 854652).

LONGNIDDRY. **Longniddry Golf Club Ltd**, The Clubhouse, Links Road, Longniddry EH32 0NL (Longniddry (0875) 52228). *Location:* from Edinburgh by A1, left for Longniddry, A198 at Wallyford roundabout or left off A1 one mile after MacMerry. 18 holes, 6219 yards, 5678 metres. S.S.S. 70. Practice ground and putting green. *Green Fees:* weekdays £22.00 per round, £32.00 per day. *Eating facilities:* every day, bar snacks only on Fridays. *Visitors:* Monday to Thursday parties booked, otherwise Monday to Friday casual bookings within the previous seven days except on Public Holidays and competition days. *Society Meetings:* catered for (except Friday – Sunday). Professional: John Gray (0875 52228). Secretary: G.C. Dempster, C.A. (0875 52141).

MUSSELBURGH. **Musselburgh Golf Club**, Monktonhall, Musselburgh EH21 6SA (031-665 2005). *Location:* from the A1 end of the Edinburgh City bypass, on the B6415 to Musselburgh. Wooded parkland, rivers. 18 holes, 6614 yards. S.S.S. 72. *Green Fees:* on application. *Eating facilities:* catering available except Tuesdays. *Visitors:* welcome with reservation. *Society Meetings:* catered for. Professional: T. Stangoe (031-665 7055). Secretary: S.Sullivan (031-665 2005). Administrator (for bookings): G. Finlay.

NEWBRIDGE. **Ratho Park Golf Club Ltd**, Ratho, Newbridge EH28 8NX (031-333 1252). *Location:* eight miles west of Edinburgh G.P.O., access from A71 or A8. Flat parkland. 18 holes, 5900 yards, 5398 metres. S.S.S. 68. *Green Fees:* weekdays £17.50 per round, £27.00 per day; weekends £30.00 per day. *Eating facilities:* full catering available. *Visitors:* welcome without reservation. *Society Meetings:* catered for Tuesdays, Wednesdays and Thursdays. Professional: Alan Pate (031-333 1406). Secretary: J.C. McLafferty (031-333 1752).

NORTH BERWICK. **Glen Golf Club**, East Links, Tantallon Terrace, North Berwick EH39 4LE (0620 2221). *Location:* off A198 one mile east of Railway Station. Seaside links with impressive panoramic views. 18 holes, 6089 yards. S.S.S. 69. *Green Fees:* weekdays £11.00 per round, £16.00 per day; weekends £14.00 per round, £20.00 per day. (Composite tickets available from hotels in East Lothian). Half price for Senior Citizens and Juniors weekdays. *Eating facilities:* full facilities available. *Visitors:* welcome anytime, no restrictions. *Society Meetings:* catered for with advance booking. Professional: (shop only). Secretary: D.R. Montgomery (0620 2221; Fax: 0620 5228). Starter: (0620 2726).

EDINBURGH AND THE LOTHIANS *Scotland*   **THE GOLF GUIDE 1994**

NORTH BERWICK. **North Berwick Golf Club,** New Clubhouse, Beach Road, North Berwick EH39 4BB (0620 4766; Fax: 0620 3274). *Location:* golf course stretches along the coast. First tee five minutes from town centre. Accessible from A198. Seaside links. 18 holes, 5960 yards. S.S.S. 70. Practice facilities. *Green Fees:* weekdays £20.00 per round, £30.00 per day (March to October); £15.00 per day (November to February). Weekends and Public Holidays £30.00 per round, £40.00 per day (March to October); £20.00 per day (November to February). *Eating facilities:* dining-rooms and bar/snacks available. *Visitors:* welcome without restrictions, book ahead Saturdays – restricted when there are club fixtures. *Society Meetings:* catered for by arrangement. Professional: D. Huish (0620 3233). Secretary: William Gray (0620 5040). Advance Bookings: (0620 2135).

PENICUIK. **Glencorse Golf Club,** Milton Bridge, Penicuik EH26 0RD (0968 677177). *Location:* A701 nine miles south of Edinburgh on Peebles Road. Parkland course with stream affecting 10 holes. 18 holes, 5217 yards. S.S.S. 66. *Green Fees:* weekdays £15.00 per round, £20.00 per day, weekends £20.00 per round. *Eating facilities:* full catering and bar. *Visitors:* welcome most days and times subject to Club Competitions. *Society Meetings:* catered for Tuesdays, most Wednesdays, Thursdays, most Fridays. Professional: C. Jones (0968 676481). Secretary: D.A. McNiven (0968 677189).

PRESTONPANS. **Royal Musselburgh Golf Club,** Prestongrange House, Prestonpans EH32 9RP (Prestonpans (0875) 810276). *Location:* A198 North Berwick road near Prestonpans. Parkland. 18 holes, 6237 yards. S.S.S. 70. *Green Fees:* weekdays £16.50 per round, £27.50 per day; weekends £27.50 per round, no day tickets. *Eating facilities:* full catering and licence. *Visitors:* welcome weekdays, not before 9.30am, not after 3pm, not Friday afternoons. *Society Meetings:* catered for weekdays only – book in advance. Professional: John Henderson (0875 810139). Secretary: T.H. Hardie.

SOUTH QUEENSFERRY. **Dundas Parks Golf Club,** Dundas Estate, South Queensferry, West Lothian. *Location:* five miles west of Edinburgh, on South Queensferry to Kirkliston road on right of A8000. Parkland course in open countryside. 9 holes (x 2). Small practice area. *Green Fees:* £8.00. *Eating facilities:* not available. *Visitors:* welcome with member, or by prior arrangement with Secretary. *Society Meetings:* by prior arrangement with Secretary. Secretary: Keith D. Love (031-331 1416).

UPHALL. **Uphall Golf Club,** Uphall, West Lothian EH52 6JT (0506 856404). *Location:* 8 miles west of Edinburgh Airport on the A89 Edinburgh to Glasgow road to the west of Uphall. Established parkland course. 18 holes. S.S.S. 67. *Green Fees:* weekdays £14.00 per round, £19.00 per day. Weekends £19.00 per round, £29.00 per day. *Visitors:* welcome weekdays without reservation. A booking through the Professional is required at weekends. *Eating facilities:* hot and cold snacks, lunches, high teas and bars. *Society Meetings:* catered for. Professional: Gordon Law (0506 855553). Manager: Tony Flood (0506 856404).

Blenheim House Hotel

Situated overlooking the sea and the 1st tee of North Berwick's famous West Course, you are assured of a warm and friendly welcome when you stay at the Blenheim.

Please ask about our special winter golfing breaks. We are only too happy to organise any individual package to suit your requirements on any of the 14 local courses, all within half an hour's drive.

For further information write to:
Blenheim House Hotel,
Westgate, North Berwick, East Lothian
Tel: (0620) 2385 Fax: (0620) 4010

AA★★

POINT GARRY HOTEL, NORTH BERWICK

Only 100 yards from the first tee of North Berwick West Golf Club, this Hotel commands one of the finest views in North Berwick. The stately Victorian house has a restful and happy atmosphere; 16 pleasantly appointed rooms, 12 with private facilities. Full central heating. Cocktail Bar and Billiard Room. The Diningroom overlooks the sea and offers good food and an excellent wine cellar. An ideal centre for golfers – within a five-mile radius of another eight golf courses. Edinburgh only 22 miles away. Full details from Resident Proprietors, **Point Garry Hotel, West Bay Road, North Berwick EH39 4AW.**
Telephone: North Berwick (0620) 2380; Fax: (0620) 2848.

Tee off from your own holiday home.

Rhodes Tantallon Caravan and Camping park is currently undergoing a development programme and we are now able to offer luxurious caravan holiday homes for sale.

East Lothian is an area renowned for its natural beauty and of course its golf courses. So golfers, get rid of the handicap of booking into a hotel. Tee off from your very own 19th.

NORTH BERWICK EAST LOTHIAN

RHODES TANTALLON CARAVAN & CAMPING PARK

(0620) 3348

For further details/brochure contact: Rhodes Tantallon Caravan and Camping Park, Lime Grove, North Berwick East Lothian Tel/Fax 0620 893348

Caravan Holiday homes for hire, tourers and motor homes welcome.

DINNER BED & BREAKFAST (5 DAYS) AND COMPOSITE WEEKLY GOLF TICKET FOR 5 ROUNDS OF GOLF: £195 PER PERSON

THIS IS GOLF COUNTRY!

NETHER ABBEY
Hotel & Restaurant, North Berwick

You'll probably know that North Berwick and the surrounding area is more than adequately served by 16 excellent golf courses, there are 12 courses in a 12 mile radius. They range from the Open Championship links at Muirfield to one of the oldest courses in Scotland at Musselburgh and also Gullane and North Berwick West, with prices and standards of skill to suit golfers of every type. We go out of our way to give you a warm welcome and pride ourselves on our service to customers who visit from all over the world. Over 16 bedrooms deliver a high degree of comfort with modern facilities. Enjoy superb cuisine in our spacious restaurant and relax in the Fly Half bar which offers a fine range of cask-conditioned ales. What more could you ask for?

AA ★★   RAC ★★   STB

WHY NOT CONTACT US NOW
TELEPHONE (0620) 2802 or FAX (0620) 5298 FOR FURTHER DETAILS
DIRLETON AVENUE, NORTH BERWICK, SCOTLAND EH39 4BQ

EDINBURGH AND THE LOTHIANS / FIFE   Scotland   THE GOLF GUIDE 1994

WEST CALDER. **Harburn Golf Club,** Harburn, West Calder EH55 8RS (West Calder (0506) 871256). *Location:* two miles south of West Calder on B7008. Parkland course. 18 holes, 5853 yards, 5436 metres. S.S.S. 68. Practice ground. *Green Fees:* £12.50 per round, £18.50 per day weekdays; £18.50 per round, £25.00 per day weekends. *Eating facilities:* full catering and bar service except Tuesdays. *Visitors:* welcome any time – no restrictions. *Society Meetings:* catered for by advance arrangement. Professional: Stuart Crookston (0506 871582). Secretary: Frank Vinter (0506 871131).

WHITBURN. **Polkemmet Golf Course,** Polkemmet Country Park, Whitburn, West Lothian (Whitburn (0501) 743905). *Location:* off B7066, one mile west of Whitburn. Inland course set within old private estate, mature varied woodland with belts of Rhododendrons. 9 holes, 2969 metres. Par 37. Driving range. *Green Fees:* Monday to Saturday £2.40 adults, Juvenile/Senior Citizens/Concessions £1.30; Sunday £3.10 adults, Juvenile/Senior Citizens/Concessions £1.80. *Eating facilities:* restaurant and bar complex. *Visitors:* welcome. Facilities include bowling green, picnic areas, etc. Caddy Cart hire 70p. Secretary: West Lothian District Council, Department of Leisure and Recreation, County Buildings, Linlithgow.

WINCHBURGH. **Niddry Castle Golf Club,** Castle Road, Winchburgh EH52 6RQ (0506 891097). *Location:* 10 miles west of Edinburgh on A803 between Kirkliston and Linlithgow. Wooded, natural parkland. 9 holes, 5450 yards. S.S.S. 67. *Green Fees:* £7.50 weekdays; £10.00 weekends. *Eating facilities:* none – but bar lunches available in village. *Visitors:* welcome anytime but not until 2pm on Saturdays of club competitions. *Society Meetings:* by arrangement. Secretary: A. Brockbank.

Fife

ABERDOUR. **Aberdour Golf Club,** Seaside Place, Aberdour KY3 0TX (0383 860688). *Location:* take Shore Road from centre of village. Parkland course situated along the shoreline of the River Forth. 18 holes, 5460 yards. S.S.S. 67. *Green Fees:* £15.00 per round, £22.00 per day. *Eating facilities:* full catering. *Visitors:* welcome on weekdays. *Society Meetings:* catered for on weekdays and Sundays. On Sundays, maximum size of group 24. Professional: Gordon McCallum (0383 860256). Secretary: John Train (0383 860080).

ANSTRUTHER. **Anstruther Golf Club,** Marsfield, Shore Road, Anstruther KY10 3DZ (0333 310956). *Location:* nine miles south of St. Andrews, west side of Anstruther. Seaside links course. 9 holes, 4144 metres. S.S.S. 63. *Green Fees:* weekdays £10.00; weekends £14.00. *Eating facilities:* lounge bar and dining room. *Visitors:* welcome except during club competitions. *Society Meetings:* outwith May/September and competition days. Secretary: A.B. Cleary (0333 310956/312283).

BURNTISLAND. **Burntisland Golf House Club,** Dodhead, Burntisland KY3 9EY (Burntisland (0592) 873247). *Location:* on B923, one mile north-east of town centre. Parkland with some hills. 18 holes, 5497 yards. S.S.S. 69. Practice net. *Green Fees:* weekdays £15.00 per round, £21.00 per day; weekends £25.00 per round, £35.00 per day. *Eating facilities:* full catering facilities. *Visitors:* welcome. Parties limited to 24 at weekends apart from club competitions. Changing room. *Society Meetings:* welcome with advance bookings. Professional: J. Montgomery (0592 873247). Secretary: Ian McLean (0592 874093).

CARDENDEN. **Auchterderran Golf Club,** Woodend Road, Cardenden (0592 721579). *Location:* six miles north of Kirkcaldy. Flat course. 9 holes, 5252 yards S.S.S. 66. *Green Fees:* weekdays £7.00; weekends £9.00. Concessionary ticket available. *Visitors:* welcome at all times, check with course for members' tournaments. *Society Meetings:* all bookings accepted. Secretary: Michael Dois (0592 721877).

STB●●●● Commended

The Inchview Hotel

AA ★★

Forming part of a curving terrace overlooking Burntisland Links and the Forth Estuary, and situated on the Fife coastal tourist route, **The Inchview Hotel gives the discerning golfer the choice of playing some of the most testing and beautiful courses in the area.** Our restaurant has a reputation for fine food, specialising in flambé dishes prepared at the table. Lounge bar offers at least 4 traditional real ales. If weekend Party Golf Bookings required please give substantial notice.
Send for brochure to Mr Peter Black, The Inchview Hotel, 69 Kinghorn Road, Burntisland, Fife KY3 9EB. Tel: 0592 872239. Fax: 0592 874866.

THE GOLF GUIDE 1994

Scotland FIFE

CRAIL. Crail Golfing Society, Balcomie Clubhouse, Fifeness, Crail KY10 3XN (Crail (0333) 50278). Instituted 1786. *Location:* eleven miles south-east of St. Andrews on A917. Parkland/seaside links. 18 holes, 5720 yards. S.S.S. 68. Practice ground. *Green Fees:* weekdays £16.00 per round, £24.00 per day; weekends £20.00 per round, £30.00 per day. 3/4/5 day £16.00 per day, Fortnightly £128. (except Sundays). *Eating facilities:* quality catering and bar. *Visitors:* welcome. *Society Meetings:* advance booking available for parties. Professional: Graeme Lennie (0333) 50960). Secretary: Mrs C.W. Penhale (0333) 50686).

CUPAR. **Cupar Golf Club,** Hilltarvit, Cupar (Cupar (0334) 53549). *Location:* near cemetery on Ceres Road. Hillside/parkland course. 9 holes, 5074 yards.

S.S.S. 65. Practice putting green. *Green Fees:* weekdays £10.00; Sundays £12.00. *Eating facilities:* full catering/bar. *Visitors:* welcome, except Saturdays, weekends after 5pm. *Society Meetings:* very welcome except Saturdays. Secretary: C.J. McCulloch (0334 52176).

DUNFERMLINE. **Canmore Golf Club,** Venture Fair, Dunfermline (Dunfermline (0383) 724969). *Location:* one mile north of town centre on A823. Parkland, undulating. 18 holes, 5347 yards. S.S.S. 66. *Green Fees:* weekdays £12.00 per round, £18.00 per day; weekends £25.00 per day. *Eating facilities:* full catering and bar. *Visitors:* welcome except on weekends. *Society Meetings:* visiting societies with prior reservation (not at weekends). Professional: John Hamlin (0383 728416). Secretary: J.C. Duncan (0383 726098).

GOLF AT CRAIL

Enjoy playing at Balcomie Golf Course, Fifeness, Crail. Every hole is within sight of the sea. Full clubhouse facilities including bar and quality catering. 11 miles south-east of ST ANDREWS.

Pro/Starter Tel: (0333) 50960 Clubhouse/Steward Tel: (0333) 50278
Secretary Tel: (0333) 50686 for party bookings.

MYRECAIRNIE FARM HOUSE
By CUPAR, FIFE KY15 4QD

Our Special Golfers' Breakfasts will set you up for the day before you tackle one of the 50 excellent courses within a 35-mile radius of our very comfortable farmhouse, eg. St. Andrews, Carnoustie, Ladybank. B&B only £17.00 per person.
Contact LILIAS SMITH   Tel: (0334) 53266 (From July 1994: Tel: 0334 653266)

The Centre of a Golfing Paradise

Centrally located in the Kingdom of Fife, with St. Andrews the Home of Golf just 10 minutes' drive and 15 other courses less than 30 minutes away. Within an hour one can reach over 50 courses, so Eden House is an ideal base for your golfing holiday. Paul and Louise, the proprietors, take pride in assisting with booking tee times, agendas, transport, etc., to make your holiday one to be remembered. Eden House has en-suite facilities, tea/coffee making facilities, direct dial telephones. Inclusive rates available.

EDEN HOUSE HOTEL — Licensed Hotel & Restaurant

Pitscottie Road, Cupar, Fife KY15 4HF Tel & Fax: (0334) 52510

Welcome to Todhall House

An ideal base for golfers wishing to play some of Scotland's finest courses – all within easy reach of Todhall. Situated between Cupar and St. Andrews, near the village of Dairsie (A91), Todhall House is a traditional Scottish country home surrounded by superb scenery and offering guests warm hospitality and the opportunity to unwind. Comfortable ensuite bedrooms have the usual facilities. Elegant lounge. Laundry. Safe storage for clubs and equipment. Ample parking. Garden with single hole putting green and practice net. Bed & Breakfast from £17.50. Dinner by arrangement. Sorry, no smoking. Telephone for brochure/reservation.

John & Gill Donald, Todhall House, Dairsie, by Cupar, Fife KY15 4RQ Tel: (0334) 56244

FIFE *Scotland*   THE GOLF GUIDE 1994

Crossford Hotels (Dunfermline) Ltd.
The Pitfirrane Arms Hotel   AA*** RAC*** STB ♛♛♛♛ Commended
CROSSFORD, DUNFERMLINE, FIFE KY12 8NJ
Telephone: 0383 736132   Fax: 0383 621760

The Hotel is conveniently situated for touring, within easy access of Edinburgh, Glasgow and the M90 motorway. We have 38 comfortable bedrooms, 16 twin, 12 double and 10 single bedded rooms. All rooms have private ensuite facilities, colour television, tea/coffee makers, telephone and radio. Daily fresh fruit and biscuits. We have 10 golf courses within 10 miles!

THE HOTEL FOR GOLFERS

Outstanding value golf and golf tuition packages inclusive of golf on a wide variety of first class links courses. 25 courses within half hour drive (St. Andrews only 10 miles away).
FREE golf on adjacent Elie 9 hole golf course (ideal for practice and beginners).
Special discount terms for societies and groups of 12 and over.
Good food, '19th hole', comfy bedrooms and a warm welcome.
Phone for brochure (0333) 330209 or fax (0333) 330381.

the **Golf Hotel**
ELIE, FIFE

STB COMMENDED ♛♛♛
AA RECOMMENDED *QQQ*

· **THE ELMS** ·
Park Place, Elie, Fife KY9 1DH

Centrally located between St. Andrews (15 mins), Leven and Ladybank, and with 9 and 18 hole courses across the road. Family-run hotel with en-suite facilities. Real home cooking with comfortable accommodation. Residential licence. Dinner, Bed and Breakfast from £28.50 for parties, plus free golf on 9 hole course. Phone for brochure (0333) 330404.

The Lomond Hills Hotel
Freuchie, near Glenrothes, Fife

Situated at the foot of the Lomond Hills, this old inn is an ideal place to stay when visiting Fife. The Hotel is close to many golf courses. Comfortable bedrooms with TV, radio, central heating, teamakers, etc; all with full facilities. Candlelit restaurant. Small leisure centre now open. 4 DAY GOLF BREAK from £150.
STB ♛♛♛ *Commended*   Tel: (0337) 57329   Exechotel

The Forest Hills Hotel
The Square, Auchtermuchty, Fife

Traditional Inn in the square of this Royal Burgh (once a busy weaving centre surrounded by forests and hills which were a favourite venue for deer and boar hunting by noblemen visiting nearby Falkland Palace). Ten bright bedrooms with central heating, teamakers, TV, radio, and all facilities. Cocktail bar; comfortable lounge; bistro, intimate restaurant. Leisure facilities available at sister hotel in Freuchie. 2 day golf break from £70.
STB ♛♛ *Commended*   Tel: (0337) 28318   Exechotel

THE GOLF GUIDE 1994

Scotland FIFE

DUNFERMLINE. Dunfermline Golf Club, Pitfirrane, Crossford, By Dunfermline KY12 8QV (01383 723534). *Location:* two miles west of Dunfermline on A994 to Kincardine Bridge. Undulating parkland. 18 holes, 6237 yards, 5739 metres. S.S.S. 70. Short 9 hole course and practice area. *Green Fees:* £18.00 per round, £25.00 per day weekdays. *Eating facilities:* full catering except Sunday evenings and Mondays, bar snacks available. *Visitors:* welcome weekdays 10am to 12 noon and 2pm to 4pm. Must have official club handicap. *Society Meetings:* accepted weekdays by prior arrangement. Professional: Steve Craig (01383 723534). Secretary: Hamish Matheson (01383 723534).

DUNFERMLINE. Pitreavie (Dunfermline) Golf Club, Queensferry Road, Dunfermline KY11 5PR (0383 722591). *Location:* M90 Edinburgh/Perth, leave at Junction 2 for Dunfermline. Undulating parkland with views across Firth of Forth. 18 holes, 6086 yards. S.S.S. 69. Practice ground. *Green Fees:* weekdays £13.00 per round, £18.00 per day; weekends £24.00 per day. Subject to review. *Eating facilities:* full catering and bar facilities available. *Visitors:* welcome except Competition Days. Please phone in advance, must have recognised Golf Union Handicap. *Society Meetings:* catered for, must be booked through Secretary. Professional: Jim Forrester (Tel & Fax: 0383 723151). Secretary: Mr D. Carter (0383 722591).

DUNFERMLINE. Saline Golf Club, Kinneddar Hill, Saline (New Oakley) (0383) 852591). *Location:* Dollar, turn left at Junction 4 M90. Hillside course. 9 holes, 5302 yards. S.S.S. 66. *Green Fees:* weekdays £8.00; weekends £10.00. *Eating facilities:* bar snacks; meals by prior arrangement. *Visitors:* welcome, no restrictions except Saturdays. *Society Meetings:* catered for mid-week or Sundays; maximum 24. Secretary: R. Hutchison (0383 852344).

ELIE. Earlsferry Thistle Golf Club, Rotton Row, Elie (0333 310053). 18 holes, 6250 yards. S.S.S. 70. *Green Fees:* set by Elie Golf House Club, on application. *Visitors:* welcome mid-week. Secretary: (0334 76770).

The course belongs to Elie Golf House Club, Earlsferry Thistle play the same course.

ELIE. Golf House Club, Elie KY9 1AS (0333 330327; Fax: 0333 330895). *Location:* 10 miles south of St Andrews on A917. Links course. 18 holes, 6253 yards. S.S.S. 70. *Green Fees:* (1993) weekdays £22.00 per round, £30.00 per day; weekends £33.00 per round, £42.00 per day. *Eating facilities:* lunches, teas, etc. *Visitors:* welcome with reservation. Elie Sports Centre nearby with leisure facilities and cafeteria. *Society Meetings:* catered for except at weekends. Professional: Robin Wilson (0333 330955). Secretary: A. Sneddon (0333 330301).

FALKLAND. Falkland Golf Club, The Myre, Falkland KY7 7AA (0337 57404). *Location:* entrance on A912, 12 miles from Kirkcaldy – approximately 20 minutes from St. Andrews. Lies at the foot of East Lomond Hills. Flat meadowland, beautiful views. 9 holes, 2608 yards, 2384 metres. S.S.S. 66 for 18 holes. *Green Fees:* £7.00 per day weekdays; £10.00 weekends. Weekly ticket £25.00. Contact 0337 57404 after 6pm. *Eating facilities:* meals by arrangement (evenings and weekends only), bar available for golfers. *Visitors:* welcome, no problem during weekdays, phone for availability weekends. *Society Meetings:* must book in advance. Secretary: Mrs H.H. Horsburgh (0337 756075).

GLENROTHES. Glenrothes Golf Club, Golf Course Road, Glenrothes KY6 2LA (Glenrothes (0592) 758686). *Location:* at the western end of town, near airfield. Hilly wooded parkland with burn crossing four fairways. 18 holes, 6444 yards. S.S.S. 71. *Green Fees:* weekdays £8.00 per round, £13.50 per day; weekends £10.00 per round, £15.00 per day. Reductions for Senior Citizens and Juniors. *Eating facilities:* two licensed lounges, dining room. Temporary day membership of club available to visitors. *Visitors:* welcome, some restrictions weekends. *Society Meetings:* welcome, contact Secretary. Hon. Secretary: Mrs P.V. Lanbells (0592 754561).

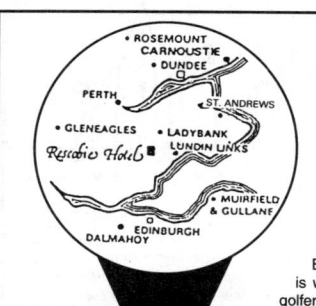

Rescobie Hotel

Valley Drive, Leslie, Fife KY6 3BQ
Telephone: 0592 742143 Fax: 0592 620231
RAC ★★ AA   STB 🌂🌂🌂🌂 Commended

Rescobie is a small country house hotel set in two acres of secluded gardens a mile away from Glenrothes golf course in the heart of Fife. Each of the 10 bedrooms has private bath or shower, colour TV, direct-dial telephone, tea/coffee making facilities, room bar etc. The hotel is comfortably appointed and the service is friendly and attentive. Much emphasis is placed on the quality of cuisine, for which the restaurant holds an AA rosette and an RAC Merit Award.
Equidistant between Carnoustie, Dalmahoy, Gleneagles and St Andrews, the hotel is within easy drive of over 100 golf courses. Special DB&B rates are available for golfers and golf programmes and/or tee times are arranged free of charge.

FIFE   *Scotland*

KINCARDINE. **Tulliallan Golf Club,** Alloa Road, Kincardine, by Alloa (0259 30396). *Location:* on A908 five miles east of Alloa, one mile north of Kincardine Bridge. Parkland slightly wooded, burn winds through the course. 18 holes, 5892 yards, 5463 metres. S.S.S. 69. *Green Fees:* information not provided. *Eating facilities:* diningroom, bar 11am to 11pm. *Visitors:* no visting parties on Fridays, Saturdays or on local holidays. *Society Meetings:* catered for with reservation, 24 limit on Sundays. Professional: Steven Kelly (0259 30798). Secretary: J.S. McDowall(0324 485420).

KINGHORN. **Kinghorn Municipal Golf Club,** MacD·ff Crescent, Kinghorn (0592 890345/80242). *Location:* bus stop at course, railway station three minutes. 18 holes, 5217 yards. S.S.S. 67. *Green Fees:* weekdays £8.00 per round, £13.50 per day; weekends £10.00 per round, £15.50 per day. *Eating facilities:* meals at clubhouse, local hotels. *Visitors:* welcome with prior reservation if large party (up to 30). *Society Meetings:* catered for by arrangement. Hon. Secretary: J.P. Robertson (0592 890345).

KIRKCALDY. **Dunnikier Park Golf Club,** Dunnikier Way, Kirkcaldy KY1 3LP (Kirkcaldy (0592) 261599). *Location:* one mile off A92 on the A910. Parkland course. 18 holes, 6601 yards, 6036 metres. S.S.S. 72. Practice ground adjacent. *Green Fees:* weekdays £8.00 per round, £13.50 per day; weekends £10.00 per round, £15.50 per day. *Eating facilities:* full catering facilities, licensed bar. *Visitors:* welcome by arrangement with Secretary, no restrictions. Adjacent to private hotel. *Society Meetings:* catered for. Professional: Jacky Montgomery (0592 205916). Secretary: Robert A. Waddell (0592 200627).

KIRKCALDY. **Kirkcaldy Golf Club,** Balwearie Road, Kirkcaldy KY2 5LT (0592 260370). *Location:* west end of town adjacent to Beveridge Park. Wooded parkland with stream. 18 holes, 6004 yards. S.S.S. 70. Small practice area. *Green Fees:* weekdays £15.00 per round, £20.00 per day; weekends £18.00 per round, £25.00 per day. *Eating facilities:* full catering facilities available. *Visitors:* welcome except Saturdays, limited Tuesdays. Professional's shop. *Society Meetings:* catered for. Professional: Paul Hodgson (0592 203258). Secretary: J.I. Brodley (0592 205240).

LADYBANK. **Ladybank Golf Club,** Annsmuir, Ladybank KY7 7RA (0337 30814). *Location:* on B9129 off A91, 15 miles St. Andrews. Wooded heathland. 18 holes, 6641 yards. S.S.S. 72. Practice ground. *Green Fees:* weekdays £24.00 per round, £32.00 per day; weekends £26.00 per round, £35.00 per day. *Eating facilities:* full catering facilities and bar. *Visitors:* welcome without reservation. Party bookings by arrangement with Secretary. *Society Meetings:* by arrangement. Professional: Martin J. Gray (0337 30725). Secretary: A.M. Dick (0337 30814).

LESLIE. **Leslie Golf Club,** Balsillie Laws, Leslie, Glenrothes KY6 3LR (0592 620040). Parkland with small stream running through some fairways. 9 holes, 4940 yards. S.S.S. 64. *Green Fees:* £6.00 weekdays, £10.00 weekends. *Eating facilities:* bar open each evening 7.30pm to 11pm, weekends 12 noon to 5pm and 7.30pm to 11pm. *Visitors:* always welcome, some restrictions on competition days. Secretary: M.G. Burns (0592 741449).

Greenside Hotel
AA★★
**High Street, Leslie,
Glenrothes, Fife, Scotland**
Telephone Glenrothes **(0592) 743453**
Proprietors: **Tommy & Mary Smith**

Our 12 bedroom family-run Hotel offers friendly and efficient service, ensuring our guests have a comfortable, enjoyable stay. Nine of the bedrooms have private bathrooms, TV, telephone and radio alarms. Picturesque views of the Lomond Hills to the north. Within easy reach of many golf courses and activity facilities.

Fernie Castle Hotel
Letham, Near Cupar, Fife KY7 7RU
Telephone: 033-781 381 Fax: 033-781 422
Superbly situated for golf – Ladybank Golf Club (2 miles) – excellent golf at reasonable charges. St. Andrews – 20 minutes by car – and many other famous courses within a 25 mile radius. Shooting and fishing can be arranged locally. Edinburgh 50 minutes. Dundee 20 minutes. Perth 30 minutes. Reduced prices for golfing parties with extra-special rates for numbers of 15-30!
Set in 25 acres of mature woodland with a private loch, Fernie Castle has excellent comfortably appointed rooms, all with private bath or shower room and a first class reputation for food and wine. You can relax over an aperitif in the historic 'Keep Bar' and enjoy our creative traditional Scottish menus either in our elegant first-floor Dining Room or in the relaxed atmosphere of Antoinettes. Our pleasant and attentive staff are here to make your stay an enjoyable one.
OFF SEASON BREAKS AVAILABLE: Dinner, Bed and Breakfast from £39.50 per person nightly. **Rates reduced for children.**

THE GOLF GUIDE 1994

Scotland FIFE

LEUCHARS. St. Michaels Golf Club, Gallowhill, Leuchars KY16 0DX (0334 839365). *Location:* quarter of a mile outside Leuchars on A919 towards Dundee. Undulating parkland course surround by plantations. 9 holes, 5158 yards. S.S.S. 66. *Green Fees:* £12.00 day ticket, Juniors £6.00. Five day ticket Monday to Friday £40.00. *Eating facilities:* bar facilities and meals available. *Visitors:* welcome anytime but not before 1pm Sundays. Changing rooms and showers. *Society Meetings:* by prior arrangement. A booking fee is payable before confirmation of reservation. Secretary: Major L.M. McIntosh (0334 55328 after 6pm).

LEVEN. Leven Golfing Society, Links Road, Leven KY8 4HS (Leven (0333) 426096). *Location:* nine miles east of Kirkcaldy on the A955. Links course, flat. 18 holes, 6434 yards, 5939 metres. S.S.S. 71. *Green Fees:* weekdays £18.00 round, £26.00 day; weekends £24.00 round, £36.00 day. *Eating facilities:* full catering available. *Visitors:* welcome (except Saturdays). *Society Meetings:* by arrangement (0333 428859). Parties of under 12 persons (0333 421390). Links Secretary: Mr B. Jackson (0333 428859).

LEVEN. Leven Thistle Golf Club, Balfour Street, Leven (0333 426397). *Location:* eight miles east of links, top championship links used for national and international events including Open qualifying. 18 holes, 6434 yards. S.S.S. 71. *Green Fees:* weekdays £18.00 per round, £24.00 per day; weekends £20.00 per round, £30.00 per day. *Eating facilities:* full catering available, two bars, function hall. *Visitors:* welcome without reservation, except Saturdays. *Society Meetings:* for group bookings contact Leven Links Joint Committee, Promenade, Leven, Fife KY8 4HS (0333 428859). Secretary: J. Scott.

LEVEN. Lundin Golf Club, Golf Road, Lundin Links KY8 6BA (0333 320202). *Location:* three miles east of Leven on the A915 (Leven to St. Andrews). Seaside links. 18 holes, 6377 yards. S.S.S. 71. Practice ground.

Green Fees: £18.00 per round, £27.00 per day weekdays; Saturdays after 2.30pm £25.00 per round. *Eating facilities:* bar and diningroom. *Visitors:* welcome Monday/Thursday 9am to 3.30pm; Friday 9am to 3pm; Saturdays no visitors before 2.30pm; Sundays no visitors. *Society Meetings:* limited numbers. Professional: David K. Webster (0333 320051). Secretary: A.C. McBride (0333 320202).

LEVEN. Scoonie Golf Club, North Links, Leven KY8 4SP (0333 427057). *Location:* on St. Andrews Road, Coast Road. Not a proper links course, course rather flat, typical seaside bunkers. 18 holes, 5600 yards, 5000 metres. S.S.S. 66. *Green Fees:* weekdays £8.00 per round, £10.00 per day; weekends £12.00 per round, £15.00 per day. *Eating facilities:* one bar, meals and bar snacks available all day. *Visitors:* welcome anytime (Saturday club competitions). *Society Meetings:* all welcome. Secretary: S. Kuczerepa (0333 351426).

LOCHGELLY. Lochgelly Golf Club, Cartmore Road, Lochgelly (Lochgelly (0592) 780174). *Location:* take M90 to Junction 4 Halbeath Interchange, follow signs. Parkland. 18 holes, 5491 yards, 5063 metres. S.S.S. 67. *Green Fees:* £9.50 per round weekdays; £14.50 per round weekends. *Eating facilities:* catering available. *Visitors:* welcome, no restrictions weekdays, weekends parties limited to 24. Secretary: R.F. Stuart (0383 512238).

LUNDIN LINKS. Lundin Ladies Golf Club, Woodielea Road, Lundin Links KY8 6AR (0333 320832). *Location:* off Leven Road. Excellent parkland course, picturesque. 9 holes, 2365 yards. S.S.S. 67. Practice net, putting green. *Green Fees:* weekdays £6.00 per day; weekends £7.50 per day. *Eating facilities:* tea making facilities. *Visitors:* welcome. Secretary: Eliz Davidson (0333 320490).

MARKINCH. Balbirnie Park Golf Club, The Clubhouse, Balbirnie Park, Markinch, Glenrothes KY7 6DD

GOLFING PACKAGE HOLIDAYS ARE OUR SPECIALITY
Let *US* organise your holiday
by arranging your golf times
**ONLY 11 MILES FROM ST ANDREWS
& 40 MINUTES FROM EDINBURGH**

IAN LADD & LYN BARRON-LADD
Resident Proprietors

One of the longest-established, and probably the friendliest hotel in Fife. 35 Golf Courses within a 20 mile radius, superb links courses in abundance with one of the top courses in Scotland next door. 18 superbly equipped en-suite rooms, top cuisine and traditional style bars. Some self-catering accommodation also available.

THE BEST VALUE FOR MONEY FOR MILES
The Lundin Links Hotel
LUNDIN LINKS, FIFE KY8 6AP, SCOTLAND
Telephone: Lundin Links (0333) 320207 Fax: (0333) 320930

BALBIRNIE HOUSE

AA ★★★★   Deluxe   RAC ★★★★

Balbirnie is an outstanding luxury country house hotel set amidst a beautiful 416 acre courntry park. The hotel is only yards away from the first tee of Balbirnie Park Golf Course, a splendid 18 hole parkland course. 100 golf courses within one hours drive.

See our colour display advertisement on page 8.

Balbirnie House, Balbrinie Park, Markinch, Glenrothes, Fife KY7 6NE. Tel: 0592 610066 Fax: 0592 610529

FIFE Scotland   THE GOLF GUIDE 1994

BELL CRAIG HOUSE
AA Listed   **RAC Acclaimed**

A small comfortable house under the personal supervision of the proprietors. Only a few minutes' walk from the world famous 'Old Course'. Ideal for a break in the home of golf. All bedrooms are ensuite and have colour TV, tea/coffee facilities and shaver/hairdryer points. Close to beach, amusements, shops and other amenities. Enjoy the 'home from home' atmosphere. Contact Sheila Black for more details.

Bell Craig House, 8 Murray Park, St. Andrews, Fife KY16 9AW. Telephone: 0334 72962

Rufflets Country House Hotel

Outstanding Country House Hotel set in 10 acres of gardens. Only one and a quarter miles from Golf Courses. 25 tastefully decorated bedrooms, attractive public rooms and restaurant, renowned for good food, using fresh local produce. St Andrews offers 5 courses – sixteen other courses within 30 minutes' drive.

Strathkinness Low Road, St Andrews, Fife KY16 9TX. Tel: (0334) 72594

ST. ANDREWS GOLF HOTEL

A Most Comfortable, Privately Owned 3-Star Hotel Offering Every Modern Facility.

- Sea front location only 200 yards from the famous "Old Course".
- Superb restaurant with gourmet food & fine wines.
- Golfing arrangements our speciality.
- "Golf Week" in October.
- All inclusive golf packages throughout the year.

FOR RESERVATIONS & BROCHURE TELEPHONE: (0334) 72611 OR FAX: (0334) 72188

The Russell Hotel

Situated on THE SCORES overlooking St. Andrews Bay, this small friendly hotel personally run by Gordon and Fiona de Vries offers good food and comfortable accommodation with 10 twin/double rooms, all with private facilities; satellite TV, telephones, tea/coffee making. Just two minutes' walk from 1st tee of the OLD COURSE and equally convenient for town centre and beaches. The RUSSELL has acquired a fine reputation for excellent cuisine and exceptional service. Golf Parties welcome. Major Credit Cards Accepted. AA★★. Enquiries to:

THE RUSSELL HOTEL, THE SCORES, ST. ANDREWS. TEL: 0334 73447. Fax: 0334 78279

HEAVEN ON EARTH

Overlooking the R&A Clubhouse and St. Andrews Bay, this famous 3-Star, 30 bedroom hotel is literally only yards from the 1st tee of the Old Course and minutes from the other St. Andrews courses. Adjacent to the hotel is The British Golf Museum and the town centre is only a short stroll away. This is a golfers paradise!

All bedrooms are ensuite and hotel facilities include two bars, a restaurant and an all day coffee shop. Special Dinner, Bed and Breakfast rates are offered, and we can assist in making golf arrangements in St. Andrews and at most of Fife's famous courses. We will be delighted to send you our brochure and other details.

SCORES HOTEL ST ANDREWS

The Scores Hotel, St. Andrews, Fife KY16 9BB, Scotland. Tel: (0334) 72451. Fax: (0334) 73947.

Sporting Laird Hotel & Apartments
5 PLAYFAIR TERRACE
St. ANDREWS KY16 9HX
Tel: (0334) 75906 Fax: (0334) 73881
RAC Acclaimed STB ❀❀ Commended
Old Course – 200 yards

A 2 day weekend / 2 nights DB&B / 3 days Golf (3 day golf ticket at St. Andrews) – £150
B 3 day weekend / 3 nights DB&B / 3 days Golf – £185
C 3 day midweek / 3 nights DB&B / 3 days Golf – £185
D 4 day midweek / 4 nights DB&B / 3 days Golf plus green fees at Lundin Links/Elie/Ladybank – £245
Further golf packages available for 3, 5 and 7 days – prices from £180.

(0592 752006). *Location:* outside Markinch near the A92. Wooded parkland course. 18 holes, 6210 yards. S.S.S. 71. *Green Fees:* weekdays £18.00 per round, £25.00 per day; weekends £26.00 per round, £32.00 per day. *Eating facilities:* snacks, lunch, high tea and full meals available during clubhouse hours. *Visitors:* no restrictions at present other than maximum number of 24 at weekends and no visitors before 10am weekends. *Society Meetings:* welcome. Secretary: W.A. Black.

ST. ANDREWS. **Balgove Course,** St. Andrews. *Location:* outskirts of St. Andrews on Dundee Road. 9 hole, beginners' course. *Green Fees:* £5.00. *Eating facilities:* hotels and restaurants in the vicinity. *Visitors:* welcome without reservation. Golf Manager: John Lindsey, Links Management Committee of St. Andrews (0334 75757).

ST. ANDREWS. **Eden Course,** St. Andrews (Starter – 0334 74269). *Location:* follow A91 trunk road to St. Andrews, directions to golf courses are clearly marked. Seaside links. 18 holes, 6122 yards. S.S.S. 70. Practice facilities. *Green Fees:* £16.00 per round weekdays. *Eating facilities:* hotels and restaurants in the vicinity. *Visitors:* welcome with or without reservation. *Society Meetings:* catered for except Saturday. Golf Manager: John Lindsey, Links Management Committee of St. Andrews (0334 75757).

ST. ANDREWS. **Jubilee Course,** West Sands, St. Andrews KY16 9JA (Starter (0334) 73938). *Location:* follow A91 trunk road to St. Andrews, directions to golf course are clearly marked. Seaside links. 18 holes, 6805 yards. S.S.S. 73. Practice facilities available. *Green Fees:* £16.00 per round weekdays. *Eating facilities:* hotels and restaurants in the vicinity. *Visitors:* welcome with or without reservation. *Society Meetings:* catered for except Saturday. Secretary: John Lindsey, Links Management Committee of St. Andrews (0334) 75757).

ST. ANDREWS. **New Course,** West Sands, St. Andrews (Starter (0334) 73938). 18 holes, 6604 yards, 6036 metres. S.S.S. 72. *Green Fees:* £18.00. *Eating facilities:* hotels and restaurants in vicinity. *Visitors:* welcome with or without reservation. *Society Meetings:* catered for except Saturday. Golf Manager: John Lindsey, Links Management Committee of St. Andrews (0334 75757).

ST. ANDREWS. **St. Andrews Links,** Old Course, St. Andrews KY16 9JA (0334 73393). Seaside links. 18 holes, 6566 yards. S.S.S. 72. Practice area and driving range available. *Green Fees:* £40.00. *Visitors:* welcome, closed Sundays. Handicap Certificate required. *Society Meetings:* welcome except Saturday. Golf Manager: John Lindsey (0334 75757).

ST. ANDREWS. **The Old Course,** St. Andrews KY16 9JA (0334 73393). *Location:* follow A91 trunk road to St. Andrews – directions to golf course are clearly marked. Seaside links. 18 holes, 6566 yards, 6004 metres. S.S.S. 72. Practice facilities. *Green Fees:* £40.00. *Visitors:* Handicap Certificate or letter of introduction required from recognised golf club. *Society Meetings:* welcome except Saturday. Golf Manager: John Lindsey (0334 75757).

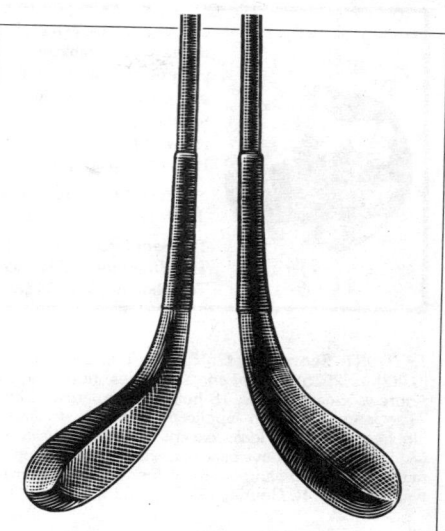

TAKE THE FAMILY FOR A WALK ROUND THE WOODS.

There are five hundred years of golfing history, and a great day out waiting to be discovered at the British Golf Museum. Enjoy the journey, as the latest Philips CD-i and touch-screen displays guide you through the game's history with stories of famous golfers and tournaments.

See the royal, the ancient, and the modern champion's golf clubs, clothing and memorabilia. Discover why a King banned the game. Learn the difference between a mashie and a spoon. Then finish the round at our gift shop.

British Golf Museum
St Andrews

The British Golf Museum,
Bruce Embankment, St Andrews, Fife KY16 9AB. Telephone: 0334 78880.

The Sandford

Conveniently located near to St Andrews (7 miles), and with 34 other golf courses within a comfortable drive – including Scotscraig, Ladybank and Carnoustie – this picturesque, listed, Country House Hotel, provides an ideal venue for those wishing to play golf in The Kingdom of Fife.

Set in seven acres of private grounds, the 16 en-suite bedroom Sandford Hotel, is renowned for its traditional style and warm, friendly service. Fine Scottish and European cuisine is the hallmark of Head Chef Steven Johnstone.

STB Four Crown Highly Commended, member of 'A Taste of Scotland' and 'Where to Eat in Scotland'.

The Sandford Country House Hotel, Newton Hill, Wormit, near Dundee, The Kingdom of Fife, Scotland DD6 8RG.
Telephone: 0382 541802 Fax: 0382 542136

TAYPORT. **Scotscraig Golf Club,** Tayport (Dundee (0382) 552515). *Location:* ten miles north of St Andrews. Seaside links. 18 holes, 6496 yards. S.S.S. 71. *Green Fees:* on application. *Eating facilities:* lunches and high teas, except Tuesdays. *Visitors:* welcome on weekdays or weekends by prior arrangement. *Society Meetings:* catered for subject to approval. Secretary: K. Gourlay (0382 552515).

THORNTON. **Thornton Golf Club,** Thornton KY1 4DW (Glenrothes (0592) 771111). *Location:* south east Fife located off A92, midway between Glenrothes and Kirkcaldy. Undulating, wooded, parkland. 18 holes, 6177 yards. S.S.S. 69. *Green Fees:* weekdays £11.00 per round, £17.00 per day; weekends £16.00 per round, £25.00 per day. *Eating facilities:* full catering service and bar. *Visitors:* welcome, restricted weekends before 10am and between 12 noon and 2.30pm. *Society Meetings:* catered for. Secretary: Neil Robertson.

Glasgow & District

GLASGOW. **Alexandra Golf Club,** Alexandra Park, Alexandra Parade, Glasgow G31 3SE (041-554 1204). *Location:* M8 off ramp to Alexandra Parade. Wooded parkland. 9 holes, 1965 yards. S.S.S. 35. Practice area. *Green Fees:* weekdays adults £1.70, weekends £2.00. Juniors 90p, Senior Citizens and UB40 55p. *Eating facilities:* bar, rooms available for functions. *Visitors:* welcome anytime. Blind Club, Unemployed Club. Bowling greens. Professional: S. Wilson. Secretary: A. Clark.

GLASGOW. **Bearsden Golf Club,** Thorn Road, Bearsden, Glasgow G61 4BP (041-942 2351). *Location:* seven miles north-west of Glasgow. Parkland. 9 holes, 6014 yards. S.S.S. 69. *Green Fees:* information not provided. *Visitors:* welcome, but must be accompanied by member. Secretary: J.R. Mercer (041-942 2381).

GLASGOW. **Bishopbriggs Golf Club,** Brackenbrae Road, Bishopbriggs G64 2DX (041-772 1810). *Location:* quarter mile from Bishopbriggs Cross off Glasgow-Kirkintilloch road. Fairly flat parkland course. 18 holes, 6041 yards. S.S.S. 69. *Green Fees:* information not provided. *Eating facilities:* full service always available. *Visitors:* weekends/Public Holidays with member only, other times apply to Secretary. *Society Meetings:* catered for Tuesdays and Thursdays by applicaton to committee at least one month in advance. Secretary: John Magin (041-772 8938).

GLASGOW. **Blairbeth Golf Club,** Fernhill, Rutherglen, Glasgow (041-634 3355). *Location:* two miles south of Rutherglen off Stonelaw Road. Parkland. 18 holes, 5800 yards. S.S.S. 67. *Green Fees:* information not provided. *Eating facilities:* available. *Visitors:* welcome with reservation, by introduction. *Society Meetings:* not catered for. Secretary: F.T. Henderson (041-632 0604).

GLASGOW. **Bonnyton Golf Club,** Eaglesham, Glasgow G76 0QA (03553 2645). *Location:* B764. Moorland. 18 holes, 6252 yards. S.S.S. 71. *Green Fees:* £25.00 per day. *Eating facilities:* full diningroom and snack facilities. *Visitors:* welcome except weekends. Professional: Robert Crerar (03553 2256). Secretary: (03553 2781).

THE GOLF GUIDE 1994

Scotland   GLASGOW & DISTRICT

GLASGOW. **Bothwell Castle Golf Club**, Blantyre Road, Bothwell G71 (0698 853177). *Location:* adjacent to M74, three miles north of Hamilton. Parkland course. 18 holes, 6243 yards, 5606 metres. S.S.S. 70. Golf clubs and caddy cars for hire. Practice fields. *Green Fees:* weekdays (8.00am to 3.30pm) £18.00 per round, £25.00 per day. (Playing times must be booked with Professional). *Eating facilities:* lunches, bar snacks and dinners available, bar. *Visitors:* welcome weekdays 9.30am to 3.30pm only. *Society Meetings:* catered for, courtesy granted by application on Tuesdays only. Professional: William Walker (0698 852052). Secretary: A.D.C. Watson (0698 852395).

GLASGOW. **Buchanan Castle Golf Club**, Buchanan Estate, Drymen, Glasgow G63 0HY (0360 60369). *Location:* Glasgow/Drymen road, half a mile short of village. Flat parkland course. 18 holes, 6086 yards. S.S.S. 69. 9 hole putting area. *Green Fees:* weekdays £25.00, all day £35.00. *Eating facilities:* full catering available. *Visitors:* welcome, Thursdays – official visiting day, Wednesday maximum 12. *Society Meetings:* welcome, maximum 12. Professional: Keith Baxter (0360 60330). Secretary: Richard Kinsella (0360 60307).

GLASGOW. **Cambuslang Golf Club**, 30 Westburn Drive, Cambuslang (041-641 3130). *Location:* half a mile north of Cambuslang main street. 9 holes, 6146 yards. S.S.S. 69. *Green Fees:* weekdays £10.00. *Eating facilities:* bar snacks, lunches, evening meals. *Visitors:* welcome Mondays, Wednesdays, Thursdays and Fridays on written application to the Secretary. *Society Meetings:* by arrangement. Secretary: William Lilly (041-641 1498).

GLASGOW. **Cathcart Castle Golf Club**, Mearns Road, Clarkston, Glasgow G76 7YL (041-638 0082). *Location:* A77, one and a half miles from Clarkston Toll. Undulating parkland course. 18 holes, 5832 yards. S.S.S. 68. *Green Fees:* £17.00 per round, £25.00 per day. *Eating facilities:* full catering available, lounge bar. *Visitors:* welcome weekdays by prior arrangement. *Society Meetings:* on Tuesdays and Thursdays by application. Professional: David Naylor (041-638 3436). Secretary: D.A. Howe (041-638 9449).

GLASGOW. **Cathkin Braes Golf Club**, Cathkin Road, Rutherglen, Glasgow G73 4SE (041-634 6605). 18 holes, 6208 yards. S.S.S. 71. Practice ground. *Green Fees:* £16.00 per round, £25.00 per day. *Eating facilities:* available. *Visitors:* welcome Monday to Friday by prior arrangement. *Society Meetings:* catered for. Professional: Stephen Bree (041-634 0650). Secretary/Treasurer: G.L. Stevenson.

GLASGOW. **Cawder Golf Club**, Cadder Road, Bishopbriggs, Glasgow G64 3QD (041-772 7101; Fax: 041-772 4463). *Location:* A803 north of city. Parkland. Cawder: 18 holes, 6305 yards, 5737 metres. S.S.S. 71. Keir: 18 holes, 5891 yards, 5373 metres. S.S.S. 68. Practice area. *Green Fees:* £22.00. *Eating facilities:* lunches, high teas, dinners available. *Visitors:* welcome when playing with member. *Society Meetings:* catered for mid-week. Professional: Ken Stevely (041-772 7102). Secretary: G.T. Stoddart (041-772 5167).

GLASGOW. **Clober Golf Club**, Craigton Road, Milngavie G62 7HP (041-956 1685). *Location:* five minutes from Milngavie centre, seven miles from Glasgow city centre. 18 holes, 5068 yards. S.S.S. 69. *Green Fees:* weekdays £9.00 per round. *Eating facilities:* morning coffee, lunches, high teas. *Visitors:* welcome weekdays before 4.30pm (Fridays 4.00pm), weekends if introduced by a member. *Society Meetings:* catered for. Secretary: J. Anderson (041-956 2499).

GLASGOW. **Cowglen Golf Club**, 301 Barrhead Road, Glasgow G43 1AA (041-632 0556). *Location:* south-west Glasgow, near the Burrell Collection. Undulating parkland course. 18 holes, 6033 yards. S.S.S. 69. Practice area. *Green Fees:* weekdays £17.00 per round, £25.00 per day. *Eating facilities:* full catering facilities available. *Visitors:* welcome when introduced by a member. Lockers and showers available. *Society Meetings:* restricted numbers, apply to Secretary. Professional: John McTear (041-649 9401). Secretary: R.J.G. Jamieson, C.A. (0292 266600).

GLASGOW. **Crow Wood Golf Club**, Garnkirk House, Cumbernauld Road, Muirhead G69 9JF (041-779 2011). *Location:* on A80 on Stirling Road, six miles north east of Glasgow. Wooded parkland. 18 holes, 6249 yards. S.S.S. 70. Practice area. *Green Fees:*

SPECTACULAR SCENERY IN THE LOCH LOMOND, STIRLING & TROSSACHS AREA

CULCREUCH CASTLE

Fintry, Glasgow G63 0LW Tel: (036086) 228 Fax: (036086) 555

Hidden away in breathtaking 1600-acre parkland grounds with salmon river and two small coarse fishing lochs. Free fishing and boating for guests. Glasgow 19 miles, Stirling and motorway 17 miles, Edinburgh 55 miles.

· 8 en-suite bedrooms including four posters & family suite · Log fires · Six foot thick walls · Battlements · 8 Scandinavian-style lodges for self-catering · Candlelit Evening Meals in the Panelled Dining Room · Dungeons Bar · Baby Listening · Squash Courts & Indoor Bowling · Colour Castle Brochure and Golfing Brochure available.

40 GOLF COURSES IN 25 MILE RADIUS
ROMANTIC 700 YEAR OLD ANCESTRAL HOME OF CLAN GALBRAITH

GLASGOW & DISTRICT Scotland

weekdays £16.00 per round, £24.00 per day. *Eating facilities:* fully licensed, snacks or full meals served all day. *Visitors:* welcome weekdays except Bank Holidays and only by arrangement with Secretary. *Society Meetings:* catered for as visitors. Professional: Alan Kershaw (041-779 1943). Secretary: Ian McInnes (041-779 4954).

GLASGOW. **Deaconsbank Golf Course,** Rouken Glen Golf Centre, Stewarton Road, Thornliebank, Glasgow G46 7UZ (041-638 7044 or 041-620 0826). *Location:* on Stewarton Road at Rouken Glen Park, only 250 yards from the A726. Parkland with wooded features, designed by James Braid. 18 holes, 4800 yards. S.S.S. 63 (Par 64). 15-bay floodlit driving range. *Green Fees:* weekdays £6.00; weekends and Public Holidays £7.00; Day Ticket £11.00. *Eating facilities:* catering and bar facilities available. *Visitors:* welcome all year round. Shop, club hire, etc. *Society Meetings:* catered for all year round. Professional: (041-638 7044). Secretary: Christine Cosh (041-620 0826).

GLASGOW. **Dougalston Golf Course,** Strathblane Road, Milngavie, Glasgow G62 (041-956 5750). *Location:* A81 half a mile Milngavie. Wooded – water; three ponds. 18 holes, 6683 yards. S.S.S. 72. Practice ground. *Green Fees:* information not provided. *Eating facilities:* diningroom and bar meals. *Visitors:* no restrictions, open to the general public. Golf Manager: W. McInnes.

GLASGOW. **Douglas Park Golf Club,** Hillfoot, Bearsden (041-942 2220). *Location:* adjacent to railway station, Hillfoot, Bearsden, 20 yards past traffic lights at Milngavie Road/Boclair Road. 18 holes. S.S.S. 69. *Green Fees:* information not provided. *Eating facilities:* full service available. *Visitors:* must be introduced and play with member. *Society Meetings:* Wednesdays and Thursdays on application to Secretary. Professional: David B. Scott. Secretary: D.N. Nicolson.

GLASGOW. **Dullatur Golf Club,** Dullatur, Glasgow G68 0AR (0236 723230). *Location:* 12 miles east of Glasgow, north of Cumbernauld on Kilsyth road via Dullatur. 18 holes, 6229 yards. S.S.S. 70. *Green Fees:* £25.00 per day, £15.00 per round after 1.30pm. *Visitors:* welcome weekdays. Professional: Duncan Sinclair.

GLASGOW. **East Kilbride Golf Club,** Chapelside Road, Nerston, East Kilbride G74 4PF (03552 20913). Parkland course with variable topography. 18 holes, 6419 yards. S.S.S. 71. *Green Fees:* weekdays £14.00 per round, £20.00 per day. *Eating facilities:* full catering except Tuesdays and Thursdays (bar snacks). *Visitors:* welcome weekdays on application. Letter of introduction from own Club Secretary required for smaller groups in advance of visits. Weekends no visitors unless accompanied by a member. *Society Meetings:* catered for on application, minimum 12, maximum 30. Professional: A.R. Taylor (03552 22192). Secretary: W.G. Gray (03552 47728).

GLASGOW. **Eastwood Golf Club,** Loganswell, Newton Mearns, Glasgow G77 6RX (035-55 261). *Location:* on main A77 road to Kilmarnock two miles south of Newton Mearns. Parkland. 18 holes, 5864 yards. S.S.S. 68. Practice area. *Green Fees:* £18.00 per round. *Eating facilities:* snacks or full meals available. *Visitors:* welcome weekdays on application to Secretary. *Visiting parties:* welcomed on prior application. Professional: S. Campbell (035-55 285). Secretary: C.B. Scouler (035-55 280).

GLASGOW. **Glasgow Golf Club,** Killermont, Bearsden, Glasgow G61 2TW (041-942 1713). *Location:* taking Maryhill Road out of Glasgow turn right at Killermont Avenue, half a mile before Canniesburn Toll. Tree-lined parkland. 18 holes, 5968 yards. S.S.S. 69. Members only. *Visitors:* only if introduced by member. *Society Meetings:* by application to Club Secretary. Professional: Jack Steven (041-942 8507). Secretary: D.W. Deas (041-942 2011; Fax: 041-942 0770).

GLASGOW. **Haggs Castle Golf Club,** Dumbreck Road, Dumbreck, Glasgow G41 4SN (041-427 0480). *Location:* straight ahead at roundabout at end of M77 from Glasgow. Flat, tree-lined course. 18 holes, 6464 yards. S.S.S. 71. Practice area and putting green. *Green Fees:* weekdays £24.00 per round, £36.00 per day. Weekends, members only. *Eating facilities:* full catering available. *Visitors:* welcome, must book through Professional, golf shoes must be worn. *Society Meetings:* by arrangement through Secretary. Professional: J. McAlister (041-427 3355). Secretary: I. Harvey (041-427 1157).

GLASGOW. **Hayston Golf Club,** Campsie Road, Kirkintilloch, Glasgow G66 1RN (041-776 1244). *Location:* 10 miles north-east of Glasgow and one mile north of Kirkintilloch. Parkland course with tree-lined fairways. 18 holes, 6042 yards. S.S.S. 69. Practice area. *Green Fees:* weekdays £15.00 per round, £20.00 per day. *Eating facilities:* lunches, dinners, bar snacks. *Visitors:* welcome weekdays before 4.30pm with letter of introduction from own club. Weekends only if introduced by member. *Society Meetings:* Tuesdays/Thursdays on application to Secretary. Professional: Steve Barnett (041-775 0882). Secretary: J.V. Carmichael (041-775 0723).

GLASGOW. **Hilton Park Golf Club,** Stockiemuir Road, Milngavie, Glasgow G62 7HB (041-956 5124). *Location:* on A809. Moorland courses. Allander course: 18 holes, 5374 yards. S.S.S. 67. Hilton course: 18 holes, 6007 yards. S.S.S. 70. Practice area. *Green Fees:* £18.00 per round, £24.00 per day. *Eating facilities:* full catering and bar. *Visitors:* on application to the Secretary (not at weekends). *Society Meetings:* as visitors. Professional: W. McCondichie (041-956 5125). Secretary: Mrs J.A. Warnock (041-956 4657).

GLASGOW. **Kirkhill Golf Club,** Cambuslang, Glasgow (041-641 3083 or 8499). 18 holes, 5862 yards. S.S.S. 69. *Green Fees:* £12.00 per round, £20.00 per day weekdays. *Eating facilities:* dining room and bar snacks. *Visitors:* welcome when introduced by member; only introduced visitors at weekends. *Society Meetings:* welcome on written application to the Secretary. Secretary: H.G. Marshall.

274

THE GOLF GUIDE 1994 *Scotland* GLASGOW & DISTRICT

GLASGOW. **Knightswood Golf Club,** Lincoln Avenue, Glasgow G13 (041-959 2131). *Location:* close to Great Western Road, Glasgow. Parkland course. 9 holes, 2717 yards. S.S.S. 66 (33). *Green Fees:* £1.75 weekdays; £1.95 weekends. Unemployed, Juniors, Senior Citizens 55p. *Visitors:* welcome anytime. Secretary: Mr Neil McCuaig (041-950 1235).

GLASGOW. **Letham Hill Municipal Golf Club,** 1240 Cumbernauld Road, Glasgow G33 1AH (041-770 6220). *Location:* 100 yards off M8 Junction 28. Parkland, some holes with views of Hogganfield Loch. 18 holes, 6073 yards. S.S.S. 68. Pitch and putt course (18 holes). *Green Fees:* weekdays £3.25 adult, £1.85 Junior; weekends £3.80. Passport to Recreation concession £1.15. Season tickets available. *Visitors:* welcome at all times – this is a public course. *Society Meetings:* details available from Course Marker. Secretary: J. Wilson.

GLASGOW. **Linn Park Golf Club,** Simshill Road, Glasgow G44 (041-637 5871). *Location:* five miles south of city centre. Parkland. 18 holes, 4952 yards. S.S.S. 65. Practice nets, putting green. *Green Fees:* weekdays £4.00 adults, £2.10 Juniors; weekends £4.00. *Visitors:* welcome without restrictions. *Society Meetings:* not catered for. Secretary: Robert Flanagan.

GLASGOW. **Littlehill Golf Club,** Auchinairn Road, Bishopbriggs, Glasgow G64. *Location:* from Glasgow on A803, turn off for Stobhill Hospital. Flat, parkland. 18 holes, 6364 yards. S.S.S. 70. Small practice area. *Green Fees:* £4.00 per round/day. Special rates for Senior Citizens, Juniors and unemployed. *Eating facilities:* canteen open five days in season, three outwith. *Visitors:* welcome without reservation – pay and play. *Society Meetings:* no restrictions. Professional: Kevin Hughes (041-762 3998). Secretary: W. Burke (041-762 3998).

GLASGOW. **Milngavie Golf Club,** Laigh Park, Milngavie, Glasgow (041-956 1619). *Location:* situated off Glasgow to Drymen road approximately one mile past Stockiemuir Service Station, turn right at signpost. 18 holes, 5818 yards. S.S.S. 68. *Green Fees:* information not provided. *Eating facilities:* catering available. *Visitors:* welcome when introduced by member only. *Society Meetings:* catered for. Secretary: Mrs A.J.W. Ness.

GLASGOW. **Pollok Golf Club,** 90 Barrhead Road, Glasgow G43 1BG (041-632 1080). *Location:* A736, four miles south of Glasgow, near end of M77. Wooded parkland. 18 holes, 6257 yards. S.S.S. 70. *Green Fees:* £26.00 per round, £33.00 per day. *Eating facilities:* dining room and bar. *Visitors:* welcome with reservation by letter to Secretary. No visitors Saturday or Sunday. No Ladies. *Society Meetings:* catered for by letter. Secretary: A Mathison Boyd (041-632 1453).

GLASGOW. **Sandyhills Golf Club,** 223 Sandyhills Road, Glasgow G32 9NA (041-778 1179). *Location:* three miles east from centre of Glasgow. Parkland. 18 holes, 6253 yards. S.S.S. 70. *Green Fees:* £20.00. *Eating facilities:* lunches at club except Mondays, order in advance. *Visitors:* welcome when introduced by a member. *Society Meetings:* welcome by prior arrangement. Secretary: Paul Ward.

GLASGOW. **The Whitecraigs Golf Club,** 72 Ayr Road, Giffnock, Glasgow G46 6SW (041-639 1681). *Location:* on A77 south of city. Parkland course, 18 holes. *Green Fees:* £23.00 per round, £29.00 per day. *Eating facilities:* diningroom, lounge bar. *Visitors:* letter of introduction required. *Society Meetings:* catered for Wednesday only. Professional: William Watson (041-639 2140). Secretary: R.W. Miller (041-639 4530).

GLASGOW. **Williamwood Golf Club,** Clarkston Road, Glasgow G44 (041-637 1783). *Location:* beside Clarkston Toll on Clarkston Road. Attractive parkland course designed by James Braid. 18 holes, 5878 yards. S.S.S. 68. Practice area and putting. *Green Fees:* information not provided. *Eating facilities:* meals must be ordered. *Visitors:* must be introduced by, and play with, a member. *Society Meetings:* weekdays only by arrangement. Professional: J. Gardner (041-637 2715). Secretary: R.G. Cuthbert CA (041-226 4311).

GLASGOW. **Windyhill Golf Club,** Baljaffray Road, Bearsden, Glasgow G61 4QQ (041-942 2349). *Location:* eight miles north-west of Glasgow. Undulating parkland, moorland course. 18 holes, 6254 yards. S.S.S. 70. Practice area. *Green Fees:* £15.00; weekends with member only. *Eating facilities:* full catering and bar. *Visitors:* welcome weekdays, by prior arrangement with Secretary. *Society Meetings:* welcome weekdays by arrangement. Professional: R. Collinson (041-942 7157). Secretary: A.J. Miller (041-942 2349).

KILSYTH. **Kilsyth Lennox Golf Club,** Tak-Ma-Doon Road, Kilsyth, Glasgow G65 0RS (Kilsyth (0236) 822190). *Location:* 12 miles from Glasgow on A80. Parkland/moorland, undulating ground with superb views across central Scotland. 9 holes, 5934 yards. S.S.S. 69. (Second 9 holes currently under construction). *Green Fees:* information not provided. *Eating facilities:* bar and lounge, bar snacks available. *Visitors:* welcome weekdays up to 5.00pm, Saturdays after 5.00pm, not Sundays. Professional: R. Abercrombie. Secretary: R. Hay (0236 823525).

NEWTON MEARNS. **East Renfrewshire Golf Club,** Pilmuir, Newton Mearns, Glasgow G77 6RT (035 55 256). *Location:* on A77, one and a half miles south of Newton Mearns. Moorland course. 18 holes, 6097 yards, 5577 metres. S.S.S. 70. *Green Fees:* weekdays £20.00 per round, £30.00 per day. *Eating facilities:* by prior arrangment with Clubmaster. *Visitors:* welcome except Saturdays but always by prior arrangement with Professional. *Society Meetings:* welcome by prior arrangement with Secretary. Professional: Gordon D. Clark (035 55 206). Secretary: A. Lindsay Gillespie (041 226 4311).

Inverness-shire

ARISAIG. **Traigh Golf Course**, Traigh Farm, Arisaig. *Location:* on A830 Fort William to Mallaig Road, between Arisaig and Morar: Seaside links. 9 holes, 2400 yards. S.S.S 66. (Course being extended and improved). *Green Fees:* £9.00. *Eating facilities:* unlicensed, soft drinks and confectionery only. *Visitors:* welcome at all times. Clubs may be hired. *Society Meetings:* by arrangement. Manager: Bill Henderson (06875 234).

BEAULY by. **Aigas Golf Course**, By Beauly IV4 7AD (0463 782942 or 782423). *Location:* A831, five miles from Beauly village. Challenging 9 hole course uniquely set in beautiful Strathglass beside the River Beauly. 9 holes, 2439 yards, S.S.S. 64 (2 x 9 holes). *Green Fees:* weekdays £8.00 per day; weekends £10.00 per day.

BOAT OF GARTEN. **Boat of Garten Golf and Tennis Club**, Boat of Garten PH24 3BQ (047983 351). *Location:* A9 six miles north of Aviemore. Wooded birch tree-lined fairways, very scenic, overlooking Cairngorm Mountains. 18 holes, 5837 yards. S.S.S. 69. Practice net. *Green Fees:* weekdays £15.00; weekends £20.00. *Eating facilities:* catering facilities open 9.30am to 9pm, bar open 11am to 11pm daily. *Visitors:* welcome 9.30am to 5.30pm. *Society Meetings:* catered for. Secretary: J.R. Ingram (047983 282; Fax: 047983 523).

CARRBRIDGE. **Carrbridge Golf Club**, Carrbridge (0474 984 674). *Location:* eight miles north of Aviemore adjacent to A9, 23 miles south of Inverness. Moorland/parkland. 9 holes, 2630 yards. S.S.S. 66. *Green Fees:* weekdays £8.00 per day; weekends £10.00 per day. *Eating facilities:* snacks, coffee etc. No bar. *Visitors:* unrestricted except competition days (mainly Sundays). Secretary: E.G. Drayson (047984 674).

FORT AUGUSTUS. **Fort Augustus Golf Club**, Markethill, Fort Augustus (0320 6460). *Location:* one mile from village on Fort William road. Moorland course with tree lined canal to north and heather and birch covered hills to the south. 9 holes (18 tees), 5454 yards. S.S.S. 68. *Green Fees:* on request. *Eating facilities:* soft drinks. *Visitors:* welcome anytime except Tuesdays and Wednesdays after 6pm and Saturday afternoons from 1.30pm to 5pm. *Society Meetings:* catered for. Secretary: I. Aitchison (0320 6460).

AIGAS GOLF COURSE

Challenging 9-hole course uniquely set in beautiful Strathglass beside the River Beauly. On A831, five miles from Beauly village. 2439 yards, SSS 64 (2 x 9 holes). Self catering accommodation available in the most attractive houses. Perfect base for touring, walking or simply 'staying put' and unwinding.
Green fees £8.00 weekdays, £10.00 weekends.

**Aigas Golf Course, by Beauly, Inverness-shire IV4 7AD
Telephone: 0463 782942/782423**

GLENAVON HOUSE

Boat of Garten, Inverness-shire PH24 3BP   Tel:/Fax: (0479) 831213

✻ Ideal situation, 3 minutes walk from the first tee of Boat of Garten Golf Club.
✻ Five delightful Highland Courses within 30 minutes drive.
✻ Six bedrooms, each with private facilities, including satellite TV.
✻ Excellent and renowned cuisine, specialising in local salmon, game and shellfish.
✻ A "dram or two" before and after dinner in the log-fired sitting room.

GLENAVON HOUSE, a superb, family run private hotel offers discerning golfers all the above, and is the perfect location for small golfing parties.

Please phone or fax for colour brochure and further information.

THE GOLF GUIDE 1994 *Scotland* **INVERNESS-SHIRE**

Skye of Curr HOTEL
Skye of Curr Road, Dulnain Bridge, Inverness-shire PH26 3PA
Tel: Dulnain Bridge (047 985) 345

A small country hotel set in the heart of the Spey Valley, within easy driving distance of many of the North's golf courses, an ideal base for the discerning golf addict. Self catering accommodation for parties of up to fifteen also available.

THE BOAT HOTEL
BOAT OF GARTEN
GOLF WEEKS & TEE BREAKS
AA ★★★ RAC

Situated overlooking the beautiful but challenging Boat of Garten Golf Course – the 'Gleneagles' of the Highlands – the Boat Hotel offers you both Tuition and Competition Weeks with our resident Professionals, or, the superb value 'Tee Break' holidays with golf on any of six local courses. Tee times confirmed.

Please contact: Golf Desk, The Boat Hotel, Boat of Garten, Inverness-shire PH24 3BH
Telephone 047 983 258   Fax 047 983 414

DALRACHNEY LODGE Hotel

RAC ★★★   Scottish Tourist Board HIGHLY COMMENDED
and
KEEPER'S HOUSE HOTEL

CARRBRIDGE,
Inverness-shire PH23 3AT
Tel: 0479 84 252 Fax: 0479 84 382

Country House Hotel set in 16 acres, originally a Hunting Lodge dating from 1845. Excellent central location in Carrbridge with fast access to many fine courses and situated directly opposite the Village Golf Course. Ten minutes from Boat of Garten. Eleven courses within easy range. Let us quote for your Golf Weekend or Group outing.

On request we shall forward our brochures which describe accommodation ranging from spacious well-equipped self-catering houses and comfortable rooms in **Keeper's House** *to large luxurious en-suite rooms in* **The Lodge** *overlooking the Cairngorm Mountains.*

Accent on the finest food prepared by professional chefs. Choose from three menus daily in Stalker's Bar and the candlelit Lodge Restaurant. Well stocked Bar with over 200 wines, malts and liqueurs. AA, RAC, "Taste of Scotland".

Privately owned by, and under the personal supervision of, Helen and Grant Swanney.

Fairwinds Hotel & Chalets

What is important to a Golfer? Golf Courses. We have 7 within easy reach. But after the game . . . what then? Friendly welcome. Good food. Relaxation. Pleasant comfortable surroundings. High standards of personal attention. All these and more await you at FAIRWINDS. All our bedrooms are ensuite. We pride ourselves on our varied menus. Vegetarian meals and packed lunches are available by arrangement. 2 and 3 bedroom Chalets and Studio Apartment also available.
STB ♦♦♦ Highly Commended   AA Selected   RAC Highly Acclaimed

Please write or phone for further details to:
**Mrs E. Reed, Fairwinds Hotel, Carrbridge,
Inverness-shire PH23 3AA
Tel: Carrbridge (047984) 240**

INVERNESS-SHIRE *Scotland* THE GOLF GUIDE 1994

INVERNESS. **Inverness Golf Club**, The Clubhouse, Culcabock Road, Inverness IV2 3XQ (Inverness (0463) 233422). *Location:* one mile south of town centre. Parkland course. 18 holes, 6226 yards. S.S.S. 70. Two practice grounds. *Green Fees:* weekdays £15.00 per round, £20.00 per day; weekends and Bank Holidays £18.00 per round, £22.00 per day. *Eating facilities:* sandwiches, lunches, high teas and dinners served at club. *Visitors:* welcome except Saturdays from 25th March to 20th October. *Society Meetings;* catered for, pre-booking preferred. Professional: A.P. Thomson (0463 231989). Secretary: J. McGill (0463 239882).

INVERNESS. **Torvean Golf Club**, Glenurquhart Road, Inverness (0463 236648). *Location:* A82 towards Fort William, approximately one mile from town centre. Parkland course. 18 holes, 5784 yards, 5288 metres. S.S.S. 68. *Green Fees:* weekdays £8.50; weekends £9.50. *Eating facilities:* snacks and bar available; summer season 11am – 11pm. *Visitors:* booking preferred, especially at weekends – telephone 0463 711434. *Society Meetings:* welcome with advance booking through Inverness District Council. Secretary: Mrs K.M. Gray (0463 225651).

KINGUSSIE. **Kingussie Golf Club**, Gynack Road, Kingussie PH21 1LR (0540 661 374). *Location:* turn at Duke of Gordon Hotel, half a mile up road (signposted). Hill type course. 18 holes, 5555 yards, 5079 metres. S.S.S. 67. *Green Fees:* weekdays £10.50 per round, £13.50 per day; weekends £12.50 per round, £16.50 per day. *Eating facilities:* bar, catering provided. *Visitors:* welcome, tee reserved for members 8.30am – 9.30am, 12.30pm – 2pm and 5.30pm – 6.30pm at weekends, otherwise no restrictions. Caravan site. *Society Meetings:* welcome. Secretary: Norman Mac-William (0540 661 600).

NETHYBRIDGE. **Abernethy Golf Club**, Nethybridge PH25 3DE (0479 821305). *Location:* 10 miles from Aviemore lying on the B970 between Boat-of-Garten and Grantown on Spey. Delightful nine hole course close to pine woods and with commanding view of the valley of the River Spey. 9 holes, 4986 yards. S.S.S. 66. *Green Fees:* £8.00 weekdays; £12.00 weekends. *Eating facilities:* clubhouse is unlicensed but there are full catering facilities available. *Visitors:* welcome subject to short restrictions when club competitions being held. *Society Meetings:* by arrangement with the Secretary. Secretary: Bill Templeton (0479 821214).

Golfing holiday on a 13,000 acre Highland Estate. Board and self catering accommodation available. Many leisure activities to enjoy. Golf on any one of six 18-hole courses within a short drive of Alvie.
See our colour display advertisement on page 9.

ALVIE ESTATE
SCOTTISH HIGHLAND GOLFING HOLIDAYS
Alvie Estate Office (Ref APG1), Kincraig, by Kingussie, Inverness-shire PH21 1NE
Telephone: 0540 651255/651249 Fax: 0540 651380

AUCHENDEAN LODGE HOTEL
DULNAIN BRIDGE, GRANTOWN-ON-SPEY PH26 3LU TEL: (047 985) 347
Enjoy Highland hospitality at its best here at AUCHENDEAN LODGE in a dramatic scenic setting with 8 golf courses within easy reach. DINNER, BED & BREAKFAST £35 - £62 GOOD HOTEL GUIDE
GOOD FOOD GUIDE. STB ✿✿✿ Highly Commended. EGON RONAY.
See also our full colour advertisement on page 9

BALAVOULIN HOTEL
RAC Highly Acclaimed
LES ROUTIERS
COMMENDED

We'll take good care of you

A friendly welcome awaits you at "The Balavoulin" – a small family-run hotel with all the comforts of home.

All bedrooms are en-suite and have colour TV; Satellite Channel; Direct-Dial Telephone; Tea/Coffee making facility. The hotel is centrally-heated and double-glazed.

Fully licensed with excellent bar-lunches and suppers and with a superb restaurant offering a choice of table d'hôte, à la carte or vegetarian menus.

The hotel is open all year round and offers a wide selection of special activity packages or ideal or for just a relaxing mid-week or weekend break. *Special rates for Dinner, Bed and Breakfast.* Just phone or write for our full colour brochure – you won't be disappointed!

Grampian Road · Aviemore · Inverness-shire PH22 1RL · Tel (0479) 810672 · Fax (0479) 811575

Scotland INVERNESS-SHIRE / KINCARDINE / KINROSS

NEWTONMORE. **Newtonmore Golf Club,** Golf Course Road, Newtonmore PH20 1AT (0540 673328). *Location:* turn off A9 at Newtonmore, course in centre of village, 45 miles south of Inverness. Mainly flat course runs along banks of River Spey amidst beautiful scenery. 18 holes, 5880 yards. S.S.S. 68. Practice green. *Green Fees:* weekdays £10.00 per round, £13.00 per day; weekends £13.00 per round, £16.00 per day. *Eating facilities:* full catering and bar facilities. *Visitors:* welcome, restrictions during open competitions and society days. Locker and shower facilities. *Society Meetings:* welcome by appointment with Secretary. Professional: Robert Henderson. Secretary: R.J. Cheyne (0540 673878).

SPEAN BRIDGE. **Spean Bridge Golf Club,** Station Road, Spean Bridge PH34 4EU (039781 340). *Location:* off A92 at Spean Bridge Hotel. Wooded course set on the hillside, lovely views. 9 holes, 2203 yards. S.S.S. 62. *Green Fees:* weekdays £7.00 per day. *Eating facilities:* Hotel nearby. *Visitors:* welcome, Tuesdays from 5pm reserved for members, competitions some weekends. Secretary: John MacLennan (0397703 379).

Kincardineshire

BANCHORY. **Banchory Golf Club,** Kinneskie Road, Banchory AB31 3TA (Banchory (03302) 2365). *Location:* 18 miles west of Aberdeen on Deeside, 100 yards south west Banchory town centre. Parkland. 18 holes, 5245 yards, 4795 metres. S.S.S. 66. *Green Fees:* weekdays £19.00; weekends £21.00. *Eating facilities:* full catering service and lounge bar. *Visitors:* welcome. *Society Meetings:* catered for except Thursdays and weekends. Professional: Mr J. Charles Dernie (Tel & Fax: 03302 2447). Admin. Secretary: Mrs Anne Smith (03302 2365).

STONEHAVEN. **Stonehaven Golf Club,** Cowie, Stonehaven AB3 2RH (Stonehaven (0569) 62124). *Location:* A92, one mile north of town. 18 holes, 5128 yards. S.S.S. 65. *Green Fees:* £13.00 weekdays, £18.00 weekends. *Eating facilities:* full catering including bar lunches. *Visitors:* welcome, only a few with reservation. *Society Meetings:* catered for except for Saturday. Secretary: E.A. Ferguson. Club Manager: R.O. Blair.

Kinross-shire

KINNESSWOOD. **Bishopshire Golf Club,** Kinnesswood, By Kinross. *Location:* take road to Glenrothes from M90, three miles. Course has panoramic views overlooking Loch Leven. 10 holes, 4700 yards, 2151 metres. S.S.S. 64. *Green Fees:* weekdays £5.00; weekends £6.00. *Eating facilities:* by arrangement or available at the hotel 400 yards away. *Visitors:* welcome without restriction. *Society Meetings:* by arrangement. Secretary: John Proudfoot (0592 780203).

GOLF IN FIFE & PERTHSHIRE

**FROM £33 PER DAY
DINNER, ROOM EN-SUITE,
SCOTTISH BREAKFAST**

Play on Scotland's greatest courses, 100 within an hour's drive from this cosy family-run hotel overlooking Loch Leven. Fresh food, real ales, helpful people. We are happy to help you with your course planning and bookings. 9 hole course adjacent to hotel. Eight seater vehicle available for hire.

THE LOMOND
COUNTRY INN
Kinnesswood,
by Loch Leven KY13 7HN

Call David Adams. Tel: 0592 84253 Fax: 0592 84693

AA ★★ (Rosette)   STB 🌸🌸🌸 Commended

PITCH UP TO THE GREEN

JUST A SHORT IRON FROM THE FRONT DOOR YOU WILL FIND THE FIRST TEES OF OUR OWN TWO SCENIC GOLF COURSES. BOTH OFFER AN ENJOYABLE AND STIMULATING CHALLENGE WHETHER YOU'RE A HOLIDAY GOLFER OR LOW HANDICAP PLAYER.
OUR 47 MODERN SPACIOUS BEDROOMS ARE ALL WELL APPOINTED AND INCLUDE SATELLITE TV. INDOOR LEISURE COMPLEX FEATURES INDOOR POOL, SAUNA, SOLARIUM, SQUASH COURT AND FITNESS AREA.
OVER 50 OTHER GREAT COURSES WITHIN AN HOUR'S EASY DRIVE INCLUDING ST. ANDREWS, GLENEAGLES AND CARNOUSTIE.

THE GREEN HOTEL

2 The Muirs, Kinross, Scotland, KY13 7AS. Tel: 0577 863467. Fax: 0577 863180.

KINROSS. **Green Hotel Golf Course,** Green Hotel, The Muirs, Kinross KY13 7AS (0577 62237). *Location:* turn left in Kinross off M90 Junction 6, course 500 yards on right. Reasonably flat wooded parkland. Two courses: Blue 18 holes, 6456 yards, 5905 metres. S.S.S. TBA; Red 18 holes, 6257 yards, 5719 metres. S.S.S. TBA. Practice ground. *Green Fees:* weekdays £14.00 per round, £20.00 per day; weekends £20.00 per round, £30.00 per day. *Eating facilities:* in clubhouse and hotel. *Visitors:* welcome, booking recommended. *Society Meetings:* catered for by arrangement. Professional: Stuart Geraghty (0577 63467). Secretary: Mrs S.M. Stewart (0577 63467).

LAURENCEKIRK. **Auchenblae Golf Club,** Auchenblae, Laurencekirk AB30 1BU. *Location:* five miles north of Laurencekirk, on A94, two miles west of Fordoun. Parkland. 9 holes, 2174 yards. S.S.S. 30. *Green Fees:* Mondays to Fridays £6.00; Saturdays £6.50, Sunday £7.00. Juniors and Senior Citizens half price at all times. *Eating facilities:* two hotels in nearby village. *Visitors:* restrictions Wednesday and Friday evenings (competitions); very busy Sundays. *Society Meetings:* small groups welcome. Secretary: A.I. Robertson (0561 378869).

MILNATHORT. **Milnathort Golf Club Ltd,** South Street, Milnathort (Kinross (0577) 864069). Parkland course. 9 holes, 5969 yards. S.S.S. 69. *Green Fees:* weekdays £10.00 per day; weekends £15.00 per day. *Eating facilities:* by arrangement. *Visitors:* welcome without reservation. *Society Meetings:* must be booked in advance. All enquiries phone Clubhouse.

Kirkcudbrightshire

CASTLE DOUGLAS. **Castle Douglas Golf Club,** Abercromby Road, Castle Douglas (0556 2801). *Location:* half a mile from town centre on A713 Castle Douglas to Ayr Road. Parkland. 9 holes, 5408 yards. S.S.S. 66. *Green Fees:* £10.00 per round or day. *Eating facilities:* catering during summer season. *Visitors:* welcome without reservation, except Tuesdays or Thursdays after 4pm and competition days. *Society Meetings:* by arrangement. Secretary: A.D. Millar (0556 2099).

SOLWAYSIDE HOUSE HOTEL
Auchencairn, By Castle Douglas DG7 1QU   ✦✦✦✦ Commended

Family-run. Comfortable accommodation and excellent Restaurant. Choice home cooked food. Superb sea/country views in unspoilt coastal village. Ideal for 'unexplored' golfing area including Championship Southerness links. BARGAIN GREEN FEES. Starting times arranged. All 8 bedrooms are en-suite and have colour TV, telephone, tea/coffee making. Putting, games room. 20 courses within one hour. 3-6 days short break from £31 per person per night for Dinner, Bed and Breakfast. **Tel: (055-664) 280.**

THE GOLF GUIDE 1994 *Scotland* KIRKCUDBRIGHTSHIRE

DALBEATTIE. Colvend Golf Club, Sandyhills, Colvend, By Dalbeattie (0556-63 398). *Location:* six miles from Dalbeattie on the A710, Solway Coast road, between Dalbeattie and Dumfries. Picturesque seaside course on a hill. 9 holes (visitors' tees), 2240 yards. S.S.S. 63. *Green Fees:* £10.00 per day; Juniors £5.00 (full fee Saturday and Sundays). *Eating facilities:* excellent catering available. *Visitors:* welcome almost anytime. Course must be vacated by 2pm on Tuesdays and 5.30pm on Thursdays, also some Sundays (competitions), from April to September. Secretary: J.B. Henderson (0556 610878).

GATEHOUSE OF FLEET. Gatehouse of Fleet Golf Club, Laurieston Road, Gatehouse of Fleet, Castle Douglas. *Location:* quarter of a mile from Gatehouse. Sloping and wooded. 9 holes, 2500 yards. S.S.S. 63. *Green Fees:* £10.00. *Visitors:* welcome at all times except Sunday mornings to 11.30am. Secretary: Peter Colville (0557 814734).

KIRKCUDBRIGHT. Kirkcudbright Golf Club, Stirling Crescent, Kirkcudbright DG6 4EZ (0557 30314). *Location:* signposted near centre of town. Hilly parkland. 18 holes, 5598 yards. S.S.S. 67. *Green Fees:* £15.00 per round, £20.00 per day. Reductions for parties of 20 or more. *Eating facilities:* coffee, lunch, evening meal (not Mondays), usual bar hours. *Visitors:* welcome without reservation most days; Tuesdays Ladies' Day, Wednesday Men's. Phone and check. *Society Meetings:* welcome, advance bookings. Secretary: John H. Sommerville.

NEW GALLOWAY. New Galloway Golf Club, New Galloway, Castle Douglas (06443 455). *Location:* one mile off A731, Ayr to Dumfries road. Scenic with fine turf. 9 holes, 5058 yards. S.S.S. 65. *Green Fees:* £10.00 per round/day. *Eating facilities:* bar. *Visitors:* welcome without reservation. Accommodation and meals available in village. *Society Meetings:* by arrangement. Secretary: Alan R. Brown (06443 455).

CLONYARD HOUSE HOTEL
Colvend – Dalbeattie – Dumfries & Galloway – Scotland DG5 4QW

The family-run Hotel for your Solway Holiday. Four golf courses within ten miles. Full restaurant facilities; cocktail bar; bar lunches and suppers. Fifteen bedrooms, all with full facilities; twelve on ground floor with private patios; one suite. Set in secluded wooded grounds.
Telephone: Rockcliffe (055663) 372; Fax: (055663) 422

GORDON HOUSE HOTEL
HIGH STREET, KIRKCUDBRIGHT, DUMFRIESSHIRE DG6 4JQ

We extend a warm welcome to all visitors here at GORDON HOUSE. Local 18-hole course three minutes away with a further selection of courses at CASTLE DOUGLAS, GATEHOUSE, GLENLUCE, DUMFRIES, NEW GALLOWAY and NEWTON STEWART. Further afield there are Championship Courses at TROON, PRESTWICK, SOUTHERNESS and TURNBERRY. Special 2-night Golf Breaks: Golf, Dinner, Bed & Breakfast from £70.00 per person. Details on request.
Telephone: (0557) 30670

Selkirk Arms Hotel
Kirkcudbright, Galloway Tel: (0557) 30402 Fax: (0557) 31639
Where Robert Burns wrote 'The Selkirk Grace'

AA ★★ RAC

Historic 18th century Hotel, now newly refurbished, in picturesque town. Ideal for business or family holidays. Golf, squash, sailing, fishing, sea-angling all nearby. Exciting à la carte menu prepared using finest fresh local ingredients. All rooms have private facilities. TV and telephone. Large secluded gardens.

HIGHLY COMMENDED

LEAMINGTON HOTEL
High Street, NEW GALLOWAY, Kirkcudbrightshire

Enjoy the warmest welcome at this family-run ten bedroomed 17th century Hotel. Ideally situated for watersports, fishing, stalking, walking, golf – LOCAL SCENIC COURSE – and touring in Bonnie Galloway. Ensuite rooms, very popular licensed restaurant offering excellent fare at reasonable prices. Weekly, family and 3-day rates. BED & BREAKFAST from £14.

STB ♛♛♛ Commended   **Telephone 06442 327**

Lanarkshire (including the Clyde Valley)

AIRDRIE. **Airdrie Golf Club,** Glenmavis Road, Airdrie (Airdrie (0236) 762195). *Location:* one mile north of Airdrie Cross. 18 holes, 6004 yards. S.S.S. 69. *Green Fees:* £12.00 per round, £20.00 per day (both inclusive of VAT). *Eating facilities:* available. *Visitors:* welcome only on application to the Secretary. Professional: A. McCloskey (0236 754360). Secretary: D.M. Hardie.

AIRDRIE. **Easter Mofffat Golf Club,** Plains, Airdrie ML6 8NP (0236 842878). *Location:* three miles east of Airdrie on old Edinburgh Road. 18 holes, 6221 yards. S.S.S. 70. Practice ground. *Green Fees:* £12.00 per round, £18.00 per day (lower rate if visited previous year). *Eating facilities:* bar and dining room. *Visitors:* welcome except weekends. *Society Meetings:* welcome. Professional: Brian Dunbar (0236 843015). Secretary: J.G. Timmons (0236 761440).

BELLSHILL. **Bellshill Golf Club,** Community Road, Orbiston, Bellshill ML4 2RZ (Bellshill (0698) 745124). *Location:* Bellshill to Motherwell road, turn right. Parkland course. 18 holes, 6494 yards. S.S.S. 71. *Green Fees:* weekdays £11.00, weekends £15.00. *Visitors:* casual visitors welcome; parties by prior application (not competition days or Sundays). Secretary: William McLenachan.

BIGGAR. **Biggar Golf Club,** Broughton Road, Biggar ML12 6HA (0899 20618).*Location:* from Edinburgh A702, from Glasgow A74 or M8, turn off at Newhouse. Flat, scenic parkland course. 18 holes, 5416 yards. S.S.S. 66. *Green Fees:* weekdays £8.50, weekends £11.00. Reductions for Juniors and Senior Citizens. *Eating facilities:* all day licence, full catering (not Mondays). *Visitors:* unrestricted, casual dress – no jeans. All weather tennis courts and caravan park. *Society Meetings:* welcome, early reservation essential. Secretary: W.S. Turnbull (0899 20566). Tee Reservations: (0899 20319).

CARLUKE. **Carluke Golf Club,** Maudslie Road, Hallcraig, Carluke ML8 5HG (0555 771070). *Location:* one and a quarter miles from Carluke Cross, through Clyde Street. Parkland course. 18 holes, 5800 yards. S.S.S. 68. Practice area. *Green Fees:* £12.00 per round, £18.00 per day weekdays. *Eating facilities:* available. *Visitors:* till 4pm weekdays, no visitors weekends. Tuition. *Society Meetings:* by written application to the Secretary. Professional: A. Brooks (0555 751053). Secretary: J.H. Muir (0555 770620).

COATBRIDGE. **Drumpellier Golf Club,** Drumpellier Avenue, Coatbridge ML5 1RX (0236 428723). *Location:* one mile from town centre. Parkland, wooded. 18 holes, 6227 yards. S.S.S. 70. Practice area. *Green Fees:* £18.00 per round, £25.00 per day weekdays. *Eating facilities:* catering available except Thursdays. *Visitors:* welcome with reservation. *Society Meetings:* catered for by arrangement. Professional: K. Hutton (0236 432971). Secretary: W. Brownlie (0236 423065).

DOUGLAS WATER. **Douglas Water Golf Club,** Ayr Road, Rigside, Lanark (055588 361). *Location:* five miles south of Lanark on A70 – turn right at Hyndford Bridge. Hilly course, small greens. 9 holes, 2947 yards, 2694 metres. S.S.S. 69. *Green Fees:* weekdays £5.00; weekends £7.00. *Eating facilities:* snacks. *Visitors:* welcome any time, with reservation on Saturdays for competitions. *Society Meetings:* contact Secretary. Secretary: Mr R.McMillan (0555 2295).

EAST KILBRIDE. **Torrance House Golf Club,** Calderglen Country Park, Strathaven Road, East Kilbride G75 0QZ (03552 49720). *Location:* East Kilbride boundary on main Strathaven road. Parkland. 18 holes, 6423 yards. S.S.S. 71. Practice area. *Green Fees:* information on request. *Eating facilities:* private clubhouse. *Visitors:* welcome mid-week only. *Society Meetings:* details on request. Secretary: Duncan A. MacIver (03552 49720). Booking Office: (03552 48636).

GARTCOSH. **Mount Ellen Golf Club,** Johnstone Road, Gartcosh (Glenboig (0236) 872277). *Location:* approximately six miles north-east of Glasgow, near old Gartcosh steelworks. Flatland. 18 holes, 5525 yards. S.S.S. 68. *Green Fees:* weekdays £10.00 per round. *Eating facilities:* bar and full catering service. *Visitors:* welcome weekdays from 9am to 4pm, no weekend visitors. *Society Meetings:* by arrangement with Secretary. Professional: G. Reilly (0236 872632). Secretary: W.J. Dickson.

HAMILTON. **Hamilton Golf Club,** Riccarton, Ferniegair, Hamilton ML3 7PZ (0698 282872). *Location:* off M74 Hamilton turn-off, one and a half miles up Larkhall road. Parkland course. 18 holes, 6700 yards. S.S.S. 70. *Green Fees:* information not provided. *Eating facilities:* meals must be ordered. *Visitors:* must be accompanied by a member. *Society Meetings:* by arrangement with Secretary. Professional: M.J. Moir (0698 282324). Secretary: P.E. Soutter (0698 286131).

CARMICHAEL COUNTRY COTTAGES

Our stone cottages nestle in fine countryside three miles south of Lanark, with five other courses within six miles. Private tennis, walking trails, fishing and orienteering, restaurant/farm shop. 12 cottages, 25 bedrooms. Open all year. Easily accessible. £160-£425 per week.

Richard & Patricia Carmichael, Carmichael Country Cottages, Carmichael by Biggar, Clydesdale ML12 6PG. Telephone: 08993 336 Fax: 08993 481

Highly Commended

THE GOLF GUIDE 1994　　　　　　　　　　　　*Scotland*　LANARKSHIRE

HAMILTON. **Strathclyde Park Golf Club,** Mote Hill, Hamilton ML3 6BY (0698 266155 ext. 154). *Location:* M74 north, Hamilton, Motherwell exit, to roundabout second exit, to roundabout second exit, pass ice rink, golf course straight ahead (about one mile from motorway turn off to course). Parkland, wooded course. 9 holes, 3147 yards. S.S.S. 70. Large practice area and driving range (24 bays). *Green Fees:* adults approximately £2.20. Juniors £1.10, Senior Citizens 60p. *Eating facilities:* bar and cafe available. *Visitors:* welcome, same day booking system in operation; phone lines open 8.45am. *Society Meetings:* welcome. Professional: Ken Davidson (0698 283994). Secretary: Kevin Will (0698 825363).

LANARK. **Carnwath Golf Club,** 1 Main Street, Carnwath (Carnwath (0555) 840251). Fairly hilly inland course. 18 holes, 5860 yards. S.S.S. 69. *Green Fees:* £17.00 per day; Sundays and Bank Holidays £20.00. *Eating facilities:* lounge bar and dining room daily. *Visitors:* welcome Mondays, Wednesdays, Fridays and Sundays with prior booking. *Society Meetings:* catered for by prior arrangement. Secretary: Donald Craig (0698 425249). Bookings: (0555 840854).

LANARK. **Lanark Golf Club,** The Moor, Whitelees Road, Lanark ML11 7RX (Lanark (0555) 663219). *Location:* off A73. Tough moorland course. 18 holes, 6423 yards. S.S.S. 71. Also 9-hole course. Two practice grounds. *Green Fees:* £18.00 per round, £28.00 per day weekdays. *Eating facilities:* full catering and bar. *Visitors:* welcome daily until 4pm, no visitors weekends. *Society Meetings:* groups of 24 and over catered for Mondays and Tuesdays. Professional: Ron Wallace (0555 661456). Secretary: G.H. Cuthill.

LANARK. **Mouse Valley Golf Course,** East End, Cleghorn, Lanark ML11 (0555 870015). *Location:* 5 miles from Carluke on A721 Peebles Road. Pay as you play. Links style course, inland undulating terrain. Mouse Water (river) runs through the course. 18 holes, 6600 yards. Par 70. Practice ground. Driving range. *Green Fees:* £8. *Eating facilities:* Full bar and catering. *Visitors:* welcome. *Society meetings:* welcome at all times. Company days. Contact: (0662 366236).

LARKHALL. **Larkhall Golf Club,** Burnhead Road, Larkhall (0698 881113). *Location:* on A74, close to M74. Parkland. 9 holes, 6684 yards. S.S.S. 72. *Green Fees:* information not provided. *Eating facilities:* meals weekends; bar normal hours. *Visitors:* welcome, but check beforehand; every second Saturday course closed to visitors. Secretary: I. Gilmour (0698 881755).

LEADHILLS. **Leadhills Golf Club,** Leadhills, Biggar (0659 74222). *Location:* seven miles south of Abington on B797. This short but testing course is the highest in Britain. 9 holes, 2400 yards. S.S.S. 62. *Green Fees:* £4.00. *Eating facilities:* not available. *Visitors:* welcome any time. *Society Meetings:* welcome. Secretary: Graham Shaw.

LESMAHAGOW. **Hollandbush Golf Club,** Acretophead, Lesmahagow (Lesmahagow (0555) 893484). *Location:* off M74 between Lesmahagow and Coalburn. 18 holes, 6110 yards. S.S.S. 70. Practice area. *Green Fees:* £9.00 weekdays; £11.00 weekends. (Special tourist rates available). *Eating facilities:* meals at club. *Visitors:* welcome without restriction. *Society Meetings:* catered for. Professional: Ian Rae (0555 893646). Secretary: James Hamilton (055 582 222).

MOTHERWELL. **Colville Park Golf Club,** Jerviston Estate, Merry Street, Motherwell ML1 4UG (0698 263017). *Location:* one mile from station (Merry Street, Motherwell). Parkland, wooded first six holes. 18 holes, 6265 yards. S.S.S. 70. *Green Fees:* £20.00. *Eating facilities:* full facilities. *Visitors:* welcome weekdays only and by prior written arrangement or accompanied by member. *Society Meetings:* by prior written arrangement. Professional: (0698 265779). Secretary: Scott Connacher.

SHOTTS. **Shotts Golf Club,** Blairhead, Benhar Road, Shotts ML7 5BJ (Shotts (0501) 820431). *Location:* off M8 at junction B7057, one and a half miles on Benhar Road. Semi-flat moorland/wooded course. 18 holes, 6125 yards. S.S.S. 70. Practice area. *Green Fees:* weekdays £14.00 per day (off season £10.00); weekends £16.00 per day (off season £12.00). *Eating facilities:* full catering, all day licence. *Visitors:* welcome anytime except Saturdays before 4.30pm and Sundays or Public Holidays. *Society Meetings:* weekdays only. Professional: Jim Forrester (0501 822658). Secretary: Jack McDermott (0501 820431).

PAY AS YOU PLAY

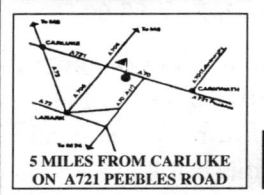

5 MILES FROM CARLUKE ON A721 PEEBLES ROAD

MOUSE VALLEY GOLF COURSE

6,600 yards Home of the Infamous Par 3 Short Hole – Oh Dear!

9 Holes – £8.00 incl. VAT • 18 Holes – £12.50 incl. VAT

Day Ticket – £18.00 incl. VAT • Limited Membership Available.

PARTY BOOKINGS 1993/94

Saturdays, Sundays & Weekdays

Coffee/Bacon Roll • Soup/Filled Roll Lunch • Evening Meal

Two Rounds of Golf **£30** per person

For further information and to book tee-off time please contact:

HELEN HOWITT ON **0555 870015**

STRATHAVEN. **Strathaven Golf Club**, Overton Avenue, Glasgow Road, Strathaven ML10 6NR (Strathaven (0357) 20539). *Location:* on A726 on outskirts of town. 18 holes, 6226 yards. S.S.S. 70. *Green Fees:* please contact Secretary for information. *Eating facilities:* full catering and bar. *Visitors:* welcome weekdays, casual visitors before 4pm; party bookings Tuesdays only by prior arrangement. Professional: M.R. McCrorie (0357 21812). Secretary: A.W. Wallace (0357 20421).

UDDINGSTON. **Calderbraes Golf Club**, 57 Roundknowe Road, Uddingston (Uddingston (0698) 813425). *Location:* at end of M74, overlooking Calderpark Zoo. 9 holes, 3425 yards. S.S.S. 67. *Green Fees:* weekdays £10.00. *Eating facilities:* catering available at all times. *Visitors:* welcome weekdays only; must be off course by 5pm. *Society Meetings:* welcome, contact Secretary. Secretary: S. McGuigan.

WISHAW. **Wishaw Golf Club**, 55 Cleland Road, Wishaw (Wishaw (0698) 372869). *Location:* centre of town, five miles from M74. Tree-lined parkland course. 18 holes, 6137 yards. S.S.S. 69. Practice area. *Green Fees:* weekdays £12.00 per round, £20.00 per day; weekends £25.00 per day. *Eating facilities:* full catering and two bars. *Visitors:* welcome before 4pm weekdays, after 11am Sundays. *Society Meetings:* by application to Secretary. Professional: J.G. Campbell (0698 358247). Secretary: D.D. Gallacher (0698 372869).

Morayshire

ELGIN. **Elgin Golf Club**, Hardhillock, Birnie Road, Elgin IV30 3SX (Elgin (0343) 542338). *Location:* half a mile south of Elgin on Birnie Road. Undulating parkland on sandy subsoil. 18 holes, 6401 yards, 5853 metres. S.S.S. 71. Practice ground and net. *Green Fees:* weekdays £14.00 per round, £20.00 per day; weekends £20.00 per round, £28.00 per day. *Eating facilities:* bar and catering every day. *Visitors:* no restrictions but parties should book with Secretary. *Society Meetings:* by arrangement with Secretary. Early booking advised. Professional: Ian Rodger (0343 542884). Secretary: Derek J. Chambers.

ELGIN. **Hopeman Golf Club**, Hopeman, Elgin IV30 2YA (Hopeman (0343) 830578). *Location:* 7 miles north-east of Elgin on B9012. Seaside links, with spectacular 12th hole. 18 holes, 5474 yards, 5003 metres. S.S.S. 67. *Green Fees:* weekdays £10.00 per day; weekends £15.00 per day. Reductions for Senior Citizens. *Eating facilities:* bar, catering. *Visitors:* welcome, some restrictions weekends. *Society Meetings:* by arrangement. Secretary: W.H. Dumbar (0343 830687).

FOCHABERS. **Garmouth & Kingston Golf Club**, Garmouth, Fochabers (0343 87388). *Location:* west bank of River Spey, 300 yards from North Sea. Flat

---

LOOKING FOR A GUIDE?

If you have found *THE GOLF GUIDE* useful, you will also enjoy other titles in the FHG range including:

Recommended Country Hotels of Britain	£3.60
Recommended Wayside Inns of Britain	£3.60
Recommended Short Break Holidays in Britain	£3.60

You'll find our guides in most bookshops and in larger newsagents. In case of difficulty you can post or fax your order direct to FHG Publications in Paisley. You'll find an Order Form showing all prices, including postage, on the back pages of this book.

THE GOLF GUIDE 1994   *Scotland* MORAYSHIRE

parkland/part links. 18 holes, 5656 yards. S.S.S. 67. *Green Fees:* weekdays £10.00 per round, £12.00 per day; weekends £14.00 per round, £18.00 per day. Reductions for parties over 20. *Eating facilities:* by arrangement, bar and snacks from 1st May to September 11am to 11pm. *Visitors:* welcome, except during local competitions. Local hotel caters for golfing holidays. *Society Meetings:* by arrangement with Secretary, very welcome. Secretary: A. Robertson (0343 87231).

FOCHABERS. **Spey Bay Golf Club,** Spey Bay Hotel, Spey Bay, Fochabers IV32 7PJ (0343 820424 Hotel). *Location:* halfway between Inverness and Aberdeen. Seaside links, wooded (gorse bushes). 18 holes, 6064 yards. S.S.S. 69. Driving range, practice area and putting green. *Green Fees:* Monday to Saturday £8.00 per round, Sundays £9.50. Parties of eight or more - two rounds and food £16.00 Monday to Friday, Sundays £18.00. *Eating facilities:* all meals available at the adjoining hotel. *Visitors:* welcome weekdays without reservation, advise prior phone call on Sundays. *Society Meetings:* catered for by prior arrangement. Special weekend terms including full board and golf available. Any enquiries to the Hotel Manager: Michael Dann. Secretary: Arthur Mitchell (0343 820459).

FORRES. **Forres Golf Club,** Muiryshade, Forres IV36 0RD (0309 672949). *Location:* one mile south from clock tower in town centre. Parkland, part wooded. 18 holes, 6203 yards. S.S.S. 69. Practice ground and putting green. *Green Fees:* weekdays £13.00 per day;

weekends £18.00. *Eating facilities:* bar and catering all day every day. *Visitors:* welcome without reservation – difficult at weekends due to competitions. *Society Meetings:* welcome. Professional: Sandy Aird (0309 672250). Secretary: D.F. Black (0309 672949).

GRANTOWN-ON-SPEY. **Grantown-on-Spey Golf Club,** The Clubhouse, Golf Course Road, Grantown-on-Spey PH26 3HY (Grantown-on-Spey (0479) 2079). *Location:* situated at north end of town, A9 to A95, then turn right opposite police station. Parkland and woodland. 18 holes, 5715 yards. S.S.S. 67. Practice area and putting green. *Green Fees:* weekdays £13.00 per day; weekends £16.00. *Eating facilities:* bar and full catering available April to December inclusive. *Visitors:* welcome weekdays, reserved for members 5.30pm – 6.30pm, Saturdays and Sundays between 8am and 10am, 1pm and 2pm, 5pm and 6pm. *Society Meetings:* catered for. Professional: W. Mitchell (0479 2398). Secretary: D. Elms (0479 2715).

LOSSIEMOUTH. **Moray Golf Club,** Stotfield Road, Lossiemouth IV31 6QS (034-381 2018). *Location:* six miles north of Elgin. Old Course 18 holes, 6643 yards, 6074 metres. S.S.S. 72. New Course 18 holes, 6005 yards, 5491 metres. S.S.S. 69. *Green Fees:* on request. *Eating facilities:* full catering and bar facilities. *Visitors:* welcome weekdays after 9.30am (except between 1-2pm). Weekends: Saturday (New Course only), Sunday not before 10.30am and not between 1-2pm. *Society Meetings:* all welcome. Handicap Certificate required. Professional: Alastair Thomson (034-381 3330). Secretary: James Hamilton (034-381 2018).

SPEY BAY HOTEL, FOCHABERS, MORAY IV32 7JP

FREE unlimited golf to residents, full board packages or self-catering available. Caravan site adjacent. Tennis, putting, children's play area. 16-bay Golf Driving Range on site. Numerous golf courses within 10-mile radius. Ideal base for touring North-East. Excellent food; accommodation with en-suite facilities, TV.   *Write or phone the Manager:* **SPEY BAY (0343) 820424.**

Best of Highland Hospitality at
THE ARDLARIG, GRANTOWN ON SPEY

Four courses nearby. Tee times arranged for Grantown on Spey and Boat of Garten Golf Clubs. Residential Licence – Private Car Parking. All meals home cooked – sumptuous breakfasts. Colour TVs & courtesy trays in rooms. 2/3 Day Breaks (inc. dinner) from £24 daily.

TASTE OF SCOTLAND
STB COMMENDED

For brochure/tariff and all enquiries call Sue or Mike on 0479 873245

STOTFIELD HOTEL
Lossiemouth, Moray IV31 6QS
Tel: 0343 812011
Fax: 0343 814820

GROUPS AND SOCIETIES WELCOMED
CONFIRMED TEE TIMES ARRANGED
Victorian Hotel with en-suite bedrooms, sauna and mini-gym. Excellent food and comprehensive wine list. American bar and grill
Also see colour advertisement on page 9.

NAIRNSHIRE *Scotland* THE GOLF GUIDE 1994

Nairnshire

CAWDOR CASTLE. **Cawdor Castle Golf Club,** Cawdor Castle, Nairn IV12 5RD (06677 615; Fax: 06677 674). *Location:* situated between Inverness and Nairn on the B9090 off A96. Parkland. 9 holes, 1161 yards. S.S.S. 32. *Green Fees:* weekdays £2.00 per round; weekends £3.00 per round. *Eating facilities:* licensed restaurant in Castle, snack bar in grounds. *Visitors:* welcome every day from 11am to 5pm May 1st to October 2nd.

NAIRN. **Nairn Dunbar Golf Club,** Lochloy Road, Nairn IV12 5AE (0667 52741). *Location:* on A96, one mile east of town. Seaside links. 18 holes, 6431 yards. S.S.S. 71. *Green Fees:* weekdays £15.00 per round, £20.00 per day; weekends £20.00 per round, £25.00 per day. *Eating facilities:* available. *Visitors:* welcome. *Society Meetings:* catered for. Professional: B. Mason (0667 53964). Secretary: Mrs S.J. MacLennan.

NAIRN. **The Nairn Golf Club,** Seabank Road, Nairn IV12 4HB (0667 53208). *Location:* Nairn West Shore, on the southern shore of the Moray Firth, 16 miles east of Inverness, five miles from Inverness Airport. Seaside links. 18 holes, 6772 yards. S.S.S. 72. Also 9 hole course (Newton Course). Large practice ground. *Green Fees:* weekdays £25.00 per round, £35.00 per day; weekends £30.00 per round, £40.00 per day. Fees subject to review. *Eating facilities:* full catering and bar available. *Visitors:* welcome, no jeans in clubhouse, Handicap Certificate required, restricted times at weekends. Full size snooker table. *Society Meetings:* bookings in advance through Secretary. Professional: Robin Fyfe (0667 52787). Secretary: Mr Jim Somerville (0667 53208; Fax: 0667 56328). Clubmaster: (0667 52103).

Ideally located overlooking the Moray Firth and situated midway between Nairn's two Championship Courses.
If you like peace and quiet here is the place to relax. Set in private grounds with own path to sandy beach.
Excellent food and accommodation. All rooms with private facilities and colour television available.
Send for colour brochure or phone
PAUL & BARBARA WILKIE
on
Nairn 0667 52039

Invernairne Hotel
Thurlow Road
Nairn IV12 4EZ
Scotland
Telephone: Nairn (0667) 52039

GOLF PACKAGES
3 Days, DB&B from £160
(2 days golf, 2 courses)
7 Days DB&B from £330
(5 days golf, 5 courses)
Individual packages arranged on request

The Links Hotel
Nairn

Elegant Victorian Hotel overlooking sea, within walking distance of Nairn Championship Course and Nairn Dunbar. Special Golf Breaks include a daily round of golf, with booked tee times, at any of the 20 local courses (list supplied) plus Dinner, Bed and full Highland Breakfast. All rooms ensuite with central heating, colour TV and tea/coffee facilities. Golfers' Niblick Bar; excellent food and wine; log fires. Ask for details of Special 3 night Golf Breaks. Open all year. 3 flights daily from Heathrow/Inverness; car hire arranged. Golf Parties and Societies up to 20 welcome.
Call today – *0667 53321.*

Scotland NAIRNSHIRE

alton burn hotel

This superb family hotel is set in its own secluded surroundings away from the hustle and bustle of everyday life. Overlooking Nairn West Championship Golf Course the hotel has 25 bedrooms – all with private bathrooms – practice golf area, putting green, tennis court, games room and heated outdoor swimming pool.

For colour brochure and full tariff send S.A.E. to:–
MRS J. McDONALD

NAIRN, SCOTLAND. TELEPHONE: (0667) 53325/52051

NAIRN DUNBAR GOLF SHOP
NAIRN DUNBAR CHAMPIONSHIP COURSE

The Best Drives finish here!

Main Sayers/Glenmuir Stockist

**Nairn Dunbar Golf Club, Lochloy Road, Nairn
TELEPHONE: BRIAN MASON (0667) 53964**

PEEBLES-SHIRE *Scotland*

Peebles-shire

PEEBLES. **Innerleithen Golf Club,** Leithen Water, Leithen Road, Innerleithen (0896 830951). *Location:* 25 miles south of Edinburgh, just south of Peebles. Situated in valley, easy walking but challenging. 9 holes, 2992 yards (x 2). S.S.S. 69. *Green Fees:* weekdays £9.00 per day; weekends £11.00 per day. *Eating facilities:* by prior arrangement. *Visitors:* welcome without reservation. *Society Meetings:* catered for by arrangement, limit 40. Secretary: S. Wyse (0896 830071).

PEEBLES. **Peebles Golf Club,** Kirkland Street, Peebles (0721 20197). *Location:* 51 miles from Glasgow, off A72 at west side of town, 23 miles from Edinburgh. 18 holes, 6137 yards. S.S.S. 69. *Green Fees:* weekdays £12.00 per round, £18.00 per day; weekends £18.00 per round, £25.00 per day. *Eating facilities:* full catering daily except Tuesdays. *Visitors:* welcome subject to tee availability. *Society Meetings:* catered for subject to prior bookings, limited to 24 players in party. Secretary: Hugh Gilmore.

WEST LINTON. **West Linton Golf Club,** West Linton EH46 7HN (0968 60463). *Location:* A702 road 17 miles south west of Edinburgh. Scenic moorland course. 18 holes, 6132 yards, 5607 metres. S.S.S. 69. Two practice areas. *Green Fees:* weekdays £14.00 per round, £20.00 per day; weekends £22.00 per round. Weekly ticket (Mon-Fri) £75.00. Fees subject to review. *Eating facilities:* catering except Tuesdays; lunches, bar snacks, high teas, morning coffee, bar. *Visitors:* welcome at all times except on Medal days and weekends before 1pm. *Society Meetings:* catered for weekdays except Tuesdays. Professional: Ricky Forrest (0968 60256). Secretary: Grahame Scott (0968 60970).

A natural choice for golfers . . .

. . . as a centre for golf, this privately-owned Edwardian Country House Hotel on the River Tweed is a natural choice. Enjoy quiet countryside golf on up to 17 scenic courses. No need for tee-times on most and few handicap restrictions. Arrangements for tuition may be made from the hotel. Inclusive rates with golf available for long or short breaks. Quiet, friendly and comfortable, the hotel has all rooms en-suite and a noteworthy reputation for good food with salmon, trout, venison and specialities from our own smokehouse.

For non-golfers many activities can be organised from the hotel, including fishing, walking, riding, clay pigeon shooting. There is a sauna and mini-gym and all rooms have tea and coffee tray, colour television, hairdryer and direct dial telephone. There are tartan, wool and cashmere shopping discounts for guests. Contact Keith or Charles Miller.

TWEED VALLEY HOTEL & RESTAURANT
Walkerburn, Near Peebles, Peeblesshire EH43 6AA
Telephone: 089687 636   Fax: 089687 639

STB 🌸🌸🌸 Commended   AA Hospitality Service Award   RAC ★★★

PERTHSHIRE Scotland

Perthshire

ABERFELDY. **Aberfeldy Golf Club,** Taybridge Road, Aberfeldy PH15 2BH (Aberfeldy (0887) 820535). *Location:* A9 to Ballinluig. Riverside course. 9 holes, 2733 yards, 2655 metres. S.S.S. 67. *Green Fees:* £10.00 per round. *Eating facilities:* snacks and bar. *Visitors:* welcome anytime. *Society Meetings:* catered for. Contact the Secretary at Aberfeldy Golf Club. Secretary: Angus M. Stewart (0887 820117).

ABERFELDY. **Kenmore Golf Course,** Mains of Taymouth, Kenmore, Aberfeldy PH15 2HN (0887 830226). *Location:* west off A9 at Ballingluig on A827, six and a half miles west of Aberfeldy through village of Kenmore on RHS. Mildly undulating natural terrain, well kept, nestled in Tay Valley. 9 holes, 6052 yards. S.S.S. 69. Practice facilities. *Green Fees:* weekdays £10.00 per 18 holes, £16.00 per day; weekends

Coshieville Hotel and Restaurant

Situated 3 miles from Kenmore and at the entrance to Glen Lyon, this small country hotel provides excellent food and accommodation. All bedrooms have private bathrooms, tea/coffee making facilities, colour TV and central heating throughout. Closely situated to the Hotel is Taymouth Castle and golf course, also Aberfeldy, Killin & Strathtay courses. Special rates for 2/3 Day and Weekly Stays throughout the year.

**COSHIEVILLE HOTEL, BY ABERFELDY, PERTHSHIRE PH15 2NE
Tel: 0887 830319   Hosts: Dougie Harkness and Annemarie Carr**

The name Coshieville is an anglicisation of 'Coeddi failthe', gaelic for 'the welcoming place of Coeddi', a monk who came down Glen Lyon from Iona and set up a hospice here. The present building stands on the site used as an Inn for over 1000 years.

Delightful waterside hotel has 38 bedrooms, all ensuite with colour TV. Situated in the beautiful village of Kenmore this hotel offers golfing and fishing breaks. Local produce is heavily relied upon in the Kenmore's kitchen with fresh salmon and seasonal game. Swimming pool and sauna available for residents. There are a variety of golf courses to enjoy nearby. Hotel residents can enjoy a 50% discount on green fees at Taymouth Castle Golf Club. Self catering units available.

**Kenmore Hotel, Kenmore, Perthshire PH15 2NU
Tel: 0887 830205 Fax: 0887 830262**

TAYMOUTH HOLIDAY CENTRE and KENMORE GOLF COURSE

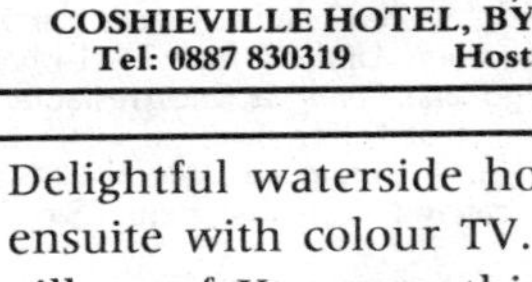

Taymouth Holiday Centre is situated in the heart of Perthshire amongst the beautiful surroundings of the Tay Valley at the head of the Loch. Holiday accommodation is available in self-catering farm cottages furnished and equipped to the Tourist Board's ＷＷＷＷ Commended standards. There is also a quiet and secluded caravan and camping park (Four Pennants) nearby, with shop and ample children's play areas. The "Byre Bistro" overlooking the first tee offers delicious bar meals, served all day, and there are many other excellent places to dine in the area. The centre's own KENMORE GOLF COURSE (6030 yards, 9 holes) offers a challenging game on excellent greens. Caddy cars and clubs can be hired and changing rooms are available. As well as golf at this or any of the other 29 courses in Perthshire, visitors can enjoy walking, fishing, cycling and all watersports at the nearby water sports centre.
Brochure available from D. Menzies & Partners, Taymouth Holiday Centre, Kenmore, Aberfeldy, Perthshire PH15 2HN Tel: 0887 830226 Fax: 0887 830211

PERTHSHIRE Scotland

£11.00 per 18 holes, £18.00 per day. Junior rates available, rates for parties on application. *Eating facilities:* full bar and catering facilities in pleasant surroundings. *Visitors:* welcome anytime. STB 4 Crown Cottages to let and group accommodation available (self catering included). Pro shop; club and trolley hire; changing and shower facilities. *Society Meetings:* up to 50 welcome. Secretary: Robin Menzies.

ABERFELDY. **Taymouth Castle Golf Course,** Kenmore, by Aberfeldy PH15 2NT (0887 830397). *Location:* six miles west of Aberfeldy. Flat parkland set in scenic mountain terrain. 18 holes, 6066 yards. S.S.S. 69. Practice area. *Green Fees:* weekdays £14.00 per round, £22.00 per day; weekends and Bank Holidays, £18.00 per round. Half-price for Juniors (under 15). Subject to review. *Eating facilities:* restaurant and bar. *Visitors:* welcome except competition days, tee reservations necessary (phone or letter). Tuition available, motorised buggies. *Society Meetings:* catered for by previous arrangement only. Professional: Alex Marshall (0887 820910). Director of Golf: Michael Mulcahey (0887 830228).

AUCHTERARDER. **Auchterarder Golf Club,** Orchil Road, Auchterarder PH3 1DW (Auchterarder (0764) 662804). *Location:* off A9 to south-west of town, next to Gleneagles. Flat parkland, part wooded. 18 holes, 5778 yards. S.S.S. 68. Small practice area. *Green Fees:* weekdays £13.00 per round, £18.00 per day; weekends £19.00 per round, £26.00 per day. *Eating facilities:* full catering and bar. *Visitors:* welcome without reservation except major competition days. *Society Meetings:* welcome, must book 3 months in advance. Professional: Gavin Baxter (0764 663711). Secretary: W.M. Campbell (0764 662804).

AUCHTERARDER. **Gleneagles Hotel Golf Courses,** Auchterarder PH3 1NF (Auchterarder (0764) 62231; Telex 76105; Fax: 0764 62134). *Location:* A9 from Perth, 16 miles south-west: bus meets trains at Gleneagles Station. Gleneagles offers two moorland 18 hole courses. **King's Course: 6125 yards par 69; **Queen's Course: 5660 yards par 67. Also Monarch's Course (18 holes) and a new 9 hole course, The Wee Course: 1481 yards par 27. *Green Fees:* on request. *Eating facilities:* at Dormy House (Bar & Restaurant) and The Gleneagles Hotel. *Visitors:* strictly Hotel residents, and members. Professional: Billy Marchbank. Hotel General Manager: Peter Lederer (0764 62231). Golf Co-ordinator: Suzanne Mailer (0764 663543; Fax: 0764 664440).

BLAIR ATHOLL. **Blair Atholl Golf Club,** Blair Atholl, Pitlochry PH18 5TG (0796) 481407). *Location:* off A9, seven miles north of Pitlochry. Flat parkland. 9 holes. S.S.S. 69. Clubs for hire. *Green Fees:* weekdays £10.00 per day; weekends £11.00 per day. *Eating facilities:* bar meals and snacks. *Visitors:* welcome at all times. *Society Meetings:* by arrangement with Secretary, not Sundays. Secretary: Mr J.A. McGregor (0796 481274).

BLAIRGOWRIE. **Alyth Golf Club,** Alyth, Blairgowrie (Alyth (08283) 2268). *Location:* A926 or A927 to Alyth, B954 one mile to Club (five miles from Blairgowrie/Coupar Angus). 18 holes, 6226 yards. S.S.S. 70. *Green Fees:* weekdays £17.00 per round, £22.00 per day; weekends £22.00 per round, £27.00 per day. *Eating facilities:* full catering facilities. *Visitors:* welcome with reservation. *Society Meetings:* catered for. Professional: Tom Melville. Secretary: Roy Davidson.

BLAIRGOWRIE. **Blairgowrie Golf Club,** Rosemount, Blairgowrie PH10 6LG (0250 872383; Fax: 0250 875451). *Location:* take A923 out of Perth, turn right at "Rosemount" sign. Flat wooded moorland. Rosemount Course: 18 holes, 6588 yards. S.S.S. 72. Lansdowne Course: 18 holes, 6895 yards. S.S.S. 73. Wee Course: 9 holes, 2307 yards. S.S.S. 65. Three practice grounds. *Green Fees:* on application. No advance booking Wednesdays/Saturdays/Sundays. *Eating facilities:* full catering available. *Visitors:* advance booking Mon/Tues/Thurs/part Fri, 8.30am-4.00pm, (through Secretary). Handicap Certificate required. *Society Meetings:* catered for by application to the Secretary. (Maximum 32 without prior permission.) Professional: Gordon Kinnoch (0250 873116). Secretary/Manager: John N. Simpson (0250 872622).

BLAIRGOWRIE. **Dalmunzie Golf Course,** Spittal O' Glenshee, Blairgowrie PH10 7QG (0250 885226). *Location:* A93 Blairgowrie to Braemar road, left at Spittal O' Glenshee. A small well-kept hill course amid glorious scenery. 9 holes, 2035 yards. Practice area. *Green Fees:* on application. Under 7 free, 7 – 14 half price (we like young golfers.) *Eating facilities:* restaurant facilities at Dalmunzie Hotel. Bar. *Visitors:* welcome without reservation. Self-catering cottages available. *Society Meetings:* catered for. Secretary: Simon Winton.

CALLANDER. **Callander Golf Club,** Aveland Road, Callander FK17 8EN (0877 30090). *Location:* M9 (Stirling) leave by Crianlarich exit on to A84 to Callander, at east end of town, just off Main Street. Parkland, partly wooded with panoramic views. 18 holes, 5125 yards. S.S.S. 66. Small practice ground. *Green Fees:* weekdays £12.00 per round, £17.00 per day; weekends £16.00 per round, £21.00 per day. *Eating facilities:* bar snacks, lunches, high teas, dinners by arrangement. *Visitors:* welcome, no restrictions. Handicap Certificate required Wednesdays and Sundays. *Society Meetings:* welcome, book nine months in advance, arrange with Secretary. Professional: W. Kelly (0877 30975). Secretary: J. McClements (0877 30090). Booking Secretary: 10.00am to 2.00pm (0877 30090), 7.00pm to 9.00pm (0877 30866).

CRIEFF. **Comrie Golf Club,** Comrie (Comrie (0764) 670055). *Location:* six miles from Crieff on Crieff/Lochearnhead Road at east end of Comrie village. 9 holes, 5966 yards. S.S.S. 69. *Green Fees:* weekdays £8.00, weekends £12.00. *Eating facilities:* light refreshments during summer months. *Visitors:* welcome without reservation. *Society Meetings:* by arrangement with Secretary. Secretary: D.G. McGlashan (0764 670544).

THE GOLF GUIDE 1994

Scotland PERTHSHIRE

YOUR ONLY WORRY WILL BE CHOOSING WHERE TO PLAY...

Situated in the heart of Scotland's golfing country, yet only 35 minutes from Edinburgh, this friendly and popular hotel is the perfect setting for your golf break. With contacts at many clubs, we are happy to organise all your golfing requirements. Our busy group package service includes discounted rates, full itinerary planning and a complimentary putter for the organiser.

Real ale bar ★ extensive bar menu ★ candlelit restaurant ★ all bedrooms ensuite ★ tea/coffee making ★ colour TV inc. Sky. Write or phone for our informative golfing brochure which includes extensive information on courses, green fees and a range of packages. 2-day bargain breaks from £59.

CARNOUSTIE · **Ladybank** · Crail ·
Scotscraig · ST ANDREWS · **Downfield**
· GLENEAGLES · **Taymouth Castle** ·
DALMAHOY · **Lundin Links** ·
ROSEMOUNT · **Elie** · **Crieff**

... The golfers hotel ...

THE GLENFARG HOTEL
GLENFARG, PERTHSHIRE PH2 9NU.
TEL: (0577) 830241.

COMMENDED   AA ★★

AUCHTERARDER GOLF CLUB

Delightful country course near to Gleneagles. 18 holes. Visitors welcome. Bar lunches and Evening meals. **GREEN FEES:** Midweek – £18 per day, £13 per round
Weekend – £26 per day, £19 per round

Orchil Road, Auchterarder PH13 1LS. Tel: Clubhouse (0764) 662804, Professional (0764) 663711

The Angus Hotel

BLAIRGOWRIE, PERTHSHIRE PH10 6NQ
Telephone: Blairgowrie (0250) 872838/872455

Carnoustie, St. Andrews, Rosemount, Downfield – need we say more?

All rooms with private facilities. Indoor heated pool, spa bath, sauna, solarium. Ample free parking.

5 days (Half Board) – £35 per day
(inc VAT at 17½%).

ST ANDREWS   CARNOUSTIE   BLAIRGOWRIE
and 55 other courses in easy reach
FIVE DAYS GOLF + B&B £170
GOLF SOCIETY SPECIALISTS
INDIVIDUALLY DESIGNED HOLIDAYS
The Alyth Hotel
Alyth, Blairgowrie Tel: 08283 2447

Nine challenging holes set on a privately owned 6000-acre estate in spectacular and beautiful scenery. The course has been owned and maintained by the Winton family for over 40 years, alongside Dalmunzie House Hotel and Highland Cottages. Why not come to stay, and enjoy carefree golf in spectacular surroundings? Send for details to Simon Winton.

DALMUNZIE GOLF COURSE
SPITTAL OF GLENSHEE, BLAIRGOWRIE, PERTHSHIRE PH10 7QG   TEL: 0250 885226

Achray House Hotel
Lochearn, St. Fillans, Perthshire PH6 2NF
Tel: 0764 685231   Fax: 0764 685320

Stunning lochside position in St. Fillans – an area of outstanding natural beauty. Well established, family run hotel, known for its wide selection of good food and caring service that brings people back year after year. The perfect base for golf, walking, sightseeing and watersports.
From £28 per night en-suite, Bed and Breakfast.

Contact Tony or Jane Ross for more details.

EGON RONAY'S GUIDES

LOCHEARNHEAD HOTEL
Escape to Perthshire – A family run Hotel with luxury self-catering Chalets overlooking LOCHEARN. Ideal golfing centre, with 7 Golf Courses within 20 miles and many more within an hour's drive. Play local 5 courses in 5 days for approximately £40. Also an ideal centre for touring, water sports (we have our own moorings and slipway), hillwalking, fishing and sailing. Enjoy superb Scottish cooking and stunning views. Families and dogs welcome. Fully licensed. 3 Day and 5 Day midweek breaks available.
Write or phone for brochure to: Lochearnhead Hotel, Lochearnhead, Perthshire
Telephone: 0567 830229   Fax: 0567 830364

Murraypark Hotel

Connaught Terrace, Crieff, Perthshire PH7 3DJ
Telephone: 0764 65 3731
Fax: 0764 5311
AA · RAC

Crieff is an important Golf centre and The Murraypark an important Golf hotel. We specialise in good food and good cheer, a friendly welcome, quiet comfort and golfers are specially welcome.
Contact Ann and Noel Scott for details.
SCOTLAND'S COMMENDED HOTEL · TASTE OF SCOTLAND

TORMAUKIN HOTEL

A friendly, comfortable Inn, set in peaceful countryside, with over 40 golf courses within a short radius. Centrally situated, with Edinburgh only 45 minutes' away.

Ten bedrooms all en-suite with TV, telephone, etc;
superb restaurant and excellent bar meals –
Egon Ronay & Johansens recommended.
Please telephone for brochure.
Tormaukin Hotel, Glendevon by Dollar,
Perthshire FK14 7JY.
Tel: 0259 781252. Fax: 0259 781526.

Scottish Tourist Board COMMENDED

WESTER RIECHIP, Butterstone, Dunkeld
Enjoy the freedom of self catering on your next Golfing Holiday.
This STB ♛♛♛♛ Deluxe Graded house accommodates 8 people in comfort. Centrally situated for access to 30 famous and popular courses in Perthshire and beyond. Cottages and flats also available for smaller groups.
Brochures from: Laighwood Holidays, Butterstone, Dunkeld, Perthshire PH8 0HB. Tel: 0350 724241

Scotland — PERTHSHIRE

CRIEFF. Crieff Golf Club, Perth Road, Crieff PH7 3LR (Crieff (0764) 652397). *Location:* A85 north-east outskirts of Crieff. Ferntower Course – 18 holes, 6402 yards. S.S.S. 71. Dornock Course – 9 holes, 2386 yards. S.S.S. 63. Two practice areas. *Green Fees:* Ferntower: weekdays £16.00 per round, £27.00 per day; weekends £20.00 per round. Dornock – per 18 holes: weekdays £11.00; weekends £13.00. *Eating facilities:* full restaurant facilities by arrangement (phone 0764 652397) and bar snacks. *Visitors:* welcome with reservation, prior arrangement advisable by phone. *Society Meetings:* book by phone and confirm in writing. Senior Professional: John Stark (0764 652909). Club Professional: David Murchie. Secretary: L.J. Rundle (0764 652397).

CRIEFF. Muthill Golf Club, Peat Road, Muthill, Crieff PH5 2AD (0764 81523). *Location:* 500 yards off main Crieff/Stirling Road at west end of village. Parkland (noted for panoramic views of Strathearn). 9 holes, 2350 yards. S.S.S. 63 for 18 holes. *Green Fees:* weekdays £8.00 per day; weekends £12.00. Fees subject to review. *Eating facilities:* tea, coffee, soft drinks only. *Visitors:* restricted when competition and matches are being played, notice displayed at clubhouse. Changing and toilet facilities available. Secretary: W.H. Gordon (0764 653319).

CRIEFF. St. Fillans Golf Club, South Loch Earn Road, St. Fillans PH6 2NG (0764 685312). *Location:* thirteen miles west of Crieff on A85 between Crieff and Lochearnhead. M9 nearest motorway. Parkland with one small hill. 9 holes, 5866 yards. S.S.S. 68 (18 holes). Practice net. *Green Fees:* weekdays £8.00 per round, £12.00 per day; weekends £10.00 per round, £14.00 per day. *Eating facilities:* light meals, teas, coffees, snacks. No bar. *Visitors:* welcome at all times. *Society Meetings:* welcome with advance booking (not July and August). Maximum 24. Hon. Professional: John Stark. Secretary: J. Allison (0764 670951).

DUNBLANE. Dunblane New Golf Club, Perth Road, Dunblane FK15 0DU (Dunblane (0786) 823711). *Location:* on main Dunblane Road at Fourways Roundabout. Parkland/undulating. 18 holes, 5939 yards. S.S.S. 68. *Green Fees:* weekdays £16.00 per round. *Eating facilities:* available. *Visitors:* welcome, but restricted at weekends. *Society Meetings:* catered for Mondays and Thursdays only. Professional: R.M. Jamieson (Fax: 0786 825946). Secretary: R.S. Macrae.

DUNKELD. Dunkeld and Birnam Golf Club, Fungarth, Dunkeld PH8 0HU (0350 727524). *Location:* turn right one mile north of Dunkeld onto A923. Heathland course with panoramic views, testing. 9 holes, 5264 yards. S.S.S. 66. *Green Fees:* on application. *Eating facilities:* meals available and bar. *Visitors:* welcome. *Society Meetings:* catered for. Secretary: Mrs W.A. Sinclair (0350 727524).

DUNNING. Dunning Golf Club, Rollo Park, Dunning (076484 684747). *Location:* 10 miles west of Perth. Parkland, softly undulating. 9 holes, 4836 yards. S.S.S. 64. *Green Fees:* £7.00 per day adults, £3.50 per day Juniors. *Eating facilities:* tea/coffee, soft drinks, snacks. *Visitors:* welcome weekdays but no visitors after 5pm unless accompanied by member; no visitors before 4pm Saturday, Sundays no visitors before 1pm. *Society Meetings:* welcome weekdays. Secretary: Miss C. Westwood (076484 684312).

KILLIN. Killin Golf Club, Killin (0567 820312). *Location:* west end of Loch Tay. Hilly parkland amongst beautiful scenery. 9 holes, 2510 yards. S.S.S. 65. Small practice area includes bunker and net. *Green Fees:* £9.00 per round, £12.00 per day. *Eating facilities:* available all day. *Visitors:* welcome. *Society Meetings:* catered for by arrangement. Secretary: Sandy Chisholm (08383 235).

THE ROYAL DUNKELD HOTEL

A former Coaching Inn, THE ROYAL DUNKELD HOTEL, some 170 years old is now a comfortable, modern hotel set in the beautiful Cathedral town of Dunkeld. We are members of the Logis of Great Britain group and our restaurant offers excellent value and now boasts membership of the Taste of Scotland scheme. Outstanding bar suppers and a warm, friendly welcome are always assured in our bar. 35 bedrooms, all ensuite. Open all year, we are perfectly situated to tour very many of Scotland's most famous golf courses.

Dunkeld, Perthshire PH8 0AR. Telephone: (0350) 727322 for reservations. Fax: (0350) 728989

LOCH TAY HIGHLAND LODGES – *SUPERB SELF CATERING*

Our luxury lodges, on the shore of Loch Tay in the heart of Scotland, are fully equipped and heated for all-year occupation with spacious comfort for 4 to 6 people.

Golfers can enjoy a local 5-day/5-course ticket at £35, or travel a little further to Kenmore, Gleneagles or Rosemount.

Our on-site facilities include riding centre, salmon and trout fishing, pleasure cruising, mini-leisure centre and putting green.

For brochure and details contact:– Pamela and Clive Booth, Loch Tay Highland Lodges, Milton Morenish, by Killin, Perthshire FK21 8TY Tel: 0567 820323 Fax: 0567 820581

♥♥♥♥ HIGHLY COMMENDED TO ♥♥♥♥♥ DELUXE

— THE — MURRAYSHALL
COUNTRY HOUSE HOTEL, RESTAURANT AND GOLF COURSE

SCONE, PERTH, SCOTLAND
Tel: 0738 51171. Fax: 0738 52595

19 Bedrooms with immaculate 18 Hole Par 73 Golf Course. A variety of Holes, Tree Lined Fairways and Water Holes, all make a real sporty challenge to the discerning Golfer.
Green Fees £20.00 – £40.00
Golf Societies, Company Golf Days welcome
Golf Packages available Overseas/Country
Membership available £117.50 pa.
Telephone for our Brochure and Tariff

PERTH. **Craigie Hill Golf Club (1982) Ltd,** Cherrybank, Perth PH2 0NE (Perth (0738) 24377). *Location:* at west end of town, easy access from M90 and A9. Hilly course with lovely scenery. 18 holes, 5379 yards. S.S.S. 66. Practice ground and putting green. *Green Fees:* weekdays £10.00 per round, £15.00 per day; Sundays £20.00 per day. Visitors with member £5.00, Juniors (weekdays) £3.00 per round. *Eating facilities:* full catering and bar. *Visitors:* welcome Mondays to Fridays and Sundays by arrangement. *Society Meetings:* catered for by written application in first instance. Professional: Frank L. Smith (0738 22644). Secretary: William A. Miller (0738 20829).

PERTH. **King James VI Golf Club,** Moncrieffe Island, Perth PH2 8NR (Perth (0738) 25170). Starter (0738 32460). *Location:* situated on Island in River Tay, access by Footbridge alongside railway from Tay Street, Perth. Parkland course. 18 holes, 6026 yards. S.S.S. 68. Practice nets, green, ground. *Green Fees:* weekdays £13.00 per round, £20.00 per day; weekends £15.00 per round after 10am, £27 per day. Subject to review. *Eating facilities:* full catering, bar. *Visitors:* welcome, phone for reservation, restricted on Saturdays. *Society Meetings:* catered for by prior booking. Fully stocked golf shop. Professional: Tony Coles (0738 32460). Secretary: Dorothy Barraclough (0738 32460).

PITLOCHRY. **Pitlochry Golf Course,** Pitlochry (Pitlochry (0796) 2792). *Location:* half mile from centre of Pitlochry on A9. 18 holes, 5811 yards, S.S.S. 68. *Green Fees: 1st April to 31st October:* weekdays £14.00 per day (£3.00 juniors); Saturdays £17.00 per day (£5.00 juniors); Sundays £17.00 per day. Restricted course (1st November to 31st March). Day ticket (any day) Adult £6.00, Junior £1.50. *Eating facilities:* catering and refreshments available in licensed clubhouse, except mid-October to end of March. *Visitors:* welcome. Caddy cars available for hire. *Society Meetings:* catered for. Professional: George Hampton (0796 2792). Secretary: D.C.M. McKenzie (0796 2114 for Group bookings). Fax: 0796 473599.

SCONE. **Murrayshall Golf Course,** Murrayshall, Scone PH2 7PH (0738 51171; Fax: 0738 52595). *Location:* three miles north of Perth on Coupar Angus Road. Undulating wooded parkland. 18 holes, 6460 yards. S.S.S. 70. Golf range. *Green Fees:* weekdays £20.00 per round, £30.00 per day; weekends £25.00 per round, £40.00 per day. *Eating facilities:* clubhouse open all day. *Visitors:* welcome at all times, no restrictions – advance booking advisable. Hotel; buggies, clubs for hire. *Society Meetings:* welcome – must book. Professional: Neil I.M. MacKintosh (0738 52784).

STRATHTAY. **Strathtay Golf Club,** Strathtay, by Pitlochry. *Location:* two miles west from Ballinluig on A9, four miles east from Aberfeldy. Wooded, mainly hilly course with beautiful panoramic views. 9 holes, 4082 yards. S.S.S. 63. *Green Fees:* £8.00 weekdays (Juniors £2.00); £10.00 weekends (Juniors £3.00). Five day ticket £25.00. *Eating facilities:* cafe and bar five minutes walk. *Visitors:* pre-teenagers MUST have adult supervision. NO visitors on Sundays 12.30pm to 5pm May to August. Open mixed foursomes every Tuesday evening April/October. New changing room, toilets. *Society Meetings:* must be arranged in advance. Secretary: J.B. Armstrong-Payne (0887 840367).

Renfrewshire

BARRHEAD. **Fereneze Golf Club,** Fereneze Avenue, Barrhead, Glasgow (041-881 1519). *Location:* nine miles south west of Glasgow. Parkland. 18 holes, 5962 yards. S.S.S. 69. *Green Fees:* on application. *Eating facilities:* lunches served at club except Mondays, order in advance. *Visitors:* welcome by arrangement. *Society Meetings:* welcome, bookings arranged in advance. Professional: Darren Robinson (041-880 7058). Secretary: A.D. Gourley C.A. (041-221 6394; Fax: 041-221 0135).

BISHOPTON. **Erskine Golf Club,** Bishopton PA7 5PH (0505 862302). *Location:* north of M8, leave M8 at Bridge Toll barrier and turn left along B815 for one mile approximately. Parkland course. 18 holes, 6298 yards. S.S.S. 70. Putting green and practice area. *Green Fees:* £20.00 per round, £30.00 per day ticket. *Eating facilities:* restaurant and bar, lunches, teas and dinners served at club. *Visitors:* welcome but must play with a member or be introduced. Professional: Peter Thomson. Secretary: T.A. McKillop.

Scotland RENFREWSHIRE

BRIDGE OF WEIR. **Old Course Ranfurly Golf Club Ltd,** Ranfurly Place, Bridge of Weir PA11 3DE (0505 613612). *Location:* five miles west of Glasgow Airport. Moorland course. 18 holes, 6089 yards. S.S.S. 69. *Green Fees:* weekdays £15.00 per round, £25.00 per day; weekends only if introduced by a member and playing with them. *Eating facilities:* restricted catering Mondays and Tuesdays. *Visitors:* welcome weekdays, should contact club beforehand. Must be members of recognised golf clubs with Handicap Certificates. *Society Meetings:* on written application only. Secretary: R. Mitchell (0505 613214).

BRIDGE OF WEIR. **Ranfurly Castle Golf Club Ltd,** Golf Road, Bridge of Weir PA11 3HN (0505 612609). *Location:* M8 from Glasgow exit Junction 29, A240 and A761 to Bridge of Weir. Moorland. 18 holes, 6284 yards. S.S.S. 70. Practice ground. *Green Fees:* weekdays £22.00 per round, £27.00 day ticket. *Eating facilities:* bar snacks all day; lunches, high teas, etc by arrangement. *Visitors:* welcome weekdays, at weekends only if accompanied by member. *Society Meetings:* catered for Tuesdays only. Professional: Alastair Forrow (0505 614795). Secretary: Mr J. Walker (0505 612609).

ELDERSLIE. **Elderslie Golf Club,** 63 Main Road, Elderslie PA5 9AZ (0505 22835). *Location:* off M8 at Linwood turn-off, continue to roundabout, follow Elderslie signs A737. Club on main road. Woodland course. 18 holes, 6031 yards. S.S.S. 69. Large practice area. *Green Fees:* £16.10 per round, £22.00 per day weekdays. *Eating facilities:* diningroom, bar and bar snacks. *Visitors:* welcome weekdays, no visitors weekends. *Society Meetings:* welcome weekdays, book through Secretary. Professional: (0505 20032). Secretary: Anne Anderson (0505 23956).

GOUROCK. **Gourock Golf Club,** Cowal View, Gourock (0475 31001). *Location:* two miles west of Gourock Station above Yacht Club. 18 holes, 6492 yards. S.S.S. 71. *Green Fees:* on application. *Eating facilities:* restaurant, full meals also bar snacks. *Visitors:* welcome with letter of introduction. *Society Meetings:* catered for on application. Professional: Robert M. Collinson. Secretary: C.M. Campbell.

GREENOCK. **Greenock Golf Club,** Forsyth Street, Greenock PA16 8RE (0475 20793). *Location:* one mile from town centre. Moorland course. 18 holes, 5835 yards. S.S.S. 68. *Green Fees:* £15.00 weekdays; £20.00 weekends. *Eating facilities:* available. *Visitors:* welcome weekdays, not Saturdays. *Society Meetings:* advance booking required. Professional: Graham Ross (0475 87236). Secretary: Eric J. Black (0475 26819).

GREENOCK. **Greenock Whinhill Golf Club,** Beith Road, Greenock (0475 24694). *Location:* 26 miles from Glasgow. Municipal course. 18 holes, 5454 yards. S.S.S. 68. *Green Fees:* information not provided. Secretary: D. McConnell.

JOHNSTONE. **Cochrane Castle Golf Club,** Craigston, Johnstone PA5 OHF (0505 22010). *Location:* A737 off Beith Road, Johnstone. Parkland course. 18 holes, 6226 yards. S.S.S. 70. Practice ground. *Green Fees:* weekdays £20.00 per day, £15.00 per round.

Eating facilities: full catering and bar snacks. *Visitors:* welcome weekdays, maximum 32 players. *Society Meetings:* catered for by arrangement, weekdays only. Professional: Stuart H. Campbell (0505 28465). Secretary: J.C. Cowan (0505 20146).

KILMACOLM. **Kilmacolm Golf Club,** Porterfield Road, Kilmacolm PA13 4PD (Kilmacolm (050 587) 2139). *Location:* A761. Moorland course. 18 holes, 5964 yards. S.S.S. 68. Practice area. *Green Fees:* £18.00 per round, £24.00 per day. *Eating facilities:* diningroom and bar. *Visitors:* welcome on weekdays. *Society Meetings:* catered for. Professional: D. Stewart (050 587 2695). Secretary: R.F. McDonald.

LANGBANK. **Gleddoch Golf and Country Club,** Langbank PA14 6YG (047554 304). *Location:* M8 west of Glasgow, past airport to Langbank, Langbank and Gleddoch House are both signposted. Moorland, woodland and parkland. 18 holes, 6332 yards. S.S.S. 71. Practice area, indoor driving bay and putting green. *Green Fees:* £25.00 day ticket. Hotel residents £12.50. *Eating facilities:* bar, lounge and restaurant open all day. *Visitors:* welcome all week. Gleddoch House Hotel, 33 bedrooms. *Society Meetings:* welcome weekdays only. Professional: Keith Campbell (047554 704). Secretary: David Tierney (047554 304).

LOCHWINNOCH. **Lochwinnoch Golf Club,** Burnfoot Road, Lochwinnoch PA12 4AN (0505 842153). *Location:* between Johnstone and Beith, off A737 on Largs road A760. Parkland, extremely scenic, set in quiet country village. 18 holes, 6202 yards. S.S.S. 70. Practice area. *Green Fees:* weekdays £20.00 per day. *Eating facilities:* licensed bar and catering, except Mondays. *Visitors:* no visitors weekends or Public Holidays. *Society Meetings:* welcome weekdays. Professional: Gerry Reilly (0505 843029). Secretary: Mrs Evelyn McBride.

PAISLEY. **Barshaw Golf Club,** Barshaw Park, Glasgow Road, Paisley (041-889 2908). *Location:* one mile from Paisley Cross travelling east towards Glasgow (Glasgow Road). Parkland course, flat/hilly. 18 holes, 5703 yards. S.S.S. 68. Putting green. *Green Fees:* £6.00; Senior Citizens and Juniors £3.00. Unemployed £3.00 (proof to be shown). *Eating facilities:* mobile van rear of clubhouse. *Visitors:* welcome anytime, must have a bag of clubs. *Society Meetings:* apply to Superintendent Parks Department (Leisure and Recreation). Secretary: W. Collins (041-884.2533).

PAISLEY. **Paisley Golf Club,** Braehead, Paisley PA2 8TZ (041-884 2292). *Location:* up Causeyside Street, Neilston Road, turn right into Glenburn, left at roundabout. Moorland – exposed course. 18 holes, 6220 yards. S.S.S. 70. Practice area. *Green Fees:* weekdays £16.00 per round, £24.00 per day. *Eating facilities:* bar snacks and full meals. *Visitors:* welcome by prior arrangement mid-week until 4pm. No Public Holidays or weekends. *Society Meetings:* catered for by prior arrangement. Professional: Grant Gilmour (041-884 4114). Secretary: W.J. Cunningham (041-884 3903).

PAISLEY. **Ralston Golf Club,** Strathmore Avenue, Ralston, Paisley PA1 3DT (041-882 1349). *Location:* two miles east of Paisley. *Green Fees:* information not provided. *Visitors:* welcome by introduction by members only. *Society Meetings:* catered for on application. Professional: John Scott (041-810 4925). Secretary: John W. Horne (041-883 7045).

PORT GLASGOW. **Port Glasgow Golf Club,** Devol Road, Port Glasgow PA14 5XE (0475 704181). *Location:* M8 to Newark Castle to roundabout, follow signs for Industrial Estate. Heathland. 18 holes, 5712 yards, 5224 metres. S.S.S. 68. *Green Fees:* weekdays £12.00 per round, £18.00 per day. *Eating facilities:* meals by arrangement. *Visitors:* welcome weekdays until 4pm, weekends must be introduced. *Society Meetings:* welcome weekdays. Secretary: N.L. Mitchell (0475 706273).

RENFREW. **Renfrew Golf Club,** Blythswood Estate, Inchinnan Road, Renfrew PA4 9EG (041-886 6692). *Location:* A8 Renfrew, turn in at Stakis Normandy Hotel. Flat parkland, wooded. 18 holes, 6818 yards, 6231 metres. S.S.S. 72. *Green Fees:* information not provided. *Eating facilities:* daily restaurant facilities and bar. *Visitors:* welcome on introduction by members. Visiting parties by arrangement. *Society Meetings:* catered for on Mondays, Tuesdays and Thursdays only by written application to Secretary. Professional: Mr David Grant (041-885 1754). Secretary: Alan Brockie.

UPLAWMOOR. **Caldwell Golf Club,** Uplawmoor, Glasgow G78 4AU (050585 329). *Location:* five miles south of Barrhead, Glasgow on A736 Irvine Road/A739. Parkland bounded by mature trees and a natural water hazard. 18 holes, 6046 yards, 5526 metres. S.S.S. 69. Practice area. *Green Fees:* £16.00 per round, £24.00 per day weekdays. *Eating facilities:* every day bar menu – filled rolls on Thursdays. *Visitors:* welcome weekdays only before 4.30pm, not weekends and Public Holidays (local and national). *Society Meetings:* weekdays only by prior arrangement. Professional: Stephen Forbes (Tel & Fax: 050585 616). Secretary: H.I.F. Harper (Tel & Fax: 050585 366).

Ross-shire

ALNESS. **Alness Golf Club,** Ardross Road, Alness (0349 883877). *Location:* on A9 ten miles north east of Dingwall. 9 holes, 2359 yards (twice round 4718 yards). S.S.S. 63. *Green Fees:* information not available. *Eating facilities;* licensed bar and snacks served. *Visitors:* welcome without reservation. *Society Meetings:* catered for if notice given. Secretary: J.G. Miller (0349 883877).

FEARN. **Tarbat Golf Club,** Tarbatness Road, Portmahomack, Fearn IV20 1YB (086 287 236). *Location:* 10 miles east of Tain. B9165 off A9. Seaside links course. 9 holes, 5054 yards. S.S.S. 65. Practice area. *Green Fees:* weekdays £5.00; weekends £6.00. £20.00 per week. *Eating facilities:* none, local hotels. *Visitors:* welcome without reservation, restrictions Saturdays. *Society Meetings:* welcome, please telephone Secretary. Secretary: D.C. Wilson (086 287 236; Fax: 0349 852131).

FORTROSE. **Fortrose and Rosemarkie Golf Club,** Ness Road East, Fortrose (Fortrose (0381) 20529). *Location:* on the Black Isle. A9 north from Inverness, across Kessock Bridge, through Munlochy, follow signs to Fortrose. Good links course, sea both sides. 18 holes, 5973 yards. S.S.S. 69. Practice area available Summer. *Green Fees:* weekdays £12.00 per round, £17.00 per day; weekends £17.00 per round. Five Day (Mon-Fri) £45.00; 10 Day (Mon-Fri) £70.00. Subject to review. *Eating facilities:* catering available. *Visitors:* welcome without reservation. *Society Meetings:* catered for. Professional: Graham Philp (0381 20733). Secretary: Mrs M. Collier.

GAIRLOCH. **Gairloch Golf Club,** Gairloch IV21 2BE (Gairloch (0445) 2407). *Location:* 75 miles west of Inverness on the A832. Seaside links, extensive views. 9 holes, 2093 yards, 1770 metres. S.S.S. 63 over 18 holes. *Green Fees:* daily £10.00, £5.00 per day for Senior Citizens and Juniors; £45.00 weekly. *Visitors:* welcome, no restrictions or reservations. Secretary: A. Shinkins (044 586 346).

THE ROYAL HOTEL

Friendly Highland Hotel with 10 bedrooms, 5 ensuite. Dining room, public and lounge bars and comfortable residents' lounge. Nearby are tennis courts, an excellent 18-hole golf course, sheltered beach and play area. 20 minutes from Inverness, ideal for touring the Highlands. Lots to do and see locally. Many other golf courses within easy reach.
ROYAL HOTEL, FORTROSE IV10 8SU. TELEPHONE: 0381 620536

Morangie House Hotel

Quite simply... a different place to stay or dine

MORANGIE ROAD · TAIN · ROSS-SHIRE · IV19 1PY
TEL: TAIN (0862) 892281

The Morangie House Hotel is only ten minutes from the famous Royal Dornoch Golf Club. Discounted green fees are available for residents wishing to play the excellent Tain Golf Course.

We offer quality Weekend Breaks and generous discounts for small parties.

Under the personal supervision of the proprietors at all times. 13 luxury bedrooms, all en suite with TV, radio, etc. Cuisine of the highest standard prepared by our award-winning chef. Restaurant open 7 days a week to non-residents.

Ashley Courtenay Award Winners
Les Routiers Recommended

INVERGORDON. **Invergordon Golf Club,** King George Street, Invergordon (0349 852715). *Location:* two miles from A9. 9 holes, 3000 yards. S.S.S. 69 over 18 holes. *Green Fees:* information not provided. *Eating facilities:* bar lunches. New clubhouse with bar facilities. Changing rooms with showers. *Visitors:* welcome without reservation. *Society Meetings:* catered for. Secretary: Bruce Gibson.

LOCHCARRON. **Lochcarron Golf Club,** Lochcarron, Wester Ross. *Location:* one mile east of Lochcarron village. Seaside links course – very interesting 2nd hole, a short course but great accuracy required. 9 holes, 1750 yards. S.S.S. 60. *Green Fees:* £5.00. *Eating facilities:* three hotels within two miles of course. *Visitors:* welcome anytime except Saturday afternoons (club matches). Secretary: G. Weighill (05202 257).

MUIR OF ORD. **The Muir of Ord Golf Club,** Great North Road, Muir of Ord IV6 7SX (0463 870825). *Location:* 15 miles north of Inverness beside A862, 12 miles north of Inverness on A9/A832. Heathland, moorland course, excellent greens. 18 holes, 5202 yards. S.S.S. 65 Medal. Practice area. *Green Fees:* October to March weekdays £12.00; weekends £15.00. Weekly tickets – six day £30.00. Monthly – seven days £100. *Eating facilities:* snacks, bar lunches; lounge and bar. *Visitors:* visiting parties welcome, weekends times by arrangement. *Society Meetings:* catered for. Professional: Mr G. Vivers (0463 871311). Secretary: Mr R. Ewart (Urray 333). Administrator: Mrs C. Moir (0463 870825).

STRATHPEFFER. **Strathpeffer Spa Golf Club,** Strathpeffer IV14 9AS (0997 421129). *Location:* 20 minutes north of Inverness by A9, 5 miles west of Dingwall, quarter of a mile north of Strathpeffer Square (signposted). Upland course, panoramic views of moorland and mountain. No bunkers but plenty of natural hazards. 18 holes, 4792 yards. S.S.S. 65. Small practice area. *Green Fees:* weekdays £10.00 per round, £15.00 per day; weekends £12.00 per round, £18.00 per day. *Eating facilities:* snacks, morning coffee, lunches, high teas (bookings required for high teas). Bar open seven days. *Visitors:* welcome without reservation, but check weekends and competition days. *Society Meetings:* catered for by arrangement. Secretary: Norman Roxburgh (0997 21396).

TAIN. **Tain Golf Club,** Chapel Road, Tain IV19 1PA (Tain (0862) 892314). *Location:* off A9, 38 miles north of Inverness. Travelling north, turn right in middle of High Street – Golf Club one mile. Parkland and seaside links. 18 holes, 6238 yards. S.S.S. 70. Practice putting green. *Green Fees:* weekdays £12.00 per round, £18.00 per two rounds; weekends £18.00 per round, £24.00 per two rounds. Special rates for parties over 10. *Eating facilities:* bar and catering. *Visitors:* welcome, depending on availability. *Society Meetings:* catered for. Professional: (0862 893313). Secretary: Mrs Kathleen Ross.

Roxburghshire

HAWICK. **Hawick Golf Club,** Vertish Hill, Hawick (0450 72293). *Location:* north along A7 from Carlisle for 40 miles or south on A7 from Edinburgh for 50 miles. Wooded parkland. 18 holes, 5929 yards. S.S.S. 69. Restricted practice area. *Green Fees:* weekdays £12.00 per round, £18.00 per day; weekends £18.00 per day only. Fees subject to review. *Eating facilities:* available all day. *Visitors:* welcome weekdays, weekends by arrangement. *Society Meetings:* catered for – contact Secretary. Hon. Secretary: Mr Jim Reilly (0450 75594).

HAWICK. **Minto Golf Club,** Denholm, Hawick TD9 8SH (Hawick (0450) 87220). *Location:* five miles north-east of Hawick leaving A698 at Denholm village. Parkland, trees, no bunkers. 18 holes, 5460 yards, 4992 metres. S.S.S. 68. Practice area. *Green Fees:* weekdays £12.00 per round, £18.00 per day; weekends £18.00 per round, £25.00 per day. Half price for under 18s. *Eating facilities:* new clubhouse with full facilities, catering. *Visitors:* welcome, with prior booking. *Society Meetings:* accepted with prior booking (weekends difficult). Secretary: Ian Todd.

ROXBURGHSHIRE Scotland

JEDBURGH. **Jedburgh Golf Club,** Dunion Road, Jedburgh, Roxburghshire TD8 6LA (0835 63587). *Location:* three quarters of a mile south of Jedburgh on the road to Hawick. Undulating, with young trees. 9 holes, 5555 yards. S.S.S. 67. *Green Fees:* £10.00. *Eating facilities:* bar from 7.30pm on May to September, meals Friday and weekend evenings. *Visitors:* welcome weekdays, weekends depending on competitions. *Society Meetings:* welcome, if notice given. Secretary: R. Strachan (0835 64175).

KELSO. **Kelso Golf Club,** Berrymoss, Kelso (0573 223009). *Location:* one mile north-east of town within Kelso Racecourse. Flat parkland. 18 holes, 6066 yards. S.S.S. 69. Practice ground. *Green Fees:* weekdays £12.00 per round, £18.00 per day; weekends £16.00 per round, £25.00 per day. *Eating facilities:* catering Wednesday to Sunday. *Visitors:* welcome without reservation. *Society Meetings:* welcome with reservation. Secretary: J.P. Payne (0573 223259).

MELROSE. **Melrose Golf Club,** Dingleton, Melrose (Melrose (089682) 2855). *Location:* A68 Edinburgh – Carlisle A7/Newcastle A68 roads. Wooded/sloping course. 9 holes, 5579 yards, 5098 metres. S.S.S. 68. Practice area. *Green Fees:* £12.00 per round/day.

Juniors half price. *Eating facilities:* by arrangement. *Visitors:* welcome anytime when no competitions taking place, Ladies Day Tuesdays. No visitor to tee off after 4pm April to October. Locker room, shower. *Society Meetings:* welcome by arrangement. Secretary: W.G. MacRae (089682 2391; Fax: 089682 2960).

NEWCASTLETON. **Newcastleton Golf Club,** Holm Hill, Newcastleton. *Location:* A7 Carlisle to Hawick road, Newcastleton is on B6357. Hilly course with splendid views. 9 holes, 5748 yards. S.S.S. 68. *Green Fees:* £6.00. *Eating facilities:* by arrangement. *Visitors:* welcome, no restrictions except competition days. *Society Meetings:* welcome. Secretary: F.J. Ewart (03873 75257).

ST. BOSWELLS. **St. Boswells Golf Club,** St. Boswells, Melrose TD6 0AT (0835 22359). *Location:* quarter of a mile off trunk route A68 at St. Boswells Green. Flat attractive scenery along the banks of the River Tweed. 9 holes, 5250 yards. S.S.S. 65. *Green Fees:* £10.00 (subject to review). *Visitors:* no visitors after 4pm on a weekday and when competitions are being held. Secretary: G.B. Ovens (0835 22359).

A choice of 14 courses before dinner — Tasty 4 courses for dinner!

On our 2, 3 or 5 night breaks you can try a fresh course everyday.
Afterwards you can enjoy a first rate dinner with our complimentary ½ bottle of wine..
At our friendly, family run hotel we make you genuinely welcome.

Cross Keys Hotel

Please ask for further details:
36 The Square, Kelso
Roxburghshire TD5 7HL
Tel: 0573 223303
Fax: 0573 225792

AA★★★
RAC★★★

Situated in the picturesque village of St. Boswells, this former coaching inn has 17 en-suite bedrooms, restaurant and lounge bar. The Borders can boast of 14 golf courses, all within a 12 mile radius of the hotel, including the 9 hole course in St. Boswells itself. Contact Louise Johnston or Sue Dodds for colour brochure and further information.

St. Boswells, Roxburghshire   Tel: (0835) 22243

RAILWAY HOTEL

Situated on the main A68 Newcastle/Edinburgh road in lovely Border countryside. Open seven days, meals available at all times. Breakfast, bar lunches, afternoon teas, high teas and supper. Live music every Saturday. Comfortable accommodation. Close to St. Boswells Golf Club, with a variety of other courses nearby.

Newton St. Boswells, Roxburghshire Telephone: (0835) 23797

Selkirkshire

ASHKIRK. **The Woll Golf Course,** The Woll Estate, Woll House, Ashkirk (0750 32222). *Location:* half a mile from the village of Ashkirk on the A7. Challenging course (opened in 1993) in natural parkland setting of outstanding beauty incorporating the Woll Burn; flat. 9 holes, 6446 yards. S.S.S. 71. Practice area. *Green Fees:* weekdays £7.00 per day; weekends £10.00. *Eating facilities:* none but pub and self catering accommodation in village. *Visitors:* welcome. Enquiries to: Ms C.I. Amos.

GALASHIELS. **Galashiels Golf Club,** Ladhope Recreation Ground, Galashiels TD1 2NJ (Galashiels (0896) 3724). *Location:* north end of town. quarter of a mile off A7 on Ladhope Drive. Parkland, hilly – municipal course. 18 holes, 5185 yards. S.S.S. 66. Practice area. *Green Fees:* weekdays £8.00 per round, £12.00 per day; weekends £12.00 per round, £16.00 per day. *Eating facilities:* catering, at weekends bar. *Visitors:* welcome without restriction. *Society Meetings:* catered for. Secretary: W.D. Millar (0750 21669).

GALASHIELS. **Torwoodlee Golf Club,** Edinburgh Road, Galashiels (Galashiels (0896) 2260). *Location:* leave Galashiels on A7 for Edinburgh. Entrance to course one mile on left. Parkland with wooded greens alongside river and splendid par 5. Designed by Braid. 9 holes, 5720 yards. S.S.S. 68. Extending to 18 holes during 1994. *Green Fees:* weekdays £10.00 per round, £14.00 per day; weekends £12.00 per round, £18.00 per day. *Eating facilities:* bar, dining room. *Visitors:* welcome without reservation. Restriction Saturday and Thurday after 1pm. Showers available. *Society Meetings:* catered for weekdays, booking required. Secretary: A. Wilson (089-682 2146).

SELKIRK. **Selkirk Golf Club,** The Hill, Selkirk (Selkirk (0750) 20621). *Location:* one mile south of Selkirk on A7 road. Undulating moorland with superb views. 9 holes, 5620 yards. S.S.S. 67. *Green Fees:* £10.00 per day (under review). *Eating facilities:* bar summer evenings and weekends. *Visitors:* ladies only Mondays 2pm onwards, members only weekends and from 5pm Fridays. *Society Meetings:* catered for by arrangement weekdays, meal arranged through Secretary. Secretary: R. Davies (0750 20427).

Stirlingshire

ABERFOYLE. **Aberfoyle Golf Club,** Braeval, Aberfoyle, By Stirling FK8 3UY (Aberfoyle (08772) 493). *Location:* A81 Glasgow – Stirling. Parkland. 18 holes, 5204 yards. S.S.S. 66. Practice facilities available. *Green Fees:* weekdays £12.00 per round, £16.00 per day; weekends £16.00 per round, £24.00 per day. *Eating facilities:* catering by arrangement. *Visitors:* welcome anytime but must not tee off before 10.30am at weekends. Secretary: R.D. Steele (08772 638).

DRYMEN. **Strathendrick Golf Club,** Glasgow Road, Drymen, Glasgow G63 (0360 40582). *Location:* one mile south of Drymen on Glasgow Road. Inland – hilly course. 9 holes, 4962 yards. S.S.S. 65. *Green Fees:* information not provided. *Visitors:* accompanied by a member welcome all week, restrictions on competition days. Secretary: Ronald H. Smith (0360 40582).

FALKIRK. **Bonnybridge Golf Club,** Larbert Road, Bonnybridge FK4 1NV (0324 812645). *Location:* five miles west of Falkirk. Parkland. 9 holes, 6060 yards. S.S.S. 69. Practice area. *Green Fees:* weekdays £8.00 per round. *Eating facilities:* catering by arrangement. *Visitors:* welcome with prior permission, no unaccompanied visitors. Secretary: C. Munn (0324 813694).

FALKIRK. **Falkirk Golf Club,** 136 Stirling Road, Camelon, Falkirk (Falkirk (0324) 611061). *Location:* one and a half miles west of town centre on A9. Parkland with streams. 18 holes, 6282 yards. S.S.S. 69. Large practice area. *Green Fees:* weekdays £10.00 per round, £20.00 per day; weekends £25.00 per day. *Eating facilities:* full catering and bar facilities. *Visitors:* welcome Monday to Friday up to 4.00pm unaccompanied, with member only at weekends. *Society Meetings:* weekdays except Wednesdays, Sundays after 10.30am. Make arrangements with Clubmaster. Secretary: John Elliott (0324 34118).

FALKIRK. **Polmont Golf Club,** Manvelrigg, Maddiston, Falkirk FK2 0LS (Polmont (0324) 711277). *Location:* first turn to the right past Fire Brigade HQ in Maddiston. Undulating course. 9 holes, 6603 yards. S.S.S. 70. *Green Fees:* weekdays £5.00 per round; Saturday £10.00 after 5pm, Sunday £10.00. *Eating facilities:* lunches and high teas. *Visitors:* welcome without reservation, no visitors after 5pm weekdays. *Society Meetings:* catered for. Secretary: Peter Lars.

LARBERT. **Falkirk Tryst Golf Club,** 86 Burnhead Road, Stenhousemuir, Larbert FK5 4BD (Larbert (0324) 562415). *Location:* three miles from Falkirk (M9), one mile from Larbert Station. Flat/seaside links style surface. 18 holes, 6053 yards, 5533 metres. S.S.S. 69. Practice area. *Green Fees:* weekdays £11.00 per round, £16.00 per day. *Eating facilities:* full catering – lunches, high teas, bar service. *Visitors:* welcome weekdays, not weekends. *Society Meetings:* catered for Mondays (except Bank Holidays), Tuesdays, Thursdays and Fridays only. Professional: Steven Dunsmore (0324 562091). Secretary: R.D. Wallace (0324 562054).

STIRLINGSHIRE Scotland

LARBERT. **Glenbervie Golf Club Ltd,** Stirling Road, Larbert FK5 4SJ (Larbert (0324) 562983). *Location:* one mile north of Larbert on A9 Falkirk to Stirling road. Parkland course. 18 holes, 6402 yards. S.S.S. 71. Two practice areas. *Green Fees:* £20.00 per round, £30.00 for day ticket. *Eating facilities:* lunches and high teas, bar snacks. *Visitors:* welcome weekdays only with reservation, letter of introduction. Weekends as members' guests only. *Society Meetings:* up to 40 competitors catered for, Tuesdays and Thursdays only. Professional: Mr John Chillas (0324 562725). Secretary: Mrs Mary Purves (0324 562605).

LENNOXTOWN. **Campsie Golf Club,** Crow Road, Lennoxtown, Glasgow G65 7HX (0360 310244). *Location:* on B822 out of Lennoxtown. Hillside course with panoramic views. 18 holes, 5517 yards, 5045 metres. S.S.S. 67. Practice fairway and putting green. *Green Fees:* weekdays £10.00 per round, £15.00 per day; weekends £12.50 per round. Reduced rates for pre-booked parties of over 12. *Eating facilities:* full catering available. *Visitors:* welcome, weekdays unrestricted, weekends by prior arrangement. *Society Meetings:* catered for. Professional: Mark Brennan (0360 310920). Secretary: J. M. Donaldson (0360 312249).

POLMONT. **Grangemouth Golf Club,** Polmont Hill, Polmont, Falkirk FK2 0YA (0324 711500). *Location:* quarter of a mile north of Junction 4 M9 motorway. Parkland course. 18 holes, 6314 yards. S.S.S. 71.

Practice area. *Green Fees:* £6.30 per round weekdays; £8.40 per round weekends. *Eating facilities:* catering and bar facilities available. *Visitors:* welcome, no restrictions. *Society Meetings:* welcome any day except Saturday. Professional: Stuart Campbell (0324 714355). Secretary: Iain Hutton (0324 712585).

STIRLING. **Bridge Of Allan Golf Club,** Sunnylaw, Bridge of Allan (Bridge of Allan (0786) 832432). *Location:* from Stirling, three miles, turn right at Bridge, keep taking the high road. Hilly course. 9 holes, 4932 yards, 4508 metres. S.S.S. 65. *Green Fees:* information not provided. *Eating facilities:* by arrangement, licensed bar. *Visitors:* welcome without reservation, no visitors on Saturdays. *Society Meetings:* catered for by arrangement. Secretary: A.M. Donoghue (0786 832007).

STIRLING. **Stirling Golf Club,** Queen's Road, Stirling FK8 2QY (Stirling (0786) 473801). *Location:* one mile from town centre, rail and bus stations; two miles from Junction 10 M9. Parkland (undulating) with superb views of mountains and castle. 18 holes, 6095 yards. S.S.S. 69. Practice area. *Green Fees:* on application. *Eating facilities:* full bar and dining facilities. *Visitors:* welcome except at weekends; casual visitors by arrangement with Pro Shop. *Society Meetings:* welcome by arrangement. Professional: Ian Collins (0786 471490). Secretary: W. McArthur (0786 464098).

RED LION HOTEL

Come and stay at this attractive hotel which has much to offer keen golfers. Set amidst the scenic countryside of Stirlingshire with its many golf courses, we are the ideal choice for anyone wanting an enjoyable break whilst playing their favourite sport. Good food all day at family prices.

2 Stirling Road, Larbert FK5 4AF.   Telephone: 0324 562886

SPECTACULAR SCENERY IN THE LOCH LOMOND, STIRLING & TROSSACHS AREA

40 GOLF COURSES IN 25 MILE RADIUS
ROMANTIC 700 YEAR OLD ANCESTRAL HOME OF CLAN GALBRAITH

CULCREUCH CASTLE

Fintry, Glasgow G63 0LW Tel: (036086) 228 Fax: (036086) 555

Hidden away in breathtaking 1600-acre parkland grounds with salmon river and two small coarse fishing lochs. Free fishing and boating for guests. Glasgow 19 miles, Stirling and motorway 17 miles, Edinburgh 55 miles.

· 8 en-suite bedrooms including four posters & family suite · Log fires
· Six foot thick walls · Battlements · 8 Scandinavian-style lodges for self-catering · Candlelit Evening Meals in the Panelled Dining Room
· Dungeons Bar · Baby Listening · Squash Courts & Indoor Bowling
· Colour Castle Brochure and Golfing Brochure available.

"MIA-ROO"
BED & BREAKFAST
Tel: **(0786) 473979**
37 Snowdon Place, Stirling FK8 2JP
Proprietors: Mr & Mrs I. L. Love

Within a 30-mile radius of over 25 courses and only five minutes from Stirling Golf Course, this family-owned Guest House is ideally placed for golfing holidays. Centrally situated for: EDINBURGH, GLASGOW, GLENEAGLES, ST. ANDREWS.

A warm welcome is assured.

Sutherland

BONAR BRIDGE. **Bonar Bridge-Ardgay Golf Club,** Market Stance, Migdale Road, Bonar Bridge. *Location:* off the A9, driving north cross Bonar Bridge, straight up hill for half a mile. Wooded heathland. 9 holes, 4626 yards. S.S.S. 63. *Green Fees:* £8.00 per day. Reduced rates for week/fortnight. *Eating facilities:* not available. *Visitors:* always welcome. *Society Meetings:* limited to weekdays. Joint Secretaries: A. Turner (054-982 248)/J. Reid (08632 750).

BRORA. **Brora Golf Club,** Golf Road, Brora KW9 6QS (0408 621417). *Location:* approximately 65 miles north of Inverness on the A9. Seaside links, 18 holes, 6110 yards. S.S.S. 69. Practice ground available. *Green Fees:* £15.00 per day, £65.00 per week. *Eating facilities:* lunches and snacks May to August. *Visitors:* welcome, only restriction on tournament days. Welcome to participate in opens with Certificate of Handicap. *Society Meetings:* catered for by arrangement. Secretary: H. Baillie (0408 621417).

DORNOCH. **Royal Dornoch Golf Club,** Golf Road, Dornoch (0862 810219; Fax: 0862 810792). *Location:* one mile from A9 to Wick. Seaside links. Championship course and Struie Course. Championship – 18 holes, 6581 yards. S.S.S. 72; Struie – 18 holes, 5221 yards. S.S.S. 68. Practice area. *Green Fees:* on request. *Eating facilities:* available. *Visitors:* welcome, no major restrictions other than competitions – bookings can be heavy. Handicap Certificates – men 24, women 35. *Society Meetings:* must be arranged through the Secretary. Professional: W.E. Skinner (0862 810902). Secretary/Manager: I.C.R. Walker (0862 810219).

DURNESS. **Durness Golf Club,** Balnakiel, Durness. *Location:* 57 miles north-west of Lairg on A838. Links course with final hole played over deep gully. 9 greens, 18 tees, 5545 yards. S.S.S 68. *Green Fees:* £8.00 per day. Weekly ticket £30.00. *Eating facilities:* snacks available 12-5pm June to September. *Visitors:* welcome without reservation, only restriction on Sunday Mornings. Course closed during lambing season (April 20th to May 14th approximately). *Society Meetings:* by arrangement. Secretary: Lucy MacKay (0971 511364).

DORNOCH CASTLE
DORNOCH, SUTHERLAND, IV25 3SD
Tel: **(0862) 810216** Fax: **(0862) 810981**   Commended

Only 5 minutes' walk from the famous Royal Dornoch Championship Course, this charming hotel has now one of the best restaurants in the area with a wine-list to match. Venison and Salmon (when in season) and other traditional Highland fare are regular features on the menu (recommended by "The Taste of Scotland"). Elegant lounges, character bar and sunny terrace overlooking the well-kept formal garden. Golf courses and lovely beaches within walking distance. Regular performances of the Dornoch Pipe Band in summer. Golf-Packages available. A member of "Scotland's Commended" Hotels.

Brochure & tariff (from £30.50 for Bed and Breakfast) from resident proprietor M. Ketchin.

CAPE WRATH HOTEL
DURNESS   Telephone: **(0971) 511212**   Fax: **(0971) 511313**

Cape Wrath Hotel enjoys an envied reputation for superb food. An extensive list of quality wines, a warm and friendly atmosphere and traditional Scottish hospitality.

Fishing: Salmon • Sea Trout • Brown Trout
Other activities: Golf • Bird Watching • Hill Walking, etc.

STAGS HEAD HOTEL

Golspie, Sutherland KW10 6TG. Telephone: GOLSPIE (0408) 633245

The Hotel has 5 bedrooms, all with ensuite facilities, colour TV, tea/coffee. Three bars, Restaurant, Function/Conference Hall. Minutes away from Golspie golf course and easy driving distance to Brora, Dornoch and Tain golf courses.

Colour Brochure and Prices on application.

Proprietors:
RONNIE & EILEEN SUTHERLAND

GOLSPIE. **Golspie Golf Club,** Ferry Road, Golspie KW10 6ST (Golspie (0408) 633266). *Location:* off A9 half a mile from Golspie. Fairly flat course, seaside links and wooded. 18 holes, 5836 yards. S.S.S. 68. Practice area available. *Green Fees:* £15.00 per day. *Eating facilities:* bar and catering service. *Visitors:* welcome, no restrictions except on competition days. *Society Meetings:* welcome by prior arrangement. Admin Secretary: Mrs Marie MacLeod.

HELMSDALE. **Helmsdale Golf Club,** Golf Road, Helmsdale KW8 6JA (04312 240). *Location:* on A9, 28 miles north of Dornoch. Parkland course. 9 holes, 1825 yards. S.S.S. 62 (2 x 9 holes). *Green Fees:* £3.00 per round, £5.00 per day. £15.00 weekly, £25.00 fortnightly. *Eating facilities:* local restaurants, bars. *Visitors:* welcome at all times. *Society Meetings:* welcome. Secretary: David Bishop (04312 339).

Wigtownshire

NEWTON STEWART. **Newton Stewart Golf Club,** Kirroughtree Avenue, Minnigaff, Newton Stewart DG8 6PF (0671 2172). *Location:* from South leave A75 at sign to Minnigaff village. Parkland, mainly flat, set in Galloway hills and with a forest backdrop. 19 holes, 5646 yards, 5160 metres, S.S.S. 69, Par 68. Additional 9 holes planned for 1994. *Green Fees:* weekdays £14.00; weekends and Bank Holidays £20.00 per day. *Eating facilities:* bar lounge, bar snacks and meals available. *Visitors:* welcome without restriction, but busy at weekends. *Society Meetings:* all welcome. Discounts available. Secretary: D.C. Matthewson (0671 3236).

NEWTON STEWART. **Wigtownshire County Golf Club,** Mains of Park, Glenluce, Newton Stewart DG8 0NN (Glenluce (05813) 420). *Location:* A75 two miles west Glenluce, eight miles east Stranraer. Seaside links.

18 holes, 5723 yards. S.S.S. 68. Practice ground. *Green Fees:* weekdays £12.00 per round, £16.00 per day; weekends £14.00 per round, £18.00 per day. *Eating facilities:* available all year round. *Visitors:* unrestricted except Wednesday evenings. *Society Meetings:* catered for. Secretary: R. McCubbin (05813 589).

PORT WILLIAM. **St. Medan Golf Club,** Monreith, Newton Stewart DG8 8NJ (09887-358). *Location:* on A747, four miles south of Port William. Seaside links course with panoramic views of Mull of Galloway and Isle of Man. 9 holes, 4552 yards. S.S.S. 62. *Green Fees:* 9 holes £6.00, £10.00 per day. £40.00 per week. *Eating facilities:* full catering and all day licence available April to October. *Visitors:* welcome, restrictions only during competitions. *Society Meetings:* welcome, please telephone the Secretary. Secretary: D. O'Neill (0988 500555).

SHENNANTON HOUSE

A grand country mansion set in a 2000 acre private estate, near to around 20 golf courses and with four par 3 golf holes in the grounds.

We also have a billiard room with a full sized antique snooker table. We offer free private river and loch fishing.

Shennanton has superb bedroom suites, many with en-suite jacuzzi baths.

We have excellent self catering accommodation suitable for family or sporting groups, or we can provide maid and meal service.

For brochure and reservations please phone (0671) 830494.

Kirkcowan, Near Newton Stewart, Wigtownshire, Scotland DG8 0EG
Tel: (0671) 830494 Fax: (0671) 830445
STB ♛♛♛♛ Deluxe
TERMS FROM AS LITTLE AS £19pp PER NIGHT

PORTPATRICK. **Portpatrick (Dunskey) Golf Club,** Golf Course Road, Portpatrick DG9 8TB (Portpatrick (0776 81273). *Location:* A75 or A77 to Stranraer then A77 to Portpatrick, fork right at War Memorial, then signposted on right. Cliff top links-type course. 18 holes, 5771 yards. S.S.S. 68. Also short 9 hole course, 1504 yards. S.S.S. 27. Practice ground. *Green Fees:* 18 hole course – weekdays £13.00 per round, £20.00 per day; weekends £16.00 per round, £24.00 per day. 9 hole course – £5.00 per round (18 tees), £10.00 per day. *Eating facilities:* full meals all week mid-March to mid-October. *Visitors:* prior booking essential. Handicap Certificate required for 18 hole course. *Society Meetings:* catered for by prior arrangement. Hon Secretary: J.A. Horberry (0776 81273).

STRANRAER. **Stranraer Golf Club,** Low Creachmore, Leswalt, Stranraer DG9 0LF (0776 87245). *Location:* three miles from Stranraer on the Kirkcolm Road (A718). Parkland, seaside – the last course James Braid designed before he died. 18 holes, 6308 yards. S.S.S. 71. 9 hole putting green. *Green Fees:* weekdays £15.75 per round, £21.00 per day; weekends £21.00 per round, £26.00 per day. Fees subject to review. *Eating facilities:* meals available, order in advance. *Visitors:* welcome, please contact the Starter at golf club or the Steward. *Society Meetings:* catered for. Secretary: W.I. Wilson C.A. (0776 3539).

WIGTOWN. **Wigtown and Bladnoch Golf Club,** Wigtown (09884 3354). *Location:* 200 yards from square in Wigtown. Parkland course. 9 holes, 5400 yards. S.S.S. 67. Green Fees: weekdays £7.00; Sundays £10.00. *Eating facilities:* bar only. *Visitors:* welcome any time. *Society Meetings:* welcome by arrangement. Secretary: L. Duxbury (098 84 273).

Scottish Islands

ARRAN

BLACKWATERFOOT. **Shiskine Golf and Tennis Club,** Blackwaterfoot, Shiskine. *Location:* off B880 at Blackwaterfoot. Seaside links with only Par 5 on island. 12 holes, 2990 yards. S.S.S. 42. Putting green, nets. *Green Fees:* £8.00 per round, £10.00 per day except July and August. *Eating facilities:* teas, lunches (no bar). *Visitors:* welcome, preferably with Club Handicap. Tennis and bowls. Shop open Easter – October. *Society Meetings:* on application, preferably with Handicap. Match Secretary: Joe Faulkner (0770 860392). Secretary: Fiona Crawford (0770 860293).

BRODICK. **Brodick Golf Club,** Brodick (Brodick (0770) 302349). *Location:* one mile north of pier. Flat seaside course. 18 holes, 4404 yards. S.S.S. 62. Practice area. *Green Fees:* weekdays £8.00 per round, £11.00 per day; weekends £9.00 per round, £12.00 per day. Subject to review. *Eating facilities:* bar snacks available. *Visitors:* welcome without restriction. *Society Meetings:* welcome with reservation by letter. Professional: P.S. McCalla (0770 302513). Secretary: H.M. Macrae (0770 302181).

CORRIE. **Corrie Golf Club,** Sannox, Corrie KA27 8JD (0770 810223). *Location:* seven miles north of Brodick. Hilly course. 9 holes, 1948 yards. S.S.S. 61. *Green Fees:* £6.00 daily. *Eating facilities:* meals available March to October. *Visitors:* very welcome except Saturday afternoon. *Society Meetings:* catered for by arrangement. Secretary: Robert Stevenson (0770 810268).

LAMLASH. **Lamlash Golf Club,** Lamlash KA27 8JU (Lamlash (0770) 600296). *Location:* A841 three miles south of Brodick Pier ferry terminal. Undulating heathland course. 18 holes, 4611 yards. S.S.S. 63. *Green Fees:* weekdays £8.00 per day, Senior Citizens £6.00 anytime. Rates subject to review. *Eating facilities:* tearoom, clubhouse bar. *Visitors:* welcome, no restrictions. *Society Meetings:* catered for. Secretary: J. Henderson (0770 600272).

Blackwaterfoot Hotel
Blackwaterfoot, Isle of Arran Tel: Shiskine (0770) 860202

This spacious, family-run hotel is situated just 50 yards from the harbour at Blackwaterfoot and only five minutes' stroll from the Blackwaterfoot/Shiskine Golf Course. Providing a warm, welcoming home from home, the hotel has 10 bedrooms, seven of which are ensuite and have hot drink making facilities, central heating and colour TV. Licensed Restaurant.
Brochure available from Proprietors John and Veronica Fowler

SCOTTISH ISLANDS *Scotland*

LOCHRANZA. **Lochranza Golf,** Isle of Arran KA27 8HL (Tel & Fax: 0770 830273). *Location:* at north end of Island of Arran in Lochranza village. Challenging course in spectacular setting. 18 holes, 5454 yards, 5033 metres. S.S.S. 70. *Green Fees:* £7.00. *Eating facilities:* tearoom, meals and snacks. Home cooking. *Visitors:* welcome daily 8th May to 30th September. Golf packages can be arranged throughout the summer. Caravans to let on adjacent site. *Society Meetings:* catered for by arrangement, short notice if necessary. Secretary: I.M. Robertson.

MACHRIE. **Machrie Bay Golf Club,** Machrie, Near Brodick KA27 8HP (077-085 261). *Location:* on A841, three and a half miles north from Blackwaterfoot. Flat seaside course. 9 holes, 2082 yards. S.S.S. 32. *Green Fees:* £5.00 per round/day. *Eating facilities:* available Summer season. Tennis court. *Visitors:* welcome, no restriction except on club competition days. *Society Meetings:* can be arranged if pre-booked. Secretary: A.M. Blair (077-085 261).

WHITING BAY. **Whiting Bay Golf Club,** Golf Course Road, Whiting Bay, Brodick (0770 700487). *Location:* through Whiting village, turn right at signpost. Undulating parkland. 18 holes, 4405 yards. S.S.S. 63. *Green Fees:* £6.00 per round; weekends (Friday to Sunday) £17.50. 10% discount for parties of 10 or over. *Eating facilities:* catering and bar. *Visitors:* welcome anytime. Clubhouse, shower, snooker and pool rooms. *Society Meetings:* by prior booking. Secretary: Irene l'Anson (0770 700307).

BUTE

ISLE OF BUTE. **Bute Golf Club,** West Shore Sands, Stravanan, Kingarth. *Location:* 8 miles from Rothesay on the A845, situated on shores of Stravanan Bay. Flat seaside links in beautiful setting. 9 holes, 2497 yards, 2284 metres. S.S.S. 64 (18 holes). *Green Fees:* £5.00 adults, £1.00 Juniors. *Visitors:* welcome any day, Saturdays after 12.30pm. *Society Meetings:* catered for by arrangement. Secretary: J.M. Burnside (070 083 648).

THE GOLF GUIDE 1994

ROTHESAY. **Port Bannatyne Golf Club,** Bannatyne Mains Road, Port Bannatyne. *Location:* two miles north of Rothesay (ferry terminal). Hill course overlooking bays and sea lochs. 13 holes, 4730 yards. S.S.S. 63. *Green Fees:* £7.50 per day, weekly £30.00, 14-day £50.00. *Eating facilities:* in village, quarter-of-a-mile from course. *Visitors:* welcome – almost unrestricted. *Society Meetings:* very welcome. Secretary: Iain L. MacLeod (0700 502009).

ROTHESAY. **Rothesay Golf Club,** Canada Hill, Rothesay PA20 (0700 502244). *Location:* island in the Firth of Clyde, ferry terminal Wemyss Bay, 35 miles south west of Glasgow. One of Scotland's most scenic island courses, designed by James Braid and Ben Sayers. 18 holes, 5370 yards. S.S.S. 67. Practice area. *Green Fees:* on application to Professional. *Eating facilities:* full facilities at clubhouse. *Visitors:* very welcome, but at weekends by prior booking through Professional. *Society Meetings:* welcome by arrangement. PGA Professional: James M. Dougal (0700 503554). Secretary: John Barker (0700 503744).

COLONSAY

ISLE OF COLONSAY. **Colonsay Golf Club,** Isle of Colonsay PA61 7YP. *Location:* two miles west of pier. Traditional links course, reputedly 200 years old. 18 holes, 4775 yards. *Green Fees:* information not available. *Eating facilities:* none. *Visitors:* always welcome. Secretary: Kevin Byrne (09512 316).

CUMBRAE

MILLPORT. **Millport Golf Club,** Golf Road, Millport (Millport (0475) 530311). *Location:* Caledonian McBrayne car ferry Largs slip to Cumbrae slip (seven minutes). On hill overlooking Firth of Clyde over Bute and Arran to Mull of Kintyre. 18 holes, 5831 yards. S.S.S. 68. Large practice area. *Green Fees:* weekdays £11.00 per round, £15.00 per day; weekends and Bank Holidays £15.00 per round, £20.00 per day. *Eating facilities:* full catering facilities. *Visitors:* welcome without reservation. Tee reservations available for parties. Well stocked Professional's shop, tuition available. Starter's telephone (0475 530305). *Society Meetings:* catered for. Special open amateur competition, Cumbrae Cup. Secretary: W.D. Patrick C.A. (0475 530308).

If you are writing, a stamped, addressed envelope is always appreciated.

Scotland SCOTTISH ISLANDS

ISLE OF GIGHA

ISLE OF GIGHA. **Gigha Golf Club.** 9-hole scenic course on this peaceful and picturesque island served by ferry from Tayinloan on the Kintyre Peninsula of south-west Argyll. Secretary: Mr M. Tart (05835 287).

ISLAY

PORT ELLEN. **Machrie Golf Club,** The Machrie Hotel and Golf Links, Port Ellen PA42 7AN (0496 2310; Golfax: 0496 2404). *Location:* adjacent Airport. Classic links. 18 holes, 6226 yards. S.S.S. 70. *Green Fees:* information not provided. *Eating facilities:* full service in hotel. *Visitors:* welcome any day without reservation. *Society Meetings:* any number catered for. Golf packages available. Secretary: M.R. MacPherson. Proprietor: Murdo MacPherson.

LEWIS

STORNOWAY. **Stornoway Golf Club,** Lady Lever Park, Stornoway, Isle of Lewis (0851 70 2240). *Location:* close proximity to town of Stornoway, in grounds of Lewis Castle. Inland course, hilly parkland, scenic. 18 holes, 5178 yards. S.S.S. 66. *Green Fees:* £10.00 per day. Weekly tickets £30.00; fortnightly ticket £50.00. Subject to alteration. *Eating facilities:* available. *Visitors:* welcome except Wednesday evenings and weekends. Car ferry daily (except Sunday) from Ullapool. British Airways service daily (except Sunday) from Glasgow and Inverness. *Society Meetings:* welcome, book through Secretary. Secretary: Mr J.D.F. Watson.

MULL

ISLE OF MULL. **Craignure Golf Club,** Scallastle, Craignure (Craignure (06802) 370). *Location:* one mile from ferry terminal at Craignure. Seaside links. 9 holes, 2218 metres. S.S.S. 64. *Green Fees:* £6.00. *Eating facilities:* not available. *Visitors:* always welcome, no restrictions except on competition days which are usually Sundays. Hon. Secretary: Sheila M. Campbell (06802 370).

TOBERMORY. **Tobermory Golf Club,** Tobermory PA75 6PE. *Location:* situated on the cliffs above the town to the north west. Panoramic views of Sound of Mull; testing terrain, not suitable for trolleys. 9 holes, 4921 yards, 4362 metres. S.S.S. 64. *Green Fees:* £9.00 per day, £30.00 per week. *Eating facilities:* none available. *Visitors:* unrestricted except for some competition days. *Society Meetings:* welcome. Secretary: Dr W.H. Clegg (0688 2013 or 2020).

ORKNEYS

KIRKWALL. **Orkney Golf Club Ltd,** Grainbank, Kirkwall (0856 872457). *Location:* half-a-mile west of Kirkwall. Parkland with good views over Kirkwall Bay and North Isles. 18 holes, 5406 yards. S.S.S. 68. Practice area. *Green Fees:* £10.00 per day. Weekly £35.00, fortnightly £50.00. *Eating facilities:* available at new clubhouse. *Visitors:* welcome at all times, restrictions only during competitions. *Society Meetings:* welcome, booking avoids clashing with competitions. Secretary: L. Howard.

The Isle of Gigha Hotel

Relax and unwind in the tranquil atmosphere of Gigha – the fairest Isle in the Hebrides. Now under new management, **Gigha Hotel** offers you a delightful stay, excellent international cuisine and a warm Island welcome.
Sample the **Gigha Golf Club** nine hole course, scene of many an island tournament. Take a break between holes to admire the magnificent views. For a more leisurely pace of life, stroll along our sandy beaches, or visit the legendary gardens of Achamore.

We look forward to welcoming you.

For reservations please call: (05835) 254

Gigha is only 20 minutes away from the mainland by car ferry from Tayinloan.

SCOTTISH ISLANDS *Scotland*

STROMNESS. **Stromness Golf Club Ltd,** Ness, Stromness (0856 850772). *Location:* on the outskirts of Stromness. Parkland/seaside links course. 18 holes, 4762 yards. S.S.S 64. *Green Fees:* £8.00 per day. £30.00 weekly ticket. *Eating facilities:* bar; hotels nearby. *Visitors:* welcome, no restrictions. *Society Meetings:* by arrangement through Secretary. Secretary: F.J. Groundwater (0856 850622).

WESTRAY. **Westray Golf Club,** Westray, Orkney Islands. *Location:* near Pierowall Village, Westray, Orkney. Seaside links course. 9 holes. *Green Fees:* £3.00 per day, Juniors £1.50; £15.00 per week, Juniors £7.50. *Visitors:* welcome anytime. Captain: Mr Stephen Hagan (08577 226). Secretary: Mr Michael Harcus (08577 516).

SHETLAND

LERWICK. **Shetland Golf Club,** PO Box 18, Lerwick (0595 84369). *Location:* four miles north of Lerwick on main road. Hilly, undulating course. Excellent greens. 18 holes, 5776 yards. S.S.S 70. *Green Fees:* £8.00. *Eating facilities:* bar snacks. *Visitors:* welcome, no restrictions except on days of open competitions. *Society Meetings:* arrange through Secretary. Secretary: D.C. Gray (0595 2691).

SKYE

SCONSER. **Isle of Skye Golf Club,** Sconser. *Location:* 20 miles from ferry on road to Portree. Seaside course with spectacular views. 9 holes (18 tees), 4798 yards, 4385 metres. S.S.S. 63. *Green Fees:* £7.00 per day. *Visitors:* no restrictions. Changing and toilet facilities. Secretary: I. Stephen (0478 2000).

SKEABOST BRIDGE. **Skeabost Golf Club,** Skeabost House Hotel, Skeabost Bridge IV51 9NP (047032 202; Fax: 047032 454). *Location:* A850 Portree to Dunvegan Road. Wooded course. 9 holes, 3335 yards. S.S.S. 58 (for 18 holes). *Green Fees:* weekdays £6.00. Free play to hotel residents staying three or more days. *Eating facilities:* buffet lunch, evening meals in hotel; bar food in public bar. *Visitors:* welcome, under 13's must be accompanied by an adult. *Society Meetings:* accepted. Club Captain: J.R. Stuart. Secretary: D.J. Matheson (047032 360).

SOUTH UIST

LOCHBOISDALE. **Askernish Golf Club,** Askernish, Lochboisdale. *Location:* three miles from Lochboisdale ferry terminal. Seaside links, designed by Tom Morris Senior 1891. 9 holes, 5042 yards. S.S.S. 68. *Green Fees:* £3.50. *Eating facilities:* local hotels. *Visitors:* welcome. Secretary: A.L. MacDonald (08784 541).

TIREE

SCARINISH. **Vaul Golf Club,** Scarinish, Isle of Tiree PA77 6XH. *Location:* two miles from Scarinish and half a mile from Lodge Hotel, ferry from Oban four hours and plane from Glasgow 45 minutes. Links course with crystal white beaches to north and south. 9 holes, 5822 yards (18 holes). S.S.S. 70 (18 holes). *Green Fees:* £4.00 daily. *Eating facilities:* at the Lodge Hotel. *Visitors:* welcome, no restrictions, no Sunday golf. *Society Meetings:* catered for, arrangement with Lodge Hotel. Secretary: N.J. MacArthur (0879 2339).

Golf in Wales
WHERE TO PLAY • WHERE TO STAY

THE OLDEST golf course in Wales is Tenby, founded in 1888 and now part of the Pembrokeshire Coast National Park. All but the last four holes at "The Burrows" as it is known, are in the links tradition. From the 15th inward the holes are on the other side of a railway line and more parkland in nature. Both the 17th and 18th have elevated tees giving superb views.

For any golf visitor to Wales Ashburnham is a must. It is situated at Pembrey – five miles west of the famous rugby town of Llanelli. The course is a tough one especially when the wind is blowing but it can be enjoyed not only by the low handicap players but also by golfers of a more modest standard. Ashburnham is long – some 7016 yards – and has a standard scratch score of 74.

Golfing at Royal St. David's, Harlech.

With the bunkers strategically placed around the course accuracy is of paramount importance.

Along the Bristol Channel, the courses are legend. Southerndown, Royal Porthcawl, Pyle and Kenfig, The Glamorganshire (five miles from Cardiff) plus a host of others not quite so well known but all offering challenges in differing ways.

Two miles on the Welsh side of the Severn Bridge St. Pierre, as every golfer will know, has been the venue for many top professional tournaments with Seve Ballesteros and Bernhard Langer being visitors. There are two courses – the old and the new – both picturesque and tree-lined with some hidden hazards for the unsuspecting and the wayward.

If you want a short break in Wales with activities other than golf also available you could do no better than book in at the delightful St. Pierre Golf and Country Club.

Inland and almost in the centre of Wales between the rolling hills of Plynlimon and the sprawling Radnor Forest lies the Victorian Spa Town of Llandrindod Wells. Here lies a golf course, carpeted with springy mountain turf begging the ball to be given a resounding clout.

Royal Porthcawl and Royal St. David's, Harlech, are the two courses that enter the conversation at a very early stage when one is discussing Welsh golf outside of Wales. Between them they have hosted dozens of championships over the years – both Welsh and British – and are undoubtedly two of the finest links courses in the country.

Royal St. David's is a quite delightful course, full of natural hazards used to full advantage in the original design. It is not long by championship standards, just 6,496 yards, but it is one of those rare links, where the par is three shots less than the standard scratch.

Twenty or so miles further south, a mile north of the town of Dolgellau is a real family golf course. It is quite short, just a 2,310 yard nine holes, set in undulating parkland and absolutely ideal for the middle to high handicap golfer.

More serious golf is played even further down the coast at the truly beautiful championship links at Aberdovey at the mouth of the Dovey Estuary. There are some fine holes, particularly the 3rd, the short 12th and the 15th. Its standing among the golfing fraternity is such that those who have discovered its charm make an annual pilgrimage to enjoy the course and the club hospitality.

Before leaving North Wales, mention must be made of Criccieth, the hilly course on the Lleyn Peninsula not far from Porthmadog offering gorgeous views over the bay. There is also a popular seaside course at Porthmadog itself. Out on the Lleyn Peninsula, the yachting resort of Abersoch has a seaside nine hole course ideal for the social golfer and nearby Pwllheli and Nefyn both welcome visitors to their eighteen hole coastal courses.

The Isle of Anglesey has four private golf courses, all adjacent to the coast at Rhosneigr, Bull Bay, Baron Hill and Holyhead as well as a nine hole public course at Llangefni.

Interested in Holidays in Wales?

You'll find hundreds of different holiday accommodation contacts in such other FHG Publications titles as *Farm Holiday Guide England & Wales, Bed & Breakfast Stops, Self-Catering & Furnished Holidays* and our *Guide to Caravan & Camping Holidays*. All available from bookshops and larger newsagents or from the Publisher in case of difficulty. Our Order Form is at the back of this book.

Clwyd

ABERGELE. **Abergele and Pensarn Golf Club,** Tan-y-Gopa Road, Abergele LL22 8DS (Abergele (0745) 824034). *Location:* below Gwrych Castle, Abergele. Parkland in scenic setting. 18 holes, 6520 yards, 5961 metres. S.S.S. 71. Practice area. *Green Fees:* £22.00 weekdays; £27.00 weekends. *Eating facilities:* full catering facilities except Mondays, two bars. *Visitors:* welcome weekdays, Bank Holidays and weekends with official club Handicap. *Society Meetings:* catered for, by arrangement with Secretary. Professional: I. Runcie (0745 823813). Secretary: Edgar Richards.

COLWYN. **Old Colwyn Golf Club,** The Clubhouse, Woodland Avenue, Old Colwyn LL29 9NL (Colwyn Bay (0492) 515581). *Location:* signposted at main Abergele road, Old Colwyn. Parkland. 9 holes (x 2), 5268 yards. S.S.S. 66. Practice area. *Green Fees:* information not provided. *Eating facilities:* bar and meals by arrangement. *Visitors:* welcome except Saturday afternoons or Wednesday evenings. *Society Meetings:* welcome by arrangement with Secretary. Secretary: D. Jones.

DENBIGH. **Denbigh Golf Club,** Henllan Road, Denbigh LL16 5AA (Denbigh (0745) 813888). *Location:* one mile from Denbigh town centre on the B5382 road. Parkland with excellent views. 18 holes, 5582 yards. S.S.S. 67. *Green Fees:* weekdays £15.00 per round, £18.00 per day; weekends and Bank Holidays £20.00 per round, £24.00 per day. *Eating facilities:* catering daily, bar. *Visitors:* welcome, no restrictions except Thursdays/Saturdays after 10.30am. *Society Meetings:* by arrangement. Professional: M.D. Jones (0745 814159). Secretary: G.C. Parry (0745 816669).

DENBIGH near. **Bryn Morfydd Hotel Golf Club,** Llanrhaeadr, Near Denbigh LL16 4NP (0745 78280; Fax: 0745 78488). *Location:* south off A525 between Denbigh and Ruthin. Peter Allis designed mature parkland course overlooking the Vale of Clwyd. Two courses. The Duchess Course – 9 holes, 1146 yards. Par 27; The Duke's Course – 18 holes, 5144 yards. S.S.S. 65, Par 70. Practice area. *Green Fees:* for 18 holes £8.00 weekdays, £9.00 weekends. *Eating facilities:* courses attached to Country House Hotel, two restaurants and two bars. *Visitors:* welcome all year. Home of British School of Golf. Hotel accommodation – 30 rooms en-suite, outdoor swimming pool. *Society Meetings:* welcome by arrangement all year. Professional: Nigel H. Lloyd. Secretary/Director of Golf: C.S. Henderson. Proprietor: D. Muirhead.

FLINT. **Flint Golf Club,** Cornist Park, Flint CH6 5HJ (0352 732327). *Location:* A548 coast road, one mile from town centre. Hilly parkland. 9 holes, 5927 yards. S.S.S. 69. Practice area. *Green Fees:* weekdays £12.00 per day; weekends with member. Special rate for golf parties numbering 12 or more. *Eating facilities:* bar; snacks and evening meals by arrangement. *Visitors:* welcome weekdays (no restrictions), weekends with member only. *Society Meetings;* welcome by arrangement. Secretary: A. Ryland (0352 733995).

HAWARDEN. **Hawarden Golf Club,** Groomsdale Lane, Hawarden, Deeside CH5 3EH (Hawarden (0244) 531447). *Location:* A55, first left at Hawarden Station going west. Undulating parkland. 9 holes, 5630 yards, 5200 metres. S.S.S. 67. *Green Fees:* weekdays £15.00. *Eating facilities:* full catering available. *Visitors:* weekdays by appointment with Secretary, otherwise must be playing with a member. *Society Meetings:* catered for by arrangement with Secretary. Professional: A. Davies. Secretary: T. Hinks-Edwards.

HOLYWELL. **Holywell Golf Club,** Brynford, Near Holywell CH8 8LQ (0352 713937). *Location:* turn off A55 at Springfield Hotel onto A5206, turn at traffic lights, up hill for one and a half miles, turn right at crossroads. Flat natural terrain, links type course. 18 holes, 6005 yards. S.S.S. 69. Par 70. *Green Fees:* weekdays £13.00; weekends and Bank Holidays £20.00. *Eating facilities:* full bar facilities and catering on request. *Visitors:* welcome weekdays without reservation; Bank Holidays and weekends by prior arrangement with Secretary. Snooker table. *Society Meetings:* by prior arrangement with Secretary. Professional: Martin Carty (0352 710040). Secretary: E.K. Carney (0352 713937).

WALES TOURIST BOARD — COMMENDED

Monksweir Hotel

ON THE BORDER OF CLYWD & GWYNEDD, RHOS-ON-SEA

Delightfully positioned. Warm welcome assured. Special Golfing Offers out of holiday season. Rooms mostly ensuite, with colour TV, tea/coffee facilities. Table licence. Self contained flat on second floor. Contact Paul or Ann Townley for brochure/tariff.
66 Colwyn Avenue, Rhos-on-Sea, Clywd, North Wales LL28 4NN. Tel: (0492) 549420

CLWYD *Wales* THE GOLF GUIDE 1994

LLANGOLLEN. **Vale of Llangollen Golf Club**, The Clubhouse, Llangollen (Llangollen (0978) 860613). *Location:* one mile east of town on the A5. 18 holes, S.S.S. 72. *Green Fees:* on application. *Eating facilities:* full catering service. *Visitors:* welcome. *Society Meetings:* welcome. Professional: D.I. Vaughan (0978 860040). Secretary: T.F. Ellis (0978 860040).

MOLD. **Mold Golf Club**, Cilcian Road, Pantymwyn, Mold CH7 1LW (Mold (0352) 740318). *Location:* three miles from Mold. Undulating course. 18 holes, 5548 yards. S.S.S. 67. Practice ground. *Green Fees:* weekdays £16.00; weekends and Bank Holidays £21.00. *Eating facilities:* bar and diningroom. *Visitors:* welcome at all times subject to tee availability. *Society Meetings:* written application. Professional: Martin Carty (0352 740318) (Lessons by appointment). Secretary: A. Newall (0352 741513).

MOLD. **Padeswood and Buckley Golf Club**, The Caia, Station Lane, Padeswood, Mold CH7 4JD (0244 550537). *Location:* A5118, near Castle Cement Works – one mile. Flat, parkland. 18 holes, 5823 yards. S.S.S. 68. *Green Fees:* weekdays £20.00 for 18 holes, £25.00 for 27 holes; Saturdays and Bank Holidays £25.00. *Eating facilities:* by arrangement with Caterer (0244 550537). *Visitors:* welcome except on Sundays. *Society Meetings:* welcome, enquiries through Secretary. Professional: David Ashton (0244 543636). Secretary: J.G. Peters (0244 550537).

PADESWOOD. **Old Padeswood Golf Club Ltd**, Station Road, Padeswood, Near Mold CH7 4JL (Buckley (0244) 547401). *Location:* off A5118 Chester to Mold road, eight miles from Chester and three miles from Mold. Situated in the beautiful Alyn Valley – nine holes flat parkland, nine holes slightly undulating. 18 holes, 6668 yards, 6079 metres. S.S.S. 72/Ladies 73. Par 3 9 hole course. 968 yards. Practice ground. *Green Fees:* weekdays £16.00 per round; weekends £20.00 per round. Par 3 weekdays £2.00; weekends £3.00. *Eating facilities:* diningroom, bar meals – two bars. *Visitors:* welcome anytime subject to tee availability. *Society Meetings:* welcome, written applications to Co. Secretary. Professional: Tony Davies (0244 547401). Co Secretary: B. Jones (0244 550414). Club Secretary: B. Hellen (0352 770506).

PRESTATYN. **Prestatyn Golf Club**, Marine Road East, Prestatyn LL19 7HS (0745 854320). *Location:* A548, on approaching Prestatyn from Chester direction turn right at sign for Pontins Holiday Village and follow club sign. Seaside links Championship course. 18 holes, 6517 yards, 5959 metres. S.S.S. 72. Practice areas. *Green Fees:* £18.00 weekdays; £25.00 weekends and Bank Holidays. *Eating facilities:* full catering available, bar. *Visitors:* members of golf club, with Handicap Certificate. *Society Meetings:* special "all-in" arrangement for 27 holes. Professional: M. Staton (0745 854320). Secretary: Roy Woodruff (0745 888353).

PRESTATYN. **St. Melyd Golf Club**, The Paddock, Meliden Road, Prestatyn LL19 9NB (0745 854405). *Location:* beside Prestatyn to Rhuddlan main road (near Meliden village). Parkland, beautifully set. 18 holes, 5811 yards. S.S.S. 68. *Green Fees:* weekdays £16.00; weekends £18.00. *Eating facilities:* full range of catering facilities except Tuesdays. *Visitors:* welcome. *Society Meetings:* catered for by arrangement with Secretary (various golf packages). Professional: Richard Bradbury (0745 888858). Secretary: Mr Peter M. Storey (0745 853574).

RHUDDLAN. **Rhuddlan Golf Club**, Meliden Road, Rhuddlan LL18 6LB (0745 590217). *Location:* leave A55 at St. Asaph for Rhuddlan, clubhouse 100m from roundabout on Rhyl side of Rhuddlan. Gently undulating, parkland course with natural hazards. 18 holes, 6482 yards. S.S.S. 71. Extensive practice ground. *Green Fees:* £20.00 per day weekdays; £25.00 per round weekends and Bank Holidays. *Eating facilities:* available daily. *Visitors:* welcome at all times when course demand permits. Sundays with member only. No denim. Snooker table. *Society Meetings:* weekdays only, maximum 50. Professional: Ian Worsley (0745 590898). Secretary: David Morris (0745 590217).

RHYL. **Rhyl Golf Club**, Coast Road, Rhyl LL18 3RE (Rhyl (0745) 353171). *Location:* one mile east of Rhyl on A548. Seaside links. 9 holes, 6153 yards. S.S.S. 69. Practice ground. *Green Fees:* weekdays £12.00 (9 holes £9.00); weekends £15.00. Discounts for parties over 15. *Eating facilities:* bar snacks and meals available, licensed bar. *Visitors:* welcome any time except when competitions in progress. *Society Meetings:*

GLYN VALLEY HOTEL

This family run hotel dates from 1835, yet has all modern facilities. The comfortable lounge bar has a beamed ceiling and open fire. Full English Breakfast and an extensive menu are offered in the attractive dining room. Glyn Ceiriog is an ideal base for exploring North Wales, with many fine golf courses within easy reach. Pony trekking, fishing, and parascending can be arranged. Pets welcome. Reductions for children under 12. Singles from £17.50, and Doubles from £34.00. The Glyn Valley offers good food, accommodation and friendly service at modest prices.

Mike and Janet Gilchrist, Glyn Valley Hotel, Glyn Ceiriog, llangollen, Clywd LL20 7EU. Telephone: 0691 718998

catered for by prior arrangement with Secretary. Professional: Martin Carty, C/o Mold Golf Club. Secretary: Mr F. Bass.

RUTHIN. **Ruthin Pwllglas Golf Club,** Pwllglas, Near Ruthin (Ruthin (0824) 702296). *Location:* Corwen Road (A494), two miles south of Ruthin. Hilly parkland. 10 holes, 5418 yards. S.S.S. 66. Practice area. *Green Fees:* weekdays £10.00, weekends and Bank Holidays £15.00 (with member £8.00). *Eating facilities:* none. Secretary can arrange catering for parties. *Visitors:* welcome without reservation, phone call advisable in high season and at weekends. *Society Meetings:* catered for midweek. Hon. Secretary: Ken Roberts (0824 703427).

WREXHAM. **Wrexham Golf Club,** Holt Road, Wrexham LL13 9SB (0978 261033). *Location:* A543 north east of Wrexham. 18 holes, 6139 yards. S.S.S. 69. Practice facilities. *Green Fees:* weekdays £17.00, weekends £22.00. *Eating facilities:* daily, subject to functions and visiting Societies. *Visitors:* welcome, subject to competitions and Society bookings. Proof of Golf Club membership and/or Handicap Certificate required. *Society Meetings:* catered for, Mondays and Fridays preferred. Professional: D.A. Larvin (0978 351476). Secretary: K.B. Fisher (0978 364268).

Dyfed

ABERYSTWYTH. **Aberystwyth Golf Club,** Brynymor Road, Aberystwyth (Aberystwyth (0970) 615104). *Location:* north end of Promenade, access near to cliff railway. Undulating meadowland. 18 holes, 6150 yards. S.S.S. 71. Practice ground. *Green Fees:* Summer: £15.00 per round, £18.00 per day weekdays; £18.00 per round, £20.00 per day weekends. 50% reduction for Juniors. *Eating facilities:* restaurant and bar. *Visitors:* welcome at all times, pre-booking helpful. *Society Meetings:* welcome, Special Deals available. Professional: Kevin Bayliss (0970 625301). Secretary: Barrie Thomas.

AMMANFORD. **Glynhir Golf Club,** Glynhir Road, Llandybie, Ammanford SA18 2TF (Llandybie (0269) 850472). *Location:* seven miles from end of M4, between Ammanford and Llandybie on the A483. Turn right up Glynhir Road and proceed for about two miles. Undulating wooded parkland course. 18 holes, 5952 yards, 5442 metres. S.S.S. 69. *Green Fees:* £15.00 (£10.00 in Winter) weekdays; £20.00 (£12.00 in Winter) weekends and Bank Holidays. *Eating facilities:* full catering available. *Visitors:* welcome but preferably on weekdays. Not Sundays. *Society Meetings:* welcome weekdays by prior arrangement with Secretary. Accommodation available. Bed and Breakfast at clubhouse (6 to 8 persons). Professional: Ian M. Roberts (0269 851010). Secretary: E.P. Rees (0269 592345).

BORTH. **Borth and Ynyslas Golf Club Ltd,** Borth SY24 5JS (Borth (0970) 871202). *Location:* turn off A487 between Aberystwyth and Machynlleth, course is north of Borth village. Championship standard links course with natural hazards (oldest 18 hole course in Wales). 18 holes, 6116 yards. S.S.S. 70. Practice area. *Green Fees:* weekdays £15.00 (August £20.00); weekends £20.00 per day. Reduced rates November to March. *Eating facilities:* full catering facilities provided advance booking made; bar open 12 noon to 2.30pm and 5pm to 8.30pm. *Visitors:* welcome at all times but should check with Professional that tee off times are available. *Society Meetings:* by prior arrangement with the Secretary. Professional: J.G. Lewis (0970 871557). Secretary: Sue Wilson (0654 781 334).

CARDIGAN. **Cardigan Golf Club,** Gwbert-on-Sea, Cardigan SA43 1PR (Cardigan (0239) 612035). *Location:* three miles north-west of Cardigan. Seaside links course. 18 holes, 6641 yards. S.S.S. 72. *Green Fees:* £15.00 per day weekdays, £20.00 per day weekends and Bank Holidays. *Eating facilities:* catering and bar facilities available. *Visitors:* welcome. Tee reserved for members 1 – 2pm. *Society Meetings:* very welcome. Professional: Colin Parsons. Hon. Secretary: J. Rhapps (0239 612035).

The Mill at Glynhir

AA ★★

LLANDYBIE, NR. AMMANFORD, DYFED SA18 2TE   Telephone: (0269) 850672
Originally a XVIIth-century mill, now converted to a small secluded luxury hotel. Extensive views over River Loughor valley and adjacent **18-hole golf course – free to residents**. Indoor swimming pool. All rooms with private spa baths and colour TV. Ideal for touring Brecons and SW Wales as well as walking and pony trekking.

HIGHCLIFFE HOTEL
School Road, Aberporth, Dyfed SA43 2DA. Tel & Fax: (0239) 810534
The hotel sits on a superb stretch of coastline, with sandy beaches and coves within easy reach. 14 ensuite bedrooms. Log fires, beamed bar and excellent cuisine. Car Park and Sky TV. Drying facilities. Golf course 6 miles.

Call Derek and Pat Conway for further details.

DYFED Wales

CARMARTHEN. **Carmarthen Golf Club**, Blaenycoed Road, Carmarthen SA33 6EH (0267 87214). Location: four miles north-west of town. Undulating parkland. 18 holes, 6210 yards. S.S.S. 71. Practice ground. Green Fees: weekdays £15.00; weekends £20.00. £5.00 reduction if with a member. Eating facilities: full catering every day except Wednesday. Visitors: welcome with proof of Handicap. Society Meetings: by arrangement. Professional: Pat Gillis (0267 87493). Secretary: Jonathan Coe (0267 87588).

HAVERFORDWEST. **Haverfordwest Golf Club**, Arnolds Down, Haverfordwest SA61 2XQ (Haverfordwest (0437) 763565). Location: one mile east of Haverfordwest on A40. S.S.S. 69. Practice fairway and putting green. Green Fees: £16.00 weekdays (£13.00 playing with a member); £23.00 weekends (£16.00 playing with member). Eating facilities: bar snacks available, meals by arrangement – 40 seater diningroom (food 8.30am to 9.30pm). Visitors: bona fide golfers welcome. Society Meetings: catered for by arrangement. Professional: A.J. Pile (0437 768409). Secretary: M.A. Harding (0437 764523).

LAMPETER. **Cilgwyn Golf Club**, Llangybi, Lampeter SA48 8NN (057045 286). Location: five miles north-east of Lampeter, off A485 at Llangybi. Flat parkland course. 9 holes, 5318 yards. S.S.S. 67. Practice area. Green Fees: weekdays £9.00, £5.00 with a member; weekends £14.00, £7.00 with a member. Weekly £60.00. Eating facilities: full bar and catering. Visitors: welcome without reservation, please telephone at weekends during summer. Golf shop. Pool table.

Caravan parking and golf for Caravan Club members. Society Meetings: catered for, Thursdays and Fridays. Secretary: L. Evans.

LLANELLI. **Ashburnham Golf Club**, Cliffe Terrace, Burry Port SA16 0HN (0554 832466). Location: south side of A484, four miles west of Llanelli. Seaside links with Championship status. 18 holes, 6627 yards. S.S.S. 72. Practice area. Green Fees: weekdays £22.50 per round; weekends and Bank Holidays £30.00 per round. Eating facilities: catering except Mondays, two bars. Visitors: welcome, starting times available from the Secretary. Society Meetings: by arrangement with Secretary. Professional: Robert A. Ryder (0554 833846). Secretary: D.K. Williams (0554 832269).

LLANRHYSTYD. **Penrhos Golf and Country Club**, Llanrhystyd SY23 5AY (Tel & Fax: 0974 202999). Location: nine miles south of Aberystwyth on A487. Parkland and meadowland with lakes and terrific views. 18 holes, 6641 yards. S.S.S. 72. Practice ground. Green Fees: weekdays £12.00 per round; weekends £18.00 per round. Eating facilities: bar meals and à la carte restaurant. Visitors: welcome at all times. Accommodation in Holiday Park, full leisure facilities. Society Meetings: welcome. Professional: Paul Diamond. Secretary: R. Rees-Evans.

MILFORD HAVEN. **Milford Haven Golf Club**, Woodbine House, Hubberston, Milford Haven (Milford Haven [0646] 692368). Location: one mile from Milford Haven on Dale Road. Parkland overlooking magnificent harbour. 18 holes, 6071 yards. S.S.S. 70.

TREVACCOON FARM

Trevaccoon is a 17th century grade II listed building made from local stone and steeped in history. There are four large family rooms and one double room, all are en-suite, with spectacular sea views. Children welcome. There is fishing, surfing, pony trekking and swimming nearby.
FREE GOLF IS OFFERED TO GUESTS NEARBY
Enquiries and bookings contact Vikki, Trevaccoon Farm.
St. Davids, Haverfordwest, Pembrokeshire SA62 6DP Tel: 0348 831438

Tyglyn Aeron Country Hotel

A lovely, family run hotel, renowned for its high standard of food and comfort. Relax after a challenging round by our inglenook fireplace or on the patio. All ten bedrooms are ensuite, with colour TV, tea/coffee facilities and central heating. Large gardens and car park. Wales Tourist Board ❦❦❦ Commended.
Mrs Thomas, Tyglyn Aeron Country Hotel, Ciliau Aeron, Dyfed. Telephone: 0570 470625

Pen-y-Castell Farm Guest House

Conveniently situated for a number of clubs along the Cardigan Bay coast, in a secluded spot with magnificent views over the bay. All bedrooms ensuite and attractively furnished. Excellent meals, Italian a speciality. Well-stocked bar and two lounges. Ample parking. Fly fishing lake. WTB ❦❦❦ Highly Commended AA *QQQ*
Pen-y-Castell Farm Guest House, Llanrhystyd, Dyfed SY23 5BZ. Tel: (0974) 272922

MILFORD HAVEN GOLF CLUB LIMITED

Attractive, well-kept 18 hole golf course with beautiful views of the Milford Haven Waterway. Visitors welcome at all times, societies by arrangement. M.H. G.C.
Full catering, bar facilities and Pro Shop. Telephone for further details.
Woodbine House, Clay Lane, Milford Haven SA73 3RX.
Telephone: (0646) 692368

Wales DYFED

Green Fees: weekdays £13.00 per day; weekends and Bank Holidays £18.00. Half price if with a member. *Eating facilities:* lunches, bar snacks; dinners available at clubhouse. *Visitors:* welcome at all times. *Society Meetings:* welcome, special rates depending on numbers. Professional: Stephen Laidler (0646 697762). Secretary: I.S. Harvey (0646 692368, 0646 693234 evenings; Fax: 0646 697018 evenings).

NEWPORT. **Newport (Pembs) Golf Club,** The Golf Club, Newport SA42 0MR (Newport [Dyfed] (0239) 820244). *Location:* two miles off A487 Cardigan-Fishguard at Newport, Dyfed. Flat seaside links course with mountain views. 9 holes, 5815 yards. S.S.S. 68. *Green Fees:* £12.50 per day. *Eating facilities:* full catering and bar facilities available. *Visitors:* welcome at all times, please telephone at weekends and Bank Holidays. Self-catering accommodation available adjoining clubhouse. *Society Meetings:* catered for at any time by arrangement with the Secretary. Professional: Mr Colin Parsons. Secretary: A.R.T. Dietrich.

PEMBROKE. **South Pembrokeshire Golf Club,** Defensible Barracks, Pembroke Dock, Pembroke (Pembroke (0646) 683817). *Location:* on hilltop overlooking Pembroke Dock and Milford Haven waterway, near western end of A477. Parkland. 9 holes, 5804 yards. S.S.S. 69. *Green Fees:* £10.00 per day. Weekly (Mondays to Fridays) £30.00. *Eating facilities:* bar, meals by prior arrangement. *Visitors:* welcome. *Society Meetings:* catered for by arrangement. Secretary: W.D. Owen (0646 682650).

ST. DAVIDS. **St. Davids City Golf Club,** Whitsands Bay, St. Davids SA62 6QY (0437 721751). *Location:* follow signs to Whitesands Bay on Fishguard Road out of St. Davids, for two miles. Car park is situated on crossroads with club sign at entrance. If you reach the beach you've gone too far! Seaside links course with spectacular panoramic views over Whitesands Bay and St. Davids Head. 9 holes, 5961 yards. S.S.S. 70. *Green Fees:* £11.00 per day. *Eating facilities:* available at our 19th Hole in Hotel adjacent to course. *Visitors:* welcome at all times but please check at weekends and Bank Holidays; Ladies' Day Friday afternoons. *Society Meetings:* welcome, book with Secretary. Secretary: C.W.J. Snushall (0437 720312).

TENBY. **Tenby Golf Club,** The Burrows, Tenby SA70 7NP (Tenby (0834) 842787). *Location:* on A478, near Tenby Railway Station. Seaside links, Championship course, oldest club in Wales. 18 holes, 6330 yards. S.S.S. 71. Practice area. *Green Fees:* weekdays £18.00; weekends £22.50. Reduced fees in winter and for Societies booked in advance. *Eating facilities:* complete dining facilities; licensed bars, snacks. *Visitors:* always welcome, subject to club competitions. Must produced Handicap Certificate. Billiards room available. *Society Meetings:* catered for by advance booking. Professional: Terence Mountford (0834 844447). Manager: Lt Cdr T.C. Peake (0834 842978).

FOR THE MUTUAL GUIDANCE OF GUEST AND HOST

Every year literally thousands of holidays, short-breaks and overnight stops are arranged through our guides, the vast majority without any problems at all. In a handful of cases, however, difficulties do arise about bookings, which often could have been prevented from the outset.

It is important to remember that when accommodation has been booked, both parties — guests and hosts — have entered into a form of contract. We hope that the following points will provide helpful guidance.

GUESTS: When enquiring about accommodation, be as precise as possible. Give exact dates, numbers in your party and the ages of any children. State the number and type of rooms wanted and also what catering you require — bed and breakfast, full board, etc. Make sure that the position about evening meals is clear — and about pets, reductions for children or any other special points.

Read our reviews carefully to ensure that the proprietors you are going to contact can supply what you want. Ask for a letter confirming all arrangements, if possible.

If you have to cancel, do so as soon as possible. Proprietors do have the right to retain deposits and under certain circumstances to charge for cancelled holidays if adequate notice is not given and they cannot re-let the accommodation.

HOSTS: Give details about your facilities and about any special conditions. Explain your deposit system clearly and arrangements for cancellations, charges, etc, and whether or not your terms include VAT.

If for any reason you are unable to fulfil an agreed booking without adequate notice, you may be under an obligation to arrange alternative suitable accommodation or to make some form of compensation.

While every effort is made to ensure accuracy, we regret that FHG Publications cannot accept responsibility for errors, omissions or misrepresentation in our entries or any consequences thereof. Prices in particular should be checked because we go to press early. We will follow up complaints but cannot act as arbiters or agents for either party.

Mid-Glamorgan

ABERDARE. **Aberdare Golf Club,** Abernant, Aberdare (0685 871188). *Location:* half a mile from town centre. Mountain course with parkland features and view of whole Cynon Valley. 18 holes, 5875 yards. S.S.S. 69. *Green Fees:* weekdays £14.00, (with member £8.00); weekends £18.00, (with member £10.00). *Eating facilities:* bar, lounge and diningroom. *Visitors:* welcome without reservation weekdays. Saturdays with member only. Handicap Certificates required. Snooker room, ladies' lounge and changing room. *Society Meetings:* catered for by prior arrangement with Secretary. Professional: A. Palmer (0685 878735). Secretary: L. Adler (0685 872797).

BARGOED. **Bargoed Golf Club,** Heolddu, Bargoed CF8 9GF (0443 830143). *Location:* A469 to Bargoed town centre – Moorland Road. Mountain top course. 18 holes, 6012 yards. S.S.S. 69. *Green Fees:* weekdays £10.00/£15.00; weekends with a member. *Eating facilities:* lunches, dinners and snacks. *Visitors:* welcome, only with member at weekends, no other restrictions. *Society Meetings:* catered for weekdays, not at weekends. Secretary: W.R. Coleman (0443 830143 or 822377).

BRIDGEND. **Southerndown Golf Club,** Ewenny, Bridgend CF32 0QP (Southerndown (0656) 880326). *Location:* three miles from Bridgend on the Ogmore Road. Downland overlooking Bristol Channel. 18 holes, 6417 yards, 5868 metres. S.S.S. 73. Practice area. *Green Fees:* £24.00 weekdays; £30.00 weekends. £18.00 after 2pm. *Eating facilities:* full diningroom and bar facilities. *Visitors:* welcome any time except on competitions days (check with Secretary). Handicap Certificate required. *Society Meetings:* catered for on Tuesdays and Thursdays or by arrangement with Secretary. Special rates dependent on number. Professional: D. McMonagle (0656 880326). Secretary: K.R. Wilcox (0656 880476).

CAERPHILLY. **Caerphilly Golf Club,** Pencapel, Mountain Road, Caerphilly CF8 1HJ (Caerphilly (0222) 883481). *Location:* seven miles north of Cardiff on A469, 250 yards south of both railway and bus stations opposite Magistrates' Court. Mountainside course with undulating features and areas of woodland. 14 holes, 6028 yards. S.S.S. 71 (course is in development stage of 18 holes scheduled for play in summer 1994). Limited practice facilities. *Green Fees:* weekdays £20.00, £10.00 with a member; weekends only if playing with a member £13.00. *Eating facilities:* men's bar, mixed lounge, ladies' lounge, dining area (by arrangement). *Visitors:* welcome weekdays only, weekends and Bank Holidays by arrangement if with a member. *Society Meetings:* only a limited number by arrangement. Professional: Richard Barter (0222 869104). Secretary: H.M. Matthews (0222 863441).

CAERPHILLY. **Castell Heights Public Golf Course,** Blaengwynlais CF8 1NG (0222 861128). *Location:* approximately four miles north of Cardiff on A469, two miles south of Caerphilly. 9 holes, 2688

COED-Y-MWSTWR HOTEL
Coychurch, Near Bridgend, Mid-Glamorgan CF35 6AF (0656-860621)
An elegant, listed hotel with spacious rooms, imaginative cuisine and an excellent cellar.
See our Display entry in the Colour Section, page 18.
FOR THE GOLF COURSES OF WALES

HERONSTON HOTEL
BRIDGEND   MID-GLAMORGAN CF35 5AW
Telephone 0656 668811   Telex 498232   Fax 0656 767391
LUXURY HOTEL WITH 76 SUPERB SUITES
Situated 4 miles off the M4.
Three Golf Championship Courses within 3 miles of Hotel.
Indoor and Outdoor Heated Swimming Pool, Sauna, Steam Room, Solarium, Jacuzzi, Snooker Room.
Special Terms for Weekend Breaks with Golf at St. Mary's Golf Club Pencoed (within 3 miles).
Transportation can be arranged to various activities.
THE HOTEL WITH THE PERSONAL TOUCH

THE GOLF GUIDE 1994

Wales MID-GLAMORGAN

yards. S.S.S. 66 for 18 holes. *Green Fees:* information not provided. *Eating facilities:* snacks, lunches and afternoon tea available. Restaurant meals booking only (0222 886686). *Visitors:* welcome, booked times only. Professional: S. Bebb. Secretary: A.H. Godsall.

CAERPHILLY. **Mountain Lakes Golf and Country Club,** Caerphilly CF8 1NG (0222 886686). *Location:* approximately four miles north of Cardiff on A469, two miles south of Caerphilly. M4 Junction 32. Part parkland, part wooded, undulating. 20 water hazards, large penncross greens. 18 holes, 6550 yards. S.S.S. 73. 20 bay driving range. *Green Fees:* weekdays £15.00 (£10.00 with member); weekends £15.00. *Eating facilities:* full restaurant and three bars. *Visitors:* welcome at all times but must have registered handicap. *Society Meetings:* welcome at all times but must have registered handicap. Professional: Sion Bebb (0222 886696). Golf Secretary: R.S. Smith (0222 627041). Company Secretary of Proprietors Club: Jean Bull (0222 861128; Fax: 0222 869030).

HENGOED. **Bryn Meadows Golf and Country Hotel,** The Bryn, Near Hengoed CF8 7SM (0495 225590/224103; Fax: 0495 228272). *Location:* A472 between from Ystrad Mynach to Blackwood, turn up lane at Texaco Service Station at Crown roundabout. Parkland course. 18 holes, 6200 yards. S.S.S. 69. *Green Fees:* weekdays £17.50; weekends £22.50. *Eating facilities:* restaurant, 70 covers. Functions up to 120. Conferences catered for from five to 120. Bar snacks served daily. *Visitors:* welcome, but not Sunday mornings. The "Fairways" Leisure Club including – indoor heated swimming pool, jacuzzi, sauna and steam rooms and "state of the art" multigym available. *Society Meetings:* welcome Tuesdays and Thursdays. Professional: B. Hunter (0495 221905). Secretary: B. Mayo.

KENFIG. **Pyle and Kenfig Golf Club,** Waun-y-Mer, Kenfig CF33 4PU (0656 782060). *Location:* one mile off M4 at Junction 37. Seaside links and downland course. 18 holes, 6650 yards, 6081 metres. S.S.S. 73. Five practice holes, practice driving range. *Green Fees:* weekdays £25.00 per round, £30.00 day; weekends only as a member's guest £15.00. *Eating facilities:* full bar and catering facilities. *Visitors:* welcome weekdays by arrangement, proof of membership of a club and Handicap Certificate required. *Society Meetings:* welcome Tuesdays and Fridays. Professional: R. Evans (Tel & Fax: 0656 772446). Secretary: Roger Thomas (0656 783093).

MAESTEG. **Maesteg Golf Club,** Mount Pleasant, Neath Road, Maesteg CF34 9PR (0656 732037). *Location:* half a mile out of Maesteg town centre on the Port Talbot road (B4282). Reasonably flat hilltop course with scenic views over wooded hills and valleys down to Swansea Bay. 18 holes, 5900 yards. S.S.S. 69. *Green Fees:* weekdays £15.00; weekends £20.00. Special rates for Societies. *Eating facilities:* bar and dining facilities available daily 11am to 11pm. *Visitors:* welcome without reservation, groups of more than 12 by arrangement. *Society Meetings:* catered for weekdays only by arrangement. Professional: Bill Evans (0656 735742). Secretary: W.H. Hanford (0656 734106).

MERTHYR TYDFIL. **Merthyr Tydfil (Cilsanws) Golf Club,** Cloth Hall Lane, Cefn Coed, Merthyr Tydfil (0685 723308). *Location:* off A470 two miles north of Merthyr Tydfil town centre. Mountain course in National Park area with outstanding views. 11 holes, 5957 yards. S.S.S. 69. *Green Fees:* £12.00 weekdays; £15.00 weekends. Half price playing with member. *Eating facilities:* weekends only. *Visitors:* welcome anytime except competition days (usually Sundays). *Society Meetings:* catered for by prior arrangement. Secretary: Vivian Price.

MERTHYR TYDFIL. **Morlais Castle Golf Club,** Pant, Dowlais, Merthyr Tydfil CF48 2UY (0685 722822). *Location:* near 'Heads of Valley Road', Dowlais roundabout, follow signs for Brecon Mountain Railway. Very pleasant moorland course with excellent views. 18 holes, 6320 yards, 5744 metres. S.S.S. 71. Practice area. *Green Fees:* weekdays £14.00 per day, £8.00 with member; weekends £16.00, £10.00 with a member. *Eating facilities:* bar meals, for other meals contact Stewardess. *Visitors:* welcome, weekends by prior arrangement with/or by application to the Secretary. *Society Meetings:* weekdays only, please contact Secretary. Secretary: Mr J.N. Powell.

MOUNTAIN ASH. **Mountain Ash Golf Club,** Cefn Pennar, Mountain Ash (Mountain Ash (0443) 472265). *Location:* A470 Pontypridd to Aberdare road, approximately 10 miles from Pontypridd, four miles north of Abercynon. Partly wooded course. 18 holes, 5553 yards. S.S.S. 68. *Green Fees:* weekdays £18.00, £10.00 with member, weekends and Bank Holidays £18.00 only with member. *Eating facilities:* catering at club. *Visitors:* welcome any time without reservation. *Society Meetings:* catered for. Professional: Ceri Hiscox (0443 478770). Secretary: Geoffrey Matthews.

NELSON. **Whitehall Golf Club,** The Pavilion, Nelson, Treharris CF46 6ST (0443 740245). *Location:* 15 miles north of Cardiff, take A4054 off A470. Hillside course with pelasant views. 9 holes (x2), 5666 yards. S.S.S. 68. *Green Fees:* on application. *Eating facilities:* available, contact Steward for cooked meals. *Visitors:* welcome weekdays, weekends with members. *Society Meetings:* by prior arrangement. Secretary: V.E. Davies.

PONTYCLUN. **Llantrisant and Pontyclun Golf Club,** The Clubhouse, Talbot Green, Pontyclun (Llantrisant (0443) 222148). *Location:* 10 miles north of Cardiff, two miles north of Junction 34 M4. Parkland. 12 holes, 5712 yards. S.S.S. 68. *Green Fees:* weekdays £20.00, £8.00 with member; weekends and Bank Holidays £10.00 with member only. *Eating facilities:* by arrangement with Steward. *Visitors:* welcome with proof of membership and weekends with member only. *Society Meetings:* catered for by arrangement. Professional: Nick Watson (0443 228169). Secretary: John Williams (0443 224601).

PONTYPRIDD. **Pontypridd Golf Club,** Ty Gwyn Road, Pontypridd CF37 4DJ (Pontypridd (0443) 402359). *Location:* east side of town centre, off A470, 12 miles from Cardiff. Wooded mountain course. 18 holes, 5650 yards, 5166 metres. S.S.S. 68. *Green Fees:*

315

FAIRWAYS HOTEL & THE PORTHCAWL HOTEL

SEAFRONT, PORTHCAWL
MID GLAMORGAN CF36 3LS

The Porthcawl is situated in the main shopping centre close to the seafront whilst Fairways commands a magnificent panoramic view southwards across the adjacent foreshore and over the Bristol Channel towards the Devon hills.

Both hotels have first class facilities and serve excellent food and are licensed. The Porthcawl also has a nightclub and health club. Within easy reach of Royal Porthcawl Golf Club and Pyle & Kenfig Golf Club. Brochure available.

Telephone: (0656) 782085 or 783544.   Fax: (0656) 785351.

---

information not provided. *Eating facilities:* dining facilities and bar snacks. *Visitors:* welcome weekdays without member, weekends with member only. Must be member of recognised golf club. *Society Meetings:* catered for with prior reservation. Professional: (0443 491210). Secretary: J.G. Graham (0443 409904).

PORTHCAWL. **Royal Porthcawl Golf Club,** Rest Bay, Porthcawl CF36 3UW (0656 782251; Fax: 0656 771687). *Location:* 25 miles west of Cardiff off Junction 37 M4, 14 miles east of Swansea. Seaside links. 18 holes, 6691 yards. S.S.S. 74. 27 acre practice area. *Green Fees:* £30.00 weekdays, £45.00 weekends. *Eating facilities:* full catering and bar facilities. *Visitors:* playing with member only at weekends, reservations required and must have Handicap Certificate. *Society Meetings:* by arrangement. Professional: Mr Peter Evans (0656 773702). Secretary: A.W. Woolcott.

RHONDDA. **Rhondda Golf Club,** Golf House, Penrhys, Ferndale, Rhondda CF43 3PW (Tonypandy (0443) 433204). *Location:* on the Penrhys road joining Rhondda Fach and Rhondda Fawr. Mountain course. 18 holes, 6206 yards. S.S.S. 70. *Green Fees:* £15.00 weekdays, £10.00 with a member; £20.00 weekends, £15.00 with member. *Eating facilities:* all facilities daily except Mondays. *Visitors:* welcome without reservation weekdays. Handicap Certificate required. Telephone for weekend availability. *Society Meetings:* welcome on written application. Professional: Rhys Davies (0443 441385). Secretary: G. Rees (Tel & Fax: 0443 441384).

South Glamorgan

BARRY. **Brynhill (Barry) Golf Club,** Port Road East, Colcot, Barry CF6 7PN (Barry (0446) 735061). *Location:* leave M4 at Junction 33 (A4232), follow signs for Barry and Cardiff (Wales) Airport onto the A4050. Club on right of road. Undulating meadowland course. 18 holes, 6077 yards. S.S.S. 69. Par 71. *Green Fees:* weekdays: £20.00 per day, £9.00 with member; Saturdays and Bank Holidays: £25.00, £9.00 with member. Societies £17.00. With County Cards £9.00. Juniors £7.00. *Eating facilities:* the Steward Mr Barrie Cahill and his wife Ann extend a warm welcome, and will provide morning coffee, lunches between 12 noon and 2.00pm. Afternoon teas and dinner from 4.30 pm. Your order prior to playing is requested. *Visitors:* welcome, except Sundays; must produce membership card and Handicap Certificate. *Society Meetings:* by arrangement with Secretary – no weekends, must be members of a golf club. Professional: Peter Fountain (0446 733660). Secretary: Keith Atkinson (0446 720277).

BARRY. **RAF St. Athan Golf Club,** Flemingstone Road, St. Athan, Barry CF6 9WA (0446 797186). *Location:* eight miles from Barry, turn left through St. Athan Village. Parkland. 9 holes, 6290 yards. S.S.S. 72. Practice area and nets. *Green Fees:* £8.00/£10.00 weekdays; £10.00/£15.00 weekends with or without member. *Eating facilities:* available except Mondays. *Visitors:* welcome except Sunday mornings, telephone for information. Handicap Certificate required. *Society Meetings:* apply through the Secretary. Professional: Neil Gillette (0222 373923). Secretary: P.F. Woodhouse (0446 751043).

CARDIFF. **Cardiff Golf Club,** Sherborne Avenue, Cyncoed, Cardiff (Cardiff (0222) 753067). *Location:* two miles north of city centre or M4, A48 or A48M from east to Pentwyn exit on Eastern Avenue, and take Pentwyn Industrial Road to top of hill at Cyncoed Village, turn left at Spar shop into Sherborne Avenue. Undulating parkland, all greens bunkered. 18 holes. S.S.S. 70. *Green Fees:* £28.00. Winter rate 1st October to 31st March £20.00. *Eating facilities:* catering available lunchtime and evening weekdays except Mondays. *Visitors:* welcome; Saturdays must play with a member. Professional: Terry Hanson (0222 754772). Secretary: Keith Lloyd (0222 753320).

CARDIFF. **Creigiau Golf Club,** Cardiff Road, Creigiau, Cardiff CF4 8NN (Cardiff (0222) 890263). *Location:* seven miles north-west of Cardiff, two miles Exit 34 M4. 18 holes, 5979 yards. S.S.S. 69. *Green Fees:* £21.00 per day (£10.00 with member). *Eating facilities:* meals on request. *Visitors:* welcome without reservation except weekends when with members only. *Society Meetings:* catered for by arrangement. Professional: Mark Maddison (0222 891909). Secretary/Manager: D. Bryan Jones (0222 890263).

CARDIFF. **Llanishen Golf Club,** Cwm, Lisvane, Cardiff CF4 5UD (Cardiff (0222) 752205). *Location:* five miles north of Cardiff city centre, one mile north of Llanishen village. Wooded mountain course with spectacular views. 18 holes, 5296 yards, 4844 metres. S.S.S. 66. *Green Fees:* £22.00. Special rates for County Cards or playing with member weekdays except Bank Holidays. *Eating facilities:* full bar and catering except Mondays. *Visitors:* welcome weekdays; weekends only with member. Handicap Certificate required. *Society Meetings:* catered for Thursday only on written application. Visitors must be bona fide members of a golf club. Professional: R.A. Jones (0222 755076). Secretary/Manager: Elfed Davies (0222 755078).

CARDIFF. **Radyr Golf Club,** Drysgol Road, Radyr, Cardiff CF4 8BS (Cardiff (0222) 842442). *Location:* junction 32 M4, A470 to Merthyr Tydfil, first exit. Parkland course. 18 holes, 6015 yards. S.S.S. 70. *Green Fees:* £25.00 weekdays. *Eating facilities:* snacks, lunches and evening meals. Please order in advance (0222 842735). *Visitors:* welcome except weekends, Handicap Certificate from recognised club required. *Society Meetings:* catered for Wednesdays, Thursdays and Fridays only. Professional/Manager: Steve Gough (0222 842476/842408).

CARDIFF. **St. Mellons Golf Club,** St. Mellons, Cardiff CF3 8XS (Castleton (0633) 680401). *Location:* just off M4 at Junction 28 on to A48. Parkland. 18 holes, 6225 yards. S.S.S. 70. *Green Fees:* £25.00 weekdays. *Eating facilities:* available. *Visitors:* welcome with Handicap Certificates weekdays only, weekends with member only. *Society Meetings:* catered for on written application. Professional: Barry Thomas (0633 680101). Secretary: Mrs K. Newling (0633 680408).

CARDIFF. **Wenvoe Castle Golf Club Ltd,** Wenvoe, Cardiff CF5 6BE (Cardiff (0222) 591094). *Location:* exit Junction 33 M4, follow signs for Cardiff Airport. Parkland. 18 holes, 6422 yards. S.S.S. 71. *Green Fees:* weekdays £20.00; weekends £12.00 with a member only. *Eating facilities:* bar snacks and restaurant meals. *Visitors:* welcome weekdays only. *Society Meetings:* catered for Monday to Thursday, parties of 16 or more. Professional: R. Day (0222 593649). Secretary: Mr M. Burke (0222 594371).

CARDIFF. **Whitchurch (Cardiff) Golf Club,** Pantmawr Road, Whitchurch, Cardiff CF4 6XD (0222 620125; Fax: 0222 529860). *Location:* Junction 32 M4. 18 holes, 6319 yards. S.S.S. 70. *Green Fees:* £23.00 weekdays, £30.00 weekends and Bank Holidays. *Eating facilities:* restaurant and two bars. *Visitors:* welcome everyday, limited over weekends. *Society Meetings:* catered for Thursdays only. Professional: Eddie Clark (0222 614660). Secretary/Manager: Lieutenant Commander R.G. Burley (0222 620985).

DINAS POWIS. **Dinas Powis Golf Club,** Golf House, Old Highwalls, Dinas Powis CF64 4AJ (Cardiff (0222) 512157). *Location:* M4 Cardiff, thereafter signposted Dinas Powis, Penarth and Barry. Mostly parkland, three holes quite hilly. 18 holes, 5151 yards. S.S.S. 66. Limited practice. *Green Fees:* weekdays £20.00; weekends £25.00. Half fee if playing with a member. Reduced rates for societies depending on numbers. *Eating facilities:* diningroom/bar snacks except Mondays. *Visitors:* welcome weekdays, weekends by arrangement. *Society Meetings:* welcome, no restrictions. Professional: G. Bennett (0222 513682). Secretary: J.D. Hughes (0222 512727).

PENARTH. **Glamorganshire Golf Club,** Lavernock Road, Penarth CF64 5UP (0222 707048). *Location:* five miles west Cardiff, one mile west Penarth Centre. Parkland course overlooking Bristol Channel. 18 holes, 6150 yards. S.S.S. 70. *Green Fees:* weekdays £24.00; weekends and Bank Holidays £30.00. *Eating facilities:* full restaurant and bar snacks, Men's bar and mixed lounge bar. *Visitors:* welcome providing no competitions in progress and/or Societies on course. Telephone call recommended. All visitors must possess current Handicap Certificate. *Society Meetings:* write to Secretary/Manager. Professional: Mr A.K. Smith (0222 707401). Secretary/Manager: W.G. Davies (0222 701185).

West Glamorgan

CLYDACH. **Inco Golf Club,** Clydach (0792 844216). *Location:* outskirts of Swansea, easily accessible from M4. Flat, tree-lined course, with river. 12 holes, 6230 yards. S.S.S. 70. *Green Fees:* information not available. *Eating facilities:* none. Bar only. *Visitors:* welcome. *Society Meetings:* catered for by arrangement through Secretary: Mr S. Murdoch (0792 843336).

GLYNNEATH. **Glynneath Golf Club,** 'Penygraig', Pontneathvaughan, Near Glynneath SA11 5UH (Glynneath (0639) 720452). *Location:* A465 Trunk road to Glynneath onto B4242 to Pontneathvaughan. Picturesque hillside course overlooking the Vale of Neath, fairly flat, half parkland, half wooded in Brecon Beacons National Park. 18 holes, 5566 yards. S.S.S.

WEST GLAMORGAN Wales

67. *Green Fees:* weekdays £12.00 per round, £15.00 per day; weekends £18.00 per day. *Eating facilities:* snacks, hot drinks and bar. *Visitors:* welcome no restrictions weekdays, restricted times weekends. *Society Meetings:* welcome by arrangement. Secretary: R.M. Ellis.

NEATH. **Neath Golf Club,** Cadoxton, Neath SA10 8AH (Neath (0639) 643615). *Location:* two miles from Neath town centre. 18 holes, 6492 yards. S.S.S. 72. *Green Fees:* weekdays £17.00. £5.00 reduction if playing with a member. *Eating facilities:* available except Monday. *Visitors:* welcome weekdays, weekends with a member only. *Society Meetings:* Wednesday, Thursday and Friday by arrangement with Secretary. Professional: E.M. Bennett. Secretary: D.M. Hughes (0639 632759).

NEATH. **Swansea Bay Golf Club,** Jersey Marine, Neath SA10 6JP (Skewen (0792) 812198). *Location:* half a mile south east of Jersey Marine village. Take B4290 turning off A483 then first right. Seaside links. 18 holes, 6605 yards. S.S.S. 72. *Green Fees:* weekdays £16.00; weekends and Bank Holidays £22.00. *Eating facilities:* bar/catering available every day from 10.30am; dinners by arrangement. *Visitors:* welcome without reservation. Indoor bowling stadium available for private hire summer months. *Society Meetings:* by arrangement. Professional: M. Day (0792 816159). Secretary: Mrs D. Goatcher (0792 814153).

SWANSEA. **Clyne Golf Club,** 120 Owls Lodge Lane, The Mayals, Swansea SA3 5DP (0792 401989). *Location:* west of Swansea, South Gower road before Mumbles. Moorland course. 18 holes, 6323 yards. S.S.S. 71. Large practice area and 9 holes putting green. *Green Fees:* weekdays £20.00; weekends £25.00. *Eating facilities:* full catering available and fully licensed. *Visitors:* welcome. *Society Meetings:* welcome by application. Professional: Mark Bevan (0792 402094). Secretary: K. Crawford.

SWANSEA. **Fairwood Park Golf Club Ltd,** Blackhills Lane, Upper Killay, Swansea SA2 7JN (Swansea (0792) 203648). *Location:* A4118 road – follow signs to "Sketty" and "Killay"; road to club opposite Swansea Airport. Parkland, many new trees planted, five lakes. Championship course. 18 holes, 6741 yards. S.S.S. 72. Practice field and net. *Green Fees:* £20.00 per day weekdays; £25.00 weekends and Bank Holidays. *Eating facilities:* full range, from bar snacks to three course meals, licensed bar. *Visitors:* welcome, large parties by appointment. If playing with a member £1.00 reduction. *Society Meetings:* welcome all through the year. Apply to Professional. Professional: Mark Evans (0792 299194). Secretary: Mrs C.J. Beer (0792 297849). Administrator: Bryn Morgan (0792 297849). Steward: J. Pettifer (0792 203648).

THE GOLF GUIDE 1994

SWANSEA. **Langland Bay Golf Club,** Langland Road, Langland, Swansea (0792) 366023). *Location:* Swansea main road to Mumbles, followed by Langland Bay. 18 holes, 5830 yards. S.S.S. 69. *Green Fees:* weekdays £24.00; weekends and Bank Holidays £26.00. *Eating facilities:* lunches, teas and supper, also bar snacks. *Visitors:* welcome without reservation. *Society Meetings:* restricted, by arrangement, £18.00, 12 or more in number. Professional: T. Lynch (0792 366186). Secretary: T.J. Jenkins (0792 361721).

SWANSEA. **Morriston Golf Club,** 160 Clasemont Road, Morriston, Swansea SA6 6AJ (Swansea (0792) 771079). *Location:* off Junction 46 M4, turn first left follow road for one mile, clubhouse on left hand side of road. Parkland course, rather difficult. 18 holes, 5785 yards. S.S.S. 68. *Green Fees:* weekdays £18.00, £12.00 with a member; weekends and Bank Holidays £25.00, £16.00 with member. Special rates for parties of 10 or over with prior notice. *Eating facilities:* catering by arrangement with caterer (0792 700310), three bars. *Visitors:* welcome, restrictions only at weekends and Bank Holidays. *Society Meetings:* welcome. Professional: D.A. Rees (0792 772335). Secretary: W.A. Jefford (0792 796528).

SWANSEA. **Palleg Golf Club,** Lower Cwmtwrch, Swansea SA9 2QQ (Glantawe (0639) 842193). *Location:* off A4067 (A4068) north of Swansea 14 miles, 25 miles Brecon. 9 holes, 6510 yards. S.S.S. 72. *Green Fees:* information not provided. *Eating facilities:* evening bar meals Tuesday, Thursday, weekend lunches. *Visitors:* welcome, restrictions Saturday (Summer) and Sunday mornings (Winter). *Society Meetings:* welcome if arranged. Secretary: Mr D.W. Moses (0792 862303).

SWANSEA. **Pennard Golf Club,** 2 Southgate Road, Southgate, Swansea SA3 2BT (0792 233131). *Location:* eight miles west of Swansea A4067, B4436. Seaside links. 18 holes, 6289 yards. S.S.S. 71. Practice areas. *Green Fees:* weekdays £18.00, with a member £12.00; weekends and Bank Holidays £22.00, with a member £15.00. *Eating facilities:* dining room and two bars. *Visitors:* welcome at any time. Squash courts, snooker room. *Society Meetings:* catered for weekdays only. Professional: M.V. Bennett (0792 233451). Secretary: E.M. Howell (0792 233131).

SWANSEA. **Pontardawe Golf Club,** Cefn Llan, Pontardawe, Swansea SA8 4SH (0792 863118). *Location:* four miles north of M4 Junction 45 on A4067 Swansea-Brecon road. Wooded course. 18 holes, 6162 yards. S.S.S. 70. *Green Fees:* £18.00 weekdays, £27.50 weekends. *Eating facilities:* restaurant open daily except Mondays. *Visitors:* welcome, weekends by prior arrangement only. Handicap Certificate required. *Society Meetings:* catered for by application/appointment. Professional: G. Hopkins (0792 830977). Secretary: Lyn Jones (0792 830041).

Gwent

ABERGAVENNY. **Monmouthshire Golf Club,** Llanfoist, Abergavenny NP7 9HE (0873 853171). *Location:* two miles out of Abergavenny on Llanfoist to Llanellen Road (A40). Parkland with scenic mountain views. 18 holes, 6045 yards. S.S.S. 69. Practice ground. *Green Fees:* weekdays £21.00, weekends and Bank Holidays £26.00. *Eating facilities:* full catering except Tuesday when bar snacks available. *Visitors:* welcome. Proof of membership of recognised golf club required. *Society Meetings:* catered for. Booking to be confirmed before Jan. 31st each year. Professional: P. Worthing (0873 852532). Secretary: G.J. Swayne (0873 852606).

BLACKWOOD. **Blackwood Golf Club,** Cwmgelli, Blackwood (0495 223152). *Location:* one mile north of Blackwood on Tredegar road A494. 9 holes, 5350 yards. S.S.S. 66. *Green Fees:* weekdays £12.50; weekends and Bank Holidays £15.00. *Visitors:* welcome weekdays only. *Society Meetings:* by arrangement. Secretary: A.M. Reed-Gibbs.

CAERLEON. **Caerleon Public Golf Course,** The Broadway, Caerleon, Newport (Caerleon (0633) 420342). *Location:* three miles off M4 at turnoff for Caerleon. Flat parkland. 9 holes, 3000 yards. S.S.S. 68. Driving range. *Green Fees:* weekdays £3.00; weekends £3.80. Senior Citizens and Juniors £2.20. *Eating facilities:* cafe and bar. *Visitors:* welcome. *Society Meetings:* welcome. Professional: Alex Campbell. Secretary: R. Morgan.

CHEPSTOW. **St. Pierre Hotel Golf and Country Club Ltd,** St. Pierre Park, Chepstow NP6 6YA (0291 625261; Fax: 0291 629975). *Location:* five minutes from M4/Severn Bridge on A48 to Newport. Two courses set in 400 acre deer park, 11 acre lake. One of the toughest finishing holes in Golf – 18th on Old Course. Old Course 18 holes, Championship/Medal 6700 yards, S.S.S. 73; standard tees 6285 yards, S.S.S. 71. Mathern Course 18 holes, 5762 yards, S.S.S. 68. *Green Fees:* Old Course – weekdays £40.00, weekends £50.00; Mathern Course weekdays £25.00, weekends £30.00. *Eating facilities:* two restaurants, bar snacks, three bars. *Visitors:* welcome with current membership of a bona fide golf club. *Society Meetings:* weekdays only, except when resident in hotel which has 150 bedrooms with bathrooms, including 42 executive lodge bedrooms, conference rooms and extensive leisure facilities. Professional: Renton Doig. Secretary: T.J. Cleary. Golf Manager: Thomas A. Davidson.

CWMBRAN. **Greenmeadow Golf and Country Club,** Treherbert Road, Croesyceiliog, Cwmbran NP44 2BZ (0633 869321). *Location:* M4 Junction 26 north on A4042. Turn right off Croesyceiliog by-pass. Next to Gwent Crematorium. Parkland course. 18 holes, 5606 yards. S.S.S. 69. Practice green and putting area. *Green Fees:* weekdays £14.00; weekends £19.00. *Eating facilities:* diningroom with 80 covers, patio restaurant 50 covers. *Visitors:* welcome weekdays, weekends by prior notice. No jeans allowed and golf shoes must be worn. *Society Meetings:* always welcome, bookings via our Professional. Package deals with meals available. Professional: C. Coombs (0633 862626). Secretary: David Williams (Fax: 0633 868430).

CWMBRAN. **Pontnewydd Golf Club,** West Pontnewydd, Cwmbran (Cwmbran (0633) 482170). *Location:* two miles north of Cwmbran on B4244. 9 holes, 5403 yards. S.S.S. 67. *Green Fees:* weekdays £16.00; weekends £16.00 only with a member. *Visitors:* welcome all week, must play with member at weekends. *Society Meetings:* not catered for. Secretary: H. R. Gabe.

LLANWERN. **Llanwern Golf Club,** Tennyson Avenue, Llanwern NP6 2DY (Newport (0633) 412380). *Location:* four miles east of Newport, one mile from M4 Junction 24. Parkland. 18 holes, 6202 yards, 5581 metres. S.S.S. 70. 9 holes, 5674 yards, 5186 metres. S.S.S. 69. Large practice area. *Green Fees:* £20.00 weekdays. *Eating facilities:* full catering and bar. *Visitors:* welcome weekdays and Thursdays especially, must have Handicap Certificate. No casual visitors at weekends. *Society Meetings:* catered for by arrangement. Professional: S. Price (0633 413233). Secretary: D.J. Peak (0633 412029).

MONMOUTH. **Monmouth Golf Club,** Leasbrook Lane, Monmouth (Monmouth (0600) 712212). *Location:* outskirts of town on Monmouth – Ross-on-Wye dual carriageway, entrance 100 yards past roundabout; signposted. Undulating parkland. 18 holes, 5700 yards. S.S.S. 67. Small practice area. *Green Fees:* £15.00 per day. Weekly ticket (Monday/Friday inclusive) £35.00. *Eating facilities:* lunch and evening meals provided each day. *Visitors:* welcome, no restrictions. *Society Meetings:* contact the Secretary in advance. Secretary: P.C. Harris (0600 712941).

ST PIERRE HOTEL, GOLF AND COUNTRY CLUB
St Pierre Park, Chepstow, Gwent NP6 6YA. Tel: 0291 625261 Fax: 0291 629975

The premier golf and conference resort in Wales, set in 400 acres of parkland with 11 acre lake. A multi-million pound refurbishment programme of the 146 ensuite bedrooms and public areas will be completed February 1994. Conference rooms, restaurant and coffee shop. Two challenging 18 hole golf courses, including one which currently plays host to the Gary Player Classic.

See our Colour Display Advertisement on page 17

GWENT/GWYNEDD *Wales*

MONMOUTH. **The Rolls of Monmouth Golf Club,** The Hendre, Monmouth NP5 4HG (0600 715353; Fax: 0600 713115). *Location:* four miles west of Monmouth on the B4233 Monmouth/Abergavenny road. Wooded, hilly parkland course on private estate. 18 holes, 6723 yards. S.S.S. 72. Practice area, practice net, putting green. *Green Fees:* on request. *Eating facilities:* full catering. *Visitors:* welcome any day. *Society Meetings:* welcome on any day including weekends. Secretary: J.D. Ross.

NANTYGLO. **West Monmouthshire Golf Club,** Pond Road, Nantyglo, Brynmawr NP3 4QT (Brynmawr (0495) 310233). *Location:* Heads of the Valleys Road to Brynmawr, roundabout to Nantyglo, signposted. Mountain and heathland course. 18 holes, 6118 yards. S.S.S. 69. *Green Fees:* Mondays to Saturdays £12.00; Sundays £17.00 guests only; £2.00 reduction if playing with member. *Eating facilities:* 24 hours notice required. *Visitors:* welcome except Sundays. *Society Meetings:* catered for by appointment only. Secretary: Colin Lewis (0495 312746).

NEWPORT. **Newport Golf Club,** Great Oak, Rogerstone, Newport NP1 9FX (Newport (0633) 892683; Fax: 0633 896676). *Location:* four miles west of Newport, one and a half miles west of exit 27 of M4 (signposted Highcross), on B4591. Parkland. 18 holes, 6314 yards, 5830 metres. S.S.S. 71. Two practice areas. *Green Fees:* £30.00 weekdays, £40.00 weekends. *Eating facilities:* full dining facilities at club. *Visitors:* welcome weekdays without reservation. *Society Meetings:* catered for weekdays (except Tuesdays). Professional: Roy Skuse (0633 893271). Secretary: (0633 892643 and 896794).

NEWPORT. **Tredegar Park Golf Club Ltd,** Bassaleg Road, Newport NP9 3PX (Newport (0633) 895219). *Location:* Junction 28 M4. Mature parkland course with River Ebbw running across. 18 holes, 6095 yards, 5626 metres. S.S.S. 70. Practice area. *Green Fees:* weekdays £25.00; weekends and Bank Holidays £30.00. *Eating facilities:* restaurant and bar. *Visitors:* welcome, must be member of affiliated club. *Society Meetings:* groups of 16 and over catered for; Package at £35 per head. Professional: M.L. Morgan (0633 894517). Secretary: Mr R.T. Howell (0633 894433; Fax: 0633 897152).

PONTYPOOL. **Pontypool Golf Club,** Lasgarn Lane, Trevethin, Pontypool NP4 8TR (Pontypool (0495) 763655). *Location:* Pontypool A4042 to St. Cadoc's Church, Trevethin. Undulating hillside course, with mountain turf and fine views. 18 holes, 6046 yards. S.S.S. 69. Practice area. *Green Fees:* £16.50 weekdays, £22.50 weekends and Bank Holidays. *Eating facilities:* diningroom and bar snacks. *Visitors:* welcome with Handicap Certificates. *Society Meetings:* catered for by arrangement. Professional: Jim Howard (0495 755544). Secretary: Mrs E. Wilce (0495 763655).

RHYMNEY. **Tredegar and Rhymney Golf Club,** Cwmtysswg, Rhymney NP2 3BQ (0685 840743). *Location:* junction of A4048 and A465 Heads of the Valley road. Mountain course. 9 holes, 5564 yards. S.S.S. 68. *Green Fees:* weekdays £10.00 (with member £7.50); weekends and Bank Holidays £12.50 (with member £10.00). *Eating facilities:* bar snacks. *Visitors:* welcome without reservation. *Society Meetings:* catered for without reservation. Secretary: V. Davies (049525 6096).

Gwynedd

ABERDOVEY. **Aberdovey Golf Club,** Aberdovey LL35 0RT (0654 767210). *Location:* west end of Aberdovey on A493, adjacent to railway station. Championship links. 18 holes, 6445 yards. S.S.S. 71. Practice area. *Green Fees:* on application. *Eating facilities:* restaurant and bar. *Visitors:* welcome on production of Handicap Certificate. *Society Meetings:* catered for by prior arrangement (not August or Bank Holidays). Professional: J. Davies (0654 767602). Secretary: J.M. Griffiths (0654 767493).

ANGLESEY. **Baron Hill Golf Club,** Beaumaris, Anglesey (Beaumaris (0248) 810231). *Location:* turn left on approach to Beaumaris from Menai Bridge on A545. Parkland. 9 holes, 5062 metres. S.S.S. 67. *Green Fees:* weekdays £12.00, £5.00 with a member.

BODFOR HOTEL

A comfortable family run licensed hotel, centrally situated opposite beach and car park. Most bedrooms are enuite and all have TV, telephone and tea making facilities. Restaurant offers table d'hôte and à la carte menus. Golf parties catered for, concessionary green fees offered. Special breaks midweek or weekends.

Bodfor Hotel, Seafront, Aberdovey, Gwynedd LL35 0EA. Telephone: 0654 767475 Fax: 0654 767679

WTB ✿✿✿✿
RAC ★★★
AA ★★★

TREFEDDIAN HOTEL
ABERDOVEY

Telephone
Aberdovey
(0654) 767213

In a magnificent setting overlooking the golf links and sandy beach in Cardigan Bay. Facilities include games room, putting green, tennis court, indoor swimming pool. Ample parking in spacious grounds. Golf. Sailing. Fishing and pony trekking in district. Send for Golf Brochure.

THE GOLF GUIDE 1994 — Wales GWYNEDD

Weekly £45.00. *Eating facilities:* clubhouse destroyed by fire – hope to resume full facility in near future. *Visitors:* welcome, competitions most Sundays, tee reserved for ladies on Tuesdays 10.30 – 12.30. *Society Meetings:* welcome, by prior arrangement with Secretary. Secretary: A. Pleming.

ANGLESEY. **Bull Bay Golf Club Ltd,** Bull Bay, Amlwch, Anglesey LL68 9RY (Amlwch (0407) 830213). *Location:* A5025 coast road, one mile west of Amlwch. Seaside heathland with stunning views – Wales' northernmost golf course. 18 holes, 6160 yards. S.S.S. 70. Practice ground and putting green. *Green Fees:* £15.00 per round, £20.00 per day weekdays; £20.00 per round, £25.00 per day weekends (including Fridays) and Bank Holidays. Discount for parties of 12 and over. *Eating facilities:* bar snacks, dining room; limited facilities on Tuesdays. *Visitors:* welcome, competitions permitting; advance bookings advised. *Society Meetings:* welcome (not usually on Saturdays), booking mandatory. Professional: Neil Dunroe PGA (0407 831188). Secretary: David W. Lewis OBE (0407 830960).

BALA. **Bala Golf Club,** Penlan, Bala (0678 520359). *Location:* turn right before coming to Bala Lake on the main Bala-Dolgellau road. Upland course with superb views in the Snowdonia National Park. 10 holes, 4970 yards, 4512 metres. S.S.S. 64. *Green Fees:* weekdays £10.00; weekends and Bank Holidays £10.00 per day. Weekly tickets £30.00. *Eating facilities:* bar with snacks available. *Visitors:* welcome all year, some restrictions on Bank Holidays and weekends. Snooker table and small golf shop. *Society Meetings:* very welcome by prior arrangement. Professional: David Larvin (visiting). Secretary/Manager: G. Davis (0678 520359 9am to 12 noon).

BANGOR. **St. Deiniol Golf Club,** Penybryn, Bangor LL57 1PX (Bangor (0248) 353098). *Location:* at A5/A55 intersection, follow A5122 for one mile to eastern outskirts of Bangor. Parkland course with magnificent views. 18 holes, 5545 yards, 5068 metres. S.S.S. 67. *Green Fees:* £10.00 per day weekdays; £15.00 weekends and Bank Holidays. *Eating facilities:* two bars; full catering Mondays excepted. *Visitors:* welcome without reservation, restrictions at weekends. *Society Meetings:* welcome by prior arrangement. Secretary: J.R. Harries.

BETWS-Y-COED. **Betws-y-Coed Golf Club,** The Clubhouse, Betws-y-Coed LL24 0AL (Betws-y-Coed (0690) 710556). *Location:* turn north off A5 in village. Parkland, flat scenic course on valley floor of River Conwy. 9 holes, 4996 yards. S.S.S. 64. *Green Fees:* £12.50 weekdays, £17.50 weekends. Rates for parties negotiable. *Eating facilities:* catering, bar 12 – 2pm and from 4.30pm. *Visitors:* no restrictions provided there are no club competitions. *Society Meetings:* catered for. Secretary: F.R. Slater (0492 641663).

CAERNARFON. **Caernarfon Golf Club,** Aberforeshore, Llanfaglan, Caernarfon (0286 673783). *Location:* two miles from town along the Menai Straits. Parkland course in superb sea and mountain setting. 18 holes, 5869 yards. S.S.S. 69. *Green Fees:* weekdays £15.00; weekends £18.00. Special rates for visiting parties, weekdays only. *Eating facilities:* excellent

---

The British Hotel
Bangor
Gwynedd
LL57 1NP

Bangor's largest hotel, all 52 bedrooms have private bathroom and toilet, colour TV, trouser press and hospitality tray. 60-seater dining room, banqueting facilities up to 140 and syndicate room for 40. Carvery; Buttery Bar; comfortable spacious lounges. Separate pub serves many fine beers. Car parking for 100. Lift to all floors. Bed & Breakfast from £13. Residents' 3 course dinner £7.50. A la carte menu also available.

Tel: 0248 364911 Fax: 0248 370569   WTB ♛♛♛ Recommended

Eryl Mor Hotel
WTB ♛♛♛ Commended

This comfortable well appointed hotel is situated overlooking Bangor's Victorian pier, with splendid views across the Menai Straits to the Great Orme, Puffin Island and Snowdonia.

The hotel rooms (mostly ensuite) have colour TV, tea and coffee facilities, radio alarm and direct dial telephone. Laundry can be arranged, and the hotel has ample drying facilities and adequate secure storage for equipment.

Eryl Mor is fully licensed with two bars, and serves delicious wholesome meals in the restaurant and bars. The whole hotel is fully centrally heated. Both managing partners are experienced golfers, and look forward to passing on advice on golf courses in North Wales.

Bangor is ideally situated as a base for a golfing break in North Wales with many challenging courses within easy reach. Please phone or fax for our comprehensive Golfing Breaks brochure with full details of over 20 courses. Our staff will arrange your complete package including liaison with golf clubs on your behalf.

We overlook nothing but the Menai Straits   Eryl Mor Hotel, Upper Garth Road, Bangor, Gwynedd LL57 2SR Tel & Fax: (0248) 353789

GLAN ABER HOTEL
HOLYHEAD ROAD, BETWS-Y-COED LL24 0AB TELEPHONE: 0690 710325 FAX: 0690 710700

Situated in the middle of the beautiful village of Betws-y-Coed. Close to scenic parkland course, 18 hole. Many other courses within easy reach. En-suite rooms have TV and teamakers. Choice of bars, games room and drying room. Car parking. Call for further details.

catering and bar facilities. *Visitors:* welcome Monday to Friday. *Society Meetings:* welcome, subject to pre-arranged bookings. Secretary: J.O. Morgan (0286 678359).

CONWY. **Conwy (Caernarvonshire) Golf Club,** Morfa, Conwy LL32 8ER (Aberconwy (0492) 593400). *Location:* follow signs for Conwy Marina off A55. Seaside links. 18 holes, 6647 yards. S.S.S. 72. Practice facilities. *Green Fees:* weekdays £22.00; weekends and Bank Holidays £27.00. Weekly ticket £88.00 (Monday to Friday). *Eating facilities:* available except Monday evening and all day Tuesday. *Visitors:* welcome with reservation, restrictions at weekends. *Society Meetings:* catered for on application to Secretary. Professional: Peter Lees (0492 593225). Secretary: E.C. Roberts (0492 592423).

CRICCIETH. **Criccieth Golf Club,** Ednyfed Hill, Criccieth (Criccieth (0766) 522154). *Location:* in High Street (A497) turn right past Memorial Hall, keep going up lane to Club. 18 holes, 5755 yards. S.S.S. 68. *Green Fees:* £10.00 weekdays; £15.00 weekends. *Eating facilities:* light meals available April to September. *Visitors:* welcome without reservation. *Society Meetings:* catered for with prior reservation. Secretary: M.G. Hamilton (0766 522697).

DOLGELLAU. **Dolgellau Golf Club,** Ffordd Pencefn, Dolgellau (0341 422603). *Location:* half-a-mile from town centre. 9 holes, 4671 yards. S.S.S. 63. *Green Fees:* weekdays £12.00; weekends £15.00. *Eating facilities:* bar and catering facilities available. *Visitors:* welcome without reservation. *Society Meetings:* catered for. Secretary: H.M. Edwards (0341 422603).

FFESTINIOG. **Ffestiniog Golf Club,** Y Cefn, Ffestiniog (0766 762637). *Location:* located on B4391, one mile from Ffestiniog village. Upland course. 9 holes, 5032 yards. S.S.S. 66. *Green Fees:* approximately £8.00. *Eating facilities:* available by prior arrangement. *Visitors:* welcome at any time, some restrictions mainly at weekends during club competitions. *Society Meetings:* by prior arrangement. Secretary: Andrew M. Roberts (0766 831829).

HARLECH. **Royal St. David's Golf Club,** Harlech LL46 2UB (0766 780203). *Location:* A496 lower Harlech road below castle. Seaside links. Championship links in an area of outstanding natural beauty. 18 holes, 6427 yards. S.S.S. 71. Large practice ground. *Green Fees:* weekdays £23.00 per day; weekends £28.00 per day (subject to review). *Eating facilities:* full catering and bar facilities available. *Visitors:* must be members of bona fide golf clubs with handicap – booking advisable. *Society Meetings:* catered for by prior arrangement. Professional: John Barnett (0766 780857). Secretary: R.I. Jones (0766 780361).

LLANDUDNO. **Llandudno Golf Club (Maesdu) Ltd,** Hospital Road, Llandudno LL30 1HU (0492 876016; Fax: 0492 871570). *Location:* Llandudno General Hospital. A55 and then A470. Parkland. 18 holes, 6513 yards. S.S.S. 72. *Green Fees:* weekdays £20.00 per day; weekends and Bank Holidays £25.00 per day. *Eating facilities:* full catering, bar (large) available. *Visitors:* welcome every day, tee reservations for members. *Society Meetings:* must be booked, catered for. Professional: S. Boulden (0492 875195). Secretary: George Dean (0492 876450).

LLANDUDNO. **North Wales Golf Club Ltd,** 72 Bryniau Road, West Shore, Llandudno LL30 2DZ (Llandudno (0492) 875325). *Location:* one-and-a-half miles from Llandudno town centre on West Shore. Seaside links. 18 holes, 6132 yards, 5580 metres. S.S.S. 69. *Green Fees:* weekdays £20.00 per day; weekends and Bank Holidays £25.00 per day. Inclusive package available November to March. *Eating facilities:* full bar and catering facilities. *Visitors:* welcome with reservation after 9.45am. Some other time restrictions. Current Handicap Certificate required. *Society Meetings:* catered for by arrangement. Professional: R.A. Bradbury (0492 876878). Secretary: G.D. Harwood (0492 875325).

LLANDUDNO. **Rhos-on-Sea Residential Golf Club,** Penrhyn Bay, Llandudno LL30 3PU (Llandudno (0492) 549100). *Location:* A55 to Colwyn Bay follow signs to Rhos-on-Sea, one mile past Rhos-on-Sea on coast road in Penrhyn Bay. Flat seaside parkland course. 18 holes, 6064 yards. S.S.S. 69. *Green Fees:* £15.00 weekdays; £20.00 weekends. *Eating facilities:* available, bar meals 12 - 2pm, teas, coffees, snacks available all day. Evening meals by arrangement. Licensed bar open 11am - 3pm lunch, 5.30pm - 11pm evenings; Sundays 12 - 2pm lunch, 7pm - 10.30pm evenings. *Visitors:* all welcome any time, prior booking required particularly weekends. 18 bedrooms, two full size snooker tables, small TV lounge. Two £100 jackpot

DEGANWY CASTLE HOTEL

Situated between Llandudno and Conwy, overlooking the estuary and Conwy Castle, with three Championship Golf courses close by. The Deganwy Castle Hotel can cater for all occasions. Excellent food and bar. Short Breaks, Weddings, Conferences, and Golfing Breaks. 32 Rooms, all en-suite. Telephone for brochure.

RAC ★★ Deganwy, Conwy,
Gwynedd LL31 9DA
Telephone: (0492) 583555

Overlooked by the ancient fortress of Harlech Castle, **THE RUM HOLE HOTEL** is directly opposite the famous Royal St David's Golf Course and is centrally situated for the Porthmadog, Criccieth, Pwllheli and Nefyn Golf Courses. En-suite accommodation, colour TV, satellite, video facilities, central heating, tea & coffee making and direct dial telephone all rooms.
GOLF PACKAGES PLAYING ROYAL ST DAVID'S, NESYN & PORTHMADOG.

Rum Hole Hotel
Ffordd Newydd
HARLECH
Gwynedd . Wales
LL46 2UB

Telephone :
Harlech (0766) 780477

ST. DAVID'S HOTEL
Harlech, Gwynedd LL46 2PT
Tel: (0766) 780366; Fax: (0766) 780820

* Overlooking Royal St. David's Golf Course
* WTB 🏵🏵🏵🏵 rating, RAC Acclaimed
* 60 bedrooms, all en suite with colour TV, telephone and tea/coffee making facilities
* Swimming pool   * 2 Bars   * Snooker room
* Golf packages playing Royal St. David's, Porthmadog and Nefyn Courses
* Societies welcomed

DUNOON HOTEL
LLANDUDNO
TELEPHONE 0492 860787
AA & RAC ★★   🏵🏵🏵 Highly Commended

Beautifully appointed Victorian Hotel with today's comforts and excellent food. Family run over 40 years. 60 bedrooms en-suite, colour TV/satellite, teamaking, telephone, radio, central heating. Oak panelled Bar and Restaurant, lounges with open fire, lift, car park. An ideal base for golfing or touring or a short break.
Open March to end October, please write or telephone for brochure.

ESPLANADE HOTEL
Glan-y-Mor Parade, Promenade, Llandudno
Tel: (0492) 860300 (5 lines)   Fax: (0492) 860418

SPECIAL ATTENTION GIVEN TO GOLFING PARTIES
MEMBERSHIPS FOR NORTH WALES GOLF CLUB

Premier seafront position. Ideally situated for town and leisure facilities. 60 rooms all with bathroom and toilet en-suite, tea/coffee making facilities, colour TV, radio, intercom and baby listening service, direct dial telephones. Central heating throughout. Car Park. Fully licensed. Lift. Small ballroom. Open all year. Christmas and New Year festivities. Spring and Autumn breaks.

WTB 🏵🏵🏵 Highly Commended ## TAN LAN HOTEL

Elegant family-run hotel situated on West Shore, close to Maesdu and North Wales Golf Courses. Beautifully appointed hotel offering a warm welcome, excellent meals and service. 18 comfortably furnished en-suite rooms, with colour TV, teamaking, clock/radio and central heating. Cosy bar and comfortable lounges. Private parking. Ideal base for golfing, touring, or a short relaxing break.
Open March to end October. Write or phone for brochure.
Great Orme's Road, West Shore, Llandudno LL30 2AR Telephone: 0492 860221 Fax: 0492 860221

fruit machines. *Society Meetings:* catered for. Professional: Mr Matthew Jones (0492 548115). Secretary: Mr Graham J. Robinson (0492 544551). Stewards: Mr and Mrs J. John.

LLANFAIRFECHAN. **Llanfairfechan Golf Club,** Llannerch Road, Llanfairfechan LL33 0EB (0248 680144). *Location:* signposted off old A55, 300 yards west of traffic lights. Hillside parkland. 9 holes, 3119 yards. S.S.S. 57. *Green Fees:* weekdays £6.00; weekends £10.00. *Eating facilities:* no eating facilities, bar open weekends and weekday evenings. *Visitors:* welcome anytime except Sundays. *Society Meetings:* by arrangement, weekdays only in Summer. Secretary: M.J. Charlesworth (0248 680524).

LLANGEFNI. **Llangefni Public Golf Course,** Llangefni, Isle of Anglesey. Short, parkland course. 9 holes, 1467 yards, 1342 metres. S.S.S. 28. Practice net. *Green Fees:* information not provided. Reduced rates Juniors and Senior Citizens. *Eating facilities:* light refreshments only. *Visitors:* welcome at all times, no booking. Golf equipment available for hire. Professional: Paul Lovell (0248 722193).

MORFA BYCHAN. **Porthmadog Golf Club,** Morfa Bychan, Porthmadog LL49 9UU (0766 512037). *Location:* turn in Porthmadog High Street at Woolworths towards Black Rock Sands, club on left hand side of road one mile west. Part parkland, part seaside links. 18 holes, 6240 yards. S.S.S. 70. Practice area. *Green Fees:* £15.00 weekdays, £20.00 weekends, £25.00 Bank Holidays. *Eating facilities:* new clubhouse with much enlarged dining facilities; lunches, teas and evening meals; two bars serving bar snacks. *Visitors:* welcome, no restrictions except for competition days. Snooker. *Society Meetings:* catered for by prior arrangement. Bookings via Match Secretary. Professional: Peter Bright (0766 513828). Secretary: Glyn Humphreys (0766 514124). Match Secretary: Dennis Morrow (0766 514286 evenings).

NEFYN. **Nefyn and District Golf Club,** Golf Road, Morfa Nefyn, Pwllheli LL53 6DA (Nefyn (0758) 720218). *Location:* north coast Lleyn Peninsula, two miles west of Nefyn, 20 miles west of Caernarfon. Seaside course. 27 holes, 6335 yards. S.S.S. 71. Practice area. *Green Fees:* weekdays £17.50 per round, £22.50 per day; weekends and Bank Holidays £25.00 per round, £30.00 per day. 10% discount for 12 or more players. *Eating facilities:* full restaurant facilities and two bars. *Visitors:* welcome without reservation, except club competition days. Billiards room available. *Society Meetings:* catered for by arrangement with Secretary. Professional: J.R. Pilkington (0758 720218). Secretary: Lt Col R.W. Parry (Tel & Fax: 0758 720966).

PENMAENMAWR. **Penmaenmawr Golf Club,** Conwy Old Road, Penmaenmawr LL34 6RD (Penmaenmawr (0492) 623330). *Location:* A55 expressway three miles west of Conwy. Parkland with panoramic views. 9 holes (18 tees), 5306 yards. S.S.S. 67. Two practice areas. *Green Fees:* £15.00 weekdays, £18.00 weekends. *Eating facilities:* bar and bar snacks, meals

DRIVE OFF TO NORTH WALES

... and spend your next golf break on a challenging course in the soft air of the lovely Lleyn Peninsula.

3 to 5 day packages arranged from Easter till 31 October includes 5 course Dinner, Bed and Breakfast and a full day's golf. Cocktail bar, comfortable lounge, colour TV and recreation rooms, plus tennis and putting green in secluded gardens. 16 in party – special rates.

**CAEAU CAPEL HOTEL   NEFYN   GWYNEDD   LL53 6EB
TELEPHONE: 0758 720240**

DEUCOCH HOTEL

WTB ♛♛♛ Commended   AA/RAC ★★

Golfing breaks are our speciality. Peaceful setting with magnificent views across Cardigan Bay to Snowdonia. Ensuite bedrooms with radio and TV (satellite) and beverage tray. Excellent restaurant and well stocked bar with fine collection of rare malt whiskies. Golf packages include Dinner, Bed and Breakfast and Green Fees at a choice of six coastal courses on the Lleyn Peninsula including Nefyn, Pwllheli and Royal St. David's at Harlech. Please write or telephone Barbara White for a brochure and tariff. Ashley Courtenay Recommended.

**Deucoch Hotel, Abersoch, Pwllheli LL53 7LD
Telephone: 0758 712680**

by arrangement. *Visitors:* welcome anytime except Saturdays. *Society Meetings:* welcome by arrangement (not Saturdays). Secretary: Mrs J. Dryhurst Jones (0492 623330).

PWLLHELI. **Abersoch Golf Club,** Golf Road, Abersoch, Pwllheli (0758 812622). *Location:* on left beyond village along the shore. Parkland and seaside links course. 18 holes, 5881 yards. S.S.S. 69. *Green Fees:* £15.00. *Eating facilities:* catering, bar. *Visitors:* welcome, booking required. Handicap Certificate required. Shop. *Society Meetings:* catered for. Secretary: Brian Guest.

PWLLHELI. **Pwllheli Golf Club,** Golf Road, Pwllheli LL53 5PS. *Location:* A499 from Caernarvon (20 miles). Parkland/seaside links. 18 holes. 6091 yards. S.S.S. 69. Two practice areas and putting green. *Green Fees:* £20.00 per day weekdays; £25.00 weekends. Reductions for parties. *Eating facilities:* two large lounge bars and diningroom. Steward: (0758 701633). *Visitors:* welcome without reservation. Pro shop. *Society Meetings:* catered for by prior arrangement. Professional: G.D. Verity (0758 612520). Secretary: R. Eric Williams (0758 701644).

RHOSNEIGR. **The Anglesey Golf Club Ltd,** Station Road, Rhosneigr, Anglesey (Rhosneigr (0407) 810219). *Location:* turn south off A5 between Gwalchmai and Bryngwram onto A4080. In about three miles turn right at Llanfaelog church about one mile from course. Links course. 18 holes, 5713 yards. S.S.S. 68. *Green Fees:* information not provided. *Eating facilities:* bar meals and restaurant. *Visitors:* welcome, preferably after 10am and 1.30pm. Handicap Certificate required. *Society Meetings:* catered for, reservation advised. Professional: Paul Lovell (0407 811202). Manager: Mr Arfon Jones (0407 810930/810219).

TREARDDUR BAY. **Holyhead Golf Club,** Lom Carreg Fawr, Trearddur Bay, Anglesey (0407 762119). *Location:* two miles from Holyhead. Seaside moorland with heavy gorse cover. 18 holes, 6058 yards. S.S.S. 70. *Green Fees:* weekdays £17.00 per round, £20.00 per day; weekends £20.00 per round, £25.00 per day. *Eating facilities:* all catering – restaurant and bar snacks. *Visitors:* welcome, must possess current Handicap and have third party public liability insurance (available from Professional). *Society Meetings:* catered for if members of bona fide golf clubs. Dormy house accommodation available for up to 12. Professional: Paul Capper (0407 762022). Secretary: D. Entwistle (0407 763279).

Powys

BRECON. **Brecon Golf Club,** Newton Park, Brecon (Brecon (0874) 2004). *Location:* on A40 west of town, half a mile from centre. 9 holes, 5218 yards. S.S.S. 66. *Green Fees:* £8.00 at all times. *Visitors:* welcome without reservation. *Society Meetings:* catered for. Secretary: D.H.E. Roderick.

BUILTH WELLS. **Builth Wells Golf Club,** Golf Club Road, Builth Wells LD2 3NF (Builth Wells (0982) 552737). *Location:* off A483, on outskirts of town on Llandovery Road. Parkland, reasonably flat. 18 holes, 5386 yards. S.S.S. 67. Practice area. *Green Fees:* £15.00 per day weekdays, £20.00 weekends and Bank Holidays. Five day and seven day tickets available. *Eating facilities:* catering all day, two bars. *Visitors:* welcome, Handicap Certificate required. *Society Meetings:* welcome, Handicap Certificate required. Professional: Bill Evans (0982 553293). Secretary: Ainsleigh Jones (0982 553296).

BUILTH WELLS. **Rhosgoch Golf Club,** Rhosgoch, Builth Wells LD2 3JY (0497 851251). *Location:* near Hay-on-Wye. Parkland course. 9 holes, 4842 yards. S.S.S. 64. *Green Fees:* £7.00 weekdays, £10.00 weekends. *Eating facilities:* bar/restaurant meals, two bars. *Visitors:* welcome anytime. Accommodation available. *Society Meetings:* anytime. Secretary: C. Dance (054422 286).

CRADOC. **Cradoc Golf Club,** Penoyre Park, Cradoc, Brecon LD3 9LP (Brecon (0874) 623658). *Location:* about two miles north of the market town of Brecon, off B4520 Upper Chapel Road (signposted) past Brecon Cathedral. Attractive parkland course situated in the Brecon Beacons National Park. 18 holes, 6301 yards. S.S.S. 71. Separate practice ground. *Green Fees:* £17.00 weekdays, £20.00 weekends. *Eating facilities:* full catering facilities daily except Mondays. *Visitors:* welcome daily but restricted on Sundays when must be playing with a member. *Society Meetings:* welcome during weekdays. Professional: Douglas Beattie (0874 625524). Secretary: G.S.W. Davies. Host of 1982 Welsh Stroke Play Championships. Home of the Welsh Brewers Champion of Champions Tournament.

CRICKHOWELL. **Old Rectory Hotel and Golf Club,** Llangattock, Crickhowell NP8 1PH (Crickhowell (0873) 810373). *Location:* Crickhowell is between Abergavenny and Brecon. Course is on a hill with spectacular views. 9 holes, 2878 yards. S.S.S. 54. *Green Fees:* information not provided. *Eating facilities:* restaurant, bar meals, two bars. *Visitors:* welcome at all times. Accommodation available, outdoor swimming pool.

POWYS *Wales*   THE GOLF GUIDE 1994

BEACONS GUEST HOUSE
WTB Commended   **AA Listed**

16 Bridge Street, Brecon, LD3 8AH. Tel: (0874) 623339

Barbara and Jonathon Cox assure you of a friendly welcome at their licensed guest house within the Brecon Beacons National Park. Close to many local golf courses. Special Breaks offered and groups catered for. Ensuite bedrooms with beverage trays and colour TV. Exellent food – Taste of Wales Recommended. Private parking.

The Lansdowne Hotel & Restaurant
The Watton, Brecon, Powys LD3 7EG   Tel: 0874 623321

Situated 5 minutes' drive from the beautiful CRADOC GOLF CLUB, with outstanding views of the Brecon Beacons National Park, The Lansdowne is a carefully restored and furnished Georgian Hotel overlooking a small park, a short walk from the town centre and all amenities. Great emphasis is placed on the creation of a warm, friendly atmosphere and providing personal service at all times. Centrally heated throughout, the Hotel offers individually designed ensuite bedrooms, all with colour TV, telephone, clock radio and tea/coffee making facilities. The licensed restaurant caters for all tastes with à la carte, table d'hôte and house speciality menus, complemented by a carefully chosen wine list. Two residents' lounges, where guests can relax over coffee or drinks from our well-stocked bar, complete the Hotel's facilities. GOLFERS and GOLF PARTIES ESPECIALLY WELCOME AND CATERED FOR.

The Red Lion Hotel

Sheila & Ron Rosier welcome you to their friendly 18th century village inn. Golf courses within 8 to 15 miles, including beautiful Cradoc Golf Club, makes the Red Lion an ideal venue. Good homemade food, fine wines and real ales are on offer in our stonewalled bars and cosy restaurant. Ensuite bedrooms have central heating, beverage tray and colour TV. Open all year. Short Breaks from £56.

Llangorse, Brecon, Powys LD3 7TY. Telephone (087484) 238

LION HOTEL
AA ★★ RAC   **WALES TOURIST BOARD**

Builth Wells, Powys, LD2 3DT. Tel: (0982) 553670

RUN BY GOLFERS FOR GOLFERS

A warm welcome, comfortable accommodation, and the finest food in Wales.
SPECIAL TERMS FOR GOLFERS – 2 NIGHT STAY from £75 inclusive of dinner, bed and breakfast, and Sunday lunch.

Caer Beris Manor

Escape to the Heart of Wales for a few days relaxation. Set in 27 acres of parkland surrounded by the River Irfon, Caer Beris Manor is the perfect hideaway. Relax in front of our log fires or enjoy a candlelit dinner in the oak panelled restaurant. All bedrooms are ensuite and have colour TV and direct-dial telephone. Play golf on some of the friendliest courses imaginable, with a lovely 18-hole parkland course adjacent. There are also several other courses nearby, including the championship course at Cradoc. Every modern convenience is offered in a setting of old world charm. A variety of holiday packages are available, including golfing, fishing and activity.

Caer Beris Manor, Builth Wells LD2 3NP. Tel: 0982 552601 Fax: 0982 552586   AA ★★★   WTB

THE GOLF GUIDE 1994　　　　　　　　　　　　　　　　　　　Wales　POWYS

KNIGHTON. **Knighton Golf Club,** Ffryd Wood, Knighton LD7 1DG (Knighton (0547) 528646). *Location:* on ring road of town, turn left off Ffryd Road. Hill course, wooded. 9 holes, 5320 yards, 5014 metres. S.S.S. 66. *Green Fees:* weekdays £8.00; weekends £10.00. *Eating facilities:* bar open in evenings, Saturday and Sunday lunch hour. *Visitors:* welcome every day except Saturday and Sunday afternoons. *Society Meetings:* catered for by arrangement. Secretary: E.J.P. Bright (0547 528684).

LLANDRINDOD WELLS. **Llandrindod Wells Golf Club,** Llandrindod Wells LD1 5NY (Llandrindod Wells (0597) 822010). *Location:* well signposted from A483 and centre of town. Hill top course with beautiful views, designed by Harry Vardon. 18 holes, 5687 yards. S.S.S. 68. *Green Fees:* £12.00 weekdays, £18.00 weekends and Bank Holidays. Parties of eight or more £1.00 per person reduction. *Eating facilities:* every day (except Tuesday), order in person. *Visitors:* welcome, advisable to book in advance. *Society Meetings:* welcome, special day packages, must book in advance. Secretary/Manager: Mr F.T. James (0597 823873).

LLANIDLOES. **St. Idloes Golf Club,** Penrallt, Llanidloes (05512 2559). *Location;* take road to Trefeglwys from Llanidloes for one mile, turn left at house on extreme bend near top of hill. Slightly undulating terrain. 9 holes (x2), 5320 yards. S.S.S. 66. *Green Fees:* weekdays £10.00; weekends £12.00. *Eating facilities:* bar, snacks. *Visitors:* welcome Monday to Saturdays. *Society Meetings:* welcome weekdays and Saturdays. Secretary: J.C. Green (05516 479).

MACHYNLLETH. **Machynlleth Golf Club,** Ffordd Drenewydd, Machynlleth SY20 8UH (0654 702000). *Location:* A489 from Newtown, left hand turn before the speed restriction sign on entering Machynlleth. Undulating meadowland course. 9 holes, 5726 yards, 5285 metres. S.S.S. 67. Small practice area. *Green Fees:* weekdays £12.00; weekends £15.00. £7.00 with a member. *Eating facilities:* by arrangement. Bar. *Visitors:* welcome except during competition days. *Society Meetings:* welcome.

NEWTOWN. **St. Giles Golf Club,** Pool Road, Newtown (Newtown (0686) 625844). *Location:* convenient to town centre, quarter-of-a-mile on Welshpool Road from Newtown. Pleasant riverside course. 9 holes, 5936 yards. S.S.S. 68. *Green Fees:* weekdays £12.50 per day, weekends and Bank Holidays £15.00 per day. *Eating facilities:* bar and catering facilities, no catering on Mondays except Bank Holidays. *Visitors:* welcome, with reservation Saturday afternoons and Sunday mornings. Handicap Certificate required. Golf shop and Professional. *Society Meetings:* catered for. Professional: Mr D.P. Owen. Secretary: Mr T.A. Hall (0686 622223).

WELSHPOOL. **Welshpool Golf Club,** Y Golfa, Welshpool (0938 83249). *Location:* A458 West from Welshpool 4 miles, signpost on right at junction with main road. Rather hilly but very beautiful scenery. 18 holes, 5708 yards. S.S.S. 69. *Green Fees:* £10.00 weekdays; £20.00 weekends. *Eating facilities:* open most of the day for food and drink. *Visitors:* welcome weekdays, must contact the Steward for weekend starting times. *Society Meetings:* must contact Mr F. Knight. Secretary: D.B. Pritchard (0938 552215).

Severn Arms Hotel

A small family run hotel. All rooms ensuite with colour TV, radio, direct dial telephone. A la carte restaurant with excellent wine list. Brochure from resident owners Geoff and Tessa Lloyd. **Concessionary rates on 2 golf courses.**
Severn Arms Hotel, Penybont, Llandrindod Wells, Powys LD1 5UA. Tel: 0597 851224 Fax: 0597 851693
AA ★★ RAC　Les Routiers　Egon Ronay Recommended　WTB

THE LION HOTEL & RESTAURANT
Berriew, Near Welshpool, Powys
Tel: (0686) 640452 Fax: (0686) 640844

17th century inn situated in Wales' best kept village. Golf Courses within 7, 9 and 15 miles; enjoy a new challenge every day on our 3-day inclusive break: Bed, Breakfast & Dinner £150 per person. En-suite.
WTB　AA ★★　Welsh Rarebits　Les Routiers

GOLF IN IRELAND

Royal Portrush.

Golf in Northern Ireland

Antrim

ANTRIM. **Massereene Golf Club,** 51 Lough Road, Antrim BT41 4DQ (Antrim (08494) 29293). *Location:* one mile S.W. of town, 3 miles from Aldergrove Airport, situated alongside the shores of Lough Neagh. 18 holes, 6440 yards. S.S.S. 71. *Green Fees:* weekdays £16.00; weekends £20.00. *Eating facilities:* Full catering facilities 12 noon till 9.00pm. *Visitors:* welcome. *Society Meetings:* catered for. Secretary: Mrs Marie Agnew (08494 28096). Professional: Jim Smyth (08494 64074).

BALLYCASTLE. **Ballycastle Golf Club,** Cushendall Road, Ballycastle (Ballycastle (02657) 62536). *Location:* approximately 50 miles along the coast road west of Larne Harbour. Seaside links/undulating. 18 holes, 5662 yards, 5177 metres. S.S.S. 68. *Green Fees:* (1993) weekdays £12.00 (with member £7.00); weekends and Public Holidays £17.00 (with member £9.00). *Eating facilities:* catering by arrangement. *Visitors:* welcome, best days during the week, no particular restrictions. *Society Meetings:* by arrangement. Professional: T. Stewart (02657 62506). Hon. Secretaries: T.J. Sheehan and M.E. Page (02657 62536).

BALLYCLARE. **Ballyclare Golf Club,** 25 Springvale Road, Ballyclare BT39 9JW (Ballyclare (09603) 42352). *Location:* two miles north of Ballyclare. Parkland, lakes and river. 18 holes, 5840 metres. S.S.S. 71. *Green Fees:* weekdays £12.00; weekends £18.00. *Eating facilities:* catering available. *Visitors:* welcome weekdays except Thursday. *Society Meetings:* catered for. Secretary: H. McConnell (09603 22696).

BALLYMENA. **Ballymena Golf Club,** 128 Raceview Road, Ballymena (Ballymena (0266) 861207). *Location:* two miles north-east of town on A42. Flat/parkland. 18 holes, 5245 metres. S.S.S. 67. *Green Fees:* weekdays £12.00 (£7.50 with member). Weekends £15.00 (£9.00 with member). *Eating facilities:* restaurant and bar snacks. *Visitors:* welcome except Tuesdays and Saturdays. *Society Meetings:* catered for except Tuesdays and Saturdays. Professional: J. Gallagher (0266 861652). Secretary: M.J. MacCrory (0266 861487).

BELFAST. **Cliftonville Golf Club,** 44 Westland Road, Belfast BT14 6NH (Belfast (0232) 744158). Parkland with rivers bisecting three fairways. 9 holes, 6210 yards, 5672 metres. S.S.S. 70. Practice fairway and nets. *Green Fees:* weekdays £12.00, playing with a member £8.00; weekends £15.00, playing with a member £10.00. Special rates – 25% discount for parties of 20 or over. *Eating facilities:* bars, catering on request. *Visitors:* no visitors after 5pm weekdays, until 6pm Saturdays and after 12 noon Sundays. *Society Meetings:* very welcome, especially by arrangement. Hon. Secretary: Martin Henderson (0232 746595).

BELFAST. **Dunmurry Golf Club,** 91 Dunmurry Lane, Dunmurry, Belfast BT17 9JS (Belfast (0232) 621402). *Location:* one mile off M1 (Dunmurry cut-off). Parkland – partially wooded. 18 holes, 5333 metres. S.S.S. 68. Practice area. *Green Fees:* weekdays £14.00; weekends £20.00. *Eating facilities:* restaurant and bar snacks every day except Monday. *Visitors:* welcome except Friday and Saturday. *Society Meetings:* catered for. Professional: Paul Leonard (0232 621314). Secretary/Manager: Allan Taylor (0232 610834).

BELFAST. **Fortwilliam Golf Club,** Downview Avenue, Belfast BT15 4EZ (0232 776798). *Location:* one mile Fortwilliam Junction M2. Parkland. 18 holes, 5933 yards. S.S.S. 68. *Green Fees:* information not provided. *Eating facilities:* available. *Visitors:* welcome most days. *Society Meetings:* catered for Tuesdays and Thursdays. Professional: Peter Hanna (0232 770980). Secretary: R.J. Campbell (0232 370770).

BELFAST. **Gilnahirk Golf Club,** Manns Corner, Upper Braniel Road, Gilnahirk, Belfast (0232 448351). *Location:* two miles from city centre, east Belfast. Parkland. 9 holes, 2699 metres. S.S.S. 68. Practice area and putting green. *Green Fees:* £3.50 weekdays for 9 holes; £4.35 weekends for 9 holes. *Visitors:* welcome, no restrictions. *Society Meetings:* all welcome. Professional: Mr K. Gray (0232 448477). Secretary: Mr H. Moore (0232 659653).

BELFAST. **Malone Golf Club,** 240 Upper Malone Road, Dunmurry, Belfast BT17 9LB (Belfast (0232) 612695). *Location:* three miles south of Belfast. Parkland, wooded course with large lake. 18 holes, 6476 yards. S.S.S. 71. 9 holes, 2895 yards. S.S.S. 72. Two practice grounds. *Green Fees:* £23.00 weekdays (except Wednesday when fee is £26.00); £26.00 weekends and Bank Holidays. *Visitors:* welcome weekdays except Wednesdays. After 5pm Saturdays and time sheet on Sundays. Dress code observed on course and in clubhouse. *Society Meetings:* Mondays and Thursdays. Professional: Michael McGee (0232 614917). Secretary: Thomas H. Young (0232 612758; Fax: 0232 431394).

BUSHMILLS. **Bushmills Golf Club,** Bushfoot Road, Portballintrae, Bushmills BT57 8RR (Bushmills (02657) 31969). *Location:* one mile north of Bushmills. Links course. 9 holes, 5218 yards. S.S.S. 68. Pitch and putt. *Green Fees:* £12.00 weekdays; £15.00 weekends. Special rates as guest of member. *Eating facilities:* bars and restaurant available. *Visitors:* welcome weekdays, Saturday restrictions during competition season, Sundays only welcome if space permits. *Society Meetings:* welcome weekdays, weekends subject to availability. Secretary/Manager: J. Knox Thompson.

ANTRIM Northern Ireland

CARRICKFERGUS. Carrickfergus Golf Club, 35 North Road, Carrickfergus BT38 8LP (Carrickfergus (09603) 62203). *Location:* north road, one mile from main shore road. Fairly flat parkland course, partially wooded. 18 holes, 5752 yards. S.S.S. 68. *Green Fees:* weekdays £14.00; weekends £19.00. Societies £12.00. *Eating facilities:* full catering and bar facilities. *Visitors:* welcome except on Saturdays. *Society Meetings:* catered for on weekdays but not after 1pm on Fridays. Professional: Ray Stevenson (09603 51803). Hon. Secretary: I.D. Jardine (09603 63713).

CARRICKFERGUS. Greenisland Golf Club, 156 Upper Road, Greenisland, Carrickfergus BT38 8RW (Whiteabbey (0232) 862236). 9 holes, 5596 metres. S.S.S. 69. *Green Fees:* weekdays £10.00, Sundays £15.00. *Eating facilities:* lunches at club, order in advance. *Visitors:* welcome except before 5.30pm Saturdays. Secretary: J. Wyness.

CARRICKFERGUS. Whitehead Golf Club, McCrae's Brae, Whitehead, Carrickfergus (Whitehead (0960) 353792). *Location:* Whitehead 15 miles from Belfast, 10 miles from Larne. 18 holes, 6362 yards. S.S.S. 71. *Green Fees:* weekdays £11.00; weekends with a member only £7.00. *Eating facilities:* by arrangement with Steward. *Visitors:* welcome Monday to Friday, weekends with a member only. *Society Meetings:* by prior arrangement. Professional: T. Loughran (0960 353118). Secretary/Manager: J.M. Niblock (0960 353631 9am – 1pm).

CUSHENDALL. Cushendall Golf Club, Shore Road, Cushendall (Cushendall (02667) 71318). *Location:* 25 miles north on Antrim coast road from Larne Harbour. Seaside – wooded. River comes into play in seven out of nine holes. 9 holes, 4678 yards, 4030 metres. S.S.S. 63. *Green Fees:* weekdays £9.00 per day, weekends and Bank Holidays £11.00; £3.00 concession if playing with member. *Eating facilities:* normal bar hours – by arrangement with caterers. *Visitors:* welcome without reservation, time sheet in operation on Sundays. *Society Meetings:* by arrangement. Hon. Secretary: Shaun McLaughlin (0266 73366).

LARNE. Cairndhu Golf Club Ltd, 192 Coast Road, Ballygally, Larne BT40 2QG (0574 583248). *Location:* four miles north of Larne. Parkland course. 18 holes, 6122 yards, 5598 metres. S.S.S. 69. Practice area. *Green Fees:* £12.00 weekdays; £18.00 weekends. *Eating facilities:* dining and bar facilities available. *Visitors:* welcome except Saturdays. *Society Meetings:* welcome. Professional: R. Walker (0574 583417). Secretary: Mrs Josephine Robinson (0574 583324).

LARNE. Larne Golf Club, 54 Ferris Bay Road, Islandmagee, Larne BT40 3RT (0960 382228). *Location:* six miles north of Whitehead on Browns Bay Road. Part links, part parkland. 9 holes, 6066 yards. S.S.S. 69. Practice ground. *Green Fees:* weekdays £8.00, with a member £4.00; weekends £15.00, with a member £8. *Eating facilities:* bar, restaurant. *Visitors:* welcome Mondays to Thursdays, and Sundays. Snooker table. *Society Meetings:* welcome on application (not Friday or Saturday). 10% reduction for societies of 20 or more. Secretary: J.B. Stewart.

THE GOLF GUIDE 1994

LISBURN. Lisburn Golf Club, Blairs Lodge, 68 Eglantine Road, Lisburn BT27 5QR (0846 677216; Fax: 0846 603608). *Location:* three miles south of Lisburn on A1. Parkland. 18 holes, 6101 metres. S.S.S. 72. Practice area. *Green Fees:* £20.00 weekdays; weekends £30.00. *Eating facilities:* bar and restaurant. *Visitors:* welcome weekdays, Tuesdays Ladies have preference. Saturday after 5.30pm only, Sundays with member only. Snooker room. *Society Meetings:* catered for Mondays, Thursdays and Fridays. Professional: B.R. Campbell (0846 677217). Secretary: G. Graham (0846 677216).

NEWTOWNABBEY. Ballyearl Golf and Leisure Centre, 585 Doagh Road, Newtownabbey BT36 8RZ (0232 848287). *Location:* six miles north of Belfast on M2, then main road to Larne, first right onto Doagh Road. Parkland. 9 holes, 2402 yards, 2196 metres. Par 3. 36 bay floodlit driving range. *Green Fees:* weekdays adult £3.00, Junior £2.00, Senior Citizen £1.50; weekends adult £4.00, Junior £3.00, Senior Citizen £2.00. *Eating facilities:* private bar, can be signed in. *Visitors:* no restrictions – pay and play. Professional: Jim Robinson and Wesley Ramsey (0232 840899). Secretary: Alan Bevan.

PORTBALLINTRAE. Bushfoot Golf Club, 50 Bushfoot Road, Portballintrae BT57 8RR (02657 31317). *Location:* off Ballaghmore Road, Portballintrae. Seaside links course. 9 holes, 5054 yards. S.S.S 68. *Green Fees:* weekdays £12.00; weekends £15.00. *Eating facilities:* full diningroom, bars. *Visitors:* welcome, restrictions weekends June to September. *Society Meetings:* all welcome weekdays. Secretary: J. Knox Thompson.

PORTRUSH. Rathmore Golf Club, Bushmills Road, Portrush BT56 8JG (0265 822285). *Location:* north east coast – six miles from Coleraine, beside roundabout on road to Bushmills. Flat seaside links. 18 holes, 6273 yards. S.S.S. 71. *Green Fees:* £16.00 weekdays; £20.00 weekends. *Eating facilities:* bar but no eating facilities. *Visitors:* Saturday and Sunday 1.30 to 2.30pm, Monday to Friday no restrictions except Tuesday after 11am September to March. *Society Meetings:* must register at Royal Portrush Golf Club and green fees paid before commencement of play. Professional: Dai Stevenson (R.P.G.C.) (0265 823335). Secretary: Derek Ross Williamson (0265 822996).

PORTRUSH. Royal Portrush Golf Club, Dunluce Road, Portrush BT56 8JQ (Portrush (0265) 822311). *Location:* one mile from Portrush on the main Portrush/Bushmills Road. Dunluce Course – natural seaside links. 18 holes, 6794 yards. S.S.S. 73. Valley Course – flat seaside links. 18 holes, 6273 yards. S.S.S. 71. Two practice grounds. *Green Fees:* Dunluce: £35.00 per day weekdays; £40.00 per day weekends Valley: £15.00 per day weekdays; £20.00 per day weekends. *Eating facilities:* three bars, restaurant with snacks and à la carte. *Visitors:* Dunluce Course: must contact Secretary prior to visit. Restrictions Wednesday and Friday afternoons and Saturday and Sunday mornings. Valley Course: welcome weekdays, plus limited tee times at weekends. *Society Meetings:* accepted with prior booking. Professional: Dai Stevenson (0265 823335). Secretary: Miss W. Erskine (0265 822311; Fax: 0265 823139).

Armagh

ARMAGH. County Armagh Golf Club, The Demesne, Newry Road, Armagh BT60 1EN (Armagh (0861) 522501). *Location:* Newry Road out of Armagh. Parkland. 18 holes, 6157 yards, 5649 metres. S.S.S. 70. Practice area available. *Green Fees:* £10.00 weekdays, £15.00 weekends. During the months of November to February (inclusive) reduction of £1.00. *Eating facilities:* diningroom/bar meals Tuesdays to Sundays, bar facilities daily. *Visitors:* welcome by arrangement. Not Saturdays or Thursdays. *Society Meetings:* welcome by arrangement except Saturdays or Thursdays. Professional: Alan Rankin (0861 525864). Secretary: June McParland (0861 525861).

CRAIGAVON. Craigavon Golf and Ski Club, Turmoyra Lane, Lurgan, Craigavon (Lurgan (0762) 326606; Fax: 0762 347272). *Location:* half a mile from motorway, one mile from town centre, adjacent to ski slope. Parkland/wooded. 18 holes, 5901 metres. S.S.S. 72. 9 hole Par 3; 12 hole pitch and putt. Driving range. *Green Fees:* weekdays £8.00; weekends £11.00. *Eating facilities:* full restaurant facilities. *Visitors:* always welcome. Modern clubhouse, showers and lockers. *Society Meetings:* welcome – book beforehand. Professional: D. Paul.

CULLYHANNA. Ashfield Golf Club, Freeduff, Cullyhanna (0693 868 180). *Location:* two miles from Crossmaglen, 15 miles from Newry. Parkland course. 18 holes, 5616 yards. S.S.S. 67. Par 69. Driving range. *Green Fees:* weekdays £8.00; weekends £10.00. *Eating facilities:* fully licensed restaurant. *Visitors:* welcome at all times except before 11am on Sundays. *Society Meetings:* welcome, special rates available. Secretary: Noel McConville.

LURGAN. Lurgan Golf Club, The Demesne, Lurgan, Craigavon BT67 9BN (Lurgan (0762) 322087). *Location:* one mile from motorway, half a mile from Town Centre. Parkland. 18 holes, 5561 metres. S.S.S. 70. Small practice area, putting green. *Green Fees:* weekdays £15.00; weekends £20.00. Reductions if playing with a member. Students £10.00, under 18's £5.00. *Eating facilities:* restaurant and lounge bar. Caterer: (0762 322337). *Visitors:* welcome Mondays, Tuesdays, Thursdays, Fridays and Sundays; Saturdays after 4pm. *Society Meetings:* welcome as per visitors. Professional: D. Paul (0762 321068). Secretary: Mrs G. Turkington (0762 322087).

PORTADOWN. Portadown Golf Club, 192 Gilford Road, Portadown, Craigavon BT63 5LF (Portadown (0762) 355356). *Location:* A59 south east of Portadown for two miles, entrance on right. Parkland. 18 holes, 5621 metres. S.S.S. 70 off white tees; 68 off green tees, 67 off yellow tees. Practice net. *Green Fees:* weekdays £15.00 (men), £12.00 (ladies); weekends and Bank Holidays £18.00 (men), £15.00 (ladies). Eating facilities: bar snacks, restaurant, members' bar and lounge. *Visitors:* welcome at all times except Tuesdays and Saturdays. Squash, indoor bowling and snooker. *Society Meetings:* catered for. Professional: Paul Stevenson (0762 334655). Secretary: Mrs Lily Holloway (0762 355356).

TANDRAGEE. **Tandragee Golf Club,** Markethill Road, Tandragee, Craigavon BT62 2GR (0762 840727). *Location:* approximately five miles from Portadown on road to Newry and Dublin. Hilly parkland and wooded. 18 holes, 5519 metres. S.S.S. 69. Practice area and net. *Green Fees:* weekdays £10.00 (£8.00 ladies). Weekends £15.00. *Eating facilities:* full catering and bars. *Visitors:* welcome all days except Thursdays (Ladies Day) and Saturdays (competition day). *Society Meetings:* welcome by arrangement, except Saturdays. Professional: E. Maney (0762 841761). Secretary: H. McCready (0762 841272).

Down

ARDGLASS. Ardglass Golf Club, 4 Castle Place, Ardglass BT32 3UR (0396 841219; Fax: 0396 841841). *Location:* nearest town – Downpatrick. Situated on the coast 30 miles due south of Belfast. Seaside links. 18 holes, 5515 metres. S.S.S. 69. *Green Fees:* weekdays £13.00; weekends £18.00. *Eating facilities:* bar and diningroom. *Visitors:* welcome. *Society Meetings:* catered for. Advance booking necessary. Professional: Kevin Dorrian (0396 841022). Secretary: Alan Cannon (0396 841219).

BALLYNAHINCH. Spa Golf Club, 20 Grove Road, Ballynahinch BT24 8PN (Ballynahinch (0238) 562365). *Location:* Ballynahinch half mile, Belfast 11 miles. Parkland, wooded. 18 holes, 5938 yards. S.S.S. 72. Practice area. *Green Fees:* weekdays £15.00, playing with member £8.00; £20.00 Sundays. Societies, playing with a member £10.00 weekdays, £13.00 Sundays £20.00. Reductions for parties over 25 in number. *Eating facilities:* meals/bar snacks. *Visitors:* welcome Mondays, Tuesdays and Thursdays. Sundays with member only and Wednesdays not after 3.00pm. *Society Meetings:* welcome Monday, Tuesday, Thursday; Sunday 10.30 to 12.30pm. Secretary: John M. Glass (0232 812340).

BANBRIDGE. Banbridge Golf Club, Huntly Road, Banbridge BT32 3UR (Banbridge (08206) 62342). *Location:* half-a-mile out of Banbridge on Huntly Road. Parkland. 18 holes, 5453 yards, 5003 metres. S.S.S. 67. Practice ground. *Green Fees:* weekdays £7.00, with a member £5.00; weekends £12.00, with a member £6.00. *Eating facilities:* bar facilities. Meals for Societies by arrangement. *Visitors:* welcome. Restrictions on Ladies' Day (Tuesday) and Men's Competition (Saturday). *Society Meetings:* catered for. Arrange with Secretary/Manager. Secretary/Manager: Thomas F. Fee (08206 23831).

BANGOR. **Bangor Golf Club,** Broadway, Bangor BT20 4RH (Bangor (0247) 465133). *Location:* one mile from town centre off Donaghadee Road. Parkland. 18 holes, 6424 yards. S.S.S. 71. Practice facilities. *Green Fees:* weekdays £16.00; weekends £22.00. *Eating facilities:* diningroom (booking essential), lunches and evening meals, bar snacks. *Visitors:* welcome Monday and Wednesday, Tuesdays Ladies' Day; not Saturdays. *Society Meetings:* advance booking necessary. Professional: Norman Drew (0247 462164). Secretary: Tom Russell (0247 270922).

BANGOR. **Carnalea Golf Club,** Station Road, Bangor BT19 1EZ (Bangor (0247) 465004). *Location:* one minute walk from Carnalea Railway Station. Seaside parkland. 18 holes, 5574 yards. S.S.S. 67. *Green Fees:* weekdays £10.00; weekends £13.00. *Eating facilities:* full restaurant and two bars. *Visitors:* welcome without reservation. *Society Meetings:* catered for. Parties over 20 persons – £9.00 each. Professional: M. McGee (0247 270122). Secretary: J.H. Crozier (0247 270368; Fax: 0247 273989).

BANGOR. **Helen's Bay Golf Club,** Golf Road, Helen's Bay, Bangor BT19 1TL (Helen's Bay (0247) 852601). *Location:* A2 from Belfast – 9 miles. Parkland. 9 holes, 5176 yards. S.S.S. 67. *Green Fees:* weekdays £12.00; weekends £15.00. *Eating facilities:* available – full restaurant, bar and lounge bar. *Visitors:* welcome Monday, Wednesday and Friday; Tuesday is Ladies' Day. *Society Meetings:* catered for by prior booking confirmed by the Hon. Secretary (maximum 40). Hon. Secretary: (0247 852815).

BELFAST. **Balmoral Golf Club Ltd,** 518 Lisburn Road, Belfast BT9 6GX (Belfast (0232) 668540). *Location:* two miles south of Belfast City Centre, next door to King's Hall. Parkland course. 18 holes, 5702 metres. S.S.S. 70. *Green Fees:* weekdays £15.00 (Wednesdays £18.00); weekends £22.50. *Eating facilities:* mixed lounge, Fred Daly Bar and restaurant. *Visitors:* welcome except Saturdays. *Society Meetings:* Mondays and Thursdays only. Professional: G. Bleakley (0232 667747; Fax: 0232 669505). Secretary: Robert McConkey (0232 381514).

BELFAST. **Belvoir Park Golf Club,** 73 Church Road, Newtownbreda, Belfast BT8 4AN (0232 491693; Fax: 0232 646113). *Location:* three miles from city centre on road to Newcastle. Parkland – well wooded. 18 holes, 6501 yards, 5943 metres. S.S.S. 71. Practice area. *Green Fees:* weekdays (excluding Wednesday) £27.00; weekends and Wednesdays £32.00. *Eating facilities:* dining and snack meals – bar. *Visitors:* welcome except Saturday. *Society Meetings:* by prior booking only. Professional: M. Kelly (0232 646714). Secretary: Kenneth H. Graham (0232 692817).

BELFAST. **Knock Golf Club,** Summerfield, Dundonald, Belfast BT16 0QX (0232 482249). *Location:* Upper Newtownards Road in east of the city of Belfast. Parkland with huge trees, large bunkers and a stream running through the course. 18 holes, 6435 yards. S.S.S. 71. Limited practice. *Green Fees:* weekdays £17.00, weekends and Bank Holidays £22.00. Fees subject to review. Parties over 25 or more (must book in advance) £15.00 per player. *Eating facilities:* full catering and bar facilities available. *Visitors:* welcome except Saturday but it is advisable to ring Professional first. *Society Meetings:* catered for Mondays and Thursdays. Professional: G. Fairweather (0232 483825). Secretary/Manager: S.G. Managh (0232 483251).

BELFAST. **Knockbracken Golf and Country Club,** 20-24 Ballymaconaghy Road, Knockbracken, Belfast BT8 4SB (0232 792100). *Location:* south from the centre of Belfast on the Ormeau Road to "Four Winds" public house and restaurant, half a mile out on Ballymaconaghy Road, on left by ski slopes. Parkland on undulating ground. 18 holes, 5391 yards. S.S.S. 68. *Green Fees:* £9.00 weekdays, £8.00 with member; £11.00 weekends and Public Holidays, £9.00 with member. *Eating facilities:* full meals and snacks served. *Visitors:* welcome anytime, weekends advised to check availability of tee times. *Society Meetings:* weekdays anytime, not on Saturdays/after 10.30am on Sundays. Professional: David Jones (0232 795666). Secretary: M. Grose (0232 401811).

BELFAST. **Mahee Island Golf Club,** Comber, Newtownards, Belfast BT23 6ET (Killinchy (0238) 541234). *Location:* Comber/Killyleagh Road. After half a mile turn left signpost Ardmillan. Keep left for six miles to course. Parkland/seaside. 9 holes, 5588 yards, 5108 metres. S.S.S. 67. Par 68 over 18 holes. Practice net, green and chipping area. *Green Fees:* weekdays £10.00; weekends £14.00. *Eating facilities:* eating by prior arrangement with caterer (Dundonald 484038). *Visitors:* welcome, restricted Wednesdays after 4pm and Saturdays until 5pm. *Society Meetings:* welcome, by prior arrangement. 50p reduction when 16 or more. Professional: (Shop) Archie McCracken (0238 541234). Hon. Secretary: T. Reid (0396 830613).

BELFAST. **Ormeau Golf Club,** 50 Park Road, Belfast BT7 2FX (Belfast (0232) 641069). *Location:* Belfast south/east; Ravenhill Road. Parkland course. 9 holes, 2678 yards, 2447 metres. S.S.S. 65. *Green Fees:* £8.00 weekdays, £10.00 weekends and Holidays. *Eating facilities:* bars and restaurant. *Visitors:* welcome, restrictions on Tuesdays and Saturdays. *Society Meetings:* welcome Thursdays or Sundays. Professional: M. Kelly (0232 640999). Secretary/Manager: G.E. McVeigh (0232 640700). Caterer: (0232 641999).

BELFAST. **Shandon Park Golf Club,** 73 Shandon Park, Belfast BT5 6NY (Belfast (0232) 793730). Parkland. 18 holes, 5714 metres. S.S.S. 70. *Green Fees:* weekdays £18.00 per round; weekends £25.00 per round. *Eating facilities:* restaurant facilities, bar snacks. *Visitors:* welcome everyday subject to advance clearance by Professional. *Society Meetings:* Mondays and Fridays only. Professional: Barry Wilson (0232 797859). Secretary: Mr Michael Corsar (0232 401856; Fax: 0232 402773).

DONAGHADEE. **Donaghadee Golf Club,** 84 Warren Road, Donaghadee BT21 0PQ (0247 888697; Fax: 0247 888891). *Location:* five miles south of Bangor on coast road. Part links and inland open, magnificent views over Copeland Islands to Scottish coast. 18 holes, 6100 yards, 5561 metres. S.S.S. 69. Practice ground. *Green Fees:* weekdays £13.50; Sundays £17.00. *Eating facilities:* restaurant, bar and

THE GOLF GUIDE 1994 — Northern Ireland DOWN

snacks except Mondays. *Visitors:* welcome any day except on Saturdays. *Society Meetings:* welcome, reductions for Society over 24. Professional: Gordon Drew (0247 882392). Secretary/Manager: M.E. Dilley (0247 883624).

DOWNPATRICK. **Bright Castle Golf Club**, 14 Coniamstown Road, Bright, Downpatrick BT30 8LU (0396 841319). *Location:* off the main Downpatrick Killough Road approximately two and a half miles off main road. Parkland – excellent fairways and greens, plenty trees. 18 holes, 7143 yards. S.S.S. 74. Putting green. *Green Fees:* information not provided. *Eating facilities:* snacks available. *Visitors:* very welcome, no restrictions. *Society Meetings:* very welcome, tee must be reserved. Secretary: Raymond Reid.

DOWNPATRICK. **Downpatrick Golf Club**, 43 Saul Road, Downpatrick BT30 6PA (Downpatrick (0396) 612152). *Location:* one and a half miles from town centre, south-east direction. Parkland, challenging upland course. 18 holes, 6400 yards. S.S.S. 69. Putting area. *Green Fees:* weekdays £13.00; weekends £18.00. 20% discount on weekdays for groups of 20 plus. *Eating facilities:* two lounges, diningroom and snack bar. Catering: (0396 615244). *Visitors:* welcome. Snooker room. *Society Meetings:* catered for by prior arrangement. Professional: (0396 615167). Secretary: Daniel McGreevy (0396 615947).

HOLYWOOD. **Holywood Golf Club**, Demesne Road, Holywood (Holywood (023 17) 2138). 18 holes, 5885 yards. *Green Fees:* information not provided. *Eating facilities:* bars and restaurant. *Visitors:* welcome. Professional: Michael Bannon. General Manager: Robin Kirk.

HOLYWOOD. **The Royal Belfast Golf Club**, Craigavad, Holywood BT18 0BP (0232 422368). *Location:* two miles past Holywood, off main Belfast to Bangor Road. Mainly parkland, bordering shores of Belfast Lough. 18 holes, 5963 yards. S.S.S. 69. Practice ground. *Green Fees:* weekdays £20.00; Saturday after 4.30pm and Sundays £25.00. *Eating facilities:* full catering and bar facilities. *Visitors:* with letter of introduction and by arrangement only. *Society Meetings:* by arrangement. Professional: D.H. Carson (0232 428586). Secretary: I.M. Piggot (0232 428165).

KILKEEL. **Kilkeel Golf Club**, Mourne Park, Kilkeel (Kilkeel (06937) 62296). *Location:* 16 miles from Newcastle and three miles from Kilkeel on main road to Newry. Parkland, wooded, undulating. 18 holes, 6650 metres. S.S.S. 72. Practice area available. *Green Fees:* weekdays £16.00 for 18 holes; weekends £18.00 for 18 holes. *Eating facilities:* full catering services on application, bar facilities. *Visitors:* welcome all week except Saturdays. *Society Meetings:* catered for by prior arrangement. Secretary: S.C. McBride (06937 63787).

LISBURN. **Down Royal Park**, Dunygarton Road, Maze, Lisburn BT27 5RT (0846 621339). *Location:* inside Maze Racecourse. Heathland. 18 holes, 6824 yards. *Green Fees:* weekdays £11.00; Saturdays £13.00; Sundays £17.00. *Eating facilities:* licensed restaurant. *Visitors:* welcome at all times. *Society Meetings:* welcome. Secretary: N.F. Ewing (acting).

NEWCASTLE. **Royal County Down Golf Club**, Newcastle BT33 0AN. *Location:* adjacent to north side of Newcastle, approach from town centre. Championship Course: 18 holes, 6968 yards. Course: 18 holes, 4100 yards. S.S.S. 60. *Green Fees:* weekdays Summer £40.00, Winter £30.00; weekends Summer £50.00, Winter £40.00. *Eating facilities:* light lunches and bar, weekdays only. *Visitors:* welcome with prior reservation. *Society Meetings:* catered for. Professional: Kevan J. Whitson (03967 22419). Secretary: P.E. Rolph (03967 23314).

NEWTOWNARDS. **Clandeboye Golf Club**, Tower Road, Conlig, Newtownards BT23 3PN (0247 271767). *Location:* Conlig village off A21 between Bangor and Newtownards. Wooded, undulating parkland/heathland. 18 holes, 5915 metres, S.S.S. 72. 18 holes, 5172 metres, S.S.S. 68. Practice ground. *Green Fees:* weekdays £17.50 and £14.00; weekends £23.00 and £17.50. *Eating facilities:* full catering and bar. *Visitors:* welcome weekdays; Saturdays and Sundays must be accompanied by member. (Thursday ladies' day). *Society Meetings:* welcome weekdays except Thursdays (in winter Mondays and Wednesdays only). Reduced rates for parties over 20. Professional: Peter Gregory (0247 271750). Secretary/Manager: Ian Marks (0247 271767).

NEWTOWNARDS. **Kirkistown Castle Golf Club**, 142 Main Road, Cloughey, Newtownards (02477 71353). *Location:* A20 west of Belfast then B173. Seaside links. 18 holes, 6176 yards. S.S.S. 70. *Green Fees:* £10.00 weekdays; £17.00 weekends and Public Holidays. Subject to review. *Eating facilities:* full catering and snacks. *Visitors:* welcome. *Society Meetings:* catered for. Professional: Jonathan Peden (Tel & Fax: 02477 71004). Secretary: D.J. Ryan (02477 71233; Fax: 02477 71699).

NEWTOWNARDS. **Scrabo Golf Club**, 233 Scrabo Road, Newtownards BT23 4SL (0247 812355). *Location:* approximately 10 miles from Belfast off main Belfast to Newtownards dual carriageway. Upland course. 18 holes, 5699 metres. S.S.S. 71. *Green Fees:* weekdays £15.00; weekends £20.00. Societies weekdays £14.00; weekends £19.00. *Eating facilities:* highly recommended full catering facilities. *Visitors:* welcome except Saturdays. *Society Meetings:* over 20 players, welcome. Professional: G. Fairweather (0247 817848) Secretary: James Fraser (0247 812355).

WARRENPOINT. **Warrenpoint Golf Club**, Lower Dromore Road, Warrenpoint (Warrenpoint (06937) 52219). *Location:* five miles south of Newry on coast road. Parkland. 18 holes, 5640 metres. S.S.S. 70. *Green Fees:* weekdays £15.00, weekends £21.00. *Eating facilities:* full catering and bar facilities. *Visitors:* welcome Sunday, Monday, Thursday, Friday. Squash, snooker facilities available. *Society Meetings:* catered for by prior arrangement. Professional: Nigel Shaw (06937 52371). Secretary: John McMahon (06937 53695; Fax: 06937 52918).

Fermanagh

ENNISKILLEN. Ashwoods Golf Centre, Ashwoods, Enniskillen (0365 325321). *Location:* one and a half miles west of Enniskillen on main road to Sligo. Meadowland, wooded and landscaped. 9 holes, 1250 yards. Golf driving range. *Green Fees:* weekdays £3.00; weekends £4.00. *Eating facilities:* available. *Visitors:* welcome, no restrictions. 12 bedroomed guesthouse (licensed). Golf clubs available for hire. *Society Meetings:* welcome, bookings in advance. Professional: Thomas Loughran. Secretary: Mrs Peggy McManus.

ENNISKILLEN. Castle Hume Golf Club, Castle Hume, Enniskillen (0365 327077). *Location:* Belleek Road, Enniskillen. Parkland course; 11th fairway, 15th green and 16th tee are situated on the lough shore. 18 holes, 5941 metres. S.S.S. 72. Putting green and practice area. *Green Fees:* weekdays £8.00; weekends £10.00. Excess of 12 players £2.00 reduction per person. *Eating facilities:* available by arrangement. *Visitors:* welcome, no restrictions. *Society Meetings:* all welcome. Secretary: Daphne Gibson.

ENNISKILLEN. Enniskillen Golf Club, Castlecoole, Enniskillen BT74 6HZ (0365 325250). *Location:* off Enniskillen to Tempo Road on outskirts of town. Undulating parkland with many mature trees. 18 holes, 5990 yards, 5574 metres. S.S.S. 70. *Green Fees:* weekdays £10.00; weekends £12.00. *Eating facilities:* bar snacks daily - full catering by arrangement. *Visitors:* welcome at all times, Ladies have priority on Tuesdays. *Society Meetings:* welcome. Special rates. Hon. Secretary: W.J. Hamilton (0365 323206).

Londonderry

CASTLEROCK. Castlerock Golf Club, 65 Circular Road, Castlerock, Coleraine BT51 4TJ (Coleraine (0265) 848215). *Location:* A2, six miles west of Coleraine. Seaside links, stream in play at four holes. 18 holes, 6687 yards. S.S.S. 72. 9 holes, 2457 metres. S.S.S. 67. Practice area. *Green Fees:* weekdays £15.00 per round; weekends £25.00. *Eating facilities:* full restaurant facilities, two bars. *Visitors:* weekdays no restrictions; casual green fees welcome Sundays. *Society Meetings:* welcome weekdays. Professional: R. Kelly (0265 848314). Secretary: R.G. McBride (0265 848314).

COLERAINE. Brown Trout Golf and Country Club, 209 Agivey Road, Aghadowey, Near Coleraine (0265 868209; Fax: 0265 868878). *Location:* on A54 between Kilrea and Coleraine. Parkland course, heavily wooded, crossing water seven times in nine holes. 9 holes, 2755 metres. S.S.S. 68. *Green Fees:* weekdays £7.00; weekends £10.00. *Eating facilities:* à la carte restaurant, bar snacks, barbecues. *Visitors:* always welcome. 15 new luxurious en suite bedrooms available. *Society Meetings:* welcome. Professional: Ken Revie. Secretary/Manager: Bill O'Hara.

LIMAVADY. Benone Golf Course, 53 Benone Avenue, Benone, Limavady (05047 22226; Fax: 05047 22010). *Location:* situated on the A2 coast road, 12 miles from Limavady. Parkland course with characteristic stream. 9 holes, 1427 yards, 1305 metres. S.S.S. 27. Practice range, putting green. *Green Fees:* weekdays £3.00 adults, £1.75 juniors; weekends £3.50 adults, £2.50 juniors. *Eating facilities:* coffee shop open July/August, restaurants within one mile. *Visitors:* welcome. Secretary: The Warden.

MAGHERAFELT. Moyola Park Golf Club, Shanemullagh, Castledawson, Magherafelt BT45 8DG (0648 68468). *Location:* 40 miles north of Belfast on M2. Attractive, spacious mature parkland. 18 holes, 6517 yards. S.S.S. 71. Practice ground, putting green. *Green Fees:* £12.00 weekdays; £20.00 weekends. *Eating facilities:* bars and restaurant. *Visitors:* welcome, Wednesday is Ladies Day and Sundays only 1.30pm to 2.30pm. *Society Meetings:* only after prior notice. Professional: Mr V. Teague (0648 68830). Secretary: Mr L.W.P. Hastings (0648 32796/31271).

PORTSTEWART. Portstewart Golf Club, Strand Head, Portstewart (Portstewart (026583) 2015). Coastal links. Strand (No. 1) course 18 holes. Town (No. 2) course 18 holes, Strand 6784 yards, S.S.S. 72; Town 4733 yards, S.S.S. 63. *Green Fees:* information not available. *Eating facilities:* meals available – advance orders. *Visitors:* welcome Mondays to Fridays with reservation. *Society Meetings:* catered for. Professional: A. Hunter (026583 2601). Secretary: Michael Moss.

PREHEN. City of Derry Golf Club, 49 Victoria Road, Prehen BT47 2PU (0504 311610). *Location:* three miles from city centre on the road to Strabane – follow the river Foyle. Parkland, wooded. 18 holes, 6362 yards. S.S.S. 71. Also 9 hole course, 4708 yards. S.S.S. 63. Practice area. *Green Fees:* information not provided. *Eating facilities:* catering and bar facilities available. *Visitors:* welcome on weekdays up to 4.30pm, weekends please contact Professional. Convenient for hotel and guest houses. *Society Meetings:* welcome, please contact Secretary. Professional: M. Doherty (0504 46696). Secretary: P.J. Doherty (0504 46369).

BROWN TROUT GOLF AND COUNTRY INN

Attractive parkland course, heavily wooded and crossing water seven times in nine holes. A la carte restaurant, bar snacks and barbecues. Well appointed bedrooms. Bill, Gerry and Jenny welcome enquiries at Northern Ireland's only Golf Hotel.

Brown Trout Golf and Country Inn, 209 Agivey Road, Aghadowey, near Coleraine.
Telephone: 0265 868209

THE GOLF GUIDE 1994 *Northern Ireland*

The links at Portstewart.

TYRONE *Northern Ireland*

Tyrone

COOKSTOWN. **Killymoon Golf Club**, Killymoon Road, Cookstown (Cookstown (06487) 62254). *Location:* private road off A29. Signposted at Dungannon end of town opposite Drum Road. Mainly flat parkland. 18 holes, 5513 metres. S.S.S. 69. Practice area. *Green Fees:* weekdays £13.00; weekends and Bank Holidays £17.00, not Saturday afternoons. *Eating facilities:* full catering at club (large groups please book). *Visitors:* welcome except Saturday until 3pm, Thursdays Ladies Day, booking essential. *Society Meetings:* Sundays limit 32, Saturdays none, weekdays welcome but ladies have priority Thursdays. Societies of 20 or more £11.00 weekdays, £15.00 weekends. Professional: Barry Hamill (06487 63460). Secretary: Les Hodgett (06487 63762).

DUNGANNON. **Dungannon Golf Club**, 34 Springfield Lane, Dungannon BT70 1QX (08687 27338). *Location:* one mile west of Dungannon, to right of Dungannon to Donaghmore Road. Flat first nine holes, hilly last nine holes. 18 holes, 5904 yards. S.S.S. 68. Putting area. *Green Fees:* £10.00 weekdays; £13.00 weekends and Bank Holidays. £2.00 discount if playing with a member. *Eating facilities:* catering by prior arrangement. *Visitors:* welcome, precluded by timesheets weekends/competitions. *Society Meetings:* welcome, especially mid week. Secretary: L.R.P Agnew (08687 22098).

FINTONA. **Fintona Golf Club**, Kiln Street, Ecclesville, Demesne, Fintona (0662 841480). *Location:* eight miles south of Omagh, county town of Tyrone. Parkland with a river running through the course. 9 holes, 5716 metres. S.S.S. 70. *Green Fees:* information not provided. *Eating facilities:* bar food. *Visitors:* welcome daily but check by telephoning at weekends. Snooker tables. *Society Meetings:* catered for by advance booking. Secretary: G. McNulty (0662 841514).

NEWTOWNSTEWART. **Newtownstewart Golf Club**, 38 Golf Course Road, Newtownstewart, Omagh BT78 4HH (Newtownstewart (06626) 61466). *Location:* signposted from Strabane Road (A57) at Newtownstewart, two miles west of Newtownstewart on B84. Parkland and wooded course. 18 holes, 5869 yards, 5341 metres. S.S.S. 69. Practice ground adjacent to clubhouse. *Green Fees:* weekdays £8.00; weekends £12.00. Weekly £40.00. Monthly £70. *Eating facilities:* available. *Visitors:* welcome at all times except during club competitions. Accommodation available in chalets beside clubhouse. *Society Meetings:* all welcome but should be affiliated to G.U. Secretary: Mr J.E. Mackin. Secretary/Manageress: Miss D. Magee.

OMAGH. **Omagh Golf Club**, 83a Dublin Road, Omagh BT78 1HQ (Omagh (0662) 243160). *Location:* one mile from Omagh town centre on Belfast/Dublin Road. Parkland. 18 holes, 4972 metres. S.S.S. 67. *Green Fees:* weekdays £10.00; weekends and Bank Holidays £15.00. £2.00 reduction if playing with a member, Senior Citizens half price. *Eating facilities:* snacks and bar facilities. *Visitors:* welcome any day except Tuesday and Saturday. Special arrangements with Royal Arms Hotel for guests. *Society Meetings:* welcome. Hon. Secretary: Joseph A. McElholm. Secretary: Florence E.A. Caldwell (0662 241442).

STRABANE. **Strabane Golf Club**, Ballycolman Road, Strabane (0504 382271). *Location:* Omagh – Strabane main road. Parkland. 18 holes, 5552 metres. S.S.S. 69. *Green Fees:* weekdays £10.00, £8.00 with a member; weekends £12.00, £10.00 with a member. *Eating facilities:* two bars, catering by arrangement. *Visitors:* welcome by arrangement. *Society Meetings:* by arrangement with Secretary. Secretary: Terry Doherty (0504 382007).

Republic of Ireland

COUNTY CARLOW

CARLOW. **Carlow Golf Club**, Deer Park, Carlow (0503 31695). *Location:* 52 miles south of Dublin, two miles north of Carlow town on N9. Parkland. 18 holes, 5844 metres. S.S.S. 70. *Green Fees:* IR£20.00. Weekly ticket IR£70.00. Groups of 12 or more IR£17.00 each (weekdays only). *Eating facilities:* restaurant open all day, bar open from 9.30am – 12 midnight. *Visitors:* welcome Monday to Friday, avoid Tuesday (Ladies Day), Saturdays difficult, Sundays impossible – pre booking advisable. *Society Meetings:* must be pre booked with Secretary. Professional: Andrew Gilbert (0503 41745). Secretary: Margaret Meaney (0503 31695; Fax: 0503 40065).

COUNTY CAVAN

BLACKLION. **Blacklion Golf Club**, Toam, Blacklion, via Sligo (072 53024; from the UK 010 353 72 53024). *Location:* Blacklion/Belcoo on Enniskillen to Sligo Road. Flat parkland wooded copses, lake partially in play, scenic. 9 holes, 6175 yards, 5614 metres. S.S.S. 69. *Green Fees:* IR£5.00 weekdays; IR£8.00 weekends. Group rates by prior arrangement. *Eating facilities:* bar with bar snacks. *Visitors:* welcome weekdays, Sundays after 4pm. *Society Meetings:* by arrangement. Hon. Secretary: Robert Thompson.

DRUMELIS. **County Cavan Golf Club**, Aranmore House, Drumelis (049 312 83). *Location:* county town of Cavan. Parkland course. 18 holes, 5519 metres. S.S.S 69. *Green Fees:* information not provided. *Eating facilities:* available. *Visitors:* welcome throughout the year. *Society Meetings:* welcome with pre-booking. Secretary: Donal Crotty (049 31643).

COUNTY CLARE

LAHINCH. **Lahinch Golf Club**, Lahinch (065 81003; Fax: 065 81592). *Location:* 30 miles north west of Shannon Airport, 200 yards from Lahinch Village on Lisconner Road. Links course. Old Course – 18 holes, 6699 yards. S.S.S. 67. *Green Fees:* on application. *Visitors:* weekdays only, by arrangement. *Society Meetings:* catered for by arrangement. Professional: R. McCavery (065 81408). Secretary: M. Murphy.

COUNTY CORK

CARRIGROHANE. **Muskerry Golf Club**, Carrigrohane (021 385104). *Location:* seven and a half miles north west of Cork City. Parkland/wooded. 18 holes, 5786 metres. S.S.S. 70. *Green Fees:* information not provided. *Eating facilities:* available. *Visitors:* welcome weekdays – Monday and Tuesday all day, Wednesday up to 11.30am, Thursday after 12.30pm and Friday up to 3.30pm. *Society Meetings:* welcome. Professional: W.M. Lehane (021 385104). Secretary: J.J. Moynihan (021 385297).

CASTLETOWNBERE. **Berehaven Golf Links**, Filane, Castletownbere, Beara. *Location:* by the main Castletownbere – Glengarriff Road. Seaside links. 9 holes, 4748 metres. S.S.S. 64. *Green Fees:* £8.00 weekdays; £10.00 weekends. *Visitors:* welcome at all times. Tennis and swimming facilities. *Society Meetings:* all welcome – £6. Secretary: A. Hanley (027 70469 home or 70164 work).

CHARLEVILLE. **Charleville Golf Club**, Ardmore, Charleville (063 81257; Fax: 063 81274). *Location:* main road from Limerick to Cork, 25 miles from Limerick. Parkland, very wooded. 18 holes, 6430 yards. S.S.S. 70. *Green Fees:* weekdays £12.00; weekends £15.00. *Eating facilities:* full eating facilities and bar. *Visitors:* welcome except weekends. *Society Meetings:* welcomed except weekends, £10.00 per person. Secretary: James A. Murphy (063 81257).

DOUGLAS. **Douglas Golf Club**, Douglas (021 891086; Fax: 021 895297). *Location:* in Douglas Village, three miles to the south of Cork City. Parkland course – very flat. 18 holes, 5664 yards. S.S.S. 69. *Green Fees:* weekdays £17.00 (18 holes); weekends £19.00; additional round same day half price. *Eating facilities:* full restaurant and bar available. *Visitors:* Monday, Wednesday, Thursday, Friday mornings, preferably mid-morning; Saturday and Sunday after 2pm. Advisable to check in advance. *Society Meetings:* welcome but bookings are made in January each year. Professional: Gary Nicholson (021 362055). Secretary: Brian Barrett (021 895297).

LITTLE ISLAND. **Cork Golf Club**, Little Island (021 353451; Fax: 021 353410). *Location:* five miles east of Cork City N25, signposted. Parkland, very scenic championship course. 18 holes, 6065 metres. S.S.S. 72, 70. Practice ground. *Green Fees:* weekdays £23.00; weekends £26.00. Special rates for groups of 20 or more: Monday and Tuesday £18.00, Friday, Saturday and Sunday £20.00. *Eating facilities:* full catering facilities, bar. *Visitors:* welcome Mondays, Tuesdays, Wednesdays and Fridays except 12.30 to 2pm; Thursday, weekends ring in advance. *Society*

Republic of Ireland

Meetings: catered for, arrange with Secretary/Manager. Professional: (021 353451). Secretary: Matt Sands (021 353037).

LITTLE ISLAND. **Harbour Point Golf Club,** Clash Road, Little Island (021 353094; Fax: 021 354408). *Location:* enter Little Island by taking a right off the main Cork/Rosslare Road, then take your next left and then right. Parkland course by banks of River Lee. 18 holes, 6630 yards, 6063 metres. S.S.S. 72. 21 bay floodlit driving range. *Green Fees:* £20.00. £11.00 before 11am Monday, Wednesday, Thursday and Friday. *Eating facilities:* full restaurant and bar facilities. *Visitors:* welcome anytime by appointment except Sunday before 11am. *Society Meetings:* welcome every day; £15.00 per person for groups of 20 or more.

TIVOLI. **Silver Springs Golf Club,** Tivoli (021 507533). *Location:* five minutes from Cork city centre. 9 holes, 4680 yards. S.S.S. 62 for 18 holes, Par 34 (68). *Green Fees:* information not provided. Special rates for groups of 20 or more. *Eating facilities:* full catering facilities, bar. *Visitors:* welcome, ring beforehand. Hotel on site, accommodation available. Full sports centre, indoor pool, squash, indoor tennis, sauna & steam bath, gym. Manager: Ian Foulger.

YOUGHAL. **Youghal Golf Club,** Knockaverry, Youghal (024 92787). *Location:* N25 main road from Rosslare to Cork. Seaside course with panoramic views of Youghal Bay/Blackwater Estuary. 18 holes, 6300 yards. S.S.S. 69. *Green Fees:* £14.00 IR. *Eating facilities:* full kitchen facilities. *Visitors:* phone re weekends and Wednesdays (ladies' day). *Society Meetings:* welcome, please phone. Special rates available. Professional: Liam Burns (024 92590). Secretary: Kieran Quill.

COUNTY DONEGAL

BUNDORAN. **Bundoran Golf Club,** Great Northern Hotel, Bundoran (072 41302). *Location:* 25 miles from Sligo on edge of Bundoran Town. Parkland, seaside; not wooded. 18 holes, 6121 yards, 5599 metres. S.S.S. 70. Practice ground. *Green Fees:* weekdays £12.00; weekends £14. *Eating facilities:* snacks in bar. *Visitors:*

THE GOLF GUIDE 1994

preferably weekdays but always welcome. Locker rooms. *Society Meetings:* very welcome with due notice. Professional: David Robinson (072 41302). Secretary: Liam M. Devitt.

LETTERKENNY. **Dunfanaghy Golf Club,** Dunfanaghy, Letterkenny (074 36335). *Location:* on main Letterkenny to Dunfanaghy Road – N56. Seaside links. 18 holes, 5066 metres. S.S.S. 66. *Green Fees:* IR£10.00 weekdays; IR£12.00 weekends. *Eating facilities:* bar snacks – soup, tea and sandwiches. *Visitors:* welcome at all times, restriction on weekend mornings. *Society Meetings:* welcome most days by booking. Club Secretary: Mary Quinn.

LETTERKENNY. **Portsalon Golf Club,** Portsalon, Letterkenny (074 59459). *Location:* 20 miles north of Letterkenny. Seaside links. 18 holes, 5878 yards, 5379 metres. S.S.S. 68, Par 69. *Green Fees:* £10.00. Weekly ticket £50.00. *Eating facilities:* diningroom and bar in clubhouse. *Visitors:* welcome. *Society Meetings:* welcome weekdays and some weekends. Secretary: C. Toland (074 53266).

COUNTY DUBLIN

BALBRIGGAN. **Balbriggan Golf Club,** Blackhall, Balbriggan (8412173). *Location:* quarter of a mile south of Balbriggan on main Belfast/Dublin Road. Parkland course with fine views of Cooley Peninsula and Mourne Mountains. 18 holes, 2968 metres. S.S.S. 71. *Green Fees:* £14.00 weekdays; £18.00 weekends. *Eating facilities:* full restaurant and snacks. *Visitors:* welcome, Tuesday Ladies' Day, Saturdays and Sundays not good as club competitions take place. *Society Meetings:* catered for Mondays, Wednesdays, Thursdays and Fridays. Secretary: Michael O'Halloran (8412229).

DONABATE. **Corballis Public Golf Course,** Donabate (8436583). *Location:* main Dublin to Belfast Road. Links course. 18 holes, 4791 yards. S.S.S. 64. *Green Fees:* £7.00 weekdays; £8.00 weekends. Unemployed, Senior Citizens and Students £3.00. *Eating facilities:* snack food. *Visitors:* welcome anytime. *Society Meetings:* welcome. Secretary: P.J. Boylan.

At Harbour Point there's always a special welcome for visitors.

● Superb 18-hole championship parkland course by the banks of the River Lee ● 21-bay all weather floodlit driving range ● Full bar and restaurant facilities ● Fully stocked Golf Store ● Situated only five miles from Cork city
● Half price green fees before 11am Monday, Wednesday, Thursday & Friday
● Ring for bookings.

Clash Road, Little Island, Co. Cork. From Britain Tel: 010-353-21-353094 or from Ireland 021-353094. Fax: 021-354408

THE GOLF GUIDE 1994 — *Republic of Ireland*

DUBLIN. **Elm Park Golf and Sports Club,** Nutley House, Donnybrook, Dublin 4 (0001 2693438; Fax: 2694505). *Location:* between R.T.E. and St. Vincent's Hospital. Flat parkland course. 18 holes, 5929 yards, 5422 metres. S.S.S. 68. *Green Fees:* £30.00 weekdays; £35.00 weekends. Subject to review. *Eating facilities:* full bar and dining facilities. *Visitors:* welcome but must telephone to arrange times with Professional. *Society Meetings:* by special arrangement. Professional: S. Green (0001 2692650). Secretary: A. McCormack.

DUBLIN. **The Royal Dublin Golf Club,** North Bull Island, Dollymount, Dublin 3 (0001 337153). *Location:* three and a half miles north east of city centre on coast road to Howth. Seaside links. 18 holes, 6850 yards, 6262 metres. S.S.S. 71. Large practice ground. *Green Fees:* weekdays £35.00 IR; weekends £45.00 IR. *Eating facilities:* grill room, restaurant, two bars. *Visitors:* Monday, Tuesday, Thursday, Friday and Sunday 10.30 to 12.30. *Society Meetings:* catered for, written application must be made. Tournament Professional: Christy O'Connor. Professional: Leonard Owens (0001 336477). Secretary: J.A. Lambe (0001 336346; Fax: 0001 336504).

DUN LAOGHAIRE. **Dun Laoghaire Golf Club,** Eglinton Park, Tivoli Road, Dun Laoghaire (01 2805116). *Location:* half a mile from town centre. Parkland. 18 holes, 5495 metres. S.S.S. 68. *Green Fees:* weekdays IR£25.00; weekends with a member. *Eating facilities:* bar, snacks, evening meals. *Visitors:* welcome weekdays. *Society Meetings:* welcome. Professional: Owen Mulhall (01 2801694). Secretary: Terry Stewart (01 2803916; Fax: 01 2804868).

FOXROCK. **Leopardstown Golf Course,** Foxrock Village, Dublin 18 (01 2895341). *Location:* five miles south of Dublin city centre, situated in Leopardstown race course. Flat parkland. 18 holes, 5300 yards. S.S.S. 69. 80 bay floodlit driving range. *Green Fees:* weekdays £IR6.50; weekends £IR9.00. *Eating facilities:* restaurant. *Visitors:* welcome. *Society Meetings:* welcome. Professional: Mr Dominic Reilly (01 2893511). Manager: Michael Hoey.

HOWTH. **Deer Park Hotel and Golf Courses,** Howth (010 3531 322624). *Location:* follow coast road via Fairview, Clontarf to Howth, nine miles from city centre. Parkland course set in the grounds of Howth Castle, spectacular views of the coast. 18 holes, 6647 yards, 6078 metres. S.S.S. 72. *Green Fees:* on application. *Eating facilities:* light meals available all day; lounge bar; restaurant. *Visitors:* welcome seven days, non residents must expect delays. Residents may book the tee. 48 bedroomed hotel. *Society Meetings:* welcome. Managers: David and Antoinette Tighe.

PORTMARNOCK. **Portmarnock Golf Club,** Portmarnock (0001 8462969; Fax: 0001 8462601). *Location:* 8 miles NE of Dublin along north coast, four miles from Airport. Seaside links – winds. Three courses: 'A' – 27 holes, 7097 yards. S.S.S. 75. 'B' – 7047 yards. S.S.S. 75. 'C' – 6596 yards. S.S.S. 74. Practice area. *Green Fees:* £40.00 IR weekdays (Ladies £25.00 IR); £50.00 IR weekends. *Eating facilities:* available. *Visitors:* by arrangement, restriction weekends and Bank Holidays. *Society Meetings:* on application, 12 or more Mondays, Tuesdays and Fridays only. Professional: J. Purcell (0001 8462634). Secretary: W. Bornemann (0001 8462968).

ST. MARGARET'S. **St. Margaret's Golf Club,** Skephubble, St. Margaret's (8640400; Fax: 8640289). *Location:* one mile east of Ashbourne Road at the Ward; eight miles north of Dublin City centre; three miles to Dublin Airport. Parkland, ultra-modern design by Craddock and Ruddy. 18 holes, 6900 yards. Extensive practice areas. *Green Fees:* £25.00 weekdays; £30.00 weekends. *Eating facilities:* full range of services. *Visitors:* welcome to all golfers. Golf Shop (8640416). *Society Meetings:* welcome. Secretary: Denis Kane.

SUTTON. **Howth Golf Club,** St. Fintan's, Carrickbrack Road, Sutton (01 323055; Fax: 01 321793). *Location:* one and a half miles from Sutton Cross on city side of hill of Howth. Moorland course with scenic views of Dublin Bay – very hilly. 18 holes, 5419 metres. S.S.S. 68. *Green Fees:* weekdays £16.00. *Eating facilities:* bar snacks from 11am. *Visitors:* welcome weekdays except Wednesdays. *Society Meetings:* bookings accepted by arrangement with Secretary. Professional: John McGuirk (01 322844). Secretary: Mrs Ann MacNeice.

COUNTY GALWAY

CLIFDEN. **Connemara Golf Club,** Aillebrack, Ballyconneely, Near Clifden (095 23502; Fax: 095 23662). *Location:* nine miles south west of Clifden. Seaside links. Championship course: 18 holes, 6790 yards, 6173 metres. S.S.S. 73. Medal course: 18 holes, 6173 metres. S.S.S. 73. Practice fairway. *Green Fees:* £16.00 per round. *Eating facilities:* à la carte restaurant and bar. *Visitors:* Monday to Saturday preferable, booking in advance advised particularly during Summer. *Society Meetings:* groups of 20 or more £9.00 per person (rate does not apply from June to September inclusive). Secretary: Matt Killilea.

LOUGHREA. **Loughrea Golf Club,** Loughrea (091 41049). Location: one and a half miles north east of town, on New Inn Road. Parkland, undulating, with beautiful views of town and Sl. Aughty Mountains in background. 18 holes, 5613 yards. Par 69. Practice area. *Green Fees:* information not provided. *Eating facilities:* light snacks and bar. *Visitors:* welcome weekdays and open days. *Society Meetings:* welcome, please telephone. Secretary: Brendan Blake (091 41339).

COUNTY KERRY

BALLYBUNION. **Ballybunion Golf Club,** Saudhill Road, Ballybunion (068 27146; Fax: 068 27387). *Location:* 20 miles from Tralee, 10 miles from Listowl. Seaside links. Two courses. 36 holes, 6800 yards. S.S.S. 71. *Green Fees:* £30.00 single round; £40.00 to play both courses. *Eating facilities:* full bar and catering facilities. *Visitors:* welcome, subject to availability. *Society Meetings:* catered for. Professional: Brian O'Callaghan (068 27146). Secretary: Jim McKenna (068 27146).

BALLYFERRITER. **Ceann Sibeal (Dingle) Golf Club,** Ballyferriter (066 56255; Fax: 066 56409). *Location:* turn right quarter of a mile after Ballyferriter. Traditional links, most westerly golf course in Europe. 18 holes, 6550 yards. S.S.S. 71. Practice ground. *Green Fees:* £16.00 per round, £21.00 per day. *Eating facilities:* diningroom, bar, full facilities. *Visitors:* welcome at all times, book in advance. Hotel adjacent. *Society Meetings:* all welcome. Professional: Dermot O'Connor. Secretary: Garry Partington.

KILLARNEY. **Killarney Golf and Fishing Club,** Mahony's Point, Killarney (064 31034; Fax: 064 33065). *Location:* Killarney town, two miles west on Ring of Kerry road. Undulating parkland courses – lakeside. Mahony's Point: 18 holes, 6152 metres. S.S.S. 72. Killeen: 18 holes, 6457 yards. S.S.S. 73. Practice area. *Green Fees:* information on request. *Eating facilities:* available all day. *Visitors:* welcome at all times, reservations in advance, Handicap Certificate required. *Society Meetings:* welcome. Professional: T. Coveney (064 31615). Secretary: T. Prendergast.

SNEEM. **Parknasilla Golf Club,** Parknasilla, Sneem (064 45122). *Location:* on the Ring of Kerry route, two miles east of Sneem Village. Hilly seaside course, wooded. 9 holes, 4894 yards. S.S.S. 65. *Green Fees:* £9.00. *Eating facilities:* available at Great Southern hotel, 10 minutes' walk. *Visitors:* welcome, no restrictions. *Society Meetings:* contact 064 45122. Professional: Charlie McCarthy. Secretary: Maurice Walsh (064 45233).

TRALEE. **Tralee Golf Club,** West Barrow, Ardfert, Tralee (066 36379). *Location:* Tralee to Barrow via the Spa and Churchill. Seaside links. 18 holes, 6252 metres. S.S.S. 72. *Green Fees:* £25.00 weekdays, £30.00 weekends. *Eating facilities:* bar and restaurant. *Visitors:* unrestricted except Wednesdays and weekends. *Society Meetings:* by arrangement. Secretary: Peter Colleran (066 36379; Fax: 066 36008).

COUNTY KILDARE

CURRAGH. **The Curragh Golf Club,** Newbridge (045 41238). *Location:* three miles south of Newbridge. Hilly heathland course. 18 holes, 6003 metres. S.S.S. 71. Practice ground. *Green Fees:* weekdays £13.00; weekends and Bank Holidays £16.00. *Eating facilities:* bar and restaurant. *Visitors:* restricted, please check in advance for course availability. *Society Meetings:* by appointment. Professional: Mr Phil Lawlor (045 41896). Secretary: Ann Culleton (045 41714).

DONADEA. **Knockanally Golf and Country Club,** Donadea, North Kildare (Tel & Fax: 045 69322). *Location:* three miles off N4 between Enfield and Kilcock. Parkland. 18 holes, 6495 yards. S.S.S. 72. *Green Fees:* IR£15.00 weekdays; IR£18.00 weekends. *Eating facilities:* available. *Visitors:* welcome, no restrictions. *Society Meetings:* by arrangement. Professional: Peter Hickey. Secretary: Noel A. Lyons (045 69322/ 6287716).

COUNTY KILKENNY

THOMASTOWN. **Mount Juliet Golf Club,** Thomastown (056 24725; Fax: 056 24828). *Location:* Thomastown – on main Dublin to Waterford Road. Parkland, designed by Jack Nicklaus, home of the 1993 Carrolls Irish Open. 18 holes, 7142 yards, 6493 metres. S.S.S. 74. 3 hole teaching academy and driving range. *Green Fees:* £57.00. Group rate £41.00 weekdays, £46.00 weekends. *Eating facilities:* full catering and bar facilities. *Visitors:* welcome, no restrictions but please book in advance. 32 bedroom de luxe Hotel. *Society Meetings:* please book in advance. Professional: Keith Mongan. Director of Golf: Katherine MacCann.

Castlerosse Hotel, Killarney

County Kerry, Ireland
Tel: 010 353 64 31134
Fax: 010 353 64 31331
Telex: 73910

"I personally look forward to ensuring your stay with us will be a memorable one."
Joe Leonard, Manager, Castlerosse Hotel

Overlooking Killarney's lakes and mountains, 5 minutes from the town centre and adjacent to Killarney's 2 championship golf courses, the Castlerosse Hotel offers you first class accommodation and the friendliest hotel in South West Ireland.

Facilities include:
- Gym • Saunas • Snooker • Putting Green
- Miles of Walking Paths and Jogging Trails

Concession green fees are available for a variety of golf clubs. The Castlerosse also encourages you to leave all the work to them – so contact them now and they will not only reserve your accommodation but also your tee times.

COUNTY LAOIS

PORTLAOISE. **The Heath Golf Club,** The Heath, Portlaoise, Co Laois (0502 46533). *Location:* three and a half miles north east of Portlaoise. Relatively flat with furze and gorse. 18 holes, 5721 metres. S.S.S. 70 white, 69 Green. 10 bay floodlit driving range. *Green Fees:* weekdays £10.00; weekends £16.00. 50% reduction if with a member. *Eating facilities:* full bar and catering facilities available. *Visitors:* welcome at all times but advance booking required for weekends and Public Holidays. *Society Meetings:* welcome by prior arrangement. Professional: Eddie Doyle (0502 46622). Secretary: Patrick A. Malone (0502 21074).

LOUTH

DROGHEDA. **County Louth Golf Club,** Baltray, Drogheda (041 22327). *Location:* Drogheda, five miles north east. Championship links course. 18 holes, 6783 yards. S.S.S. 72. *Green Fees:* weekdays £27.00; weekends £33.00. *Eating facilities:* restaurant, coffee shop and bar. *Visitors:* welcome weekdays except Tuesdays on application, weekends restricted. Accommodation available for 20 persons. *Society Meetings:* on application. Professional: Paddy McGuirk (041 22444). Secretary: Michael Delany (041 22329; Fax: 041 22969).

DUNDALK. **Dundalk Golf Club,** Blackrock, Dundalk (042 21379; Fax: 042 22022). *Location:* Dundalk coast road to Blackrock, three miles. Parkland. 18 holes, 5504 yards, 6115 metres. S.S.S. 72 (Par 72). Six acre field practice ground. *Green Fees:* weekdays £18.00; weekends £20.00. *Eating facilities:* full restaurant and bar. *Visitors:* welcome Mondays, Wednesdays, Thursdays and Fridays, restrictions Tuesdays and weekends. *Society Meetings:* welcome except Tuesdays and Sundays. Professional: James Cassidy. Secretary: Joe Carroll (042 21731).

LIMERICK

CASTLETROY. **Castletroy Golf Club,** Castletroy, Co. Limerick (061 335261; Fax: 061-335373). *Location:* three miles from Limerick City on N7 (Dublin Road). Parkland with numerous trees. 18 holes, 6330 yards. S.S.S. 71. *Green Fees:* weekdays £20.00; weekends with a member only, £12.00. *Eating facilities:* full catering service, bar. *Visitors:* welcome, most weekdays, restrictions weekends and Thursday afternoons, Tuesdays is Ladies' Day – advisable to phone. *Society Meetings:* welcome Mondays, Wednesdays and Fridays, group rates available. Professional: M. Cassidy (061 338283). Secretary: Laurence Hayes (061 335753).

COUNTY MAYO

ACHILL. **Achill Golf Club,** Keel, Achill. *Location:* N59 from Westport and R319 from Mulranny to Achill. Seaside links in scenic setting. 9 holes, 2723 yards, 2489 metres. S.S.S. 66. *Green Fees:* on application. *Visitors:* welcome at all times, no restrictions. *Society Meetings:* by prior arrangement. Secretary: Patrick Lavelle.

BALLINROBE. **Ballinrobe Golf Club,** Castleton Road, Ballinrobe (Tel & Fax: 092 41448). *Location:* one mile from town on the Castleton road. Flatland with four holes in the middle of a racecourse. 9 holes, 5540 metres. S.S.S. 68. Practice ground. *Green Fees:* £8.00. *Eating facilities:* snacks and bar facilities. *Visitors:* welcome at all times except Tuesday evenings and Sundays. Excellent shooting and beside two of the best trout fishing lakes in Europe. *Society Meetings:* welcome. Secretary: Pat Holian (092 41659).

BALLINROBE GOLF CLUB

Ballinrobe is one of Ireland's oldest Golf Clubs and can proudly claim to have provided a century of golf for members and visitors on its nine-hole flatland course. Bar and restaurant during Summer. Visitors welcome by arrangement. Societies welcome. Call Secretary Pat Holian for details.

Ballinrobe Golf Club, Castlebar Road, Ballinrobe, Co. Mayo.
Telephone: 092 41659. From UK: 010 353 92 41659

COUNTY MEATH

NAVAN. **Royal Tara Golf Club,** Bellinter, Navan (046 25244). *Location:* 25 miles north of Dublin off National Primary Route N3. Parkland, private course. 18 holes, 5757 yards. S.S.S. 70. 9 hole course, 3184 yards. S.S.S. 35. *Green Fees:* IR£14.00 weekdays; IR£18.00 weekends. *Eating facilities:* bar and full catering facilities. *Visitors:* welcome, Tuesday Ladies Day, please check with club in advance. *Society Meetings:* welcomed Monday, Thursday, Friday and Saturday. Professional: Mr Adam Whiston (046 25244). Secretary: Mr Paddy O'Brien (046 25508).

COUNTY MONAGHAN

CASTLEBLAYNEY. **Castleblayney Golf Club,** Onomy, Castleblayney (042 46194). *Location:* Hope Castle Estate, 500 yards from town centre. Scenic parkland course with lakes and forest in centre of Leisure Park. 9 holes, 5345 yards. S.S.S. 66. *Green Fees:* £5.00 weekdays; £8.00 weekends. *Eating facilities:* restaurant and bar. *Visitors:* welcome at all times except during major competitions. Accommodation in Hope Castle Complex. *Society Meetings:* welcome. Secretary: Des McGlynn (042 40197).

COUNTY ROSCOMMON

ROSCOMMON. **Roscommon Golf Club,** Mote Park, Roscommon (0903 26382). *Location:* half a mile south of Roscommon town. Parkland/wooded. 9 holes, 5784 metres. S.S.S. 70. Practice ground. *Green Fees:* £10.00, Saturdays only by arrangement. £6.00 for Societies. *Eating facilities:* full bar, snacks, teas, coffee, etc. *Visitors:* welcome all year round, Saturdays by arrangement and no visitors Sundays except on open days. *Society Meetings:* welcome. Secretary: Cathal McConn (0903 26062).

COUNTY SLIGO

ENNISCRONE. **Enniscrone Golf Club,** Enniscrone (096 36657). *Location:* on coast road from Sligo to Ballina, about nine miles from Ballina. Championship links course – host to the Irish Close Championship 1993. 18 holes, 6570 yards. S.S.S. 72. Practice area and putting green. *Green Fees:* information not provided. *Eating facilities:* bar and full catering facilities. *Visitors:* welcome. *Society Meetings:* groups of 12 or more, Green Fee £10.00. Professional: Charlie McGoldrick. Secretary: John Fleming.

COUNTY TIPPERARY

CARRICK-ON-SUIR. **Carrick-on-Suir Golf Club,** Garravoone, Carrick-on-Suir (051 40047). *Location:* one mile from Carrick-on-Suir on Dungarvan Road. Scenic 9 hole course on elevated ground close to town. 9 holes, 5948 yards. S.S.S. 68. *Green Fees:* £10.00. *Eating facilities:* full meals and bar snacks available by prior arrangement. *Visitors:* welcome Monday to Saturday, avoid Tuesday and Wednesday evenings in summer (competitions). Special rates for groups. *Society Meetings:* all welcome by prior arrangement. Secretary: Francis Comerford (051 43328).

CLONMEL. **Clonmel Golf Club,** Lyreanearla, Mountain Road, Clonmel (052 21138). *Location:* set in the scenic slopes of the Comeragh Mountains, just a short distance from the town of Clonmel. 18 holes, 5785 metres. S.S.S. 70 white, 69 green. *Green Fees:* £12.00 weekdays; £15.00 weekends. *Eating facilities:* full catering and bar. *Visitors:* always welcome. Golf range across the road with B&B accommodation. *Society Meetings:* welcomed, except weekends – contact Secretary/Manager for prior arrangement. Professional: Mr Robert Hayes (052 24050). Secretary: Ms Aine Myles Keating (052 24050).

COUNTY WATERFORD

LISMORE. **Lismore Golf Club,** Ballyin, Lismore (058 54026). *Location:* one kilometre north of Lismore Heritage Town, just off the N72. Undulating parkland with mature trees, course surrounded by woodlands. 9 holes, 5196 metres. S.S.S. 67. *Green Fees:* £8.00 weekdays; £10.00 weekends and Bank Holidays. Reductions for Societies. *Eating facilities:* tea, coffee, snacks. *Visitors:* welcome weekdays, restriction may apply on Wednesday (Ladies' day). *Society Meetings:* welcome weekdays except Wednesday. Secretary: Patrick Norris.

COUNTY WICKLOW

BRITTAS BAY. **The European Club,** Brittas Bay, Wicklow (Dublin 2804077/0404 47346). *Location:* one mile south of main Brittas Bay beach on coast road, 40 miles south of Dublin City Centre. Rolling linksland overlooking Arklow Bay, designed and owned by Pat Ruddy. 18 holes, 6900 yards. S.S.S. 72. Extensive practice areas. *Green Fees:* IR£20.00 weekdays; IR£25.00 weekends. Discounts for groups of 20 plus. *Eating facilities:* full services. *Visitors:* welcome to all golfers, advisable to book. *Society Meetings:* welcome. Secretary: Pat Ruddy (01 2804077; Fax: 01 2808457).

Isle of Man

DOUGLAS. **Douglas Golf Club,** Pulrose Golf Course, Pulrose Road, Douglas (0624 675952). *Location:* one mile from town centre, next to power station. Undulating parkland. 18 holes, 5922 yards. S.S.S. 68. Practice and putting area. *Green Fees:* information not provided. *Eating facilities:* light meals available in licensed bar. *Visitors:* welcome, no restriction. *Society Meetings:* catered for by arrangement with Professional. Professional: K. Parry (0624 661558). Secretary: Mr G. Allen.

DOUGLAS. **Pulrose Golf Course,** Douglas. *Location:* one mile from town centre, next to power station. Undulating parkland with memorable 17th hole. 18 holes, 5922 yards. S.S.S. 68. Putting and practice area. *Green Fees:* information not provided. *Eating facilities:* bar; meals available at all times. *Visitors:* welcome, no restrictions. *Society Meetings:* by arrangement with Professional. Professional: K. Parry (0624 75952). Secretary: G. Allen.

FORT ISLAND. **Castletown Golf Club,** Castletown Golf Links Hotel, Fort Island, Derbyhaven (Castletown (0624) 822201). *Location:* 12 miles from Douglas. Three miles from Ronaldsway airport. Seaside links course. 18 holes, 6731 yards. S.S.S. 73. *Green Fees:* weekdays £19.00 per person per day; weekends £25.00 per person per day. *Eating facilities:* table d'hôte/à la carte restaurant, daytime and evening bistro snacks. *Visitors:* welcome without reservation. Accommodation available, plus sauna, sunbeds, swimming pool, changing rooms. *Society Meetings:* catered for. Professional: Murray S. Crowe (0624 822211). General Manager: Miss J.M. Mitchell (0624 822201). Hon. Secretary: Mr A. Karran.

ONCHAN. **King Edward Bay Golf Club,** Groudle Road, Howstrake, Onchan (0624 620430). *Location:* north headland of Douglas Bay. Stunning views from Headland links course. Watered greens, excellent fairways. 18 holes, 5450 yards. S.S.S. 67. Practice area. *Green Fees:* weekdays £12.00; weekends £16.00. *Eating facilities:* full catering available, three bars. *Visitors:* welcome without reservation but not before 9.30am Sundays. *Society Meetings:* most welcome by arrangement. Special rates. Professional: Donald Jones (0624 672709). Secretary: Miss C. Nightingale (Tel & Fax: 0624 676794).

PEEL. **Peel Golf Club,** Rheast Lane, Peel (0624 842227). *Location:* outskirts of Peel on main Douglas Road. Combination of links and heathland. 18 holes, 5914 yards. S.S.S. 68. Practice ground. *Green Fees:* weekdays £13.00 per day; weekends £17.00. *Eating facilities:* full bar service and meals. *Visitors:* welcome, but check in advance for weekend availability. *Society Meetings:* catered for, check in advance. Pro Shop. Professional: R. Garrard (0624 844232). Secretary: T.P. Kissack (0624 843456).

PORT ERIN. **Rowany Golf Club,** Rowany Drive, Port Erin (0624 834108). *Location:* off the Promenade. Hilly setting and meadowland. 18 holes, 5480 yards. S.S.S. 69. Practice ground. *Green Fees:* £12.00 per day weekdays; £17.00 weekends. 25% discount for parties of 20 and over. *Eating facilities:* restaurant and bar meals. *Visitors:* welcome by arrangement. Accommodation can be arranged. *Society Meetings:* welcome. Professional: Calum Wilson (0624 834108). Secretary: W.H. Vincent (0624 834072).

PORT ST. MARY. **Port St. Mary Golf Club,** Point Road, Port St. Mary (0624 834932). *Location:* clearly signposted after entering Port St. Mary. Seaside links with beautiful panoramic views. 9 holes, 2754 yards. S.S.S. 66. *Green Fees:* weekdays £7.00; weekends £10.00. 10% reductions for Societies. *Eating facilities:* restaurant and bar open all day. *Visitors:* welcome at all times, only restrictions weekends between 8am to 10.30am. Handicap Certificate required. Secretary: T.M. Boyle (0624 832274).

RAMSEY. **Ramsey Golf Club,** Brookfield (0624 813365). *Location:* west boundary of Ramsey. Parkland. 18 holes, 6019 yards. S.S.S. 69. Practice ground. *Green Fees:* weekdays £10.00 winter, £15.00 summer; weekends £12.00 winter, £18.00 summer. *Eating facilities:* bar snacks and lunches available every day, à la carte restaurant available Thursday, Friday and Saturday. *Visitors:* welcome, teeing off between 10am – 12 noon and 2pm – 4pm only. *Society Meetings:* welcome weekdays only. Professional: Mr Peter Lowey (0624 814736). Secretary: Mrs S.J. Birchall (0624 812244).

CASTLETOWN GOLF LINKS HOTEL

* Superb 18 hole Championship Links Course   * Luxurious on-course hotel.
* Sauna, Solarium, Swimming Pool, Snooker Room.
* Free Membership to Palace Hotel Casino with admission to Toffs Night Club.

Castletown Golf Links Hotel, Fort Island, Derbyhaven, Isle of Man
Telephone (0624) 822201   Fax 824693
Also see colour advertisement on page 18.

Channel Islands

La Moye, Jersey.

THE GOLF GUIDE 1994

Channel Islands

ALDERNEY. Alderney Golf Club, Route des Carrieres, Alderney (0481 822835). *Location:* one mile east of St. Anne. Seaside links with sea views from every hole. 9 holes, 2528 yards. S.S.S. 65. Putting and practice area. *Green Fees:* weekdays £15.00, £10.00 with a member; weekends £20.00, £15.00 with a member. *Eating facilities:* bar and meals. *Visitors:* welcome all year. Parties over 4 must contact Club for availability. *Society Meetings:* welcome by arrangement. Secretary: Nigel Soane-Sands (0481 822835). Manager: (Fax: 0481 823609).

GUERNSEY. Royal Guernsey Golf Club, L'Ancresse, Vale, Guernsey (0481 47022). *Location:* three miles north of St. Peter Port. Seaside links. 18 holes, 6206 yards. S.S.S. 70. Practice ground. *Green Fees:* £25.00, £15.00 playing with a member. *Eating facilities:* restaurant and bar. *Visitors:* welcome except Thursday and Saturday afternoons and Sundays unless playing with a member. Must have Handicap Certificate. *Society Meetings:* October to March only, by prior arrangement. Professional: Norman Wood (0481 45070). Secretary: M. De Laune (0481 46523; Fax: 0481 43960).

GUERNSEY. St. Pierre Park Golf Club, Rohais, St. Peter Port, Guernsey (0481 728282 ext 564). *Location:* 10 minutes from St. Peter Port. Wooded parkland with numerous lakes. 9 holes, 2511 yards. S.S.S. 27. Driving range, putting green. *Green Fees:* information not provided. *Eating facilities:* two restaurants and two bars in hotel. *Visitors:* welcome subject to rules and regulations on display. Hotel accommodation in 135 luxurious rooms and suites. Pro shop. Shop Manager: R. Corbet.

JERSEY. Jersey Recreation Grounds, Greve D'Azette, St. Clement, Jersey (0534 21938). *Location:* inner coast road near St. Helier. Flat course with some water hazards. 9 holes, 2244 yards. S.S.S. 30. Practice range and putting green. *Green Fees:* information not provided. *Eating facilities:* licensed buffet. *Visitors:* welcome at all times. *Society Meetings:* welcome. Managing Director: P.A.O. Graham.

JERSEY. La Moye Golf Club, St. Brelade, Jersey (0534 42701). *Location:* on road to Corbiere Lighthouse at La Moye, St. Brelade. Turn right at airport crossroads, right again at crossroads traffic lights. Seaside links championship course. 18 holes, 6512 yards. S.S.S. 72. Practice ground. *Green Fees:* on application. *Eating facilities:* full restaurant/snack facilities, three bars. *Visitors:* weekdays 9.30-11am and 2-3.30pm, weekends 2.30pm onwards. Must have Handicap Certificate. *Society Meetings:* by prior appointment only. Professional: Mr Mike Deeley (0534 43130). Secretary: Mr Pat Clash (0534 43401).

JERSEY. Les Mielles Golf Course, The Mount, Val de la Mare, St. Ouen's, Jersey JE3 2PQ (0534 82787; Fax: 0534 83739). *Location:* centre of St. Ouen's Bay. 12 holes (extending to 18 holes in the near future). Driving range. *Green Fees:* information not provided. Secretary: J.E. Hurley.

JERSEY. Royal Jersey Golf Club, Grouville, Jersey (0534 854416; Fax: 0534 854684). *Location:* take coast road from St. Helier, head towards Gorey. Seaside links course. 18 holes, 6059 yards. S.S.S. 70. *Green Fees:* weekdays £30.00 per round; weekends and Bank Holidays £35.00 per round (after 2.30pm). *Eating facilities:* bar snacks. *Visitors:* welcome weekdays between 10am and 12 noon or 2pm to 4pm; weekends after 2.30pm. Handicap Certificate required. *Society Meetings:* welcome by prior arrangement. Professional: Tommy A. Horton (0534 852234). Secretary: R.C. Leader.

HOLIDAY BUNGALOWS

3 bungalows, all near beach, at Grouville and close to bus stop, shops and golf course. Accommodate 2-8 people. Everything supplied including linen. Cot. Children and pets welcome. Open all year. Terms from £80 to £290 per week all told. Jersey is a beautiful place to visit all year round. Excellent restaurants, shops (no VAT) and entertainment. Trips to France or other Channel Islands easily arranged.

Write for further details from:
Mrs. P. Johnson, 'Mon Repos', Coast Road, Grouville, Jersey (0534) 853333

Les Arches HOTEL

Hotel Register ○○○ A.A. R.A.C.

OPEN ALL YEAR ROUND

Overlooking the French Coast. Private access to Beach. All rooms en-suite with satellite T.V. Close to the Royal Jersey Golf Club. Heated pool and pretty garden. Nightclub; Tennis Court; Sauna; Mini Gym; Bars. English and Continental cuisine. Bed & Breakfast from £32.

Archirondel Bay, Jersey, Channel Islands JE3 6DR.
Telephone (0534) 853839 Fax (0534) 856640

Golf in France
WHERE TO PLAY • WHERE TO STAY
by Michael Gedye

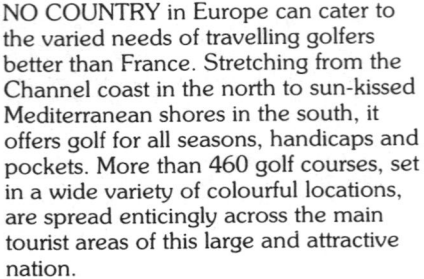

NO COUNTRY in Europe can cater to the varied needs of travelling golfers better than France. Stretching from the Channel coast in the north to sun-kissed Mediterranean shores in the south, it offers golf for all seasons, handicaps and pockets. More than 460 golf courses, set in a wide variety of colourful locations, are spread enticingly across the main tourist areas of this large and attractive nation.

Whether nestling greenly in the shadow of an ancient chateau, rambling along a sandy shoreline or carved from a pine-clad mountainside, all the golf courses we have selected are in interesting locations, in good condition, present an exciting challenge to golfers of all handicaps and offer full facilities with a warm welcome. For convenience, they are grouped into seven regions.

The **North** comprises those areas nearest Britain, the region just across the Channel formed the original holiday golfing playgrounds in the early part of this century. Nord, Pas-de-Calais, Picardy and Normandy offer such historic golfing gems as Wimereux, Granville, Le

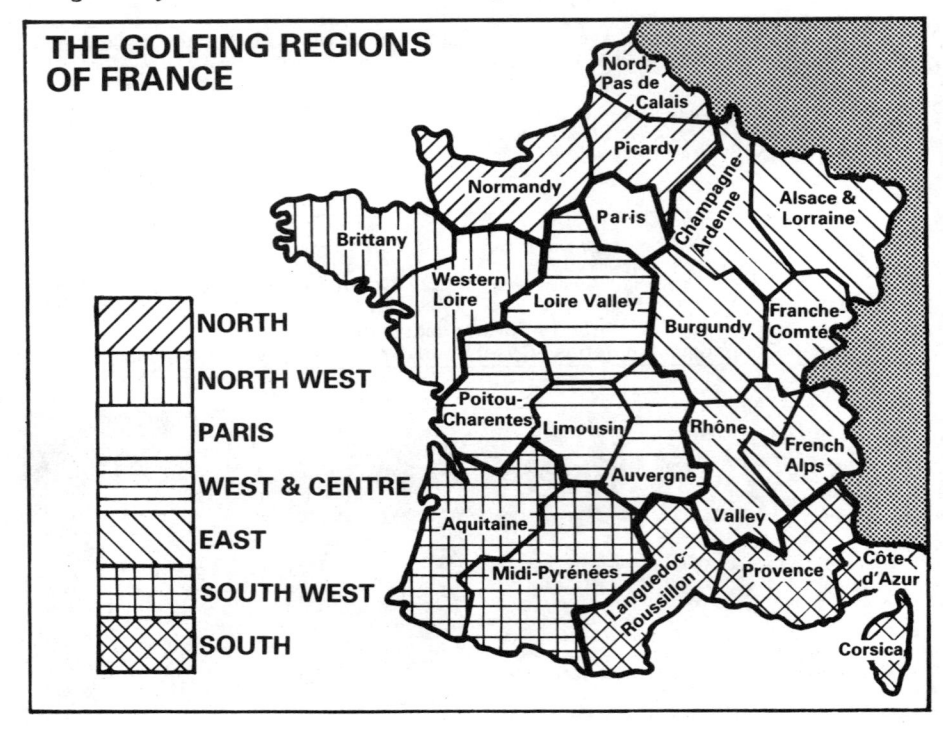

THE GOLFING REGIONS OF FRANCE

- NORTH
- NORTH WEST
- PARIS
- WEST & CENTRE
- EAST
- SOUTH WEST
- SOUTH

Touquet, Hardelot and Deauville alongside more recent additions such as Champe de Bataille and Omaha Beach.

The **North West** area of Brittany and the Western Loire has long been a golfing favourite for its ease of access by ferry and car and the timeless ambience of its southern reaches plus a unique microclimate. Golf in Brittany tends to follow the coast, with such treats as St. Malo Le Tronchet, Brest Iroise, L'Odet and St. Laurent. Inland, Rennes has three courses, of which La Freslonnière is well worth a detour for its understated charm. The chateau and wine regions of the Western Loire yield further rich bounty, notably La Baule and La Bretesche near the coast in the north, St. Jean de Monts and La Domangère similarly further south plus the Anjou Country Club and Golf de Sablé inland near Angers.

For those visiting the capital, **Paris** can offer golf to the visitor, often of very high quality. Tigers will want to flex their skills on the fairways of Golf National, home of the French Open. Lesser lights can enjoy the wooded beauty of Yvelines.

The **West & Centre** region includes the Loire Valley, Poitou-Charente, Limousin and Auvergne. For a real test, visit Les Bordes with its many hazards in a sylvan setting or for sheer magnificence, tackle the plunging fairways of Royan near the sea.

The largest geographic region is undoubtedly the **East**, which includes Champagne-Ardennes, Lorraine, Alsace, Burgundy, Franche-Comte, French Alps and the Rhone Valley. Players at Chamonix hole out under the eternal snows of Mont Blanc while those embraced by the luxuries of Evian have the vista of Lake Leman.

Golf began, as far as Continental Europe is concerned, in the **South West** and the coast from Bordeaux to Biarritz is rich with choice. Golf du Medoc and Chateau des Vigiers offer golf in vinified style, Pessac and Gujan pure holiday enjoyment while further down the coast the litany of old and new delights include Moliets, Seignosse, Hossegor, Chiberta, Biarritz, Arcangues and Nivelle – a superb selection along the seashore.

Finally, in the **South**, one can discover the sun-splashed greens of Languedoc-Roussillon, Provence and Cote d'Azur, where natural beauty and elegance go hand in hand. Contrast the rugged, strategic slopes of Golf de Frégate and Les Baux with the manicured excellence of Cannes and St. Raphael or, for a real examination, visit the trilogy of Massane, La Grande Motte and Nimes, fine championship courses that have tested the best. A fitting finale to a selection geared to all tastes and talents.

NORTH

BAYEUX. **Omaha Beach Golf Club,** Ferme St. Sauveur, 14520 Port-en-Bessin (31.21.72.94). *Location:* from Paris, autoroute de Normandy A13 towards Caen. Don't go into the city, take the peripheral highway towards Bayeux, follow signs to Port en Bessin. Hilly course. 18 holes, 6229 metres, S.S.S. 72. 9 holes, 2875 metres, S.S.S. 35. Driving range. *Green Fees:* on application. *Eating facilities:* bar and restaurant (31.21.32.32). *Visitors:* welcome. Professional: Marc Eve. Secretary: (31.21.72.94; Fax: 31.51.79.61).

BOULOGNE. **Golf de Wimereux,** Route d'Ambleteuse, 62930 Wimereux (21.32.43.20). *Location:* north of Wimereux on the D940 approximately seven km north of Boulogne. Venerable Scottish-style links course with broad fairways between sea and dunes. 18 holes, 6150 metres, Par 72. Practice ground, putting green. *Eating facilities:* clubhouse, bar and restaurant. Trolley and club hire.

CAEN. **Golf de Caen,** Le Vallon, 14112 Biéville-Beauville (31.43.98.93; Fax: 31.47.45.30). *Location:* follow road to Guistreham car ferries, first on your right to Château de Beauregard. A hilly course, wooded. 18 holes, 6155 metres, Par 72. Practice, pitch and putt. *Green Fees:* weekdays 190f; weekends 240f. *Eating facilities:* available except for Tuesdays. Pro shop.

Golf in France **THE GOLF GUIDE 1994**

DEAUVILLE. **Golf de St Gatien Deauville,** Le Mont Saint Jean, 14130 Saint-Gatien-des-Bois (31.65.19.99; Fax: 31.65.11.24). *Location:* about eight km inland and eight km east of Deauville. An interesting course with 9 holes, sloping steeply through woodland, plenty of sand and strategic water. 18 holes, 6200 metres, Par 72. 9 holes, 3035 metres, Par 36. Driving range, putting green. *Eating facilities:* bar and restaurant in rustic 18th century clubhouse. Pro shop; cart, trolley and club hire.

DEAUVILLE. **New Golf Lucien Barriere Deauville,** 14800 Deauville, Saint-Arnoult (31.88.20.53; Fax: 31.88.75.99). *Location:* on the south-western side of Deauville with the sea to the north. A scenic and varied course, hilly in part with fast greens. 18 holes, 5934 metres, Par 71. 9 holes, 3033 metres, Par 36. Practice ground and putting green. *Eating facilities:* bar and restaurant in clubhouse; all facilities at the adjoining Golf Hotel. Pro shop; club, cart and trolley hire.

GRANVILLE. **Association du Golf de Granville,** Route de la Plage, 50290 Breville-sur-Mer (33.50.23.06; Fax: 33.61.91.87). *Location:* near Granville, towards Coutances and Cherbourg. Seaside links. 18 holes, 5854 metres, Par 71. 9 holes, 2323 metres, Par 33. Driving range, putting green. *Green Fees:* weekdays 140f; weekends 200f, Holidays 220f. *Eating facilities:* bar and restaurant in clubhouse. Pro shop; trolley and club hire. *Visitors:* welcome, no restrictions. Special rates for groups over 10.

HARDELOT. **Golf d'Hardelot "Les Dunes",** Avenue Edouard VII, 62152 Hardelot Plage (21.91.90.90; Fax: 21.33.26.40). *Location:* at Hardelot Plage, 15km south of Boulogne. Undulating dunes with attractive pine trees. 18 holes, 6014 metres, Par 73. Golf Academy. *Green Fees:* weekdays Summer 260f; Winter 200f; weekends Summer 300f, Winter 260f. *Eating facilities:* clubhouse. *Visitors:* welcome. Handicap Certificate required. *Society Meetings:* welcome. Professional: Peter Dawson/Louis Maisonnave. Secretary: S. Devilliers.

HARDELOT. **Golf d'Hardelot "Les Pins",** 3 Avenue du Golf, 62152 Hardelot Plage (21.83.73.10; Fax: 21.83.24.33). *Location:* the beach-resort of Hardelot Plage is 15 km south of Boulogne. Attractive course carved through a pine forest. 18 holes, 5870 metres, Par 72. Practice ground, putting green. *Eating facilities:* clubhouse with bar and fine restaurant. Handicap Certificate required. Pro shop; club and trolley hire.

LAON. **Golf de l'Ailette,** 02860 Cerny-en-Laonnois (23.24.83.99; Fax: 23.24.84.66). *Location:* about 10km south of Laon. An interesting course laid out on the edge of a forest flanked by large areas of water. 18 holes, 6127 metres, Par 72. 9 holes, 1165 metres, Par 28. Driving range, putting green. *Eating facilities:* bar and restaurant in clubhouse. Pro shop; trolley and club hire.

LE TOUQUET. **Golf du Touquet,** Avenue du Golf, 62520 Le Touquet (21.05.68.47). *Location:* on the coast, two km south of Le Touquet. The Forest Course – in the heart of an old pine forest. 18 holes, 5912 metres, Par 71. The Sea Course – a championship links course bordered by sand dunes. 18 holes, 6082 metres, Par 72. Also a 9-hole beginners' course. Practice ground and putting green. *Green Fees:* from 180ff to 320ff depending on season. *Eating facilities:* bar and restaurant in clubhouse. Pro shop; trolley and club hire. Professional: P. Philippon.

LILLE. **Golf de Bondues,** Château de la Vigne, BP 54, 59587 Bondues Cedex (20.23.13.85). *Location:* about 10km north of Lille, west of the N17. In the grounds of an 18th century château, the courses have well protected greens with deep bunkers and several water hazards. 18 holes, 6261 metres, Par 73. 18 holes, 6000 metres, Par 72. Driving range, putting green. *Eating facilities:* bar and restaurant in clubhouse. Pro shop, trolley hire. Professional: (20.23.13.97). Secretary: (20.23.20.62; Fax: 20.23.24.11).

DEAUVILLE SAINT-GATIEN GOLF CLUB

Typical and ancient Normandy timbered clubhouse offers golfers a warm welcome. Splendid views over the Seine Estuary.

27 holes.   Open seven days.

**Deauville Saint-Gatien Golf Club,
14130 Saint-Gatien-Des-Bois
Telephone: 31.65.19.99 Fax: 31.65.11.24**

348

THE GOLF GUIDE 1994

Golf in France

NEUBOURG. **Golf Club du Champ de Bataille,** 27110 Le Neubourg (32.35.03.72; Fax: 32.35.83.10). *Location:* south-west of Rouen, about 28km north-west of Evreux. A fine test of golf attractively laid out through the wooded estate of the elegant château. Par 3 holes. 18 holes, 6575 yards, 5983 metres, Par 72. Driving range, putting green. *Green Fees:* weekdays 220f (full season); weekends 330f (full season). Special rates to tour operators under contract with the club. *Eating facilities:* bar and restaurant in château clubhouse. *Visitors:* welcome, no restrictions. Pro shop; cart, trolley and club hire. Guest rooms available in the château. *Society Meetings:* welcome.

ST. OMER. **Aa Saint-Omer Golf Club,** Chemin des Bois, Acquin-Westbecourt, 62380 Lumbres (21.38.59.90; Fax: 21.38.59.90). *Location:* from Calais take A26 auto route, Junction 3 St. Omer, right onto RN42 Expressway, first exit Acquin/Lumbres (30 minutes from Calais). Undulating parkland and mature trees overlooking the valley of the River Aa. 18 holes, 6400 metres, Par 72. 9 holes, 2003 metres, Par 31. Practice ground and putting green. *Eating facilities:* clubhouse bar and restaurant. Pro shop; trolley and club hire.

NORTH WEST

ANGERS. **Anjou Golf and Country Club,** Route de Cheffes, 49330 Champigne (41.42.01.01; Fax: 41.42.04.37). *Location:* about 20km north of Angers, from Paris A11, exit Durtal. Flat course with a few lakes and trees. 18 holes, 6227 metres, Par 72. Short 6 hole course, 750 metres, Par 19. Practice facilities. *Green Fees:* weekdays 200/160f; weekends 160/120f. Discount for hotel residents. *Eating facilities:* bar and restaurant in clubhouse. *Visitors:* welcome. Starting times must be booked in advance. Professional: D. Dalies. Secretary: F. Guel. Pro shop; cart, trolley and club hire.

ANGERS. **Golf de Sablé-Solesmes,** Domaine de l'Outinière, Route de Pince1, 72300 Sablé-sur-Sarthe (43.95.28.78; Fax: 43.92.39.05). *Location:* east of the A11, about 40km north of Angers, south-east of Le Mans. Three totally different 9's – Forest and River: 18 holes, 6207 metres, Par 72; Waterfall: 9 holes, 3069 metres, Par 36, radiate from the large clubhouse. Testing and spectacular with park, woodland and lakeside holes. Driving range, putting green. *Green*

Fees: weekdays 180 – 230f; weekends 260 – 320f. *Eating facilities:* bar and restaurant in clubhouse. Pro shop; cart, trolley and club hire. Professional: Olivier Gaudin. Secretary: Angèle Goyer. Director: Moraly Michel.

AURAY. **Golf de Baden,** Kernic, 56870 Baden (97.57.18.96; Fax: 97.57.22.05). *Location:* between the village of Baden and the sea, south of the RN 165 at Auray exit. Undulating course partly through pine woods and around lakes. 18 holes, 6112 metres, Par 72. 3 hole, 535 metre pitch and putt course. Practice, putting green, green d'approche. *Green Fees:* on application. *Eating facilities:* bar and snacks in clubhouse. Pro shop; trolley and club hire; club repair. Neighbouring hotels "Le Gavrinis" and "du Loch" offer year-round golfing breaks.

AURAY. **Golf de Saint Laurent,** 56400 Auray, Ploemel (97.56.85.18; Fax: 97.56.89.99). *Location:* about five km west of Auray and not far from Carnac with its ancient standing stones. High quality championship course, undulating through mature trees. 18 holes, 6112 metres, Par 72. 9 hole course, 2705 metres, Par 35. *Green Fees:* 18 holes 150f – 230f; 9 holes 100f – 150f. *Eating facilities:* bar and restaurant in on-course Fairway Hotel St. Laurent; also on-course "Maeve" self catering cottages available. Pro shop; cart, trolley and club hire. Professionals: Paul Braun, Dominique Jouan.

BENODET. **Golf de l'Odet,** Menez Groas, Clohars-Fouesnant, 29950 Bénodet (98.54.87.88; Fax: 98.54.61.40). *Location:* south of Quimper, towards the sea at Bénodet. An undulating partly wooded course. 18 holes, 6235 metres, Par 72. 9 holes, 1100 metres, Par 27. Driving range, putting green, pitching green. *Eating facilities:* bar, restaurant and on-site Hotel Eurogreen, whose residents have reduced green fees. *Visitors:* welcome, no restrictions but advisable to book tee times. Other accommodation nearby. Pro shop; cart, trolley and club hire. Professional: Yva Bechu. Secretary: J.P. Chaton (98.54.87.88; Fax: 98.52.61.40).

BREST. **Golf de Brest Iroise,** Parc de Loisirs de Lann Rohou, 29800 Landerneau (98.85.16.17; Fax: 98.21.52.08). *Location:* east of Brest, five km south of Landerneau. A tough course, open to the breeze in a beautiful natural setting. 18 holes, 5885 metres, Par 72. 9 holes, 3329 metres, Par 37. Driving range, putting green. *Eating facilities:* bar and restaurant and all facilities at the Golf Hotel d'Iroise. Pro shop; cart, trolley and club hire.

Hôtel de la Plage

Lovely hotel on sandy beach, with splendid ocean views. Extensive range of leisure facilities. Plenty to entertain children at this pleasant resort. A variety of golf courses nearby.

See our colour display advertisement on page 36.

2 avenue de la mer, 85690 Notre-Dame-de-Monts, Vendée, France.
Telephone: 51 58 83 09 Fax: 51 58 97 12

Golf in France THE GOLF GUIDE 1994

LA BAULE. **Golf de la Baule,** Domaine de St. Denac, 44117 St. André-des-Eaux (40.60.46.18; Fax: 40.60.41.41). *Location:* to the east of La Baule, 3km from St. André des Eaux. A parkland course winding through mature trees with hills and a large lake affecting the back nine. 18 holes, 6700 yards, 6157 metres, S.S.S. 73, Par 72. Practice ground and putting greens. *Green Fees:* from 170f – 320f depending on time of year. 20% reduction for groups of 15 or more. *Eating facilities:* bar and restaurant. *Visitors:* welcome by reservation booked the day before. Pro shop; cart, club and trolley hire. *Society Meetings:* welcome by arrangement. Professional: Eric Mauger (40.60.34.04). Secretary: Eric Stoquer.

LA BAULE. **Golf de la Bretesche,** Domaine de la Bretesche, 44780 Missillac (40.88.30.05). *Location:* 20km north-east of La Baule; 50km north-west of Nantes on the N165. In a wooded parkland with narrow fairways. 18 holes, 6080 metres, S.S.S. 72. Practice ground, putting green, training bunker, pitch and putt. *Green Fees:* 140ff – 280ff. 20% reduction for residents in the hotel. *Eating facilities:* bar and restaurant. *Visitors:* welcome. *Society Meetings:* welcome. Professional: Thierry Mathon (40.88.30.03; Fax: 40.88.36.28). Secretary: Isabelle Moreau (40.88.30.03; Fax: 40.88.36.28).

LA ROCHE-SUR-YON. **Golf Club de la Domangère,** Route de Nesmy, 85310 Nesmy (51.07.60.15; Fax: 51.07.64.09). *Location:* approximately 10km south of La Roche-sur-Yon east of the D747. A long and majestic course with plenty of strategic water, mature trees and bordered by the River Yon. 18 holes, 6480 metres, Par 72. 4 hole practice course, driving range, putting green. *Eating facilities:* bar, grill-room and restaurant in the on-site Hotel de la Domangère. Club, cart and trolley hire.

LORIENT. **Golf du Val Quéven,** Kerrousseau RD 6, 56530 Quéven (97.05.17.96; Fax: 97.05.19.18). *Location:* at Pont Scorff near Quéven off the RN 165 shortly after Lorient. A varied course, wooded and with water hazards. 18 holes, 6140 metres, Par 72. Driving range, putting green. *Green Fees:* 150f, 190, 230f. *Eating facilities:* bar and restaurant. Pro shop; club and trolley hire. Professional: Luc Miriel. Secretaries: R. Deltour, S. Jochnans.

LORIENT. **Golf Ploemeur Ocean,** Saint Jude-Kerham, 56270 Ploemeur (97.32.81.82; Fax: 97.32.80.90). *Location:* main route Rennes-Lorient, exit Ploemeur. Seaside course, huge American style greens, water hazards. 18 holes, 5957 metres, S.S.S. 72. Covered driving range. *Green Fees:* from 140f – 230f depending on season. 20% reduction for tour operators. *Eating facilities:* bar and restaurant. *Visitors:* welcome. Hotels in immediate surroundings. *Society Meetings:* managed by the SEM of Ploemeur. Professionals: M. Zimmermann and M. Queffelec. Secretary: Mlle Le Cloirec. Manager: M. Jean-Luc Bernard.

RENNES. **Golf de la Freslonnière,** 35650 Le Rheu (33.99.14.84.09; Fax: 33.99.14.94.98). *Location:* three km from Rennes towards Lorient. Woodland course with water features and banks of rhododendrons. 18 holes, 5671 metres, Par 71. Practice ground and putting green. *Green Fees:* weekdays 200f; weekends 230f. *Eating facilities:* clubhouse, restaurant and bar. Golf holiday packages from nearby Novotel Rennes. Pro shop; club, cart and trolley hire. Professional: Richard Triaire.

RENNES. **Golf de Rennes,** St. Jacques de la Lande, 35136 Rennes (99.31.52.52). *Location:* eight km south of Rennes, off the D177 to Redon. Set amongst mature woodland with several water hazards; a new course to enjoy. 18 holes, 6150 metres, Par 72. 9 holes, 2068 metres, Par 32. Short 9 hole course. *Green Fees:* weekdays 190f; weekends 230f. *Eating facilities:* bar and restaurant in clubhouse. *Visitors:* welcome, no restrictions. Pro shop; trolley and club hire.

ST. MALO. **Golf de St-Malo-le-Tronchet,** Le Tronchet, 35540 Miniac Morvan (99.58.96.69). *Location:* 23km south of St. Malo, 12km east of Dinan, south of the N176. Rolling parkland designed on a grand scale with vast greens and sand traps, strategic water. 18 holes, 6046 metres, Par 72. 9 holes, 2684 metres, Par 36. Driving range, putting green. *Green Fees:* £220f. Reduced rates for students. *Eating facilities:* bar and restaurant. *Visitors:* welcome. "Hostellerie Abbatiale" close by the course with all hotel facilities and golf holiday packages. Pro shop; trolley and club hire. *Society Meetings:* welcome, bookings required. Professional: M. Cyril Bourakhowitch. Secretary: Mme Raquel Watbot.

ST.-JEAN-DE-MONTS. **Golf Club de St. Jean-de-Monts,** Avenue des Pays de Monts, 85160 St. Jean-de-Monts (51.58.82.73; Fax: 51.59.18.32). *Location:* a partly links-style course along the seaside with pine trees and dunes. On the Atlantic coast some 60/70km south-west of Nantes. 18 holes, 5962 metres, Par 72. Short 5 hole course. Practice ground and putting greens. *Eating facilities:* clubhouse with bar and restaurant. The Hotel de la Plage in nearby Notre Dame de Monts offers golfing breaks. Pro shop; cart, club and trolley hire.

PARIS

PARIS. **Golf de Forges-les-Bains,** Rue de Général Leclerc, 91470 Forges-les-Bains (64.91.48.18; Fax: 64.91.40.52). *Location:* A10 Orleans, exit Les Ulis then towards Limours and Forges-les-Bains. Wooded course. 18 holes, 6207 metres, Par 72. Driving range, practice area. *Green Fees:* weekdays 200f; weekends 300f. *Eating facilities:* bar and restaurant in clubhouse. *Visitors:* welcome, no restrictions but reservations preferred. Pro shop; trolley and club hire. Professionals: Sydney Kershaw, Martino Proenca. Secretary: Fabrice Gicquiaud.

PARIS. **Golf de la Vaucouleurs,** 78910 Civry-la-Forêt (34.87.76.04). *Location:* off the A13 at the Mantes interchange, south off the road to Houdan. Two 18 hole courses. "The River" – very varied with trees, water and hills, 6298 metres, Par 73; "The Little Valley" – a links-type course, 5638 metres, Par 70. Practice ground, putting green. *Green Fees:* weekdays 350f, weekends 200f. *Eating facilities:* bar and restaurant in clubhouse; also at nearby Hotel la Dousseine at Anet. Pro shop; club and trolley hire. Professional: Raymond Marro (34.87.62.29; Fax: 34.87.70.09).

PARIS. **Golf des Yvelines,** Château de la Couharde, 78940 La Queue-les-Yvelines (34.86.48.89; Fax: 34.86.50.31). *Location:* about 45km west of Paris by N12, near Montfort-l'Amaury. Built around the elegant château, with fairways cut through thick woods. 18 holes, 6344 metres, S.S.S. 72. 9 holes, 2065 metres, S.S.S. 31. Practice ground, putting green. *Green Fees:* weekdays 200ff, weekends 350ff. *Eating facilities:* bar and restaurant. *Visitors:* all visitors welcome. Club and trolley hire. Professional: Jean Paul Chardonnet.

PARIS. **Golf National,** 2 Avenue du Golf, 78280 Guyancourt (30.43.36.00; Fax: 34.43.85.58). *Location:* about 25km south-west of Paris off the D91. A public facility of 45 holes laid out in three courses. "The Albatross" (now the venue for the French Open) – 18 holes, 6500 metres championship course with severe water hazards and winding fairways, Par 72; "The Eagle" – 18 holes, 6000 metres, Par 72 for experienced players; "The Birdie" – 9 hole, 2100 metres beginners' course, Par 32 and driving range; "The Par" – a warm-up, practice course. Putting greens. *Green Fees:* weekdays 200ff, weekends 300ff. *Eating facilities:* on-site Hotel Novotel. Cart, club and trolley hire.

WEST & CENTRE

CHEVERNY. **Golf du Château de Cheverny,** La Rousselière, 41700 Contres (54.79.24.70; Fax: 54.79.25.52). *Location:* on the south of Cheverny 15km south of Blois. Built over the former hunting grounds of the Château with large well-kept greens. 18 holes, 6272 metres, Par 71. 3 hole practice course, driving range and putting green. *Eating facilities:* bar and restaurant in clubhouse. *Visitors:* welcome. Pro shop; club and trolley hire. *Society Meetings:* 20% reduction on fees.

COGNAC. **Golf du Cognac,** Saint-Brice, 16100 Cognac (45.35.38.50; Fax: 45.35.10.76). *Location:* five km east of Cognac, north of the N141 across the River Charente. Undulating fairways with views of vineyards and the river; some water hazards. 18 holes, 6122 metres, Par 72. 4 hole practice course, putting green and driving range. *Green Fees:* 200f. *Eating facilities:* clubhouse with restaurant and bar. Pro shop; cart, club and trolley hire. Professional: Jean-Marc Lecuona (45.32.37.60). Secretary: Emmanuel Ballongue (45.32.18.17).

LOUDUN. **Golf Public Saint-Hilaire,** 86120 Roiffe (49.98.78.06; Fax: 49.98.72.57). *Location:* 15km north of Loudun towards Saumur on the D147. An attractive woodland course with water hazards. 18 holes, 6280 metres, Par 72. 6 hole practice course, driving range and putting green. *Eating facilities:* clubhouse with restaurant and bar. Pro shop; trolley and club hire.

ORLÉANS. **"Les Bordes" Golf International,** 41220 St-Laurent Nouan (54.87.72.13; Fax: 54.87.78.61). *Location:* from Paris motorway A10 exit Meung sur Loire. Laid out on a former hunting park. 18 holes, 7041 yards, 6412 metres,Par 72. Driving range, putting green. *Green Fees:* weekdays 400f; weekends and Holidays 700f. *Eating facilities:* bar and restaurant in clubhouse. *Visitors:* welcome every day. Pro shop; carts, trolley and clubs for hire. Professional: M. Masahiko Kitamura.

POITIERS. **Golf du Haut-Poitou,** Parc de Loisirs de St. Cyr, 86130 Jaunay-Clan (49.62.53.62). *Location:* 20km north of Poitiers and 15km south of Chatellerault. Undulating course with a lake and water hazards and wooded hills. 18 holes, 6590 metres, S.S.S. 73. 9 holes, 1800 metres, Par 31. Practice ground, driving range, putting and pitching greens. *Green Fees:* weekdays 9 hole course 120ff, 18 hole course 170ff; weekends 9 hole course 130ff, 18 hole course 200ff. *Eating facilities:* clubhouse with restaurant and bar. *Visitors:* welcome without restriction. Pro shop and equipment hire. *Society Meetings:* welcome. Professional: David Maxwell. Secretaries: Catherine Marchais and B. Guignard (49.62.53.62; Fax: 49.60.28.58).

ROYAN. **Golf de Royan,** Maine-Gaudin, La Palud, 17420 St.-Palais-sur-Mer (46.23.40.80). *Location:* on the D25 coast road, six km north-west of Royan. An exciting course with narrow fairways undulating through tall pines. 18 holes, 6033 metres, Par 71. 6 hole pitch and putt, practice ground with driving range, putting green. *Green Fees:* weekdays 170f – 230f; weekends 190f – 230f. *Eating facilities:* restaurant and bar in clubhouse. Pro shop with equipment hire.

TOURS. **Golf d'Ardrée,** B P 1, 37360 St.-Antoine-du-Rocher (97.56.77.38; Fax: 47.56.79.96). *Location:* 10km north of Tours. An attractive parkland course with strategic water and sand. 18 holes, 5507 metres, Par 70. Practice ground and putting green. *Green Fees:* weekdays 210f; weekends 260f. Special rates for groups of 20 or more (20% discount). *Eating facilities:* restaurant and bar in clubhouse. *Visitors:* welcome. Pro shop; club and trolley hire.

TOURS. **Golf du Château des Sept Tours,** 37330 Courcelles de Tourraine (47.24.69.75; Fax: 47.24.23.74). *Location:* on the D34 between Château la Vallière and Langeais. A long demanding course with attractive woods and water. 18 holes, 6194 metres, Par 73. Practice ground and putting green. *Green Fees:* weekdays 180f; weekends 240f. *Eating facilities:* bar and restaurant in on-site Hotel Château des Sept Tours. Pro shop; club and trolley hire. Professionals: Brian Sparks/Yannick Sailllour.

EAST

AIX-LES-BAINS. Golf Club d'Aix-les-Bains, Avenue de Golf, 73100 Aix-les-Bains (79.61.23.35; Fax: 79.34.06.01). *Location:* three km south of Aix by the Lac du Bourget. An attractive parkland course on sloping land surrounded by wooded hills. 18 holes, 5595 metres, Par 71. Driving range, putting green. *Eating facilities:* bar and restaurant in clubhouse. Pro shop; trolley and club hire.

CHAMONIX. **Golf de Chamonix,** 35 Route du Golf, BP 31, 74400 Chamonix (50.53.23.27; Fax: 50.53.15.85). *Location:* on the N506 three km north of Chamonix. Green fairways follow the valley floor with streams and trees. Spectacular mountain views including Mont Blanc. 18 holes, 6076 metres, S.S.S. 72. Driving range, putting green. *Green Fees:* weekdays 200f; weekends 250f. July/August 300f per day. *Eating facilities:* restaurant. *Visitors:* welcome every day with a Handicap Certificate. Pro shop; cart, trolley and club hire. *Society Meeting:* welcome, 10% reduction. Professional: Jean Claude Bonnaz. Secretary: Caroline de Chardon (50.53.06.28; Fax: 50.53.38.69).

EVIAN. **Royal Golf Club d'Evian,** Rive Sud du Lac de Genève, 74500 Evian-les-Bains (50.26.85.00; Fax: 50.75.38.40). *Location:* on high ground above Evian, 8km from Thonon, 45km west of Geneva. Hilly fairways overlooking Lake Leman, sloping greens guarded by deep bunkers. 18 holes, 6674 yards, 6006 metres, Par 72. Covered and uncovered practice range, two putting greens, chipping green, pitching green, training bunkers, pitch and putt. *Green Fees:* weekdays 190/350f according to season; weekends 290/380f according to season. Free to hotels' guests – guaranteed tee times. *Eating facilities:* restaurant and bar: Le Chalet du Golf. *Visitors:* welcome, Handicap 35 or course authorization. Pro shop – clubs, bags and carts. *Society Meetings:* welcome (no more than 120 people). Professionals: Jean-Marc Bochaton (lessons) and Lamberto Capoccia (courses). Secretary: Sylvie Martin. Director: Valérie Pamard.

GRENOBLE. **Golf International de Grenoble,** Route de Montavie, 38320 Eybens (76.73.65.00). *Location:* five km south of Grenoble. A long course with winding fairways, small lakes, trees – architect Robert Trent Jones Jnr. 18 holes, 6410 metres, Par 72. Practice ground and putting green. *Green Fees:* weekdays 220f, weekends 250f. *Eating facilities:* clubhouse and nearby hotel. Pro shop; cart, trolley and club hire.

LYON. **Golf Club de Lyon,** 38280 Vilette d'Anthon (78.31.11.33; Fax: 72.02.48.27). *Location:* Lyon, motorway A42 exit Balan. Brocards – flat, wooded; Sangliers – hilly, wooded. Brocards 18 holes, 6167 metres, S.S.S. 72; Sangliers 18 holes, 6727 metres. S.S.S 72. Practice ground, putting green, 7 holes pitch and putt. *Green Fees:* weekdays 200f; weekends 300f. *Eating facilities:* bar and restaurant in clubhouse. *Visitors:* welcome anytime. Pro shop; equipment hire.

ST. JULIEN (Geneva). **Golf and Country Club de Bossey,** Château de Crevin, Bossey, 74160 St.-Julien-en-Genevois. *Location:* just near the main road between St. Julien en Genevois and Annemasse about five miles from each of these towns. Just in France on the southern outskirts of Geneva. Challenging mountain golf with fine views. Well wooded with water hazards. 18 holes, 6002 metres, Par 72. Driving range, putting green. *Green Fees:* weekdays only, on application. *Eating facilities:* bar and restaurant in château clubhouse. *Visitors:* welcome weekdays only, maximum of three times a year. Maximum handicap 35. No jeans allowed on course. Contact General Manager for details. Pro shop; cart, trolley and club hire. *Society Meetings:* catered for, contact General Manager. Professional: Mark Cobley (50.43.65.66). Secretary: (50.43.75.25; Fax: 50.95.32.57).

SOUTH WEST

ANGLET. **Golf de Chiberta,** 104 Boulevard des Plages, 64600 Anglet (59.63.83.20; Fax: 59.63.30.56). *Location:* three km north-east of Biarritz. A well-established combination of seashore and wooded parkland. 18 holes, 5650 metres, Par 70. Driving range, putting green. *Eating facilities:* bar and restaurant in clubhouse. Pro shop; trolley and club hire.

ARCACHON. **Golf de Gujan Mestras,** B P 74, Route de Sanguinet, 33470 Gujan Mestras (56.66.86.36; Fax: 56.66.10.93). *Location:* a spectacular course with well-located water obstacles. 12 km east of Arcachon, 40km west of Bordeaux, north of the A66. 18 holes, 6225 metres, Par 72. 9 holes, 2630 metres, Par 35. *Eating facilities:* restaurant, clubhouse and at nearby hotel. Pro shop; equipment and trolley hire.

BANDOL. **Fregate Golf Club,** RD 559, 83270 St-Cyr-sur-Mer (94.32.50.50; Fax: 94.29.96.94). *Location:* about 7km from St-Cyr-sur-Mer on the road to Bandol on the right hand side. A dramatic new course in a vineyard setting overlooking the Mediteranean. 18 holes, 6500 metres. Par 72. Also 9 holes, 1500 metres. Par 29. Practice ground and putting green. *Green Fees:* information not provided. *Eating facilities:* bar and restaurant. Also on-site hotel by 18th green. Pro shop, club, cart and trolley hire.

BAYONNE. **Golf de la Côte d'Argent,** 40660 Moliets (58.48.54.65; Fax: 58.48.54.88). *Location:* about 30km north of Bayonne on the Atlantic coast at Moliets. Part of a leisure seaside complex with links and wooded inland holes. 18 holes, 6164 metres, Par 72. 9 holes, 1905 metres, Par 31. Practice ground, putting green. *Green Fees:* 210f (270f in July). *Eating facilities:* bar and restaurant in clubhouse and in on-site hotels. *Visitors:* welcome. Pro shop; cart, club and trolley hire; tennis, archery. *Society Meetings:* welcome. Professionals: Franck Duiousso, Patrick Talon.

THE GOLF GUIDE 1994 *Golf in France*

BAYONNE. **Golf de Seignosse,** Carrefour de Bocau, 40510 Seignosse (58.43.17.32; Fax: 58.43.16.67). *Location:* about 25km north of Bayonne on the D79 north of Hossegor. Very hilly, exciting and undulating course, a pleasure to look at as well as play. 18 holes, 6140 metres, Par 72. Practice ground. *Green Fees:* High Season 300f, Low Season 220f. *Eating facilities:* bar and restaurant; Hotel. Pro shop; cart, club and trolley hire. *Visitors:* welcome.

BIARRITZ. **Golf d'Arcangues,** Argelous, 64200 Arcangues (59.43.10.56; Fax: 59.41.12.36). *Location:* three km south-east of Biarritz. A fine rolling test in modern but natural style. Mounded bunkers and strategic water. 18 holes, 6142 metres, Par 72. *Eating facilities:* bar and restaurant in clubhouse. Pro shop and equipment hire.

BIARRITZ. **Golf de Biarritz Le Phare,** 2 Avenue Edith Cavell, 64200 Biarritz (59.03.71.33). *Location:* in Biarritz, facing the ocean with cooling breezes. A historic course (1888) with fast greens, level, many bunkers. 18 holes, 5379 metres, S.S.S. 69. Practice ground, putting green. *Green Fees:* off season 220ff, main season 300ff. *Eating facilities:* bar and restaurant in clubhouse, the nearby Hôtel du Palais and other hotels. Pro shop; club and trolley hire. Secretary: (59.03.71.80; Fax: 59.03.26.74).

BORDEAUX. **Golf de Bordeaux Cameyrac,** 33450 St. Sulpice et Cameyrac (56.72.96.79; Fax: 56.72.86.56). *Location:* 15km from Bordeaux N89 (Exit no. 15) close to the famous vineyards of St. Emilion and Pomerol. Fairways run through forest, alongside ponds and vineyards. 18 holes, 5972 metres, Par 72. 9 holes, 1188 metres, Par 28. Practice ground, putting green. *Green Fees:* weekdays 150f for 18 holes, 110f for 9 holes; weekends 200f for 18 holes, 140f for 9 holes. *Eating facilities:* bar and restaurant (56.72.94.51). *Visitors:* welcome every day 8.30am to 7.30pm. Pro shop; equipment hire. *Society Meetings:* welcome. Professional/Manager: Mr Christian Chabrier. Secretary: Mr Alexis Champion.

BORDEAUX. **Golf de Pessac,** Rue de la Princesse, 33600 Pessac (56.36.24.47; Fax: 56.36.52.89). *Location:* on the western outskirts of Bordeaux, four km from the city and close to the airport. St. Jean d'Illiac road. A level course with large bunkers and some water. 27 holes providing alternative 9 hole layouts plus 9 hole practice course. 18 holes, 6300 metres, all Par 72. Driving range, putting green. *Green Fees:* weekdays 200f; weekends 260f. *Eating facilities:* restaurant and bar. *Visitors:* welcome. *Society Meetings:* welcome. Pro shop; cart, club and trolley hire. Professional: S. Scursoglio. Secretary: P. Passemard.

BORDEAUX. **Golf du Médoc,** Chemin de Courmateau, 33290 Le Pian Médoc (56.72.01.10; Fax: 56.72.03.44). *Location:* 15km to the north-west of Bordeaux by the River Garonne. Two courses, the original with widespread fairways, water and banks; 18 holes, 6316 metres. S.S.S. 71. The newer course "Des Vignes" winding through lakes and pine trees, has each of its 18 holes named after a Meldoc wine château: 6291 metres, Par 70. Practice ground, pitching and putting greens. *Eating facilities:* clubhouse with bar and quality restaurant. Pro shop; cart, club and trolley hire.

CASTELJALOUX. **Golf de Casteljaloux,** Route de Mont-de-Marsan, 47700 Casteljaloux (53.93.51.60; Fax: 53.93.04.10). *Location:* situated on the D933 facing Lake Clarens on the road to Mont-de-Marsan, 15km from the exit of the motorway, 90km from Bordeaux, 170km from Toulouse. Gentle slopes and some difficult greens. 18 holes, 5916 metres, Par 72. Practice holes, bunkers and tees, driving range and putting green. *Green Fees:* weekdays low season 150f, high season 180f; weekends low season 200f, high season 220f. *Eating facilities:* bar and restaurant in clubhouse with fine views. *Visitors:* welcome. Pro shop; club and trolley hire. *Society Meetings:* by arrangement. Professional: Francois Thollon Pommerol. Secretary: Véronique Huix.

DORDOGNE. **Château des Vigiers Golf and Country Club,** 24240 Monestier (53.61.50.00; Fax: 53.61.50.20). *Location:* about an hour's drive east of Bordeaux on D936, bearing right on D18 at Ste-Foy-la-Grande. New course, rolling past orchards, vineyards, woods, lakes surrounding charming 16th century château clubhouse which is also a luxury hotel. 18 holes, 6003 metres. Par 72. 9 hole practice course, driving range and putting green. *Green Fees:* information not provided. *Eating facilities:* restaurant and bar. Pro shop, club, cart and trolley rental.

HOSSEGOR. **Golf d'Hossegor,** Avenue du Golf, 40150 Hossegor (58.43.56.99; Fax: 58.43.98.52). *Location:* about 15km north of Bayonne just west of the A63. Fine classic test of golf over gently undulating, heavily wooded land. 18 holes, 5867 metres, Par 71. Driving range, putting green. *Eating facilities:* bar and restaurant in clubhouse. Pro shop; trolley and club hire.

PAU. **Pau Golf Club,** Rue du Golf, 64140 Billère (59.32.02.33; Fax: 59.62.42.57). *Location:* RN 117 Commune de Billère 5km from Pau towards Bayonne. The first course in continental Europe (1856). Flat, wooded, along the River Gave. 18 holes, 5312 metres, S.S.S. 69. Practice facilities including three practice holes. *Green Fees:* weekdays 200f; weekends 250f. Special rates available on request. *Eating facilities:* bar

---

HÔTEL DU PALAIS
Biarritz
Sister city with Augusta, Georgia
1 avenue de l'Imperatrice, 64200,
Biarritz, France
Tel: (010 33) 59.41.64.00
Fax: (010 33) 59.24.36.84
London Office: 071-630 1704

Enjoy the dignified luxury of this prestigious Hotel on the Basque coast, the 'Mecca' of golf in France. Within easy reach of 6 of France's leading courses, catering for all levels of golf, the Hôtel du Palais offers the very best to golfers and their families. Tennis, riding and Casino nearby, and magnificent seafront location.
See also our colour display advertisement on page 33.

Golf in France   **THE GOLF GUIDE 1994**

and restaurant in clubhouse. *Visitors:* welcome. *Society Meetings:* by arrangement. Professional: D. Loustalet (59.32.79.24). Secretary: Mme Nicole Larre (59.32.02.33).

SAINT-JEAN-DE-LUZ. **Golf de la Nivelle,** Place William Sharp, 64500 Ciboure (59.47.18.99; Fax: 59.47.21.16). *Location:* two km south of Saint-Jean, on the banks of the River Nivelle. A "town" course; classic parkland with mature trees and harbour views. 18 holes, 5513 metres, Par 70. Practice ground, putting green. *Green Fees:* weekdays 200ff, weekends 250ff. *Eating facilities:* bar and restaurant in clubhouse. Self catering flats on golf course. Pro shop; equipment hire.

TOULOUSE. **Golf International de Toulouse Seilh,** Route de Grenade, 31840 Seilh (61.42.59.30; Fax: 61.42.34.17). *Location:* about 12km north-west of Toulouse near the A62. "Yellow" Course of moderate difficulty, 18 holes, 4202 metres, Par 64; "Red" Course of competitionstandard, 18 holes, 6200 metres, Par 72. Extensive practice and training facilities. *Eating facilities:* bar and restaurant in clubhouse. Pro shop; club, cart and trolley hire.

VILLENEUVE-SUR-LOT. **Golf de Castelnaud,** "La Menuisiére", 47290 Castelnaud de Gratecambe (53.01.74.64; Fax: 53.01.78.99). *Location:* on the N21 10km north of Villeneuve, between the scenic valleys of the Lot and the Dordogne. Inland course with water and many trees. 18 holes, 6322 metres, Par 72. 9 hole practice course, 1092 metres, Par 27. Practice ground, putting green. *Eating facilities:* the clubhouse is an 18th century manor house with what is reputed to be the best golf course restaurant in France. Pro shop; equipment hire.

SOUTH

AIX-EN-PROVENCE. **Golf International de Château L'Arc,** Domaine de Château L'Arc, 13710 Fuveau (42.53.28.38; Fax: 42.29.08.41). *Location:* about 15km south-east of Aix-en-Provence just south of the A8. A challenging course of varying terrain through trees, sloping fairways and water hazards. 18 holes, 6300 metres, Par 73. Driving range, putting green. *Eating facilities:* bar and restaurant in clubhouse. Pro shop; cart, trolley and club hire.

AVIGNON. **Golf des Baux de Provence,** Domaine de Manville, 13520 Les Baux de Provence (0800 890 033 90.54.37.02; Fax: 0800 890 033 90.54.40.93). *Location:* 25km from Avignon, 18km from Arles, 80km from Marseille (Airport), the course is on the D27 between Les Baux and Maussane-les-Alpilles. Designed by the British architect Martin Hawtree, the course is set between pines, olive trees and scented lavender. 9 holes, 2842 metres. Par 36. Practice, putting green, 9 hole pitch and putt course 836 metres, Par 27. *Green Fees:* weekdays 160ff; weekends 210ff. Special rates for pairs, Juniors and for 9 holes. *Eating facilities:* bar and restaurant in clubhouse. *Visitors:* always welcome. Hire of clubs, trolleys and golf cars. *Society Meetings:* welcome by arrangement. Professional: Frédéric Monréal. Secretary: Sylvie Martin-Raget.

BÉZIERS. **Golf du Cap d'Agde,** 4 Avenue des Alizés, 34300 Cap d'Agde (67.26.54.40; Fax: 67.26.97.00). *Location:* on the coast, about 60km south-west of Montpellier and 20km east of Béziers. Seaside links. 18 holes, 6301 metres, Par 72. Practice ground, 9 hole pitch and putt. *Green Fees:* weekdays 200f; weekends 250f. *Eating facilities:* bar and restaurant in clubhouse. *Visitors:* welcome, no restrictions. Club, trolley and cart hire. *Society Meetings:* welcome by reservation. Professionals: Xavier Bernard, Vincent Denis. Secretary: Marguerite Bouvier.

CANNES. **Golf Club de Cannes-Mandelieu,** Route de Golf, 06210 Mandelieu-la-Napoule (93.49.55.39; Fax: 93.49.92.90). *Location:* across the mouth of the small River Siagne, abouth seven km west of Cannes, south of the A8. A short, level course, third oldest and most popular in France. 18 holes, 5867 metres, Par 71. 9 holes, 2409 metres, Par 34. Practice ground, putting green. *Eating facilities:* bar and restaurant in attractive clubhouse. Pro shop; club, cart and trolley hire.

CANNES. **Golf Country Club de Cannes-Mougins,** 175 Route d'Antibes, 06250 Mougins (93.75.79.13; Fax: 93.75.27.60). *Location:* eight km north of Cannes, near the A8. A high-class private course, undulating through wooded hills, part of the annual Volvo Tour. 18 holes, 6304 metres, S.S.S. 74. Driving range, putting green. *Green Fees:* weekdays 310f; weekends 360f. *Eating facilities:* restaurant, bar, snacks. *Visitors:* welcome, no restrictions. Sauna. Pro shop; cart, trolley and club hire. Professionals: Michel Damiano, Patrick Lemaire, Richard Sorrell. Secretary: D. Menager.

CANNES. **Riviera Golf Club,** Avenue des Amazones, 06210 Mandelieu (92.97.66.33). *Location:* less than five km west of Cannes, just south of the A8. A new 18 hole course by American master Robert Trent Jones; mostly level, some hills and lakes. 18 holes, 6080 metres, Par 72. Driving range, putting green. *Eating facilities:* in clubhouse. Pro shop; equipment hire.

CORSICA. **Golf de Sperone,** Domaine de Sperone, 20169 Bonifacio (95.73.17.13; Fax: 95.73.17.85). *Location:* near Bonifacio, southern point of Corsica. Another new Trent Jones creation, part on rocky maquis inland, part overlooking the Mediterranean. 18 holes, 6130 metres, Par 73. Practice facilities. *Green Fees:* 330f to 390f. *Eating facilities:* bar and restaurant in the clubhouse. *Visitors:* welcome every day, please make a reservation. Pro shop. *Society Meetings:* welcome except July and August. Professional: Philippe Allain. Secretaries: A. Blanc and S. Biondi.

FREJUS. **Golf de Roquebrune,** CD 7, 83520 Roquebrune-sur-Argens (94.82.92.91; Fax: 94.82.94.74). *Location:* inland, midway between Cannes and St. Tropez. A natural and attractive course, hilly and with water traps. 18 holes, 6241 metres, Par 71. Large 3 hole practice area, driving range and putting green. *Eating facilities:* bar and restaurant in clubhouse. Pro shop; club and trolley hire.

THE GOLF GUIDE 1994

Golf in France

GRASSE. **Golf de la Grande Bastide,** Chemin des Picholines, 06740 Chateauneuf de Grasse (93.77.70.08; Fax: 93.77.72.36). *Location:* just northeast of Grasse about 12km from coast. Gently rolling, of equal challenge to all grades of player. A new 18 hole course, 6710 yards, 6105 metres, Par 72. Driving range, putting green. *Green Fees:* weekdays 240f; weekends 270f. *Eating facilities:* bar and restaurant in clubhouse. *Visitors:* welcome anytime. Trolley and club hire. *Society Meetings:* welcome.

MARSEILLES. **Golf d'Aix Marseille,** Domaine de Riquetti, 13290 Les Milles (42.24.20.41; Fax: 42.39.91.48). *Location:* between Marseille and Aix-en-Provence, west of the A51. A mature parkland course in a natural setting with a wealth of established trees. 18 holes, 6291 metres, Par 73. Driving range, putting green. *Green Fees:* weekdays 220f; weekends 300f. From 15th July to 31 August 200f. *Eating facilities:* bar and restaurant in clubhouse. *Visitors:* welcome, closed Tuesdays. Pro shop; trolley and club hire.

MONTE CARLO. **Monte Carlo Golf Club,** Route du Mont Agel, 06320 La Turbie (Tel & Fax: 93.41.09.11). *Location:* from Nice, take autoroute A8 towards Genova and exit for La Turbie. Signpost at end of town, left turn for Mont Agel. Golf course entrance after 5 kms. Picturesque course with exceptional views of the Mediterranean and southern Alps. 18 holes, 5700 metres, Par 71. Driving range, practice, putting green. *Green Fees:* weekdays 350f; weekends 450f. *Eating facilities:* bar and restaurant. *Visitors:* welcome, Handicap Certificate required. Pro shop; cart, trolley and club hire. *Society Meetings:* welcome by prior arrangement. Professionals: E. Ruffier-Meray, J.M. Loustalan. Secretary: C. Houtart.

MONTPELIER. **Golf de la Grande-Motte,** BP16, 34280 La Grande-Motte (33.67.72.87.78; Fax: 67.29.18.84). *Location:* on the coast, east of Montpelier. Former marshland, now a 42 hole complex with fast greens, water, trees and bunkers. "The Pink Flamingos" – 18 competition class holes, 6161 metres, Par 72; "The Seagulls" – 3220 metres, Par 58; and 9 hole practice green, 560 metres, Par 19. Practice ground, putting green. *Green Fees:* weekdays 180/100/60frs; weekends 220/120/60frs. *Eating facilities:* bar and restaurant in clubhouse and on-course Golf Hotel. Pro shop; trolley and cart hire. Professionals: V. Etchevers, P. Etchevers, A. Milhau and A. Schneider.

MONTPELLIER. **Golf Club de Fontcaude,** Domaine de Fontcaude, 34990 Juvignac (67.03.34.30; Fax: 67.03.34.51). *Location:* at Juvignac, six km west of Montpellier. Undulating over a rolling, scrub-covered landscape, this course provides a fair and interesting challenge. 18 holes, 6292 metres, Par 72. 9 holes, 1290 metres, Par 29. Driving range, putting green. *Green Fees:* weekdays 170f; weekends 230f. *Eating facilities:* bar and restaurant in clubhouse. *Visitors:* welcome, no restrictions. Pro shop; cart, trolley and club hire. *Society Meetings:* welcome. Professional: Stéphane Mourgue. Secretaries: Cathy Laniboire, Nathalie Rossi.

MONTPELLIER. **Golf de Massane,** Domaine de Massane, 34670 Baillargues (67.87.87.89; Fax: 67.87.87.90). *Location:* seven km from airport, 10km from Montpellier and two km from autoroute. Tough championship layout which hosts the annual Volvo Tour qualifying. Elevated greens protected by sand and water. 18 holes, 6375 metres, Par 72. 9 hole compact course. Extensive teaching school with large driving range, pitching and putting greens. *Green Fees:* weekdays 195ff; weekends 270ff. *Eating facilities:* bar and restaurant in clubhouse, hotel on course. Pro shop. *Society Meetings:* welcome. Professional: Nicolas Armand (67.87.87.91). Secretary: Chantal Tisserand (67.87.87.89).

NIMES. **Golf de Nîmes-Campagne,** Route de Saint-Gilles, 30900 Nîmes (66.70.17.37). *Location:* about three km south of Nîmes, by the airport. A classic parkland course of championship calibre built around a hill. 18 holes, 6135 metres, Par 72. Driving range, putting green. *Eating facilities:* bar and excellent restaurant in imposing hilltop clubhouse. Pro shop; cart, trolley and club hire.

NIMES. **Golf des Hauts de Nîmes,** Vacquerolles, Route de Sauve, 30900 Nîmes (66.23.33.33). *Location:* on the north-west outskirts of Nîmes. New course running up a valley and over steeply wooded hills. 18 holes, 6286 metres, Par 72. Driving range, putting green. *Eating facilities:* bar and restaurant in clubhouse. Pro shop; trolley and club hire.

PERPIGNAN. **Golf de St-Cyprien,** Mas d'Huston, 66750 Saint-Cyprien Plage, Perpignan (68.21.01.71; Fax: 68.21.11.33.). *Location:* just south of Perpignan, a renowned course between sea and lake with the Pyrenees mountains in the background. Challenging championship course with water hazards. 18 holes, 6480 metres, Par 73. Golf Course – 9 holes, 2724 metres, Par 35. *Green Fees:* information not provided. *Eating facilities:* bar at clubhouse. Bars, restaurants and accommodation at Le Mas d'Huston, on-course hotel. Open all year. Pro shop, golf clinic.

Le Mas d'Huston

Luxury hotel with 50 large and spacious bedrooms, all individually decorated. Shops, bars and restaurants. Tennis, pool and water sports. Championship golf. Fine cuisine. Peace and relaxation. Studios and apartments for self-catering, with all hotel facilities. See colour advertisement on page 35.

Le Mas d'Huston, Golf de Saint-Cyprien, 66750 Saint Cyprien Plage
Telephone: 68.21.01.71 Fax: 68.21.11.33
or Telephone: 68.37.63.63 Fax: 68.37.64.64 (from 1st March 1994)

Golf in France   **THE GOLF GUIDE 1994**

LATITUDES VALESCURE
SEE COLOUR DISPLAY ADVERTISEMENT ON PAGE 34.
LATITUDES VALESCURE, AVENUE DU GOLF, 83700 SAINT RAPHAEL, COTE D'AZUR
TELEPHONE: 94 82 42 42   FAX: 94 44 61 37

ST. RAPHAÈL. **Golf de l'Estérel,** Avenue du Golf, 83700 St. Raphaèl (94.82.47.88; Fax: 94.44.64.61). *Location:* inland just a few metres north of St. Raphaèl, close to Golf de Valescure. Not long but rated difficult; many trees, narrow fairways and water hazards protecting beautiful greens. 18 holes, 5941 metres, Par 71. 9 holes, 1400 metres, Par 29. Driving range, 9 hole school. *Green Fees:* weekdays 260f; weekends 290f. *Eating facilities:* bar, clubhouse and restaurant. On-site Hotel Latitudes-Valescure (30% reduction in green fees for residents). Pro shop; club, cart and trolley hire.

ST. RAPHAÈL. **Golf et Tennis Club de Valescure,** BP451, Route de Golf, 83700 St.-Raphael (94.82.40.46; Fax: 94.82.41.42). *Location:* about five km east of St.-Raphaèl. An established course (1895), winding attractively through the umbrella pine trees. 18 holes, 5067 metres, Par 68. Driving range, putting green. *Eating facilities:* bar and restaurant in period clubhouse. Also at golf hotel nearby. Pro shop; trolley and club hire.

Golf in Portugal
WHERE TO PLAY • WHERE TO STAY
by Michael Gedye

FOR THE visiting golfer, there are two major regions to consider – the holiday coasts either side of Lisbon and the southern sunshine strip of the Algarve. Elsewhere, golf is available in the north, the Azores and the semi-tropical island of Madeira.

The **Costa Verde** in the north offers three courses – the Oporto Golf Club (where Portuguese golf started in 1890), Miramar and the latest links-style test of Estela, at Povoa de Varzim.

Better known, although still under-visited is the **Costa de Liboa**, which divides fairly neatly into the area west of the city (the Costa do Estoril) and that to the south of the Tagus river, the Costa Azul. In the former, pride of place goes to the classic Mackenzie Ross test of Estoril, now sadly bisected by the new coastal motorway. It is supported by five other courses, the best being the new 18-hole layout of Penha Longa, built on a palatial royal estate, with a clubhouse to match.

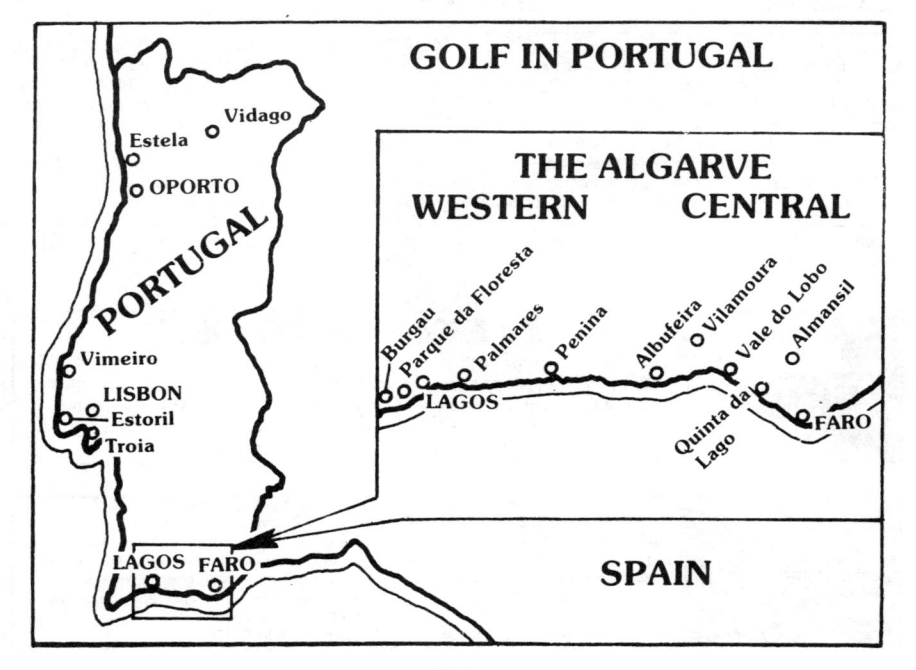

Visit the Costa Azul and you are in for a treat. Three fine courses, each in a differing location, each of particular interest. The Portuguese Country Club at Aroeira is an unheralded masterpiece by English architect Frank Pennink. Carved through a natural pine forest, it represents fine golf for all levels and a haven of peace only a short drive from the city. Montado, the newest course, flanks working vineyards near Setubal and adds a link in the golfing chain which runs south to Troia. Built by Trent Jones on a pine-encrusted sandbar, Troia is a tough, often breezy test indeed and, with Aroeira, among the very best.

Down in the sunny **Algarve,** nearly half of the country's golf courses are situated along a coast of stunning white beaches, sheer cliffs and rolling orchards. At the western end, six golfing locations include the dramatic challenge of Parque da Floresta, the popular slopes of Palmares and the famous international examination of Penina. Newcomers include the Alto Club and two courses at Carvoeiro, with the 18-hole Vale da Pinta an excellent layout through mature olive groves.

Centrally, near Albufeira, are three golfing locations, the largest being the extensive Vilamoura complex, with three courses and 63 holes in play. Near neighbours are the excellent Vila Sol, a great course in excellent condition, and Pine Cliffs, with shots to match its name.

Nearer Faro are the best collection of golf courses in the Algarve. Vale do Lobo, Quinta do Lago, San Lorenzo and now Pinheiros Altos – a grand total of 99 holes laid out over a rolling, sandy, pine-sprinkled landscape with sparkling sea views. Manicured greens and fairways, splashes of white sand, tempting strategic water – here is a holiday golfer's dream.

ALGARVE

ALBUFEIRA. **Pine Cliffs Golf and Country Club,** Pinhal do Concelho, 8200 Albufeira (010 351 89 501090; Fax: 010 351 89501200). *Location:* seven km from Vilamoura, situated outside Olhos d'Agua. Seaside links. 9 holes, 2557 yards, 2324 metres, Par (equivalent) 67. 9 hole Par 3 course. *Green Fees:* 4,000 for 9 holes. Discounts for hotel guests. *Eating facilities:* bar, restaurant. *Visitors:* welcome, advance booking required. Golf academy, changing facilities. *Society Meetings:* all groups welcome. Professional/Golf Director: David J. Marsh.

ALMANSIL. **San Lorenzo Golf Club,** Quinta do Lago, 8135 Almansil, Loule 8100 (010 351 89 396522; Fax: 010 351 89 396908). *Location:* 20km from Faro Airport towards west. Parkland with seaside view surrounded by wildlife and umbrella pine trees. 18 holes, 6238 metres. S.S.S. 73. Practice range. *Green Fees:* 2500esc. Free to Hotel Dona Filipa guests. *Eating facilities:* bar and restaurant. *Visitors:* welcome, please reserve a day before wishing to play. *Society Meetings:* welcome if staying in Dona Filipa Hotel. Professional: A. Rodrigues. Secretary: Antonio Santos (010 351 89 396534).

LITTLE EAGLES
Tastefully modernised cottage in Alfeicao Hills. Two double bedrooms and child's loft. Luxuriously equipped for **all seasons.** Seven acres of grounds, large swimming pool and panoramic views. 3 miles west of Loule and short drive to Faro Airport.
Easy access to all **golf courses** and coastal amenities.
Details from Pam Emmerson. Telephone: 0959 573752

VILLA VIVALDI
Luxury villa with modern interior including artwork. Private grounds, panoramic views, pool and barbecue. Large living room with fireplace. Open plan dining room and modern kitchen. Two double ensuite bedrooms and one twin bedroom with shower room. Several sofabeds available. Garage. Maid service. Short drive to Loule, Algarve beaches, golf courses and Faro. Long/short lets from £400 to £675 per week.
Telephone Pam Emmerson: 0959 573752

THE GOLF GUIDE 1994

Golf in Portugal

ALMANSIL. **Sociedade do Golfe da Quinta do Lago,** Quinta do Lago, 8135 Almansil (089 396002/3; Fax: 089 394013). *Location:* 15 minutes west of Faro Airport, nearest town Almansil. Gently undulating sandy land covered with umbrella pines, wild flowers and lakes. 4 courses – A,B,C,D. A/D 6850 yards, A/C 7040 yards, B/C 7137 yards, B/D 6915 yards. S.S.S. A/D 73, A/C 73, B/D 73, B/C 73. Driving range. *Green Fees:* Visitors: 10,000 esc; Residents: 7,500 esc. *Eating facilities:* clubhouse restaurant and bar; snack bar on course. *Visitors:* welcome subject to availability. Pro Shop, boutique and golf academy. Professional: Domingos Silva (089 394529). Secretary: Jose A. Capele (089 394529).

ALMANSIL. **Vale do Lobo Golf Club,** Vale do Lobo, Almansil, Loule 8137 (089 393939; Fax: 089 394713; Telex: 56842). *Location:* on the cliff edge, overlooking the sea, 15 minutes' drive west from Faro. 27 holes, three loops of 9; average 18-hole length 6600 yards. S.S.S. 72. *Green Fees:* 10,000esc. *Facilities:* clubhouse with restaurant, bar and shop. Nearby the 5 star Dona Filipa Hotel and luxury villa estate with leisure complexes. Professional: Steven Walker. Secretary: J.A. Walker.

ALVOR. **Alto Golf Club,** Quinto do Alto do Poco, Alvor, 8500 Portimao (082 416913; Fax: 082 401046). *Location:* in Alvor, overlooking the Atlantic ocean and the Bay of Lagos. A parkland course designed by Sir Henry Cotton with gently undulating fairways and challenging sloping greens. Stunning views of the Monchique Mountains in the background. 18 holes, 6125 metres, Par 72. Driving range, putting green. *Eating facilities:* bar and restaurant in clubhouse. Pro shop; cart, trolley and club hire.

BUDENS/SALEMA. **Parque da Floresta Golf and Country Club,** Vale do Poco, Budens, 8650 Vila do Bispo (082 65333/4; Fax: 082 65157). *Location:* follow N125 west through Logos,following signs to Sagres. Located just past Budens on right. Undulating course. 18 holes, 6020 metres. S.S.S. 72. Large practice ground, driving range, putting green. *Green Fees:* on application. *Eating facilities:* restaurant and bar. *Visitors:* most welcome with no restrictions. Advisable to book starting times by phone. Pro shop. *Society Meetings:* catered for by arrangement with Golf Manager. Golf Manager: Thomas A. Pidd.

LAGOA. **Carvoeiro Golf and Country Club,** Carvoeiro, Apartado 24, 8400 Lagoa (82 52670; Fax: 82 341459). *Location:* just inland from Carvoeiro. A superb course undulating through olive groves. Challenging Par 3's and excellent well-protected greens. 18 holes, 5861 metres, Par 72. Also Gramacho course – 9 holes, 5919 metres (holes played twice but with alternate tees and greens) Par 72. Driving range, putting green. *Green Fees:* information not provided. *Eating facilities:* bar and snacks in clubhouse. Pro shop; club, cart and trolley hire.

LAGOA. **Quinta do Gramacho,** Carvoeiro Golfe, Apartado 24, 8400 Lagoa (082 52610; Fax: 082 52649). *Location:* just inland from Carvoeiro. An innovative course on an attractive compact site, with 18 greens and a selection of different tees linking with 9 fairways. Interesting and highly playable. 18 holes, 5919 metres, Par 72. Driving range, putting green. *Green Fees:* 18 holes, 8000esc; 9 holes, 5000esc. *Eating facilities:* in timber clubhouse. Pro shop; trolley and club hire.

LAGOA. **Vale da Pinta,** Carvoeiro Golfe (2nd course), Apt. 24, 8400 Lagoa (351 82 52670; Fax: 351 82 52649). *Location:* 2kms south of Lagoa on the Estrada Nacional 125, follow roadsigns. Parkland in ancient olive groves with trees 600/700 years old. 18 holes, 5861 metres. S.S.S. 71, Par 71. *Green Fees:* 8000esc. *Eating facilities:* restaurant and bar plus magnificent terrace. *Visitors:* welcome any time, after booking starting times. Staff in reception speak seven different languages. Accommodation available locally (351 82 357262). *Society Meetings:* welcome anytime by arrangement. Professional: Roel H. Gritter. Director of Golf: Aart C. Spaans.

LAGOS. **Palmares Golf Club,** Meia Praia, Lagos 8600 (082 762961; Fax: 082 762534). *Location:* five kilometres from centre of Lagos on main Meia Praia beach. Five link type holes – very scenic. 18 holes, 5961 metres. S.S.S. 72. Driving range, putting green, pitch and putt. *Green Fees:* 7,000.00 escudos. *Eating facilities:* restaurant and bar. *Visitors:* always welcome. *Society Meetings:* always welcome by prior arrangement. Professional: Luis Espadinha. Secretary: Dennis Garvey (082 762953).

PORTIMAO/PENINA. **Penina Golf Club,** Penina Golf Resort Hotel, PO Box 146, Penina, 8502 Portimao (082 415415; Fax: 082 415000). *Location:* five km from Portimao, 12km from Lagos. Long, flat course with lakes, trees and bunkers. 18 holes (plus two 9 hole courses), 7041 yards, 6439 metres. S.S.S. 73. Also Monchique Course 9 holes, 3268 yards, 2987 metres, S.S.S. 35 and Quinta Course 9 holes, 2035 yards, 1851 metres, S.S.S. 31. Golf academy, putting greens. *Green Fees:* Championship course 9.500Esc; Monchique course 6.000Esc; Quinta 5.000Esc. Special tickets June, July, August. *Eating facilities:* clubhouse and Hotel restaurants. *Visitors:* welcome, Handicap Certificate required to play Championship Course. Professional: Jose Lourenco and Robin Liddle. Secretary: Leonel Rio.

QUINTA DO LAGO. **Pinheiros Altos Golf Club,** Quinta do Lago, 8135 Almansil, Algarve (89 394340; Fax: 89 394392). *Location:* south of Almansil just east of the Quinta do Lago and San Lorenzo courses. A combination of elevated holes through pines and low lying marshland with strategic water. 18 holes, 5624 metres. Par 71. Teaching academy, practice ground and putting green. *Green Fees:* information not provided. *Eating facilities:* bar and snacks. Pro shop, club, car and trolley hire.

VILAMOURA. **Golf Vila Sol,** Vila Sol, Alto do Semino (089 302144; Fax: 089 302147). *Location:* just east of Vilamoura off the road leading down to Quarteira. An excellent natural course undulating through umbrella pines with good water hazards and superb greens. 18 holes, 6183 metres, Par 72. Driving range, putting green. *Eating facilities:* bar and restaurant in clubhouse. Pro shop; cart, trolley and club hire.

VILAMOURA. **Vilamoura One (The Old Course)**, Vilamoura, Quarteira 8125 (089 321652; Telex: 56914 LUGOLF). *Location:* 20km from Faro Airport, 25km from Faro. Narrow fairways through pine woods, sea views. 18 holes, 6331 metres. S.S.S. 72. Practice and putting greens. *Green Fees:* information on request. *Eating facilities:* restaurant and bar. *Visitors:* course open to all players with Handicap Certificate. Pro shop, hire of trolleys. Professional: Joaquim Catarino (089 321652). Sales Director: Susete Calado (089 380726).

VILAMOURA. **Vilamoura Three and Four**, Vilamoura – 8125 Quarteira (089 380724; Telex: 56018 VIGOLF; Fax: 089 380726). *Location:* 20 kms from Faro Airport – 25 kms from Faro. 27 challenging holes set up overlooking the sea, although not particularly long for a modern layout; its 10 different lakes being the principal hazards. 3 x 9-holes. Driving range, putting green. *Green Fees:* on request. *Eating facilities:* restaurant and bar. *Visitors:* Vilamoura Three is open to players with Handicap Certificate, Vilamoura Four is open to beginners all year round. *Society Meetings:* welcome at all times. Professional: Abilio Coelho (089 380724). Sales Director: Susete Calado (089 380726).

VILAMOURA. **Vilamoura Two (The New Course)**, as Vilamoura One (089 314470). *Location:* as Vilamoura One. Pine wood setting. Sea views. 18 holes, 6256 metres. S.S.S 71. Driving range. *Green Fees:* on request. *Eating facilities:* bar and restaurant. *Visitors:* open to players with Handicap Certificate all year round. *Society Meetings:* welcome at any time. Professional: Manuel Pardal (089 321562). Secretary: Eduard Sousa (089 322704). Sales Director: Susete Calado (089 380726).

LISBON

AROEIRA. **Clube de Campo de Portugal**, Herdade de Aroeira, Fonte da Telha, 2825 Monte de Caparica, Aroeira, Costa Lisboa (01 2971314; Fax: 01 2971358). *Location:* just 20 minutes south of Lisbon behind the cliffs running down from the seaside resort of Caparica. This well-established course remains one of Portugal's best kept secrets. A superb test through a floral pine forest by Frank Pennink; one for purists to savour. 18 holes, 6040 metres, Par 72. Driving range, putting green. *Eating facilities:* bar and restaurant in clubhouse. Pro shop; cart, trolley and club hire.

ESTORIL. **Estoril Palacio Golf Course**, Estoril (4680400). *Location:* an undulating links course with views of the Atlantic, north west of Lisbon. Pine trees and natural hazards. 27 holes including 18-hole championship course, 5700 yards. S.S.S. 69. *Facilities:* clubhouse with restaurant, bar and swimming pool. The 5 star Hotel Palacio one mile away with superb amenities. Hotel's guests are entitled to special privileges at the Estoril Palacio. Golf Director: E. Pinheira.

ESTORIL. **International Golf Academy**, Estoril Sol Golf Club, Quinta do Outeiro, Linho, Sintra 2710 (351-1-9232461; Telex: 12624). *Location:* take the main Cascais-Sintra road and turn left at the village of Linho towards Lagoa Azul. 18 holes, 3341 metres. S.S.S. 62. Purpose-built golf academy – practice facility, chipping greens, putting green. *Green Fees:* 3,900 esc. *Eating facilities:* restaurant and bar. *Visitors:* no restrictions. *Society Meetings:* welcome. Professionals: Tom Lister/Antonio Dantas Jr. Secretary: Nuno Texeira Bastos.

ESTORIL. **Penha Longa Golf Club**, Lagoa Azul, Linho, 2710 Sintra (01 9240320; Fax: 01 9240388). *Location:* half an hour west of Lisbon, just north of Estoril on the main road to Sintra. A new course of quality laid out over craggy hills, wooded slopes and valleys surrounding an ancient royal palace. 18 holes, 6170 metres, Par 72. Driving range, three putting greens. *Eating facilities:* bar and restaurant in palatial new clubhouse. Pro shop; cart, trolley and club hire.

ESTORIL. **Quinta da Marinha Golf Club**, Casa 36, Quinta da Marinha, Cascais 2750 (4869881). *Location:* 30 km north west of Lisbon, close to Estoril and Cascais. Championship golf course designed by Robert Trent Jones. Open sandy course with pine trees, lakes and spectacular views over the mountains and ocean. 18 holes, 6684 yards. S.S.S. 71. *Green Fees:* on application. *Eating facilities:* clubhouse with bar and restaurant. Accommodation in luxury villas and townhouses surrounding the golf course. Professional: Antomio Damtas. Secretary: Numo Texeira Bastos.

HOTEL PALACIO

Estoril

Rua do Parque 2765 ESTORIL/PORTUGAL (near Lisbon)
Tel: (010-351)-1-4680400; Telex 12757 PLAGE
Fax: (010-351)-1-4684867

The HOTEL PALACIO . . . a modern symbol of luxury and comfort in the tradition of the Old World . . . 200 rooms and suites of quiet elegance . . . Conference and Meeting Rooms, plus full convention facilities . . . swimming pool in spacious garden . . . magnificent beach . . . special privileges for international championship golf course . . . 18 clay tennis courts, nearby . . . Gambling Casino.
See also our colour display on page 32.

Golf in Portugal

LISBON. **Lisbon Sports Club,** Casal da Carregueira, Belas, Queluz 2745 (01 4310077). *Location:* 25 km from Lisbon. Parkland. 18 holes, 5278 metres. S.S.S. 69. *Green Fees:* 5,000esc weekdays, 6,000esc weekends. 10% discount for groups. *Eating facilities:* clubhouse with restaurant, bar and swimming pool. *Visitors:* welcome weekdays, Handicap Certificate required. Professional: Jose Baltazar (01 4321474). Secretary: Mrs Manuela De Sousa (Tel & Fax: 01 4312482).

PRAIA DE MIRAMAR. **Clube de Golf de Miramar,** Av. Sacadura Cabral, Miramar, Valadares 4405 (02 7622067; Fax: 02 7627859). *Location:* approximately 13 km south of Oporto. Flat coastal course amongst dunes alongside the beach. 9 holes, 5146 metres. S.S.S. 67. *Green Fees:* 9.000esc. *Eating facilities:* clubhouse with restaurant and bar. Hotels, restaurants and casino nearby. Pro Shop. 50% discount on green fees given by some hotels. Professional: Manuel Ribeiro/Joao Couto. Secretary: Manuela Pinto Leite.

TROIA. **Troia Golf Club,** Troia, Setubal 2900 (065 4412; Fax: 065 44162; Telex: 18138). *Location:* on the Troia Peninsula, 42 km south of Lisbon by motorway. Seaside links, small greens, long fairways and sandy roughs. 18 holes. S.S.S. 74. Two putting areas and driving range. *Green Fees:* on application. Special rates for Hotel Magnoliamar guests. *Eating facilities:* clubhouse with bar/restaurant. *Visitors:* welcome, no restrictions all year round. Golf/Hotel Special Packages available. *Society Meetings:* welcome, special rates. Secretaries: Madalena O'Neil, Pinheiro de Mello (065 44151).

VIMEIRO. **Vimeiro Golf Club,** Praia do Porto Novo, Vimeiro, Torres Vedras 25600 (98157; Telex: 43353). *Location:* approximately 70 km north of Lisbon, overlooking the sea. A level course, divided by a river and sheltered by rocky cliffs. 9 holes with 18 tees, 5228 yards. S.S.S. 67. *Facilities:* the neighbouring Hotel Golf Mar offers all facilities.

OPORTO

ESPINHO. **Oporto Golf Club,** Lugar do Sisto, Paramos, Espinho 4500 (351 02 722008; Fax: 351 02 726895). *Location:* 18 miles south of Oporto, one mile south of Espinho. Seaside links, few trees, founded in 1890. 18 holes, 6500 yards. S.S.S. 70. Practice ground. *Green Fees:* 8,000 esc per round, half price for guests of hotels mentioned below. *Eating facilities:* bar with snacks (restaurant – members only). *Visitors:* welcome Tuesdays to Fridays (closed Mondays); weekends and Bank Holidays till 10am. Handicap Certificate required. Beach, hotels – Hotel Solverde, Hotel Praia – Golf, casino nearby. Professional: Eduardo Maganinho. Secretary: Margarida Moreira.

ESTELA. **Estela Golf Club,** Rio Alto-Estela, 4490 Povoa de Varzim (52 601567/612400; Fax: 52 612701; Telex: 25654). *Location:* 30 km north of Oporto, 24 km from the international airport. Seaside links. 18 holes, 6095 metres. S.S.S. 73. *Green Fees:* 6,000esc. *Eating facilities:* full bar and catering facilities. *Visitors:* welcome anytime when no competitions taking place. Sopete Hotel guests entitled to special privileges. *Society Meetings:* by arrangement. Professionals: Carlos Alberto, Carlos Henrique. Secretary/Manager: Salete Correia.

MADEIRA

MADEIRA. **Campo de Golfe da Madeira,** Santo Antonio da Serra, 9100 Santa Cruz (091 552345; Fax: 091 552367). *Location:* main highway to Airport (Santa Cruz) Machilo. Wooded, mountainous with view over Atlantic Ocean. 27 holes, 6082 metres. Driving range, putting and chipping green. *Green Fees:* 7000esc 18 holes. *Eating facilities:* restaurant, snack bar, lounge bar. *Visitors:* welcome to play in tournaments except PGA Madeira Island Open (January). Pro shop; cart, trolley and club hire. Professional: Joao Sousa. Secretary: Anthony Barton (acting).

NOTE

All the information in this book is given in good faith in the belief that it is correct. However, the publishers cannot guarantee the facts given in these pages, neither are they responsible for changes in policy, ownership or terms that may take place after the date of going to press. Readers should always satisfy themselves that the facilities they require are available and that the terms, if quoted, still apply.

Golf in Spain
WHERE TO PLAY • WHERE TO STAY
by Michael Gedye

SPAIN occupies a unique place in golf development. Nowhere else in the world, outside of parts of the United States, is there a country where the major proportion of its golf courses have been built in coastal vacation areas, primarily aimed at visiting holiday golfers from abroad. Of the 230-odd courses which have been opened to date, most fringe the Mediterranean coast and the attendant Ballearic islands, with the density increasing as one moves south-west towards Gilbraltar and the Atlantic coast of Andalucia.

Our selection has concentrated on four of the most popular areas for resort golf – the Costa del Sol and other coastal areas of Andalucia in the south; the central-eastern regions of Murcia and Valencia plus the sunshine island of Majorca. A total of thirty-eight courses, all offering a warm welcome to the visitor and golf of excellent calibre.

The vast region of ANDALUCIA can have the golf along its coastal plains subdivided into three sections – West, Central and East. To the West, one can find a contrast between well-established and new, with all offering golf of quality. Cadiz now has Montecastillo and Novo Sancti Petri while just to the east of Gibraltar, the new complex of San Roque has joined the mature and highly revered layouts of Sotogrande and Valderrama.

The Central area clusters around Marbella and spreads east to just beyond Malaga, a rich vein of golf with a history dating back to 1925. The first of the true resort golf courses was Guadalmina, opened in 1959, leading a steadily increasing trend of development over the intervening years until the region can now offer a concentration of holiday golf to rival Myrtle Beach or Florida. There is golf for all tastes here, from the world-famous championship holes of Las Brisas to the dramatic subtlety of Torrequebrada; from the understated class of Rio Real to the spectacular mountainous challenge of Monte Mayor. Many are carved from the river valleys and low hills which lie inland from the strips of beach hotels, running back up towards the blue shadow of the mountain ranges of Sierra Nevada and Ronda, rugged terrain which has tested the course designer and placed a premium on earth-moving for the constructor and accuracy for the player.

Golf along the Costa del Sol offers a wider selection than you can ever hope to play, with a full range of attendant practice facilities, golf academies and even, for insomniacs, a 9-hole floodlit course of 2,700 metres par 36 open 24 hours a day! A number of major championships have been played here. The World Cups of 1973 and 1989 were both held over Las Brisas, as were the Spanish Opens of 1970 and 1983. Other courses which have hosted the Open are Sotogrande (1966) and Torrequebrada (1979), while the end-of-season Volvo Masters is held each year at Valderrama.

Plenty of courses to test the tiger but there are also others of more gentle character to capture the interest of the handicap player. East of Malaga lies Almeria and the pleasant resort location of Almerimar – golf and much more right by the sea.

Golf in Spain

HOLIDAY GOLF IN SPAIN

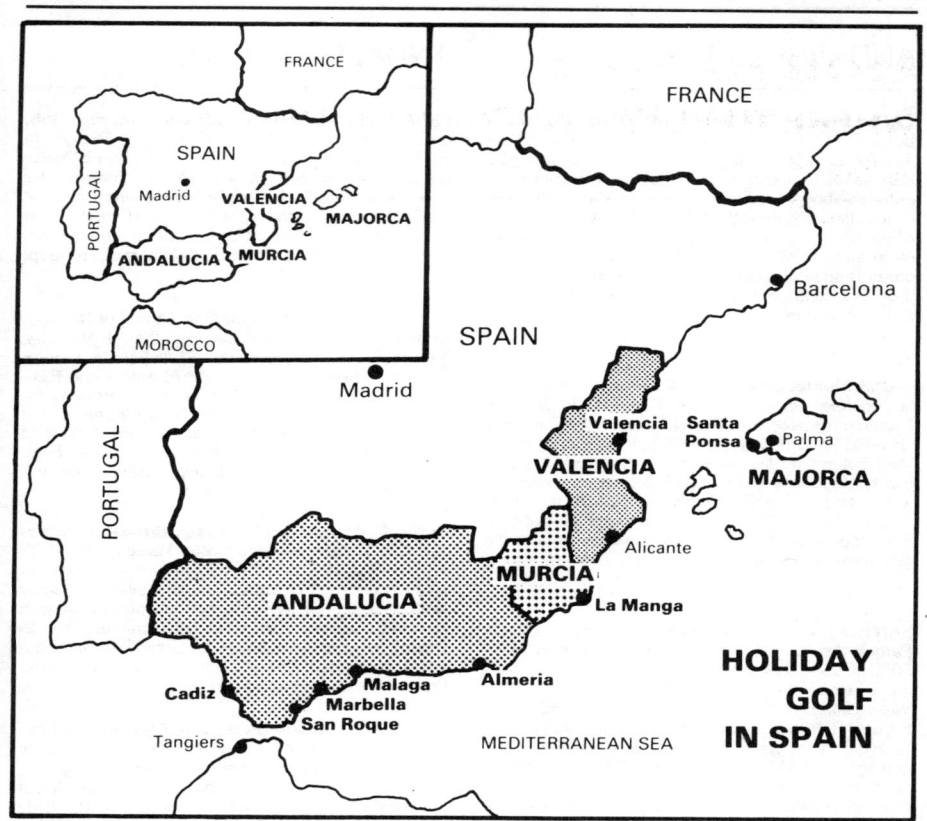

In MURCIA, pride of place must go to the La Manga Club. Host to five Spanish Opens between 1973 and 1977, the complex now boasts three fine courses to head the wide range of leisure and sporting activity available. Shielded by a crescent of low hills, with views down to the Mar Menor and the sea beyond, it offers a genuine self-contained golf and sports resort, a landmark for Europe.

A little further north through Alicante to VALENCIA, lie a string of golfing gems of rare quality. El Saler, which has twice held the Spanish Open, is arguably (with St. Andrews and Carnoustie) one of the finest public course tests of golf anywhere. Add in Golf Escorpion (Spanish Open 1980) and the more recent examples of El Bosque and Villamartin, as well as others along the way, and here is a further 'golfing' coast establishing itself on the tourism map.

Finally the island of MAJORCA, where golf goes hand in hand with the general range of holiday activities and benefits from the mild year-round climate. The best courses are found at Santa Ponsa, where two 18-hole layouts undulate gently past trees and water not too far from the sea.

A careful selection of top holiday golf, something for everyone, to suit all levels of fitness and ability, all in regions generally blessed with good weather and all catering to the needs of the holiday visitor.

ANDALUCIA: West

CADIZ. **Club de Golf Novo Sancti Petri**, Playa de la Barrosa, 11130 Chiclana de la Frontera, Cadiz (956-49 44 50; Fax: 956-49 43 50). *Location:* end of the La Barrosa road at Chiclana. This is a 27 hole layout along a stretch of virgin coastline. Mostly parkland with lakes which affect play on eight holes. Fairly flat with a wealth of young trees. 27 hole – M&C 6466 metres, M&P 6476 metres, P&C 6510 metres, all Par 72. Practice ground and putting green. *Green Fees:* information not provided. *Eating facilities:* bar and restaurant. Pro shop; club, cart and trolley hire.

CADIZ. **Montecastillo**, Ctra de Arcos, 11406 Jerez de la Frontera (956-18 92 29; Fax: 956-30 95 70). *Location:* situated next to the Formula 1 Grand Prix circuit at km 9.600 on Jerez-Arcos road. A relatively level but rolling layout with a distinct links flavour. Plenty of mounds and elevated tees, vast bunkers and water. 18 holes, 6424 metres, Par 72. Driving range and putting green. *Green Fees:* information not provided. *Eating facilities:* bar and restaurant in hotel castle clubhouse. Pro shop; club, car and trolley hire.

SAN ROQUE. **Club de Golf Sotogrande**, Paseo del Parque, Apartado 14, 11310 Sotogrande (956-79 50 50; Fax: 956-79 50 29). *Location:* right at Sotogrande entrance off N340 going west; then 2.5 km towards sea. Well established (1964) and a major golfing landmark in Europe. Rolling slopes and strategic water are offset by cork oak, eucalyptus, palm and pine. A demanding golfing feast. 18 holes, 6224 metres, Par 72. Also 9 hole short course. Practice ground and putting green. *Green Fees:* information not provided. *Eating facilities:* bar and restaurant. Pro shop; club, cart and trolley hire. Telephone in advance.

SAN ROQUE. **Club de Golf Valderrama**, Avda Los Cortijos, s/n, 11310 Sotogrande (956-79 57 75; Fax: 956-79 60 28). *Location:* access through the main Sotogrande entrance (right of N340 going west); then 2.5 km inland. Over heavily rolling hills with a commitment to excellence, this is a course to savour and appreciate. 18 holes, 6311 metres, Par 71. Practice ground and putting green. *Green Fees:* information not provided. *Eating facilities:* bar and restaurant. *Visitors:* must book in advance. Pro shop.

SAN ROQUE. **San Roque Club**, Apartado de Correos 127, 11360 San Roque (956-61 30 30; Fax: 956-61 30 12). *Location:* go west on N340 past Sotogrande 3 km and turn right at sign. Telephone first. The good variety of challenging holes of championship calibre are lined with olive trees and strategic water. 18 holes, 6440 metres, Par 72. Practice ground and putting green. *Eating facilities:* bar and restaurant. Pro shop; club, cart and trolley hire.

ANDALUCIA: Central

BENAHAVIS. **La Quinta Golf and Country Club**, Carratera de Ronda, Benahavis, Marbella (952-78 34 62; Fax: 952-78 34 66). *Location:* inland from Puerto Banus, 11 km west of Marbella. Neat and narrow, this new course has a fine clubhouse overlooking the Marbella region and the sea. 18 holes, 5413 metres, Par 71. Also 9 further holes. *Green Fees:* information not provided. *Eating facilities:* bar and restaurant. Pro shop; club, cart and trolley hire.

BENAHAVIS. **Monte Mayor Golf Club**, Los Naranjos Country Club, Nueva Andalucia, 29660 Marbella, Malaga (952-81 08 05; Fax: 952-81 48 54). *Location:* in the hills between San Pedro de Alcantara and Estepona; inland from Ctra. N-340, km. 165.6. Possibly the Costa del Sol's most spectacular course, a challenging layout over mountainous terrain for the bold and accurate. 18 holes, 5593 metres, Par 70. *Green Fees:* information not provided. *Eating facilities:* bar and restaurant in clubhouse. Cart hire.

BENALMADENA. **Golf Torrequebrada**, Apartado 120, 29630 Benalmadena-Costa, Malaga (952-44 27 42; Fax: 952-56 11 29). *Location:* north of the Malaga-Cadiz coast road at km 220. A dramatic and highly strategic test, not too long but full of interest with elevated sea views. 18 holes, 5806 metres, Par 72. Driving range and putting green. *Green Fees:* information not provided. *Eating facilities:* bar and restaurant. Pro shop; club, cart and trolley hire.

ESTEPONA. **Atalaya Park**, Estepona-Malaga, Crta. Benahavis, 29680 Estepona, Malaga. *Location:* between Marbella and Estepona, off N340 going west, turn inland for Benahavis just past Guadalmina. One of the coast's well-established courses (1966). The fairly open parkland holes are lined with eucalyptus and pine. 18 holes, 6177 metres, Par 72. Large practice ground and putting greens. *Green Fees:* information not provided. *Eating facilities:* bar and restaurant in Swiss chalet style clubhouse. Pro shop; club, cart and trolley hire.

ESTEPONA. **Golf El Paraiso**, Carretera de Cadiz-Malaga, 29680 Estepona, Malaga. *Location:* west on N340, turn right at Benavista then inland 3 km. A fine rolling parkland style course opened in 1974. The holes run over and around a hill surmounted by the El Paraiso Hotel. 18 holes, 6116 metres, Par 71. Practice ground and putting green. *Green Fees:* information not provided. *Eating facilities:* bar and restaurant. Pro shop; club, cart and trolley hire.

MALAGA. **Guadalhorce Club de Golf**, Ctra de Cartama, Apartado 48, 28950 Campanillas, Malaga (952-24 36 82; Fax: 952-24 16 78). *Location:* east towards Malaga on N340 past airport; turn right at sugar refinery taking underpass towards Bacardi distillery. A combination of classic parkland on level land with sculptured holes with raised greens and strategic water. 18 holes, 6194 metres, Par 72. Practice ground and putting green. Also 9 short holes. *Green Fees:* informa-

THE GOLF GUIDE 1994

Golf in Spain

tion not provided. *Eating facilities:* bar and restaurant in classical 19th century Andalucian manor house. Pro shop; club, cart and trolley hire.

MARBELLA. **Aloha Golf,** Nueva Andalucia, 29660 Marbella, Malaga (952-81 37 50; Fax: 952-81 23 89). *Location:* 3 km inland from Puerto Banus, 8 km east of Marbella. A fine course, opened in 1975. Tight fairways with numerous trees running through mountain valleys. 18 holes, 6261 metres, Par 72. Practice ground and putting green. *Green Fees:* information not provided. *Eating facilities:* bar and restaurant. Pro shop; club, cart and trolley hire.

MARBELLA. **Club de Golf Las Brisas,** Apartado 147, Nueva Andalucia, 29660 Marbella, Malaga (952-81 08 75; Fax: 952-81 55 18). *Location:* turn right of N340 at Puerto Banus. Over hill past bullring, then right and follow signs to Hotel Golf Plaza. A fine course which has played host to two World Cups and numerous other major Opens. Tough, with plenty of water and fast, sloping greens. 18 holes, 6163 metres, Par 72. Practice ground and putting green. *Green Fees:* information not provided. *Eating facilities:* bar and restaurant. Pro shop; club, cart and trolley hire.

MARBELLA. **Golf Rio Real,** Apartado 82, 29600 Marbella (952-77 37 76; Fax: 952-77 21 40). *Location:* 5km east from Marbella on N340, take overpass to Incosol and follow signs for 2.5km. A relatively gentle test of golf amongst mature and exotic trees. Well-cared for and closely linked to Hotel Los Monteros and Incosol Clinic. 18 holes, 6057 metres, Par 72. Practice ground and putting green. *Green Fees:* information not provided. *Eating facilities:* bar.

MARBELLA. **Guadalmina Club de Golf,** Guadalmina Alta, San Pedro de Alcantara, 29678 Marbella (952-88 33 75; Fax: 952-88 54 79). *Location:* turn right off N340 approximately 2km west of Sand Pedro de Alcantara. A development which now boast 45 holes – the original South course, the North which is more open despite some strategic water, and a short 9 hole layout. North: 18 holes, 6065 metres, Par 71. South: 18 holes, 5825 metres, Par 71. Driving range and putting greens. *Green Fees:* information not provided. *Eating facilities:* bar and restaurant. Pro shop; club, cart and trolley hire.

MARBELLA. **Los Naranjos Golf Club,** Apartado 64, 29660 Nueva Andalucia, Malaga (952-81 52 06; Fax: 952-81 14 28). *Location:* turn right of N340 (going west) at Puerto Banus. Past bullring and over hill for 2km. The sister course to Las Brisas. The front nine run through fragrant orange groves while later holes are tougher and more undulating. 18 holes, 6437 metres, Par 72. Practice ground and putting green. *Green Fees:* information not provided. *Eating facilities:* bar and restaurant in grand new clubhouse. Pro shop; club, cart and trolley hire.

MIJAS. **Club de Golf de Mijas,** Apartado 145, 29640 Fuengirola (952-47 68 43; Fax: 952-46 79 43). *Location:* from Fuengirola on N340 take the Fuengirola bypass and turn left at underpass. Then 2 km before turning right. Two excellent courses: Los Lagos – 18 holes, 6348 metres, Par 71; and Los Olivos – 18 holes, 5896 metres, Par 72. The former course is relatively open although the greens are well protected by sand and water; the latter is narrower with smaller greens, favouring finesse over power. Driving range and putting green. *Green Fees:* information not provided. *Eating facilities:* bar and restaurant. Pro shop; club, cart and trolley hire.

MIJAS. **Golf del Chaparral,** Urbanizacion El Chaparral, CN-340, 29648 Mijas-Costa, Malaga (952-49 34 50; Fax: 952-49 34 51). *Location:* on CN 340 driving east, turn left at km 203. A new course in steeply undulating land; tough with elevated tees, winding pine-lined valleys and superb views over the Mediterranean. 18 holes, 5700 metres, Par 72. Practice ground and putting green. *Green Fees:* information not provided. *Eating facilities:* bar and restaurant. Pro shop; club, cart and trolley hire.

MIJAS. **La Cala Golf and Country Club,** La Cala de Mijas, 29647 Mijas Costa (95-2589100; Fax: 95-2589105). *Location:* from La Cala del Moral between Fuengirola and Marbella, turn inland for about 5km on unmade road. Set in a high inland valley, La Cala offers elevated greens, large bunkers, plenty of thinking holes and some magnificent views. 18 holes, 5982 metres, Par 71. Also a further 18 holes and 6 hole Par 3 course. Golf academy and putting green. *Green Fees:* information not provided. *Eating facilities:* bar and restaurant. Pro shop; club, cart and trolley hire.

RINCON DE LA VICTORIA. **Anoreta Golf,** Urbanizacion Anoreta Golf Avda. del Golf s/n, 29730 Rincon de la Victoria, Malaga (952-40 40 00; Fax: 952-40 40 50). *Location:* 12 km east of Malaga at Rincon de la Victoria, only second course to be built east of Malaga. Fairly open parkland at present, with water hazards on 11 holes. 18 holes, 5976 metres, Par 72. Driving range and putting green. *Green Fees:* information not provided. *Eating facilities:* bar and restaurant. Pro shop; club, cart and trolley hire.

ANDALUCIA: East

ALMERIA. **Golf Almerimar,** Golf Hotel Almerimar, El Ejido, 04700 Almeria (951-48 02 34; Fax: 951-48 46 19). *Location:* 7 km from El Ejido, which is some 35 km from Almeria on the main Malaga road. This is a well-established course in a relatively level situation, with a wealth of trees and the chance of a breeze from the sea alongside. 18 holes, 6111 metres, Par 72. Practice ground and putting green. *Green Fees:* information not provided. *Eating facilities:* bar and restaurant. Pro shop; club, cart and trolley hire.

MURCIA

MURCIA. **La Manga Club,** Los Belones, Cartagena, 30385 Murcia (968-56 45 11; Fax: 968-56 47 50). *Location:* 30 km from Cartagena, 75 km from Murcia and 100 km from Alicante airport. Access off road to Murcia Airport. A true sporting resort in all aspects, with 54 holes of palm-lined golf backed by low hills as well as tennis, squash, bowls, health club and watersports at the Mar Menor close by. Five star La Manga Club hotel on site. Three courses: North 18 holes, 5780 metres, Par 71; South 18 holes, 6361 metres, Par 72; La Princesa 18 holes, 5971 metres, Par 72. Driving range and putting green. *Green Fees:* information not provided. *Eating facilities:* bar and restaurant. Pro shop; club, cart and trolley hire.

VALENCIA

BETERA. **Club de Golf Escorpion,** Apartado 1, 46117 Betera, Valencia (96-160 12 11; Fax: 96-169 01 87). *Location:* take the road from Valencia to Liria, turning off at San Antonio de Benageber. Go 4 km to the right, direction Betera. A fine private club offering parkland-style golf with a mountain backdrop. Tree-lined and interesting. 18 holes, 6319 metres, Par 72. Driving range and putting green. *Green Fees:* information not provided. *Eating facilities:* bar and restaurant. Pro shop; club, cart and trolley hire.

CHIVA. **Club de Golf El Bosque,** Carretera Godelleta, 46370 Chiva-Valencia (96-180 41 42; Fax: 96-180 40 09). *Location:* take the Nacional III road (Madrid-Valencia) to km 324, turn off for Godelleta. Modern American design in an attractive location backed by wooded hills. Plenty of strategic sand. A course kept in excellent condition. 18 holes, 6276 metres, Par 72. Driving range and putting green. *Green Fees:* information not provided. *Eating facilities:* bar, restaurant and coffee shop. Pro shop; club, cart and trolley hire.

ORIHUELA. **Campo de Golf Villamartin,** Apartado 35, Torrevieja, 03300 Orihuela, Alicante (96-676 03 50; Fax: 96-676 03 58). *Location:* on the Torrevieja-Cartagena road at km 7.6, near San Javier Airport and El Alted. Two courses laid out on interesting coastal sandy land with some pines. A good test of golf, open to the breeze. 18 holes, 6132 metres, Par 72; 18 holes, 5770 metres, Par 72. Driving range and putting green. *Green Fees:* information not provided. *Eating facilities:* bar, coffee shop and restaurant. Pro shop; club, cart and trolley hire.

VALENCIA. **Campo de Golf El Saler,** Parador Nacional "Luis Vives", El Saler, Valencia (96-161 11 86; Fax: 96-162 70 16). *Location:* at km 18 on the road from Nazaret to Oliva, right by the sea. One of the great Spanish tests of golf, with open links fairways and tight holes lined with umbrella pine; a public facility offering true seaside conditions. 18 holes, 6355 metres, Par 72. Driving range and putting green. *Green Fees:* information not provided. *Eating facilities:* bar, restaurant and coffee shop. Pro shop; club, cart and trolley hire.

MAJORCA

CALA D'OR. **Vall D'Or Golf Club,** Apartado 23, 07660 Cala D'Or (971 837001; Fax: 971 837299). *Location:* approximately 60km east of Palma on the road from Porto Colom to Cala D'Or. Undulating, winding course, with trees. 18 holes, 5881 metres. S.S.S. 71. Driving range, club hire. *Green Fees:* on application. 10% discount if player comes with a card from hotel. *Eating facilities:* clubhouse, bar and restaurant. *Visitors:* welcome with Handicap. Nearby hotels include Cala D'Or, Rocador, Rocador Playa. Professional: Antonio Gonzalez (971 837001). Secretary: Celestino Padial (971 837068).

MAGALLUF. **Poniente Golf Club,** Crta. Cala Figuera S/N, Costa de Calvia (03471 130148). *Location:* 18km west of Palma, one km from Magalluf on the Andraix Road. The course is considered long and difficult surrounded by trees and water, with large and fast greens. 18 holes, 6430 metres. S.S.S. 72. Driving range, putting green. *Green Fees:* information not provided. *Eating facilities:* clubhouse, restaurant and bar. Nearby hotels include Son Callu, Club Galatzo.

PALMA. **Real Golf de Bendinat,** Campoamor S/N, 07015 Calvia, Baleares (3471 405200; Fax: 3471 700786). *Location:* five km west from Palma centre. A short, hilly but interesting course. 9 holes, 4988 metres. S.S.S. 68. Driving range, putting green. *Green Fees:* 5000ptas. *Eating facilities:* snack bar and Restaurant "Hoyo 10". *Visitors:* welcome, 20% discount for large groups. Please reserve tee-off times through our Fax No: (3471 700786). Professional: Ricardo Galiano (3471 405450). Secretary: Beatriz Arnau (3471 405200).

PALMA. **Son Vida Golf,** Urb. Son Vida, 07013 Palma de Mallorca (0034-(9)71-79.12.10; Fax: 79.11.27). *Location:* five km north-west of Palma. Majorca's first course (1964) winding through trees and estate villas

*Villas overlooking
Santa Ponsa Club.*

Golf in Majorca

with lakes and gentle slopes. 18 holes, 6276 yards. S.S.S. 71. Driving range, Pro Shops, car, trolley and club rental. *Green Fees:* on application. *Eating facilities:* snacks and lunches in the comfortable clubhouse, excellent restaurant El Pato (The Duck) overlooking 18th hole. *Visitors:* welcome. Nearby hotels (20 %% discount on green fees) include Arabella Golf Hotel (5 stars), Hotel Son Vida (5 stars) on the course, Victoria Sol (5 stars) Palma, Bonanza Playa Illestas, Son Caliu. Manager: Peter Haider.

POLLENSA. **Golf Pollensa,** Ctra. Palma Pollensa, 07460 Pollensa (00-34-71 533216; Fax: 00-34-71 533265). *Location:* in the north of the Island of Mallorca, 45 km from Palma Airport and 2 km from Pollensa. On the south side of a hill with smooth and beautiful undulations and sea views. 9 holes, 5304 metres. S.S.S. 70. Driving range. *Green Fees:* 5300pts. Groups (more than 10 people) 10% discount. *Eating facilities:* snack bar. *Visitors:* welcome, tee reservation recommended. Changing room, swimming pool. *Society Meetings:* welcome. Professional: Carlos Insua.

SANTA PONSA. **Santa Ponsa Golf Club One,** Santa Ponsa, 07184 Calvia (690211; Fax: 693364). *Location:* 18km on motorway from Palma to Andratix, turn off roundabout Santa Ponsa. Gently sloping fairways with water hazards. 18 holes, 6170 metres. S.S.S. 72 men, 73 ladies. Practice range, two putting greens. *Green Fees:* 6200pts. Subject to review. *Eating facilities:* restaurant and bar in clubhouse, also small bar on golf course. *Visitors:* welcome; maximum Handicaps - 28 men, 36 ladies. Accommodation available, swimming pool, paddling pool, tennis. *Society Meetings:* welcome. Professionals: Diego Lopez/George Oosterlynck. Director: Jose M. Comez.

SANTA PONSA. **Santa Ponsa Golf Club Two,** Santa Ponza, Calvia (690211/102732; Fax: 693364/ 102732). *Location:* as Sant Ponza One. A very interesting and enjoyable course, it has a mixture of holes, some with very tight fairways and others with many water hazards. Designed by Jose Gancedo. White Stakes – 6036 metres, Par 72; Yellow Stakes – 5672 metres, Par 70; Blue Stakes – 5144 metres, Par 72; Red Stakes – 4883 metres, Par 70. S.S.S. 72. Practice range, putting green. *Green Fees:* on request. *Eating facilities:* as Santa Ponza One. *Visitors:* at moment only open for shareholders.

SON SERVERA. **Son Servera Golf Club,** Costa de los Pinos, 07550 Son Servera (56.78.02; Fax: 56.81.46). *Location:* Palma – Manacor – San Llorens – Son Servera. Fairly flat, narrow, seaside course, set among pine trees. 9 holes, 2978 metres. S.S.S. 72. *Green Fees:* 5000pts. Groups of four persons 20% discount. *Eating facilities:* bar and restaurant. *Visitors:* welcome, no restrictions. Nearby hotels include Eurotel Golf Punta Roja, Rotja, Flamenco, Royal Mediterranea, Gran Sol. Professional: Santiago Sota Bedia. Secretary: Pedro Canellas Ramis.

**FEDERACION BALEAR DE GOLF
BALEARIC ISLANDS GOLF FEDERATION**

Driving Ranges
in Britain & Ireland

Driving Ranges

LONDON

CHINGFORD. **Chingford Golf Range**, Waltham Way, Chingford E4 8AQ (081-529 2409). *Location:* two miles south of Junction 26 M25. 23 bay two tier driving range. *Fees:* information not provided. *Opening hours:* 9.30am to 10pm. Practice putting green, practice bunker; new multi-level practice mat; video, tuition available at all times. Professional: Gordon Goldie PGA and Susan Wood WPGA.

LONDON. **Docklands Golf Range Ltd.**, Brunswick Wharf, Leamouth Road, London E14 2NL (071-712 9944). *Location:* follow City Airport signs from Tower of London through the Limehouse Link Tunnel and pick up signs to golf range. 30 bay covered floodlit range. *Fees:* £2.00 for 45 balls. *Eating facilities:* full bar and cafe facilities. *Opening hours:* 7.30am to 10.30pm Mondays to Saturdays, 8.30am to 9.30pm Sundays. Fully qualified PGA coaching staff, group and individual tuition available.

LONDON. **Ealing Golf Range**, Rowdell Road, Northolt, Middlesex UB5 6AG (081-845 4967). *Location:* A40 Target roundabout, Northolt. Golf range with 40 floodlit bays – 36 covered and 4 open. *Fees:* £1.00 for 28 balls. *Eating facilities:* bar and catering. *Opening hours:* 10am to 10pm. Four teaching professionals. Shop open 10am to 10pm weekdays, 10am to 8pm weekends. Squash club, gymnasium and function room. Head Professional: David Elliott (081-845 4967).

AVON

BRISTOL. **Bristol Golf Academy**, Common Mead Lane, Filton Road, Bristol BS16 1QQ (0272 701116/7; Fax: 0272 701118). *Location:* behind Crest Hotel on Junction 1 of the M32. 26 bay range, grass putting green, bunker, Astroturf putting green. *Fees:* information not provided. *Eating facilities:* public bar and restaurant. *Opening hours:* 9am to 10.30pm weekdays; 8am to 10.30pm weekends. Large comprehensive golf shop. Professional: Mark Pierce.

BEDFORDSHIRE

LEIGHTON BUZZARD. **Aylesbury Vale Golf Club**, Wing, Leighton Buzzard LU7 0UJ (0525 240196). *Location:* four miles west of Leighton Buzzard and half a mile south of Stewkley Village. 10 covered, floodlit bays, Astroturf, 90 compression balls. *Fees:* £1.50 for 65 balls. *Eating facilities:* downstairs bar and restaurant, upstairs bar, balcony with views over course. *Opening hours:* 7.30am to 10pm. Indoor golf simulator. Professional: Lee Scarbrow (0525 240197). Secretary/Manager: Chris Wright (0525 240196).

BERKSHIRE

MAIDENHEAD. **Hawthorn Hill Golf Centre**, Drift Road, Hawthorn Hill, Near Maidenhead SL6 3ST (0344 75588/26035). *Location:* on A330 Ascot to Maidenhead road. 36 covered, floodlit bays. 18 hole 'pay and play' course. Professionals. Tuition. *Fees:* information not provided. *Opening hours:* 8am to 10pm daily. *Eating facilities:* "Racecourse Restaurant" and Golfers bar and terrace.

WOKINGHAM. **Downshire Driving Range**, Easthampstead Park, Wokingham RG11 3DH (0344 302030). *Location:* between Bracknell and Wokingham, off the Nine Mile Ride. 30 bay covered floodlit driving range. *Fees:* £1.50 bucket. *Eating facilities:* bar and restaurant, bar snacks available. *Opening hours:* 7.30am to 10pm. Tuition, 18 hole course, 9 hole pitch and putt; golf superstore. Societies welcome.

WOKINGHAM. **Sindlesham Driving Range**, Mole Road, Wokingham RG11 5DJ (0734 788494). *Location:* two minutes from M4 Junction 11. 25 covered, floodlit bays. Professional tuition available. *Fees:* £2.00 per bucket. *Opening hours:* 7am to 10pm. *Eating facilities:* restaurant and bar. *Visitors:* open to the public. Health club and squash club. Professional: Andrew R. Wild (0734 788494).

BUCKINGHAMSHIRE

COLNBROOK. **Colnbrook Golf Range**, Galleymead Road, Colnbrook SL3 0EN (0753 682670). *Location:* one mile from Junction 5 M4, one mile Junction 14 M25. 27 bay floodlit, covered, grassed range. *Fees:* information not provided. *Eating facilities:* fully licensed bar 11am to 11pm six days a week, catering, anything from snacks to full à la carte – excellent resident chef. *Opening hours:* 9am to 10.30pm. Professional: Graham Hepworth; Assistant: Paul Leycock. Very well equipped golf shop. Full tuition, video assisted lessons given.

MILTON KEYNES. **Windmill Hill Golf Range,** Tattenhoe Lane, Bletchley, Milton Keynes MK3 7RB (0908 378623). *Location:* off A421 at Bletchley. 23 bay covered floodlit driving range. *Fees:* half bucket (46 balls) £1.60; 92 balls £3.00. *Eating facilities:* public bar and catering. *Opening hours:* 9am to 9pm weekdays, 8am to 8pm weekends. Professional, tuition, public course – 18 holes, Par 73.

STOWE. **Silverstone Golf Club,** Silverstone Road, Stowe MK18 5LH (0280 850005). 12 bay covered range. *Fees:* weekdays £8.00; weekends £12.00. Membership available. *Eating facilities:* licensed bar, good food. *Opening hours:* dawn to 11pm. Tuition available – group or private.

CAMBRIDGESHIRE

ROYSTON. **Whaddon Golf Centre,** Whaddon, Royston SG8 5RX (0223 207285). *Location:* four miles north of Royston off A1198, nine miles south of Cambridge off A603. 9 open bays, 14 bays covered, floodlit and grassed. *Fees:* £1.00 for 50 balls. *Eating facilities:* available. *Opening hours:* 8am to 9pm weekdays, 8am to dusk weekends. Three Professionals — coaching by appointment. Putting green and Par 3 approach course.

ST. NEOTS. **Abbotsley Golf and Squash Club,** Eynesbury, Hardwicke, St Neots PE19 4XN (0480 215153/474000). *Location:* A45 St. Neots bypass to Abbotsley, south east of St. Neots Junction 13 M11. 21 bay range and grass. *Fees:* £2.00 per bucket (80 balls). *Opening hours:* 8am to 10pm. *Eating facilities:* bar and food available all day. Two courses (36 holes), residential golf school, shop, tuition; residential schools for golf with Vivien Sanders and John Stirling. 15 bedroom hotel, 6 squash courts, snooker, 2 sun beds, sauna.

CHESHIRE

STOCKPORT. **Cranford Golf Centre,** Harwood Road, Heaton Mersey, Stockport SK4 3AW (061-432 8242). *Location:* five minutes from M63 and M56 motorways. 43 all weather covered tees, fully floodlit. *Fees:* £2.50 per bucket (50 balls). No booking or membership required. *Eating facilities:* drinks and snacks available. *Opening hours:* seven days a week 10am to 11pm. Two indoor bunkers, 9 hole indoor putting course, changing rooms and golf shop. Group facilities and lessons available. Professional: Anthony Murray.

CORNWALL

REDRUTH. **Radnor Golf and Ski Centre,** Radnor Road, Redruth TR16 5EL (0209 211059). *Location:* follow signs from Old Redruth by-pass (A3047) or cross roads at north country. 18 bay covered floodlit driving range. *Fees:* £1.40 for 50 balls. Subject to review. *Eating facilities:* bar available. *Opening hours:* weekdays 8.30am to 9pm; weekends and Bank Holidays 8.30am to 6pm. PGA Approved. Teaching, club repairs, shop. Indoor ski machine, snooker. 9 hole Par 3 course.

TRURO. **Killiow Golf Club Driving Range,** Killiow Golf Park, Kea, Truro (0872 70246). *Location:* take A39 from Truro directed to Falmouth, 2.75 miles. Large sign on right into park. All weather floodlit driving range with bunker and putting facilities. *Fees:* information on request. *Visitors:* some restrictions – check with Reception. Secretary: John Crowson (0872 72768).

DERBYSHIRE

CHESTERFIELD. **Grassmoor Golf Centre,** North Wingfield Road, Grassmoor, Chesterfield S42 5EA (0246 856 044). *Location:* M1 Junction 29 or A61 near Chesterfield. 26 bay covered, floodlit range. *Fees:* per bucket (approximately 80 balls) £1.50 members, £2.00 non-members. *Eating facilities:* catering available 8am to 11pm weekdays, 7.30am to 11pm weekends; bar open 11am to 11pm weekdays, till 10.30pm weekends. *Opening hours:* seven days a week 9am to 9.30pm. Golf lessons £9.50 with video.

ESSEX

BRAINTREE. **Towerlands Driving Range,** Panfield Road, Braintree CM7 5BJ (0376 326802). *Location:* off A120 in Braintree then B1053. 6 grassed bays. *Fees:* £1.25 for 50 balls. *Opening hours:* 8.30am till dark. *Eating facilities:* full bar and restaurant. 9 hole course, professional tuition, indoor bowls, squash, full sports hall and equestrian facilities. Professional: Andrew Boulter.

COLCHESTER. **Colchester Golf Range,** Old Ipswich Road, Ardleigh, Colchester (0206 230974). *Location:* next to the Crown Inn, Old Ipswich Road. Covered, floodlit range, 12 bays. Professional tuition available. Putting green. *Fees:* £1.75 for 50 balls. *Opening hours:* weekdays 10am to 9pm, weekends 10am to 5pm. *Eating facilities:* The Crown Inn, 50 yards from golf range.

Driving Ranges

COLCHESTER. **Earls Colne Golf and Leisure Centre,** Earls Colne, Colchester CO6 2NS (0787 224466; Fax: 0787 224410). *Location:* B1024 between A120 and A606 Earls Colne. 20 bay covered floodlit driving range. *Fees:* £1.75 for 50 balls. *Eating facilities:* full restaurant and bar facilities. *Opening hours:* 9am to 10pm seven days a week. Tuition available. 18 hole and 9 hole courses, 4 hole teaching course. Leisure centre – swimming pool, gym, sun beds, beauty parlour, spa bath. Creche. Professional: Owen McKenna.

ILFORD. **Fairlop Waters,** Forest Road, Barkingside, Ilford IG6 3JA (081-500 9911). *Location:* two miles north of Ilford, half a mile from A12, one and a half miles from southern end of M11. Covered, floodlit range, 36 bays. 18 hole golf course, 9 hole Par 3 course. Individual or group tuition available. *Fees:* information not provided. *Opening hours:* 9am to 10pm. *Eating facilities:* bars and American Diner. Banqueting facilities and conferences. 38 acre sailing lake, 25 acre country park, children's play area. Professional: Tony Bowers (081-501 1881). Manager: Keith Robson.

GLOUCESTERSHIRE

GLOUCESTER. **Gloucester Hotel and Country Club,** Robinswood Hill, Matson Lane, Gloucester GL4 9EA (0452 525653). 12 bays covered and floodlit. *Fees:* £1.00 per basket of balls for driving range. *Opening hours:* 9am to 9.30pm. *Eating facilities:* available. Five professional instructors, private and group tuition available. Sebastian Coe Health Park, dry ski slope, golf course, indoor swimming pool, sauna, solarium, gymnasium, 6 squash courts, two tennis courts, snooker, pool, skittles etc.

HAMPSHIRE

BORDON near. **Kingsley Golf Club,** Main Road, Kingsley, Near Bordon GU35 9NG (04203 88195). *Location:* B3004 off A325 Farnham to Petersfield road. *Fees:* information not provided. Indoor computerised driving bay, equipment store, golf school for tuition. Professional/Acting Secretary: Richard Adams.

HEREFORD & WORCESTER

LEOMINSTER. **The Grove Golf Centre,** Fordbridge, Leominster HR6 0LE (0568 611804). *Location:* adjacent to Leominster Golf Club, three miles south of Leominster on A49. 18 bay floodlit range (four outdoor). *Fees:* £1.00 per 30 balls. *Opening hours:* 8am to 9pm. Also 9 hole putting green, practice bunker, club hire, tuition available. Professional: Gareth Bebb.

THE GOLF GUIDE 1994

HERTFORDSHIRE

WARE. **Whitehill Golf Centre,** Dane End, Ware SG12 0JS (0920 438495; Fax: 0920 438891). *Location:* turn at Happy Eater, High Cross on A10 north of Ware. 25 bays covered, floodlit, grassed. *Fees:* £1.50 45 balls, £2.50 90 balls. *Eating facilities:* bar and food. *Opening hours:* Wednesday to Friday 7am to 10pm, Tuesday 10am to 10pm, Monday 7am to 10pm, weekends and Bank Holidays 7am to dusk. Professional tuition, 18 hole golf course, practice bunkers, snooker.

WELWYN GARDEN CITY. **Gosling Golf Range,** Gosling Sports Park, Stanborough Road, Welwyn Garden City AL8 6XE (0707 331056). *Location:* A1(M) Junction 4, follow signs for Welwyn Garden City. 22 bays covered floodlit driving range. *Fees:* £1.90 bucket of 48 balls non members, members £1.65. *Opening hours:* 9am to 10pm weekdays, weekends 9am to 8pm. *Eating facilities:* extensive bar/catering within Sports Park. Resident Professional, tuition and shop. Extensive facilities with ski-ing, tennis, athletics, bowls, cycling, badminton. Health suite, etc. Brochure available.

HUMBERSIDE

SCUNTHORPE. **Grange Park Golf Range,** Butterwick Road, Messingham, Scunthorpe DN17 3PP (0724 764478). *Location:* five miles south of Scunthorpe between Messingham and East Butterwick, four miles south of Junction 3 of M180. 20 bay covered floodlit driving range. *Fees:* £1.25 for 50 balls. *Opening hours:* 9am to 10pm weekdays, 9am to 9pm weekends. Large Pro shop and exclusive golf ladies' wear shop. Professional available. 9 hole pay and play course on site.

KENT

CHATHAM. **Chatham Golf Centre,** Street End Road, Chatham ME5 0BG. *Location:* five minutes' drive from Rochester Airport. Covered, floodlit range, 30 bays. Tuition available. *Fees:* £2.00 per 65 balls. *Opening hours:* 10am to 10pm. *Eating facilities:* licensed snack bar. Fully stocked Pro Shop. Competitive prices. Professional: Colin Bentley (0634 848925). Secretary: R. Burden (0634 848907).

THE GOLF GUIDE 1994

Driving Ranges

MAIDSTONE. **Langley Park Driving Range**, Sutton Road, Langley, Maidstone ME17 3NQ (0622 863163). *Location:* south of Maidstone on A274, first turning after Park Wood Industrial Estate. 26 covered, floodlit bays. *Fees:* £1.40 for 42 balls. *Eating facilities:* licensed bar, snacks available. *Opening hours:* 10am to 10pm. PGA tuition, computerised putting machine – £1 per 9 holes, putting green.

ORPINGTON. **Ruxley Park Golf Centre**, Sandy Lane, St. Pauls Cray, Orpington BR5 3HY (0689 871490; Fax: 0689 891428). *Location:* off old A20 at Ruxley Corner. 24 bays, covered, floodlit, grassed. *Fees:* information not provided. *Opening hours:* 9am to 10.30pm. *Eating facilities:* breakfast, lunch available, bar open all day. 18 hole Par 71 golf course.

LANCASHIRE

BLACKPOOL. **Herons Reach Driving Range**, The Village Hotel and Leisure Club, East Park Drive, Blackpool FY3 8LL (0253 838866). *Location:* from Junction 4 off M55 follow signs for Blackpool Zoo, complex is opposite Stanley Park and next to the Zoo. 18 bay covered, floodlit range. *Fees:* £2.00 for multiples for 50 balls. *Eating facilities:* Spikes Bar, leisure bar, grill restaurant. *Opening Hours:* 8am to 10pm, open to the general public. *Visitors:* welcome. Must hold current Handicap Certificate. 166 bedroomed hotel, leisure facilities, conference and banqueting facilities. Hotel Reservations (0253 838866; Fax: 0253 798800). *Society Meetings:* welcome. Golf Packages available. Group and individual tuition, all standards, video aids. Golf trolleys and buggies for hire. Professional: Richard Hudson. Golf Manager: David Hughes.

KEARSLEY. **Kearsley Golf Driving Range**, Moss Lane, Kearsley, Bolton BL4 8SF (Farnworth (0204) 75726). *Location:* Manchester to Bolton A666. Small 9 hole pitch and putt attached. *Fees:* £1.40 for multiples of 25 balls. *Opening hours:* weekdays 11am to 9.30pm; weekends 11am to 4.30pm. *Eating facilities:* bar and snack bar. *Visitors:* welcome. Professional: E. Raymond Warburton.

NORTHAMPTONSHIRE

NORTHAMPTON. **Delapre Golf Complex**, Eagle Drive, Nene Valley Way, Northampton NN4 0DU (0604 763957 or 764036). *Location:* three miles from M1 Junction 15 towards Wellingborough. 40 covered, floodlit bays plus 30 grassed areas. *Fees:* practice balls dispensed at £2.00 per unit. *Opening hours:* 7am to 10.30pm. *Eating facilities:* cooked meals served. PGA qualified teaching professionals available, 18 and 9 hole golf courses and 9 hole pitch and putt.

NOTTINGHAMSHIRE

CALVERTON. **Ramsdale Park Golf Centre**, Oxton Road, Calverton NG14 6NU (0602 655600). *Location:* north east Nottingham city, on B6386 Oxton Road. 25 bay covered floodlit range. *Fees:* small £2.00, medium £3.00, large £3.75. *Eating facilities:* available. *Opening hours:* 7.30am to 10pm. Professional tuition, 18 hole main course and 18 hole Par 3 course.

NOTTINGHAM. **Carlton Forum Leisure Centre (South)**, Foxhill Road, Carlton, Nottingham NG4 1RL (0602 612949). *Location:* east side of Nottingham. 28 bay covered, floodlit range. *Fees:* £2.30 per basket (approximately 80 balls). *Eating facilities:* bar, restaurant. *Opening hours:* Monday noon to 10.30pm, Tuesday-Sunday 9.30am to 10.30pm. Golf shop, snooker, indoor bowls, ski-ing, sledging, all outdoor pitches. Newly formed golf society, new members most welcome, all standards. Professional: Mr John Down.

SURREY

CHESSINGTON. **Chessington Golf Centre**, Garrison Lane, Chessington KT9 2LW (081-391 0948). *Location:* as Chessington Course entry. Covered, floodlit range, 18 bays. 9 hole course. Private and group tuition available. *Fees:* information not provided. *Opening hours:* 9am to 10pm. *Eating facilities:* available.

COBHAM. **Silvermere Driving Range**, Redhill Road, Cobham KT11 1EF (0932 867275). *Location:* half a mile from Junction 10 on M25, take B366. Covered, floodlit range, 34 bays. 18 hole course. Teaching available. *Fees:* information not provided. *Opening hours:* 9am to 10pm. *Eating facilities:* full facilities.

CROYDON. **Croydon Driving Range**, 175 Long Lane, Addiscombe, Croydon CR0 7TE (081-654 7859). *Location:* on A222 about two miles east of Croydon. 24-bay driving range. *Fees:* information not provided. *Eating facilities:* licensed bar and snacks available. *Visitors:* very welcome at all times, open to the public. Professional: Nick Parfrement (081-656 1690).

ESHER. **Sandown Golf Centre**, More Lane, Esher KT10 8AN (0372 463340). *Location:* centre of Sandown Park Racecourse. 33 bay covered floodlit range plus grassed area. *Fees:* information not provided. *Eating facilities:* coffee shop and bar. *Opening hours:* 10am to 10pm weekdays; 10am to 9pm weekends. Three PGA Professionals. Snooker club.

LEATHERHEAD. **Pachesham Golf Centre**, Oaklawn Road, Leatherhead KT22 0BT (0372 843453). *Location:* half a mile outside Leatherhead, just off A244. Junction 9 M25. 33 bay covered floodlit range. *Fees:* 30 balls £1.00, 60 balls £1.75, 90 balls £2.00. *Eating facilities:* available. *Opening hours:* weekdays 9am to 10pm, weekends 9am to 9pm. PGA teaching professional, 9 hole golf course.

373

OLD WOKING. **Hoebridge Golf Centre,** Old Woking Road, Old Woking GU22 8JH (0483 722611). Covered, floodlit range. 25 bays. Two 18 hole courses and 9 hole course. *Fees:* information not provided. *Opening hours:* dawn to dusk in summer, 8am to 11pm in winter. *Eating facilities:* available.

RICHMOND. **Richmond Golf Centre,** The Athletic Ground, Kew Foot Road, Richmond TW9 2SS (081-940 5570). *Location:* next to Richmond swimming pool on the 316 road. Covered, floodlit driving range, 23 bay and grassed area. *Fees:* information not provided. *Opening hours:* 9.30am to 9.30pm. *Eating facilities:* some catering. Professional tuition available.

EAST SUSSEX

HELLINGLY. **Wellshurst Golf and Country Club,** North Street, Hellingly BN27 4EE (04353 3456). *Location:* two miles from the A22 London to Eastbourne Road on A267. 16 bay covered, floodlit range. *Fees:* £2.00 per large bucket of quality two piece balls. *Eating facilities:* full bar and catering facilities available at all times. *Opening hours:* 7.30am to 9.30pm. Full professional staff for lessons, well stocked pro shop, 18 hole course, two sand bunker bays.

HORAM. **Horam Park Golf Course and Floodlit Driving Range,** Chiddingly Road, Horam TN21 0JJ (04353 3477; Fax: 04353 3677). *Location:* 13 miles north of Eastbourne, 7 miles east of Uckfield. Covered, floodlit, Astroturf range. 16 bays. 5 PGA Golf Professionals, lessons and tuition available. Golf shop. *Fees:* £2.00 per bucket; £1.00 after 8.30pm. *Opening hours:* weekdays 8am to 10.30pm. *Eating facilities:* restaurant bar and spike bar.

SEDLESCOMBE. **Aldershaw Golf Club,** Kent Street, Sedlescombe TN33 0SD (0424 870898; Fax: 0424 870855). *Location:* A21 near Sedlescombe. Driving range. *Fees:* £2.00 per bucket, £1.00 after 8.30pm. *Eating facilities:* drinks and snacks available all day.

WEST SUSSEX

CRAWLEY. **Gatwick Manor Golf Club,** Gatwick Manor Hotel, London Road, Lowfield Heath, Crawley RH10 2ST (0293 526310 (Hotel); 0293 538587 (club)). *Location:* A23 Crawley to Gatwick Airport on London Road on right. 9 grassed tees. *Fees:* £3 for 9 holes. *Eating facilities:* hotel facilities at Gatwick Manor. *Opening hours:* 9am to 8.00pm seven days a week.

LITTLEHAMPTON near. **Rustington Golf Centre,** Golfers Lane, Rustington, Near Littlehampton BN16 4NB (0903 850786/850790). *Location:* on A259 at Rustington, near Littlehampton. 30 bay covered, floodlit, grassed range. *Fees:* £2.95 basket of balls, £1 club hire. *Eating facilities:* coffee shop. *Opening hours:* 9am to 9pm seven days. Teaching Professional, well stocked golf shop.

TYNE AND WEAR

NEWCASTLE-UPON-TYNE. **Gosforth Park Golfing Complex Ltd,** High Gosforth Park, Newcastle-Upon-Tyne NE3 5HQ (091-236 4480). *Location:* off A1 for Gosforth Park. 45 bay covered, floodlit range. 18 hole golf course and 9 hole pitch and putt. Professional tuition available. *Fees:* information not provided. *Opening hours:* 8am to 10.30pm. *Eating facilities:* bar and restaurant.

WASHINGTON. **Washington Moat House Golf Club,** Stone Cellar Road, High Usworth, District 12, Washington NE37 1PH (091-417 2626). *Location:* just off A1(M), take A194 then exit A195 Washington. 21 bay floodlit grassed range. 18 hole pitch and putt. *Fees:* information on request. *Eating facilities:* Bunkers Bar 9am to 11pm, serves snacks. Buffets etc by arrangement. *Opening hours:* 9.30am to 10pm. Golf professional, tuition available. Leisure club with sauna, pool, solarium, multi gym, spa and squash.

WARWICKSHIRE

COVENTRY. **John Reay Golf Centres,** Sandpits Lane, Keresley, Coventry CV7 8NJ (0203 333920). *Location:* three miles from Coventry city centre along A51 Tamworth Road. Covered, floodlit driving range. 30 bays. Golf club repair facility. Teaching professionals using latest video techniques. *Fees:* 45 balls £1. *Opening hours:* weekdays 9am to 10pm. *Eating facilities:* Hogan's Bar & Bistro open every day. *Visitors:* open to the public. Large Golf Shop with all the leading brands of golf equipment. Professional: John Reay (0203 333920/333405).

WARWICK. **Warwick Golf Centre,** The Racecourse, Warwick CV34 6HW (0926 494316). *Location:* Racecourse, Warwick. 28 bay covered, floodlit range. *Fees:* large basket £2.30, medium basket £2.00 and small basket £1.30. *Opening hours:* 10am to 9pm. *Eating facilities:* bar only. Professional tuition, 9 hole golf course open to the public.

WEST MIDLANDS

DUDLEY near. **Swindon Ridge Golf Driving Range,** Bridgnorth Road, Swindon, Near Dudley DY3 4PU (0902 896191). *Location:* B4176 Bridgnorth/Dudley Road, three miles from Himley A449 Junction. 27 bay floodlit range (22 covered). *Fees:* £1.40 for small bucket, £2.20 for large bucket, £2.95 for extra-large bucket. Tuition £8.00 per half hour with large bucket free. *Opening hours:* 9am to 9.30pm weekdays, 8.30am to 6pm weekends. *Eating facilities:* licensed bar and restaurant. 18 hole private golf club on site plus 9 hole Par 3. Two snooker tables in bar.

WOLVERHAMPTON. **Three Hammers Golf Complex,** Old Stafford Road, Coven, Wolverhampton WV10 7PP (0902 790428). *Location:* Junction 2 M54 north on A449, one mile on right. 24 covered floodlit bays. *Fees:* balls from £1.00. *Eating facilities:* bookings taken from 10.30am, details on (0902 791917). *Opening hours:* weekdays £9.30am to 10pm, Saturdays 9.30am to 6pm, Sundays 9.30am to 5.30pm. 18 hole Par 3 course, two teaching Professionals.

WILTSHIRE

SWINDON. **Broome Manor Golf Complex,** Pipers Way, Swindon SN3 1RG (0793 532403/495761). *Location:* two miles from Junction 15 on M4, follow signs for Golf Complex. 35 bays, 30 covered, five uncovered, floodlit range. *Fees:* large basket £2.75, standard £2.00. *Eating facilities:* full service available. *Opening hours:* 8am to 9pm. 18 hole course, 9 hole course, short game practice area, pitch and putt. Professional tuition available.

WESTBURY near. **Thomstone Park Golf Club and Driving Range,** Chapmanslade, Near Westbury BA13 4AQ (0373 832825). *Location:* three miles north-west of Warminster on A36. 20 bay covered floodlit, grassed range. *Fees:* £2.00 per 50 balls, £3.00 per 100 balls. *Eating facilities:* coffee shop and bar in clubhouse. *Opening hours:* weekdays and Saturdays 8am to 9pm, Sundays 8am to 6pm. Professional available for lessons, Pro shop, 18 hole course, sauna, solarium.

WEST YORKSHIRE

BRADFORD. **Shay Grange Golf Centre,** Long Lane, Off Bingley Road, Heaton, Bradford BD9 6RX (0274 483955). *Location:* take the A650 Bradford to Bingley road, turn left at Cottingley lights; the Centre will be found on the left after two miles. 32 bay covered, floodlit, grassed range. *Fees:* £2.00 for 60 balls. *Eating facilities:* coffee shop. *Opening hours:* weekdays 9am to 10pm, weekends 9am to 7pm. Golf instruction school, all weather putting green, sand bunker. Discount golf shop. Professional: Steve Dixon.

LEEDS. **Leeds Golf Centre,** Wike Ridge Lane, Shadwell, Leeds LS17 9JW (0532 886186). *Location:* eight miles north of Leeds in village of Wike. 18 bay covered, floodlit, grassed range; artificial turf mats. *Fees:* information not provided. *Eating facilities:* available. Brochure gives full details of facilities available.

CHANNEL ISLANDS

ST. OUEN'S. **Les Mielles Golf Course,** St. Ouen's Bay, Jersey (0534 482787). *Location:* centre of St. Ouen's Bay. 36 bay grassed driving range. *Fees:* information not provided. *Opening hours:* dawn till dusk. *Eating facilities:* kiosk. Grade A PGA Professional Terry Le Brocq. Crazy golf, public golf facility. Manager: J.A. Le Brun.

SCOTLAND

ABERDEENSHIRE

ABERDEEN. **Kings Links Golf Centre,** Golf Road, Aberdeen AB2 1RZ (0224 641577; Fax: 0224 639410). *Location:* behind Pittodrie Stadium, on the Kings Links, by the beach. 44 bay covered, floodlit range. *Fees:* £1.60 per 40 balls. *Eating facilities:* sandwiches at lunchtime, vended drinks and snacks. *Opening hours:* 8.30am to 10pm weekdays, 8am to 5pm weekends. Adjoins Kings Links Golf Course, PGA qualified Professionals for tuition and club repair. Short game area (bunkers and putting) and putting green. Concessions available for Senior Citizens and under 14's.

EDINBURGH & LOTHIANS

DALKEITH near. **Melville Golf Range,** South Melville, Lasswade EH18 1AN (031-663 8038). *Location:* three minutes from Edinburgh City Bypass (Exit A7 Galashiels); on number 8 LRT bus route. 22 covered bays plus 12 outdoor mats. Floodlit. *Fees:* top quality two piece balls from £1.60 for 50, various concessions. *Eating facilities:* hot and cold beverages available. *Opening hours:* weekdays 9am to 10pm; weekends 9am to 8pm. Club hire and repairs, golf shop, ladies' and gents' equipment and golf wear, trial clubs, synthetic grass mats. Resident Professional. Putting area new for 1994.

EDINBURGH. **Port Royal Golf Range,** Eastfield Road, Ingliston, Edinburgh EH28 8TR (031-333 4377). *Location:* follow signs to Edinburgh Airport, on slip road approximately 100 yards from airport entrance. Five miles from centre of Edinburgh. 36 bays, 24 covered, floodlit and 12 grassed. 1000 square yard putting green and 9 hole Par 3 golf course. Pro shop, Professional and tuition. *Fees:* £1.40 per basket. *Eating facilities;* bar and lounge area, bar meals all day. *Opening hours:* 10am to 10pm. Open all year.

ARMAGH

CRAIGAVON. **Craigavon Golf and Ski Centre,** Turmoyra Lane, Silverwood, Lurgan, Craigavon BT66 6NE (0762 326606; Fax: 0762 347272). *Location:* A76 off M1 motorway. Floodlit driving range with 10 covered and 10 grassed bays. *Fees:* £1.60 per bucket. *Eating facilities:* full restuarant. *Opening hours:* 9am to 9pm. Professional, equipment hire, ski slope.

GLASGOW & DISTRICT

UDDINGSTON. **Clydeway Golf Centre,** Blantyre Farm Road, Uddingston G71 7RR (041-641 8899). *Location:* B758 off Main Street, Uddingston, near Glasgow Zoo. 25 covered floodlit bays. *Fees:* £1.70 for 60 balls. *Opening hours:* 10am 5.30pm (8.30pm April to September). Tuition and repairs, very large modern shop including ladies' department.

COUNTY DOWN

KNOCKBRACKEN. **Knockbracken Golf Centre,** 24 Ballymaconaghy Road, Knockbracken, Belfast BT8 4SB (0232 792108). *Location:* outskirts of Belfast, approximately three miles from centre along Ormeau Road near "Four Winds" Restaurant and Public House. 36 bays covered, floodlit and grassed. *Fees:* £2.20 for 100 balls, £1.80 for 70 balls, £1.25 for 40 balls. *Opening hours:* 9am to 11pm. *Eating facilities:* bar open seven days a week during normal opening hours, catering available seven days a week 11am to 10pm. Tuition available at Golf Academy by PGA Professionals. Snooker, playing machines, ski slope in season, equipment hire available, bowling (indoors).

RENFREWSHIRE

RENFREW. **Normandy Golf Range,** Inchinnan Road, Renfrew PA4 9EG (041-886 7377). *Location:* take M8; turn-off Glasgow Airport turn off; take Renfrew Road one mile away. 25 bays covered, floodlit. *Fees:* £1.00 token for 40 balls. *Opening hours:* 9.30am to 10.00pm seven days. *Eating facilities:* full hotel facilities. Professional, assistants, tuition anytime. Adjacent to Renfrew Golf Club. Large comprehensive stock of all leading golf equipment.

FERMANAGH

ENNISKILLEN. **Ashwoods Golf Centre,** Ashwoods, Sligo Road, Enniskillen (0365 325321 or 322908). *Location:* one and a half miles west of Enniskillen on main Sligo Road. 7 bay covered, floodlit range. *Fees:* £2.00 per bucket of 70 balls. *Eating facilities:* none on site, available 300 yards away. *Opening hours:* 9am to 10pm summer, 9am to 8pm winter. Resident Professional, 9 hole Par 3 course, club hire available.

NORTHERN IRELAND

ANTRIM

NEWTOWNABBEY. **Ballyearl Golf and Leisure Centre,** 585 Doagh Road, Newtownabbey BT36 8RZ (0232 848287). *Location:* six miles north of Belfast on M2 then first right onto Doagh Road from Belfast to Larne Road. 32 bay covered, floodlit range, 20 grassed bays. *Fees:* £2.00 small bucket (70 balls), £2.70 large bucket (110 balls). *Eating facilities:* bar – may be signed in. *Opening hours:* 9am to 10.15pm. Professional: Jim Robinson. Five squash courts, sunbed, theatre, golf, fitness suite and art classes. Various courses available.

REPUBLIC OF IRELAND

DUBLIN

FOXROCK. **Leopardstown Driving Range,** Foxrock (01 895341). *Location:* five miles south of Dublin city centre situated in Leopardstown race course. 38 indoor, 38 outdoor floodlit bays. *Fees:* information not provided. *Opening hours:* 9am to 10pm. *Eating facilities:* restaurant. Professional tuition – practice green. 9 hole golf course and 18 hole par 3.

Index

AA Saint-Omer Golf Club ST.OMER 349
Abbey Hill Golf Club MILTON KEYNES 69
Abbey Park Golf & Country Club REDDITCH 122
Abbeydale Golf Club Ltd. SHEFFIELD 222
Abbotsley Golf and Squash Club ST NEOTS 371
Aberdare Golf Club ABERDARE 314
Aberdour Golf Club ABERDOUR 264
Aberdovey Golf Club ABERDOVEY 320
Aberfeldy Golf Club ABERFELDY 289
Aberfoyle Golf Club ABERFOYLE 299
Abergele & Pensarn Golf Club ABERGELE 309
Abernethy Golf Club NETHYBRIDGE 278
Abersoch Golf Club PWLLHELI 325
Aberystwyth Golf Club ABERYSTWYTH 311
Aboyne Golf Club ABOYNE 235
Abridge Golf & Country Club STAPLEFORD TAWNEY 112
Accrington and District Golf Club ACCRINGTON 141
Achill Golf Club ACHILL 341
Acre Gate Golf Club FLIXTON 154
Addington Court Golf Courses CROYDON 190
Addington Palace Golf Club CROYDON 190
Aigas Golf Club BEAULY 276
Airdrie Golf Club AIRDRIE 282
Airlinks Golf Club HOUNSLOW 57
Aldeburgh Golf Club ALDEBURGH 186
Aldenham Golf & Country Club WATFORD 128
Alderley Edge Golf Club ALDERLEY EDGE 72
Alderney Golf Club ALDERNEY 345
Aldershaw Golf Club SEDLESCOMBE 200
Aldershaw Golf Club SEDLESCOMBE 374
Aldwark Manor Golf Hotel ALDWARK 216
Alexandra Golf Club GLASGOW 272
Alford Golf Club ALFORD 235
Alfreton Golf Club ALFRETON 92
Allendale Golf Club HEXHAM 172
Allerton Park Golf Club LIVERPOOL 160
Allestree Park Golf Club DERBY 93
Alloa Golf Club ALLOA 251
Alness Golf Club ALNESS 296
Alnmouth Golf Club Ltd. ALNMOUTH 170
Alnmouth Village Golf Club ALNMOUTH 170
Alnwick Golf Club ALNWICK 170
Aloha Golf Club MARBELLA 365
Alresford Golf Club ALRESFORD 115
Alsager Golf and Country Club ALSAGER 72
Alston Moor Golf Club ALSTON 87

Alto Golf Club ALVOR 359
Alton Golf Club ALTON 116
Altrincham Golf Course ALTRINCHAM 152
Alva Golf Club ALVA 251
Alwoodley Golf Club LEEDS 227
Alyth Golf Club BLAIRGOWRIE 290
Ampfield Par Three Golf & Country Club AMPFIELD 116
Andover Golf Club ANDOVER 116
Anglesey Golf Club Ltd. RHOSNEIGR 325
Anjou Golf and Country Club ANGERS 349
Annanhill Golf Club KILMARNOCK 245
Anoreta Golf RINCON DE VICTORIA 365
Anstruther Golf Club ANSTRUTHER 264
Ansty Golf Centre COVENTRY 209
Appleby Golf Club APPLEBY 87
Aquarius Golf Club SOUTHWARK 59
Arbroath Golf Course ARBROATH 237
Arcot Hall Golf Club Ltd. NEWCASTLE 172
Ardeer Golf Club STEVENSTON 246
Ardglass Golf Club ARDGLASS 331
Arkley Golf Club BARNET 124
Army Golf Club ALDERSHOT 115
Arrowe Park Golf Course BIRKENHEAD 158
Ashbourne Golf Club ASHBOURNE 92
Ashburnham Golf Club LLANELLI 312
Ashdown Forest Hotel FOREST ROW 199
Ashfield Golf Club CULLYHANNA 331
Ashford (Kent) Golf Club ASHFORD 133
Ashford Manor Golf Club ASHFORD 55
Ashley Wood Golf Club BLANDFORD 101
Ashridge Golf Club BERKHAMSTED 124
Ashton & Lea Golf Club Ltd. PRESTON 145
Ashton-in-Makerfield Golf Club Ltd ASHTON-IN-MAKERFIELD 152
Ashton-on-Mersey Golf Club SALE 156
Ashton-under-Lyne Golf Club ASHTON-UNDER-LYNE 152
Ashwoods Golf Centre ENNISKILLEN 334
Ashwoods Golf Centre ENNISKILLEN 376
Askernish Golf Club LOCHBOISDALE 306
Aspley Guise and Woburn Sands ASPLEY GUISE 65
Association du Golf de Granville GRANVILLE 348
Astbury Golf Club CONGLETON 73
Atalaya Park ESTEPONA 364
Atherstone Golf Club ATHERSTONE 206
Auchenblae Golf Club LAURENCEKIRK 280

INDEX

THE GOLF GUIDE 1994

Auchmill Golf Course ABERDEEN 234
Auchterarder Golf Club AUCHTERARDER 290
Auchterderran Golf Club CARDENDEN 264
Austerfield Park Golf Club DONCASTER 221
Austin Lodge Golf Club EYNSFORD 135
Axe Cliff Golf Club AXMOUTH 95
Aycliffe Golf Club NEWTON AYCLIFFE 107
Aylesbury Vale Golf Club LEIGHTON BUZZARD 370
Aylesbury Vale Golf Club LEIGHTON BUZZARD 64

Baberton Golf Club EDINBURGH 257
Backworth Golf Club SHIREMOOR 205
Bacup Golf Club BACUP 141
Badgemore Park Golf Club HENLEY-ON-THAMES 177
Baildon Golf Club SHIPLEY 229
Bakewell Golf Club BAKEWELL 92
Bala Golf Club BALA 321
Balbirnie Park Golf Club MARKINCH 269
Balbriggan Golf Club BALBRIGGAN 338
Balgove Course ST ANDREWS 271
Ballards Gore Golf Club ROCHFORD 111
Ballater Golf Club BALLATER 235
Ballinrobe Golf Club BALLINROBE 341
Ballochmyle Golf Club MAUCHLINE 245
Ballybunion Golf Club BALLYBUNION 340
Ballycastle Golf Club BALLYCASTLE 329
Ballyclare Golf Club BALLYCLARE 329
Ballyearl Golf and Leisure Centre NEWTOWNABBEY 376
Ballyearl Golf and Leisure Centre NEWTOWNABBEY 330
Ballymena Golf Club BALLYMENA 329
Balmoral Golf Club Ltd BELFAST 332
Balnagask Golf Course ABERDEEN 234
Bamburgh Castle Golf Club BAMBURGH 171
Banbridge Golf Club BANBRIDGE 331
Banchory Golf Club BANCHORY 279
Bangor Golf Club BANGOR 332
Banstead Downs Golf Club SUTTON 196
Bargoed Golf Club BARGOED 314
Barlaston Golf Club BARLASTON 183
Barnard Castle Golf Club BARNARD CASTLE 106
Barnehurst Golf Club BEXLEY HEATH 55
Barnham Broom Hotel Golf Club NORWICH 166
Barnsley Golf Club BARNSLEY 221
Baron Hill Golf Club ANGLESEY 320
Barrow Golf Club BARROW-IN-FURNESS 87
Barrow Hill Golf Club CHERTSEY 189
Barshaw Golf Club PAISLEY 295
Barton-on-Sea Golf Club BARTON-ON-SEA 116
Basildon Golf Club BASILDON 108
Basingstoke Golf Club BASINGSTOKE 116

Batchwood Hall Golf Club ST. ALBANS 127
Bath Golf Club BATH 61
Bathgate Golf Club BATHGATE 256
Bawburgh Golf Club NORWICH 166
Beacon Park Golf Centre SKERMERSDALE 146
Beaconsfield Golf Club Ltd BEACONSFIELD 67
Beadlow Manor Hotel, Golf & Country Club BEADLOW 63
Beamish Park Golf Club STANLEY 107
Bearsden Golf Club GLASGOW 272
Bearsted Golf Club MAIDSTONE 137
Bearwood Golf Club SINDLESHAM 67
Beau Desert Golf Club Ltd. CANNOCK 183
Beauchief Golf Club SHEFFIELD 222
Beauport Park Golf Club HASTINGS 199
Beckenham Place Park Golf Club BECKENHAM 133
Bedale Golf Club BEDALE 216
Bedford and County Golf Club BEDFORD 64
Bedfordshire Golf Club BEDFORD 64
Bedlingtonshire Golf Club BEDLINGTON 171
Beeston Fields Golf Club NOTTINGHAM 174
Beith Golf Club BEITH 244
Belfairs Golf Club LEIGH-ON-SEA 110
Belford Golf Club BELFORD 171
Belfry Golf Club WISHAW 213
Belhus Park Golf Club OCKENDON 111
Belleisle Golf Course AYR 242
Bellingham Golf Club HEXHAM 172
Bellshill Golf Club BELLSHILL 282
Belmont Lodge and Golf Course BELMONT 120
Belton Park Golf Club GRANTHAM 148
Belton Woods Hotel and Country Club GRANTHAM 149
Belvoir Park Golf Club BELFAST 332
Ben Rhydding Golf Club ILKLEY 226
Benone Golf Course LIMAVADY 334
Bentham Golf Club BENTHAM 216
Bentley Golf Club BRENTWOOD 108
Berehaven Golf Club CASTLETOWNBERE 337
Berkhamsted Golf Club BERKHAMSTED 124
Berkshire Golf Club ASCOT 65
Berwick-upon-Tweed (Goswick) BERWICK-UPON-TWEED 171
Betchworth Park Golf Club (Dorking) Ltd DORKING 192
Betws-y-Coed Golf Club BETWS-Y-COED 321
Beverley and East Riding Golf Club BEVERLEY 129
Bexley Heath Golf Club BEXLEY HEATH 133
Bidston Golf Club MORETON 161
Bigbury Golf Club Ltd. BIGBURY 95
Biggar Golf Club BIGGAR 282
Billingham Golf Club BILLINGHAM 77
Bingley (St. Ives) Golf Club BINGLEY 224
Birch Grove Golf Club COLCHESTER 109

378

THE GOLF GUIDE 1994   INDEX

Birchwood Golf Club WARRINGTON 76
Birley Wood Golf Club SHEFFIELD 223
Birstall Golf Club BIRSTALL 146
Birtley Golf Club BIRTLEY 204
Bishop Auckland Golf Club BISHOP AUCKLAND 106
Bishop's Stortford Golf Club BISHOP'S STORTFORD 124
Bishopbriggs Golf Club GLASGOW 272
Bishopshire Golf Club KINNESSWOOD 279
Bishopswood Golf Club BASINGSTOKE 116
Blackburn Golf Club BLACKBURN 141
Blackley Golf Club MANCHESTER 154
Blacklion Golf Club BLACKLION 337
Blackmoor Golf Club BORDON 117
Blackpool North Shore Golf Club BLACKPOOL 142
Blackpool Park Golf Club BLACKPOOL 142
Blackwell Golf Club BLACKWELL 120
Blackwell Grange Golf Club DARLINGTON 106
Blackwood Golf Club BLACKWOOD 319
Blair Atholl Golf Club BLAIR ATHOLL 290
Blairbeth Golf Club GLASGOW 272
Blairgowrie Golf Club BLAIRGOWRIE 290
Blairmore and Strone Golf Club DUNOON 241
Blankney Golf Club LINCOLN 149
Bletchingley Golf Club BLETCHINGLEY 189
Bloxwich Golf Club WALSALL 212
Blyth Golf Club Ltd. BLYTH 171
Boat of Garten Golf and Tennis Club BOAT OF GARTEN 276
Bognor Regis Golf Club BOGNOR REGIS 201
Boldmere Municipal Golf Club SUTTON COLDFIELD 212
Boldon Golf Club Ltd. EAST BOLDON 204
Bolton Golf Club Ltd. BOLTON 152
Bolton Municipal Golf Course BOLTON 143
Bon Accord Municipal Golf Club ABERDEEN 234
Bonar Bridge-Ardgay Golf Club BONAR BRIDGE 301
Bonnybridge Golf Club FALKIRK 299
Bonnyton Golf Club GLASGOW 272
Boothferry Golf Club HOWDEN 130
Bootle Golf Club BOOTLE 159
Borth and Ynyslas Golf Club Ltd BORTH 311
Boston Golf Club Ltd. BOSTON 148
Bothwell Castle Golf Club GLASGOW 273
Botley Park Golf Club SOUTHAMPTON 119
Bournemouth & Meyrick Park Golf Club BOURNEMOUTH 101
Bowood Golf Club CAMELFORD 79
Bowood Golf and Country Club CALNE 214
Bowring Golf Club HUYTON 160
Boxmoor Golf Club HEMEL HEMPSTEAD 126

Boyce Hill Golf Club Ltd SOUTH BENFLEET 111
Brackenwood Golf Club WIRRAL 163
Brackley Golf Club SALFORD 156
Bradford Golf Club GUISELEY 225
Bradford Moor Golf Club POLLARD LANE 229
Bradley Hall Golf Club HALIFAX 225
Bradley Park Golf Course HUDDERSFIELD 226
Braehead Golf Club ALLOA 251
Braemar Golf Club BRAEMAR 235
Braeside Golf Club BECKENHAM 133
Braids United Golf Club EDINBURGH 257
Brailes Golf Club Ltd BRAILLES 206
Braintree Golf Club BRAINTREE 108
Bramall Park Golf Club STOCKPORT 157
Bramhall Golf Club BRAMHALL 153
Bramley Golf Club GUILDFORD 193
Brampton Golf Club BRAMPTON 88
Brampton Park Golf Club HUNTINGDON 70
Bramshaw Golf Club LYNDHURST 118
Brancepeth Castle Golf Club BRANCEPETH 106
Brandhall Golf Club BIRMINGHAM 208
Brandon Wood Golf Course COVENTRY 209
Bransford Golf Club BRANSFORD 120
Branshaw Golf Club KEIGHLEY 226
Branston Golf Club BURTON-ON-TRENT 183
Breadsall Priory Hotel Golf & Country Club DERBY 93
Brean Golf Club BURNHAM-ON-SEA 181
Brechin Golf and Squash Club BRECHIN 238
Brecon Golf Club BRECON 325
Breightmet Golf Club BOLTON 152
Brickendon Grange Golf and Country Club HERTFORD 126
Bridge of Allan Golf Club STIRLING 300
Bridgnorth Golf Club BRIDGNORTH 177
Bridlington Golf Club BRIDLINGTON 129
Bridport & West Dorset Golf Club BRIDPORT 102
Bright Castle Golf Club DOWNPATRICK 333
Brighton and Hove Golf Club BRIGHTON 197
Bristol Golf Academy BRISTOL 370
Bristol and Clifton Golf Club BRISTOL 61
Broadstone (Dorset) Golf Club BROADSTONE 103
Broadway Golf Club BROADWAY 112
Brocton Hall Golf Club STAFFORD 184
Brodick Golf Club BRODICK 303
Brokenhurst Manor Golf Club BROCKENHURST 117
Bromborough Golf Club BRONBOROUGH 159
Bromley Golf Club BROMLEY 55
Brookdale Golf Club Ltd. MANCHESTER 154
Brookmans Park Golf Club HATFIELD 126
Broome Manor Golf Complex SWINDON 215
Broome Manor Golf Complex SWINDON 375

INDEX   THE GOLF GUIDE 1994

Broome Park Golf & Country Club CANTERBURY 134
Broomieknowe Golf Club Ltd EDINBURGH 257
Brora Golf Club BRORA 301
Brough Golf Club BROUGH 129
Broughty Golf Club MONIFIETH 238
Brown Trout Golf and Country Club COLAINE 334
Bruntsfield Links Golfing Soc. EDINBURGH 257
Bryn Meadows Golf and Country Hotel HENGOED 315
Bryn Morfydd Hotel Golf Club DENBIGH 309
Brynhill (Barry) Golf Club BARRY 316
Buchanan Castle Golf Club GLASGOW 273
Buckingham Golf Club BUCKINGHAM 68
Buckpool Golf Club (Buckie) BUCKIE 248
Bude and North Cornwall Golf Club BUDE 79
Budock Vean Golf and Country House Hotel FALMOUTH 79
Builth Wells Golf Club BUILTH WELLS 325
Bulbury Woods Golf Club POOLE 104
Bull Bay Golf Club Ltd. ANGLESEY 321
Bulwell Forest Golf Club BULWELL 173
Bundoran Golf Club BUNDORAN 338
Bungay and Waveney Valley Golf Club BUNGAY 186
Bunsay Downs Golf Club MALDON 110
Burford Golf Club BURFORD 176
Burghill Valley Golf Club HEREFORD 121
Burghley Park (Stamford) Golf Club STAMFORD 150
Burhill Golf Club WALTON-ON-THAMES 196
Burley Golf Club RINGWOOD 119
Burnham Beeches Golf Club BURNHAM 68
Burnham and Berrow Golf Club BURNHAM-ON-SEA 181
Burnham-on-Crouch Golf Club Ltd BURNHAM-ON-CROUCH 109
Burnley Golf Club BURNLEY 143
Burntisland Golf House Club BURNTISLAND 264
Burslem Golf Club Ltd. STOKE-ON-TRENT 185
Burton-on-Trent Golf Club BURTON-ON-TRENT 92
Bury Golf Club Ltd. BURY 153
Bury St. Edmunds Golf Club BURY ST. EDMUNDS 186
Bush Hill Park Golf Club WINCHMORE HILL 60
Bushey Hall Golf Club BUSHEY 124
Bushfoot Golf Club PORTBALLINTRAE 330
Bushmills Golf Club BUSHMILLS 329
Bute Golf Club ISLE OF BUTE 304
Buxton and High Peak Golf Club BUXTON 92

Caerleon Public Golf Course CAERLEON 319
Caernarfon Golf Club CAERNARFON 321

Caerphilly Golf Club CAERPHILLY 314
Caird Park Golf Club DUNDEE 238
Cairndhu Golf Club Ltd. LARNE 330
Calcot Park Golf Club READING 66
Caldecott Hall Golf Club GREAT YARMOUTH 164
Calderbraes Golf Club UDDINGSTON 284
Calderfields Golf Club Ltd WALSALL 212
Caldwell Golf Club UPLAWMOOR 296
Caldy Golf Club Ltd WIRRAL 163
Caledonian Golf Club ABERDEEN 234
Callander Golf Club CALLANDER 290
Calverley Golf Club LEEDS 227
Camberley Heath Golf Club CAMBERLEY 189
Cambridgeshire Moat House Hotel Golf Club CAMBRIDGE 70
Cambuslang Golf Club GLASGOW 273
Came Down Golf Club DORCHESTER 103
Camperdown Golf Club DUNDEE 238
Campo de Golf El Saler VALENCIA 366
Campo de Golf Villamartin ORIHUELA 366
Campo de Golfe da Madeira MADEIRA 361
Campsie Golf Club LENNOXTOWN 300
Canmore Golf Club DUNFERMLINE 265
Cannock Park Golf Club CANNOCK 184
Canons Brook Golf Club HARLOW 110
Canterbury Golf Club CANTERBURY 134
Canwick Park Golf Club LINCOLN 149
Cape Cornwall Golf and Country Club PENZANCE 82
Caprington Golf Club KILMARNOCK 245
Cardiff Golf Club CARDIFF 316
Cardigan Golf Club CARDIGAN 311
Cardross Golf Club CARDROSS 253
Carholme Golf Club LINCOLN 149
Carlisle Golf Club CARLISLE 88
Carlow Golf Club CARLOW 337
Carlton Forum Leisure Centre (South). NOTTINGHAM 373
Carluke Golf Club CARLUKE 282
Carlyon Bay Hotel Golf Course ST AUSTELL 85
Carmarthen Golf Club CARMARTHEN 312
Carnalea Golf Club BANGOR 332
Carnoustie Golf Links CARNOUSTIE 238
Carnwath Golf Club LANARK 283
Carradale Golf Club CARRADALE 241
Carrbridge Golf Club CARRBRIDGE 276
Carrick-on-Suir Golf Club CARRICK-ON-SUIR 342
Carrickfergus Golf Club CARRICKFERGUS 330
Carvoeiro Golf and Country Club LAGOA 359
Carvynick Golf and Country Club NEWQUAY 81
Castell Heights Public Golf Course CAERPHILLY 314
Castle Combe Golf Club CASTLE COMBE 214

THE GOLF GUIDE 1994　　　　　　　　　　　　　　　　　　　　　　　　　　INDEX

Castle Douglas Golf Club CASTLE DOUGLAS 280
Castle Eden & Peterlee Golf Club HARTLEPOOL 77
Castle Hume Golf Club ENNISKILLEN 334
Castle Point Golf Club CANVEY ISLAND 109
Castleblayney Golf Club CASTLEBLANEY 342
Castlefields Golf Club BRIGHOUSE 225
Castlerock Golf Club CASTLEROCK 334
Castletown Golf Club FORT ISLAND 343
Castletroy Golf Club CASTLEROY 341
Cathcart Castle Golf Club GLASGOW 273
Cathkin Braes Golf Club GLASGOW 273
Catterick Garrison Golf Club CATTERICK 216
Cave Castle Hotel Golf Club BROUGH 129
Cavendish Golf Club Ltd. BUXTON 92
Cawder Golf Club GLASGOW 273
Cawdor Castle Golf Club CAWDOR CASTLE 286
Ceann Sibeal Golf Club BALLYFERRITER 340
Chadwell Springs Golf Club WARE 128
Channels Golf Club CHELMSFORD 109
Chapel-en-le-Frith Golf Club CHAPEL-EN-LE-FRITH 92
Charleville Golf Club CHARLEVILLE 337
Charnwood Forest Golf Club LOUGHBOROUGH 147
Chart Hills Golf Club ASHFORD 133
Chartham Park Golf Club EAST GRINSTEAD 202
Chartridge Park Golf Club CHESHAM 68
Chateau des Vigiers Golf & Country Club DORDOGNE 353
Chatham Golf Centre CHATHAM 372
Cheadle Golf Club CHEADLE 153
Chelmsford Golf Club CHELMSFORD 109
Cherry Lodge Golf Club BIGGIN HILL 133
Cherwell Edge Golf club BANBURY 176
Chesfield Downs Family Golf Centre GRAVELEY 124
Chesham and Ley Hill CHESHAM 68
Cheshunt Golf Club WALTHAM CROSS 128
Chessington Golf Centre CHESSINGTON 373
Chessington Golf Club CHESSINGTON 189
Chester Golf Club CHESTER 72
Chester-Le-Street Golf Club CHESTER-LE-STREET 106
Chesterfield Golf Club Ltd. CHESTERFIELD 92
Chesterfield Municipal Golf Course CHESTERFIELD 92
Chesterton Golf Club BICESTER 176
Chestfield (Whitstable) Golf Club WHISTABLE 141
Chevin Golf Club DUFFIELD 93
Chigwell Golf Club CHIGWELL 109
Childwall Golf Club Ltd LIVERPOOL 160

Chiltern Forest Golf Club AYLESBURY 67
Chilwell Manor Golf Club NOTTINGHAM 174
Chingford Golf Club CHINGFORD 55
Chingford Golf Range CHINGFORD 370
Chippenham Golf Club CHIPPENHAM 214
Chipping Norton Golf Club CHIPPING NORTON 176
Chipping Sodbury Golf Club BRISTOL 61
Chipstead Golf Club CHIPSTEAD 190
Chislehurst Golf Club CHISLEHURST 134
Chorley Golf Club CHORLEY 143
Chorleywood Golf Club Ltd. CHORLEYWOOD 124
Chorlton-cum-Hardy Golf Club MANCHESTER 154
Chulmleigh Golf Course CHULMLEIGH 96
Church Stretton Golf Club CHURCH STRETTON 177
Churchill & Blakedown Golf Club BLAKEDOWN 120
Churston Golf Club Ltd BRIXHAM 95
Cilgwyn Golf Club LAMPETER 312
Cirencester Golf Club CIRENCESTER 113
City Of Newcastle Golf Club NEWCASTLE-UPON-TYNE 204
City of Coventry Golf Club COVENTRY 210
City of Derry Golf Club PREHEN 334
City of Wakefield Golf Club WAKEFIELD 230
Clacton Golf Club CLACTON 109
Clandeboye Golf Club NEWTOWNARDS 333
Clandon Regis Golf Club WEST CLANDON 196
Clayton Golf Club BRADFORD 224
Cleckheaton and District Golf Club Ltd CLECKHEATON 225
Cleethorpes Golf Club Ltd CLEETHORPES 129
Cleeve Cloud Golf Club CHELTENHAM 112
Clevedon Golf Club CLEVEDON 63
Cleveland Golf Club REDCAR 77
Cliftonville Golf Club BELFAST 329
Clitheroe Golf Club CLITHEROE 143
Clober Golf Club GLASGOW 273
Clonmel Golf Club CLONMEL 342
Close House Golf Club HEDDON-ON-THE-WALL 204
Clovelly Golf and Country Club BIDEFORD 95
Club de Golf El Bosque CHIVA 366
Club de Golf Escorpion BETERA 366
Club de Golf Las Brisas MARBELLA 365
Club de Golf Novo Sancti Petri CADIZ 364
Club de Golf Sotogrande SAN ROQUE 364
Club de Golf Valderrama SAN ROQUE 364
Club de Golf de Mijas MIJAS 365
Clube de Campo de Portugal AROEIRA 360
Clube de Golf de Miramar PRAIA DE MIRAMAR 361

INDEX THE GOLF GUIDE 1994

Clydebank & District Golf Club CLYDEBANK 253
Clydebank Municipal Golf Course CLYDEBANK 253
Clydeway Golf Centre UDDINGSTON 376
Clyne Golf Club SWANSEA 318
Cobtree Manor Park Golf Club MAIDSTONE 137
Cochrane Castle Golf Club JOHNSTONE 295
Cockermouth Golf Club EMBLETON 89
Cocks Moors Woods Golf Club BIRMINGHAM 208
Colchester Golf Club COLCHESTER 109
Colchester Golf Range COLCHESTER 371
Cold Ashby Golf Club NORTHAMPTON 168
Collingtree Park Golf Club NORTHAMPTON 169
Colnbrook Golf Range COLNBROOK 370
Colne Golf Club COLNE 144
Colonsay Golf Club ISLE OF COLONSAY 304
Colvend Golf Club DALBEATTIE 281
Colville Park Golf Club MOTHERWELL 283
Comrie Golf Club CRIEFF 290
Concord Park Golf Club SHEFFIELD 223
Congleton Golf Club CONGLETON 73
Connemara Golf Club CLIFDEN 339
Consett & District Golf Club CONSETT 106
Conwy (Caernarvonshire) Golf Club CONWY 322
Cooden Beach Golf Club BEXHILL-ON-SEA 197
Coombe Hill Golf Club KINGSTON-UPON-THAMES 194
Coombe Wood Golf Club KINGSTON-UPON-THAMES 194
Copt Heath Golf Club SOLIHULL 211
Copthorne Golf Club CRAWLEY 201
Corballis Public Golf Course DONABATE 338
Corby Public Golf Course CORBY 168
Corhampton Golf Club SOUTHAMPTON 120
Corinthian Golf Club DARTFORD 134
Cork Golf Club LITTLE ISLAND 337
Corrie Golf Club CORRIE 303
Cosby Golf Club COSBY 146
Costessey Park Golf Course NORWICH 166
Cotswold Edge Golf Club WOTTON-UNDER-EDGE 115
Cotswold Hills Golf Club Ltd CHELTENHAM 113
Cottesmore Golf & Country Club CRAWLEY 201
Coulsdon Court Golf Course COULSDON 190
County Armagh Golf Club ARMAGH 331
County Cavan Golf club DRUMELIS 337
County Louth Golf Club DROGHEDA 341
Coventry Golf Club COVENTRY 210
Coventry Hearsall Golf Club COVENTRY 210
Cowal Golf Club DUNOON 241
Cowdray Park Golf Club MIDHURST 203
Cowes Golf Club COWES 132
Cowglen Golf Club GLASGOW 273

Coxmoor Golf Club MANSFIELD 174
Cradoc Golf Club CRADOC 325
Craigavon Golf & Ski Club CRAIGAVON 331
Craigavon Golf & Ski Club CRAIGAVON 376
Craigie Hill Golf Club (1982) Ltd PERTH 294
Craigmillar Park Golf Club EDINBURGH 257
Craignure Golf Club CRAIGNURE 305
Crail Golfing Society CRAIL 265
Cranbrook Golf Club Ltd CRANBROOK 134
Crane Valley Golf Club VERWOOD 105
Cranford Golf Centre STOCKPORT 371
Cray Valley Golf Club ORPINGTON 137
Craythorne Golf Centre BURTON-ON-TRENT 183
Creigiau Golf Club CARDIFF 317
Cretingham Golf Club FRAMLINGHAM 186
Crewe Golf Club Ltd CREWE 73
Crews Hill Golf Club ENFIELD 56
Criccieth Golf Club CRICCIETH 322
Crichton Royal Golf Club DUMFRIES 251
Crieff Golf Club CRIEFF 293
Crimple Valley Golf Club HARROGATE 217
Croham Hurst Golf Club CROYDON 192
Crompton and Royton Golf Club Ltd OLDHAM 156
Crook Golf Club CROOK 106
Crookhill Park (Municipal) Golf Club DONCASTER 221
Crosland Heath Golf Club Ltd HUDDERSFIELD 226
Crow Wood Golf Club GLASGOW 273
Crowborough Beacon Golf Club CROWBOROUGH 198
Croydon Driving Range CROYDON 373
Cruden Bay Golf Club PETERHEAD 236
Cuddington (Banstead) Golf Club BANSTEAD 189
Cullen Golf Club CULLEN 249
Cupar Golf Club CUPAR 265
Curragh Golf Club CURRAGH 340
Cushendall Golf Club CUSHENDALL 330

Dainton Park Golf Club NEWTON ABOTT 98
Dalbeattie Golf Club DALBEATTIE 251
Dale Hill Golf Club WADHURST 201
Dalmahoy Hotel, Golf & Country Club KIRKNEWTON 260
Dalmally Golf Club DALMALLY 241
Dalmilling (Municipal) Golf Club AYR 242
Dalmunzie Golf Course BALIRGOWRIE 290
Dalston Hall Golf Club CARLISLE 88
Darenth Valley Golf Course SEVENOAKS 139
Darlington Golf Club Ltd DARLINGTON 107
Dartford Golf Club Ltd DARTFORD 135
Dartmouth Golf Club WEST BROMWICH 213
Dartmouth Golf and Country Club TOTNES 100

THE GOLF GUIDE 1994 INDEX

Darwen Golf Club DARWEN 144
Datchet Golf Club SLOUGH 67
Davenport Golf Club STOCKPORT 75
Daventry and District Golf Club DAVENTRY 168
Davyhulme Park Golf Club DAVYHULME 153
Deaconsbank Golf Course GLASGOW 274
Dean Wood Golf Club UPHOLLAND 146
Deane Golf Club BOLTON 152
Deangate Ridge Golf Club DEANGATE 135
Deer Park Golf & Country Club LIVINGSTON 261
Deer Park Hotel & Golf Courses HOWTH 339
Deeside Golf Club ABERDEEN 234
Delamere Forest Golf Club NORTHWICH 74
Delapre Golf Complex NORTHAMPTON 373
Delapre Park Golf Club NORTHAMPTON 169
Denbigh Golf Club DENBIGH 309
Denham Golf Club DENHAM 68
Denton Golf Club DENTON 153
Derby Golf Club SINFIN 94
Dereham Golf Club DEREHAM 164
Dewlands Manor golf Course ROTHERFIELD 200
Dewsbury District Golf Club MIRFIELD 229
Dibden Golf Centre DIBDEN 117
Didsbury Golf Club Ltd MANCHESTER 154
Dinas Powis Golf Club DINAS POWIS 317
Dinsdale Spa Golf Club DARLINGTON 106
Disley Golf Club STOCKPORT 157
Diss Golf Club DISS 164
Docklands Golf Range Ltd LONDON 370
Dolgellau Golf Club DOLGELLAU 322
Dollar Golf Club DOLLAR 251
Donaghadee Golf Club DONNAGHADEE 332
Doncaster Town Moor Golf Club DONCASTER 221
Doon Valley Golf Club PATNA 246
Dore and Totley Golf Club SHEFFIELD 223
Dorking Golf Club DORKING 192
Douglas Golf Club DOUGLAS 343
Douglas Golf Club DOUGLAS 337
Douglas Park Golf Club GLASGOW 274
Douglas Water Golf Club DOUGLAS WATER 282
Douglaston Golf Course GLASGOW 274
Down Royal Park LISBURN 333
Downes Crediton Golf Club CREDITON 96
Downfield Golf Club DUNDEE 238
Downpatrick Golf Club DOWNPATRICK 333
Downshire Driving Range WOKINGHAM 370
Downshire Golf Course WOKINGHAM 67
Drayton Park Golf Club TAMWORTH 185
Driffield Golf Club DRIFFIELD 130
Drift Golf Club EAST HORSLEY 192
Droitwich Golf & Country Club DROITWICH 121
Druids Heath Golf Club WALSALL 213

Drumpellier Golf Club COATBRIDGE 282
Duddingston Golf Club Ltd EDINBURGH 258
Dudley Golf Club LIVERPOOL 160
Dudley Golf Club Ltd. DUDLEY 210
Dudsbury Golf Club FERNWOOD 103
Duff House Royal Golf Club BANFF 248
Dufftown Golf Club DUFFTOWN 249
Dukinfield Golf Club DUKINFIELD 154
Dullatur Golf Club GLASGOW 274
Dulwich & Sydenham Hill Golf Club DULWICH 55
Dumbarton Golf Club DUMBARTON 254
Dumfries & Galloway Golf Club DUMFRIES 252
Dumfries and County Golf Club DUMFRIES 252
Dun Laoghaire Golf Club DUN LAOGHAIRE 339
Dunaverty Golf Club SOUTHEND 242
Dunbar Golf Club DUNBAR 256
Dunblane New Golf Club DUNBLANE 293
Dundalk Golf Club DUNDALK 341
Dundas Parks Golf Club SOUTH QUEENSFERRY 262
Dunfanaghy Golf Club LETTERKENNY 338
Dunfermline Golf Club DUNFERMLINE 267
Dungannon Golf Club DUNGANNON 336
Dunham Forest Golf & Country Club ALTRINCHAM 152
Dunkeld & Birnam Golf Club DUNKELD 293
Dunmurry Golf Club BELFAST 329
Dunnerholme Golf Club ASKAM-IN-FURNESS 87
Dunnikier Park Golf Club KIRKCALDY 268
Dunning Golf Club DUNNING 293
Duns Golf Club DUNS 249
Dunscar Golf Club Ltd. BOLTON 152
Dunstable Downs Golf Club DUNSTABLE 64
Dunstanburgh Castle Golf Club ALNWICK 170
Dunwood Manor Golf Club ROMSEY 119
Durham City Golf Club DURHAM 107
Durness Golf Club DURNESS 301
Duxbury Park Golf Club (Municipal) CHORLEY 143
Dyke Golf Club BRIGHTON 197

Eagles Golf club KINGS LYNN 165
Eaglescliffe Golf Club EAGLESCLIFFE 77
Ealing Golf Club GREENFORD 56
Ealing Golf Range LONDON 370
Earls Colne Golf and Leisure Centre COLCHESTER 109
Earls Colne Golf and Leisure Centre COLCHESTER 372
Earlsferry Thistle Golf Club ELIE 267
Easingwold Golf Club EASINGWOLD 217
East Berkshire Golf Club CROWTHORNE 65
East Bierley Golf Club BRADFORD 224
East Brighton Golf Club BRIGHTON 198

INDEX

THE GOLF GUIDE 1994

East Devon Golf Club SALTERTON 96
East Dorset Golf Club WAREHAM 105
East Herts Golf Club Ltd BUNTINGFORD 124
East Kilbride Golf Club GLASGOW 274
East Renfrewshire Golf Club NEWTON MEARNS 275
East Sussex National Golf Club UCKFIELD 200
Eastbourne Downs Golf Club EASTBOURNE 199
Eastbourne Golfing Park EASTBOURNE 199
Easter Moffat Golf Club AIRDRIE 282
Eastham Lodge Golf Club EASTHAM 159
Eastwood Golf Club GLASGOW 274
Eaton (Norwich) Golf Club NORWICH 166
Eden Course ST ANDREWS 271
Edenbridge Golf and Country Club EDENBRIDGE 135
Edgbaston Golf Club Ltd BIRMINGHAM 208
Edwalton Municipal Golf & Social Club EDWALTON 173
Edzell Golf Club EDZELL 238
Effingham Golf Club EFFINGHAM 192
Effingham Park Golf Club EFFINGHAM 202
Elderslie Golf Club ELDERSLIE 295
Elfordleigh Hotel Golf & Country Club PLYMOUTH 98
Elgin Golf Club ELGIN 284
Elland Golf Club ELLAND 225
Ellesborough Golf Club AYLESBURY 67
Ellesmere Golf Club MANCHESTER 154
Ellesmere Port Golf Club SOUTH WIRRAL 75
Elm Park Golf and Sports Club DUBLIN 339
Elsham Golf Club BRIGG 129
Eltham Warren Golf Club ELTHAM 56
Elton Furze Golf Club PETERBOROUGH 71
Ely City Golf Course Ltd. ELY 70
Enderby Golf Club ENDERBY 146
Enfield Golf Club ENFIELD 56
Enmore Park Golf Club BRIDGWATER 181
Enniscrone Golf Club ENNISCRONE 342
Enniskillen Golf Club ENNISKILLEN 334
Entry Hill Golf Club BATH 61
Enville Golf Club Ltd STOURBRIDGE 185
Epsom Golf Club EPSOM 192
Erewash Valley Golf Club ILKESTON 93
Erlestoke Sands Golf club DEVIZES 214
Erskine Golf Club BISHOPTON 294
Estela Golf Club ESTELA 361
Estoril Palacio Golf Course ESTORIL 360
Evesham Golf Club EVESHAM 121
Exeter Golf & Country Club EXETER 96
Eyemouth Golf Club EYEMOUTH 249

Fairfield Golf and Sailing Club AUDENSHAW 154
Fairhaven Golf Club Ltd. LYTHAM ST. ANNES 144
Fairlop Waters ILFORD 110
Fairlop Waters ILFORD 372
Fairwood Park Golf Club Ltd. SWANSEA 318
Fakenham Golf Club FAKENHAM 164
Falkirk Golf Club FALKIRK 299
Falkirk Tryst Golf Club LARBERT 299
Falkland Golf Club FALKLAND 267
Falmouth Golf Club FALMOUTH 81
Farnham Golf Club Ltd FARNHAM 193
Farnham Park Municipal Golf Course SLOUGH 69
Faversham Golf Club Ltd FAVERSHAM 136
Felixstowe Ferry Golf Club FELIXSTOWE 186
Fereneze Golf Club BARRHEAD 294
Ferndown Golf Club FERNDOWN 103
Fernfell Golf and Country Club CRANLEIGH 190
Ferrybridge "C" P.S. Golf Club KNOTTINGLEY 227
Ffestiniog Golf Club FFESTINIOG 322
Filey Golf Club FILEY 217
Filton Golf Club BRISTOL 61
Finchley Golf Club Ltd. FINCHLEY 56
Fingle Glen Golf and Leisure Complex EXETER 96
Fintona Golf Club FINTONA 336
Fishwick Hall Golf Club PRESTON 145
Flackwell Heath Golf Club Ltd. HIGH WYCOMBE 68
Flamborough Head Golf Club BRIDLINGTON 129
Fleetlands Golf Club GOSPORT 118
Fleetwood Golf Club Ltd FLEETWOOD 144
Fleming Park Golf Club EASTLEIGH 117
Flempton Golf Club BURY ST. EDMUNDS 186
Flint Golf Club FLINT 309
Flixton Golf Club URMSTON 155
Forest Hills Golf Club Ltd COLEFORD 113
Forest Park Golf Club YORK 220
Forest of Arden Hotel, Golf and Country Club COVENTRY 210
Forfar Golf Club FORFAR 238
Formby Golf Club FORMBY 159
Formby Ladies' Golf Club FORMBY 159
Fornham Park Golf & Country Club BURY ST. EDMUNDS 186
Forres Golf Club FORRES 285
Forrester Park Golf and Tennis Club MALDON 110
Fort Augustus Golf Club FORT AUGUSTUS 276
Fortrose and Rosemarkie Golf Club FORTROSE 296
Fortwilliam Golf Club BELFAST 329
Fosseway Country Club and Centurion Hotel BATH 61
Foxhills Country Club OTTERSHAW 194
Fraserburgh Golf Club FRASERBURGH 235

THE GOLF GUIDE 1994   INDEX

Fregate Golf Club BANDOL 352
Freshwater Bay Golf Club FRESHWATER 132
Frilford Heath Golf Club ABINGDON 176
Frinton Golf Club FRINTON-ON-SEA 110
Frodsham Golf Club FRODSHAM 73
Fulford (York) Golf Club Ltd. YORK 220
Fulford Heath Golf Club WYTHALL 123
Fulneck Golf Club Ltd. PUDSEY 229
Fulwell Golf Club HAMPTON HILL 57
Furness Golf Club BARROW-IN-FURNESS 87
Fynn Valley Golf Club IPSWICH 187

G.P.T Golf Club COVENTRY 210
Gainsborough Golf Club GAINSBOROUGH 148
Gairloch Golf Club GAIRLOCH 296
Galashiels Golf Club GALASHIELS 299
Ganstead Park Golf Club CONISTON 129
Ganton Golf Club Ltd SCARBOROUGH 219
Garesfield Golf Club CHOPWELL 204
Garforth Golf Club Ltd. LEEDS 227
Garmouth & Kingston Golf Club FOCHABERS 284
Gatehouse of Fleet Golf Club GATEHOUSE OF FLEET 281
Gathurst Golf Club Ltd. WIGAN 158
Gatley Golf Club Ltd. CHEADLE 72
Gatton Manor Hotel, Golf & Country Club DORKING 192
Gatwick Manor Golf Club CRAWLEY 374
Gay Hill Golf Club BIRMINGHAM 208
Gedney Hill Golf Course SPALDING 150
Gerrards Cross Golf Club GERRARDS CROSS 68
Ghyll Golf Club THORNTON IN CRAVEN 220
Gifford Golf Club HADDINGTON 260
Gillingham Golf Club Ltd GILLINGHAM 136
Gilnahirk Golf Club BELFAST 329
Girton Golf Club CAMBRIDGE 70
Girvan Golf Club GIRVAN 244
Glamorganshire Golf Club PENARTH 317
Glasgow Golf Club IRVINE 244
Glasgow Golf Club GLASGOW 274
Gleddoch Golf & Country Club LANGBANK 295
Glen Golf Club NORTH BERWICK 261
Glenbervie Golf Club Ltd LARBERT 300
Glencorse Golf Club PENICUIK 262
Glencruitten Golf Club OBAN 242
Gleneagles Hotel Golf Courses AUCHTERARDER 290
Glengorse Golf Club OADBY 148
Glenrothes Golf Club GLENROTHES 267
Glossop and District Golf Club GLOSSOP 93
Gloucester Hotel & Country Club GLOUCESTER 114
Gloucester Hotel &, Country Club GLOUCESTER 372

Glynhir Golf Club AMMANFORD 311
Glynneath Golf Club GLYNNEATH 317
Goal Farm Golf Club PIRBRIGHT 195
Gog Magog Golf Club CAMBRIDGE 70
Golf Almerimar ALMERIA 365
Golf Club d'Aix-les-Bains AIX-LES-BAINS 352
Golf Club de Cannes-Mandelieu CANNES 354
Golf Club de Fontcaude MONTPELLIER 355
Golf Club de St. Jean-de-Monts ST. JEAN-DE-MONTS 350
Golf Club de la Domangere LA-ROCHE-SUR-YON 350
Golf Club du Champ de Bataille NEUBOURG 349
Golf Country Club de Cannes-Mougins CANNES 354
Golf El Paraiso ESTEPONA 364
Golf House Club ELIE 267
Golf International de Chateau L'Arc AIX-EN-PROVENCE 354
Golf International de Grenoble GRENOBLE 352
Golf International de Toulouse Seilh TOULOUSE 354
Golf National PARIS 351
Golf Ploemeur Ocean LORIENT 350
Golf Pollensa POLLENSA 368
Golf Public Saint-Hilaire LOUDUN 351
Golf Rio Real MARBELLA 365
Golf Torrequebrada BENALMADENA 364
Golf Vila Sol VILAMOURA 359
Golf and Country Club de Bossey ST.JULIEN 352
Golf d'Aix Marseilles MARSEILLES 355
Golf d'Arcangues BIARRITZ 353
Golf d'Ardree TOURS 351
Golf d'Hardelot "Les Dunes" HARDELOT 348
Golf d'Hardelot "Les Pins" HARDELOT 348
Golf d'Hossegor HOSSEGOR 353
Golf de Baden AURAY 349
Golf de Biarritz Le Phare BIARRITZ 353
Golf de Bondues LILLE 348
Golf de Bordeaux Cameyrac BORDEAUX 353
Golf de Brest Iroise BREST 349
Golf de Caen CAEN 347
Golf de Cap d'Agde BEZIERS 354
Golf de Casteljaloux CASTELJALOUX 353
Golf de Castelnaud VILLENEUVE-SUR-LUT 354
Golf de Chamonix CHAMONIX 352
Golf de Chiberta ANGLET 352
Golf de Forges-les-Bains PARIS 350
Golf de Gujan Mestras ARCACHON 352
Golf de Lyon LYON 352
Golf de Massane MONTPELLIER 355
Golf de Nimes-Campagne NIMES 355
Golf de Pessac BORDEAUX 353
Golf de Rennes RENNES 350

INDEX

Golf de Roquebrune FREJUS 354
Golf de Royan ROYAN 351
Golf de Sable-Solesmes ANGERS 349
Golf de Saint Laurent AURAY 349
Golf de Seignosse BAYONNE 353
Golf de Sperone CORSICA 354
Golf de St Gatien Deauville DEAUVILLE 348
Golf de St-Cyprien PERPIGNAN 355
Golf de St-Malo-le-Tronchet ST.MALO 350
Golf de Wimereux BOULOGNE 347
Golf de l'Ailette LAON 348
Golf de l'Esterel ST-RAPHAEL 356
Golf de l'Odet BENODET 349
Golf de la Baule LA BAULE 350
Golf de la Bretesche LA BAULE 350
Golf de la Cote d'Argent BAYONNE 352
Golf de la Freslonniere RENNES 350
Golf de la Grande Bastide GRASSE 355
Golf de la Grande-Motte MONTPELLIER 355
Golf de la Nivelle SAINT-JEAN-DE-LUZ 354
Golf de la Vaucouleurs PARIS 351
Golf del Chaparral MIJAS 365
Golf des Baux de Provence AVIGNON 354
Golf des Hauts de Nimes NIMES 355
Golf des Yvelines PARIS 351
Golf du Chateau de Cheverny CHEVERNY 351
Golf du Chateau des Sept Tours TOURS 351
Golf du Cognac COGNAC 351
Golf du Haut-Poitou POITIERS 351
Golf du Medoc BORDEAUX 353
Golf du Touquet LE TOUQUET 348
Golf du Val Queven LORIENT 350
Golf et Tennis Club de Valescure ST-RAPHAEL 356
Golspie Golf Club GOLSPIE 302
Goodwood Golf Club CHICHESTER 201
Goring and Streatley Golf Club STREATLEY ON THAMES 67
Gorleston Golf Club GREAT YARMOUTH 165
Gosforth Golf Club Ltd. NEWCASTLE-UPON-TYNE 204
Gosforth Park Golfing Complex Ltd NEWCASTLE-UPON-TYNE 374
Gosling Golf Range WELLWYN GARDEN CITY 372
Gosport & Stokes Golf Club GOSPORT 118
Gotts Park Municipal Golf Club LEEDS 227
Gourock Golf Club GOUROCK 295
Grange Fell Golf Club GRANGE-OVER-SANDS 89
Grange Park Golf Club ST. HELENS 163
Grange Park Golf Club ROTHERHAM 222
Grange Park Golf Range SCUNTHORPE 130
Grange Park Golf Range SCUNTHORPE 372
Grange-over-Sands Golf Club GRANGE-OVER-SANDS 89

THE GOLF GUIDE 1994

Grangemouth Golf Club POLMONT 300
Grantown-on-Spey Golf Club GRANTOWN-ON-SPEY 285
Grassmoor Golf Centre CHESTERFIELD 92
Grassmoor Golf Centre CHESTERFIELD 371
Great Barr Golf Club BIRMINGHAM 208
Great Harwood Golf Club BLACKBURN 142
Great Lever and Farnworth Golf BOLTON 152
Great Salterns Municipal Golf Course PORTSMOUTH 119
Great Yarmouth and Caister Golf Club GREAT YARMOUTH 165
Green Haworth Golf Club ACCRINGTON 141
Green Hotel Golf Course KINROSS 280
Greenburn Golf Club FAULDHOUSE 259
Greenisland Golf Club CARRICKFERGUS 330
Greenmeadow Golf and Country Club CWMBRAN 319
Greenmount Golf Club BURY 153
Greenock Golf Club GREENOCK 295
Greenock Whinhill Golf Club GREENOCK 295
Grim's Dyke Golf Club PINNER 58
Grimsby Golf Club Ltd GRIMSBY 130
Guadalhorce Club de Golf MALAGA 364
Guadalmina Club de Golf MARBELLA 365
Guildford Golf Club GUILDFORD 193
Gullane Golf Club GULLANE 259

Habberley Golf Club KIDDERMINSTER 122
Haddington Golf Club HADDINGTON 260
Hadley Wood Golf Course BARNET 124
Haggs Castle Golf Club GLASGOW 274
Hagley Country Club Golf Club HAGLEY 121
Haigh Hall Golf Club WIGAN 158
Hainault Forest Golf Club CHIGWELL 109
Hainsworth Park Golf Club BEVERLEY 129
Hale Golf Club ALTRINCHAM 72
Halesowen Golf Club HALESOWEN 211
Halifax Golf Club Ltd HALIFAX 225
Hallamshire Golf Club Ltd SHEFFIELD 223
Hallowes Golf Club SHEFFIELD 223
Haltwhistle Golf Course CARLISLE 171
Ham Manor Golf Club Ltd ANGMERING 201
Hamilton Golf Club HAMILTON 282
Hampstead Golf Club HAMPSTEAD 56
Hamptworth Golf and Country Club SALISBURY 215
Handsworth Golf Club BIRMINGHAM 208
Hanging Heaton Golf Club DEWSBURY 225
Hankley Common Golf Club FARNHAM 193
Harborne (Church Farm) Golf Club BIRMINGHAM 209
Harborne Golf Club BIRMINGHAM 209
Harborne Municipal Golf Club BIRMINGHAM 209
Harbour Point Golf Club LITTLE ISLAND 338

THE GOLF GUIDE 1994   INDEX

Harburn Golf Club WEST CALDER 264
Harewood Downs Golf Club CHALFONT ST. GILES 68
Harpenden Common Golf Club HARPENDEN 126
Harpenden Golf Club HARPENDEN 126
Harrogate Golf Club Ltd HARROGATE 217
Hartlepool Golf Club Ltd HARTLEPOOL 77
Hartley Wintney Golf Club FLEET 117
Hartsbourne Golf and Country Club BUSHEY HEATH 124
Hartswood Golf Club BRENTWOOD 108
Harwich and Dovercourt Golf Club HARWICH 110
Harwood Golf Club BOLTON 153
Hatchford Brook Golf Club BIRMINGHAM 209
Hatfield London Country Club HATFIELD 126
Haverfordwest Golf Club HAVERFORDWEST 312
Haverhill Golf Club Ltd HAVERHILL 187
Hawarden Golf Club HAWARDEN 309
Hawick Golf Club HAWICK 297
Hawkhurst Golf Club HAWKHURST 136
Hawkstone Park Hotel SHREWSBURY 179
Hawthorn Hill Golf Centre MAIDENHEAD 66
Hawthorn Hill Golf Centre MAIDENHEAD 370
Haydock Park Golf Club NEWTON-LE-WILLOWS 161
Hayling Golf Club HAYLING ISLAND 118
Hayston Golf Club GLASGOW 274
Haywards Heath Golf Club HAYWARDS HEATH 202
Hazel Grove Golf Club STOCKPORT 157
Hazlehead Golf Course ABERDEEN 234
Hazlemere Golf & Country Club HIGH WYCOMBE 68
Headingley Golf Club LEEDS 227
Headley Golf Club BRADFORD 224
Heaton Moor Golf Club STOCKPORT 157
Heaton Park Golf Club MANCHESTER 155
Hebden Bridge Golf Club HEBDEN BRIDGE 226
Helen's Bay Golf Club BANGOR 332
Helensburgh Golf Club HELENSBURGH 254
Hellidon Lakes Golf Club HELLIDON 168
Helmsdale Golf Club HELMSDALE 302
Helsby Golf Club HELSBY 73
Henbury Golf Club BRISTOL 61
Hendon Golf Club HENDON 57
Henley Golf Club HENLEY-ON-THAMES 177
Herefordshire Golf Club HEREFORD 121
Herne Bay Golf Club HERNE BAY 136
Herons Reach Driving Range BLACKPOOL 373
Herons Reach Golf Club BLACKPOOL 142
Hesketh Golf Club SOUTHPORT 161
Hessle Golf Club COTTINGHAM 129
Heswall Golf Club HESWALL 159

Hever Golf Club HEVER 136
Hewitts Golf Centre ORPINGTON 137
Heworth Golf Club GATESHEAD 204
Heworth Golf Club YORK 221
Hexham Golf Club HEXHAM 172
Heysham Golf Club HEYSHAM 144
Hickleton Golf Club DONCASTER 221
High Elms Golf Club FARNBOROUGH 135
High Post Golf Club Ltd SALISBURY 215
Highbullen Hotel Golf Course UMBERLEIGH 100
Highcliffe Castle Golf Club CHRISTCHURCH 103
Highgate Golf Club HIGHGATE 57
Highwoods Golf Club BEXHILL-ON-SEA 197
Highworth Community Golf Centre HIGHWORTH 215
Hill Barn Golf Course WORTHING 203
Hill Valley Golf & Country Club WHITCHURCH 180
Hillingdon Golf Club HILLINGDON 57
Hillsborough Golf Club Ltd. SHEFFIELD 223
Hillside Golf Club SOUTHPORT 161
Hilltop Public Golf Course BIRMINGHAM 209
Hilton Park Golf Club GLASGOW 274
Himley Hall Golf Centre DUDLEY 211
Hinckley Golf Club HINCKLEY 146
Hindhead Golf Club HINDHEAD 194
Hindley Hall Golf Club WIGAN 158
Hintlesham Hall Golf Club IPSWICH 187
Hirsel Golf Club COLDSTREAM 249
Hobson Municipal Golf Club NEWCASTLE-UPON-TYNE 205
Hockley Golf Club WINCHESTER 120
Hoebridge Golf Centre WOKING 197
Hoebridge Golf Centre OLD WOKING 374
Holiday Inns Golf Club WEST DRAYTON 60
Hollandbush Golf Club LESMAHAGOW 283
Hollingbury Park Golf Club BRIGHTON 198
Holme Hall Golf Club SCUNTHORPE 131
Holsworthy Golf Club HOLSWORTHY 97
Holtye Golf Club EAST GRINSTEAD 202
Holyhead Golf Club TREARDDUR BAY 325
Holywell Golf Club HOLYWELL 309
Holywood Golf Club HOLYWOOD 333
Home Park Golf Club HAMPTON WICK 57
Honiton Golf Club HONITON 97
Hopeman Golf Club ELGIN 284
Horam Park Golf Course HEATHFIELD 199
Horam Park Golf Course HORAM 374
Horncastle Golf Club HORNCASTLE 149
Hornsea Golf Club HORNSEA 130
Horsenden Hill Golf Club GREENFORD 56
Horsforth Golf Club Ltd. LEEDS 227
Horsle Lodge Golf Club HORSLEY 93
Horton Park Country Club EPSOM 193

387

INDEX

THE GOLF GUIDE 1994

Houghton-le-Spring Golf Club HOUGHTON-LE-SPRING 204
Houldsworth Golf Club Ltd. MANCHESTER 155
Hounslow Heath Municipal Golf Course HOUNSLOW 57
Howley Hall Golf Club Ltd. LEEDS 227
Howth Golf Club SUTTON 339
Hoylake Golf Club WIRRAL 163
Huddersfield Golf Club HUDDERSFIELD 226
Hull Golf Club (1921) Ltd HULL 130
Humberstone Heights Golf Club LEICESTER 147
Hunley Hall Golf Club BROTTON 77
Hunstanton Golf Club HUNSTANTON 165
Huntercombe Golf Club HENLEY-ON-THAMES 177
Huntly Golf Club HUNTLY 235
Hurdwick Golf club TAVISTOCK 98
Hurst Golf Club READING 66
Hurtmore Golf Club GODALMING 193
Huyton and Prescot Golf Club Ltd HUYTON 160
Hythe Imperial Golf Club HYTHE 136

Ifield Golf and Country Club CRAWLEY 202
Iford Bridge Golf Club CHRISTCHURCH 103
Ilford Golf Club ILFORD 110
Ilfracombe Golf Club ILFRACOMBE 97
Ilkeston Borough Golf Club ILKESTON 93
Ilkley Golf Club ILKLEY 226
Immingham Golf Club IMMINGHAM 130
Inco Golf Club CLYDACH 317
Ingestre Park Golf Club STAFFORD 184
Ingol Golf & Squash Club PRESTON 145
Innellan Golf Club DUNOON 241
Innerleithen Golf Club PEEBLES 288
Insch Golf Club INSCH 235
International Golf Academy ESTORIL 360
Inverallochy Golf Club INVERALLOCHY 236
Inverclyde National Golf Training Centre LARGS 245
Invergordon Golf Club INVERGORDON 297
Inverness Golf Club INVERNESS 278
Inverurie Golf Club INVERURIE 236
Ipswich Golf Club IPSWICH 187
Irvine Golf Club IRVINE 244
Irvine Ravenspark Golf Club IRVINE 244
Isle of Gigha Golf Club ISLE OF GIGHA 305
Isle of Purbeck Golf Club STUDLAND 104
Isle of Skye Golf Club SCONSER 306
Isles of Scilly Golf Club ST. MARY'S 86
Iver Golf Course IVER 68
Ivinghoe Golf Club LEIGHTON BUZZARD 64

Jedburgh Golf Club JEDBURGH 298
Jersey Recreation Grounds JERSEY 345
John O'Gaunt Golf Club SANDY 65
John Reay Golf Centres COVENTRY 374

Jubilee Course ST ANDREWS 271

Kearsley Golf Driving Range KEARSLEY 373
Kedleston Park Golf Club QUARNDON 94
Keighley Golf Club KEIGHLEY 226
Keith Golf Club KEITH 249
Kelso Golf Club KELSO 298
Kemnay Golf Club KEMNAY 236
Kendal Golf Club KENDAL 89
Kenilworth Golf Club KENILWORTH 206
Kenmore Golf Course ABERFELDY 289
Keswick Golf Club KESWICK 89
Kettering Golf Club KETTERING 168
Kibworth Golf Club Ltd. LEICESTER 147
Kidderminster Golf Club KIDDERMINSTER 122
Kilbirnie Place Golf Club KILBIRNIE 245
Kilkeel Golf Club KILKEEL 333
Killarney Golf and Fishing Club KILLARNEY 340
Killin Golf Club KILLIN 293
Killiow Golf Club TRURO 86
Killiow Golf Club TRURO 371
Killymoon Golf Club COOKSTOWN 336
Kilmacolm Golf Club KILMACOLM 295
Kilmarnock (Barassie) Golf Club TROON 246
Kilspindie Golf Club ABERLADY 256
Kilsyth Lennox Golf Club KILSYTH 275
Kilton Forest Golf Club WORKSOP 175
King Edward Bay Golf Club ONCHAN 343
King James VI Golf Club PERTH 294
King's Lynn Golf Club KING'S LYNN 165
Kinghorn Municipal Golf Club KINGHORN 268
Kings Links Golf Centre ABERDEEN 375
Kings Norton Golf Club Ltd. BIRMINGHAM 209
Kingsdown Golf Club CORSHAM 214
Kingsknowe Golf Club EDINBURGH 258
Kingsley Golf Club BORDON 117
Kingsley Golf Club BORDON 372
Kingsthorpe Golf Club NORTHAMPTON 169
Kingswood Golf & Country Club Ltd KINGSWOOD 194
Kington Golf Club KINGTON 122
Kingussie Golf Club KINGUSSIE 278
Kingweston Golf Club STREET 182
Kintore Golf Club INVERURIE 236
Kirby Muxloe Golf Club KIRKBY MUXLOE 146
Kirkby Lonsdale Golf Club KIRKBY LONSDALE 89
Kirkbymoorside Golf Club KIRKBYMOORSIDE 218
Kirkcaldy Golf Club KIRKCALDY 268
Kirkcudbright Golf Club KIRKCUDBRIGHT 281
Kirkhill Golf Club GLASGOW 274
Kirkintilloch Golf Club KIRKINTILLOCH 254
Kirkistown Castle Golf Club NEWTOWNARDS 333
Kirriemuir Golf Club Ltd. KIRRIEMUIR 238

THE GOLF GUIDE 1994   INDEX

Knaresborough Golf Club KNARESBOROUGH 218
Knebworth Golf Club KNEBWORTH 126
Knighton Golf Club KNIGHTON 327
Knighton Heath Golf Club BOURNEMOUTH 101
Knights Grange Golf Course WINSFORD 76
Knightswood Golf Club GLASGOW 275
Knock Golf Club BELFAST 332
Knockanally golf and Country Club DONADEA 340
Knockbracken Golf Centre KNOCKBRACKEN 376
Knockbracken Golf and Country Club BELFAST 332
Knole Park Golf Club SEVENOAKS 139
Knott End Golf Club BLACKPOOL 142
Knowle Golf Club BRISTOL 61
Knutsford Golf Club KNUTSFORD 73
Kyles Of Bute Golf Club TIGHNABRUAICH 242

La Cala Golf and Country Club MIJAS 365
La Manga Club MURCIA 366
La Moye Golf Club JERSEY 345
La Quinta Golf and Country Club BENAHAVIS 364
Ladbrook Park Golf Club Ltd SOLIHULL 211
Ladybank Golf Club LADYBANK 268
Lahinch Golf Club LAHINCH 337
Lakeside Golf Club RUGELEY 184
Lakeside Lodge Golf Club HUNTINGDON 71
Laleham Golf Club CHERTSEY 189
Lamberhurst Golf Club TUNBRIDGE WELLS 140
Lambourne Golf Club BURNHAM 68
Lamlash Golf Club LAMLASH 303
Lanark Golf Club LANARK 283
Lancaster Golf and Country Club Ltd LANCASTER 144
Langholm Golf Club LANGHOLM 283
Langland Bay Golf Club SWANSEA 318
Langley Park Driving Range MAIDSTONE 373
Langley Park Golf Club BECKENHAM 133
Lanhydrock Golf Club BODMIN 79
Lansdown Golf Club BATH 61
Lansil Golf Club LANCASTER 144
Largs Golf Club LARGS 245
Larkhall Golf Club LARKHALL 283
Larne Golf Club LARNE 330
Lauder Golf Club LAUDER 249
Launceston Golf Club LAUNCESTON 81
Lavender Park Golf Centre ASCOT 65
Leadhills Golf Club LEADHILLS 283
Leamington and County Golf Club LEAMINGTON SPA 207
Leaside Golf Club EDMONTON 55
Leasowe Golf Club MORETON 161

Leatherhead Golf Club LEATHERHEAD 194
Lee Park Golf Club LIVERPOOL 160
Lee Valley Leisure Golf Course EDMONTON 55
Lee-on-the-Solent Golf Club LEE-ON-THE-SOLENT 118
Leeds Castle Golf Course MAIDSTONE 137
Leeds Golf Centre LEEDS 227
Leeds Golf Centre LEEDS 375
Leeds Golf Club LEEDS 228
Leek Golf Club LEEK 184
Lees Hall Golf Club Ltd. SHEFFIELD 223
Leicestershire Golf Club LEICESTER 147
Leigh Golf Club WARRINGTON 76
Leighton Buzzard Golf Club LEIGHTON BUZZARD 64
Lenzie Golf Club LENZIE 254
Leominster Golf Club LEOMINSTER 122
Leopardstown Golf Course FOXROCK 339
Leopardstown Golf Course FOXROCK 376
Les Bordes Golf International ORLEANS 351
Les Mielles Golf Course JERSEY 345
Les Mielles Golf Course ST. OUEN'S 375
Leslie Golf Club LESLIE 268
Letchworth Golf Club LETCHWORTH 126
Letham Hill Municipal Golf Club GLASGOW 275
Leven Golfing Society LEVEN 269
Leven Thistle Golf Club LEVEN 269
Lewes Golf Club LEWES 200
Leyland Golf Club Ltd LEYLAND 144
Libbaton Golf Club UMBERLEIGH 100
Liberton Golf Club EDINBURGH 258
Lickey Hills (Municipal) Golf Club REDNAL 211
Lightcliffe Golf Club HALIFAX 225
Lilleshall Hall Golf Club NEWPORT 179
Lilley Brook Golf Club CHELTENHAM 112
Limpsfield Chart Golf Club WEYBRIDGE 195
Lincoln Golf Club LINCOLN 149
Lindrick Golf Club WORKSOP 175
Lingdale Golf Club WOODHOUSE EAVES 148
Lingfield Park Golf Club LINGFIELD 194
Links Country Park Hotel and Golf Club CROMER 164
Links Golf Club NEWMARKET 187
Linlithgow Golf Club LINLITHGOW 260
Linn Park Golf Club GLASGOW 275
Liphook Golf Club LIPHOOK 118
Lisbon Sports Club LISBON 361
Lisburn Golf Club LISBURN 330
Lismore Golf Club LISMORE 342
Little Aston Golf Club STREETLY 185
Little Chalfont Golf Club LITTLE CHALFONT 69
Little Hay Golf Complex HEMEL HEMPSTEAD 126
Little Lakes Golf Club BEWDLEY 120
Littlehampton Golf Club LITTLEHAMPTON 203
Littlehill Golf Club GLASGOW 275

389

INDEX THE GOLF GUIDE 1994

Littlestone Golf Club NEW ROMNEY 137
Llandrindod Wells Golf Club LLANDRINDOD WELLS 327
Llandudno Golf Club (Maesdu) Ltd LLANDUDNO 322
Llanfairfechan Golf Club LLANFAIRFECHAN 324
Llangefni Public Golf Course LLANGEFNI 324
Llanishen Golf Club CARDIFF 317
Llantrisant and Pontyclun Golf Club PONTYCLUN 315
Llanwern Golf Club LLANWERN 319
Llanymynech Golf Club OSWESTRY 179
Lobden Golf Club ROCHDALE 156
Lochcarron Golf Club LOCHCARRON 297
Lochgelly Golf Club LOCHGELLY 269
Lochgilphead Golf Club LOCHGILPHEAD 241
Lochmaben Golf Club LOCKERBIE 252
Lochranza Golf LOCHRANZA 304
Lochwinnoch Golf Club LOCHWINNOCH 295
Lockerbie Golf Club LOCKERBIE 252
London Scottish Golf Club LONDON 57
Longcliffe Golf Club LOUGHBOROUGH 147
Longley Park Golf Club HUDDERSFIELD 226
Longniddry Golf Club Ltd LONGNIDDRY 261
Longridge Golf Club PRESTON 145
Looe Golf Club LOOE 81
Los Naranjos Golf Club MARBELLA 365
Lothianburn Golf Club EDINBURGH 258
Loudoun Gowf Club GALSTON 244
Loughrea Golf Club LOUGHREA 339
Loughton Golf Club LOUGHTON 110
Louth Golf Club LOUTH 149
Low Laithes Golf Club Ltd. WAKEFIELD 230
Lowes Park Golf Club Ltd BURY 153
Ludlow Golf Club LUDLOW 177
Luffenham Heath Golf Club STAMFORD 150
Luffness New Golf Club ABERLADY 256
Lullingstone Park Golf Club ORPINGTON 58
Lundin Golf Club LEVEN 269
Lundin Ladies Golf Club LUNDIN LINKS 269
Lurgan Golf Club LURGAN 331
Lutterworth Golf Club LUTTERWORTH 146
Lybster Golf Club LYBSTER 250
Lydney Golf Club LYDNEY 114
Lyme Regis Golf Club LYME REGIS 104
Lymm Golf Club LYMM 74
Lyneham Golf Club CHIPPING NORTON 176
Lyons Gate Golf Course DORCHESTER 103
Lytham Green Drive Golf Club LYTHAM ST. ANNES 144

Macclesfield Golf Club MACCLESFIELD 74
Machrie Bay Golf Club MACHRIE 304
Machrie Golf Club PORT ELLEN 305
Machrihanish Golf Club CAMPBELTOWN 241

Machynlleth Golf Club MACHYNLLETH 327
Maesteg Golf Club MAESTEG 315
Magdalene Fields Golf Club BERWICK-UPON-TWEED 171
Magpie Hall Lane Municipal Golf Club BROMLEY 134
Mahee Island Golf Club BELFAST 332
Maidenhead Golf Club MAIDENHEAD 66
Malden Golf Club NEW MALDEN 194
Maldon Golf Club MALDON 111
Malkins Bank Golf Club SANBACH 75
Malone Golf Club BELFAST 329
Malton and Norton Golf Club MALTON 218
Manchester Golf Club MANCHESTER 155
Mangotsfield Golf Club BRISTOL 61
Mannings Heath Golf Club HORSHAM 202
Manor Golf Club BRADFORD 224
Manor House Hotel and Golf Course MORETONHAMPSTEAD 98
Mansfield Woodhouse Golf Club MANSFIELD 174
Mapledurham Golf Club MAPLEDURHAM 177
Mapperley Golf Club MAPPERLEY 174
March Golf Club MARCH 71
Market Drayton Golf Club MARKET DRAYTON 179
Market Harborough Golf Club MARKET HARBOROUGH 147
Market Rasen and District Golf Club MARKET RASEN 150
Marlborough Golf Club MARLBOROUGH 215
Marple Golf Club MARPLE 156
Marsden Golf Club HUDDERSFIELD 226
Marsden Park Golf Club NELSON 145
Maryport Golf Club MARYPORT 89
Masham Golf Club RIPON 218
Massereene Golf Club ANTRIM 329
Matlock Golf Club Ltd. MATLOCK 94
Maxstoke Park Golf Club BIRMINGHAM 209
Maybole Golf Club MAYBOLE 246
Maylands Golf and Country Club ROMFORD 111
McDonald Golf Club ELLON 235
Mellor and Towncliffe Golf Club STOCKPORT 157
Melrose Golf Club MELROSE 298
Meltham Golf Club MELTHAM 229
Melton Mowbray Golf Club MELTON MOWBRAY 148
Melville Golf Range DALKEITH 375
Mendip Golf Club Ltd. SHEPTON MALLET 182
Mentmore Golf and Country Club LEIGHTON BUZZARD 64
Meon Valley Hotel, Golf and Country Club SOUTHAMPTON 119
Merchants of Edinburgh Golf Club EDINBURGH 258

THE GOLF GUIDE 1994 — INDEX

Mere Golf and Country Club KNUTSFORD 73
Merlin Golf Club NEWQUAY 81
Merthyr Tydfil (Cilsanws) Golf Club MERTHYR TYDFIL 315
Mickleover Golf Club MICKLEOVER 94
Mid-Dorset Golf Club OKEFORD FITZPAIGNE 104
Mid-Herts Golf Club ST. ALBANS 127
Mid-Kent Golf Club GRAVESEND 136
Middlesbrough Golf Club MIDDLESBROUGH 77
Middlesbrough Golf Municipal Centre MIDDLESBROUGH 77
Middleton Park (Municipal) Golf Club LEEDS 228
Milford Haven Golf Club MILFORD HAVEN 312
Mill Hill Golf Club LONDON 58
Mill Ride Golf Club NORTH ASCOT 66
Millbrook Golf Course AMPTHILL 63
Millport Golf Club MILLPORT 304
Milnathort Golf Club MILNATHORT 280
Milngavie Golf Club GLASGOW 275
Minchinhampton Golf Club MINCHINHAMPTON 115
Minehead & West Somerset Golf Club MINEHEAD 182
Minto Golf Club HAWICK 297
Mitcham Golf Club MITCHAM 194
Moffat Golf Club MOFFAT 253
Mold Golf Club MOLD 310
Monifieth Golf Links MONIFIETH 238
Monmouth Golf Club MONMOUTH 319
Monmouthshire Golf Club ABERGAVENNY 319
Monte Carlo Golf Club MONTE CARLO 355
Monte Mayor Golf Club BENAHAVIS 364
Montecastillo CADIZ 364
Montrose Links Trust MONTROSE 240
Moor Allerton Golf Club LEEDS 228
Moor Hall Golf Club Ltd SUTTON COLDFIELD 212
Moor Park Golf Club RICKMANSWORTH 127
Moore Place Golf Club ESHER 193
Moors Valley Golf Centre RINGWOOD 119
Moortown Golf Club LEEDS 228
Moray Golf Club LOSSIEMOUTH 285
Morecambe Golf Club Ltd. MORECAMBE 145
Morlais Castle Golf Club MERTHYR TYDFIL 315
Morpeth Golf Club MORPETH 172
Morriston Golf Club SWANSEA 318
Mortonhall Golf Club EDINBURGH 258
Moseley Golf Club BIRMINGHAM 209
Mottram Hall Golf Course PRESTBURY 75
Mount Ellen Golf Club GARTCOSH 282
Mount Juliet Golf Club THOMASTOWN 340
Mount Oswald Golf Club DURHAM 107
Mountain Ash Golf Club MOUNTAIN ASH 315
Mountain Lakes Golf and Country Club CAERPHILLY 315

Mouse Valley Golf Course LANARK 283
Mowsbury Golf Club BEDFORD 64
Moyola Park Golf Club MAGHERAFELT 334
Muckhart Golf Club DOLLAR 251
Muir of Ord Golf Club MUIR OF ORD 297
Mullion Golf Club HELSTON 81
Mundesley Golf Club NOWRICH 166
Murcar Golf Club ABERDEEN 234
Murrayfield Golf Club EDINBURGH 258
Murrayshall Golf Course SCONE 294
Muskerry Golf Club CARRICROHANE 337
Musselburgh Golf Club MUSSELBURGH 261
Muswell Hill Golf Club WOOD GREEN 60
Muthill Golf Club CRIEFF 293

Nairn Dunbar Golf Club NAIRN 286
Nairn Golf Club NAIRN 286
Neath Golf Club NEATH 318
Nefyn District Golf Club NEFYN 324
Nelson Golf Club NELSON 145
Nevill Golf Club TUNBRIDGE WELLS 140
New Course ST ANDREWS 271
New Cumnock Golf Club NEW CUMMOCK 246
New Forest Golf Club LYNDHURST 119
New Galloway Golf Club NEW GALLOWAY 281
New Golf Lucien Barriere Deauville DEAUVILLE 348
New Mills Golf Club STOCKPORT 94
New North Manchester Golf Club Ltd MANCHESTER 155
New Zealand Golf Club Addlestone 196
Newark Golf Club NEWARK 174
Newbattle Golf Club Ltd DALKEITH 256
Newbiggin-by-the-Sea Golf Club Ltd NEWBIGGIN-BY-THE-SEA 172
Newbold Comyn Golf Club LEAMINGTON SPA 207
Newburgh-on-Ythan Golf Club ELLON 235
Newbury & Crookham Golf Club NEWBURY 66
Newby Grange Golf Club CARLISLE 88
Newcastle United Golf Club NEWCASTLE-UPON-TYNE 204
Newcastle-under-Lyme Golf Club NEWCASTLE UNDER LYME 184
Newcastle-under-Lyme Municipal Golf Club NEWCASTLE-UNDER-LYME 184
Newcastleton Golf Club NEWCASTLETON 298
Newmachar Golf Club MEWMACHAR 236
Newport (I.O.W.) Golf Club NEWPORT 132
Newport (Pembs) Golf Club NEWPORT 313
Newport Golf Club NEWPORT 320
Newquay Golf Club NEWQUAY 82
Newton Abbot (Stover) Golf Club NEWTON ABBOT 98
Newton Green Golf Club SUDBURY 188

INDEX

Newton Stewart Golf Club NEWTON STEWART 302
Newtonmore Golf Club NEWTONMORE 279
Newtownstewart Golf Club NEWTOWNSTEWART 336
Niddry Castle Golf Club WINCHBURGH 264
Nigg Bay Golf club ABERDEEN 234
Nizels Golf Club TONBRIDGE 140
Normanby Hall Golf Club SCUNTHORPE 131
Normandy Golf Range RENFREW 376
Normanton Golf Club NORMANTON 229
North Berwick Golf Club NORTH BERWICK 262
North Downs Golf Club WOLDINGHAM 197
North Foreland Golf Club BROADSTAIRS 133
North Hants Golf Club FLEET 117
North Middlesex Golf Club BARNET 55
North Oxford Golf Club OXFORD 177
North Shore Hotel and Golf Club SKEGNESS 150
North Wales Golf Club Ltd LLANDUDNO 322
North Warwickshire Golf Club Ltd COVENTRY 210
North Wilts Golf Club DEVIZES 214
North Worcestershire Golf Club BIRMINGHAM 209
Northampton Golf Club NORTHAMPTON 169
Northamptonshire County Golf Club NORTHAMPTON 170
Northcliffe Golf Club BRADFORD 224
Northenden Golf Club MANCHESTER 155
Northern Golf Club ABERDEEN 234
Northwood Golf Club NORTHWOOD 58
Nottingham City Golf Club NOTTINGHAM 174
Notts. Golf Club Ltd. KIRKBY IN ASHFIELD 174
Nuneaton Golf Club NUNEATON 207

Oadby Golf Club OADBY 148
Oak Park Golfing Complex CRONDALL 117
Oakdale Golf Club HARROGATE 218
Oake Manor Golf Club TAUNTON 182
Oaklands Golf Club TARPORLEY 76
Oakmere Park SOUTHWELL 175
Oaks Sport Centre Ltd CARSHALTON 189
Oastpark Golf Club SNODLAND 140
Okehampton Golf Club OKEHAMPTON 98
Old Colwyn Golf Club COLWYN 309
Old Course ST ANDREWS 271
Old Course Ranfurly Golf Club BRIDGE OF WIER 295
Old Fold Manor Golf Club BARNET 55
Old Links (Bolton) Ltd. BOLTON 153
Old Padeswood Golf Club Ltd PADESWOOD 310
Old Rectory Hotel & Golf Club CRICKHOWELL 325
Old Thorns Golf Course & Hotel LIPHOOK 118

Oldham Golf Club OLDHAM 156
Oldmeldrum Golf Club OLDMELDRUM 236
Olton Golf Club Ltd. SOLIHULL 211
Omagh Golf Club OMAGH 336
Omaha Beach Golf Club BAYEUX 347
Ombersley Golf Club DROITWICH 121
Onneley Golf Club CREWE 73
Oporto Golf Club ESPINHO 361
Orkney Golf Club KIRKWALL 305
Ormeau Golf Club BELFAST 332
Ormonde Fields Golf Club CODNOR 93
Ormskirk Golf Club ORMSKIRK 145
Orsett Golf Club ORSETT 111
Orton Meadows Golf Club PETERBOROUGH 71
Osborne Golf Club EAST COWES 132
Oswestry Golf Club OSWESTRY 179
Otley Golf Club OTLEY 229
Oundle Golf Club OUNDLE 170
Outlane Golf Club OUTLANE 229
Oxley Park Golf Club Ltd WOLVERHAMPTON 213

Pachesham Golf Centre LEATHERHEAD 194
Pachesham Golf Centre LEATHERHEAD 373
Padbrook Park Golf Club CULLOMPTON 96
Padeswood & Buckley Golf Club MOLD 310
Painswick Golf Club PAINSWICK 115
Painthorpe House Golf and Country Club WAKEFIELD 230
Paisley Golf Club PAISLEY 295
Palacerigg Golf Club CUMMBERNAULD 254
Palleg Golf Club SWANSEA 318
Palmares Golf Club LAGOS 359
Panmure Golf Club BARRY 237
Pannal Golf Club HARROGATE 218
Panshanger Golf Complex WELWYN GARDEN CITY 128
Park Golf Club SOUTHPORT 161
Parkhall Golf Course STOKE ON TRENT 184
Parklands Golf Club NEWCASTLE-UPON-TYNE 205
Parknasilla Golf Club SNEEM 340
Parkstone Golf Club POOLE 104
Parque da Floresta Golf and Country Club BUDENS/SALEMA 359
Pastures Golf Club MICKLEOVER 94
Patshull Park Hotel Golf and Country Club WOLVERHAMPTON 180
Pau Golf Club PAU 353
Peacehaven Golf Club NEWHAVEN 200
Peebles Golf Club PEEBLES 288
Peel Golf Club Ltd. PEEL 343
Penha Longa Golf Club ESTORIL 360
Penina Golf Club PORTIMAO/PENINA 359
Penmaenmawr Golf Club PENMAENMAWR 324
Penn Golf Club WOLVERHAMPTON 213

THE GOLF GUIDE 1994

INDEX

Pennard Golf Club SWANSEA 318
Pennington Golf Club (Municipal) LEIGH 154
Pennyhill Park Country Club BAGSHOT 189
Penrhos Golf and Country Club LLANRHYSTYD 312
Penrith Golf Club PENRITH 89
Penwortham Golf Club PRESTON 145
Perivale Park Golf Club GREENFORD 56
Perranporth Golf Club PERRANPORTH 85
Perton Park Golf Club WOLVERHAMPTON 214
Peterborough Milton Golf Club PETERBOROUGH 71
Peterhead Golf Club PETERHEAD 236
Petersfield Golf Club PETERSFIELD 119
Phoenix Golf Club ROTHERHAM 222
Pike Hills Golf Club YORK 221
Pikefold Golf Club MANCHESTER 155
Piltdown Golf Club UCKFIELD 200
Pine Cliffs Golf & Country Club ALBUFEIRA 358
Pinheiros Altos Golf Club QUINTA DO LAGO 359
Pinner Hill Golf Club PINNER 58
Pipps Hill Golf Club BASILDON 108
Pitlochry Golf Course PITLOCHRY 294
Pitreavie (Dunfermline) Golf Club DUNFERMLINE 267
Pleasington Golf Club BLACKBURN 142
Polkemmet Golf Course WHITBURN 264
Pollok Golf Club GLASGOW 275
Polmont Golf Club FALKIRK 299
Poniente Golf Club MAGALUFFCALVIA 366
Pontardawe Golf Club SWANSEA 318
Pontefract & District Golf Club PONTEFRACT 229
Ponteland Golf Club NEWCASTLE-UPON-TYNE 172
Pontnewydd Golf Club CWMBRAN 319
Pontypool Golf Club PONTYPOOL 320
Pontypridd Golf Club PONTYPRIDD 315
Port Bannatyne Golf Club ROTHESAY 304
Port Glasgow Golf Club PORT GLASGOW 296
Port Royal Golf Range EDINBURGH 376
Port St. Mary Golf Club PORT ST. MARY 343
Portadown Golf Club PORTADOWN 331
Porters Park Golf Club RADLETT 126
Porthmadog Golf Club MORFA BYCHAN 324
Portmarnock Golf Club PORTMARNOCK 339
Portobello Golf Club EDINBURGH 258
Portpatrick (Dunskey) Golf Club PORTPATRICK 303
Portsalon Golf Club LETTERKENNY 338
Portsmouth Golf Club (1926) PORTSMOUTH 119
Portstewart Golf Club PORTSTEWART 334
Potters Bar Golf Club POTTERS BAR 126

Poult Wood Public Golf Course TONBRIDGE 140
Poulton Park Golf Club Ltd. WARRINGTON 76
Poulton-le-Fylde Golf Club BLACKPOOL 142
Powfoot Golf Club ANNAN 251
Praa Sands Golf Club PENZANCE 82
Prenton Golf Club BIRKENHEAD 158
Prestatyn Golf Club PRESTATYN 310
Prestbury Golf Club MACCLESFIELD 74
Preston Golf Club PRESTON 145
Prestonfield Golf Club EDINBURGH 258
Prestwich Golf Club MANCHESTER 155
Prestwick Golf Club PRESTWICK 246
Prestwick St Cuthbert Golf Club PRESTWICK 246
Prestwick St Nicholas Golf Club PRESTWICK 246
Prince's Golf Club SANDWICH BAY 138
Priors Hall Golf Club CORBY 168
Prudhoe Golf Club PRUDHOE 172
Pulrose Golf Course DOUGLAS 343
Pumpherston Golf Club LIVINGSTON 261
Purley Chase Golf & Country Club "1990" NORTH WARWICKSHIRE 207
Purley Downs Golf Club PURLEY 195
Puttenham Golf Club GUILDFORD 193
Pwllheli Golf Club PWLLHELI 325
Pyecombe Golf Club BRIGHTON 198
Pyle & Kenfig Golf Club KENFIG 315
Pype Hayes Golf Club SUTTON COLDFIELD 212

Queen's Park Bournemouth GC BOURNEMOUTH 102
Queens Park Golf Course CREWE 73
Queensbury Golf Club BRADFORD 224
Quietwaters Hotel, Golf and Country Club MALDON 111
Quinta Do Gramacho Golf Club LAGOA 359
Quinta da Marinha Golf Club ESTORIL 360

RAF Benson WALLINGFORD 177
RAF St. Athan Golf Club BARRY 316
Radcliffe-on-Trent Golf Club RADCLIFFE-ON-TRENT 175
Radnor Golf and Ski Centre REDRUTH 85
Radnor Golf and Ski Centre REDRUTH 371
Radyr Golf Club CARDIFF 317
Ralston Golf Club PAISLEY 296
Ramsdale Park Golf Centre CALVERTON 173
Ramsdale Park Golf Centre CALVERTON 373
Ramsey Golf Club HUNTINGDON 71
Ramsey Golf Club RAMSEY 343
Ranfurly Castle Golf Club Ltd BRIDGE OF WEIR 295
Rathmore Golf Club PORTRUSH 330

INDEX

Ratho Park Golf Club NEWBRIDGE 261
Ravelston Golf Club Ltd EDINBURGH 258
Raven Hall Country House Hotel GC SCARBOROUGH 219
Ravensworth Golf Club Ltd. GATESHEAD 204
Rawdon Golf & Lawn Tennis Club LEEDS 228
Reading Golf Club READING 66
Real Golf de Bendinat PALMA 366
Reay Golf Club THURSO 250
Redbourn Golf Club ST. ALBANS 128
Reddish Vale Golf Club STOCKPORT 157
Redditch Golf Club REDDITCH 122
Redditch Kingfisher Golf Club REDDITCH 123
Redhill and Reigate Golf Club REDHILL 195
Regent Park Golf Club Ltd BOLTON 153
Reigate Heath Golf Club REIGATE 195
Renfrew Golf Club RENFREW 296
Renishaw Park Golf Club SHEFFIELD 94
Retford Golf Club Ltd. RETFORD 175
Rhondda Golf Club RHONDDA 316
Rhos-on-Sea Residential Golf Club LLANDUDNO 322
Rhosgoch Golf Club BUILTH WELLS 325
Rhuddlan Golf Club RHUDDLAN 310
Rhyl Golf Club RHYL 310
Richmond (Yorkshire) Golf Club RICHMOND 218
Richmond Golf Centre RICHMOND 374
Richmond Golf Club RICHMOND 195
Rickmansworth Public Golf Course RICKMANSWORTH 127
Riddlesden Golf Club KEIGHLEY 227
Ringway Golf Club ALTRINCHAM 152
Ripon City Golf Club RIPON 219
Risebridge Golf Centre ROMFORD 111
Rishton Golf Club BLACKBURN 142
Riviera Golf Club CANNES 354
Robin Hood Golf Club SOLIHULL 211
Rochdale Golf Club ROCHDALE 156
Rochester and Cobham Park Golf Club ROCHESTER 138
Roehampton Club Ltd. ROEHAMPTON 58
Rolls Of Monmouth Golf Club MONMOUTH 320
Romanby Golf Course NORTHALLERTON 218
Romiley Golf Club STOCKPORT 157
Romney Warren Golf Club NEW ROMNEY 137
Rookery Park Golf Club LOWESTOFT 187
Roscommon Golf Club ROSCOMMON 342
Rose Hill Golf Club BIRMINGHAM 209
Roseberry Grange Golf Club CHESTER-LE-STREET 106
Rosehearty Golf Club ROSEHEARTY 236
Ross-on-Wye Golf Club ROSS-ON-WYE 123
Rossendale Golf Club Ltd. ROSSENDALE 146
Rothbury Golf Club ROTHBURY 172
Rotherham Golf Club Ltd ROTHERHAM 222
Rothesay Golf Club ROTHESAY 304

THE GOLF GUIDE 1994

Rothley Park Golf Club ROTHLEY 148
Roundhay Golf Club LEEDS 228
Routenburn Golf Club LARGS 245
Rowany Golf Club PORT ERIN 343
Rowlands Castle Golf Club HAVANT 118
Royal Aberdeen Golf Club ABERDEEN 234
Royal Ascot Golf Club ASCOT 65
Royal Ashdown Forest Golf Club (Old Course) EAST GRINSTEAD 198
Royal Belfast Golf Club HOLYWOOD 333
Royal Birkdale Golf Club SOUTHPORT 161
Royal Blackheath Golf Club ELTHAM 56
Royal Burgess Golfing Society of Edinburgh EDINBURGH 258
Royal Cinque Ports Golf Club DEAL 135
Royal County Down Golf Club NEWCASTLE 333
Royal Cromer Golf Club CROMER 164
Royal Dornoch Golf Club DORNOCH 301
Royal Dublin Golf Club DUBLIN 339
Royal Eastbourne Golf Club EASTBOURNE 199
Royal Epping Forest Golf Club CHINGFORD 55
Royal Forest of Dean Golf Club COLEFORD 114
Royal Golf Club d'Evian EVIAN-LES-BAINS 352
Royal Guernsey Golf Club GUERNSEY 345
Royal Jersey Golf Club JERSEY 345
Royal Liverpool Golf Club HOYLAKE 160
Royal Lytham & St. Annes Golf LYTHAM ST. ANNES 144
Royal Mid-Surrey Golf Club RICHMOND 195
Royal Montrose Golf Club MONTROSE 240
Royal Musselburgh Golf Club PRESTONPANS 262
Royal North Devon Golf Club WESTWARD HO 101
Royal Norwich Golf Club HELLESDON 165
Royal Porthcawl Golf Club PORTHCAWL 316
Royal Portrush Golf Club PORTRUSH 330
Royal St David's Golf Club HARLECH 322
Royal St. Georges Golf Club SANDWICH 139
Royal Tara Golf club NAVAN 342
Royal Tarlair Golf Club MACDUFF 249
Royal Troon Golf Club TROON 247
Royal West Norfolk Golf Club KING'S LYNN 165
Royal Wimbledon Golf Club WIMBLEDON 60
Royal Winchester Golf Club WINCHESTER 120
Royal Worlington and Newmarket Golf Club BURY ST. EDMUNDS 186
Royston Golf Club ROYSTON 127
Ruddington Grange Golf Club NOTTINGHAM 175
Rugby Golf Club RUGBY 207
Ruislip Golf Club RUISLIP 59
Runcorn Golf Club RUNCORN 75
Rushcliffe Golf Club EASTLAKE 173
Rushden Golf Club RUSHDEN 170

THE GOLF GUIDE 1994　　　　　　　　　　　　　　　　　　　　　　　　　　　　　　　INDEX

Rushmere Golf Club IPSWICH 187
Rustington Golf Centre LITTLEHAMPTON 374
Ruthin Pwllglas Golf Club RUTHIN 311
Rutland County Golf Club STAMFORD 151
Ruxley Park Golf Centre ORPINGTON 137
Ruxley Park Golf Centre ORPINGTON 373
Ryburn Golf Club HALIFAX 225
Ryde Golf Club RYDE 132
Rye Golf Course RYE 200
Ryston Park Golf Club DOWNHAM MARKET 164
Ryton Golf Club RYTON 205

Saddleworth Golf Club OLDHAM 156
Saffron Walden Golf Club SAFFRON WALDEN 110
Sale Golf Club SALE 156
Saline Golf Club DUNFERMLINE 267
Salisbury & South Wilts Golf Club SALISBURY 215
Saltburn by the Sea Golf Club Ltd SALTBURN BY THE SEA 78
Saltford Golf Club SALTFORD 63
San Lorenzo Golf Club ALMANSIL 358
San Roque Club SAN ROQUE 364
Sand Moor Golf Club Ltd. LEEDS 228
Sandbach Golf Club SANDBACH 75
Sandford Springs Golf Club BASINGSTOKE 116
Sandilands Golf Club MABLETHORPE 149
Sandiway Golf Club NORTHWICH 75
Sandown Golf Centre ESHER 193
Sandown Golf Centre ESHER 373
Sandwell Park Golf Club WEST BROMWICH 213
Sandy Lodge Golf Club NORTHWOOD 58
Sandyhills Golf Club GLASGOW 275
Sanquhar Golf Club SANQUHAR 253
Santa Ponsa Golf Club One SANTA PONSA 368
Santa Ponsa Golf Club Two SANTA PONSA 368
Sapey Golf Club BROMYARD 121
Saunton Golf Club BRAUNTON 95
Scarborough North Cliff Golf Club SCARBOROUGH 219
Scarborough South Cliff Golf Club Ltd SCARBOROUGH 219
Scarcroft Golf Club LEEDS 228
Scoonie Golf Club LEVEN 269
Scotscraig Golf Club TAYPORT 272
Scrabo Golf Club NEWTOWNARDS 333
Scraptoft Golf Club LEICESTER 147
Scunthorpe Golf Club SCUNTHORPE 131
Seacroft Golf Club SKEGNESS 150
Seafield Golf Course AYR 244
Seaford Golf Club SEAFORD 200
Seaham Golf Club SEAHAM 107
Seahouses Golf Club SEAHOUSES 173
Seascale Golf Club SEASCALE 90

Seaton Carew Golf Club HARTLEPOOL 77
Sedbergh Golf Club SEDBERGH 90
Sedgley Golf Centre DUDLEY 211
Seedy Mill Golf Club LICHFIELD 184
Selby Golf Club SELBY 219
Selkirk Golf Club SELKIRK 299
Selsdon Park Hotel Golf Course CROYDON 192
Selsey Golf Club CHICHESTER 201
Sene Valley Golf Club FOLKESTONE 136
Serlby Park Golf Club DONCASTER 222
Settle Golf Club SETTLE 220
Shandon Park Golf Club BELFAST 332
Shanklin & Sandown Golf Club SANDOWN 132
Shaw Hill Hotel Golf & Country Club CHORLEY 143
Shay Grange Golf Centre BRADFORD 375
Sheerness Golf Club SHEERNESS 139
Sherborne Golf Club SHERBORNE 104
Sherdley Park Golf Club ST HELENS 163
Sheringham Golf Club SHERINGHAM 167
Sherwood Forest Golf Club MANSFIELD 174
Shetland Golf Club LERWICK 306
Shifnal Golf Club SHIFNAL 179
Shillinglee Park Golf Club CHIDDINGFOLD 189
Shipley Golf Club BRADFORD 224
Shirehampton Park Golf Club BRISTOL 62
Shirland Golf Club SHIRLAND 94
Shirley Golf Club SHIRLEY 211
Shirley Park Golf Club Ltd. CROYDON 192
Shiskine Golf & Tennis Club BLACKWATERFOOT 303
Shooters Hill Golf Club SHOOTERS HILL 59
Shortlands Golf Club BROMLEY 133
Shotts Golf Club SHOTTS 283
Shrewsbury Golf Club SHREWSBURY 179
Shrigley Hall Golf and Country Club MACCLESFIELD 74
Shrivenham Park Golf Course SHRIVENHAM 215
Sickleholme Golf Club SHEFFIELD 94
Sidcup Golf Club (1926) Ltd. SIDCUP 140
Sidmouth Golf Club SIDMOUTH 98
Silecroft Golf Club MILLOM 89
Silkstone Golf Club BARNSLEY 221
Silloth On Solway Golf Club SILLOTH 90
Silsden Golf Club KEIGHLEY 227
Silver Springs Golf Club TIVOLI 338
Silverdale Golf Club CARNFORTH 143
Silverknowes Golf Club EDINBURGH 259
Silvermere Driving Range COBHAM 373
Silvermere Golf & Leisure Complex COBHAM 190
Silverstone Golf Club STOWE 70
Silverstone Golf Club STOWE 371
Sindlesham Driving Range WOKINGHAM 370
Singing Hills Golf Course Ltd ALBOURNE 201

INDEX

Sittingbourne and Milton Regis SITTINGBOURNE 140
Sitwell Park Golf Club ROTHERHAM 222
Skeabost Golf Club SKEABOST BRIDGE 306
Skelmorlie Golf Club SKELMORLIE 246
Skipton Golf Club SKIPTON 220
Sleaford Golf Club SLEAFORD 150
Slinfold Park Golf and Country Club HORSHAM 203
Sociedade do Golfe da Quinta do Lago S.A. ALMANSIL 359
Son Servera Golf Club SON SERVERA 368
Son Vida Golf Club PALMA 366
Sonning Golf Club SONNING 66
South Beds. Golf Club LUTON 64
South Bradford Golf Club BRADFORD 224
South Herts Golf Club TOTTERIDGE 59
South Kyme Golf Club SOUTH KYME 150
South Leeds Golf Club LEEDS 228
South Moor Golf Club STANLEY 107
South Pembrokeshire Golf Club PEMBROKE 313
South Shields Golf Club Ltd. SOUTH SHIELDS 205
South Staffordshire Golf Club WOLVERHAMPTON 214
Southend-on-Sea Golf Club SOUTHEND-ON-SEA 111
Southerndown Golf Club BRIDGEND 314
Southerness Golf Club DUMFRIES 252
Southfield Golf Club OXFORD 177
Southport & Ainsdale Golf Club SOUTHPORT 162
Southport Municipal Golf Club SOUTHPORT 162
Southport Old Links Golf Club SOUTHPORT 162
Southsea Golf Club PORTSMOUTH 119
Southwick Park Golf Club FAREHAM 117
Southwold Golf Club SOUTHWOLD 188
Southwood Golf Course FARNBOROUGH 117
Spa Golf Club BALLYNAHINCH 331
Spalding Golf Club SPALDING 150
Spean Bridge Golf Club SPEAN BRIDGE 279
Spey Bay Golf Club FOCHABERS 285
Springfield Park Golf Club LONDON 58
Springfield Park Golf Club ROCHDALE 156
Springhead Park Golf Club HULL 130
Sprowston Park Golf Club NORWICH 167
St Deiniol Golf Club BANGOR 321
St. Cleres Golf Club STANFORD LE HOPE 112
St. Andrews Links ST ANDREWS 271
St. Annes Old Links Golf Club LYTHAM ST. ANNES 145
St. Augustine's Golf Club RAMSGATE 138
St. Austell Golf Club ST. AUSTELL 85
St. Bees Golf Club WHITEHAVEN 90

THE GOLF GUIDE 1994

St. Boswells Golf Club ST. BOSWELLS 298
St. David's City Golf Club ST. DAVID'S 313
St. Enodoc Golf Club WADEBRIDGE 86
St. Fillans Golf Club CRIEFF 293
St. George's Hill Golf Club WEYBRIDGE 197
St. Giles Golf Club NEWTOWN 327
St. Idloes Golf Club LLANIDLOES 327
St. Ives (Hunts) Golf Club ST. IVES 71
St. Margaret's Golf Club ST. MARGARETS 339
St. Medan Golf Club PORT WILLIAM 302
St. Mellion Golf and Country Club SALTASH 85
St. Mellons Golf Club CARDIFF 317
St. Melyd Golf Club PRESTATYN 310
St. Michael's Jubilee Golf Club WIDNES 76
St. Michaels Golf Club LEUCHARS 269
St. Neots Golf Club ST. NEOTS 71
St. Pierre Hotel Golf & Country Club Ltd CHEPSTOW 319
St. Pierre Park Golf Club GUERNSEY 345
Staddon Heights Golf Club PLYMOUTH 98
Stafford Castle Golf Club STAFFORD 184
Stamford Golf Club STALYBRIDGE 75
Stand Golf Club MANCHESTER 155
Stanedge Golf Club CHESTERFIELD 93
Stanmore Golf Club STANMORE 59
Stanton-on-the-Wolds Golf Club STANTON-ON-THE-WOLDS 175
Stapleford Abbotts Golf Club STAPLEFORD ABBOTTS 112
Staverton Park Hotel and Golf Club DAVENTRY 168
Stevenage Golf Centre STEVENAGE 128
Stinchcombe Hill Golf Club DURSLEY 114
Stirling Golf Club STIRLING 300
Stock Brook Manor Golf Club BILLERICAY 108
Stockport Golf Club Ltd. STOCKPORT 157
Stocksbridge and District Golf Club Ltd SHEFFIELD 223
Stocksfield Golf Club STOCKSFIELD 173
Stockwood Park Golf Club LUTON 65
Stoke By Nayland Golf Club COLCHESTER 186
Stoke Poges Golf Club STOKE POGES 69
Stoke Rochford Golf Club GRANTHAM 149
Stone Golf Club STONE 185
Stoneham Golf Club SOUTHAMPTON 120
Stonehaven Golf Club STONEHAVEN 279
Stoneyholme Municipal Golf Club CARLISLE 88
Stornoway Golf Club STORNOWAY 305
Stourbridge Golf Club STOURBRIDGE 212
Stowe Golf Club STOWE 70
Stowmarket Golf Club Ltd STOWMARKET 188
Strabane Golf Club STRABANE 336
Stranraer Golf Club STRANRAER 303
Stratford Oaks Golf Club STRATFORD UPON AVON 207

THE GOLF GUIDE 1994 INDEX

Stratford-on-Avon Golf Club STRATFORD-UPON-AVON 207
Strathaven Golf Club STRATHAVEN 284
Strathclyde Park Golf Club HAMILTON 283
Strathendrick Golf Club DRYMAN 299
Strathlene Golf Club BUCKIE 249
Strathpeffer Spa Golf Club STRATHPEFFER 297
Strathtay Golf Club STRATHTAY 294
Strawberry Hill Golf Club TWICKENHAM 59
Stressholme Golf Club DARLINGTON 107
Stromness Golf Club Ltd STROMNESS 306
Sturminster Marshall Golf Club WIMBORNE 105
Sudbury Golf Club Ltd. WEMBLEY 60
Sunbury Golf Club SHEPPERTON 59
Sundridge Park Golf Club BROMLEY 133
Sunningdale Golf Club SUNNINGDALE 195
Sunningdale Ladies Golf Club SUNNINGDALE 67
Surbiton Golf Club CHESSINGTON 189
Sutton Bridge Golf Club SPALDING 150
Sutton Coldfield Golf Club SUTTON COLDFIELD 212
Sutton Park Municipal Golf Club HULL 130
Swaffham Golf Club SWAFFHAM 167
Swansea Bay Golf Club NEATH 318
Swanston Golf Club EDINBURGH 259
Swindon Golf Club DUDLEY 211
Swindon Golf Club SWINDON 215
Swindon Ridge Golf Driving Range DUDLEY 211
Swindon Ridge Golf Driving Range DUDLEY 375
Swinley Forest Golf Club ASCOT 65
Swinton Park Golf Club MANCHESTER 155

Tadmarton Heath Golf Club BANBURY 176
Tain Golf Club TAIN 297
Tall Pines Golf Club BRISTOL 62
Tamworth Municipal Golf Club TAMWORTH 185
Tandragee Golf Club TANDRAGEE 331
Tandridge Golf Club OXTED 195
Tankersley Park Golf Club SHEFFIELD 223
Tapton Park Golf Club CHESTERFIELD 93
Tarbat Golf Club FEARN 296
Tarbert Golf Club TARBERT 242
Tarland Golf Club ABERDEEN 235
Taunton Golf Club TAUNTON 182
Taunton and Pickeridge Golf Club TAUNTON 182
Tavistock Golf Club TAVISTOCK 98
Taymouth Castle Golf Course ABERFELDY 290
Taynuilt Golf Club TAYNUILT 242
Teesside Golf Club STOCKTON-ON-TEES 78
Tehidy Park Golf Club CAMBORNE 79
Teignmouth Golf Club TEIGNMOUTH 98
Telford Hotel Golf & Country Club TELFORD 179
Temple Golf Club MAIDENHEAD 66

Temple Newsam Golf Club LEEDS 229
Tenby Golf Club TENBY 313
Tenterden Golf Club TENTERDEN 140
Test Valley Golf Club BASINGSTOKE 116
Tewkesbury Park Hotel, Golf & Country Club TEWKESBURY 115
Thames Ditton & Esher Golf Club ESHER 193
The European Club BRITTAS BAY 342
The Grove Golf Centre LEOMINSTER 372
The Heath Golf Club PORTLAOISE 341
The Honourable Company of Edinburgh Golfers GULLANE 260
The Langdon Hills Golf Club BULPHAN 108
The London Golf Centre NORTHOLT 58
The Long Ashton Golf Club BRISTOL 62
The Manor of Groves Golf and Country Club SAWBRIDGEWORTH 127
The Northumberland Golf Club Ltd NEWCASTLE-UPON-TYNE 205
The Vale Golf and Country Club PERSHORE 122
The Warley Park Golf Club BRENTWOOD 108
The Warrington Golf Club APPLETON 72
The Wirral Ladies Golf Club Ltd BIRKENHEAD 158
The Woll Golf Course ASHKIRK 299
The Worcestershire Golf Club MALVERN WELLS 122
Thetford Golf Club THETFORD 167
Theydon Bois Golf Club EPPING 110
Thirsk and Northallerton Golf Club THIRSK 220
Thomstone Park Golf Club and Driving Range WESTBURY 375
Thorndon Park Golf Club Ltd. BRENTWOOD 108
Thorne Golf Club DONCASTER 222
Thornhill Golf Club THORNHILL 253
Thornton Golf Club THORNTON 272
Thorpe Hall Golf Club SOUTHEND-ON-SEA 112
Thorpe Wood Golf Course PETERBOROUGH 71
Thorpeness Golf Club Hotel THORPENESS 188
Thoulstone Park Golf Club WESTBURY 216
Three Hammers Golf Complex WOLVERHAMPTON 375
Three Locks Golf Club MILTON KEYNES 69
Three Rivers Golf & Country Club CHELMSFORD 110
Thurlestone Golf Club THURLESTONE 99
Thurso Golf Club THURSO 250
Tidworth Garrison Golf Club TIDWORTH 216
Tilgate Forest Golf Centre CRAWLEY 202
Tillicoultry Golf Club STIRLING 251
Tilsworth Golf Centre LEIGHTON BUZZARD 64
Tinsley Park Golf Club (Municipal) SHEFFIELD 223
Tiverton Golf Club TIVERTON 100
Tobermory Golf Club TOBERMORY 305

INDEX

Todmorden Golf Club TODMORDEN 230
Tolladine Golf Club WORCESTER 123
Toot Hill Golf Club ONGAR 111
Torphin Hill Golf Club EDINBURGH 259
Torphins Golf Club TORPHINS 236
Torquay Golf Club TORQUAY 100
Torrance House Golf Club EAST KILBRIDE 282
Torrington Golf Club TORRINGTON 100
Torvean Golf Club INVERNESS 278
Torwoodlee Golf Club GALASHIELS 299
Towerlands Golf Club BRAINTREE 108
Towerlands Golf Club BRAINTREE 371
Towneley Golf Club BURNLEY 143
Tracy Park Golf and Country Club BRISTOL 62
Traigh Golf Course ARISAIG 276
Tralee Golf Club TRALEE 340
Tredegar & Rhymney Golf Club RHYMNEY 320
Tredegar Park Golf Club NEWPORT 320
Tregenna Castle Hotel Golf Club ST. IVES 85
Treloy Golf Club NEWQUAY 82
Trent Park Golf Club LONDON 58
Trentham Golf Club STOKE-ON-TRENT 185
Trentham Park Golf Club STOKE-ON-TRENT 185
Trevose Golf and Country Club PADSTOW 82
Troia Golf Club TROIA 361
Troon Municipal Golf Course TROON 247
Truro Golf Club TRURO 86
Tudor Park Golf and Country Club MAIDSTONE 137
Tulliallan Golf Club KINCARDINE 268
Tunbridge Wells Golf Club TUNBRIDGE WELLS 141
Turnberry Hotel Golf Courses TURNBERRY 247
Turnhouse Golf Club EDINBURGH 259
Turriff Golf Club TURRIFF 237
Turton Golf Club BOLTON 153
Twickenham Golf Course TWICKENHAM 60
Tylney Park Golf Club BASINGSTOKE 116
Tynedale Golf Club HEXHAM 172
Tynemouth Golf Club Ltd. TYNEMOUTH 173
Tyneside Golf Club Ltd NEWCASTLE-UPON-TYNE 205
Tyrrells Wood Golf Club Ltd LEATHERHEAD 194
Tytherington Golf Club MACCLESFIELD 74

Ufford Park Hotel Golf & Leisure WOODBRIDGE 188
Ullesthorpe Court Golf Club LUTTERWORTH 147
Ulverston Golf Club Ltd ULVERSTON 90
Upavon (RAF) Golf Club PEWSEY 215
Upchurch River Valley Golf Courses SITTINGBOURNE 140
Uphall Golf Club UPHALL 262
Upminster Golf Club UPMINSTER 60
Upton-By-Chester Golf Club CHESTER 72
Uttoxeter Golf Club UTTOXETER 185
Uxbridge Golf Course UXBRIDGE 60

Vale da Pinta LAGOA 359
Vale do Lobo Golf Club ALMANSIL 359
Vale of Leven Golf Club ALEXANDRIA 253
Vale of Llangollen Golf Club LLANGOLLEN 310
Vall D'Or Golf Club CALA D'OR 366
Vaul Golf Club SCARINISH 306
Ventnor Golf Club VENTNOR 132
Verulam Golf Club ST. ALBANS 127
Vicars Cross Golf Club CHESTER 72
Vilamoura One (The Old Course) VILAMOURA 360
Vilamoura Three and Four VILAMOURA 360
Vilamoura Two (The New Course) VILAMOURA 360
Vimeiro Golf Club VIMEIRO 361
Vivary Park Public Golf Course TAUNTON 182

Wakefield Golf Club WAKEFIELD 230
Waldringfield Heath Golf Club WOODBRIDGE 188
Wallasey Golf Club WALLASEY 163
Wallsend Golf Club WALLSEND 206
Walmer and Kingsdown Golf Club DEAL 135
Walmersley Golf Club BURY 153
Walmley Golf Club SUTTON COLDFIELD 212
Walsall Golf Club WALSALL 213
Walton Hall Golf Club WARRINGTON 76
Walton Heath Golf Club TADWORTH 196
Wanstead Golf Club WANSTEAD 60
Wareham Golf Club WAREHAM 105
Warkworth Golf Club MORPETH 172
Warley Golf Club WARLEY 213
Warren Golf Club DAWLISH 96
Warren Golf Club MALDON 111
Warren Golf Club WALLASEY 163
Warrenpoint Golf Club WARRENPOINT 333
Warwick Golf Centre WARWICK 208
Warwick Golf Centre WARWICK 374
Washington Moat House Golf Club WASHINGTON 206
Washington Moat House Golf Club WASHINGTON 374
Waterhall Golf Club BRIGHTON 198
Waterlooville Golf Club PORTSMOUTH 119
Wath Golf Club ROTHERHAM 222
Wavendon Golf Centre MILTON KEYNES 69
Weald of Kent Golf Course HEADCORN 136
Wearside Golf Club SUNDERLAND 205
Welcombe Hotel Golf Course STRATFORD UPON AVON 208

THE GOLF GUIDE 1994 — INDEX

Wellingborough Golf Club WELLINGBOROUGH 170
Wells (Somerset) Golf Club Ltd WELLS 183
Wellshurst Golf and Country Club HAILSHAM 199
Wellshurst Golf and Country Club HELLINGLY 374
Welshpool Golf Club WELSHPOOL 327
Welwyn Garden City Golf Club Ltd WELWYN GARDEN CITY 128
Wensum Valley Golf Club NORWICH 167
Wentworth Club Ltd VIRGINIA WATER 196
Wenvoe Castle Golf Club CARDIFF 317
Wergs Golf Club WOLVERHAMPTON 214
Werneth Golf Club OLDHAM 156
Werneth Low Golf Club HYDE 154
Wessex Golf Centre WEYMOUTH 105
West Berkshire Golf Club NEWBURY 66
West Bowling Golf Club Ltd. BRADFORD 224
West Bradford Golf Club Ltd BRADFORD 225
West Byfleet Golf Club WEST BYFLEET 196
West Chiltington Golf Club WEST CHILTINGTON 203
West Cornwall Golf Club ST. IVES 85
West Derby Golf Club LIVERPOOL 161
West End Golf Club (Halifax) Ltd HALIFAX 225
West Essex Golf Club CHINGFORD 55
West Herts Golf Club WATFORD 128
West Hill Golf Club BROOKWOOD 189
West Hove Golf Club HOVE 200
West Kent Golf Club ORPINGTON 138
West Kilbride Golf Club WEST KILBRIDE 247
West Lancashire Golf Club BLUNDELL SANDS 159
West Linton Golf Club WEST LINTON 288
West Lothian Golf Club LINLITHGOW 261
West Malling Golf Club MAIDSTONE 137
West Middlesex Golf Club SOUTHALL 59
West Monmouthshire Golf Club NANTYGLO 320
West Park Golf and Country Club TOWCESTER 170
West Surrey Golf Club GODALMING 193
West Sussex Golf Club PULBOROUGH 203
West Wilts Golf Club WARMINSTER 216
Westerhope Golf Club NEWCASTLE-UPON-TYNE 205
Western Gailes Golf Club IRVINE 245
Western Park Golf Club LEICESTER 147
Westerwood Golf Club CUMBERNAULD 254
Westgate and Birchington Golf Club WESTGATE ON SEA 141
Westhill Golf Club WESTHILL 237
Westhoughton Golf Club WESTHOUGHTON 157
Weston Turville Golf and Squash Club AYLESBURY 67

Weston-Super-Mare Golf Club WESTON-SUPER-MARE 63
Westonbirt Golf Club TETBURY 115
Westray Golf Club WESTRAY 306
Westwood Golf Club LEEK 184
Wetherby Golf Club WETHERBY 230
Wexham Park Golf Course WEXHAM 70
Weymouth Golf Club Ltd WEYMOUTH 105
Whaddon Golf Centre ROYSTON 371
Whalley Golf Club BLACKBURN 142
Wheatley Golf Club DONCASTER 222
Whetstone Golf Club and Driving Range LEICESTER 147
Whickham Golf Club Ltd. NEWCASTLE-UPON-TYNE 205
Whipsnade Park Golf Club DAGNALL 124
Whitburn Golf Club SOUTH SHIELDS 205
Whitby Golf Club WHITBY 220
Whitchurch (Cardiff) Golf Club CARDIFF 317
Whitecraigs Golf Club GLASGOW 275
Whitefield Golf Club WHITEFIELD 158
Whitehall Golf Club NELSON 315
Whitehead Golf Club CARRICKFERGUS 330
Whitehill Golf Club WARE 128
Whitehill Golf Club WARE 372
Whitelakes Golf Club SOLIHULL 212
Whiteleaf Golf Club PRINCES RISBOROUGH 69
Whitewebbs Golf Club ENFIELD 56
Whiting Bay Golf Club WHITING BAY 304
Whitley Bay Golf Club WHITLEY BAY 206
Whitsand Bay Hotel Golf Club TORPOINT 85
Whitstable and Seasalter Golf Club WHITSTABLE 141
Whittaker Golf Club LITTLEBOROUGH 154
Whittington Barracks Golf Club LICHFIELD 184
Wick Golf Club WICK 250
Widnes Golf Club WIDNES 76
Widnes Municipal WIDNES 76
Widney Manor Golf Club SOLIHULL 212
Wigan Golf Club WIGAN 158
Wigtown and Bladnoch Golf Club WIGTOWN 303
Wigtownshire County Golf Club NEWTOWN STEWART 302
Wildernesse Golf Club SEVENOAKS 139
Willesley Park Golf Club ASHBY DE LA ZOUCH 146
William Wroe Municipal Golf Course TRAFFORD 157
Williamwood Golf Club GLASGOW 275
Willingdon Golf Club EASTBOURNE 199
Wilmslow Golf Club KNUTSFORD 74
Wilpshire Golf Club Ltd BLACKBURN 142
Wilton Golf Club REDCAR 78
Wimbledon Common Golf Club WIMBLEDON 60

399

INDEX

Wimbledon Park Golf Club WIMBLEDON 60
Windermere Golf Club WINDERMERE 90
Windlemere Golf Club WOKING 197
Windmill Hill Golf Course MILTON KEYNES 69
Windmill Hill Golf Course MILTON KEYNES 371
Windmill Village Hotel and Golf Club COVENTRY 210
Windwhistle Golf, Squash and Country Club Ltd CHARD 181
Windyhill Golf Club GLASGOW 275
Winter Hill Golf Club MAIDENHEAD 66
Winterfield Golf Club DUNBAR 257
Wishaw Golf Club WISHAW 284
Withernsea Golf Club WITHERNSEA 131
Withington Golf Club Ltd. MANCHESTER 156
Woburn Golf and Country Club MILTON KEYNES 69
Woking Golf Club WOKING 197
Wollaton Park Golf Club NOTTINGHAM 175
Wolstanton Golf Club WOLSTANTON 185
Wood Valley (Beccles) Golf Club BECCLES 186
Woodbridge Golf Club WOODBRIDGE 188
Woodbury Park Golf and Country Club EXETER 96
Woodcote Park Golf Club Ltd. COULSDON 190
Woodford Golf Club WOODFORD GREEN 112
Woodhall Hills Golf Club Ltd. PUDSEY 229
Woodhall Spa Golf Club WOODHALL SPA 151

Woodham Golf and Country Club NEWTOWN AYCLIFFE 107
Woodlands Manor Golf Club SEVENOAKS 139
Woodsome Hall Golf Club HUDDERSFIELD 226
Wooler Golf Club WOOLER 173
Woolton Golf Club LIVERPOOL 161
Worcester Golf and Country Club WORCESTER 123
Worfield Golf Club WORFIELD 180
Workington Golf Club WORKINGTON 90
Worksop Golf Club WORKSOP 175
Worlebury Golf Club WESTON-SUPER-MARE 63
Worplesdon Golf Club WOKING 197
Worsley Golf Club ECCLES 154
Worthing Golf Club WORTHING 203
Wortley Golf Club SHEFFIELD 223
Wrag Barn Golf Club HIGHWORTH 215
Wrangaton Golf Club SOUTH BRENT 98
Wrekin Golf Club TELFORD 180
Wrexham Golf Club WREXHAM 311
Wrotham Heath Golf Club SEVENOAKS 139
Wyboston Lakes Golf Club WYBOSTON 65
Wyke Green Golf Club ISLEWORTH 57

Yelverton Golf Club YELVERTON 101
Yeovil Golf Club YEOVIL 183
York Golf Club YORK 221
Youghal Golf Club YOUGHAL 338

THE GOLF GUIDE 1994

Index to Advertisers

Abbey Park Golf & Country Club 22,122
Achray House Hotel 292
Airlinks Golf Club 57
Aladdins Cave of Golf 54
Aldwark Manor Golf Hotel 216
Alma Lodge Hotel 157
Alsager Golf and Country Club 72
Alton Burn Hotel 287
Alvie Estate Office 9,278
Alyth Hotel 291
The Anchor Inn 182
Angus Hotel 291
Annandale Arms 253
Annanhill Golf Club 245
Appleby Manor Hotel 87
Ardchonnel Farm 242
The Ardlarig 285
Argyll Arms 241
Aston Hotel 217
Atlantic Hotel 162
Auchendean Lodge 9,278
Auchterarder Golf Club 291
Ayrshire Tourist Board 243

Balavoulin Hotel 278
Balbirnie House Hotel 8,269
Ballinrobe Golf Club 341
Barn Hill Farmhouse 115
Barnham Broom Hotel 166
Batch Farm Country Hotel 17,181
Battleborough Grange Country Club 182
Beacons Guest House 326
Beadlow Manor Hotel 63
Beaumaris Hotel 167
Beechmount 113
The Bel Alp Hotel 99
The Belfry 213
Belgravia Hotel 162
The Bell Craig Guest House 270
Royal Forest of Dean Golf Club 114
Belton Woods Hotel 25,149
Bissets Hotel 259

Black Lion Hotel 78
The Blacksmiths Arms 88
Blackwaterfoot Hotel 303
Blenheim House Hotel 262
Blue Bell Hotel 171
The Boat Hotel 277
Bodfor Hotel 320
Boothferry Borough Council 130
Boscawen 82
Braemar Hotel 241
Bridport Arms Hotel 102
Briggate Lodge Inn 131
Briggens House Hotel 128
The British Hotel 321
British Golf Museum 271
Broadsands Links Hotel 95
Broome Park Golf & Country Club 134
Brown Trout Golf & Country Club 334
Buccleuch Arms Hotel 298
Burnham and Berrow Golf Club 181
Busbiehill Guest House 245
Butts Hill Farm 139
Buxton Hotel 213

Caddy Matic 4
Caer Beris Manor Hotel 326
Caeu Capel Hotel 324
Cairndale Hotel 252
Calder House Private Hotel 91
Caledonian Thistle Hotel 8,234
Cape Wrath Hotel 301
Carlyon Bay Hotel 11,84
Carmichael Country Cottages 282
Castlerosse Hotel 340
Castletown Golf Links Hotel 18,343
Charlton Kings Hotel 113
Chartham Park Golf Club 202
Chequers Hotel 199
Chesfield Downs Fam Golf Centre 125
Clonyard House Hotel 281
Coast and Country Caravans 138
Cobblers Cottage 80
Coed-y-Mwstwr Hotel 18,314

INDEX   THE GOLF GUIDE 1994

Collingtree Park Golf Course 169
The Commodore Hotel 62
Coshieville Hotel 289
Cottesmore Golf and Country Club 202
Country Club Hotels 6,44
The Courtyard 100
The Courtyard 257
Craigesk Guest House 261
Craiglea Hotel 247
Crail Golfing Society 265
Crescent Lodge Hotel 59
Cross Keys Hotel 298
Crown and Cushion Hotel 176,207
Cruden Bay Golf Club 236
Culcreuch Castle Hotel 273,300

Dale Hill Golf Club 29,200
Dalmunzie House Hotel 291
Dalrachney Lodge Hotel 277
Dalston Hall Caravan Park 88
Darnley Hotel 97
Deauville Saint Gatien Glf Club 348
Deganwy Castle Hotel 322
Delaine Hotel 217
Deucoch Hotel 324
The Dormy 103
Dornoch Castle Hotel 301
The Dower House Hotel 151
Dukes Folly Hotel 162
Dunoon Hotel 323

East Dorset Golf Club 105
Eden House Hotel 265
The Elms Guest House 266
The Elms Court Hotel 242
Enfield Golf Club 56
Eryl Mor Hotel 321
Esplanade Hotel 323

Fairways Hotel 316
Fairwinds Hotel 277
Farringford Hotel 132
Fern House 136
Fernfell Golf and Country Club 190
Fernie Castle Hotel 268
Finlayson Arms Hotel 244
The Fircroft Hotel 102
Floyde Hotel 97
Forest of Arden Hotel, Golf & C.C 210

Forrest Hills Hotel 266
Four Poster Lodge 220
Friarn Court Hotel 181

Gatton Manor Hotel, Golf & C.C 192
Glan Aber Hotel 321
Glenavon House 276
Glencoe Hotel 239
The Glenesk Hotel 239
The Glenfarg Hotel 291
Gloucester Hotel & Country Club 21,114
Glyn Valley Hotel 310
Goldenstones Hotel 256
The Golf Hotel 256
Golf Hotel 261
The Golf Hotel 266
Gordon House Hotel 281
The Green Hotel 280
Greens of Scotland 233
Greenside Hotel 268

Hadley Wood Golf Club 123
Hagley Country Golf Club 121
Harbour Point Golf Club 338
The Harewood Arms Hotel 228
The Harvesters' Hotel 260
Hawkstone Park Hotel 23,179
Heathside Hotel 195
Hellidon Lakes Hotel & C.C. 168
The Heronston Hotel 314
Highcliffe Hotel 311
Hillhouse Farm 245
The Hillside Hotel 257
Hintlesham Hall 187
Hotel Palacio 32,360
Hotel Du Palais 33,353
Hotel Le Mas D'Huston 35,355
Hotel De La Plage 36,349
Hunley Hall Golf Club 78

The Inchview Hotel 264
Invernairne Hotel 286
Isle of Gigha Hotel 305
Ivyside Hotel 28,141

Kenmore Hotel 289
Kersbrook Hotel and Restaurant 104
King's Gap Court Hotel 160
King William IV 134

THE GOLF GUIDE 1994 INDEX

Kyle and Carrick District Council 243

The Langham Hotel 217
Lanhydrock Golf Club 79
Lansdowne Hotel 198
Lansdowne Hotel and Restaurant 326
Lanteglos Country House Hotel 12,79
Latitudes Valescure 34,356
Le Strange Arms Hotel 165
Leamington Hotel 281
Les Arches Hotel 345
The Links Hotel 173
Links Country Park Hotel & G.C. 164
The Links Hotel 286
The Links Hotel 240
The Lion Hotel 326
The Lion Hotel & Restaurant 327
Little Eagles 358
Loch Tay Holiday Lodges 293
Lochearnhead Hotel 292
The Lodge Hotel 165
The Lomond Country Inn 279
Lomond Hill Hotel 266
Looe Golf Club 81
Lostwithiel Golf & Country Club 80
The Lundin Links Hotel 269

Macclesfield Golf Club 74
Mains of Aigas 276
The Mallard 259
The Manor of Groves Golf & C.C. 127
Manor Park Hotel 246
The Manor House Hotel & Golf Crs. 15,99
Marine Hotel 248
Mayrose Farm 80
Melville Golf Range 255
Mere Golf and Country Club 73
Merlin Court Hotel 97
Metropole Hotel 161
Mia-Roo 300
Middle Ruddings Country Inn 89
Milford Haven Golf Club 312
The Mill at Glynhir 311
Mon Repos 345
Monksweir Hotel 309
Montrose Links Trust 240
Moorlands Hotel 73
Morangie House Hotel 297
Mottram Hall 75

Mouse Valley Golf Course 283
Moxhull Hall Hotel 212
Murraypark Hotel 292
Murrayshall Country Hse Hotel 294
Myrecairnie Farm House 265

Nairn Dunbar Golf Shop 287
Nether Abbey Hotel 263
Newquay Golf Club 81
Nizels Ltd 29,140
Normandy Arms 100
Northern Hotel 239

Old Thorns Hotel 26,118
Orillia House 220

Panmure Arms Hotel 239
Park Hotel 240
Patshull Park Hotel 180
Paul Jones Hotel 252
Pedn Olva Hotel 13,85
Pen-y-Castell Farm Guest House 312
Penmere Manor Hotel 80
Penny Farthing Hotel 118
Penscot Farmhouse Hotel 62
Petwood Hotel 24,151
Pine Lodge Hotel 174
Pitfirrane Arms Hotel 266
Point Garry Hotel 262
Poolway House Hotel & Rest. 113
Port Gaverne Hotel 84
The Porthcawl Hotel 316
Power Shift 232
Praa Sands Golf Club 82
Purley Chase Golf & Country Club 207

The Queen's Hotel 260

Railway Hotel 298
Raven Hall Country House Hotel 219
Red House Farm 166
Red Lion Hotel 300
The Red Lion Hotel 326
Redheugh Hotel 257
Rescobie Hotel and Restaurant 267
Rhodes Tantallon Car & Camp Park 263
The Riverside Hotel 183
The Roblin Hotel 244
Rocks Place Hotel 123

INDEX

The Royal Hotel 219
The Royal Dunkeld Hotel 293
Royal Hotel 296
Royal Hotel 250
Royal Liverpool Golf Club 160
Rudding Park Holiday Cottages 218
Rufflets Country House Hotel 270
Rum Hole Hotel 323
The Russell Hotel 270

Sandford Hotel 272
Scawfell Hotel 91
The Scores Hotel 270
The Seafield Arms Hotel 248
Hotel Seaforth 237
Selkirk Arms Hotel 281
Selsdon Park Hotel 191
The Severn Arms Hotel 327
Shaw Hill Hotel & Country Club 143
Shennanton House 302
Skye of Curr Hotel 277
Solwayside House Hotel 280
South Lodge Hotel 203
South Beach Hotel 247
Spey Bay Hotel 284
Sporting Laird Hotel 270
Springfield Country Hotel 104
Sprowston Park Golf Club 167
St. Andrews Golf Hotel 270
St. Brannock's House Hotel 97
St. Davids Hotel 323
St. Enodoc Hotel 86
St. Nicholas Hotel 246
St. Pierre Hotel Golf & Country Club 17,319
Stags Head Hotel 302
Stanley Arms Hotel 91
Station Hotel 239
Stotfield Hotel 9,285
Sutherland House Private Hotel 135
The Swan Revived Hotel 69

Tan Lan Hotel 323
The Tanner of Wingham Restaurant 134
Tarn End Hotel & Restaurant 88
G. Taylor Associates 233
Taymouth Holiday Centre 289
Telford Hotel Golf & Ctry Club 178
Todhall House 265
Tormaukin Hotel 292
Tralee Hotel 101
Tree Tops Restaurant and Motel 159
Trefeddian Hotel 320
Tregenna Castle Hotel 16,85
Trevaccoon Farm 312
Trevose Golf and Country Club 82
Tweed Valley Hotel 288
Tyglyn Aeron Country Hotel 312
Tytherington Golf Club 19,74

Ufford Park Hotel Golf & Leis. 188

Venn Ottery Barton Hotel 96
Verulam Golf Club 127
Villa Vivaldi 358
Village Leisure Hotels Ltd 19,142

Washington Moat House 206
The Watersplash Hotel 117
The Weigh Inn Motel 250
Wentworth Club Ltd 196
West Farm 105
West Ridge 16,95
Wester Riechip 292
Westerwood Hotel, Country Club 254
The Wheatsheaf 116
Wheel Farm Country Cottages 16,99
The White Hart Hotel 80
The White Lodge Hotel 83
Wild Boar Hotel 91

Yelverton Golf Club 101

The Countryman
comes from the country

THE COUNTRYMAN COMES FROM THE HEART OF THE BRITISH COUNTRYSIDE

The Countryman is unique - every other month this magazine will bring you all the peoples and places, crafts, characters and customs, wildlife and waysides of the British countryside.

Whatever your interests and wherever you live **The Countryman** is the ideal way to learn about the heritage that belongs to all of us. It will show you places to visit, reveal the history and traditions of everyday life and discuss the changes that are affecting our countryside.

Whether for yourself, a relative or friend **The Countryman** is the ideal gift. An attractive greetings card will be sent with a gift subscription to say that it is from you.

Subscribe now using the coupon overleaf and wherever you are **The Countryman** will bring the heart of the countryside a lot closer.

The Countryman
comes from the country

FROM THE HEART OF THE BRITISH COUNTRYSIDE DIRECTLY TO YOUR DOOR

A subscription to **The Countryman** costs -

	1 Year	2 Years
UK	❏ £12.00	❏ £22.00
Europe Airmail	❏ £14.00	❏ £26.00
Overseas Surface	❏ £14.00	❏ £26.00
Overseas Airmail	❏ £21.00	❏ £40.00

Please start my subscription with the next available issue -

Mr/Mrs/Miss/Ms..

Address ....

.... Postcode...........................

Country .... Telephone No.........................

Please send **The Countryman** to -

Mr/Mrs/Miss/Ms..

Address ....

....

Postcode........................... Country ....

It will be announced in your name with an attractive greetings card.

❏ I enclose a cheque/international money order for £............... pounds sterling, made payable to *Link House Magazines Ltd*.

Please debit my ❏ Visa ❏ Access ❏ Amex

Card No __ __ __ __ __ __ __ __ __ __ __ __

Expiry date .... Signature....................................... Date ....

Return to: The Countryman Subscriptions, 120-126 Lavender Avenue, Mitcham, Surrey, CR6 3TH, Great Britain.

Data Protection Act:
Occasionally we may make names and addresses available to carefully vetted companies who sell goods and services by mail that we believe may be of interest to our readers. If you would prefer not to receive such mailings please tick this box. ❏

C4GOG

CREDIT CARD HOTLINE 081 646 6672

ORDER NOW! *See Overleaf*

407

ONE FOR YOUR FRIEND 1994

FHG Publications have a large range of attractive holiday accommodation guides for all kinds of holiday opportunities throughout Britain. They also make useful gifts at any time of year. Our guides are available in most bookshops and larger newsagents but we will be happy to post you a copy direct if you have any difficulty. We will also post abroad but have to charge separately for post or freight.

The inclusive cost of posting and packing the guides to you or your friends in the UK is as follows:

Farm Holiday Guide ENGLAND, WALES and IRELAND
Board, Self-catering, Caravans/Camping, Activity Holidays. Over 400 pages. **£4.50**

Farm Holiday Guide SCOTLAND
All kinds of holiday accommodation. **£3.00**

SELF-CATERING & FURNISHED HOLIDAYS
Over 1000 addresses throughout for Self-catering and caravans in Britain. **£3.80**

BRITAIN'S BEST HOLIDAYS
A quick-reference general guide for all kinds of holidays. **£3.00**

The FHG Guide to CARAVAN & CAMPING HOLIDAYS
Caravans for hire, sites and holiday parks and centres. **£3.00**

BED AND BREAKFAST STOPS
Over 1000 friendly and comfortable overnight stops. Non-smoking, The Disabled and Special Diets Supplements. **£3.80**

CHILDREN WELCOME! FAMILY HOLIDAY GUIDE
Family holidays with details of amenities for children and babies. **£4.00**

Recommended SHORT BREAK HOLIDAYS IN BRITAIN
'Approved' accommodation for quality bargain breaks. Introduced by John Carter. **£4.00**

Recommended COUNTRY HOTELS OF BRITAIN
Including Country Houses, for the discriminating. **£4.00**

Recommended WAYSIDE INNS OF BRITAIN
Pubs, Inns and small hotels. **£4.00**

PGA GOLF GUIDE Where to play and where to stay
Over 2000 golf courses in Britain with convenient accommodation. Endorsed by the PGA. Holiday Golf in France, Portugal and Majorca. **£8.50**

PETS WELCOME!
The unique guide for holidays for pet owners and their pets. **£4.00**

BED AND BREAKFAST IN BRITAIN
Over 1000 choices for touring and holidays throughout Britain. Airports and Ferries Supplement. **£3.00**

THE FRENCH FARM AND VILLAGE HOLIDAY GUIDE
The official guide to self-catering holidays in the 'Gîtes de France'. **£8.50**

Tick your choice and send your order and payment to FHG PUBLICATIONS, ABBEY MILL BUSINESS CENTRE, SEEDHILL, PAISLEY PA1 1TJ (TEL: 041-887 0428. FAX: 041-889 7204). **Deduct** 10% for 2/3 titles or copies; 20% for 4 or more.

Send to: NAME ....

ADDRESS ....

....

.... POST CODE ....

I enclose Cheque/Postal Order for £ ....

SIGNATURE .... DATE ....

A
B
C
D
E
F
G
SHETLAND ISLANDS
YELL
MAINLAND
Lerwick
Sumburgh
ORKNEY
MAINLAND
Kirkwall
Stromness
HOY
0 10 20 30 40 50 Kilometres
0 10 20 30 Miles
Grid interval is 30 miles
Durness
Thurso
John o'Groats
Bettyhill
Tongue
Scourie
Wick
Lochinver
Lairg
Helmsdale
Golspie
Ullapool
Bonar Bridge
Dornoch
Tain
Gairloch
Poolewe
LEWIS
WESTERN ISLES
Dingwall
Rosemarkie
HIGHLAND
Cullen
Banff
Fraserburgh
Elgin
Fochabers
Keith
Forres
Nairn
Beauly
Inverness
Daviot
Peterhead
Huntly
Portree
RAASAY
SKYE
Kyle of Lochalsh
Kyleakin
Dornie
Broadford
Grantown-on-Spey
Carrbridge
Tomintoul
Aviemore
GRAMPIAN
Inverurie
Aberdeen
Fort Augustus
Kingussie
Mallaig
Braemar
Banchory
Stonehaven
INNER HEBRIDES
Fort William
Kinlochleven
Ballachulish
Glencoe
Kinloch Rannoch
Pitlochry
Brechin
Montrose
Tobermory
Aberfeldy
TAYSIDE
Forfar
Arbroath
Dunkeld
Blairgowrie
Carnoustie
Dundee
MULL
Oban
Taynuilt
Dalmally
Killin
Crianlarich
Lochearnhead
Perth
Crieff
Cupar
St Andrews
Inveraray
Callander
Auchterarder
FIFE
Arrochar
Tarbet
Aberfoyle
Kinross
CENTRAL
Stirling
Dunfermline
Kirkcaldy
North Berwick
Lochgilphead
Luss
Drymen
JURA
Ardrishaig
Dunoon
Gourock
Balloch
Dumbarton
EDINBURGH
Dunbar
Greenock
Dalkeith
Haddington
Tarbert
Glasgow
Rothesay
Paisley
LOTHIAN
Eyemouth
ISLAY
Largs
Chirnside
Berwick upon Tweed
STRATHCLYDE
Hamilton
Lauder
Duns
Coldstream
Cornhill-on-Tweed
Ardrossan
Kilmarnock
Lanark
Peebles
Galashiels
Irvine
Kelso
Wooler
Bamburgh
KINTYRE
Brodick
Lamlash
Troon
Prestwick
Biggar
Selkirk
Seahouses
Campbeltown
Ayr
Abington
New Cumnock
BORDERS
Jedburgh
ARRAN
Hawick
Alnwick
Maybole
Moffat
Beattock
Girvan
NORTHUMBERLAND
Langholm
Bellingham
Morpeth
DUMFRIES & GALLOWAY
Whitley Bay
New Galloway
Dumfries
Gretna
Longtown
Newton Stewart
Castle Douglas
Annan
Newcastle-upon-Tyne
Stranraer
Carlisle
Greenhead
Hexham
Corbridge
Portpatrick
Gatehouse of Fleet
Wigtown
Silloth
Kirkcudbright
Port William
CUMBRIA
Alston
Durham
Bassenthwaite
Penrith
5
6
1
2
3
4
5
6
7
8
9
10
11

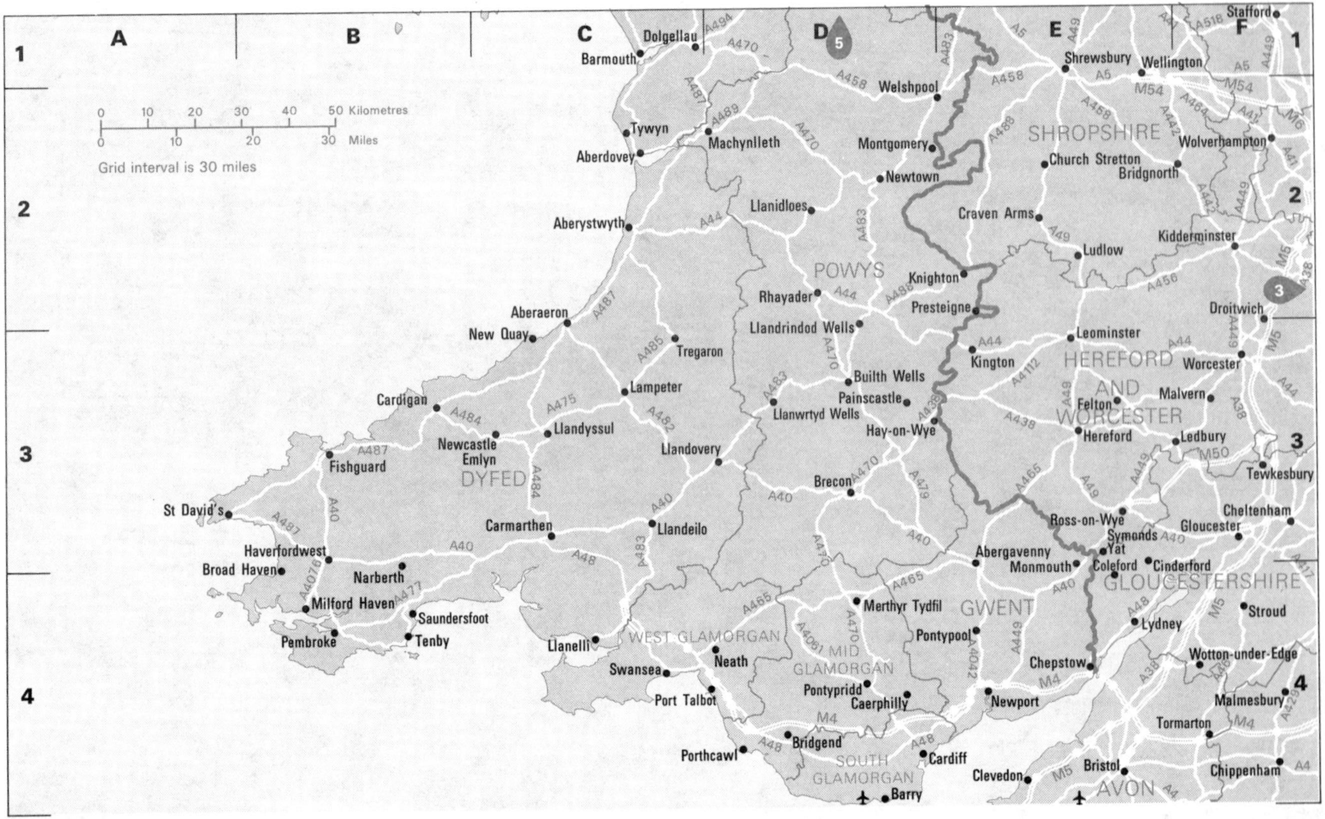

0 10 20 30 40 50 Kilometres
0 10 20 30 Miles
Grid interval is 30 miles
SHROPSHIRE
POWYS
DYFED
HEREFORD AND WORCESTER
GWENT
GLOUCESTERSHIRE
WEST GLAMORGAN
MID GLAMORGAN
SOUTH GLAMORGAN
AVON
Barmouth
Dolgellau
Tywyn
Aberdovey
Machynlleth
Welshpool
Montgomery
Newtown
Llanidloes
Aberystwyth
Aberaeron
New Quay
Tregaron
Lampeter
Cardigan
Newcastle Emlyn
Llandyssul
Fishguard
St David's
Haverfordwest
Broad Haven
Narberth
Milford Haven
Saundersfoot
Pembroke
Tenby
Carmarthen
Llandeilo
Llandovery
Llanelli
Swansea
Neath
Port Talbot
Porthcawl
Bridgend
Pontypridd
Caerphilly
Cardiff
Barry
Merthyr Tydfil
Pontypool
Newport
Clevedon
Bristol
Chepstow
Abergavenny
Monmouth
Coleford
Symonds Yat
Ross-on-Wye
Cinderford
Lydney
Gloucester
Cheltenham
Stroud
Wotton-under-Edge
Tormarton
Malmesbury
Chippenham
Tewkesbury
Ledbury
Malvern
Hereford
Felton
Worcester
Droitwich
Kidderminster
Leominster
Kington
Presteigne
Knighton
Rhayader
Llandrindod Wells
Builth Wells
Painscastle
Llanwrtyd Wells
Hay-on-Wye
Brecon
Ludlow
Craven Arms
Church Stretton
Bridgnorth
Wolverhampton
Shrewsbury
Wellington
Stafford

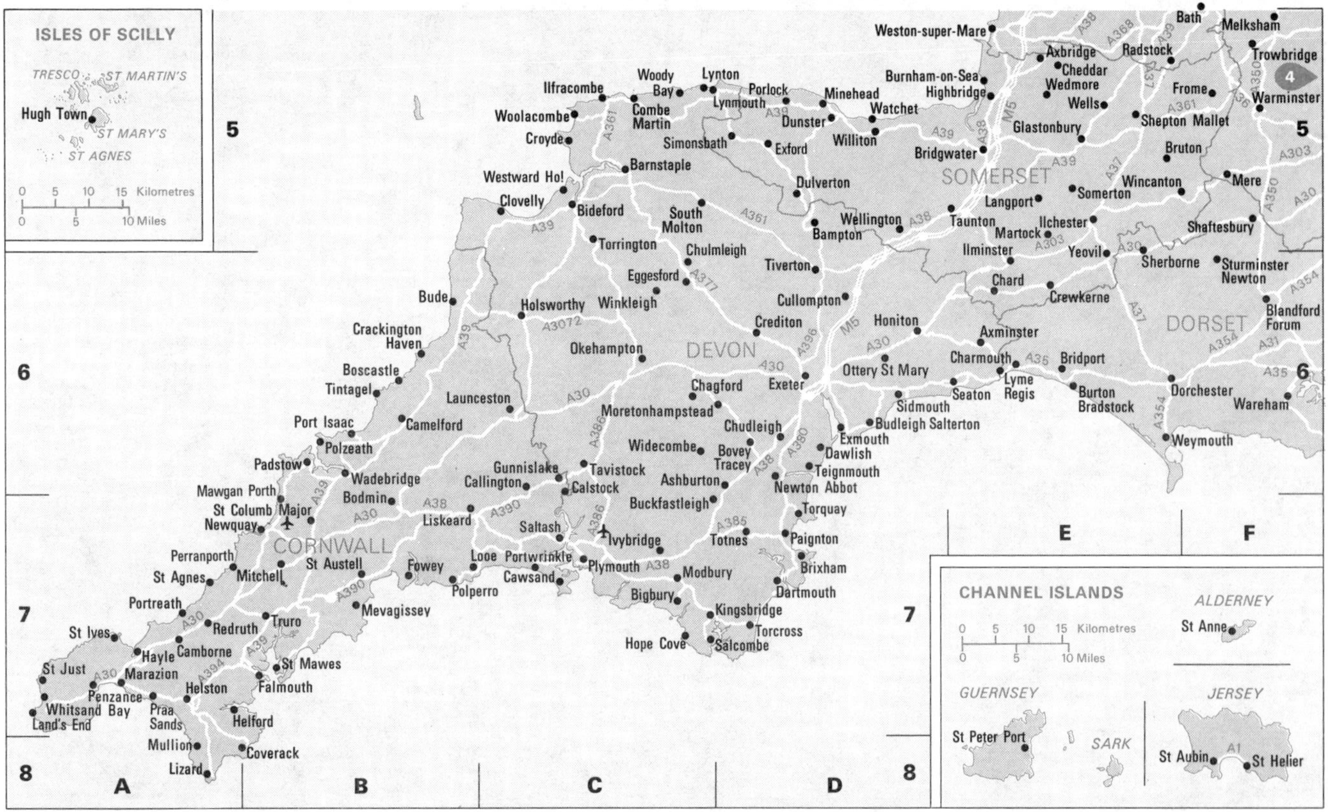
ISLES OF SCILLY
TRESCO
ST MARTIN'S
Hugh Town
ST MARY'S
ST AGNES
0 5 10 15 Kilometres
0 5 10 Miles
CHANNEL ISLANDS
ALDERNEY
St Anne
GUERNSEY
St Peter Port
SARK
JERSEY
St Aubin
St Helier
A1
CORNWALL
DEVON
SOMERSET
DORSET
A B C D E F
5 6 7 8
4
Weston-super-Mare
Bath
Melksham
Trowbridge
Warminster
Radstock
Axbridge
Cheddar
Wedmore
Wells
Frome
Shepton Mallet
Burnham-on-Sea
Highbridge
Glastonbury
Bruton
Mere
Bridgwater
Wincanton
Somerton
Langport
Taunton
Martock
Ilchester
Yeovil
Sherborne
Shaftesbury
Sturminster Newton
Blandford Forum
Ilminster
Chard
Crewkerne
Axminster
Charmouth
Lyme Regis
Bridport
Burton Bradstock
Dorchester
Wareham
Weymouth
Seaton
Sidmouth
Budleigh Salterton
Exmouth
Dawlish
Teignmouth
Newton Abbot
Torquay
Paignton
Brixham
Dartmouth
Ottery St Mary
Honiton
Exeter
Cullompton
Crediton
Tiverton
Wellington
Bampton
Dulverton
Minehead
Watchet
Williton
Dunster
Porlock
Exford
Lynton
Lynmouth
Simonsbath
Woody Bay
Combe Martin
Ilfracombe
Woolacombe
Croyde
Barnstaple
Westward Ho!
Clovelly
Bideford
South Molton
Torrington
Chulmleigh
Eggesford
Winkleigh
Holsworthy
Okehampton
Chagford
Moretonhampstead
Chudleigh
Widecombe
Bovey Tracey
Ashburton
Buckfastleigh
Totnes
Modbury
Kingsbridge
Torcross
Salcombe
Hope Cove
Bigbury
Ivybridge
Plymouth
Tavistock
Gunnislake
Calstock
Callington
Saltash
Cawsand
Portwrinkle
Looe
Polperro
Fowey
Liskeard
Launceston
Bude
Crackington Haven
Boscastle
Tintagel
Camelford
Port Isaac
Polzeath
Padstow
Wadebridge
Bodmin
Mawgan Porth
St Columb Major
Newquay
Perranporth
St Agnes
Mitchell
St Austell
Mevagissey
Portreath
Truro
Redruth
Camborne
St Ives
Hayle
St Mawes
Falmouth
St Just
Marazion
Penzance
Helston
Whitsand Bay
Land's End
Praa Sands
Helford
Mullion
Coverack
Lizard
A30
A38
A39
A35
A37
A303
A361
A386
A390
A396
A3072
A377
A380
A385
A394
A354
A350
A368
A36
A31
M5

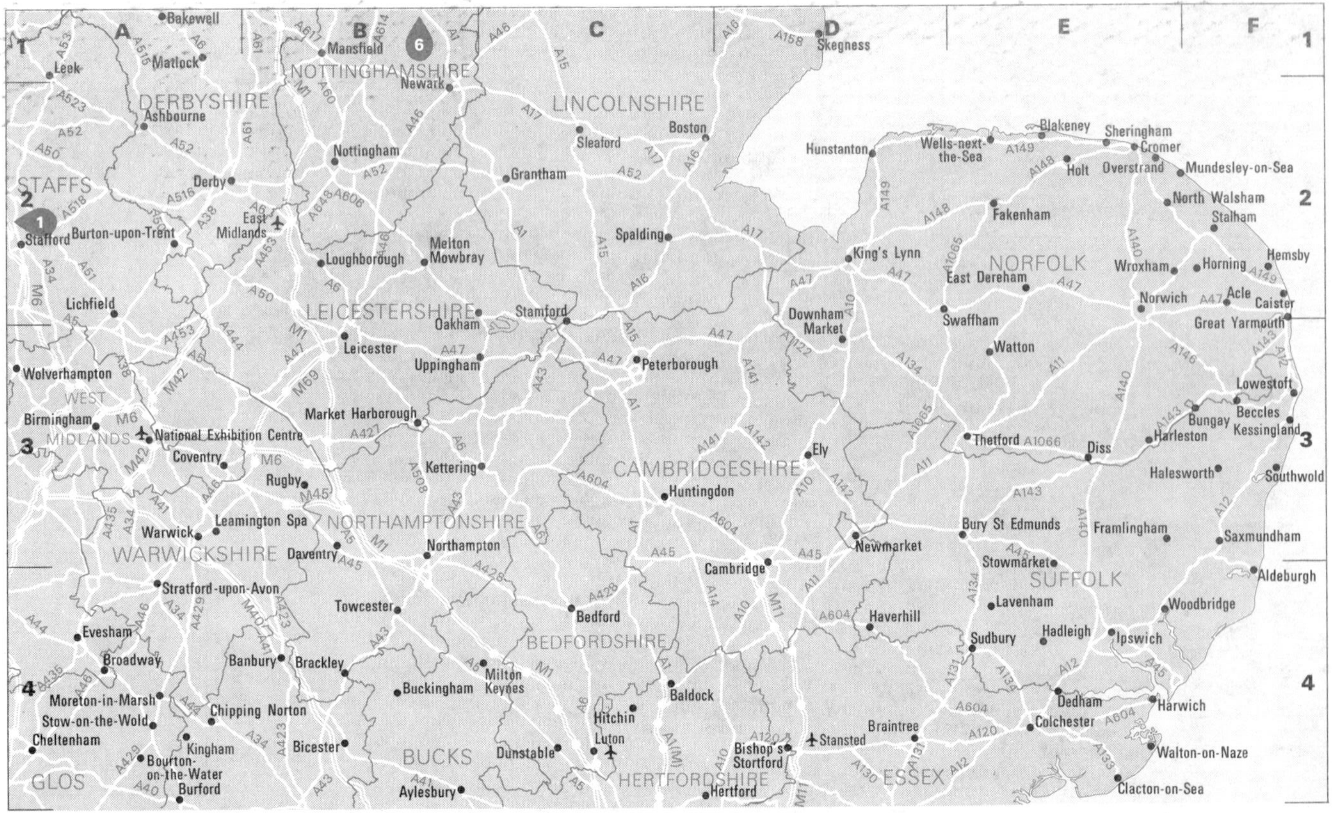

A
B
C
D
E
F
1
2
3
4
Bakewell
Matlock
Leek
Mansfield
NOTTINGHAMSHIRE
Newark
Skegness
DERBYSHIRE
Ashbourne
LINCOLNSHIRE
Boston
Sleaford
Nottingham
Derby
Grantham
STAFFS
Stafford
Burton-upon-Trent
East Midlands
Melton Mowbray
Loughborough
Spalding
Hunstanton
Wells-next-the-Sea
Blakeney
Sheringham
Cromer
Holt
Overstrand
Mundesley-on-Sea
North Walsham
Stalham
Fakenham
King's Lynn
NORFOLK
Wroxham
Horning
Hemsby
East Dereham
Norwich
Acle
Caister
Great Yarmouth
Swaffham
Downham Market
Watton
Lichfield
LEICESTERSHIRE
Oakham
Stamford
Leicester
Uppingham
Peterborough
Wolverhampton
WEST MIDLANDS
Birmingham
National Exhibition Centre
Coventry
Rugby
Market Harborough
Kettering
CAMBRIDGESHIRE
Huntingdon
Ely
Thetford
Diss
Harleston
Bungay
Beccles
Lowestoft
Kessingland
Halesworth
Southwold
Leamington Spa
Warwick
WARWICKSHIRE
NORTHAMPTONSHIRE
Daventry
Northampton
Cambridge
Newmarket
Bury St Edmunds
Framlingham
Saxmundham
Stowmarket
SUFFOLK
Aldeburgh
Stratford-upon-Avon
Towcester
Bedford
Haverhill
Lavenham
Woodbridge
Evesham
BEDFORDSHIRE
Sudbury
Hadleigh
Ipswich
Broadway
Banbury
Brackley
Milton Keynes
Buckingham
Baldock
Dedham
Harwich
Moreton-in-Marsh
Stow-on-the-Wold
Chipping Norton
Cheltenham
Kingham
Bourton-on-the-Water
Burford
GLOS
Bicester
BUCKS
Dunstable
Luton
Hitchin
Bishop's Stortford
Stansted
Braintree
Colchester
Walton-on-Naze
Clacton-on-Sea
ESSEX
HERTFORDSHIRE
Hertford
Aylesbury

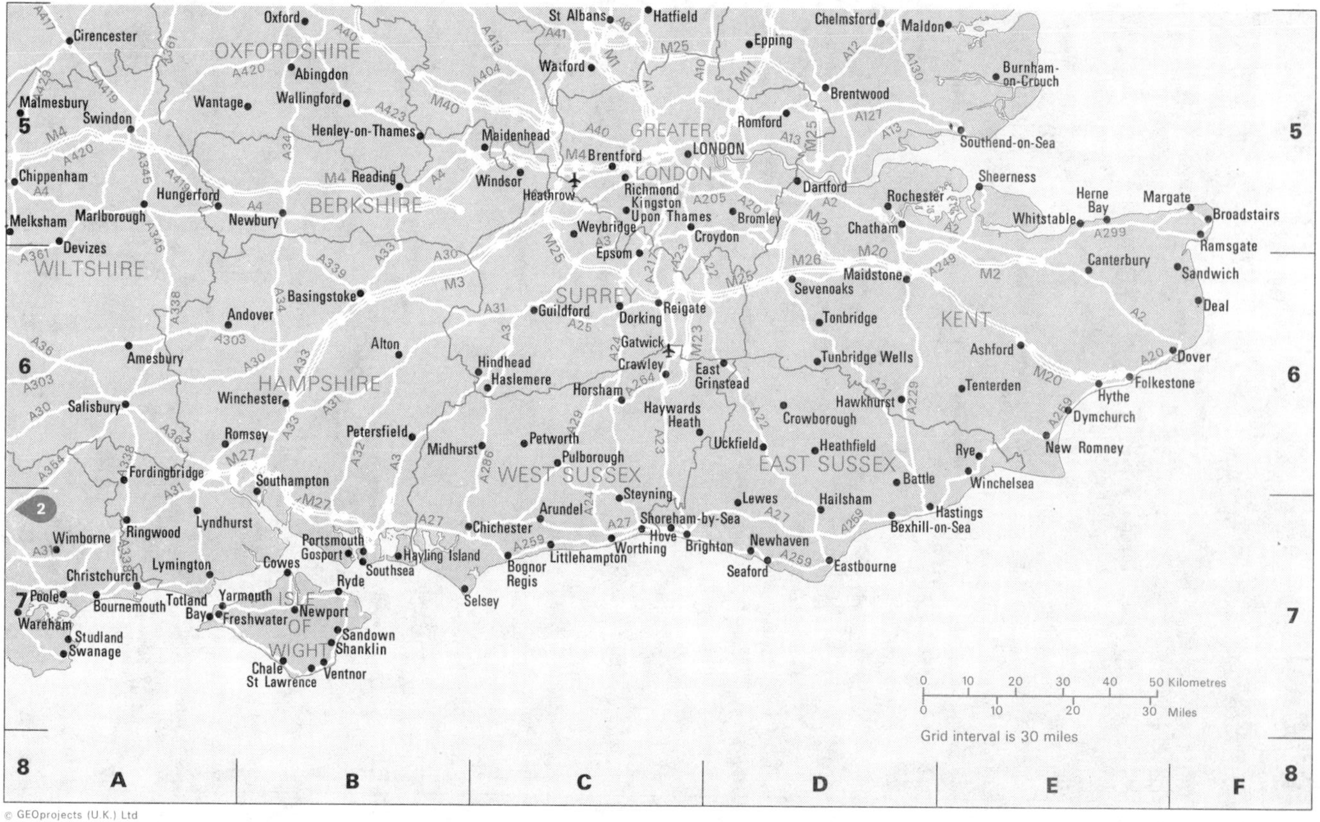
OXFORDSHIRE
BERKSHIRE
WILTSHIRE
HAMPSHIRE
SURREY
GREATER LONDON
KENT
WEST SUSSEX
EAST SUSSEX
ISLE OF WIGHT
Oxford
Cirencester
Abingdon
Wantage
Wallingford
Malmesbury
Swindon
Henley-on-Thames
Maidenhead
Chippenham
Hungerford
Reading
Windsor
Heathrow
Melksham
Marlborough
Newbury
Devizes
Basingstoke
Andover
Amesbury
Alton
Salisbury
Winchester
Romsey
Petersfield
Fordingbridge
Southampton
Lyndhurst
Ringwood
Wimborne
Christchurch
Lymington
Cowes
Portsmouth
Gosport
Southsea
Hayling Island
Ryde
Poole
Bournemouth
Totland Bay
Yarmouth
Freshwater
Newport
Wareham
Studland
Swanage
Sandown
Shanklin
Chale
St Lawrence
Ventnor
St Albans
Hatfield
Watford
Epping
Chelmsford
Maldon
Burnham-on-Crouch
Brentwood
Romford
LONDON
Brentford
Richmond
Kingston Upon Thames
Weybridge
Epsom
Croydon
Bromley
Dartford
Southend-on-Sea
Sheerness
Rochester
Chatham
Whitstable
Herne Bay
Margate
Broadstairs
Ramsgate
Canterbury
Sandwich
Deal
Maidstone
Sevenoaks
Guildford
Dorking
Reigate
Gatwick
Crawley
East Grinstead
Tonbridge
Tunbridge Wells
Ashford
Dover
Folkestone
Hythe
Tenterden
Hindhead
Haslemere
Horsham
Haywards Heath
Crowborough
Hawkhurst
Dymchurch
New Romney
Midhurst
Petworth
Pulborough
Uckfield
Heathfield
Rye
Winchelsea
Battle
Steyning
Lewes
Hailsham
Hastings
Bexhill-on-Sea
Arundel
Chichester
Shoreham-by-Sea
Hove
Brighton
Worthing
Littlehampton
Bognor Regis
Selsey
Newhaven
Seaford
Eastbourne
M4
M40
M25
M1
M11
M3
M27
M20
M26
M2
M23
A417
A429
A419
A420
A361
A4
A345
A346
A338
A303
A30
A36
A354
A31
A34
A339
A33
A32
A3
A31
A25
A24
A29
A286
A27
A259
A264
A23
A22
A217
A205
A20
A21
A229
A249
A299
A2
A13
A127
A12
A130
A10
A41
A6
A413
A404
A423
A40
0 10 20 30 40 50 Kilometres
0 10 20 30 Miles
Grid interval is 30 miles
A B C D E F
5 6 7 8

A
B
C
D
1
2
3
4
5
6
7
7
DUMFRIES AND GALLOWAY
NORTH
CUMBRIA
ISLE OF MAN
LANCASHIRE
GREATER MANCHESTER
MERSEYSIDE
ANGLESEY
CHESHIRE
CLWYD
GWYNEDD
SHROPSHIRE
POWYS
Girvan
Langholm
Bellingham
New Galloway
Dumfries
Newton Stewart
Annan
Gretna
Longtown
Greenhead
Brampton
Castle Douglas
Gatehouse of Fleet
Carlisle
Wigtown
Silloth
Kirkcudbright
Wigton
Alston
Port William
Maryport
Cockermouth
Bassenthwaite
Penrith
Workington
Keswick
Brampton
Appleby
Whitehaven
Ennerdale Bridge
Ullswater
Shap
Kirkby Stephen
Little Langdale
Ambleside
Hawkshead
Gosforth
Seascale
Windermere
Coniston
Kendal
Ramsey
Sedbergh
Broughton-in-Furness
Newby Bridge
Peel
Kirkby Lonsdale
Millom
Ulverston
Grange-over-Sands
Ingleton
Douglas
Port Erin
Castletown
Port St Mary
Barrow-in-Furness
Morecambe
Lancaster
Settle
Fleetwood
Clitheroe
Blackpool
Lytham St Annes
Preston
Blackburn
Southport
Chorley
Formby
Bolton
Wigan
Manchester
Amlwch
Liverpool
Hoylake
Birkenhead
Holyhead
Llanerchymedd
Llandudno
Colwyn Bay
Prestatyn
Rhyl
Menai Bridge
Beaumaris
Conwy
Knutsford
Llangefni
Abergele
Northwich
Bangor
Chester
Denbigh
Caernarvon
Llanrwst
Llanberis
Ruthin
Betws-y-Coed
Nantwich
Wrexham
Corwen
Newcastle-under-Lyme
Portmadoc
Ffestiniog
Llangollen
Nefyn
Criccieth
Penrhyndeudraeth
Bala
Pwllheli
Llanbedrog
Harlech
Wem
Market Drayton
Oswestry
Abersoch
Aberdaron
Dolgellau
Barmouth
Wellington
Welshpool
Shrewsbury
Tywyn
Machynlleth
A77
A713
A76
A701
A74
A7
A68
A75
A69
A74
A686
A689
A596
A595
M6
A6
A686
A66
A5086
A596
A66
A595
A591
A685
A6
A592
A684
A595
M6
A590
A65
A6
A683
A6
A585
M55
M6
A59
A59
A666
A570
A565
A59
M61
A6
M58
M62
M53
M56
M6
A537
A54
A49
A50
A55
A41
A51
A483
A494
A4
A1
A18
A5
A4
A5
A5
A5
A55
A470
A487
A5
A470
A5
A494
A470
A495
A5
A483
A49
A53
A526
A51
A53
A41
A518
A458
A5
M54
A458
A464
A5
A493
A487
A483
A49

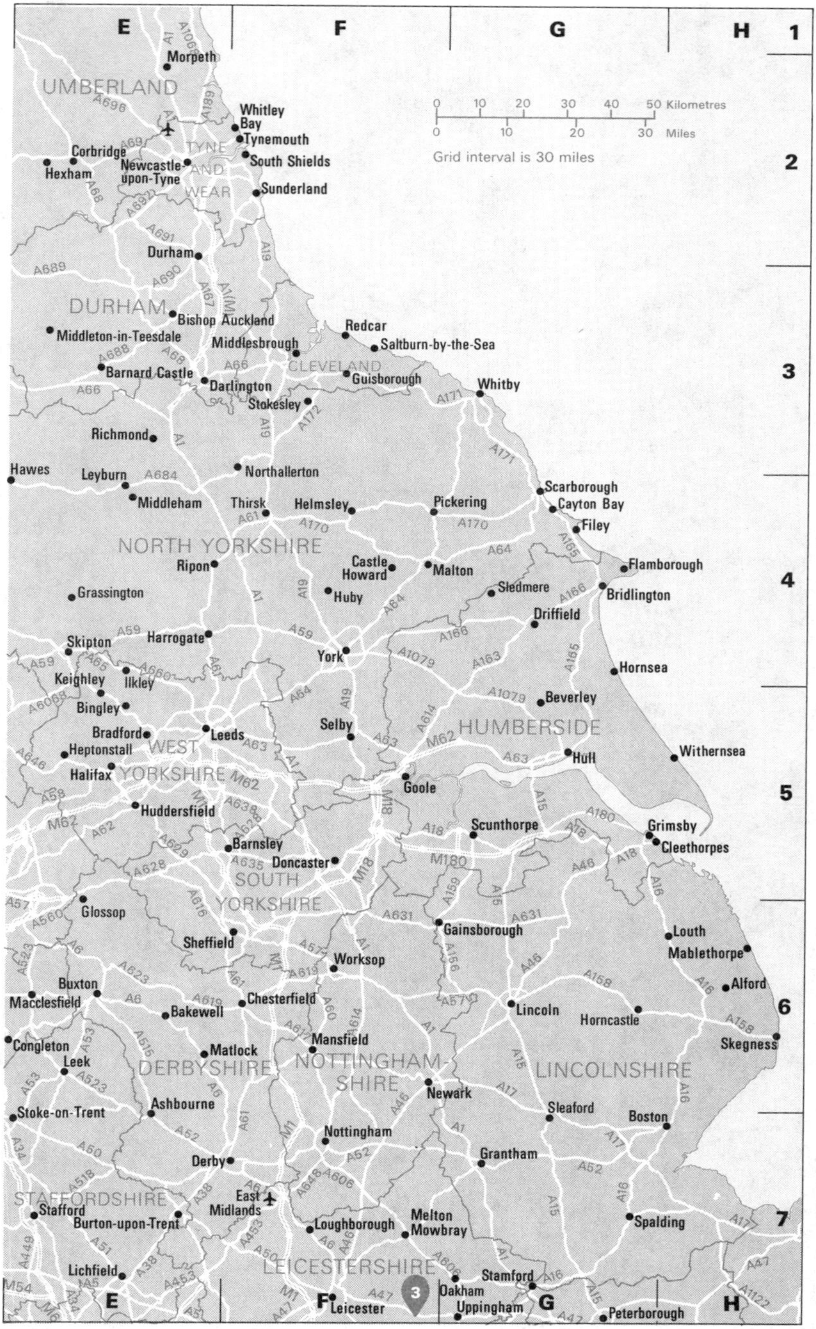
E
F
G
H
1
2
3
4
5
6
7
0 10 20 30 40 50 Kilometres
0 10 20 30 Miles
Grid interval is 30 miles
UMBERLAND
Morpeth
Whitley Bay
Tynemouth
South Shields
Corbridge
Hexham
Newcastle-upon-Tyne
TYNE AND WEAR
Sunderland
Durham
DURHAM
Bishop Auckland
Middleton-in-Teesdale
Middlesbrough
Redcar
Saltburn-by-the-Sea
CLEVELAND
Guisborough
Barnard Castle
Darlington
Stokesley
Whitby
Richmond
Northallerton
Hawes
Leyburn
Middleham
Thirsk
Helmsley
Pickering
Scarborough
Cayton Bay
Filey
NORTH YORKSHIRE
Ripon
Castle Howard
Malton
Flamborough
Bridlington
Grassington
Huby
Sledmere
Driffield
Skipton
Harrogate
York
Hornsea
Keighley
Ilkley
Bingley
Beverley
Bradford
Leeds
Selby
HUMBERSIDE
Heptonstall
WEST YORKSHIRE
Halifax
Hull
Withernsea
Goole
Huddersfield
Scunthorpe
Grimsby
Cleethorpes
Barnsley
Doncaster
SOUTH YORKSHIRE
Glossop
Gainsborough
Sheffield
Louth
Mablethorpe
Worksop
Buxton
Alford
Macclesfield
Chesterfield
Lincoln
Horncastle
Bakewell
Congleton
Mansfield
Skegness
Matlock
Leek
DERBYSHIRE
NOTTINGHAMSHIRE
LINCOLNSHIRE
Newark
Ashbourne
Stoke-on-Trent
Sleaford
Boston
Nottingham
Grantham
Derby
STAFFORDSHIRE
East Midlands
Stafford
Burton-upon-Trent
Loughborough
Melton Mowbray
Spalding
LEICESTERSHIRE
Lichfield
Stamford
Oakham
Leicester
Uppingham
Peterborough
3
A1
A1068
A696
A189
A69
A68
A692
A691
A19
A689
A690
A167
A1(M)
A688
A66
A171
A172
A684
A61
A170
A64
A165
A166
A59
A65
A660
A6068
A1079
A163
A614
A63
M62
A646
A58
A638
A628
A629
A635
M18
A18
A180
M180
A46
A15
A159
A57
A560
A616
A631
A6
A523
A623
A619
A60
A614
A158
A16
A53
A515
A617
A1
A17
A52
A50
A518
A38
A648
A606
A46
A453
A449
A51
A5
M54
M6
A34
M1
A47
A1122

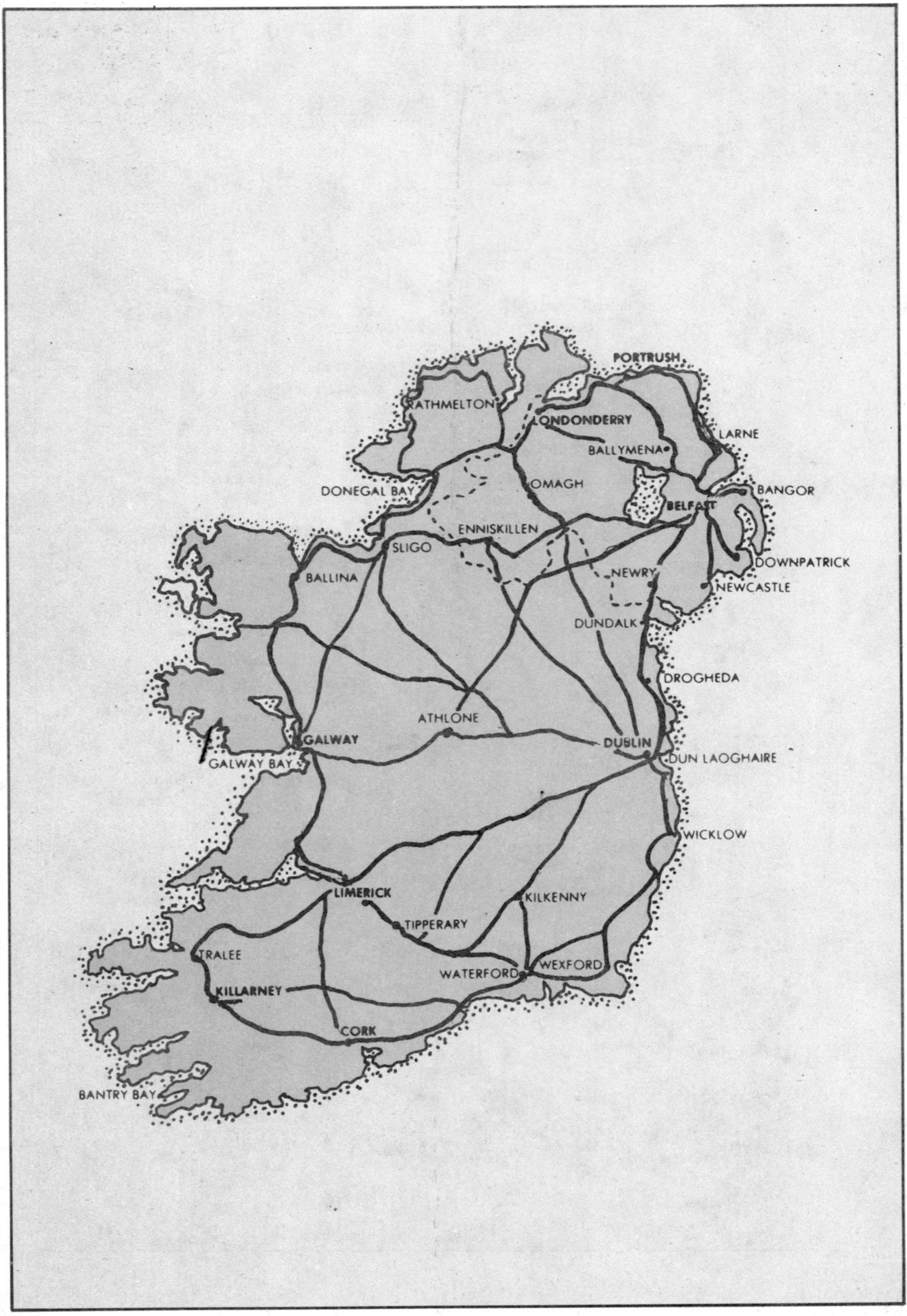
PORTRUSH
RATHMELTON
LONDONDERRY
LARNE
BALLYMENA
DONEGAL BAY
OMAGH
BANGOR
BELFAST
ENNISKILLEN
SLIGO
DOWNPATRICK
BALLINA
NEWRY
NEWCASTLE
DUNDALK
DROGHEDA
ATHLONE
GALWAY
DUBLIN
DUN LAOGHAIRE
GALWAY BAY
WICKLOW
LIMERICK
KILKENNY
TIPPERARY
TRALEE
WEXFORD
WATERFORD
KILLARNEY
CORK
BANTRY BAY